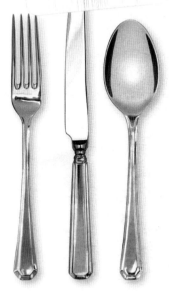

THE GOOD FOOD GUIDE

2013

Distributed by Littlehampton Book Services Ltd
Faraday Close, Durrington, Worthing, West Sussex, BN13 3RB

Copyright © Which? Ltd, 2012

Base mapping by Cosmographics Ltd
Data management and export by AMA DataSet Ltd, Preston
Printed and bound by Charterhouse, Hatfield

A catalogue record for this book is available from the British Library

ISBN: 978 1 84490 136 4

Consultant Editor: Elizabeth Carter
Managing Editor: Rochelle Venables
Assistant Editor: Francesca Bashall

The Good Food Guide makes every effort to be as accurate and up to date as possible.
All inspections are anonymous, but every Main Entry has been contacted separately
for details.

As we are an annual Guide, we have strict guidelines for fact-checking information
ahead of going to press, so some restaurants were dropped if they failed to provide the
information we required. Readers should still check details at the time of booking,
particularly if they have any special requirements.

Please send updates to: editors@thegoodfoodguide.co.uk or The Good Food Guide,
2 Marylebone Road, London, NW1 4DF

We would love to hear your feedback on any restaurant. To have your say, join us at
www.thegoodfoodguide.co.uk

"You can corrupt one man.
You can't bribe an army."

Raymond Postgate, founder of
The Good Food Guide, 1951

Please turn to the page number listed to find restaurant reviews for the corresponding region.

		Page
1	Bedfordshire	177
2	Berkshire	180
3	Borders	479
4	Buckinghamshire	188
5	Cambridgeshire	195
6	Central Scotland	504
7	Channel Islands	563
8	Cheshire	201
9	Cornwall	206
10	Cumbria	220
11	Derbyshire	231
12	Devon	237
13	Dorset	252
14	Dumfries & Galloway	482
15	Durham	258
16	East Sussex	405
17	Essex	262
18	Fife	506
19	Glamorgan	529
20	Gloucestershire & Bristol	265
21	Grampian	514
22	Greater Manchester	281
23	Gwent	537
24	Hampshire	289
25	Herefordshire	304
26	Hertfordshire	307
27	Highlands & Islands	517
28	Isle of Wight	292
29	Kent	313
30	Lancashire	325
31	Leicestershire & Rutland	331
32	Lincolnshire	336
33	London	17
34	Lothians	483
35	Merseyside	341
36	Mid-Wales	541
37	Norfolk	347
38	North-East Wales	545
39	North-West Wales	547
40	Northamptonshire	355
41	Northern Ireland	571
42	Northumberland	358
43	Nottinghamshire	361
44	Oxfordshire	366
45	Shropshire	376
46	Somerset	380
47	Staffordshire	391
48	Strathclyde	495
49	Suffolk	393
50	Surrey	401
51	Tayside	510
52	Tyne & Wear	421
53	Warwickshire	425
54	West Midlands	429
55	West Sussex	414
56	West Wales	556
57	Wiltshire	435
58	Worcestershire	443
59	Yorkshire	445

Contents

UK overview map	4
Introduction	6
Editors' Awards	9
Readers' Awards	11
Longest-serving restaurants	12
Top 50 restaurants 2013	13
How to use the Guide	14
London explained	16
LONDON - Central	28
LONDON - North	83
LONDON - East	94
LONDON - South	116
LONDON - West	133
LONDON - Greater	165
ENGLAND	175
SCOTLAND	477
WALES	527
CHANNEL ISLANDS	563
NORTHERN IRELAND	571
UK atlas maps	580
Index – town	600
Index – restaurant	605
Reader thanks	617
Special thanks	623

Introduction

Britain's bestselling restaurant guide continues to thrive, 62 years since its birth, casting its expert eye over cafés, pubs and restaurants throughout the UK. But why, when we are bombarded with advice from blogs, tweets, forums and websites, do we depend on an annual guide like *The Good Food Guide*? The simple answer is – the Guide can be trusted. Its perennial strength is that every entry represents a whole range of meals eaten by genuine restaurant customers, whether in celebration, on holiday, or in the normal course of business. These are people who claim no freebies, special service, recompense or reward, and our many years of success have depended on their support. Each year every entry is assessed afresh, based on feedback from readers and backed up by anonymous, expert inspections. And in a year when public confidence in political institutions, banking and journalism has been eroded, the integrity of independent voices like *The Good Food Guide* is now more important than ever.

British cooking comes of age

The past year has been a cracker for the reputation of British food abroad. British chefs in Paris were celebrated in *Le Figaro*, while the *International Herald Tribune* got 'on the trail of the new "English cuisine"'. In London, a heady culinary optimism is attracting substantial numbers of food tourists – and judging by our feedback, Londoners love eating out more than ever before. There has been an explosion of new ideas right across the city: from high-end openings (Cut at 45 Park Lane, Alyn Williams at the Westbury), to boomtown Soho (Ducksoup, 10 Greek Street, a revitalised Quo Vadis). Even touristy Covent Garden has benefited from the Soho ripple effect, with first the Opera Tavern and now the Delaunay and Mishkin's challenging the area's bland chains. The London street-food scene continues to expand, churning out good, inexpensive food from cheerful vans, carts and stalls, peddling anything from meaty burgers, hand-rolled pizza and Scotch eggs to paella, Korean sliders and custard tarts. Some have even become restaurants: Meatwagon has become the grunge-tastic, long-of-queue Meat Liquor, whilst Pitt Cue has moved its pulled-pork operation from a van under Hungerford

Londoners have been eating out more than ever before, and there has been an explosion of new ideas right across the city.

Bridge to bricks and mortar in Soho. Both join the ultra-democratic, no-reservations group of hip urban restaurants responding to a public desire for good cooking in casual, unconventional settings.

Outside the London bubble…

This edition of the Guide comes out in increasingly difficult times. The resurgence of pride in British cooking and produce continues, but away from the London bubble, many places are facing a brutal reality. Readers have sent disturbing reports of restaurants with only two tables taken on a Saturday night and noted how much easier it is to book at short notice at weekends. The Hungry Monk, proud inventor of the banoffi pie and a Guide stalwart of 41 years, has gone from these pages; it is not the only one to give up. Others have told us they are up for sale, quietly struggling on until a buyer is found.

But nevertheless, there are reasons to be cheerful. The 1999 edition of *The Good Food Guide* was the last time more than one restaurant scored a perfect 10. Now, fourteen years later, Simon Rogan's L'Enclume in Cumbria joins Heston Blumenthal's Fat Duck in that elite club. Here are two brilliantly artistic, entrepreneurial and very modern chefs with totally different philosophies: the cerebral Blumenthal, whose witty cooking is based on surprises, clever deceptions and sheer theatre; and Rogan, whose farm-to-table cooking is never less than a sheer, sensual delight – a celebration of the Cumbrian seasons. We salute them both for perfecting the art of giving such tremendous pleasure through their skill and vision.

Here are two brilliantly artistic and very modern chefs with totally different philosophies.

Elsewhere, a new breed of hostelry is beginning to stand out from the masses, with designer details and doses of luxury at wallet-friendly rates. The time is right for these unpretentious and lively places with their emphasis on hospitality. The Gunton Arms in Norfolk, the Wheatsheaf Inn at Northleach, and the Beckford Arms at Fonthill Gifford are establishing a gold standard with their warm, quirky and cleverly furnished country-house style. Their bedrooms offer the comforts of a deluxe country house hotel without the premium prices, while their kitchens pursue a philosophy of very good seasonal food, offering great Britishness in all its forms, from sausage rolls in the bar to whole roast chickens for Sunday lunch. They may not be doing something new, but they are making a virtue of high standards and good value at a time when there is an ever-increasing demand for it.

We can't do it without you...

The Good Food Guide's major remit has always been to agitate for ever-higher standards of catering and hospitality. There has never been a better time to eat out, whether in a restaurant listed in the Guide's Top 50, a mid-range restaurant offering value for money in this new age of austerity, or a fantastic country pub. *The Good Food Guide,* however, remains a book of exceptions, and to eat out in this country is to know that disappointments are all too frequent. That is why we need

> *The Good Food Guide's major remit has always been to agitate for ever higher standards of catering and hospitality.*

your help: we need you to tell us about your restaurant experiences, both good and bad. So next time you go out to eat, please log on to www.thegoodfoodguide. co.uk and tell us about it. And while you are there, you can sample a veritable smorgasbord of restaurant news, features, chef interviews and competitions, as well as the opportunity to subscribe to *The Good Food Guide* online and enjoy a host of membership benefits. But most importantly, please remember that we read every piece of feedback you send us – and we may well use your recommendations in next year's Guide.

Elizabeth Carter, Consultant Editor

Editors' Awards

Every year The Good Food Guide team recognises excellence across the restaurant industry with its Editors' Awards. For the 2013 edition, the team is delighted to confer the following awards:

Chef of the Year
Clare Smyth (Restaurant Gordon Ramsay)

Chef to Watch
Dave Watts, Cotswold House, Chipping Campden

Best New Entry
The Gunton Arms, Thorpe Market, Norfolk

Pub of the Year
The Plough Inn, Longparish, Hampshire

Wine List of the Year
Drake's Restaurant, Ripley, Surrey

Best Seafood
The Seahorse, Dartmouth, Devon

Best Value for Money
Create, Leeds

Best Café
Food by Breda Murphy, Whalley, Lancashire

Readers' Awards

The Good Food Guide Readers' Restaurant of the Year Awards, run annually in the spring, give our readers the chance to nominate their favourite local restaurant. This year over 44,500 nominations flooded into The Good Food Guide, as diners across the UK rushed to recognise the top-notch food and fantastic service being offered by their neighbourhood eateries. Consultant Editor Elizabeth Carter says, 'What makes these awards so special is that they are based on feedback from The Good Food Guide readers – the people who are out there eating and enjoying food every day. What higher compliment could there be?' From a stellar shortlist of regional winners, The Good Food Guide editors picked an overall Restaurant of the Year – Van Zeller, in Harrogate, whose award was presented by The Good Food Guide's Chef of the Year for 2012, Angela Hartnett.

The Readers' Restaurant of the Year 2013
Van Zeller, Harrogate

Regional Restaurant of the Year Winners

1. **Wales**
   Y Polyn, Carmarthen

2. **East England**
   Maison Bleue,
   Bury St Edmunds

3. **London**
   Charlotte's Place, Ealing

4. **North East**
   Van Zeller, Harrogate

5. **South East**
   Jeremy's Restaurant,
   Haywards Heath

6. **South West**
   The Swan, Wedmore

7. **Midlands**
   The Bluebell,
   Henley-in-Arden

8. **Scotland**
   Ubiquitous Chip, Glasgow

9. **North West**
   Grenache, Manchester

10. **Northern Ireland**
    Mourne Seafood Bar,
    Belfast

Longest-serving restaurants

The Good Food Guide was founded in 1951. The following restaurants have appeared consistently since their first entry into the Guide.

The Connaught, London, 60 years

Gravetye Manor, East Grinstead, 56 years

Porth Tocyn Hotel, Abersoch, 56 years

Sharrow Bay, Ullswater, 52 years

Le Gavroche, London, 43 years

Ubiquitous Chip, Glasgow, 41 years

Plumber Manor, Sturminster Newton, 40 years

The Druidstone, Broad Haven, 40 years

The Waterside Inn, Bray, 40 years

Airds Hotel, Port Appin, 37 years

Farlam Hall, Brampton, 36 years

Corse Lawn House Hotel, Corse Lawn, 34 years

Hambleton Hall, Hambleton, 34 years

The Pier at Harwich, Harbourside Restaurant, Harwich, 34 years

Magpie Café, Whitby, 33 years

RSJ, London, 32 years

The Seafood Restaurant, Padstow, 32 years

The Sir Charles Napier, Chinnor, 32 years

Kalpna, Edinburgh, 31 years

Le Caprice, London, 31 years

Little Barwick House, Barwick, 31 years

Inverlochy Castle, Fort William, 30 years

Ostlers Close, Cupar, 30 years

The Cellar, Anstruther, 29 years

Brilliant, London, 28 years

Clarke's, London, 28 years

Le Manoir aux Quat'Saisons, Great Milton, 28 years

Roade House, Roade, 28 years

Blostin's, Shepton Mallet, 27 years

Read's, Faversham, 27 years

The Castle at Taunton, Taunton, 27 years

The Three Chimneys, Isle of Skye, 27 years

Wallett's Court, St Margaret's-at-Cliffe, 27 years

Northcote, Langho, 26 years

ramsons, Ramsbottom, 26 years

Weavers, Haworth, 25 years

The Old Vicarage, Ridgeway, 25 years

Le Champignon Sauvage, Cheltenham, 24 years

Kensington Place, London, 24 years

Quince & Medlar, Cockermouth, 24 years

Silver Darling, Aberdeen, 24 years

Bibendum, London, 23 years

The Great House, Lavenham, 23 years

Ynyshir Hall, Eglwysfach, 23 years

Dylanwad Da, Dolgellau, 23 years

Top 50 restaurants 2013

A placing within *The Good Food Guide*'s Top 50 listing is greatly coveted by chefs and restaurateurs. This year, we have seen something very interesting at the top...

1. The Fat Duck, Berkshire (10)
2. L'Enclume, Cumbria (10)
3. Restaurant Sat Bains, Nottinghamshire (9)
4. Restaurant Gordon Ramsay, Royal Hospital Road, London (9)
5. Restaurant Nathan Outlaw, Cornwall (9)
6. Pollen Street Social, London (9)
7. Le Manoir aux Quat'Saisons, Oxfordshire (8)
8. Hibiscus, London (8)
9. The Square, London (8)
10. The Ledbury, London (8)
11. Marcus Wareing at the Berkeley, London (8)
12. Le Champignon Sauvage, Gloucestershire (8)
13. Adam Simmonds at Danesfield House, Buckinghamshire (8)
14. Le Gavroche, London (8)
15. Alain Ducasse at the Dorchester, London (8)
16. Whatley Manor, The Dining Room, Wiltshire (8)
17. The Waterside Inn, Berkshire (7)
18. Midsummer House, Cambridgeshire (7)
19. Dinner by Heston Blumenthal, London (7)
20. Pied-à-Terre, London (7)
21. The Kitchin, Edinburgh (7)
22. Murano, London (7)
23. Restaurant Martin Wishart, Edinburgh (7)
24. Gidleigh Park, Devon (7)
25. Fraiche, Merseyside (7)
26. Robert Thompson at the Hambrough, Isle of Wight (7)
27. The Crown at Whitebrook, Gwent (7)
28. The Pass, West Sussex (7)
29. Michael Wignall, the Latymer at Pennyhill Park Hotel, Surrey (7)
30. Fischer's Baslow Hall, Derbyshire (7)
31. Hambleton Hall, Rutland (7)
32. The Peat Inn, Fife (7)
33. Andrew Fairlie at Gleneagles, Tayside (7)
34. The Old Vicarage, Derbyshire (7)
35. The Artichoke, Buckinghamshire (7)
36. The Hand & Flowers, Buckinghamshire (6)
37. Purnell's, West Midlands (6)
38. Tyddyn Llan, Denbighshire (6)
39. Mr Underhill's, Shropshire (6)
40. Bohemia, Jersey (6)
41. The Sportsman, Kent (6)
42. The Creel, Orkney (6)
43. Simon Radley at the Chester Grosvenor, Cheshire (6)
44. The Yorke Arms, Ramsgill, North Yorkshire (6)
45. The Royal Oak, Paley Street, Berkshire (6)
46. Galvin La Chapelle, London (6)
47. Paul Ainsworth at No. 6, Cornwall (6)
48. The Box Tree, West Yorkshire (6)
49. Castle Terrace, Edinburgh (6)
50. Tuddenham Mill, Suffolk (6)

How to use the Guide

Each year *The Good Food Guide* is completely rewritten and compiled from scratch.
Our research list is based on the huge volume of feedback we receive from readers; the list
of many of our contributors at the back of the book is testimony to their dedication. This
feedback, together with anonymous inspections, ensures that every entry is assessed afresh.
To everyone who has used our feedback system (www.thegoodfoodguide.co.uk/feedback)
over the last year, many thanks, and please keep the reports coming in.

Symbols

Restaurants that may be given Main Entry or Also Recommended status are contacted
ahead of publication and asked to provide key information about their opening hours and
facilities. They are also invited to participate in the £5 voucher scheme. The symbols on these
entries are based on this feedback from restaurants, and are intended for quick, at-a-glance
identification. This year, our wine-bottle accolade recognises restaurants whose wine lists
might be outstanding for one of a number of reasons, be it strong options by the glass, an
in-depth focus on a particular region, or attractive margins on fine wines. For more detailed
notes, please visit www.thegoodfoodguide.co.uk

    🛏   Accommodation is available.

    £30   It is possible to have three courses (excluding wine) at the restaurant
    ▼   for less than £30.

    V   The restaurant has a separate vegetarian menu.

    £5   The restaurant is participating in our £5 voucher scheme.
    OFF   (Please see the vouchers at the end of the book for terms and conditions.)

    🍾   The restaurant has a wine list that our wine expert has deemed
    outstanding. Please visit www.thegoodfoodguide.co.uk for notes on
    the individual restaurants.

    £XX   The price indicated on each review represents the average price of a
    three-course dinner, excluding wine.

Scoring

In our opinion the restaurants included in *The Good Food Guide* are the very best in the UK; this means that simply getting an entry is an accomplishment to be proud of, and a Score 1 or above is a significant achievement.

We reject many restaurants during the compilation of the Guide. There are always subjective aspects to rating systems, but our inspectors are equipped with extensive scoring guidelines to ensure that restaurant bench-marking around the UK is accurate. We also take into account the reader feedback that we receive for each restaurant, so that any given review is based on several meals.

Score 1   Capable cooking, with simple food combinations and clear flavours, but some inconsistencies.

Score 2   Decent cooking, displaying good basic technical skills and interesting combinations and flavours. Occasional inconsistencies.

Score 3   Good cooking, showing sound technical skills and using quality ingredients.

Score 4   Dedicated, focused approach to cooking; good classical skills and high-quality ingredients.

Score 5   Exact cooking techniques and a degree of ambition; showing balance and depth of flavour in dishes, while using quality ingredients.

Score 6   Exemplary cooking skills, innovative ideas, impeccable ingredients and an element of excitement.

Score 7   High level of ambition and individuality, attention to the smallest detail, accurate and vibrant dishes.

Score 8   A kitchen cooking close to or at the top of its game – highly individual, showing faultless technique and impressive artistry in dishes that are perfectly balanced for flavour, combination and texture. There is little room for disappointment here.

Score 9   This mark is for cooking that has reached a pinnacle of achievement, making it a hugely memorable experience for the diner.

Score 10   It is extremely rare that a restaurant can achieve perfect dishes on a consistent basis.

'New chef' in place of a score indicates that the restaurant has had a recent change of chef; we particularly welcome reports on these restaurants. Also Recommended reviews are not scored but our inspectors think they are worth considering if you are in the area. Readers Recommend reviews are supplied by readers. These entries are the local, up-and-coming places to watch and represent the voice of our thousands of loyal followers.

London Explained

London is split into six regions: Central, North, East, South, West and Greater. Restaurants within each region are listed alphabetically. Each Main Entry and Also Recommended entry has a map reference.

The lists below are a guide to the areas covered in each region.

London — Central
Belgravia, Bloomsbury, Covent Garden, Fitzrovia, Holborn, Hyde Park, Lancaster Gate, Leicester Square, Marble Arch, Marylebone, Mayfair, Oxford Circus, Piccadilly, Soho, Trafalgar Square, Westminster

London — North
Archway, Belsize Park, Camden, Euston, Golders Green, Hampstead, Islington, Kentish Town, King's Cross, Neasden, Primrose Hill, Stoke Newington, Swiss Cottage, West Hampstead, Willesden

London — East
Arnold Circus, Barbican, Bethnal Green, Blackfriars, Canary Wharf, City, Clerkenwell, Dalston, Farringdon, Hackney, Hackney Wick, Moorgate, St Paul's, Shoreditch, Spitalfields, Tower Hill, Wapping, Whitechapel

London — South
Balham, Battersea, Bermondsey, Blackheath, Borough, Brixton, Camberwell, Clapham, East Dulwich, Elephant and Castle, Forest Hill, Greenwich, Putney, South Bank, Southwark, Stockwell, Tooting, Vauxhall, Wandsworth, Wimbledon

London — West
Belgravia, Chelsea, Chiswick, Earl's Court, Ealing, Fulham, Hammersmith, Kensal Rise, Kensington, Knightsbridge, Ladbroke Grove, Notting Hill, Olympia, Pimlico, Shepherd's Bush, South Kensington

London — Greater
Barnes, Croydon, Crystal Palace, East Sheen, Gants Hill, Harrow-on-the-Hill, Kew, Richmond, Southall, Surbiton, Sutton, Teddington, Twickenham, Walthamstow, Wood Green

LONDON

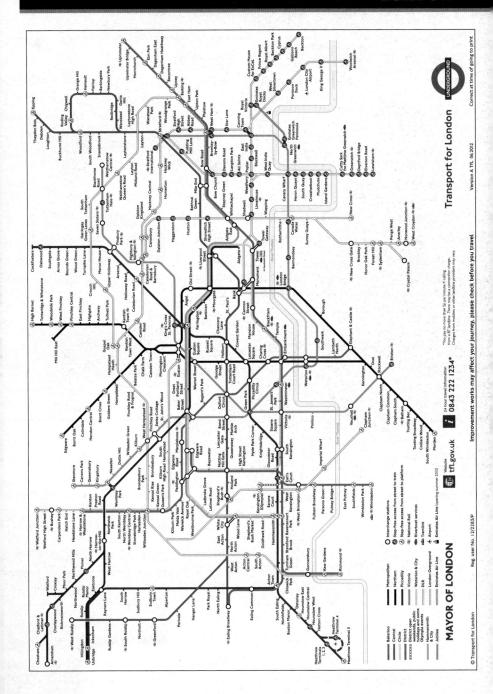

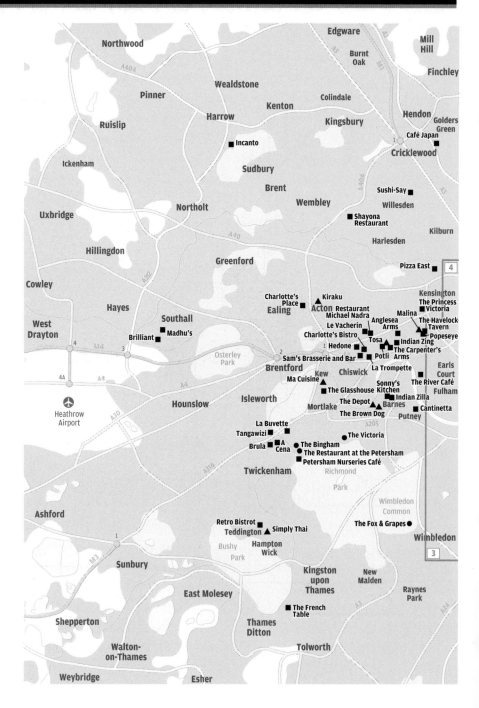

Northwood

Edgware

Mill Hill

Finchley

Burnt Oak

Wealdstone

Pinner

Kenton

Colindale

Hendon

Golders Green

Harrow

Kingsbury

Café Japan

Ruislip

Cricklewood

Ickenham

■ Incanto

Sudbury

Brent

Sushi-Say ■

Uxbridge

Northolt

Wembley

Willesden

■ Shayona Restaurant

Kilburn

Hillingdon

Harlesden

Greenford

Cowley

Pizza East ■

4

Hayes

Kensington
The Princess Victoria

West Drayton

Southall

Charlotte's Place

Kiraku

Acton

Restaurant Michael Nadra

Malina

The Havelock Tavern

Brilliant ■ Madhu's

Ealing

Le Vacherin

Anglesea Arms

Popeseye

Charlotte's Bistro

Tosa

Indian Zing

Hedone

The Carpenter's Arms

Sam's Brasserie and Bar ■

Potli

La Trompette

Earls Court
The River Café

Brentford

Kew

Chiswick

Ma Cuisine

Sonny's Kitchen

Osterley Park

The Glasshouse

Indian Zilla

Fulham

Heathrow Airport

Isleworth

The Depot

Barnes

Cantinetta

Hounslow

Mortlake

The Brown Dog

Putney

La Buvette

Tangawizi

The Victoria

Brula

A Cena

The Bingham
The Restaurant at the Petersham
Petersham Nurseries Café

Twickenham

Richmond Park

Wimbledon Common

Ashford

Retro Bistrot
Teddington

Simply Thai

The Fox & Grapes ●

Wimbledon

Hampton Wick

Bushy Park

3

Sunbury

Kingston upon Thames

New Malden

Raynes Park

East Molesey

■ The French Table

Shepperton

Thames Ditton

Tolworth

Walton-on-Thames

Weybridge

Esher

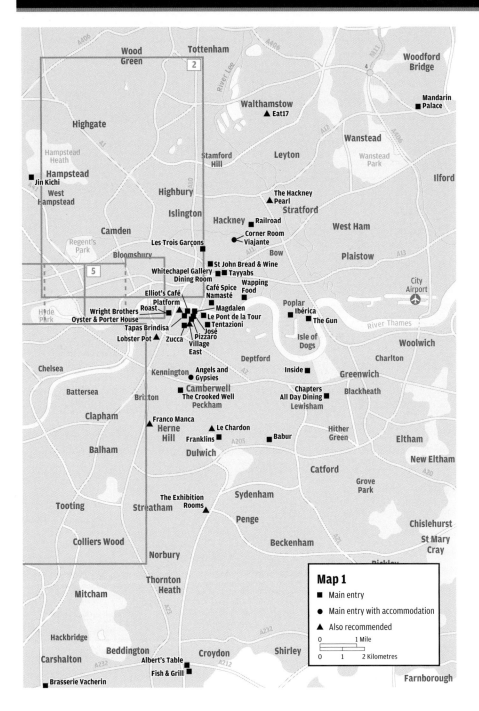

Map 1

■ Main entry

● Main entry with accommodation

▲ Also recommended

0   1 Mile

0   1   2 Kilometres

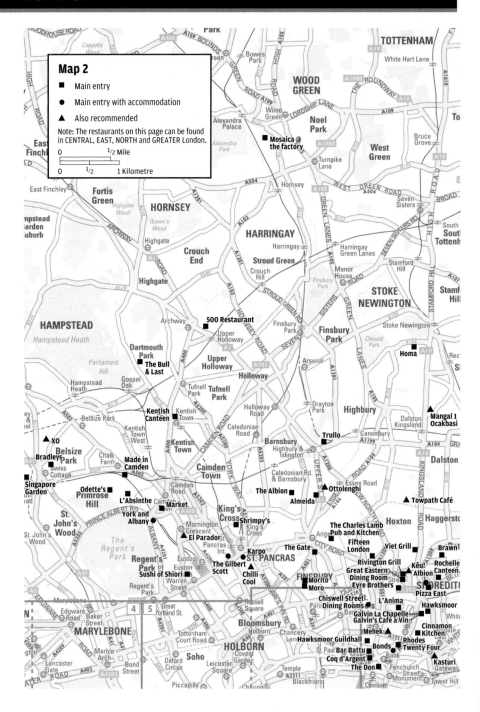

Map 2

- ■ Main entry
- ● Main entry with accommodation
- ▲ Also recommended

Note: The restaurants on this page can be found in CENTRAL, EAST, NORTH and GREATER London.

0   1/2 Mile

0   1/2   1 Kilometre

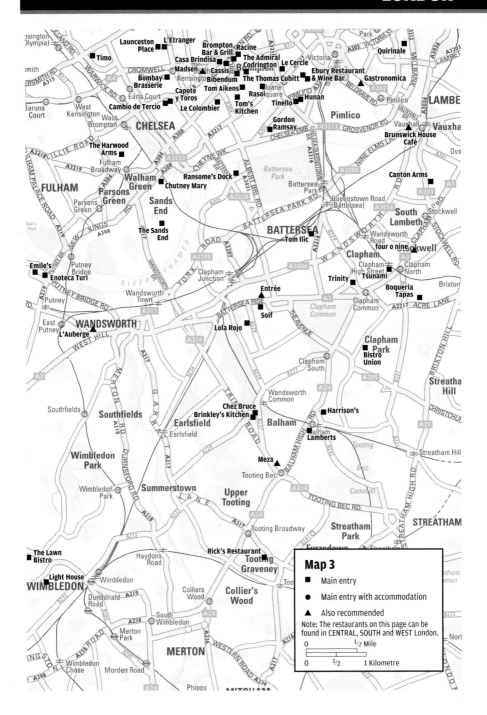

Map 3 showing London restaurant locations including areas: Kensington (Olympia), Chelsea, Fulham, Battersea, Clapham, Wandsworth, Wimbledon, Balham, Tooting, Streatham, Merton, Pimlico, Vauxhall, Lambeth, Brixton.

Restaurant labels on map:

Timo, Launceston Place, L'Etranger, Brompton Bar & Grill, Racine, Casa Brindisa, The Admiral Codrington, Le Cercle, Victoria, Quirinale, Madsen, Cassis, Bombay Brasserie, Kensington, Bibendum, The Thomas Cubitt, Ebury Restaurant & Wine Bar, Gastronomica, Tom Aikens, Capote y Toros, Rasoi, Hunan, Cambio de Tercio, Le Colombier, Tom's Kitchen, Tinello, Gordon Ramsay, Pimlico, Brunswick House Café, The Harwood Arms, Fulham Broadway, Walham Green, Ransome's Dock, Chutney Mary, Canton Arms, Parsons Green, Sands End, Battersea, Queenstown Road (Battersea), South Lambeth, Stockwell, The Sands End, Tom Ilic, Wandsworth Road, four o nine, Emile's, Enoteca Turi, Putney Bridge, Clapham Junction, Clapham, Tsunami, Trinity, Boqueria Tapas, Brixton, Entrée, Soif, L'Auberge, Lola Rojo, Clapham Park, Bistro Union, Streatham Hill, Chez Bruce, Brinkley's Kitchen, Harrison's, Southfields, Earlsfield, Balham, Lamberts, Wimbledon Park, Meza, Summerstown, Upper Tooting, The Lawn Bistro, Rick's Restaurant, Tooting Graveney, Light House, Collier's Wood, Streatham Park, WIMBLEDON, MERTON, STREATHAM

Map 3

- ■ Main entry
- ● Main entry with accommodation
- ▲ Also recommended

Note: The restaurants on this page can be found in CENTRAL, SOUTH and WEST London.

0 — 1/2 Mile

0 — 1/2 — 1 Kilometre

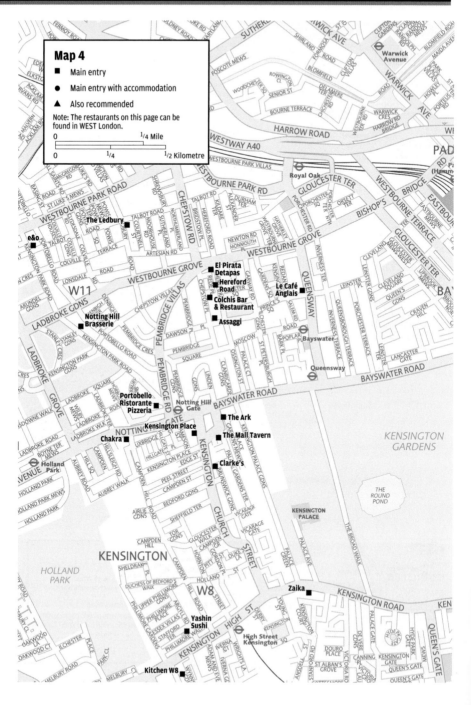

Map 4

■ Main entry

● Main entry with accommodation

▲ Also recommended

Note: The restaurants on this page can be found in WEST London.

| 0 | | ¼ Mile |
| 0 | ¼ | ½ Kilometre |

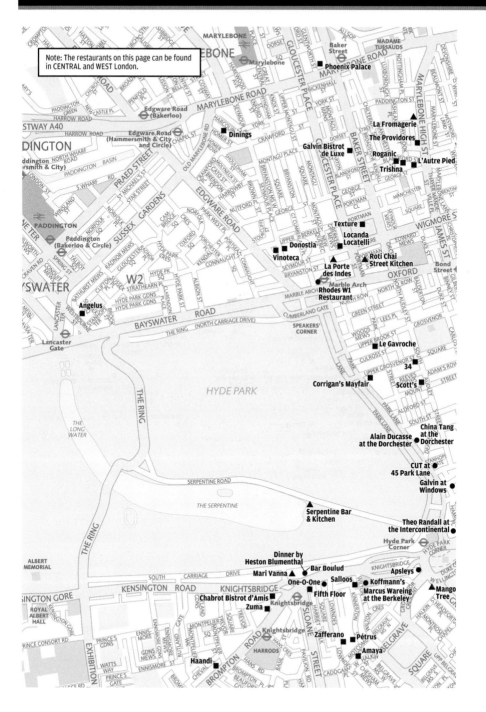

Note: The restaurants on this page can be found in CENTRAL and WEST London.

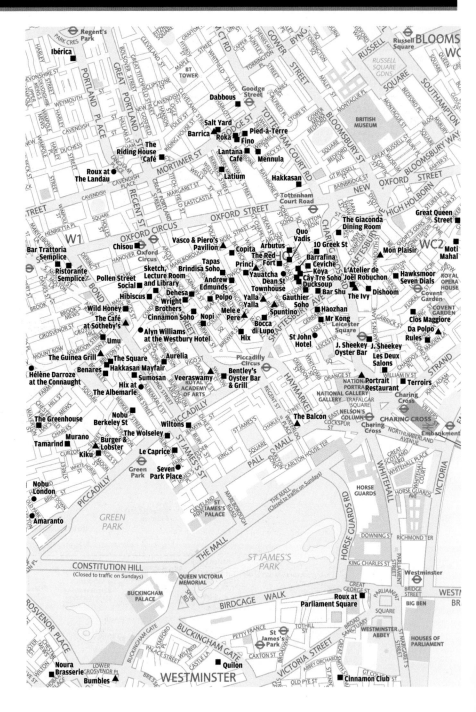

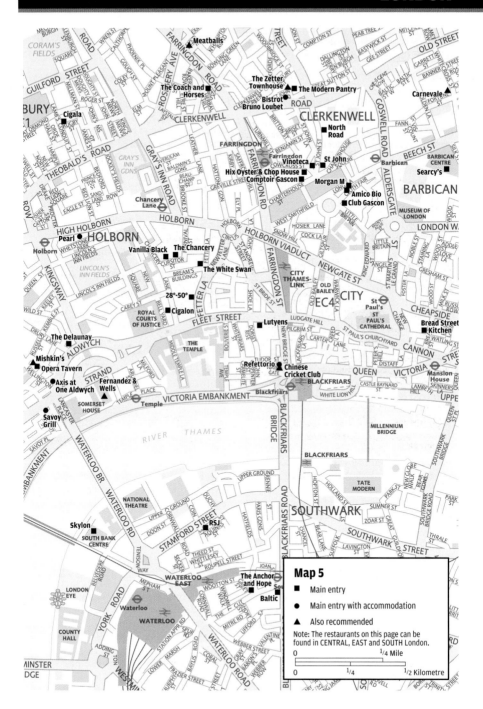

Map 5

- ■ Main entry
- ● Main entry with accommodation
- ▲ Also recommended

Note: The restaurants on this page can be found in CENTRAL, EAST and SOUTH London.

0   ¼ Mile

0   ¼   ½ Kilometre

★ TOP 50 ★

Alain Ducasse at the Dorchester

A corner of France on Park Lane
The Dorchester Hotel, 53 Park Lane, Hyde Park, W1K 1QA
Tel no: (020) 7629 8866
www.alainducasse-dorchester.com
⊖ Hyde Park Corner, map 4
Modern French | £85
Cooking score: 8

Behind half-frosted windows opposite Hyde Park, the Alain Ducasse restaurant at the Dorchester is the hotel's very own corner of France. Here, in a room divided by organically shaped screens and with a prevailing tone of very pale green, the menus speak another language, though with translations (the English for 'cookpot' turns out to be 'cookpot'). Ducasse's food has never been about breathless avant-garderie, but is nonetheless confident in bringing together elements of a dish that remain unfamiliar to British tradition. A *sauté gourmand* of lobster is partnered with chicken quenelles and homemade pasta for a starter on the main carte, and might be followed by sea bass seasoned with citrus and accompanied by chards in two colours – green and white. The dual-colour motif turns up again in a meat course, this time in the form of orange and yellow carrots to go with loin of milk-fed Limousin veal. The Lunch Hour menu, with its almost provocatively simple dishes – a soft-boiled egg with artichoke, seared Arctic char with fennel – is still capable of turning up rich and exciting flavours. Among desserts, the 'Baba like in Monte Carlo' may have lost something in translation, but is actually a bespoke exercise in which you get to choose your own rum. For a more palate-sharpening twang, go for the quince and grapefruit tart, which comes with a perfumed Earl Grey sorbet. The classical wine list starts at £25 for reds, £35 for whites. If you have the resources, sign up for the sommelier's wine flights, which

are largely (though not quite exclusively) about celebrating the treasures of the French vineyards.
Chef/s: Jocelyn Herland. **Open:** Tue to Fri L 12 to 2, Tue to Sat D 6.30 to 10. **Closed:** Sun, Mon, 26 to 30 Dec, 6 to 9 Apr, 2 to 5 Jun, 14 Aug to 5 Sept. **Meals:** Set L £55. Set D £60 (2 courses) to £85. Tasting menu £120 (8 courses) to £180. **Service:** 12.5%. **Details:** 82 seats. Separate bar. Wheelchair access. Music. Children over 10 yrs only.

NEW ENTRY
Alyn Williams at the Westbury

Wareing's right-hand man goes solo
The Westbury Hotel, 37 Conduit Street, Mayfair, W1S 2YF
Tel no: (020) 7629 7755
www.westburymayfair.com
⊖ Oxford Circus, map 5
Modern British | £45
Cooking score: 5

Having bided his time as Marcus Wareing's right-hand man at the Berkeley for five years, Alyn Williams now has his own name above the door of a five-star hotel restaurant. Alyn Williams at the Westbury sends out mixed messages: the rosewood panelling, generously spaced tables and handsome, glass-fronted 'wine salon' (private dining room) at centre stage bespeak serious fine dining, while the sparkly carpet, jovial staff and quirky desserts (e.g. 'walnut whip' with marshmallow and walnut ice cream) suggest something more offbeat. Williams has hit his creative stride immediately. Combinations from the carte such as sand carrot, liquorice and foie gras or, to follow, Cotswold white chicken, girolles, smoked egg and charred leek are modish but not over-complex. The tasting menu (£55), meanwhile, ticks off a few food trends ('beach vegetables' with cod; foie gras 'semifreddo' with frozen yoghurt) without foregoing gravitas. Presentation is precise, portions small. Vegetarians come up trumps – they get a tasting menu and a carte – alongside the same plus set lunch for the omnivores.

Cherry-picking from the menus is allowed – just one of several guest-friendly touches we applaud. Plenty of interest at the lower reaches of the heavyweight wine list (from £19.50) is another.
Chef/s: Alyn Williams. **Open:** Mon to Fri L 12 to 2.30, Mon to Sat D 6 to 10.30. **Closed:** 25 and 26 Dec. **Meals:** Set L £20 (2 courses) to £24. Set D £40 (2 courses) to £45. **Service:** 12.5%. **Details:** 54 seats. No music. Wheelchair access. Car parking.

Amaranto

Sultry opulence and souped-up Italian cuisine
Four Seasons Hotel, Hamilton Place, Park Lane, Mayfair, W1J 7DR
Tel no: (020) 7319 5206
www.fourseasons.com
⊖ Hyde Park Corner, Green Park, map 5
Italian | £70
Cooking score: 4

⊨ V

Money is no object at this all-inclusive lounge-bar-restaurant hybrid on the ground floor of the revamped Four Seasons Hotel – as you might expect from the glitzy address. Shades of blood-red amaranth (the plant that gives the restaurant its name) mingle with black lacquering and shiny marble surfaces to create a sultry vision of opulence. The restaurant deals in artfully souped-up Italian cuisine: pasta is a sure-fire hit and the kitchen rolls out some inspired variations on the theme, from wild boar ravioli with silky pumpkin 'vellutata', chestnuts and guanciale (cured pig's cheek) to egg-free rigatoni 'alla carbonara Prosecco'. Moving on, high levels of technical prowess are also required for, say, veal fillet with pecorino and ricotta on braised pearl barley and red Moscato grapes with black cabbage purée. To conclude, submit to the chocolate-based excesses of 'six little sins'. Virtually everything on the vast, all-Italian wine list is available by the glass, but expect to pay upwards of £10 a shot for the privilege.
Chef/s: Adriano Cavagnini and Davide Degiovanni. **Open:** all week L 12 to 2, D 6 to 10.30. **Meals:** alc (main courses £11 to £30). Set L £19.50 (2 courses)

to £26. Tasting menu £95 (6 courses). **Service:** 15%. **Details:** 52 seats. 30 seats outside. Separate bar. Wheelchair access. Music.

Andrew Edmunds

Wine-loving Soho stalwart
46 Lexington Street, Soho, W1F 0LW
Tel no: (020) 7437 5708
⊖ Oxford Circus, Piccadilly Circus, map 5
Modern European | £35
Cooking score: 2
🍾

This wine-loving stalwart is part of the Soho old guard, right down to its candlelit Dickensian interiors, floral displays and cramped pew seating (upstairs and down). It might feel like a 70s throwback, but the crowds keep piling in to imbibe and feed on generous plates of colourfully eclectic food – cauliflower fritters with coriander yoghurt, roast octopus with new potatoes and wilted wild garlic, spatchcock quail with roast beetroot, chickpea and cumin salad. The line-up is tweaked every session, with patriotic puds such as rhubarb fool or damson and sloe gin ice cream bringing up the rear. Owner Andrew Edmunds is a knowledgeable and passionate wine buff, and his quirky list is full of oddball discoveries, boutique bottles and bargains galore – with painless mark-ups to boot. Prices start at £17.50 (£5 a glass).
Chef/s: Roberto Piaggesi. **Open:** all week L 12.30 to 3 (1 to 3 Sat, 1 to 3.30 Sun), D 6 to 10.45 (10.30 Sun). **Closed:** 24 Dec to 2 Jan, Easter, Aug bank hol. **Meals:** alc (main courses £11 to £22). **Service:** 12.5%. **Details:** 45 seats. 4 seats outside. No music.

Angelus

A corner of France in London
4 Bathurst Street, Lancaster Gate, W2 2SD
Tel no: (020) 7402 0083
www.angelusrestaurant.co.uk
⊖ Lancaster Gate, map 4
Modern French | £55
Cooking score: 4

'A unique corner of France in London' is one
verdict on this smart, professionally run venue
in Lancaster Gate. Indeed, in an area poorly
served by quality restaurants, intimate, elegant
Angelus has settled into a very nice groove. A
lot of effort has gone into creating a mood that
is 'incredibly warm, comfortable and
unpretentious'. The kitchen takes British raw
ingredients and treats them with French
subtlety: as in escabèche of Cornish mackerel
(with celeriac and apple) or slow-roasted
shoulder of Elwy salt marsh lamb (with caper
berries, cauliflower gratin and honey-glazed
carrots). The house speciality of foie gras
crème brûlée continues to draw praise, as does
the excellent value prix-fixe lunch menu, and
the outside seating (with heaters) is a bonus.
The extensive wine list shows owner Thierry
Tomasin's great knowledge of wine – it is full
of interesting surprises, with some off-the-
beaten-track gems alongside the classics.
Prices from £25.
Chef/s: Martin Nisbet. **Open:** all week 10am to 11pm
(10pm Sun). **Closed:** 24 Dec to 2 Jan. **Meals:** alc
(main courses £20 to £32). Set L £42.
Service: 12.5%. **Details:** 40 seats. 12 seats outside.
Separate bar. Music.

Symbols

🛏 Accommodation is available

💷30 Three courses for less than £30

V Separate vegetarian menu

£5 OFF £5-off voucher scheme

🍾 Notable wine list

Apsleys

Glamour, thrills and fabulous Italian flavours
The Lanesborough, Hyde Park Corner, Hyde Park,
SW1X 7TA
Tel no: (020) 7333 7254
www.lanesborough.com
⊖ Hyde Park Corner, map 4
Italian | £60
Cooking score: 6

It may take its title from nearby Apsley House
(one-time home of the Duke of Wellington),
but this is undeniably a Heinz Beck restaurant,
fronted by the German über-chef. It's a
glamorous dining room, with Art Deco
flourishes and three extraordinary chandeliers
suspended from a glass atrium, while the
cooking inhabits the same heady, extravagant
world as Beck's star-spangled eatery in Rome.
The prestige seasonal tasting menu is a seven-
course display of technical virtuosity peppered
with 'high-grade ingredients' and fabulously
defined flavours. Thrills are many and artfully
contrived, from a brilliant slow-cooked egg
with amaranth and Alba truffle to fabulously
rich game tortellini with pumpkin and
Parmesan cream, or a delightful take on the
Wellington theme involving beautifully
cooked Anjou pigeon coated with a silky
mustard seed sauce and a thin layer of pastry.
Elsewhere, the menu delivers some of the best
antipasti in town – from veal terrine
croquettes to scallops with asparagus (plus
some extra Sturia caviar) – as well as a near-
legendary retread of pasta carbonara involving
bite-sized parcels of fagottelli filled with
luscious creamy sauce. To conclude, the
sweetness of an Amedei 'Chuao' chocolate
dome is hard to resist. Uniformed staff play it
suitably cool; the wine list goes with the
immoderate financial flow, peddling
European big hitters from £35 upwards.
Chef/s: Heros de Agostinis. **Open:** all week L 12.30
to 1.30, D 7 to 10 (7.30 to 10 Sat and Sun).
Meals: alc (main courses £29 to £38). Set L £25 (2
courses) to £35. Set D £45. Tasting menu £65 (5

courses) to £85 (7 courses). **Service:** 12.5%.
Details: 110 seats. Separate bar. Wheelchair access.
Music. Car parking.

Arbutus

Groundbreaking Soho eatery
63-64 Frith Street, Soho, W1D 3JW
Tel no: (020) 7734 4545
www.arbutusrestaurant.co.uk
⊖ Tottenham Court Road, map 5
Modern European | £32
Cooking score: 5

Back in the late noughties, Arbutus was the
talk of the town – an uncompromising star
performer famed for its rigorous seasonal
sourcing, butch ingredients and pioneering
attitude to wine. Fast-forward a few years and
the place seems to have lost some of its sheen
and virtuosic oomph, with reports of 'matter-
of-fact cooking' on the increase. That said,
noisy crowds still pack the elbow-to-elbow
dining room for seasonal triumphs including
a 'pretty springtime salmagundi' of fresh goats'
cheese, peas, broad beans and marjoram
draped with young radishes – stems, leaves
and all. In meatier territory, a 'very fine' two-
part rabbit dish involving roast saddle and a
cottage pie offers rustic nourishment for the
inner man, likewise a bowl of melting pork
'petit salé' with some pungent saucisse, Puy
lentils and dark greens. Sadly, other ideas sit
less comfortably on the palate – witness an
off-key pairing of roast cod and sticky chicken
wings with a dollop of potent pink grapefruit,
ginger and honey conserve ('like X-rated
marmalade'). But all is forgiven when the
kitchen wheels out its masterstroke – a
seriously wobbly, nutmeg-tinged custard tart
embellished with plump sultanas and pine
nuts ('sheer perfection'). Be warned: meals
often proceed at break-neck speed and service
seems to be becoming increasingly unreliable,
with uninterested staff prone to 'idle chat and
clock-watching'. Thankfully, the lively wine
list still makes its point, with everything
available by the 250ml carafe and bottles
from £17.50.

Chef/s: Anthony Demetre and Alan Christie. **Open:**
all week L 12 to 2.30 (3 Sun), D 5 to 11 (10.30 Sun).
Closed: 25 and 26 Dec, 1 Jan. **Meals:** alc (main
courses £16 to £23). Set L £17.95 (2 courses) to
£19.95. Pre-theatre set D £18.95 (2 courses) to
£20.95. **Service:** 12.5%. **Details:** 70 seats. No music.

L'Atelier de Joël Robuchon

Technical marvels and classic French modes
13-15 West Street, Covent Garden, WC2H 9NE
Tel no: (020) 7010 8600
www.joel-robuchon.com
⊖ Leicester Square, map 5
Modern French | £72
Cooking score: 6

V

Putting his menu where his mouth is, Joël
Robuchon describes London as 'the
gastronomic capital of Europe', and here, at a
discreetly fronted venue in the West End, he is
an enthusiastic participant in the action. It all
extends over three levels: a bar at the top, a
conventional dining room on the first floor,
and, on the ground floor, counter seating on
stools with views into the kitchen. A plethora
of menus includes mix-and-match formats at
various fixed prices, small taster portions, the
main carte (plus veggie version), and the
'Découverte' tasting menus. The influences are
many and varied, so a Spanish-inspired starter
of jamón Ibérico de Bellota with toasted
tomato bread may be followed by Japanese-
style cod in yuzu broth with lily bulbs. There
are technical marvels too, in the form perhaps
of a soft-poached egg 'battered' in crispy rice
with osciètre caviar, as well as dishes that lean
to classical French modes; a main-course quail
stuffed with foie gras, served with truffled
mash, for example. Desserts may then go
typically tropical for passion fruit and banana
crémeux with rum granité and coconut foam.
France leads the wines, with shorter shrift
given elsewhere. Bottles start at £26 (£6 a
glass).

Chef/s: Olivier Limousin. **Open:** all week L 12 to
2.30, D 5.30 to 10.30. **Closed:** 25 and 26 Dec, 1 Jan,
Aug bank hol. **Meals:** alc (main courses £19 to £32).
Set L and pre-theatre D £28 (2 courses) to £40.

Tasting menu £125 (10 courses). **Service:** 12.5%. **Details:** 43 seats. Separate bar. Wheelchair access. Music. Car parking.

NEW ENTRY

Aurelia

Wildly delicious Mediterranean flavours in Mayfair

13-14 Cork Street, Mayfair, W1S 3NS
Tel no: (020) 7409 1370
www.aurelialondon.co.uk
⊖ Piccadilly Circus, Green Park, map 5
Mediterranean | £40
Cooking score: 4

£5
OFF

The window boxes outside Cork Street's Aurelia are planted with neatly clipped rosemary. That tells you something about the new restaurant in the Roka/Zuma stable: there's an impulse to tame the Mediterranean's rugged ingredients for Mayfair's cashmere-clad diners. But you can't keep such wildly delicious flavours down. If the dishes (many cooked on the rotisserie in the basement dining room's open kitchen) look prim at times, they taste anything but. 'Courgette fritti' become something special garnished with excellent Parmesan and lemon, while Moroccan-style lamb cutlets – prettily scattered with dried rose petals – are juicy and generous, even at £23 with nothing on the side. Limoncello semifreddo with blood orange is a good finish. Everything is designed to be shared and is served 'as and when' (which suits only some dishes and some customers). Bills quickly mount up, aided by a Mediterranean wine list at Mayfair prices. Wine starts at £24.
Chef/s: Alex Simone. **Open:** all week L 12 to 3, D 6 to 11.30 (10 Sun). **Closed:** 25 and 26 Dec. **Meals:** alc (main courses £15 to £28). **Service:** 12.5%. **Details:** 80 seats. Separate bar. Wheelchair access. Music.

L'Autre Pied

Genuinely exciting big-city cooking

5-7 Blandford Street, Marylebone, W1U 3DB
Tel no: (020) 7486 9696
www.lautrepied.co.uk
⊖ Bond Street, map 4
Modern European | £44
Cooking score: 6

£5
OFF

Over the last 12 months, it has been all change in the kitchens of this confident little Marylebone flyer and its aristocratic elder sibling Pied-à-Terre (see entry), although each restaurant now seems at ease with its new main players. Both venues are still under David Moore's wing, but there have been some subtle and significant shifts of emphasis at L'Autre Pied since chef Marcus Eaves' departure: the moody black-walled space of yore has been replaced by a bland, comfortable interior; the menu no longer ambushes customers with hidden costs for extras; and portions have become distinctly generous. New boy Andrew McFadden is a 'master of complementary flavours' and can deliver some genuinely exciting dishes from the lexicon of big-city blockbusters: frothy Jerusalem artichoke soup with an amazing range of textures and lingering notes of toasted hazelnut and burnt Roscoff onion; a harmonious pairing of crunchy, spice-crusted brill with mussel cream, blobs of intense aubergine purée, sea purslane and tiny florets of pickled cauliflower. Readers have also drooled over beautifully composed plates of roast partridge with cabbage cannelloni, cavolo nero, caramelised onion and a 'lip-sticking' jus. Desserts are intricate and full of fine components, although some diners have found them too finicky for their own good – lime and vodka parfait with mandarin sorbet, coconut foam and chocolate streusel, for example. Attentive, professional service receives its share of plaudits, likewise the excellent selection of wines by the glass on the stylish, cosmopolitan list. Bottles from £25.

Chef/s: Andrew McFadden. **Open:** all week L 12 to 2.45 (2.30 Sat, 3.30 Sun), Mon to Sat D 6 to 10.45. **Closed:** 24 to 28 Dec. **Meals:** alc (main courses £16 to £33). Set L £18.95 (2 courses) to £22.50. Sun L £29.50. Tasting menu £67.50 (9 courses). **Service:** 12.5%. **Details:** 53 seats. 9 seats outside. Music.

Axis at One Aldwych

Thrilling interiors and satisfying food
1 Aldwych, Covent Garden, WC2B 4BZ
Tel no: (020) 7300 0300
www.onealdwych.com
⊖ Covent Garden, map 5
Modern British | £40
Cooking score: 2
£5 OFF 🍴 V

With modish design features and Thai silk panels, this dramatic subterranean dining room beneath One Aldwych is still something of a 'hidden gem', according to one devotee. The kitchen satisfies fans of Welsh rarebit and char-grilled Galloway ribeye, as well as those who like their food in the zeitgeist zone – think seared scallops with wild garlic risotto and nettle dressing or saddle of rabbit stuffed with langoustines alongside pickled carrots and rabbit scratchings. Bite-sized duck parcels have also gone down well, while dessert might bring gingerbread soufflé with banana ice cream. Polite service runs at a steady pace, and the well-spread wine list starts at £22.50.
Chef/s: Dominic Teague. **Open:** Tue to Fri L 12 to 2.30, Tue to Sat D 5.30 to 10.30 (5 Sat). **Closed:** Sun, Mon, 19 Dec to 10 Jan, bank hols. **Meals:** alc (main courses £14 to £24). Set L and D £18.75 (2 courses) to £21.75. **Service:** 12.5%. **Details:** 120 seats. Separate bar. Wheelchair access. Music.

🍴 **Average Price**

The average price listed in main-entry reviews denotes the price of a three-course meal, without wine.

ALSO RECOMMENDED

▲ The Balcon

Sofitel St James Hotel, 8 Pall Mall, St James's, SW1Y 5NG
Tel no: (020) 7968 2900
www.thebalconlondon.com
⊖ Piccadilly Circus, Charing Cross, map 5
Modern European

The Balcon appears very grand, with its Parisian brasserie good looks and prices that match its prime Mayfair location (it's part of the Sofitel St James Hotel). But while it's not cheap, it does cosset. The all-day menu is long enough to ensure most tastes are catered for. It offers an odd mix of French classics and English tradition, as in brioche 'toad-in-the-hole' with Lyonnaise pistachio sausage and garlic confit chicken jus (£9.75) or Scottish beef and foie gras cottage pie with chanterelle mushrooms (£23). Wines from £28. Open all week.

Bar Shu

Red-hot Szechuan firecracker
28 Frith Street, Soho, W1D 5LF
Tel no: (020) 7287 8822
www.bar-shu.co.uk
⊖ Leicester Square, map 5
Chinese | £25
Cooking score: 4
£30

King of the hill when it comes to Szechuan cuisine in Soho, this smart-casual firecracker remains a red-hot ticket for those who like their food dosed with scary anatomical offcuts and 'mouth-numbing' chillies. The hefty pictorial menu certainly delivers what it promises, be it stridently spiced platters of shredded dried beef ('like earthy biltong'), stewed duck tongues, gargantuan slow-cooked pork knuckle in a powerfully zesty dong-po gravy or slithery aubergine with a smoky, blazing-red sauce. But it's not all agony and ecstasy: the kitchen can also produce tip-top renditions of gentler favourites such as bouncy 'gobstopper' kung-po prawns bobbing in seafood broth. Veggies

should beware the 'meatless' dishes cooked in meat stock, and mild-mannered souls may be cowed by stern-faced 'good cop, bad cop' service, but this place still yields ample rewards. Wines (from £21.90) are heavily marked up, so stick to soothing green-tea drinks. Sibling Ba Shan is at 24 Romilly Street, while Baozi Inn at 25 Newport Court is tailor-made for a speedy, cut-price fix.
Chef/s: Zhang Xiao Chung. **Open:** all week 12 to 11 (12 to 11.30 Fri and Sat). **Closed:** 24 and 25 Dec. **Meals:** alc (main courses £10 to £33). **Service:** 12.5%. **Details:** 100 seats. Wheelchair access. Music.

Bar Trattoria Semplice
Flavour is everything
22-23 Woodstock Street, Mayfair, W1C 2AR
Tel no: (020) 7491 8638
www.bartrattoriasemplice.com
⊖ Bond Street, map 5
Italian | £30
Cooking score: 2

Bar Trattoria Semplice is an offshoot of Ristorante Semplice (see entry) just round the corner. The décor is upmarket café (lots of blond wood and elbow-to-elbow tables), matched by a menu of straightforward food made from fine ingredients treated simply. Flavour is everything in dishes such as octopus and potato salad with lemon dressing, ravioli filled with sheep's ricotta and spinach and served with butter and sage, or a classic lasagne (something of a house speciality). There's also lamb shank or ribeye steak, as well as a simple tiramisu or Italian cheeseboard to finish. The Italian wine list starts at £14.50.
Chef/s: Mariano Russo. **Open:** Mon to Fri L 12 to 4, D 5 to 10.30. Sat 12 to 11. Sun 12 to 9.30. **Closed:** 25 and 26 Dec. **Meals:** alc (main courses £15 to £22). Set L £19.50. **Service:** 12.5%. **Details:** 50 seats. Separate bar. Music.

▮▮● Also Recommended
Also recommended entries are not scored but we think they are worth a visit.

Barrafina
Crammed with good things
54 Frith Street, Soho, W1D 4SL
Tel no: (020) 7813 8016
www.barrafina.co.uk
⊖ Tottenham Court Road, map 5
Spanish | £25
Cooking score: 4

£30

'Not a dud dish' reports one enthusiastic reader of repeated visits to Sam and Eddie Hart's pint-sized tapas bar. Good things are crammed into this small Soho space; pans, chefs and glassware jostle with oils, vinegars and the excellent Spanish produce which, year on year, safeguards Barrafina's reputation. Chef Nieves Barragán Mohacho's knack with flavour extends beyond staples like ham croquetas or toast with allioli to a 'gorgeous' roast pork shoulder with sherry and quince jus or morcilla with piquillo peppers and quail eggs. Finish with Santiago tart or teeth-sticking turrón. None of the 23 stools at the bar can be reserved, so at busy times it can be difficult to see the jamón for the queue; to be assured of a seat, arrive before you're hungry. You can start drinking and nibbling while you stand and wait; the neat Spanish wine list starts at £18 and includes plenty of sherry.
Chef/s: Nieves Barragán Mohacho. **Open:** all week L 12 to 3 (1 to 3.30 Sun), D 5 to 11 (5.30 to 10 Sun). **Closed:** 25 and 26 Dec, 1 and 2 Jan, bank hols. **Meals:** alc (tapas £6 to £16). **Service:** 12.5%. **Details:** 23 seats. 12 seats outside.

ALSO RECOMMENDED
▲ Barrica
62 Goodge Street, Fitzrovia, W1T 4NE
Tel no: (020) 7436 9448
www.barrica.co.uk
⊖ Goodge Street, map 5
Spanish £5 off

Tables at the back of this deep, narrow room may be a little more relaxed than the stools around the bustling bar, but the authentic tapas on offer here is enjoyable wherever you can find a space. Well-sourced quality ingredients take centre-stage, whether it's Villarejo (rosemary Manchego made from ewes' milk, from £4) or daily specials such as braised lamb's breast with anchovy (£6.50). From the charcoal grill, try John Dory with asparagus (£6.95). House wine £15. Closed Sun.

Benares

Lovely treats and unforgettable Indian flavours
12a Berkeley Square, Mayfair, W1J 6BS
Tel no: (020) 7629 8886
www.benaresrestaurant.com
◉ Green Park, map 5
Indian | £55
Cooking score: 4

V

'A true delight', writes one excited correspondent – in fact re-energised Benares seems to be on a roll, delivering 'lovely treats' and waves of unforgettable flavours. The set-up now includes a chef's table and a ritzy bar for 'mind-blowing' cocktails (try the passion fruit and chutney martini), although the main business still takes place in the classy (if slightly 'austere') dining room. Gastro-guru Atul Kochhar's refined take on Indian cooking is typified by hirtan boti (a superlative, 'melting' dish of roast roe deer fillet partnered by venison pickle, peanut-sesame sauce and broccoli stir-fry), but his confident fusion of Asian spicing and European culinary technique also yields extravagant butter-poached lobster masala 'two ways' and slow-braised dum gosht (lamb shoulder with apricot, cumin and tangy sweet potatoes). Framing the main event is a list of crafty appetisers (spice-crusted scallops with cauliflower purée and piccalilli) and fascinating crossover desserts (star anise tarte Tatin with fennel and salted butter caramel). The 60-page wine list is designed for food matching, but intimidating prices (from £22) may deter cavalier experimentation.
Chef/s: Atul Kochhar. **Open:** Mon to Sat L 12 to 2.30, D 5.30 to 11. **Closed:** Sun, 24 to 27 Dec, 1 Jan. **Meals:** alc (main courses £24 to £54). Set L and D £25 (3 courses). **Service:** 12.5%. **Details:** 80 seats. Separate bar. Wheelchair access. Music. No children after 7.30.

Bentley's Oyster Bar & Grill

'Consistently excellent' food and polished service
11-15 Swallow Street, Piccadilly, W1B 4DG
Tel no: (020) 7734 4756
www.bentleys.org
◉ Piccadilly Circus, map 5
Seafood | £45
Cooking score: 4

As soon as Irish chef Richard Corrigan stepped aboard the deck of this venerable gastronomic galleon back in 2005, it took on a breezy new lease of life. The street-level oyster bar is an upbeat, marble-hued haven for those who like their crustaceans and bivalves *au naturel*, although the main action takes place in the clubby upstairs grill – a study in maritime blues and whites, with fishy paintings and William Morris fabrics. Shrewdly sourced seafood receives open-minded treatment, but there's also respect for the old ways: pots of Cornish mussels, lobster bisque and fish pie sit easily alongside stuffed squid with chorizo and feta or monkfish saltimbocca with morcilla, quince and kale. Meanwhile carnivores get their kicks from hefty mixed grills, veal T-bones and saddle of rabbit with black pudding. The food is 'consistently excellent' and polished service knows its ps and qs; however, there are issues with the cost of it all. The globetrotting, food-friendly wine list comes with a heavy price tag; that said, the quality is high and producers have been chosen with real care. Around 20 cracking selections by the glass or 500ml carafe (from £17) offer the best value.
Chef/s: Michael Lynch and Richard Corrigan. **Open:** all week L 12 to 3, D 6 to 11 (10 Sun). **Closed:** 25 Dec. **Meals:** alc (main courses £22 to £29). Set L £24.95. Sun L £45. **Service:** 12.5%. **Details:** 95 seats. 24 seats outside. Music.

Bocca di Lupo

Stunning plates bursting with Italian flavours
12 Archer Street, Piccadilly, W1D 7BB
Tel no: (020) 7734 2223
www.boccadilupo.com
⊖ **Piccadilly Circus, map 5**
Italian | £45
Cooking score: 4

This confident Italian in the heart of theatreland continues to thrive on accessibility, fair value and seriously considered cooking. Inside, it forgoes edgy statements in favour of a long, stool-lined bar and elbow-to-elbow bare wooden tables, with smart but affable service that matches the easy-going vibe. Forget conventional courses – on offer is a stunning line-up of small and large plates bursting with regional flavours. From Puglia there could be a raw broad bean salad with sheep's ricotta, pea shoots, lemon zest and mint, or 'very good' orecchiette with 'nduja (pork sausage), red onion, tomato and rocket from Calabria. But that's just the beginning. The cornucopia of delights might include veal tongue served with homemade and cured sausage, bread and bone marrow polenta, home-candied mostarda and salsa verde, and a selection of gelati from Gelupo, the firm's gelateria across the road. The modern wine list explores Italy with insightful selections and offers plenty by the glass or carafe, with bottles from £16.
Chef/s: Jacob Kenedy. **Open:** all week L 12.15 to 3 (12.30 Sun), Mon to Sat D 5.15 to 11 (5.30 Sun). **Closed:** Christmas period. **Meals:** alc (main courses £9 to £30). **Service:** 12.5%. **Details:** 62 seats. Wheelchair access. Music.

ALSO RECOMMENDED

▲ Bumbles

16 Buckingham Palace Road, Belgravia, SW1W 0QP
Tel no: (020) 7828 2903
www.bumbles1950.com
⊖ **Victoria, map 5**
Modern British £5 OFF

Victoria's most venerable restaurant is well into its sixth decade and it continues to offer 'great value in a handy location'. Chicken liver parfait, Gloucester Old Spot sausages with mash and 'a warm, gooey' chocolate brownie are typical of the £10 menu. Elsewhere you'll find Morecambe Bay shrimps and snail lasagne, duck breast and confit leg or tandoori-spiced bass with potato gnocchi, yoghurt and marinated cucumber at £19.50 for two courses and £23.50 for three. Wines from £13.50. Closed Sat L and Sun.

▲ Burger & Lobster

29 Clarges Street, Mayfair, W1J 7EF
Tel no: (020) 7409 1699
www.burgerandlobster.com
⊖ **Green Park, map 5**
North American

It's fun. It's got pizazz – an all-day eatery offering just three things: burgers, lobster rolls, grilled or boiled whole lobsters (desserts are a token gesture), with chips, salad, and bottles of Hellmann's mayo and Heinz tomato ketchup, for £20. Expensive for the burger, but most are here for lobster. The dining area jostles for space with the bar, you eat cheek-by-jowl, there's no booking and yet it's constantly rammed. Cheerful service is fast-paced. Good beers, wines from £22. Closed Sun D.

▲ The Café at Sotheby's
34–35 New Bond Street, Mayfair, W1A 2AA
Tel no: (020) 7293 5077
www.sothebys.com
⊖ Bond Street, Oxford Circus, map 5
Modern European

A darling of the art crowd, this appendage to
Sotheby's spills over into the foyer of the
auction house. The main bids are for lobster
club sandwiches at lunchtime, but the eclectic
daily menu also takes in anything from
marinated quail with pearl barley and broad
bean salad (£8.50) to herb-crusted hake with
saffron-braised fennel and salsa verde
(£18.50). Handy for breakfast and afternoon
tea, too. Wines (from £28.90) have been
chosen by the auction house's very own Serena
Sutcliffe, MW. Open Mon to Fri.

Le Caprice
Famous Mayfair brasserie with loyal fans
Arlington House, Arlington Street, Mayfair,
SW1A 1RJ
Tel no: (020) 7629 2239
www.le-caprice.co.uk
⊖ Green Park, map 5
Modern British | £35
Cooking score: 4

Le Caprice provides a welcome break from the
whirl of activity outside. The room is black
and white with monochrome photographs, a
long bar, and simple table settings. The food
may be unambitious – no more than modern
brasserie food – but every care is taken with
ingredients and the output is consistent.
Indeed, customers are a loyal bunch, drawn
back time and time again for dressed Dorset
crab, steak tartare, and salmon fishcakes with
buttered spinach and sorrel sauce, all served in
a slick, approachable manner. 'Cauliflower
soup with small blue cheese-filled dumplings
and a traditional calf's liver dish were both
good' was the verdict of one who went for
Sunday brunch, while others have applauded
the Welsh rarebit and iced zabaglione with
roasted Ruby plums. What is not liked is the

£2-a-head cover charge levied on each table.
The wine list is a rangy global affair, with
bottles starting at £24.50.
Chef/s: Andrew McLay. **Open:** Mon to Sat L 12 to 3
(4 Fri and Sat), D 5.30 to 12. Sun 11.30 to 11. **Closed:**
25 Dec. **Meals:** alc (main courses £16 to £27). Set D
£17.25 (2 courses) to £22.25. **Service:** 12.5%.
Details: 74 seats. Separate bar. Wheelchair access.
Music. Car parking.

NEW ENTRY
Cây Tre Soho
Modish Vietnamese
42-43 Dean Street, Soho, W1D 2PZ
Tel no: (020) 7317 9118
www.caytresoho.co.uk
⊖ Leicester Square, map 5
Vietnamese | £16
Cooking score: 2

This outlet from a restaurant group based in
Hoxton sets itself apart from other Vietnamese
places with its 'great fit-out', so dining takes
place in a modish monochromatic space with
bleached wood panels. Phos and rice plates
feature strongly on the menu. At inspection, a
small plate of Hanoi sweet potato and whole
shrimp fritter, and a translucent white crab
and mixed herbs crêpe, outflanked a main
course of wok-fried Indochine lamb rump,
which arrived with 'enough garlic to ward off
vampires'. Exotic ice creams (jackfruit or
soursop) are a good way to end. Wines
from £18.
Chef/s: Binh. **Open:** all week L 12 to 5, D 5 to 11
(11.30 Fri and Sat, 10 Sun). **Closed:** 25 and 26 Dec.
Meals: alc (main courses £8 to £12). **Service:** 12.5%.
Details: 90 seats. No music.

Visit us Online
To find out more about
The Good Food Guide, please visit
www.thegoodfoodguide.co.uk

NEW ENTRY
Ceviche
Fabulous Peruvian flavour explosions
17 Frith Street, Soho, W1D 4RG
Tel no: (020) 7292 2040
www.cevicheuk.com
⊖ Tottenham Court Road, map 5
Peruvian | £28
Cooking score: 2

Frith Street is developing a terrific reputation for interesting, high-quality little concept restaurants – and this Peruvian 'can hold its head up with the best'. The bar is long, thin and lined with diners eating cheek-by-jowl, while at the back is the equally cramped dining room. For complexity, texture and a sheer flavour explosion, newcomers should start with a dish from the ceviche bar, say sea bass in 'tiger's milk' (the lime-based marinade used to make ceviche) with red onions. Follow with a small plate like causa mar (squid, prawns and avocado on a Peruvian potato cake) and then anticuchos (grilled skewers of steak, chicken or salmon). Drink pisco sours, or South American wines from £17 a bottle.
Chef/s: Gregor Funcke. **Open:** all week 12 to 11.30 (10.15 Sun). **Closed:** 25 Dec. **Meals:** Ceviche from £5.25, alc (main courses £5.75 to £12.50). **Service:** 12.5%. **Details:** 80 seats. 4 seats outside. Separate bar. Music.

The Chancery
Stylish sustenance in lawyerland
9 Cursitor Street, Holborn, EC4A 1LL
Tel no: (020) 7831 4000
www.thechancery.co.uk
⊖ Chancery Lane, map 5
Modern European | £35
Cooking score: 3

A corner site in bustling Holborn comprises a set of sparely styled dining rooms over ground floor and basement, with a couple of optimistic outdoor tables for those who like to enjoy the London traffic. Brisk corporate business may take priority over private pairs and parties, but there's a good buzz to the place. Mladen Vidaković took over in 2012, and maintains the surprisingly finely detailed style forged by his predecessor. Expect impressive hot-smoked salmon with orange-poached endive, samphire and pressed cucumber, sea bass with samphire, char-grilled fennel and clam butter, and a duo of crisp pork belly and glazed cheek with curried cauliflower purée in prune jus. A spin on classic chocolate-sauced profiteroles incorporates honey and lavender cream. House French on a kindly priced list is £17.50.
Chef/s: Mladen Vidaković. **Open:** Mon to Fri L 12 to 2.30, Mon to Sat D 6 to 10.30. **Closed:** Sun, 23 Dec to 4 Jan. **Meals:** Set L and D £28.50 (2 courses) to £35. **Service:** 12.5%. **Details:** 70 seats. 12 seats outside. Separate bar. Music.

China Tang at the Dorchester
Scintillating Shanghai glitz
The Dorchester Hotel, 53 Park Lane, Hyde Park, W1K 1QA
Tel no: (020) 7629 9988
www.thedorchester.com
⊖ Hyde Park Corner, map 4
Chinese | £50
Cooking score: 3

Ostentatiously glamorous, sleek, and as slinky as a night in old Shanghai, this scintillating dining room in the bowels of the Dorchester has glitz sprinkled like stardust over every silken swathe and chinoiserie artefact. The backdrop may be flamboyantly OTT, but the kitchen plays it conventional – plates of wok-fried prawns, braised beef in oyster sauce, lobster with noodles and suchlike. Prices are not for the faint-hearted – bird's nest chicken soup is £60, beansprouts will set you back £8, and the overstuffed wine list takes no prisoners (bottles start at £26). That said, there are more affordable deals to be had, especially if you're a fan of dim sum.
Chef/s: Chong Choi Fong. **Open:** all week 12 to 12. **Closed:** 24 and 25 Dec. **Meals:** alc (main courses £14 to £150). Set L £23. Set D from £75 (5 courses). **Service:** 12.5%. **Details:** 200 seats. Separate bar. No music. Wheelchair access. Car parking.

Chisou

Pleasant, affordable Japanese eatery
4 Princes Street, Mayfair, W1B 2LE
Tel no: (020) 7629 3931
www.chisourestaurant.com
⊖ Oxford Circus, map 5
Japanese | £40
Cooking score: 4

£5 OFF

It's quite a treat to find a pleasant, affordable Japanese restaurant so close to Oxford Circus. Stylistic simplicity is the order of the day – lots of wood, neutral colours – while the feel is that of a casual Tokyo eatery. The kitchen offers a range of Japanese cooking styles: luscious sashimi and sushi will not disappoint, there are the usual teriyaki dishes, which take in mackerel, salmon, chicken and beef, good tempura choices (the squid has been praised) as well as pork tonkatsu and a handful of soup and udon choices. Familiar appetisers from edamame to deep-fried soft-shell crab with ponzu dip open proceedings, the chef's specials are worth exploring, and the set lunch is good value. Wine from £14.90. Further branches are at 31 Beauchamp Place, Knightsbridge; tel: (020) 3155 0005, and 1-4 Barley Mow Passage, Chiswick; tel (020) 8994 3636.
Chef/s: Kodituwakku. **Open:** Mon to Sat L 12 to 2.30 (12.30 to 3 Sat), D 6 to 10.15. **Closed:** Sun, 23 Dec to 3 Jan, bank hols. **Meals:** alc (main courses £10 to £26). Set L £14.50 (2 courses) to £19.50.
Service: 12.5%. **Details:** 72 seats. 4 seats outside. Music.

❚❙❘ Please send us your feedback

To register your opinion about any restaurant listed in the Guide, or a new restaurant that you wish to bring to our attention, please visit the web address at the bottom of the page. Your feedback informs the content of the book and will be used to compile next year's reviews.

Cigala

Gregarious Spanish hangout
54 Lamb's Conduit Street, Bloomsbury, WC1N 3LW
Tel no: (020) 7405 1717
www.cigala.co.uk
⊖ Holborn, Russell Square, map 5
Spanish | £26
Cooking score: 1

£30

A tapas trailblazer in its early days, Cigala still keeps the faith by offering the real thing in a gregarious setting devoid of castanet clichés. Enjoy plates of jamón, albondigas and croquetas in the roistering downstairs bar or bag a table in the street-level dining room for something more ambitious – perhaps roast duck breast with giant judion beans and Seville oranges or a saffron-tinged stew of octopus, monkfish and mussels. Paellas are great for sharing and the all-Spanish wine list is a cracker, with prices from £12 a carafe.
Chef/s: Jake Hodges. **Open:** all week 12 to 10.45 (12.30 to 9.45 Sun). **Closed:** 24 to 26 Dec, Easter. **Meals:** alc (main courses £14 to £20). Set L £17.50 (2 courses). **Service:** 12.5%. **Details:** 60 seats. 20 seats outside. Separate bar. No music.

Cigalon

Platefuls of Provence
115 Chancery Lane, Holborn, WC2A 1PP
Tel no: (020) 7242 8373
www.cigalon.co.uk
⊖ Chancery Lane, map 5
French | £29
Cooking score: 3

£5 OFF 🍾 £30

'A quiet evening brought attentive managerial service and a warm welcome; banquette seat; good truffle risotto and salade niçoise followed by ox cheek and, for me, a truly delicious pissaladière'. Pascal Aussignac's resolutely French restaurant reminds visitors of the kind of place they used to find years ago on holiday in the Var. Although the kitchen has its heart in Provence, the repertoire is fleshed out with ideas from Corsica, the whole admirably interpreted by Julien Carlon, a former head chef at Comptoir Gascon (see entry). Flavours are strong; recommendations have been enthusiastic for aïoli of salt cod in a vegetable broth, grilled onglet with gnocchi and oxtail 'daube', and iced nougat with poached rhubarb. Drink wines from Provence and Corsica; prices from £19.50.

Chef/s: Julien Carlon. **Open:** Mon to Fri L 12 to 2.30, D 6 to 10. **Closed:** Sat, Sun, Christmas and New Year, bank hols. **Meals:** alc (main courses £9 to 22). Set L and D £19.50 (2 courses) to £24.50. **Service:** 12.5%. **Details:** 68 seats. Music.

Cinnamon Club

Electrifying new-wave Indian
30-32 Great Smith Street, Westminster, SW1P 3BU
Tel no: (020) 7222 2555
www.cinnamonclub.com
⊖ Westminster, map 5
Indian | £47
Cooking score: 3
£5
OFF

Housed in the Old Westminster Library, the Cinnamon Club is now into its second decade of bringing electrifying new-wave Indian cooking to the capital. The place is festooned with private areas for celebrations, but the main dining room has lost none of its dynamic buzz. Guest dishes by French chef Eric Chavot (including a fine crab risotto in truffled cappuccino) are there for those who don't quite feel able to face the exhilarating challenge of the main menu. Here, tandoori pigeon breast with chickpeas and tamarind may be followed by seared sea bass with curried blackeyed peas, green mango and coconut chutney, then rice kheer and caramelised milk dumplings in rasmalai sauce to finish. Prices may reflect the location, but genuine efforts have been made to compile a wine list that's capable of standing up to the often demanding cooking. Floral Gewürztraminers, spangling Sauvignons and muscular Shiraz are what it's about. Bottles start at £22.

Chef/s: Vivek Singh. **Open:** Mon to Sat L 12 to 2.45, D 6 to 10.30. **Closed:** Sun, 25 and 26 Aug, 7 May, 25 to 27 Aug. **Meals:** alc (main courses £15 to £95). Set

L £22 (2 courses) to £24. **Service:** 12.5%. **Details:** 125 seats. Separate bar. No music. Wheelchair access.

NEW ENTRY

Cinnamon Soho

Passionate and exciting Indian cooking
Kingly Street, Soho, W1B 5PF
Tel no: (020) 7437 1664
www.cinnamonsoho.com
⊖ Oxford Circus, map 5
Indian | £28
Cooking score: 3

Cinnamon Soho is the third London project of chef Vivek Singh, who's seen success with Westminster's Cinnamon Club and east London's Cinnamon Kitchen (see entries). Singh is among an elite of highly influential Indian chefs credited with revolutionising Indian cuisine in the UK by applying a fine dining approach to their native cooking and merging traditional spicing with prime British ingredients. Cinnamon Soho is more of a fun, informal project, with a slick, contemporary interior and an emphasis on cocktails and small plates. The menu is diverse; dishes vary from daringly Indian and regional (bheja fry of lamb brains in mince curry), to Anglo-Indian creations (Bangla Scotch egg). Keralan seafood pie comprises perfectly cooked smoked haddock, prawn, squid and mussels swimming in fragrant coconut, ginger and curry leaf sauce and topped with a light flaky-pastry lid, while garlic naan and old Delhi-style fenugreek chicken 'just sing'. Wines start at £11.20 for a carafe.

Chef/s: Vivek Singh. **Open:** all week L 12 to 2.30 (3 Sun), Mon to Sat D 5.30 to 11. **Closed:** 25 and 26 Dec, 7 May, 27 Aug. **Meals:** alc (main courses £12 to £18). Set L £15 (2 courses) to £18. **Service:** 12.5%. **Details:** 75 seats. Wheelchair access. Music.

Clos Maggiore
Flexible French restaurant
33 King Street, Covent Garden, WC2E 8JD
Tel no: (020) 7379 9696
www.closmaggiore.com
⊖ Covent Garden, map 5
French | £38
Cooking score: 2

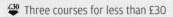 V

Just off the Covent Garden piazza, Clos Maggiore aims to re-create the feel of a country inn in Provence, with framed pictures, low-lit rooms and overhanging blossoms, as well as an old-school approach to intimate dining. The entire gamut of menus is offered, from lingering tasters to pre- and post-theatre deals and vegetarian options. Modern French standbys include starters of seared scallops and brandade, or pressed partridge and foie gras, followed by honey-glazed duck with plum and endive in port sauce. Finish with Valrhona and griottine cherry fondant with griottine sorbet. A fabulous wine list doesn't expend all its labours in France, but painstakingly divides Italy and California into their regions as well, with gold-standard growers tumbling out all over. Prices do get giddy, but there is affordable drinking too, with bottles from £18.50 (£4.75 a glass). **Chef/s:** Marcellin Marc. **Open:** all week L 12 to 2.30, D 5 to 11 (10 Sun). **Closed:** 24 and 25 Dec. **Meals:** alc (main courses £18 to £22). Set L and D £15.50 (2 courses) to £19.50. Sun L £22.50. **Service:** 12.5%. **Details:** 70 seats. Music. Children at L only.

Symbols
🛏 Accommodation is available

£30 Three courses for less than £30

V Separate vegetarian menu

£5 OFF £5-off voucher scheme

 Notable wine list

NEW ENTRY
Copita
Bite-size portions with big flavours
27 d'Arblay Street, Soho, W1F 8EP
Tel no: (020) 7287 7797
www.copita.co.uk
⊖ Oxford Circus, Tottenham Court Road, map 5
Spanish | £30
Cooking score: 3

Perilously high stools, whirring ceiling fans and high decibels are the hallmarks of Copita – a small tapas outfit causing a stir on Soho's d'Arblay Street. Though the post-work media crowds come primarily to plunder the Spanish wine list, the kitchen is also a force to be reckoned with. Portions are small in scale but big on flavours – alongside chorizo, croquetas et al, there might be anchovy fillet with broad bean ice cream, or duck egg yolk galvanised by piquillo peppers and hazelnut. Inspection saw some virtuoso moments (a masterly dish of Galician beef rump with foie gras and mash); however, we probably won't be the last to grumble that, while dishes may be bite-size, prices aren't. Some redemption comes in the authoritative wine list, which starts at £18. **Chef/s:** Ignacio Pinilla. **Open:** Mon to Fri L 12 to 4, D 5.30 to 10.30. Sat 1pm to 10.30. **Closed:** Sun, bank hols. **Meals:** alc (tapas dishes £2 to £14). **Service:** 12.5%. **Details:** 40 seats. 6 seats outside. Music.

Corrigan's Mayfair
Magical food at a Mayfair five-star
28 Upper Grosvenor Street, Mayfair, W1K 7EH
Tel no: (020) 7499 9943
www.corrigansmayfair.com
⊖ Marble Arch, map 4
Modern British | £54
Cooking score: 6

V

Chef Richard Corrigan is an Irish farmer's son at heart but – oh! – he does like a bit of glamour. His restaurant off Park Lane is just what one would expect in a Mayfair five-star: a lively bar (places set for eating), waiters

evocatively clad in starched white jackets, sparkling crystal, even the tinkling of live piano from time to time. When Corrigan's is on song, such touches enliven what is actually a rather sombre room; when the service is 'off' (and it is the service that has riled readers), they mean nothing. At inspection, we found the service lacking in confidence and in the magic that the food deserves. The cooking is as impressive as ever, characterised by powerful British ingredients (including game and wild fish) and confident global strokes. Begin, perhaps, with cured wild trout, wasabi mayonnaise and mooli, then a main of roasted squab, crispy leg, pickled cherries and endive – both pretty on the plate and impeccably executed. Rose-water parfait, raspberries, rose petals and yoghurt is a typically inspired dessert. Lunch menus are cheaper but somewhat skimpily portioned, so splash out if you can – ideally reserving part of your budget for the excellent modern wine list (from £25).
Chef/s: Richard Corrigan and Chris McGowan. **Open:** Sun to Fri L 12 to 3 (4 Sun), all week D 6 to 11 (9.30 Sun). **Closed:** 25 Dec, 1 Jan. **Meals:** alc (main courses £23 to £44). Set L £27. **Service:** 12.5%. **Details:** 70 seats. Separate bar. Wheelchair access. Music.

NEW ENTRY

CUT at 45 Park Lane
Culinary superstar's eatery is a cut above
45 Park Lane, Mayfair, W1K 1PN
Tel no: (020) 7493 4545
www.45parklane.com
⊖ **Hyde Park Corner, map 4**
American | £85
Cooking score: 4

Somebody at CUT at 45 Park Lane can bake, judging by all the carb-obsessed feedback. But let's not dwell on the 'outstanding' breads and the pastry basket at 'the best American breakfast in town': CUT is culinary superstar Wolfgang Puck's first European restaurant and, like the Los Angeles original, it's all about steak. The cuts range from Casterbridge filet

mignon to Chilean Wagyu, 'cooked to perfection' and served with a comprehensive choice of sauces and sides ('fantastic' tempura onion rings or 'amazing' creamed spinach with fried egg). Meat aside, composed salads or scallop carpaccio make a light, California-style start to proceedings, while banana cream pie for pudding is the other extreme. The glossy, mirrored room, with Hyde Park views and an upstairs bar, flows from the lobby and feels 'very New York'. It doesn't come cheap, certainly not the US-favouring wine list (from £25), but few readers express regret.
Chef/s: David McIntyre. **Open:** all week L 12 to 2.30 (11 to 3 Sun), D 6 to 10.45 (10.30 Sun). **Meals:** alc (main courses £30 to £85). Set L £55. Sun L £55 to £85. **Service:** 12.5%. **Details:** 70 seats. Separate bar. Wheelchair access. Music. Car parking.

ALSO RECOMMENDED

▲ Da Polpo
6 Maiden Lane, Covent Garden, WC2E 7NA
Tel no: (020) 7836 8448
www.dapolpo.co.uk
⊖ **Covent Garden, map 5**
Italian-American

Out of the Russell Norman stable of Polpo, Polpetto, Spuntino and Mishkins (see entries) comes this lively Covent Garden eatery. The menu takes its cue from the original Polpo; in other words Italian-American comfort food that is firmly in touch: 'gorgeous meatballs', a generous salad of beetroot, rocket and walnut pesto (£6), plates of fritto misto (£9), and belly pork with radicchio and hazelnuts, then Nutella pizzetta for dessert. Good service. Wines from £18. Open all week.

NEW ENTRY

Dabbous

A-list contender
39 Whitfield Street, Fitzrovia, W1T 2SF
Tel no: (020) 7323 1544
www.dabbous.co.uk
⊖ Goodge Street, map 5
Modern European | £45
Cooking score: 5

£5
OFF

Currently London's hardest-to-book restaurant, Ollie Dabbous's monochrome concrete and metal venue on a grungy Fitzrovia street zipped into the superleague when the *Evening Standard*'s Fay Maschler awarded it her top mark two weeks after it opened. The diminutive size explains the pressure on tables, and there's no doubting the chef's talent. Standouts have been mixed alliums in a chilled pine infusion, pea and mint (a deeply satisfying amalgamation of pea purée, whole pea pods, pea shoots, and delicate mint flavours), 'top drawer' coddled egg with woodland mushrooms and smoked butter, a Japanese-style bowl of squid with seaweed, radishes and toasted buckwheat in a light broth, and Ibérico pork with a 'pleasing, smoky finish'. However, results aren't always on target, judging by one reporter's underwhelming braised veal shin with spelt, celery and kinome, and 'palate cleanser-sized' lovage granita, the only sweet offering on the set-lunch menu (although from the carte others have praised a light chocolate ganache with basil moss and sheep's milk ice cream). Things also need to be calmer, more considerate, especially the service. But you can't quibble with the prices. The modern wine list, which puts quality above showiness, starts at £17.50.
Chef/s: Ollie Dabbous. **Open:** Tue to Sat L 12 to 2.30, D 6 to 10. **Closed:** Sun, Mon, 2 weeks Aug, 2 weeks Christmas. **Meals:** alc (main courses £11 to £14). Set L £21 to £24 (4 courses). Tasting menu £49 (7 courses). **Service:** 12.5%. **Details:** 40 seats. Separate bar. Music.

Dean Street Townhouse

Teeming open-all-hours eatery
69-71 Dean Street, Soho, W1D 3SE
Tel no: (020) 7434 1775
www.deanstreettownhouse.com
⊖ Tottenham Court Road, map 5
Modern British | £40
Cooking score: 3

 V

From the full-English brigade at breakfast to the post-theatre crowd teeming in after 11pm, there's no typical Dean Street customer – it's the very image of an open-all-hours London eatery. Style-wise, it forgoes edgy Soho fashion statements in favour of close-packed white-clothed tables, with added gloss from chandeliers and red leather banquettes. A long zinc bar adds to the buzz (though it can often feel manic at peak times). Come here if your palate warms to straight-talking British staples of Lancashire cheese and onion tart, helpings of salt beef with caraway dumplings, or roast chicken with sage and onion stuffing. There's fish too, perhaps whole grilled Rye Bay plaice, and elderflower and strawberry jelly with buttermilk pudding for afters. Wines are a sound international jumble, with prices from £18.50.
Chef/s: Stephen Tonkin. **Open:** all week 12 to 11.30 (12am Fri and Sat, 10.30 Sun). **Meals:** alc (main courses £14 to £26). Set early D £16.50 (2 courses) to £19.50. Sun L £24 (2 courses) to £28. **Service:** 12.5%. **Details:** 115 seats. 25 seats outside. Separate bar. Wheelchair access. Music.

Dehesa

Agreeable tapas pit-stop
25 Ganton Street, Oxford Circus, W1F 9BP
Tel no: (020) 7494 4170
www.dehesa.co.uk
⊖ Oxford Circus, map 5
Spanish/Italian | £30
Cooking score: 2

'Handsome dark wood, you do sit very close to people; popular place, not easy to get a table.' So run the notes of one reporter on this lively Soho tapas bar that's twinned with Salt

Yard and the Opera Tavern (see entries). Perch at the bar or sit at communal tables and tuck into satisfying pan-fried hake with Arbequina olive oil mash, surf clams and chorizo, salt marsh lamb chops with lamb's tongue, pied de mouton mushrooms and mint aïoli, or spinach and ricotta-stuffed malfatti. Date pannacotta with rhubarb is a typical dessert. Service is casual but efficient. Wines from £16. **Chef/s:** Giancarlo Vatteroni. **Open:** Mon to Fri L 12 to 3, D 5 to 11. Sat 12 to 11, Sun 12 to 5. **Closed:** 24 to 26 Dec, 31 Dec to 2 Jan. **Meals:** alc (tapas £4 to £10). **Service:** 12.5%. **Details:** 40 seats. 28 seats outside. Music.

NEW ENTRY
The Delaunay
Tremendous Grand Central European-style café
55 Aldwych, Covent Garden, WC2B 4BB
Tel no: (020) 7499 8558
www.thedelaunay.com
⊖ Temple, map 5
Modern European | £32
Cooking score: 4

🍷 V

Dream-team restaurateurs Chris Corbin and Jeremy King have done it again. Their new darling of the London restaurant scene looks as if it has been here for ever, and the reworking of the former Bank restaurant – buffed up with wood panelling and projecting an ambience reminiscent of the grand cafés of Central Europe – has been hailed as 'a brilliant job'. A typical day starts with superb breakfast viennoiserie and weaves all the way through to dinner. The menu looks back with affection, reintroducing classics such as wieners (perhaps a superb cheesy käsekrainer with potato salad, sauerkraut and caramelised onions), schnitzels, tarte flambée and a creamy fillet of beef stroganoff (better than a fondly remembered original for one reporter). Skill and attention are evident in the sweets, with a 'fluffy and melting' Salzburg soufflé offset by apricot compote. The cooking upstages older sister the Wolseley (see entry). Wines from £19.50.

Chef/s: Lee Ward. **Open:** all week 11.30 to 12 (11pm Sun). **Closed:** 25 Dec. **Meals:** alc (main courses £10 to £28). **Service:** 12.5%. **Details:** 175 seats. Separate bar. No music. Wheelchair access.

Les Deux Salons
Barnstorming French brasserie
40-42 William IV Street, Covent Garden, WC2N 4DD
Tel no: (020) 7420 2050
www.lesdeuxsalons.co.uk
⊖ Charing Cross, map 5
French | £35
Cooking score: 4

Dynamic duo Will Smith and Anthony Demetre (see Arbutus and Wild Honey) have nailed the French brasserie with this two-tiered barnstormer – an emphatically Gallic mélange of mosaic floors, dark panelling, green leather banquettes and brass fittings. Les Deux Salons does plush sobriety and sociable hubbub with equal aplomb, although pedestrian, lackadaisical staff continue to irritate time-pressed theatre-goers. Despite a 'silver-service attitude' out front, the kitchen knows how to deliver some really vigorous food: asparagus with a beautifully balanced egg and spring onion sauce is richness personified; a springy salad of broad beans and shaved radishes is all about sap-rising seasonality. The Josper grill handles anything from thick Barnsley chops to andouillette de troyes (a chitterling/tripe sausage). Navarin of lamb and succulent rabbit à la moutarde emphasise the owners' love affair with humble cuts, while desserts are classics ranging from îles flottantes to Paris Brest. As for the ancillaries, there's crusty country bread, the cheeses would do a Parisian fromagerie proud, and everything on the attractive wine list is available by the 250ml 'pot lyonnais'; bottles from £16.

Chef/s: Craig Johnston. **Open:** all week 12 to 11 (10am to 10.30pm Sun). **Closed:** 25 and 26 Dec, 1 Jan. **Meals:** alc (main courses £15 to £23). Set L £15.50. Pre-theatre D £15.95. **Service:** 12.5%. **Details:** 150 seats. No music. Wheelchair access.

Dinings

Seriously skilled modern Japanese food
22 Harcourt Street, Marylebone, W1H 4HH
Tel no: (020) 7723 0666
www.dinings.co.uk
◉ Marylebone, map 4
Japanese | £60
Cooking score: 3

The décor may be spartan at this restaurant shoehorned into the ground floor and basement of a Marylebone townhouse, but the sushi and sashimi are gleaming and sea-fresh – the focus is firmly on the food. The modern Japanese menu may be a revelation to people whose experience is limited to sushi bars; Tomonari Chiba and head chef Masaki Sugisaki have created dishes that mix traditional Japanese elements with Western technique. The starting point is a form of tapas, say crispy belly pork with chogochu-jang sauce and apple salsa. Seasonal specialities of Scottish lobster and mixed seafood miso bouillabaisse, and char-grilled rack of lamb with Korean spicy miso and spring vegetables have been highlights. Prices are high, but the ingredients are top-drawer, the skills serious. Wines from £19.
Chef/s: Masaki Sugisaki. **Open:** Mon to Fri L 12 to 2.30, Mon to Sat D 6 to 10.30. **Closed:** Sun, 25 Dec to 3 Jan. **Meals:** alc (main courses £7 to £30). **Service:** 11.5%. **Details:** 28 seats. Music.

Dishoom

Funky all-day Indian café
12 Upper St Martin's Lane, Covent Garden, WC2H 9FB
Tel no: (020) 7420 9320
www.dishoom.com
◉ Leicester Square, Covent Garden, map 5
Indian | £20
Cooking score: 2

A chip off the old Bombay block, Dishoom brings something of the subcontinent's faded café culture to savvy Covent Garden, peddling all-day fodder in a bright setting of marble-topped tables, chequer-board

flooring, dangling lamps and kitsch Bollywood flourishes. Bacon naan rolls laced with chilli jam hit the button for breakfast, while hot grills on cool, fragrant salads and a raft of 'small plates' do the business later on: try the 'fantastically light', crunchy bhel puris, desi fish fingers or keema pau (spiced minced lamb with hot buttered bread). Chicken 'berry' biryani and the daily 'Ruby Murray' are recommended if you require something more filling. 'Lovely staff and brilliant cocktails' too. Wines start at £18.90.
Chef/s: Naved Nasir. **Open:** all week 8am to 11pm (8 to 12 Fri, 10 to 12 Sat, 10 to 10 Sun). **Closed:** 25 Dec, 1 Jan. **Meals:** alc (main courses £7 to £12). Set L and D £27.50. **Service:** 12.5%. **Details:** 140 seats. 20 seats outside. Separate bar. Wheelchair access. Music.

NEW ENTRY

Ducksoup

A waiting game with tasty rewards
41 Dean Street, Soho, W1D 4PR
Tel no: (020) 7287 4599
www.ducksoupsoho.co.uk
◉ Tottenham Court Road, map 5
Modern European | £25
Cooking score: 3

This corridor of a restaurant with its dive-bar vibe and sparse, distressed décor reflects the increasing degree to which good cooking pops up in the casual, unconventional settings that many food lovers prefer. The daily menu plays off the seasons with Eurozone-inspired dishes, say wild rabbit ragù and wet polenta or a very good bollito misto with aïoli and green sauce. The food is comforting, big-flavoured and it relies more on quality ingredients than precise technique. But intense noise and cramped tables make it hard to relax, and you have to be in the mood for the record player (bring your own vinyls). Expect to queue for the popular ground floor – the hard-to-fathom booking policy may stick you in the basement dining room. House wine is £25.

Chef/s: Julian Biggs. **Open:** all week L 12 to 3, Mon to Sat D 6 to 10.30. **Closed:** 25 and 26 Dec. **Meals:** alc (main courses £7 to £14). **Details:** 60 seats. Music.

ALSO RECOMMENDED
▲ Fernandez & Wells
Somerset House, Strand, Covent Garden, WC2R 0RN
Tel no: (020) 7420 9408
www.fernandezandwells.com
⊖ Temple, map 5

The latest addition to a lively family of tapas bar-cum-cafés, Fernandez & Wells offers an enclave of Latin-cool amidst the stately environs of Somerset House. It is set just off the courtyard; high Victorian ceilings and whitewashed walls fit surprisingly well with the mandatory dangling jamón and shuffling world music. The menu shows an equally harmonious touch in the kitchen – a plate of piquant Alejandro chorizo matched with crumbly Manchego makes for decent grazing. Wines from £21. Open all week.

Fino
Big-hitting tapas restaurant
33 Charlotte Street (entrance in Rathbone Street), Fitzrovia, W1T 1RR
Tel no: (020) 7813 8010
www.finorestaurant.com
⊖ Goodge Street, map 5
Spanish | £35
Cooking score: 3

Hopes rarely rise when descending to a basement restaurant, but since the Hart brothers opened Fino in 2003, their big-hitting tapas venue has never lacked for enthusiastic, solid support. This is partly what lends it its air of confidence and assurance. Add a lively atmosphere, efficient service and straightforward cooking and it makes an appealing package. From the 'powerful punch' of arroz negro to the 'full-on flavours' of butter, garlic and coriander accompanying 'superb' razor clams, there's a real taste of the Mediterranean about the food. Expect

'delicately flavoured' crisp belly pork (though accompanying patatas bravas in the shape of 'thin, over-salty French fries' sounded a duff note), and chocolate soup with caramelised pumpkin seeds for a fine finale. An all-Spanish wine list opens at £18.
Chef/s: Nieves Barragan Mohacho. **Open:** Mon to Fri L 12 to 2.30, Mon to Sat D 6 to 10.30. **Closed:** Sun, bank hols. **Meals:** alc (tapas £10 to £28). **Service:** 12.5%. **Details:** 85 seats. Separate bar. Wheelchair access. Music.

ALSO RECOMMENDED
▲ La Fromagerie
2-6 Moxon Street, Marylebone, W1U 4EW
Tel no: (020) 7935 0341
www.lafromagerie.co.uk
⊖ Baker Street, Bond Street, map 4
Modern European

With a name like La Fromagerie you'd expect this specialist café to be all about cheese. And it is – to a point. Explore the awesome walk-in cheese room before sampling French, Italian or Spanish cheeseboards or sharing a Vacherin Mont d'Or (£18). But there's more. The place is open for boiled eggs and Poilâne soldiers before work, lunches of soups, charcuterie plates, and confit duck leg with haricots tarbais (£9.50). Homemade cakes fill the gaps. House wine is £18.65. Closed D.

Galvin at Windows
Ambitious French cuisine and spectacular views
Hilton Hotel, 22 Park Lane, Mayfair, W1K 1BE
Tel no: (020) 7208 4021
www.galvinatwindows.com
⊖ Hyde Park Corner, Green Park, map 4
French | £65
Cooking score: 6

If you haven't got tickets for the London Eye, the next-best aerial gig in town is the 28th-floor restaurant at the Park Lane Hilton. The food's better, for one thing. There's something about having the whole of London spread out below you that really piques the appetite, and André Garrett's contemporary stylings certainly rise to the occasion. The flagship Menu Prestige does a comprehensive job of rounding up the likes of Loch Duart salmon and Cornish crab for a first course with avocado purée and fennel compote, or Yorkshire rhubarb (poached in Banyuls) as a garnish for seared foie gras and ras-el-hanout seed crunch. Herdwick lamb saddle and braised shoulder form the centrepieces of a main course dish that also incorporates a tiny shepherd's pie, with puntarelle, lardo and capers, and there's white Cotswold chicken with a little onion tart, puréed mushrooms and hazelnut jus. It all ends with a witty flourish: end-of-the-pier desserts such as banana milkshake with hazelnut and chocolate croquette, or peanut butter parfait with a caramel centre and popcorn ice cream. A comprehensive wine list contains an embarrassment of riches, for much of which you'll need to be embarrassingly rich. Prices open at £18 (£4 for a small glass).

Chef/s: André Garrett. **Open:** Sun to Fri L 12 to 2.30 (11.45 to 3.30 Sun), Mon to Sat D 6 to 10.30 (11 Thur to Sat). **Meals:** Set L £25 (2 courses) to £29. Set D £65. **Service:** 12.5%. **Details:** 109 seats. Separate bar. No music. Wheelchair access. Car parking.

Galvin Bistrot de Luxe
Reverie-inspiring French menus
66 Baker Street, Marylebone, W1U 7DJ
Tel no: (020) 7935 4007
www.galvinrestaurants.com
⊖ Baker Street, map 4
French | £36
Cooking score: 5

'Very good food, full of flavour and a busy Saturday night atmosphere', observed a reporter of this enduringly popular restaurant where a mere glance at the day's menu inspires the true foodie to reverie. For the food and the whole business are part of the Galvin brothers' love affair with the Paris brasserie – the cooking here waves the French flag with pride and is not afraid to do things in a straightforward fashion. Nor does it flinch at good ingredients. It is this immediacy and quality that is the main appeal: oysters, steak

tartare, charcuterie, beef bourguignon, cassoulet, crème brûlée, tarte Tatin, the list may be predictable, but they are still done memorably. An avidly reported meal proves the point: after escabèche of yellowfin tuna with aubergine purée and herb salad, and a 'particularly good' salmon ravioli, the happy recipients got their fill of 'excellent' caramelised veal brains with beurre noisette, as well as pot-roast Landaise chicken breast, and pavé of cod with piperade tartelette and anchoïade dressing. The set lunch and dinner are real deals and wines (from £19.75) are French, with a few tasty interlopers from elsewhere.

Chef/s: Luigi Vespero. **Open:** all week L 12 to 2.30 (3 Sun), D 6 to 10.30 (11 Thur to Sat, 9.30 Sun). **Closed:** 25 and 26 Dec, 1 Jan. **Meals:** alc (main courses £17 to £21). Set L £19.50. Set D £20.50. **Service:** 12.5%. **Details:** 128 seats. 12 seats outside. Separate bar.

Gauthier Soho
Picture-pretty 'plats' at canny prices
21 Romilly Street, Soho, W1D 5AF
Tel no: (020) 7494 3111
www.gauthiersoho.co.uk
⊖ Leicester Square, map 5
Modern French | £40
Cooking score: 6
£5 OFF 🍷 V

Once you have rung the doorbell, gained admittance to this topiary-fronted townhouse and ascended the stairs to the becalmed waters of the creamy-white dining room, you are safe from the neighbourhood's trendily raffish bedlam. Such is Gauthier Soho – a 'warmly embracing' restaurant of the modern French school, where superbly attentive service is a given and the food is a procession of miniature, picture-pretty 'plats'. Chef-proprietor Alexis Gauthier turned heads when he was at Roussillon, and has settled comfortably since decamping to W1. To begin, his detailing, poise and near-flawless technique might yield a bijou assemblage of yuzu and miso curd with crustacean fricassee and smoked broth, or the myriad textures of foie gras with apple and crispy artichokes, vinegar-tinged red shallots and port reduction. Moving on, there might be a more orthodox dish of roasted wild sea bass in brown butter with toasted salsify, sautéed cos lettuce and morel velouté or a big-spender's collation of Wagyu beef with larded Kentish carrots, 'round fries' and a classic beef jus. Prices are remarkably canny, and all dishes are virtuously calorie-counted – until you reach wicked desserts such as the ever-wonderful Golden Louis XV with praline soufflé. Gauthier's perennial fascination with vegetables shows in a genuinely creative veggie menu, and readers appreciate his sensitivity to dietary issues. Ace sommelier Roberto Della Pietra also receives plaudits aplenty, and his highly idiosyncratic wine list (complete with poems and wine lovers' eulogies) is a peerless in-depth exploration of France with some lesser-known additions from elsewhere. Bottles from £22 (£4.25 a glass).

Chef/s: Alexis Gauthier and Gerard Virolle. **Open:** Mon to Sat L 12 to 2.30, D 5.30 to 10.30. **Closed:** Sun, 25 and 26 Dec, bank hols. **Meals:** Set L £18 (2 courses) to £40. Pre-theatre D £18 (2 courses) to £50 (4 courses). Tasting menu D £60 (5 courses). **Service:** 12.5% (optional). **Details:** 45 seats. Music. Children over 8 yrs only.

★ TOP 50 ★

Le Gavroche

Foursquare London favourite
43 Upper Brook Street, Mayfair, W1K 7QR
Tel no: (020) 7408 0881
www.le-gavroche.co.uk
⊖ Marble Arch, map 4
French | £100
Cooking score: 8

The dear old Gavroche, one of London gastronomy's firmest friends, has stood foursquare through the decades, like the ancient trees in nearby Hyde Park, acquiring another ring of venerability with each passing season. Most readers feel at home in its green, subterranean room, not stifled, but enveloped in a warm embrace. The world could have ended up there, and you would still find your napkin courteously refolded for you when you returned to your seat, perhaps just in time to greet the arrival of your côte de veau in creamed morels. If there is any evolution in the menus, it happens at a pace that's too glacial for the naked eye to detect. The artichoke heart with truffled chicken mousse and foie gras remains, as do the lobster mousse with caviar in Champagne butter, and the grilled Dover sole on the bone with langoustine. These are classical dishes of course, but executed with flair and freshness, quite as though they were freshly minted only last week. Very occasionally we receive a report that doesn't get the food, finding it bland or unambitious: a serving of braised milk-fed lamb lacking depth; the red pepper coulis with a small fillet of mackerel poorly seasoned. It's possible that the shock-tactic food on offer throughout British catering today has thrown classical cooking into the shadows. What could be more *classique* than an omelette for pudding, named after Baron de Rothschild and filled with apricots and Cointreau? Gianduja chocolate praline is the opulent accompaniment to raspberry mille-feuille. The Gavroche is not in the habit of sending us its wine list. Those who have managed to smuggle reports back tell us it's full of glorious bottles at substantial mark-ups. There's a thing. Whites start at £22, reds at £30.

Chef/s: Rachel Humphrey. **Open:** Mon to Fri L 12 to 2, Mon to Sat D 6.30 to 11. **Closed:** Sun, 23 Dec to 3 Jan, bank hols. **Meals:** alc (main courses £27 to £48). Set L £52. Tasting menu £100. **Service:** 12.5%. **Details:** 65 seats. Separate bar. No music.

⫲● Please send us your feedback

To register your opinion about any restaurant listed in the Guide, or a new restaurant that you wish to bring to our attention, please visit the web address at the bottom of the page. Your feedback informs the content of the book and will be used to compile next year's reviews.

The Giaconda Dining Room
Perky Tin Pan Alley eatery
9 Denmark Street, Soho, WC2 H8LS
Tel no: (020) 7240 3334
www.giacondadining.com
⊖ Tottenham Court Road, map 5
Modern European | £30
Cooking score: 3

Denmark Street (aka Tin Pan Alley) is London's rock star thoroughfare, synonymous with the Sex Pistols and Jimi Hendrix – and in more recent times the Giaconda Dining Room, Paul Merrony's formerly perky, pint-sized restaurant (as we went to press we learned that the restaurant would be revamped and enlarged). It is named after a rambunctious rockers' café that previously occupied the premises; these days it's a much better-behaved operation altogether. Seasonal risotto and pasta starters make for rousing opening acts, while the mains represent a greatest hits compilation of French bistro cooking – think along the lines of steak tartare with chips, or duck confit with Lyonnaise potatoes. Eton Mess stages a minor British invasion among the desserts, while a surprisingly affordable stash of wines opens at £19.50.
Chef/s: Paul Merrony. **Open:** Tue to Fri L 12 to 2.15, Tue to Sat D 6 to 9.15. **Closed:** Sun, Mon, 1 week Christmas, 3 weeks Aug. **Meals:** alc (main courses £14 to £21). **Service:** not inc. **Details:** 32 seats.

Great Queen Street
Fair prices and no frills
32 Great Queen Street, Covent Garden, WC2B 5AA
Tel no: (020) 7242 0622
⊖ Covent Garden, map 5
British | £26
Cooking score: 1

A pioneer, with sibling the Anchor & Hope (see entry), of the take-as-you-find approach, Great Queen Street remains resolutely simple, fast-moving and offline. You can, at least, book a table and expect to be brought fairly priced British food with a seasonal bent. Onion soup with Stinking Bishop cheese could be followed, from a wide range of deliberately plain mains, by roast Old Spot pork with choucroute. Desserts tend towards the soft and creamy; flavoured custards or buttermilk pudding are a constant. Wine from £14.
Chef/s: Tom Norrington-Davies and Sam Hutchins. **Open:** all week L 12 to 2.30 (1 to 4 Sun), Mon to Sat D 6 to 10.30. **Closed:** Christmas, Easter, bank hols. **Meals:** alc (main courses £6 to £21). Feasting menu £32. **Service:** not inc. **Details:** 60 seats. 8 seats outside. Separate bar. No music. Wheelchair access.

The Greenhouse
Rarefied Mayfair restaurant
27a Hay's Mews, Green Park, W1J 5NX
Tel no: (020) 7499 3331
www.greenhouserestaurant.co.uk
⊖ Green Park, map 5
French | £75
Cooking score: 4

Chefs have come and gone at the Greenhouse, and the relatively long residency of Antonin Bonnet ended in spring 2012, when Arnaud Bignon took up the reins. People appreciate the rarefied air of approaching through a decked garden, and the dining room's fresh green tones and supremely accomplished service are relaxing. First impressions of the new regime have been mixed. Tandoori-spiced scallops with rolled leaves of Savoy cabbage and a ginger beurre blanc are a pleasant opener, though the bowl of puréed, acridly smoked potato that conceals oysters and pickled shallot, topped with green romaine foam, offers little to get your teeth into. Fine Dorset lamb from the carte, seasoned with ras-el-hanout and served with red pepper purée, works well, but a brick of Dombes duck breast with three baby beetroots is more prosaic. Rhubarb, variously poached and jellied, comes with excellent ginger ice cream. An exhaustive wine collection has plenty by the glass (from £8), but forbidding prices.

Chef/s: Arnaud Bignon. **Open:** Mon to Fri L 12 to 2.30, Mon to Sat D 6.30 to 11. **Closed:** Sun, 25 Dec to 2 Jan, bank hols. **Meals:** Set L £25 (2 courses) to £29. Set D £65 (2 courses) to £75. **Service:** 12.5%. **Details:** 60 seats. Separate bar. No music. Wheelchair access.

ALSO RECOMMENDED
▲ The Guinea Grill
30 Bruton Place, Mayfair, W1J 6NL
Tel no: (020) 7409 1728
www.theguinea.co.uk
⊖ Bond Street, map 5
British

This ancient Mayfair hostelry is cramped, faded and utterly traditional; the cooking draws on a curious past of steaks, seafood, and the famous steak and kidney pie, but it pleases nonetheless. Highlights can be as refreshingly simple as grilled sardines (£7.50) and the Guinea mixed grill (£24.50). Such uncomplicated cookery requires spot-on ingredients and the kitchen certainly obliges – its beef, in particular, is considered among the best in town. Wines from £21. Closed Sat L and Sun.

Hakkasan
Thrillingly seductive new-Cantonese food
8 Hanway Place, Fitzrovia, W1T 1HD
Tel no: (020) 7927 7000
www.hakkasan.com
⊖ Tottenham Court Road, map 5
Chinese | £65
Cooking score: 5

Despite its grubby location in a back alley off Tottenham Court Road, jet-setting Hakkasan seems a world away from today's economic hard times. A trailblazing fixture of London's Chinese scene since 2001, it continues to preach its sexy oriental gospel in a smouldering, subterranean space that mixes the backstage flurry of a fashion show with the shrouded exclusivity of a private club. Moody indigo lighting, lattice screens and black lacquered panels might suggest some designer opium den (minus the soporific smoke),

although thrillingly seductive new-Cantonese food is the drug here. During the day, chattering crowds are lured by the prospect of ambrosial dim sum, ranging from steamed quail dumplings and fried oyster salad roll to three-style mushroom cheung fun, venison puffs and sticky rice rolls. As for the inspirational full menu, the kitchen blends regional rustic themes (Hakka lamb stew, jasmine tea-smoked chicken) with platinum-priced plates for the high rollers (grilled Wagyu beef with enoki mushrooms) – although the real stars are sophisticated seafood specialities such as grilled Chilean sea bass in Chinese honey, stir-fried New Zealand blue abalone or spicy prawns with lily bulbs and almonds. Sexy cocktails bring roistering crowds to the bar, saké is available by the carafe, and the wine list offers a winning selection of classy bottles tailored to the food – although prices (from £34) may deter serious experimentation.
Chef/s: Tong Chee Hwee. **Open:** all week L 12 to 3.15 (4.15 Sat and Sun), D 6 to 11 (11.45 Thur to Sat). **Closed:** 25 Dec. **Meals:** alc (main courses £17 to £61). **Service:** 13%. **Details:** 210 seats. Wheelchair access. Music.

Hakkasan Mayfair
Slinky Chinese opulence
17 Bruton Street, Mayfair, W1J 6QB
Tel no: (020) 7907 1888
www.hakkasan.com
⊖ Green Park, Bond Street, map 5
Chinese | £70
Cooking score: 4
 V

Even more vampish and exclusive than the Hanway Place original (see entry), Hakkasan Mayfair shows off its intoxicating, big-money charms with a cacophonous cocktail bar and a glamorous dining room overlaid with flashes of slinky, ice-cool minimalism. Devotees of the worldly Hakkasan style will find much to enjoy here – from the revelatory 'small eats' (homemade pumpkin tofu or sesame prawn toast with foie gras, anyone?) to jasmine tea-smoked chicken or spicy venison stir-fry with eryngii mushrooms, baby leeks and dried chilli. The new kid also has some new tricks up its oriental sleeve – perhaps steamed New Zealand lobster tails wrapped in glass vermicelli with rice wine, truffle-roast duck with 'tea plant' fungi or sweet-and-sour Duke of Berkshire pork with pomegranate. As for dessert, expect east/west culture clashes such as baked lemon tart with roasted sesame meringue and tahini honey. If your wallet can stand the pain, it's also worth investing in the seriously pricey (but endlessly fascinating) wine list. Bottles start at £31.

Chef/s: Tong Chee Hwee. **Open:** all week L 12 to 3.15 (4.15 Sat and Sun), D 6 to 12 (12.30 Thur to Sat). **Closed:** 24 and 25 Dec. **Meals:** alc (main courses £16 to £80). Set L £50. Set D £65 to £130 (10 courses). **Service:** 13%. **Details:** 211 seats. Separate bar. Wheelchair access. Music.

Haozhan

Contemporary Chinatown eatery
8 Gerrard Street, Soho, W1D 5PJ
Tel no: (020) 7434 3838
www.haozhan.co.uk
⊖ Leicester Square, map 5
Chinese | £25
Cooking score: 1

£5 OFF £30 ▼

Haozhan announces itself as 'modern oriental dining' and inside it's a far cry from all-you-can-eat buffets and dangling paper lanterns of Chinatown yore, with its modish black décor and luminous green lighting. The pan-Asian menu, too, largely shuns sweet-and-sour clichés. A signature starter of sautéed quail in chilli-smothered batter impresses, although an inspection revealed a few inconsistencies among the mains. The fairly priced wine list, starting at £15, is a welcome touch; the tedious, meandering piano music on the stereo is not.

Chef/s: Weng Kong Wong. **Open:** all week L 12 to 5, D 5 to 11.30 (12 Fri and Sat, 11 Sun). **Closed:** 24 and 25 Dec. **Meals:** alc (main courses £10 to £41). **Service:** 12.5%. **Details:** 80 seats. Music.

NEW ENTRY

Hawksmoor Seven Dials

British beef at its best
11 Langley Street, Covent Garden, WC2H 9JG
Tel no: (020) 7420 9390
www.thehawksmoor.com
⊖ Covent Garden, map 5
British | £65
Cooking score: 4

'I've lost my heart to Hawksmoor!' chimed one reader after a blisteringly good evening at the Covent Garden branch of this revivalist steakhouse mini-chain. Like its siblings in the City and Guildhall (see entries), Seven Dials mixes dark-wood clubbiness, industrial-chic paraphernalia and noisy *Mad Men* vibes with a tub-thumping approach to British beef. Check the huge blackboards for special cuts or take advice from the garrulously persuasive servers. Premium prices do little to dampen the sheer pleasure of gorging on huge plates of thickly carved bone-in ribs, porterhouse steaks, D-rumps and sirloins, supplemented by ample sides of sticky bone marrow gravy, duck-fat chips and dollops of spicy ketchup. The rest of the menu covers all bases, from crab and samphire salad, grilled chicken, macaroni cheese and meatballs with grits to sticky orange pudding with custard. Hawksmoor also scores with its fabulous low-lit bar and extensive collection of brilliant cocktails for every time of day; otherwise, well-chosen beefy wines start at £19.

Chef/s: Oliver Clark. **Open:** all week L 12 to 3 (4.30 Sun), Mon to Sat D 5 to 10.30 (11 Fri and Sat). **Closed:** 24 to 26 Dec. **Meals:** alc (main courses £11 to £50). **Service:** 12.5%. **Details:** 194 seats. Separate bar. Wheelchair access. Music.

Visit us Online
To find out more about *The Good Food Guide*, please visit www.thegoodfoodguide.co.uk

Hélène Darroze at the Connaught

Complex avant-garde thrills
16 Carlos Place, Mayfair, W1K 2AL
Tel no: (020) 3147 7200
www.the-connaught.co.uk
⊖ Bond Street, Green Park, map 5
Modern French | £80
Cooking score: 6

🍴 V

The arrival of *femme merveille* Hélène Darroze in 2008 signalled a wave of Gallic incursions into this bastion of Mayfair conservatism. From the antique Berkel meat slicer to the frosted Baccarat water tumblers, delicate silver cutlery and golden chandelier, the pastel-hued dining room now has a muted, playful feel – although hush-hush murmurs are still the order of the day. Against this backdrop, diners can expect to pay top dollar for some highly abstruse (but impressively potent) renditions of the new haute cuisine, underpinned by flavours from Darroze's beloved Landes. Her calling cards tell their own tale: Fines de Claire oyster tartare with Sologne caviar and white bean velouté; a regional marriage of confit foie gras terrine with Jurançon wine, banana purée, celeriac and Japanese gomashio seasoning with crispy gingerbread toast; roast Limousin veal larded with Taggiasca olives alongside crispy polenta, broad beans, spring onion and confit tomato, all bathed in a light jus pointed up with Cantabrique anchovies. By contrast, desserts such as Manjari chocolate ganache with hazelnut gianduja biscuit and galangal cream may lack the high-flying innovation or thrills of their savoury cousins, although the petits fours are a dream (don't miss the absolutely fabulous piña colada macaroons). Top-drawer service comes courtesy of a battalion of dutiful and very beautiful French staff with accents as thick as rouille and an obsessive line in minutiae; the only blip for one reader was 'being charged £28 for a glass of Champagne from the trolley'. Yes, wine prices will make your head spin, even before you have taken a sip: be

prepared to shell out upwards of £30 for anything serious from the aristocratic Francophile list.
Chef/s: Hélène Darroze. **Open:** Tue to Sat L 12 to 2.30 (brunch 11 to 2.30 Sat), D 6.30 to 10.30. **Closed:** Sun, Mon, first week Jan, 2 weeks Aug. **Meals:** Set L £35. Set D £80. Tasting menu £92 (6 courses) to £115 (9 courses). **Service:** 12.5%. **Details:** 60 seats. Separate bar. No music. Wheelchair access.

★ TOP 50 ★

Hibiscus

Wildly creative, knockout dishes from a master
29 Maddox Street, Mayfair, W1S 2PA
Tel no: (020) 7629 2999
www.hibiscusrestaurant.co.uk
⊖ Oxford Circus, map 5
Modern French | £80
Cooking score: 8

🍴 V

Claude Bosi's cooking has always pushed at the boundaries. Now, in a bold move, the chef has abandoned the concept of conventional menus, adapting his food to the best ingredients available that day. Just tell your waiter what you can't or won't eat from a list of ingredients provided, decide whether to have three, six or eight courses, and sit back and prepare for a succession of wildly creative dishes. Although his cooking is grounded in France, Bosi reaches around the world in search of radical ideas and obscure ingredients. Rich, sensuous roast foie gras is delivered with a dash of ayam sioh (tamarind sauce) with confit shallots, a dab of coriander purée, and a single cockle (with the instruction to eat last), to create an interplay of sweet, salt and tart that couldn't be more finely orchestrated. In the spiny shell of a violet sea urchin, he layers urchin mousse and jelly in a briny-sweet riff that underscores his fondness for supple, silky textures. His cod, too, is almost like a set cream, the fork slips so smoothly through the flesh. It is invigorated by a rice-less risotto of celeriac, celery and razor clam and by the citrus zing of pomelo. And meat? In addition to slow-barbecued grilled kid, an accompanying cottage pie delivers a memorable salty tang from the addition of winkles. These are knockout dishes, no question, and that extends to a pre-dessert of apple purée, celeriac jelly and chestnut cream – perfectly displaying Bosi's skill at packing intriguing ingredients into one composition and coaxing all into harmony. And as a finale, his blood-orange and marjoram givré is beautifully realised, at once silky and dense and accessorised with a superb orange-soaked polenta cake. Bosi seals the deal with a treasure trove of a wine list – around 85 per cent biodynamic. With scores of desirable bottles, small producers galore, as well as good choices at lower prices (from £26), diners can readily get however much direction they require from the three sommeliers. And there's good news for those who find the dining room dull – a bold revamp is planned in January 2013.

Chef/s: Claude Bosi. **Open:** Mon to Sat L 12 to 2.30, D 6.30 to 10 (6 Fri and Sat). **Closed:** Sun, 10 days Dec to Jan, bank hols. **Meals:** Set L £29.50 (2 courses) to £34.95. Set D £80. Tasting menu £90 (6 courses), £100 (8 courses). **Service:** 12.5%. **Details:** 45 seats. No music. Wheelchair access.

Hix

Über-cool Brit brasserie
66-70 Brewer Street, Soho, W1F 9UP
Tel no: (020) 7292 3518
www.hixsoho.co.uk
⊖ Piccadilly Circus, map 5
British | £35
Cooking score: 3

Mark Hix's über-cool restaurant and basement bar packs in a cheerful throng of hipsters and foodies. This patriotic brasserie strives to source the UK's finest seasonal foodstuffs and present them simply. Foraged greens lend an intriguing twist to dishes, say fleshy sea purslane as a foil for fish. An awe-inspiring platter of raw Manx queenies marinated with cucumber and wild chervil opened one spring dinner. Most mains feature a chunk of protein with sparse adornments; expect a fat, juicy sea bass fillet on lemon butter with a stem of blanched sea kale and a

sprinkle of shelled Morecambe shrimps, or a hefty rose veal chop char-grilled and slathered with sage butter. Desserts include seriously moist cherry bakewell with almond ice cream. House wine is £20.

Chef/s: Simon Hicks. **Open:** all week 12 to 11. **Closed:** 25 and 26 Dec. **Meals:** alc (main courses £15 to £37). Set L and D £17.50 (2 courses) to £22.50. **Service:** 12.5%. **Details:** 80 seats. Separate bar. Wheelchair access. Music.

Hix at the Albemarle

Old-school charm and regional goodies
Brown's Hotel, 30 Albemarle Street, Mayfair, W1S 4BP
Tel no: (020) 7518 4004
www.thealbemarlerestaurant.com
⊖ Green Park, map 5
British | £33
Cooking score: 4

⟲ V

Brown's Hotel first opened its doors in 1837, the year that Queen Victoria ascended the throne, and it has stood for a brand of aristocratic English hospitality ever since. Regional food crusader Mark Hix has pedigree to spare, so it seems apt that he should set up camp here, re-energising the dining room's dark-panelled, clubby masculinity with some on-trend Brit Art and spotlighting the newly discovered seasonal flavours of our green and pleasant land. How about a plate of char-grilled Cornish cuttlefish with Bath Pig chorizo and sea purslane, or Dorset snails with Peter Gott's wild boar bacon and Cumbrian black pudding, or even wild rabbit braised in Burrow Hill cider with hedgerow garlic? The dishes come thick and fast, from potted Morecambe Bay shrimps to Williams pear and custard tart, via roasts from the trolley, Lancashire hotpot, hay-baked lamb and savouries such as Scotch woodcock. Artisan British beers pay tribute to the food; otherwise dip into the high-flown international wine list (from £28).

Chef/s: Lee Streeton. **Open:** all week L 12 to 3 (4 Sat and Sun), D 5.30 to 11 (7 to 10.30 Sun). **Meals:** alc (main courses £16 to £69). Set L and D

£27.50 (2 courses) to £32.50. Sun L £37.50. **Service:** 12.5%. **Details:** 80 seats. Separate bar. No music. Wheelchair access.

Ibérica

Classic and modern tapas with verve
195 Great Portland Street, Fitzrovia, W1W 5PS
Tel no: (020) 7636 8650
www.ibericalondon.com
⊖ Regent's Park, Great Portland Street, map 5
Spanish | £35
Cooking score: 3

Large plate-glass windows entice the curious into the two-tiered room that is, to give it its full name, Ibérica Food and Culture. The dramatic space is divided up well, offset by spectacular hanging lamps and intricately patterned tiles. It's the kind of look that demands big personality from its incumbents, and that's what it gets. The kitchen team specialises in assembling classic and modern tapas, and does so with verve: witness octopus Gallego with potatoes and paprika; mini-burgers made with Secreto Ibérico pork; impressive charcuterie and cheeses, and superb Sunday paellas. Staff aren't shy either, confidently answering queries and exceptionally proud of their delicious caramelised rice pudding. They can also talk guests through an exciting wine list (from £20.90) that is, of course, all Spanish. **Chef/s:** Cesar Garcia. **Open:** all week 11.30 to 11.00 (12 to 4 Sun). **Closed:** 25 and 26 Dec. **Meals:** alc (main courses £7 to £15). Set L £15 (two courses). **Service:** 12.5%. **Details:** 130 seats. Wheelchair access. Music.

ALSO RECOMMENDED
▲ The Ivy

1-5 West Street, Covent Garden, WC2H 9NQ
Tel no: (020) 7836 4751
www.the-ivy.co.uk
⊖ Leicester Square, map 5
Modern European

When they rebuilt the Ivy in the 1920s, it was to the initial alarm of regulars such as Noël Coward. Its starry, theatrical clientele remains undimmed to this day, which is why it's still hard to secure a table for the dependable brasserie food: perhaps tuna and kingfish sashimi in white soy (£15.75), crisp belly pork with garlic mash and scrumpy sauce (£18), and Congolese Virunga chocolate pudding with Turkish delight ice cream (£8.75). Wines from £24.25. Open all week.

J. Sheekey

Theatreland's seafood star
28-32 St Martin's Court, Covent Garden,
WC2N 4AL
Tel no: (020) 7240 2565
www.j-sheekey.co.uk
⊖ Leicester Square, map 5
Seafood | £37
Cooking score: 4
V

'This is one of our favourite West End restaurants' pronounced one reader, and such praise is echoed in many other reports. Given the plum location just off Leicester Square and the low-key glitz of the surroundings (a clubby wood-panelled interior hung with photos of theatre luminaries), it's no wonder that this theatreland veteran continues to play to packed houses. Regulars keep coming back in their droves for the surefire mix of cosseting atmosphere, slick service and consistently well-prepared seafood. There's a modern-classic feel to the food, but it doesn't get overly predictable: there's not only crab bisque, devilled whitebait, and the 'superlative' fish pie, but also fried cod tongues with peas and smoked bacon, roasted monkfish with borlotti beans, Datterini tomatoes and green sauce, and sea trout with caramelised chicory and citrus dressing. A slate of British cheeses and sweet things, such as double chocolate soufflé pudding with pistachio, conclude things satisfyingly. Wines from £20. **Chef/s:** James Cornwell. **Open:** all week L 12 to 3 (3.30 Sun), D 5.30 to 12 (6 to 11 Sun). **Closed:** 25 Dec. **Meals:** alc (main courses £15 to £40). Sun L £26.50. **Service:** 12.5%. **Details:** 93 seats.

J. Sheekey Oyster Bar
Sheekey offspring with speciality seafood
33-34 St Martin's Court, Covent Garden,
WC2N 4AL
Tel no: (020) 7240 2565
www.j-sheekey.co.uk
⊖ Leicester Square, map 5
Seafood | £26
Cooking score: 4

The Oyster Bar opened cheek by jowl with the original J. Sheekey (see entry) in 2008. It displays a marked family resemblance in the panelled walls covered with framed celebrity photos, and a bar that extends over three sides of a square, where comfortable seating permits a fast and productive encounter with the seafood specialities in which the place trades. Oysters and Champagne are where many will start, but less obvious byways worth exploring include smoked anchovies with confit beetroot and horseradish, a shrimp and scallop burger with spicy mayo, or monkfish and tiger prawn curry with butternut squash and almonds on basmati rice. The beating heart of the operation, though, remains the old-school platters of fruits de mer, the steamed or grilled market fish and the famous fish pie, for which happy Covent Gardeners drop in any time of the afternoon or evening. House wines are £17.50.
Chef/s: James Cornwell. **Open:** all week 12 to 12 (11pm Sun). **Closed:** 25 Dec. **Meals:** alc (main courses £6 to £13). **Service:** 12.5%. **Details:** 32 seats. Wheelchair access. Music.

Kiku
Bastion of cultured Japanese cuisine
17 Half Moon Street, Mayfair, W1J 7BE
Tel no: (020) 7499 4208
www.kikurestaurant.co.uk
⊖ Green Park, map 5
Japanese | £40
Cooking score: 4

Kiku's measured pace, clean lines, stone floors and oriental blinds create a mood of Zen-like calm that no doubt soothes the work-driven salarymen and Mayfair business suits who frequent this bastion of cultured Japanese cuisine. Aficionados of refined, high-art sushi should proceed to the expansive bar, where fastidious chefs create sparkling-fresh nigiri, maki rolls and sashimi. Otherwise, move into the dining room and partake of an exquisitely formal kaiseki banquet or pick your way through the carte; either way, marvel at the clarity of zensai appetisers such as tsukimi natto (fermented beancurd with quail's egg yolk) or ikura oroshi (salmon roe on grated mooli) before sampling una-jyu (grilled eel on rice served in a box with miso soup), satoimo nasu (taro and aubergine casserole) or some assorted tempura. Sukiyaki, shabu-shabu hotpots and udonsuki (various ingredients and wheat noodles in seasoned broth) are good for sharing, and there are dainty daifuku rice cakes to finish. Wines from £15.50.
Chef/s: H Shiraishi, Y Hattori and M Anayama. **Open:** Mon to Sat L 12 to 2.30, all week D 6 to 10.15 (5.30 to 9.45 Sun). **Closed:** 25 to 27 Dec, 1 Jan. **Meals:** alc (main courses £12 to £39). Set L £15 (2 courses) to £20. Set D £20 (2 courses) to £50 (8 courses). **Service:** 12.5%. **Details:** 100 seats. No music. Wheelchair access.

Koya
Noodles with oodles of love and care
49 Frith Street, Soho, W1D 4SG
Tel no: (020) 7434 4463
www.koya.co.uk
⊖ Tottenham Court Road, map 5
Japanese | £15
Cooking score: 2

These premises were once home to groundbreaking Alastair Little (the visionary chef who changed the way Britain ate in the 1990s), and the same ambience of café-like informality behind a grey frontage pervades this Japanese fast-food place. Udon noodles are the speciality, with smoked mackerel, vegetable tempura or pork and miso, either hot or cold in hot broth, or served with pouring or dipping sauces. Small plates such as kakuni (cider-braised belly pork), and mixed kaiso seaweed salad, as well as rice bowl dishes of duck or beef, flesh out the menus. Don't expect dessert; it isn't the point. There is wine at £23, as well as saké, shochu and Kirin beer. **Chef/s:** Junya Yamasaki and Shuko Oda. **Open:** all week L 12 to 3, D 5.30 to 10.30 (10 Sun). **Closed:** 25 Dec, 1 Jan. **Meals:** alc (main courses £7 to £14). **Service:** 10%. **Details:** 48 seats. No music.

Lantana Café

Lively Aussie brunch star
13 Charlotte Place, Fitzrovia, W1T 1SN
Tel no: (020) 7637 3347
www.lantanacafe.co.uk
⊖ Goodge Street, Tottenham Court Road, map 5
Australian | £15
Cooking score: 1

Don't be put off by the scruffy décor or weekend queues: this all-day eatery serves big, bold food with an Aussie accent and a keen eye for value. Corn fritters star at breakfast, but maple French toast with bacon, banana and candied pecans comes a close second. The daily repertoire takes in the likes of confit chicken salad with chicory, pear and blue cheese dressing or oxtail, rocket and white onion risotto, delivered by good-natured staff. House wine is £17. **Chef/s:** George Notley. **Open:** Mon to Fri B 8 to 11.30 (Brunch 9 to 3 Sat and Sun). All week L 12 to 3. **Closed:** 25 Dec to 2 Jan. **Meals:** alc (main courses £5 to £13). **Service:** not inc. **Details:** 30 seats. 10 seats outside. Music.

Latium

Smart Fitzrovia Italian
21 Berners Street, Fitzrovia, W1T 3LP
Tel no: (020) 7323 9123
www.latiumrestaurant.com
⊖ Goodge Street, Oxford Circus, map 5
Italian | £36
Cooking score: 3

It may be named after the region around Rome, but Latium treads a culinary path right across chef-proprietor Maurizio Morelli's boot-shaped homeland. Cured tuna loin with camomile, chives and lemon dressing is a typically zingy opener, while pasta might include tagliolini with Sicilian octopus, black olives and chicory, tagliatelle with Sardinian artichokes or something from the renowned ravioli selection. After that, consider wild sea bass with pumpkin sauce and turnip tops or slow-cooked belly pork with Savoy cabbage, spring onions and balsamic vinegar. Conclude with fruity, ricotta-filled cannoli – or even one of the intriguing sweet ravioli. The interior is a smart, Fitzrovia-friendly mix of vivid artwork and cappuccino tones, with Venetian blinds at the windows. The wine list is dominated by patrician regional Italians from £16 (£4.50 a glass). **Chef/s:** Maurizio Morelli. **Open:** Mon to Fri L 12 to 3, Mon to Sat D 6.30 to 10.30 (11.30 Sat). **Closed:** Sun, 24 to 26 Dec, bank hols. **Meals:** alc (main courses £15 to £21). Set L £16.50 (2 courses) to 22.50. Set D £29.50 (2 courses) to £35.50. **Service:** 12.5%. **Details:** 55 seats. No music. Wheelchair access.

Locanda Locatelli
Classic Italian flagship
8 Seymour Street, Marble Arch, W1H 7JZ
Tel no: (020) 7935 9088
www.locandalocatelli.com
⊖ Marble Arch, map 4
Italian | £57
Cooking score: 4

At Giorgio Locatelli's restaurant on the fringes of Marylebone, soothing russet and sandy tones predominate, and the menus follow the classic Italian format. You may begin with an antipasto of beans, red onions, almonds and Parmesan, or go straight on to pasta, which shouldn't be missed, even when it's as simple as spaghetti with tuna, tomato and garlic. The memorable mains are roasted meats and fish, such as rabbit leg in Parma ham with polenta and radicchio, or monkfish on samphire and rocket, 'a dish as beautiful to see as it was to consume'. Finish with textbook tiramisu. There is scarcely a better chance in London to drink Italian, from the exhaustive tour of the viticultural regions to passiti dessert wines, Marsalas and grappas. Prices open at a mere £12.50 (£3.50 a glass) for a fresh Sicilian Catarratto.
Chef/s: Giorgio Locatelli. **Open:** all week L 12 to 3 (3.30 Sat and Sun), D 6.45 to 11 (11.30 Fri and Sat, 10.15 Sun). **Closed:** 24 to 27 Dec. **Meals:** alc (main courses £9 to £33). **Service:** not inc. **Details:** 83 seats. No music. Wheelchair access.

ALSO RECOMMENDED
▲ Mango Tree
46 Grosvenor Place, Belgravia, SW1X 7EQ
Tel no: (020) 7823 1888
www.mangotree.org.uk
⊖ Victoria, Hyde Park Corner, map 4
Thai

This opulent Belgravia venue has been flying the flag for Thai cooking for a decade. It's certainly out to impress with its spacious, clean-cut décor, and it offers an extensive menu that takes in familiar items like spicy fishcakes, som tum salad, roast duck curry and stir-fries such as chicken fillets with fresh chilli. Expect excellent-value set deals, too, including lunch and pre- and post-theatre menus at £17 for two courses and £20 for three. The five-course Taste of Thailand menu is £48. House wine £19. Open all week.

▲ Mele e Pere
46 Brewer Street, Soho, W1F 9TF
Tel no: (020) 7096 2096
www.meleepere.co.uk
⊖ Piccadilly Circus, map 5
Italian

This basement trattoria not far from Piccadilly Circus comes with a bar area that 'could be used to great effect just as a wine bar'. The main dining room is casual in a lots-of-wood-and-mismatched-tables kind of way. The kitchen offers gutsy Italian standards such as minestrone soup (£6), 'lovely and rich' tripe with tomatoes and Parmesan, and spaghetti carbonara (£10), while Amalfi lemon sorbet provides 'great lemon flavour'. The all-Italian wine list is an absolute gem; bottles from £16.50. Closed Sun.

Mennula
A hearty Sicilian workout
10 Charlotte Street, Fitzrovia, W1T 2LT
Tel no: (020) 7636 2833
www.mennula.com
⊖ Goodge Street, map 5
Italian | £35
Cooking score: 3
£5 OFF

Sicily, known as 'God's kitchen' for its abundance of beautiful ingredients, is the inspiration behind Mennula in London's medialand. Mennula isn't exclusively Sicilian, but it's the likes of blood-orange, fennel, mint and bottarga salad, spaghetti with sardines, pine nuts, sultanas and saffron and – of course – the joyous Sicilian desserts (sweet ricotta-filled cannoli, cassata etc.) that immediately leap out from the modern Italian menu. Sicilian stuzzichini (snacks) make a good start, even if you then branch out geographically for wild boar maltagliati (random-shaped) pasta or roast belly pork with honey, black truffle and cavolo nero. The business crowd rates the 'very professional' service and chic interiors, though seating can be cramped. Sicilian wineries get top billing on the 'pricey' wine list (from £16).

Chef/s: Santino Busciglio. **Open:** Mon to Fri L 12 to 3, all week D 6 to 11 (10 Sun). **Meals:** alc (main courses £18 to £36). Set L and D £17.95. Tasting menu £59.95. **Service:** 12.5%. **Details:** 40 seats. 10 seats outside. Music.

ALSO RECOMMENDED

▲ Mishkin's

25 Catherine Street, Covent Garden, WC2B 5JS
Tel no: (020) 7240 2078
www.mishkins.co.uk
⊖ Covent Garden, map 5
American-Jewish

Russell Norman's fifth eatery maintains the family resemblance (distressed brick walls, industrial ducting, bare tables) but this time explores American-Jewish cooking (not kosher), with varying success. Highlights are whopping sandwiches with big fat, American-sized fillings – choose from Reuben on rye or salt beef (both £9) – meatballs (say lamb and pistachio) and mac and cheese. Chicken matzo ball soup (£5) lacked body, and it's back to the drawing board for latkes and blintzes. Pleasant, casual service. Wines from £18. Open all week.

▲ Mon Plaisir

21 Monmouth Street, Covent Garden, WC2H 9DD
Tel no: (020) 7836 7243
www.monplaisir.co.uk
⊖ Covent Garden, map 5
French

London's oldest French restaurant crams a hundred souls into four rooms and is no-nonsense, relatively quick and convenient for theatres. However, the cooking is from a menu of basic French restaurant staples; gratinée à l'oignon (£6.75), coq au vin (£17.50), and baba au rhum are typical. 'OK for quickest of bites pre-theatre' is one verdict, but others have enjoyed scallops 'cooked to perfection', a well-made steak tartare, and moreish gratin dauphinois. House French is £18. Closed Sun.

Moti Mahal

Indian regional cook's tour

45 Great Queen Street, Covent Garden, WC2B 5AA
Tel no: (020) 7240 9329
www.motimahal-uk.com
⊖ Covent Garden, map 5
Indian | £45
Cooking score: 3

£5 OFF V

Born in Delhi and now trading in Covent Garden, Moti Mahal brings an informed regional sensibility to its food. The action is spread over two vividly decorated floors and the menu takes visitors on a fascinating cook's tour along the mighty 2,500km Grand Trunk Road – an ancient highway that runs from Bengal to the North-West Frontier. It's a convoluted trek, but eager staff are happy to act as navigators while diners work their way through inspired, artfully spiced offerings such as stir-fried lambs' brains with coriander on masala bread (from Lahore), a trio of Punjabi tikkas, an Amritsari dish of John Dory with cracked pepper and star fruit salad, or classic Lucknow biryanis cooked in sealed pots. House wine is £28. Note that the menus and wine list were being updated as we went to press.

Chef/s: Anirudh Arora. **Open:** Mon to Fri L 12 to 3, Mon to Sat D 5.30 to 11. **Closed:** Sun, 25 to 26 Dec. **Meals:** alc (main courses £8 to £25). Set D £19 (2 courses) to £23. Tasting menu £49. **Service:** 12.5%. **Details:** 90 seats. Wheelchair access. Music.

Also Recommended
Also recommended entries are not scored but we think they are worth a visit.

Mr Kong

Redoubtable Chinatown beacon
21 Lisle Street, Soho, WC2H 7BA
Tel no: (020) 7437 7341
www.mrkongrestaurant.com
⊖ Leicester Square, map 5
Chinese | £20
Cooking score: 2

V

Over the last 25 years, members of the Kong family dynasty have turned this old warhorse into a redoubtable beacon of Cantonese cooking in ever-changing, increasingly touristy Chinatown. The regional tag means that seafood is a strong suit, so look for chef's specials such as steamed crab in rice wine with noodles, fried cuttlefish cakes with garlic sprouts or braised turbot with bitter melon and beancurd sticks. The heavy-duty menu also touts roast meats, hotpots (belly pork with yams), sizzlers and Westernised classics ranging from won ton soup to chicken in black bean sauce – not forgetting an unusually extensive range of vegetarian specialities. House wine is £10.50.
Chef/s: Kwai Kong and Y Wai Lo. **Open:** all week noon to 2.45am (1.45am Sun). **Closed:** 24 and 25 Dec. **Meals:** alc (main courses £8 to £28). Set L and D £11 (2 courses) to £24.80 (4 courses). **Service:** 10%. **Details:** 110 seats. No music.

★ TOP 50 ★

Murano

Paradigm of Mayfair exclusivity
20 Queen Street, Mayfair, W1J 5PP
Tel no: (020) 7495 1127
www.muranolondon.com
⊖ Green Park, map 5
Italian | £65
Cooking score: 7

V

When Angela Hartnett MBE acquired this paradigm of Mayfair exclusivity from Gordon Ramsay, she inherited not only a room of her own, but also all the beige-tinted trappings of corporate nicety. Fancy Murano glassware, frivolous chandeliers, mirrored walls, discreet curtains and thick carpets add gravitas to the restaurant's hushed and very proper demeanour. The surrounds may lack zest, but Angela's cooking remains triumphant – a 'seriously distinguished' take on contemporary Italian cuisine seen through a Kentish woman's eyes. Her gastronomic love affair has lost none of its ardour or intensity as her star has waxed ever stronger, and there are dishes to prove it: a disarmingly simple and refreshing salad of peaches, apples and artichokes; signature pumpkin ravioli with amaretti crumbled over the top; handmade linguine with prawns, garlic and just enough chilli to tingle the throat; duck cooked rare with lemon cream and mustard fruits. Her ingredients-led seasonal adventures have also yielded a silkily potent zuppa di pesce, and impeccably timed fillet of Cumbrian beef served with mint, courgettes and garlic purée. Good quality in-between offers of arancini and bread with Italian meats are a nice touch, cheeses are 'second to none', and desserts include a truly sublime milk chocolate ganache, and a great espresso soufflé 'with a perfect rise and texture'. Regulars have also applauded the terrific-value set lunch. Dashing staff in dapper waistcoats remain charming, courteous and unfailingly approachable – 'not pompous in any way'. The 30-page wine list has quality and depth, but its comprehensive tour through France, Italy and the Iberian Peninsula comes at a cost; prices start at £29.50 (£6.50 for a 125ml glass).
Chef/s: Angela Hartnett. **Open:** Mon to Sat L 12 to 3, D 6 to 11. **Closed:** Sun, 24 to 27 Dec. **Meals:** Set L and D £50 (2 courses) to £65. Tasting menu £85. **Service:** 12.5%. **Details:** 55 seats. No music. Wheelchair access.

🍴 **Average Price**
The average price listed in main-entry reviews denotes the price of a three-course meal, without wine.

ALSO RECOMMENDED

▲ National Portrait Gallery, Portrait Restaurant

St Martin's Place, Trafalgar Square, WC2H 0HE
Tel no: (020) 7312 2490
www.searcys.co.uk
⊖ Leicester Square, Charing Cross, map 5
Modern British £5 OFF

Picture-perfect rooftop views ensure a fast flow of custom through the National Portrait Gallery's third-floor restaurant. Food is, not surprisingly, British, though readers report that some dishes are slightly lacking in pride, national or otherwise. To start, a simple mackerel pâté comes with pickled cucumber, radishes and Nordic bread (£7), while belly pork with braised red cabbage, parsnips and pear sauce (£17.50) is ample fuel for further cultural endeavours. House wine from £18.85. Closed Mon to Wed and Sun D.

Nobu Berkeley St

High-gloss hangout
15 Berkeley Street, Mayfair, W1J 8DY
Tel no: (020) 7290 9222
www.noburestaurants.com
⊖ Green Park, map 5
Japanese | £70
Cooking score: 4

'Bring some F1 earplugs' advises a reporter who was greeted by a thunderous babble when he visited this über-cool Mayfair hangout. A stream of catwalk queens and A-list fashionistas swan up and down the sweeping staircase that leads to the high-gloss, modishly designed dining room, and they are here for the glamour as much as the food. Sadly, the kitchen can sometimes lose sight of the finer points of detailing and presentation in a rush to feed the throngs: 'it's all rather predictable and formulaic' noted one reader who knows what the Nobu brand can deliver. Sushi and sashimi are ozone-fresh but lack that extra zing – although the fabulous o-toro (fatty tuna) fully warrants its cult status. The needlessly convoluted menu also promises a host of 'classics' from crispy Latin-inspired

tacos to cubes of sublimely sweet belly pork in thick miso. In the evening, specialities from the wood-fired oven are a must: try the duck breast with wasabi salsa or the Ibérico pork with spicy ponzu. 'Osusume' specials such as baby artichoke salad with lobster are also worth noting. Rare sakés abound, and the swanky, gold-standard wine list brings peerless growers and great vintages to the table, but at an eye-watering price: bottles start at around £36.
Chef/s: Mark Edwards. **Open:** Mon to Fri L 12 to 2.15, all week D 6 to 11 (12.45 Thur to Sat, 10.30 Sun). **Closed:** 25 and 26 Dec, bank hols. **Meals:** alc (main courses £5 to £40). Set L £26 to £29. Set D £24 to £33.50. Tasting menu £70 to £90 (6 courses). **Service:** 15%. **Details:** 180 seats. Separate bar. Wheelchair access. Music. No children in the bar.

Nobu London

Japanese fusion pioneer
Metropolitan Hotel, 19 Old Park Lane, Mayfair, W1K 1LB
Tel no: (020) 7447 4747
www.noburestaurants.com
⊖ Hyde Park Corner, map 5
Japanese | £75
Cooking score: 4

There's no doubt that when the global Nobu brand rolled into Mayfair in 1997, it heralded a new wave of A-list dining in the capital. Most of the celebs now get their kicks at its sibling on Berkeley Street (see entry), and with whispers of a ritzy new Nobu hotel in the pipeline, the original may find it hard to compete. For now, this rather severe, white-walled dining room continues to offer trademark high-end Japanese cooking with Latin add-ons – although the results seem less startling or innovative than they did back in the noughties. A cavalcade of fine-tuned old-style sushi and new-style sashimi shares the billing with tartares, ceviches, blistering South-American anticuchos skewers and specialities ranging from salmon kelp rolls to beef tenderloin tataki with ponzu and garlic chips – not forgetting the now-iconic

caramelised black cod in miso and some wildly freaky crossover desserts. Be warned: eating here may feel like a Japanese assembly line, especially as table-turning is enforced with samurai-like rigour. Also take a deep breath before opening the seriously heavyweight wine list: growers and vintages are second to none, but with a 125ml glass of Kiwi Sauvignon Blanc weighing in at £8.50, it's definitely not for everyday imbibing.
Chef/s: Mark Edwards. **Open:** all week L 12 to 2.15 (12.30 to 2.30 Sat and Sun), D 6 to 10.15 (11 Fri and Sat, 10 Sun). **Closed:** 25 and 26 Dec, 1 Jan. **Meals:** alc (main courses £10 to £42). Set L £28.50. Set D £33.50. Tasting menu L £60 to £70 (5 courses). Tasting menu D £80 to £95 (6 courses). **Service:** 15%. **Details:** 150 seats. Wheelchair access. Music.

Nopi

All-day food to be fought over
21-22 Warwick Street, Soho, W1B 5NE
Tel no: (020) 7494 9584
www.nopi-restaurant.com
⊖ Piccadilly Circus, map 5
Middle Eastern/Mediterranean | £40
Cooking score: 3

Readers wonder how Nopi chef Ramael Scully can take ordinary ingredients and turn them into something to be fought over. This is, perhaps, the secret of the Ottolenghi empire and (if diners can remain mannerly) the reason why Nopi dishes are built to share. The surroundings, all white-painted bricks and glowing bowls of flowers, embody lo-fi style and fit the all-day ethos very well. Breakfast speaks of Ottolenghi's signature style with shakshuka (braised eggs with spiced tomato sauce and smoked labneh), and reports suggest that non-meat choices like burrata with blood-orange and coriander seeds, or cauliflower, chilli and coconut fritters work better than fish dishes such as baby octopus with ras-el-hanout spices. Sweets like caramel and roast peanut ice cream with chocolate sauce hit the spot every time. 'Heart-

stoppingly superb' coffee is a highlight, with something stronger from £22 for a bottle of house wine. Unexpectedly, there's saké too.
Chef/s: Yotam Ottolenghi and Ramael Scully. **Open:** Mon to Fri 8am to 2.45, D 5.30 to 11.30. Sat 10am to 5.30pm, Sun 10am to 4pm. **Meals:** alc (main courses £8 to £13). **Service:** 12.5%. **Details:** 85 seats. Separate bar. Music.

Noura Brasserie

Tasty, traditional Lebanese favourite
16 Hobart Place, Belgravia, SW1W 0HH
Tel no: (020) 7235 9444
www.noura.co.uk
⊖ Victoria, map 5
Lebanese | £35
Cooking score: 2

£5 OFF **V**

The Bou Antoun brothers opened this well-heeled brasserie in 1999 – the first of a central London-based mini-chain (see website for branches). The key to its success is simple: all-day opening and a comprehensive menu of mostly traditional Lebanese cooking. Hot and cold meze ('good and tasty') take in everything from falafel, tabbouleh and foul medames (fava beans in tomatoes, garlic and olive oil) to sujuk (spicy sausage) with eggs, and chicken livers marinated in lemon and garlic. The char-grill turns out mains of chunky-skewered meats, and baklava is a sure-fire sticky-sweet finish. Service is 'pleasant'. House wines £22.
Chef/s: Badih El Asmar. **Open:** all week 11am to 11pm (10.30 Sun). **Meals:** alc (main courses £13 to £25). Set L £22.50. Set D £32. Sun L £32. **Service:** 12.5%. **Details:** 130 seats. 30 seats outside. Wheelchair access. Music.

Opera Tavern

Vibrant theatreland venue with lively tapas
23 Catherine Street, Covent Garden, WC2B 5JS
Tel no: (020) 7836 3680
www.operatavern.co.uk
⊖ Covent Garden, map 5
Spanish/Italian | £35
Cooking score: 4

'Tried to book Mishkin's next door, failed. Had heard some decent things about the Opera Tavern so took a punt. Overall it was excellent.' So notes one reporter, happy to find this vibrant theatreland venue lived up to expectations. This place is proud of its wares. The lively tapas assortment manages to be seasonal and creative (pistachio-crusted gurnard with baby artichokes, blood orange and mint) and nostalgic (classic tortilla, patatas fritas – 'just really good chips' – with aïoli and bravas sauce). Highlights have been chorizo with piquillo peppers, 'some really excellent quality jamón Ibérico de Bellota', and the mini-Ibérico pork and foie gras burger – delivered in an unfussy style that echoes the surroundings. The ground floor, with its long bar and open grill, has the best atmosphere, and service is roundly applauded. The enticing list of Italian and Spanish wines, arranged by style and thoughtfully annotated, opens at £16.
Chef/s: James Thickett and Ben Tish. **Open:** all week L 12 to 3, Mon to Sat D 5 to 11.30. **Closed:** 24 to 26 Dec, 1 and 2 Jan. **Meals:** alc (tapas £4 to £14). **Service:** 12.5%. **Details:** 76 seats. 8 seats outside. Wheelchair access. Music. Children allowed in upstairs restaurant only.

Symbols

🛏 Accommodation is available

💷³⁰ Three courses for less than £30

V Separate vegetarian menu

💷⁵ £5-off voucher scheme

🍷 Notable wine list

Pearl

A slice of decadence
252 High Holborn, Holborn, WC1V 7EN
Tel no: (020) 7829 7000
www.pearl-restaurant.com
⊖ Holborn, map 5
Modern French | £60
Cooking score: 5

Romantically named Pearl inhabits a world of Ionic columns, marble-clad walls and walnut panelling, with intricate strings of pearly beads dangling seductively from its lofty ceilings. Once home to the Pearl Assurance banking hall, it is now a sophisticated bar and dining room offering a slice of decadence for those with an appetite for daringly beautiful, modern French cooking. Jun Tanaka certainly knows how to impress: consider a fastidious, ingenious starter involving cauliflower custard with Périgord truffle, hazelnut pesto and shimeji mushrooms, or a bigger dish of turbot baked in a seaweed crust with squid tagliatelle, cockles, sea vegetables and lemongrass consommé. 'Amazingly consistent', razor-sharp technique is a given, even when the results are tailored to more conservative palates – as in loin of rabbit with prunes and smoked bacon, mischievously accompanied by a sausage roll and piccalilli or Elwy Valley lamb Wellington, lifted to new seasonal heights with salt-baked kohlrabi, roast Jerusalem artichokes and trompettes de mort. Desserts may sound a touch ordinary – banana and chocolate pudding, almond pannacotta with plum compote and honey ice cream – but the plates are so pretty and the detailing so exact that no one is ever disappointed. The heavyweight wine list is pitched squarely at Holborn's legal and money men; prices jet skywards from £20.
Chef/s: Jun Tanaka. **Open:** Mon to Fri L 12 to 2.30, Mon to Sat D 6 to 10. **Closed:** Sun, bank hols. **Meals:** Set L £19 (2 courses) to £23. Set D £50 (2 courses) to £60. Tasting menu £70. **Service:** 12.5%. **Details:** 80 seats. Separate bar. Wheelchair access. Music.

Phoenix Palace

Hong Kong opulence and fresh dim sum
3-5 Glentworth Street, Marylebone, NW1 5PG
Tel no: (020) 7486 3515
www.phoenixpalace.co.uk
⊖ **Baker Street, map 4**
Chinese | £35
Cooking score: 2

£5
OFF

A splash of Hong Kong opulence beneath a vast apartment block just off Baker Street, the mighty Phoenix Palace is a riot of gaudy colours, dragon motifs, antique carved furniture and screens. Freshly made dim sum is the main daytime attraction; hordes of staff in gold waistcoats deliver commendable versions of steamed Shanghai dumplings, deep-fried octopus patties with vinaigrette, crispy dough sticks, slithery chicken cheung fun and more besides. The full 200-dish menu tours the Chinese regions for hot-and-sour soup, eel fillet with 'briny' mustard greens in black bean sauce, Szechuan pork chops and steamed sea bass with Tientsin cabbage. House wine is £17.

Chef/s: Marco Li. **Open:** all week 12 to 11 (11 to 10 Sun). **Closed:** 25 Dec. **Meals:** alc (main courses £8 to £36). Set D £30.50. **Service:** 12.5%. **Details:** 280 seats. Separate bar. Wheelchair access. Music.

★ TOP 50 ★

Pied-à-Terre

As accomplished as it's ever been
34 Charlotte Street, Fitzrovia, W1T 2NH
Tel no: (020) 7636 1178
www.pied-a-terre.co.uk
⊖ **Goodge Street, map 5**
Modern French | £75
Cooking score: 7

🍷 V

After two decades of delivering high-end French cuisine on Charlotte Street, this 'small but precise' restaurant is still eliciting reams of fan mail from readers. David Moore has nurtured a succession of talented chefs over the years; Marcus Eaves trained here under previous incumbent Shane Osborn before taking the top job at the Marylebone sister restaurant L'Autre Pied (see entry). Now he is back at the mothership, cooking in a similar style to his mentor − 'every bit as good', according to one regular. The results are innovative, assured and accomplished. This year's inspection found the diminutive dining room abuzz with a lively, joyful hubbub, exuding a relaxed, welcoming vibe. Highlights included a startlingly clean-tasting chervil and asparagus soup poured over a delicate ragoût of just-cooked baby broad beans topped with a soft-poached quail's egg, and a generous portion of subtly marinated raw scallops paired with caramelised nuggets of celeriac, a scattering of toasted hazelnuts and a deeply pungent hazelnut mayonnaise. Veal rump arrived as an impressively soft and juicy cylinder of rosy-pink flesh, rolled in a vividly green and fresh-tasting herb crust, topped with spears of braised celery and white asparagus. Globe artichoke purée lent a rich, earthy note, balanced by dabs of zesty, lemongrass-scented jus. A fruit soup billed as lemon posset, confit clementine and blood-orange consommé delivered an intriguing interplay of flavours and textures, with an explosive citrus punch. To round things off, a beguiling Earl Grey tea tart was teamed with strident bergamot ice cream and little pearl-like globes of vanilla and orange gel. 'Suggested wine' is a good way into a list that starts at £20 a bottle (£5.50 a glass).

Chef/s: Marcus Eaves. **Open:** Mon to Fri L 12.15 to 2.30, Mon to Sat D 6 to 10.45. **Closed:** Sun, 22 Dec to 5 Jan. **Meals:** alc (main courses £42). Set L £27.50 (2 courses) to £33.50. Set D £60 (2 courses) to £75. Tasting menu £99. **Service:** 12.5%. **Details:** 40 seats. Separate bar. No music. Wheelchair access.

Average Price

The average price listed in main-entry reviews denotes the price of a three-course meal, without wine.

★ TOP 50 ★

Pollen Street Social

Utterly brilliant uptown eatery
8-13 Pollen Street, Mayfair, W1S 1NQ
Tel no: (020) 7290 7600
www.pollenstreetsocial.com
⊖ Oxford Circus, map 5
Modern British | £55
Cooking score: 9
🍷 V

Since launching early in 2011, Jason Atherton's brilliantly conceived gaff in deepest Mayfair has reached new peaks of creativity, confidence and sheer joie de vivre. Whether you pitch up in the bar for some cocktails and tapas or book into the classy metropolitan dining room with its leather and wooden trim, contemporary artworks and clearly visible kitchen, this place 'hits exactly the right note' in every department. Social by name and social by nature, it feels openly gregarious, but never modishly trendy. Atherton isn't one to stand still and is forever evolving new ideas (often launched on the good-value set lunch). For one reader, autumnal heaven arrived in the shape of exquisitely cooked Yorkshire partridge with plum jam, compressed apple, kale and a little boat of bread sauce. Another, eating in high summer, got a seasonal kick from a super-fresh, zingy scallop ceviche amalgamated with crunchy apple, cucumber and red radish and a light soy and yuzu dressing, alongside a pile of evanescent horseradish 'snow'. And, across the board, the rolling carnival of dishes tells its own thrilling story: tartare of fallow deer with pickled beetroot and broken egg sauce; roast red mullet with Spanish prawn rice, cockles, samphire and instantly moreish seaweed potatoes; rack of Cotswold lamb with braised shoulder, goats' curd, creamed aubergine and olive reduction suffused with aromatic Middle Eastern spice. Even when it's close to the edge, this is scintillating, exuberant cooking that never intimidates. Then it's on to the dessert bar – the venue's final trump card. Grab a stool and marvel as the crew slice, drizzle, scoop and conjure up all manner of delights, from strawberry and beetroot sorbet half-concealed by shards of basil-ash meringue or pineapple and Kaffir lime granita topped with lychee foam, to a decadent tiramisu doused in coffee and chocolate sauce poured from a cafetière. Pollen Street couldn't function without its committed staff, who provide exactly the right kind of approachable service – a mix of professionalism, common courtesy and sheer energetic style. As for wine, sommelier Laure Patry is a miracle-worker when it comes to teasing out recommendations from the high-class wine list: don't refuse the extraordinary 'wild ferment' Assyrtiko, Gaia from Santorini if it's offered. Prices start at £25 (£6.50 a glass).

Chef/s: Jason Atherton. **Open:** Mon to Sat L 12 to 2.30, D 6 to 10.30. **Closed:** Sun, 25 Dec, bank hols. **Meals:** alc (main courses £20 to £30). Set L £22 (2 courses) to £25.50. Tasting menu £69 (7 courses). **Service:** 12.5%. **Details:** 100 seats. Separate bar. Music.

Polpo

Venetian-inspired eatery
41 Beak Street, Soho, W1F 9SB
Tel no: (020) 7734 4479
www.polpo.co.uk
⊖ Piccadilly Circus, Oxford Circus, map 5
Italian | £18
Cooking score: 1
 £30

Trendy or too cool for school? Reports of 'slapdash cooking' and service that veers from 'really snappy and engaged' to 'amateurish' mean the jury is out for Russell Norman's Venetian-inspired refuelling joint, although 'excellent' arancini, a 'perky salad of flat-leaf parsley, radishes, capers et al', plus top-notch grilled carta di musica (flatbread) and cotechino with cabbage and mustard redeemed a hit-and-miss test meal. Bookings are only taken for lunch, but in the evening you can wait for a table in the new Campari bar downstairs. Wine from £18.

Chef/s: Tom Oldroyd and Diogo Santos. Open: all week L 12 to 3 (4 Sat and Sun), Mon to Sat D 5.30 to 11. Closed: 25 Dec to 1 Jan. Meals: alc (tapas £5 to £9). Service: 12.5%. Details: 60 seats. Separate bar.

ALSO RECOMMENDED
▲ La Porte des Indes

32 Bryanston Street, Marble Arch, W1H 7EG
Tel no: (020) 7224 0055
www.laportedesindes.com
⊖ Marble Arch, map 4
Indian

Bollywood meets Disney World at this flamboyant Indian old-stager, with its luxuriant tropical palms, flowing drapes, cascading waterfalls and kitsch OTT décor. Bombay chaat (£7.95), tandooris, Goan pork vindaloo, saffron-tinged Hyderabadi lamb biryani (£17.50) and other favourites from the subcontinental foodie trail are outshone by a roster of Creole-style specialities from 'Les Indes Françaises' – think grilled poulet rouge marinated in 'red spices', prawns in mild coconut curry with green mangoes or stir-fried guinea fowl with dried chillies. Four-course Sunday brunch buffets are also worth noting. Wines from £21. Open all week.

▲ Princi

135 Wardour Street, Soho, W1F OUT
Tel no: (020) 7478 8888
www.princi.co.uk
⊖ Tottenham Court Road, Piccadilly Circus, map 5
Italian

Though there are bars and eateries aplenty in Wardour Street, there's nothing quite like Princi, Alan Yau and Rocco Princi's little bit of *spirito di Milano* in the heart of Soho. Achingly elegant for what is basically a self-service café, it's good for daytime bonhomie as well as a quick-fix lunch or dinner: heritage tomato salad with buffalo mozzarella (£7.50), baked pasta, meaty stews and pizzas (from £6.50), plus pastries and excellent espresso. Wines from £20. Open all week.

The Providores
Fusion trailblazer
109 Marylebone High Street, Marylebone, W1U 4RX
Tel no: (020) 7935 6175
www.theprovidores.co.uk
⊖ Baker Street, Bond Street, map 4
Fusion | £46
Cooking score: 2

Elbow through the 'noise and chaos' of the ground floor café/tapas bar to reach the calmer first-floor restaurant. Nowadays, Peter Gordon has the fusion market pretty much to himself, but tasting portions of, say, Massaman curry-spiced oxtail crépinette with garam masala root vegetables and goats' curd have been described as 'flavourless and underseasoned' – poor value when bills are high. Providores has to regain trust. Sweet potato and miso dumplings (with saké-mirin braised cherry tomatoes, green papaya, cucumber and coriander salad with lime coconut milk and crushed salted peanuts) is a step in the right direction. New Zealand wines open at £24.50.

Chef/s: Karl Calvert. Open: all week L 12 to 3, D 6 to 10. Closed: 24 Dec to 4 Jan, Easter Mon. Meals: Set D £33 (two courses) to £63 (five courses). Service: 12.5%. Details: 40 seats. 6 seats outside. Music.

Quilon
Spot-on south Indian flavours
41 Buckingham Gate, Westminster, SW1E 6AF
Tel no: (020) 7821 1899
www.quilon.co.uk
⊖ St James's Park, Victoria, map 5
Indian | £48
Cooking score: 4

The refurbishment of this long-standing Indian restaurant has worked well; the browns, caramels, creams and golds make it look less like a corporate hotel dining room and more like an attractive space. Sriram Aylur continues to preside over an inventive menu of modern south Indian cooking and his spicing, as well as timing and presentation, is spot-on.

Ingredients are of excellent quality, with seafood a strength, be it char-grilled scallops topped with mango chilli relish or a 'delicate and utterly delicious' whole Goan-spiced sea bass, served filleted and topped with green and red masala. Meticulous cooking is shown, too, in a cauliflower chilli fry (dry, crunchy florets tossed with yoghurt, green chilli and curry leaves) and Mangalorean chicken (cooked in a spicy coconut sauce). Breads are unusually good, as are rice dishes and, for dessert, hot vermicelli kheer is recommended. There are spice-friendly wines (from £22), but note the great selection of international beers.
Chef/s: Sriram Aylur. **Open:** all week L 12 to 2.30 (12.30 to 3.30 Sat and Sun), D 6 to 11 (10.30 Sun). **Closed:** 25 Dec. **Meals:** alc (main courses £16 to £29). Set L £24. Set D £41. Sun L £24. **Service:** 10%. **Details:** 81 seats. Separate bar. Wheelchair access. Music.

Quirinale

Intimate Westminster Italian
1 Great Peter Street, Westminster, SW1P 3LL
Tel no: (020) 7222 7080
www.quirinale.co.uk
⊖ Westminster, map 3
Italian | £30
Cooking score: 3

MPs may be watching their expenses these days, but political bigwigs and correspondents from the nearby Houses of Parliament still convene in this intimate basement dining room to take advantage of its large leather banquettes, cleverly spaced tables (no chance of eavesdropping here) and thoughtful, seasonally attuned Italian cooking. Smoked tuna with fennel salad, lime dressing and coriander oil is a zingy starter; pasta could run to spaghetti with clams and bottarga or Sardinian malloreddus shells with sausage and pecorino. Mains span everything from amaretti-crusted saddle of venison to halibut with Tropea onion marmalade and orange dressing. Desserts such as semolina pudding with rhubarb and mint are sure to get the vote,

while pre-*Question Time* lubrication comes from a predominantly Italian list with prices from £19.
Chef/s: Stefano Savio. **Open:** Mon to Fri L 12 to 2.30, D 6 to 10.30. **Closed:** Sat, Sun, 24 Dec to first Mon in Jan, Aug, bank hols. **Meals:** alc (main courses £17 to £28). Set L and early D £19 (2 courses) to £23. **Service:** 12.5%. **Details:** 52 seats. Music.

Quo Vadis

Rekindled British cooking of the best sort
26-29 Dean Street, Soho, W1D 3LL
Tel no: (020) 7437 9585
www.quovadissoho.co.uk
⊖ Tottenham Court Road, map 5
British | £32
Cooking score: 4

From the moment you swing through the revolving doors and cruise past the huge pannier of citrus fruits, you know this re-energised Soho grandee is a class outfit. The dining room now looks sharp as a pin, with clean lines, distressed mirrors and Art Deco fittings, and the kitchen is on hot form – thanks to new frontman Jeremy Lee (ex-Blueprint Café). The daily menu is great fun, with its jolly Hogarth-meets-Hockney sketches, the weather forecast and little boxes advertising 'bites' (bloater paste, say), 'today's braise' and smoked eel toasties spiked with eye-wateringly pungent horseradish. Other spiffing platefuls yield jellied pork terrine with pickled prunes; a daisy-fresh combo of milky charred squid, crunchy fennel, broad beans and wild garlic leaves; and thick, fleshy roast duck breast atop a crisp potato cake with a gratifying casserole of peas, shallots and bacon. After that, lemon posset with quince purée is simplicity itself. This is rekindled British cooking of the best sort – emphatically seasonal grub full of vigour, character and 'leave-well-alone' clarity. Oh-so-cool service is pure 'new Soho' – all sharp outfits, ponytails and curls (and that's just the boys). The wine list moves upwards from £10.50 a carafe.

Chef/s: Jeremy Lee. **Open:** Mon to Sat L 12 to 3, D 5.30 to 11. **Closed:** Sun, bank hols. **Meals:** alc (main courses £14 to £25). Theatre set menu £17.50 (2 courses) to £19. **Service:** 12.5%. **Details:** 85 seats. 20 seats outside. Separate bar. No music.

The Red Fort
Indian 'new wave' veteran
77 Dean Street, Soho, W1D 3SH
Tel no: (020) 7437 2525
www.redfort.co.uk
➔ **Tottenham Court Road, map 5**
Indian | £40
Cooking score: 2
£5 OFF **V**

A standard-bearer for 'new wave' Indian cuisine during the 80s, the Red Fort has settled into a more orthodox role. However, it has added a few funky twists: at lunchtime, the front of the restaurant becomes a cut-price brasserie, while the basement Zenna bar is a glitzy night-time haunt for spiced cocktails and Asian canapés. Otherwise, the place deals in luxury, with flamboyant interiors, sharp service and a steeply priced menu of 'Mughal court cooking'. Typical shouts might include monkfish tikka with ginger and saffron, grilled lamb chops with star anise and pomegranate sauce, or roast rabbit spiked with mustard, chilli and fennel. Biryanis are the real thing. Flashy wines start at £25.
Chef/s: MA Rahman. **Open:** Mon to Fri L 12 to 4, all week D 5.30 to 11.30 (10.30 Sun). **Closed:** 25 Dec. **Meals:** alc (main courses £16 to £36). Set L £14 (2 courses) to £25. Set D £18 (2 courses) to £30. **Service:** 12.5%. **Details:** 80 seats. Separate bar. Wheelchair access. Music.

Rhodes W1 Restaurant
Nouvelle cuisine, with some real delights
Great Cumberland Place, Marble Arch, W1H 7DL
Tel no: (020) 7616 5930
www.rhodesw1.com
➔ **Marble Arch, map 4**
Anglo-French | £50
Cooking score: 3

It may surprise the out-of-town special occasion crowd who head for this celebrity chef-led hotel restaurant, but British food champion Gary Rhodes here offers a throwback to 1980s nouvelle cuisine. There are some real delights: an amuse-bouche of deconstructed BLT (jellied tomato consommé, lettuce mousse and crispy bacon dust), and a main of poussin 'various ways' (roasted, poached, fried, and confit) which made 'a beautifully comforting dish, if not entirely filling'. Others are less successful; witness pollack with a bitter olive froth and a dull tomato-based sauce. However, puddings – lemon curd with crisp meringues, hot Valrhona tart with Bushmills ice cream – follow a pattern of clever ideas, careful presentation, punchy flavours and delicate portions. The tome-like wine list starts at £24, but the sky's the limit.
Chef/s: Paul Welburn. **Open:** Tue to Fri L 12 to 2, Tue to Sat D 7 to 10. **Closed:** Mon, Sun, 2 weeks Dec, 2 weeks Aug. **Meals:** Set L £25.95 (2 courses) to £32.95. Set D £39.90 (2 courses) to £49.90. Tasting menu £75 (7 courses). **Service:** 12.5%. **Details:** 42 seats. Separate bar. Wheelchair access. Music.

NEW ENTRY
The Riding House Café
All-day food everybody loves to eat
43 Great Titchfield Street, Fitzrovia, W1W 7PQ
Tel no: (020) 7927 0840
www.ridinghousecafe.co.uk
⊖ Oxford Circus, map 5
Modern British | £28
Cooking score: 3

This all-day brasserie certainly pulls in the crowds. Get in whenever you can – it's open for eggs Benedict before work, through till the evening's last mouthful – and offers a lively, uplifting, clattery ambience, great service, and a menu with the kind of comfort food everybody likes to eat, from cheeseburgers and fish and chips to steak béarnaise and Sunday roasts. There are flourishes of ambition, too: small sharing plates of crumbed lamb breast with sauce gribiche or salt cod fritter with red pepper aïoli; whole roast turbot served with braised salsify, pancetta and red wine sauce to share. Puddings like cinnamon doughnuts with chocolate sauce keep the comfort factor high. Cocktails fit the bill, and the short, global wine list starts at £16.50.
Chef/s: Paul Daniel. **Open:** Mon to Fri 7.30 to 10, Sat and Sun 9 to 10 (9.30 Sun). **Closed:** 25 Dec. **Meals:** alc (main courses £10.50 to £25). **Service:** 12.5%. **Details:** 130 seats. Separate bar. Music.

Ristorante Semplice
Top-end Italian with enticing deals
9-10 Blenheim Street, Mayfair, W1S 1LJ
Tel no: (020) 7495 1509
www.ristorantesemplice.com
⊖ Bond Street, Green Park, map 5
Italian | £47
Cooking score: 5

The restaurant name may translate as 'simple', but there's precious little that's everyday about this top-end Italian. With its gold-frescoed walls, slinky leather furnishings and walnut panelling, Semplice exudes suave

metropolitan chic – no wonder enticingly priced set deals attract bevies of Bond Street ladies who lunch. Those who prefer to dip into the carte can expect a high-end repertoire of regional dishes inspired by prime ingredients imported from the mother country. A starter of grilled octopus with potato passata, black olives and parsley sauce has been praised to the skies, likewise a signature plate of roasted and pan-fried Italian rabbit with glazed baby carrots and artichoke sauce – although few can resist the Fassone beef carpaccio or the Amarone-soaked risotto with quail and radicchio. Elsewhere, the kitchen rolls out some stunningly creative pasta, ranging from squid-ink tagliolini with gurnard, romanesco, olives and tomato bread to a classic pairing of Gragnano spaghetti with aged pecorino, Sarawak black pepper and Italian mountain butter that is the essence of 'semplice'. Milk-fed lamb, Alba truffles and Piedmontese veal have their say, and the kitchen's open-minded approach to sourcing also brings in Ibérico pork loin and Cornish sea bass. Desserts such as apple fritters with cinnamon custard and apple jelly show a deft touch. The stellar wine list is a connoisseur's tour through the regional vineyards of Italy with superstars, artisan gems and quality drinking from £19.50.
Chef/s: Marco Torri. **Open:** Mon to Fri L 12 to 2.30, Mon to Sat D 6.30 to 10.30. **Closed:** Sun, 24 Dec to 1 Jan, bank hols. **Meals:** alc (main courses £25 to £29). Set L £23 (2 courses) to £27.50. Tasting menu £85 (7 courses). **Service:** 12.5%. **Details:** 75 seats. Wheelchair access. Music.

NEW ENTRY
Roganic
For a short time only...
19 Blandford Street, Marylebone, W1U 3DH
Tel no: (020) 7486 0380
www.roganic.co.uk
⊖ Marylebone, Bond Street, map 4
Modern British | £55
Cooking score: 6

Although Simon Rogan's tiny pop-up restaurant (it closes June 2013) has a stark, spare look, it has a complex taste – Andy Tomlinson interprets the L'Enclume style of his boss with considerable skill (see entry, Cumbria). The cooking is bold, ultra-modern, yet rustic. One minute you're nibbling on a crisp hay-smoked eel and pork belly croquette, the next you're spooning up pickled celery from a fabulous carrot concoction flavoured with ham fat and wild basil. It's a busy, highly worked approach; dishes are defined by their look-at-me artistry, but every detail makes sense, from the subtle hits of sweet and sour in a delicate sea scallop with oyster, seaweed, watercress and tiny diced apple, via the L'Enclume classic 'grown-up yolk from a golden egg', to the intense flavours of lemon sole with smoked marrow and roasted bone sauce. Equally deft is the umami hit of buffalo curds in a mushroom broth flavoured with salsify and water mint, the richness of Reg's duck breast with red orach, English mace and crispy sweetbreads, and the fact that whenever a dish threatens to be too indulgent, a tart, astringent note flickers, reining everything in. Desserts are clever and innovative – macerated strawberries with buttermilk, sweet cicely and yoghurt was a complete winner at inspection. The mainly French wine list starts high at £28.

Chef/s: Simon Rogan and Andy Tomlinson. **Open:** Tue to Sat L 12 to 2, D 6.30 to 9. **Closed:** Sun, Mon, Christmas and New Year, Easter. **Meals:** Set L £29. Set D £55 (6 courses) to £80 (10 courses). **Service:** 12.5%. **Details:** 28 seats. No music. Children at L only.

Roka

Stylish urban Japanese eating
37 Charlotte Street, Fitzrovia, W1T 1RR
Tel no: (020) 7580 6464
www.rokarestaurant.com
⊖ **Goodge Street, map 5**
Japanese | £50
Cooking score: 4

With branches in Canary Wharf and Hong Kong, Roka has its finger on the pulse of urban Japanese eating, exhibiting all the design style we have come to expect. Full-drop windows open up to Charlotte Street in good weather, while the interior is all exotic woods, right up to the burled counter that surrounds the centre of the action – the robata grill where chefs perform in animatronic efficiency from the stroke of noon through till late evening. Grilled fish (sea bass, bream, salmon) with umami-rich dressings (yuzu, miso, wasabi) are the hub, along with konbu-smoked duck, baby back ribs, and Wagyu beef with eryngii mushrooms and ponzu for the splashers. Gyoza, hotpots, tempura, maki rolls and sushi are all on hand too, and there are opulent tasting menus. Wines from £24 (£5.90 a glass) are supplemented by serious saké and shochu listings.

Chef/s: Darren Johnson. **Open:** all week L 12 to 3.30 (12.30 to 4 Sat and Sun), D 5.30 to 11.30 (10.30 Sun). **Closed:** 25 Dec. **Meals:** alc (dishes from £5 to £15). **Service:** 13.5%. **Details:** 88 seats. 24 seats outside. Separate bar. Wheelchair access. Music.

ALSO RECOMMENDED

▲ Roti Chai Street Kitchen

3 Portman Mews South, Marylebone, W1H 6HS
Tel no: (020) 7408 0101
www.rotichai.com
⊖ **Marble Arch, Bond Street, map 4**
Indian

A boon for shoppers, this cheerful, canteen-style all-day Indian eatery offers a mix of bonhomie and fairly priced, fast-paced sustenance. Found directly behind the Marble Arch M&S, Roti Chai deals in instantly appealing food along the lines of good bhel puri (£3.90), a 'superb, melting' railway lamb curry (£8.50), chicken curry with steamed rice or a delicately spiced rice with cauliflower, nuts and paneer. There's a more formal Indian restaurant in the basement. Wines from £18.50. Open all week.

Roux at Parliament Square

Assured Anglo-French cooking
12 Great George Street, Parliament Square,
Westminster, SW1P 3AD
Tel no: (020) 7334 3737
www.rouxatparliamentsquare.co.uk
⊖ Westminster, St James's Park, map 5
Anglo-French | £47
Cooking score: 4

The stately surroundings of the Royal
Institution of Chartered Surveyors make a
fitting backdrop for this accommodating
outpost of the Roux empire. Original
fireplaces stand their ground in the pastel-
toned dining room, leather-bound books line
the walls and the tables are dressed to impress
Westminster's politicos. Michel Jnr and co
aren't actively involved in the kitchen, but
lieutenant Toby Stuart knows how to marry
all that classical *savoir faire* with judiciously
sourced British ingredients. 'Stunning
presentation' is a feature of everything from a
luxurious starter of Cornish crab ravioli with
an etuvée of leeks and Champagne velouté to a
sweet conceit involving Yorkshire rhubarb
soufflé, oat crumble, blood-orange compote
and custard ice cream. In between, don't be
surprised to see saddle of rabbit stuffed with
apple and black pudding, or Arctic char with
Jersey Royals, white asparagus and an
emulsion of sea vegetables. The Francophile
wine list features some notable bottles chosen
by Albert and Michel themselves; prices start
at £20.
Chef/s: Toby Stuart. **Open:** Mon to Fri L 12 to 2, D
6.30 to 10. **Closed:** Sat, Sun, 24 Dec to 2 Jan, bank
hols. **Meals:** alc (main courses £18 to £26). Set L
£25. **Service:** 12.5%. **Details:** 56 seats. Separate
bar. No music. Wheelchair access.

Roux at the Landau

Grand hotel restaurant with modern menus
Langham Hotel, Portland Place, Oxford Circus,
W1B 1JA
Tel no: (020) 7965 0165
www.thelandau.com
⊖ Oxford Circus, map 5
Modern European | £45
Cooking score: 4

£5 OFF 🍴 V

As the restaurant of the grand Langham Hotel,
Roux at the Landau cuts an equally grand
pose. The oval room, fashioned from the old
Victorian ballroom, is wood-panelled, with
modern chandeliers and immaculate table
settings. An outpost of the Roux empire, the
kitchen deals in modern, classically based
cuisine, fashioned around seasonality and
quality ingredients. The cooking is not the
most adventurous around but its scope is
broad, taking in contemporary ideas (rare
roast squab pigeon breast with buttermilk
dressing, pickled green tomatoes and summer
lettuces) alongside more traditional treatments
(Dover sole meunière). Equally good for a pre-
theatre dine-and-dash, the early menu
delivered, at a June meal, fresh pea velouté
with spiced chorizo croquettes and herb salad,
seared sea bass with violet artichokes barigoule
and wet garlic tartine, and roast almond
parfait with fresh apricot and green almond
salad. Service is, as ever, first-class. Wines
from £30.
Chef/s: Chris King. **Open:** Mon to Fri L 12.30 to 2.30,
Mon to Sat D 5.30 to 10.30. **Closed:** Sun. **Meals:** alc
(main courses £22 to £45). Set L and D £47.50.
Service: 12.5%. **Details:** 82 seats. Separate bar.
Wheelchair access. Music. Car parking.

Rules

New chef sticks to the Rules
35 Maiden Lane, Covent Garden, WC2E 7LB
Tel no: (020) 7836 5314
www.rules.co.uk
⊖ Covent Garden, Leicester Square, map 5
British | £44
Cooking score: 3

Chef David Stafford (ex Galvin Café à Vin) has joined Rules but, rest assured, has not rocked the boat at London's oldest restaurant. You can still have your steak and kidney pie, your classically garnished game, your syrup sponge and custard. Roast quail with chanterelles, heaped on toast spread with the bird's liver, made a lip-smacking, rib-sticking start – pure Rules territory. Less convincing was a pretty, contemporary dish of venison fillet with beetroot, ruby chard and hazelnuts that simply didn't 'gel'. The spellbound tourists and theatre-folk, who come for the cosseting warmth of the characterful room and the flamboyant service as much as for the food, do well to stick with tradition – rib of beef, saddle of lamb and the like. Wines from £24.50.
Chef/s: David Stafford. **Open:** all week 12 to 11.30 (10.30 Sun). **Closed:** 25 and 26 Dec. **Meals:** alc (main courses £20 to £32). **Service:** 12.5%. **Details:** 95 seats. Separate bar. No music.

Salt Yard

Versatile tapas hot spot
54 Goodge Street, Fitzrovia, W1T 4NA
Tel no: (020) 7637 0657
www.saltyard.co.uk
⊖ Goodge Street, map 5
Spanish/Italian | £30
Cooking score: 2

Open-minded versatility is the key to this charcuterie bar and restaurant in freewheeling Fitzrovia. Sit outside with a glass of wine and some cheese, nibble smoked almonds and boquerones at the jam-packed bar, or take advantage of the kitchen's full repertoire – a tapas-fuelled, Spanish/Italian hybrid that runs all the way from jamón Ibérico to Piedmontese Gorgonzola. An 'amazing' dish of poached egg with Manchego, faro, Swiss chard and red pepper dressing wowed one reader, but the choice also extends to smoked eel brandade with beetroot and puntarelle (chicory) or roasted chorizo with apples and Moscatel. A snappy list of geographically appropriate wines starts at £16.
Chef/s: Andrew Clarke and Ben Tish. **Open:** Mon to Fri L 12 to 3, Mon to Sat D 5 to 11. **Closed:** Sun, 24 Dec to 4 Jan, bank hols. **Meals:** alc (tapas £4 to £15). **Service:** 12.5%. **Details:** 60 seats. 14 seats outside. Music. Children allowed downstairs only.

Savoy Grill

An evocation of flavours past
The Savoy, Strand, Covent Garden, WC2R 0EU
Tel no: (020) 7592 1600
www.gordonramsay.com
⊖ Charing Cross, map 5
Anglo-French | £40
Cooking score: 4
🛏 V

The Savoy may look newly minted after its life-changing refit, but this iconic dining room feels almost as glamorous as it did back in the 'good old days'. Star quality drips from every tortoiseshell panel, velvet banquette and opulent Art Deco flourish, while the cooking is a forthright evocation of flavours past. Here are mighty grills, heroic pies, casseroles and roasts with assorted accompaniments courtesy of *Larousse* or Mrs Beeton – think steamed steak and ale pudding with onion sauce, sea bass 'en papillote' with Swiss chard, salsify and Sauternes sauce, lobster thermidor, blanquette of veal, and steaks with béarnaise or marrow bone and shallot sauce. Recent samplings also suggest that desserts are on-the-money – satisfying banana and blackberry Eton mess and a classily rendered chocolate fondant with pistachio ice cream, for example. On the down side, the set lunch has been decidedly underwhelming and some customers feel let down by chaotic service. France looms large on the blue-blooded wine list; prices open at £31.

Chef/s: Andy Cook. Open: all week L 12 to 3 (4 Sun), D 6 to 10.30. Meals: alc (main courses £12 to £38). Set L £26. Service: 12.5%. Details: 40 seats. Wheelchair access. Music.

Scott's
It's about luxury, comfort and indulgence
20 Mount Street, Mayfair, W1K 2HE
Tel no: (020) 7495 7309
www.scotts-restaurant.com
⊖ Green Park, map 4
Seafood | £45
Cooking score: 4

Once past the doorman, the extremely smart first impression of Scott's is sustained, from the rich wood walls and the striking paintings that cover them, to the white starchery and the bevy of staff. The food pampers. It's not about surprise or innovation, but luxury, comfort and indulgence; the extensive menu choice runs from buttery white asparagus to Sevruga caviar among starters, and then lobster thermidor or Dover sole for mains. There's a no-nonsense feel; each dish has a central taste and others support it without any, or very little, fashionable chi-chi. Fish is exceptionally well-handled – sea trout with globe artichokes, capers and tomato, and cod with crab risotto have been praised. Meat is of the finest – perhaps Cornish lamb or Black Mount venison with roasted beets and horseradish mash. Desserts follow a familiar route: Cox's pippin apple pie or baked rhubarb and custard. Wines from £24.
Chef/s: David McCarthy. Open: all week 12 to 10.30 (10 Sun). Closed: 25 Dec. Meals: alc (main courses £17 to £29). Service: 12.5%. Details: 120 seats. 28 seats outside. Separate bar. No music. Wheelchair access.

┃┃┃ Also
┃┃┃ Recommended
Also recommended entries are not scored but we think they are worth a visit.

▲ Serpentine Bar & Kitchen
Serpentine Road, Hyde Park, W2 2UH
Tel no: (020) 7706 8114
www.serpentinebarandkitchen.com
⊖ Hyde Park Corner, map 4
Modern British

The mix of stunning modern building and great location on the eastern edge of the Serpentine draws both tourists and Londoners to this venue, with its fair-weather terrace overlooking the lake and a splendidly informal, light-filled space inside. The cooking showcases all things British, from breakfast to dinner, taking in fish finger butty with tartare sauce (£7), sausage and mash, steak and chips (£17.50), and cakes for tea, backed up by good wood-fired pizzas. Wines from £16. Open all week.

Seven Park Place
Wonderful, fastidiously detailed food
St James's Hotel and Club, 7-8 Park Place, Mayfair, SW1A 1LS
Tel no: (020) 7316 1600
www.stjameshotelandclub.com
⊖ Green Park, map 5
Modern French | £58
Cooking score: 6

Visiting Seven Park Place is like putting on evening dress: you look immaculate but are constrained by its smartness. There is a lack of freedom in the 'dense dining room' where tables are perhaps too close together and the impact of patterned carpets, patterned banquettes and boldly patterned wallpaper in a smallish space can induce a 'slightly claustrophobic' feeling. But the food placed in front of you can be wonderful. William Drabble is now well established in his own gaff in the five-star setting of the St James's Hotel. He marries classical French technique with some classic modern British ideas; the result is highly fastidious cooking that makes its mark through painstaking detail, seen in dishes such as baked fillet of red mullet with

garlic, parsley and mullet liver sauce, or an exquisite combination of seared foie gras with caramelised pears and ginger syrup. Readers praise meltingly tender saddle of Lune Valley lamb with turnips and thyme, the equally gentle roasted veal sweetbreads that come with a casserole of ceps, onions and bacon, and a very good version of burnt lemon cream. Drinkers can look forward to top-drawer quaffing from a list that shimmers with class, though prices rise skywards from £29.
Chef/s: William Drabble. **Open:** Tue to Sat L 12 to 2, D 7 to 10. **Closed:** Sun, Mon. **Meals:** Set L £24.50 (2 courses) to £29. Set D £52 (2 courses) to £58. **Service:** 12.5%. **Details:** 34 seats. Separate bar. No music.

READERS RECOMMEND
Siam Café
Thai
5 Walkers Court, Soho, W1F 0BT
Tel no: (020) 3384 0580
www.siamsohocafe.com
'This place is such good value for money and it tastes great; a refreshing alternative to the more expensive Asian franchise restaurants in central London. The menu may be small, but the taste, freshness and generous helpings prove size doesn't matter.'

Sketch, Lecture Room & Library
An extravagant pleasure palace
9 Conduit Street, Mayfair, W1S 2XG
Tel no: (020) 7659 4500
www.sketch.uk.com
⊖ Oxford Circus, map 5
Modern European | £100
Cooking score: 6

V

Assaulting the senses, confounding the expectations, has always been what the multi-faceted Sketch is about, right down to the crystal caverns that are the lavatories, and the roped-off entrance that screams 'You can't afford it!' Indeed, you probably can't. Pierre Gagnaire's concept dishes, deconstructed to

the extent of each of the elements appearing on a separate little plate, are hilariously expensive (though less so than they once were). Expect convocations of ingredients such as Gillardeau oysters in sorrel bouillon, white crab with avocado and citrus jelly, and a langoustine, with langoustine bisque and shrimp butter. Alternatively a main course that combines saddle of Quercy lamb with cabbage, stuffed grapes, olives and garlic sablé, as well as its oregano-scented rack with turnips in port, the sweetbreads, a tomato tartlet, sheep's milk yoghurt, Roquefort and a dried apricot. The Gourmet Rapide lunches are the bargain option, the wines less gouging than you might anticipate. There are glasses from £5.50, and legions of halves. Bottles start at £21.
Chef/s: Pierre Gagnaire. **Open:** Tue to Fri L 12 to 2.30, Tue to Sat D 6.30 to 10.30. **Closed:** Sun, Mon, 2 weeks Dec, 2 weeks Aug. **Meals:** alc (main courses £37 to £55). Set L £30 (2 courses) to £35. **Service:** 12.5%. **Details:** 48 seats. Separate bar. Music.

ALSO RECOMMENDED
▲ Spuntino
61 Rupert Street, Soho, W1D 7PW
www.spuntino.co.uk
⊖ Piccadilly Circus, map 5
North American

'You could walk right past it, so inconspicuous is the frontage', notes a regular to Russell Norman's oh-so-chilled eatery. With the careworn steel, wood and ceramic of the tiny interior and long queues (no telephone, no booking), this could be a bar in Brooklyn's hip Williamsburg. Small Italian-American themed sharing plates run from mac and cheese (£8), via sliders (mini-burgers) and steak and eggs (£10), to spicy sausage and Cheddar grits and shoestring fries. House wine £16.50. Open all week.

The Square

World-class gastronomy
6-10 Bruton Street, Mayfair, W1J 6PU
Tel no: (020) 7495 7100
www.squarerestaurant.com
⊖ Green Park, map 5
Modern French | £80
Cooking score: 8

The seeming paradox of the restaurant's appearance, an extensive façade in the middle of Mayfair that nonetheless manages to look rather discreet in its dark-toned, semi-frosted way, is in many ways emblematic of its whole philosophy. Philip Howard has maintained an impressive commitment to superlatively refined gastronomy ever since the early St James's Square days. Inside, the place feels expansive, the kind of wide canvas you might come across among the Manhattan elite, with subtle lighting, oceans of parquet space between tables, and excellent large abstracts offsetting the neutral decorative tones. Howard and his team have continued to uphold the essential balance between continuity and innovation that characterises the highest achievers. Working his way through the nine-course taster in summer, with accompanying wine options, a reporter wrote that it was 'worth every penny, and as good a meal as we have had anywhere'. The roll call took in artichoke salad with Wagyu beef and truffle cream, salt-cured foie gras terrine with apricot and Sauternes jelly, John Dory with girolles and thyme, and spring lamb with garlic and olive gnocchi in aged balsamic – and the recipient found every dish 'absolutely world-class'. The willingness to experiment is reflected in the gradual evolution of signature dishes, which have included a beginner of sautéed langoustine and barbecued pork ribs, best-dressed in lardo di Colonnata, grapefruit, honey and soy; the superb assiette of Pyrenean lamb with ewe's curd ravioli in new season's olive oil, garnished with pine nuts and raisins; and the long-running Brillat-Savarin cheesecake, a rich proposition sheared through by the cutting edges of passion fruit and lime. A cheese trolley of legendary proportions might so bewilder that the one cheese in the tasting menu – perhaps Wigmore with truffle honey and apricot – suffices. Bigger still is the extremely fine wine list, where the undisputed pedigree of the producers, which we might take for granted, is underwritten by some relatively fair pricing at the lower end. The glass price minimum of £9.50 may seem high, but that buys you a fine mature Fleurie. Bottles start at £25.

Chef/s: Philip Howard. **Open:** Mon to Fri L 12 to 2.45, all week D 6.30 to 10 (10.30 Fri and Sat, 9.30 Sun). **Closed:** 25 and 26 Dec, 1 Jan. **Meals:** Set L £30 (2 courses) to £35. Set D £80. Tasting menu £105 (9 courses). **Service:** 12.5%. **Details:** 75 seats. No music. Wheelchair access.

St John Hotel

Flat-out excellent Brit meat
1 Leicester Street, Leicester Square, WC2H 7BL
Tel no: (020) 3301 8069
www.stjohnhotellondon.com
⊖ Leicester Square, map 5
British | £40
Cooking score: 4

The burgeoning St John group now incorporates this stripped-down modern hotel on the cusp of Chinatown and Leicester Square, where, in an atmosphere of almost antiseptic clean minimalism, you are offered the group's trademark British food. The menus are stern in their terseness, but orchestrate a wealth and depth of flavour from slow-cooking techniques, the fashionably unfashionable cuts of meat (cheeks, chops and hearts) and the flat-out excellence of the raw materials. Start with a pairing of devilled pig skin and smoked cod roe, or grilled clams with wild fennel and lemon, and then gird your taste-buds for sweetbreads with butter beans and sea beet, or a Middle White pork chop with lentils and mustard. It's as robust and fortifying as it sounds, with a queen of puddings on hand to fill any remaining gaps.

The old-school Britishness of it all is emphasised by an entirely French wine list, opening at £20.50.
Chef/s: Tom Harris. **Open:** all week L 12 to 3, D 5.30 to 12am. **Meals:** alc (main courses £15 to £25). Set L and early D £17.50 (2 courses) to £22.50. **Service:** 12.5%. **Details:** 54 seats. Separate bar. No music. Wheelchair access.

Sumosan

Glamorous modern Japanese
26b Albemarle Street, Mayfair, W1S 4HY
Tel no: (020) 7495 5999
www.sumosan.com
⊖ Green Park, map 5
Japanese | £60
Cooking score: 4

Deep in gilt-edged Mayfair, Sumosan picks up its trade from hedge-fund managers, wealthy expats, A-listers and auction-house dilettantes – a late-night crowd who are unlikely to flinch at bonsai portions or sumo-sized bills. This glamorous venue is part of a Moscow-based chain, so expect a distinctive, multinational take on Japanese cuisine that deploys fusion flavours and luxury ingredients with a degree of dexterity. Top-notch sushi and sashimi look the part – check out the famous T&T (tuna and truffle hand roll) – and the kitchen moves quickly from oysters with ponzu dressing, glass noodle salads and rock shrimp tempura into the realms of teppanyaki duck breast with buckwheat risotto, or Wagyu beef with wasabi sauce and artichokes. 'Weight loss' and 'healthy balance' menus are aimed at starlets who want to keep in shape. The slinky J Bar downstairs is perfect for cocktails, but saké is the drink of choice – ask the sommelier for advice. Wines start at £31.
Chef/s: Bubker Belkhit. **Open:** Mon to Fri L 12 to 2.45, all week D 6 to 11.30 (10.30 Sun). **Closed:** 25 and 26 Dec. **Meals:** alc (main courses £8 to £65). Set menus from £24.90. **Service:** 15%. **Details:** 100 seats. Separate bar. Music.

Tamarind

A benchmark for high-end Moghul cuisine
20 Queen Street, Mayfair, W1J 5PR
Tel no: (020) 7629 3561
www.tamarindrestaurant.com
⊖ Green Park, map 5
Indian | £60
Cooking score: 5

£5 OFF **V**

'Still a class act' notes a reporter on this Guide stalwart, adding it 'may no longer be at the vanguard of Indian cooking, but it's still a benchmark for high-end, high-quality Moghul cuisine'. The gaudy décor of the low-ceilinged basement dining room and the ambient lounge muzak are 'not to everyone's taste', but it's plush, unfussy and comfortable with a welcoming vibe, ample elbow room and gold-star service that goes a long way to justifying the premium prices. Alfred Prasad's menu incorporates luxury ingredients into its essentially classic north Indian repertoire, from a standout starter featuring three enormous, just-cooked scallops on a mouth-tingling smoked tomato chutney spiked with chilli, black pepper, fennel and anise, to the flavour of lobster shining cleanly through its rich, vibrantly spiced pink peppercorn masala – a commendable balancing act. Grilled meats are equally impressive, not least a superlatively juicy quartet of two-inch-thick lamb cutlets: French-trimmed, marinated in papaya, garlic, chilli and cream, and lightly charred over a charcoal flame. Vegetable dishes have garnered praise, while naan bread stuffed with dates, coconut and poppy seeds is almost as sweet as the excellent mango kulfi. A heavyweight wine list – with typical Mayfair mark-ups – opens at £28, but there's Cobra beer, too.
Chef/s: Alfred Prasad. **Open:** Sun to Fri L 12 to 2.30, all week D 5.30 to 10.30 (10.15 Sun). **Closed:** 25 to 27 Dec, 1 Jan. **Meals:** alc (main courses £18 to £28). Set L £18.50 (2 courses) to £21.50. Set D £56. Sun L £32. **Service:** 12.5%. **Details:** 84 seats. Music. No children after 7pm.

Tapas Brindisa Soho
Top-drawer Spanish provisions
46 Broadwick Street, Soho, W1F 7AF
Tel no: (020) 7534 1690
www.tierrabrindisa.com
⊖ Oxford Circus, map 5
Spanish | £25
Cooking score: 3

Spanish produce supplier Brindisa, the owner of this small, trailblazing chain of tapas restaurants, has pitched them to perfection, and this Soho branch is no exception. Top-drawer charcuterie (including acorn-fed jamón Ibérico and chorizo Leon), regional cheeses, Nardin boquerones, air-cured tuna loin and other artisan provisions pepper the menu. Order several items from a list that might include courgettes stuffed with Ibérico pork, served with a piquillo pepper sauce and goats' cheese, and classic pulpo a la gallega. Little details count – Gordal olives with orange and oregano, patatas bravas with spicy tomato sauce – and you can feel at home with desserts such as turrón mousse with raisins soaked in Pedro Ximénez sherry. The sound selections on the all-Spanish wine list start at £17.50.
Chef/s: Ismael Playan. **Open:** all week 12 to 11 (4 to 9 Sun). **Closed:** 25 and 26 Dec, 1 Jan. **Meals:** alc (tapas £5 to £11). **Service:** 12.5%. **Details:** 48 seats. 4 seats outside. Separate bar.

NEW ENTRY
10 Greek Street
Nice vibes, sharp cooking, no reservations
10 Greek Street, Soho, W1D 4DH
Tel no: (020) 7734 4677
www.10greekstreet.com
⊖ Tottenham Court Road, map 5
Modern European | £27
Cooking score: 4

At a glance, 10 Greek Street looks like it might be a rather humourless operation: an austere black frontage, stark walls, a policy of no-reservations at dinner. Yet this is a restaurant that is big-hearted and garrulous, whose generous food and unfussy staff have earned it no end of critical overtures since it opened in spring 2012. Trendy though the Soho address may be, dishes go in for minimum posturing – an inspection starter of pickled herring, broad beans, peas and chilli made for a punchy, uncluttered ensemble of flavours. Mains can be equally effervescent – a hefty slab of 'crumbled' braised lamb atop chickpeas and purple-sprouting broccoli, or perhaps pitch-perfect whole lemon sole, in full voice with cherry tomatoes, samphire, watercress and tapenade. Desserts don't try any clever stunts; think along the lines of crème caramel with prunes. The concise wine list starts at £16, and rarely ventures north of £30.
Chef/s: Cameron Emirali. **Open:** Mon to Sat L 12 to 2.30, D 5.30 to 10.45. **Closed:** Sun. **Meals:** alc (main courses £12 to £18). **Service:** not inc. **Details:** 35 seats. Music.

Terroirs
Crowd-pulling bistro with great wines
5 William IV Street, Covent Garden, WC2N 4DW
Tel no: (020) 7036 0660
www.terroirswinebar.com
⊖ Charing Cross, map 5
Modern European | £25
Cooking score: 3

'Still a real gem', writes a regular of this Charing Cross hot spot, which launched in 2009. The busy, bustling interior of this little piece of France is testament to its popularity. The split-level ground-floor room is filled with posters, Parisian street signs and close-set tables; the laid-back basement restaurant is all brick walls and wooden tables, with a wider menu. Just about every dish begs to be ordered: duck rillettes are a star turn, but oxtail ragù with chestnuts and gnocchi, a main course lamb broth with wild garlic and radishes, and bitter chocolate pot have pleased reporters. The wine list is startlingly good – it motors through the vineyards of small artisan growers, mainly in France and Italy, with bantering commentary and realistic prices. Bottles from £17, but there's a fantastic selection by the glass or pot lyonnaise. **Chef/s:** Pascal Wiedemann. **Open:** Mon to Sat L 12 to 3, D 5.30 to 11. **Closed:** Sun, 25 and 26 Dec. **Meals:** alc (main courses £15 to £17). **Service:** 12.5%. **Details:** 130 seats. 6 seats outside. Music.

Texture

Cool Nordic restaurant with surprising food
34 Portman Street, Marble Arch, W1H 7BY
Tel no: (020) 7224 0028
www.texture-restaurant.co.uk
⊖ Marble Arch, map 4
Modern French/Nordic | £55
Cooking score: 4

The magnificent, ornately plastered white dining room still feels cool and contemporary five years after opening. Agnar Sverrisson, Icelandic by birth, continues to bring his new Nordic focus to the menu, rejecting butter and cream and combining unusual flavourings that bring vigour and surprise. Top-quality ingredients lie at the heart of things: Cornish king crab is partnered with Périgord truffle, Icelandic herbs and Jerusalem artichokes, Pyrenean lamb makes a seasonal appearance, and Icelandic lightly salted cod arrives with barley risotto, prawns, grapefruit and shellfish jus. A standout dessert is chocolate parfait with candied beetroot, crumbs and yoghurt ice cream. Choose from the carte or go for the six- or seven-course tasting menus; however, prices are high – the set lunch may be the best option. France claims the lion's share on Xavier Rousset's impeccable wine list, though the rest picks out interesting wines from around the globe. Prices start at £29.
Chef/s: Agnar Sverrisson. **Open:** Tue to Sat L 12 to 2.30, D 6.30 to 10.30. **Closed:** Sun, Mon, 23 Dec to 9 Jan, 1 to 15 Aug. **Meals:** alc (main courses £28 to £35). Set L £19.90 (2 courses) to £24. Tasting menu £76 (7 courses). **Service:** 12.5%. **Details:** 52 seats. Separate bar. Wheelchair access. Music.

Theo Randall at the InterContinental

Plate-lickingly good Italian food
InterContinental London Hotel, 1 Hamilton Place, Mayfair, W1J 7QY
Tel no: (020) 7318 8747
www.theorandall.com
⊖ Hyde Park Corner, map 4
Italian | £60
Cooking score: 6

'A definite thumbs-up for this place after an evening that was better than expected from a Mayfair hotel restaurant'. That's one verdict on Theo Randall's homage to rustic Italian regional cooking, set in a five-star slice of real estate. Indeed, Randall's food regularly hits the high notes, as you would expect from a chef who sources top-drawer ingredients and is steeped in the sensual world of spaghetti with Dorset blue lobster and wood-roasted turbot. His cooking is built on meticulous detail, although he never forgets that flavour comes first: a startlingly fresh buffalo mozzarella with black olives and artichokes, and a ricotta and spinach ravioli with a sage and butter sauce saw reporters tempted to lick every morsel off the plate. Spot-on cooking, too, in an 'extremely hearty portion' of Anjou pigeon, marinated and wood-roasted on pagnotta bruschetta with trevisse tardivo, pancetta and lentils di Castelluccio, which gave a 'much-welcome, deeper flavour than anticipated'. To finish, the Amalfi lemon tart is worth a punt; otherwise consider pannacotta with prunes d'Agen and almond croquante. Service has travelled from 'slow at times' via 'a little too serious' to 'effortless'. The list is a wine lover's tour of the Italian regions, with international back-up; prices from £25.
Chef/s: Theo Randall. **Open:** Mon to Fri L 12 to 3, Mon to Sat D 6 to 11. **Closed:** Sun, 1 Jan, bank hols. **Meals:** alc (main courses £28 to £38). Set L and D £27 (2 courses) to £33. **Service:** 12.5%. **Details:** 180 seats. Separate bar. Wheelchair access. Music. Car parking.

NEW ENTRY

34

Opulence and thrilling grilling in Mayfair
34 Grosvenor Square (Entrance on South Audley
Street), Mayfair, W1K 2HD
Tel no: (020) 3350 3434
www.34-restaurant.co.uk
Bond Street, Green Park, map 4
Modern British | £37
Cooking score: 2

Richard Caring's latest opening is a
characteristically opulent riff on London's
current steakhouse craze. The décor evokes
Manhattan, but the dining experience is
quintessentially Mayfair. There are salads and
seafood, but beef is the star: flame-grilled on a
South American-style parilla to produce a
slightly bitter, well-charred crust. With dry-
aged Scots Angus, USDA prime, Australian
Wagyu and cuts of wet-aged Argentinian
bifes, plus a range of sauces, 34 offers umpteen
ways to have your pound of flesh. To finish, a
chocolate and mint bombe is a masterpiece of
showmanship: hot fudge sauce poured on to a
chocolate sphere that melts to reveal ice cream.
Wines from £22.50.
Chef/s: Paul Brown. **Open:** all week 12 to 10.30.
Closed: 25 Dec. **Meals:** alc (main courses £19 to
£85). **Service:** 12.5%. **Details:** 96 seats. Separate
bar. Music.

Trishna

Indian seafood star
15-17 Blandford Street, Marylebone, W1U 3DG
Tel no: (020) 7935 5624
www.trishnalondon.com
Marylebone, Bond Street, map 4
Indian/Seafood | £30
Cooking score: 3

Born out of a legendary seafood restaurant of
the same name in Mumbai, Trishna courts
Marylebone's foodie throngs with its suave
looks, welcoming surrounds and creative fish
cookery. There is much to enjoy here, from
starters of koliwada shrimps, carom seeds and
sweet red chilli chutney to hariyali bream
pointed up with green chilli, coriander and
tomato kachumber or Dorset brown crab

enriched with butter, pepper and garlic. Meat
and veggie alternatives also satisfy, be it guinea
fowl tikka with masoor lentils or char-grilled
'kati meeti' aubergine with paneer and onion
seeds. Seafood biryani comes highly
recommended from the bargain 'lunch bites'
offer, and service gets a big thumbs-up too.
Wine is taken seriously, with several 'flights' on
offer and classy recommendations by-the-
glass alongside every dish on the menu.
Bottles from £19.50.
Chef/s: Karam Sethi. **Open:** all week L 12 to 2.45
(12.30 to 3.15 Sun), D 6 to 10.45 (6.30 to 9.45 Sun).
Closed: 25 to 27 Dec, 1 and 2 Jan. **Meals:** alc (main
courses £8 to £20). Set L £15 (2 courses) to £18.50.
Early D £20 (4 courses). Tasting menu £38.50 (5
courses) to £47.50 (7 courses). **Service:** 12.5%.
Details: 65 seats. 10 seats outside. Music.

Umu

Gilt-edged Kyoto cuisine
14-16 Bruton Place, Mayfair, W1J 6LX
Tel no: (020) 7499 8881
www.umurestaurant.com
Green Park, Bond Street, map 5
Japanese | £90
Cooking score: 5

The imperial Kyoto stylings of Umu come
wrapped in elegant contemporary design to
ensure that your encounter with the place is as
feather-light as the pressure you apply to the
touchpad at the door to get in. An interior
hewn from wood in various finishes and
textures conjures a feeling of relaxation, the
tranquillity deepened by the geometrically
flawless floral displays, the dangling shards of
Murano glass, and the mesmeric sight of sushi
chefs chopping and slicing in Zen-like silence.
There are bento lunches for those on the go,
but it's in the kaiseki tasting menus that Umu
really shows its paces. These offer a series of
small dishes, whose clean, intense flavours are
intended to be experienced independently,
with none of the cumulative impact that
Western cooking provides. An abalone
steamed over saké arrives with a blob of sea
jelly. Soup of John Dory and turnip is
sharpened with kumquat and ginger. The sea

urchin with foie gras custard is a celebrated dish, while the meat course may offer mallard jibuni (flour-coated meat in a mirin-based sauce) with pumpkin purée. There's fruit or ice cream to finish and wines by the glass from £7, but cups of saké are the way to go.
Chef/s: Yoshinori Ishii. **Open:** Mon to Fri L 12 to 3, Mon to Sat D 6 to 11. **Closed:** Sun, 25 Dec to 3 Jan. **Meals:** alc (main courses £18 to £65). Set L from £25. Tasting menu £95. **Service:** 12.5%. **Details:** 64 seats. Wheelchair access. Music.

ALSO RECOMMENDED
▲ Vasco & Piero's Pavilion
15 Poland Street, Soho, W1F 8QE
Tel no: (020) 7437 8774
www.vascosfood.com
⊖ Oxford Circus, map 5
Italian

A family-run Italian veteran from the days of 'old Soho', Vasco & Piero's continues to nourish, comfort and satisfy with a repertoire of traditional dishes drawn mainly from Umbria and its environs. Handmade pasta is a dependable shout (try aubergine tortellini or spaghettini with calamari), but the rolling menu also takes in everything from Umbrian ham with pecorino and rocket (£10.50) to rare beef tagliata or grilled tuna with lentils and spinach (£22.50). House wine is £17.50. Closed Sat L and Sun.

▲ Veeraswamy
Victory House, 99-101 Regent Street (entrance on Swallow Street), Piccadilly, W1B 4RS
Tel no: (020) 7734 1401
www.veeraswamy.com
⊖ Piccadilly Circus, map 5
Indian

Britain's oldest Indian (born in 1926) flaunts its heritage against a lavish backdrop of Mughal carpets, Maharaja turbans and antique Bengali paintings – although fibre-optic lighting, black granite surfaces and silver jali screens signal that it's also in tune with the times. The cooking is on-trend too; Keralan prawns and rogan josh now play second fiddle to venison

kebabs stuffed with dates and tamarind (£10.50), whole sea bass marinated in mint and cumin (£22.50) or lamb chops with saffron and star anise. Wines from £25. Open all week.

Vinoteca
Welcoming, buzzy brasserie
15 Seymour Place, Marylebone, W1H 5BD
Tel no: (020) 7724 7288
www.vinoteca.co.uk
⊖ Marble Arch, map 4
Modern European | £28
Cooking score: 2

Vinoteca's concept suits the way London wants to eat and drink these days, with an atmosphere of warm informality, menus that allow for nibbling as much as three-coursing it, and a heroic wine list that encourages exploration. The kitchen is as dab a hand at turning out Middle White pork cracklings to crunch on as it is at brasserie fare such as broccoli and Stilton pie, fried chicken livers and duck hearts with fried egg on toast, or lemon sole with capers and brown butter. The wine list is a constant work in progress. Bottles start at £14.50 (£3.80 a glass).
Chef/s: William Leigh. **Open:** all week L 12 to 3 (4 Sun), Mon to Sat D 6 to 10. **Closed:** 25 Dec to 1 Jan. **Meals:** alc (main courses £10 to £18). **Service:** 12.5%. **Details:** 60 seats. 6 seats outside. Separate bar. Music.

The White Swan
Hugely popular foodie boozer
108 Fetter Lane, Holborn, EC4A 1ES
Tel no: (020) 7242 9696
www.thewhiteswanlondon.com
⊖ Chancery Lane, map 5
British | £35
Cooking score: 3

Ten years on, the White Swan remains a hugely popular local rendezvous and has never strayed from its avowed aims – which is why drinkers pack the ground-floor bar, enjoying its pub vibes. It's also why the hungry continue to mount the staircase to the top floor for the unexpected, sophisticated feel of the restaurant and the eclectic modern food. Rustic pork terrine or new season's asparagus teamed with Dorset crab and Irish white pudding might give way to roast rump of Herdwick hogget with its grilled liver, spinach, wild garlic, violet artichoke and roast onion tortellini, or Cornish brill paired with ox cheek ravioli. Walnut and honey tart with mascarpone sorbet is a fitting finale. The global wine list opens at £16.50.

Chef/s: John Tremayne. **Open:** Mon to Fri L 12 to 3, D 6 to 10. **Closed:** Sat, Sun, 25 and 26 Dec, bank hols. **Meals:** alc (main courses £13 to £21). Set L £24 (2 courses) to £31. Bar menu also available. **Service:** 12.5%. **Details:** 52 seats. Separate bar. Music.

Wild Honey

Well-heeled Francocentric bistro
12 St George Street, Mayfair, W1S 2FB
Tel no: (020) 7758 9160
www.wildhoneyrestaurant.co.uk
⊖ Oxford Circus, Bond Street, map 5
Modern European | £35
Cooking score: 5

Even well-heeled Mayfair needs a local bistro, a place with stools at the bar, banquettes, booths and close-packed tables – and Will Smith and Anthony Demetre's clubby, oak-panelled dining room is it. Seasonality is a characteristic of the daily output, taking in a salad of fresh goats' curd, Anya potatoes and peas in spring, and pheasant with potted cabbage, prunes and Armagnac in autumn. The food may not have quite the direct and earthy appeal of its earlier days, but skilful cooking such as this, applied to fine materials, ensures a high success rate. A portion of creamy lamb sweetbreads with a dollop of sheep's ricotta and a tangle of English spinach, fennel and mint delivers a richly sweet collation, although traditionalists may prefer to start with the restrained thrills of rabbit, pork and apricot terrine with fruit relish and pickled carrots. Fish is well-treated too,

judging by fresh, accurately timed cod fillet (with potato gnocchi, peas, broad beans and monk's beard – a type of chicory). Desserts are a delight, especially the never-off-the-menu wild-honey ice cream and honeycomb. Just about everything on the carefully assembled, good-value wine list is available by the 250ml carafe; bottles from £16.50.

Chef/s: Colin Kelly. **Open:** all week L 12 to 2.30 (3 Sun), D 5 to 11 (10.30 Sun). **Closed:** 25 and 26 Dec, 1 Jan. **Meals:** alc (main courses £15 to £23). Set L £18.95. Set early D £21.95. Sun L £24.50. **Service:** 12.5%. **Details:** 60 seats. No music.

Wiltons

Bastion of St James' tradition
55 Jermyn Street, Mayfair, SW1Y 6LX
Tel no: (020) 7629 9955
www.wiltons.co.uk
⊖ Green Park, map 5
British | £60
Cooking score: 4

A moment's respects: we were sad to hear of the death in January 2012 of Patrick Flaherty, Wilton's long-serving oyster bar tender, just as he was about to embark on a half-century season at this bastion of St James' tradition. Wiltons has been looking after the great and the good among London diners since George II was on the throne, with properly dressed seafood (lobster cocktails, crab and avocado, those oysters) and seasonal game (teal, woodcock, partridge) its strongest selling points. Meats from the carving trolley change by day – Thursday brings honey-glazed gammon – and for those whose eyes are trained forwards, not back, the kitchen offers some more modern tasting dishes, such as Angus beef and oxtail with morels in red wine. An early evening menu ensures you'll get to theatreland on time, and not have to do without a portion of apple and raisin crumble with Calvados. Wine starts at £30.

Chef/s: Daniel Kent. **Open:** Mon to Fri L 12 to 2.30, D 5.30 to 10.30. **Closed:** Sat, Sun, 22 Dec to 7 Jan, bank hols. **Meals:** alc (main courses £18 to £60). Set L and early D £35 (2 courses) to £45. Set D £55.

Tasting L £48. Tasting D £80 (5 courses) to £90. **Service:** 12.5%. **Details:** 100 seats. Separate bar. No music. Wheelchair access.

The Wolseley
High-impact all-day brasserie
160 Piccadilly, Mayfair, W1J 9EB
Tel no: (020) 7499 6996
www.thewolseley.com
⊖ **Green Park, map 5**
Modern European | £35
Cooking score: 2

'Food is always very good, service sometimes hit-and-miss, atmosphere always excellent' just about sums up Corbin and King's high-impact all-day brasserie. Styled on the grand cafés of central Europe, it plays to the crowds and reporters don't seem to mind the tightly packed tables and high decibel levels. The repertoire of tried-and-true stalwarts ranges from dressed Cornish crab via duck confit and boiled salt beef (with herb dumplings) to herrings with pumpernickel, and Wiener schnitzel. It's a handy spot for breakfasts and afternoon teas, too, but getting in can be a headache so do book ahead. Wines from £19.50.
Chef/s: Lawrence Keogh. **Open:** all week L 12 to 3 (3.30 Sat and Sun), D 5.30 to 12 (11 Sun). **Closed:** 25 Dec, August bank hol. **Meals:** alc (main courses £12 to £33). **Service:** 12.5%. **Details:** 150 seats. Separate bar. No music. Wheelchair access.

NEW ENTRY
Wright Brothers
Soho oyster house
13 Kingly Street, Soho, W1B 5PW
Tel no: (020) 7434 3611
www.thewrightbrothers.co.uk
⊖ **Oxford Circus, map 5**
Seafood | £30
Cooking score: 2

Nothing to do with their airborne namesakes, these Wright brothers occupy themselves with things that swim in the sea. They own a Cornish oyster farm, and have set up this Soho reboot of an old-school London oyster house – complete with clattering bar stools and ceramic-tiled walls – plus a more sedate restaurant upstairs. Molluscs are the mainstay; varieties from all corners of the British Isles feature, both 'naked' and dressed, along with some French ambassadors. Elsewhere, dishes stick to the seafood script – think whitebait and tartare, fish pie and a perfectly executed moules marinière. A French-dominated wine list starts at £19. See also Wright Brothers in Southwark.
Chef/s: Jai Parkinson. **Open:** all week L 12 to 3 (3.30 Sat, 4 Sun), Mon to Sat D 5.30 to 10.45. **Closed:** 24 to 28 Dec, 1 and 2 Jan, bank hols. **Meals:** alc (main courses £12 to £16). Set L £14.50 (2 courses) to £16.50. Set D £16.50 (2 courses) to £18.50. **Service:** not inc. **Details:** 96 seats. 26 seats outside. Separate bar. Wheelchair access. Music.

ALSO RECOMMENDED
▲ Yalla Yalla
1 Green's Court, Piccadilly, W1F 0HA
Tel no: (020) 7287 7663
www.yalla-yalla.co.uk
⊖ **Piccadilly Circus, map 5**
Lebanese

This tiny gaff up an alley off Brewer Street is made to look bigger by 'comically tiny stools' at the tables. But 'stupendous' Lebanese street food is the draw, from wraps and pastries to meze and grilled meats. Sujuk (£4.75) are excellent little lamb sausages with tomato, parsley and lemon juice, there are feta and haloumi cheese pastries, and slow-cooked lamb shoulder with seven-spiced rice (£10.75). Open all week. Wines from £18. Also at 12 Winsley Street, W1W 8HQ; tel (020) 7637 4748, and a counter on the mezzanine level at King's Cross station.

Yauatcha

Drop-dead cool Chinese venue
15-17 Broadwick Street, Soho, W1F ODL
Tel no: (020) 7494 8888
www.yauatcha.com
⊖ Tottenham Court Road, map 5
Chinese | £50
Cooking score: 3

V

As drop-dead cool as its big brother Hakkasan (see entries), Yauatcha divides into a hip street-level space for roistering, café-style fun and a slinky basement where moody lighting and lacquered screens lend a clubby exclusivity to proceedings. Either way, expect thunderous chatter, whirling service and a dim sum menu that ventures where few similar outfits fear to tread: scallop siu mai and glutinous rice are rapidly eclipsed by thrilling plates of roast duck and pumpkin puffs, lobster dumplings with tobiko caviar, jasmine tea-smoked ribs and homemade tofu with salted radish. After that, dip into the pleasure-seeking world of coconut and white chocolate charlotte with mint, basil and mango. For heady kicks of another kind, drop by for one of Yauatcha's uplifting teas and a couple of funky macaroons. Ultra-trendy global wines from £25.
Chef/s: Tong Chee Hwee. **Open:** all week 12 to 11.30 (12 to 11.45 Fri and Sat, 10.30 Sun). **Closed:** 24 and 25 Dec. **Meals:** alc (dishes £9 to £29).
Service: 12.5%. **Details:** 180 seats. Separate bar. Wheelchair access. Music.

Zafferano

Top Italian performer
15 Lowndes Street, Belgravia, SW1X 9EY
Tel no: (020) 7235 5800
www.londonfinedininggroup.com
⊖ Knightsbridge, Hyde Park Corner, map 4
Italian | £47
Cooking score: 6

'Nobody does it better in London', affirmed a long-time supporter of Zafferano's 'white truffle season' – a revelatory fungal celebration that adds extra warmth and earthy richness to this top Italian performer. As a loyal Knightsbridge servant since the mid 90s, it maintains a serious pose and sophisticated demeanour without puffing itself up: effortless chic is the style and the dining room keeps its cool with stone floors, brick walls and sleek banquettes. The kitchen proves its pedigree by following the calendar unerringly and treating seasonal ingredients with proper consideration. As ever, elegantly fashioned homemade pasta remains a star turn: lobster linguine always gets plenty of votes, but the choice might also extend to veal shin ravioli with saffron or twisted strozzapreti with Tropea onions and tomato. Invitingly fresh, seasonally attuned salads are another strong suit (fresh peas and broad beans with salted ricotta, or cuttlefish with green beans and Taggiasche olives, for example), and there is much to cheer when it come to the main events. Rib of beef with artichokes and mash did the business for one reader, but the kitchen can also deliver knock-out plates of calf's liver with Swiss chard and balsamic vinegar, or char-grilled monkfish with courgettes and sweet chilli. To finish, tortino di cioccolato (chocolate fondant) is worth the 12-minute wait; otherwise go straight for the vanilla pannacotta or citrusy cannoli with pistachios. The top-end wine list is an Italian regional blockbuster with serious pickings but unapologetic Knightsbridge prices; bottles start at £32.
Chef/s: Andy Needham. **Open:** all week L 12 to 3, D 6 to 11. **Meals:** alc L (main courses £9 to £25). Set L £21 (2 courses) to £26. Set D £36.50 (2 courses) to £46.50. **Service:** 13.5%. **Details:** 100 seats. Separate bar. No music. Wheelchair access.

Symbols

🛏 Accommodation is available

£30 Three courses for less than £30

V Separate vegetarian menu

£5 OFF £5-off voucher scheme

🍶 Notable wine list

L'Absinthe
Cracking classics and stonking good value
40 Chalcot Road, Primrose Hill, NW1 8LS
Tel no: (020) 7483 4848
www.labsinthe.co.uk
⊖ Chalk Farm, map 2
French | £25
Cooking score: 3

'We left with a warm glow about this establishment' revealed one couple, smitten by the cheery vibes and energetic staff at this small French restaurant. They also loved the reasonable prices (lunch, in particular, is stonking good value). The kitchen belts out cracking French regional classics like escargots, leeks vinaigrette with poached egg, and salade Lyonnaise. It's a tried-and-trusted repertoire at main course stage too, with robust versions of boeuf bourguignon, and Toulouse sausage with Lyonnaise potatoes and mustard sauce. Desserts play it straight with crêpes suzette and tarte Tatin. L'Absinthe runs its own wine shop, and everything on the (almost) all-French list is offered at retail price with a standard £10 surcharge for drinking at table. Vin de pays is £15.50.
Chef/s: Christophe Fabre. **Open:** Tue to Sun L 12 to 2.30 (4 Sat and Sun), D 6 to 10.30 (9.30 Sun). **Closed:** Mon, 1 week Christmas, 2 weeks Aug. **Meals:** alc (main courses £10 to £18). Set L £10.95 (2 courses) to £13.95. Sun L £15.95 (2 courses) to £19.50. **Service:** 12.5%. **Details:** 75 seats. 14 seats outside. No music.

The Albion
Lively local with no-frills Brit food
10 Thornhill Road, Islington, N1 1HW
Tel no: (020) 7607 7450
www.the-albion.co.uk
⊖ Angel, Highbury & Islington, map 2
British | £30
Cooking score: 2

£5
OFF

'A nice place to have on your doorstep' noted a visitor to this pretty, wisteria-covered Georgian pub. The Albion takes a dressed-down, casual approach to things, with wood floors, polished tables and animated local vibes. Winter fires and a summer walled garden cover the seasons perfectly. The regularly changing menu trumpets no-frills, British dishes along the lines of cauliflower cheese soup or Hansen & Lydersen smoked salmon with buttered spelt bread. There's good choice from the grill, including impressive steaks, or there's brown trout with horseradish potatoes, heritage beetroot and crème fraîche, and chicken, leek and mushroom pie. Wines from £16.50.
Chef/s: David Johnson. **Open:** Mon to Sat L 12 to 3 (4 Sat), D 6 to 10. Sun 12 to 9. **Meals:** alc (main courses £10 to £25). **Service:** 10%. **Details:** 130 seats. 130 seats outside. Wheelchair access. Music.

Almeida
Long-running Islington performer
30 Almeida Street, Islington, N1 1AD
Tel no: (020) 7354 4777
www.almeida-restaurant.co.uk
⊖ Angel, Highbury & Islington, map 2
French | £30
Cooking score: 3

Playing out its culinary scenarios across the road from the namesake Almeida Theatre, this long-running Islington performer is a smart-looker with its sleek minimalist lines, abstract artwork and open-to-view kitchen. And smart bistro cooking is the order of the day, as Alan Jones and his team turn their hand to chicory, Roquefort, walnut and poached pear salad, Denham Estate venison bourguignon or poached brill with Jersey Royals, samphire and Champagne velouté. A pot-au-feu of Vendée black-leg chicken has been rich, satisfying and deeply savoury, while desserts might deliver hot chocolate fondant with honeycomb ice cream. The odd dish can disappoint and the interior can sometimes feel a bit like a '90s hotel dining room' when it's bereft of theatre-goers, but there's always plenty to applaud on the thoughtfully compiled wine list – not least the page of house recommendations by the glass or 460ml 'pot'. France is the main contender, although it's also worth looking for interesting names from Italy and Spain; bottles start at £17.50. **Chef/s:** Alan Jones. **Open:** Tue to Sun L 12 to 2.15 (2.30 Sat, 3.30 Sun), Mon to Sat D 5.30 to 10.30. **Meals:** alc (£11 to £22). Set L and D £15.95 (2 courses) to £18.95. **Service:** 12.5%. **Details:** 100 seats. 16 seats outside. Separate bar. No music. Wheelchair access.

Bradleys

Long-running French favourite
25 Winchester Road, Swiss Cottage, NW3 3NR
Tel no: (020) 7722 3457
www.bradleysnw3.co.uk
⊖ Swiss Cottage, map 2
French | £40
Cooking score: 3

Simon Bradley has plenty to be proud of as he celebrates 20 years of serving simple, well-made seasonal bistro food to the Swiss Cottage crowd. Bradleys is a pretty space in dove-grey and burgundy, opening to a garden at the back. It's around the corner from the Hampstead Theatre and can get packed in the early evening with pre-curtain eaters, but settles into calm civility later. Fish starters are usually reliable (perhaps red mullet with artichoke, tomato galette and tapenade) as are mains such as beautifully timed turbot with violet artichoke barigoule and spinach. Meats might include veal rump with creamed leeks, salsify and morel sauce. Sensational rhubarb soufflé is among well-reported desserts, and the user-friendly wine list features sound global selections. House Chardonnay and Merlot are £17.50. **Chef/s:** Simon Bradley. **Open:** Sun to Fri L 12 to 3, Mon to Sat D 6 to 11. **Meals:** Set L £13.50 (2 courses) to £17.50. Set D £24.50. Sun L £23. **Service:** 12.5%. **Details:** 60 seats. No music.

ᚹ Also Recommended

Also recommended entries are not scored but we think they are worth a visit.

The Bull & Last

Tried-and-true modern Brit dishes
168 Highgate Road, Hampstead, NW5 1QS
Tel no: (020) 7267 3641
www.thebullandlast.co.uk
⊖ Tufnell Park, Kentish Town, map 2
Modern British | £30
Cooking score: 3

The Bull and Last is a listed building (or an old pub, if you prefer) close to Parliament Hill. The spacious, breezy ambience of the place suits the mood of the food – a cavalcade of tried-and-true modern Brit dishes. Nibbling some vegetable fritto misto in the bar while dithering over the menu is a good way to kick things off. The meatier mains also score highly, whether for a haunch of venison and braised shoulder with salsify, pistachio and blackberries or slow-cooked pig's cheek with choucroute, black pudding and cider prunes. There's a comforting familiarity about starters such as brown crab macaroni with tomato, chilli and crème fraîche, and puddings of apple crumble or baked chocolate mousse. Wines from £16. **Chef/s:** Oliver Pudney. **Open:** all week L 12 to 3 (4 Sat, 12.30 to 4 Sun), D 6.30 to 10 (9 Sun). **Closed:** 24 and 25 Dec. **Meals:** alc (main courses £15 to £28). **Service:** not inc. **Details:** 130 seats. 30 seats outside. Separate bar. Music. Car parking.

Café Japan

Good sushi at fair prices
626 Finchley Road, Golders Green, NW11 7RR
Tel no: (020) 8455 6854
⊖ Golders Green, map 1
Japanese | £25
Cooking score: 3

Good sushi at fair prices is the formula on which Café Japan has built its reputation, and this Golders Green stalwart is emphatically still 'worth schlepping across London for' according to one veteran customer. Unlike its high-fashion counterparts in Mayfair, little time is squandered on cosmetic appearances; the small dining room is dressed in plain,

blond wood (although there are mutterings of a refurb). The focus instead lies on fresh produce and precise preparation. Set menus offer good guidance, although toro (fatty tuna) sashimi, perfectly textured tempura and the signature age-roll – crispy fried fish with spicy mayo – have been singled out by glowing reports. The wine list is limited to a handful of whites and reds (from £14); green tea, saké and Japanese beer are also present and correct.
Chef/s: BH Min. **Open:** Tue to Sun L 12 to 2.30 (3 Sat and Sun), D 6 to 10.30 (10 Sun). **Closed:** Mon, 1 week Christmas, 1 week Aug. **Meals:** alc (main courses £11 to £28). Set L £8.50 (2 courses) to £13.50. Set D £14 (2 courses) to £28. Sun L £8.50. **Service:** not inc. **Details:** 35 seats. Music.

NEW ENTRY

The Charles Lamb Pub and Kitchen

Affable local with to-the-point food
16 Elia Street, Islington, N1 8DE
Tel no: (020) 7837 5040
www.thecharleslambpub.com
⊖ Angel, map 2
Modern British | £23
Cooking score: 2

A canny retreat from the boutique boozers of Upper Street, the Charles Lamb is an affable neighbourhood pub squirrelled away down a side street behind Angel tube. Inside, wainscotted walls, tatty board games and a vague whiff of Victoriana sit comfortably with the gutsy, to-the-point menu. Among the ranks of mains you might find a steak, mushroom and Guinness pie with mash. Elsewhere, asparagus, sweet potato and chickpea tagine nods to Islington media types. The wine list makes a point of being exclusively Old World (from £14), but ales on tap are equally distinguished – try Dark Star Hophead.

Chef/s: Claire Roberson. **Open:** Wed to Sun L 12 to 3 (4 Sat, 6 Sun), Mon to Sat D 6 to 9.30. **Closed:** 24 Dec to 1 Jan. **Meals:** alc (main courses £10 to £13). **Service:** not inc. **Details:** 40 seats. 30 seats outside. Separate bar. Music.

ALSO RECOMMENDED

▲ Chilli Cool

15 Leigh Street, King's Cross, WC1H 9EW
Tel no: (020) 7383 3135
www.chillicool.com
⊖ Russell Square, King's Cross, map 2
Chinese

Better-than-usual Szechuan cooking is to be had at this modest Bloomsbury address. The kitchen aims for a fast turnaround, pleasing a mixed crowd with generous portions and fair prices. For a full-on assault on the senses, try fiery appetisers such as aubergine with red and green chopped chilli (£5.20) and chef's specials such as gong hao chilli chicken with peanuts (£7.50). Pork figures enterprisingly (hot and chilli crispy pork intestine; hot and spicy pig's feet). Wines from £9.90. Open all week.

500 Restaurant

Genuine neighbourhood Italian
782 Holloway Road, Archway, N19 3JH
Tel no: (020) 7272 3406
www.500restaurant.co.uk
⊖ Archway, map 2
Italian | £25
Cooking score: 2

Its Archway address and bare-wood interiors aren't much to shout about, but 500 still does the business as a genuine neighbourhood Italian. Honest regional cooking is the kitchen's stock-in-trade; it knocks out generous versions of *cucina povera* in the shape of, say, pumpkin and chestnut soup, duck ravioli, a risotto with Verona celery and Gorgonzola, or char-grilled lamb cutlets with Jerusalem artichokes and bagna cauda (hot dipping sauce). After that, the signature 'coppa 500' might yield caramelised pears with cinnamon ice cream, while the wine list picks up some tasty Italian regional stuff from £13.50. The name 500? It refers to the owners' passion for the dinky Fiat Cinquecento car. **Chef/s:** Mario Magli. **Open:** Fri and Sat L 12 to 3, Mon to Sat D 6 to 10.30. Sun 12 to 9.30. **Closed:** 2 weeks Christmas, 2 weeks summer. **Meals:** alc (main courses £11 to £17). **Service:** not inc. **Details:** 40 seats. Music.

NEW ENTRY

The Gate

Easy-eating vegetarian
370 St John Street, Islington, EC1V 4NN
Tel no: (020) 7278 5483
www.thegaterestaurants.com
⊖ Angel, map 2
Vegetarian | £25
Cooking score: 1

V

Competition for casual eateries is fierce in Islington, but this vegetarian – an offshoot of the long-established Gate in Hammersmith which, at the time of going to press, was closed for refurbishment – is just about holding its own, valued for its location opposite Sadler's Wells. Halloumi in a tikka marinade, Thai salad, with a 'nicely tart' sweet-sour dressing, and a rich couscous-crusted aubergine layered with green pesto and cream cheese on a beetroot and chickpea base are typical choices. Pressed chocolate and chilli cake with crème fraiche wraps things up nicely, while a globe trotting wine list kicks off at £16.25. **Chef/s:** Adrian Daniel. **Open:** all week L 12 to 2.30, D 6 to 10.30, Sat and Sun brunch 10 to 3. **Meals:** alc (main courses £11 to £16). Set L and D £12.50 (2 courses) to £15. **Service:** 12.5%. **Details:** 90 seats. Separate bar. Wheelchair access. Music.

The Gilbert Scott

Opulent surroundings and patriotic victuals
St Pancras Renaissance Hotel, Euston Road, Euston, NW1 2AR
Tel no: (020) 7278 3888
www.thegilbertscott.co.uk
⊖ King's Cross St Pancras, map 2
British | £35
Cooking score: 1

 V

Mulligatawny soup, Mrs Beeton's spatchcock chicken, faggots, pease pudding, Lord Mayor's trifle...welcome to the born-again world of British gastronomy, dusted off for twenty-first century palates and served in the opulent Victorian Gothic surrounds of the revitalised St Pancras Renaissance Hotel (originally designed by George Gilbert Scott). This is Marcus Wareing's tribute to patriotic victuals and fancy conceits, delivered by his deputy Oliver Wilson and served in a lofty, pillared room that can feel cramped and noisy despite its grandiose proportions. The cooking generally passes muster, but the £2 service charge can grate and the wine list has nothing below £25. Reports please. **Chef/s:** Oliver Wilson. **Open:** Mon to Sat L 12 to 3, D 5.30 to 11. Sun 12 to 10. **Meals:** alc (main courses £16 to £28). Set L and D £22 (2 courses) to £27. Sun L £27. **Service:** 12.5%. **Details:** 110 seats. Separate bar. No music. Wheelchair access.

READERS RECOMMEND

Gung-Ho

Chinese
328-332 West End Lane, West Hampstead, NW6 1LN
Tel no: (020) 7794 1444
'Really hits the spot. A neighbourhood Chinese restaurant with big ideas – and fantastic spring rolls!'

Homa

Trendy brasserie with sunny food
71-73 Stoke Newington Church Street, Stoke
Newington, N16 0AS
Tel no: (020) 7254 2072
www.homalondon.co.uk
⊖ Arsenal, map 2
Modern European | £26
Cooking score: 3

Run by an Italian-Turkish couple, Homa is a
lively Mediterranean-crossbreed brasserie
currently doing a roaring trade in Stoke
Newington. Interiors are dressed for the
trendy postcode – cue artfully dangling light
fittings and mandatory bare floorboards. The
menu is a bit less fashion-conscious; sound
ingredients are allowed to speak for
themselves in simple combinations. Try a
starter of marinated artichokes with Serrano
ham, pecorino cheese and shallot dressing.
Mains, too, show a steady hand – an
inspection bavette of beef was perfectly
cooked, skilfully paired with wet polenta,
cavolo nero and wild mushrooms. Homa is
equally in its element fending off hangovers
with a formidable brunch menu at weekends,
and crowd-pleasing pizzas fill stomachs from
3pm on weekdays. House wines start
at £15.50.
Chef/s: Phil Jones. **Open:** all week L 12 to 3 (4 Sat
and Sun), D 6 to 10.30 (10 Sun). **Closed:** 25 and 26
Dec. **Meals:** alc (main courses £12 to £19).
Service: not inc. **Details:** 80 seats. 30 seats outside.
Separate bar. Music.

Symbols

⇤ Accommodation is available

£30 Three courses for less than £30

V Separate vegetarian menu

£5 OFF £5-off voucher scheme

🍷 Notable wine list

Jin Kichi

Japanese hangout with lots of choice
73 Heath Street, Hampstead, NW3 6UG
Tel no: (020) 7794 6158
www.jinkichi.com
⊖ Hampstead, map 1
Japanese | £25
Cooking score: 1

V

Hampstead locals might think they've
stumbled on to Tokyo's mean streets when
they arrive at this cramped Japanese hangout.
The best seats are around the robata grill,
which turns out teriyakis and yakitori skewers
(try duck with spring onion or chicken skin
with salt) but there's ample choice if you prefer
your food raw, deep-fried or simmered, with a
full contingent of nigiri sushi, hand rolls and
sashimi, tempura and udon noodles. Wines
(from £28) are minimal; drink tea, beer or
chilled saké.
Chef/s: Ray Shimazu. **Open:** Tue to Sun L 12.30 to 2,
D 6 to 11 (10 Sun). **Closed:** Mon, 25 Dec, Tue after
bank hols. **Meals:** alc (main courses £5 to £16).
Service: 12.5%. **Details:** 42 seats. Music.

NEW ENTRY

Karpo

A terrific addition to King's Cross
23 Euston Road, King's Cross, NW1 2SD
Tel no: (020) 7843 2221
www.karpo.co.uk
⊖ King's Cross, map 2
Eclectic | £30
Cooking score: 1

The punk-themed exterior is all huge graphics
and neon colours, there are pastries piled in the
window and a pseudo-industrial interior
offering a flexible menu that sprawls in all
culinary directions – 'a bit exhausting' but this
all-day eatery fits the bill for the transient
custom at King's Cross. Karpo is open from
breakfast to dinner. Expect beef tataki, steaks
from the wood-fired oven or pan-fried cod,

cockles and braised fennel, and pecan tart with bourbon and orange ice cream. Wines from £16.
Open: all week 7am to 11pm. **Meals:** alc (main courses £9 to £22). **Service:** 12.5%. **Details:** 140 seats. Separate bar. Music.

Kentish Canteen
Populist, urban-minded eatery
300 Kentish Town Road, Kentish Town, NW5 2TG
Tel no: (020) 7485 7331
www.kentishcanteen.co.uk
⊖ Kentish Town, map 2
Modern European | £19
Cooking score: 2

The Kentish of the name refers to Kentish Town, rather than the Garden of England, while 'canteen' emphasises that this is a populist, urban-minded eatery with bags of vigour. Inside, a counter loaded with tapas-style goodies sets the tone, and proceedings kick off with breakfast/brunch taking in anything from French toast to eggs every which way. After that, it's a free-roaming, Euro-accented run through mackerel ceviche, Champagne risotto with tempura artichokes, pollack fillet with braised lentils, and grilled chorizo with roasted sweet potato. Burgers, steaks and salads also feature, while desserts promise the likes of pistachio rice pudding or lavender crème brûlée. Wines from £15.95. Downstairs is a funky, Irish-themed 'shebeen' bar.
Chef/s: Julian Legge. **Open:** all week 10am to 10.30pm (9 to 8 Sun). **Closed:** 25 and 26 Dec. **Meals:** alc (main courses £9 to £16). Set L £13.95 (2 courses) to £16.95. Set D £15.95 (2 courses) to £18.95. **Service:** 12.5%. **Details:** 70 seats. 20 seats outside. Separate bar. Wheelchair access. Music.

¦¦¦ Also Recommended
Also recommended entries are not scored but we think they are worth a visit.

Made in Camden
A kaleidoscope of captivating sharing plates
Roundhouse, Chalk Farm Road, Camden, NW1 8EH
Tel no: (020) 7424 8495
www.madeincamden.com
⊖ Chalk Farm, map 2
Fusion | £25
new chef

'There are few places of this quality in north west London – the food is exciting, innovative and delicious' enthuses a supporter of the Roundhouse's casual, unpretentious eatery. Josh Katz has left, but the kitchen continues to raise the bar, pumping out a kaleidoscope of ingredients and flavours via a series of captivating sharing plates; previously these have included an 'amazing' soft-shell crab tempura with nori salt and jalapeño dressing, a stunning belly pork with braised red cabbage and quince, garlic and maple purée, and sweet potato and ricotta gnocchi with burnt aubergine and pangrattato (toasted breadcrumbs). Sassy desserts put a brave new spin on the classics – walnut and caramelised pear tiramisu or sweet-spiced chestnut bread-and-butter pudding, for instance. Brunch is recommended, too. House wine is £17.50.
Open: Tue to Sun L 12 to 2.30 (10.30 to 3 Sat and Sun), D 6 to 10.30. **Closed:** Mon, 25 and 26 Dec. **Meals:** alc (main courses £6 to £16). Set L £10 (2 courses). **Service:** 12.5%. **Details:** 54 seats. Separate bar. Wheelchair access. Music.

ALSO RECOMMENDED
▲ Mangal 1 Ocakbasi
10 Arcola Street, Stoke Newington, E8 2DJ
Tel no: (020) 7275 8981
www.mangal1.com
⊖ Dalston Kingsland, map 2
Turkish

Quite a fixture on the Stoke Newington scene, this cheap and busy ocakbasi values the simple approach – grills from the sizzling ocak, backed up by salads, pide and sac bread. Starters (£2 to £5) include hummus, lahmacun (Turkish pizza topped with mince and onions), and grilled aubergine and peppers with yoghurt and butter sauce. Skewered mains (£9 to £10) could be anything from lamb chops and chicken wings to quail. House wine is £13, but you can BYO. Open all week.

Market

Trendy eatery with plucky Brit food
43 Parkway, Camden, NW1 7PN
Tel no: (020) 7267 9700
www.marketrestaurant.co.uk
⊖ Camden Town, map 2
British | £27
Cooking score: 2

Don't be fooled by the name: the wares on offer at this trendy little eatery are a world away from the wacky goods peddled by Camden's market traders. Blasted brick walls and zinc-topped tables create just the right utilitarian mood for a daily menu that resounds with pared-down but plucky British flavours. Come here for plates of pig's cheeks with black pudding and peas, lamb's sweetbreads with lentils or pollack with mash, leeks, mussels and cockles. Alternatively, fill up with a trencherman chicken and ham pie or onglet steak and fries, before bowing out with sticky toffee pud or jam sponge and custard. Gluggable wines start at £17.20.
Chef/s: Alan Turner. **Open:** all week L 12 to 2.30 (1 to 3.30 Sun), Mon to Sat D 6 to 10.30. **Closed:** 24 Dec to 1 Jan, bank hols. **Meals:** alc (main courses £13 to £17). Set L £10 (2 courses). Set D £17.50 (2 courses). **Service:** 12.5%. **Details:** 38 seats. 4 seats outside. Music.

Odette's

Letting quality ingredients do the talking
130 Regents Park Road, Primrose Hill, NW1 8XL
Tel no: (020) 7586 8569
www.odettesprimrosehill.com
⊖ Chalk Farm, map 2
Modern British | £40
Cooking score: 5

A reliable favourite in a smart Victorian street, Odette's may fit like an old glove, but there's nothing dowdy or dull here. Smart wrought iron chandeliers, thick carpet and boldly patterned wallpaper adorn the room, giving diners a soothing, cosseted feeling, and quietening down the busy chatter to a happy hubbub. Odette's diners know what they're about and, in the hands of chef-proprietor Bryn Williams, the restaurant's culinary star is still in the firmament. The seasonally changing menu is pleasingly unfussy, allowing quality ingredients to do the talking: asparagus, generously sprinkled with white truffle, is served with a perfectly dippy deep-fried duck egg, and a pile of celeriac rémoulade to give the dish substance; rich and indulgent crab lasagne piles on the luxury with a bisque-like sauce, delicate tendrils of chilli-fried squid adding textural contrast; a picture-perfect saddle of rabbit is served with its tiny rack of ribs, the accompanying mustard gnocchi adding a veneer of down-to-earth peasantry. Puds are just as ambitious; a bright green pistachio cake with caramelised apple and sweet crisp is not to be missed. House wines (from £19.50 a bottle) are pretty ordinary, but there's plenty of scope to indulge further down the list.
Chef/s: Bryn Williams. **Open:** all week L 12 to 2.30 (3 Sat and Sun), D 6 to 10.30. **Closed:** 24 to 26 Dec, 1 Jan. **Meals:** alc (main courses £16 to £25). Set L £17 (2 courses) to £20. Set D £22 (2 courses) to £25. **Service:** 12.5%. **Details:** 50 seats. 30 seats outside. Separate bar. Music.

ALSO RECOMMENDED

▲ Ottolenghi

287 Upper Street, Islington, N1 2TZ
Tel no: (020) 7288 1454
www.ottolenghi.co.uk
⊖ Angel, Highbury & Islington, map 2
Mediterranean/Asian

Islington's chattering classes pep up their
polenta these days with the fusion flavours of
cook and *Guardian* columnist Yotam
Ottolenghi. This is the most restaurant-like of
his four-strong Ottolenghi café chain, serving
breakfast, lunch and dinner every day at
communal tables. Frightfully chic white
interiors set off technicolour salads and
Mediterranean, Middle Eastern and Asian-
inspired 'meze' to perfection: think roasted
aubergine with turmeric yoghurt and
pomegranate (£9), then prawns with pomelo,
pickled endive and tamarind (£11.50). Wine
from £19.

▲ El Parador

245 Eversholt Street, Camden, NW1 1BA
Tel no: (020) 7387 2789
www.elparadorlondon.com
⊖ Mornington Crescent, map 2
Tapas

Locals are loyal to this evergreen tapas
restaurant for good reason, and it's worth
knowing about if you're in the
neighbourhood. It's warm, busy and the
imaginative tapas selection delivers value for
money. Good things to be had range from
simple grilled squid (£6.20) or sardines with
sea salt, black pepper and olive oil to duck
breast goujons marinated with mint and garlic
and served with honey, figs and roasted
piquillo peppers (£6.90). House wine is £15.
Closed Sat and Sun L.

NEW ENTRY
Shayona Restaurant

Indian veggie with bargain buffet lunches
56-62 Meadow Garth, Neasden, NW10 8HD
Tel no: (020) 8965 3365
www.shayonarestaurants.com
⊖ Stonebridge Park, map 1
Indian vegetarian | £13
Cooking score: 1

Owned by the magnificent Swaminarayan
Hindu temple across the road, Shayona is
dedicated to Indian sattvic cooking (a
vegetarian cuisine that bans garlic and onions).
Its warehouse-like shell hides a surprisingly
smart dining area with chandeliers and
colourful paintings. Dishes hail from across
India, incorporating snacks such as Punjabi
samosas or Rajasthani stuffed puris, as well as
South Indian dosas and rich curries. The
Gujarati lunchtime buffet (£7.99) is a bargain;
a food shop and sweets bar next door add to
the draw. No alcohol.
Chef/s: Anop Singh. **Open:** Mon to Fri 11.30 to 10
(Sat and Sun 11 to 10). **Meals:** alc (main courses £5
to £7). Buffet L £7.99. **Service:** not inc. **Details:** 150
seats. Separate bar. Wheelchair access. Music. Car
parking.

NEW ENTRY
Shrimpy's

Cool American-style pop-up diner
The King's Cross Filling Station, Goods Way, King's
Cross, N1C 4UR
Tel no: (020) 8880 6111
www.shrimpys.co.uk
⊖ King's Cross, map 2
Californian-Mexican | £35
Cooking score: 2

You'd be forgiven if you mistook this smart
new American-style diner for an art
installation, with its undulating fibreglass
screen and neon signage. The team behind
Hackney's Bistrotheque has turned this one-
time dingy petrol station into a colourful slice
of Americana overlooking Regent's canal,
where it serves fancy interpretations of

Californian-Mexican cuisine. The soft-shell crab burger, legs akimbo on a bun, has reserved cult status, though delicate plates are skilfully done, too. Bar and booths are furnished with linen and crystal; here those craving clean flavours can sample Peruvian ceviche, and heartier appetites can savour fried chicken, or skirt steak with chimichurri. A knockout chocolate brownie and pistachio sundae makes an indulgent finish. Wines start at £19. Cards only.

Chef/s: Tom Collins. **Open:** all week 11 to 10.30 (11 Fri and Sat). **Meals:** alc (main courses £16 to £28). **Service:** 12.5%. **Details:** 50 seats. Separate bar.

Singapore Garden

Long-running oriental eatery
83 Fairfax Road, Swiss Cottage, NW6 4DY
Tel no: (020) 7328 5314
www.singaporegarden.co.uk
⊖ Swiss Cottage, map 2
Chinese/Malaysian | £35
Cooking score: 2

The fact that Singapore Garden has been run by the same family since 1983 says a lot about its staying power – and north London's enduring appetite for zesty oriental food. Inside, it puts on quite a show, with exotic vegetation and chinoiserie adding some faraway romance to the vibrant dining room. Meanwhile, the kitchen treks over China, Malaysia and Singapore for a host of strongly flavoured, pungent dishes ranging from wok-fried pork dumplings to plates of mee goreng noodles. Also make a beeline for the specials – perhaps otak-otak (Malaysian-style fishcakes), or spiced leg of beef with Chinese herbs. House wine is £18.

Chef/s: Kok Sum Toh. **Open:** all week L 12 to 3 (5 Sun), D 6 to 11 (11.30 Fri and Sat). **Closed:** 4 days at Christmas. **Meals:** alc (main courses £9 to £30). Set D £35 (4 courses). **Service:** 12.5%. **Details:** 85 seats. 12 seats outside. Wheelchair access. Music.

Sushi-Say

Japanese delicacies from a sushi master
33b Walm Lane, Willesden, NW2 5SH
Tel no: (020) 8459 7512
⊖ Willesden Green, map 1
Japanese | £28
Cooking score: 4

It's not exactly a first choice for foodie adventurers, but Willesden Green does have one ace up its sleeve. Katsuharu and Yuko Shimizu's honourable eatery has been holding firm here since 1995, and the couple deserve a cheer for bringing sushi and other Japanese delicacies to the backwaters of NW2. The narrow, contemporary dining room looks modest enough, but the kitchen can compete with the best in town – thanks to high-quality produce and considerable culinary technique. Mr Shimizu is a sushi master, and he applies his talents to top-notch nigiri (fatty tuna, marinated mackerel with kelp, surf clams, salmon roe) as well as overseeing other textbook offerings from the traditional repertoire. Zensai appetisers of grilled aubergine with bonito flakes, savoury chawan mushi custard and sliced turbot with sticky fermented soya beans sharpen the taste-buds, ahead of salmon teriyaki, soft-shell crab tempura, deep-fried pork katsu and assorted noodles. Exclusive imported saké is the drink of choice, although there are a few wines from £18.60.

Chef/s: Katsuharu Shimizu. **Open:** Sat and Sun L 12 to 3, Wed to Sun D 6.30 to 10 (6 to 9.30 Sun). **Closed:** Mon, Tue, 25, 26 and 31 Dec, 1 and 2 Jan, 2 weeks Feb/Mar, 1 week Easter, 10 days Aug. **Meals:** alc (main courses £10 to £27). Set L £13.50 to £21. Set D £26.20 (6 courses) to £44.50 (8 courses). **Service:** not inc. **Details:** 41 seats. No music. Wheelchair access.

Sushi of Shiori

Simple, succulent sushi and sashimi
144 Drummond Street, Euston, NW1 2PA
Tel no: (020) 7388 9962
www.sushiofshiori.co.uk
⊖ Warren Street, Euston Square, map 2
Japanese | £25
Cooking score: 2

With one chef and eight no-nonsense counter-style seats, it's no surprise that simplicity is the watchword here – this diminutive Japanese eatery remains a trusted place for deliciously fresh nigiri sushi and sashimi. Sushi, such as sake (salmon), toro (fatty tuna) and suzuki (sea bass) are of good quality, succulent and prepared with obvious care, but the menu also takes in maki rolls, miso soup, donburi (rice bowls topped with fish), and yakitori (grilled chicken skewers). Lunchtime set menus are good value. Drink saké from a well-considered selection (300ml from £16.50), beer or tea; the token wines start at a whopping £32.
Chef/s: Takashi Takagi. **Open:** Tue to Sat L 11.30 to 2.30, D 5.30 to 10. **Closed:** Sun, Mon, 2 weeks Christmas and New Year, Easter, 2 weeks Aug. **Meals:** alc (main courses £12 to £28). Set L £15 (2 courses) to £20. Set D £40 (5 courses) to £70 (8 courses). **Details:** 8 seats. Wheelchair access. Music.

Trullo

Effortlessly likeable Italian eatery
300-302 St Paul's Road, Islington, N1 2LH
Tel no: (020) 7226 2733
www.trullorestaurant.com
⊖ Highbury and Islington, map 2
Italian | £30
Cooking score: 3

Positioned, not auspiciously, between a key-cutter's and a fried chicken take-away, it's easy to miss Trullo, Highbury Corner's effortlessly likeable Italian eatery. The low-key black frontage is, however, all part of Trullo's humble charm, along with a sparse, trattoria-like dining room and simple Italian dishes constructed on solid foundations of scrupulous sourcing. Antipasti might involve nothing more complicated than pairing buffalo mozzarella with roast quail, or salumi with marinated Puglian olives. Mains shift up a gear or two, with clear, bold flavours emerging – think lamb rump nuanced with slow-cooked purple sprouting broccoli, anchovy and garlic, or perhaps bream fillet with cannellini beans and hot olive sauce. A swoon-inducing caramel and vanilla pannacotta stars among the desserts. The Italian-accented wine list starts at £20.
Chef/s: Tim Siadatan. **Open:** all week L 12.30 to 2.45, Mon to Sat D 6 to 10.15. **Closed:** 24 Dec to 4 Jan. **Meals:** alc (main courses £12 to £21). Set L £12. Sun L £30. **Service:** 12.5% for parties of 6 or more. **Details:** 80 seats. Separate bar. Music.

ALSO RECOMMENDED

▲ XO

29 Belsize Lane, Belsize Park, NW3 5AS
Tel no: (020) 7433 0888
www.rickerrestaurants.com/xo
⊖ Belsize Park, map 2
Pan-Asian

Booth seating amid a minimal green vibe under light fittings like Calder mobiles is the setting for the Belsize Park branch of Will Ricker's pan-Asian restaurant group. It's an uplifting, chattery, family-friendly place, in which you might zip from dim sum like chilli salt squid (£7) or prawn har-gau, through chicken, aubergine and lychee green curry (£12.75) or whole grilled bream in garlic and chilli (£16.50), to orange pudding with bitter chocolate sorbet (£5.50). Wines from £16. Open all week.

Also Recommended
Also recommended entries are not scored but we think they are worth a visit.

The York & Albany
Metropolitan food for big-city palates
127-129 Parkway, Camden, NW1 7PS
Tel no: (020) 7388 3344
www.gordonramsay.com
⊖ Camden Town, map 2
Modern European | £30
Cooking score: 4

🛏 V

When it opened in the majestic John Nash building, the York & Albany was originally billed as 'the complete lifestyle experience', but thankfully there's less bombast about the place these days. The notion of a please-all town house hotel combining an all-day bar and events space with luxury bedrooms, bespoke picnics and a restaurant still captivates the local smart set, and the sedate dining room has enough culinary thrills to keep regulars interested. The menu sports a mixed bag of smart-casual metropolitan dishes for big-city palates – a host of wood-fired pizzas, pastas, burgers, ribeye steaks and more swanky culinary riffs, ranging from sea bream with Jerusalem artichokes, salsify and chanterelles to Creedy Carver duck with leek and thyme boulangère, white onion purée and Hispi cabbage. For dessert, the kitchen contents itself with the likes of salt caramel parfait with peanuts and dark chocolate. The trademark Gordon Ramsay wine list offers a terrific selection of varietals from around the globe at prices that will please everyday drinkers and connoisseurs alike. A dozen house selections start at £18.50.
Chef/s: Simon Gregory. **Open:** Mon to Sat L 12 to 3 (12.15 Sat), D 6 to 11. Sun 12 to 8.30. **Meals:** alc (main courses £15 to £27). Set D £18 (2 courses) to £21. Sun L £17. **Service:** 12.5%. **Details:** 120 seats. Wheelchair access. Music.

BRUNO LOUBET
Bistrot Bruno Loubet

When did you realise you wanted to be a chef?
Food was a big part of my family life and we grew or raised almost everything ourselves. When we had family gatherings at my grandmother's farm, I was always drawn to the kitchen.

Give us a quick culinary tip
Always prep ahead of time to avoid putting yourself under pressure.

Which chefs do you admire, and why?
Jamie Oliver is someone that I hugely admire for his drive, his commitment to bringing decent food to the masses and for challenging the status quo.

What's always in your fridge?
Fresh eggs. They can be used in so many ways, for anything from a sabayon or soufflé to a simple omelette.

What's your earliest food memory?
At five years old, being caught sitting in the middle of my neighbours' strawberry patch, enjoying their delicious wild strawberries.

What would you be if you weren't a chef?
A farmer. I spend my days off tending to my veggie patch.

Albion

Trendy all-day British café
2-4 Boundary Street, Shoreditch, E2 7DD
Tel no: (020) 7729 1051
www.albioncaff.co.uk
⊖ Shoreditch, Liverpool Street, Old Street, map
2
British | £25
Cooking score: 2

This smart caff, part of Terence Conran's
Boundary project, is strategically designed
with a food shop and bakery upfront, drawing
hungry mouths into the light-filled dining
space. The simple menu offers all-day
breakfast and shepherd's pie, and comforting
puddings like plum crumble. For a late-night
bite try Welsh rarebit with a cool beer. Albion
won't win accolades for culinary wizardry
(and the Albion breakfast needs attention), but
glory can be found in its baked goods – the
baker announces what's just emerged from the
oven on Twitter. Service could be friendlier,
but pricing is fair. Wines start at £18.
Chef/s: Alex Umeh. **Open:** all week 8am to 11.30pm.
Meals: alc (main courses £9 to £13) Set L and D £18
(2 courses) to £25. **Service:** 12.5%. **Details:** 60
seats. 12 seats outside. Wheelchair access. Music.

Amico Bio

Agreeable Italian vegetarian in the City
44 Cloth Fair, Barbican, EC1A 7JQ
Tel no: (020) 7600 7778
www.amicobio.co.uk
⊖ Barbican, map 5
Italian vegetarian | £22
Cooking score: 1

V

Occupying a handsome Georgian shop near
Smithfield market, Amico Bio is an agreeable
bastion of veggie cooking that has somehow
found favour with the steak-guzzling suits of
the City. Despite announcing itself as
London's first vegetarian-organic-Italian
restaurant, local sourcing doesn't enter into the
equation. Ingredients are shipped from the
family farm in Italy, ending up in secondi such

as borlotti bean ragù with roasted pumpkin,
or a decidedly un–Italian vegetable tempura
served with sweet-and-sour sauce. Organic
vintages dominate the wine list, from £13.50.
Chef/s: Pasquale Amico. **Open:** Mon to Fri 12 to
10.30, Sat 5 to 10.30. **Closed:** Sun, 25 and 26 Dec,
bank hols, 1 week August. **Meals:** alc (main courses
£7 to £9). **Service:** not inc. **Details:** 40 seats. Music.

L'Anima

Gorgeous modern Italian food
1 Snowden Street, City, EC2A 2DQ
Tel no: (020) 7422 7000
www.lanima.co.uk
⊖ Liverpool Street, map 2
Italian | £48
Cooking score: 5

When chef/patron Francesco Mazzei isn't in
the kitchen crafting 'gorgeous' modern Italian
food, he can sometimes be found front-of-
house talking to guests. 'He's a wonderful host'
who 'never forgets [his customers] have a
choice where to spend their money'. Judging
by the glowing reports this year, the City's
expense-account diners would probably even
hand over their own cash at L'Anima. The
high-spec glass, stone and marble space near
Liverpool Street is 'unique' and 'stylish –
especially for the City'. Calabrian Mazzei is
praised for exciting menus packed with 'novel
but not over-trendy combinations'. That
might mean burrata cheese with smoked
aubergine, hazelnuts and red onion jam to
start, homemade malloreddus (Sardinian
pasta) with clams, colatura ('anchovy water'),
tomato and bottarga (salted fish roe), or sea
bass with garum and cime di rapa. (Furrowed
brows may have to refer to the menu's brief
glossary for translations.) L'Anima regulars
stick to their favourites – often beef carpaccio
with truffle sauce, 'faultless' fritto misto,
linguine with fresh crab, and Calabrian iced
truffle. The experience doesn't come cheap
and, try as you might, you won't want to stick
to the cheapest wine (£18) from an 'evolving',
all-Italian list featuring 'more than the usual
suspects'.

Chef/s: Francesco Mazzei and Luca Terraneo. **Open:** Mon to Fri L 11.45 to 3, Mon to Sat D 5.30 to 11 (11.30 Sat). **Closed:** Sun, bank hols. **Meals:** alc (main courses £13 to £36). Set L £24.50 (2 courses) to £28.50. **Service:** 12.5%. **Details:** 120 seats. Separate bar. Wheelchair access. Music.

Bar Battu

Tasty treats and interesting tipples
48 Gresham Street, City, EC2V 7AY
Tel no: (020) 7036 6100
www.barbattu.com
⊖ Bank, map 2
Modern European | £25
Cooking score: 2

This vibrant City wine bar, run by staff who are passionate about wine and food, is regularly rammed with enthusiasts seeking an interesting tipple. The quality wine list offers exemplary choice by the glass or carafe. Alternatively choose a bottle (from £17.50) to go with tasty treats from the menu, where culinary influences jostle: Spanish cured meats alongside bresaola, baby squid à la plancha next to asparagus with hollandaise. Mains might include boudin noir with mash, glazed apple and Calvados jus or polenta with smoked ricotta and baby onions. Finish with chocolate fondant. In the same stable is Luc's Brasserie, a dyed-in-the-wool Gallic eatery in Leadenhall Market (www.lucsbrasserie.com). **Chef/s:** Ruben Estrella. **Open:** Mon to Fri L 12 to 3 (4 Mon), Tue to Fri D 4 to 10. **Closed:** Sat, Sun, 24 Dec to 2 Jan, bank hols. **Meals:** alc (main courses £13 to £25). Set L and D £17.50 to £19.50. **Service:** 12.5%. **Details:** 110 seats. Separate bar. Wheelchair access. Music.

Bistrot Bruno Loubet

Clever cooking from a starry chef
The Zetter Hotel, 86-88 Clerkenwell Road, Clerkenwell, EC1M 5RJ
Tel no: (020) 7324 4455
www.bistrotbrunoloubet.com
⊖ Farringdon, Barbican, map 5
Modern French | £32
Cooking score: 4

Starry chef Bruno Loubet is now firmly ensconced at his 'bistrot' on the ground floor of Clerkenwell's funky Zetter Hotel. Although the name may suggest check cloths and dripping candles, the lofty room cuts quite a dash, with its huge floor-to-ceiling windows, metallic *objets d'art* and curious hybrid furniture. Bruno's clever cooking is also a few notches above beef bourguignon – just consider a dish of flame-grilled mackerel with smoked cod's roe, apple compote and seaweed oil, or grilled rose veal rump with carrot and ginger purée, greens and lemon thyme jus. Also expect some technically astute renditions of the bourgeois classics, from Mauricette snails (made to his mother's recipe) with dinky meatballs and wild mushrooms to hare royale revisited, bowls of bouillabaisse with traditional accoutrements or lamb osso buco on Roquefort risotto. Sharply executed desserts play the field too, from bitter chocolate délice with coffee sabayon to citrus gratin with pistachio crumble. France tops the bill on the reasonably priced wine list, with bottles from £15.95. **Chef/s:** Bruno Loubet and Dominique Goitinger. **Open:** all week L 12 to 2.30 (3 Sun), D 6 to 10.30 (10 Sun). **Closed:** 25 and 26 Dec. **Meals:** alc (main courses £16 to £20). Set L £20 (2 courses) to £23. **Service:** 12.5%. **Details:** 88 seats. 44 seats outside. Separate bar. Wheelchair access. Music.

Bonds

Solid City pleaser
Threadneedle Hotel, 5 Threadneedle Street, City,
EC2R 8AY
Tel no: (020) 7657 8088
www.theetoncollection.co.uk
⊖ Bank, map 2
Modern British | £42
Cooking score: 4

This spacious dining room with its towering
columns feels as solid as the nearby Bank of
England building, although any formality is
softened by clever lighting and contemporary
finishes. Stephen Smith now heads the
kitchen, but continues to offer full-throttle
contemporary food – basically a marriage of
classical French techniques with some ideas
out of the modern British stable. Soft and
creamy seared Scottish scallops, for example,
are served with tiny cubes of caramelised
pineapple and given an added dimension by a
light curry oil, while Highfield ribeye beef is
paired with girolles and pommes Maxim and
rounded off by well-judged bordelaise sauce.
A mango parfait ('like sunshine on a plate') is a
fitting finale. The service can struggle at times
– it needs to be more consistent, given the
prices. The wine list is extensive; there are
even some relatively affordable bottles
amongst the big-ticket labels, with prices
kicking off at £19.
Chef/s: Stephen Smith. **Open:** Mon to Fri L 12 to 2,
D 6 to 10. **Closed:** Sat, Sun, 22 to 26 Dec. **Meals:** alc
(main courses £13 to £28). Set L £19.95 (2 courses)
to £23.95. Set D £23.95. **Service:** 12.5%. **Details:** 80
seats. Separate bar. Wheelchair access. Music.

Brawn

Unbuttoned neighbourhood eatery
49 Columbia Road, Shoreditch, E2 7RG
Tel no: (020) 7729 5692
www.brawn.co.uk
⊖ Shoreditch, map 2
French | £30
Cooking score: 4

'Old building, kind of factory style' is one way
to describe this muscular neighbourhood
eatery from the team behind Terroirs and Soif
(see entries) and it fits the Columbia Road
location to a T. As you might expect, the food
is as plain as the restaurant itself. Big, bold
flavours prevail on a menu that emphasises
seasonality and lets well-sourced ingredients
shine – from impeccable charcuterie to the
likes of spatchcock quail with harissa,
aubergine and coriander. There's thrifty use of
all those overlooked bits of meat: brawn
(potted pig's head), of course, as well as veal's
brain (with sauce ravigote) and caillette (pork
tripe sausage) with chips. Crêpes with salted
butter caramel are the dessert of choice.
Modest prices extend to the illuminating
modern wine list; mainly French with a side
trip to Italy, it opens with a superb selection by
the glass and 500ml carafe. Bottles
from £16.50.
Chef/s: Owen Kenworthy. **Open:** Thur-Sun L 12 to 3
(4 Sun), Mon to Sat D 6 to 11. **Closed:** 25 Dec to 2
Jan, bank hols. **Meals:** alc (main courses £9 to £15).
Sun L £25. **Service:** 12.5%. **Details:** 70 seats.
Wheelchair access. Music.

NEW ENTRY
Bread Street Kitchen
Gordon's buzzy all-dayer
One New Change, 10 Bread Street, St Paul's,
EC4M 9AB
Tel no: (020) 3030 4050
www.breadstreetkitchen.com
⊖ St Paul's, map 5
Modern British | £39
Cooking score: 2

The Gordon Ramsay group now brings us this vast, pillared warehouse space with booth seating, best experienced when in full cry. There's take-out coffee and cake in the bar, and breakfast from 7am. The main menu offers starters of crisp-skinned chicken wings, and potted salt brisket with piccalilli, and mains like ribeye with marrow bone or yellowfin tuna with parsnip mash in black pepper sauce. Dishes are substantial enough that finishing with impressive bread-and-butter pudding or blood-orange baked Alaska seems like self-indulgence. House selections by the glass (from £5), half-bottle (from £10) or bottle (from £18.50) head a good wine list.
Chef/s: Erion Karaj. **Open:** Mon to Sat L 11.30 to 3, D 5.30 to 11. Sun 11 to 8. **Meals:** alc (main courses £12 to £30). **Service:** 12.5%. **Details:** 275 seats. Separate bar. Wheelchair access. Music.

Café Spice Namasté
Classy, modern Indian
16 Prescot Street, Tower Hill, E1 8AZ
Tel no: (020) 7488 9242
www.cafespice.co.uk
⊖ Tower Hill, map 1
Indian | £30
Cooking score: 2

'I have eaten there a number of times – the real test of a good restaurant' notes a fan of this 'very classy and modern' Indian not far from Brick Lane. Detailed menu notes give the origins of every dish, from the usual favourites (chicken tikka, tarka dhal) to 'dynamite' peri peri spiced squid. Other choices include home-grown classics like beef curry à la Dada (seemingly so popular it's impossible to remove from the menu) and vegetarian dishes

such as kozambu (spinach and split-pea dumplings). A modest selection of wines starts at £17.95 a bottle.
Chef/s: Cyrus Todiwala. **Open:** Mon to Fri L 12 to 3, Mon to Sat D 6.15 to 10.30 (6.30 Sat). **Closed:** Sun, 25 Dec to 1 Jan, bank hols. **Meals:** alc (main courses £15 to £20). Set L and D £25 (2 courses) to £30. **Service:** 12.5%. **Details:** 140 seats. Wheelchair access. Music.

ALSO RECOMMENDED

▲ Carnevale
135 Whitecross Street, Barbican, EC1Y 8JL
Tel no: (020) 7250 3452
www.carnevalerestaurant.com
⊖ Barbican, map 5
Vegetarian

This deli-cum-café is easy to miss, and first-timers venturing into the deli are amazed to find a few tables tucked away at the back with diners enjoying lively vegetarian dishes that pull together ideas from all over the Mediterranean. Goats' cheese parcels with orange and almond salad (£6.25) might be followed by chickpea, lentil and spinach curry served with marinated haloumi and fig kebabs with yoghurt and mint dressing (£12.50). Soups and starters could make a satisfying lunch. Wines from £16. Closed Sat L and Sun.

▲ Chinese Cricket Club
Crowne Plaza, 19 New Bridge Street, Blackfriars, EC4V 6DB
Tel no: (020) 7438 8051
www.chinesecricketclub.com
⊖ Temple, Mansion House, St Paul's, map 5
Chinese £5 OFF

'A fantastic find' was one reporter's verdict on this restaurant, named in honour of the Chinese cricket team. It's hidden away within the corporate setting of a Crowne Plaza Hotel; atmosphere may not be high on the agenda, but the cooking certainly makes up for it. Warm up with chicken in sweet vinegar (£9.50) and finish your innings with fried sea bass in sweet-and-sour sauce (£16) or steamed lobster in Szechuan butter (£31). House wine £19.50. Closed Sun.

NEW ENTRY
Chiswell Street Dining Rooms
Polished, clubby spot for City lunching
56 Chiswell Street, City, EC1Y 4SA
Tel no: (020) 7614 0177
www.chiswellstreetdining.com
⊖ Moorgate, map 2
Modern British | £45
Cooking score: 2

Tom and Ed Martin are known for their collection of London boozers; they haven't strayed far from their safe-but-successful formula for this polished new bar and restaurant at the Montcalm London City hotel – though it's anything but pubby. Spread over three window-lined rooms, with painted panelled walls and olive leather chairs, it's an attractive, clubby spot, suited to City lunching. Make no mistake, the food is rich. Gently wobbling baked crab tart, lamb rump with flageolet purée and ginger sponge with rhubarb compote cry out for wine (of the fine French variety) and a lie-down. The former starts at £16.50.
Chef/s: Richard O'Connell. **Open:** all week L 12 to 3, D 6 to 11. **Meals:** alc (main courses £15 to £28). Set D £38. **Service:** 12.5%. **Details:** 78 seats. Separate bar. Wheelchair access. Music.

Cinnamon Kitchen
Suited-and-booted City Indian
9 Devonshire Square, City, EC2M 4YL
Tel no: (020) 7626 5000
www.cinnamon-kitchen.com
⊖ Liverpool Street, map 2
Indian | £35
Cooking score: 4
£5 OFF

In 2008, Westminster's Cinnamon Club spawned an offspring that got all suited and booted and headed east into the City, to no less

a venue than the East India Company's original spice warehouse. Executive chef Vivek Singh has worked his magic here too, to produce a style of innovative pan-Indian cooking that is alive with the precision of individual spices, often brought to bear on traditionally Western ingredients. Cumin-tempered artichoke soup with masala toast gives the old soup-and-bread idea a refreshing spin; English asparagus might appear grilled in kadhai spices. A tandoor oven turns out richly succulent rump of Kentish lamb, or there may be red deer roasted in the Rajasthani fashion, accompanied by stir-fried beetroot. Desserts such as Indian banana tarte Tatin with thandai ice cream (based on the traditional Peshwari spiced milk) maintain the pace. A wine list that mirrors the ambitious dynamism of the food includes aromatic Greek, Austrian and Alsatian whites, and plenty of spice-friendly reds. Prices open at £19.
Chef/s: Vivek Singh. **Open:** Mon to Fri L 12 to 2.45, Mon to Sat D 6 to 10.45. **Closed:** Sun, 25 and 26 Dec, 7 May, 27 Aug. **Meals:** alc (main courses £13 to £32). Set L £15 (2 courses) to £18. **Service:** 12.5%. **Details:** 110 seats. 60 seats outside. Separate bar. Wheelchair access. Music.

Club Gascon
A lively sea of surrealist cooking
57 West Smithfield, City, EC1A 9DS
Tel no: (020) 7796 0600
www.clubgascon.com
⊖ Barbican, Farringdon, St Paul's, map 5
Modern French | £50
Cooking score: 6
£5 OFF V

You might have thought that the Club Gascon concept – taster portions of radically aestheticised French haute cuisine distantly based on the earthiness of south-western cooking – would have had its five minutes in the London limelight, and then been blown away on the next breeze of fashion. Not so. Pascal Aussignac's restaurant, on the ground floor of an ornate Victorian City building, endures, not least by virtue of Aussignac's restless culinary intellect, which achieves striking results by means of the kind of surrealist approach that can all too easily come unstuck. The classifications of the menu help a little with orientation, but you soon set sail on a lively sea. Crackled capon wings, scallops ballottine, nuts and lovage might be juxtaposed with venison carpaccio and winkles with peas, broad beans and horseradish snow. For veg, eucalyptus crush and smoked elderflower adds aromatic lift to white asparagus, while the roll call of foie gras variations includes a terrine of pine-smoked squirrel foie, pointed with frosted Worcestershire sauce. Don't expect the respite of a trad cheese plate, when the Ossau-Iraty ewes' milk cheese comes with rose shavings, crunchy grapes, muesli and verjus, and the final flourish is administered at dessert, with the likes of confit rhubarb and strawberries with green pepper, maize fondant and poppy liquor. Finding wine matches for that lot requires some expertise, but there's a good sommelier on hand, and the list itself is an inspired exploration of the peripheral French regions, from dry Jurançon to sweet Gaillac. Wines by the glass (from £5) are good, but a few more wouldn't come amiss. Bottles start at £22.

Chef/s: Pascal Aussignac. **Open:** Mon to Fri L 12 to 2, Mon to Sat D 7 to 10 (10.30 Fri and Sat). **Closed:** Sun, 24 Dec to 3 Jan, bank hols. **Meals:** alc (main courses £13 to £23). Set L £25. Tasting menu £55 (5 courses). **Service:** 12.5%. **Details:** 37 seats.

The Coach & Horses
Belt-busting British pub grub
26-28 Ray Street, Clerkenwell, EC1R 3DJ
Tel no: (020) 7278 8990
www.thecoachandhorses.com
⊖ Farringdon, map 5
Modern British | £23
Cooking score: 2

£5 OFF

A handsome Victorian bolt-hole tucked away in Clerkenwell, the Coach and Horses sets out its stall with no-frills British fare. The stripped-back décor belies the cosy

atmosphere, and although the kitchen seems to have lost its sense of adventure of late, it still sends out confident, well-priced classics. Regular big-flavoured fixtures that continue to please include roast beef sandwich, beer-battered fish and (excellent) chips, and the pub's signature Scotch eggs. Pear and almond tart with crème fraîche is a typical pud. Staff are obliging, and beer connoisseurs are well catered for with plentiful real ales. Wines from £14.25.

Open: Sun to Fri L 12 to 3 (12.30 to 4 Sun), Mon to Sat D 6 to 10. **Closed:** 24 Dec to 2 Jan, bank hols. **Meals:** alc (main courses £9 to £15). **Service:** 12.5%. **Details:** 80 seats. 50 seats outside. Separate bar. Music.

Comptoir Gascon
Earnest, brasserie-style Gallic cooking
61-63 Charterhouse Street, Clerkenwell, EC1M 6HJ
Tel no: (020) 7608 0851
www.comptoirgascon.com
⊖ Farringdon, Barbican, map 5
French | £27
Cooking score: 4

£30

A worthy understudy to Club Gascon (see entry), Comptoir Gascon skips the showboating cuisine beloved of its big brother on the opposite side of Smithfield Market, instead trading in earnest, brasserie-style Gallic cooking. Brick walls, scruffy blackboards and tightly packed tables sit perfectly with the straight-talking menu – start with grilled duck hearts, potato cake and crème forte, or 'piggy treats' – an abidingly popular charcuterie spread. True to the restaurant's Gascon roots, duck is the headline act among mains; it stars in everything from the deluxe duck burger to a masterly Toulousain cassoulet. However, there are lots of dishes to satisfy those who aren't quackers about canard – roasted haddock, black lentils and mussel stew, for example, typifies a rustic simplicity in the kitchen's approach. Finish with Gascon mess – a boozy reinvention of

Eton's famous pudding. An affordable and concise wine list doesn't stray beyond French borders and starts at £16.50.

Chef/s: Pascal Aussignac. **Open:** Tue to Sat L 12 to 2, D 6 to 10. **Closed:** Sun, Mon, 22 Dec to 3 Jan, Easter. **Meals:** alc (main courses £8 to £15). Set L £14.50. **Service:** 12.5%. **Details:** 40 seats. 8 seats outside. Wheelchair access. Music.

Coq d'Argent
Slick rooftop dining with spectacular views
1 Poultry, City, EC2R 8EJ
Tel no: (020) 7395 5000
www.coqdargent.co.uk
⊖ Bank, map 2
French | £40
Cooking score: 2

The view's the thing at this dizzily located restaurant atop 1 Poultry; the panoramic cityscape is best enjoyed over drinks on the terrace. Customers are loyal, drawn back by the well-oiled, well-established feel to both the garden bar/brasserie and the slick dining room, and by the vigorous French bourgeois cooking. Strong on classics like foie gras with pain d'épices, beef tartare and coq au vin, the kitchen is equally adept at modern dishes such as honey and red wine-glazed pork cheeks with truffle mash, buttered root vegetables and pig's ear crisp. Desserts are a strength. The huge wine list opens at £21.

Chef/s: Mickael Weiss. **Open:** Sun to Fri L 11.30 to 3 (12 Sun), Mon to Sat D 6 to 10 (6.30 Sat). **Closed:** bank hols. **Meals:** alc (main courses £16 to £34). Set L and D £25 (2 courses) to £30. Sun L £25 (2 courses) to £28. **Service:** 12.5%. **Details:** 150 seats. 100 seats outside. Separate bar. Wheelchair access.

NEW ENTRY
Corner Room
Trendy food and bang-for-buck
Town Hall Hotel, Patriot Square, Bethnal Green, E2 9NF
Tel no: (020) 7871 0460
www.cornerroom.co.uk
⊖ Bethnal Green, map 1
Modern European | £25
Cooking score: 4

Just because it's cosy and candlelit doesn't mean it can't be gastronomically challenging. Nuno Mendes' walk-in only Corner Room at Bethnal Green's Town Hall Hotel is what the French would call a 'neo bistro', which – roughly translated – means trendy food and bang-for-buck. As at his fine-dining Viajante downstairs (see entry), Mendes draws inspiration from all over the world. Venison in ash with fridge-cold salsify and dabs of date purée was a poor start, but once that was over with, the rest was pleasure: Chinese-style short ribs so soft you could eat them with a spoon, with mushroom caramel, a delicate version of ham hock and pickle, and, for dessert, dark chocolate and peanut butter ice cream. Wines are limited to five whites and four reds, but they're clever, sub-£35 choices. N.B. Tables are allocated for just 90 minutes. The fashionably frosty staff had us in and out well within that time.

Chef/s: Nuno Mendes. **Open:** Mon to Fri L 12 to 3.30, D 6 to 10.30. Sat and Sun 12 to 10.30. **Meals:** alc (main courses £12 to £15). Set L £15 (2 courses) to £19. **Service:** 12.5%. **Details:** 30 seats. Separate bar. Wheelchair access. Music.

The Don
Fine wines and enterprising cooking
The Courtyard, 20 St Swithin's Lane, City,
EC4N 8AD
Tel no: (020) 7626 2606
www.thedonrestaurant.co.uk
⊖ Bank, Cannon Street, map 2
Modern European | £36
Cooking score: 2

£5
OFF

For 170 years until the late 1960s, these premises were the bottling cellars for Sandeman's ports and sherries, making the Don a fitting venue for some of the City's soundest and finest drinking. If you're in the market for some solid sustenance too, there's a menu of enterprising modern European cooking in the ground-floor restaurant (trad fish soup, scallops in the shell in vanilla-lime beurre blanc, black Bigorre pig three ways on Bramley apple and rosemary compote in Calvados sauce, poached pear with chocolate and hazelnut cream), and a more bustling basement bistro. Sooner or later, the wine list calls with its many-tongued siren voice, offering quality across the stylistic spectrum, from Massena's thunderous Howling Dog Petite Sirah from the Barossa to lace-delicate German Rieslings. Bottles start at £19.25 (£5.50 a glass).
Chef/s: Matthew Burns. **Open:** Mon to Fri L 12 to 2.30, D 6 to 10. **Closed:** Sat, Sun, 23 Dec to 4 Jan, bank hols. **Meals:** alc (main courses £15 to £33). **Service:** 12.5%. **Details:** 100 seats. Separate bar. No music.

Eyre Brothers
Broad-shouldered and beautiful Iberian cuisine
68-70 Leonard Street, Shoreditch, EC2A 4QX
Tel no: (020) 7613 5346
www.eyrebrothers.co.uk
⊖ Old Street, map 2
Spanish/Portuguese | £35
Cooking score: 4

Eleven years on, Eyre Brothers continues to enjoy faithful support. Located in the hinterland around Old Street tube station, it's a surprisingly classy place, sleekly done out in white and dark wood. Informal, helpful service contributes to a laid-back feel. The ethnic guidepost is Iberian – broad-shouldered but beautifully executed plates of regional Spanish and Portuguese cuisine. Impeccable ingredients star in dishes such as Portuguese hare with smoked toucinho (bacon) and red wine soup, and Palourde clams with jamón Serrano, onions, fino sherry, parsley and fried potatoes. Mains deliver 'big-mouth flavours in hearty portions', say grilled fillet of acorn-fed pig, marinated with smoked paprika, thyme and garlic, and served with patatas pobres. Desserts (if you have room) don't stray far from the realms of caramelised apple tart. The all-Iberian wine list is great value (right down to the sherries and ports), with cracking house selections by the glass; bottles from £19.
Chef/s: David Eyre and João Cleto. **Open:** Mon to Fri L 12 to 2.30, Mon to Sat D 6 to 11 (7 Sat). **Closed:** Sun, Christmas to New Year, bank hols. **Meals:** alc (main courses £10 to £30). **Service:** 12.5%. **Details:** 70 seats. Separate bar. Wheelchair access. Music.

Fifteen London
Jamie's thriving trattoria
15 Westland Place, Shoreditch, N1 7LP
Tel no: (020) 3375 1515
www.fifteen.net
⊖ Old Street, map 2
Italian | £46
Cooking score: 3

Jamie Oliver's great idea of setting up a restaurant to provide underprivileged kids with gainful employment and to get them enthused about food is now a well-established and thriving business, just entering a second decade. Its utilitarian and urban warehouse setting is an energetic, edgy space, offering vibrant Italianate dishes based on fresh seasonal ingredients and delivered in an unfussy style that perfectly echoes the bare boards and unadorned tables. Work your way through burrata with char-grilled Conference pears and mixed spring leaves, seafood risotto

with white wine and samphire or very good linguine carbonara, then free-range Norfolk chicken alla Diavola with fregola, purple sprouting broccoli and salsa rossa piccante. Wines from £16.75.
Chef/s: Andrew Parkinson. **Open:** all week L 12 to 3, D 6 to 10. **Closed:** 25 Dec. **Meals:** alc (main courses £19 to £29). Set L £24 (2 courses) to £34. **Service:** 12.5%. **Details:** 65 seats.

★ TOP 50 ★

Galvin La Chapelle

Head-turning French class
35 Spital Square, Spitalfields, E1 6DY
Tel no: (020) 7299 0400
www.galvinrestaurants.com
⊖ Liverpool Street, map 2
Modern French | £48
Cooking score: 6

'Bonjour French sophistication, au revoir Sunday blues!' quipped one weekender after a blisteringly good lunch at the Galvin brothers' magnum opus. Occupying what was St Botolph's Hall (a girls' school in deepest Spitalfields), it wows with its soaring vaulted ceilings, stone arches and fabulous marble columns. The stunningly restored interior is matched by a 'head-turning' prix-fixe menu that has delivered real class in the shape of silky sweetcorn velouté with mussels and croûtons, 'stunningly simple' roast pavé of hake with 'creamily comforting' pomme purée and samphire, and a wedge of Chaource rouzaire cheese accompanied by a salad of organic beetroot and roasted plums. The kitchen also knows how to dazzle on a higher plane, serving spice-crusted Bresse pigeon tagine with couscous, aubergine purée and harissa sauce, risottos enlivened with Périgord truffles or spring vegetables, and roast fillet of Scotch beef with glazed short rib, fondant potato, navets (turnips) and a deep, fulsome Hermitage jus. To conclude, try the textbook tarte Tatin or the seasonal blackberry soufflé. Details such as fresh sourdough bread and zingy raspberry macaroons are much appreciated, likewise the considerable and French-accented wine list, which naturally

includes sublime rarities from La Chapelle – the jewel of Maison Jaboulet in the Rhône Valley. House selections start at £23.
Chef/s: Jeff Galvin and Zac Whittle. **Open:** all week L 12 to 2.30 (3 Sun), D 6 to 10.30 (9.30 Sun). **Closed:** 25 and 26 Dec, 1 Jan. **Meals:** alc (main courses £23 to £33). Set L £26.50. Early set D £29.50. Tasting menu £70 (7 courses). **Service:** 12.5%. **Details:** 108 seats. 32 seats outside. Separate bar. No music. Wheelchair access.

Galvin's Café à Vin

Good-value Galvin offshoot
35 Spital Square, Spitalfields, E1 6DY
Tel no: (020) 7299 0404
www.galvinrestaurants.com
⊖ Liverpool Street, map 2
Modern European | £28
Cooking score: 4

£30

Chris and Jeff Galvin's unpretentious French café is a useful place with an informal way of doing things, a great alfresco terrace, not too dear and quite with-it in the kitchen department. The style is a typical London café-cum-brasserie; unlike the brothers' swish La Chapelle next door (see entry), the interior is simple, in a dark-wood-and-zinc-bar kind of way, with tightly packed tables and a direct approach to public eating. The menu stays short, with some constants – steak tartare, garlicky snails à la bourguignonne and superb tarte flambée, as well as a couple of imaginative pizzas from the wood-fired oven, and baba au rhum with Chantilly cream. The hallmark of the cooking is high flavour applied to first-class seasonal ingredients: say wood-roast John Dory with braised fennel and lemon or char-grilled pork ribeye with pommes Anna, Hispi cabbage and mustard jus. The set lunch remains exceptional value. Wines from £23.
Chef/s: Jack Boast. **Open:** all week L 12 to 2.30 (3 Sun), 6 to 10.30 (9.30 Sun). **Closed:** 25 and 26 Dec, 1 Jan. **Meals:** alc (main courses £13 to £22). Set L and early D £14.95. Sun L £14.95. **Service:** 12.5%. **Details:** 50 seats. 110 seats outside. Wheelchair access. Music.

Great Eastern Dining Room

Hip pan-Asian favourite
54-56 Great Eastern Street, Shoreditch, EC2A 3QR
Tel no: (020) 7613 4545
www.rickerrestaurants.com
⊖ Old Street, map 2
Pan-Asian | £27
Cooking score: 2

'An old favourite, I just keep coming back for consistently stunning fusion food' trumpets a supporter of this Hoxton outpost of Will Ricker's pan-Asian empire. The cool contemporary warehouse conversion continues to draw the crowds, not least for the atmosphere and the cocktails. As for the food, there's no clear distinction between first and main courses, so meals can be flexible; sharing is *de rigueur* – all the better for ensuring maximum coverage of dim sum such as prawn har-gau or pumpkin gyoza. Then move on to sweet shrimp tempura, blackened salmon with sweet miso or lamb rendang. Wines from £16.50.
Chef/s: Kon Dyugay. **Open:** Mon to Fri L 12 to 3.30, Mon to Sat D 6 to 10.45. **Closed:** Sun, bank hols. **Meals:** alc (main courses £10 to £20). Set L and D £24 (2 courses) to £30/£38. **Service:** 12.5%. **Details:** 65 seats. Separate bar. Music.

The Gun

Laid-back Docklands pub with good ingredients
27 Coldharbour, Canary Wharf, E14 9NS
Tel no: (020) 7515 5222
www.thegundocklands.com
⊖ Canary Wharf, map 1
British | £30
Cooking score: 2

'The Gun is a beautiful pub', thought one first-time visitor, wowed by the view across the Thames to the O2. An early eighteenth-century hostelry, originally used by dockers and boatmen, it is now a refreshingly laid-back venue best known for cooking that sees good British ingredients treated with minimum fuss. Expect smoked haddock, mussel and saffron soup, and roast cod given a pleasing zip with chorizo, borlotti bean and confit garlic stew or tried-and-tested aged Black Angus ribeye with béarnaise sauce. The bar does a great line in snacks (fish finger sandwich, black pudding Scotch egg). Wines from £16.50.
Chef/s: Mark Fines. **Open:** all week L 12 to 3 (4 Sat and Sun), D 6 to 10.30 (6.30 to 9.30 Sun). **Closed:** 25 and 26 Dec. **Meals:** alc (main courses £14 to £28). **Service:** 12.5%. **Details:** 40 seats. 40 seats outside. Separate bar. Wheelchair access. Music. No children after 8.

ALSO RECOMMENDED

▲ The Hackney Pearl

11 Prince Edward Road, Hackney Wick, E9 5LX
Tel no: (020) 8510 3605
www.thehackneypearl.com
⊖ Hackney Wick, map 1
Modern British

A blend of new-Brit culinary cool and cheeky Aussie bravado, this all-purpose café-bar has stepped up to the mark as Hackney Wick's arty hub. Its easy-going offer of Formica tables, coffee and cakes, brunch deals and honest tucker yields snacks, salads and sturdy dishes ranging from home-pickled herrings with mustard cream (£6.20) to lamb loin chops with creamy mash and beetroot tzatziki or a brace of slip soles with Pink Fir Apple potatoes and sage butter (£15). Locally brewed real ales, classic cocktails and wines from £9.80 a 500ml carafe. Open all week.

NEW ENTRY

Hawksmoor Guildhall

Expertly aged, exquisitely prepared prime beef
10-12 Basinghall Street, City, EC2V 5BQ
Tel no: (020) 7397 8120
www.thehawksmoor.com
⊖ Bank, map 2
British | £65
Cooking score: 4

Like its older siblings in Spitalfields and Seven Dials (see entries), this enormous, buzzing, low-lit basement restaurant is a place that's all about meat, serving some of the most expertly aged and exquisitely prepared prime beef in London – at (well-worth-it) premium prices. But while cuts of Yorkshire-reared Longhorn beef range from 55 day-aged D-rump – served, perhaps, with béarnaise and a heap of crunchy, addictive triple-cooked chips – to sublime chateaubriand, you can also eat spectacular veal chops and, should you want to tread more lightly, grilled free-range chicken and native lobster. Start with potted smoked mackerel or meatball and grits, and enjoy a sticky orange pudding for dessert. Do find time to try what is probably the best weekday breakfast in the City (7am to 10am). Like the beef, the décor is aged to perfection, service can't be praised highly enough, and the wine list opens at £19.

Chef/s: William Kirwan. **Open:** Mon to Fri L 12 to 3, D 5 to 10.30. **Closed:** Sat and Sun, 24 Dec to 2 Jan. **Meals:** alc (main courses £13 to £48). Set L and D £55. **Service:** 12.5%. **Details:** 253 seats. Separate bar. Wheelchair access. Music.

Hawksmoor
Prime British steakhouse
157 Commercial Street, City, E1 6BJ
Tel no: (020) 7247 7392
www.thehawksmoor.co.uk
⊖ Liverpool Street, Aldgate East, map 2
British | £65
Cooking score: 3

Hawksmoor's newer branches (in Covent Garden and Guildhall) are a polished take on this, its original British steakhouse in Spitalfields – 'an amazing restaurant from the moment you walk in'. 'Second to none' dry-aged Longhorn beef from Yorkshire, cooked over charcoal, and two types of chips (triple-cooked and beef dripping, both terrific) have local suits and hipsters alike salivating. If bone-in sirloin or porterhouse, sides of creamed spinach and 'extras' like bone marrow and Stilton hollandaise don't get your juices flowing, you're in the wrong place (though there are daily grilled fish specials and starters such as asparagus with duck egg hollandaise).

Wines (from £19) are, unsurprisingly, steak-friendly and there's a new basement bar for cocktails or a burger and local beer.
Chef/s: Lewis Hannaford. **Open:** all week L 12 to 2.30 (4.30 Sun), Mon to Sat D 6 to 10.30. **Closed:** 24 Dec to 2 Jan. **Meals:** alc (main courses £11 to £35). **Service:** 12.5%. **Details:** 240 seats. Separate bar. Wheelchair access. Music.

Hix Oyster & Chop House
Popular place where provenance is everything
35-37 Greenhill Rents, Cowcross Street, Clerkenwell, EC1M 6BN
Tel no: (020) 7017 1930
www.hixoysterandchophouse.co.uk
⊖ Farringdon, map 5
British | £45
Cooking score: 4
V

Mark Hix has made a success of providing sensible dishes in that no-frills modern British style. This, his original restaurant, is a hugely popular place where tiled walls, bare boards and closely packed tables help crank up the volume, and the food deserves credit for its lack of ostentation. Dishes follow the seasons beadily, and whether it's West Country fish, seasonal game or foraged pickings, provenance is everything. The result is a vivid repertoire that promises several types of oysters, St George's mushrooms on toast with ramsons (wild garlic) or wild sea kale, Morecambe Bay shrimps and capers, ahead of a meaty veal chop with sage butter or whole lemon sole with béarnaise sauce. Desserts will tempt, even if you didn't think you needed one: hazelnut and Amedei chocolate meringue or just a shot of Beefeater sloe gin jelly. Drinks cover all bases, from beer and cider to comprehensive wines (from £20).
Chef/s: Martin Sweeney. **Open:** Sun to Fri L 12 to 3 (2 Sun), all week D 6 to 11. **Closed:** 25 and 26 Dec, bank hols. **Meals:** alc (main courses £15 to £36). Set L and D £17.50 (2 courses) to £22.50. Sun L £27.50 (2 courses) to £32. **Service:** 12.5%. **Details:** 65 seats. 12 seats outside. Music.

NEW ENTRY
Ibérica
Top-tier tapas in Docklands
10 Cabot Square, Canary Wharf, E14 4QQ
Tel no: (020) 7636 8650
www.ibericalondon.co.uk
⊖ Canary Wharf, map 1
Spanish | £35
Cooking score: 3

For its second branch, Fitzrovia conquistador Ibérica has journeyed to Docklands. Its butch looks – studded leather chairs, bull's head, iron chandeliers and legs of ham – have gone down well with Canary Wharf 'masters of the universe' who share a taste for Ibérica's top-tier tapas and Spanish fine wines. The alternately classic and creative menu is designed by top Spanish chef Nacho Manzano, and executed by Cesar Garcia. Fried artichokes and white asparagus with sea urchin aïoli and a (heavy-going) gazpacho of berries, beetroot and anchovy demonstrate the kitchen's wilder streak, while excellent cheese croquetas, mini-Ibérico pork burgers and lovingly presented jamón play safer but hit the bullseye. Caramelised Spanish rice pudding could round things off. Service is infectiously enthusiastic. House wine from £20.90.
Chef/s: Cesar Garcia. **Open:** all week 11.30am to 11.00pm (Sun 12 to 4). **Closed:** 25 and 26 Dec. **Meals:** alc (main courses £7 to £15). **Service:** 12.5%. **Details:** 145 seats. Wheelchair access. Music.

ALSO RECOMMENDED
▲ Kasturi
57 Aldgate High Street, Whitechapel, EC3N 1AL
Tel no: (020) 7480 7402
www.kasturi-restaurant.co.uk
⊖ Aldgate, map 2
Indian £5 OFF

Among Aldgate's towering financial landmarks, this flashily appointed City Indian cuts quite a dash with its Art Deco interiors and skilfully executed repertoire of regional dishes from the North West Frontier. Tip-top tandooris and traditional biryanis (from £10.50) line up alongside more ambitious specialities that are several notches above the average curry house offerings, say chicken bhuna Hyderabadi (£9.95). Old favourites of dhansaks and vindaloos are also served and there is plenty to please vegetarians. House wine £16.50. Closed Sun

▲ Kêu!
332 Old Street, Shoreditch, EC1V 9DR
Tel no: (020) 7739 1164
www.keudeli.co.uk
⊖ Old Street, map 2
Vietnamese

Join the fast-moving queue of Shoreditch office workers at this trendy Vietnamese sandwich bar, from the same stable as nearby Viet Grill. Banh mi (French-inspired Vietnamese baguettes) are the top pick; the 'classic' (£5) with belly pork, ham terrine and chicken liver pâté, fragrant herbs and pickled vegetables is the one to try. Summer rolls (£3), some soups, salads and specials supplement the sandwich menu. Take away or eat in at (limited) counter seating, with a Vietnamese beer or iced coffee. Closed Sundays.

Lutyens
Smooth, seductive Conran classic
85 Fleet Street, City, EC4Y 1AE
Tel no: (020) 7583 8385
www.lutyens-restaurant.com
⊖ Chancery Lane, St Paul's, Temple, map 5
French | £45
Cooking score: 4

This Sir Terence Conran/Peter Prescott venture occupies a grand building designed by Sir Edwin Lutyens. Suits are very much in evidence, unsurprising in the heart of the legal district, but the atmosphere is smooth and inviting, with well-drilled service. A changing of the guard in the kitchen took place in the spring of 2012, but the Conran house style of populist brasserie cooking is maintained. Menus are long enough to ensure most tastes are catered for; they show occasional inventive touches but generally play it safe with a repertoire of well-rehearsed dishes in which prime ingredients (lobster mayonnaise, fillet steak bordelaise) produce seductive results. The classical French background also delivers humbler items such as leek and potato soup with wild garlic persillade and duck confit, while the evening menu compris offers exceptional value with its three courses, wine, coffee and petits fours deal. Wines from £20. **Chef/s:** Henrik Ritzen. **Open:** Mon to Fri L 12 to 3, D 6 to 10. **Closed:** Sat, Sun, 24 Dec to 4 Jan, 30 Jul to 10 Aug, bank hols. **Meals:** alc (main courses £16 to £36). Set L (bar) £16.50 (2 courses) to £19.50. Set D (menu compris) £39.50. **Service:** 13.5%. **Details:** 125 seats. 14 seats outside. Separate bar. Wheelchair access. Music.

ALSO RECOMMENDED

▲ Meatballs

The Quality Chop House, 92-94 Farringdon Road, Clerkenwell, EC1R 3EA
Tel no: (020) 3490 6228
www.meatballs.co.uk
⊖ Farringdon, map 5
Italian-American

Didn't think you could build a menu around the humble meatball? Think again. In the historic setting of this late nineteenth-century chop house, you can mix and match three 'balls' for £4.95 (or three sliders for £5.95); choice ranges from pork and rosemary to Thai chilli chicken, and lamb with cucumber, dill and yoghurt sauce. Bonus balls are £1.95, 'underneath' takes in buttered spaghetti (£2.25) or mash; 'on the side' includes peas with lettuce, spring onions and cream. With puddings such as egg custard under £5, it makes for wallet-friendly dining. Wines from £14.25. Open all week.

▲ Mehek

45 London Wall, Moorgate, EC2M 5TE
Tel no: (020) 7588 5043
www.mehek.co.uk
⊖ Moorgate, Liverpool Street, map 2
Indian £5 OFF

Polished wood floors, a long bar, yellow walls, artefacts galore… Mehek cuts quite a dash on historic London Wall, and the cooking tries to live up to its auspicious, overtly snazzy surroundings. The name means 'fragrance', and the kitchen delivers aromatic hits in the shape of king prawn puris (£7.50), Kashmiri chicken with pineapple (£14.90), home-style Lahore lamb with boiled egg and other regionally inspired dishes – plus a roster of familiar dhansaks, bhunas, biryanis et al. House wine is £16.95. Open Mon to Fri.

The Modern Pantry

Flexible fusion in Clerkenwell
47-48 St John's Square, Clerkenwell, EC1V 4JJ
Tel no: (020) 7553 9210
www.themodernpantry.co.uk
⊖ Farringdon, map 5
Fusion | £40
Cooking score: 3

An exercise in Clerkenwell minimalism, with a roistering vibe that extends from the casual café to the spacious upstairs dining room, Anna Hansen's converted Georgian townhouse is also a hotbed of flexible fusion food. Unframed sketches line the walls, the din seldom subsides and the menu is a riot of flavours garnered from the world larder. Seaweed tartare sauce is applied to smoked haddock and chickpea fish fingers, onglet steak is marinated in miso, and the kitchen ups the ante with fizzy, shopping-list combos ranging from seared scallops with cauliflower and wasabi purée, tobiko, pink peppercorns and pickled ginger salsa to confit duck leg with aubergine, coriander and cumin relish, udon noodles and ponzu dressing. Breakfast, weekend brunch and afternoon tea are popular shouts, too. Free-roaming global wines start at £18.

Chef/s: Anna Hansen and Robert McLeary. **Open:** Mon to Fri 12 to 10.30 (10 Mon). Sat and Sun 10 to 4, 6 to 10.30. **Closed:** 24 to 27 Dec. **Meals:** alc (main courses £16 to £22). Set weekday L £20 (2 courses). Sun L £25. **Service:** 12.5%. **Details:** 112 seats. 36 seats outside. Separate bar. Wheelchair access. Music.

NEW ENTRY
Morgan M
French sophistication and precision
50 Long Lane, Barbican, EC1A 9EJ
Tel no: (020) 7609 3560
www.morganm.com
➔ Barbican, map 5
Modern French | £44
Cooking score: 5

V

Morgan Meunier's exclusive London concern has now relocated from Islington to Barbican. Directly opposite Smithfield market, it's a split-level job, with the principal business happening on the ground floor and a more informal bistro down below. The former is done in muted hues of soft apple-green and ivory, with mellow lighting, pine floors and smartly attired tables. From here, turn your attention to the colourful, innovative cuisine that Meunier has made his signature. Yellowfin tuna tartare with cumin-scented aubergine caviar, grapefruit and red pepper sorbet is a starter to make you sit up and take notice, even if its combined effect is a little jangly; mains might offer superb honey-glazed quail with a Brussels sprout-sized spinach parcel of the leg-meat, accompanied by fine lemon couscous, or sea bass with carrot and ginger risotto in saffron and lemon broth. Dessert may see a silver jug of dark chocolate soup decanted over lightly caramelised pistachios for a winning performance, while passion-fruit soufflé rises to the occasion, along with its sorbet and crème anglaise. The wine list opens at £19 (£4.50 a small glass), before galloping off round the French regions. **Chef/s:** Morgan Meunier. **Open:** Mon to Fri L 12 to 2.45, Mon to Sat D 6 to 10.30. **Closed:** Sun, 24 to 30 Dec. **Meals:** alc (main courses £22 to £29). Set L and

D £21.50 (2 courses) to £25.50. Tasting menu £50 (6 courses). **Service:** 12.5%. **Details:** 59 seats. Separate bar. Wheelchair access. Music.

Morito
Tip-top tapas
32 Exmouth Market, Clerkenwell, EC1R 4QL
Tel no: (020) 7278 7007
www.morito.co.uk
➔ Farringdon, map 2
Tapas | £20
Cooking score: 4

Moro's pint-sized tapas bar, next door to its illustrious sibling (see entry), has quite a swagger considering there's not much in the way of décor, the few tables are tightly packed, and there's a no-booking policy. But the buzz is great and the food makes amends with its freshness, punch and flavours, kicking off simply with Padrón peppers, plates of jamón Ibérico de Bellota and quails' eggs with cumin and salt. Sam and Sam Clark know their way around the byways of Spanish and North African cuisine, so they avoid all the tapas clichés. They make the most of top-notch ingredients – big-on-flavour lamb chops with cumin and paprika, or slow-roasted belly pork with cumin and lemon, and 'sensational' fried chickpeas with pumpkin, coriander and tahini sauce are typical of the kitchen's impressive output. Consider a glass of sherry before hitting the excellent, though compact, Iberian wine list; prices from £16. **Chef/s:** Samuel and Samantha Clark. **Open:** all week L 12 to 4, Mon to Sat D 5 to 11. **Closed:** Christmas week, bank hols. **Meals:** alc (tapas from £3 to £9). **Service:** 12.5%. **Details:** 35 seats. 12 seats outside. Wheelchair access. Music.

Visit us Online
To find out more about *The Good Food Guide*, please visit www.thegoodfoodguide.co.uk

Moro

Getting even hotter
34-36 Exmouth Market, Clerkenwell, EC1R 4QE
Tel no: (020) 7833 8336
www.moro.co.uk
⊖ Farringdon, map 2
Spanish/North African | £32
Cooking score: 4

Samuel and Samantha Clark have been plying their spirited Moorish trade at this rousing Clerkenwell favourite for 15 years, but regulars confirm that Moro is as hot as ever – in fact the cooking seems to be getting even better. Their earthy fusion of Spanish and North African flavours has lost none of its vibrancy or impact as the kitchen piles on the sweet, savoury and aromatic delights. The char-grill delivers 'spectacularly flavoursome' lamb chops with a rich aubergine and red onion stew, or sea bass with 'six grains', sweet herbs and turnip salad, while the output of the wood-fired oven might run from roasted pork with braised chard and Amalfi lemon to whole bream with fino sauce, purple sprouting broccoli and crispy capers. To start, morsels of mojama (air-dried tuna) 'explode in the mouth', and there are perfectly simple desserts such as Malaga raisin ice cream to finish. Gorgeous sherry flights suit the food; otherwise cruise through the drinkable pan-Iberian pleasures of the helpfully annotated wine list. Prices start at £16 (£4.50 a glass).
Chef/s: Samuel and Samantha Clark. **Open:** all week L 12.30 to 2.30 (12 to 2.45 Sun), Mon to Sat D 6 to 10.30. **Closed:** 24 Dec to 4 Jan, bank hols. **Meals:** alc (main courses £16 to £20). **Service:** 12.5%. **Details:** 90 seats. 20 seats outside. No music. Wheelchair access.

Average Price

The average price listed in main-entry reviews denotes the price of a three-course meal, without wine.

NEW ENTRY
North Road

Foraged fare and hints of Scandinavia
69-73 St John Street, Clerkenwell, EC1M 4AY
Tel no: (020) 3217 0033
www.northroadrestaurant.co.uk
⊖ Barbican, map 5
Modern European | £39
Cooking score: 4

£5 OFF

The most fashionable things in food right now, namely foraged ingredients and hints of Copenhagen's Noma (the world's best restaurant, allegedly), are offered at Danish chef Christoffer Hruskova's Clerkenwell restaurant. An admirably short menu of four starters, four mains and four puddings (plus tasting menu option) piques the interest immediately with talk of a starter of Scottish scallops with carrot, sea buckthorn and sea urchin and, to follow, Dorset turbot and bakskud (salted smoked dab) with sea kale and nettle. Poor bread accompanied by a solid ball of clarified brown butter made a worryingly weak start, but some strong cooking followed, including a pretty, powerful assembly of Herdwick lamb heart, wild garlic and yoghurt with pickled elderberries, and a wittily presented, assertive green rhubarb dessert with caramelised milk sorbet. There were quibbles: ill-thought-out plating that 'hid' key flavours; heavy salt usage; and garbled descriptions from the otherwise strong service team. The striking bar and dining room follows the Scandinavian theme, with tactile materials and Danish design, though the feel is somewhat spare – more conducive to business than pleasure (in contrast to the food). The intelligent and gently priced wine list (from £25) inspires you to try something new.
Chef/s: Christoffer Hruskova. **Open:** Mon to Fri L 12 to 2.45, Mon to Sat D 6 to 10.45 (11 Fri and Sat). **Closed:** Sun, 25 Dec to first week Jan, bank hols. **Meals:** alc (main courses £19 to £24). Set L £22 (2 courses) to £25. **Service:** 12.5%. **Details:** Separate bar. Music.

Pizza East

Oh-so-cool Italian eatery
56 Shoreditch High Street, Shoreditch, E1 6JJ
Tel no: (020) 7729 1888
www.pizzaeast.com
⊖ Liverpool Street, Old Street, map 2
Italian-American | £24
Cooking score: 2

 £30

The epicentre of East-End chic is the perfect location for this oh-so-cool eatery on the ground floor of the former Lipton's tea warehouse. Exposed brick, concrete and scuffed floorboards make a utilitarian but sharply contemporary setting. Regulars return repeatedly for the big-on-flavour blend of Italian-American cooking that majors in wood-fired pizzas ('the potato, pancetta, puzzone one was an absolute knockout') and more. Top-drawer ingredients define the repertoire, especially Italian charcuterie and cheeses, and reporters have praised beef lasagne, crispy belly pork, lamb meatballs, and salted chocolate caramel tart. Wines from £17.59. Big brother to Pizza East Portobello (see entry).
Chef/s: Brian McGowan. **Open:** all week L 12 to 5 (10am Sat and Sun), D 5 to 11 (12am Thur, 1am Fri and Sat). **Closed:** 24 to 26 Dec. **Meals:** alc (main courses £8 to £17). **Service:** 12.5%. **Details:** 136 seats. Separate bar. Wheelchair access. Music.

NEW ENTRY

Railroad

Gem with innovative global food
120-122 Morning Lane, Hackney, E9 6LH
Tel no: (020) 8985 2858
www.railroadhackney.co.uk
⊖ Bethnal Green, map 1
Eclectic | £22
Cooking score: 2

 £30

A trip down Morning Lane sounds promising, but then you find yourself on a grim Hackney street and feel duped – until you find this gem. The small café-bar-restaurant has communal tables and a brief menu that changes daily.

Much effort goes into sourcing and the food is innovative and global: Vietnamese banh mi – a spicy minced pork and pickled vegetable sandwich – or a 'stand-out' cauliflower and yoghurt soup, for example. You can have dinner from Wednesday to Saturday; pork shoulder slow-cooked in chillies, bay, allspice and tomato is a typical main, pressed chocolate cake a good ending. Wines from £15.
Chef/s: Lizzie Parle. **Open:** all week L 12 to 3.30 (10am Sat and Sun), Wed to Sat D 7 to 9.30. **Closed:** 24 Dec to 7 Jan. **Meals:** alc (main courses £11 to £16). **Service:** not inc. **Details:** 34 seats. Music.

Refettorio

Convivial City Italian
Crowne Plaza Hotel, 19 New Bridge Street, City, EC4V 6DB
Tel no: (020) 7438 8052
www.refettorio.com
⊖ Blackfriars, map 5
Italian | £30
Cooking score: 2

At lunchtime, this capacious Italian within the Crowne Plaza Hotel is an ever-popular meeting ground for the smart City crowd, who convene around huge refectory tables for assorted 'convivia' (sharing plates of charcuterie and regional cheeses topped up with rustic breads, homemade pickles and salads). The set-up is driven by superstar Giorgio Locatelli, and his culinary lieutenants also deliver a full menu of perky antipasti (endive salad with pear and Gorgonzola), plentiful handmade pastas (paccheri with prawns and cherry tomatoes, say) and rustic mains of pork chop with braised black cabbage and chestnuts or sea bass with braised fennel and celeriac purée. The all-Italian wine list starts at £18.50.
Chef/s: Alessandro Bay. **Open:** Mon to Fri L 12 to 2.30, Mon to Sat D 6 to 10.30 (10 Fri and Sat). **Closed:** Sun, 24 to 30 Dec, Good Fri, Easter Mon. **Meals:** alc (main courses £12 to £24). Set L and D £18 (2 courses) to £25. **Service:** 12.5%. **Details:** 100 seats. Separate bar. Wheelchair access. Music.

Rhodes Twenty Four

Cityscapes and re-imagined heritage cooking
Tower 42, 25 Old Broad Street, City, EC2N 1HQ
Tel no: (020) 7877 7703
www.rhodes24.co.uk
⊖ **Liverpool Street, map 2**
British | £55
Cooking score: 4

All the world's great cities have restaurants up
in the clouds, and Gary Rhodes's venue on the
24th floor of Tower 42, one of the City's
reference works of look-at-me modern
architecture, enjoys views as imperious as you
might imagine – and then some. The blond-
wood-and-mauve décor is a trifle bland, but
the prospect over the capital and the re-
imagined heritage cooking more than
compensate. Game pie with buttered celeriac
gets the ball rolling with a robust kick, or
there's Lincolnshire smoked eel with beetroot,
goats' curd and watercress. Fish dishes are more
involved than the fish and chips you may be
expecting – as when halibut turns up with
braised veal risotto – but steamed mutton and
onion suet pudding with crushed swede
should reassure the thoroughgoing
traditionalists. Overseas visitors can go native
with bread-and-butter pudding. A wine list of
vigorously marked-up classics starts at £24.
Chef/s: Gary Rhodes. **Open:** Mon to Fri L 12 to 2.15,
D 6 to 9.15. **Closed:** Sat, Sun, 25 Dec, 1 Jan, bank
hols. **Meals:** alc (main courses £18 to £30). Tasting
menu £75 (5 courses). **Service:** 12.5%. **Details:** 75
seats. Separate bar. Wheelchair access. Music.

Rivington Grill

Nostalgic British grill and bistro
28-30 Rivington Street, Shoreditch, EC2A 3DZ
Tel no: (020) 7729 7053
www.rivingtongrill.co.uk
⊖ **Old Street, map 2**
Modern British | £27
Cooking score: 2

£30

Rivington Street in Shoreditch may be
tipping the scales in the trend stakes, but this
smart British bistro has remained resolutely

unfazed. Nostalgia is the restaurant's
lifeblood; the all-day menu is a sentimental
tour of British regions and traditional dishes.
Expect every dish to be given a geographical
credit, from Isle of Mull diver scallops to
Speyside flat-iron steak from the grill and
even native potatoes. Unfussy and robust
dishes garner most praise, particularly brunch
fare and the burger. Save room for Trinity
House burnt cream. Staff nonchalance has
struck a dud note, and lacklustre flavours
could be sharpened up. Wines from £15.
Chef/s: Simon Wadham. **Open:** all week L 12 to 3 (11
to 4 Sat and Sun), D 6 to 11 (10 Sun). **Closed:** 25
Dec, 1 Jan. **Meals:** alc (main courses £14 to £30).
Service: 12.5%. **Details:** 80 seats. Separate bar. No
music. Wheelchair access.

Rochelle Canteen

Quirky East End hideaway
Rochelle School, Arnold Circus, London, E2 7ES
Tel no: (020) 7729 5677
www.arnoldandhenderson.com
⊖ **Liverpool Street, map 2**
British | £23
Cooking score: 2

It's quirky: an old bike shed, hidden behind
the high walls of an ex-school, with
communal tables, no alcohol licence and
restricted opening hours, but owners Margot
Henderson and Melanie Arnold make it work.
'Very few local restaurants care about their
food like these guys' enthused one fan. The
short, terse menu is defined by seasonal
pickings and the nose-to-tail philosophy of
Fergus Henderson's St John (see entry). Those
in the know pack in for rabbit offal on toast,
grilled mackerel with new potatoes and dulse
(seaweed), and blood-orange posset. Excellent
alfresco opportunities. BYO, with
corkage £5.
Chef/s: James Ferguson. **Open:** Mon to Fri 9.30am
to 4.30pm. **Closed:** Sat, Sun, 25 Dec to 1 Jan, bank
hols. **Meals:** alc (main courses £10 to £17).
Service: not inc. **Details:** 36 seats. 20 seats outside.
No music. Wheelchair access.

St John

Provenance-driven nose-to-tail adventures
26 St John Street, Clerkenwell, EC1M 4AY
Tel no: (020) 3301 8069
www.stjohnrestaurant.com
⊖ **Farringdon, map 5**
British | £32
Cooking score: 5

Still strangely alluring after all these years, St John remains one of London's foodie paradoxes – a restaurant that garners plaudits by serving reinvented 'poorhouse victuals' in the bare-bones surrounds of a minimally converted smokehouse. The interior exudes a white-walled austerity that chimes perfectly with the kitchen's provenance-driven nose-to-tail adventures. Founder Fergus Henderson has never shied away from anatomically challenging ideas, and the place remains a mecca for those wanting to gorge on curious bits from 'slightly less-trodden animals'. These days, no one bats an eyelid if the menu offers crispy pig's skin or duck hearts, but the devil is in the detail (or the uncompromising lack of it) and devotees continue to relish the gut-busting honesty and unadulterated earthiness of it all. The talk is of indulgent plates of chitterlings, fabulously juicy mixed offal on toast, snails 'as good as anything in Paris', melting roast hare with mashed swede or 'superbly salty' ox tongue with spinach. If blood and guts isn't your thing, the kitchen can roll out smoked herring with beetroot tops and horseradish or a veggie combo of celeriac and baked eggs. To finish, the cinnamon-spiked apple crumble with custard is 'truly astounding', likewise the marmalade ice cream. Perversely, the wine list hops over to France for its regional input; prices from £24.
Chef/s: Chris Gillard. **Open:** Sun to Fri L 12 to 3 (1 to 3 Sun), Mon to Sat D 6 to 11. **Closed:** 1 week Christmas. **Meals:** alc (main courses £13 to £30). **Service:** 12.5%. **Details:** 110 seats. Separate bar. No music.

St John Bread & Wine

Spitalfields humdinger
94-96 Commercial Street, Spitalfields, E1 6LZ
Tel no: (020) 3301 8069
www.stjohnbreadandwine.com
⊖ **Liverpool Street, map 1**
British | £28
Cooking score: 3

The laid-back baby brother of St John (see entry), this Spitalfields humdinger is also a defiant nose-to-tail campaigner, with the bonus of splendid artisan breads from its own bakery. There's plenty to applaud here, and regulars have a habit of reeling off their favourites: foie gras and duck liver on toast ('a great treat'); superb lamb's fry (testicles to you and me); sea bass baked in salt; 'challenging but enjoyably pink' roast grouse or woodcock in season; glorious mallard legs with parsnip and pickled walnut; goats' cheese with beetroot and lentils... and so forth. To finish, the steamed treacle sponge is a must ('if you can be carried home in a cushioned palanquin'); otherwise, freshen up with a spiky apple sorbet laced with vodka. The wine list is a French love affair, with prices from £24.
Chef/s: Lee Tiernan. **Open:** all week L 12 to 4, D 6 to 10.30 (9 Sun). **Closed:** Christmas to New Year. **Meals:** alc (main courses £11 to £17). **Service:** not inc. **Details:** 60 seats. No music.

Searcy's

Pitch-perfect favourites, wickedly good puds
Level 2, Barbican Centre, Silk Street, Barbican, EC2Y 8DS
Tel no: (020) 7588 3008
www.searcys.co.uk
⊖ **Barbican, Moorgate, map 5**
Modern European | £28
Cooking score: 3

In contrast to the somewhat 'stark, sterile feel' of the Barbican itself, this stylish restaurant promises airy comfort. Judging by reports, the kitchen seems to work best when it's on familiar ground – sending out pitch-perfect renditions of calf's liver with crushed Jersey Royals, spinach and salsa verde or grilled onglet steak with twice-cooked chips and horseradish sauce, plus some wickedly good desserts including summer pudding and chocolate nemesis seasonally embellished with Scottish strawberries, red wine syrup, vanilla and crème fraîche. By contrast, more ambitious outings such as Andalucian garlic and saffron soup with salt cod and chorizo can sometimes flounder. Thankfully, Searcy's can always be relied on when it comes to wine, and the accessible, cosmopolitan list offers consistently satisfying drinking from £18 (£4.50 a glass).

Chef/s: Darren Archer. **Open:** Mon to Fri L 12 to 2.30, Mon to Sat D 5 to 10.30. **Closed:** Sun, 24 to 26 Dec, bank hols. **Meals:** alc (main courses £13 to £20). Set L £18.50 (2 courses) to £22.50. **Service:** not inc. **Details:** 72 seats. Separate bar. Wheelchair access. Music. Car parking.

Tayyabs
Rollicking Punjabi canteen with wicked spicing
89 Fieldgate Street, Whitechapel, E1 1JU
Tel no: (020) 7247 6400/9543
www.tayyabs.co.uk
⊖ Whitechapel, Aldgate East, map 1
Indian/Pakistani | £20
Cooking score: 2

V £30

'Every year we fly over from our home in Germany to eat at Tayyabs', confess a couple who are addicted to this legendary canteen's gastronomic thrills. Trade also comes from nearer home, of course, and the owners recently added a first-floor extension to accommodate everyone. Opened in 1972, this rollicking place has grafted on some arty Whitechapel chic over the years, but has lost none of its edge – or indeed its talent for conjuring up wickedly spiced tandooris and punchy curries such as karahi keema, 'dry meat', sag aloo and dhal karela (lentils with bitter gourd). The results may challenge your waistline, but never your wallet. Unlicensed – so BYO booze.

Chef/s: Wasim Tayyab. **Open:** all week L 12 to 3, D 4 to 11.30. **Meals:** alc (main courses £6 to £13). **Service:** not inc. **Details:** 370 seats. Wheelchair access. Music.

ALSO RECOMMENDED
▲ Towpath Café
42 De Beauvoir Crescent, Dalston, N1 5SB
www.towpathcafe.wordpress.com
⊖ Old Street, map 2
Modern European

On the Regent's Canal between the Angel and Broadway market, this seasonal café (March to end Oct) is at its best in fair weather – there's little space under cover. Lori De Mori and Jason Lowe's quirky hole-in-the-wall opens from breakfast (porridge, granola with yoghurt, superb coffee) till dusk. Tables are communal, ideas simple, ingredients impeccable: fennel and blood-orange salad (£5.50), toasted Montgomery Cheddar cheese sandwich (£6), rhubarb and frangipane tart. Wine from £19. Open Tue to Sun.

Les Trois Garçons
High-camp and vigorous French cooking
1 Club Row, Shoreditch, E1 6JX
Tel no: (020) 7613 1924
www.lestroisgarcons.com
⊖ Liverpool Street, map 1
French | £47
Cooking score: 2

The garçons are a Malaysian-French-Swedish triumvirate who acquired a Shoreditch Victorian boozer in 1996, moved in and have presided over its gradual transformation into a contemporary restaurant, complete with chef's table and décor of dangling handbags. The vigorously modern French cuisine doesn't stint on vivid juxtapositions. Start with sea bass roulade with red mullet escabèche, accompanied by a salad of baby gem, pickled mooli and papaya, then marinated and braised venison with Savoy, salsify and puréed beetroot in Madeira jus, and ease down with

crème brûlée and lavender sorbet. Wines start at £24.50 (£6.50 a glass) for a Picpoul de Pinet.
Chef/s: Michael Chan. **Open:** Mon to Fri L 12 to 2.30, Mon to Sat D 6 to 9.30 (10 Thur, 10.30 Fri and Sat). **Closed:** 24 Dec to 4 Jan, bank hols. **Meals:** Set L £17.50 (2 courses) to £22. Set D £40.50 (2 courses) to £47. Tasting menu £75. **Service:** 12.5%. **Details:** 65 seats. Wheelchair access. Music. Children at L and early D only.

28°-50°
Dedicated to the fruit of the vine
140 Fetter Lane, City, EC4A 1BT
Tel no: (020) 7242 8877
www.2850.co.uk
⊖ **Chancery Lane, map 5**
French | £29
Cooking score: 3
🍾 £30

'We arrived early for lunch to an empty restaurant,' a reader reports. 'Fifteen minutes later, it was heaving.' This basement venue, with its light wood floor, bare tables and single-minded dedication to the fruit of the vine, works to a winning formula. Truffled tagliatelle, followed by a main course risotto served in a roast squash, stood out on that occasion. There are other sound bistro dishes such as duck rillettes with cornichons and toast, and onglet with chips and sauce Choron, with indulgent finishers like chocolate and blood-orange trifle. Wines are served in dinky 75ml, small 125ml and large 250ml measures. And they have bottles, too. The list covers a lot of ground in a short span, from the Arbois to Mendoza, the Alentejo to Marlborough, with sound growers all over. If it's caution you're throwing to the winds, look to the Collectors' List. Otherwise, prices open at £19.50 for bottles of Puglian Fiano and Sicilian Nero d'Avola.
Chef/s: Ben Mellor. **Open:** Mon to Fri L 12 to 2.30, D 6 to 9.30. **Closed:** Sat, Sun, 25 Dec to 2 Jan. **Meals:** alc (main courses £15 to £17). Set L £15.95. **Service:** 12.5%. **Details:** 60 seats. Separate bar. Music.

Vanilla Black
Proper cooking for neglected veggies
17-18 Tooks Court, Farringdon, EC4A 1LB
Tel no: (020) 7242 2622
www.vanillablack.co.uk
⊖ **Chancery Lane, map 5**
Vegetarian | £33
Cooking score: 2
V

'Eating out a lot as a vegetarian can become tiresome very quickly... Vanilla Black is the antidote. It's as if you are finally being treated to proper food.' So says one reporter, who is delighted that Andrew Dargue moved from Yorkshire to London with his innovative take on vegetarian food. The cooking delivers a galaxy of flavours, from an opening poached duck egg yolk with whipped spinach, crispy bread, seeds and mustard oil, via warm celery pannacotta with blue Wensleydale profiteroles, charred celery, carrots and apple sauce, to white chocolate and cep tart with a cornflake cake, Picpoul sorbet and crispy tarragon. Wines from £16.50. All-day sibling Orchard is at 11 Sicilian Avenue, Holborn; tel: (020) 7831 2715.
Chef/s: Andrew Dargue. **Open:** Mon to Fri L 12 to 2.30, Mon to Sat D 6 to 10. **Closed:** Sun, 2 weeks Christmas and New Year, bank hols. **Meals:** (alc (main courses £12 to £15). Set L £18.50 (2 courses) to £23.50. Set D £24.50 (2 courses) to £32.50. **Service:** 12.5%. **Details:** 45 seats. Music.

Viajante
Truly original food that makes a splash
Patriot Square, Bethnal Green, E2 9NF
Tel no: (020) 7871 0461
www.viajante.co.uk
⊖ **Bethnal Green, map 1**
Modern European | £65
Cooking score: 5
🛏 V

The restaurant on the ground floor of Bethnal Green's Victorian town hall – now a boutique hotel – looks coolly urbane and modern, in stark contrast to the gritty urban street outside. Attention is focused on the open kitchen, which forms part of the double dining room; ceremony is little stood upon here, it is the food that makes the splash. Portuguese-born Nuno Mendes aims to make a strong impression with his truly original cooking, which combines the subtlest flavours of East and West, underpinned by a mastery of sous-vide and low-temperature cooking techniques. To get a glimpse, the three-course lunch menu at £28 is a good intro; otherwise menus of six, nine and twelve 'tiny offerings' (quipped one reader) begin with a salvo of intensely flavoured canapés, among them Thai Explosion II (chicken mousse heady with coconut and Thai spices sandwiched between crisp chicken skin) and toasted amaranth (gluten-free grain) biscuits with an earthy wood sorrel purée. A great meat dish of obviously Iberian influence is duck breast, heart and tongue with carrots and crosnes (an artichoke-like root vegetable). Desserts such as pickled and raw cucumber with reduced milk sorbet play with sweet and savoury tastes. Modern wines start at £30.

Chef/s: Nuno Mendes. **Open:** Fri to Sun L 12 to 2, all week D 6 to 9.30. **Closed:** bank hols. **Meals:** Set L £28 (3 courses), £50 (6 courses) to £65 (9 courses). Set D £65 (6 courses) to £90 (12 courses). **Service:** 12.5%. **Details:** 35 seats. Separate bar. Wheelchair access. Music. No children under 11 yrs.

Viet Grill

Tasty, satisfying street food
58 Kingsland Road, Shoreditch, E2 8DP
Tel no: (020) 7739 6686
www.vietnamesekitchen.co.uk
⊖ **Old Street, map 2**
Vietnamese | £22
Cooking score: 2

Of all the canteen-style restaurants on the Kingsland Road, Viet Grill has the best décor – a nifty modern look that references Vietnam's French colonial past. The restaurant has won legions of fans with its flexible, appealing menu, which takes in sociable plates of tasty street food and all manner of salads (spicy green mango with dried squid, daikon

and knotweed), meat dishes (Tamworth belly pork in caramelised coconut juice) and fish (banana leaf whole-roasted mackerel). Elsewhere, a bowl of pho or dish of stir-fried noodles and seafood ratchet up the satisfaction factor. Wines, chosen by Malcolm Gluck, start at £18.

Chef/s: Vinh Vu. **Open:** Mon to Sat 12 to 11 (11.30 Fri and Sat). Sun 12 to 10.30. **Closed:** Christmas and New Year. **Meals:** alc (main courses £7 to £25). **Service:** 12.5%. **Details:** 140 seats. Separate bar. Music.

Vinoteca

Mediterranean flavours and interesting tipples
7 St John Street, Farringdon, EC1M 4AA
Tel no: (020) 7253 8786
www.vinoteca.co.uk
⊖ **Farringdon, Barbican, map 5**
Modern European | £28
Cooking score: 3

In the five years it has been open, this unassuming wine bar has gathered something of a following. It's all rollickingly informal, the emphasis firmly on food with a Mediterranean flavour, with lots of interesting tipples to sample. Ingredients are impeccable and the menu encourages experimentation. Settle down with a bottle of something from the worldwide list of 300 bins and share a plate of Jabugo cured meats, almonds and olives, or go for bold flavour combinations in keenly priced dishes such as deep-fried n'duja sausage with pearl barley, Savoy cabbage, pancetta and sage crumble, or whole roasted pigeon with beetroot, squash and farro (a nutty grain). Wines from £14.50. Offshoots in Marylebone (see entry) and at 53-55 Beak Street, Soho; tel: (020) 3544 7411.

Chef/s: John Cook. **Open:** Mon to Sat L 12 to 2.45 (4 Sat), D 5.45 to 10. **Closed:** Sun, 24 Dec to 3 Jan. **Meals:** alc (main courses £10 to £16). Set L £8.95 (1 course). **Service:** 12.5%. **Details:** 35 seats. 6 seats outside. Separate bar. Music.

Wapping Food

Skilful food in an old power station
Wapping Hydraulic Power Station, Wapping Walk,
Wapping, E1W 3SG
Tel no: (020) 7680 2080
www.thewappingproject.com
⊖ Wapping, map 1
Modern European | £35
Cooking score: 3
£5
OFF

The run-down warehouse exterior and café-like interior belie Wapping Food's skilfully rendered food and friendly service. One reporter commented that the restaurant had just been inserted into the shell of the hydraulic station, among the machinery and dangling hooks and chains – not a criticism; this light-filled, soaring space has 'a great vibe'. The menu taps into the UK's regional network, and offers mainly no-frills dishes such as wood pigeon with braised red cabbage and watercress, and roast rabbit saddle with swede and carrot mash. The package also runs to a blinding weekend brunch (10 to 12.30) with possibly the best American-style pancakes in town. House wine £19.
Chef/s: Matthew Young. **Open:** Sat and Sun brunch 10 to 12.30, L 1 to 3.30 (4 Sun), Mon to Sat D 6.30 to 11 (7 Sat). **Closed:** 24 Dec to 3 Jan, bank hols. **Meals:** alc (main courses £16 to £23). Set L and D £37.50 to £53.50. **Service:** 12.5%. **Details:** 120 seats. 60 seats outside. Wheelchair access. Music. Car parking.

Whitechapel Gallery Dining Room

Good value and flavours that sing
77-82 Whitechapel High Street, Whitechapel,
E1 7QX
Tel no: (020) 7522 7896
www.whitechapelgallery.org/dining-room
⊖ Aldgate East, map 1
Modern European | £30
Cooking score: 3

The small, light, street-facing room, part of the landmark art gallery, comes with tightly packed tables and a menu that champions

seasonal British produce. It's a zesty assortment – Montgomery Cheddar, Dedham Vale beef, Cornish sardines, Portland crab, English asparagus – that's been given a homely Italian flavour courtesy of consultant chef Angela Hartnett. Flavours are allowed to sing in simply marvellous dishes such as roasted beets with toasted walnut and mustard leaves, and braised rabbit leg, smoked pancetta, heritage carrots and Dijon sauce. Rhubarb fool with sugared almonds or some British cheeses could close the show. Readers have appreciated the good value of it all and have also praised the friendly service. Wines from £14.95.
Chef/s: Emma Duggan. **Open:** Tue to Fri and Sun L 12 to 3 (3.45 Sun), Wed to Fri D 6 to 9.30, Sat 12 to 9.30. **Closed:** Mon, 25 Dec to 3 Jan. **Meals:** alc (main courses £12 to £17). Sun L £14.95. **Service:** 12.5%. **Details:** 36 seats. Wheelchair access. Music.

ALSO RECOMMENDED

▲ The Zetter Townhouse

49-50 St John's Square, Clerkenwell, EC1M 5RJ
Tel no: (020) 7324 4444
www.thezettertownhouse.com
⊖ Farringdon, map 5
Global

Round the corner from Bistrot Bruno Loubet at the Zetter Hotel (see entry), this discreet Georgian townhouse feels like a 'secret club'. The sultry cocktail lounge serves red-hot cocktails and nibbles in a dimly lit setting of knick-knacks and books. Loubet oversees a menu of satisfying 'small eats', from spot-on Scotch eggs with mustard mayo (£4.50) to 'fiercely good' pan-fried haloumi with lemon, chilli and oregano. Otherwise, feast on an English 'supper bowl' of wild rabbit casserole or ham hock and split-pea stew (£7.50). Wines from £15.95.

¶¶¶ Also Recommended
Also recommended entries are not scored but we think they are worth a visit.

The Anchor & Hope
Hearty stuff from a foodie boozer
36 The Cut, South Bank, SE1 8LP
Tel no: (020) 7928 9898
⊖ Waterloo, Southwark, map 5
British | £25
Cooking score: 3
£30

This foodie boozer has flourished triumphantly since launching in 2003 and now has a reputation that has spread far beyond its locale. Crowds may pack the bar, you can't book (except on Sundays), and the food is as plain and unadulterated as the dining room itself – battered, cramped, with the barest of comforts. But, in trademark fashion, the kitchen makes the most of meaty cheap cuts (perhaps slow-baked lamb neck and gratin dauphinois) and the tersely written menu bristles with unfettered modern food, whether warm snail and bacon salad, Middle White faggot and chips or a simple grilled lemon sole with salsify, brown shrimps and almonds. Hearty stuff, so a scoop of candied blood-orange ice cream may be the perfect finish. Wines from £15.
Chef/s: Jonathan Jones. **Open:** Tue to Sat L 12 to 2.30, Sun L 2 (1 sitting), Mon to Sat D 6 to 10.30. **Closed:** Christmas, New Year, 2 weeks Aug, bank hols. **Meals:** alc (main courses £11 to £24). Sun L £30. **Service:** not inc. **Details:** 45 seats. 20 seats outside. Separate bar. Wheelchair access. Music.

NEW ENTRY
Angels and Gypsies
Take a pew for saintly tapas
33 Camberwell Church Street, Camberwell, SE5 8TR
Tel no: (020) 7703 5984
www.angelsandgypsies.com
map 1
Spanish | £30
Cooking score: 3
🛏

Don't be fooled by the pews, prayer chairs and stained glass, this is a shrine to more earthy delights: legs of jamón hang proudly in the window, and a wood-fired oven churns out devilishly good organic sourdough. A sanctuary from the grit and grime of Camberwell, Angels and Gypsies draws a loyal congregation. They love its 'attentive service' and laid-back menu of rustic Iberian plates, with avant-garde touches and a colourful Latin-American vibe borrowed from the boutique hotel upstairs. Though classic tapas such as tortilla and croquetas are constants, highlights include cuttlefish stew and an heirloom tomato salad hailing from the daily specials board, and the produce-led vegetarian offerings. The horseshoe bar serves plentiful, good-value French and Spanish wines (from £16), and a selection of Latin rums.
Chef/s: Mel Raido. **Open:** all week L 12 to 3 (3.30 Sat, 4 Sun), D 6 to 10.30 (11 Fri and Sat). **Closed:** 24 and 25 Dec, Easter Mon. **Meals:** alc (tapas £4 to £11). **Service:** not inc. **Details:** 74 seats. Music.

ALSO RECOMMENDED
▲ L'Auberge
22 Upper Richmond Road, Putney, SW15 2RX
Tel no: (020) 8874 3593
www.ardillys.com
⊖ East Putney, map 3
French

French-owned and run, Pascal Ardilly's small neighbourhood bistro wins new friends with its warm welcome and personal attention. It also manages to produce food that is familiar (boeuf bourguignon, cassoulet) but up-to-date enough to appeal to today's tastes. Start with scallops with broad bean purée and Parmesan crumble (£8.50), go on to venison fillet with red wine, chestnuts and cranberry jus (£17.50) and finish with caramelised orange tart and peppercorn sorbet. Wines from £15.95. Tue to Sat D only.

Babur

Creative surroundings and creative cooking
119 Brockley Rise, Forest Hill, SE23 1JP
Tel no: (020) 8291 2400
www.babur.info
map 1
Indian | £25
Cooking score: 2
£5 OFF £30

Famed for its creative approach to art and design, this classy-looking Indian proves the point with ethnic triptychs, hand-woven kantha table-runners and a handwritten kalamkari horoscope by the entrance. Against a backdrop of exposed brick, glass and veneered timber, customers can also sample creative dishes that show flashes of innovation and respect for the subcontinent's regional traditions. Pan-seared mackerel with apple and coriander salsa, clove-smoked ostrich, and spice-crusted shoulder of lamb with beetroot khichdi share the billing with goat patties, chicken biryani and twice-marinated tandoori prawns with 'prawn pickle' purée. Sunday lunch is a leisurely family buffet, cocktails are worth sipping and wines start at £16.50.
Chef/s: Praveen Kumar Gupta. **Open:** all week L 12 to 2.30 (4 Sun), D 6 to 11.30. **Closed:** 26 Dec. **Meals:** alc (main courses £12 to £17). Sun L £11.95. **Service:** not inc. **Details:** 72 seats. Music. Car parking.

Baltic

Eastern European chic
74 Blackfriars Road, Southwark, SE1 8HA
Tel no: (020) 7928 1111
www.balticrestaurant.co.uk
⊖ Southwark, map 5
Eastern European | £26
Cooking score: 2
£5 OFF £30

With its gleaming white walls, cool bar, skylights and galleries, Baltic brings some eastern European chic to an eighteenth-century coachbuilder's workshop. That said, the kitchen takes a few liberties with geography: it plunders Siberia for generous, winter-warming pelmeni dumplings; heads to sunnier climes for char-grilled lamb shashlik with smoked aubergine salad; and keeps up nationalist appearances with marinated herrings, blinis, roast goose, cod with kasza (buckwheat), and golabki (stuffed cabbage leaves with cranberry sauce). After all that, finish off with makowiec (poppy seed and honey cake with fruit compote). To drink, high-proof vodkas await; otherwise pick something topographically suitable from the wine list – prices from £17.
Chef/s: Piotr Repinski. **Open:** Tue to Sat L 12 to 3.15, Mon to Sat D 5.30 to 11.15. Sun 12 to 10.15. **Closed:** 24 to 27 Dec. **Meals:** alc (main courses £15 to £22). Set L and D £14.50 (2 courses) to £17.50. Sun L £17.50 (2 courses) to £20.50. **Service:** 12.5%. **Details:** 150 seats. Separate bar. Wheelchair access. Music.

NEW ENTRY

Bistro Union

Proper British neighbourhood bistro
40 Abbeville Road, Clapham, SW4 9NG
Tel no: (020) 7042 6400
www.bistrounion.co.uk
⊖ Clapham South, map 3
British | £26
Cooking score: 2
£30

This Adam Byatt restaurant is not far from his high-achieving Trinity (see entry), but is an altogether more casual affair. The shoestring décor carries a sense of style, nonetheless, and the cooking is fashionably simple – a patriotic fish finger sarnie pops up on the bar menu, while a summery 'allotment box' comes with six different vegetables and a fantastic bespoke salad cream. Typical of the style, too, is roast quail with gem lettuce, anchovy and Berkswell cheese, while proper tapioca with raspberry jam and a tub of gold-top milk helps to erase memories of school versions ('frogspawn'). Wines start from £17, but you can also fly the flag with Freedom lager or Orchard Pig cider.

Chef/s: Karl Goward. **Open:** all week L 12 to 3 (4 Sun), Mon to Sat D 6 to 10. **Closed:** 24 to 28 Dec. **Meals:** alc (main courses £10 to £22). **Service:** 12.5%. **Details:** 47 seats. 12 seats outside. No music. Wheelchair access.

NEW ENTRY

Boqueria Tapas

Sparklingly fresh, authentic tapas
192 Acre Lane, Brixton, SW2 5UL
Tel no: (020) 7733 4408
www.boqueriatapas.com
⊖ Clapham North, Brixton, map 3
Spanish | £20
Cooking score: 3

Named after the famous covered food market in Barcelona, the Brixton Boqueria is more smart-central-London than cutesy-neighbourhood – but with distinctly non-central prices. There's a chic, minimalist interior; a bar at the front gives way to a softly lit, wooden-floored dining room. Tapas classics include immaculate croquetas, calamari and paellas – perhaps black rice with squid and mussels – as well as more contemporary dishes such as deliciously crispy, melting suckling pig with zingy lemon sorbet and parsnip crisps, and aubergine cannelloni with creamy goats' cheese. Service is well-informed and the mostly Spanish wine list starts at a very reasonable £13.50.
Chef/s: Enrique Canadas. **Open:** Mon to Thur 5 to 11, Fri to Sun 12.30 to 11 (10pm Sun). **Meals:** alc (tapas £4 to £9). **Service:** not inc. **Details:** 55 seats. Separate bar. Wheelchair access. Music.

Symbols

🛏 Accommodation is available

£30 Three courses for less than £30

V Separate vegetarian menu

£5 OFF £5-off voucher scheme

🍾 Notable wine list

Brinkley's Kitchen

Vibrant food at well-pitched prices
35 Bellevue Road, Wandsworth, SW17 7EF
Tel no: (020) 8672 5888
www.brinkleys.com
⊖ Balham, map 3
Modern European | £28
Cooking score: 1

This buzzing neighbourhood brasserie overlooks leafy Wandsworth Common and it continues to appeal to a lively mix of residents and local workers. From the open kitchen a vibrant, internationally inspired menu of dishes aims to please everybody and prices are well pitched. Choices might include: char-grilled calamari with red chilli, rocket and lemon; pan-fried haddock fillet with spinach, poached egg and hollandaise; or wild mushroom ravioli with cream, parsley and Parmesan. Finish with lemon tart and crème fraîche. House wine from £14.50.
Chef/s: Malcom Hamala. **Open:** all week L 12 to 4 (11 to 4 Sat and Sun), Mon to Sat D 6 to 11. **Closed:** 25 and 26 Dec. **Meals:** alc (main courses £11 to £23). Set L £13.50. Set D £18.50. **Service:** 12.5%. **Details:** 92 seats. 28 seats outside. Separate bar. Wheelchair access. Music.

ALSO RECOMMENDED

▲ Brunswick House Café

Brunswick House, 30 Wandsworth Road,
Vauxhall, SW8 2LG
Tel no: (020) 7720 2926
www.brunswickhousecafe.co.uk
⊖ Vauxhall, map 3
Modern British

'Reclamation, ornament and curiosities' fill this eighteenth-century mansion, and the café resembles a props department: 'a bit shabby, a bit battered, a bit temporary'. Everything is for sale, so it feels like the chandeliers, 1950s signs and tumblers of tulips could be whisked away. But it's a great local asset, popular for breakfast. The short, seasonal menu offers exceptional value, from warm chorizo and aïoli bap (£5) to spring chicken, garlic, giant couscous and herbs (£13.40). Wines from £16. Open all week.

Cantinetta
Informal Italian eating with brio
162-164 Lower Richmond Road, Putney, SW15 1LY
Tel no: (020) 8780 3131
www.cantinetta.co.uk
⊖ Putney Bridge, map 1
Italian | £27
Cooking score: 3
 £30

A fresh, airy space hung with mirrors and minimalist pictures, and with a half-open terrace for warm weather dining, Cantinetta brings informal Italian eating to well-heeled Putney. Classic dishes are cooked with brio and flair, whether it's buffalo mozzarella with puntarelle and bottarga in anchovy dressing, vincisgrassi (a rich truffly take on lasagne from the Marche), cod with borlotti beans, or calf's liver veneziana with soft polenta. To finish, there's textbook tiramisu, or perhaps apple fritters with cinnamon ice cream. An all-Italian wine list (bar the Champagnes) kicks off with Sicilian house wines at £14.50 (£3.75 a glass).
Chef/s: Mariano Bressan. **Open:** Sun L 12 to 4, Tue to Fri D 6 to 10.30 (11 Fri). Sat 12 to 11. **Closed:** Mon, bank hols. **Meals:** alc (main courses £14 to £18). Set L and D £12.50 (2 courses) to £15.50. Set D £14.50 (2 courses) to £17.50. Sun L £18.50. **Service:** 12.5%. **Details:** 96 seats. 56 seats outside. Separate bar. Wheelchair access. Music.

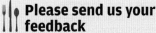
Please send us your feedback
To register your opinion about any restaurant listed in the Guide, or a new restaurant that you wish to bring to our attention, please visit the web address at the bottom of the page. Your feedback informs the content of the book and will be used to compile next year's reviews.

Canton Arms
A great local asset
177 South Lambeth Road, Stockwell, SW8 1XP
Tel no: (020) 7582 8710
www.cantonarms.com
⊖ Stockwell, map 3
Modern British | £23
Cooking score: 1
 £30

'It's an old south London boozer all right', remarked one who noted the local drinking crew watching football in the front bar. Out back it's more Clapham: the cosy dining room sporting a wall of books and 'full of laid-back, rather well-to-do couples'. The menu offers English and Mediterranean ways: ham hock or smoked herring and potato salad alongside the likes of baked gurnard, potato, olives and rosemary, and salt marsh lamb shoulder. Conclude with marmalade bread-and-butter pudding. Wines from £13.60.
Chef/s: Trish Hilferty. **Open:** Tue to Sun L 12 to 2.30 (4 Sun), Mon to Sat D 6 to 10. **Closed:** 25 Dec to 2 Jan, bank hols. **Meals:** alc (main courses £11 to £16). **Service:** not inc. **Details:** 60 seats. 30 seats outside. Separate bar. Wheelchair access. Music.

Chapters All Day Dining
Good stuff at keen prices
43-45 Montpelier Vale, Blackheath, SE3 OTJ
Tel no: (020) 8333 2666
www.chaptersrestaurants.com
map 1
Modern British | £25
Cooking score: 3
 £30

A neighbourly vibe and flexible menus make an appealing package at this dressed-down brasserie (think lots of wood, mirrors, exposed brickwork). From scrambled eggs and almond croissants before work, through to the evening's last mouthful of crème brûlée, there's plenty of good stuff on offer at keen prices. Chicken liver parfait with red onion marmalade, various risottos, daube of beef with sweet potato purée and Savoy cabbage, and spatchcock chicken with lemon and thyme have all been praised, although the kitchen can also rustle up textbook steaks with a choice of sauces (the peppercorn is popular). Finish with warm sticky toffee pudding. Wines are from £15.80, with plenty of choice by the glass and pichet.

Chef/s: Alexander Tyndall. **Open:** all week B from 8 (9 Sun), L 12 to 3 (11 Sat, 11 to 4 Sun), D 6 to 11 (9 Sun). **Closed:** 2 and 3 Jan. **Meals:** alc (main courses £10 to £26). **Service:** 12.5%. **Details:** 100 seats. 16 seats outside. Separate bar. Wheelchair access. Music.

ALSO RECOMMENDED
▲ Le Chardon
65 Lordship Lane, East Dulwich, SE22 8EP
Tel no: (020) 8299 1921
www.lechardon.co.uk
map 1
French £5 OFF

A *chardon* is a thistle, as you might guess from the prickly-themed tiles all around this former grocer's. It's been serving real French bistro food to East Dulwich since 1998; typical are duck foie gras with prune and red onion chutney (£11.45), whole roast sea bass in olive oil, lemon and herbs and spices (£14.75) and tarte Tatin flamed with Calvados (£6.45). Wines from £16.95. Open all week. The other Chardon is at 32 Abbeville Road, Clapham; tel: (020) 8673 9300.

Chez Bruce
A treat worth sharing
2 Bellevue Road, Wandsworth, SW17 7EG
Tel no: (020) 8672 0114
www.chezbruce.co.uk
⊖ Balham, map 3
Modern British | £45
Cooking score: 6

It may be one of the most lauded restaurants in London, but the crowded bistro-style dining room is much more suited in character, style and cuisine to its leafy suburban address than it would be to a grand central London

destination. The customers, mostly locals with a smattering of trophy hunters, are an artfully casual crowd, comfortably dressed, out for a treat they feel is worth sharing with family and friends. Chef-proprietor Bruce Poole has developed his own style, combining classic techniques with modern flavours. A beautifully presented, generous starter of grilled mackerel served with crisp-fried king prawns, for example, is given zing with a vibrant combination of pomegranate, lime and tarragon; thinly sliced veal and asparagus salad is given texture and added luxury by the accompanying truffled polenta chips. Main courses follow the eclectic Anglo-Mediterranean path – a wonderfully aromatic tagine made of lamb breast is accompanied by some deeply savoury lamb rump and kofta. Those who can bear to skip the deservedly famous cheeseboard find sophisticated, beautifully presented desserts: hot chocolate tart with praline parfait, according to one reporter, 'will have us returning for more'. The sommeliers are good at keeping diners' budgets in mind when giving advice and are graceful about recommending house selections, from £20 a bottle.

Chef/s: Matt Christmas. **Open:** all week L 12 to 2.30 (3 Sat and Sun), D 6.30 to 10 (10.30 Fri and Sat, 7 to 9.30 Sun). **Closed:** 24 to 26 Dec. **Meals:** Set L Mon to Fri £23.50 (2 courses) to £27.50. Set L Sat and Sun £29.50 (2 courses) to £35. Set D £34.50 (2 courses) to £45. **Service:** 12.5%. **Details:** 100 seats. No music. Wheelchair access. Children at L only

NEW ENTRY
The Crooked Well
Fast becoming a local favourite
16 Grove Lane, Camberwell, SE5 8SY
Tel no: (020) 7252 7798
www.thecrookedwell.com
map 1
Modern British | £35
Cooking score: 3
£5 OFF

The Crooked Well team met while working for the Hotel du Vin chain, and went it alone in 2011, taking on and reviving the fortunes of this down-at-heel boozer. Wedged between Camberwell and Grove Lane, the pub is making a name as a new-wave dining venue with a strong community vibe – locals love the family Sunday roast platters, sharing dishes (rabbit and bacon pie), fish and chips to take away, and the BYO wine dinners. There's an elegant Art Deco feel to the bar-cum-dining room, where the likes of fried duck egg, asparagus and wild garlic and truffle mayonnaise, hake with shrimp ravioli, beurre blanc and fennel ceviche, and almond and gooseberry cake with vanilla pannacotta could be on the daily changing menu. House wine £14.50.

Chef/s: Matt Green-Armytage. **Open:** Tue to Sun L 12.30 to 2.30 (4 Sun), all week D 6.30 to 10 (9.30 Sun and Mon, 10.30 Fri and Sat). **Closed:** 25 and 26 Dec. **Meals:** alc (main courses £11 to £18). **Service:** 10%. **Details:** 40 seats. 42 seats outside. Wheelchair access. Music. No children after 10.30.

NEW ENTRY
Elliot's Café
On-trend foodie canteen
12 Stoney Street, Borough, SE1 9AD
Tel no: (020) 7403 7436
www.elliotscafe.com
⊖ London Bridge, map 1
British | £30
Cooking score: 1

Wedged into a rough-hewn space underneath the arches, this on-trend canteen is custom-built for the local crowd and Borough Market's foodie throngs. The place is alive with chat, service is charm personified and the daily menu promises plates of comforting cauliflower fondue ('sinful in the extreme'), full-flavoured clams with bacon, buttermilk-fried chicken with cucumber salad, and naughty puds including malt cake with spiced pumpkin sherbet. Drinks run from craft beers to a clutch of oddball wines (from £19.50). A dedicated bar is in the offing.

Chef/s: Brett Redman. **Open:** all week L 12 to 3 (4 Sat and Sun), Mon to Sat D 6 to 10. **Meals:** alc (main courses £10 to £19). Set L and D £25 (2 courses) to £30. **Service:** not inc. **Details:** 50 seats. 9 seats outside. Music.

Emile's
Long-serving Putney favourite
96-98 Felsham Road, Putney, SW15 1DQ
Tel no: (020) 8789 3323
www.emilesrestaurant.co.uk
⊖ Putney Bridge, map 3
Anglo-French | £29
Cooking score: 1

Diners continue to sing the praises of Emil Fahmy and Andrew Sherlock's long-established restaurant near the river. Favourites like beef wellington and treacle tart are fixtures on wide-choice dinner menus priced for two or three courses. However, the kitchen also tries unusual combinations: witness a starter of guinea fowl boudin with haricot bean and baby onion stew and an Earl Grey fumet, or a main course mackerel fillet with smoked cod's roe, crushed potatoes, spinach and seaweed oil. House wine is £15.40.

Chef/s: Andrew Sherlock and Sam Stafford. **Open:** Mon to Sat D only 7.30 to 11. **Closed:** Sun, 24 to 30 Dec, 2 Jan, Easter Sat, bank hols. **Meals:** Set D £25 (2 courses) to £28.50. **Service:** not inc. **Details:** 90 seats. Music.

Enoteca Turi
Smart Italian with impeccable food
28 Putney High Street, Putney, SW15 1SQ
Tel no: (020) 8785 4449
www.enotecaturi.com
⊖ Putney Bridge, map 3
Italian | £39
Cooking score: 3

Over the years Enoteca Turi seems to have settled into an easy familiarity with its smart surroundings – and when a place works this well, that's no bad thing. There is a new chef, but Giuseppe Turi has always overseen the kitchen and things continue unabated. The cooking is bright and modern, with strong seasonal flavours – impeccably sourced British and Italian materials are the mainstay of menus that are compact and easy to digest. Roast quail wrapped in pancetta might start, while pasta options include ravioli filled with beetroot and ricotta with a butter and poppy seed sauce. Simple main courses might be Roman-style braised oxtail, roast and braised rabbit, or grilled Angus ribeye with roasted bone marrow. Finish with prune and almond tart. The 300-bin wine list is a glorious collection from all corners of Italy; it effortlessly cherry-picks the best in all the regions, but does not exclude those on smaller budgets (with prices from £17.50).

Chef/s: Giuseppe Turi and Baldo Amodio. **Open:** Mon to Sat L 12 to 2.30, D 7 to 10.30 (11 Fri and Sat). **Closed:** Sun, 25 and 26 Dec, 1 Jan. **Meals:** alc (main courses £12 to £27). Set L £17.50 (2 courses) to £20.50. Set D £27.50 (2 courses) to £32.50. **Service:** 12.5%. **Details:** 103 seats. Wheelchair access. Music.

ALSO RECOMMENDED
▲ Entrée
2 Battersea Rise, Battersea, SW11 1ED
Tel no: (020) 7223 5147
www.entreebattersea.co.uk
⊖ Clapham South, map 3
Modern European £5 OFF

Combining a funky ground-floor piano bar with a smart upstairs brasserie, Entrée has a lot to offer Clapham's good-time crowd and local foodies in search of some neatly trimmed French and Italian cooking. Typical offerings range from wood pigeon in filo pastry or mushroom arancini with trompette vinaigrette (£6.50) to Old Spot belly pork with chicory, black pudding and crispy polenta (£17) and seared rainbow trout with leek fondue. Wines from £18 (£4.75 a glass). Restaurant open Sat and Sun L, all week D.

▲ four o nine
409 Clapham Road, Clapham, SW9 9BT
Tel no: (020) 7737 0722
www.fouronine.co.uk
⊖ Clapham North, map 3
Modern European

As befits a room hidden above a pub, you enter speakeasy-style: buzz to get in, climb stairs, cross a decked terrace. There's a bar and dining room, and it makes a thumping good neighbourhood destination. The no-airs-and-graces food is a zesty Euro-inspired assortment: from monkfish with morteau sausage, Puy lentils and pickled rhubarb (£10), and dry-aged 28-day steak (from £18) to Champagne-poached sole fillets, and duck breast with foie gras (£19). Wines from £17. Open Sat and Sun L, all week D.

The Fox & Grapes
Cut-above pub classics
9 Camp Road, Wimbledon, SW19 4UN
Tel no: (020) 8619 1300
www.foxandgrapeswimbledon.co.uk
⊖ Wimbledon, map 1
British | £35
Cooking score: 2

It may be a proper pub with barstools and beer pumps, but most people are here to eat. Claude Bosi of Hibiscus fame (see entry) is the owner, with his manager-brother Cedric, and regulars rightly expect the cooking to be a cut above. Pub classics are writ large on the menu (and very good they are, too) – fish and chips, ploughman's, pies, and steak aged for 28 days, with triple-cooked chips, salad and proper béarnaise. Puddings like pear Tatin and sticky toffee can be eaten with relish. The wine list has a huge selection by the glass; bottles from £19.50.

Chef/s: Julian Ward. **Open:** Mon to Sat L 12 to 3, D 6 to 9.30. Sun 12 to 8.30. **Closed:** 25 Dec. **Meals:** alc (main courses £14 to £32). Set L (Mon to Fri) £17.50 (2 courses) to £19.50. **Service:** 12.5%. **Details:** 80 seats. Separate bar. Wheelchair access. Music.

ALSO RECOMMENDED
▲ Franco Manca
4 Market Row, Brixton, SW9 8LD
Tel no: (020) 7738 3021
www.francomanca.co.uk
⊖ Brixton, map 1
Italian

The key to Franco Manca's success lies in the detail: the specially constructed wood-burning oven, the sourdough base rested for 20 hours, the carefully sourced toppings for just six choices – from tomato, garlic and oregano (£4) to home-cured Gloucester Old Spot ham with mozzarella, buffalo ricotta and wild mushrooms (£6.85). Even the wines are organic (from £13.95). Open all week, except D Mon to Wed. Offshoots at 144 Chiswick High Road; tel (020) 8747 4822, and Unit 2003, The Balcony, Westfield Stratford City; tel (020) 8522 6669.

Franklins
Hugely likeable veteran bistro
157 Lordship Lane, East Dulwich, SE22 8HX
Tel no: (020) 8299 9598
www.franklinsrestaurant.com
map 1
British | £28
Cooking score: 2
£5 OFF £30

A snappy, pared-back interior of wood and reclaimed furniture sets the tone for a refreshingly unpretentious slice of high-street dining. Hugely likeable in a simple, low-key way, this veteran bistro has won many followers over the years. The kitchen takes full advantage of strong supply lines, with a seasonally charged menu that digs its heels into the British soil. Ox heart with chicory, capers and seed mustard, and rabbit with cider, button onions and turnips define the style, with extra possibilities in the shape of, say, whole plaice and tartare sauce, and custard tart with red wine pear. House wine is £14.50.

Chef/s: Ralf Wittig. **Open:** all week 11 to 10.30 (12 to 10 Sun). **Closed:** 25 and 26 Dec, 1 Jan. **Meals:** alc (main courses £11 to £21). Set L £13.95 (2 courses) to £16.95. **Service:** not inc. **Details:** 72 seats. 16 seats outside. No music. Wheelchair access.

Harrison's
Buzzing local brasserie
15-19 Bedford Hill, Balham, SW12 9EX
Tel no: (020) 8675 6900
www.harrisonsbalham.co.uk
⊖ Balham, map 3
Modern British | £28
Cooking score: 1
£30

Sam Harrison's second gaff (see entry, Sam's Brasserie) has quite a swagger. Big windows give lots of light and street views, and those lured into the lively bar and dining room don't leave disappointed. The big attraction is good-value menus that aim to please all-comers. Alongside standard fare such as tempura tiger prawns or confit duck leg, there are some interesting options – say seared salmon fillet burger with wasabi mayo and spicy green papaya salad. Wines from £16.
Chef/s: Peter Murray. **Open:** all week L 12 to 3 (12.15 to 4 Sat and Sun), D 6 to 10.30 (6.30 Sat, 6.30 to 10 Sun). **Closed:** 24 to 27 Dec. **Meals:** alc (main courses £11 to £21). Set L and D £13.50 (2 courses) to £16.50. Sun L £19.50 (2 courses) to £22.50. **Service:** 12.5%. **Details:** 80 seats. 12 seats outside. Separate bar. Wheelchair access. Music.

Inside
Stylish, buzzy neighbourhood bistro
19 Greenwich South Street, Greenwich, SE10 8NW
Tel no: (020) 8265 5060
www.insiderestaurant.co.uk
⊖ Greenwich, map 1
Modern European | £28
Cooking score: 1
£30

'Good food, well priced' was the verdict of one visitor to this stylish neighbourhood bistro, which has been a welcome addition to the Greenwich scene for more than a decade. The attractively priced menus are matched by a buzzy atmosphere and modern European dishes with bold flavours. Pheasant pithiviers, spinach, oyster mushrooms and port jus might be followed by wild sea bass, shallot purée, fondant potato and chive velouté. Finish with cardamom crème brûlée. House wines from Languedoc are £16.30.

Chef/s: Guy Awford and Brian Sargeant. **Open:** Tue to Sun L 12 to 2.30 (3 Sun), Tue to Sat D 6.30 to 11. **Closed:** Mon, 24 to 27 Dec. **Meals:** alc (main courses £13 to £18). Set L £12.95 (2 courses) to £17.95. Set D £17.95 (2 courses) to £24.95. Sun L £18.95 (two courses) to £23.95. **Service:** not inc. **Details:** 38 seats. Wheelchair access. Music.

NEW ENTRY

José
Stand up for triumphantly simple tapas
104 Bermondsey Street, Bermondsey, SE1 3UB
Tel no: (020) 7403 4902
www.josepizarro.com
⊖ London Bridge, Borough, map 1
Spanish | £17
Cooking score: 3

José Pizarro's tapas joint, his first since leaving the Brindisa fold, is emphatically a bar, not a restaurant, so prepare to stand or perch while you graze. The spirit of Madrid's neighbourhood sherry bars is heartily embraced and the kitchen dishes out impeccable morsels – plentiful porky treats and hand-carved jamón, alongside classics such as croquetas and tortilla. From the daily specials board comes 'stunning' rare-grilled Ibérico pork from the plancha, or razor clams. Desserts are a footnote (not listed on the menu), but ask and you may find yourself delving into a chocolate pot with olive oil and sea salt, or a rice pudding. The adventurous sherry list encourages exploration; knowledgeable staff are eager to recommend sherry and tapas pairings. Wines start at £18.

Chef/s: José Pizarro. **Open:** all week 12 to 10.30 (5.30pm Sun). **Closed:** 24 to 27 Dec. **Meals:** alc (tapas £4 to £9). **Service:** not inc. **Details:** 17 seats. Wheelchair access. Music.

Lamberts
Good-natured local asset
2 Station Parade, Balham High Road, Balham, SW12 9AZ
Tel no: (020) 8675 2233
www.lambertsrestaurant.com
⊖ Balham, map 3
Modern British | £30
Cooking score: 2

£5 OFF

The inhabitants of Balham look kindly on Joe Lambert's gregarious, good-natured eatery, and it's easy to see why. A neighbourly vibe is one of its attributes, although there is much to be said for the capably crafted seasonal food, too. Drop by in January and you might be treated to a boudin of Longhorn beef with spinach, then Telmara duck breast with an offal pasty and caramelised chicory; in April you could order a duck egg with purple sprouting broccoli ahead of rare-breed Ryeland lamb with spring vegetables. The wine list opens with house selections from £18 (£7.50 a 300ml decanter). Some alfresco seating is in the pipeline.

Chef/s: Ryan Lowery. **Open:** Sat and Sun L 12 to 2.30 (5 Sun), Tue to Sat D 7 to 10. **Closed:** Mon, 25 and 26 Dec, bank hols. **Meals:** Set L £17 (2 courses) to £20. Set D £25 (2 courses) to £30. Sun L £24. **Service:** 12.5%. **Details:** 53 seats. Separate bar. Music.

NEW ENTRY

The Lawn Bistro
The perfect bistro
67 High Street, Wimbledon Village, Wimbledon, SW19 5EE
Tel no: (020) 8947 8278
www.thelawnbistro.co.uk
⊖ Wimbledon, map 3
Modern British | £35
Cooking score: 3

Chef-proprietor Ollie Couillard has an impressive pedigree in modern Anglo-French cooking and his unassuming bistro has become a magnet for food-conscious locals. He delivers generous portions of interesting but approachable food, based on classic techniques. Grilled aubergine and courgette with goats' curd, broad beans, pomegranate and mint is 'memorably beautiful', with the right balance of sweetness and acidity. To follow, steamed plaice with fennel and peas is 'an elegant, delicate dish for a summer's evening', but an excellent Gloucester Old Spot chop with anchovy and sage butter and forestière potatoes is on hand for heavier weather. Puds, like apple croustade with ice cream, are mostly big enough to share. The global wine list offers plenty under £25. Lawn Bakery, at 9 High Street, is a bakery/café offshoot for breakfast, lunches and afternoon tea.

Chef/s: Ollie Couillard. **Open:** all week L 12 to 2.30 (3 Sun), Mon to Sat D 6.30 to 10.30. **Meals:** Set L £19.50 (2 courses) to £22.50. Set D £29.50 (2 courses) to £34.50. Sun L £29.50. **Service:** 12.5%. **Details:** 70 seats. No music. Wheelchair access.

Light House
Buzzy neighbourhood restaurant
75-77 Ridgway, Wimbledon, SW19 4ST
Tel no: (020) 8944 6338
www.lighthousewimbledon.com
⊖ Wimbledon, map 3
Modern European | £29
Cooking score: 2
£5 OFF £30

The modern décor (with artful bowls of fruit and veg on the counters) helps sell the menu before the efficient staff even tell customers what's on offer. No surprise, then, that it's usually buzzy here. When on form, the kitchen delivers crisp-fried, perfectly timed black bream with parsley and red onion salad, say – but attention to detail can slip. The dressing for a Serrano ham salad with artichoke, egg and caperberries might be forgotten; chips accompanying beautifully cooked calf's liver could be soggy from lying too long in the sauce. But chocolate brownie and lemon curd parfait are pure indulgences. Wines from £14.75.

Chef/s: Chris Casey. **Open:** all week L 12 to 2.45 (3.30 Sun), Mon to Sat D 6 to 10.30. **Closed:** 25 to 27 Dec, 1 Jan. **Meals:** alc (main courses £13 to £18). Set L £13.95 (2 courses) to £16.95. Set D £25. Sun L £23. **Service:** 12.5%. **Details:** 80 seats. Wheelchair access. Music.

ALSO RECOMMENDED
▲ Lobster Pot
3 Kennington Lane, Elephant and Castle, SE11 4RG
Tel no: (020) 7582 5556
www.lobsterpotrestaurant.co.uk
⊖ Kennington, map 1
Seafood £5 OFF

Now in its 22nd year, Hervé Régent's quirky, nautical-themed fish restaurant continues to bring a smile to the face of diners with its backdrop of Brittany seascapes, lifebelts and maritime sound effects. The menu is unashamedly and uncompromisingly old-school French – homemade fish soup (£10.50) could lead on to fillet of monkfish with wild mushrooms and Pernod sauce (£20.50) or duck stew (£19.50). Profiteroles are typical of the familiar and comforting desserts. House wine is £18.50. Closed Sun and Mon.

NEW ENTRY
Lola Rojo
Contemporary and creative tapas
78 Northcote Road, Battersea, SW11 6QL
Tel no: (020) 7350 2262
www.lolarojo.net
⊖ Clapham South, map 3
Spanish | £26
Cooking score: 2
£5 OFF £30

Cristina Garcia and Antonio Belles are from Barcelona, and they serve attractive, contemporary tapas in their pretty dining room and tiny wraparound terrace. The kitchen does have a penchant for coating things in batter – scallop medallions were not advertised as deep-fried, and, soft and tasty as they were, we found ourselves extracting them from batter cases. Elsewhere, there's sweet Ibérico ham or black rice with squid, plus playful battered chorizo lollipops, and sweet piquillo peppers topped with garlic-fried prawns and spinach leaves. A small selection of sherries opens at £4.50 a glass; the notable regional Spanish wine list starts at £20 (£4.95 a glass).

Chef/s: Antonio Belles. **Open:** Mon to Thur L 12 to 3, D 6 to 10.30. Fri to Sun 12 to 12. **Closed:** 25 and 26 Dec, 1 Jan. **Meals:** alc (main courses £8 to £16). Set L £9.50. Sun L £15. **Service:** 12.5%. **Details:** 50 seats. 17 seats outside. No music.

Magdalen

Dependable bolt-hole with polished food
152 Tooley Street, Southwark, SE1 2TU
Tel no: (020) 7403 1342
www.magdalenrestaurant.co.uk
⊖ London Bridge, map 1
Modern British | £32
Cooking score: 3

Magdalen looks like it might be more at home in Montmartre than beside a busy A-road near London Bridge. It has been plying its trade as a dependable neighbourhood bolt-hole for over five years. The dining room exudes a hushed sophistication a world away from the hubbub outside – crimson walls, crisp white linen and polished floors are the backdrop against which an equally polished menu flourishes. Starters fit largely into comfort-food territory: Devon crab mayonnaise, say, or lamb sweetbreads and green sauce, which were faultless at inspection. Mains may be just as hearty – a rich fish stew of bream, skate and clams – but can still yield the occasional surprise, perhaps sauté of kid offal with bacon, mash and sherry vinegar. A Francophile wine list opens at £19.

Chef/s: James Faulks. **Open:** Mon to Fri L 12 to 2.30, Mon to Sat D 6.30 to 9.30. **Closed:** Sun, 22 Dec to 3 Jan, bank hols. **Meals:** alc (main courses £14 to £21). Set L £15.50 (2 courses) to £18.50. **Service:** 12.5%. **Details:** 90 seats. No music. Wheelchair access.

▲ Meza

34 Trinity Road, Tooting, SW17 7RE
Tel no: (07722) 111299
⊖ Tooting Bec, map 3
Lebanese

Meza is a simple, honest Lebanese restaurant that's 'compact and buzzing'. 'Book well in advance to get a table' say regulars, but it does 'a roaring trade in take-aways' if plans go awry. A great array of starters, from 'amazingly creamy', 'superb' hummus (£3.25) to labneh open proceedings, then generous mains such as lahem meshwi (grilled skewers of lamb cubes, £9.50) or sea bass grilled with cumin and olive oil. Wine is Lebanese white, red or rosé (£15). Cash only.

NEW ENTRY
Pizarro

Thrilling fare from a Spanish food hero
194 Bermondsey Street, Southwark, SE1 3TQ
Tel no: (020) 7378 9455
www.josepizarro.com
⊖ London Bridge, Borough, map 1
Spanish | £26
Cooking score: 4

Bermondsey is a hotbed of culinary talent, and one of its brightest stars is José Pizarro. Following hot on the heels of his sherry bar (José, see entry), Pizarro's restaurant proper is an elegant wood-panelled space filled with communal benches, tables at the back and bar stools with a view of the open kitchen. Spanish food is not just about tapas, and Pizarro explores its culinary heritage and his Extremadura roots with a rustic ingredients-led menu. With simple techniques and an abundance of lesser-known cuts, mains might include succulent lamb's tongue or slow-cooked Ibérico pig's cheek with sweet potato and almonds. Elsewhere, delicate spring vegetable soup with clams or meaty cod cheeks showcase impeccably fresh seafood. Puddings are 'lovely, but not revolutionary'. Enthusiastic front-of-house staff ooze

Hispanic charm, but be prepared to wait, as queues are likely. The attractively priced all-Spanish wine list opens at £18.
Chef/s: José Pizarro. **Open:** Mon to Fri L 12 to 3, D 6 to 11. Sat 12 to 11, Sun 12 to 10. **Closed:** 24 to 27 Dec. **Meals:** alc (main courses £12 to £16). **Service:** not inc. **Details:** 80 seats. Separate bar. Wheelchair access. Music.

ALSO RECOMMENDED
▲ Platform

56-58 Tooley Street, Southwark, SE1 2SZ
Tel no: (020) 7403 6388
www.platformse1.co.uk
⊖ London Bridge, map 1
Modern British

Underneath the arches below Platform One of London Bridge station, Platform is a confident operator, with a downstairs bar that 'can get quite lairy of an evening', an extensive drinks list and a flexible menu. The upstairs brasserie majors in quality and seasonality, does a great line in 'sharers' like the 'not-to-be-missed' quail Scotch eggs with salad cream (£4.50) and bangs out starters of devilled lamb's kidneys, mains of roast pollack with chorizo (£14) and luscious desserts. Wines from £19.50. Closed Sun.

Le Pont de la Tour
Thoroughly satisfying, seductive French favourite
36d Shad Thames, Bermondsey, SE1 2YE
Tel no: (020) 7403 8403
www.lepontdelatour.com
⊖ Tower Hill, London Bridge, map 1
Modern French | £45
Cooking score: 3

Their location on Butler's Wharf has always been one of the strongest cards in this restaurant's hand. To sit on the river terrace with Tower Bridge rising in the middle distance offers the kind of cityscape to seduce London newbies. What you'll eat is efficiently prepared brasserie cuisine, with starters such as crab tian and foie gras ballottine supplementing the excellent shellfish. Mains

take in whole grilled Dover sole meunière, roasted duck breast with chou farci in Madeira jus, or wild mushroom pithiviers with celeriac, shallots and truffle for the veggies. Add a couple of sides, a dessert such as traditional crêpes suzette or Valrhona chocolate assiette, and have a drink, and the bill will gracefully ascend into the realms of myth. Be prepared, and it's a thoroughly satisfying experience, the more so as the wines are great. Glass prices start at £7, and there are micro-servings of classic wines down to 50ml (a couple of mouthfuls of JN Gagnard's Bâtard-Montrachet are £14, but at least you get to taste it). Bottles open at £24, then shoot into a dazzling stratosphere where mere mortals have rarely trodden.
Chef/s: Tom Cook. **Open:** all week L 12 to 3 (5 Sat, 4 Sun), D 6 to 11. **Meals:** Set L £26.50 (2 courses) to £31.50. Set D £44.50. Sun L £28.50. **Service:** not inc. **Details:** 110 seats. 70 seats outside.

Ransome's Dock
A fine neighbourhood restaurant
35-37 Parkgate Road, Battersea, SW11 4NP
Tel no: (020) 7223 1611
www.ransomesdock.co.uk
map 3
Modern British | £33
Cooking score: 3
£5 OFF

In 2012, Martin and Vanessa Lam celebrated 20 years of running their fine neighbourhood restaurant on the southern shore of the Thames. They were among the first to offer what is now the London style of modern European cooking: invigorating menus with plenty of choice and specialising in straightforward dishes made from top-quality ingredients. Dorset crab cakes with papaya and lime salsa get the ball rolling, while mains run the gamut from braised oxtail with horseradish mash to sea bass with grilled peppers, courgettes and tomatoes, and saffron potatoes. Finish with warm chocolate and damson tart and crème fraîche. The wine list signposts all the byways that others leave

unexplored, at prices that undercut many similar places outside London. Bottles from £16.50 (£3.50 a glass).
Chef/s: Martin and Vanessa Lam. **Open:** all week L 12 to 5 (3.30 Sun), Mon to Sat D 5 to 11. **Closed:** 24 to 27 Dec, Aug bank hol. **Meals:** alc (main courses £13 to £24). Set L £16 (2 courses). Sun L £22.50. **Service:** 12.5%. **Details:** 56 seats. 24 seats outside. Separate bar. Wheelchair access. Music.

Rick's Restaurant

Tiny Tooting treasure
122 Mitcham Road, Tooting, SW17 9NH
Tel no: (020) 8767 5219
www.ricks-restaurant.co.uk
⊖ Tooting Broadway, map 3
Modern European | £22
Cooking score: 1

£5 OFF £30

Rick's has dropped the 'café' tag, but this 'absolutely tiny' eatery still wins the day with its splendidly animated buzz, huge welcome and accommodating prices. Spanish influences show in the bottles of sherry, cava and tapas-style small plates (such as top-notch anchovies on toast). The kitchen also wins friends with its twice-baked goats' cheese soufflé and plum compote, grilled squid with polenta, and confit duck with spiced lentils. To finish, try poached pears or steamed ginger pud with custard. Wines from sunny southern climes start at £13.75 (£3.75 a glass).
Chef/s: Ricardo Gibbs. **Open:** Tue to Fri L 12 to 3, Mon to Fri D 6 to 11 (9 Mon). Sat 10 to 11. Sun 10 to 9. **Closed:** 25 Dec, 1 Jan. **Meals:** alc (main courses £8 to £15). **Service:** 12.5%. **Details:** 40 seats. Wheelchair access. Music.

Symbols

🛏 Accommodation is available

£30 Three courses for less than £30

V Separate vegetarian menu

£5 OFF £5-off voucher scheme

🍾 Notable wine list

Roast

Great views and big flavours
Floral Hall, Stoney Street, Southwark, SE1 1TL
Tel no: (0845) 034 7300
www.roast-restaurant.com
⊖ London Bridge, map 1
British | £42
Cooking score: 2

Once touted as battling on the frontline of modern British gastronomy, signs are that Roast has lost some of its heat recently, with grumbles of disproportionate, wallet-roasting prices. Fortunately, the location can still set temperatures soaring, with commanding views over Borough Market from the old Floral Hall. A recent inspection saw a few punches pulled by a kitchen that usually prides itself on big, bruising flavours – scallops with whipped cauliflower and hazelnut butter made an apologetic starter. However, a main of roasted Goosnargh duck with chicory, apple and golden raisin slaw heralded a return to form. House wines from £19.
Chef/s: Marcus Verberne. **Open:** Mon to Sat L 12 to 3.45 (2.45 Mon and Tue), D 5.30 to 10.45 (6 Sat.) Sun 12 to 9.45. **Closed:** 25 Dec and 26 Dec, 1 Jan. **Meals:** alc (main courses £15 to £36). Set L and D £28. Sun L £32. **Service:** 12.5%. **Details:** 120 seats. Separate bar. Wheelchair access. Music.

RSJ

Excellent-value food and astonishing wines
33 Coin Street, Southwark, SE1 9NR
Tel no: (020) 7928 4554
www.rsj.uk.com
⊖ Waterloo, Southwark, map 5
Modern European | £32
Cooking score: 3

£5 OFF 🍾 V

As robust, resilient and reliable as the rolled steel joists after which it is named, RSJ continues to please legions of South Bank regulars. 'I've been coming here for 15 years' admits one devotee, who loves the courteous, long-serving staff, the cracking French wines and the excellent-value food. Theatre-goers take full advantage of the speedy fixed-price menu, but the Euro-accented carte also has plenty to offer. Crab and avocado ravioli with chilli and soft herb bisque, or devilled chicken livers on brioche might set the scene for pan-fried sea bass with mussel and saffron broth or rump of new season Welsh lamb with ratatouille, mint and balsamic jus. To finish, Bramley apple crumble squeezes in between buttermilk pannacotta and iced chestnut parfait with poached pear. However, RSJ's pride and joy is its astonishing selection of wines from the Loire valley – a treasured and tantalising collection running to some 250 bins. There are also some choice pickings from other French regions, with prices from £17.50.

Chef/s: Ian Stabler and Ajo Plunkett. **Open:** Mon to Fri L 12 to 2.30, Mon to Sat D 5.30 to 11. **Closed:** Sun, 24 to 27 Dec, bank hols. **Meals:** alc (main courses £16 to £21). Set L and D £16.95 (2 courses) to £19.95. **Service:** 12.5%. **Details:** 90 seats. 12 seats outside. Music.

Skylon

Bags of trendy snap, crackle and pop
Southbank Centre, Belvedere Road, South Bank, SE1 8XX
Tel no: (020) 7654 7800
www.skylon-restaurant.co.uk
⊖ **Waterloo, map 5**
Modern European | £45
Cooking score: 2

A spectacular riverside tribute to the Festival of Britain, Skylon spreads itself over the third floor of the Southbank Centre – but there's no hint of austerity about Helena Puolakka's cooking. Expect bags of trendy snap, crackle and pop in the shape of wild halibut carpaccio with dried cranberries, capers and lemony fennel drizzle, or confit duck salad with shaved foie gras, French beans and Cassis dressing, plus indulgent sweetness from desserts such as lemongrass pannacotta with elderflower jelly. The adjoining all-day brasserie majors on grills and the likes of

steamed salmon with pesto; the snazzy bar deals in cocktails. Wines from £21.50 (£6 a glass).

Chef/s: Helena Puolakka. **Open:** all week L 12 to 2.30 (4 Sun), Mon to Sat D 5.30 to 10.30. **Closed:** 25 Dec. **Meals:** Set L £24.50 (2 courses) to £28.50. Set D £40 (2 courses) to £45. Sun L £29.50. Tasting menu £59 (7 courses). **Service:** 12.5%. **Details:** 80 seats. Separate bar. Wheelchair access. Music.

NEW ENTRY
Soif

A chip off a fine block
27 Battersea Rise, Battersea, SW11 1HG
Tel no: (020) 7223 1112
⊖ **Clapham South, map 3**
Modern European | £28
Cooking score: 2

The team behind Terroirs and Brawn (see entries) has opened a third big-hearted wine bar-cum-eatery that enthusiastically embraces the group philosophy of rustic, flavour-driven food and terrific wines. This one is comprised of a split-level room done functionally in wood tones, with a busy front bar and similarly clamorous dining room at the back. Short menus change regularly; rillettes and chicken liver with pancetta and dandelion are typical of the simple, big-on-flavour starters. Braised beef with red cabbage and horseradish makes a generous impact, and chestnut cake with crème fraîche rounds things off nicely. The enthusiastically informed wine list, which includes lots of biodynamics, starts at £17.

Chef/s: Colin Westal. **Open:** Thur to Sun L 12 to 3 (11 Sat, 11 to 4 Sun), Mon to Sat D 6 to 10. **Meals:** alc (main courses £13 to £17). Set L £10 (1 course). **Service:** 12.5%. **Details:** 60 seats. 10 seats outside. Separate bar. Music.

Tapas Brindisa
A little taste of Spain
18-20 Southwark Street, Southwark, SE1 1TJ
Tel no: (020) 7357 8880
www.tapasbrindisa.com
⊖ London Bridge, map 1
Spanish | £20
Cooking score: 3

 £30

Brindisa is a Spanish produce supplier and
should be heartily congratulated for bringing a
little taste of Spain to various parts of London
(see Casa Brindisa and Tapas Brindisa Soho).
This, the original, is the most functional, but
concrete floors, tightly packed tables and table
mats that double as menus produce a
convincing Spanish atmosphere. There are
plenty of interesting specialities, ranging from
first-rate acorn-fed jamón Ibérico and perfect
regional charcuterie and cheeses, via
marinated Cantabrian white anchovies and
Gordal olives, to classic tapas like Padrón
peppers, patatas bravas and croquetas de
jamón. Elsewhere, there are more evolved
dishes – lentil stew with pan-fried foie gras
and crispy ham or asparagus with duck egg,
romesco sauce and Serrano ham. The all-
Spanish wine list opens at £17.50.
Chef/s: Roberto Castro. **Open:** Mon to Sat L 12 to 3
(4 Fri and Sat), D 5.30 to 11. Sun 12 to 10. **Closed:** 25
and 26 Dec, 1 Jan. **Meals:** alc (tapas £4 to £10).
Service: 12.5%. **Details:** 36 seats. 20 seats outside.
Wheelchair access. Music.

Tentazioni
Enjoyable and popular Italian
Lloyds Wharf, 2 Mill Street, Bermondsey, SE1 2BD
Tel no: (020) 7237 1100
www.tentazioni.co.uk
⊖ Bermondsey, London Bridge, map 1
Italian | £35
Cooking score: 3

 £5 OFF

Riccardo Giacomini's narrow, colourful
restaurant tucked away in a former warehouse
near Tower Bridge has proved an enjoyable
and popular venue over the years. The kitchen

understands the subtleties of Italian food, and
this is obvious in dishes like sea bass tartare
with crushed black pepper, venere black rice
and raw almond – no gimmickry, everything
perfectly fresh. A light three-colour potato
gnocchi served with a white ragù sauce, fresh
peas and truffle, and a Sardinian-inspired dish
of spaghettini with creamy mullet roe have
been satisfying second courses. Even when
there are no surprises, the cooking is
accomplished; witness crusted rack of lamb
that arrives with a potato timbale and mint
sauce. The reasonable Italian wine list opens at
£12.50. Note the excellent gluten-free menu.
Chef/s: Riccardo Giacomini and Alessandro Cattani.
Open: Mon to Fri L 12 to 2.45, Mon to Sat D 6 to
10.45. **Closed:** Sun, 24 to 26 Dec, bank hols.
Meals: alc (main courses £15 to £25). Set L £11.95 (2
courses) to £15. Set D £37.95. Tasting menu £48.50
(7 courses). **Service:** 12.5%. **Details:** 50 seats.
Music.

Tom Ilic
Gutsy meat cookery and good value
123 Queenstown Road, Battersea, SW8 3RH
Tel no: (020) 7622 0555
www.tomilic.com
map 3
Modern European | £34
Cooking score: 2

This is what is meant by a neighbourhood
restaurant: a convivial, welcoming place that
has a good local following. Value for money is
a big plus. Tom Ilic cooks a modern brasserie
menu – mackerel with celeriac rémoulade and
marinated beetroot, risottos, sea bass – but the
real star of the show is his gutsy meat cookery.
Whether it's deftly handled honey-glazed
pork belly and sautéed fillet with home-
pickled cabbage, or aged Kettyle beef served
with chips and horseradish soufflé, he puts the
emphasis on unfussy flavours and top-quality
ingredients. Wines from £19.50.
Chef/s: Tom Ilic. **Open:** Wed to Sun L 12 to 2.30
(3.30 Sun), Tue to Sat D 6 to 10.30. **Closed:** Mon, 26
to 30 Dec, 1 week Aug, bank hols. **Meals:** alc (main
courses £14 to £20). Set L £15.50 (2 courses) to
£19.50. **Service:** 12.5%. **Details:** 60 seats.

Trinity

Truly wonderful neighbourhood restaurant
4 The Polygon, Clapham, SW4 0JG
Tel no: (020) 7622 1199
www.trinityrestaurant.co.uk
⊖ Clapham Common, map 3
Modern British | £40
Cooking score: 5

Adam Byatt has cemented his position as top dog in Clapham with the recent launch of Bistro Union (see entry), but Trinity remains his flagship – a 'truly wonderful' neighbourhood restaurant and a high-achiever into the bargain. Regulars love the conversational mood of the place, its telling blend of intimacy and bonhomie, and staff with that caring touch – although coming here is mainly about the food. Byatt's pedigree is a given, and he proves his mettle with subtle invention as well as big-hearted flavours: pepper-crusted beef fillet with pickled onions, sorrel and beer mayonnaise is in tune with the down-home revivalist zeitgeist, while Cornish sea bass with mussel emulsion, shellfish and monk's beard shows respect for the traditions of classic cuisine. Readers have also singled out a 'splendid-looking' terrine of chicken, foie gras and artichokes with pickled apple and brioche on the side, and the 'absolutely sensational' pig's trotter on sourdough with crackling and sauce gribiche. Finally, classy desserts such as Vacherin cheesecake with quince and walnuts or rhubarb crumble soufflé with stem ginger ice cream are presented with thoughtfulness and courtesy – 'we were even offered some fresh honeycomb to try'. A £2 cover charge pays for bread, water and canapés, and the accommodating wine list has plenty of well-considered drinking from £12 a carafe (£4.50 a glass).
Chef/s: Adam Byatt. **Open:** Tue to Sun L 12.30 to 2.30 (2 Sat, 4 Sun), Mon to Sat D 6.30 to 10. **Closed:** 24 to 26 Dec. **Meals:** alc (main courses £17 to £28). Set L £20 (2 courses) to £25. Sun L £35. **Service:** 12.5%. **Details:** 53 seats. No music. Wheelchair access.

Tsunami

High-gloss Japanese fusion favourite
5-7 Voltaire Road, Clapham, SW4 6DQ
Tel no: (020) 7978 1610
www.tsunamirestaurant.co.uk
⊖ Clapham North, map 3
Japanese | £35
Cooking score: 3

A sliver of oriental glamour down by Clapham's railway sidings, sleek Tsunami is a hot ticket for the local smart set, with its glass-ceilinged interior, floral displays and sultry colour schemes. Food-wise, the kitchen flatters its savvy audience with oyster and saké shooters, baby back ribs with chilli-chocolate and coffee sauce, Korean-style lamb cutlets and other fusion hits, as well as exploring the traditional Japanese repertoire in some depth. Expect high-gloss nigiri, maki rolls and luxury 'sets' alongside crowd-pullers such as beef tataki salad, sizzling teriyaki plates and king crab tempura with yuzu butter. To drink, get into the groove with some serious saké or one of the snazzy cocktails; otherwise, the wine list offers cosmopolitan drinking from £17.50. There's a West End branch at 93 Charlotte Street; tel: (020) 7637 0050.
Chef/s: Tommy Cheung. **Open:** Sat and Sun L 12.30 to 3.30, all week D 5.30 to 10.30 (11 Fri and Sat, 10 Sun). **Closed:** 24 to 26 Dec. **Meals:** alc (main courses £8 to £23). Set L £15 (2 courses). Set D £37. **Service:** 12.5%. **Details:** 96 seats. 20 seats outside. Separate bar. Wheelchair access. Music.

ALSO RECOMMENDED
▲ Village East

171-173 Bermondsey Street, Southwark, SE1 3UW
Tel no: (020) 7357 6082
www.villageeast.co.uk
⊖ London Bridge, map 1
Modern European

Nowhere better exemplifies how Londoners eat and drink today than hip brasserie Village East. The flexible all-day menu works hard, going from international breakfasts and artisan coffee to steaks and cool cocktails at night, with modern 'diner' and European classics in between. Warm squid and chorizo salad (£7.50/£13) is one of several to come in a choice of sizes, while Longhorn beef burger with foie gras (£14.70) performs both lunch and dinner duty. Wines from £17. Open seven days.

Wright Brothers Oyster & Porter House

Bivalves and 'black stuff'
11 Stoney Street, Southwark, SE1 9AD
Tel no: (020) 7403 9554
www.wrightbrothersoysterhouse.com
⊖ London Bridge, map 1
Seafood | £30
Cooking score: 2

The name may be a rose-tinted reference to impoverished days gone by, but this spit-and-sawdust 'oyster and porter house' is in the business of peddling bivalves to fish-loving foodies with Champagne tastes and bulging wallets. Sit at the counter, squeeze around one of the communal tables or bag a barrel in the boisterous, brick-walled room. Cornish natives from the owners' oyster beds by the Helston river slip down well with a pint of the 'black stuff', although the blackboard might also advertise wild mussels, potted shrimps, winkles and whelks, and a smattering of hot dishes ranging from devilled whitebait to beef, Guinness and oyster pie. Wines from £13 a carafe.
Chef/s: Phillip Coulter. **Open:** all week L 12 to 3 (4 Sat, 7 Sun), Mon to Sat D 6 to 10. **Meals:** alc (main courses £11 to £22). **Service:** not inc. **Details:** 40 seats. 10 seats outside. No music. Wheelchair access.

Zucca

Get-stuck-in, good-value Italian cooking
184 Bermondsey Street, Bermondsey, SE1 3TQ
Tel no: (020) 7378 6809
www.zuccalondon.com
⊖ London Bridge, Borough, map 1
Italian | £25
Cooking score: 3
 £30

Not far from London Bridge, Zucca has all the accoutrements of a modern city eatery – the glass frontage, the open-plan kitchen, the café ambience perfect for kicking back – but without the big city prices. Its informal, get-stuck-in Italian cooking can be erratic as to portion size (one of you might get an enormous hake slab with cime di rapa and salsa verde, while the other has a little serving of belly pork with artichokes) but the flavours and seasonings are sharp and enlivening. The mountain of deep-fried pumpkin (zucca) is a popular (if oily) starter, and any gaps will surely be plugged by a monster hunk of plum cake to finish. The textbook pannacotta is a lighter bite. A fine Italian wine list, with runs of particularly good producers (Altare in Piedmont, Ornellaia in Tuscany, Montevetrano in Campania), is worth exploring. Prices start at £20 (£5.20 a glass).
Chef/s: Sam Harris. **Open:** Tue to Sun L 12 to 3 (3.30 Sat and Sun), Tue to Sat D 6 to 10. **Closed:** Mon. **Meals:** alc (main courses £14 to £16). **Service:** not inc. **Details:** 60 seats. No music. Wheelchair access.

Abu Zaad

Middle Eastern
29 Uxbridge Road, Shepherd's Bush, W12 8LH
Tel no: (020) 8749 5107
www.abuzaad.co.uk
'We both agreed that it was money extremely well spent, the food leaving a lasting positive impression.'

The Admiral Codrington

Chelsea pub with rewarding food
17 Mossop Street, Chelsea, SW3 2LY
Tel no: (020) 7581 0005
www.theadmiralcodrington.co.uk
⊖ South Kensington, map 3
Modern British | £30
Cooking score: 3

To the unassuming eye, the Cod is just another west London pub stuffed full of suits, sporting a crowd-pleasing but unadventurous menu of pub classics. But appearances can be deceiving. While the dark-wood bar is often heaving, the cream dining room to the rear is a much more tranquil affair, where diners will find themselves rewarded by a kitchen that takes exceptional pride in its craft. Dishes include flawlessly crispy chilli-salt squid, herb-crusted cod in a creamy white wine sauce, and what is surely one of the best burgers in west London, coated with smoked raclette cheese and served up in a shiny brioche bun. Wines start at £15 on a list that includes some bargain bottles and excellent English fizz by the glass.
Chef/s: Fred Smith. **Open:** Mon to Sat L 12 to 2.30 (3.30 Sat), D 6.30 to 11 (7 Sat). Sun 12 to 9. **Closed:** 24 to 26 Dec. **Meals:** alc (main courses £14 to £28). **Service:** 12.5%. **Details:** 55 seats. 20 seats outside. Separate bar. Wheelchair access. Music.

Also Recommended

Also recommended entries are not scored but we think they are worth a visit.

Amaya

Sleek Indian with tapas-style tasting plates
15 Halkin Arcade, Motcomb Street, Knightsbridge, SW1X 8JT
Tel no: (020) 7823 1166
www.realindianfood.com
⊖ Knightsbridge, map 4
Indian | £46
Cooking score: 3
V

Amaya occupies a desirable slice of Belgravia real estate and is a hugely ambitious affair: sleek, slinky and with a penchant for glamour. Locals flock to sample the wares in its vast, triangular dining area – a riotous mix of bold colours, vibrant murals and polished metal. The 'theatre kitchen' delivers a raft of tapas-style tasting plates from the tandoori oven, sigri grill and tawa skillet, with dishes arriving in waves when they are ready. Typically appetising options might include griddled scallops with green herb sauce, monkfish tikka or Punjabi chicken wing lollipops spiced with chilli and lime, plus Keralan biryanis and curries such as slow-cooked shabdeg gosht (lamb shank with turnips) to follow. Expert Matthew Jukes is the brains behind the spice-friendly wine list; prices from £25.
Chef/s: Karunesh Khanna. **Open:** all week L 12.30 to 2.15 (2.45 Sun), D 6.30 to 11.30 (10.30 Sun). **Meals:** alc (main courses £11 to £32). Set L £19.50 (2 courses). **Service:** 12.5%. **Details:** 100 seats. Separate bar. Wheelchair access. Music. No children after 6.30.

Anglesea Arms

Veteran crowd-pleaser
35 Wingate Road, Shepherd's Bush, W6 0UR
Tel no: (020) 8749 1291
www.anglesea-arms.com
⊖ Ravenscourt Park, map 1
Modern British | £30
Cooking score: 2

This lively, shabby-chic Victorian pub is a veteran when it comes to pleasing both drinkers and food fans. Navigate the bustling front bar and bag a table in the homely,

vintage-styled restaurant facing the open kitchen. Although some dishes have a Mediterranean edge, the twice-daily changing menu is essentially modern British. A punchy starter of seared ox heart with endive and red wine vinaigrette might be followed by a more delicate grilled turbot with romanesco broccoli and herb butter sauce. Ricotta doughnuts with butterscotch sauce are a popular pud. There are 20 well-considered wines by the glass; bottles from £16.50.
Open: all week L 12.30 to 2.45 (3 Sat, 3.30 Sun), D 7 to 10.30 (6.30 to 9.30 Sun). **Closed:** 23 to 28 Dec. **Meals:** alc (main courses £9 to £25). **Service:** 12.5%. **Details:** 90 seats. 20 seats outside. Separate bar. No music.

The Ark
Quintessential neighbourhood Italian
122 Palace Gardens Terrace, Notting Hill, W8 4RT
Tel no: (020) 7229 4024
www.ark-restaurant.com
⊖ Notting Hill Gate, map 4
Italian | £35
Cooking score: 2

With its sloping roof and skylights, this quintessential neighbourhood Italian feels more like a greenhouse than anything nautical – although the sought-after decked terrace might suggest something different. A new chef is at the helm, but the Ark continues to cruise through familiar waters, sending out full-blooded dishes 'bursting with generosity'. Homemade pasta is a top shout, judging by reports of fragrant tagliolini with crab, and buttery porcini ravioli dressed with rosemary oil. Salty-sweet grilled razor clams have also pleased. The kitchen also produces sizeable helpings of braised oxtail with celery or pan-fried cod with lentils and salsa verde. Italian regional wines from £17.
Chef/s: Kiri Pegasiou. **Open:** Tue to Sat L 12 to 3, Mon to Sat D 6.30 to 11. **Closed:** Sun, bank hols. **Meals:** alc (main courses £15 to £23). Set L £13.50 (2 courses) to £17. **Service:** 12.5%. **Details:** 60 seats. 12 seats outside. Separate bar. Music.

Assaggi
Very good Italian cooking indeed
39 Chepstow Place, Notting Hill, W2 4TS
Tel no: (020) 7792 5501
⊖ Notting Hill Gate, map 4
Italian | £60
Cooking score: 4
V

'This is very good cooking indeed' noted a visitor to this modest Italian dining room on the first floor of a former pub. The peach-and-blue interior is not the most comfortable, and it can be 'a noisy, clattering place when busy', but Assaggi is a likeable restaurant noted for hospitable service and rustic food majoring in the boldest of flavours. Grilled Mediterranean vegetables are a guaranteed treat, served with top-notch olive oil, or there's capunti pasta with salsiccia sausage, packed with the flavours of Puglia. This paves the way for 'superb' rack of lamb with caponata, or turbot fillet with a medley of peas and broad beans, lifted by ultra-thin lemon peel. Cheeses are in prime condition, and the lovely, sweet flavour of an Amaretto parfait inspires memories of lazy days in the sun – which may be the reason for its success. An all-Italian wine list starts at £23.95.
Chef/s: Nino Sassu. **Open:** Mon to Sat L 12.30 to 2.30 (1 to 2.30 Sat), D 7.30 to 11. **Closed:** Sun, 2 weeks Christmas, bank hols. **Meals:** alc (main courses £9 to £30). **Service:** not inc. **Details:** 35 seats. No music.

Bar Boulud
Glamour and finger-lickingly delicious food
Mandarin Oriental Hyde Park, 66 Knightsbridge, Knightsbridge, SW1X 7LA
Tel no: (020) 7201 3899
www.barboulud.com
⊖ Knightsbridge, map 4
French | £40
Cooking score: 4

'Incredibly consistent, although I make it easy for them by always having the same things' confessed a fan, adding that Daniel Boulud's glamorously sleek, high-gloss brasserie is 'a model on how to run a large-cover restaurant'. It continues to be a firm favourite with readers, who love the 'wonderful bistro feel' and the fact that it is a place where you can be 'as formal as you like with the gorgeous dim lighting and foie gras' or dress-down casual with 'finger-licking delicious' burgers ('especially the piggie'). There's also 'divine' charcuterie, oysters, escargots de bourgogne, very good steaks, coq au vin and boudin noir with celeriac purée and caramelised apple. Those who make it to dessert can expect île flottante or a chestnut and rum soufflé. Service is 'exemplary'. Wines are knowledgeably sourced, but lofty prices reflect the snazzy address; bottles from £22.50.

Chef/s: Dean Yasharian. **Open:** all week L 12 to 2.45, D 5.30 to 10.45 (9.45 Sun). **Meals:** alc (main courses £9 to £30). Set L and pre-theatre £23. **Service:** 12.5%. **Details:** 165 seats. Separate bar. Wheelchair access. Music.

Bibendum
Delightful design icon with seasonal classics
Michelin House, 81 Fulham Road, South Kensington, SW3 6RD
Tel no: (020) 7581 5817
www.bibendum.co.uk
⊖ South Kensington, map 3
French | £49
Cooking score: 4

V

Bibendum is the kind of neighbourhood restaurant that inspires loyalty – the draw is Matthew Harris's seasonal menus packed with classic French and modern European-inspired dishes. The first-floor dining room is a delight, too – especially in daylight but also in the evening – with its large stained-glass Michelin man window and high ceiling. On the food front, you could take the well-tried route with soupe de poissons, escargots, roast chicken with tarragon and fillet steak au poivre. Otherwise, try scallops with blood-orange, cucumber and dill salad before cod with red lentil, coconut and coriander dhal – all are of a consistently high standard. To

finish, there's usually crème brûlée or tarte fine aux pommes with vanilla ice cream. Grand French vintages dominate the global wine list, though the real everyday treasures are to be found among the house selections, which offer fine drinking from £19.95.

Chef/s: Matthew Harris. **Open:** all week L 12 to 2.30 (12.30 to 3 Sat and Sun), D 7 to 11 (10.30 Sun). **Closed:** 25 and 26 Dec, 1 Jan. **Meals:** alc (main courses £19 to £30). Set L £26.50 (2 courses) to £30. Sun L and D £30. **Service:** 12.5%. **Details:** 90 seats. Separate bar. No music.

NEW ENTRY
Bombay Brasserie
Some of London's best Indian food
Courtfield Road, South Kensington, SW7 4QH
Tel no: (020) 7370 4040
www.bombaybrasserielondon.com
⊖ Gloucester Road, map 3
Indian | £35
Cooking score: 3

Perhaps because of its longevity – it opened in 1982 – Bombay Brasserie is sometimes overlooked in discussions about London's upscale Indian restaurants. It shouldn't be. With its soaring ceilings, twinkling chandeliers and rejuvenated colonial grandeur, it's now serving 'some of the most delicious Indian food in the capital'. The menu, which reflects the diversity of the region's cuisine, is now overseen by Sriram Aylur of sister restaurant Quilon (see entry), and it sings with quality produce. But it's the Indian staples that shine: 'chicken tikka, gobi mutter and naans here are as good as just about anywhere in India' says one reporter. The lamb shank and saffron curry stands out for its perfectly flaking meat and deep, rich cumin, saffron, cardamom and cashew nut-enriched sauce. Carafes of wine from £11.

Chef/s: Sriram Aylur, Prahlad Hegde. **Open:** all week L 12 to 3, D 7 to 11.30 (10.30 Sun). **Meals:** alc (main courses £6 to £29). Set L £22. Set D £43. Sun L £26. **Service:** 10%. **Details:** 80 seats. 100 seats outside. Separate bar. Wheelchair access. Music.

Brompton Bar & Grill

Seductive neighbourhood bistro
243 Brompton Road, South Kensington, SW3 2EP
Tel no: (020) 7589 8005
www.bromptonbarandgrill.com
⊖ South Kensington, map 3
Anglo-French | £30
Cooking score: 2

'An incredible experience' sums up readers' affection for this busy bistro, with its touch of Knightsbridge glamour. It strikes just the right note for a neighbourhood restaurant, and keeps regulars returning with a changing menu that straddles classic French and modern British cooking, and sharp service. The set-up continues to deliver well-rehearsed dishes in which prime ingredients (dressed Dorset crab and mayonnaise, say) produce seductive results. The French background also yields humbler items: devilled kidneys and bubble and squeak partnering Elwy Valley double lamb chop, for instance. Sticky toffee pudding with clotted cream ice cream is a favourite. Wines from £14.50.
Chef/s: Gary Durrant. **Open:** all week L 12 to 3 (3.30 Sat and Sun), D 6 to 10.30 (10 Sun). **Closed:** 25 Dec. **Meals:** alc (main courses £13 to £37). Set L and early D £15.50 (2 courses) to £18.50. Sun L £21.50. **Service:** 12.5%. **Details:** 50 seats. Separate bar. Music.

Le Café Anglais

Big-hearted brasserie pleasures
8 Porchester Gardens, Notting Hill, W2 4DB
Tel no: (020) 7221 1415
www.lecafeanglais.co.uk
⊖ Bayswater, map 4
Anglo-French | £50
Cooking score: 4

A brasserie on a grand scale, Le Café Anglais occupies a gorgeously appointed, light-filled room with echoes of an Art Deco salon in its satin drapes and leather banquettes. Rowley Leigh's open-to-view kitchen majors in big-hearted Anglo-French pleasures, cooked with panache, gusto and an eye for seasonal details. The near-legendary hors d'oeuvre selection delivers winning versions of brawn with sauce ravigote, salsify fritters, mortadella with celeriac rémoulade and more besides, ahead of meaty rotisserie treats (roast rump of veal persillade) and generous plates of fried cod with pea purée or grilled pork chops with polenta and apples. After that, check out the cheese trolley or take the sweet route for 'Black Forest revisited' or bitter chocolate soufflé with hazelnut ice cream. The venue also accommodates an all-day oyster bar, where punters can chill out over some crustacea. The Euro-accented wine list shows a touch of class, with serious names in abundance and fine drinking from £19.50.
Chef/s: Rowley Leigh. **Open:** all week L 12 to 3.30, D 6.30 to 10.30 (11 Fri and Sat, 10 Sun). **Closed:** 25 to 27 Dec, 1 Jan. **Meals:** alc (main courses £15 to £33). Set L and D £20 (2 courses) to £25. Sun L £25 (2 courses) to £30. **Service:** 12.5%. **Details:** 130 seats. Separate bar. No music. Wheelchair access. Car parking.

Cambio de Tercio

Impressive, high-octane Spaniard
163 Old Brompton Road, Earl's Court, SW5 0LJ
Tel no: (020) 7244 8970
www.cambiodetercio.co.uk
⊖ Gloucester Road, map 3
Spanish | £45
Cooking score: 5

With offshoot Capote y Toros (see entry) all-but next door, this stretch of the Old Brompton Road has been a recipe for success for Cambio de Tercio. The bold, high-decibel Spaniard has been impressing the neighbourhood and beyond for many years and shows no sign of taking its foot off the pedal in these penny-pinching times. Indeed, the animated, elbow-to-elbow interior has seen some changes of late, and now offers a contemporary cocktail bar/lounge (plus a few additional covers) after extending into the adjacent property, and there's a new kitchen in the basement. Here Alberto Criado punches well above his weight when it comes to his highly personal take on modern Spanish cooking. A glance at the menu is enough to have you salivating: whether traditional calamares fritos, pulpo gallego or pimientos de Padrón; a cleverly worked caramelised mille-feuille of foie gras with smoked eel and baked apple; or 'good for sharing' main courses like grilled Spanish salt cod teamed with braised pig's head, baby onions and orange 'air'. Afterwards, the caramelised bread pudding with crema catalana ice cream should provide a sweet hit. The formidable wine list opens with a staggering 110 sherries, while 350 all-Spanish wines (from £22) include classics, smaller appellations and new discoveries. **Chef/s:** Alberto Criado. **Open:** all week L 12 to 2.30 (3 Sat and Sun), D 6.30 to 11.30 (11 Sun). **Closed:** 22 Dec to 3 Jan. **Meals:** alc (main courses £18 to £23). Set L and D £18 (2 courses) to £25. Sun L £22. **Service:** 12.5%. **Details:** 55 seats. 8 seats outside. Separate bar. Music.

NEW ENTRY
Capote y Toros
Show-stopping sherry and tapas bar
157 Old Brompton Road, South Kensington, SW5 0LJ
Tel no: (020) 7373 0567
www.cambiodetercio.co.uk
⊖ Gloucester Road, map 3
Spanish | £20
Cooking score: 3

'Soooo much fun' enthused a visitor to this offshoot of nearby Cambio de Tercio (see entry). The effervescent Capote – a ham, tapas and sherry bar – is a diminutive hot-ticket local: think sunny colours, matador photos, racks of wine and sherry and dangling Ibérico hams. Roll up and wait your turn for a table (if busy) over a glass of amontillado at the counter or bar. The menu keeps things simple and produce-led; traditional tapas line up alongside top-notch hams and charcuterie, so expect spicy Andalusian chorizo cooked with fino or pork meatballs with an oloroso sauce, served alongside wonderful acorn-fed Ibérico ham and seafood offerings like Galician octopus with potato and sweet paprika. There's

a 'show-stopping' 110 sherries on offer, while the all-Spanish wines similarly impress, with 350 bins from £21.50.
Chef/s: Luis Navacerrada. **Open:** Tue to Sat D only 6 to 11.30. **Closed:** Sun, Mon, 22 Dec to 4 Jan. **Meals:** alc (tapas £4 to £11). **Service:** 12.5%. **Details:** 20 seats. 2 seats outside. Separate bar. Music.

The Carpenter's Arms
Jolly local with please-all food
89-91 Black Lion Lane, Hammersmith, W6 9BG
Tel no: (020) 8741 8386
www.carpentersarmsw6.co.uk
⊖ Stamford Brook, Ravenscourt Park, map 1
Modern European | £27
Cooking score: 2

With its enviably pretty beer garden, pared-down interiors and jolly bonhomie, the Carpenter's Arms is just the ticket for Hammersmith's dressed-down locals. The cooking is a deft mix of British and European ways, with a touch of the Orient here and there – so expect beer-battered haddock and slow-roast belly pork with braised red cabbage, alongside the likes of lobster salad with mango, chilli and coriander, rabbit and chorizo crépinettes or roasted poussin with sautéed shallots and sugar snaps. The Carpenter's offerings also extend to deli-style sharing platters with home-baked bread and a commendable choice of wines (from £16.50) – although real ales are in short supply. **Chef/s:** Nilton Campos. **Open:** all week L 12 to 3 (4 Sat and Sun), D 6 to 10 (9 Sun). **Closed:** 26 to 30 Dec. **Meals:** alc (main courses £12 to £20). **Service:** 12.5%. **Details:** 40 seats. 40 seats outside. Music.

⫴ **Average Price**
The average price listed in main-entry reviews denotes the price of a three-course meal, without wine.

Casa Brindisa

Authentic Spanish venue
7-9 Exhibition Road, South Kensington, SW7 2HQ
Tel no: (020) 7590 0008
www.brindisa.com/restaurants
⊖ South Kensington, map 3
Spanish | £25
Cooking score: 3

 £30

Brindisa's South Kensington branch maintains the Spanish produce supplier's reputation for running one of the most authentic Spanish venues in town. Much of the repertoire is driven by top-drawer ingredients imported from the home country: acorn-fed jamón Ibérico, cured Catalan sausage, Catalan flatbread, goats' and sheep's milk cheeses – the list goes on. Elsewhere, there are house specialities of xató – salt cod, anchovy and frisée salad with romesco dressing – and acorn-fed duck breast with pumpkin chutney and Pedro Ximénez reduction, as well as tried-and-trusted classics such as potato tortilla, croquetas of ham and chicken, gambas al ajillo, and a nostalgic crema catalana for dessert. A comprehensive Spanish wine list opens with Macabeo and Garnacha house selections from £17.50.
Chef/s: Leonardo Rivera. **Open:** all week 12 to 11. **Closed:** 24 to 27 Dec, 1 and 2 Jan. **Meals:** alc (tapas £7 to £14). **Service:** 12.5%. **Details:** 65 seats. 16 seats outside. Separate bar. Wheelchair access. Music.

Cassis

An authentic taste of Provence
232-236 Brompton Road, South Kensington, SW3 2BB
Tel no: (020) 7581 1101
www.cassisbistro.co.uk
⊖ South Kensington, map 3
French | £25
Cooking score: 4

 £30

The general bonhomie between staff and regular customers quickly builds the image of a user-friendly, cheerful restaurant with a relaxing, light interior. Cassis is intended to look like a modern French brasserie, though the view through floor-to-ceiling plate-glass windows is of the busy Brompton Road. But fear not, the blue horizons and shaded squares of Provence are soon summoned by the imagination and by the food. Petites bouchées are carefully crafted – the pastis-flambéed snails in puff pastry with garlic butter left one enthusiast doubting whether he had had better in France – while bouillabaisse, roast Landes duck breast with chickpea galette and niçoise olive sauce, and a Grand Marnier and orange soufflé large enough to share reveal a sincere exploration of Provençal cuisine. Immense care has gone into the wine list; French regional classics take star billing, but there is also much to seduce elsewhere. Prices from £17.
Chef/s: David Escobar. **Open:** all week 12 to 11, (11.30am Sat, 10.30pm Sun). **Closed:** 25 and 26 Dec. **Meals:** alc (main courses £14 to £34). Set L £17 (2 courses) to £20. **Service:** 12.5%. **Details:** 90 seats. 10 seats outside. Separate bar. Wheelchair access. Music.

Le Cercle

Intense mouthfuls of pleasure
1 Wilbraham Place, Belgravia, SW1X 9AE
Tel no: (020) 7901 9999
www.lecercle.co.uk
⊖ Sloane Square, map 3
Modern French | £32
Cooking score: 3

£5 OFF

Owners Pascal Aussignac and Vincent Labeyrie built their reputation on their native Gascon cuisine (Club Gascon, see entry), but though there is a smattering of foie gras and charcuterie on the menu at this elegant basement restaurant, it encompasses a much wider range of flavours. Some of the cooking is inspired – a starter of baby squid maki has the young cephalopod wrapped around fine batons of carrot and ginger, delivering sensationally light but intense mouthfuls of pleasure. Other dishes are slightly more workaday – terrine of rabbit is good, rather

than exceptional; beautifully cooked lamb chump is served with a rich tomato coulis. Lovely ice creams (violet, hibiscus), good cheese and the likes of crème brûlée complete the picture. The well-heeled wine list starts at £20.
Chef/s: Pierre Mirepoix. **Open:** Tue to Sat L 12 to 2, D 5.30 to 10.45. **Closed:** Sun, Mon, 2 weeks Christmas and New Year. **Meals:** alc (main courses £13 to £24). Set L and D £18.50 (2 courses) to £23.50. **Service:** 12.5%. **Details:** 60 seats. Wheelchair access. Music.

Chabrot Bistrot d'Amis
Diminutive bistrot with lots to like
9 Knightsbridge Green, Knightsbridge, SW1X 7QL
Tel no: (020) 7225 2238
www.chabrot.co.uk
⊖ **Knightsbridge, map 4**
French | £35
Cooking score: 5
£5
OFF

Regulars are clearly delighted to have this diminutive two-floored bistrot close to home ('or was I in south-west France somewhere?') and most are drawn here by the food. Certainly, there are no fine-dining trappings to detract from the robust regional cooking – tables couldn't be more tightly packed – but for lovers of French food, there's much to like. A typical route in might be beetroot salad with fresh goats' cheese; confit duck leg with green beans, shallots and warm potato salad; and baba flavoured with Armagnac syrup. The menu barely changes, apart from a few seasonal tweaks, but it is built around established standards, which brings people back because they know the quality won't waver from one visit to the next. Escargots in parsley butter, foie gras terrine, jambon de Bayonne are all present and correct, but a swerve off the beaten track at main course might bring something like baby monkfish fillets with paprika, crushed potatoes and artichokes or a splendid roasted Pyrenean baby lamb shoulder with spices, dried fruit and herb couscous for two to share. Service is very

French, charming and efficient. Drinking is mostly French, too, with prices starting at £19.50.
Chef/s: Thierry Laborde. **Open:** all week L 12 to 3, D 6.30 to 11 (10 Sun). **Closed:** 25 and 26 Dec, bank hols. **Meals:** alc (main courses £13 to £34). Set L £15.50 (2 courses). Set D £19.50 (2 courses) to £21.50. Sun L £19.50. **Service:** 12.5%. **Details:** 65 seats. Music.

NEW ENTRY
Chakra
Authentic Indian delicacies to share
157-159 Notting Hill Gate, Notting Hill, W11 3LF
Tel no: (020) 7229 2115
www.chakralondon.com
⊖ **Notting Hill Gate, map 4**
Indian | £55
Cooking score: 3

Andy Varma, ex-chef of Chelsea's once-celebrated Vama, has reappeared at flash W11 newcomer Chakra. Chakra's luxurious cuisine draws inspiration from India's royal kitchens and legendary chefs, which might mean patiala chaap (tender Punjabi lamb chops) or, from Lucknow, venison kakori kebab. 'London' touches come in the form of tandoor-roasted black cod and a not-entirely-convincing 'curry patta burrata', the creamy Italian cheese, dusted with spices alongside aubergine and tomatoes. Varma is nothing if not creative. Like its customers, Chakra is dressed to impress: the all-cream front room, padded walls and chandeliers wouldn't look out of place in a Dubai nightclub; the skylit back room is considerably easier on the eye. Service, alas, has some catching up to do. Wines start at £21.
Chef/s: Andy Varma. **Open:** all week L 12 to 3, D 6 to 11. **Closed:** 25 and 26 Dec. **Meals:** alc (main courses £9 to £27). Set L £30 (2 courses) to £40. Set D £50. Sun L £22.50. Gourmand menu £65 (6 courses). **Service:** 12.5%. **Details:** 75 seats. 12 seats outside. Wheelchair access. Music.

Charlotte's Bistro

Slick neighbourhood eatery
6 Turnham Green Terrace, Chiswick, W4 1QP
Tel no: (020) 8742 3590
www.charlottes.co.uk
⊖ Turnham Green, map 1
Modern British | £29
Cooking score: 2

This perennially buzzy bar-cum-restaurant manages to be a magnet both for drinkers, who enjoy 'popping in for a cocktail or two in the evening', and for those seeking more substantial sustenance. The menus cut and paste the modes of the moment into an invigorating range of choice, presenting mackerel with a little white crab meat and ponzo dressing, or partnering a main-course crispy belly pork with smoked mash and pig's cheek faggot. The set-price lunch has been described as 'quality food at an exceptional price', and service copes well. House wine is £18. Sister to Charlotte's Place in Ealing (see entry).
Chef/s: Wesley Smalley. **Open:** Mon to Sat L 12 to 3, D 5.30 to 10, Sun 12 to 9. **Closed:** 26 Dec, 1 Jan. **Meals:** alc (main courses £15 to £17). Set L £12.95 (2 courses) to £15.95. Sun L £18.50 (2 courses) to £22.50. **Service:** 12.5%. **Details:** 60 seats. Separate bar. Music.

★ READERS' RESTAURANT OF THE YEAR ★
LONDON

Charlotte's Place

Dependable, pleasing cooking and great value
16 St Matthew's Road, Ealing, W5 3JT
Tel no: (020) 8567 7541
www.charlottes.co.uk
⊖ Ealing Broadway, Ealing Common, map 1
Modern European | £29
Cooking score: 4

'I love this restaurant and think the people of Ealing are so lucky to have it on their doorstep' sums up our readers' affection for this friendly neighbourhood venue overlooking Ealing Common. Recession-defying prices (the set lunch is very good value) and dependable cooking that mixes and matches diverse European techniques are reasons enough to seek it out, not to mention the spot-on service. The kitchen runs with the seasons and pleases with the likes of smoked haddock and leek croquette, served with a poached duck egg, spinach and hollandaise, or beef ragù raviolo. Roast hake with white and borlotti bean ragoût, chorizo and salsa verde, and navarin of lamb are decent main course shouts. Desserts might bring an 'outstanding' blood-orange sorbet or dark chocolate and Baileys marquise with praline ice cream, but it's worth checking out the superb selection of cheeses from La Fromagerie. Wines from £18.
Chef/s: Greg Martin. **Open:** Mon to Sat L 12 to 2.30, D 6 to 9.30, Sun 12 to 9. **Closed:** 26 Dec to 3 Jan. **Meals:** Set L £14.95 (2 courses) to £17.95. Set D £24.95 (2 courses) to £29.95. Sun L £19.95 (2 courses) to £23.95. **Service:** 12.5%. **Details:** 54 seats. 16 seats outside. Music.

Chutney Mary

Culinary adventures at a sumptuous Indian
535 King's Road, Fulham, SW10 0SZ
Tel no: (020) 7351 3113
www.chutneymary.com
⊖ Fulham Broadway, map 3
Indian | £34
Cooking score: 3

£5
OFF

Goan-spiced oyster bhajias, baked paneer and wild mushroom terrine or Normandy foie gras with a green papaya glaze aren't the sort of dishes you expect to see on a curry house menu – but Chutney Mary isn't your average vindaloo and lager hangout. Named after fashion-conscious Indian ladies from the days of the Empire, this sumptuous piece of work spreads itself over three floors emblazoned with bejewelled tapestries, palm trees and silks – exactly the right backdrop for Siddharth Krishna's open-minded culinary adventures. British ingredients get a good airing (Sandringham venison pops up in ginger-spiced samosas; lamb from Little Braxted Hall might appear with caramelised beetroot), and there's room for a few evergreens such as butter chicken masala or sealed pots of Hyderabadi biryani. The wine list (from £25) fits the food. **Chef/s:** Siddharth Krishna. **Open:** Sat and Sun L 12.30 to 2.45, all week D 6.30 to 11.30 (10.30 Sun). **Meals:** alc (main courses £17 to £32). Sun L £24. **Service:** 12.5%. **Details:** 110 seats. Music. Children over 3 yrs only; over 10 yrs after 8.

Clarke's

Landmark London eating address
124 Kensington Church Street, Notting Hill, W8 4BH
Tel no: (020) 7221 9225
www.sallyclarke.com
⊖ Notting Hill Gate, map 4
Modern British | £43
Cooking score: 4

The restaurant (and bakery and shop) on Kensington Church Street has been one of the landmark addresses of London eating since the 1980s, when its style of simple, direct, ingredients-led cookery helped to see off the last pomposities of French-orientated nouvelle cuisine. The daily changing menus have expanded into full à la carte format, but the sharp focus and uncomplicated balance of dishes remain intact. A winter dinner opened with black rice and roasted fennel salad with anchovies, olives, rocket and caper salsa verde to set the taste-buds at attention. Mains offered a range from turbot fillets with baked artichoke in chive cream, to lamb rump with braised Castelluccio lentils and cavolo nero in yoghurt and coriander. An intermediate cheese trio leads nicely into the likes of passion-fruit cheesecake with mango and toasted coconut. The wine list has always been one of the glories of Clarke's, with concise but superb selections from around the world, including a special section of old treasures from California's Ridge Vineyards. Prices start at £19 a bottle (£6.75 a small glass).

Chef/s: Sally Clarke. **Open:** all week L 12.30 to 2 (12 Sat), Mon to Sat D 6.30 to 10. **Closed:** Christmas, first week Jan, 1 week Aug. **Meals:** alc (main courses £20 to £23). Set D £42.50. **Service:** 12.5%. **Details:** 80 seats. No music.

NEW ENTRY
Colchis Bar and Restaurant

Explore the world of Georgian cuisine
39 Chepstow Place, Notting Hill, W2 4TS
Tel no: (020) 7221 7620
www.colchisrestaurant.co.uk
⊖ Notting Hill Gate, map 4
Georgian | £27
Cooking score: 1
 £30

Easy-going Colchis is a comfortable, contemporary venue that pays homage to the earthy world of Georgian cuisine. A board of moreish flatbread filled with cheese, chanakhi (casseroled lamb with potatoes and aubergine in rich tomato sauce), then lamb shashlyk (kebab) with sour plum and spicy red pepper dipping sauces have all hit the spot. But heavy-duty khinkali (dumplings with minced beef and pork) are more reminiscent of eastern Europe back in the day. Pleasant staff are a plus. Georgian wines start at £23 a bottle before the wine list goes global. **Chef/s:** Manana Chighvinadze. **Open:** Tue to Sun L 12 to 4, D 6 to 11 (10 Sun). **Closed:** Mon, 24 to 26 Dec. **Meals:** alc (main courses £10 to £23). **Service:** 12.5%. **Details:** 32 seats. 8 seats outside. Separate bar. Music.

Le Colombier

Pleasing French classics
145 Dovehouse Street, Chelsea, SW3 6LB
Tel no: (020) 7351 1155
www.le-colombier-restaurant.co.uk
⊖ South Kensington, map 3
French | £40
Cooking score: 2

You don't have to be French to run a note-perfect Parisian-style bistro, but it helps. Didier Garnier's Colombier earns repeat business for its 'pleasant buzz', spotless presentation and 'charming without being sycophantic' waiters. 'It's a fun place to be', inside and out. The menu is pleasingly classic; oeufs en meurette (poached eggs in red wine sauce), veal kidneys with mustard cream sauce and oeufs à la neige make regular appearances. The two-course set lunch at £19.50 with coffee is 'remarkable' value for SW3. A regular suggests taking advice on the all-French wine list, adding: 'They have never let me down'.

Chef/s: Philippe Tamet. **Open:** all week L 12 to 3 (3.30 Sun), D 6.30 to 10.30 (10 Sun). **Meals:** alc (main courses £18 to £35). Set L £19.50 (2 courses). Sun L £23. **Service:** 12.5%. **Details:** 45 seats. 25 seats outside. No music.

★ TOP 50 ★

Dinner by Heston Blumenthal
A taste of history
Mandarin Oriental Hyde Park, 66 Knightsbridge, Knightsbridge, SW1X 7LA
Tel no: (020) 7201 3833
www.dinnerbyheston.com
⊖ Knightsbridge, map 4
British | £55
Cooking score: 7

'Great food in a great restaurant' seems to be the consensus as Heston Blumenthal's effusively hyped Knightsbridge blockbuster settles into its stride. It may be a world away from the celestial gastronomy and sheer genius of the Fat Duck (see entry), but Dinner has its own patriotic trumpet to blow and the whole place is undoubtedly big box-office. That said, the dining room plays it low key – a rather masculine, square space with windows overlooking Hyde Park, leather panels, cartoonish jelly-mould lampshades on the walls and a spectacular glass-fronted kitchen providing the *coup de théâtre*: just look at the whole pineapples turning on spits powered by a giant wristwatch mechanism. Blumenthal has raided the lost archives and delivered a time-traveller's sweep through six centuries of British food history, although the results are

re-engineered retro-originals rather than faint replicas: your average medieval peasant would be gobsmacked by 'rice and flesh' (a lavish, saffron-soaked risotto with calf's tail braised in red wine); likewise, it's hard to imagine anyone in blitzed wartime London sitting in their Anderson shelter with a plate of 'cod in cider' (a soothing collation of pearly-white fish in a boozy sauce with chard and mussels). Think *Back to the Future* rather than *Remembrance of Things Past*, with technically majestic, show-stopping contributions from 'banging fresh' roast halibut, cockle ketchup and chicory leaves (c.1830), exquisitely plump 'powdered' (ie salt-cured) duck breast with confit fennel and 'umbles', hay-smoked mackerel on a gently pickled lemon salad with Gentleman's Relish, and some truly revelatory desserts – notably the rose-tinted 'taffety' tart and a sublime, eighteenth-century 'chocolate bar' with tangy passion-fruit jam running through it and a blob of ginger ice cream on the side. Of course, not everyone buys into Blumenthal's arcane sorcery, with some readers citing 'the Emperor's new clothes' and 'serious disappointment' along the way. The wing rib of Irish Angus beef has outshone the Hereford ribeye for flavour and quality, and the skinny, limp fries have reminded more than one reporter of a big-brand burger chain. Service is tickety-boo, with enough knowledge and nous to keep obsessive bloggers and scholastic foodies happy, but expect to pay handsomely for the experience. In particular, the connoisseur's wine list is reckoned to be 'eye-gougingly expensive', although it offers real class, pedigree and star names in every department; bottles start at £35.

Chef/s: Ashley Palmer-Watts. **Open:** all week L 12 to 2.30, D 6.30 to 10.30. **Meals:** alc (main courses £23 to £33). Set L £32. **Service:** 12.5%. **Details:** 103 seats. Separate bar. No music. Wheelchair access.

e&o

Global flavours and good desserts
14 Blenheim Crescent, Notting Hill, W11 1NN
Tel no: (020) 7229 5454
www.rickerrestaurants.com
⊖ **Ladbroke Grove, map 4**
Pan-Asian | £40
Cooking score: 2

When it launched in 2002, Will Ricker's hip 'Eastern and Oriental' grazing concept was manna for every self-respecting Notting Hillbilly out on the town. But e&o's fortunes seem to be flatlining as hard times come calling and new trends descend on W11. Its global mix of dim sum, sushi, curries, salads and BBQ nibbles seems more 'one-dimensional' these days – witness rather laboured versions of peppered tuna with miso aïoli, prawn laksa and 'bland' Singapore noodles. But there are still good things to be had – from deep-fried whole sea bass to coconut and peanut sambal chicken. East/west desserts are also good, judging by a fired-up ginger cheesecake. The globetrotting wine list starts at £18.
Chef/s: Simon Treadway. **Open:** Mon to Fri L 12 to 3, D 6 to 11. Sat 12 to 11. Sun 12.30 to 10.30. **Closed:** 25 and 26 Dec, Aug bank hol. **Meals:** alc (main courses £11 to £36). Set L £19. **Service:** 12.5%. **Details:** 86 seats. 22 seats outside. Separate bar. Music.

Ebury Restaurant & Wine Bar

Passionate commitment to enjoyment
139 Ebury Street, Belgravia, SW1W 9QU
Tel no: (020) 7730 5447
www.eburyrestaurant.co.uk
⊖ **Victoria, map 3**
Modern European | £33
Cooking score: 2

£5 OFF **V**

It's possible that owner Nigel Windridge's much-frequented wine bar and restaurant continues to enjoy faithful support because of its superior wine list and passionate commitment to drinking pleasure and enjoyment. But the food and the warm ambience induced by closely-packed tables and timeworn gentleman's club décor are equally strong magnets. The cooking is not the most adventurous, but the scope is broad, taking in contemporary ideas (spiced pigeon breast with oriental salad) alongside more traditional requirements (steaks, calf's liver and bacon) and rustic dishes (sausages with wholegrain mustard mash). Top marks, too, for gluten- and dairy-free menus. Wines from £16.
Chef/s: Bernard Dumonteil. **Open:** all week L 12 to 3, D 6 to 10.15. **Closed:** 24 Dec to 2 Jan. **Meals:** alc (main courses £14 to £30). Set L and D £19 (2 courses) to £25. **Service:** 12.5%. **Details:** 70 seats. Separate bar. Music.

L'Etranger

Idiosyncratic Franco-Japanese creations
36 Gloucester Road, South Kensington, SW7 4QT
Tel no: (020) 7584 1118
www.etranger.co.uk
⊖ **Gloucester Road, South Kensington, map 3**
Modern French | £55
Cooking score: 4

A Franco-Japanese amalgam, decoratively inspired by Albert Camus' existentialist novel of the same name, L'Etranger insists on its own peculiar kind of distinctiveness. Exposed wood floors and a palette of lilac and grey sets the understated tone, the better to spotlight the idiosyncratic creations of Jérôme Tauvron, who has worked under Michel Guérard, Pierre Gagnaire and Alain Ducasse. A typical starter is tuna tataki with foie gras shavings and truffled ponzu jelly, but dishes can be either straightforwardly east Asian (crispy squid with chilli and spring onion) or haute française, as in a main course of smoked duck breast with cep ravioli and garlic spinach. Truffles are virtually everywhere, although not in the Japanese classic black cod caramelised in miso, which comes with sushi rice and pickled ginger. Finish with Nobu-style chocolate fondant and green tea ice cream. A gargantuan wine list of more than 80 pages opens with reams of Champagnes, and includes a listing of premium sakés, as well as

top-credential growers from all over the show, notably the California regions, Burgundy and Italy. Dig deep, though. House wines start at £22 for red and £24 white.
Chef/s: Jérôme Tauvron. **Open:** all week L 12 to 3, D 5.30 to 11 (10 Sun). **Meals:** alc (main courses £15 to £65). Set L £14.50 (2 courses) to £19.50. Set D £48. Sun L £22 (2 courses) to £24. **Service:** 12.5%. **Details:** 64 seats. Separate bar. Music.

Fifth Floor

Cool foodie package
Harvey Nichols, 109-125 Knightsbridge, Knightsbridge, SW1X 7RJ
Tel no: (020) 7235 5250
www.harveynichols.com
⊖ Knightsbridge, map 4
Modern European | £40
Cooking score: 3

The fifth floor of the Harvey Nichols store is a cool amalgam of food emporium, all-day café, slinky bar and smart restaurant, the latter much improved by a makeover that has added contemporary clean looks and a more relaxed feel. Chef Jonas Karlsson's menu is a European-influenced tribute to good British produce, with a healthy balance between familiarity and innovation. Take the well-tried route of dressed Cornish crab salad with avocado and mango vinaigrette, and braised pork cheeks, boulangère potatoes, leeks and truffle jus. Otherwise, explore the world of whipped goats' cheese, beetroot soil and pickled vegetables, then hake tournedos, choucroute, morteau sausage and red wine fumet. Blood-orange sorbet with coconut and chocolate sticks might provide the final thrill. Wines from £22.50.
Chef/s: Jonas Karlsson. **Open:** all week L 12 to 3 (5 Sun), Mon to Sat D 6 to 11. **Closed:** 25 Dec. **Meals:** alc (main courses £11 to £32). Set L and D £20 (2 courses) to £25. **Service:** 12.5%. **Details:** 80 seats. Separate bar. Wheelchair access. Music.

ALSO RECOMMENDED
▲ Gastronomica

45 Tachbrook Street, Pimlico, SW1V 2LZ
Tel no: (020) 7407 4488
www.gastronomica.co.uk
⊖ Pimlico, Victoria, map 3
Italian £5 OFF

The smell of fresh bread is a draw, and this busy deli is a good place to pop in for simple Italian rustic cooking that uses properly sourced ingredients (Gastronomica is an importer of Italian produce). Grab a seat at the communal tables and tuck into Parmesan, Parma ham and grilled vegetables (£6.50), tagliatelle with cherry tomato sauce (£7) or gnocchi that's 'the best I've had outside Italy'. Finish with homemade sponge cake (£4). Service comes with easy Italian charm. Wines from £18.

Haandi

Indian dishes heady with subtle spices
136 Brompton Road, Knightsbridge, SW3 1HY
Tel no: (020) 7823 7373
www.haandi-restaurants.com
⊖ Knightsbridge, map 4
North Indian | £26
Cooking score: 3
£5 OFF **V** £30

Seek out the Cheval Place entrance to this East African-Indian, which brings you to a small bar area with views of the restaurant beyond. A glass-fronted kitchen lends a modern note to an otherwise dated room stuffed with cane furniture and oversized pot plants. Watch as the chefs prepare the dishes of the north Indian frontier: rich masalas; tandoor-cooked seekh kebabs; and aromatic rogan josh. Subtle yet complex spicing is Haandi's stock-in-trade, perfectly exemplified in the jeera chicken, a Kenyan speciality heady with the scent of toasted cinnamon, cloves and coriander. Naan has been underwhelming, though chilli paneer is fresh and zingy. Service can be patchy and forgetful. Wines from £18.50.

Chef/s: Ratan Singh. **Open:** all week L 12 to 3, D 5.30 to 11. **Closed:** 25 Dec. **Meals:** alc (main courses £7 to £16). Set L £11.95. **Service:** 12.5%. **Details:** 65 seats. Music.

The Harwood Arms
Gastronomic excellence and a fine wine list
Walham Grove, Fulham, SW6 1QP
Tel no: (020) 7386 1847
www.harwoodarms.com
⊖ Fulham Broadway, map 3
British | £35
Cooking score: 5

The Harwood is a self-styled 'rural haven in the middle of Fulham', a place that cleverly marries the ethos of a good country inn, with its close-knit ties to local supply lines, with that of the best kind of urban pub, where gastronomic excellence and a fine wine list combine to raise the game. A bare-boarded floor and lilac colour scheme help the mood of airy expansiveness, and Barry Fitzgerald's cooking mobilises some top-drawer British artisanal produce in productive ways. The palate-pleasing depth and complexity achieved are often sensational, as in the brilliantly textured deep-fried battered oysters to start, or a satisfying combination of pheasant terrine with pheasant and celeriac soup. There are nods to domestic tradition in mains such as a properly moist stuffed chicken leg cooked in mead with layered black pudding and potato, or plaice roasted on the bone, served with potted shrimp butter and baby gem. Doughnuts appear in various guises at dessert, perhaps as brown sugar specimens with sea buckthorn curd and sour cream, while a traditional biscuit revival brings on baked lemon thyme custard with apple sorbet and custard creams. Cheeses come with hemp biscuits and Welsh cakes. A fine selection of wines by the glass opens at £4, bottles at £16, on a well-annotated and distinguished list.
Chef/s: Barry Fitzgerald. **Open:** Tue to Sun L 12 to 3 (12.30 to 4 Sun), all week D 6.30 to 9.30 (7 to 9 Sun). **Closed:** 24 to 28 Dec, 1 Jan. **Meals:** alc (main courses £17 to £19). Set L £18.50 (2 courses) to £22.50. Tasting menu £50. **Service:** 12.5%. **Details:** 45 seats. Separate bar. Music.

The Havelock Tavern
Pleasing local with good pub food
57 Masbro Road, Shepherd's Bush, W14 0LS
Tel no: (020) 7603 5374
www.havelocktavern.com
⊖ Shepherd's Bush, Olympia, map 1
Modern British | £30
Cooking score: 2

'Still one of the best pubs in the area' reckons a regular of this Shepherd's Bush local. Covered in cobalt-blue tiles outside, spacious and laid-back inside, and with a terrace, it serves good, straightforward modern pub cooking. Expect salt-and-pepper squid with lime and chilli sauce, then char-grilled bavette steak with chips and tomato and tarragon butter, or roast cod in mussel and spinach sauce. Pannacotta with biscotti is the lighter alternative to getting stuck into sticky toffee pudding with vanilla ice cream and toffee sauce. Plenty of wines by the glass from £4.15 make for cheery drinking. Bottles start at £15.50.
Chef/s: James Howarth. **Open:** all week L 12.30 to 2.30 (3 Sun), D 7 to 10 (9.30 Sun). **Closed:** 25 and 26 Dec. **Meals:** alc (£9 to £14). **Service:** not inc. **Details:** 80 seats. 32 seats outside. Separate bar. No music.

NEW ENTRY
Hedone
Top-notch design and the best ingredients
301-303 Chiswick High Road, Chiswick, W4 4HH
Tel no: (020) 8747 0377
www.hedonerestaurant.com
⊖ Chiswick Park, map 1
Modern European | £50
Cooking score: 4

The 'foodie' set has lost its heart to former food blogger Mikael Jonsson's brave Chiswick venture. That's not an unreasonable response to this exciting neighbourhood restaurant, with its 'top notch' design (arty and informal with an open kitchen), and some wonderful,

wonderful dishes. However, it has left expectations high. 'Grossly overpriced', one reader complains, disappointed by just a single daily menu (offered as a four, five or seven courser) 'with few variations'. The approach, however, suits Jonsson and his pursuit of the best ingredients bar none – beef from O'Shea's and a Sika deer dish induce something like ecstasy. Portions are 'tiny' (or minimalist if you're feeling kind). Menus are constantly evolving, but you can rejoice if they feature anything resembling the crab sandwich amuse-bouche ('Wow!'), 'superb' mackerel and lettuce starter or refreshing poached quetsch plum dessert. Wines are intelligently chosen, but start high at £30.

Chef/s: Mikael Jonsson. **Open:** Fri and Sat L 12.30 to 2.15, Tue to Sat D 6.30 to 9.30. **Closed:** Sun, Mon, 2 weeks Christmas and New Year. **Meals:** Set L £30. Set D £50 (4 courses). Tasting menu £75. **Service:** 12.5%. **Details:** 40 seats. Separate bar. No music. Wheelchair access. No babies at D.

Hereford Road

Flag-waving Brit fare
3 Hereford Road, Notting Hill, W2 4AB
Tel no: (020) 7727 1144
www.herefordroad.org
⊖ Bayswater, map 4
British | £26
Cooking score: 2

Set in an ex-butcher's shop amidst the tidy squares and prim Victorian townhouses of Bayswater, Hereford Road lives up to its meaty heritage with an appropriately carnivorous menu. Captaining the kitchen is Tom Pemberton, formerly of St John (see entry), who has made a career serving up bulldog British fare. A test meal suggested this patriotic fervour had gone off the boil somewhat: potted crab tasted insipid: and pot-roast rabbit with fennel and bacon felt like a hastily arranged marriage of ingredients. But elsewhere there's good sea bass and Hereford lamb. Nostalgic desserts include buttermilk pudding and poached pear. Wines from £18.

Chef/s: Tom Pemberton. **Open:** all week L 12 to 3 (4 Sun), D 6 to 10.30 (10 Sun). **Closed:** Christmas. **Meals:** alc (main courses £10 to £16). Set L £13 (2 courses) to £15.50. **Service:** 12.5%. **Details:** 66 seats. 6 seats outside. No music. Wheelchair access.

Hunan

Chinese regional surprises
51 Pimlico Road, Chelsea, SW1W 8NE
Tel no: (020) 7730 5712
www.hunanlondon.com
⊖ Sloane Square, map 3
Chinese | £60
Cooking score: 3

The drill at this wholly idiosyncratic restaurant is a succession of pan-Chinese 'tapas', some of them Hunanese-inspired, but most more obviously Taiwanese. There is no menu as such. What turns up will be made from anything you haven't specifically said you don't like. Steamed bamboo cup soup might set the ball rolling, followed in rapid succession by mussels in black bean sauce, steamed quail with its hard-boiled egg and winter melon, stir-fried aged ribeye, sublime crispy frogs' legs with fermented bamboo shoots and chilli, or the signature hearty broth of minced pork, Chinese mushrooms and ginger. Sweet things may include red bean pancakes. Then again, the meal may just involve none of the above. It's a genuine *menu surprise*. A stylistically arranged wine list is full of pedigree growers to delight posh Londoners, but there is ample quality choice below £30. Prices open at £17.

Chef/s: Michael Peng. **Open:** Mon to Sat L 12.30 to 2, D 6.30 to 10.30. **Closed:** Sun, 2 weeks Christmas, 1 week Aug, bank hols. **Meals:** Set L £29.80. Set D £43.80. **Service:** 12.5%. **Details:** 50 seats. No music.

Indian Zing

Cool place, hot food
236 King Street, Hammersmith, W6 0RF
Tel no: (020) 8748 5959
www.indianzing.co.uk
⊖ Ravenscourt Park, map 1
Indian | £27
Cooking score: 4

 V

The harmonious mystical principles of Vastu Shastra inform the interiors of Manoj Vasaikar's purple-fronted Indian – although it's a pity that the notion of 'cool' also extends to a 'draughty' tented space at the rear of the dining room. That said, this is a top spot, known for its creative, enlightened cooking, as well as its commitment to free-range and organic produce. Marinated 'gymkhana' lamb chops are reckoned to be 'the greatest on earth', but forthright spicing and exciting flavours also shine through in everything from lobster balchao sweetened with Goan jaggery (unrefined cane sugar) to banana flower and colocasia-leaf kofta in a delicate pumpkin gravy. Indian Zing also plays its part when it comes to healthy eating, offering refreshingly 'zingy' root vegetable and sprouted bean tikki, Maharashtrian vegetable bhanavia (a baked/griddled version of the ubiquitous onion bhajia) and a 'scrumptious' multi-seed take on masala bread-and-butter pudding. Well-chosen, spice-friendly wines start at £16 – note the organic labels and the bottles from India's Sula Vineyard.
Chef/s: Manoj Vasaikar. **Open:** all week L 12 to 3 (1 to 4 Sun), D 6 to 11 (10 Sun). **Meals:** alc (main courses £9 to £20). Set L £12 (2 courses) to £15. **Service:** 12.5%. **Details:** 51 seats. 32 seats outside. Wheelchair access. Music.

Kensington Place

Popular long-standing brasserie
201-209 Kensington Church Street, Notting Hill, W8 7LX
Tel no: (020) 7727 3184
www.kensingtonplace-restaurant.co.uk
⊖ Notting Hill Gate, map 4
Modern British | £25
Cooking score: 2

£30

This popular, lively and noisy dining room virtually defined the London brasserie scene in the late 1980s, and it continues on its merry way, serving food and drink in the cavernous, glass-fronted space overlooking Kensington Church Street. Nowadays the kitchen deals in straightforward Modern British brasserie cooking – a mix of classics (confit duck leg or fish and chips) and more modern ideas such as sea bass with herb gnocchi and brown shrimp velouté. Seasonal tweaks may deliver the likes of new season's lamb with braised lettuce and crushed peas, and rhubarb posset with shortbread. Wine starts at £19.
Chef/s: Daniel Loftin. **Open:** Tue to Sun L 12 to 3 (4 Sun), Mon to Thurs D 6.30 to 10.30 (11 Fri and Sat). **Meals:** alc (main courses £11 to £24). Set L £17 (2 courses) to £20. **Service:** 12.5%. **Details:** 110 seats. Separate bar. Wheelchair access. Music.

READERS RECOMMEND

Kerbisher & Malt

Fish & Chips
164 Shepherd's Bush Road, Hammersmith, W6 7PB
Tel no: (020) 3556 0228
'Really fresh fish and the best chips, it sets a new standard for London chippies. Don't forget to try the pickled onion rings!'

ALSO RECOMMENDED
▲ Kiraku

8 Station Parade, Uxbridge Road, Ealing, W5 3LD
Tel no: (020) 8992 2848
www.kiraku.co.uk
⊖ Ealing Common, map 1
Japanese

Kiraku provides Ealing commuters with a genuine Japanese fix in pared-back, easy-on-the-eye surroundings. The kitchen takes a whistle-stop tour through the country's traditional cuisine, stopping off for zensai appetisers, udon noodles, yakitori skewers, tempura and teriyaki, and a full complement of sushi and sashimi. Don't miss the zany deep-fried pork, Camembert and miso maki rolls (£9.20) or the green-tea sponge cake with kuri ice (£6.20). Saké, shochu and Sapporo beer are better bets than the house wine (£15). Closed Mon.

Kitchen W8

Big-city brio and neighbourhood glitz
11 Abingdon Road, Kensington, W8 6AH
Tel no: (020) 7937 0120
www.kitchenw8.com
⊖ High Street Kensington, map 4
Modern European | £40
Cooking score: 5

Combining the virtues of a special-occasion treat and a 'fabulous' local eatery, Kitchen W8 is proving its worth as a rip-roaring Kensington destination, despite the stripped-bare name and the cool, smartly turned-out interiors (think muted colours and big round mirrors against chic wallpaper). This is a place that happily accommodates all-comers – 'we took six of the pickiest eaters in the world, aged from 5 to 78, and they were delighted', reported one diner. Expect sharply tuned flavours, with touches of new-minted Brit and some Mediterranean sunshine applied to the kitchen's Euro-accented labours. A superbly balanced raviolo of oxtail with bone marrow and chestnut mushrooms impressed one reader, likewise a dish of venison with a powerful beetroot jus. Big-city brio is also the hallmark of roast Orkney scallop with clementine purée and crushed pumpkin or a dish of duck with spiced bread purée, rhubarb, stem ginger and glazed turnips. To finish, a gloriously whiffy cheeseboard awaits – unless you fancy bowing out with, say, bitter chocolate mousse with salted caramel ice cream and thyme purée. W8's wonderfully dedicated, on-the-ball staff deserve a lot of credit, too. The cosmopolitan wine list is a fine match for the food, with prices from £19 (£4.75 a glass) – note that you can BYO on Sunday evenings.

Chef/s: Mark Kempson. **Open:** all week L 12 to 2.30 (12.30 to 3 Sun), D 6 to 10.30 (6.30 to 9.30 Sun). **Closed:** 25 and 26 Dec, bank hols. **Meals:** alc (main courses £18 to £30). Set L £17.50 (2 courses) to £19.50. Set D £21.50 (2 courses) to £24.50. Sun L £29.50. **Service:** 12.5%. **Details:** 75 seats. No music. Wheelchair access.

Koffmann's

The old master is back
The Berkeley, Wilton Place, Belgravia, SW1X 7RL
Tel no: (020) 7235 1010
www.the-berkeley.co.uk
⊖ Knightsbridge, Hyde Park Corner, map 4
French | £55
Cooking score: 5

Pierre Koffmann's was a name to conjure with in the wave of innovative French gastronomy that overtook London in the 1980s, when his La Tante Claire was a reference restaurant. His triumphal return to premises in the Berkeley hotel has been welcomed by many. The pleasantly light basement room is run with polished solicitude by excellent staff, and the cooking, much of which harks back to the chef's Gascon roots, produces many satisfactions. Boudin noir with Bethmale cheese, onions and beetroot is an earthy, no-nonsense starter, and this robust approach is also seen in the pasta-like ribbons of squid that come in a richly reduced bolognaise sauce. Main courses are graceful renditions of hearty peasant cooking: baked skate with herb butter and olives; veal kidneys with wild

mushrooms; beef cheeks braised in red wine; and, of course, the legendary pig trotter, boned and pot-roasted in veal jus, filled with a chicken-based mousse of sweetbreads and morels and served with velvety pomme purée garnished with crackling. Desserts take in classic lemon tart with matching sorbet, and pain perdu served with a roasted banana. Wine prices are quite high, but the selections include some of south west France's star names: Cahors, Gaillac, Madiran, Fronton, Irouléguy. Whites start at £24, reds £26.
Chef/s: Pierre Koffmann. **Open:** all week L 12 to 2.30, D 6 to 10.30. **Meals:** alc (main courses £22 to £60). Set L £21.50 (2 courses) to £25.50. **Service:** 12.5%. **Details:** 115 seats. Separate bar. Wheelchair access. Music.

Launceston Place
Safe, urbane cuisine
1a Launceston Place, South Kensington, W8 5RL
Tel no: (020) 7937 6912
www.launcestonplace-restaurant.co.uk
⊖ Gloucester Road, map 3
Modern British | £46
Cooking score: 4

Deep in residential Kensington, this long-established bastion of the London dining scene offers clever lighting and modern pictures to give the place a chic London club air, offset by a 'quirky English' feel – 'a bit higgledy and the antithesis of the modern fashion'. The cooking is reliable, with nothing to frighten the horses: a mouthful or two of aromatic mushroom froth to get the juices going; a cleverly viscous yolk of a slow-poached duck egg, served with a light asparagus velouté; pork tenderloin keeping company with a deconstructed choucroute, a deep-fried ball of slow-cooked pig's head to further surprise and delight; a very good chocolate and raspberry soufflé (the pudding of choice for most tables). Service is precise and professional to a well-heeled clientele, for whom the house wine (from £25) would be an unlikely choice, given the variety and extent of the cellar.

Chef/s: Tim Allen. **Open:** Tue to Sun L 12 to 2.30 (3 Sun), all week D 6 to 10 (6.30 to 9.45 Sun). **Closed:** 25 and 26 Dec. **Meals:** Set L £19 (2 courses) to £23. Set D £40 (2 courses) to £46. Sun L £27. **Service:** 12.5%. **Details:** 60 seats. Wheelchair access. Music.

★ TOP 50 ★

The Ledbury
Ingenious cooking from a huge talent
127 Ledbury Road, Notting Hill, W11 2AQ
Tel no: (020) 7792 9090
www.theledbury.com
⊖ Notting Hill Gate, Westbourne Park, map 4
Modern French | £80
Cooking score: 8
♦ V

Plying its trade well away from the capital's centres of gastronomic gravity, the über-cool Ledbury is camped between W11's desirable hedge-fund terraces and off-limits high-rise blocks. Famously attacked during the summer riots of 2011, it's a bastion of tasteful affluence – all shades of charcoal grey and cream, with trimmed topiary hiding its city-meets-country terrace, inviting awnings and glimpses of the high-ceilinged dining room from the road. In a cocooned, soigné setting of mirrored walls, arty chandeliers and leather chairs, where everyone is courteously accommodated by a smart, knowledgeable crew. Behind it all is Aussie star Brett Graham, who cooks with astonishing vigour, authority and a master's touch, belting out ingeniously inventive ideas and constantly refining his best-known riffs – few can resist his flame-grilled mackerel with mackerel tartare, avocado and shiso, or his loin of Sika deer resplendent among fronds of resinous Douglas fir. Graham's feel for game in all its seasonal glory also shows in barnstorming combos of pigeon and woodcock served with pretty 'red' accompaniments – beetroot, plums and even cherries (if appropriate). And there's brilliance in the fish department too: how about a tranche of turbot paired with crab, pine nuts, cauliflower and blood-orange? But it isn't all designer brio: a many-coloured

starter of heritage tomatoes with dried olive, green tomato juice and crisp pastry tubes filled with goats' curd is 'a lesson in absolute clarity and intensity', while unabashed simplicity is the key to a staggeringly fine plate involving three cuts of spectacular lamb (thickly sliced loin, soft gooey shoulder and potently rich shank) offset by a slab of luscious aubergine glazed in black sugar and garlic. Occasionally Graham's creative efforts have been known to misfire. Why offer a gorgeous, purple-hued dried-flower parfait adorned with floral whimsies and jewel-like fruit alongside dollops of warm school-dinner tapioca – especially when the kitchen can deliver faultless, light-as-air soufflés, beautifully astringent rhubarb mille-feuille with clementine leaf ice cream, and illuminating variations on olive-oil pannacotta (perhaps with wild strawberries, white chocolate 'snow' and black olive caramel). The deeply serious, cosmopolitan wine list kicks off with a page of top recommendations by the glass, before scouring the globe for majestic Burgundies, Spanish treasures, whizz-bang Aussies and more. Bottles start at £25. Also note the splendid line-up of world beers.
Chef/s: Brett Graham. **Open:** Tue to Sun L 12 to 2 (2.30 Sun), all week D 6.30 to 10.15 (7 to 10 Sun). **Closed:** 25 and 26 Dec, Aug bank hol. **Meals:** alc (main courses £28 to £33). Set L £30 (2 courses) to £35. Set D £80. Sun L £50. Tasting menu £105 (10 courses). **Service:** 12.5%. **Details:** 62 seats. 28 seats outside. No music. Wheelchair access.

READERS RECOMMEND

Lola & Simon
International
278 King Street, Hammersmith, W6 0SP
Tel no: (020) 8563 0300
www.lolaandsimon.co.uk
'The food was so fresh and well presented, and the restaurant itself was very nice on the eye.'

ALSO RECOMMENDED
▲ Madsen
20 Old Brompton Road, South Kensington, SW7 3DL
Tel no: (020) 7225 2772
www.madsenrestaurant.com
⊖ South Kensington, map 3
Scandinavian

Hooked on *The Killing*, *Borgen* and *The Bridge*? Now try the food at this Scandinavian restaurant, a lingonberry's throw from South Kensington tube. Lunch can be as simple as smushi (small versions of the Danish open sandwich); dinner can bring classic onion-marinated herring (£7.95), pork and veal meatballs with red cabbage (£13.50) and a Swedish chocolate cake topped with orange ganache and lingonberry ice cream. Weekend brunch is popular (try the cinnamon rolls), service is attentive, and wines start at £18.50. Closed Sun D.

▲ Malina
166 Shepherd's Bush Road, Hammersmith, W6 7PB
Tel no: (020) 7603 8881
www.malinarestaurant.com
⊖ Hammersmith, map 1
Polish

From the duo who once ran Polish veteran Daquise, Malina is an agreeable neighbourhood drop-in complete with homespun parlour furniture and giant raspberry (malina) motifs on ivory walls. Savoury and sweet pierogi dumplings are typical of a heavy-duty, rustic menu that also offers crisp, warm blinis, beetroot soup (£4.50), and old-fashioned rib-stickers ranging from gypsy pancakes and 'huge' trout baked in sour cucumber brine with dill (£13.90) to bigos stew with sauerkraut and sausage. Shots of vodka and Polish mead are alternatives to the basic wine list (from £13.90). Closed Mon to Fri L.

The Mall Tavern
Buzzing foodie hot spot
71-73 Palace Gardens Terrace, Notting Hill,
W8 4RU
Tel no: (020) 7229 3374
www.themalltavern.com
⊖ Notting Hill Gate, High Street Kensington,
map 4
Modern British | £30
Cooking score: 3

The overriding decorative impression is of
rough-and-ready functionality – close-
packed tables in particular – though locals
have quickly adopted this Victorian tavern as
their ideal neighbourhood eatery. However,
your first request (at dinner) might be for a
torch rather than a drink; as much as we all
love gentle lighting, the dining room is so dim
it's hard to read the menu. But your second
entreaty should be for some fresh, warm soda
bread. And while, at times, the cooking can be
hit and miss, there are good things to be had
on the no-frills British menu, from slow-
cooked egg with salt cod and parsley dressing
via the never-off-the-menu cow pie to
venison and pork meatballs with popped corn.
Seasonal themes also point up desserts such as
Champagne rhubarb trifle. Wines from £17.
Chef/s: Jesse Dunford Wood. **Open:** all week 12 to
10. **Closed:** 1 week Christmas to New Year.
Meals: alc (main courses £13 to £36).
Service: 12.5%. **Details:** 80 seats. 26 seats outside.
Separate bar. Music.

¶|♦ Please send us your feedback
To register your opinion about any
restaurant listed in the Guide, or a new
restaurant that you wish to bring to our
attention, please visit the web address at
the bottom of the page. Your feedback
informs the content of the book and will
be used to compile next year's reviews.

★ TOP 50 ★
Marcus Wareing at the Berkeley
Diverting menus from a stellar chef
The Berkeley, Wilton Place, Belgravia, SW1X 7RL
Tel no: (020) 7235 1200
www.marcus-wareing.com
⊖ Hyde Park Corner, Knightsbridge, map 4
Modern European | £80
Cooking score: 8

One of the most remarkable aspects of Marcus
Wareing's restaurant in this top-notch
Knightsbridge hotel is that it doesn't feel at all
as though you are in a hotel, despite the initial
trip through the lobby. The richness of the
wood panelling, the comfortable padded
chairs and the soft lighting create a cocoon-
like space that, of an evening, fairly glows.
Wareing has become one of London's busiest
consultant chefs, with many outside interests,
but the menus over which he has executive
control here are still reliably among the
capital's most diverting. There is innovation
aplenty, a dedicated team with the technical
skill to realise the more offbeat ideas
successfully, and the fun factor hardly ever
goes missing. Elements combine in a dish like
complex chords – as when seared mackerel
and a scallop escabèche are suddenly thrown
into relief by the citrusy zing of pine-nut and
yuzu sorbet. A spring dish that delighted more
than one reporter consisted of a bowl of whole
tiny peas in pea velouté with a hint of lemon
and a hint of mint, an essay in spring freshness.
Perfectly tender quail arrives with prunes and
Hispi cabbage, and a brilliant foam flavoured
with baked potato; while another bird, Anjou
pigeon this time, forms the basis of an
amalgam of sweet, sour and salt tastes, with its
garnishes of mushrooms, radicchio and
purslane in rich red wine jus. Others have been
impressed by the handling of Herdwick
mutton, its accompaniments of raisins, capers
and cabbage all linked by a thread of cumin
running through the dish. The custard tart
with blood-orange remains a star in the
dessert firmament; a composition of Horlicks

parfait, honey jelly and whisky foam seems more at the drawing-board stage. After one or two concerns in recent years, the pace and tone of service are now back to pitch perfect. Wines are a glittering array, a prolonged exploration of the regions and grapes of all the best producing countries. Even Germany is still anatomised into its regions. Prices are naturally high, but we can imagine what those Meursaults and Gevreys will taste like. House white is £35, red £40.

Chef/s: Marcus Wareing. **Open:** Mon to Fri L 12 to 2.30, Mon to Sat D 6 to 10.30. **Closed:** Sun, 1 Jan. **Meals:** Set L £30 (2 courses) to £38. Set D £80. Chef's menu £120 (7 courses). **Service:** 12.5%. **Details:** 70 seats. No music. Wheelchair access.

ALSO RECOMMENDED
▲ Mari Vanna
Wellington Court, 116 Knightsbridge, Knightsbridge, SW1X 7PJ
Tel no: (020) 7225 3122
www.marivanna.co.uk
⊖ Knightsbridge, map 4
Russian

More a café masquerading as a restaurant, Mari Vanna opens for lunch, does afternoon tea and continues until the last mouthful of smetannik (sour cream cake) has been consumed at dinner. This is Russia straight out of central casting, from the riotous décor to the hearty cooking with lashings of sour cream and the long list of vodkas. Prices can be outrageous (especially wine, from £35) so stick to meat-based borsch (£9), potato and mushroom-filled dumplings (£11) or minced beef and pork pelmeni (ravioli). Utterly charming service. Open all week.

READERS RECOMMEND
Mazi
Greek
12-14 Hillgate Street, Notting Hill, W8 7SR
Tel no: (020) 7229 3794
www.mazi.co.uk
'Fabulous place, great food, great atmosphere! Food was spot on.'

Notting Hill Brasserie
Upper-crust neighbourhood brasserie
92 Kensington Park Road, Notting Hill, W11 2PN
Tel no: (020) 7229 4481
www.nottinghillbrasserie.com
⊖ Notting Hill Gate, map 4
Modern European | £50
Cooking score: 4

There's a touch of calm, worldly sophistication about this upper-crust neighbourhood brasserie that makes it equally inviting for big-occasion bashes and cool, romantic assignations to the accompaniment of live jazz. The place occupies five elegantly appointed rooms in three knocked-together townhouses and justifies its prices with lofty corniced ceilings, cool artwork and long drapes at arched windows. It also delivers on the food front, with highly assured, Med-influenced brasserie cooking in the mould of pan-fried halibut with a risotto of chanterelles and butternut squash or an indulgent dish of roast chicken breast with creamed cabbage, girolle purée, mushroom ravioli and Parmesan. To start, there might be a terrine of foie gras, pheasant and partridge enlivened with vanilla purée. Desserts could usher in warm pear financier with cinnamon ice cream or tarte Tatin with Calvados sauce. The well-spread wine list opens with house selections from £22 (£5.50 a glass). For groovy sounds and snazzy cocktails, try the adjoining No.92 bar.

Chef/s: Karl Burdock. **Open:** Sat and Sun L 12 to 3 (4 Sun), Tue to Sun D 7 to 10.30 (11 Sat, 10 Sun). **Closed:** 25 and 26 Dec, Aug bank hol. **Meals:** alc (main courses £19 to £33). Set L £15.50 (2 courses) to £19.50. Sun L £29.50 (2 courses) to £36.50. **Service:** 12.5%. **Details:** 100 seats. Separate bar. Wheelchair access. Music.

Readers Recommend
A 'readers recommend' review is a genuine quote from a report sent in by one of our readers. We intend to follow up these suggestions throughout the year to come.

One-O-One

Top-end seafood cookery
Sheraton Park Tower, 101 Knightsbridge,
Knightsbridge, SW1X 7RN
Tel no: (020) 7290 7101
www.oneoonerestaurant.com
⊖ Knightsbridge, map 4
Seafood | £55
Cooking score: 5

One-O-One is a victim of its own reputation. For many years it was seen as a major venue by people who enjoy seafood, but things elsewhere have come on apace in recent years. There is an impression that, while Pascal Proyart's standards have not changed, others have surpassed him through the astonishing enthusiasm and dedication that pervades the UK dining scene these days. The result is that diners now arrive with more acute requirements and he has not responded. The ambience doesn't help – 'this is clearly a hotel dining room' – though the food is still good. One visitor reported on a meal that was faultless from the yellowfin tuna tartare with crispy soft-shell crab tempura, sushi rice and wasabi sorbet through to wild sea bass baked in salt with a Champagne-butter sauce. But balance this against the muddled, muted flavours of native lobster with summer vegetable macedoine salad, lobster pastilla and green pea sorbet, and a less-than-inspired dessert of minted fresh raspberry with pink Champagne jelly and white chocolate ice cream. However, meat is a comfortable bedfellow on the menu; spring English lamb fillet with olive and rosemary, green asparagus and wild garlic gnocchi was considered a real treat by one reporter. The wine list is interesting but overly expensive; from £31.
Chef/s: Pascal Proyart. **Open:** all week L 12 to 2.30 (12.30 Sat and Sun), D 6.30 to 10. **Closed:** 25 Dec, 1 Jan. **Meals:** alc (main courses £27 to £39). Set L £17 (2 courses) to £22. Tasting menu £59 (6 courses). **Service:** 12.5%. **Details:** 55 seats. Separate bar. Wheelchair access. Music. Car parking.

Pétrus

Well-crafted, flavour-packed French food
1 Kinnerton Street, Knightsbridge, SW1X 8EA
Tel no: (020) 7592 1609
www.gordonramsay.com
⊖ Knightsbridge, map 4
Modern French | £65
Cooking score: 5

The central feature of Pétrus is a glass-fronted wine store – the sommelier will happily conduct you round it if you have the time – and Pétrus claret red features in the restaurant's colour scheme. Sean Burbidge has the contemporary French style off to a T, producing well-crafted dishes that look the part and are all about contrasting intensities of flavour. Reports of the good-value lunch menu are as enthusiastic as ever: crisply cooked red mullet with a bouillabaisse poured over it; beef carpaccio with foie gras; breast and stuffed leg of lamb with wild mushrooms and a brilliant dauphinois are all mentioned in dispatches. At dinner, the ante is upped and dishes become exhilaratingly creative and complex, starting perhaps with langoustine fricassee with snails, chicken wing and parsley cream, then red-leg partridge with pancetta, ceps and chestnuts. One pair were urged to order the signature dessert, a chocolate sphere filled with milk ice-cream and garnished with honeycomb; they opted instead for superb pistachio parfait with sour cherries and elderflower foam and got a taster of the sphere anyway with petits fours. The weighty wine list is a classicist's dream, but may call for one of those bank loans you can't get any more. Whites start at £23, reds at £30.
Chef/s: Sean Burbidge. **Open:** Mon to Sat L 12 to 2.30, D 6.30 to 10.30. **Closed:** Sun. **Meals:** Set L £30. Set D £65. Tasting menu £75 (7 courses). **Service:** 12.5%. **Details:** 55 seats. Separate bar. No music. Wheelchair access.

El Pirata Detapas
Funky vibes and trendy tapas
115 Westbourne Grove, Notting Hill, W2 4UP
Tel no: (020) 7727 5000
www.elpiratadetapas.co.uk
⊖ Notting Hill Gate, Bayswater, map 4
Spanish | £20
Cooking score: 3

Sleek, funky and polished, this white-tiled offshoot of El Pirata in Mayfair is spread over two levels, with a private basement room showcasing legs of Iberian ham. Tapas chart-toppers such as crispy fried squid, grilled chorizo and toasted bread with tomatoes share the billing with more experimental ideas inspired by the Iberian new wave. Executive chef Omar Allibhoy spent time with Spanish master Ferran Adrià, so expect flashes of El Bulli élan when it comes to octopus carpaccio with dots of clementine 'caviar', capers, paprika and Albequina olive oil, six-hour belly pork with red-wine pear and parsnip purée, or chicken roulade with walnuts and herby mojo verde. Paellas are fine for sharing. Finish with a combo of chocolate truffles, chocolate mousse and saffron toffee. Terrific Spanish regional wines (from £15) too.
Chef/s: Neftali Cumplido and Omar Allibhoy. **Open:** Mon to Fri L 12 to 3, D 6 to 11, Sat and Sun 12 to 11. **Closed:** 25 to 28 Dec, 1 Jan, Aug bank hol. **Meals:** alc (tapas £3 to £20). Set L £9.95 (2 courses) to £21. Set D £12 (2 courses) to £21. Chef's menu £25. **Service:** 12.5%. **Details:** 90 seats. Wheelchair access. Music.

🍴 Please send us your feedback

To register your opinion about any restaurant listed in the Guide, or a new restaurant that you wish to bring to our attention, please visit the web address at the bottom of the page. Your feedback informs the content of the book and will be used to compile next year's reviews.

NEW ENTRY
Pizza East Portobello
Crowd-pulling pizzas come west
310 Portobello Road, Ladbroke Grove, W10 5TA
Tel no: (020) 8969 4500
www.pizzaeastportobello.com
⊖ Ladbroke Grove, map 1
Italian-American | £22
Cooking score: 2

Pizza East Portobello is a much more intimate affair than the vast Shoreditch original (see entry, Pizza East). The pseudo-industrial vibe continues, albeit softened by a bright corner site decked out in stripped wood and tiles. Expert pizzas steal the headlines on the Italian-American menu – the sage, veal meatballs and cream option alone is worth the trip – but the wood oven also kicks out a great veal bone marrow starter as well as mac 'n' cheese and crispy belly pork with lentils. The cured meat selection deserves an honourable mention, while salted chocolate caramel tart stands out among the desserts. Wines from £17.50.
Chef/s: Tim Fuller and Kyle Boyce. **Open:** all week 8am to 11.30pm (12am Fri and Sat, 10pm Sun). **Closed:** 25 Dec. **Meals:** alc (main courses £7 to £17). **Service:** 12.5%. **Details:** 139 seats. 26 seats outside. Separate bar. Wheelchair access. Music.

Popeseye
Sticking to steak
108 Blythe Road, Olympia, W14 0HD
Tel no: (020) 7610 4578
www.popeseye.com
⊖ Olympia, map 1
Steaks | £20
Cooking score: 1

The steak, the whole steak and nothing but the steak – that's the promise at this red-blooded eatery. Ian Hutchinson was dealing in slabs of properly aged, grass-fed Aberdeen Angus long before meat-fests became trendy, and he keeps it simple: just three cuts – sirloin, fillet and rump (aka popeseye) – grilled to

order and served with chips and optional salad. That's it, apart from farmhouse cheeses and a few puds. Wine from £13.50. Also at 277 Upper Richmond Road, Putney; tel (020) 8788 7733.
Chef/s: Ian Hutchinson. **Open:** Mon to Sat D only 6.45 to 10. **Closed:** Sun, 24 Dec to 3 Jan. **Meals:** alc (steaks £10 to £46). **Service:** 12.5%. **Details:** Cash only. 34 seats. No music.

Portobello Ristorante Pizzeria
Eat-me pizza for sharing
7 Ladbroke Road, Notting Hill, W11 3PA
Tel no: (020) 7221 1373
www.portobellolondon.co.uk
⊖ Notting Hill Gate, map 4
Italian | £35
Cooking score: 1

'Much better than your average pizzeria' pronounced a reporter of this regulation neighbourhood haunt, which peddles 'pizzametro' – pizza by the half and whole metre – noted for thin crusts and good ingredients. Other dishes can ratchet up the earthiness, from well-reported pasta (perhaps spaghetti alla vongole) to char-grilled Italian sausage with roast potatoes and diavola sauce. It's cramped, but the atmosphere is easy-going and the front terrace is a great place to enjoy a lazy summer lunch. Wines from £17.
Chef/s: Andrea Ippolito. **Open:** all week 12 to 11.30 (10.30 Sun). **Closed:** 25 and 26 Dec. **Meals:** alc (main courses £9 to £20). Set L £12.50.
Service: 12.5%. **Details:** 60 seats. 28 seats outside.

Symbols
🛏 Accommodation is available
£30 Three courses for less than £30
V Separate vegetarian menu
£5 OFF £5-off voucher scheme
🍾 Notable wine list

NEW ENTRY
Potli
Authentic Indian street food
319-321 King Street, Hammersmith, W6 9NH
Tel no: (020) 8741 4328
www.potli.co.uk
⊖ Ravenscourt Park, Stamford Brook, map 1
Indian | £24
Cooking score: 3

West London locals should be cock-a-hoop that this unpretentious Indian has pitched up on their doorstep – it deserves to be packed out nightly. Interiors keep it simple: it's the authentic Indian street food that wows. Vegetarian and meat curries impress but, better still, opt for a selection of sharing starters and let the kitchen walk you through India's famous street markets, from Chowpatty to Aminabad. The likes of aloo tikki with chole (spiced potato cakes on a chickpea masala), baby fenugreek leaf bhajia, a first-rate chicken tikka selection, and marinated lamb-leg steaks slow-cooked on limestone are as authentic Indian food as you will find outside the subcontinent. Wines from £14.
Chef/s: Jay Ghosh. **Open:** all week L 12 to 2.45 (4 Sun), D 6 to 10.30 (11 Fri and Sat). **Meals:** alc (main courses £8 to £13). Set L £9.95. Sun L £10.99. **Service:** 12.5%. **Details:** 80 seats. 24 seats outside. Separate bar. Wheelchair access. Music.

The Princess Victoria
Superior pub food and glorious wines
217 Uxbridge Road, Shepherd's Bush, W12 9DH
Tel no: (020) 8749 5886
www.princessvictoria.co.uk
⊖ Shepherd's Bush Market, map 1
British | £27
Cooking score: 3

Built as a splendid gin palace in the 1820s, when Victoria was still a princess, this Shepherd's Bush pub has been restored and lightly modernised, with plenty of pictures and the odd animal head. It does superior pub food well: perhaps jugged hare on sourdough toast as a starter, followed by stone bass with saffron linguine in crab bisque, or tender Tamworth pork with potato gratin and bacon in marjoram jus. The house 'pork board' encourages the best type of pigging out, featuring everything from pâté to black pudding, rillettes to scratchings. Warm Eccles cakes come with a slab of Scottish Dunsyre Blue (a shock to Lancashire purists), while sticky toffee pudding with toffee pecan sauce is reliably weighty. The principal glory is a very fine, knowledgeable wine list, which arcs confidently across the globe at prices to welcome you in, rather than make you sigh with regret. Glasses from £3.95, bottles £15.90.

Chef/s: Matt Reuther. **Open:** all week 12 to 10.30 (9.30 Sun). **Closed:** 24 to 27 Dec, bank hols, 2 weeks August. **Meals:** alc (main courses £10 to £23). Set L £12.50 (2 courses, Mon-Fri). **Service:** not inc. **Details:** 120 seats. 25 seats outside. Separate bar. Music. Car parking.

Racine

Classic and comforting French food
239 Brompton Road, Knightsbridge, SW3 2EP
Tel no: (020) 7584 4477
www.racine-restaurant.com
⊖ Knightsbridge, South Kensington, map 3
French | £50
Cooking score: 4

Henry Harris's unpretentious Knightsbridge brasserie (think brown hues, mirrors and close-packed tables) continues to please. Although long-established, it manages to achieve a freshness of welcome and attention that wins friends, and to produce classic and comforting French cooking that is at once familiar (filet au poivre, grilled rabbit and mustard sauce) and sufficiently aware of changes of taste to have current appeal. This is a neighbourhood restaurant par excellence that has never rested on its laurels. Successes have included crab salad with herb omelette and horseradish, soft roes and sorrel on toast, excellent grilled lamb chops and a very good tête de veau with a sauce ravigote. Among

desserts, pear and chocolate profiteroles are much approved. A likeable wine list, strong on France, comes with good choice by the glass; bottles from £20.

Chef/s: Henry Harris. **Open:** all week L 12 to 3 (3.30 Sat and Sun), D 6 to 10.30 (10 Sun). **Closed:** 25 Dec. **Meals:** alc (main courses £17 to £29). Set L and D £15.50 (2 courses) to £17.75. Sun L £18 (2 courses) to £20. **Service:** 14.5%. **Details:** 60 seats. 4 seats outside. No music. Wheelchair access.

Rasoi

Luxurious Indian flagship
10 Lincoln Street, Chelsea, SW3 2TS
Tel no: (020) 7225 1881
www.rasoirestaurant.co.uk
⊖ Sloane Square, map 3
Indian | £59
Cooking score: 5
V

Ring the doorbell to gain entrance, and take the trip from upper-class Chelsea chic into a world of silk drapes, murals, ceremonial masks, temple bells and religious effigies, with the perfume of incense and aromatic spices hanging in the air. Welcome to Rasoi Vineet Bhatia – a flagship for the Indian new wave, suffused with vivacious flavours and culinary themes a world away from Friday night curry-house vindaloos. Consider this: sea bass served two ways with a beetroot and pea upma (a semolina-based dish), white tomato foam and a sauce of lemongrass and coconut, or perhaps spiced cobnut chicken with pickle-infused achari potatoes, crispy onion rings and tarka dhal sauce. Street snacks are given an inventive workout, likewise veggie specialities such as asparagus and carrot parcels with okra pilau, pineapple stew and plantain crisps. There is also a fondness for princely, gilded Mughal-style embellishments, be it a silver-crusted olive chutney with sesame-spiced cod or gold-topped gulab jamun alongside a rose petal mousse. Prices may be more eye watering than the food itself, although you can keep it tight by opting for the more affordable set lunch. Wines are also tailored for fatter wallets, but the quality is high and there is plenty to enjoy if you're after a spice-friendly tipple. Bottles start at £26 (£6 a glass).

Chef/s: Vineet Bhatia. **Open:** Sun to Fri L 12 to 2.30, all week D 6 to 10.30 (10 Sun). **Closed:** 25 and 26 Dec, 1 Jan. **Meals:** alc (main courses £24 to £35). Set L £22 (2 courses) to £27. Set D £49 (2 courses) to £59. Sun L £22. Tasting menu £87 (7 courses). **Service:** 12.5%. **Details:** 50 seats. No music.

★ CHEF OF THE YEAR 2013 – CLARE SMYTH ★
★ TOP 50 ★

Restaurant Gordon Ramsay
Graceful new dishes and glorious classics
68-69 Royal Hospital Road, Chelsea, SW3 4HP
Tel no: (020) 7352 4441
www.gordonramsay.com/royalhospitalroad
⊖ Sloane Square, map 3
Modern French | £95
Cooking score: 9

V

It's tough at the top. On the one hand, having refined what you do to such a pitch of excellence that the plaudits and the international custom keep on flowing, the temptation may be to stick rather than twist. On the other, where do consistency and tenacity become inert familiarity? Since last year's Guide, Clare Smyth and her team have been on a fact-finding mission to some of the pace-setting redoubts of the *nueva cocina* in northern Spain, and the research has paid handsome dividends. New dishes have been developed, all stamped with a gracefully light touch and an even firmer grasp of seasonality. A trio of Isle of Skye scallops appears amid a brilliant amalgam of heritage apple, walnuts, celery and an emulsified cider sauce, blending sweet and sour. Roast fillet of Cornish turbot is wrapped in Ibérico ham to give just enough salty tang, anointed with a buttery asparagus stock and decorated with a few edible flowers, a dish with more daring delicacy to it than Ramsay himself might have essayed. That said, the best of the Hospital Road classics remain: the glorious ravioli of lobster, langoustine and salmon in lemongrass and chervil velouté; the powerfully rich sautéed foie gras with roasted

veal sweetbreads, Cabernet Sauvignon vinegar and velouté of almond. The peripheral detailing clinches the deal. It's the appetiser soups and pre-dessert froths that can so often appear perfunctory in this context. Not so here. A pre-dessert of eucalyptus jelly worked through with a crunchy gravel of lime and mint, with apple sorbet, avocado mousse and the oriental waft of shiso leaf speaks of all the innovative excitement that went into its creation. When it comes to wine, there's global breadth and excellence of pedigree, and the provision of some relatively kindly priced wines at the lower end (say, below £40). Bottles start at £28, small glasses at £6, for the dependable dry white Bordeaux of Château Bauduc.

Chef/s: Clare Smyth. **Open:** Mon to Fri L 12 to 2.30, D 6.30 to 11. **Closed:** Sat, Sun, 25 and 26 Dec. **Meals:** Set L £45. Set D £95. Tasting menu £125 (7 courses). **Service:** 12.5%. **Details:** 45 seats. No music.

Restaurant Michael Nadra
Stylish and satisfying Chiswick favourite
6-8 Elliott Road, Chiswick, W4 1PE
Tel no: (020) 8742 0766
www.restaurant-michaelnadra.co.uk
⊖ Turnham Green, map 1
Modern European | £35
Cooking score: 4

Chiswick isn't short of modern European brasserie eating, and yet Michael Nadra's stylish eatery, with its chocolate-brown banquette seating, tiled floor and marine-themed pictures, makes enough of a statement to get itself noticed. A large part of its appeal is the assured, no-nonsense cooking, which mixes and matches influences to produce satisfying dishes. Serrano ham comes with Puglian burrata, wild rocket and basil, in a dazzling dressing of Kalamata olive oil and pomegranate molasses. Main courses pile in the ingredients in happy profusion: steamed sea bass and black tiger prawns arrive in chestnut velouté with pearl barley, all fired up with chilli and roasted garlic; or there could be lamb rump with flageolets and cauliflower purée in rosemary and garlic sauce. Twenty minutes' wait is rewarded with a chocolate fondant, served with salted caramel and vanilla ice cream. Wines open with a good glass selection from £4.50; bottles from £16. **Chef/s:** Michael Nadra. **Open:** all week L 12 to 2.30 (3.30 Sat and Sun), Mon to Sat D 6 to 10 (10.30 Fri and Sat). **Closed:** 24 to 26 Dec, 1 Jan. **Meals:** Set L £19.50 (2 courses) to £24. Set D £29 (2 courses) to £35. Tasting menu L £39 (6 courses). Tasting menu D £49 (6 courses). **Service:** 12.5%. **Details:** 55 seats. Music.

The River Café
Italian icon by the river
Thames Wharf, Rainville Road, Hammersmith, W6 9HA
Tel no: (020) 7386 4200
www.rivercafe.co.uk
⊖ Hammersmith, map 1
Italian | £60
Cooking score: 6
🍷

It may have been buffeted by misfortune in recent times, but the iconic River Café rolls on and, 25 years down the line, it remains one of the finest advertisements for Italian regional cooking in the capital. The riverside setting is a big plus and in fine weather it's a top choice for eating alfresco; otherwise, tables amid the high-arched ceilings, steel and glass of the bright, white dining room are at a premium. Steep prices and strictly enforced time slots rarely dampen readers' enthusiasm for food that sings with seasonal vitality. Robust homemade pasta is a winning call (perhaps ravioli stuffed with wild hops, nettles and buffalo ricotta, or taglierini with clams, chilli and zucchini flowers). The wood-fired oven and char-grill also earn their keep, however: in April you might be greeted by monkfish with anchovy and rosemary sauce, Castelluccio lentils and Florence fennel, or slow-cooked veal shin in Soave Classico with thyme, artichokes and Swiss chard; fast-forward six months and you might encounter roast Yorkshire grouse on Capezzana di Carmignano bruschetta, or pork leg wrapped in Parma ham with squash. What these disparate dishes have in common is diligent sourcing, a dedication to vigorous rustic flavours, and an intuitive feel for plants with a purpose – be it fragrant leaves or profuse veggie adornments. To finish, it's hard to trump the legendary chocolate nemesis, although the pannacotta with grappa and seasonal fruit comes a close second. Apart from Billecart-Salmon Champagne, the wine list is an unrepentantly chauvinistic tribute to the glories of Italian regional viticulture, taking in Piedmont, Tuscany, Sardinia and all points in between. Sub-£30 bottles are sparse, but you're paying for quality here. **Chef/s:** Ruth Rogers. **Open:** all week L 12.30 to 2.15 (12 Sun), Mon to Sat D 7 to 11 (11.30 Fri and Sat). **Closed:** 24 Dec to 1 Jan, bank hols. **Meals:** alc (main courses £32 to £45). **Service:** 12.5%. **Details:** 110 seats. 30 seats outside. Separate bar. No music. Wheelchair access.

Salloos
Distinguished ambassador for Pakistani cooking
62-64 Kinnerton Street, Knightsbridge, SW1X 8ER
Tel no: (020) 7235 4444
⊖ Knightsbridge, map 4
Pakistani | £40
Cooking score: 2

Set on a side street in the heart of London's embassy district, Salloos has been a distinguished ambassador for Pakistani cooking for 35 years. Its longevity means that the kitchen very much subscribes to the 'ain't broke, don't fix it' school of thought, with well-rehearsed tandoori classics spearheading the menu – expect big, muscular flavours from the signature lamb chops, shish kebabs and tikka dishes. Diners would do well to opt for Salloos' specialities, many of them cribbed from the owner's mother's recipe book; perhaps haleem akbari (shredded lamb cooked with wheatgerm, lentils and spices). A good-sized wine list starts at £20.

Chef/s: Abdul Aziz. **Open:** Mon to Sat L 12 to 2.30, D 7 to 11.15. **Closed:** Sun, 25 and 26 Dec. **Meals:** alc (main courses £16 to £20). **Service:** 12.5%. **Details:** 55 seats. No music.

Sam's Brasserie & Bar

Busy, buzzy neighbourhood brasserie
11 Barley Mow Passage, Chiswick, W4 4PH
Tel no: (020) 8987 0555
www.samsbrasserie.co.uk
⊖ Chiswick Park, Turnham Green, map 1
Modern European | £30
Cooking score: 2

Live music at the weekend, 'accommodating service' and a new lunchtime take-away menu are just three reasons why this busy, buzzy sibling of Harrison's in Balham (see entry) is a winner with the Chiswick crowd. The kitchen roams around the globe, picking up New England clam chowder, tuna tartare and a well-reported Goan fish curry along the way, although its backbone is a solid contingent of pan-European staples ranging from rabbit and foie gras terrine to mustard-crusted rack of salt marsh lamb with pea and mint risotto. To finish, banana crème brûlée and flourless chocolate cake get the nod. Wines start at £16 (£4.50 a glass).
Chef/s: Ian Leckie. **Open:** all week L 12 to 3 (4 Sat and Sun), D 6.30 to 10.30 (9.30 Sun). **Closed:** 24 to 28 Dec. **Meals:** alc (main courses £12 to £21). Mon to Fri set L and early D £13.50 (2 courses) to £16.50. **Service:** 12.5%. **Details:** 100 seats. Separate bar. Wheelchair access. Music.

The Sands End

Nicely scrubbed-up pub with spirited food
135-137 Stephendale Road, Fulham, SW6 2PR
Tel no: (020) 7731 7823
www.thesandsend.co.uk
⊖ Fulham Broadway, map 3
British | £25
Cooking score: 3

£30

A likeable pub on an unassuming residential street in Fulham, the Sands End follows the dress code for the well-appointed boozer about town – blackboards, chunky wooden tables, and real ales and superior Scotch eggs at the bar. Buoyed by the arrival of Nathan Green, the kitchen too has been scrubbing up nicely, with a good balance of butch British steaks and roasts, as well as dishes where Mediterranean sensibilities are at play, say a spicy starter of roast red pepper and plum tomato soup, drizzled with black olive oil. Mains are similarly simple but spirited: tender Wiltshire downland spring lamb with broad beans excelled on inspection; or perhaps opt for Irish sea trout with girolle mushrooms. A decent selection of wines starts at £18.
Chef/s: Nathan Green. **Open:** all week L 12 to 3, D 6 to 10. **Closed:** 25 Dec, 1 Jan. **Meals:** alc (main courses £13 to £25). Set L £13.50 (2 courses) to £16.50. Sun L £15.50. **Service:** 12.5%. **Details:** 65 seats. 16 seats outside. Separate bar. Wheelchair access. Music.

The Thomas Cubitt

Versatile Belgravia pub-cum-restaurant
44 Elizabeth Street, Belgravia, SW1W 9PA
Tel no: (020) 7730 6060
www.thethomascubitt.co.uk
⊖ Victoria, map 3
Modern British | £36
Cooking score: 3

Master builder Thomas Cubitt might be surprised to see how this Georgian townhouse has been cleverly transformed for the twenty-first century. As an all-purpose pub-cum-restaurant it does swanky Belgravia proud, with proceedings divided between the convivial bar and the more elegant first-floor dining room (think duck-egg-blue walls lined with architectural prints); there's also a new function space at the top of the building. If pints of ale, cocktails and plates of steak and Guinness pie don't appeal, head upstairs for more refined satisfaction in the shape of hot-smoked duck breast with sweet potato and pickled cherry jus, or salmon and spinach wellington with celeriac and Champagne sauce. To begin, try roast veal sweetbreads

with walnut and black pudding; to finish, consider Earl Grey brûlée with cinnamon doughnuts. House wine is £18.
Chef/s: Phillip Wilson. **Open:** all week L 12 to 3.30, D 6 to 10.30. **Closed:** 25 and 26, 31 Dec. **Meals:** alc (main courses £17 to £28). Set L £17.50 (2 courses). Sun L £17 (2 courses) to £19.50. **Service:** 12.5%. **Details:** 130 seats. 26 seats outside. Separate bar. Music.

Timo

Convivial, intimate neighbourhood Italian
343 Kensington High Street, Kensington, W8 6NW
Tel no: (020) 7603 3888
www.timorestaurant.net
↔ High Street Kensington, map 3
Italian | £38
Cooking score: 2
£5 OFF

This intimately arranged space is convivial, service is courteous and the modern Italian cooking reveals a light touch. This amounts to starters such as burrata di Andria (creamy mozzarella from Andria) with a coulis of fresh tomatoes and basil, or linguine with fresh clams, chilli, olive oil, garlic and parsley. Among main courses have been a first-rate char-grilled ribeye with rosemary roast potatoes, rocket and Parmesan shavings, and baked John Dory fillet with tarragon risotto. Typical desserts include pannacotta and tiramisu. The whole of Italy is covered by the wine list, which features some good producers; bottles from £18.50.
Chef/s: Luca Bevere. **Open:** Mon to Sat L 12 to 2.30, D 6.30 to 11. **Closed:** Sun, 23 to 27 Dec, bank hols. **Meals:** alc (main courses £7 to £23). Set L and D (6.30 to 8) £14.90 (2 courses) to £18.90. **Service:** 12.5%. **Details:** 49 seats. 2 seats outside. Separate bar. Music.

🍴 **Visit us Online**
To find out more about
The Good Food Guide, please visit
www.thegoodfoodguide.co.uk

Tinello

The Italians' Italian
87 Pimlico Road, Pimlico, SW1W 8PH
Tel no: (020) 7730 3663
www.tinello.co.uk
↔ Sloane Square, map 3
Italian | £49
Cooking score: 4

It's reassuring when Italian restaurants are frequented by Italians; Tinello is one such, so the rest of us might be wise to take the hint. But then owners Federico and Max Sali are Giorgio Locatelli protégés and they manage to encapsulate what makes Italian food so special – the basis of the menu is rooted in really good raw ingredients and the kitchen knows its techniques. Shared 'small eats' make a diverting opener, along the lines of fried courgettes, burrata cheese and pomegranate, and chicken liver crostini. You might opt for an intermediate pasta course in the Italian way – perhaps homemade pappardelle with hare ragù – or just steam straight to the main courses, where roast plaice fillet with cannellini beans and mussels or hearty bollito misto await. Desserts are a familiar line-up of tiramisu, cantucci with vin santo and ice creams. The wine list favours Italy; house selections start at £14.50.
Chef/s: Federico Sali. **Open:** all week L 12 to 2.30, D 6.15 to 10.30. **Closed:** 24 to 27 Dec, bank hols. **Meals:** alc (main courses £11 to £26). **Service:** not inc. **Details:** 76 seats. No music.

Tom Aikens

Good-looks and imagination from a Chelsea star
43 Elystan Street, Chelsea, SW3 3NT
Tel no: (020) 7584 2003
www.tomaikens.co.uk
↔ South Kensington, map 3
Modern French | £45
Cooking score: 6
£5 OFF V

'Copenhagen-meets-Chelsea' is one way of looking at Tom Aikens' proposed 'new vision' in his redesigned restaurant. The chef has plumped for an haute-cuisine version of the pseudo-industrial look favoured by many new London openings, with food quotes stencilled on monochrome walls standing in for bespoke graffiti. And it's oh-so-casual – tables are bare, and staff (charming) dressed in an Abercrombie & Fitch sort of way. Aikens has flirted with extravagant combinations, foams and daubs over the years, but his cooking now has a more orthodox bent, with the emphasis on exquisite presentation and imaginatively worked ingredients. At an early summer meal, seasonal alliances yielded poached loin of rabbit with a fantastic riff on new season's peas – whole, puréed, velouté, snow – dotted with tiny flavour bombs of intense white balsamic jelly, and sesame-coated pollack teamed with fennel purée and a delicious dill juice. There was seasonal resonance, too, in a dish of baby Cumbrian lamb 'of incredible flavour', but that was served with heavy-handed accompaniments – fiercely roasted new season's garlic, chipolino onion and rather dense aligot potato – indicating that consistency can be a bugbear. Seasoning has been uncertain, and some trendy combinations and obscure ingredients (roast and braised leeks with accompanying crispy crumbs, snow and purée) leave diners puzzled. There's praise, however, for dessert – candied beetroot (beetroot every which way with goats' curd and yoghurt) – and breads and petits fours 'are amazing'. As for the wine list, expect a trustworthy selection across the globe, with prices from £24.

Chef/s: Tom Aikens. **Open:** Mon to Fri L 12 to 2.30, Mon to Sat D 6.45 to 10.30. **Closed:** Sun, 25 to 26 Dec, bank hols. **Meals:** alc (main courses £21 to £32). Set L 24 (2 courses) to £29. Tasting menu £60 (6 courses) to £80 (8 courses). **Service:** 12.5%. **Details:** 60 seats. Wheelchair access. Music.

HÉLÈNE DARROZE
The Connaught

When did you realise you wanted to be a chef?
I am a fourth generation descendent in a long line of chefs, and was born in a region of France where the arts of living, hospitality and eating well are very important. When you mix them all you get a fate from which it is difficult to escape.

What is your biggest kitchen bugbear?
I don't like a microwave in the kitchen.

What food trends are you spotting at the moment?
I cook with my heart and my emotions and don't follow trends or fashion. I think my way of cooking gradually adapts to what my guests expect from me.

What advice would you give a chef starting their career?
My philosophy is all about respect and communication. Be organised, be sensitive to other people's emotions and work hard.

Which chefs do you admire, and why?
Michel Bras, for his talent and for being an inspiration to chefs around the world.

Sum up your cooking style in three words
Produce, authenticity and emotion.

Tom's Kitchen

Laid-back brasserie
27 Cale Street, Chelsea, SW3 3QP
Tel no: (020) 7349 0202
www.tomskitchen.co.uk
⊖ Sloane Square, South Kensington, map 3
Modern British | £40
Cooking score: 2

The burgeoning of Chelsea star Tom Aikens'
restaurant empire began in 2006 when this
offshoot opened a few hundred yards away
from the mothership. It's a former pub turned
laid-back brasserie, with a bar upstairs
equipped with cocktails and Wi-Fi. Beef from
a Devon farm appears on the menus as tartare,
grilled sandwiches, burgers and steaks, and
there's a roll-call of brasserie favourites to back
it up, from sardines niçoise to salmon
fishcakes, and veal and pork meatballs with
polenta. Finish with baked Alaska for two, or
lemon meringue pie. Wines kick off at £18.50
(£5 a glass) for house Sicilian.
Chef/s: Tom Aikens. **Open:** all week 8 to 2.30 (10 to
3.30 Sat and Sun), D 6 to 10.30 (9.30 Sun). **Closed:**
24 to 26 Dec. **Meals:** alc (main courses £14 to £30).
Service: 12.5%. **Details:** 90 seats. Separate bar.
Wheelchair access. Music.

ALSO RECOMMENDED

▲ Tosa

332 King Street, Hammersmith, W6 0RR
Tel no: (020) 8748 0002
www.tosauk.com
⊖ Ravenscourt Park, Stamford Brook, map 1
Japanese £5
OFF

With its robata grill glowing next to the
entrance, diminutive Tosa sets out its stall as a
streetwise purveyor of yakitori, kushiyaki and
other skewered morsels (from around £2 a
go). Try the pork with shiso leaf, chicken livers
and quails' eggs, or salt mackerel and salmon
cheeks. The list of esoteric sushi and
traditional specialities ranges from eel nigiri
and octopus sashimi (£9.50) to natto maki
rolls (fermented beancurd). House wine is
£13.50. Open all week. Also at 152 High
Road, East Finchley; tel (020) 8883 8850.

La Trompette

A beacon of excellence
5-7 Devonshire Road, Chiswick, W4 2EU
Tel no: (020) 8747 1836
www.latrompette.co.uk
⊖ Turnham Green, map 1
Modern European | £43
Cooking score: 5

Some 13 years since it first opened, this elegant
neighbourhood restaurant on a boutique-
lined street just off Chiswick High Road
continues to be a shining beacon of excellence
in west London. An old hand reports that 'the
menu is appealing, the dishes not too
ambitious so can be consistently cooked, and
the service is great (as is the wine list)'. The
pattern set by Anthony Boyd last year has
continued, his modern approach underpinned
by a classical theme and driven by an awareness
of the seasons and an instinctive feel for
flavour combinations that work. Tastes are
rounded; among highlights this year have
been loin and haché of venison with braised
red cabbage, onion purée and a well-made
sauce poivrade, and perfectly timed sea bass
with Jerusalem artichoke purée, parsley root,
roast salsify and red wine vinaigrette. This is
cooking that achieves what it sets out to do, be
it a rich foie gras and chicken liver parfait with
dressed lentils to start, or an exemplary Black
Forest ice cream as a finale. A thoroughgoing
comprehensiveness brings quality European
and southern hemisphere wines, as well as
oodles of posh French gear, on to a
majestically sweeping list. Prices open
at £17.50.
Chef/s: Anthony Boyd. **Open:** all week L 12 to 2.30
(12.30 to 3 Sun), D 6.30 to 10.30 (9.30 Sun). **Closed:**
24 to 26 Dec. **Meals:** Set L £23.50 (2 courses) to
£27.50. Early D £19.50. Set D £37.50 (2 courses) to
£42.50. Sun L £32.50. **Service:** 12.5%. **Details:** 72
seats. 16 seats outside. No music. Wheelchair
access.

Le Vacherin

Warmly comforting neighbourhood bistro
76-77 South Parade, Chiswick, W4 5LF
Tel no: (020) 8742 2121
www.levacherin.com
⊖ Chiswick Park, map 1
French | £35
Cooking score: 4

A well-established outpost of French civilisation in deepest Chiswick, Malcolm John's warmly comforting neighbourhood bistro sails on, oblivious to culinary trends and passing fads. The low-lit elegance of the place puts everyone in a feel-good frame of mind, and there's nothing scary about a menu that touts pigeon salad with Cassis, salt-cured foie gras, escargots de Bourgogne or frogs' legs with clams and Tamworth pork belly among its starters. After that, honest, thoughtful and generous ideas abound: a four-part assiette of hare with stuffed cabbage; char-grilled filet mignon with sautéed ceps, gnocchi and Madeira jus; confit of Gressingham duck with braised endive and sauce à l'orange. The gooey namesake cheese also makes a timely appearance in traditional company with almonds, truffles, pickles and Bayonne ham, while desserts promise spoonfuls of French provincial satisfaction in the shape of tarte Tatin, blackberry soufflé or bitter chocolate terrine with Agen prunes and Armagnac. As expected, bottles from the home country's regional highways and byways dominate the carefully chosen wine list; prices from £17.
Chef/s: Malcolm John. **Open:** Tue to Sun L 12 to 3 (4 Sun), all week D 6 to 10.30 (11 Fri and Sat, 10 Sun). **Closed:** 25 and 26 Dec, bank hols. **Meals:** alc (main courses £19 to £22). Set L £18.50 (2 courses) to £22.50. Set D £25. Sun L £25. **Service:** 12.5%. **Details:** 68 seats. 4 seats outside. Separate bar. Music.

Average Price

The average price listed in main-entry reviews denotes the price of a three-course meal, without wine.

Yashin Sushi

Sushi with a creative twist
1a Argyll Road, Kensington, W8 7DB
Tel no: (020) 7938 1536
www.yashinsushi.com
⊖ High Street Kensington, map 4
Japanese | £45
Cooking score: 3

A year after its first entry in the Guide, this smart contemporary neighbourhood restaurant continues to attract a loyal following. The menu has been expanded to show off luxury ingredients such as Wagyu strip loin with wasabi sauce, but the forte is raw fish, with sparkling-fresh sushi passing the quality test. Lightly seared salmon and spinach maki is lifted by a piquant red onion dipping sauce, there are creative touches in yellowtail tuna with French mustard and yuzu, and garoupa rubbed with black bean sauce and ginger. But best of all is a slice of soft and creamy fatty tuna with bonito flakes. Appetisers can range from edamame to smoked salmon caviar with truffle soy. The repertoire also covers salads, soups and dishes such as lamb chop marinated with saikyo miso. Prices are high, especially for wines, which rise rapidly from £28.
Chef/s: Yasuhiro Mineno and Shinya Ikeda. **Open:** all week L 12 to 3, D 6 to 11. **Closed:** Christmas, first and third Mon of every month. **Meals:** alc (dishes £6 to £25). Set L £15 (2 courses) to £20. Set D £40 (2 courses) to £50. **Service:** 12.5%. **Details:** 37 seats. Music.

Zaika

Sophisticated Indian with bold flavours
1 Kensington High Street, Kensington, W8 5NP
Tel no: (020) 7795 6533
www.zaika-restaurant.co.uk
⊖ High Street Kensington, map 4
Indian | £40
Cooking score: 3

£5
OFF

Zaika translates from Urdu as 'sophisticated flavour', and this Kensington veteran hammers home the point that it's a rung or two above your neighbourhood tandoori. It's housed in an old bank with an ornate stone façade and interiors that are heavy on bling – mahogany panelling, tinted glass and plush fabrics give advance warning of the razzle-dazzle on the menu. Expect bold flavours from the likes of tandoori titar (guinea fowl marinated in mustard seeds and curry leaves) or tikhi jhangli machli (spicy Icelandic cod steamed in banana leaf). Elsewhere, a few old favourites arrive dressed up for a big night, Herdwick lamb shank rogan josh among them. Interesting desserts include nutty chocolate samosas with caramelised banana. An Old World-weighted wine list starts at £20.

Chef/s: Jasbinder Singh. **Open:** Tue to Sun L 12 to 2.45, all week D 6 to 10.45 (9.45 Sun). **Closed:** 25 and 26 Dec. **Meals:** alc (main courses £17 to £26). Set L £18.50 (2 courses) to £22.50. Set D £22.50 (2 courses) to £27. **Service:** 12.5%. **Details:** 90 seats. Separate bar. Music.

Zuma

Slinky Knightsbridge high roller
5 Raphael Street, Knightsbridge, SW7 1DL
Tel no: (020) 7584 1010
www.zumarestaurant.com
⊖ Knightsbridge, map 4
Japanese | £75
Cooking score: 5

Dangerously seductive, debonair and relentlessly fashionable, Zuma mixes the Zen-like tranquillity of a Japanese garden with some post-industrial, *Blade Runner* edginess and spoonfuls of Knightsbridge glamour. Inspired by the four primary elements (earth, air, fire and water), it combines monolithic surfaces with rough-hewn wood, marble pillars, steel and glass – a moody backdrop for one of the capital's most moneyed playgrounds. Whether you are at the sushi counter or chilling out in the main dining room, you can expect some astonishing contemporary Japanese food – a procession of sublime, immaculately conceived tasting dishes bristling with pin-sharp flavours, textures and contrasts. To begin, there are palate-arousing plates of scallop tartare with

wasabi ponzu or crispy squid with green chilli and lime. After that, graze your way through some vegetable tempura or miso-marinated chicken roasted over cedar wood, but don't miss out on the wonder stuff from the robata grill – perhaps marinated veal chop with cucumber and Japanese umeboshi plum, king crab with lime butter or even a slab of platinum-priced Wagyu beef with garlic chips. High-art sushi and sashimi are out of the top drawer, while desserts turn westwards for, say, green tea and banana cake with coconut ice cream and peanut toffee sauce. Zuma also boasts an incomparable range of seasonal and rare sakés, while the prestigious wine list is a compendium of big-hitting classics and carefully chosen, food-friendly bottles. Prices start at £22.

Chef/s: Soon Li Ong. **Open:** all week L 12 to 2.30 (3 Fri, 12.30 to 3.30 Sat and Sun), D 6 to 11 (10.30 Sun). **Closed:** 25 Dec. **Meals:** alc (dishes £7 to £70). Tasting menu £96. **Service:** 15%. **Details:** 175 seats. Separate bar. Wheelchair access. Music.

A Cena

Attractive local Italian with reliable food
418 Richmond Road, Twickenham, TW1 2EB
Tel no: (020) 8288 0108
www.acena.co.uk
⊖ Richmond, map 1
Italian | £35
Cooking score: 2

£5
OFF

The menu options at Twickenham's attractive local Italian are 'not your run-of-the-mill choices'. Panisse with tiger prawns, risotto al Barbera d'Asti, roast pork 'wild boar style' (with red wine, celery, mushrooms and carrots) and Seville orange tart are bold and strong, but not typically 'Britalian'. Fusilli with basil and tomato or ribeye with fried potatoes are as mainstream as it gets. The service is as 'reliable' as the food, so A Cena makes a good choice for business and family occasions. The proudly Italophile wine list finds room for a few interlopers from the New World; prices from £17.50.
Chef/s: Nicola Parsons. **Open:** Tue to Sun L 12 to 2.30, Mon to Sat D 7 to 10.30. **Closed:** bank hols, Easter weekend, 25 and 26 Dec. **Meals:** alc (main courses £14 to £24). Sun L £21 (2 courses) to £25. **Service:** 12.5% for parties of 6 or more. **Details:** 55 seats. Wheelchair access. Music.

NEW ENTRY
Albert's Table

Confident and sophisticated local bistro
49C Southend, Croydon, CR0 1BF
Tel no: (020) 8680 2010
www.albertstable.co.uk
map 1
Modern British | £28
Cooking score: 3

£5   V   £30
OFF

Croydon may not strike you as a destination for great food, but Joby Wells, head chef and owner of Albert's Table, is doing his darndest to make it one. His smart eatery is notable for its friendly ambience and burgeoning local following. If providence is your thing, prepare to be amply rewarded. Wells sources

impeccable ingredients and his illustrious CV, which includes stints at The Square and La Trompette (see entries), makes its mark in skilful bistro favourites. Perhaps start with a refined and much-loved shortcrust tart of Dorset crab, followed by slow-roast thick rib of local Hereford beef with triple-cooked chips, or Atlantic cod with foraged greens. The menu's lower echelons impress; try Kentish strawberry fool with meringue and strawberry sorbet. Wines open at £16.75.
Chef/s: Joby Wells. **Open:** Tue to Sun L 12 to 2.30 (3.30 Sun), Tue to Sat D 6.30 to 10.30. **Closed:** Mon. **Meals:** Set L £16 (2 courses) to £19.50. Set D £22 (2 courses) to £27.50. Tasting menu £45 (5 courses). **Service:** 12.5%. **Details:** 64 seats. Wheelchair access. Music.

The Bingham

Heavenly contemporary cuisine
61-63 Petersham Road, Richmond, TW10 6UT
Tel no: (020) 8940 0902
www.thebingham.co.uk
⊖ Richmond, map 1
Modern British | £50
Cooking score: 6

£5   V
OFF

The view of the Thames, Richmond Bridge and weeping willows on the banks, makes the Bingham's window tables hot favourites. However, those guests relegated to the 'cheap seats', as it were, don't come off too badly: they can gaze at the chic dining room, its Venetian mirrors, chandeliers and soft gold Louis chairs, as they ponder the menu. Shay Cooper's 'heavenly' contemporary cuisine is as easy on the eye as the 'gorgeous surroundings'. With its muted watercolour palette, smoked butter risotto with pied de bleu mushrooms and Belper Knolle cheese, dotted with cubes of Muscat vinegar, has the creaminess of comfort food, but with sparks of excitement at every turn. Smoked eel carbonara – an inspired idea – to accompany roast halibut is similarly melting, but offset by green, iron-rich parsley purée, cockles and cucumber. Fans love the 'added surprises of inventive combinations' (possibly thinking of celery sorbet with lemon cheesecake?) and give Cooper's considered cooking the attention it demands. They also praise the 'excellent-value' three-course lunch at £19.50. The wine list (from £19) promises delights 'from the price of a travelcard to the price of a small car'; it roams the world with stop-offs in Brazil, Croatia and more familiar French territory. **Chef/s:** Shay Cooper. **Open:** all week L 12 to 2.30 (4 Sun), Mon to Sat D 7 to 10. **Meals:** alc (main courses £12 to £30). Set L £16 (2 courses) to £19.50. Sun L £38. Tasting menu £65. **Service:** 12.5%. **Details:** 38 seats. 14 seats outside. Separate bar. Wheelchair access. Music. Car parking.

Brasserie Vacherin
Gallic flavours from start to finish
12 High Street, Sutton, SM1 1HN
Tel no: (020) 8722 0180
www.brasserievacherin.co.uk
map 1
French | £25
Cooking score: 2

Malcolm John's all-day brasserie established a reputation for good, honest cooking soon after it opened at the end of 2009. Fans remain impressed by the comfortable interior, simply dressed tables and very good service. Starters of home-cured salmon gravadlax with fennel and pea leaves, and jambon persillé (ham hock terrine), suggest the kitchen knows how to keep things simple. Mains see first-class ingredients show up in classic French combinations: cod with petit ratatouille and basil dressing, for example, and very good steaks with béarnaise. Puddings such as crème brûlée or tarte fine aux pommes provide Gallic flavour to the end. Wines start at £15.50. **Chef/s:** Mareks Zilberts. **Open:** all week 12 to 10.30 (11pm Fri and Sat). **Closed:** 25 Dec. **Meals:** alc (main courses £10 to £18). Set L £16 (2 courses) to £17.95. Sun L £18 (2 courses) to £22.50. **Service:** 12.5%. **Details:** 70 seats. 14 seats outside. Wheelchair access. Music.

Brilliant
Curry kings' easy-going Indian
72-76 Western Road, Southall, UB2 5DZ
Tel no: (020) 8574 1928
www.brilliantrestaurant.com
⊖ Hounslow West, map 1
Indian | £25
Cooking score: 3

From humble beginnings as a 36-seater local restaurant, Brilliant has grown over the past four decades into a fully-fledged and well-oiled venue. The invigorating Punjabi cooking packs them in and ensures the Anand brothers' place as the kings of west London's curry scene. Regulars may not stray too far from the tried-and-tested lamb curry, chicken keema and masala king prawns, but low-calorie 'healthy option' choices of methi chicken and vegetable shashlik garner equal praise, as do exemplary roti breads. Reporters have noted that even at the busiest times Brilliant retains 'a very easy atmosphere' and the staff are 'always helpful' and friendly. House wine from £11; beers and lassi are also offered. **Chef/s:** Jasvinderjit Singh. **Open:** Tue to Fri L 12 to 3, Tue to Sun D 6 to 11.30. **Closed:** Mon, 25 Dec. **Meals:** alc (main courses £5 to £14). **Service:** 10%. **Details:** 220 seats. Music. Car parking.

ALSO RECOMMENDED
▲ The Brown Dog
28 Cross Street, Barnes, SW13 OAP
Tel no: (020) 8392 2200
www.thebrowndog.co.uk
map 1
Modern British

This 'backstreet gem' is a fine neighbourhood hostelry full of pubby bonhomie and cooking that's a nice mix of British and Mediterranean influences. The menu shows flair – braised bacon, Puy lentils and English mustard (£6.50) or Dorset crab salad crop up among the likes of confit duck leg with white beans, merguez sausage and chard (£15.25), and black bream with samphire and shellfish bisque. There's hot chocolate brownie sundae for afters. Wines from £16.50. Open all week.

Brula

Dependable, recession-busting local asset
43 Crown Road, St Margarets, Twickenham, TW1 3EJ
Tel no: (020) 8892 0602
www.brula.co.uk
⊖ Richmond, map 1
French | £30
Cooking score: 3

V

A devotee who has frequented Brula ever since the early days confirms that it's one of Twickenham's more dependable culinary assets, and a real charmer to boot: 'they always remember me', he confesses. It's not hard to see why the place is such a local favourite – who could resist those stained-glass windows, recession-busting prices and ever-courteous staff, not to mention the prospect of some cracking bistro food? Steak frites is an outright winner, but the kitchen also rolls out more elaborate combos ranging from pollack fillet with a warm cocoa bean salad, brown shrimps, rouille and pickled trompettes to roast chump of lamb with lentil moussaka, merguez sausage, cumin-spiced yoghurt and harissa. Finish with the 'fromage du jour' or something sweet – perhaps cherry clafoutis with Kirsch. Eighteen house selections (from £18) lead off a solid French wine list.
Chef/s: Jamie Russell. **Open:** all week L 12 to 3, Mon to Sat D 6 to 10. **Closed:** 26 Dec. **Meals:** alc (main courses £15 to £20). Set L £14 (2 courses) to £19. Set D £19 (2 courses) to £25. Sun L £19. **Service:** 12.5%. **Details:** 45 seats. No music.

⫴ Also Recommended

Also recommended entries are not scored but we think they are worth a visit.

La Buvette

Textbook French favourites
6 Church Walk, Richmond, TW9 1SN
Tel no: (020) 8940 6264
www.labuvette.co.uk
⊖ Richmond, map 1
French | £27
Cooking score: 3
£5 OFF £30

A former church refectory in a leafy spot in Richmond is as good a place as any to find a classic French bistro, its properly clothed tables neatly packed in and the views of the garden a delight in the summer. Buck Carter may not be French, but he can turn out satisfying Parisian standards with the best of them; he offers a textbook fish soup with rouille, croûtons and Gruyère, or piperade with warm Cabécou (Pyrénéan goats' cheese) to start, and follows up strongly with herb-buttered onglet steak with chips and salad, or fillet of hake with char-grilled fennel and tapenade. The deal is sealed at meal's end with strawberry Vacherin, or dark-and-white chocolate mousse cake. The short French wine list opens at £15.
Chef/s: Buck Carter. **Open:** all week L 12 to 3, D 5.45 to 10. **Closed:** 25 to 27 Dec, Good Fri, Easter Sun. **Meals:** alc (main courses £23 to £40). Set L £14.25 (2 courses) to £17. Set D £16.50 (2 courses) to £21. Sun L £17.25 (2 courses) to £20. **Service:** 12.5%. **Details:** 47 seats. 34 seats outside. No music.

ALSO RECOMMENDED
▲ The Depot

Tideway Yard, Mortlake High Street, Barnes, SW14 8SN
Tel no: (020) 8878 9462
www.depotbrasserie.co.uk
map 1
Modern European

River views from terrace and dining room make the the Depot a great shout for a relaxed meal with friends and family. Vogueish cooking and rich ingredients ramp up the sense of occasion nicely. Alongside brasserie classics of oysters, Caesar salad and steak frites there might be goats' cheese and hazelnut soufflé with saffron-poached pears (£6.50), mackerel with Chinese greens and black bean and ginger dressing (£13.95), then crème brûlée with crystallised ginger (£5.50). House wine £16.75. Open all week.

▲ Eat17

28-30 Orford Road, Walthamstow, E17 9NJ
Tel no: (020) 8521 5279
www.eat17.co.uk
⊖ Walthamstow Central, map 1
British

Velvet pouffes, marble tables and trendy lamps add a touch of West End glitz to this all-day Walthamstow eatery, although the kitchen also knows how to sate big East End appetites. Breakfast and brunch standards please the early birds, eclectic tapas-style tit-bits suit the grazing crowd, and hefty plates of Brit-inspired grub satisfy the rest. Starters of torn duck salad or scallops with pea purée (£6) give way to jerk chicken, milk-braised pork shoulder or roast duck with sticky red cabbage (£12.50). Wines from £14. Closed Sun D.

▲ The Exhibition Rooms

69-71 Westow Hill, Crystal Palace, SE19 1TX
Tel no: (020) 8761 1175
www.theexhibitionrooms.com
map 1
Modern European £5 OFF

This neighbourhood venue is a useful, attractive and relaxed place to eat, in an area not known for good restaurants. It's designed to be relatively affordable, and the food on the broad menu more than passes muster. There aren't many surprises, just sound brasserie favourites such as steak tartare or crab salad (£8.50), and rump of Herdwick lamb with crushed new potatoes, Puy lentils and sweetbread croquette (£18.50). House wine is £16. Open Fri to Sun L and all week D.

Fish & Grill

Local gem with dependable classics
48-50 South End, Croydon, CR0 1DP
Tel no: (020) 8774 4060
www.fishandgrill.co.uk
map 1
British | £35
Cooking score: 2
 £30

Malcolm John's spacious suburban brasserie attracts a loyal local following with its dependable classics. Fresh fish and crustaceans, displayed at an open fish bar, are the main attraction that keeps Croydon's diners coming back for more. Please-all bistro fare such as seared scallops and fish pie dominates, and spanking-fresh specials capitalise on the best of the daily fish supplies. Grill highlights include Aberdeen Angus rib steak and whole line-caught Cornish sea bass. Reports of inconsistencies and sloppy service suggest Malcolm John may be taking his eye off the ball as he expands his mini-empire. Reports please. Wines from £16.
Chef/s: Neil Batey. **Open:** Fri to Mon L 12 to 4 (10 to 4 Sat and Sun), D 4 to 11 (10.30 Sun, 5 to 11 Mon). **Meals:** alc (main courses £12 to £48). Set L and D £14.95 (2 courses) to £17.95. **Service:** 12.5%. **Details:** 100 seats. 6 seats outside. Separate bar. Wheelchair access. Music. Car parking.

The French Table

Fantastic neighbourhood restaurant
85 Maple Road, Surbiton, KT6 4AW
Tel no: (020) 8399 2365
www.thefrenchtable.co.uk
map 1
French | £34
Cooking score: 4

Set in a tree-lined suburban parade, Eric and Sarah Guignard's 'consistently fantastic' neighbourhood restaurant continues to attract nothing but praise from its regulars. 'We have always been impressed by the quality of the cooking and the friendly, efficient service' says one, while another notes that the place 'never lets us down'. The airy, modern surroundings are matched by accomplished, creative French cooking driven by high-quality ingredients. An 'outstanding' truffled egg with asparagus and a Parmesan biscuit base is a front-runner, while scallops might appear rolled in ventrèche (French pancetta) and served with pumpkin tortellini, leek fondue and hazelnut mousse. A classic tournedos Rossini has been hailed 'the best steak I have ever eaten' and Scottish venison comes wrapped in Bayonne ham and teamed with parsnip cannelloni and cep sauce. To finish, there's coffee crème brûlée with Amaretto ice cream. House wines start at £16.95.

Chef/s: Eric Guignard. **Open:** Tue to Sun L 12 to 2.30, Tue to Sat D 7 to 10.30. **Closed:** Mon, 25 and 26 Dec. **Meals:** alc (main courses £12 to £20). Set weekday L £19.50 (2 courses) to £23.50. Sat L £22.50. Sun L £26.50. **Service:** 12.5%. **Details:** 48 seats. Music.

The Glasshouse
Alluring high-achiever
14 Station Parade, Kew, TW9 3PZ
Tel no: (020) 8940 6777
www.glasshouserestaurant.co.uk
⊖ Kew Gardens, map 1
Modern European | £43
Cooking score: 5

The eye-catching broad glass frontage in a parade of shops a few paces from Kew Gardens tube station gives you pause – especially when you glance at the menu. One of a triumvirate of high-achieving restaurants in the Bruce Poole and Nigel Platts-Martin stable (see entries for La Trompette and Chez Bruce), the Glasshouse offers the same style of roughly French-influenced modern bistro cooking, overlaid with notes of east Asia. Scallop sashimi with ponzu dressing, prawn beignet and wasabi could be the prelude to glazed miso aubergine with edamame beans, tempura vegetables and shiitake gyoza dumplings. Otherwise, it could be silky rabbit and foie gras terrine full of gamey flavour, fine lamb shoulder with chicory, or sea bass with leeks, brown shrimps and gnocchi in vermouth velouté. For one reporter at least, they saved

the best till last, in the shape of a 'fantastically light' rum baba with peaches and crème Chantilly, doused in extra rum. Service is commended as brilliant; the outstanding achievement award goes to the sommelière, who knows her way flawlessly around the pedigree list. Bottles from the lesser-known corners of Europe and the aristocracy of the southern hemisphere add to the allure. Prices start at £20 (£5 a glass).

Chef/s: Daniel Mertl. **Open:** all week L 12 to 2.30 (3 Sun), D 6.30 to 10.30 (7 to 10 Sun). **Closed:** 24 to 26 Dec, 1 Jan. **Meals:** Set L £23.50 (2 courses) to £27.50. Set D £37.50 (2 courses) to £42.50. Sun L £27.50 (2 courses) to £32.50. Tasting menu £60. **Service:** 12.5%. **Details:** 65 seats. No music.

Incanto
Local Italian with plenty to tempt
41 High Street, Harrow-on-the-Hill, HA1 3HT
Tel no: (020) 8426 6767
www.incanto.co.uk
⊖ Harrow-on-the-Hill, map 1
Italian | £32
Cooking score: 4

An oasis in an otherwise desert-like foodie landscape, this attractively relaxed, light-filled restaurant tucked behind a mouthwatering Italian deli has the attention of every gastro-savvy diner in the neighbourhood. Customers are greeted by friendly, confident and competent staff, and presented with menus that have plenty to tempt. Be warned, the kitchen has a disposition to overcomplicate – the lack of competition means there's not much reason to rein in inventiveness, and a ballottine of chicken, served with lime, chilli and cauliflower relish is, in fact, a disparate curry. The wise stick to classic dishes – a top-quality crab risotto; the sumptuously rich paccheri pasta with long-cooked squid, white wine and leek; or the house special of superb ravioli with pancetta, duck egg and truffle. House wines are plentiful by the glass (bottles from £17.50) and though the focus is on Italy, like the menu there's plenty of input from the rest of the world.

Chef/s: Quentin Dorangeville. **Open:** Tue to Sun L 12 to 2.30 (12.30 to 4 Sun), Tue to Sat D 6.30 to 10.30. **Closed:** Mon, 25 and 26 Dec, 1 Jan, Easter Sun. **Meals:** alc (main courses £16 to £24). Set L £17.95 (2 courses) to £19.95. Set D £19.95 (2 courses) to £23.95. **Service:** 12.5%. **Details:** 65 seats. Wheelchair access. Music.

Indian Zilla
Stylish Indian with creative cooking
2-3 Rocks Lane, Barnes, SW13 0DB
Tel no: (020) 8878 3989
www.indianzilla.co.uk
map 1
Indian | £27
Cooking score: 4

Out of the same stable as Indian Zing (see entry), this stylish restaurant blends chef/proprietor Manoj Vasaikar's eye for soothing detail with some highly creative cooking. Cool interiors, angular lines and restrained colours set the mood, while the kitchen shows an admirable commitment to free-range and organic produce. Chicken might be given the Malabar treatment with mustard seeds, tamarind and coconut milk, jumbo prawns are marinated with pomegranate seeds and dill, and Nilgiri lamb is pointed up with stone-ground spices; also look for the signature banana flower and colocasia leaf kofta in a delicate pumpkin gravy. Elsewhere, readers have applauded the Karwari fish curry flavoured with native triphala (a blend of three Ayurvedic herbs). Desserts might bring a new taste experience in the shape of tandoori figs with apple and muesli crumble. To drink, order a Cobra beer or a bottle of vin de pays (£16). Manoj Vasaikar also runs Indian Zest at 21 Thames Street, Sunbury on Thames; tel (01932) 765000.
Chef/s: Manoj Vasaikar. **Open:** Sat and Sun L 12 to 3 (4 Sun), all week D 6 to 11 (10 Sun). **Closed:** 25 Dec. **Meals:** alc (main courses £9 to £20). Sun L £12 (2 courses) to £15. **Service:** 12.5%. **Details:** 75 seats. 4 seats outside. Music.

ALSO RECOMMENDED

▲ Ma Cuisine
9 Station Approach, Kew, TW9 3QB
Tel no: (020) 8332 1923
www.macuisinebistrot.co.uk
⊖ Kew Gardens, map 1
French £5 OFF

Ma Cuisine is a caricature of a French bistro, with gingham tablecloths, café tables on the street and a greatest-hits menu – cassoulet, fish soup, boudin noir. But a salad of coquilles Saint Jacques with celeriac purée and pancetta (£7.50) is carefully and elegantly prepared. More generous, but equally good, is a veal chop (£19.50) served with a good dauphinois, lashings of greens and a vinegar-heavy béarnaise. Service is cheerful and wines are priced to keep customers jolly; house white is £13.75.

Madhu's
Polished Indian that hits the spot
39 South Road, Southall, UB1 1SW
Tel no: (020) 8574 1897
www.madhusonline.com
map 1
Indian | £22
Cooking score: 3
£5 OFF V £30

Madhu's is over twenty-five years old, and now looks like a high-gloss, West End Indian – all mirrors, metal and shiny black surfaces. The cooking reaches parts that most curry house kitchens can only dream of – although the food is never modish or effete. What you get is a barrage of full-blooded, expertly timed dishes showing a deft touch with the spice box. Specialities flagged with a red M are always worth a try – perhaps pan-fried cassava with cumin, masala fish or the gloriously buttery makhani chicken – although the regular standbys seldom disappoint. Tandoori lamb chops, karahi gosht, bhindi masala and excellent 'bread preparations' are all consumed with relish by Madhu's loyal fans. House wine is £10.

Chef/s: Rakesh Verma. **Open:** Mon and Wed to Fri L 11.30 to 3, Wed to Mon D 6 to 11.30. **Closed:** Tue. **Meals:** alc (main courses £5 to £12). Set L and D £20. **Service:** 10%. **Details:** 105 seats. Wheelchair access. Music.

Mandarin Palace
Suburban Cantonese stalwart
559-561 Cranbrook Road, Gants Hill, IG2 6JZ
Tel no: (020) 8550 7661
⊖ Gants Hill, map 1
Chinese | £25
Cooking score: 2
£5 OFF **V** £30

Authentic Cantonese cooking just off the Gants Hill roundabout sounds an unlikely proposition, but this gaudily decorated Chinese stalwart continues to deliver the goods in a flamboyant setting of fans, lattice screens and artefacts. Dim sum is a top shout; tick off your selections from a list that might feature steamed pork and radish dumplings, crispy chicken croquettes, congee with grated scallop and 'sweet dew' of sago with taro. The full menu also stays true to its regional roots with a host of barbecued meats and abundant seafood (crispy eel with honey sauce, for example), plus 'sizzlers', hotpots and one-plate noodle specialities. House wine is £16. **Chef/s:** Huorong Chen. **Open:** Mon to Sat L 12 to 4, D 6.30 to 11.30. Sun 12 to 11.30. **Closed:** 25 Dec. **Meals:** alc (main courses £9 to £45). Set L £9.80. Set D £24. **Service:** 10%. **Details:** 100 seats. Separate bar. Music. Car parking.

Symbols

�: Accommodation is available
£30 Three courses for less than £30
V Separate vegetarian menu
£5 OFF £5-off voucher scheme
🍷 Notable wine list

Mosaica @ the Factory
Funky flavours in an ex-chocolate factory
Chocolate Factory, Clarendon Road, Wood Green, N22 6XJ
Tel no: (020) 8889 2400
www.mosaicarestaurants.com
⊖ Wood Green, map 2
British | £40
Cooking score: 3
£5 OFF

A former chocolate factory on an industrial estate may sound an unlikely gastronomic destination, but this 'oasis of a restaurant' continues to thrill regulars. They are drawn by 'friendly and discreet service' and the funky atmosphere of the shabby-chic, New York-style loft space with its mismatched furniture and open kitchen. This is a laid-back dining experience, although one reporter noted that 'you have to be in the mood' for all the bustle and clatter. Bold flavours and imaginative combinations permeate the menu, which might begin with Parma ham, feta, blossom honey and leaves, go on to a main course of 'amazing' 21-hour slow-roast belly pork, mustard mash and red cabbage, and end with yoghurt, mixed berries, honey and pistachio. Wines start at £14. **Chef/s:** Steven Goode. **Open:** Sun to Fri L 12 to 2.30 (1 to 4 Sun), Mon to Sat D 7 to 9.30 (10 Sat). **Meals:** alc (main courses £14 to £23). **Service:** 10%. **Details:** 80 seats. 20 seats outside. Wheelchair access. Music. Car parking.

Petersham Nurseries Café
Unusual eatery with Moroccan flavours
Church Lane, off Petersham Road, Richmond, TW10 7AG
Tel no: (020) 8605 3627
www.petershamnurseries.com
⊖ Richmond, map 1
Modern British | £45
Cooking score: 3

Those who make the effort to search out this unusual dining space are always astonished by its beauty – even the rickety chairs and dirt floors somehow manage to enhance the

charm. Since Skye Gyngell's departure in early 2012, guest chef Greg Malouf has structured a menu around Moroccan flavours with Australian overtones, and the food suits the location well, making full use of the fresh, strong flavours from the Nurseries' herb garden. A tomato and parsley salad, dressed simply with excellent olive oil and Amalfi lemon juice and decorated with viola flowers, accompanies deep-fried haloumi; fennel and coriander are a foil for hazelnut-crusted chicken liver and aïoli. Prices are high, but for an elegant lunch (and occasional supper) treat, it's almost worth it. The drinks are as fragrant as the cooking – upmarket cordials sit alongside a well-thought-out, shortish wine list; bottles from £24. More reports please.
Chef/s: Greg Malouf. **Open:** Tue to Sun L only 12 to 2.45 (3 Sat and Sun). **Closed:** Mon, 25 and 26 Dec. **Meals:** alc (main courses £19 to £33). **Service:** 12.5%. **Details:** 100 seats. 100 seats outside. No music. Wheelchair access.

The Restaurant at the Petersham
Sumptuous views and reinvented favourites
Nightingale Lane, Richmond, TW10 6UZ
Tel no: (020) 8940 7471
www.petershamhotel.co.uk
⊖ Richmond, map 1
Modern British | £45
Cooking score: 4
£5 OFF 🍴

Standing aloof on the side of Richmond Hill, with a masterful view of the Thames and the surrounding meadows, the Petersham is handy for the Royal Botanic Gardens and the rugby at Twickenham. It's Greater London at its most pastoral, and the rather grand, chandeliered hotel dining room boasts sumptuous views. Reinventions of traditional favourites are much in Alex Bentley's line, so you might start with smoked haddock on toast, complete with capers and Parmesan and topped with a cleverly crisp-textured poached egg. A leg of duck with a kind of cassoulet of smoked morteau sausage and white beans is garnished with choucroute and field

mushroom, but quite often tried-and-true preparations appear undisguised, as in Dover sole meunière or grilled beef fillet in béarnaise. Desserts spangle things up again with the likes of milk chocolate pannacotta, lime compote and Turkish delight ice cream. The French-led wine list opens at £23.50.
Chef/s: Alex Bentley. **Open:** all week L 12.15 to 2.15 (12.30 to 3.30 Sun), D 7 to 9.45 (8.45 Sun). **Closed:** 25 and 26 Dec, 1 Jan. **Meals:** alc (main courses £21 to £33). Set L £19.95 (2 courses) to £23.95. Sun L £34.50. **Service:** 12.5%. **Details:** 70 seats. Separate bar. No music. Wheelchair access. Car parking.

Retro Bistrot
Warm, buzzy French bistro
114-116 High Street, Teddington, TW11 8JB
Tel no: (020) 8977 2239
www.retrobistrot.co.uk
map 1
French | £25
Cooking score: 3
£5 OFF **V** £30

A neighbourhood venue with a staunch local following, the charming Bistrot offers simple and occasionally innovative French cooking. The 'wonderful warm, buzzy atmosphere' is commended by a reader who goes on to eulogise our host ('a fantastic character and wearer of magnificent waistcoats'). In surroundings of exposed brick and big mirrors, expect the likes of double-baked goats' cheese soufflé with beetroot and herb salad, braised halibut in mussel and clam chowder, and fried calf's liver and bacon with Lyonnaise potatoes and braised baby gem. Everyone loves the chateaubriand for two, with thick chips, French beans and béarnaise. Go all-out at dessert stage with white chocolate croquant, white chocolate and raspberry mousseline and pistachio and raspberry compote. House French is £15.50 (£4.50 a glass).
Chef/s: Andrew West. **Open:** Tue to Sun L 12 to 3.30, Tue to Sat D 6.30 to 11. **Closed:** Mon, 25 and 26 Dec, first 2 weeks Jan, first 2 weeks Aug. **Meals:** alc

(main courses £13 to £25). Set L £10.95 (2 courses) to £13.95. Set D £17.50 (2 courses) to £19.95. **Service:** 12.5%. **Details:** 120 seats. Music.

ALSO RECOMMENDED
▲ Simply Thai

196 Kingston Road, Teddington, TW11 9JD
Tel no: (020) 8943 9747
www.simplythai-restaurant.co.uk
map 1
Thai

Patria Weerapan runs a tight ship at this minimalist Thai eatery, cooking most of the food herself while keeping an eye on business out front. Specialities such as pan-roasted halibut with spicy aubergine (£14.50) brighten up a concise menu. Expect classic soups, zingy salads and 'warm starters' (satays, fishcakes, dumplings), plus stir-fries and curries including the signature 'spicy sweet' pork loin with palm sugar, coconut cream and fine beans (£8.95). Drink Singha beer or house wine (£14.95). Open all week D only.

Sonny's Kitchen

Relaunched eatery with a fired-up kitchen
94 Church Road, Barnes, SW13 0DQ
Tel no: (020) 8748 0393
www.sonnys.co.uk
map 1
Modern European | £30
Cooking score: 4

Having collaborated on Kensington's Kitchen W8 (see entry), Rebecca Mascarenhas has once again teamed up with The Square's Phil Howard to relaunch her Barnes eatery, now renamed Sonny's Kitchen. Interiors have been jazzed up – the tablecloths are gone and new tiled walls give it a more contemporary feel. At our midweek lunch the space was positively heaving – which might account for the haphazard service that meant it took half an hour and a starter course for our drinks to arrive. Yet if the front-of-house is still fine-tuning, the kitchen is firing on all cylinders, serving up refined comfort food. A starter of gazpacho with a dollop of melting sour-cream

ice cream was pitch-perfect and well-balanced, distinctive flavours continued into an innovative main of pizza bianca with smoked mozzarella, cured Wagyu beef and globe artichoke. To finish, a devilish popping-candy sundae was a delight. Wines start at £15.50.
Chef/s: Alex Marks. **Open:** all week L 12 to 4 (10am Sun), Mon to Sat D 7 to 10.30 (11 Fri and Sat). **Closed:** bank hols. **Meals:** alc (main courses £11 to £19). Set L £13.50 (2 courses) to £15.50. Set D £15.50 (2 courses) to £18.50. Sun L £20 (2 courses) to £24.50. **Service:** 12.5%. **Details:** 98 seats. 10 seats outside.

Tangawizi

Upscale local Indian
406 Richmond Road, Richmond, TW1 2EB
Tel no: (020) 8891 3737
www.tangawizi.co.uk
⊖ Richmond, **map 1**
Indian | £25
Cooking score: 2

The word tangawizi is Swahili for ginger, and this upscale Indian hard by Richmond Bridge piles on the exoticism with multi-hued purple and gold interiors, mirrored walls and the scent of incense in the air. There's also a racy vibrancy about the cooking, and the kitchen shows its ambition by adding a mango dressing to marinated grilled paneer, serving lamb on the bone with potatoes, and offering chocolate samosas to finish. It also knows how to keep hardcore curry house fans happy by dishing up dopiazas, dhansaks, biryanis and chicken tikka masala. If palate cleansing is required, try the mango and Champagne sorbet. House wine is £14.50.
Chef/s: Surat Singh Rana. **Open:** all week D only 6 to 11 (10.30 Sun). **Closed:** 25 and 26 Dec, 1 Jan. **Meals:** alc (main courses £7 to £15). **Service:** not inc. **Details:** 60 seats. Music.

The Victoria

Appealing all-rounder

10 West Temple Sheen, East Sheen, SW14 7RT

Tel no: (020) 8876 4238

www.thevictoria.net

⊖ Richmond, map 1

Modern British | £25

Cooking score: 3

The leafy suburban setting of this dining pub with rooms, and its proximity to Richmond Park, draws a mixed and very appreciative crowd. Coffee sales rocket as dog walkers mingle with mums fresh from the school run in the informal bar and sofa-filled lounge, and there's a real family atmosphere in the conservatory for Saturday brunch and Sunday lunch. Evenings are relaxed, with diners delving into Paul Merrett's appealing modern British menu, where belly pork with seared scallops, herb and green pea purée and bordelaise jus may precede a classic ribeye steak with béarnaise or pan-fried bass on sag aloo potatoes with onion bhajia, tomato chilli jam and curry oil. Warm chocolate pudding with peanut butter ice cream is a good way to finish. Wines from £16.50.

Chef/s: Paul Merrett. **Open:** all week L 12 to 2.30 (4 Sat and Sun), Mon to Sat D 6 to 10 (10.30 Sat). **Meals:** alc (main courses £13 to £18). Set L £12.50 (2 courses). Sun L £24 (2 courses) to £28. **Service:** 12.5%. **Details:** 78 seats. 50 seats outside. Music. Car parking.

¶|◦ THE AMERICAN DREAM

Indulgence comes in many forms, and the seductive power of American-style junk food cannot be denied. 'Junk' dishes can and have been improved, though, and diners-and-dives dishes done well – burgers and sliders, macaroni cheese, ribs, deep-fried chicken and chilli cheese fries – have proved as irresistible as an episode of *The Wonder Years*. Dominated by casual no-reservations joints, our favourites for fun-in-a-bun deliver a juicy comfort hit.

Our London readers like:

Meat Liquor, Marylebone
Shield your eyes. Vaulted ceilings with liberal splashes of graffiti await those who queue for chilli cheese fries, deep-fried pickles, wings, and of course, succulent burgers in sweet, soft buns.
www.meatliquor.com
Open Mon to Sat

Pitt Cue Co, Soho
Real barbecue is an art form, and Pitt Cue Co honours the tradition. Hipsters (and the rest of us) favour pulled pork and burnt end mash, topped with caramelised brisket.
www.pittcue.co.uk
Open Mon to Sat

ENGLAND

Bedfordshire, Berkshire,
Buckinghamshire, Cambridgeshire,
Cheshire, Cornwall, Cumbria, Derbyshire,
Devon, Dorset, Durham, Essex,
Gloucestershire & Bristol,
Greater Manchester,
Hampshire (inc. Isle of Wight),
Herefordshire, Hertfordshire, Kent,
Lancashire, Leicestershire and Rutland,
Lincolnshire, Merseyside, Norfolk,
Northamptonshire, Northumberland,
Nottinghamshire, Oxfordshire, Shropshire,
Somerset, Staffordshire, Suffolk, Surrey,
Sussex – East, Sussex – West,
Tyne & Wear, Warwickshire,
West Midlands, Wiltshire, Worcestershire,
Yorkshire

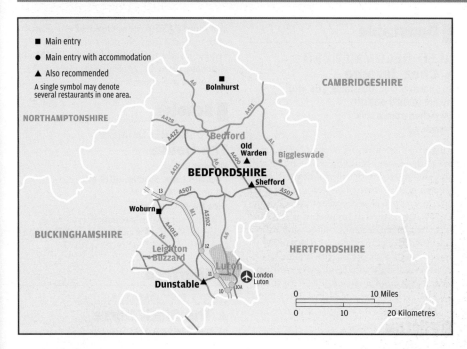

Bolnhurst

The Plough
Sunny place with an inspired chef
Kimbolton Road, Bolnhurst, MK44 2EX
Tel no: (01234) 376274
www.bolnhurst.com
Modern British | £35
Cooking score: 5

Gaily turned out in yellow and blue, with floral walls and bare-boarded floors, the Plough is a sunny-natured place – literally so if you bag a table in the oak-framed, full-windowed extension, which comes into its own in fair weather. Martin Lee is an inspired chef, cooking with precision, imagination and flair. He absorbs culinary influences from all over while capitalising on the best local produce. Nibbly appetisers are informed by tapas (boquerones, chorizo, Gordal Reina olives) but also include lamb tikka and devils on horseback. On the main menu, classical technique mingles with modern British modes, so baked crab thermidor sits alongside roast veal sweetbreads with red onion marmalade and crisp celeriac in red wine. Mains extend from roast monkfish in curried shrimp sauce with pak choi and coriander, to a slow-cooked rabbit leg with pancetta, creamed cabbage, a crisp potato galette and shallot confit. British, Irish and continental cheeses appear in splendid array; desserts beguile with the likes of frangipane tart topped with pears poached in mulled wine. A glorious wine list, the sort we all like to see, is arranged by style, concisely annotated and determined to offer fair value. Bottles start at £15.95 (£3 a small glass).

Chef/s: Martin Lee. **Open:** Tue to Sun L 12 to 2, Tue to Sat D 6.30 to 9.30. **Closed:** Mon, first two weeks Jan. **Meals:** alc (main courses £16 to £27). Set L and D £15 (2 courses) to £19. Sun L £21 (2 courses) to £25. **Service:** not inc. **Details:** 90 seats. 30 seats outside. No music. Car parking.

Dunstable

ALSO RECOMMENDED
▲ Chez Jerome
26 Church Street, Dunstable, LU5 4RU
Tel no: (01582) 603310
www.chezjerome.co.uk
French £5 OFF

This 'warm, welcoming oasis' occupies a
fifteenth-century building whose inner walls
are criss-crossed with original timbers. Here,
according to his many fans, Jerome Dehoux
provides a 'first-class', 'excellent value' dining
experience. Typical of his uncluttered Gallic
style are roasted beetroot stuffed with walnuts
and Auvergne blue cheese with balsamic
syrup, seared duck breast with orange sauce,
potatoes and vegetables, and warm rustic apple
tartlet with custard sauce (£24.95 for three
courses). Wines start at £14.25. Closed Sun D.

Flitton

READERS RECOMMEND
The White Hart
Modern British
Brook Lane, Flitton, MK45 5EJ
Tel no: (01525) 862022
www.whitehartflitton.co.uk
'This is a pub/restaurant with no pretence, but
in my view outstanding food and well worth a
detour.'

Old Warden

ALSO RECOMMENDED
▲ Hare & Hounds
High Street, Old Warden, SG18 9HQ
Tel no: (01767) 627225
www.hareandhoundsoldwarden.co.uk
Modern British

For hearty food in a relaxed environment, this
dining pub is 'spot on'. The outside looks
traditional, with fancy fascia boards, but the
interior is subtly modern. The same could be
said of the cooking, which ranges from pub
staples to a full meal of tempura tiger prawns

and squid (£7.50), slow-cooked belly pork
with buttered mash, honey-roasted root
vegetables and apple and cider sauce (£16) and
chocolate nemesis (£6.30). Wines from £13.
Open Tue to Sat and Sun L.

Scholes

READERS RECOMMEND
The House
Modern British
1 Scholes Lane, Scholes, BD19 6PA
Tel no: (01274) 870676
www.the-house.uk.com
'This is a superb little restaurant in every
respect...The food is an absolute delight and is
cooked to perfection.'

Shefford

ALSO RECOMMENDED
▲ The Black Horse
Ireland, Shefford, SG17 5QL
Tel no: (01462) 811398
www.blackhorseireland.com
Modern British

Back in the 1850s, navvies constructing
Bedfordshire's railways were fed, watered and
(occasionally) locked up at this hostelry out in
the sticks. These days, civility reigns in the
thoroughly welcoming open-plan bar/dining
room where eating is now the main business of
the day. The kitchen adds dependable pies,
grills and specials to a menu that might take
in, say, roasted red pepper and goats' cheese tart
(£7.95), pork Wellington or poached Loch
Duart salmon in olive oil with sorrel sauce
(£14.95). House wine is £15.95. No food Sun
D. Accommodation.

> ### 🍴 Also Recommended
> Also recommended entries are not scored
> but we think they are worth a visit.

▌Woburn

Paris House

Picture-perfect plates and pretty parkland
London Road, Woburn Park, Woburn, MK17 9QP
Tel no: (01525) 290692
www.parishouse.co.uk
Modern European | £67
Cooking score: 5

£5 OFF **V**

Sitting pretty amid Woburn Park's lush green acres, with meandering muntjacs for company, Paris House is a cocooned world of civilised grace and favour, overseen by a brigade of ever-courteous French staff. Visitors have much to smile about, from the kooky sculptures and voguish red chandeliers to the snatches of recipes printed on the backs of the dining chairs and the occasional gastronomic parody ('tongue in cheek Bedfordshire clanger' with smoked apple purée, anyone?). If you order 'ham, egg and chips', you'll be presented with some smoky ham hock terrine accompanied by a soft-boiled quail's egg, poached pineapple and purple potato 'crisps', but the kitchen reserves most of its efforts for more orthodox ideas – perhaps carpaccio of venison with confit egg yolk, toasted hazelnuts and blackberries, or roast sirloin of beef with red onion tart, braised snails and a blue cheese beignet. Fish has also been well received. Dessert might bring a 'boozy' riff on Black Forest gâteau or mandarin cheesecake with digestive-biscuit crumble. As a protégé of empire-building restaurateur Alan Murchison, chef Phil Fanning knows how to deliver highly accomplished, elaborately worked plates of picture-perfect contemporary food – although the results can sometimes seem like 'fine dining by numbers'. The international wine list (from £22) also lacks that 'wow' factor.
Chef/s: Phil Fanning. **Open:** Wed to Sun L 12 to 2, Tue to Sat D 7 to 9. **Closed:** Mon, 25 Dec to 7 Jan. **Meals:** Set L £25 (2 courses) to £30. Set D £54 (2 courses) to £67. Sun L £30. Tasting menus from £71 (8 courses) to £95 (10 courses). **Service:** 12.5%. **Details:** 40 seats. Separate bar. Wheelchair access. Music. Car parking.

🍴 ALYN WILLIAMS
Alyn Williams at the Westbury

Which chefs do you admire, and why?
Simon Rogan for his fresh approach to cooking and his commitment to using his own produce. Paul Bocuse for his longevity and unwavering dedication to hospitality.

Give us a quick culinary tip
Always make sure you are well prepared before you start cooking.

What food trends are you spotting at the moment?
A lot of chefs are following the current Nordic cooking style, with lots of foraging and very local produce.

What advice would you give a chef starting their career?
Don't give up as soon as the going gets tough. Immerse yourself in the discipline.

What's your earliest food memory?
Farley's rusks soaked in warm milk, followed by my dad's minestrone.

What would you be if you weren't a chef?
A pro snowboarder or a lounge singer.

Sum up your cooking style in three words
Simple, tasty, considered.

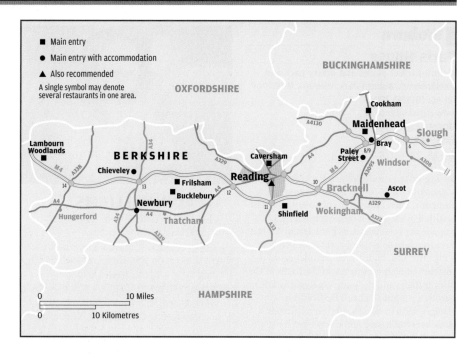

Ascot

Restaurant Coworth Park

Contemporary magnificence and expert service
Coworth Park, London Road, Ascot, SL5 7SE
Tel no: (01344) 876600
www.coworthpark.com
Modern European | £60
new chef

The hotel in its sprawling grounds abutting Windsor Great Park is part of the Sultan of Brunei's Dorchester group, so habitués of other-worldly magnificence who have wearied of Park Lane hubbub can decamp to the countryside, where the clunk of polo mallets announces a different pace altogether. There's magnificence here too, though of a distinctly more contemporary kind, with up-to-the-minute spa technologies and a serene glassed-in dining room overlooking the balustraded terrace and the lawns, with comfortable caramel-coloured seating and expertly poised service. The kitchen has been in something of a state of flux recently, with Brian Hughson, formerly of The Grill at the Dorchester, named as successor to the former incumbent, John Campbell, as we went to press. On the wine front, a French-led wine list exudes pedigree and maturity. To split hairs, prices are toppy, but not quite as toppy as they could be in the circumstances (assuming you don't head straight for the Mouton). The starting point is £28. Reports, please.

Chef/s: Brian Hughson. **Open:** Tue to Sun L 12.30 to 2.30 (3 Sun), Tue to Sat D 6.30 to 9.30. **Closed:** Mon. **Meals:** Set L £29.95. Sun L £45. **Service:** 12.5%. **Details:** 70 seats. Separate bar. Wheelchair access. Music. Car parking.

Average Price

The average price listed in main-entry reviews denotes the price of a three-course meal, without wine.

Bray

★ TOP 50 ★

The Fat Duck

The experience of a lifetime
1 High Street, Bray, SL6 2AQ
Tel no: (01628) 580333
www.thefatduck.co.uk
Modern British | £180
Cooking score: 10

V

If the success of a restaurant can truly be measured by the near-impossibility of getting in, the Fat Duck continues to be way ahead of the pack. Securing a table requires serious effort, especially now the booking system has moved online. Persevere and you will be rewarded with one of Britain's most distinctive, idiosyncratic and – it almost goes without saying – dazzlingly polished fine-dining occasions. With three addresses in Bray alone, plus Dinner in London (see entries), and an inexhaustible supply of TV work, Heston Blumenthal has a lot to do, but this is where his boldest and bravest experiments are being carried out, where the quest for culinary astonishment remains most fiercely focused. To some, what Blumenthal is doing is playing a clever postmodern conceptual game that just happens to involve food, but that is to misunderstand his fascination with the science, the mechanics and the alchemy of taste, not to mention a historian's interest in the British culinary traditions of previous centuries. Yes, there are dishes that stay on the menu from year to year, but they are in a constant process of refinement. The 'Sounds of the Sea' dish that features tapioca and dried sardine 'sand' with Japanese seaweeds now comes with Irish abalone and slivers of mackerel and halibut under a foaming wave of smoked water (together with an iPod feed of ambient marine sound). Toast sandwiches add a picnic feel to the Mad Hatter's Tea Party serving of mock-turtle soup, with its edible pocket-watch for dipping in the teapot. The famous bright green snail porridge in its lidded dish is now intensely redolent of fennel, but still buttery and luscious as ever. New ideas flow freely too, though: a single slice of luxuriously tender British Wagyu beef with piccalilli components; powdered duck, a reimagining of a Victorian recipe with gorgeously soft breast meat, a smear of black pudding purée, duck hearts and creamed Apache potato; vegetable marrow filled with horseradish royale in Marmite broth, accompanied by deep-fried marbles of sauce gribiche in a little silver cone, one of a number of brilliant vegetarian creations from the vegetarian version of the tasting menu. The constant overturning of expectations is what drives these dishes; you start out startled and end up bowled over by conviction. A dessert to see in the summer involves a row of variously sized strawberries, along with a cone of Earl Grey ice cream, a heap of chopped pistachios under a kind of picnic blanket, edible flowers and chamomile. Many of the dishes incorporate a now-indispensable performance element, as when an oak-moss table centrepiece is blasted with liquid nitrogen while you put a sliver of truffle on your tongue, and then set about quail jelly with crayfish cream, chicken liver parfait and truffle toast. Surely no restaurant staff in the country are put through such paces, and yet they look to a one as though they're doing it all for the first time at each session. The understandably heightened cost is driven further towards the stratosphere by the wine mark-ups. Glasses start at £12, bottles of white at £30, red at £45, but what treasures there are – the Silex Pouilly-Fumés of the late Didier Dagueneau, Antinori's Tignanello, Yatir from Israel. If only the banks were still lending us money.

Chef/s: Heston Blumenthal. **Open:** Tue to Sat L 12 to 2, D 7 to 9.30. **Closed:** Mon, Sun, 2 weeks Christmas. **Meals:** Tasting menu L and D £180. **Service:** 12.5%. **Details:** 40 seats. No music.

Visit us Online

To find out more about *The Good Food Guide*, please visit www.thegoodfoodguide.co.uk

The Hinds Head

The English country pub, Heston-style
High Street, Bray, SL6 2AB
Tel no: (01628) 626151
www.hindsheadbray.com
British | £38
Cooking score: 4

The venerable fifteenth-century hostelry at the heart of Bray was the second arm of Heston Blumenthal's operations here. A stone's throw from the Fat Duck (see entry above), it aims to offer the English country-pub experience in a setting of low beamed ceilings, oak panelling and proper fireplace. The food fits the ethos too, mixing modern pub cooking such as roast fillet of cod with celeriac purée, sultanas and salt cod, or chicken thigh with liver butter in a bourguignon-style sauce, with reconstructed old-school fare such as Scotch egg, devils on horseback, snail hash (from a Victorian recipe) and oxtail and kidney pudding. Sweet treats include rhubarb and custard quaking pudding (to a recipe from the time of Queen Anne), or hazelnut and chocolate truffle with blood-orange sorbet. A restaurant-style wine list, divided between Old and New Worlds, starts at £19.25 for a Côtes de Thongue Chardonnay, or £18.95 for a Sicilian red blend.

Chef/s: Kevin Love. **Open:** all week L 12 to 2.30 (4 Sun), Mon to Sat D 6.30 to 9.30. **Closed:** 25 and 26 Dec. **Meals:** alc (main courses £16 to £28). Set L £27.50. **Service:** 12.5%. **Details:** 140 seats. Separate bar. No music. Wheelchair access. Car parking.

★ TOP 50 ★

The Waterside Inn

An irresistible package
Ferry Road, Bray, SL6 2AT
Tel no: (01628) 620691
www.waterside-inn.co.uk
French | £130
Cooking score: 7

The gentle transition by which the Waterside has passed from the legendary Michel Roux, who invented Bray as a gastronomic destination in the 1970s, into the hands of his son Alain has been as admirable in its smooth professionalism as virtually everything else the place achieves. Its sensually pleasing riverside setting, the lofty but personalised approach of the service brigade, and the finely burnished, more or less traditional French cuisine add up to an irresistible package. There is no hiding the fact that it costs a fair bit – indeed, as an enamoured reporter comments, 'it's so pricey that one might weep if it failed to live up to its worldwide reputation' – but the Waterside is, for most, the complete experience. Bracing freshness characterises openers such as classic scallop ceviche, or Devon crab with melon and almonds and a single marinated prawn, while the lobster medallions done in white port with gingery vegetable julienne is practically a heritage dish now. Main course meats are handled with tender care, from initial searing to resting, so that Angus fillet is accorded all its succulence, garnished with black olives and tapenade croquettes, and sauced with a basil-scented Graves reduction so poised between strength and grace that 'it's like angels singing rock music'. A similar silkiness is conjured out of the grilled rabbit fillets that come with celeriac fondant and glazed chestnuts in Armagnac. Some have felt the dessert assiettes are not quite as up-to-snuff these days as they might be, but individual dishes such as peach in tutti-frutti Champagne nage with a strawberry-stuffed waffle lack nothing in imagination. Wines are of the old school; vertical flights of Latour, Yquem and the likes flash by as you flick through, looking for something you can afford. There are glasses from £8, and Sauvion's excellent Muscadet is only £21.50, but mainly it's a question of flying high in Birdland.

Chef/s: Alain Roux. **Open:** Wed to Sun L 12 to 2 (2.30 Sun), D 7 to 10. **Closed:** Mon, Tue, 26 Dec for four weeks. **Meals:** alc (main courses £49 to £69). Set L £42.50 (2 courses) to £58. Sun L £74. Tasting menu £147.50. **Service:** not inc. **Details:** 70 seats. Separate bar. Car parking. Children over 12 yrs only.

Bucklebury

NEW ENTRY
The Bladebone Inn
Versatile village inn
Chapel Row, Bucklebury, RG7 6PD
Tel no: (0118) 9712326
www.thebladeboneinn.com
Modern British | £25
Cooking score: 1

£30

Eclectic décor makes this a versatile village
inn; the front bar is cosily informal, the
restaurant is smarter, with modern furnishings
and a large conservatory looking on to a lush
garden. The cooking is equally flexible,
spanning everything from burgers to ling
fillet with braised baby gem lettuce, fennel
and sauce vierge. Cooking is precise, as in a
starter of tender salt-and-pepper squid. Finish
with chocolate brownie with passion-fruit
sorbet and truffles. Wines from £15.
Chef/s: Kiren Puri. **Open:** all week L 12 to 3 (4 Sun),
D 6 to 9. **Meals:** alc (main courses £11 to £18).
Service: not inc. **Details:** 48 seats. 48 seats outside.
Separate bar. Music. Car parking.

Caversham

Mya Lacarte
Popular neighbourhood restaurant
5 Prospect Street, Caversham, RG4 8JB
Tel no: (01189) 463400
www.myalacarte.co.uk
Anglo-French | £35
Cooking score: 1

£5
OFF

Familiarity breeds fondness – despite a rather
scruffy entrance and minimalist décor, Mya
Lacarte remains a popular neighbourhood
restaurant. The modern British (with a little
help from France) cooking showcases local
and seasonal produce including Berkshire
wood pigeon and Ashampstead venison.
Some tasks are handled deftly, but consistent
cooking is not guaranteed. Meltingly
delicious belly pork with crisp apple fritters
and delicate, flavoursome stuffed quail both

impressed, but a twice-baked soufflé was too
light on cheese. For desserts, try sticky toffee
pudding. Wines from £14.50.
Chef/s: Justin Le Stephany. **Open:** all week L 12 to 3
(4 Sun), Mon to Sat D 5 to 10 (10.30 Fri and Sat).
Closed: 25 and 26 Dec, 1 Jan. **Meals:** alc (main
courses £14 to £22). Set L and D £14.95 (2 courses)
to £18.95. Sun L £14.95. **Service:** not inc. **Details:** 50
seats. Music. Car parking.

Chieveley

The Crab at Chieveley
Fresh seafood, done well
Wantage Road, Chieveley, RG20 8UE
Tel no: (01635) 247550
www.crabatchieveley.com
Seafood | £50
Cooking score: 3

This picture-perfect collection of cottages,
which forms a restaurant and hotel, takes six
deliveries a week from Brixham, Newlyn and
Looe, so fresh seafood is guaranteed. And if
the fishing nets and naval paraphernalia hung
all about aren't equally contemporary, they are
appropriate. Having chosen from a table in the
snug, fish bar or restaurant, diners must choose
again; the three menus are served throughout.
Classic fish soup and bouillabaisse are done
well, and accurate timing and skilful saucing
benefit dishes like Dover sole paupiette with
vermouth cream and monkfish Wellington
with Madeira jus. At inspection, meaty roast
hake with a Parmesan crust featured in a good-
value set lunch. Desserts such as a chocolate
and praline royale are accomplished; service is
welcoming. Wines from £19.25 (£4.65 a
glass).
Chef/s: John Harrison. **Open:** all week L 12 to 2.30,
D 6 to 9.30. **Meals:** alc (main courses £20 to £38).
Set L and D £15.95 (2 courses) to £19.95. Sun L
£22.50. **Service:** 10%. **Details:** 80 seats. 24 seats
outside. Separate bar. Wheelchair access. Music.
Car parking.

Cookham

Maliks

Dynamic Home Counties Indian
High Street, Cookham, SL6 9SF
Tel no: (01628) 520085
www.maliks.co.uk
Indian | £30
Cooking score: 2

£5 OFF

It may look like an ivy-clad country boozer, but the interior of Maliks tells a very different story. A new bar and private dining area are in the pipeline, but this dynamic Indian still shows its serene class with spotless clothed tables and a soundtrack of classical ragas. The menu is also a cut above, moving swiftly from samosas, jalfrezis and chicken tikka masala to the likes of roast duck in tangy lemon and chilli sauce, tetul lamb with tamarind or delicately marinated red mullet with mushrooms and peppers. Wines start at £15. Branches at 14 Oak End Way, Gerrards Cross; tel: (01753) 880888 and 101 High Street, Marlow; tel: (01628) 482180.
Chef/s: Malik Ahmed and Shapon Miah. **Open:** all week L 12 to 2.30, D 6 to 11 (10.30 Sun). **Closed:** 25 and 26 Dec. **Meals:** alc (main courses £8 to £16). Set L £12 (2 courses) to £15. Set D £24 (2 courses) to £30. Sun L buffet £10. **Service:** 10%. **Details:** 70 seats. Wheelchair access. Music. Car parking.

NEW ENTRY

The White Oak

Pretty pub with smart but simple cooking
The Pound, Cookham, SL6 9QE
Tel no: (01628) 523043
www.thewhiteoak.co.uk
Modern British | £28
Cooking score: 3

The White Oak is a pretty pub whose coffee-and-cream restaurant, with its wood floors, ornate mirrors and white candelabra, opens on to a garden. Clive Dixon is now in charge, so you can expect sure-footed cooking with an eye for flavour and texture; witness a generous bowl of cockles and clams with chunky slices

of leek and onion and a moreishly moppable, garlicky liquor. Also impressive is his fish cookery, if turbot atop a feast of green vegetables with smooth mash and a perfectly seasoned butter and chive sauce is anything to go by. 'Really beautiful' sherry trifle with lavender custard and crunchy meringue pieces makes a fine finale. Wines from £16.
Chef/s: Clive Dixon. **Open:** all week L 12 to 2.30 (3.30 Sun), Mon to Sat D 6 to 9.30. **Meals:** alc (main courses £15 to £23). Set L and D £15 (2 courses) to £19. **Service:** not inc. **Details:** 80 seats. 30 seats outside. Separate bar. Music. Car parking.

Frilsham

The Pot Kiln

The game's up
Frilsham, RG18 0XX
Tel no: (01635) 201366
www.potkiln.org
British | £30
Cooking score: 2

£5 OFF

Mike Robinson's delightful terracotta-coloured pub lies deep in newly christened Kate Middleton country, which has always been hunting country. The local love of countryside pursuits is reflected in hunting prints and mounted trophies in the low-ceilinged, pine-filled dining room. Here, a buzz of real enjoyment pervades as an improved kitchen does full justice to some impeccably sourced produce. Locally shot venison is the star, whether in a flavoursome rabbit and roe pâté, meltingly soft braised shank of muntjac, or a succulent pavé of fallow deer. Not the right time for game? Tender sweet-and-sour ox tongue with crispy pig's cheek celebrates nose-to-tail cooking. To follow, try the excellent deep-dish treacle tart. Portions are generous, and service is young and well-informed. Wines start at £16.
Chef/s: Mike Robinson. **Open:** Wed to Mon L 12 to 2 (3 Sun), D 7 to 9 (9.30 Sat, 6 to 8.30 Sun). **Closed:** Tue, 25 Dec. **Meals:** alc (main courses £14 to £18). Set L £14.95 (2 courses) to £17.95. **Service:** 10%. **Details:** 48 seats. 100 seats outside. Separate bar. No music. Car parking.

BERKSHIRE

Great Shefford

READERS RECOMMEND
The Swan Inn
Modern British
Newbury Road, Great Shefford, RG17 7DS
Tel no: (01488) 648271
www.theswanshefford.com
'Just wow, a flavour roller-coaster. Not only is the food amazing, but the service is just so lovely.'

Lambourn Woodlands
The Hare
Coaching inn with please-all food
Ermin Street, Lambourn Woodlands, RG17 7SD
Tel no: (01488) 713860
www.theharerestaurant.co.uk
Modern British | £37
Cooking score: 2
£5 OFF

Once a refuelling point for seventeenth-century coach travellers, this Grade II-listed inn is still in the hospitality business – although most of its trade now comes from the well-to-do Berkshire racing set. Drink in the bar, carouse in the gazebo or pick one of the congenial dining areas for satisfying food with some eclectic modern accents. Duck and pistachio terrine with Asian slaw and hoisin glaze might precede grilled lemon sole with fennel or a stout plateful of local venison with a dinky suet pud, salsify and artichoke purée. To finish, try pecan pie. A handy all-day lounge menu (not Sun) touts toasted muffins, fish pie and suchlike. House wine is £18.
Chef/s: Jamie Hodson. Open: all week L 12 to 2 (2.30 Sun), D 7 to 9 (9.30 Fri and Sat). Closed: 25 and 26 Dec, 1 Jan. Meals: alc (main courses £15 to £26). Set L £21 (2 courses) to £27.50. Set D £21 (2 courses) to £37. Sun L £27.50. Service: not inc. Details: 75 seats. 70 seats outside. Separate bar. Wheelchair access. Music. Car parking.

Maidenhead
Boulters Riverside Brasserie
Stylish brasserie with gorgeous views
Boulters Lock Island, Maidenhead, SL6 8PE
Tel no: (01628) 621291
www.boultersrestaurant.co.uk
Modern British | £30
Cooking score: 2
£5 OFF

A self-proclaimed 'jewel on the Thames', Boulters stands on its own little island, with river views all around. The best vistas are from the dedicated Terrace Bar, although there is much to enjoy from the stylish brasserie below – particularly if you are partial to well-rendered contemporary food. Herefordshire snails, Berkshire muntjac and Cornish gurnard all make an appearance, but the menu also casts its net further afield for salade niçoise or Barbary duck breast with sarladaise potatoes, wilted spinach, confit garlic and Provençal jus. Desserts might usher in lemon meringue pie or tarte Tatin (made with Cox's Orange Pippins). Wines from £15.50.
Chef/s: Daniel Woodhouse. Open: Tue to Sun L 12 to 2.30, Tue to Sat D 6.30 to 9.30. Closed: Mon, 26 to 30 Dec. Meals: alc (main courses £15 to £28). Set L £15.95 (2 courses) to £19.95. Sun L £21.95 (2 courses) to £26.95. Service: 12.5%. Details: 80 seats. 20 seats outside. Separate bar. Wheelchair access. Music. Car parking.

Newbury
The Vineyard at Stockcross
Formidable French cooking and epic wines
Newbury, RG20 8JU
Tel no: (01635) 528770
www.the-vineyard.co.uk
Modern French | £72
Cooking score: 6

Think of it as a restaurant-with-rooms on a grand scale or a lavish expression of the hospitality industry in full flow; either way, the Vineyard at Stockcross is a splendidly dramatic prospect. Named in honour of owner Sir Peter Michael's elite Californian winery, this West Coast-style villa is all about ostentatious opulence, with the split-level Art Deco restaurant at the centre of things. As lights flicker and change colour throughout the evening, customers can savour some of the 'most consistent' haute cuisine in the Home Counties, courtesy of chef Daniel Galmiche. A 'sensational' scallop soufflé with shellfish sabayon blew one reporter away, and another was seduced by a dish of melting Anjou squab pigeon with confit potatoes and sherry vinegar jus. Elsewhere, formidable technical acumen is the hallmark of highly worked specialities such as confit duck foie gras pointed up with Seville orange, candied zest and almonds, or pan-roasted monkfish wrapped in pancetta alongside braised fennel, carrot and clementine purée. Billowing soufflés reappear for dessert (the passion-fruit version has been lauded), or you might fancy blackberry parfait and Earl Grey rice pudding with a sesame and nougatine biscuit. Dinner will test the thickness of your wallet, although the set lunch is a bargain for penny-watchers. Despite the kitchen's excellent endeavours, wine remains the cornerstone here, and guests can now marvel at the brand new 'vault', with a glass floor allowing glimpses of the prodigious cellar. The 'short list' (100 bins) is a rewarding way in, with plenty of serious drinking by the glass or carafe; alternatively, take time to peruse the full collection – an epic tome that explores the byways of Californian winemaking before celebrating the oenophile planet in depth. Bottles start at £20.

Chef/s: Daniel Galmiche. **Open:** all week L 12 to 2, D 7 to 10. **Meals:** Set L £23 (2 courses) to £29. Set D £62 (2 courses) to £72. Sun L £39. Tasting menu L £49, D £99 (7 courses). **Service:** not inc. **Details:** 90 seats. 20 seats outside. Separate bar. Wheelchair access. Music. Car parking.

||♦ Average Price

The average price listed in main-entry reviews denotes the price of a three-course meal, without wine.

∎ Paley Street

★ TOP 50 ★

The Royal Oak
Classy inn with fine food
Littlefield Green, Paley Street, SL6 3JN
Tel no: (01628) 620541
www.theroyaloakpaleystreet.com
British | £50
Cooking score: 6

Dubbed 'the quintessential English pub experience' by one doting regular, the Royal Oak certainly has everything you might expect from a well-to-do country hostelry: an auspicious village location; all the beams and exposed brickwork you could wish for; real ales on tap, creature comforts and even some celebrity connections (it's owned by Sir Michael Parkinson's son, Nick). But there's a lot more going on here than 'beer and skittles'. Yes, you can feast heartily on Scotch eggs, mighty pies and plates of roast beef on Sunday, but chef Dominic Chapman's cooking also raises the bar way beyond anything offered in your average local boozer. Readers' recommendations tell their own story: lasagne of rabbit, wild mushrooms and chervil ('a melt-in-the-mouth marvel'); potted Dorset crab with rosemary and sea-salt toast; Brixham lemon sole with cockles and brown shrimps; peppered haunch of venison with creamed spinach and sauce poivrade... the list goes on and on. This is re-invented, ingredients-led British cookery of a high order, and the kitchen can deliver exactly the right touch or impact when needed – sometimes trencherman hearty, sometimes light as can be. To finish, the ghosts of Mrs Beeton and Eliza Acton hover over desserts such as Yorkshire rhubarb trifle, steamed butterscotch pudding or apple, quince and blackberry crumble. Fine food demands fine wine (even in a pub), and the 380-bin list is a stunner that plunders the classic French regions and champions young contenders from the New World. Twenty-two house

selections start at £17.50 (£3 for a 125ml glass). Note: extra restaurant seating and eight bedrooms are new for late 2012.
Chef/s: Dominic Chapman. **Open:** all week L 12 to 2.30 (3.30 Sun), Mon to Sat D 6.30 to 9.30 (10 Fri and Sat). **Meals:** alc (main courses £20 to £30). Set L (Mon to Sat) £25 (2 courses) to £30. Set D (Mon to Thur) £25 (2 courses) to £30. **Service:** 12.5%. **Details:** 80 seats. 40 seats outside. Separate bar. Music. Car parking. Children over 3 yrs only.

Reading

ALSO RECOMMENDED
▲ London Street Brasserie
2-4 London Street, Reading, RG1 4SE
Tel no: (01189) 505036
www.londonstbrasserie.co.uk
Modern European

This former tollhouse alongside the river Kennet has been a well-supported fixture of Reading's scene for 13 years. 'A very pleasant experience' was the view of one regular, another praised the 'exceptional' service in this buzzy brasserie, where thoughtfully conceived modern European menus offer a high comfort factor: from honey-glazed duck leg, foie gras, champ potatoes and red wine jus (£7.90) to monkfish in Parma ham, with confit lemon, white beans and chorizo (£18). Wines from £18.50. Open all week.

Shinfield

L'ortolan
Enticing menus full of impact
Church Lane, Shinfield, RG2 9BY
Tel no: (01189) 888500
www.lortolan.com
Modern French | £48
Cooking score: 6
£5 OFF **V**

Calling Shinfield a village depends very much on what ideal dimensions you think a village ought to have. Suffice to say it's a bit more than a church, a pub and a post-box, but just far enough out of Reading to make it feel you're retreating into the countryside. L'ortolan is

buried amid leafy lanes, an attractive country house done in cool contemporary understated style, with fabric-framed mirrors and halogen lights on washing lines in a room that looks over a bit of the front garden. Alan Murchison makes important culinary waves at all the restaurants he oversees, but it's probably here that the focus is at its most intense. The menus are reliably enticing, from the simplest lunch deal to the multi-course wowsers, and dishes deliver plenty of impact. A starter of wild mushrooms, smoked eel and artichoke cream with pasta discs and mushroom tapioca crisps is a superb opener, gaining hugely from its buttery but sharp reduction sauce, and was the prelude at a spring lunch to guinea fowl breast with spring veg and slightly extraneous pink grapefruit with its purée. A big hit of voguish Indian flavour comes from pollack with lentil dhal and curried mussels, before the gentleness of strawberries with fennel cream and fromage blanc sorbet. Breads are terrific, as is the witty French service. Wines do a good job too, finding quality and value all over the vinous globe, and leading with some interesting glass selections. Prices open at £19 for white, £24 for red, with glasses from £8.
Chef/s: Alan Murchison. **Open:** Tue to Sat L 12 to 2, D 7 to 9 (9.30 Fri and Sat). **Closed:** Sun, Mon, 24 Dec to 3 Jan. **Meals:** Set L £25 (2 courses) to £29.90. Set D from £49. Gourmand menu £71.
Service: 12.5%. **Details:** 62 seats. Separate bar. Wheelchair access. Music. Car parking.

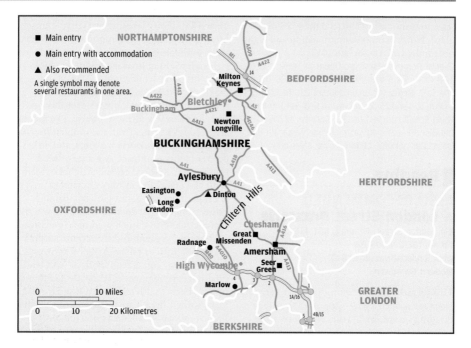

Amersham

★ TOP 50 ★

The Artichoke

Expect waves of amazement
9 Market Square, Amersham, HP7 0DF
Tel no: (01494) 726611
www.artichokerestaurant.co.uk
Modern European | £45
Cooking score: 7

Laurie and Jacquie Gear's dedication, energy and hard graft is certainly paying off. A tidily run, open kitchen focuses the eye, but the dining room's design details are also worth absorbing – top-end cutlery, lovely glassware, clever floral arrangements, subdued colours. As for the food itself, one regular nails it: 'texture, colour, contrast, impact, surprise – Laurie Gear's cooking is gaining depth as well as clarity'. Seasonality is king, and the menu is tweaked as the months roll by: in winter, a dish of creamy snail bonbons appears in company with pig's tail, crunchy grelot onions and bay-leaf emulsion; come summer, the

juicy gastropods are braised in red wine and nestled into a bed of Valencia wet rice seeded with crunchy sourdough crumbs, fresh and dehydrated young garlic and a sprouting, bonsai forest of minuscule fungi. The local landscape and its artisans are also given full rein: fennel salami from Wee Three Pigs finds its way into a salad of steamed and lightly pickled heritage carrots with carrot tops and truffled goats' curd, while sea trout is gently and warmly smoked over Pioneer hops from the Chiltern Brewery. Elsewhere a clever dish of boned and rolled skate is dressed with purple cauliflower purée and tiny pyramids of marinated green romanesco, and free-range local duck is teamed with boudin blanc, orange jelly and baby turnips. And when the petits fours arrive, they might include a single ripe cherry – a reminder of the region's fruit-growing tradition. Above all, expect 'waves of amazement' from the tiny details: a shot-glass of chilled fennel mousse dotted with blobs of crab cream; aerated goats' milk mousse with a ball of astringent sorrel sorbet suspended in it; some teardrop tarragon meringues accompanying a delectable summertime celebration of strawberries. The kitchen's confident mood is matched by a well-drilled, 'considerate' and enthusiastic team, and there's no quibbling about the prices – the five-course tasting lunch is one of the best bargains for miles around. A well-considered, knowledgeable wine list pulls together great stuff from reputable and forward-looking producers worldwide; prices start at £23. **Chef/s:** Laurie Gear. **Open:** Tue to Sat L 12 to 2.30, D 6.30 to 11. **Closed:** Sun, Mon, 1 week Christmas, 2 weeks Aug, bank hols. **Meals:** alc (main courses £19 to £22). Set L £21.50 (2 courses) to £25. Set D £38 (2 courses) to £45. Tasting menu L £35 (5 courses), D £65 (7 courses). **Service:** 12.5%. **Details:** 46 seats. Music.

ALSO RECOMMENDED
▲ Gilbey's
1 Market Square, Amersham, HP7 0DF
Tel no: (01494) 727242
www.gilbeygroup.com
Modern British

Old and new are comfortable companions in this former grammar school dating from 1600. The fresh blue interior feels modern yet classic; linen-clad tables provide seating for 50 (plus 20 in the garden on sunny days). Typical offerings are pork and pink peppercorn terrine with cider jelly and leeks vinaigrette (£8.85), sea bass with mustard Puy lentils, Parmentier potatoes and caper dressing (£18.95) and chocolate marquise with coffee bean ice cream and salted hazelnuts. Wines start at £15. Open all week.

> ### ¶|• Please send us your feedback
> To register your opinion about any restaurant listed in the Guide, or a new restaurant that you wish to bring to our attention, please visit the web address at the bottom of the page. Your feedback informs the content of the book and will be used to compile next year's reviews.

▮ Aylesbury
Hartwell House
Luxurious dining at a magnificent mansion
Oxford Road, Aylesbury, HP17 8NR
Tel no: (01296) 747444
www.hartwell-house.com
Modern European | £47
Cooking score: 3
£5 OFF 🛏

The TV vogue for country house drama has made us all look at places like Hartwell with new eyes. A magnificent Jacobean mansion in the Vale of Aylesbury, it's a model of gracious living, with sumptuous interiors including a relaxing primrose-hued dining room. Daniel Richardson does the place proud with a repertoire of luxurious grand-hotel dining that takes in the likes of seared scallops on artichoke risotto with rocket salad to start, and mains such as venison loin with swede purée, Brussels sprouts and chestnuts in red wine reduction. Finish with a passion-fruit soufflé dressed in matching sauce, accompanied by white rum and coconut sorbet. The wine list is in keeping with the surroundings, but there are many competitively priced bottles. Spanish house wines are £22.50.
Chef/s: Daniel Richardson. **Open:** all week L 12.30 to 1.45, D 7.30 to 9.45. **Meals:** alc (main courses £23 to £30). Set L £23.50 (2 courses) to £30.95. Set D £39. Sun L £33.95. **Service:** not inc. **Details:** 60 seats. Children over 5 yrs only.

▮ Dinton
ALSO RECOMMENDED
▲ La Chouette
High Street, Dinton, HP17 8UW
Tel no: (01296) 747422
www.lachouette.co.uk
Belgian £5 OFF

After more than two decades, tireless Frédéric Desmette's unorthodox 'auberge' is still a dependable and captivating refuge for fans of *cuisine ancienne*. Superb breads, 'amazing' sauces and Belgian-inflected dishes are reasons to be cheerful – try brown shrimp croquettes

(£12.50), 'huge' grilled scallops with chicory, or partridge 'in cabbage' (£18.50). Gallic diehards including rump steak with morels are also in demand. The owner's paintings of *chouettes* (owls) are a perennial talking point. Terrific Belgian beers and top-class French wines (from £16.80) captivate, too. Closed Sat L and Sun.

▌Easington
The Mole & Chicken
Attractive inn with sound cooking
nr Long Crendon, Easington, HP18 9EY
Tel no: (01844) 208387
www.themoleandchicken.co.uk
Modern British | £26
Cooking score: 1

🛏 £30

A lovely location, on a ridge overlooking countryside, makes this handsome dining pub-with-rooms popular. Inside, it's a blend of old and new; chunky wood tables co-exist with low beams and a real fire, and the restaurant rambles through several little rooms. The cooking is up-to-the-minute, with devilled lamb's kidneys on toast or crab cakes with aïoli opening proceedings. Old Spot belly pork with champ, sprouting broccoli and red cabbage is a typical main, then crème brûlée to finish. Wines from £16.50.
Chef/s: Steve Bush. **Open:** all week L 12 to 2.30 (3 Sat, 4 Sun), D 6 to 9.30 (9 Sun). **Closed:** 25 Dec. **Meals:** alc (main courses £12 to £24). Set L and D £12.95 (2 courses) to £16.95. **Service:** not inc. **Details:** 62 seats. 60 seats outside. Wheelchair access. Music. Car parking.

Symbols
🛏 Accommodation is available
£30 Three courses for less than £30
V Separate vegetarian menu
£5 £5-off voucher scheme
🍷 Notable wine list

▌Great Missenden
La Petite Auberge
Unswervingly French food
107 High Street, Great Missenden, HP16 0BB
Tel no: (01494) 865370
www.lapetiteauberge.co.uk
French | £37
Cooking score: 2

£5 OFF

Housed in an attractive little terrace on Great Missenden's well-manicured high street, La Petite Auberge's split-level dining area resembles the sitting room of a Hemel Hempstead show house: pristine, with white walls and peach carpets. However, its menu is unswervingly French, les escargots and all. So, few surprises, but no mistakes, either, in a fish soup with thick, garlicky rouille, or competently cooked ris de veau in a gravy-like chartreuse sauce with perfect veg. Pudding may veer slightly from the norm; lemon tart was a cheesecake, served with a dollop of lemon curd. Wine from an all-French list starts at £18.50.
Chef/s: Hubert Martel. **Open:** Mon to Sat D only 7 to 10. **Closed:** Sun (except Mothering Sun L), 2 weeks Christmas, 2 weeks Easter. **Meals:** alc (main courses £17 to £20). **Service:** not inc. **Details:** 30 seats. No music. Wheelchair access.

▌Long Crendon
Angel Restaurant
Ever popular all-rounder
47 Bicester Road, Long Crendon, HP18 9EE
Tel no: (01844) 208268
www.angelrestaurant.co.uk
Modern European | £28
Cooking score: 1

🛏 V £30

The transition from pub to smart restaurant occurred many years ago, and the Angel is at ease in its affluent surroundings. Dining areas include a parquet-floored, oak-beamed bar, a conservatory and a patio. Eating options are equally diverse, ranging from lunchtime sandwiches to elaborate fish specials such as roast halibut with crab and salmon crust. Set lunches are relative bargains: perhaps feta and tomato tart, then Caesar salad topped with precisely cooked salmon, and lemon tart with kiwi sorbet. Wines from £18.

Chef/s: Trevor Bosch. **Open:** all week L 12 to 2.30 (3 Sun), Mon to Sat D 7 to 9.30. **Meals:** alc (main courses £16 to £30). Set L and D £14.95 (2 courses) to £19.95. Sun L £24.95. **Service:** not inc. **Details:** 70 seats. 30 seats outside. Separate bar. Wheelchair access. Music. Car parking.

▮ Marlow

★ TOP 50 ★

Adam Simmonds at Danesfield House

Staggeringly confident food with real class
Henley Road, Marlow, SL7 2EY
Tel no: (01628) 891010
www.danesfieldhouse.co.uk
Modern European | £65
Cooking score: 8

⇦ V

As Danesfield House comes into view, its full-frontal Victorian grandeur may stop you in your tracks. There's a touch of the Gothic folly about its sparkling white castellated walls, its ornate red-brick chimneys, battlements and turrets – not to mention the horticultural excesses of its 65-acre estate, complete with sculptured topiary, beech glades and rockeries. By contrast, the sophisticated flagship restaurant aims for a more contemporary shade of pale with its bleached-oak panelling, mirrors, and lamps, all designed to lull the senses. Chef Adam Simmonds has made this dining room his own in recent times, and guests can look forward to displays of staggeringly confident cooking with bags of exuberant vitality and class. Every tiny detail and clever flourish is painstakingly orchestrated, from frivolous amuse-bouches such as a witty 'solid' Martini involving vodka jelly, sorbet and lime, to refreshing pre-desserts and dainty petits fours. In between, everything rings true as top-flight ingredients are deployed with real intelligence: how about

a masterful dish of 'deliciously rare' roast venison served with chestnuts, caraway croquettes and a pear and blue cheese purée? Or a serving of pearly white brill, arrayed with stunning Parmesan macaroni, Simmonds' trademark salt-baked celeriac, apple shavings and wisps of fennel foam? Sometimes it's the little things that matter – roasted ceps and a slow-cooked quail's egg added to a starter of roast quail breast, or perhaps a few transparent squares of pickled kohlrabi enhancing a salad combo of Cornish crab, avocado and pink grapefruit. To follow, excellent farmhouse cheeses are subjected to some tongue-in-cheek trickery, with their traditional apple and celery accompaniments cunningly appearing in the form of zingy, palate-teasing sorbets. As for dessert, buttermilk and honey ice cream with clementine, honey mousse and dried almonds is a current hit, although reporters have also been wowed by a surprise package involving lemon parfait, fennel-pollen ice cream, fennel granita and squares of olive oil jelly. It's worth noting that such labour-intensive food inevitably takes time, and dinner can proceed at a snail's pace: 'we were still exchanging pleasantries well after midnight' commented one rather exasperated reader. The high-class international wine list oozes nobility, with excellent food-matching possibilities and exhaustive coverage across the board. Fascinating 'seasonal selections' start at £24.95, and there's an admirable choice of sherries.

Chef/s: Adam Simmonds. **Open:** Thur to Sat L 12 to 3, Tue to Sat D 7 to 9.30. **Closed:** Sun, Mon, 23 Dec to 7 Jan, 18 Aug to 2 Sept. **Meals:** Set L and D £50 (2 courses) to £65. Tasting menu £82 (7 courses). **Service:** 12.5%. **Details:** 24 seats. Separate bar. No music. Wheelchair access. Car parking. Children over 12 yrs only.

▮|● Average Price

The average price listed in main-entry reviews denotes the price of a three-course meal, without wine.

The Hand & Flowers

Big-hearted, resourceful cooking
126 West Street, Marlow, SL7 2BP
Tel no: (01628) 482277
www.thehandandflowers.co.uk
Modern British | £45
Cooking score: 6

Its cottagey outlook, cramped conditions and crooked beams may suggest pubby intent, but the Hand & Flowers moved on from beer and skittles a long time ago – even though real ales still do duty at the minuscule bar. These days, Marlow's chattering classes come here to drink fizz and make merry over 'boards' of fish and chips, while others with loftier aspirations crowd round scrubbed tables for Tom Kerridge's high-end comfort food. Much of the cooking is as big-hearted as the man himself – how about a gut-busting dish involving a split beef shin bone piled with boozy braised meat and accompanied by a single carrot of epic proportions? Some readers feel that there's too much reliance on old faithfuls, pub retreads and *Great British Menu* showstoppers – the mussels with stout, the slow-cooked duck with duck-fat chips, the outrageous-looking Essex lamb 'bun' – but no one complains when the kitchen can deliver classical perfection in the shape of herb-crusted, pearly cod with pungent pastrami, asparagus spears, wrinkly morels and blue-eyed borage flowers ('one of the most beautiful, clean and satisfying dishes I've eaten in ages'). This is smart, resourceful and 'immensely pleasurable' cooking, although there's also room for the occasional blast – perhaps grassy-green parsley soup with smoked eel and Parmesan tortellini or a tricksy dessert of warm pistachio sponge with melon sorbet and marzipan ('goodness gracious me!' exclaimed one reader). Service from legions of chatty young staff always means well, but organisation can suffer when Kerridge isn't at the helm. The wine list is peppered with top names for all wallets, and there's a developing selection of organic/biodynamic labels. House selections start at £23 (£6 a glass).
Chef/s: Tom Kerridge. **Open:** all week L 12 to 2.30 (3.30 Sun), Mon to Sat D 6.30 to 10. **Closed:** 24 to 26 Dec. **Meals:** alc (main courses £19 to £33). Set L Mon to Sat £15 (2 courses) to £19.50. **Service:** not inc. **Details:** 50 seats. 20 seats outside. Music. Car parking.

The Vanilla Pod

Eminently civilised house of delights
31 West Street, Marlow, SL7 2LS
Tel no: (01628) 898101
www.thevanillapod.co.uk
Modern European | £45
Cooking score: 5

A low-key but enviably consistent performer on Marlow's replete restaurant scene, the Vanilla Pod occupies an intimate two-storey house that was once home to poet TS Eliot. These days, the smartly appointed, eminently civilised dining room makes a good-natured but unobtrusive setting for Michael Macdonald's sure-footed, erudite and technically astute cooking. His terrific-value set lunch continues to thrill readers and there's much to applaud. A 'perfect assembly' of poached quail breast with gently pickled vegetables; delicate boudin blanc (a recent arrival) dressed with apple purée and truffled apple jelly; intricately flavoured lemon sole with saffron sauce, and bittersweet chocolate fondant infused with orange – all have contributed to the genteel, feel-good effect. Macdonald's kitchen also knows how to put on the style with effortless aplomb, offering up carefully considered plates of seared scallops with Pimm's jelly and apple foam, matching pink grapefruit mousseline with local honey ('a brilliant contrast') and slow-poaching Gressingham duck breast in olive oil until it's 'almost too tender to be recognised'. Little details such as complex amuse-bouches, shots of piña colada with rum jelly and coconut foam, and even coffee with soft-textured fruit jellies mean a lot here, likewise the engaging

attentions of ever-tactful, courteous and well-drilled staff. An equally commendable, French-led wine list starts at £19.50 (£4.50 for a tiddly 125ml glass).
Chef/s: Michael Macdonald. **Open:** Tue to Sat L 12 to 2, D 7 to 10. **Closed:** Sun, Mon, 24 Dec to 3 Jan. **Meals:** Set L £15.50 (2 courses) to £19.50. Set D £40 (2 courses) to £45. Tasting menu £55 (7 courses). **Service:** not inc. **Details:** 38 seats. 10 seats outside. Separate bar. No music.

■ Milton Keynes

Taipan

Best dim sum for miles
5 Savoy Crescent, Milton Keynes, MK9 3PU
Tel no: (01908) 331883
www.taipan-mk.co.uk
Chinese | £20
Cooking score: 3

£5 OFF V £30

Taipan has been a bastion of honest Chinese food in Milton Keynes' concrete and plate-glass jungle since the 1990s. The capacious restaurant is spread over two open-plan floors in the town's Theatre District. At lunchtime, an extensive, capably handled dim sum menu pulls in local Chinese families, shoppers and suits with its top-drawer renditions of steamed scallop and spinach dumplings, slithery cheung fun, deep-fried croquettes and some more anatomically challenging specialities. Evenings are more westernised, and the cooking has its ups and downs – although fish is a reliably strong suit: try the mixed seafood hotpot, deep-fried eel with red bean sauce or the spicy Szechuan-style sea bass. Reporters also rate the hot-and-sour soup ('as good as Hong Kong'), the sizzling black pepper beef and the braised beancurd. Drink tea, Tsing Tao beer, saké or wine (from £12.95).
Chef/s: P M Lai. **Open:** Mon to Sat L 12 to 3.30, D 5.30 to 11. Sun 11.30 to 10. **Closed:** 24 to 26 Dec. **Meals:** alc (main courses £8 to £15). Set L and D £15 (2 courses) to £25. **Service:** 10%. **Details:** 120 seats. No music. Wheelchair access.

■ Newton Longville

The Crooked Billet

Regional produce and stupendous wines
2 Westbrook End, Newton Longville, MK17 0DF
Tel no: (01908) 373936
www.thebillet.co.uk
Modern British | £26
Cooking score: 2

V £30

Seriously thatched and solidly antiquated, this pristine hostelry has no truck with tags like 'gastropub', preferring to focus on the virtues of good food in its own right. Regional producers and village allotment holders make a big contribution to the kitchen's output, and there's always a lot happening on the plate: sea trout appears with wild garlic gnocchi, courgettes, oven-dried tomatoes, ricotta, lemon thyme butter and olive fritter, while roast duck breast might keep company with crispy confit, duck hash, a duck egg, pickled onions and spinach purée. But it's not all complicated stuff: you can also get sandwiches and simple classics such as devilled kidneys in the bar. The Billet's trump card, however, is its stupendous, globetrotting wine list, which offers more than 200 bins by the glass (from £4 to £48); the mighty compendium also appears in two formats, including a version devised for food matching. Bottles from £16.
Chef/s: Emma Gilchrist. **Open:** Tue to Sun L 12 to 2 (3.30 Sun), Tue to Sat D 7 to 9.45. **Closed:** Mon, 27 to 29 Dec. **Meals:** alc (main courses £11 to £27). Set L £17.50 (2 courses) to £21.50. Set D £19.50 (2 courses) to £23.50. Sun L £21.50 (2 courses) to £26. Tasting menu £65 (7 courses). **Service:** not inc. **Details:** 60 seats. 50 seats outside. Separate bar. Music. Car parking.

¶¶ Visit us Online

To find out more about *The Good Food Guide*, please visit www.thegoodfoodguide.co.uk

Radnage

The Three Horseshoes
Lovely views and sophisticated pub food
Horseshoe Road, Bennett End, Radnage,
HP14 4EB
Tel no: (01494) 483273
www.thethreehorseshoes.net
Modern British | £33
Cooking score: 3

A beautifully sited country inn with views over an unravaged Chiltern valley, the Horseshoes has been given a modern transformation, with tiled floors, pale wood beams, and tables in the garden for fair-weather dining. The kitchen trades in eclectic, sophisticated pub food. Tiger prawns with chorizo, garlic butter and rocket start things off with a zing, while mains might offer roast guinea-fowl breast with smoked bacon, baby leeks and cocotte potatoes, or the famous Fish Board, an honour-roll of gravadlax, smoked salmon and trout, crab salad, marinated anchovies and tempura prawns. Finish with lemon and lavender crème brûlée and poached blueberries. Service is generally willing, but can be prone to error, say readers. Wines start at £16.50 (£4.10 a glass) for a Chilean Merlot.
Chef/s: James Norie. Open: Tue to Sun L 12 to 2.30 (3 Sun), Mon to Sat D 6.30 to 9 (7 to 9.30 Fri and Sat). Meals: alc (main courses £12 to £20). Set L Tue to Sat £16 (2 courses) to £21. Set D Mon to Fri £16 (2 courses) to £21. Sun L £21.50 (2 courses) to £27.50. Service: 10%. Details: 70 seats. 120 seats outside. Separate bar. Wheelchair access. Music. Car parking.

Seer Green

The Jolly Cricketers
Heavenly food to bowl you over
24 Chalfont Road, Seer Green, HP9 2YG
Tel no: (01494) 676308
www.thejollycricketers.co.uk
Modern British | £30
Cooking score: 4
£5 OFF

First-timers are delivered a googly here. This gloriously retro little pub might appear fixed in the 1950s, complete with cricket memorabilia, mantelpiece clock and regulars, but the food (and, alas, the bill) is incontestably 21st century – and 'heavenly'. Order real ale and posh sandwiches in the snug bar, or head for the adjacent restaurant, equally cosy but with imaginative interpretations of traditional dishes using local ingredients. Ambrosially light mushroom soup is boosted by garlic and truffle oil, and served with mushroom Scotch egg – a gooey-yolked quail's egg encased in mushroom pâté under a crisp coating. Mains might be pheasant with root vegetable gratin, or perhaps succulent roast cod with salsify, puréed potato and salty poultry sauce, then a tangy quince crumble to conclude. At inspection, staff, though welcoming, seemed keen to maximise revenue, but culinary class won through. Small wonder that regulars are bowled over. Wine from £15.75.
Chef/s: Gerd Greaves. Open: Tue to Sun L 12 to 2.30 (3.30 Sat and Sun), Tue to Sat D 6.30 to 9. Closed: Mon, 2 weeks Jan. Meals: alc (main courses £14 to £23). Service: not inc. Details: 36 seats. 40 seats outside. Separate bar. No music. Car parking.

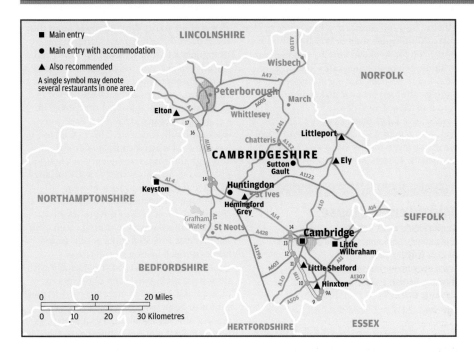

▮ Cambridge

Cotto

Faultlessly seasonal local food
183 East Road, Cambridge, CB1 1BG
Tel no: (01223) 302010
www.cottocambridge.co.uk
Modern European | £40
Cooking score: 3

German-born Hans Schweitzer's career has taken him from Munich, via Iran and Barbados, to his present berth in a former tramshed. His kitchen is supplied from East Anglian smallholdings and the city's daily market, so the focus is faultlessly seasonal, and the format is flexible enough to please the large student population. Snacky things during the day are a boon, and so are the three dinner sessions each week, when crab and crayfish tian with saffron aïoli and cucumber might precede pairings like slow-roasted cheeks of dry-aged Black Angus beef and sirloin in claret sauce, or cod with seared scallops in emulsified parsley sauce. Patisserie is a speciality, for eating in or taking away: think plum butter crumble tart and chocolate ganache cake. Wines from £17.50.
Chef/s: Hans Schweitzer. **Open:** Tue to Fri L 10 to 3, Thur to Sat D 6.30 to 10. **Closed:** Sun, Mon, 1 week Christmas, 3 weeks Aug. **Meals:** alc (main courses £12 to £20). Set D £40. **Service:** not inc. **Details:** 45 seats. Music. Car parking.

NEW ENTRY

Fitzbillies

Delightfully donnish
51-52 Trumpington Street, Cambridge, CB2 1RG
Tel no: (01223) 352500
www.fitzbillies.com
Modern British | £26
Cooking score: 1

Corduroy, cardigans and facial hair is the look for male staff at this 90-year old Cambridge favourite, plucked from recessional ruin by brave Tim Hayward and Alison Wright. Locals have cheered the return of the Fitzbillies

Chelsea bun and comforting lunchtime staples (parsnip and apple soup or Welsh rarebit). It's now open for weekend dinner – choose clams with monk's beard, then calf's liver and sauerkraut, perhaps. Baking is a highlight, so a squidgy rhubarb bostock makes a sound pudding. Wine from £16.

Chef/s: Rosie Sykes. **Open:** all week L 12 to 2.30, Fri and Sat D 6.15 to 9.30. **Closed:** 25 Dec to 2 Jan. **Meals:** alc (main courses £11 to £17). **Service:** not inc. **Details:** 45 seats. No music. Wheelchair access.

★ TOP 50 ★

Midsummer House

Cambridge's class act
Midsummer Common, Cambridge, CB4 1HA
Tel no: (01223) 369299
www.midsummerhouse.co.uk
Modern British | £75
Cooking score: 7

V

From the moment you step through the door, Daniel Clifford's entrancing Victorian villa pitched between Midsummer Common and the river Cam is an absolute joy. Enjoy drinks and watery views from the upstairs lounge bar, before descending to the recently extended conservatory dining room for equally attractive garden vistas. Welcome to Cambridge's class act – an auspicious restaurant overseen by a brigade of vigilant, well-informed staff who treat everyone with the respect that they deserve. Clifford is a prodigiously talented chef who can deliver sustenance, 'titillation' and satisfaction at every turn: cheesy gougères and Bloody Mary sorbet to whet the appetite; supremely good coffee and a veritable sweetshop of petits fours to close the show – plus some hot mini-doughnuts, if you still have room. In between, it's complexity and precision all the way, as in a single, timed-to-perfection scallop with celeriac purée, a blob of apple caramel and some julienne of apple garnished with truffles, or a serving of sea bass sandwiched between a decorative disc of fried lettuce and a slick of Jerusalem artichoke purée with a potent chicken jus and astringent pickled artichokes –

a 'clever idea' to cut through the richness. Just about everything involves cutting-edge techniques and time-consuming hard graft: consider an exacting dish of venison coated in cocoa nib and roasted pine nuts, with dried sweetcorn, parsnips and cabbage braised in Douglas Fir butter, plus shallots cooked in raspberry vinegar and a pool of dark sauce thickened with chocolate. Things tend to be less involved when it comes to desserts, although there is finesse aplenty in a textbook pistachio soufflé or a warmly exotic mélange of figs and dates accompanied by fig cannelloni, gingerbread ice cream and cinnamon. Most of the fireworks revolve around Clifford's market/tasting menus, but 'classic' deals also deliver the goods, from home-smoked mackerel with caviar, cucumber and lime to confit pork belly with slow-roast neck, swede and honey purée, cabbage and Madeira sauce. Steep prices don't appear to be an issue, judging by recent reports, although you can expect to pay handsomely if you fancy dipping into the heavyweight global wine list. Be warned: sub-£40 bottles are very thin on the ground.

Chef/s: Daniel Clifford. **Open:** Wed to Sat L 12 to 1.45, Tue to Sat D 7 to 9.30 (6.30 Fri and Sat). **Closed:** Sun, Mon, Christmas and New Year. **Meals:** Set L and D (Tue to Thur) £40 to £60 (5 courses). Tasting menus £75 (6 courses) to £95 (10 courses). **Service:** 12.5%. **Details:** 44 seats. Separate bar. No music.

Restaurant Alimentum

High-impact food at reasonable prices
152-154 Hills Road, Cambridge, CB2 8PB
Tel no: (01223) 413000
www.restaurantalimentum.co.uk
Modern European | £45
Cooking score: 6

£5 OFF

Following some refurbishment, customers can now espy the goings-on in the kitchen through a special 'feature window' – otherwise Alimentum still looks like a cool big-city brasserie. Mark Poynton's food is a smart, high-impact package defined by bold strokes and complex flavours: from richly hued ballottine of quail offset by sweetcorn and some jokey truffle popcorn, or 'superbly cooked' halibut embroidered with crisp pumpkin seeds, butternut squash purée, green cabbage and wild mushrooms, to a formidable seasonal dish of venison loin accompanied by potato terrine, sprout leaves and juniper. Meanwhile, desserts trip back to the 70s for clever new takes on Battenberg, rhubarb crumble and Black Forest gâteau (served with vanilla meringue, cherry sorbet and a chocolate tuile). Bargain set lunches also pull the crowds, and details such as top-notch home-baked breads, a knowledgeably presented, deliciously ripe cheeseboard and dreamy petits fours round off a 'totally pleasurable experience' – although chirpy, helpful and unobtrusive staff play their part too. 'Serious food at reasonable prices' is the prevailing message from readers – a plaudit that also applies to the enticing wine list (a 'nice change for those used to central London mark-ups'). Choice is global, with Puglian Primitivo 'Le Maschere' proving particularly popular with reporters. Mouthwatering house recommendations start at £19.50 (£9 a carafe.)

Chef/s: Mark Poynton. **Open:** all week L 12 to 2.30 (3 Sun), Mon to Sat D 6 to 10. **Closed:** 23 Dec to 2 Jan, bank hols. **Meals:** Set L and early D £16.50 (2 courses) to £22.50. Set menu £32.50 (2 courses) to £45. Tasting menu £65 (7 courses). **Service:** 12.5%. **Details:** 60 seats. Separate bar. Wheelchair access. Music.

Elton

ALSO RECOMMENDED
▲ The Crown Inn
8 Duck Street, Elton, PE8 6RQ
Tel no: (01832) 280232
www.thecrowninn.org
Modern British

Marcus Lamb has always taken hospitality seriously, and his thatched village inn overlooking the green functions as a centre for eating, meeting and drinking and has an appropriately informal atmosphere. The menu reflects something of the region, say pheasant and chestnut terrine (£5.50) or roasted local Aylesbury duck breast with dauphinois, braised red cabbage and a port sauce (£16.95). Apple crumble tart is a good way to finish. House wine is £15.95. No food Sun D or Mon L. Accommodation.

Ely

ALSO RECOMMENDED
▲ The Boathouse
5-5a Annesdale, Ely, CB7 4BN
Tel no: (01353) 664388
www.theboathouseely.co.uk
Modern British

Overlooking the river Ouse and just 10 minutes' walk from Ely Cathedral, the Boathouse was the starting point for the Oxford and Cambridge boat race in 1944. These days it's a trendily styled restaurant serving up classic British and European dishes such as ham hock with black pudding and duck egg salad (£5.75); pot-roasted guinea fowl breast with wild mushroom risotto and rocket (£14), and marmalade bread-and-butter pudding with chocolate sauce (£5.50). Wines from £14.75. Open all week.

Great Wilbraham

READERS RECOMMEND
The Carpenters Arms
Modern British
10 High Street, Great Wilbraham, CB21 5JD
Tel no: (01223) 882093
www.carpentersarmsgastropub.co.uk
'Excellent food overall. I have eaten from both the restaurant and bar menu and food was top quality with locally sourced ingredients.'

❙❙❙ Average Price
The average price listed in main-entry reviews denotes the price of a three-course meal, without wine.

||● HANS SCHWEITZER
Cotto

When did you realise you wanted to be a chef?
At the age of four - my parents took me out to very good restaurants in Germany, France and Belgium.

What's your biggest kitchen bugbear?
Lazy chefs who do not clear up after themselves and chefs that waste food.

What is your earliest food memory?
Eating snow-white sweetbreads with light lemon mousseline at Comme Chez Soi in Brussels.

What advice would you give a chef starting their career?
Only take this lifestyle on if you have passion, artistic flair and stamina.

What would be your last meal?
Fresh beluga caviar - as I used to eat it on the shores of the Caspian Sea, with a little lemon and Persian yoghurt.

What food trends are you spotting at the moment?
'Farm to fork'.

Sum up your cooking style in three words
Artistic, fresh, flavourful.

▮ Hemingford Grey

ALSO RECOMMENDED
▲ The Cock
47 High Street, Hemingford Grey, PE28 9BJ
Tel no: (01480) 463609
www.thecockhemingford.co.uk
Modern British

If you've come to the Cock in search of real ale and boozy distractions, enter through the door marked 'pub'; if you're after some 'stimulating' food and good-natured service, pick the door labelled 'restaurant'. The latter is an animated, open-plan space dealing in sausages, fish specials and a roster of appetising dishes running from rabbit, pancetta and pine-nut salad (£5.75), via steamed game pudding (£12) to cherry and Marsala trifle. To drink, sample one of the cracking Languedoc wines (from £19.50). Open all week.

▮ Hinxton

ALSO RECOMMENDED
▲ The Red Lion Inn
32 High Street, Hinxton, CB10 1QY
Tel no: (01799) 530601
www.redlionhinxton.co.uk
Modern British £5 OFF

A terrific pub garden complete with a dovecote is one of the selling points at this pink-washed, sixteenth-century freehouse hidden away in Cambridgeshire's southern reaches. Order a pie, burger or fishcakes in the beamed bar; otherwise graduate to the restaurant for the likes of smoked haddock and spring onion risotto (£7), best end of Denham Estate lamb or Dingley Dell pork fillet with grain-mustard mash, sage and cider jus (£17). For afters, try apricot pannacotta with peppermint jelly. House wine £14. Open all week. Accommodation.

Huntingdon
The Old Bridge Hotel
Wine lovers' oasis with seasonal food
1 High Street, Huntingdon, PE29 3TQ
Tel no: (01480) 424300
www.huntsbridge.com
Modern British | £33
Cooking score: 3

Despite its solid, worthy-looking exterior, this ivy-clad converted bank by a bridge over the Ouse has a thoroughly upbeat, smart-casual demeanour that suits its affluent aspirations. Blissful gardens run down to the riverbank, but most attention focuses on the fresh-faced conservatory dining room with its classical *trompe l'oeil* friezes, pastel-green hues and summery feel. The menu evolves with the calendar and it's a flexible compendium of British flavours with some colourful Mediterranean inserts: Portland crab is served with fennel, radicchio and pomegranate salad, venison is seasonally enriched with red cabbage, beetroot and port, while poached and roasted ballotine of rabbit is paired with pappardelle pasta and braised lettuce. Otherwise, pick Jimmy Butler's sausages or fish and chips for a quick fix, perhaps followed by pear and almond tart. Thanks to owner John Hoskins MW, the Old Bridge is also an oenophile oasis with its own wine shop and a truly top-class, global list notable for its 'flat' mark-ups and mouthwatering sense of adventure. Two-dozen brilliant house selections start at £15.95 (£4.40 a glass). **Chef/s:** James Claydon. **Open:** all week L 12 to 2, D 6.30 to 10. **Meals:** alc (main courses £14 to £30). Set L £15.95 (2 courses) to £19.95. Sun L £29.50. **Service:** not inc. **Details:** 85 seats. 40 seats outside. Separate bar. No music. Car parking.

Visit us Online
To find out more about
The Good Food Guide, please visit
www.thegoodfoodguide.co.uk

Keyston
The Pheasant
Flavours that sing out
Loop Road, Keyston, PE28 0RE
Tel no: (01832) 710241
www.thepheasant-keyston.co.uk
Modern British | £29
Cooking score: 2

The A14 can be a drag; abandon it at junction 15 to recharge at this thatched foodie haven, all beams, fires and generous welcome. Strong flavours sing out in Simon Cadge's 'staggering' food – witness the fragrant finish of truffle oil on a smooth cauliflower soup, or the pink, tender lamb's liver, its pan-fried richness cut with just-wilted spinach. Owner John Hoskins (who also owns Huntingdon's the Old Bridge Hotel, see entry), is a Master of Wine, so it's no surprise to find a wine list bursting with fresh ideas and accessible tasting notes, alongside a dozen or so by-the-glass tempters. Refreshingly fair prices start at £16.95 for a house bottle. **Chef/s:** Simon Cadge. **Open:** Tue to Sat L 12 to 2 (3.30 Sun), D 6.30 to 9.30. **Closed:** Mon, 2 to 16 Jan. **Meals:** alc (main courses £12 to £25). Set L £14.95 (2 courses) to £19.95. Sun L £25. **Service:** not inc. **Details:** 70 seats. 30 seats outside. Wheelchair access. Car parking.

Little Shelford

ALSO RECOMMENDED
▲ Sycamore House
1 Church Street, Little Shelford, CB22 5HG
Tel no: (01223) 843396
Modern British £5 OFF

Locals and incomers receive the warmest of welcomes at Michael and Susan Sharpe's beguiling restaurant, which is housed in their home. It's an immensely pleasing country venue – small and cosy, with cooking that's not over-ambitious. The short-choice, three-course dinner menu (£28.50) might include leek and Gruyère tart with olive pastry, crispy duck with cranberries and red wine, and a brandy-snap basket filled with stem ginger ice cream. Wines from £15. The evening-only dining room operates from Wed to Sat.

Little Wilbraham
The Hole in the Wall
Refreshing cooking from a MasterChef finalist
Primrose Farm Road, Little Wilbraham, CB21 5JY
Tel no: (01223) 812282
www.holeinthewallcambridge.co.uk
Modern British | £27
Cooking score: 1

It's not taken too long for *MasterChef* 2010 finalist Alex Rushmer to find a stove to call home and offer local diners delicious respite from chain-swamped Cambridge. This is refreshing cooking: roasted bone marrow with shallots and parsley is a tantalising combination of saltiness, smoothness and herbiness, while the delicacy of lemon sole is offset by crisp lemon dumplings and a scattering of oh-so-fashionable sea vegetables. End with a light-as-you-like doughnut with decadently thick chocolate dipping sauce. Wine from £16.
Chef/s: Alex Rushmer. **Open:** Wed to Sun L 12 to 2, Wed to Sat D 7 to 9. **Closed:** Mon, Tue, 26 Dec to 12 Jan, last week Sept. **Meals:** alc (main courses £12 to £20). Set L £14 (2 courses) to £16, Sun L £19.50 to £24. **Service:** not inc. **Details:** 70 seats. 20 seats outside. Separate bar. Wheelchair access. Music. Car parking.

Littleport

ALSO RECOMMENDED
▲ The Fen House
2 Lynn Road, Littleport, CB6 1QG
Tel no: (01353) 860645
Anglo-French

Despite its diminutive proportions and limited opening times, David Warne's converted Georgian residence remains a culinary beacon out in the Fens. Two evenings a week, he cooks a fixed-price menu (£40) with strong French connections – perhaps a

warm salad of sweet-and-sour veal kidney with orange and Madeira, then poached turbot with wilted spinach and ginger butter sauce. To conclude, a plate of complimentary cheese precedes desserts such as mulled wine jelly with cinnamon ice cream. House wine is £16.50. Open Fri and Sat D only.

Sutton Gault
The Anchor Inn
Lovely old pub with lots of fans
Bury Lane, Sutton Gault, CB6 2BD
Tel no: (01353) 778537
www.anchor-inn-restaurant.co.uk
Modern British | £28
Cooking score: 2

The Anchor is an engaging all-rounder, a lovely old pub next to the New Bedford River, with magnificent view over the fens. Its cheery feel, rustic interior and reasonably priced food has won many fans. In particular, they have enjoyed game croquette with oriental salad and sweet-and-sour quince dipping sauce, and sea bass with chilli, ginger and coriander couscous, as much as a straightforward fillet steak with chunky chips and Jack Daniels sauce. Hot chocolate fondant with satsuma and cardamom ice cream makes for a reliably good finish. Wines from £16.
Chef/s: Adam Pickup and Maciej Bilewski. **Open:** all week L 12 to 2 (Sun 2.30), D 7 to 9, (6.30 to 9.30 Sat, 6.30 to 8.30 Sun). **Meals:** alc (main courses £12 to £23). Set L £13.95 (2 courses) to £17.95. **Service:** not inc. **Details:** 60 seats. 18 seats outside. No music. Car parking.

¶|● Please send us your
¶|¶ feedback
To register your opinion about any restaurant listed in the Guide, or a new restaurant that you wish to bring to our attention, please visit the web address at the bottom of the page. Your feedback informs the content of the book and will be used to compile next year's reviews.

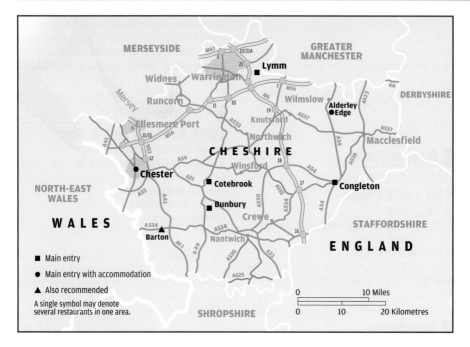

▌ Alderley Edge

Alderley Edge Hotel

Modern cuisine in traditional surroundings
Macclesfield Road, Alderley Edge, SK9 7BJ
Tel no: (01625) 583033
www.alderleyedgehotel.com
Modern British | £46
Cooking score: 3

🍴 V

A handsome Victorian Gothic façade greets
visitors to the Alderley Edge Hotel. The
restaurant – a large, 'welcoming and
comfortable' conservatory – deals in
'beautifully presented' contemporary offerings
such as lemon sole, new season peas and broad
beans with oregano and tomato, or a
'humorous' pork pie fritter with slow-cooked
belly, cider-braised cheek and apple purée.
Mains show a commitment to local sourcing
in the form of Cheshire lamb (braised neck
and wild garlic leaf) or locally reared beef
(with ox cheek), while puddings take in the
likes of rhubarb and custard or slow-poached

pears with anise ice cream. Reports are
uniform in their praise for impeccable service.
The wine list is international, with an
emphasis on France. House selections start
at £17.95.
Chef/s: Chris Holland. **Open:** all week L 12 to 2 (4
Sun), Mon to Sat D 7 to 10. **Meals:** alc (main courses
£24). Set L £23.95. Set D £34.50. Tasting menu
£58.50 (6 courses). **Service:** not inc. **Details:** 80
seats. 26 seats outside. Separate bar. Wheelchair
access. Music. Car parking.

▌ Barton

ALSO RECOMMENDED
▲ The Cock O' Barton

Barton Road, Barton, SY14 7HU
Tel no: (01829) 782277
www.thecockobarton.co.uk
Modern European

A sprawling, stylish interior belies the age of
this roadside pub, where the occasional beam
is the only real sign of its history. Nibbles are
global (edamame beans £2.50, flatbread and

dips £3.50) but most of the meal stays closer to home: smoked mackerel pâté (£6.50) could precede venison casserole with potato and root vegetable gratin and caramelised pear (£14.50). There's a good selection from the grill, and homely desserts such as spiced apple crumble (£5.75). Wines start at £14.75. Closed Mon.

Bollington

The Lord Clyde
Modern British
36 Clarke Lane, Kerridge, Bollington, SK10 5AH
Tel no: (01625) 562123
www.thelordclyde.co.uk
'Ooooh, this one is a bit of a find – a small pub with a menu that punches well above its weight.'

Bunbury

NEW ENTRY
The Yew Tree Inn
Big-hearted country local
Long Lane, Spurstow, Bunbury, CW6 9RD
Tel no: (01829) 260274
www.theyewtreebunbury.com
Modern British | £25
Cooking score: 2

Rescued from dereliction by Jon and Lindsay Cox, the Yew Tree Inn has been re-energised by a smart makeover. Part of the attraction is that it still functions as a local hostelry: local and regional ales are dispensed from the central bar, and the kitchen tips its hat to pub grub (fish and chips, local steak with béarnaise). But there are contemporary ideas, too, ranging from bestsellers like Bury black pudding hash cake with apple rösti and poached egg, to exemplary ballottine of chicken stuffed with Wirral watercress mousse and served atop creamed spring greens and bacon, and 'amazing' beetroot brownie with honeycomb ice cream. Wines from £13.95.

Chef/s: Mark Hughes. **Open:** Mon to Fri L 12 to 2.30, D 6 to 9.30 (10 Fri), Sat 12 to 10, Sun 11 to 8. **Closed:** 25 Dec. **Meals:** alc (main courses £10 to £20). **Service:** not inc. **Details:** 65 seats. 65 seats outside. Wheelchair access. Music. Car parking.

Chester

1539 Restaurant & Bar
Racing certainty for big flavours
Watergate Square, Chester, CH1 2LY
Tel no: (01244) 304611
www.restaurant1539.co.uk
Modern British | £25
Cooking score: 1

The date refers to the year horse-racing began in Chester, a fitting commemoration for this lively venue in the old city walls, overlooking the modern-day racecourse. A roof terrace adds to the allure of the brasserie cooking, which takes in Llandudno smoked salmon with pink grapefruit and sorrel, a duo of loin of rose veal and braised squid on saffron linguine with tomato foam and squid ink, and lemon meringue pie with honey syrup and whisky cream. A short wine list opens at £16. **Chef/s:** Darren Gallagher. **Open:** Mon to Fri L 12 to 3 (3.30 Fri), D 6 to 10. Sat 12 to 10.30, Sun 12 to 5. **Meals:** alc (main courses £12 to £27). Set L £10. Sun L £14.50. **Service:** not inc. **Details:** 160 seats. 50 seats outside. Separate bar. Wheelchair access. Music. Car parking.

Joseph Benjamin
Lively deli/eatery with foodie pleasures
134-140 Northgate Street, Chester, CH1 2HT
Tel no: (01244) 344295
www.josephbenjamin.co.uk
Modern European | £25
Cooking score: 2

Pitched at the heart of things, hard by Chester's historic city walls, Joe and Ben Wright's self-named deli/eatery provides a great service for shoppers, local workers and those after simple foodie pleasures. It can get

noisy, but there's no arguing with the kitchen's output – a lively compendium of ideas from near and far, based on well-sourced produce. Charcuterie plates and 'JB staples' such as Chester sausages with champ and cider sauce share the billing with flashier ideas ranging from sautéed monkfish cheeks with mango salsa and baba ganoush to confit Goosnargh duck with Puy lentils, red cabbage and rhubarb. Keenly priced wines from £14.75 (£3.95 a glass).
Chef/s: Joe Wright. **Open:** Tue to Sun L 12 to 3 (4 Sun), Thur to Sat D 6 to 9.30. **Closed:** Mon, 25 Dec to 1 Jan. **Meals:** alc (main courses £10 to £18). Sun L £16.95 (2 courses) to £19.95. **Service:** not inc. **Details:** 40 seats. 14 seats outside. Separate bar. Wheelchair access. Music.

Michael Caines at ABode Chester
High-level dining in more ways than one
Grosvenor Road, Chester, CH1 2DJ
Tel no: (01244) 347000
www.michaelcaines.com
Modern British | £35
Cooking score: 5

Michael Caines and his team are reaching for even dizzier heights, if reports for this, his most recent addition to the ABode chain, are anything to go by. Chris Cleghorn now heads the kitchen at this fifth-floor restaurant overlooking Chester racecourse after spells at the Exeter branch, and also at Caines' spiritual home Gidleigh Park (see entries). Whether you choose the à la carte, the grazing menu or a simple race-day table d'hôte, there is much to tempt: slow-cooked salmon with salmon jelly, wasabi yoghurt, honey and soy vinaigrette, or even the ubiquitous ham hock terrine, 'raised to another level' with exact seasoning and 'delightful' soused vegetables. Praise, too, for braised beef cheek with smoked buttered potato purée, roast shallot and sea bream with 'near-perfect' fennel risotto, braised fennel and fennel foam. There is no comedown at dessert either, with passion-fruit mousse and rice pudding ice cream ('a lovely fresh finish') or

perhaps salted peanut butter parfait and caramelised banana sorbet. Service, from the 'attentive and engaging' front-of-house team, is spot-on. The wine list offers much of interest, with some well-thought-out offerings by the glass. House selections start at £27.50.
Chef/s: Christopher Cleghorn. **Open:** all week L 12 to 2.30 (3 Sun), Mon to sat D 6 to 10. **Closed:** 1 to 6 Jan. **Meals:** alc (main courses £19 to £26). Set L £14.50. Set D £17.95 (2 courses) to £25. Sun L £30. **Service:** 12%. **Details:** 80 seats. 20 seats outside. Separate bar. Wheelchair access. Music. Car parking.

★ TOP 50 ★

Simon Radley at the Chester Grosvenor
Shockingly good show-stoppers
Eastgate, Chester, CH1 1LT
Tel no: (01244) 324024
www.chestergrosvenor.com
Modern European | £69
Cooking score: 6

Erected in 1865, the imperious Grosvenor is Chester's pride and joy – and among its many worldly delights is a glowing green-and-gold dining room overseen by a brigade of smartly attired waiters. This is long-standing chef Simon Radley's domain, and he is capable of delivering some 'shockingly good' dishes. Whether it's an amuse of salmon, orange and beetroot, 2cm-squared, or a dessert called 'chocolate chip' (Valrhona after-dinner mint with secret pannacotta), eating here is a trip full of surprises – even if some ideas occasionally lack that thrill factor. 'Pond life' (watercress whip with crayfish tails, garlic snails and frog's leg bonbon) remains a show-stopper, and it pays to expect the unexpected here. Readers document the results in drooling detail: an exemplary scallop presented atop salty peanut butter with some crispy piglet belly and equally crispy squid; a 'truly wonderful' chicken dish cooked three ways with egg yolk and asparagus; an

extraordinary composition of Landaise duck with ceps, polenta and raisins; a blistering 'Turkish' flavour bomb involving Manjari chocolate, pistachio cream, almond milk ice and rose jelly. And then there are the top-drawer accessories – an ad lib bread selection, a mighty cheese trolley, and a cornucopia of truffles, jellies, macaroons and fruit tartlets. The whole experience is backed up by a patrician 55-page wine list, dutifully demystified by sommelier Garry Clark: from elite Champagnes to rare stickies, it offers a palate-expanding tour through the winemaking world, with lesser-known grapes and styles in abundance. Prices start at £20.
Chef/s: Simon Radley. **Open:** Tue to Sat D only 6.30 to 9. **Closed:** Sun, Mon. **Meals:** Set D £69. Tasting menu £90 (8 courses). **Service:** 12.5%. **Details:** 45 seats. Separate bar. No music. Wheelchair access. Car parking. Children over 12 yrs only.

Congleton

L'Endroit

A warm welcome and lip-smacking food
70-72 Lawton Street, Congleton, CW12 1RS
Tel no: (01260) 299548
www.lendroit.co.uk
French | £27
Cooking score: 3

A 'hidden gem' with 'amazing food and lovely service', this classy little restaurant has scores of loyal followers. The interior is subtly French in style, the menu overtly so. Foie gras is a regular fixture – maybe pan-fried and served with honey confit carrots and sherry vinegar, or used with leg meat in a stuffing for breast of local pheasant. Other choices range from grilled rib of beef to share, with red wine sauce, to pan-fried halibut with tomato butter, mangetout and asparagus. Classic puddings include crème brûlée and marquise au chocolat. There's an excellent selection of house wines for under £14, a keenly priced international list and a separate line-up of 'special wines' offering some interesting French finds for connoisseurs.

Chef/s: Eli Leconte. **Open:** Tue to Fri L 12 to 2, D 6 to 10 (10.30 Sat). Sun L 12 to 2 (May to Sept). **Closed:** Mon, 2 weeks Feb/Mar, 1 week Jun, 1 week Sept. **Meals:** alc (main courses £14 to £18). Set L £11.95 (2 courses). **Service:** not inc. **Details:** 36 seats. 12 seats outside. Wheelchair access. Music. Car parking.

Cotebrook

Fox & Barrel

Friendly pub with inspired food
Foxbank, Cotebrook, CW6 9DZ
Tel no: (01829) 760529
www.foxandbarrel.co.uk
Modern British | £24
Cooking score: 2

Low beams, an open fire and solid oak floors make this a 'warm and inviting' pub, but it is set apart by 'excellent' cooking that 'punches well above normal pub food weight'. One reporter loved the 'superb' squid and chorizo risotto, while another praised the 'utterly fantastic' pork and chorizo meatballs with pasta and tomato sauce. Other choices range from an upmarket ploughman's to aubergine, spinach and lentil moussaka, with maybe chocolate and macadamia nut sponge pudding for dessert. Prices are deemed 'not expensive' and the international wine list follows suit, kicking off at £14.75 and offering plenty by the glass.

Chef/s: Richard Cotterill and Aaron Totty. **Open:** all week 12 to 9.30 (9 Sun). **Meals:** alc (main courses £10 to £18). **Service:** not inc. **Details:** 100 seats. 110 seats outside. Separate bar. No music. Car parking.

Symbols

🛏 Accommodation is available

💷30 Three courses for less than £30

V Separate vegetarian menu

£5 OFF £5-off voucher scheme

🍷 Notable wine list

Heatley

La Boheme

French
3 Mill Lane, Heatley, WA13 9SD
Tel no: (01925) 753657
www.laboheme.co.uk

'Imaginative menus which are changed regularly. Good food, excellent service and overall excellent value for money.'

Lymm

The Church Green

Smart pub where grilling's the thing
Higher Lane, Lymm, WA13 0AP
Tel no: (01925) 752068
www.aidenbyrne.co.uk
Modern British | £36
Cooking score: 2

V

A highfalutin tasting menu still runs at Aiden Byrne's Lymm pub, but eating activity now centres on the grills and homely dishes which have also proved a hit at his second restaurant near Chester. Readers praise the 'relaxed' ambience and, following a few tweaks, the interior seems to have settled into a smart–but–comfortable groove just right for this part of Cheshire. Inspection brought a robust, rich black pudding hash brown and smoky ribeye steak with dripping chips boasting a fabulous Sunday roast whiff, though wet–'n'–woolly grilled plaice was a low point. Puddings are evolved; a layered triple chocolate mousse worked a treat with a poached pear on warm gingerbread. Service is friendly, but can be absent–minded. House wine is £15. (Some information may be out of date as no details were provided by the restaurant.)

Chef/s: Aiden Byrne. **Open:** all week 12 to 9 (10pm Fri and Sat, 8pm Sun). **Closed:** 25 Dec. **Meals:** alc (main courses £10 to £35). Sun L £14. Tasting menu £60 (4 courses). **Service:** not inc. **Details:** 80 seats. 120 seats outside. Wheelchair access. Music. Car parking. Children allowed until 10pm

A MATCH MADE IN HEAVEN

Patricia Michelson, of specialist food shop and café **La Fromagerie**, gives us her top tips for the best cheese and wine pairings.

'It is sometimes best to choose a wine that originates from the same region as the cheese; for instance Sancerre white wine and Crottin de Chavignol goats' cheese are a perfect match, being both from the Loire region of France.

You will be surprised at just how many cheeses work well with white wines, sweeter, or off-dry style wines.

Enjoy lighter, soft or crumbly cheeses with light white wines such as Sauvignon Blanc. Match semi-hard, or hard fruity cheeses like Comté and Gruyère with fruity, acidic wines, for instance Chardonnay. For rich, soft cheeses with a sticky rind, select dry red wines with body, but avoid puckering tannins. Blue cheeses work beautifully with port, or even with Sauternes style wines, and partner powerful, earthy cheeses with a big, bold red.

Like all marriages, understanding the ways around pairing cheese and wine takes time, but once mastered it's a joy forever.'

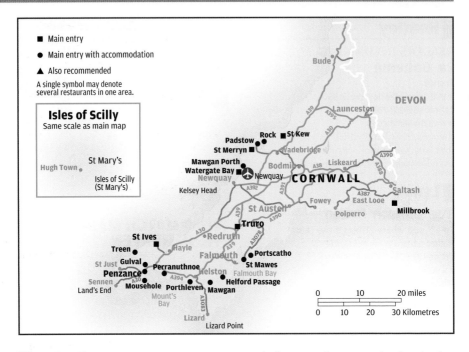

- ■ Main entry
- ● Main entry with accommodation
- ▲ Also recommended

A single symbol may denote several restaurants in one area.

Isles of Scilly
Same scale as main map

St Mary's

Hugh Town

Isles of Scilly
(St Mary's)

Gulval

NEW ENTRY
The Coldstreamer Inn
Village local with fresh flavours
Gulval, TR18 3BB
Tel no: (01736) 362072
www.coldstreamer-penzance.co.uk
Modern British | £25
Cooking score: 2

£5 OFF 🍴 £30

Located in the heart of Gulval, which is now almost a suburb of Penzance, this late-Victorian pub-with-rooms comes with an agreeably civilised feel to its spacious bar and adjoining dining room. The kitchen looks to the locality for ingredients, but also mixes influences in true modern British style: slow-cooked mackerel with rocket and black bean dressing rubs shoulders with confit belly pork with fennel, watercress and apple purée, while perfectly timed hake (teamed with homemade tagliatelle with crab, dill and shellfish cream) lines up alongside lamb chops with mint-

crushed potatoes, beetroot, spinach and red pepper salsa. To drink, there are Cornish-brewed ales and 30 or so creditable wines from £14.50.

Chef/s: Tom Penhaul. Open: all week L 12 to 3, D 6 to 9. Closed: 25 and 26 Dec. Meals: alc (main courses £11 to £18). Set L £14 (2 courses) to £16.50. Set D £21. Sun L £16.50. Service: not inc. Details: 55 seats. 12 seats outside. Separate bar. Music.

Helford Passage

Ferryboat Inn
Reinvented riverside hostelry
Helford Passage, TR11 5LB
Tel no: (01326) 250625
www.ferryboatinnhelford.com
Seafood | £30
Cooking score: 2

£5 OFF 🍴

The odd upset aside, reports on the hospitality at this 300-year-old pub set in a spectacular location overlooking the Helford estuary have been enthusiastic. The refurbishment by oyster specialists the Wright Brother (see entries, London) has worked to great effect, and the cooking has an even tone. The idea is that people can pop in for a plate of home-smoked salmon or macaroni cheese and a glass of beer, or stay for fresh-picked Cornish crab, and roast belly pork with black pudding and apple, accompanied by a well-sourced bottle (starting at £15) from the short wine list. **Chef/s:** Ben Lightfoot. **Open:** all week L 12 to 3, D 6 to 9 (8 Sun). **Meals:** alc (main courses £9 to £17). **Service:** not inc. **Details:** 70 seats. 80 seats outside. Music. Car parking.

Mawgan
New Yard Restaurant
First-rate food that reflects its surroundings
Trelowarren Estate, Mawgan, TR12 6AF
Tel no: (01326) 221595
www.trelowarren.com
Modern British | £31
Cooking score: 5

£5 OFF 🍴

Local spies reckon that this converted coach house at the heart of the Trelowarren Estate is quite a foodie destination. It's a well-bred place that glows with confidence, but there's no standing on ceremony – what you see is what you get when it comes to service and food. Local sourcing is the mantra and the food certainly reflects the surroundings. After a stunning drive along a single-track estate road through fields and woods, you will be met with menus offering the likes of woodcock with textures of shallot, and Primrose Herd pork belly with braised red cabbage and celeriac purée. Olly Jackson can deliver some seriously good stuff. There's been praise for a mackerel trio (escabèche, pan-fried, smoked), while a bestselling starter of Falmouth Bay crab tortellini with fennel purée and pea shoots, and a dish of local pheasant breast teamed with dauphinois potatoes and sprouting broccoli were components of a much-enjoyed winter lunch. To finish, there are simple strokes, say a lemon polenta cake with a crème fraîche sorbet and some lovely, zingy lemon curd, but the choice might also

run to a swanky metropolitan combo of apples: tart, parfait and doughnuts. The wine list has been constructed with care and offers good-value drinking from £18. **Chef/s:** Olly Jackson. **Open:** all week L 12 to 2 (2.30 Sun), Mon to Sat D 7 to 9. **Closed:** Mon and Tue from Sept to Whitsun. **Meals:** alc (main courses £15 to £22). Set L £20 (2 courses) to £25. Set D £27. Sun L £21. **Service:** not inc. **Details:** 50 seats. 20 seats outside. Wheelchair access. Music. Car parking.

Mawgan Porth

NEW ENTRY
The Herring
Vibrant clifftop seafooder
Bedruthan Steps Hotel, Mawgan Porth, TR8 4BU
Tel no: (01637) 860860
www.bedruthan.com
Seafood | £35
Cooking score: 4

£5 OFF 🍴

If commitment to sustainability is a concern, your conscience will be clear after a meal at the vibrantly decorated Herring, the seafood restaurant at the Bedruthan Steps Hotel, perched above the cliffs of Mawgan Porth. The kitchen may be global in outlook but nearly all the ingredients are lovingly plucked from the local hedgerows or line-caught on the inshore coastal waters. Ryan Vennings, formerly of the Porthminster Beach Café in St Ives (see entry), mixes Asian and oriental flavours with wild sea spinach, purslane, garlic and gorse flower – perhaps in a deeply satisfying red cod cheek and scallop Indonesian-style curry featuring local herbs with a hint of chilli and tamarind. Starters include blowtorched mackerel with beetroot and sumac, while far-from-token meat offerings embrace crispy veal sweetbreads and St Ives Dexter beef fillet. Desserts, including a vanilla pannacotta with strawberry sherbet, hit all the right notes. House wine from £14.95. **Chef/s:** Ryan Vennings. **Open:** all week L 11 to 5, D 5 to 9. **Closed:** 23 to 28 Dec, first 2 weeks Jan. **Meals:** alc (main courses £9 to £19). Sun L £17.50.

Service: not inc. **Details:** 200 seats. 35 seats outside. Separate bar. Wheelchair access. Music. Car parking.

■ Millbrook
The View
Outstanding clifftop package
Treninnow Cliff Road, Millbrook, PL10 1JY
Tel no: (01752) 822345
www.theview-restaurant.co.uk
Modern British | £30
Cooking score: 2

With their spectacular coastal views across Whitsand Bay, window tables at this clifftop restaurant are highly prized. 'Attentive and friendly' service adds to what one reader described as 'a very enjoyable experience in a perfect place'. Another enthused about chef/owner Matt Corner's 'passion and zero pretence'. The menu showcases local produce, with much of the seafood caught off Looe Harbour. Ingredients are handled with care and respect – hand-dived scallops arrive with beetroot and orange purée and crisp prosciutto; Cornish cod appears with a chorizo and parsley 'cassoulet'. Desserts could yield a plum clafoutis with vanilla ice cream. Wine from £15.50.
Chef/s: Matt Corner. **Open:** Wed to Sun L 12 to 1.45, D 7 to 8.45. **Closed:** Mon, Tue, Feb. **Meals:** alc (main courses £16 to £21). Set L £12.50 (2 courses) to £15. Set D £15 (2 courses) to £18.50. **Service:** not inc. **Details:** 48 seats. 24 seats outside. Music. Car parking.

■ Mousehole
NEW ENTRY
The Old Coastguard
Reborn hotel with confident local food
The Parade, Mousehole, TR19 6PR
Tel no: (01736) 731222
Modern British | £21
Cooking score: 3

This long-established hotel in the unspoilt and popular fishing village of Mousehole was acquired in early 2012 by the Inken brothers, owners of the Gurnard's Head at nearby Treen and the Felin Fach Griffin in Wales (see entries). With spectacular, sweeping views across Mount's Bay and an attractive, enclosed sub-tropical garden, tables on the terrace are highly prized when the weather cooperates. Inside, the newly refurbished dining room is all sage and sunflower yellow, with chunky wood tables and a log fireplace to enhance the relaxed, farmhouse feel. The seasonal menu might feature Newlyn smoked salmon and beetroot risotto, and a precisely cooked fillet of John Dory teamed with leeks and a curry velouté. Meat choices could include pork chop with braised Savoy cabbage and cauliflower cheese. Wines start at £16.
Chef/s: Bruce Rennie and Tom Symons. **Open:** all week L 12.30 to 2, D 6.30 to 9 (winter), 6 to 9.30 (summer). **Closed:** 24 and 25 Dec, 3 days early Jan. **Meals:** alc (main courses £11 to £12). Set L £14 (2 courses) to £17.50. **Service:** not inc. **Details:** 60 seats. 40 seats outside. Separate bar. Wheelchair access. Music. Car parking.

2 Fore Street

Harbourside restaurant with fine fish
2 Fore Street, Mousehole, TR19 6PF
Tel no: (01736) 731164
www.2forestreet.co.uk
Seafood | £27
Cooking score: 2

 £30

Close to the harbourside with its far-reaching views of the Lizard, this bright and cheery restaurant focuses on local produce, particularly fish and seafood from nearby Newlyn. The light lunch menu might offer hand-picked crab salad with pickled cucumber or a starter of shell-roasted scallops with garlic, parsley and toasted breadcrumbs. Grilled lemon sole fillets with samphire and hand-cut chips might be one of the blackboard specials, with organic beef burger offering a meatier alternative. Crème brûlée with stewed plums is a typically straightforward dessert. Wines from £14.75.
Chef/s: Joe Wardell. **Open:** all week L 12 to 3, D 6 to 9.30. **Closed:** Mon Feb and Nov, 25 and 26 Dec. **Meals:** alc (main courses £14 to £16). **Service:** not inc. **Details:** 36 seats. 22 seats outside. Music.

▌Padstow

★ TOP 50 ★

Paul Ainsworth at No. 6

Padstow's premier gastronomic address
6 Middle Street, Padstow, PL28 8AP
Tel no: (01841) 532093
www.number6inpadstow.co.uk
Modern British | £36
Cooking score: 6

V

It's just possible that Padstow is now best enjoyed on a squally winter weekend. Roll up in high summer and you haven't a hope of finding a parking space. Not that anyone's complaining. It's Cornwall's red-hot gastronomic nerve-centre after all, and Paul Ainsworth's place in among the narrow streets is its premier address. A comfortingly domestic atmosphere has settled over the various little rooms; it's a perfectly relaxing backdrop for the kind of cooking that will take your breath away. The avant-garderie extends to a menu of ingredients written in the form of a word-cloud. Choose ten, and the brigade will magic up a starter and main from them for you. If that sounds like hard work (on both sides), the main menu offers breast, gizzard and leg of Cornish duck à la Peking with spring onion and cucumber; cod with yoghurt and raisins, a cod 'bubble' and curried cauliflower; and rhubarb and tonka bean arctic roll with pain d'épices. The wine list lives up to the excitement with stimulating, imaginative choices from around the world, including Hungarian dry Furmint and Lebanese rosé. Prices open at £17 (£4.50 a glass).
Chef/s: Paul Ainsworth. **Open:** Tue to Sun L 12 to 2, D 6 to 10. **Closed:** Mon, 24 to 26 Dec, 7 to 31 Jan. **Meals:** alc (main courses £19 to £24). Set L £13 (2 courses) to £17. **Service:** not inc. **Details:** 40 seats. Music.

Rick Stein's Café

Feel-good crowd-pleaser
10 Middle Street, Padstow, PL28 8AP
Tel no: (01841) 532700
www.rickstein.com
Seafood | £25
Cooking score: 1

 £30

This simple, tightly packed café is one of the more informal eateries in the TV chef's empire. It offers straightforward cooking shored up by strong produce, rather than dazzling kitchen skills. Seafood is the main item; trademark global combinations appear in dishes such as sardines with sun-dried tomatoes and fennel seeds, or sea bass with lemongrass, spiced shrimp paste, kachumber (an Indian tomato, onion and cucumber salad) and rice. Breakfast (till 10.30am) and coffee and cake are available, too. House wine from £18.15.
Chef/s: Paul Rowley and Mark O'Hagan. **Open:** all week L 12 to 3, D 6.30 to 9.30. **Closed:** 25 and 26 Dec, 1 May. **Meals:** alc (main courses £11 to £17). Set D £22. **Service:** not inc. **Details:** 36 seats. 14 seats outside. Wheelchair access. Music.

NEW ENTRY
Rojano's in the Square
Excellent pizzas pull the crowds
9 Mill Square, Padstow, PL28 8AE
Tel no: (01841) 532796
www.rojanos.co.uk
Italian | £24
Cooking score: 2

 £30

With new owners (Paul Ainsworth at No. 6, see entry) and a new look, Padstow's long-standing Italian now plays host to tourists and locals with renewed vigour. It looks every inch the modern eatery, from the elegant grazing bar (antipasti, pizzas, sharing platters), on the first floor to the cheerful, casual dining room below. And a first-floor balcony and pleasant front terrace are perfect for outdoor eating. Food runs from white crab bruschetta, charcuterie, and classic pasta pairings to superb pizzas (the seafood-laden pescatora is highly recommended), and a very good white chocolate pannacotta. All-Italian wines from £18.45.
Chef/s: Neil Stansbridge. **Open:** all week L 12 to 3, D 5 to 10. **Closed:** 24 to 26 Dec, 3 weeks Jan. **Meals:** alc (main courses £7 to £25). **Service:** not inc. **Details:** 75 seats. 28 seats outside. Music.

St Petroc's Bistro
Stylish Padstein restaurant-with-rooms
New Street, Padstow, PL28 8EA
Tel no: (01841) 532700
www.rickstein.com
Modern European | £33
Cooking score: 1

This white-painted hotel just up from the harbour was an early addition to Rick Stein's now bulging portfolio of Padstow ventures. It's light and breezy, but reports this year have indicated some inconsistency, ranging from smoked salmon with focaccia set off by 'very good homemade horseradish' and Galician hake on a braise of potatoes, tomato and onions with caramelised garlic, to less successful Cantabrian crab and prawn salad

and 'significantly over-seasoned' vegetables. Service at inspection was minimal and inexperienced. Wines from £18.45.
Chef/s: Paul Harwood. **Open:** all week L 12 to 2, D 6.30 to 9.30. **Closed:** 25 and 26 Dec, 1 May. **Meals:** alc (main courses £15 to £26). Set L (winter only) £15 (2 courses) to £18.50. **Service:** not inc. **Details:** 56 seats. 36 seats outside. Separate bar. Wheelchair access. Music.

The Seafood Restaurant
Rick Stein's seafood original
Riverside, Padstow, PL28 8BY
Tel no: (01841) 532700
www.rickstein.com
Seafood | £60
Cooking score: 3

You can barely turn a corner in Padstow these days without seeing Rick Stein's name on some branded merchandise, but this airy restaurant-with-rooms overlooking the quay is where it all began. As 'Padstein' incarnate, it attracts droves of foodie pilgrims, and the kitchen duly obliges with the kind of muscular, globally minded cooking that has won Stein legions of devotees: stir-fried mussels with black beans, garlic and ginger; char-grilled Dover sole with salt and lime; Singapore chilli crab; hake and chips (a whopping £18). Yes, you can expect to pay handsomely for the privilege of a table here, although the circular seafood bar offers an economy-class way in for those on tight budgets. Inflated prices remain a bugbear, likewise erratic, 'unhappy' service and a lack of common courtesy. The wine list is stuffed with fish-friendly big hitters, priced from £19.75.
Chef/s: Stephane Delourme. **Open:** all week L 12 to 2.30, D 7 to 10. **Closed:** 25 and 26 Dec, 1 May. **Meals:** alc (main courses £18 to £48). Set L £29.50 (winter), £37.50 (summer). **Service:** not inc. **Details:** 90 seats. Separate bar. No music. Wheelchair access. Children over 3 yrs only.

Penzance

The Bakehouse
Funky eatery with good local food
Old Bakehouse Lane, Chapel Street, Penzance,
TR18 4AE
Tel no: (01736) 331331
www.bakehouserestaurant.co.uk
Modern European | £25
Cooking score: 3

V

'Robust, no-nonsense flavouring; splendid
use of local produce; great service' began one
commentary on this two-tiered restaurant
tucked away off Chapel Street. The Bakehouse
has been going for almost a decade – everyone
gets to know it, they like the 'funkiness' of the
place, the local art, the palm-filled courtyard,
and they return. The cooking is Anglo-
European; it appeals for well-executed
straightforwardness and majors in local Angus
beef steaks – which come with a choice of
sauces, rubs and butters – and star-spangled
seafood direct from Newlyn, perhaps
Falmouth Bay scallops with caper, lemon and
sage butter, grilled whole lemon sole or sea
bream with pesto and wild mushrooms. Finish
with hazelnut and oatmeal meringue with red
berries and clotted cream. Wines from £13.95.
Chef/s: Andy Carr. **Open:** all week D only 6.15 to 9.
Closed: Sun (Nov to Mar), 24 to 27 Dec, 1 Jan.
Meals: alc (main courses £10 to £20). Set D £13 (2
courses before 7.15). **Service:** not inc. **Details:** 56
seats. Music.

The Bay
Art, views and Cornish flavours
Hotel Penzance, Britons Hill, Penzance, TR18 3AE
Tel no: (01736) 366890
www.thebaypenzance.co.uk
Modern British | £33
Cooking score: 3

£5 OFF V

Hospitality is a plus at this Penzance fixture,
thanks to the warmth of the staff, who create a
refreshingly welcoming feel. It's a light and
modern extension to Hotel Penzance (with its
own entrance), smart and sassy inside with
simple contemporary furnishings, views of
Mounts Bay, and regularly changing art
exhibitions. A robustly seasonal menu built
around fresh, carefully sourced ingredients
more than lives up to expectations, from
'delicious fillet of skate wing' (with wood-
roasted red peppers, rocket sauce and capers)
to 'excellent local pork' (with hog's pudding,
poached apple and cider reduction and dried
apple rings). Start with steamed Fowey
mussels and finish with the well-reported
vanilla crème brûlée that comes with a
passion-fruit madeleine and dark chocolate
sorbet. The reasonably priced, wide-ranging
wine list starts at £16.75.
Chef/s: Ben Reeves. **Open:** Sun to Fri 12 to 10, Sat D
6.30 to 10. **Meals:** alc (main courses £18 to £35). Set
L £11.95 (2 courses) to £15.95. Set D £24 (2 courses)
to £33. **Service:** not inc. **Details:** 50 seats. 12 seats
outside. Separate bar. Music. Car parking.

Harris's
Old favourite with satisfying food
46 New Street, Penzance, TR18 2LZ
Tel no: (01736) 364408
www.harrissrestaurant.co.uk
Modern European | £33
Cooking score: 2

Readers continue to sing the praises of Roger
and Anne Harris's long-established town
centre restaurant, from the warm, cosy
atmosphere to cooking that will not amaze for
its adventure but will satisfy for its technique.
The style is simple, seasonally aware and uses
mainly Cornish produce. Grilled scallops on
salad leaves with a herb dressing is a favourite
starter; mains might feature roast monkfish
with mushroom risotto and white wine sauce,
or venison medallions on beetroot with
glazed pear and red wine sauce. Puddings are
old favourites: tart citron, little chocolate pot,
apple strudel. Wines from £15.90.
Chef/s: Roger Harris. **Open:** Tue to Sat L 12 to 2,
Mon to Sat D 7 to 9. **Closed:** Sun, Mon (winter only),
2 to 3 weeks Nov and Feb. **Meals:** alc (main courses
£17 to £30). **Service:** 10%. **Details:** 20 seats.
Separate bar. Music. Children over 7 yrs only.

ALSO RECOMMENDED

▲ Untitled by Robert Wright

Abbey Street, Penzance, TR18 4AR
Tel no: (01736) 448022
www.untitledbyrobertwright.com
Modern European £5 OFF

The last time this two-tiered restaurant overlooking the harbour was in the *Guide* it was called the Abbey Restaurant. Now re-named, it offers mainstream Med-inspired dishes taking in starters of salt-and-pepper squid with aïoli or pork terrine with piccalilli (£6.75). Baby monkfish fillets with braised alexanders and creamed potato (£15.75) is a typical main course. Desserts include a 'delicate and light' vanilla pannacotta served with shortbread and poached blueberries. House wine £15. Closed Sun and Mon Oct to Easter.

▌Perranuthnoe

Victoria Inn

Historic inn with appealing cooking
Perranuthnoe, TR20 9NP
Tel no: (01736) 710309
www.victoriainn-penzance.co.uk
Modern British | £27
Cooking score: 2
£5 OFF ▤ £30

'This is our favourite place by far in West Cornwall for either lunch or dinner,' is one typically effusive verdict on Anna and Stewart Eddy's ancient inn, set seductively in an unspoilt coastal village not far from Penzance. There is no posturing or frippery here, just good humour and appealing cooking that celebrates seasonal produce along the lines of Cornish crab on warm garlic toast with pickled fennel, herb salad and aïoli. Belly pork with black pudding, roasted parsnips, apple and bay leaf sauce is a cracking main course, while sticky ginger pudding with apple compote, toffee sauce and malt ice cream has been described as 'near perfect'. Wines from £14.50.

Chef/s: Stewart Eddy. **Open:** all week L 12 to 2 (2.30 Sun), Mon to Sat D 6.30 to 9. **Closed:** Mon (Oct to Easter), 25 and 26 Dec, 1 Jan, 1 week Jan. **Meals:** alc (main courses £10 to £18). **Service:** not inc. **Details:** 60 seats. 28 seats outside. Separate bar. Music. Car parking.

▌Porthleven

Kota

Enticing gem with racy flavours
Harbour Head, Porthleven, TR13 9JA
Tel no: (01326) 562407
www.kotarestaurant.co.uk
Fusion/Modern European | £30
Cooking score: 2
£5 OFF ▤

Jude and Jane Kereama's converted cornmill by Porthleven harbour is an unassuming little gem, a good-humoured restaurant-with-rooms delivering inventive, enticing food with shots of racy flavours from Jude's native New Zealand. There's much input from Cornwall's larder and local seafood is a strength. Jude gets straight to the point with starters of mussels with tamarind, chilli and coconut broth, and scallops with belly pork, soy ginger and cider apple purée. Straightforward meat dishes also tantalise, say roast lamb rump with Savoy cabbage, flageolet beans, shiitakes and roast garlic. Desserts step up with mille-feuille of rhubarb parfait and apple sorbet. Wines from £14.50.

Chef/s: Ross Sloan. **Open:** Mon to Sat D only 6 to 9 (check ahead for Mon openings). **Closed:** Sun, 25 and 26 Dec, 1 Jan to 10 Feb. **Meals:** alc (main courses £12 to £22). Early D £15. **Service:** not inc. **Details:** 30 seats. Separate bar. Wheelchair access. Music.

¡|¡ Average Price

The average price listed in main-entry reviews denotes the price of a three-course meal, without wine.

Portscatho

Driftwood

Elegant clifftop hotel with stylish food
Rosevine, Portscatho, TR2 5EW
Tel no: (01872) 580644
www.driftwoodhotel.co.uk
Modern European | £46
Cooking score: 5

The Robinsons' supremely elegant boutique hotel stands about a mile aloof of the village of Portscatho, gazing distractedly out to sea from its cliff over Gerrans Bay. Benefiting from the warm, breezy summers of the Gulf Stream, its southern coastal location also fits it to make the most of the bounty of the Cornish boats and farms. Chris Eden puts it all to good use with stylish modern dishes that are usually overlaid with his own innovative touches. Poached ray wing with pork crackling and pine nuts, as well as apple purée and shallot rings, has plenty going on, or there could be a serving of quail with its legs as confit, along with celeriac, spelt, coppa and hazelnuts. The cooking manages the increasingly elusive trick of being surprising without resorting to preposterous combinations, dressing a main course of brill with pumpkin purée, chanterelles and crab, or partnering venison loin with salsify, beetroot and green peppercorns, and onions stewed in port. Citrus tang is confidently handled in desserts such as spiced pineapple with lime and lemongrass sorbet and toasted marshmallow, or crème brûlée with blood orange and basil. House wines from France and Chile at £19 head up a short but varied list.
Chef/s: Chris Eden. **Open:** Thur to Sat L 12 to 2 (Jun to Sept only), all week D 7 to 9.30. **Closed:** early Dec to early Feb. **Meals:** Set L £28 (2 courses) to £35. Set D £38 (2 courses) to £46. **Service:** not inc. **Details:** 34 seats. Separate bar. Music. Car parking. No children under 5 yrs.

NEW ENTRY
Rosevine

Flexible seaside retreat
Rosevine, Portscatho, TR2 5EW
Tel no: (01872) 580206
www.rosevine.co.uk
Modern British | £32
Cooking score: 2

'Does B&B and rents out apartments and studios, so is something of a small holiday complex, with the restaurant providing a sort of "formal" canteen. But make no mistake, it is run on very professional lines.' So said one reporter of this grand Victorian house, which has sea views and unusual benefits – if you eat, you can use the pool. The short menu appeals with its local produce, from 'exquisite' early asparagus with a duck egg, via slow-cooked Cornish lamb confit with gratin potatoes and fine beans in herb butter, to crème brûlée and rhubarb parfait. Service is 'impeccable'. Wines from £18.
Chef/s: Tony Duce. **Open:** all week 12 to 9 (12 to 2 Sun, Nov to May). **Closed:** Jan. **Meals:** alc (main courses £14 to £20). Sun L £18.95. **Service:** not inc. **Details:** 36 seats. 18 seats outside. Separate bar. Wheelchair access. Music. Car parking.

Rock

Nathan Outlaw Seafood & Grill

A breath of fresh air
St Enodoc Hotel, Rock Road, Rock, PL27 6LA
Tel no: (01208) 863394
www.nathan-outlaw.com
Seafood | £36
Cooking score: 4

Nathan Outlaw's more informal brasserie-style restaurant is quite simply a breath of fresh air. The views over the estuary and distant fields are almost as appetising as Peter Biggs's light, fresh cooking. Local and seasonal produce form the mainstay of his short menu, and the style is reassuringly straightforward, with nothing too exotic or adventurous. Among the 'stunning' raw materials have been 'out of this world' Porthilly oysters fried in breadcrumbs, served with a dab of mayo and delicious lemon and shallot vinegar, and an outstanding fish soup 'stuffed with fresh fish'. Reporters have emerged full of praise for the simplicity of 'beautifully fresh whole plaice' with an orange and rosemary butter. They also cite the quality of the aged ribeye steak as an example of the kitchen's commitment to excellence without resorting to over-the-top combinations to keep people interested. The same goes for desserts such as a well-made citrus sponge served with a dab of intense lemon curd, offset by smooth, sweet elderflower ice cream. The short wine list is no less delightful, well chosen and keenly priced, with every bottle (from £19) available by the glass or carafe.

Chef/s: Peter Biggs. **Open:** all week L 12 to 3, D 6 to 9.30. **Closed:** 23 Dec to 3 Feb. **Meals:** alc (main courses £14 to £25). **Service:** 10%. **Details:** 40 seats. 30 seats outside. Wheelchair access. Music. Car parking. Children over 10 yrs only.

★ TOP 50 ★

Restaurant Nathan Outlaw
Awe-inspiring food from a top talent
St Enodoc Hotel, Rock Road, Rock, PL27 6LA
Tel no: (01208) 863394
www.nathan-outlaw.com
Seafood | £85
Cooking score: 9

Nathan Outlaw is a hero of the current British culinary revolution, one of the brightest talents to be let loose in a UK kitchen. Since moving to Rock in 2010 he's done some serious thinking, tasting and tweaking, and the result is extraordinary – he only cooks fish and has done away with butter and cream in savoury dishes. Resources have been aimed at creating a single, memorable experience and it is all in the detail: in the understanding that superb, seasonal ingredients (mostly Cornish) of unimpeachable quality come first; that service should be among the best you'll ever

encounter; and that the sommelier can be relied upon to give as much direction as required. Exceptional anywhere, but to find it in Cornwall is a miracle – especially when it comes via a daily changing nine-course tasting menu. The sheer breadth of the food can be gauged immediately from the terrific three-part opening salvo: salmon cured in cider, embellished with seaweed and served with a horseradish yoghurt sauce; nuggets of lobster in the most exquisite smoked paprika sauce; and the sweetness of scallops – cooked and raw – enhanced by herbs and lemon and tempered by the sharp, salty tang of capers. Elsewhere, careful consideration is given to texture. That's why mackerel is served with a light oyster tempura and a dressing of rapeseed oil, sweet vinegar and cooking juices flecked with dill and studded with tiny pieces of cucumber. That's why the tiniest pieces of apple add a sweetly acidic note to an intense bisque-like seafood sauce accompanying a mound of the freshest crabmeat. And that's why local asparagus is added to a dish of monkfish wrapped in bacon and served with charcoal mussels (coated in squid-ink breadcrumbs and deep-fried), some poached mussels and a light curry sauce. Service is perfectly paced – it needs to be, as cheeses from the cream of West Country makers are included at no extra charge (other restaurants take note). Then an almost sugarless burnt rhubarb and custard cream arrives, the perfect curtain raiser for bitter chocolate and vanilla meringue with tiny dabs of peanut, yoghurt and orange. There's an unfussy mood in the elegant dining room, sustained by engaging and genuinely committed staff. The prestigious wine list is built on interest and appeal rather than a roll call of ancient vintages, with bottles from £20.

Chef/s: Nathan Outlaw. **Open:** Tue to Sat D only 7 to 9. **Closed:** Sun, Mon, 23 Dec to 3 Feb. **Meals:** Tasting menu £85 (9 courses). **Service:** 12.5%. **Details:** 20 seats. Wheelchair access. Music. Car parking. No children.

St Ives

Alba

Ex-lifeboat house that lifts the spirits
Old Lifeboat House, Wharf Road, St Ives, TR26 1LF
Tel no: (01736) 797222
www.thealbarestaurant.com
Modern European | £29
Cooking score: 3

The setting is one to lift the spirits – a converted lifeboat house overlooking St Ives' waterfront. Alba piles on the style with its two-tier dining room, contemporary canvasses and glass-fronted kitchen, while the food is appealing on every level, from a starter of crab linguine with basil, lemon, garlic and Parmesan to mains of mackerel fillet with Asian greens, prawn tempura and crab and soba noodles. Meat dishes are also worth a punt, perhaps crispy belly pork with black pudding hash, apple purée, red cabbage and star anis jus. Desserts such as chocolate tart with Cornish sea salt caramel ice cream and peanut brittle are equally rewarding. House wines start at £12.95. **Chef/s:** Grant Nethercott. **Open:** Wed to Sun L 12 to 2, all week D 6 to 10. **Closed:** 25 and 26 Dec. **Meals:** alc (main courses £13 to £24). Set L and D £15.50 (2 courses) to £18.50. **Details:** 60 seats. Music.

Alfresco

Vibrant harbourfront venue
The Wharf, St Ives, TR26 1LF
Tel no: (01736) 793737
www.alfrescocafebar.co.uk
Modern British | £27
Cooking score: 2

Touristy seaside eateries are two a penny in these parts, but open-fronted Alfresco is a cut above the local norm, thanks to its 'fantastic' location on St Ives promenade, its scintillating vibes, bubbly staff and some highly competent fish cookery. Steamed mussels always go down well, but also look for more punchy offerings,

such as ceviche of wild sea bass with chilli, coconut and crab bonbons or rosemary salt-cured hake with cauliflower and anchovy dressing. Meat eaters often plump for crispy belly pork (perhaps with vanilla and quince purée), while a 10-strong West Country cheeseboard has the edge over desserts such as hot chocolate pudding. House wine is £14.95. **Chef/s:** Jamie Phillips. **Open:** all week L 12 to 5, D 6 to 10. **Meals:** alc (main courses £13 to £20). Set L and D £16.95 (2 courses). **Service:** not inc. **Details:** 26 seats. 12 seats outside. Wheelchair access. Music.

The Black Rock

Friendly local eatery with imaginative menus
Market Place, St Ives, TR26 1RZ
Tel no: (01736) 791911
www.theblackrockstives.co.uk
Modern European | £26
Cooking score: 2

'Very friendly and welcoming, and made you want to come back' noted one visitor to David Symons' simple, contemporary restaurant close to the Barbara Hepworth museum. The mood is relaxed, and the food taps into the fashion for ingredients-led dishes with clean-cut flavours. Beef blade braised in stout with creamed Jerusalem artichokes is a meaty big hitter, but the short menu is full of imaginative ideas, taking in everything from roasted half-shell scallops with garlic and saffron sauce, and whole plaice with clams, new potatoes and purple sprouting to rhubarb crumble with crème fraîche ice cream. Wine from £16.50. **Chef/s:** David Symons. **Open:** Mon to Sat D only 6 to 10. **Closed:** Sun, Nov, Jan. **Meals:** alc (main courses £13 to £17). Set D £15.50 (2 courses) to £17.95. **Details:** 36 seats. Separate bar. Music.

Visit us Online
To find out more about
The Good Food Guide, please visit
www.thegoodfoodguide.co.uk

Blas Burgerworks

Feel-good eco-friendly burger bar
The Warren, St Ives, TR26 2EA
Tel no: (01736) 797272
www.blasburgerworks.co.uk
Burgers | £15
Cooking score: 1

 V

'Beyond doubt the best burgers we have ever eaten'claimed one fan of this chilled-out backstreet burger bar behind St Ives Arts Club. This eco-friendly operation has a utilitarian design and a feel-good vibe. Cooked on a char-grill, burgers are made from local beef and free-range chicken, although there are vegetarian options and fish from Cornish day-boats. Get stuck into a beef burger topped with Davidstow Cheddar and Primrose Herd bacon; finish with local Willy Waller's ice cream. Wines from £14.50.
Chef/s: Sally Cuckson, Marie Dixon and Sarah Newark. **Open:** Mon to Sat D only 6 to 10, all week 12 to 10 during school hols. **Closed:** Sun, Nov to mid Feb. **Meals:** alc (main courses £8 to £11). **Service:** not inc. **Details:** 30 seats. Music.

Porthminster Beach Café

Beach hangout with enticing global dishes
Porthminster Beach, St Ives, TR26 2EB
Tel no: (01736) 795352
www.porthminstercafe.co.uk
Seafood | £35
Cooking score: 4

V

This may be a striking white Art Deco hangout on a prime Cornish beach, but Aussie chef Mick Smith's enticing and highly original global dishes owe more to the culinary hotspots of Sydney than St Ives. The stunning seafront location might encourage lesser kitchens to tread water, but Smith and his team continue to innovate, and challenge the most adventurous palates with some vibrant fusion cooking. Cornish seafood takes centre stage in main courses such as a 'deeply satisfying' Indonesian-style monkfish curry or pan-roasted turbot fillet with pink grapefruit and orange jelly, and crispy cod cheeks with chilli lime salt, snow peas, mint and broad beans. That's not to say meat dishes don't demand attention; one reporter heaped praise on 'melt in the mouth' braised pork cheeks that were served with parsnip and horseradish purée, Cornish cider and toasted pine nuts. Wines are arranged by style and start at £14.95.
Chef/s: Mick Smith. **Open:** all week L 12 to 3.45, D 6 to 10. **Closed:** Jan. **Meals:** alc (main courses £10 £24). **Service:** not inc. **Details:** 60 seats. 70 seats outside. Wheelchair access. Music.

St Andrew's Street Bistro

Vibrant eatery with Italian-inspired menus
16 St Andrew's Street, St Ives, TR26 1AH
Tel no: (01736) 797074
www.bistrostives.co.uk
Modern European | £25
Cooking score: 1

 V

'Really good, vibrant atmosphere', enthused one reporter of this eclectically decorated, two-tiered bohemian restaurant tucked down a narrow street behind the harbour. New chef Alex Redwood promises a more seasonal approach to the monthly changing, Italian-inspired menus. Duck rillettes with celeriac rémoulade and toast is a good way to kick off a meal here. It might be followed by seafood linguine packed with scallops, crab, mussels, garlic and chilli. Baked orange tart gets the thumbs-up too. House wine is £13.50.
Chef/s: Stephan Bloc. **Open:** all week D 6.30 to 9 (6 Sat). **Closed:** Nov, Jan. **Meals:** alc (main courses £12 to £19). Set D £18.95. **Service:** not inc. **Details:** 60 seats. Music.

Readers Recommend

A 'readers recommend' review is a genuine quote from a report sent in by one of our readers. We intend to follow up these suggestions throughout the year to come.

NEW ENTRY
Seagrass Restaurant
Quality seafood in a stylish setting
Fish Street, St Ives, TR26 1LT
Tel no: (01736) 793763
www.seagrass-stives.com
Modern British | £40
Cooking score: 2

Its location on Fish Street, just off the harbour at St Ives, is a clue to the focus of this light and stylish restaurant, and the quality of the local seafood here is notable. A starter of precisely grilled scallops arrives with a punchy chorizo and lime dressing and might be followed by an 'incredibly fresh' sea bass fillet teamed with crab and mussel bisque. If fish isn't your thing, try the saddle of Cornish red deer with butternut purée, wild mushrooms and fondant potato. Pineapple tarte Tatin with Malibu cream is one of several flavour-packed desserts. Wine from £13.75.
Chef/s: Lee Groves. **Open:** Mar to Nov all week L 12.30 to 2.30, D 5.30 to 9.30 (Nov to Mar D only 5.30 to 9 Tue to Sat). **Closed:** 25 Dec. **Meals:** alc (main courses £14 to £44). Set early D £15.95 (2 courses) to £19.95. **Service:** not inc. **Details:** 32 seats. Music.

READERS RECOMMEND

Halsetown Inn
Modern British
Halsetown, St Ives, TR26 3NA
Tel no: (01736) 795583
www.halsetowninn.co.uk
'From the people behind Blas Burgerworks, a pub in a small village just out of St Ives – good twice-cooked pork and rhubarb trifle.'

Porthmeor Beach Café
Tapas
Porthmeor, St Ives, TR26 1JZ
Tel no: (01736) 793366
www.porthmeor-beach.co.uk
'A terrific location and a great place to enjoy a bit of tapas and some wine as the sun sets.'

∎ St Kew
St Kew Inn
Ancient charm with a modern take
St Kew, PL30 3HB
Tel no: (01208) 841259
www.stkewinn.co.uk
Modern British | £27
Cooking score: 2

This 600-year-old pub in St Kew Churchtown is just as lovely on a winter's evening, when you can dine in front of its blazing ancient range, as it is on a midsummer's day when the meadow garden beckons. Chefs David Trainer and Martin Perkins have produced a surprisingly conservative menu that clearly aims to appeal to one and all. This makes for constraints. A shame, for 'brilliantly executed' Indian-spiced pollack with pan-fried sag aloo and delicately spiced tomato sauce revealed that they are more talented than the menu might suggest. Desserts are a triumph, from homemade ice creams to a 'light and delicious' syrup sponge. Wines from £14.95.
Chef/s: David Trainer and Martin Perkins. **Open:** all week L 12 to 2, D 6 to 9. **Closed:** 25 Dec. **Meals:** alc (main courses £10 to £20). Sun L £19.50.
Service: not inc. **Details:** 70 seats. 50 seats outside. Separate bar. No music. Car parking. Children not allowed in main bar.

∎ St Mawes
Hotel Tresanton
Stylish seaside bolt-hole
27 Lower Castle Road, St Mawes, TR2 5DR
Tel no: (01326) 270055
www.tresanton.com
Modern European | £40
Cooking score: 3

Conceived as a seaside bolt-hole for jaded townies, Olga Polizzi's Hotel Tresanton is a charming venue, even out of season. There's an air of restrained extravagance, from the seductive terrace overlooking the Fal estuary

to the cool stylishness of muted neutrals that sets a rather rarified tone in the dining room. Local and seasonal produce form the bedrock of short-choice menus that are fixed-price for lunch and dinner, with the emphasis firmly on seafood. There might be brill with lobster raviolo and carrots, followed by John Dory with monkfish, squid, pancetta and spinach; meat eaters can enjoy Cornish-bred sirloin with crispy potatoes, purple sprouting broccoli, rosemary and anchovy. Burnt English custard with raspberries is a popular dessert. Wines from £20.
Chef/s: Paul Wadham. **Open:** all week L 12.30 to 2.30, D 7 to 9.30. **Closed:** 2 weeks Jan. **Meals:** alc (main courses £18 to £23). Set L £26.50 (2 courses) to £35. Set D £43.50. Sun L £43.50. **Service:** not inc. **Details:** 60 seats. 60 seats outside. Separate bar. No music. Wheelchair access. Car parking. Children over 6 yrs only at D.

Treen
The Gurnard's Head
Clifftop pub with menus of 'sheer delight'
Treen, TR26 3DE
Tel no: (01736) 796928
www.gurnardshead.co.uk
Modern British | £28
Cooking score: 3
£5 OFF 🛏 V £30

More pleasant to look at than its famously ugly namesake, this old pub is guided in all things by its clifftop location. Pretension is kept at bay by the constant presence of hungry walkers, and the kitchen is well supplied with fish (including gurnard). Visitors tell of their 'sheer delight' in a menu that puts wild and unusual ingredients to sensible, intuitive use. Marinated mackerel comes with cucumber and wild flowers; cod with gnocchi and purple sprouting broccoli gets a lift from sorrel and cockle vinaigrette; and gurnard is served with orange-braised endive, cocotte potatoes, spinach and a sauce that captures the flavour of bouillabaisse. Puddings might be a 'perfect' lemon posset or melon soup with meringue and mint, matched with a glass of greengage liqueur. House wine is £15.95.

Chef/s: Bruce Rennie. **Open:** all week L 12.30 to 2.30 (12 Sun), D 6.30 to 9.30. **Closed:** 25 and 26 Dec, 4 days Jan. **Meals:** alc (main courses £7 to £18). Set L £14.50 (2 courses) to £17.50. **Service:** not inc. **Details:** 60 seats. 40 seats outside. Separate bar. Car parking.

Truro
Tabb's
A beguiling favourite
85 Kenwyn Street, Truro, TR1 3BZ
Tel no: (01872) 262110
www.tabbs.co.uk
Modern British | £35
Cooking score: 4
£5 OFF

Nigel Tabb's generously welcoming restaurant has been a Truro asset since late 2005. Occupying a former pub, it generates a mood of understated elegance and down-to-earth bonhomie where everyone feels at home. Nigel's stock-in-trade is a gently daring version of modern British cooking, built around bold, high-impact flavours. Grilled fillet of mackerel with potato and pepper cakes, accompanied by shredded chorizo and Jerusalem artichoke velouté is a well-conceived starter that could be followed by fillet and pot-roast shoulder of wild venison with caramelised orange, shallot cream, shredded parsnip and port reduction, or the fillet of ray wing with garlic-seared cockles that impressed one reporter. Others have enjoyed the scallops with hog's pudding, the smoked haddock soup and the courgettes in tempura batter that were 'an excellent accompaniment to a duck main course'. Praise, too, for chocolate marquise with black treacle ice cream. An accessible 40-bin wine list adds appeal; prices start at £16.95.
Chef/s: Nigel Tabb. **Open:** Tue to Fri L 12 to 2, Tue to Sat D 6.30 to 9. **Closed:** Sun, Mon. **Meals:** alc (main courses £15 to £21). Set L £19.50 (2 courses) to £26. **Service:** not inc. **Details:** 30 seats. Separate bar. Music.

Watergate Bay
Fifteen Cornwall
Zealously sourced ingredients with rustic punch
On the beach, Watergate Bay, TR8 4AA
Tel no: (01637) 861000
www.fifteencornwall.co.uk
Italian | £35
Cooking score: 4

'On the beach' overlooking one of Cornwall's hippest and most photogenic surfing destinations, this is the West Country outpost of Jamie Oliver's Foundation of Promise (a training programme for disadvantaged youngsters). 'Fab!' exclaimed a fan – and it's easy to see why. Breakfast kick-starts the day, kids get proper respect, and lunch hits the bullseye with trademark JO creations that add some right-on rustic punch to zealously sourced ingredients – think 'seaside' taglierini with crispy pangrattato breadcrumbs, chargrilled leg of locally reared lamb with Sicilian aubergine caponata, and puds such as Amalfi lemon and ricotta cheesecake with lemon curd. Dinner is a fixed-price, five-course deal that ups the ante with pukka-chic plates of char-grilled beef fillet, smashed Jerusalem artichokes, radicchio, horseradish and Fontodi olive oil, or brill saltimbocca with borlotti beans, rosemary and anchovy dressing. Jamie's homemade cola drink is a fizzy hit, and the funky wine list offers some cracking stuff from Italy, France and the New World. Prices from £19.95 (£5 a glass).
Chef/s: Andy Appleton. **Open:** all week L 12 to 2.30, D 6.15 to 9.15. **Meals:** alc L (main courses £17 to £28). Set L £28. Set D £60 (5 courses). **Service:** not inc. **Details:** 120 seats. Separate bar. Wheelchair access. Music. Car parking.

ANDY APPLETON
Fifteen, Cornwall

Give us a quick culinary tip
When making stocks for soup and risotto, make sure you cook the vegetables first, slow and over a low heat, to release the flavour. Use the best ingredients you can afford.

Which chefs do you admire, and why?
Keith Floyd: I liked watching him on TV and admire the simplicity and his passion. I also admire Jamie Oliver and the River Café chefs due to their style of cooking.

What food trends are you spotting at the moment?
We have supported local and seasonal food from the start and it is good to see other restaurants following suit.

Sum up your cooking style in three words
Seasonal, rustic, local.

What's your biggest extravagance in the kitchen?
The finest quality of food and ingredients: the best Tuscan olive oil and Italian Amedei chocolate.

What's your earliest food memory?
Catching and cooking mackerel with my dad in Cornwall.

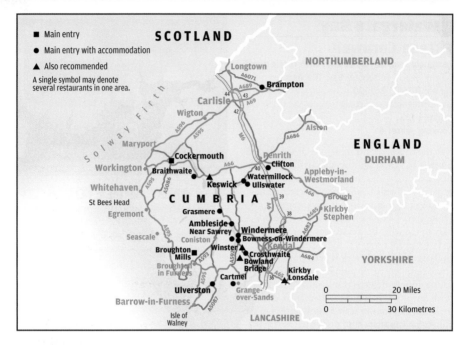

Ambleseide

The Drunken Duck Inn

Handsome inn bursting with attributes
Barngates, Ambleside, LA22 ONG
Tel no: (015394) 36347
www.drunkenduckinn.co.uk
Modern British | £35
Cooking score: 2

A handsome country inn bursting with attributes, the Drunken Duck offers glorious Lakeland views, walking and sightseeing opportunities, its own microbrewery, blazing wood fires and reams of colourful history – plus food with a strong regional flavour. Lunchtime victuals in the bar promise wild mushrooms on toast, venison suet pud and so on, while things take a fancier turn in the adjoining restaurant. Clever ideas such as wood pigeon with radish, apple, dandelion and burdock jus, or halibut with roasted artichokes, salsify and chanterelles go down well, although readers warn about 'unjustifiable' supplements on some dishes. By contrast, the impressive wine list is an all-out winner for value, with plenty to suit all palates. Around 20 house selections start at £20.50 (£5.65 a glass).
Chef/s: Jonny Watson. **Open:** all week L 12 to 4, D 6 to 9.30. **Closed:** 25 Dec. **Meals:** alc (main courses £13 to £28). **Service:** not inc. **Details:** 60 seats. 40 seats outside. Separate bar. No music. Wheelchair access. Car parking.

Please send us your feedback

To register your opinion about any restaurant listed in the Guide, or a new restaurant that you wish to bring to our attention, please visit the web address at the bottom of the page. Your feedback informs the content of the book and will be used to compile next year's reviews.

Bowland Bridge

ALSO RECOMMENDED
▲ Hare & Hounds
Bowland Bridge, LA11 6NN
Tel no: (015395) 68333
www.hareandhoundsbowlandbridge.co.uk
Modern British £5 OFF

This seventeenth-century coaching inn is hidden within the folds of the Winster Valley in the picturesque hamlet of Bowland Bridge. The sympathetically renovated rooms offer guests a bar and restaurant as well as accommodation. The menu places strong emphasis on local supplies; highlights take in Cartmel Valley smoked venison (£5.95) and Winster Valley pheasant served with a fricassee of wild garlic mushrooms and a creamy leek and Cheddar sauce (£13.50). Wines from £14.95. Open all week.

Bowness-on-Windermere

Linthwaite House
Quality cooking at a delightful hotel
Crook Road, Bowness-on-Windermere, LA23 3JA
Tel no: (015394) 88600
www.linthwaite.com
Modern British | £45
Cooking score: 5
🛏 V

An enviable setting above Windermere is not the sole reason Linthwaite House continues to delight, but it's certainly worth arriving in good time for a drink in the conservatory. Chris O'Callaghan's menu is almost as absorbing as the view and his ambitious creativity is tempered by a real ability to maximise tastes and balance texture and colour – and he has the respect for great seasonal ingredients that seems natural at this Lake District stalwart. Precise timing and beautiful presentation are the order of the day in the elegant green-and-brown dining room. To start, salmon gets a lovely whisky and beetroot cure, with a dill ice cream providing

further flattery, and moist, well-seasoned ham hock terrine works well with a smoked pepper and pickled onion garnish. Tender fillet and slow-cooked, melting shoulder of lamb is garnished with pommes Anna and al dente grilled asparagus: not unusual, but outstanding. Crisp-skinned sea bream with globe artichoke and a lively lemon purée also hits the mark. Dessert is a greater outlet for invention, as in tamarind pannacotta with elderflower jelly and carrot sorbet. For cooking of this quality, the three-course set lunch is a steal. Wines start at £24.50.
Chef/s: Chris O'Callaghan. Open: Tue to Sun L 12.30 to 2, all week D 7 to 9. Meals: Set L £14.95 (2 courses) to £19.95. Set D £52 (4 courses). Sun L £24.95. Service: not inc. Details: 54 seats. 28 seats outside. Separate bar. Car parking.

Braithwaite

NEW ENTRY
The Cottage in the Wood
Accomplished, ambitious food-with-a-view
Whinlatter Forest, Braithwaite, CA12 5TW
Tel no: (01768) 778409
www.thecottageinthewood.co.uk
Modern British | £36
Cooking score: 2
🛏 V

Nestled in England's only true mountain forest, this unassuming cottage has high culinary ambitions and a jaw-dropping vista. Teasers on a pithy menu ('Peter's furry little friend', for instance) beg tongue-in-cheek descriptions, which the Cottage's amicable host happily gives. Head chef Ryan Blackburn's team forage ingredients, but admirable intentions and delicate flavours can be lost on the plate. Starters might fail to dazzle, but mains of Herdwick hogget with wild garlic, charred onions and salsify, and John Dory with cauliflower, shrimps and Sauternes velouté exemplify triumphant pairing of impeccable produce and accomplished technique. Iced gingerbread parfait with rhubarb also impresses. Wines from £16.50.

Chef/s: Ryan Blackburn. **Open:** Tue to Sun L 12.30 to 2.30, Tue to Sat D 6 to 9. **Closed:** Mon, Jan. **Meals:** Set L £14.95 (2 courses) to £18.95. Set D £36. Sun L £25. **Service:** not inc. **Details:** 40 seats. Wheelchair access. Music. Car parking.

Brampton
Farlam Hall
Lakeland retreat with lots to love
Brampton, CA8 2NG
Tel no: (016977) 46234
www.farlamhall.co.uk
Modern British | £45
Cooking score: 3

'Everything here is done to quiet perfection,' says one fan of this 'stylish but homely' Victorian manor set in peaceful gardens, complete with ornamental lake. Run by the Quinion family for well over three decades, it benefits from a very 'hands-on' approach, with Barry Quinion in charge of the kitchen. Expect 'high-quality comfort food' along the lines of chicken liver and brandy parfait with toasted brioche and caramelised red onions, and mains of griddled veal steak with mushroom sauce and crisp West Cumbrian pancetta. Dessert-wise, there's dark chocolate crème brûlée, although 'well-varied and up-to-standard' English cheeses are a perfect alternative. The international wine list includes a good selection by the glass, with bottles starting at £20.75.
Chef/s: Barry Quinion. **Open:** all week D only 8 (1 sitting). **Closed:** 25 to 31 Dec, 3 to 17 Jan. **Meals:** Set D £45 (4 courses). **Service:** not inc. **Details:** 45 seats. Wheelchair access. Car parking. Children over 5 yrs only.

Visit us Online
To find out more about
The Good Food Guide, please visit
www.thegoodfoodguide.co.uk

Broughton Mills
Blacksmiths Arms
Quaint inn with people-pleasing food
Broughton Mills, LA20 6AX
Tel no: (01229) 716824
www.theblacksmithsarms.com
Modern British | £23
Cooking score: 2

Remote and suitably quaint, this eighteenth-century inn is rammed with original features. Served between low ceilings and stone floors, Michael Lane's food ticks off an international list, combining hearty, robust dishes and more contemporary offerings. It's done with people-pleasing skill, so slow-cooked shoulder of lamb Henry is properly tender and vast, the battered king prawns on an oriental salad are ethereally light, and a wild mushroom risotto with Parmesan is timed to the second. Well-made gratin dauphinois, duck-fat roast potatoes and griddled asparagus show a pleasing regard for vegetables. To finish, try lime and ginger brûlée. House wine from £13.50.
Chef/s: Michael Lane. **Open:** Tue to Sun L 12 to 2, all week D 6 to 9. **Closed:** 25 and 26 Dec. **Meals:** alc (main courses £11 to £17). **Service:** not inc. **Details:** 40 seats. 24 seats outside. Separate bar. No music. Car parking.

Cartmel
★ TOP 50 ★
L'Enclume
Miracles of nature
Cavendish Street, Cartmel, LA11 6PZ
Tel no: (015395) 36362
www.lenclume.co.uk
Modern British | £89
Cooking score: 10

There was a time when Cartmel's only attractions were its little racecourse and its twelfth-century priory. That was before Hampshire-born Simon Rogan moved here and took over the hewn-out stone smithy. Since then, L'Enclume has evolved into a world-class destination, serving food that is hard-wired to the Cumbrian soil. The restaurant itself has been freshened up for twenty-first century visitors – slabs of modernism, unclothed expanses of dark wood (note the softly undulating table tops). Nature is the theme: 'These ingredients will not wait,' explains Rogan, and the result is a daily 12-course menu with numerous extras built around it; a bald version is printed out as a guide. To begin, a quick-fire salvo includes the 'oyster pebble' – a riotous *trompe l'oeil* joke involving a pile of stones with one strange greyish nugget on top. In reality, it's a smooth meringue dyed with squid ink and filled with the most intense oyster cream imaginable; for maximum briny impact, you are instructed to eat it with the huge oyster leaf provided. 'Feel it in your mouth' is the message; open up those dormant taste buds, smell, savour and admire the fragrances, the pungency, the earthy realism of it all. Rogan understands wild plants and their place in the bigger scheme of things. The kitchen's deep-rooted agenda and synergistic relationship with the land also means that stuff can be grown to order – he cooks what the land can provide, nothing more, nothing less – and if you ever wondered why chefs are obsessed with foetal vegetables, just try the tiny, flavour-burst turnips served with Reg Johnson's Goosnargh chicken and some supercharged chicken offal bolognese. When it comes to orthodox cooking, Rogan can cut it with the best – witness his butter-braised turbot glazed with syrupy chicory jam and a rich bone sauce; again, the accompaniments are heaven-sent – wild red orach leaves and deep crimson beetroot (embryonic specimens again). Eating at L'Enclume is a meticulously choreographed journey, so it seems almost inappropriate to single out the blast of ice-cool, sushi freshness in slices of marinated mackerel invigorated by tiny thyme flowers, aromatic pennyroyal leaves and droplets of pungent, peppery radish 'essence'; the tartare of wild venison chopped so cleanly and finely, seasoned with smoked salt and dots of blistering yellow mustard and

embedded with beads of candied fennel; even the daily-baked breads are in a class of their own. As the whole 'tour de force' approaches its final destination, the compass swings towards sweetness. Rogan has seriously upped his game here: cherries with musky meadowsweet ice cream, hazelnut and apple; crimson raspberries on crumbled lemon verbena cake with blazing green cicely granita; a deliriously heady combo of iced chamomile, candied celery and resinous spruce syrup. Even more impressive is the fact that everyone is in tune, and it shows in highly committed, impressively informed service that manages to mix five-star professionalism with kindliness and genuine affection. Not surprisingly, the thoughtful wine list (from £23) has a strong organic and biodynamic contingent, a fondness for artisan growers and a dedication to quality – it's a perfect fit for the food. There's also a quiet little revolution going on here: Rogan's upland farm is coming on strong and he is also developing Aulis, a cutting-edge, gastronomic research space and 'kitchen table' next door. Special packages are available if you fancy exploring these purposeful holistic delights.

Chef/s: Simon Rogan. **Open:** Wed to Sun L 12 to 1.30, all week D 6.45 to 9. **Meals:** Set L £29 (3 courses). Set menu £69 (8 courses) to £89 (12 courses). **Service:** not inc. **Details:** 50 seats. No music. Wheelchair access. Car parking. No children under 10 yrs at D.

Rogan & Company
Really hitting the mark
The Square, Cartmel, LA11 6QD
Tel no: (015395) 35917
www.roganandcompany.co.uk
Modern British | £35
Cooking score: 4

Having succeeded as a high-quality brasserie, the focus at Simon Rogan's second Cartmel restaurant is now on reviving the style of dishes from the early days of L'Enclume (see entry). It's all about respect for ingredients and the careful balance of tastes and textures. To start, soused mackerel with pickled vegetables is bright and lively, while salt-baked kohlrabi with ruby chard and goats' milk curd with rocket, beetroot and radish shows flair in the absence of meat. Precise timing and accomplished saucing combine in mains of wild brill, lobster dumplings and lobster cream, and poached chicken with enoki mushrooms in a deeply flavoured jus. Dessert is equally impressive: try spiced pineapple tart or poached rhubarb with buttermilk custard. The youthful staff offer help and welcome, and house wine is from £17.

Chef/s: Simon Rogan and Danielle Barry. **Open:** Wed to Sun L 12 to 2, D 6.30 to 9. **Closed:** Mon, Tue. **Meals:** alc (main courses £15 to £21). **Service:** not inc. **Details:** 50 seats. Wheelchair access. Music.

Clifton

George & Dragon
Estate pub with strong local connections
Clifton, CA10 2ER
Tel no: (01768) 865381
www.georgeanddragonclifton.co.uk
Modern British | £25
Cooking score: 3

A partnership made in heaven – or at least on the fringes of the Lake District – this reconfigured coaching inn is a thriving adjunct to the ancient Lowther Estate, and makes full use of its organically reared meats, plus generous seasonal pickings from its woods, fields and hedgerows. It's a fruitful tie-in that regularly yields accomplished and satisfying dishes, from venison carpaccio with pear and truffle oil to the signature Shorthorn sirloin steak with hand-cut chips and béarnaise. Game fans might fancy mallard and smoked black pudding hash, fish lovers could veer towards monkfish with saffron potatoes and cucumber, and there are sweet hits from crumbles, brûlées and chocolate desserts. The pub's sympathetically restored interior has been hand-crafted from Cumbrian slate, timber, stone and other natural materials. Around 50 wines start at £14.85.

Chef/s: Paul McKinnon. **Open:** all week L 12 to 2.30, D 6 to 9. **Closed:** 26 Dec. **Meals:** alc (main courses £12 to £23). **Service:** not inc. **Details:** 100 seats. 60 seats outside. Separate bar. Wheelchair access. Music. Car parking.

Cockermouth

Quince & Medlar
A real veggie find
11-13 Castlegate, Cockermouth, CA13 9EU
Tel no: (01900) 823579
www.quinceandmedlar.co.uk
Vegetarian | £27
Cooking score: 4

Colin and Louisa Le Voi's evergreen restaurant draws folk from afar for its fresh, invigorating vegetarian food. Although it has been established for 24 years, reporters continue to consider the place a real find, and have emerged from the comfortable, traditionally decorated restaurant (think soft furnishings, soft light and polished wood) full of praise for a kitchen that shows care with details. Colin creates a raft of Mediterranean flavours from balsamic-baked red onion stuffed with saffron couscous, pine nuts, Kalamata olives and feta with spinach and a basil pesto, to Sicilian fennel and polenta with a chunky tomato sauce. Start with cheesy millet muffins with sun-dried tomato and green olive tapenade, and finish with a light and dark chocolate orange torte. Organic wines start at £15.10.

Chef/s: Colin Le Voi. **Open:** Tue to Sat D only 6.30 to 9.30. **Closed:** Sun, Mon, 24 to 26 Dec. **Meals:** alc (main courses £14). **Service:** not inc. **Details:** 26 seats. Music. Children over 5 yrs only.

Also Recommended
Also recommended entries are not scored but we think they are worth a visit.

Crosthwaite
The Punch Bowl
Keen prices and cosmopolitan ideas
Lyth Valley, Crosthwaite, LA8 8HR
Tel no: (015395) 68237
www.the-punchbowl.co.uk
Modern British | £25
Cooking score: 3

Happily straddling the roles of pub and restaurant-with-rooms, the Punch Bowl piles on the style with a gorgeous setting overlooking the Lyth Valley and a rural-chic interior of slate, polished oak floors, beams and neutral colours. The food is just the ticket, too, with keen prices and cosmopolitan ideas. Whether you fancy fish and chips or beef bourguignon, the kitchen can oblige. It also rings the changes with queenie scallops served with garlic, Gruyère and parsley sauce; sea bass in a shrimp cream sauce with potato rösti, romanesco and buttered seasonal vegetables, and treacle tart – all components of 'one of the most delicious meals I have eaten in a restaurant'. However, 'erratic service' has marred the experience for several visitors. Wines from £19.
Chef/s: Scott Fairweather. **Open:** all week 12 to 9.30. **Meals:** alc (main courses £11 to £20). Set L £12.95 (2 courses) to £15.50 (Mon to Fri). Sun L £17.95. **Service:** not inc. **Details:** 90 seats. 50 seats outside. Separate bar. Music. Car parking.

Grasmere
The Jumble Room
Big-city fusion in the Lakes
Langdale Road, Grasmere, LA22 9SU
Tel no: (015394) 35188
www.thejumbleroom.co.uk
Global | £40
Cooking score: 2

Striking pictures of cattle lowering their heads to have a sniff at what you're eating form the decorative theme of this unusual and hearteningly informal eatery, where the eclectic menu speaks more of big-city fusion than Lakeland pastoral. Dong po pork and Cullen skink kick things off, before mains oscillate wildly from lamb tagine to Emperor Choo Chee's seafood curry, a fish medley in coconut milk and Thai spices, served with basmati. Local cheeses provide the unsticky alternative to a pairing of chocolate truffle cake and poached pear. House Chilean is £16.95 (£5.50 a glass).
Chef/s: Trudy and David Clay. **Open:** Wed to Sun L 12 to 3, D 6 to 10.30. **Closed:** Mon, Tue, 14 to 27 Dec, Wed and Thur Jan. **Meals:** alc (main courses £13 to £26). **Service:** not inc. **Details:** 45 seats. Music.

Keswick

ALSO RECOMMENDED
▲ Swinside Lodge
Grange Road, Newlands, Keswick, CA12 5UE
Tel no: (017687) 72948
www.swinsidelodge-hotel.co.uk
Modern British £5

Occupying a tranquil spot just a stroll from Cat Bells fell, this pleasing Georgian residence is an archetypal family-run Lakeland retreat, right down to its lovely views out towards Derwentwater and its no-choice, four-course dinner menu (£45). Expect a nightly peppering of classic ideas and native ingredients – think Cumbrian beef fillet with parsnips, baby leeks and pickled walnuts; saffron-baked salmon with celeriac, fennel and Pernod sauce; and time-honoured country-house desserts such as warm ginger sponge with caramelised apple. Wines from £18.50. Open all week, D only.

Symbols
🛏 Accommodation is available
£30 Three courses for less than £30
V Separate vegetarian menu
£5 £5-off voucher scheme
🍷 Notable wine list

Kirkby Lonsdale

ALSO RECOMMENDED
▲ The Sun Inn
6 Market Street, Kirkby Lonsdale, LA6 2AU
Tel no: (015242) 71965
www.sun-inn.info
British

The period features of Mark and Lucy Fuller's venerable inn-with-rooms are eye-catching. The food, too, deserves attention, and the menus are pleasingly flexible. The bar offers upbeat pub grub – from nibbles of cauliflower cheese or sausage and mustard dip (£3.95) to full-size fish and chips (£9.95). Upgrade to the restaurant for intensely seasonal dishes, which in winter could mean potted crab and partridge – fried breast and pithiviers leg – with sticky red cabbage (£16.95). House wine £15.75. Closed Mon L.

Near Sawrey
Ees Wyke
Beatrix Potter bolt-hole
Near Sawrey, LA22 0JZ
Tel no: (015394) 36393
www.eeswyke.co.uk
Modern British | £35
Cooking score: 2
£5 OFF 🛏

Visitors to this neck of the woods come in search of misty-eyed, storybook nostalgia; Near Sawrey is Beatrix Potter country and Ees Wyke is right at the heart of the author's home village. Hosts Richard and Margaret Lee offers lashings of hospitality and well-tried fixed-priced dinners in true Lakeland style. Regulars appreciate Richard's consistent cooking and his unaffected use of 'superlative raw materials', from gorgeous scallops to first-rate lamb from the fells. Other recent hits have included cod and pancetta fishcakes with chilli dressing, 'fluffy' sticky toffee sponge with hot butterscotch sauce and an exemplary regional cheeseboard. House wine is £19.50 (£4.50 a glass).

Chef/s: Richard Lee. **Open:** all week D only 7.30 (1 sitting). **Meals:** Set D £35 (5 courses). **Service:** not inc. **Details:** 16 seats. No music. Car parking. Children over 12 yrs only.

Ullswater
Sharrow Bay
Country-house comfort and fine food
Ullswater, CA10 2LZ
Tel no: (01768) 486301
www.sharrowbay.co.uk
Modern British | £45
Cooking score: 5

Concerns regarding its future have not diminished the attraction of this leading Lakeland retreat. While the chintzy décor and reverential hush of the Sharrow Bay dining room might not appeal to all, there's no arguing with the seamless service and accomplished cooking. Head chef Colin Akrigg continues the culinary legacy of Francis Coulson in a classical repertoire of fad-free dishes that are finely tuned, well balanced and elegantly presented. The lunch menus offer ample choice and good value, while dinner of up to 10 courses makes more demands on the pocket and the waistband. Saucing is a particular strength, be it wild mushroom and brandy with succulent breast of quail, tomato and rosemary with perfectly timed Herdwick lamb or Noilly Prat and lemon with a beautifully fresh fillet of cod. Cold desserts can be more adventurous, but few can resist trying the 'icky' sticky toffee pudding in the dining room where it was first served. In the lounge, there's coffee and panoramic views of Ullswater alongside country-house comfort. The distinguished wine list offers a serious choice, with prices to match. A good selection by the glass starts at £5.45, with bottles from £22.50.

Chef/s: Colin Akrigg and Mark Teasdale. **Open:** all week L 12.30 (1 sitting), D 7.30 (1 sitting). **Meals:** alc (main courses £25 to £35). Set L £35. Set D £45 to £75 (6 courses). Sun L £45. **Service:** not inc.

Details: 60 seats. 15 seats outside. No music. Wheelchair access. Car parking. Children over 11 yrs only.

▌Ulverston

The Bay Horse

Glorious views, hospitality and good food
Canal Foot, Ulverston, LA12 9EL
Tel no: (01229) 583972
www.thebayhorsehotel.co.uk
Modern British | £36
Cooking score: 3

🚗 V

Hard by the Leven Estuary, with glorious views taking in the Lancashire and Cumbrian fells, Robert Lyons' handsome coaching inn draws a loyal crowd with its personable hospitality and good food. A few easy dining options are served in the bar at lunchtime. Dinner is at eight in the conservatory, and the menu, which changes monthly, seems designed for customers to eat and be pleased. Along with roast belly pork and steak casserole with sage and onion dumplings, there are a few fancier dishes, perhaps salmon escalope marinated in lime juice, ginger and red chilli, or bobotie (a South African dish of minced lamb, apricot and spices baked with a brandied egg custard). A typical dessert is dark chocolate brandy crème brûlée. Wines from £13.50.
Chef/s: Robert Lyons and Kris Hogan. **Open:** all week L 12 to 2 (4 Sat and Sun), D 7.30 for 8 (1 sitting). **Meals:** alc (main courses £22 to £27). Set D £18 (2 courses) to £31. **Service:** not inc. **Details:** 40 seats. Separate bar. Music. Car parking. Children over 9 yrs only.

🍴 SIMON ROGAN
L'Enclume

Give us a quick culinary tip
Find someone to do your washing up.

Which chefs do you admire, and why?
Pierre Gagnaire and Marc Veyrat gave me the inspiration to choose the path I took.

What food trends are you spotting at the moment?
Simple, fast food that's done really well, such as burgers, hot dogs and ribs - food with BBQ aspects.

Sum up your cooking style in three words
Natural, healthy, unique.

What advice would you give a chef starting their career?
Find a great kitchen, keep your head down and graft hard.

What's your earliest food memory?
Mum's chicken curries.

What's your 'show-off' dish?
I don't really have one. I look at the whole menu journey, not individual dishes.

What would you be if you weren't a chef?
I would be in the music industry.

NEW ENTRY
The General Burgoyne
Reborn Lakes pub
Church Road, Great Urswick, Ulverston, LA12 0SZ
Tel no: (01229) 586394
www.generalburgoyne.com
British | £28
Cooking score: 2

£5 OFF £30

Craig and Louise Sherrington have injected new life into this seventeenth-century Lakes pub. The redecorated orangery provides an airy, contemporary contrast to the oak-beamed snug rooms. The menu might seem uncomfortably extensive, but dishes are skilfully made, using good local ingredients. Be prepared to wait for generous helpings of comforting food including crisp whitebait, meltingly tender belly pork and creamy fish pie. The specials menu showcases smarter dishes including well-risen soufflé of Westmorland cheese, precisely timed rack of lamb, and imaginative desserts such as deconstructed lemon meringue pie. Service is friendly and informative, and wines start at £11.95 a bottle (£3.25 a glass).
Chef/s: Craig Sherrington. **Open:** Wed to Sat L 12 to 2, Mon to Sat D 6 to 9, Sun 12 to 8. **Closed:** First week Jan. **Meals:** alc (main courses £13 to £16), Sun L £17.95. Tasting menu £42.95. **Details:** 50 seats. 12 seats outside. Separate bar. Music. Car parking.

▮ Watermillock
Rampsbeck Country House Hotel
Gracious comforts and fine contemporary food
Watermillock, CA11 0LP
Tel no: (017684) 86442
www.rampsbeck.co.uk
Anglo-French | £55
Cooking score: 4

Surrounded by 18 acres of pristine grounds and gardens overlooking Ullswater, this seductively situated lakeside mansion never stints on the luxurious knick-knacks or opulent trappings. It may not be a place to 'let your hair down', but take time to revel in its photogenic views, gracious comforts and finely executed contemporary food. British regional ingredients are given some fancy French manners in the shape of slow-cooked belly of suckling pig with black pudding beignet and sage jus, or roast fillet of veal with a thyme rösti, butternut squash purée, seared foie gras and port sauce. The kitchen also knows how to add some zest to fish – serving John Dory with shrimp risotto and lemongrass foam, or matching wild sea bass with a langoustine brochette, noodles and tomato dressing. Finally, expect some tricks and treats when it comes to desserts – Valrhona chocolate mousse with beetroot sorbet, or rhubarb and orange consommé with lemon cake, rhubarb jam and lemon meringue ice cream. An auspicious, style-led wine list caps it all, with some intriguing stuff from elite growers worldwide. Twenty top-end house recommendations start at £18.50 (£5 a glass).
Chef/s: Andrew McGeorge. **Open:** all week L 12 to 1.45, D 7 to 9. **Closed:** first week Jan. **Meals:** Set L £26 (2 courses) to £32. Set D £54.50 to £59.95 (4 courses). **Service:** not inc. **Details:** 40 seats. Separate bar. Wheelchair access. Music. Car parking.

▮ Windermere
Gilpin Hotel & Lake House
Charming hotel with full-of-goodness local food
Crook Road, Windermere, LA23 3NE
Tel no: (015394) 88818
www.gilpinlodge.co.uk
Modern British | £59
Cooking score: 5

£5 OFF ▭ V

'The place retains its charm and maintains the standards of a top-drawer country house hotel', reported a visitor to this well-appointed Victorian Lodge a few minutes from Windermere. Friendly, personal service meets the challenge presented by multiple dining rooms – at full tilt, four are in use – and head chef Phil Cubin, promoted from within,

keeps standards high. Delicately presented and full of local goodness, his supremely confident dishes are British in tone with an engaged, thoughtful approach to the temptations of European bits and bobs. At lunchtime, there might be starters such as a salad of local quail, leek and hazelnut with quince purée, then lamb rump, gratin potato and celeriac in rosemary jus, or sea bass with basil potato purée and olive oil dressing. To finish, try liquorice pannacotta with blackberry sorbet, candied fennel and pickled blackberries, or a popular cheese plate. Dinner is a longer affair, with five courses and canapés, but skilful balance keeps things manageable. The impressive wine list has a French core, complemented by an interesting international selection. Prices start at £21 for a Chilean Riesling; since this and some other bottles are below the house wine price of £25, those on a budget should explore beyond the front pages.
Chef/s: Phil Cubin. **Open:** all week L 12 to 2, D 6.30 to 9.15. **Meals:** alc (main courses £15 to £20). Set L £30. Set D £58.50 (5 courses). Sun L £35.
Service: not inc. **Details:** 65 seats. 30 seats outside. Separate bar. No music. Wheelchair access. Car parking. Children over 7 yrs only.

Holbeck Ghyll
The finer things of life
Holbeck Lane, Windermere, LA23 1LU
Tel no: (015394) 32375
www.holbeckghyll.com
Modern British | £65
Cooking score: 5

Standing majestically above Lake Windermere and the Langdale fells, this Victorian hunting lodge has astonishing views to spare, and it's far enough away from the madding crowd to offer solace, tranquillity and a taste of the finer things of life. Chef David McLaughlin is no slouch when it comes to delivering technically accomplished food full of serious intent. Given the setting, it's no surprise that Cumbrian lamb plays a starring role (perhaps in humble company with swede purée and haggis beignets), and there are timely outings

for pigeon, oxtail and venison (sometimes in mellow, autumnal garb with pumpkin purée, braised red cabbage and herb gnocchi). To start, hand-dived Scottish scallops regularly win votes, while other starters put down an emphatic contemporary marker – witness salt cod pannacotta with pickled vegetables, or boudin blanc with sautéed langoustines and chorizo foam. Meanwhile, labour-intensive effort and complex riffs rule when it comes to sublime desserts such as a mille-feuille of rhubarb, oat and vanilla – although wholesome date pudding with caramel sauce also elicits drools of delight. The Anglo-French cheese trolley is loaded with ripe specimens, but it pales in comparison to the stupendous, ever-evolving wine list. France takes most of the honours, but also look for 'fantastic finds' from South Africa, California and Argentina; 'personal' house selections start at £28 (£6.75 a glass).
Chef/s: David McLaughlin. **Open:** all week L 12 to 2, D 7 to 9.30. **Meals:** alc L (main courses £16 to £25). Set D £65. Gourmet menu £78 (7 courses).
Service: not inc. **Details:** 55 seats. 20 seats outside. No music. Car parking. Children over 8 yrs only at D.

Jerichos at the Waverley
Robust flavours given polish and pizazz
College Road, Windermere, LA23 1BX
Tel no: (015394) 42522
www.jerichos.co.uk
Modern British | £35
Cooking score: 4

Should you seek a fine feast or need refuelling after a long walk, chef-proprietor Chris Blaydes and his wife Jo aim to please you – and they take popular pastoral fare up a notch. Housed in a handsome Victorian property in Windermere village, Jerichos takes no risks with its impeccable produce, yet shows significant skill. The favourite char-grilled mature Scotch beef with homemade French fries and Dijon butter is 'out of this world', and generous starters include Formby asparagus, local smoked organic salmon and slow-

cooked egg – an ambrosial beginning to proceedings. Sophisticated palates might opt for hake fillet on warm potato with Flookburgh shrimp and char-grilled scallop, and finish with honey, yoghurt and vanilla pannacotta with rhubarb and ginger sorbet. An exceptional, ever-evolving list groups wines by the food styles to which each is suited, and opens at £16 (£5 a glass).
Chef/s: Chris Blaydes and Tim Dalzell. **Open:** Tue and Wed, Fri to Sun D only from 7. **Closed:** Mon, Thur, 3 weeks early Dec, 24 to 26 and 31 Dec, 3 weeks Jan. **Meals:** alc (main courses £17 to £25). **Service:** not inc. **Details:** 26 seats. Music. Car parking. Children over 12 yrs only at D.

The Samling
Shining with seasonal goodness and flavour
Ambleside Road, Windermere, LA23 1LR
Tel no: (015394) 31922
www.thesamlinghotel.co.uk
Modern British | £55
new chef

Set in a secluded 67-acre private estate overlooking Lake Windermere, The Samling's modest proportions belie its grandeur and air of exclusivity. Meals begin with canapés beside the fire – or on the terrace in fine weather – before guests pass through to the small dining room (ripe for its mooted expansion). We learned of Daniel Grigg's departure too late to respond with an inspection, but chef Ian Swainson, formerly at Seaham Hall in Co Durham and La Bécasse in Ludlow before that, is likely to continue building on the impressive network of local producers for which the kitchen is noted. In the past Swainson's cooking has shone with seasonal goodness and remarkable depth of flavour and we expect regional ingredients will continue to shape the menu. Service has been described as 'well-paced', though reports suggest the ceremonial gestures could be toned down. The expansive global wine list opens at £25.

Chef/s: Ian Swainson. **Open:** all week L 12 to 2, D 6.30 to 9.30. **Meals:** alc (main courses £55 to £65). Set L £35. Set D £55. Tasting menu £70. **Service:** not inc. **Details:** 20 seats. Music. Car parking.

▌Winster

ALSO RECOMMENDED
▲ The Brown Horse Inn
Winster, LA23 3NR
Tel no: (015394) 43443
www.thebrownhorseinn.co.uk
Modern British £5 OFF

Uncluttered yet still traditional, the Brown Horse has not forsaken its pub roots – expect a fire in winter and garden drinks on sunny days. Countryside rolls out on every side. The menu takes its cue from local, seasonal ingredients – some home-grown – and offers pub classics such as meat and potato pie (£10.95), home-smoked salmon and prawn fishcake with watercress mayonnaise (£6.95) and roast Winster venison with blue-cheese creamed leeks. Wines from £14.95. Accommodation. Open all week.

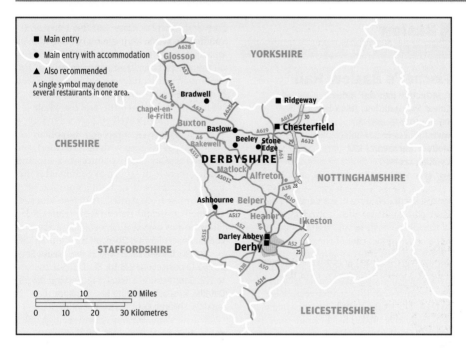

Ashbourne
The Dining Room
Finely honed seasonal food
33 St John Street, Ashbourne, DE6 1GP
Tel no: (01335) 300666
www.thediningroomashbourne.co.uk
Modern European | £40
Cooking score: 4

Don't be fooled by the wonky, beamed seventeenth-century building – as far as Peter Dale is concerned, ye olde England stops at the gate. Dinner may be one sitting with a no-choice tasting menu, but seasonal awareness (80 per cent of produce is sourced within a 35-mile radius) and vibrant contemporary strokes colour just about every finely honed dish, be it a winter opening salvo of Atlow mushrooms and Jerusalem artichokes with truffle oil powder and pearl barley, or asparagus with Spenwood ewes' cheese and sherry vinegar. Peter's classic techniques, suitably sharp and up to date, feature when he pulls Cornish halibut

brandade and Ross-shire lobster into subtle interplay with potato soup, fennel, lemon, saffron and garlic, and impresses with a dish of beef rösti and sous-vide sirloin, wild horseradish and winter vegetables.
Homemade sourdough and 'fantastic' service continue to be mentioned in dispatches.
There's a sound selection of wines from £22.
Chef/s: Peter Dale. **Open:** Tue and Wed D (by arrangement only), Thur to Sat D 7 (1 sitting). **Closed:** Sun, Mon, 1 week over Shrove Tue, 1 week Sept, last 2 weeks Dec. **Meals:** Set weekday D £40 (5 courses). Sat D £48 (8 courses). **Service:** not inc. **Details:** 16 seats. Wheelchair access. Music. Children over 12 yrs only.

Average Price
The average price listed in main-entry reviews denotes the price of a three-course meal, without wine.

Baslow

★ TOP 50 ★

Fischer's Baslow Hall
A seductive package indeed
Calver Road, Baslow, DE45 1RR
Tel no: (01246) 583259
www.fischers-baslowhall.co.uk
Modern European | £72
Cooking score: 7

An Edwardian house on the edge of a peaceful Derbyshire village, within strolling distance of the Chatsworth Estate, Baslow Hall has been in the tender care of the Fischers since 1988. Over that time, an impressively loyal fan-base has been built up, as is attested by the overwhelmingly positive reader feedback we receive each year. It's a seductive package indeed. The stone-built house, reached via a winding drive shaded by chestnut-trees, is covered in climbing foliage, and within its grounds, wonderful for wandering in, is Max Fischer's organically tended kitchen garden, which supplies Rupert Rowley with bundles of herbs, salads, fruits and veg. Rowley is an extravagantly talented chef, drawing on the best of contemporary technique while managing to avoid a lot of the modern clichés. One reporter began with a brace of scallops, cooked *à point*, the seared tops contrasting with the softer meat below, accompanied by shaved black pudding (familiar enough, perhaps), but also sliced duck hearts. 'It worked in every way' she confirmed. Another began with tempura quail breast, a study in 'beautiful tastes and textures', and followed on with brill fillet with braised chicory and chervil tuber purée, in duck roasting juices, in which the distinctive accompaniments somehow managed not to overpower the delicacy of the fish. Meat dishes include an Indian-influenced bravura performance with venison saddle, which comes with kofta, burnt aubergine purée, grilled red onion and wild rice. The sylvan setting is echoed in a dessert called Chocolate Tree Trunk, a sturdy edifice that comes with orange and chocolate mousse and lime and chocolate sorbet, or there may be a soufflé of patte de loup apples, offset with treacle-rich Pedro Ximénez ice cream. Add to all this the fact that 'from your arrival you are welcomed into a luxurious old house that feels homely and welcoming, yet has the perfect balance of professionalism', and the whole experience is pretty well guaranteed to stay with you. A fine, genuinely cosmopolitan wine list is in keeping with the classy feel, and though there are plenty of once-in-a-lifetime bottles, there is also much to commend at the more affordable end, including Foundstone Chardonnay from Australia's Berton Vineyard and the Rothschild Escudo Rojo from Chile. House wines start at £22, or £5.50 a glass.
Chef/s: Rupert Rowley. **Open:** all week L 12 to 1.30, D 7 to 8.30. **Closed:** 25, 26 and 31 Dec. **Meals:** Set L £28.50 (2 courses) to £33.50. Set D £55 (2 courses) to £72. Gourmet D £72. Sun L £42. **Service:** not inc. **Details:** 55 seats. Separate bar. No music. Car parking. Children over 10 yrs only at D.

Rowley's
Lively village brasserie
Church Lane, Baslow, DE45 1RY
Tel no: (01246) 583880
www.rowleysrestaurant.co.uk
Modern British | £28
Cooking score: 1
£5 OFF £30

Max Fischer and Rupert Rowley of nearby Baslow Hall (see entry) own this handsome converted village pub that's 'jazzed up with aubergine, lime, chocolate and dark purple, and splashy modern artwork'. Head chef Craig Skinner changes his menu regularly; dishes might include chicken and pear terrine (described as 'a triumph') with homemade chutney that delivers a pleasing kick, goats' cheese pannacotta, haddock with rarebit topping, and risotto of Derbyshire wild mushrooms. Service is informed, friendly and 'efficient without being intrusive'. The open kitchen adds to the buzzy atmosphere. House wine starts at £18.95.

Chef/s: Craig Skinner. Open: all week L 12 to 2.30 (3 Sun), Mon to Sat D 5.30 to 9 (6 to 9.30 Sat). Closed: 26 Dec. Meals: Set L £18.50 (2 courses) to £22.50. Set D £22 (2 courses) to £28. Sun L £22 (2 courses) to £26. Service: not inc. Details: 64 seats. 12 seats outside. Separate bar. Wheelchair access. Music. Car parking.

▌Beeley

The Devonshire Arms

Well-to-do country inn
Devonshire Square, Beeley, DE4 2NR
Tel no: (01629) 733259
www.devonshirebeeley.co.uk
Modern British | £28
Cooking score: 2

While there's a sophisticated, contemporary feel to this eighteenth-century coaching inn, ducal crowns woven into the carpet (a reminder that the owner is the Duke of Devonshire) and a focus on food have not obscured its original function. Real ales are still served to those who only want to pop in for a pint. Once ensconced, however, your attention may well be drawn to the great value set lunch or evening menu with its offers of bangers and mash, spit-roast poussin with fat chips and garlic mayonnaise and seasonal game from the Chatsworth Estate. House wine is £16.95.
Chef/s: Alan Hill. Open: all week L 12 to 3, D 6 to 9.30. Meals: alc (main courses £11.95 to £25). Set L £14.95 (2 courses) to £18.95. Sun L £14. Service: not inc. Details: 60 seats. 20 seats outside. Separate bar. Wheelchair access. Music. Car parking.

▌Boylestone

READERS RECOMMEND

The Lighthouse Restaurant

Modern British
New Road, Boylestone, DE6 5AA
Tel no: (01335) 330658
www.the-lighthouse-restaurant.co.uk
'The food is delicious, with beautiful flavours and delightful presentation and they never let standards slip.'

▌Bradwell

The Samuel Fox Inn

Cockle-warming country pub
Stretfield Road, Bradwell, S33 9JT
Tel no: (01433) 621562
www.samuelfox.co.uk
Modern British | £25
Cooking score: 1

Samuel Fox was a Bradwell native who invented the steel-ribbed umbrella – a century-and-a-half later, his namesake country pub follows his example, offering welcome shelter from the Peak District's harsher elements, along with a good repertoire of cockle-warming dishes. Homemade black pudding with apples and thyme is a solid opening gambit, before equally no-nonsense slow-braised lamb shoulder with creamed Savoy cabbage and mash. An honour roll of cheeses from northern England is an obvious way to conclude. Wines start at £15.
Chef/s: Charles Curran. Open: all week L 12 to 2 (6 Sat and Sun), D 6 to 9.30 (9 Sun). Meals: alc (main courses £12 to £18). Set L £10 (2 courses) to £15. Sun L £15. Service: not inc. Details: 48 seats. 20 seats outside. Wheelchair access. Music. Car parking.

Chesterfield

Non Solo Vino

Trailblazing Italian wine shop-cum-restaurant
417 Chatsworth Road, Brampton, Chesterfield,
S40 3AD
Tel no: (01246) 276760
www.nonsolovino.co.uk
Italian | £39
Cooking score: 3

£5 OFF **V**

Chesterfield got a real shot in the arm when the owners of the town's trailblazing wine emporium added a light, bright restaurant to their premises – and the result certainly lives up to its name ('not only wine'). Lunch now centres on assorted bocconcini ('tapas' plates such as roasted Taleggio in pancetta or sea bream with caponata), while evening brings a menu of sharply defined Italian dishes viewed through a contemporary pan-European lens. Capesante in tre modi (scallops three ways) involves accompaniments including wasabi mousse, while filetto di manzo sees slow-cooked and pan-roasted Derbyshire beef allied to sautéed foie gras, spinach, braised beef-shin cannelloni and tempura of smoked bone marrow. Jazz nights and wine-tasting evenings are ever-popular, with the wine side of things comprising shelves of Italian bottles, plus an Enomatic machine for sampling by the glass and a terrific list of cherry-picked regional beauties. Prices start at £17.
Chef/s: Matt Bennison. **Open:** Tue to Sun L 12 to 2.30, Tue to Sat D 6 to 10 (7 to 11 Sat). **Closed:** Mon, 25 and 26 Dec, first week Jan. **Meals:** L tapas (from £3 per item). Set D £32 to £39 (4 courses). Tasting menu £49 (7 courses) to £59 (9 courses). **Service:** 10%. **Details:** 46 seats. Separate bar. Music. Car parking.

Darley Abbey

Darleys

Tourist hot spot with capable food
Darley Abbey Mills, Haslams Lane, Darley Abbey,
DE22 1DZ
Tel no: (01332) 364987
www.darleys.com
Modern British | £35
Cooking score: 3

V

Housed in a converted cotton mill by the river Derwent, Darleys forms part of a vast World Heritage Site – so expect sightseers and nostalgia-hungry tourists aplenty. Inside, however, it's a bright, design-led contemporary space where visitors can look forward to some generally capable modern cooking with a few nods to the region. A starter of seared scallops and black pudding with cider and caramel apple purée has gone down well, likewise broccoli soup embellished with a Stilton soufflé and walnut crumbs. After that, cannon of Derbyshire beef might crop up in company with ox cheek and potato cannelloni, while fish could be represented by fillet of plaice with parsley and shrimp risotto. Grumbles about 'ordinary' food and offhand service continue, although the wine list is a rock-solid selection from £16.
Chef/s: Jonathan Hobson. **Open:** all week L 12 to 2 (2.30 Sun), Mon to Sat D 7 to 9. **Closed:** 25 Dec to 12 Jan, 1 week summer, bank hols. **Meals:** alc (main courses £17 to £22). Set L £18.95 (2 courses) to £20.95. Sun L £22.50. **Service:** not inc. **Details:** 60 seats. 16 seats outside. Separate bar. Music. Car parking.

▌ Derby

Zest

Capable local restaurant
16d George Street, Derby, DE1 1EH
Tel no: (01332) 381101
www.restaurantzest.co.uk
Modern British | £25
Cooking score: 1

£5 OFF £30

Spread over two floors in a converted stable building in Derby's bohemian Cathedral Quarter, Zest has been a noble steed of a local restaurant for 15 years. The menu capably canters through eclectic modern British and European influences; mains might see honey-glazed duck breast with cherry sauce and balsamic syrup, or pork tenderloin with parsley potatoes and Parmesan and marjoram cream. Desserts (say sticky toffee pudding and cranberry cheesecake) don't pull any punches. The wine list offers ample glugging from £13.
Chef/s: Jan Hlavac. **Open:** Mon to Sat L 12 to 3, D 6 to 10. **Closed:** Sun, 26 Dec, 1 Jan. **Meals:** alc (main courses £15 to £19). Set L £9.95 (2 courses) to £11.95. Set D £15.95 (2 courses) to £18.95. **Service:** not inc. **Details:** 60 seats. Wheelchair access. Music. No children after 8.

ALSO RECOMMENDED

▲ Masa

The Old Wesleyan Chapel, Brook Street, Derby, DE1 3PF
Tel no: (01332) 203345
www.masarestaurantwinebar.com
Modern European £5 OFF

From its original use as a Wesleyan chapel, this listed building just outside the Derby inner ring road ('careful navigation around one-way systems required') has become a 'cavernous' bar and restaurant – the many-tiered dining gallery 'reaching up towards the ceiling'. Eurozone-inspired dishes range from confit duck leg with a cassoulet of coco beans (£7.50) to herb-crusted loin of cod with sauce vierge or fillet of local beef with red wine jus

(£22.50). There's apple crème brûlée for dessert, and a global list of wines from £14.50. Closed Mon and Tue.

▲ Mumbai Chilli

28 Stenson Road, Derby, DE23 1JB
Tel no: (01332) 767090
www.mumbaichilli.com
Indian £5 OFF

Although the menu is straight out of the 'tikka masala' stable, smart, contemporary Mumbai Chilli is worth a visit for good tandooris (including top-drawer lamb chops, £8.50), a contingent of high street curries from chicken jalfrezi to prawn korma (£7.95), plus a few specials like lamb hindustani (cooked in a rich gravy with roasted almonds and aromatic spices). There are decent rice and breads (from £1.85), pleasant service, and respectable wines from £11.95. Open all week.

▌ Ridgeway

★ TOP 50 ★

The Old Vicarage

A beacon of natural-born cooking
Ridgeway Moor, Ridgeway, S12 3XW
Tel no: (0114) 2475814
www.theoldvicarage.co.uk
Modern British | £65
Cooking score: 7

£5 OFF

Tessa Bramley and her team celebrated 25 years as Guide grandees during 2012. It has been a long haul, but their enchanting converted vicarage remains a beacon of natural-born cooking and a little slice of Arcadia just eight miles from Sheffield's bright lights. Dedication and personality mean more than grand gestures here, and Tessa's belief in the virtues of culinary craftsmanship over 'experimental pseudo-science' (her words) shows in her loyalty to the seasons, her respect for native produce and her feel for what is 'right' on the plate – wild lavender with lamb, juniper with fallow deer, scallops with rhubarb and star anise, sea bass with lemon, and so on. The kitchen runs with nature and the calendar, serving butternut squash ravioli with walnut and chive dressing, conjuring up Yuletide with a dish of mallard breast, blueberry compote and candied Seville orange, and roasting locally reared Charolais beef on caraway-scented cabbage with confit chicken wings, black pudding and parsnip purée. Tessa knows how to coax a full measure of flavour from sympathetically chosen ingredients, and gently garlands her dishes with thoughtful wild pickings from the meadows and copses beyond her kitchen door. Everything connects, and desserts also show a sneaking affection for the old English ways – as in a baked chocolate pudding with chocolate fudge sauce and custard, or caramelised apple tart with caramel sauce. Carefully selected regional cheeses are served with Ridgeway's own wild-flower honey, although staff aren't always fully conversant with each specimen. Some lapses in housekeeping have been noted of late, but hopefully this is a minor blip, rather than a sign that the years are starting to take their toll. The Old Vicarage also runs its own wine business, with personal connections to some of the world's top growers; from the 'chic rustique' varietals of south-west France to full-blooded, food-friendly big hitters, it's a truly prestigious, global line-up. The owner's 'special recommendations' are always worth a punt; otherwise, prices start at £24. Also note the eclectic choice of bottled beers from home and abroad.

Chef/s: Tessa Bramley and Nathan Smith. **Open:** Tue to Fri L 12.30 to 2, Tue to Sat D 6 to 9.30 (10 Sat). **Closed:** Sun, Mon, 26 Dec to 6 Jan, 2 weeks Aug, bank hols. **Meals:** Set L £30 (2 courses) to £40. Set D £65 (4 courses). Tasting menu £70 (7 courses). **Service:** not inc. **Details:** 40 seats. 16 seats outside. Separate bar. No music. Wheelchair access. Car parking.

Stone Edge

NEW ENTRY
Red Lion Bar & Bistro
Souped-up pub classics
Peak Edge Hotel, Darley Road, Stone Edge, S45 0LW
Tel no: (01246) 566142
www.redlionpubandbistro.com
Modern British | £27
Cooking score: 2

£5 OFF | £30

'On the top of the moors, in the middle of nowhere', this sprawling roadside pub (with adjoining modern hotel) has been scrubbed to within an inch of its life, outside and in. The low ceilinged, darkly painted warren of rooms is rather gloomy by day, but 'the thing is, the chef can cook'. Souped-up pub classics include local lamb rump on gnocchi, and the ubiquitous plate of pig. The black pudding Scotch egg filled with foie gras is 'a revelation' – a surprisingly subtle, sophisticated dish; served with a chunk of still-warm homemade bread it makes a very pleasing lunch. House wine is £14.95.

Chef/s: Carl Riley. **Open:** all week 12 to 9 (9.30 Fri and Sat). **Meals:** alc (main courses £10 to £23). **Service:** not inc. **Details:** 82 seats. 20 seats outside. Separate bar. Wheelchair access. Music. Car parking.

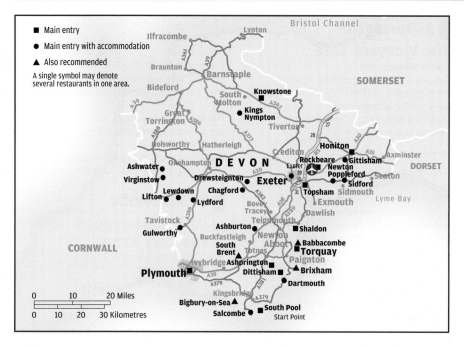

Ashburton

Agaric

Heartfelt natural cooking
30 North Street, Ashburton, TQ13 7QD
Tel no: (01364) 654478
www.agaricrestaurant.co.uk
Modern British | £35
Cooking score: 4

A dozen years on, Nick and Sophie Coiley continue to do what they do best: serving up straight-to-the-point, calendar-friendly dishes that make the most of Devon's fantastic larder. Their easy-going approach is just the ticket, too; the converted shop in the centre of Ashburton delivers an intimacy that endears it to visitors. Nick's experience at the stove is shown by a deep understanding of combinations and flavours – he's not afraid to let ingredients speak for themselves – and everything, from bread to chutneys and ice creams, is made on the premises. The menu happily name checks West Country produce in classics like a twice-baked soufflé made with Somerset-produced Ogleshield cheese, but there's also roast, spiced fillet of Brixham cod with cauliflower pakora, yoghurt and dukkah (a nut and spice blend), best-end of local herb-crusted lamb with spinach and goats' cheese gnocchi, and a fabulous hot Seville orange soufflé with a warm chocolate sauce. The short, fairly priced wine list opens at £19.50.
Chef/s: Nick Coiley. **Open:** Wed to Fri L 12 to 2, Wed to Sat D 7 to 9. **Closed:** Sun to Tue, 2 weeks Dec, 2 weeks Aug. **Meals:** alc (main courses £16 to £23). Set L £14.95 (2 courses). **Service:** not inc. **Details:** 28 seats. 16 seats outside. Separate bar. No music. Wheelchair access.

Visit us Online
To find out more about
The Good Food Guide, please visit
www.thegoodfoodguide.co.uk

Ashprington
The Vineyard Café

Quirky alfresco café
Sharpham Estate, Ashprington, TQ9 7UT
Tel no: (01803) 732178
www.thevineyardcafe.co.uk
Modern British | £25
Cooking score: 1

This quirky café, located on the Sharpham Estate, delivers the perfect alfresco experience, with stunning views over the River Dart and every climatic eventuality covered. 'A wonderful lunch in an unbeatable setting' was the verdict of one reporter. Such a lunch could take in pea, mint and cheese fritters, John Dory with slow-cooked fennel, crushed rosemary potatoes and caper, lemon butter dressing. Round things off with rhubarb and ginger steamed pudding. Wines from the Sharpham vineyard start at £13.45.
Chef/s: Charlie Godard, Rosie Weston and Angela Howard-Chappell. **Open:** all week L only 12 to 2 (3 Sat and Sun). **Closed:** Oct to Easter. **Meals:** alc (main courses £11 to £20). Set L £15 (2 courses) to £20. **Service:** not inc. **Details:** 60 seats outside. Wheelchair access. Car parking.

Ashwater
Blagdon Manor

Hospitable West Country treasure
Ashwater, EX21 5DF
Tel no: (01409) 211224
www.blagdon.com
Modern British | £38
Cooking score: 2

It's almost a dozen years since Steve and Liz Morey moved into this serenely located, Grade II-listed manor. During their stewardship they have cared lovingly for the place – it shows in every detail – and everyone is put at their ease by a mood that is as intimate and personable as can be. As you might expect, Steve taps into Devon's rich larder for his set-price dinners, starting perhaps with galantine of rabbit and pigeon with sesame-coated chicken wings and date sauce, then slow-cooked lamb shank with creamed potatoes, root vegetables and lentils. Lemon posset, lemon curd doughnut and warming mulled wine or West Country cheeses make a fine finale. Wines from £16.
Chef/s: Steve Morey. **Open:** Sun L 12 to 2, Wed to Sun D 7 to 9. **Closed:** Mon, Tue, Jan. **Meals:** Set D £40 (2 courses) to £45. Sun L £25. **Service:** not inc. **Details:** 28 seats. Separate bar. Wheelchair access. Car parking. Children over 12 yrs only.

Babbacombe

ALSO RECOMMENDED
▲ The Cary Arms

Beach Road, Babbacombe, TQ1 3LX
Tel no: (01803) 327110
www.caryarms.co.uk
Modern British

On fine days expect a scrum, as crowds make the steep descent to the Cary Arms to soak up the sun and sea views from its terraces just above the beach. Unpretentious pub food is the orientation – say warm smoked mackerel with beetroot relish and dill mayonnaise to start (£6.95), followed by roast duck breast on champ with smoked bacon and shallot sauce (£18.95), and orange and almond tart with local Yarde Farm ice cream (£6.25). Wines from £15.95. Open all week.

Bigbury-on-Sea

ALSO RECOMMENDED
▲ The Oyster Shack

Milburn Orchard Farm, Stakes Hill, Bigbury-on-Sea, TQ7 4BE
Tel no: (01548) 810876
www.oystershack.co.uk
Seafood

With a low-key, comfortable interior and a splendid sail-covered terrace, the Oyster Shack looks good in any weather, and it more than lives up to expectations. It is billed as 'that seafood place', with oysters, crabs and lobsters being the main draw, but there are also grilled sardines with tapenade (£7), moules marinière, and cod fillet with risotto nero and gremolata (£22). A lack of airs and graces and courteous, informed staff add to the sheer enjoyment. Wines from £14.95. Open all week.

Brixham

ALSO RECOMMENDED
▲ The Brixham Deli

68a Fore Street, Brixham, TQ5 8EF
Tel no: (01803) 859585
www.thebrixhamdeli.co.uk
Modern British

A double-fronted shop just off the inner harbour at Devon's fishing hub, the Deli welcomes punters in with alluringly stacked shelves and big wooden tables for sharing. The superior café menu offers up baked goats' cheese salad with beetroot and balsamic reduction (£5.95), steak burger with mozzarella and smoked bacon and chips (£8.95), seared Brixham scallops with chorizo and rocket (£7.95), and chocolate brownie with clotted cream (£3.95). There's a breakfast menu for early birds. House wine is £10.99.

Chagford

★ TOP 50 ★

Gidleigh Park

Elegant, polished country house
Chagford, TQ13 8HH
Tel no: (01647) 432367
www.gidleigh.com
Modern European | £105
Cooking score: 7

£5 OFF ⏴ V

Newcomers may be expecting a grand baronial pile soaring in turrets above acres of golf-course, but Gidleigh is more of a real home than that – albeit a fairly well-to-do one. It was built in the 1920s for an Australian shipping magnate, and sits on a Dartmoor hillside enjoying the calm, restorative views. As indeed do guests taking aperitifs on the terrace. Flawlessly maintained Arts and Crafts interiors establish a tone of formal elegance, which is sustained by precision-drilled staff. Michael Caines is still notionally head chef at Gidleigh, but is a very busy man these days, and has a highly proficient team in place to interpret his vision. That's just as well, as the cooking depends on delicate balances of ingredients and techniques to achieve its impact. A signature starter is the finely judged combination of frogs' legs, crayfish and snails on nettle and garlic risotto, praised for its gentle potency, but there may also be the unabashed French classicism of a foie gras terrine with Madeira jelly and truffled green beans. Fish main courses are subtly worked, rather than defiantly robust in the modern way, witness one reporter's John Dory with bacon and grapefruit ('one of the best dishes I have ever enjoyed'), while meats are allowed to shine amid a welter of seasonal vegetables, as in the local rose veal that comes with broad beans, button onions, mousseron mushrooms and pea purée in a sauce of sherry cream. The chocolate trio – a mousse of dark, parfait of milk with hazelnut, and ice cream of white – garners extravagant plaudits, and there's usually a beautifully rendered soufflé with matching sorbet, perhaps an intense summer raspberry version. A properly comprehensive wine list naturally has plenty of quality French product, but doesn't just dwell there. Italy and Iberia are well represented, as is South Africa, and there is a reasonable spread at the affordable end. Glasses start at £9, bottles at £26.
Chef/s: Michael Caines. **Open:** all week L 12 to 2.30, D 7 to 9.45. **Meals:** Set L £40 (2 courses) to £52. Set D £105. Tasting menu £105 (6 courses) to £125 (8 courses). **Service:** not inc. **Details:** 50 seats. Separate bar. No music. Wheelchair access. Car parking. Children 8 yrs and over only.

Also Recommended
Also recommended entries are not scored but we think they are worth a visit.

CHAGFORD

22 Mill Street
Plaudit-winning gem
22 Mill Street, Chagford, TQ13 8AW
Tel no: (01647) 432244
www.22millst.com
Modern British | £42
Cooking score: 4

Tucked away in a terrace just off Chagford's
main square, Helena King's restaurant-with-
rooms is a serenely welcoming place, with
peeps of Dartmoor through the blinded
windows of the dining room. It's hospitably
run, with a nice sense of relaxation – and
plaudits have come thick and fast for Ashley
Wright's locally sourced cooking since last
year's new entry. The fixed-price menus offer
just four options per course, yet choosing feels
agreeably difficult. Start, perhaps, with a
composition of langoustine, boudin noir,
Jerusalem artichoke and roast garlic, before
braised cheek and tail of ox with earthy, rooty
accompaniments of sprout leaves, turnip,
swede and gnocchi. Fish may be brill spiced
with ras-el-hanout. Desserts have featured an
alliterative assemblage of poached pear,
pineapple, pain perdu, pistachio and Greek
yoghurt pannacotta. Fine local cheeses are on
hand, too. The well-written wine list is fairly
priced and full of good things. Prices start
at £19.
Chef/s: Ashley Wright. **Open:** all week L 12 to 2, D 7
to 10.30. **Meals:** Set L £16.95 (2 courses) to £21.95.
Set D £36 (2 courses) to £42. **Service:** not inc.
Details: 22 seats. 6 seats outside. Music.

Average Price
The average price listed in main-entry
reviews denotes the price of a three-
course meal, without wine.

Dartmouth
The Angel
Seasoned campaigner with honest food
2 South Embankment, Dartmouth, TQ6 9BH
Tel no: (01803) 839425
www.theangeldartmouth.co.uk
Anglo-French | £33
Cooking score: 5

The latest angelic manifestation of this
seasoned campaigner on the Dartmouth
waterfront – it's been the Carved Angel, the
New Angel, Angelique and now the Angel –
feels like the best fit in a good while. It's a
bright white room (there's another upstairs)
with big windows offering views of the little
ferries plying the Dart estuary, and an open-
to-view kitchen. Crisp table linen and chatty,
knowledgeable staff help keep the tone afloat,
and the kitchen turns out honest, well-
thought-out modern eating that everybody
can understand. Fine local asparagus is tucked
under a light, fluffy blanket of lemon sabayon,
while a version of imam bayaldi strikes all the
right chords for garlicky, chillified intensity.
For omnivores, there is intensely rich chicken
liver and foie gras parfait with red onion
marmalade, crumbled almonds and brioche
toast, and simple but good bistro mains such as
lemon sole fillets on mashed potato with a
scattering of full-flavoured tiny brown
shrimps, or roast pork fillet with mustard-
fruit crust, borlotti beans and spinach.
Desserts maintain a light note, for pecan
parfait and blueberries, and even for dark
chocolate and almond tart with mascarpone
and passion-fruit coulis. A serviceable wine
list opens at £22 for whites, £24 for reds.
Chef/s: Stephen Bulmer. **Open:** Wed to Sun L 12 to 2
(3 Sun), Wed to Sat D 6.30 to 9 (9.30 Fri and Sat).
Closed: Mon, Tue. **Meals:** alc (main courses £18 to
£21). Set L £22.50 (2 courses) to £25.
Service: 12.5%. **Details:** 60 seats. Music.

★ BEST SEAFOOD ★

The Seahorse
Approachable seafood eatery par excellence
5 South Embankment, Dartmouth, TQ6 9BH
Tel no: (01803) 835147
www.seahorserestaurant.co.uk
Seafood | £33
Cooking score: 4

£5 OFF

'These guys try 24/7. Go spend, relax, inhale and enjoy' enthused one reader; another was simply seduced by the 'happy, contented buzz and smell of good food' on a winter's night. Clearly Mitch Tonks' Seahorse is the kind of approachable eatery you can make friends with. Set on Dartmouth's re-energised Embankment, it comes with lofty ceilings, Art Deco lamps and an open kitchen. Fish is Tonks' stock-in-trade, and it shows: how about ozone-fresh whole turbot roasted on the bone in the wood-fired oven, then expertly filleted at the table – or 'deliciously sweet' Lyme Bay scallops cooked 'in the shell' with garlic and white port? Elsewhere, char-grilled monkfish could appear with fennel gratin, spinach and some 'divine' garlicky potato croquettes. Desserts don't go in for pyrotechnics, but are content to satisfy cravings with dense chocolate nemesis or sticky toffee pudding. The wine list bristles with imaginative bottles from artisan producers, chosen for their affinity to the food. Italy and the Iberian Peninsula provide the best pickings, and the special Tonnix (blended by Tonks and fellow restaurateur Mark Hix) is also recommended. Prices start at £19.
Chef/s: Mitch Tonks and Mat Prowse. **Open:** Wed to Sun L 12 to 2.30 (12.30 Sun), Tue to Sat D 6 to 9.30. **Closed:** Mon, 25 and 26 Dec. **Meals:** alc (main courses £16 to £29). Set L and early D £15 (2 courses) to £20. Sun L £25. **Service:** not inc. **Details:** 40 seats. 4 seats outside. Wheelchair access. Music.

ALSO RECOMMENDED
▲ Rockfish Seafood and Chips
8 South Embankment, Dartmouth, TQ6 9BH
Tel no: (01803) 832800
www.rockfishdevon.co.uk
Seafood

Bang-slap on the quayside overlooking the Dart Estuary – where better to enjoy traditional fish 'n' chips? It's another winner from seafood aficionado Mitch Tonks (see entries the Seahorse, Dartmouth and Rockfish Grill, Bristol). The glass-fronted diner is sunnily decked out in beach-hut style, and the wide-ranging menu delivers simple seafood dishes (most landed locally at Brixham), including Devon crab cocktail (£7.95), battered red gurnard or grilled sea bass fillet with olive oil, garlic and sea salt (£11.95). Wines from £17. Open all week.

■ Dittisham

NEW ENTRY
Anchorstone Café
Seafood lovers' paradise
Manor Street, Dittisham, TQ6 0EX
Tel no: (01803) 722365
www.anchorstonecafe.co.uk
Seafood | £23
Cooking score: 3

£30

'This place gets better and better every year. The menu becomes more adventurous every time and the seafood couldn't be fresher. Very hard to get to (boat is the best way), but on a hot, sunny day, you feel like you're in paradise, with views to die for.' That was one couple's cheery judgement, heartily endorsed by others. The local seafood brings people flocking to this out-of-the-way café, where crabs and delicious side salads of 'homemade coleslaw, couscous and other goodies', vie for attention with 'terrific' whitebait, River Dart oysters – the 'creamiest I've had in the UK' – whole lemon sole, and bouillabaisse stuffed with squid, crevettes, clams, cockles and mussels, all served by staff who 'can't do enough to help'. Wines from £16.95.

Chef/s: Clare Harvey. **Open:** All week L 12 to 4, Thur to Sat D 6 to 8 (July and Aug only). **Closed:** Nov to Mar. **Meals:** alc (main courses £12 to £22). **Service:** not inc. **Details:** 28 seats. 50 seats outside. No music. Wheelchair access.

Drewsteignton

The Old Inn
Exclusive little restaurant-with-rooms
Drewsteignton, EX6 6QR
Tel no: (01647) 281276
www.old-inn.co.uk
Modern European | £43
Cooking score: 3

Since Duncan Walker moved here and donned his whites in 2009, the Old Inn has been transformed from a heavy-duty, touristy boozer into a rather exclusive little restaurant-with-rooms. Opening hours are limited and prices aren't 'cheap', but the food shows some real star quality and a sure hand at the stove. Intense, precise flavours come through strongly in a disarmingly titled 'plate of crab' and a luxurious collation of sautéed rabbit and calf's sweetbreads in mille-feuille; after that, expect more robust flavours in the shape of, say, poached guinea fowl with gnocchi in thyme and leek broth or grilled turbot fillet with smoked haddock tortellini and chives. For dessert, a 'plate of raspberry' has gone down well, or you could try prune and Armagnac soufflé. The house Pinot Blanc Rhinephalz is £25 (£6.50 a glass).

Chef/s: Duncan Walker. **Open:** Wed to Sat D only 7 to 10. **Closed:** Sun to Tue. **Meals:** Set D £37.50 (2 courses) to £42.50. **Service:** not inc. **Details:** 18 seats. No music. Children over 12 yrs only.

Exeter

Michael Caines at ABode Exeter
Certainly a polished set-up
Royal Clarence Hotel, Cathedral Yard, Exeter, EX1 1HD
Tel no: (01392) 223638
www.abodehotels.co.uk
Modern European | £50
Cooking score: 4

⇌ V

'An experience and an entertainment', according to one reader, Michael Caines' self-named restaurant at the front of the Royal Clarence Hotel also maintains 'an ambassadorial air, with standards that few can attain'. It's certainly a polished set-up, with immaculate mirrored surrounds, exemplary service and a menu that has MC's thumbprints all over it. Consider the warm salad of Devon quail with quail's egg, caramelised hazelnuts and quail vinaigrette, the salted cod fillet with smoked paprika, lemon confit, samphire, red pepper and chorizo purée, or even the sirloin of Devon beef with braised short ribs, glazed shallots, creamed celeriac and Madeira sauce – a dish that highlights Caines' more orthodox side. Ingredients are true to the region, flavours come with plenty of oomph, and the kitchen also shows its prowess with desserts such as confit orange soufflé or star anise crème brûlée with hazelnut nougatine and green apple sorbet. House wines start at £26.50 (£6.45 a glass).

Chef/s: Craig Dunn. **Open:** Mon to Sat L 12 to 2.30, D 6 to 9.45. **Closed:** Sun. **Meals:** alc (main courses £23 to £26). Set D £17.95 (2 courses) to £25. **Service:** 12%. **Details:** 75 seats. Separate bar. No music. Wheelchair access.

▌Gittisham

Combe House

Seductive hotel with seriously good dining
Gittisham, EX14 3AD
Tel no: (01404) 540400
www.combehousedevon.com
Modern British | £52
Cooking score: 5

 V

Built in Elizabethan times, Combe House is a 'delightful country house in wonderful parkland in a remote corner of Devon'. But not so remote 'that it isn't well-patronised both for lunches and dinners'. The gorgeous interiors form the backdrop of a well-run hotel ('greeting and service were exemplary'), and a dining room of serious intent. The focus is on excellent raw materials; Hadleigh Barrett befriends the best suppliers. His menus are imaginative without running riot – style never gets in the way of substance. A winter menu offering roast breast and confit leg of squab pigeon with chestnut purée, sprouts and bacon puts down a strong local marker that defines what is to follow – notably the earthy seasonal clarity of 'first-rate' venison loin on 'delicious, sweet' red cabbage, smoked mashed potato and roast turnips. In Devon there is no excuse for a poor cheeseboard; here you get a very good one, while rhubarb mousse cake with cheesecake cream is a typical dessert. As for the wine list (helpfully laid out for food matching), classic French regions provide an abundance of serious bottles, but the net is spread wide for fine drinking beyond Europe. Seasonal house selections start at £22.
Chef/s: Hadleigh Barrett. **Open:** all week L 12 to 2.30, D 7 to 9.30. **Closed:** 2 weeks Jan. **Meals:** Set L £29 (2 courses) to £33. Set D £52. Sun L £37. **Service:** not inc. **Details:** 75 seats. Separate bar. Wheelchair access. Music. Car parking.

▌Gulworthy

The Horn of Plenty

Ravishing views and confident cooking
Gulworthy, PL19 8JD
Tel no: (01822) 832528
www.thehornofplenty.co.uk
Modern European | £50
Cooking score: 3

Rural England barely gets more picture-postcard than this. The late-Georgian house stands foursquare in gardens awash with azaleas, camelias and rhododendrons, with ravishing views along the wooded Tamar Valley. Julie Leivers and Damien Pease, who took over in 2010, have retained the classic country house look and people love the way it 'makes you feel special without being patronising'. Eat in the conservatory dining room and expect Mediterranean-accented British cooking driven by local and seasonal produce: say, best end of local lamb with smoked aubergine purée, ratatouille and tapenade jus. A fixed-price lunch might see you journeying from pollack fillet with white bean and bacon chowder, through roast pork loin with black pudding, apple and tarragon, to arrive with satisfaction at mandarin tart and confit sorbet. Wines from £19.50.
Chef/s: Scott Paton. **Open:** all week L 12 to 2, D 7 to 9.30. **Meals:** Set L £19.50 (2 courses) to £24.50. Set D £49.50. **Service:** not inc. **Details:** 40 seats. 25 seats outside. Separate bar. Wheelchair access. Music. Car parking.

Honiton

The Holt
Honest pub food
178 High Street, Honiton, EX14 1LA
Tel no: (01404) 47707
www.theholt-honiton.com
Modern British | £26
Cooking score: 1

A godsend for Honiton, this well-run town-centre pub does sterling service, welcoming drinkers with local ales in the rustic bar and offering great modern pub food in the dining room upstairs. Slow-baked beef shin casserole with potato and thyme dumplings, and a well-reported confit duck leg with Puy lentils, root vegetables and chorizo (part of a 'fab dinner') may be simple, but this indicates that attention is focused where it should be – on good raw materials. Wines from £14.
Chef/s: James Baxter. **Open:** Tue to Sat L 12 to 2, D 6.30 to 9.30 (10 Fri and Sat). **Closed:** Sun, Mon, 25 and 26 Dec. **Meals:** alc (main courses £13 to £16). **Service:** not inc. **Details:** 60 seats. Separate bar. Wheelchair access. Music.

Kings Nympton

The Grove Inn
Proper country inn with local food
Kings Nympton, EX37 9ST
Tel no: (01769) 580406
www.thegroveinn.co.uk
British | £23
Cooking score: 2

The Grove hits the bullseye as a proper country inn, with thatched roof, stone walls, beamed ceilings, fires – and no medieval jukebox to drown the chat. A menu teeming with local produce is the final piece in the jigsaw; its excellence is apparent the moment you set about a bowl of spring vegetable soup with wild garlic pesto. North Devon trout with horseradish cream, wild rabbit stew, skate wing in brown caper butter, cranberry and almond tart with clotted cream: all fly the Devon flag proudly. And there are a couple of Devonian interlopers among the wines, which start at £15.
Chef/s: Deborah Smallbone. **Open:** Tue to Sun L 12 to 2 (2.30 Sun), Mon to Sat D 6.45 to 9. **Closed:** 25 Dec. **Meals:** alc (main courses £7 to £18). Sun L £13.40 (2 courses) to £16.40. **Service:** not inc. **Details:** 28 seats. 12 seats outside. Separate bar. No music. Wheelchair access.

Knowstone

The Masons Arms
Confident cooking with panache
Knowstone, EX36 4RY
Tel no: (01398) 341231
www.masonsarmsdevon.co.uk
Modern British | £41
Cooking score: 6

A little to the south of Exmoor, just off the A361, the Dodsons' little restaurant in a thatched thirteenth-century inn has bags of character. If there is a beaten track in north Devon, this is off it, but the journey is well worthwhile for Sarah's practised hospitality out front and Mark's Roux-trained culinary expertise behind the scenes. It's the kind of cooking that has the confidence to do the simple things with supreme panache, as evidenced by the booming depth of Jerusalem artichoke soup with wild mushrooms, or a well-timed smoked haddock and Parmesan risotto topped with a poached egg. Meat mains are handled well, whether for belly pork roulade with braised red cabbage and apple compote, or local beef fillet with oxtail ravioli in truffled Madeira jus. Fish could be potato-coated brill with curly kale and curried mussel ragoût. Vanilla berry trifle makes a straightforwardly satisfying finish, or explore the fine farmhouse cheeses of Devon and Somerset. A useful list of well-chosen wines opens at £14.50 (£5 a glass).
Chef/s: Mark Dodson. **Open:** Tue to Sun L 12 to 2, Tue to Sat D 7 to 9. **Closed:** Mon, first week Jan, 1 week Aug. **Meals:** alc (main courses £18 to £25). Sun L £35.50. **Service:** not inc. **Details:** 28 seats. 16 seats outside. Separate bar. Music. Car parking. Children 5 yrs and over only at D.

▌Lewdown

The Harris Arms
Generous country cooking
Portgate, Lewdown, EX20 4PZ
Tel no: (01566) 783331
www.theharrisarms.co.uk
Modern British | £25
Cooking score: 2

£5
OFF

'Best pub food in the area', pronounced one reader and such praise is echoed in many other reports for this homely, family-run pub just off the A30. Reporters have particularly liked the pub's relaxed feel, and reasonable prices, as well as the kitchen's commitment to local produce. Alongside homespun English diehards, perhaps a hearty, chunky vegetable soup or sausage, mash and onion gravy, there could be venison bourguignon or rabbit casserole with prunes in brandy, mashed potatoes and a white wine and mustard sauce. Incidentals charm: West Country cheeses, the care of customers, and the quality and commitment of the wine list (from £18).
Chef/s: Andy Whiteman. Open: Tue to Sun L 12 to 2 (2.30 Sun), D 6.30 to 9. Closed: Mon, 26 Dec. Meals: alc (main courses £10 to £18). Sun L £14 (2 courses) to £16.50. Service: not inc. Details: 52 seats. 40 seats outside.

Lewtrenchard Manor
Alchemy from an accomplished chef
Lewdown, EX20 4PN
Tel no: (01566) 783222
www.lewtrenchard.co.uk
Modern British | £51
Cooking score: 6

☜ V

Standing a little way off the north-west fringe of Dartmoor, not far from Okehampton, Lewtrenchard is a greystone Jacobean manor house. Generations of the Gould family, its one-time proprietors, are hung in oils around the place, not forgetting the Rev Sabine Baring Gould, composer of *Onward Christian Soldiers*. James and Sue Murray are back in charge, having sold to von Essen in 2003, and the ship sails on, its culinary department helmed with assurance and distinction by John Hooker, whose touch on the tiller remains steady. The style is local-larder country house in its grandeur, with much of the fresh produce grown in the grounds. A fleeting luncher who wasn't sure about the idea of vanilla in the parsnip soup was won over by its gentling effect on the rooty sweetness of the main component, the kind of alchemy that accomplished chefs specialise in. A version of Waldorf salad incorporates Devon's Vulscombe goats' cheese, while mains turn up sea bass with potted shrimps and braised cos, or Creedy Carver duck with watercress, grapes and confit shallots. Adventurers head for the Purple Carrot, the chef's table setting for dishes drawn from the main menu. West Country cheeses, or blood orange cheesecake with lime curd, end things on a high. A briskly efficient wine list opens at £23.50.
Chef/s: John Hooker. Open: all week L 12 to 2, D 7 to 9. Meals: Set L £19 (2 courses) to £24. Set D £47 (2 courses) to £50.50. Service: not inc. Details: 60 seats. Separate bar. Wheelchair access. Music. Car parking. Children over 8 yrs only at D.

▌Lifton

The Arundell Arms
Civilised sporting retreat
Fore Street, Lifton, PL16 0AA
Tel no: (01566) 784666
www.arundellarms.com
Modern British | £43
Cooking score: 4

£5
OFF ☜

An agreeable feeling of pastoral prosperity characterises this former coaching inn near Dartmoor. The place runs trippingly along under the watchful eyes of the Fox-Edwards family – who have been in possession since 1961 – and its reputation as one of England's major sporting hotels is well-deserved. It still plays its part as a busy local, with pub favourites served in the Courthouse Bar, but diners head to the smart restaurant for Steven Pidgeon's ingredients-led, straight-down-

the-line cooking. Pork tenderloin with braised cheek, Savoy cabbage and cider gravy is a meaty big-hitter, but the daily menu covers a lot of ground – everything from brill with smoked chowder or mignon of wild venison, to a casserole of Cornish sea bass, sea bream and John Dory with scallops, saffron potato, tomato and leeks. The thoughtful wine list picks fine names from France and beyond and has a fair spread of prices from £18.
Chef/s: Steven Pidgeon. **Open:** all week L 12 to 2, D 7 to 10. **Meals:** Set L £19 (2 courses) to £22.50. Set D £39 (2 courses) to £42.50. Sun L £21.50 (2 courses) to £26. **Service:** not inc. **Details:** 50 seats. 20 seats outside. Separate bar. Wheelchair access. Music. Car parking.

Lydford
The Dartmoor Inn
Banging the drum for quality
Moorside, Lydford, EX20 4AY
Tel no: (01822) 820221
www.dartmoorinn.com
Modern British | £30
Cooking score: 3

🛏 V

Fifteen years on, Philip and Karen Burgess's gentrified rural hostelry continues to bang the drum for top quality seasonal produce. People come from all over, squeezing into the cosy bar for sandwiches, a Devon Ruby burger or Cornish crab salad, or eating in the network of elegant dining rooms, where the focus is on sound traditional cooking. Falmouth Bay scallops with broccoli purée and chilli relish might open a meal, then maybe mignon of venison served with venison cottage pie and peppered sauce, or wild hake with crisp fried belly pork and wild garlic oil. Wonderful banana fritters with cocoa sugar and clotted cream stands out among straightforward comfort desserts. Real ales are on draught and a thoroughly accessible wine list opens at £16.50.
Chef/s: Andrew Honey and Philip Burgess. **Open:** Tue to Sun L 12 to 2.30, Mon to Sat D 6.45 to 9.15. **Meals:** alc (main courses £14 to £24). Set L and D

£17.50 (2 courses) to £20. Sun L £26. **Service:** not inc. **Details:** 65 seats. 15 seats outside. Separate bar. No music. Car parking.

Newton Poppleford
Moores'
Ticking all the right boxes
6 Greenbank, High Street, Newton Poppleford, EX10 0EB
Tel no: (01395) 568100
www.mooresrestaurant.co.uk
Modern British | £25
Cooking score: 1

£5 OFF 🛏 £30

This converted village shop on a raised slip road beside the High Street has been home to Jonathan and Kate Moore's intimate restaurant-with-rooms for the past seven years. The whole operation is pleasantly understated, with carefully sourced produce the starting point for some engaging cooking – reporters have singled out for praise the timbale of crab and mango, mullet fillets in chilli and coconut sauce with spinach and red rice, and ginger crème brûlée. Among meat dishes, there may be grilled lamb cutlets with dauphinois potatoes and Creedy Carver duck breast. House wine is £13.95.
Chef/s: Jonathan Moore. **Open:** Tue to Sun L 12 to 1.30 (1 Sat), Tue to Sat D 7 to 9.30. **Closed:** Mon, first 2 weeks Jan, Aug bank hol. **Meals:** Set L £15.95 (2 courses) to £21.45. Set D £18.50 (2 courses) to £24 (Sat £28.50). Sun L £15.95. **Service:** not inc. **Details:** 32 seats. 12 seats outside. Wheelchair access. Music.

Symbols
🛏 Accommodation is available
£30 Three courses for less than £30
V Separate vegetarian menu
£5 OFF £5-off voucher scheme
🍷 Notable wine list

Plymouth

Tanners

Reputable restaurant with winning ways
Prysten House, Finewell Street, Plymouth,
PL1 2AE
Tel no: (01752) 252001
www.tannersrestaurant.co.uk
Modern British | £35
Cooking score: 3

 V

The now famous Tanner brothers took over Plymouth's oldest house back in 1999, and have transformed it into a reputable eatery full of culinary zest and imagination. Consider one reporter's experience of the tasting menu: juicy seared scallops with celeriac and golden raisins; an exquisite serving of creamed butternut squash with goats' cheese fondant, tiny pieces of astringent pickled beetroot and crunchy gingerbread crumb; a barnstorming dish of Bodmin venison crusted with hazelnuts and cocoa nib, and a dreamy espresso jelly to finish. Despite its thick stone walls and flagstone floors, the fifteenth-century building never feels cold – thanks to soft lights, a cosy vibe and liberal helpings of genuine bonhomie. Visitors also appreciate 'old-fashioned personal service' from a brigade of switched-on staff. A host of commendable house wines by the glass or carafe does the wine list proud; bottles start at £14.95.
Chef/s: Martyn Compton, Chris and James Tanner.
Open: Tue to Sat L 12 to 2.30, D 7 to 9.30. **Closed:** Sun, Mon, 24 to 31 Dec, first week Jan. **Meals:** alc (main courses £16 to £25). Set L £14 (2 courses) to £18. Set D £20. Tasting menu £55 (6 courses).
Service: not inc. **Details:** 60 seats. 50 seats outside. Wheelchair access. Music.

CRAIG DUNN
Michael Caines at ABode Exeter

Which chefs do you admire, and why?
Michael Caines, for what he has achieved in the industry to date, with more to come.

What's your earliest food memory?
Coming in from school to the smell of homemade soup, I always loved that smell.

What advice would you give a chef starting their career?
Make sure you work in a kitchen with a good reputation, where you will learn from chefs who don't cut corners and are willing to teach.

What is your 'show-off' dish?
My rolled loin of rabbit dish that I did on *Britain's Best Dish* on ITV, with confit of leg and potato purée.

What would you be if you weren't a chef?
I would have loved to play in a band.

What would be your last meal?
Shepherd's pie with a pint of Guinness. Perfect.

What's your least favourite food?
I really don't like tripe and never have done; even the name sounds wrong to me.

ALSO RECOMMENDED

▲ Lemon Tree Café & Bistro

2 Haye Road South, Elburton, Plymouth, PL9 8HJ
Tel no: (01752) 481117
www.lemontreecafe.co.uk
Modern European £5 OFF

A 'charming, relaxed atmosphere and smiling, excellent service' impress reporters at this chic bistro. It's a continental café with a whiff of old Morocco, specialising in spreads of nibbly food (meze, zakuski, smörgåsbord). Blackboard specials include root vegetable soup with black pepper crème fraîche (£4.95), smoked haddock and poached egg in mustard sauce with mash (£7.95) and orange and cardamom rice pudding (£4.95). House Chilean is £13.95. Open Tue to Sat L. Mon to Sat D for private parties of 10 or more.

■ Rockbeare

The Jack in the Green

Cracking roadside pub
London Road, Rockbeare, EX5 2EE
Tel no: (01404) 822240
www.jackinthegreen.uk.com
Modern British | £30
Cooking score: 3
£5 OFF **V**

Tired and hungry travellers should take note of this roadside pub and make the short detour off the A30 for some cracking food. With some 20 years under his belt, Paul Parnell is an old hand at the hospitality game, providing pints for drinkers, pub food for lunchers and something a bit fancier in the rustic-chic dining rooms. Local sourcing is close to the kitchen's heart – in the bar there's not a word to be said against faggot with creamed potato and onion gravy or shepherd's pie. Elsewhere, menus work with the seasons, offering Jerusalem artichoke soup, whole lemon sole with morels and anchovy butter, and loin of local lamb with braised shoulder and sweetbreads. For dessert, consider rosewater crème brûlée. Wines from £16.

Chef/s: Matthew Mason. **Open:** Mon to Sat L 12 to 2, D 6 to 9 (9.30 Fri and Sat), Sun 12 to 9. **Closed:** 25 Dec to 5 Jan. **Meals:** alc (main courses £19 to £26). Set L £20 (2 courses) to £25.75. Set D £25. Sun L £20 (2 courses) to £25.75. **Service:** not inc. **Details:** 130 seats. 70 seats outside. Separate bar. Music. Car parking.

■ Salcombe

South Sands Beachside Restaurant

Seafood that's well worth seeking out
Bolt Head, Salcombe, TQ8 8LL
Tel no: (01548) 845900
www.southsands.com
Seafood | £35
Cooking score: 2
£5 OFF

It's tricky negotiating the narrow road to the little inlet of South Sands, but this boutique hotel and its Beachside Restaurant are well worth the effort. It's cool and relaxed, with pale wood floors, Lloyd Loom chairs and seashore colours, and a wall of windows opens on to a decked terrace overlooking the small beach. Seafood is the main event, delivered in a straightforward, light brasserie style – perhaps dressed Salcombe crab with garlic mayo and toasted brioche, and beer-battered Cornish hake with pea purée, chips and tartare. Meat fans may prefer beef rib with red wine butter. Wines from £17 a bottle.
Chef/s: Stuart Downie. **Open:** all week L 12 to 3, D 6 to 9.30. **Meals:** alc (main courses £15 to £28). Set L and D £15.95 (2 courses) to £20.95. Sun L £25. **Service:** not inc. **Details:** 80 seats. 48 seats outside. Separate bar. Wheelchair access. Music. Car parking.

█ Shaldon

Ode

Dazzling combinations from an organic champion

21 Fore Street, Shaldon, TQ14 ODE
Tel no: (01626) 873977
www.odetruefood.co.uk
Modern British | £38
Cooking score: 5

Few restaurants can boast better green credentials than Tim and Clare Bouget's environmentally friendly Georgian town house. The pair are seasoned campaigners for organic, local and regional British food, ethically reared meat and sustainable fish, so it comes as no surprise to find a vivid sense of seasonality about the cooking – the kitchen is never shy about showing off local allegiances. At its best, the food is boldly innovative without being outlandish. Ideas really do work on the plate, with dazzling combinations and kaleidoscopic flavours setting the tone. Faultless ingredients are the key and the kitchen manages to fuse local materials with exotica: Lyme Bay mackerel glazed with soy is served with sprouts and house-made chilli jam, while breast of Crediton duck appears teamed with clove and winter greens, spelt, and sweet-and-sour sauce. Earthier themes also surface in dishes such as slow-cooked haunch of fallow deer with red cabbage, crushed potato and glazed shallots. To follow, there are delights aplenty, whether a warm ginger pudding with spiced cracknel, gingerbread milk shake and butterscotch, or a plate of West Country cheeses. Unusual producers with an organic/biodynamic approach are championed on the short, well-priced wine list, which opens at £17. A simpler offshoot, Café Ode, is to be found in Ness Cove, Shaldon; tel: (01626) 873977.

Chef/s: Tim Bouget. **Open:** Wed to Sat D only 7 to 9.30. **Closed:** Sun to Tue, Oct, 1 week Jan, bank hols. **Meals:** alc (main courses £18 to £23). Set L £19.50 (2 courses) to £23.50. Set D £23.50 (2 courses) to £29.75. **Service:** not inc. **Details:** 24 seats. Music.

█ Sidford

The Salty Monk

Industrious cooking and personal hospitality

Church Street, Sidford, EX10 9QP
Tel no: (01395) 513174
www.saltymonk.co.uk
Modern British | £43
Cooking score: 3

Originally a salt house used by Benedictine monks, this lovely old medieval dwelling has been re-invented as a tasteful restaurant with boutique bedrooms and all mod cons, including a mini-spa/fitness studio. Annette and Andy Witheridge make a 'perfect pair' – she takes care of meeting and greeting, while he mans the stove. The cooking is industrious and skilful, although those weaned on sharp big-city food have found the results a tad 'unexceptional'. Roasted home-smoked salmon with beetroot compote is a signature starter, and fish from the day boats might also yield turbot fillet with gnocchi and a saffron sauce. Elsewhere, West Country farmers supply rare-breed pork, wild boar and Devon Hog lamb (perhaps served as a tripartite dish involving a miniature hotpot, roast loin and homemade sausage). To finish, lemon tart ('hot from the oven') with clotted cream has outclassed a rather 'disappointing' concoction of brown-sugar meringue 'mushrooms' with caramel sauce. The well-considered wine list (from £14.95) has a fair showing of organic and biodynamic bottles.

Chef/s: Andy Witheridge. **Open:** Thur to Sun L 12 to 1.30, all week D 6.30 to 9. **Closed:** Jan, 1 week Nov. **Meals:** alc (main courses £19 to £29). Set D £42.50. Sun L £29.50. **Service:** not inc. **Details:** 36 seats. 18 seats outside. Separate bar. Wheelchair access. Music. Car parking.

South Brent

ALSO RECOMMENDED
▲ The Turtley Corn Mill
Avonwick, South Brent, TQ10 9ES
Tel no: (01364) 646100
www.turtleycornmill.com
British £5 OFF

Set in six acres of gardens (complete with a lake), this converted corn mill now does duty as an upmarket B&B and all-day eatery. Devon produce gets a good outing on a daily menu that has rustic flavours in its blood: pork rillettes (£5.75) or local mussels in a creamy sauce might give way to pheasant casserole with mash and cabbage (£11.50), braised beef and Stilton pie or smoked haddock and Jerusalem artichoke bake. Steaks, burgers and battered haddock please the traditionalists. House wine is £14.50. Open all week.

South Pool
The Millbrook Inn
Proper village pub with top-notch food
South Pool, TQ7 2RW
Tel no: (01548) 531581
www.millbrookinnsouthpool.co.uk
French | £30
Cooking score: 2
£5 OFF

It's a cracking location – a delightful village next to the Salcombe Estuary. And the venerable Millbrook lives up to the billing; it's a perfect example of a village local, with real ales, a friendly atmosphere and great food. Jean-Philippe Bidart's gutsy, familiar French classics are based on the very best local and seasonal produce, from Start Bay crab bisque and river Teign mussels served in a chorizo, cream and white wine broth, to locally shot pheasant and pigeon teamed with Strasbourg sausage, choucroute and juniper jus. A 'truly great' plum and apple crumble is the perfect finish. Wines from £15.50.

Chef/s: Jean-Philippe Bidart. **Open:** all week L 12 to 2 (2.30 Sun), D 7 to 9. **Meals:** alc (main courses £11 to £25). Set L £10 (2 courses) to £12. Sun L £15. **Details:** 40 seats. 40 seats outside. Wheelchair access.

Topsham
La Petite Maison
Engaging 'auberge' with assured cooking
35 Fore Street, Topsham, EX3 0HR
Tel no: (01392) 873660
www.lapetitemaison.co.uk
Modern European | £38
Cooking score: 4
£5 OFF

True to the name, there's something of the French auberge about this 'petite maison' in trendy Topsham by the river Exe. Douglas and Elizabeth Pestell moved here in 2000 and have gradually imbued the venerable bow-windowed building with their own brand of engaging hospitality. White stucco, a Dutch fireplace and other homespun touches set the tone, while the kitchen adds some French and Mediterranean nuances to fastidiously sourced West Country ingredients without puffing itself up. An assured dish of Creedy Carver duck breast with confit leg, red cabbage, caramelised kumquat, orange and Cointreau sauce shows the style, and there's also a seasonal edge to medallions of venison with a poached pear, red cabbage, port and redcurrant jelly moistened with game jus. Locally landed seafood might include a bright starter of pan-fried squid with king prawns, chorizo and oriental citrus dressing. Desserts move into the realms of warm almond and apricot tart with Amaretto mascarpone cream. Seventy well-spread wines start at £17.75. **Chef/s:** Douglas Pestell and Sarah Bright. **Open:** Tue to Sat L 12.30 to 2 (bookings only), D 7 to 10. **Closed:** Sun, Mon, 1 week Apr, Nov, 26 to 30 Dec. **Meals:** Set L and D £31.95 (2 courses) to £37.95. **Service:** not inc. **Details:** 26 seats. Music.

Torquay

The Elephant

Extraordinary dishes from an ambitious chef
3-4 Beacon Terrace, Torquay, TQ1 2BH
Tel no: (01803) 200044
www.elephantrestaurant.co.uk
Modern British | £50
Cooking score: 5

£5
OFF

Perfectly positioned on a terrace rising away from the harbour, with boats bobbing at their moorings, Simon Hulstone's restaurant is on two levels, a smart ground-floor Brasserie, and the Room, an elegant space upstairs, all handsome polished boards, antique light fittings, big mirrors and framed menus. Hulstone appeared in the south-west heats of the *Great British Menu*, and is ambitious and infectiously creative, with strong regional loyalty and a keen eye for how dishes may be made to look extraordinary. Where others follow their instincts to jolt the unsuspecting palate, there's a gentleness to the Elephant, producing a fine starter of thin-sliced halibut in Gewürztraminer beurre blanc, with pearls of roasted cucumber, or pairing beef tartare and an oyster, alongside a sweetbread beignet and a quail egg. At main, a roundel of chicken breast and lamb, wrapped in cabbage, sits in the centre of a horizontal stripe of other ingredients – asparagus, pea shoots, shallots, roast garlic – while loin and cheek of fine local pork comes with a croquette of morcilla and pistachio, pickled veg and sage oil. That architectural skill resurfaces in a dessert consisting of a sphere of strawberries and lemon mascarpone with elderflower cream and strawberry juice. The wine list furnishes enough good bottles at keen prices to maintain interest. House wines are £17.50.
Chef/s: Simon Hulstone. **Open:** Brasserie: Tue to Sat L 12 to 2, D 6.30 to 9. Restaurant: Tue to Sat D only 7 to 9. **Closed:** Brasserie: Sun, Mon, first 2 weeks Jan. Restaurant: Sun, Mon, Oct to Apr. **Meals:** Brasserie: alc (main courses £16 to 24) Restaurant: Set D £39.50 (2 courses) to £49.50.

Tasting menu £60 (7 courses). **Service:** 10%. **Details:** 74 seats. Separate bar. Wheelchair access. Music. Children allowed in brasserie only.

Virginstow

Percy's

Excellent cooking in an alluring setting
Coombeshead Estate, Virginstow, EX21 5EA
Tel no: (01409) 211236
www.percys.co.uk
Modern British | £40
Cooking score: 4

£5
OFF

As the years pass, and it has been 17 years now, the Bricknell-Webbs' creation seems to go from strength to strength. The country hotel is part of a 130-acre organic farm that supplies much of the produce to the kitchen, and few would dispute the allure of the setting or the excellence of Tina Bricknell-Webb's cooking. Her fixed-price menu is limited in choice and backed up by industrious enterprise, which yields superb homemade bread, preserves and much more. Meats are home-reared and fish is fresh or nothing: Cornish scallops, for example, could be teamed with home-cured bacon and served with a dill, mustard and honey dressing; sea bass may arrive simply steamed with some fresh asparagus and béarnaise sauce. Lemon tart with rosemary ice cream and raspberries is a typical dessert. While output is very consistent, painful waits between courses still elicit comments in reports. Wines begin at £20.
Chef/s: Tina Bricknell-Webb. **Open:** all week D only 7 to 8.30. **Meals:** Set D £40. **Service:** not inc. **Details:** 20 seats. Separate bar. Wheelchair access. Music. Car parking. Children 10 yrs and over only.

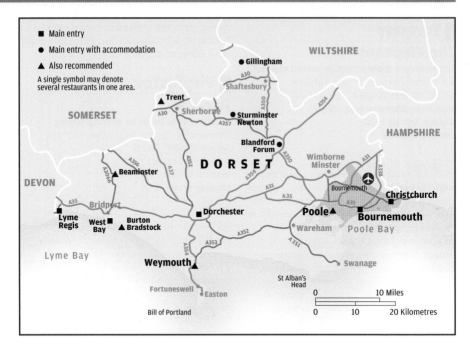

■ Beaminster

ALSO RECOMMENDED
▲ The Wild Garlic

4 The Square, Beaminster, DT8 3AS
Tel no: (01308) 861446
www.thewildgarlic.co.uk
Modern British £5 OFF

Former *MasterChef* winner Mat Follas certainly tries hard at this contemporary-rustic eatery within Beaminster's sixteenth-century tollhouse, waiting at table as well as manning the stoves. On offer is an inventory of trendy, forthright dishes running from 'cultivated' exotic mushrooms on chilli toast (£7) and 12-hour, triple-cooked belly pork with sweet potato (£18) to bitter chocolate fondant with walnut brittle. Despite good intentions, the kitchen seems to have a habit of faltering – although great-value fixed-price deals get a resounding thumbs-up. House wine is £16. Closed Sun to Tue.

■ Blandford Forum

Castleman Hotel

Hospitable dower-house hideaway
Chettle, Blandford Forum, DT11 8DB
Tel no: (01258) 830096
www.castlemanhotel.co.uk
Modern British | £26
Cooking score: 2
 £30

This peaceful country restaurant-with-rooms, a former dower house, is in an impossibly pretty location and makes for an intimate venue run with conviviality and an eye for the best regional produce. The cooking avoids risk-taking in favour of well-tried mainstream ideas: dishes such as smoked haddock and prawn pancake with dill and cheese sauce, and roast duck with grapes, bacon and thyme won't rock the world, but they are capably cooked. Start with Mediterranean-style fish soup or devilled lamb's kidneys, finish with lemon posset and rhubarb. A modest house selection (from £14) thriftily opens a wine list that features some splendid bottles.

Chef/s: Barbara Bourke and Richard Morris. **Open:** Sun L 12 to 2, all week D 7 to 10. **Closed:** 25, 26 and 31 Dec, Feb. **Meals:** alc (main courses £11 to £22). Sun L £23. **Service:** not inc. **Details:** 40 seats. Separate bar. No music. Wheelchair access. Car parking.

▌ Bournemouth

The Print Room

Art Deco glamour and global flavours
Richmond Hill, Bournemouth, BH2 6HH
Tel no: (01202) 789669
www.theprintroom-bournemouth.co.uk
Modern European | £28
Cooking score: 2

£5 £30
OFF

This majestic Art Deco building once hummed with printing presses, but now struts its stuff as a glamorous brasserie and 'grand café' – a lavish mix of mirrors, chequered floors, crushed velvet sofas and Swarovksi crystal chandeliers, with a 25m zinc bar to boot. Crustacea and charcuterie are supplemented by upmarket, globally inclined dishes running from herring roes on toast or fillet of New Forest venison with goats' cheese gnocchi to pork samosas, Thai-style monkfish with red lentil curry or Moroccan couscous with haloumi. You can also drop by for weekend breakfast, sandwiches and afternoon tea. The wine list is an admirable brasserie-style collection of well-chosen bottles at keen prices, with around a dozen by the glass or 500ml carafe. Bottles start at £16.

Chef/s: Matthew Tribouillard. **Open:** all week L 12 to 3 (4 Sun), Mon to Sat D 6 to 10. **Meals:** alc (main courses £8 to £19). Set L £12 (2 courses) to £15. Sun L £9.95. **Service:** not inc. **Details:** 150 seats. Separate bar. Wheelchair access. Music.

ALSO RECOMMENDED

▲ Dosa World

280 Old Christchurch Road, Bournemouth, BH1 1PH
Tel no: (01202) 318535
www.dosaworld.net
Indian

It's astonishing to find such authentic Sri Lankan and South Indian food hereabouts. Behind its plate-glass frontage, Dosa World is a no-frills, green-hued, town-centre café with friendly service and multicultural diners. The 117-strong menu embraces 25 types of masala dosa, a spicy 'bread biriani' of mutton kothu parotta (£5.25), and a zesty starter of devilled squid (£5.50). Prices are low, with house wine at just £8.50 a bottle; alternatively, there's the savoury thirst-quencher of yoghurty badam milk at £3.25. Open all week.

▲ WestBeach

Pier Approach, Bournemouth, BH2 5AA
Tel no: (01202) 587785
www.west-beach.co.uk
Seafood

'You can't dine any closer to the sea without getting your toes wet', say the owners of this breezy favourite hard by Bournemouth's West Beach. The seaside surrounds call for ozone-fresh fish, and the kitchen obliges with crustacean platters, fishy 'roast dinners' and dishes ranging from salmon ceviche with sour apple purée (£8.50) to hake bourguignon with spinach (£16.50). Meat fans can enjoy crispy duck salad or slow-cooked belly pork. House wine £16.50. Closed Sun and Mon D (Dec and Jan).

READERS RECOMMEND

Koh Thai Tapas

Daimler House, 38-40 Poole Hil, Bournemouth, BH2 5PS
Tel no: (01202) 294723
www.koh-thai.co.uk
'Favourite dishes are the Massaman Lamb, their magnificent satay chicken, and the spicy Thai soup with tiger prawns. Tom (yum)!'

Burton Bradstock

ALSO RECOMMENDED
▲ Hive Beach Café
Beach Road, Burton Bradstock, DT6 4RF
Tel no: (01308) 897070
www.hivebeachcafe.co.uk
Seafood

'A memorable meal in a wonderful location' gives an idea of this quintessential seafood café's enduring popularity. Perched on a shingle beach, the café is open all week for breakfast, lunch, afternoon snacks and occasional suppers. Form an orderly queue at the counter and wait for the attentive staff to bring your grilled Lyme Bay lemon sole (£17.95) or Cornish coast mussels steamed in cider, leek and cream (£14.95). Wines from £12.80. Opening hours are seasonal, so check the website.

Christchurch

NEW ENTRY
The Jetty
Slick new harbourside restaurant
Christchurch Harbour Hotel & Spa, 95 Mudeford, Christchurch, BH23 3NT
Tel no: (01202) 400950
www.thejetty.co.uk
Seafood | £35
Cooking score: 4
£5 OFF

With floor-to-ceiling glass on every side, there's no shortage of views from Alex Aitken's slick new harbourside restaurant – a wide window even lets you watch the bustling kitchen. The interior is coolly understated, with smooth surfaces and a ripple-effect ceiling that echoes the waters outside, while a smart and supremely efficient young team keeps everything well oiled. The kitchen's gutsy, unpretentious sweep through modern European cooking puts the spotlight on fine British produce – rare saddle of venison with gamey New Forest haggis, sweet red wine-poached pear and caramelised walnut was the highlight at inspection. Elsewhere there's fine

seafood: crab risotto, for example, topped with a soft-shell crab in perfectly crisp batter. The only wobble in an otherwise note-perfect performance was a passion-fruit soufflé overpowered by a puckering passion-fruit sauce. Wines from £16.50.
Chef/s: Alex Aitken. Open: Mon to Sat L 12 to 2.30, D 6 to 10. Sun 12 to 8. Meals: alc (main courses £16 to £29). Set L and D £17.95 (2 courses) to £21.95. Sun L £28.50. Service: 10%. Details: 70 seats. 30 seats outside. Separate bar. Wheelchair access. Music. Car parking.

Cranborne

READERS RECOMMEND
La Fosse at Cranborne
Modern British
London House, The Square, Cranborne, BH21 5PR
Tel no: (01725) 517604
www.la-fosse.com
'The food is excellent. I ate, for example, wonderful grilled shrimps with fresh vegetables, and the cheese plate was marvellous.'

Dorchester

Sienna
Tiny restaurant with big ideas
36 High West Street, Dorchester, DT1 1UP
Tel no: (01305) 250022
www.siennarestaurant.co.uk
Modern British | £43
Cooking score: 4

Confirming the old adage that 'size isn't everything', Russell and Eléna Brown's pint-sized restaurant makes a big impression within the tight, almost domestic confines of a converted sweet shop. Their warmly intimate dining room holds just 15 people and opening times are rather limited, but the kitchen proves its worth with some highly precise and technically assured cooking. Menus evolve with the market and the seasons, and Russell sets the bar high from the start – perhaps sending out char-grilled Jurassic Coast rose veal with white bean casserole, pickled carrots and Arbequina olive oil. Mains pick up the

pan-European theme, whether it's roast loin of Dorset lamb enriched with Jerusalem artichoke velouté and thyme jus or fillet of line-caught sea bass finished with braised endive, orange, almonds and handmade macaroni. The low-key culinary professionalism also shows in desserts such as salted toffee tart with crème fraîche sorbet and an orange reduction. Wines (from £18.50) offer quality as well as variety.
Chef/s: Russell Brown. **Open:** Wed to Sat L 12.30 to 2, Tue to Sat D 7 to 9. **Closed:** Sun, Mon, 2 weeks spring, 2 weeks autumn. **Meals:** Set L £25.50 (2 courses) to £28.50. Set D £36.50 (2 courses) to £43. Tasting menu £55 (6 courses). **Service:** not inc. **Details:** 15 seats. Music. Children over 11 yrs only.

Gillingham
Restaurant Stock Hill
Tip-top European cooking
Stock Hill House, Stock Hill, Gillingham, SP8 5NR
Tel no: (01747) 823626
www.stockhillhouse.co.uk
European | £40
Cooking score: 5

The Gillingham in north Dorset pronounces itself with a hard G, so there need be no confusion with the one in Kent. It also boasts this stone-built house in 11 acres of richly lovely gardens, which was once the home of the cartoonist Osbert Lancaster's grandfather, in case you were wondering. The Hausers have run it as a bright, elegant country hotel since the mid-1980s, and they maintain consistent standards. Peter Hauser mixes the foodways of his native Austria with classical French cookery to create a culinary alloy that commands great local loyalty. Start with marinated herring and tomato salad in red onion and white wine cream, or sautéed lamb's sweetbreads deglazed with Pernod in puff pastry, before mains of gedünsteter rostbraten (beef escalope with onions and sour cream), or pork Holstein, the breaded fillet topped with a fried egg and marinated anchovies. It all sounds deceptively straightforward, but ingredients are tip-top,

and the cooking achieves a rare depth of flavour. Dessert could be a Viennese mini-cheesecake with fig sorbet, or fürst pückler torte, a layered chocolate and red berry gâteau. Austrian Grüner Veltliner and Blaufränkisch inveigle their way among the French classics on the wine list, which starts at £24.95.
Chef/s: Peter Hauser and Lorna Connor. **Open:** all week L 12.15 to 1.30, D 7 to 8.45. **Meals:** Set L £19.50 (2 courses) to £25. Set D £40. Sun L £21.50. **Service:** not inc. **Details:** 24 seats. 8 seats outside. No music. Car parking.

Lyme Regis
Hix Oyster & Fish House
Marine cuisine and swoon-inducing views
Cobb Road, Lyme Regis, DT7 3JP
Tel no: (01297) 446910
www.hixoysterandfishhouse.co.uk
Seafood | £30
Cooking score: 3

'We arrived as the sun was setting over the harbour below the restaurant, a wonderful location' swooned a reporter, gazing down through full-drop windows at the coastal views from Mark Hix's splendidly sited seafood place. The highly skilled, youthful team helps things go with a swing, and the marine cuisine offers native oysters with local spicy sausages, gull's eggs with mayonnaise and celery salt, and sensitively cooked mains such as Portland grey mullet with shrimps and sea purslane, or a rather dashing crab and pumpkin curry served in the shell. Some have felt the dishes to be a little prosaic on occasion, but simplicity is the point. Finish with lemon curd and ginger cheesecake, and a helping of truffles made with Temperley's cider brandy. Wines start at £19.75.
Chef/s: Phil Eagle. **Open:** all week 12 to 10. **Closed:** Mon (Oct to Apr only), 25 and 26 Dec. **Meals:** alc (main courses £14 to £30). Set L and D £17 (2 courses) to £21. **Service:** 10%. **Details:** 50 seats. 20 seats outside. Wheelchair access. Music.

Poole

ALSO RECOMMENDED
▲ Guildhall Tavern
15 Market Street, Poole, BH15 1NB
Tel no: (01202) 671717
www.guildhalltavern.co.uk
French £5 OFF

Now in its second decade but by no means over the hill, this resolutely French restaurant continues to pull in a raft of locals and visitors to its warmly welcoming dining room. French onion soup (£6.25), and skate with butter and caperberries (£18.95) are tried-and-true stalwarts, designed to make you think you are on the other side of the Channel, but with 'well-executed beef bourguignon and starter and dessert punching well above the modest £14', the set lunch is a top shout too. Wines from £15.25. Closed Sun and Mon.

Sturminster Newton
Plumber Manor
'What eating out in England should be'
Sturminster Newton, DT10 2AF
Tel no: (01258) 472507
www.plumbermanor.com
Anglo-French | £35
Cooking score: 2

If you are dreaming of an escape to a country house retreat of honeyed stone, it could look pretty much like the Prideaux-Brunes' Jacobean manor house – their family home for four centuries. Visitors love everything about the place, from its dreamy gardens to dinner that's 'a first-class example of what eating out in England should be'. There's nothing here to offend or challenge: chicken liver pâté with onion marmalade, lemon sole with grapes and white wine, or chicken with lemon and tarragon, cooked by the practised hand of Brian Prideaux-Brune, deal in comfort and familiarity. Wines from £17.

Chef/s: Brian Prideaux-Brune. Open: Sun L 12 to 2, all week D 7.30 to 9. Closed: Feb. Meals: Set D £35. Sun L £25. Service: not inc. Details: 65 seats. Separate bar. No music. Wheelchair access. Car parking.

Trent

ALSO RECOMMENDED
▲ The Rose & Crown
Trent, DT9 4SL
Tel no: (01935) 850776
www.roseandcrowntrent.co.uk
Modern British

An ever-so-English setting by the church creates the right impression for visitors to this ancient thatched hostelry. Exposed stone, beams and blazing fires reinforce the mood, and the kitchen uses local ingredients for some first-class food. Lunch is a mix of sandwiches and pub classics, say pork sausages with horseradish mash (£10.95); dinner brings pigeon breast with lentils (£5.50), lamb rump or slow-roast belly pork (£13.95), and desserts like Dorset apple cake. Wines from £13.95. No food Sun D and Mon. Accommodation.

West Bay
Riverside Restaurant
Long-running favourite with heartwarming seafood
West Bay, DT6 4EZ
Tel no: (01308) 422011
www.thefishrestaurant-westbay.co.uk
Seafood | £36
Cooking score: 3
£5 OFF V

The Watsons took over the lease of the old café and post office in 1960 and have never looked back. At this rate, they'll be getting a blue plaque soon. Cross the wooden walkway to the harbourside building and settle in for some heartwarming, uncomplicated fish and seafood cookery while you gaze out over the water. It's not all traditional: you might open with seared squid served with chickpea and vine tomato compote, and follow with brill fillet on crispy spinach in sorrel sauce. But seafood platters and pancakes, generously crammed bourrides, and whole fish grilled on the bone in lemon and butter will continue to be the compass-settings for many. Staff could chill out; it shouldn't feel like a race. Wines start at £17.50 (£4.25 a glass).

Chef/s: Tony Shaw. **Open:** Tue to Sun L 12 to 2.30, Tue to Sat D 6.30 to 9. **Closed:** Mon, 1 Dec to 12 Feb. **Meals:** alc (main courses £13 to £40). Set L £19.55 (2 courses) to £26.50. **Service:** not inc. **Details:** 80 seats. 25 seats outside. Separate bar. No music. Wheelchair access.

■ Weymouth

ALSO RECOMMENDED
▲ Crab House Café

Ferryman's Way, Portland Road, Weymouth, DT4 9YU
Tel no: (01305) 788867
www.crabhousecafe.co.uk
Seafood

Forget the bib and tucker, flip-flops are more in order at this quirky wooden shack overlooking Chesil beach. The owners have their own oyster beds; the rest of the seafood is landed within 40 miles of the kitchen. The menu changes daily, but might include whole crab (£19.25), whole red gurnard with tomatoes and basil (£16.25) or whole brill, baked with lime and coriander butter (£18.50), and Dorset apple cake. Wines from £14.90. Open Wed to Sat and Sun L.

MARK JORDAN
The Atlantic Hotel,
Ocean Restaurant

When did you realise you wanted to be a chef?
I originally wanted to study animation, but then discovered a passion for cooking at the age of 15.

Which chefs do you admire, and why?
Heston Blumenthal for pushing the boundaries, Nuno Mendes for his skill and Keith Floyd for starting my career.

What food trends are you spotting at the moment?
Local seaweeds and edible herbs from the Jersey seashore.

What's your biggest extravagance in the kitchen?
My Carpigiani ice cream machine.

What is your earliest food memory?
When I was about five, waiting to lick the bowl my mum had used to make fairy cakes.

What is your 'show-off' dish?
Assiette of Jersey beef, buttered poached lobster and potato cappuccino.

What would you be if you weren't a chef?
I'd be in animation, making films like *Wallace and Gromit*!

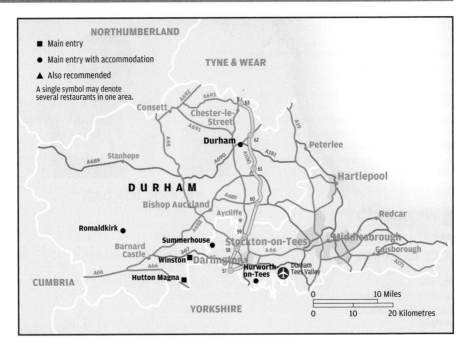

Map legend:
- ■ Main entry
- ● Main entry with accommodation
- ▲ Also recommended

A single symbol may denote several restaurants in one area.

NORTHUMBERLAND

TYNE & WEAR

Consett
Chester-le-Street
Durham
Stanhope
Peterlee
Hartlepool
DURHAM
Bishop Auckland
Aycliffe
Redcar
Romaldkirk
Summerhouse
Stockton-on-Tees
Middlesbrough
Barnard Castle
Winston
Darlington
Guisborough
Hutton Magna
Hurworth-on-Tees
Durham Tees Valley
CUMBRIA
YORKSHIRE

0   10 Miles
0   10   20 Kilometres

■ Durham

Bistro 21

Friendly bistro delivering top comfort food
Aykley Heads House, Aykley Heads, Durham,
DH1 5TS
Tel no: (0191) 3844354
www.bistrotwentyone.co.uk
Modern British | £33
Cooking score: 3

Part of the '21 Hospitality Group' owned by
local food hero Terry Laybourne, Bistro 21 is
located in an open woodland suburb close to
Durham Police headquarters. Housed in an
eighteenth-century farmhouse, it has an
open-air courtyard – a great spot for fine
weather drinks – and a spacious, rustically
stylish dining room. The classically informed
but simple cooking delivers comfort food
with that something extra – 'the food has
more oomph to it than the phrase comfort
food suggests'. Try tempura battered tiger
prawns with curried mayonnaise and pickled
cucumber salad to start, then venison
medallions with celeriac purée, roast potatoes
and bitter chocolate sauce. Pavlova-poached
rhubarb and blood oranges may be more
meringue than pavlova, but still makes a
satisfying finish. Service is 'particularly
friendly and professional'. House wines
are £16.95.

Chef/s: Gareth Lambert. **Open:** Mon to Sat L 12 to 2,
D 6 to 10. **Closed:** Sun, 25 and 26 Dec, 1 Jan, bank
hols. **Meals:** alc (main courses £12 to £27). Set L
£15.50 (2 courses) to £18. Set D £16.50 (2 courses)
to £19.50. **Service:** 10%. **Details:** 60 seats. 24 seats
outside. Separate bar. Wheelchair access. Music.
Car parking.

Symbols

⊟ Accommodation is available

£30 Three courses for less than £30

V Separate vegetarian menu

£5 OFF £5-off voucher scheme

🍷 Notable wine list

Gourmet Spot

Small restaurant with big ideas
The Avenue, Durham, DH1 4DX
Tel no: (0191) 3846655
www.gourmet-spot.co.uk
Modern European | £38
Cooking score: 3

Situated on a hill near the city centre, this ambitious restaurant with its tiny bar and small dining room nevertheless has a countryside feel. Although adjectives such as 'amazing' have peppered readers' reports, the execution doesn't always live up to the menu description, and other reporters have found the food 'poor'. At a test meal, a surf-and-turf starter of confit chicken thigh with North Coast scallops, egg yolk, wild garlic emulsion, chicory and apple was as complex as it sounds, but not totally convincing. There was also a lot going on in a main course rolled confit leg of duck with roast cured breast, confit potato, Asian-style cabbage, rhubarb and ginger foam. However, presentation is impressive and a lemon assiette with mint made a pleasing finale. Wines from £15.
Chef/s: Stephen Hardy. **Open:** Tue to Sat D only 6 to 9.30. **Closed:** Sun, Mon, 25 and 26 Dec, first week Jan. **Meals:** Set D £30 (2 courses) to £38. Tasting menu £55 (8 courses). **Service:** 12.5%. **Details:** 24 seats. Separate bar. Wheelchair access. Music. Car parking.

▮ Hurworth-on-Tees

The Bay Horse

Cut-above village pub
45 The Green, Hurworth-on-Tees, DL2 2AA
Tel no: (01325) 720663
www.thebayhorsehurworth.com
Modern British | £29
Cooking score: 3

This Grade II-listed building – dating from the fifteenth century, but refurbished in 2008 – gives the impression of being a cut above the usual village pub, with more adventurous

food than you might expect. It's run with great warmth, and Marcus Bennett is in charge of the foodie fireworks. His style is a mix of classical with contemporary flourishes; witness a starter of French black pudding teamed with quince purée and chutney, pressed pear and brandy sausage and braised and crispy celery. That might lead to slow-cooked corn-fed chicken breast with a stuffed ballotine of the leg, mushroom duxelles, Jerusalem artichokes, truffle oil and thyme and garlic jus. Lemon pannacotta makes a satisfying finale. Light lunches are simple and straightforward, and bread is freshly baked. Wines from £16.95.
Chef/s: Marcus Bennett. **Open:** all week L 12 to 2.30 (4 Sun), D 6 to 10. **Closed:** 25 and 26 Dec. **Meals:** alc (main courses £14 to £25). Set L £12.95 (2 courses) to £15.95. Sun L £14.95. **Service:** not inc. **Details:** 70 seats. 60 seats outside. Separate bar. Wheelchair access. Music. Car parking.

Kenny Atkinson at The Orangery

Gold standard cooking with panoramic views
Rockliffe Hall, Hurworth-on-Tees, DL2 2DU
Tel no: (01325) 729999
www.rockliffehall.com
Modern British | £60
Cooking score: 5

Rockliffe Hall is a country-retreat hotel with all the amenities, not far from the North York Moors. There are no fewer than three dining options, but the gold standard is Kenny Atkinson's Orangery, housed in a Victorian addition to the main building, where once was nurtured much exotic flora. With panoramic views over the gardens, the stage is set for an adventure through various tasting menus of prestige north-eastern produce. Reporters are voluble in their support, the detail of dishes lingering passionately in the memory. For one, it was Lindisfarne oyster soup, Whitby lobster with beetroot, wild mallard terrine, sea bream on crab risotto, and an array of hogget (loin, shoulder and sweetbread) with creamy mash and confit tomato. For another, the highlights were mackerel with gooseberries, lemon and mustard, turbot on Jerusalem artichoke risotto with veal sweetbread and truffle, and slow-roasted beef fillet with braised cheek, pease pudding and asparagus. The cooking hits the spot by combining formidable technical skill with flavours and textures to indulge the palate, through to seductive desserts such as Cluizel chocolate terrine with red wine pear, caramel ice cream and popcorn. Wines by the small glass from £5.50 lead off a list that provides a wealth of choice below £35. Eye-catching producers and ripe vintages abound, and there are entries from Canada, Uruguay and Wales amid the usual suspects.

Chef/s: Kenny Atkinson. **Open:** Tue to Sat D only 6.30 to 9.30. **Closed:** Sun, Mon. **Meals:** Tasting menu £59.50 (5 courses) to £85 (10 courses). **Service:** not inc. **Details:** 50 seats. Separate bar. Wheelchair access. Music. Car parking.

Hutton Magna
The Oak Tree Inn
Village hostelry with high standards
Hutton Magna, DL11 7HH
Tel no: (01833) 627371
www.theoaktreehutton.co.uk
Modern British | £31
Cooking score: 3

'Lovely little place with a high standard of cooking' enthused one fan of Alastair and Claire Ross's homely pub-cum-restaurant. It's run as a real village hostelry, with oodles of traditional character, but when it comes to food, evening menus of simple, clean-cut modern dishes punch above their weight: say beetroot and goats' cheese tart or crispy monkfish fillet teamed with aubergine and fennel. Main course highlights may include best end of lamb with a lamb and black pudding shepherd's pie, or stone bass with mussels, chorizo and new potatoes. When it comes to dessert, sticky gingerbread pudding or hot chocolate fondant go down a treat. Seven wines by the glass (from £3.55) are a welcome sight and bottles start at £14.

Chef/s: Alastair Ross. **Open:** Tue to Sun D only 6 to 9 (8 Sun). **Closed:** Mon, 24 to 27 and 31 Dec, 1 Jan. **Meals:** alc (main courses £19 to £23). **Service:** not inc. **Details:** 20 seats. Separate bar. Music. Car parking.

Romaldkirk
The Rose & Crown
Well-run village charmer
Romaldkirk, DL12 9EB
Tel no: (01833) 650213
www.rose-and-crown.co.uk
Modern British | £35
Cooking score: 2

£5 OFF

'We had dinner, bed and breakfast at this traditional English village inn, and were impressed by the way it was run'. So says one reporter of this ivy-clad eighteenth-century coaching inn on the village green, which draws the crowds with its down-to-earth bonhomie. Eat in the bar/brasserie or the oak-panelled, candlelit dining room, where your meal might start off with smoked haddock, prawn and mushroom gratin, followed by a tomato and apple soup. A main of Teesdale lamb is served three ways: confit of shoulder, shepherd's pie and pink slices. Homemade rhubarb ice cream makes a comforting dessert. Wines from £17.95.

Chef/s: Christopher Davy and Andrew Lee. **Open:** Sun L 12 to 1.45, all week D 7.30 to 9. **Closed:** 24 to 26 Dec. **Meals:** Set L £18.95. Set D £35 (4 courses). Bar menu available. **Service:** not inc. **Details:** 24 seats. 24 seats outside. Separate bar. No music. Wheelchair access. Car parking.

Please send us your feedback

To register your opinion about any restaurant listed in the Guide, or a new restaurant that you wish to bring to our attention, please visit the web address at the bottom of the page. Your feedback informs the content of the book and will be used to compile next year's reviews.

◼ Summerhouse
The Raby Hunt
Personally run restaurant-with-rooms
Summerhouse, DL2 3UD
Tel no: (01325) 374237
www.rabyhuntrestaurant.co.uk
Modern British | £40
Cooking score: 3
£5 OFF 🛏

This early nineteenth-century pub (now a restaurant-with-rooms) has been brought up to date with more than a lick of paint, and it provides an elegant setting for the contemporary cooking that is James Close's forte. While much is made of local sourcing, inspiration for dishes comes from wider-spread European roots. Readers applaud a 'stunning' starter of rack and neck of lamb with goats' cheese, Jerusalem artichoke and a spiced lamb and black olive jus, and the 'cooked to perfection' loin of venison with caramelised cauliflower textures. Desserts have been a particular highlight for many, and the rice pudding, raspberry jam and cinnamon ice cream garners as much praise as the high-quality local cheeses served with 'melt-in-the-mouth' biscuits. House wine is £14.95.
Chef/s: James Close. **Open:** Thur to Sun L 12 to 2, Wed to Sat D 6.30 to 9. **Closed:** Mon, Tue, 25 and 26 Dec, 1 Jan. **Meals:** alc (main courses £18.95 to £27.95). Set L and D £18.95 (2 courses) to £21.95. Sun L £19.50. **Service:** not inc. **Details:** 28 seats. 10 seats outside. Separate bar. Wheelchair access. Music. Car parking.

◼ Winston
The Bridgewater Arms
Character, warmth and local ingredients
Winston, DL2 3RN
Tel no: (01325) 730302
www.thebridgewaterarms.com
Modern European | £34
Cooking score: 1

A 'gem' in lovely Teesdale, this listed former schoolhouse majors on friendliness and cosy comfort. An easy-to-like menu is served in both the bar, with its bookshelves and log fire, and the candlelit restaurant. Dishes demonstrate an enthusiasm for good local seafood, including Craster smoked salmon with capers and cornichons, and grilled North Sea Dover sole, as well as the odd dalliance with Asian flavours in a dessert of lemongrass ice cream with roast pineapple. House wine is from £15.
Chef/s: Paul Grundy and Richard Vart. **Open:** Tue to Sat L 12 to 2, D 6 to 9. **Closed:** Sun, Mon, 25 to 27 Dec. **Meals:** alc (main courses £14 to £36). **Service:** not inc. **Details:** 48 seats. Music. Car parking.

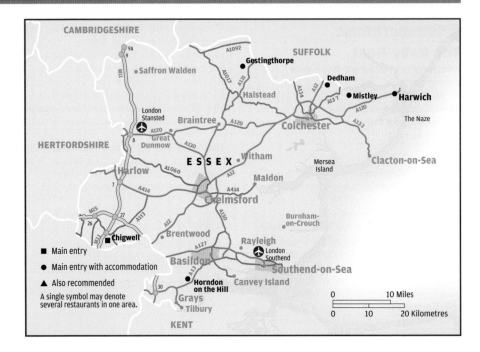

Chigwell

The Bluebell

Local asset with sterling produce
117 High Road, Chigwell, IG7 6QQ
Tel no: (020) 8500 6282
www.thebluebellrestaurant.co.uk
Modern European | £37
Cooking score: 1

A surprisingly large restaurant in the heart of
Chigwell, the Bluebell has a reputation built
on sterling British produce. Warm pheasant
salad with apple rémoulade, and main courses
of slow-cooked Gressingham duck with chilli
and coriander potatoes, wilted greens and
spiced honey jus, or wild sea bass with
boulangère potatoes, creamed leeks, baby
fennel and red wine fumé typify the style of
the all-embracing menu. For dessert, maybe
apple tarte Tatin with vanilla ice cream. Wines
from £16.50.
Chef/s: Gavin Maguire. **Open:** Tue to Sun L 12 to 2
(4 Sun), Tue to Sat D 6.45 to 9.30 (6.30 to 10.30
Sat). **Closed:** Mon, 26 and 27 Dec, 31 Dec to 4 Jan.

Meals: alc (main courses £17 to £29). Set L £16.95 (2
courses) to £19.95. Set D Tue to Thur £18.95 (2
courses) to £23.95. Sun L £18.95 (two courses) to
£23.95. **Details:** 90 seats. Separate bar. Wheelchair
access. Music.

Dedham

The Sun Inn

Splendid inn with a Mediterranean spin
High Street, Dedham, CO7 6DF
Tel no: (01206) 323351
www.thesuninndedham.com
Mediterranean | £25
Cooking score: 3

£5 OFF £30

It may be deep in Constable country, but this
splendidly revitalised fifteenth-century inn
has Mediterranean blood running through its
veins. Aperitivi and antipasti set the tone for a
menu that puts a sunny spin on native
produce: from Arborio rice with Mersea
oysters, Prosecco, shallots and tarragon, via
pheasant ravioli overlaid with lemon, thyme

and pomegranate, to White Breed beef casserole with rosemary, orange zest and wet polenta – not forgetting tremendously nourishing bowls of Italian fish stew. Eat and drink in the bar (all heavy oak boards, elm tables and real ales) or settle into the spacious restaurant; either way, expect top-drawer service from a bevy of bubbly staff. The 'superb' 100-bin wine list is driven by knowledge, enthusiasm and a dedication to fine drinking from lesser-known sources. Eloquent food-matching notes and kind prices are a bonus; bottles from £14, glasses from £3.50.
Chef/s: Ugo Simonelli. **Open:** all week L 12 to 2.30 (3 Sat and Sun), D 6.30 to 9.30 (10 Fri and Sat). **Closed:** 25 and 26 Dec. **Meals:** alc (main courses £10 to £19). Set L and D £12 (2 courses) to £15. **Service:** not inc. **Details:** 60 seats. 60 seats outside. Separate bar. Music. Car parking.

Epping

READERS RECOMMEND
The Raj
Indian
75 High Street, Epping, CM16 4BA
Tel no: (01992) 572193
www.rajindian.co.uk
'Food of the highest standard – the king prawn dishes particularly are second to none.'

Gestingthorpe

NEW ENTRY
The Pheasant
Indulge in some comfort eating
Gestingthorpe, CO9 3AU
Tel no: (01787) 461196
www.thepheasant.net
Modern British | £25
Cooking score: 1
£5 OFF 🛏 £30

Walk in the door of this country pub-with-rooms and you feel instantly at home. With small, interlinked rooms, low-beamed ceilings, wood burners and old-fashioned polished tables it has the kind of relaxed feel

that lifts the spirits. James Donoghue's unpretentious food does not suffer from a lack of quality – there's locally baked bread, estate game, ice cream from a nearby farm, even local ales . A bar menu offers Welsh rarebit or a 'fantastic' poacher's pasty 'stuffed full of pheasant', while the carte promises 'thick, beautifully flavoured' spicy orange and carrot soup, and fillet of chicken with bubble and squeak, creamed swede and carrot and parsley sauce. House wine is £14.95.
Chef/s: James Donoghue. **Open:** all week L 12 to 2.30, D 6.30 to 9. **Meals:** alc (main courses £22 to £33). Set L and D £12.50 (2 courses) to £15.50. **Service:** not inc. **Details:** 40 seats. 30 seats outside. Music. Car parking.

Harwich

The Pier at Harwich, Harbourside Restaurant
Fine seafood and estuary views
The Quay, Harwich, CO12 3HH
Tel no: (01255) 241212
www.milsomhotels.com
Seafood | £35
Cooking score: 2

As the name suggests, this welcoming hotel set firmly on Harwich quayside offers views across the Stour and Orwell estuaries from its first-floor restaurant. Seafood is the order of the day and chef Tom Bushell has quickly stamped his identity on the menus, which offer classics alongside dishes with a more contemporary slant. A starter of steamed mussels, cockles, clams, tiger prawns and langoustine in anise velouté might be followed by lobster thermidor. Meatier choices include lamb cutlets with tabbouleh, harissa and tzatziki. Finish with pear and apple tarte Tatin. House wine is £17.60. The ground-floor bistro serves simpler food.
Chef/s: Tom Bushell. **Open:** all week L 12 to 2, D 6 to 9. **Closed:** 25 and 26 Dec. **Meals:** alc (main courses £16 to £39). Set L £20.50 (2 courses) to £25. Sun L £29.50. **Service:** not inc. **Details:** 70 seats. Separate bar. Music. Car parking.

Horndon on the Hill

The Bell Inn

Medieval pub with comforting food
High Road, Horndon on the Hill, SS17 8LD
Tel no: (01375) 642463
www.bell-inn.co.uk
Modern European | £29
Cooking score: 2

The medieval Bell Inn has been run by members of the Vereker family for 75 years and still has proper English heritage to spare – no fruit machines or jukeboxes disturb the 'brilliant atmosphere' or conversational buzz in the flagstone-floored, oak-beamed bar. The place also does a decent line in food, from pubby staples such as rabbit terrine ('as good as anything in Lyon') to spot-on beef fillet with oxtail won ton and a dinky cottage pie, or pan-fried brill with sweetcorn chowder. The 'fat chips' with balsamic mayo are unmissable, and puds might include mango and white chocolate mousse with popping candy. Good-value wines from £13.95.
Chef/s: Stuart Fay. **Open:** all week L 12 to 1.45 (2.15 Sun), D 6.30 to 9.45 (6 Sat, 7 Sun). **Closed:** 25 and 26 Dec, bank hols. **Meals:** alc (main courses £12 to £25). **Service:** not inc. **Details:** 80 seats. 36 seats outside. Separate bar. No music. Wheelchair access. Car parking.

Mistley

The Mistley Thorn

Upbeat eatery with painless prices
High Street, Mistley, CO11 1HE
Tel no: (01206) 392821
www.mistleythorn.co.uk
Modern European | £24
Cooking score: 2

Readers have endorsed the comfort of the bedrooms at this modernised eighteenth-century coaching inn. Sherri Singleton's menus follow the calendar and the cooking scores with its simplicity, Mediterranean flavours and painless prices. Local oysters are a treat, fish dishes 'very good', perhaps smoked haddock chowder, followed by cioppino (a Cal-Ital-style seafood stew) or Harwich crab cakes. Otherwise, there's char-grilled Red Poll ribeye or Deben duck breast in plum-red wine sauce, and chocolate St Emilion to finish. A valuable local resource and an agreeable stopover. Wines from £14.95.
Chef/s: Sherri Singleton. **Open:** all week L 12 to 2.30 (5 Sat and Sun), D 6.30 to 9.30 (10 Fri and Sat). **Meals:** alc (main courses £9 to £17). Set L £10.95 (2 courses) to £15.95. Sun L £11.95 (2 courses) to £16.95. **Service:** not inc. **Details:** 70 seats. 12 seats outside. Separate bar. Wheelchair access. Music. Car parking.

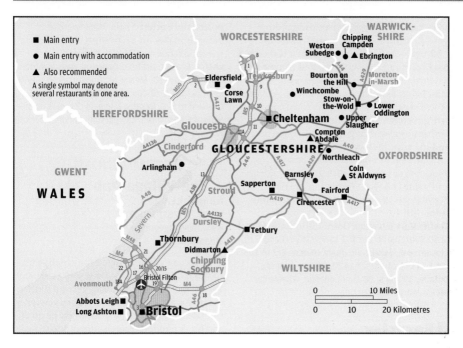

▌Abbots Leigh

NEW ENTRY
The George Inn
Smart pub with skilful local food
Manor Road, Abbots Leigh, BS8 3RP
Tel no: (01275) 372467
www.thegeorgeinn.uk.com
Modern British | £25
Cooking score: 2

£30

This smartly renovated village pub between
Bristol and Portishead has built up a strong
local reputation for no-frills pub food based
on local produce, although villagers can still
pop in for a pint. Scan the frequently changing
menu in the oak-beamed restaurant where
chef/proprietor Dan Powell's skills are evident
in a starter of 'pub-smoked' mackerel with a
crab beignet, soused cucumber, celeriac
rémoulade and chilli dressing. A fragrant,
precisely timed fillet of wild sea bass cooked
'en papillote' with soy, ginger and spring
onions may arrive with a bowl of brown

shrimp and pak choi noodles. Apple tarte Tatin
with clotted cream ice cream is 'very, very
good'. Wines start at £16.25.
Chef/s: Dan Powell. **Open:** Tue to Sun L 12 to 2.30
(3.30 Sun), Tue to Sat D 6.30 to 9.30. **Closed:** Mon,
25 Dec, bank hols. **Meals:** alc (main courses £11 to
£16). **Service:** not inc. **Details:** 40 seats. 40 seats
outside. No music. Car parking. No children in the
bar after 7.

▌Arlingham
The Old Passage
Pin-sharp seafood and fresh flavours
Passage Road, Arlingham, GL2 7JR
Tel no: (01452) 740547
www.theoldpassage.com
Seafood | £35
Cooking score: 3

£5 OFF

Many readers seem to enjoy themselves at this
restaurant-with-rooms on the banks of the
River Severn. Menus lean toward seafood,
with pin-sharp treatments seen in dishes such

as 'fantastic' scallops Mornay, 'outstanding' potted shrimps, a 'lovely meaty' plaice in butter, a 'beautifully executed roast turbot and oxtail dish', and 'possibly the best fish pie we have ever tasted'. Fresh flavours and seasonality drive the kitchen. The cooking can reveal a splendidly rustic, unrefined edge when it comes to the occasional meat dish – perhaps ox cheek faggots with mashed potato and red wine jus from the good-value lunchtime River Menu. As for dessert, chocolate tart teamed with griottine cherries and white chocolate sorbet hits the mark. Service gets rave reviews, too. House wines from £18.40.

Chef/s: Mark Redwood. **Open:** Tue to Sun L 12 to 2 (2.30 Sun), Tue to Sat D 7 to 9 (6.45 Fri and Sat). **Closed:** Mon. **Meals:** alc (main courses £17 to £45). Set L £15 (2 courses) to £20. **Service:** not inc. **Details:** 50 seats. 30 seats outside. Wheelchair access. Music. Car parking.

Barnsley

The Potager Restaurant
Rich pickings from Rosemary's garden
Barnsley House, Barnsley, GL7 5EE
Tel no: (01285) 740000
www.barnsleyhouse.com
Modern British | £40
Cooking score: 3

Formerly the home of celebrated garden designer Rosemary Verey, this Cotswold manor house is now an upmarket boutique hotel that attracts some notable guests. The Potager overlooks the gardens and has recently been tastefully revamped to make it more informal. Comfortable new banquettes along one side of the room add to the relaxed feel and gone are the starched white linen tablecloths. Head chef Graham Grafton's modern European style uses the maximum local produce, much of it from the kitchen garden. This is evident in tempura of 'just-picked' vegetables served with Thai dipping sauce, and a main of rabbit pie with mustard,

potato and buttered kale. Passion-fruit bavarois makes for a refreshing finale. House selections start at £24.50 a bottle.
Chef/s: Graham Grafton. **Open:** all week L 12 to 2.30, D 7 to 9.30. **Meals:** alc (main courses £15 to £27). Set L £22 (2 courses) to £25. Sun L £25 (2 courses) to £28. **Details:** 60 seats. 25 seats outside. Separate bar. Music. Car parking. Children over 12 yrs only at D.

ALSO RECOMMENDED

▲ The Village Pub
Barnsley, GL7 5EF
Tel no: (01285) 740421
www.thevillagepub.co.uk
Modern British

This ancient grey Cotswold stone pub-with-rooms is on the main road that snakes through the village. Inside, it's all real fires and timbers, overlaid with a twenty-first century version of rural décor. In the bar, snacks might be quail and black pudding Scotch eggs or Welsh rarebit fritters; popular options in the dining room could be Dorset crab with mayonnaise (£10.95), navarin of lamb and 'superb' steaks (£16), then chestnut and chocolate torte. Wines from £18.25. Open all week. Accommodation.

Bourton on the Hill

Horse & Groom
Excellent village inn with no-frills flavours
Bourton on the Hill, GL56 9AQ
Tel no: (01386) 700413
www.horseandgroom.info
Modern British | £26
Cooking score: 2

Perched on a hill with panoramic Cotswold views, this honey-coloured Georgian stone inn is 'consistently excellent', according to one reporter – a view echoed by another, who praised the 'wonderful' staff for their friendly efficiency. Brothers Tom and Will Greenstock have achieved the perfect balance; the pub dispenses real ale for the locals and attracts

long-distance diners with its no-frills modern dishes. A starter of 'full-flavoured' Cornish soup might be followed by spiced lamb kofta tagine, whilst steamed marmalade sponge pudding with Jersey cream is a rib-sticking way to end the meal. Wines start at £14.
Chef/s: Will Greenstock. **Open:** all week L 12 to 2 (2.30 Sun), Mon to Sat D 7 to 9 (9.30 Fri and Sat). **Closed:** 25 Dec, 31 Dec, 1 week Jan. **Meals:** alc (main courses £12 to £21). **Service:** not inc. **Details:** 75 seats. 56 seats outside. Separate bar. No music. Car parking.

▌Bristol
Bell's Diner
Local favourite with polished modern cooking
1-3 York Road, Montpelier, Bristol, BS6 5QB
Tel no: (0117) 9240357
www.bellsdiner.com
Modern British | £30
Cooking score: 4
£5 OFF

Many of the fittings date back to when a grocer's shop occupied this corner spot half a century ago, but there is nothing old-fashioned about the highly polished modern cooking at this enduring neighbourhood restaurant. Chef-patron Chris Wicks and his team have developed their own repertoire of imaginative, refined dishes in this bohemian backwater of inner-city Bristol. There is clearly a Scandinavian influence, with an increased use of interesting and foraged ingredients. Orkney Bay scallops might appear with broad beans, lemon and seaweed; locally reared kid is served with hay-infused goats' milk and 'slate' soda bread (made with charcoal powder-coated Tymsboro goats' cheese). Less experimental choices include halibut paired with salsa verde, Swiss chard, radish and asparagus, although toasted hay custard tart with beer, coffee and walnuts is one of the more ambitious desserts. An intelligent wine list starts at £18.50 and matches Old World with cutting-edge producers, including biodynamic and natural wines.

Chef/s: Christopher Wicks and Alex Collins. **Open:** Wed to Fri L 12 to 2, Tue to Sat D 7 to 9 (9.30 Fri and Sat). **Closed:** Sun, Mon, 24 to 30 Dec. **Meals:** alc (main courses £15 to £23). Tasting menu £49.50. **Service:** 12.5%. **Details:** 55 seats. Music.

Bordeaux Quay
Eco-friendly harbourside brasserie
V-Shed, Canons Way, Bristol, BS1 5UH
Tel no: (0117) 9431200
www.bordeaux-quay.co.uk
Modern European | £33
Cooking score: 2

The dust has finally settled at this eco-friendly venue after a period of change (with management and the kitchen). The former warehouse on Bristol's harbourside now operates as a brasserie downstairs, with a more formal first-floor restaurant – where local and seasonal produce forms the backbone of a menu with an increasingly Italian slant. The dishes are rustic and vibrant; bold flavours are evident in a starter of Bath chaps and Somerset spelt risotto, which might lead on to green peppercorn venison rump, smoked pear and mushroom purée. Finish with blood-orange and rhubarb pannacotta. House wine from £17.
Chef/s: Mena Iovino. **Open:** Sun L 12 to 3, Tue to Sat D 6 to 10. **Closed:** Mon, 25 and 26 Dec. **Meals:** alc (main courses £12 to £24). Set L and D £17.50 (2 courses) to £22.50. Sun L £12.50. **Service:** 10%. **Details:** 250 seats. 45 seats outside. Separate bar. Wheelchair access. Music.

Flinty Red
Livewire local restaurant
34 Cotham Hill, Bristol, BS6 6LA
Tel no: (0117) 9238755
www.flintyred.co.uk
European | £23
Cooking score: 4
£30

'My favourite place in Bristol' was the verdict of one reader, who keeps returning to this small, unassuming neighbourhood restaurant for the 'superb food and friendly staff'. Run in conjunction with an independent wine shop a few doors along the road, Flinty Red continues to impress with its thoroughly contemporary European dishes, many of which are served in two sizes to encourage sharing. The menu has a strong Italian influence and there is some impeccable sourcing of imported and local ingredients – including vegetables grown in the garden of the sister wine shop. Standout dishes have included a starter of fennel and almond ravioli with Caprino Sardo goats' cheese and a 'rich and meltingly tender' ox cheek carbonnade. Doughnuts with maple syrup and whipped yoghurt is one dessert to win praise. The vibrant modern wine list includes more than 20 by the glass and carafe, with house bottles kicking off at £16.

Chef/s: Matthew Williamson. **Open:** Tue to Sat L 12 to 3, Mon to Sat D 6.30 to 10. **Closed:** Sun, 24 to 28 Dec, first week Jan. **Meals:** alc (main courses from £13 to £16). Set L £9.95 (2 courses). **Service:** not inc. **Details:** 36 seats. Music.

Greens' Dining Room

Welcoming bistro with wonderful food
25 Zetland Road, Bristol, BS6 7AH
Tel no: (0117) 9246437
www.greensdiningroom.com
Modern European | £27
Cooking score: 3

Tucked down a leafy Bristol side street, this 'modern and clean' family-run bistro 'never disappoints'. The setting is 'very relaxed, comfortable and welcoming' and the 'simply wonderful' food references such culinary greats as Elizabeth David, Jane Grigson and Claudia Roden. A 'simple truffle pasta dish with sage and butter' delighted one reporter with its 'balance of flavour', while 'phenomenally tender aubergine fondants' served with fresh spinach and a tangy, slightly sweet chickpea tagine also got the thumbs-up. For meat eaters there might be teal and pork terrine with pickles and relish, followed by duck breast with braised red cabbage and juniper. Finish with chocolate and almond

pithiviers with vanilla ice cream. A snappy international wine list starts at £14.50 and includes lots by the glass.

Chef/s: Andrew and Simon Green. **Open:** Tue to Sat L 12.30 to 2.30, D 6.30 to 10. **Closed:** Sun, Mon, 2 weeks Christmas. **Meals:** alc (main courses £9 to £19). Set L £10 (2 courses) to £15. Set D £15 (2 courses) to £21. **Service:** not inc. **Details:** 38 seats. 12 seats outside. Music.

Lido

Aromatic food in awesome surrounds
Oakfield Place, Clifton, Bristol, BS8 2BJ
Tel no: (0117) 9339530
www.lidobristol.com
Mediterranean | £35
Cooking score: 3

'A touch of class in Bristol' commented one reader after visiting this awesome restaurant and spa complex in the city's reinvigorated Victorian lido. 'You could almost be in the Med' chirped another fan, seduced by the breezy poolside setting as well as the colourful, aromatic food on offer. Influences from Spain, North Africa and the Middle East loom large, and the kitchen calls on its wood-fired oven for everything from 'fabulous' sourdough bread and pastries to specialities such as roast mackerel with mussels, dill and pine nut and raisin pilaff, or veal loin with sage, capers, St George's mushrooms and artichokes. Tapas-style starters might include slow-cooked rabbit with morcilla and broad beans, while meze plates are great for sharing. To finish, try the 'heavenly' salted caramel ice cream. European wines start at £17.50.

Chef/s: Freddy Bird. **Open:** all week L 12 to 3, Mon to Sat D 6 to 10. **Meals:** alc (main courses £15 to £21). Set L and D £16 (2 courses) to £20. Sun L £20. **Service:** not inc. **Details:** 100 seats. 40 seats outside. Separate bar. Music.

Visit us Online
To find out more about
The Good Food Guide, please visit
www.thegoodfoodguide.co.uk

The Muset by Ronnie

Excellent value, deep flavours, loyal fans
12-16 Clifton Road, Bristol, BS8 1AF
Tel no: (0117) 9737248
www.ronnies-restaurant.co.uk
Modern European | £38
Cooking score: 4

£5 OFF

The Muset by Ronnie is off the beaten track in the leafy backstreets of Clifton, but it has already gained quite a loyal band of followers since it opened in 2011. Owner Ron Faulkner also runs Ronnies in Thornbury (see entry) and reporters have noted a similar level of 'high quality' service and 'excellent value', particularly on the set-price menus. There has been a change of chef in the first year, but Jethro Lawrence has already demonstrated that he is not afraid of coaxing some deep flavours from the carefully sourced ingredients. This was evident at inspection – in an accomplished starter of meltingly tender cider-braised pig cheek and smoked eel ravioli; in a main course of precisely cooked monkfish 'ras-el-hanout' with lentils, king prawns, cumin-flavoured cauliflower and yoghurt; and in a dessert of chocolate slice with cherries and cherry sorbet, which was light and delicate. House wines from £16.
Chef/s: Jethro Lawrence. **Open:** Tue to Sun L 12 to 2.30 (3 Sun), Tue to Sat D 6.30 to 9.30 (10.30 Fri and Sat). **Closed:** Mon, 25 to 27 Dec, 1 to 3 Jan. **Meals:** alc (main courses £14 to £22). Set L £12 (2 courses) to £14.25. Set D £16 (2 courses) to £19. Sun L £21. **Service:** 12.5%. **Details:** 72 seats. Separate bar. Wheelchair access. Music.

▌▌▌ Please send us your feedback

To register your opinion about any restaurant listed in the Guide, or a new restaurant that you wish to bring to our attention, please visit the web address at the bottom of the page. Your feedback informs the content of the book and will be used to compile next year's reviews.

NEW ENTRY
Prego

Tip-top local Italian
7 North View, Bristol, BS6 7PT
Tel no: (0117) 9730496
www.pregobar.co.uk
Italian | £25
Cooking score: 3

£30

This buzzy bistro opened two years ago in an affluent area that had been starved of good restaurants – and it has certainly won over the locals. Occupying a former shop, Prego specialises in seasonal, regional rustic Italian cooking, conjured from tip-top local and Italian ingredients. This takes the form of popular pizzas, an appealing carte or the specials board, which might offer crisp fried Cornish squid with aïoli to start, followed by skilfully made English rose veal agnolotti with Umbrian lentils and Parmesan served in a herby broth. All puddings are made on the premises and the Seville orange curd tart with roasted rhubarb, pomegranate and almonds is one of many seasonal highlights. An all-Italian wine list starts at a commendably affordable £11.45.
Chef/s: Sam Sohn-Rethel. **Open:** Tue to Sat L 12 to 2, Mon to Sat D 6 to 10 (9 Mon). **Closed:** bank hols, 25 Dec to 1 Jan. **Meals:** alc (main courses £11 to £18). Set L £12.95 (2 courses) to £15.95. **Service:** not inc. **Details:** 50 seats. 20 seats outside. Wheelchair access. Music.

The Pump House

Waterfront venue with bold seasonal food
Merchants Road, Hotwells, Bristol, BS8 4PZ
Tel no: (0117) 9272229
www.the-pumphouse.com
Modern British | £28
Cooking score: 3

£30

Housed in a grand Victorian pumping station that once controlled Bristol's swing bridges and floating harbour, this rustic-chic waterfront venue is now in the business of delivering seasonal sustenance to the local

populace. Chef/proprietor Toby Gritten's food is marked by strong, precise flavours, and he also does his bit for the foraging cause (alexanders pop up in a dish of cider-steamed hake with artichokes, mushrooms and crushed Pink Fir Apple potatoes). Winter might bring a warm salad of Wincanton wood pigeon with confit duck gizzards, followed by a 'nose-to-tail' plate of Middle White pork with Cox's apples. Desserts such as bitter chocolate and gingerbread with smoked almond and burnt-butter ice cream also show plenty of creative oomph. Drink regional real ales in the bar, or pick something from the well-spread wine list; prices from £14.
Chef/s: Toby Gritten. **Open:** Tue to Sun L 12 to 3, Mon to Sat D 6.30 to 9.30. **Closed:** 25 Dec. **Meals:** alc (main courses £14 to £20). Set L and D £17.50 (2 courses) to £20. **Service:** 10%. **Details:** 60 seats. 100 seats outside. Separate bar. Music. Car parking. No children under 14 yrs in restaurant.

riverstation
Consistently good waterfront veteran
The Grove, Bristol, BS1 4RB
Tel no: (0117) 9144434
www.riverstation.co.uk
Modern European | £28
Cooking score: 3

A veritable veteran of Bristol's ever-evolving restaurant scene, this glass-fronted former river police station continues to be one of the city's most consistent places. Downstairs there is a bustling café/bar; upstairs is the bright restaurant, with its open kitchen and waterfront views. The daily changing menu looks to the Mediterranean for inspiration, although tip-top ingredients tend to come from local producers. A starter of seared scallops with Jerusalem artichoke purée, candy beetroot salad and pancetta was 'most enjoyable', according to one contented diner, who went on to savour pan-fried halibut with samphire and cockles. A 'wonderful' salted caramel ice cream has garnered praise, too. The interesting and astute wine list starts at £14.95, with 14 served by the glass and carafe.

Chef/s: Peter Taylor and Toru Yanada. **Open:** all week L 12 to 2.30 (3 Sun), Mon to Sat D 6 to 10.30 (11 Fri and Sat). **Closed:** 24 to 26 Dec. **Meals:** alc (main courses £15 to £20). Set L £12.75 (2 courses) to £15.50. Set D £14.75 (2 courses) to £18.50. Sun L £16 (2 courses) to £19.50. **Service:** not inc. **Details:** 120 seats. 22 seats outside. Separate bar.

Rockfish Grill
Quality seafood brasserie
128-130 Whiteladies Road, Bristol, BS8 2RS
Tel no: (0117) 9737384
www.rockfishgrill.co.uk
Seafood | £37
Cooking score: 4
£5 OFF

A gentle refurbishment has resulted in a more open, lighter feel to Mitch Tonks's informal seafood brasserie and sister to the Seahorse, Dartmouth (see entry). The entrance has moved around the corner, so you now walk past the day's catch in the fishmongers en route to your table in the dining room. Sea-green leather button-back banquettes and pictures of Brixham fishermen set the scene; linen cloths on previously bare tables make the place feel classier, but 'not at all stuffy'. While it's possible to pop in for a plate of oysters and a glass of Prosecco, you will be tempted to dive into the daily changing menu, which might start with Dartmouth crab with dill, lemon and avocado. Meat dishes are not an afterthought; lamb's sweetbreads with Marsala was handled with as much care as red gurnard cooked 'al cartoccio' (in parchment paper) with garlic, rosemary and chilli. Wines from £18.
Chef/s: James Davidson. **Open:** Tue to Sat L 12 to 2.30 (3 Sat), D 6 to 10 (10.30 Fri and Sat). **Closed:** Sun, Mon, 25 Dec to 4 Jan. **Meals:** alc (main courses £13 to £22). Set L and early D £12.50 (2 courses) to £15. **Service:** not inc. **Details:** 52 seats. Music.

Seasons.Casamia

Even more culinary derring-do
38 High Street, Westbury on Trym, Bristol,
BS9 3DZ
Tel no: (0117) 9592884
www.casamiarestaurant.co.uk
Italian | £45
Cooking score: 5

The unassuming entrance might suggest a
traditional neighbourhood restaurant, but
there is nothing conventional about Casamia.
Since taking over their parents' trattoria,
Jonray and Peter Sanchez-Iglesias have put this
suburban venue well and truly on the culinary
map. Cutting-edge cooking techniques and a
desire to push the gastronomic boundaries
make a meal here a unique dining experience.
The new Seasons.Casamia concept sees the
restaurant change its appearance four times a
year, complete with seasonal smells and
sounds. From the spring menu, John Dory
poached in olive oil is paired with sea beet, a
light cider velouté, chopped hazelnuts and
mustard flowers. A rump of lamb cooked sous
vide is served with a traditional mint sauce and
a 'cannelloni' of leek leaves filled with sautéed
leeks and chives. A curtain-closing dessert of
'Easter egg' is a gossamer-thin dark chocolate
dome, smashed open to reveal white chocolate
mousse and a frozen mango sorbet 'yolk'. This
left-field approach might not be to
everybody's liking and there have been
complaints that the limited choice of three
tasting menus is 'too exclusive' and there
'should be an additional carte'. All this aside,
the cooking skills, ingredients and service at
inspection were hard to fault. Wines from £18.
Chef/s: Jonray and Peter Sanchez-Iglesias. **Open:**
Sat L 12 to 2, Tue to Sat D 7 to 9.30. **Closed:** Sun,
Mon, 25 and 26 Dec. **Meals:** Tasting menu £45 (5
courses) to £88 (11 courses). **Service:** not inc.
Details: 40 seats. Separate bar. Wheelchair access.
Music.

Cheltenham

★ TOP 50 ★

Le Champignon Sauvage

Prime ingredients and nice surprises
24-26 Suffolk Road, Cheltenham, GL50 2AQ
Tel no: (01242) 573449
www.lechampignonsauvage.co.uk
Modern French | £59
Cooking score: 8

It's now 25 years since David and Helen
Everitt-Matthias opened in the centre of
Cheltenham. Very much a product of the late-
1980s boom in exploratory gastronomy, the
Champignon, like its fungal woodland
namesake, springs up anew with the passing
seasons – or in this case, the tides of culinary
fashion. David's cooking acknowledges the
developments in restaurant food elsewhere –
it doesn't stand still – without feeling any
undue need to follow them slavishly. Here,
within the good-natured environs of a
comfortably furnished room hung with
abstract paintings, its tables well-spaced and
double-clothed, an honest-to-goodness
celebration of regional ingredients takes place,
the dishes offering nice surprises along the
way without occluding the obvious quality of
their prime materials. The tartare of Dexter
beef with corned beef is justly eulogised by
readers, the savoury tenderness of the meats
offset by Japanese condiments in the form of
wasabi cream and pickled shimejis. Odd
combinations may generally be nothing new,
but can still draw on great imaginative
resources, as when a galette of pig trotter and
whelks turns up with citrus-cured mackerel,
and when, moving on to mains, a golden
beetroot 'sauerkraut' with beetroot and
rosehip purée are the preferred
accompaniments to a serving of Winchcombe
venison. Fruit is inventively pressed into
service in main courses – perhaps baby figs
with pigeon and woodruff parsnips, or pear
with cod and caramelised cauliflower – while
desserts may drift off into the herb garden for
caramel-poached pineapple and pineapple-
verbena sorbet, or iced prune and burdock

mousse with prune-kernel ice cream. The wine list is reasonably priced throughout, and well-stocked with reliable producers. French purists will probably be most pleased, but there are some good southern-hemisphere specialists in there too: Hunter, Hamilton Russell, Clos du Val, Hackett, and more. Good house wines open with a Burgundy négociant's blend at £18.

Chef/s: David Everitt-Matthias. **Open:** Tue to Sat L 12.30 to 1.15, D 7.30 to 8.30. **Closed:** Sun, Mon, 10 days Christmas, 3 weeks Jun. **Meals:** Set L and Tue to Fri D £26 (2 courses) to £32. Sat D £48 (2 courses) to £59. **Service:** not inc. **Details:** 38 seats. No music.

Lumière
Cutting-edge cooking and classic techniques
Clarence Parade, Cheltenham, GL50 3PA
Tel no: (01242) 222200
www.lumiere.cc
Modern British | £47
Cooking score: 5
£5 OFF **V**

It is four years since Jon Howe and Helen Aubrey took over this understated central Cheltenham restaurant a short stroll from the town's Promenade. In that time, this ambitious young couple has made 'steady and careful improvements' according to one reporter, whose enthusiasm for the 'friendly service' and 'beautifully presented' food was echoed by another who enjoyed a 'stunning meal from start to finish'. The serene, contemporary dining room may trade on intimacy but there is nothing diminutive about the talent or aspirations in the kitchen, where Jon's innovative, well-defined cooking demonstrates cutting-edge ideas underpinned by a mastery of classic techniques. Superb homemade breads and inspired extras such as squid ink crackers and 'ingenious' scones with beetroot jam and truffle cream pave the way for some supremely confident cooking of well-sourced local ingredients. A winning starter of precisely cooked line-caught Cornish mackerel comes teamed with contrasting textures of sweet and earthy

beetroot, chorizo, cauliflower and sweetcorn, while a main course of impressively fresh day-boat ling arrives with cockles, clams, artichoke, spinach and quinoa. To finish, Yorkshire rhubarb trifle is taken to a higher plane by the addition of honeycomb, hibiscus and ginger. The serious wine list starts at £20 a bottle.

Chef/s: Jon Howe. **Open:** Wed to Sat L 12 to 2, Tue to Sat D 7 to 9. **Closed:** Sun, Mon, 2 weeks Jan, 2 weeks summer. **Meals:** Set L £22 (2 courses) to £26. Set D £42 (2 courses) to £47. Tasting menu L £47, D £60. **Service:** not inc. **Details:** 34 seats. Music. Children 8 yrs and over only.

ALSO RECOMMENDED

▲ The Daffodil
18-20 Suffolk Parade, Cheltenham, GL50 2AE
Tel no: (01242) 700055
www.thedaffodil.com
Modern British £5 OFF

'Great atmosphere in an old cinema' is one way of describing this beautifully refurbished Art Deco picture house, now a well-supported bar and restaurant. It's a huge, lively space, noted for courteous staff and British brasserie favourites such as salmon and pollack fishcakes with hollandaise sauce (£6.95), eggs Benedict, roasted lamb chump with charred ratatouille and fondant potato (£17.50) and good old fish and chips. Finish with lime and lemongrass pannacotta with honeycomb and honey ice cream. Wines from £15.95. Closed Sun.

▲ The Tavern
5 Royal Well Place, Cheltenham, GL50 3DN
Tel no: (01242) 221212
www.thetaverncheltenham.com
Modern British £5 OFF

It's not just the name that has changed at The (Royal Well) Tavern. What was a smart pub-meets-brasserie has been transformed into an edgy New York-style diner, complete with popcorn machine on the bar. Vintage and reclaimed furnishings add a trendy Soho vibe, as do the brown paper placemat menus that offer plenty of small bites, such as pulled pork and beetroot sliders (£4), alongside the likes of duo of duck with truffled leeks and croquette potato (£19). Wines from £16. Open all week.

Chipping Campden

★ CHEF TO WATCH ★

NEW ENTRY

Cotswold House

Beautiful food from a bright new talent
Cotswold House Hotel, The Square, Chipping
Campden, GL55 6AN
Tel no: (01386) 840330
www.cotswoldhouse.com
Modern British | £35
Cooking score: 6

This honey-stone hotel and spa, in a Regency town house off Chipping Campden's high street, appointed a bright new talent to its kitchen in 2011. Dave Watts, who trained under Raymond Blanc, produces exquisitely balanced, often complex, dishes that are beautiful to behold. The Dining Room – there's also the informal all-day Cotswold Grill – marries wood-panelling and retro chairs with arched French windows and a decorative plasterwork ceiling, the whole cheered up by flowers and modern art. Ambient music accompanies the well-practised staff. There are no borders between starters and mains: simply choose three, four or five moderately portioned courses of whatever you like. After gorgeous nibbles and a spring-like pre-starter (lemon curd, fresh goats' cheese, peas, broad beans), a luscious confit salmon was expertly balanced by crunchy pickled cucumber and a mild, creamy wasabi emulsion. Impeccable spring lamb arrived with white asparagus; deeply flavoured squab pigeon was offset by an exploration of beetroot textures. Pudding continued the intricate story: intense chocolate tart leavened by pistachio cake and made extraordinary with a salty blast of sorrel sorbet. There's enough excitement and skill

here to shake the Cotswolds from its slumbers. The sizeable global wine list (from £19) has ample choice by the glass.
Chef/s: Dave Watts. **Open:** Tue to Sat D 7 to 9.30. **Closed:** Mon, Sun, 2 weeks Christmas. **Meals:** Set D £30 (2 courses) to £55. **Service:** 12.5%. **Details:** 32 seats. Separate bar. Wheelchair access. Music. Car parking.

Cirencester

Made by Bob

Fun Italian eatery/deli
The Corn Hall, Unit 6, 26 Market Place,
Cirencester, GL7 2NY
Tel no: (01285) 641818
www.foodmadebybob.com
Mediterranean | £28
Cooking score: 3

Since it opened five years ago, this 'fun and novel' café/deli has established itself as a gastronomic hub in the self-proclaimed capital of the Cotswolds. Chef/proprietor James 'Bob' Parkinson once worked at Bibendum (see entry, London) and he can be observed at close quarters from stools around the open kitchen. Reporters have been uniform in their criticism of service, which continues to be 'disorganised' and 'in danger of lowering the overall feel', but there are no gripes about the precisely cooked modern European food. A well-reported grilled focaccia with hummus and Mediterranean vegetables might be followed by halibut with ink linguine, saffron, clams, fennel and parsley. Desserts are a strength, an example being pannacotta with sultanas in Armagnac. House wine £16.
Chef/s: Bob Parkinson. **Open:** Mon to Sat L 12 to 3, Thur and Fri D 7 to 9.30. **Closed:** Sun, 25 and 26 Dec. **Meals:** alc (main courses £11 to £19). **Service:** not inc. **Details:** 60 seats. Wheelchair access. Music.

READERS RECOMMEND
Jesse's Bistro
Modern British
The Stableyard, Black Jack Street, Cirencester,
GL7 2AA
Tel no: (01285) 641497
www.jessesbistro.co.uk
'They use local or English products, cook them simply, bake their own bread, and have an excellent English cheese selection.'

Coln St Aldwyns
ALSO RECOMMENDED
▲ The New Inn
Main Street, Coln St Aldwyns, GL7 5AN
Tel no: (01285) 750651
www.new-inn.co.uk
Modern British £5 OFF

This sixteenth-century inn bang in the middle of a picturesque village oozes character. Being off the beaten track, it has to please a variety of customers, and succeeds with a bar menu of beef burgers (£12), steaks and sandwiches, and restaurant dishes that show serious intent. Start with chicken liver parfait, go on to Cotswold lamb chump with its own mini shepherd's pie (£18.25) and finish with white chocolate and chilli cheesecake and raspberries. House wine is £17. Open all week.

Compton Abdale
ALSO RECOMMENDED
▲ The Puesdown Inn
Compton Abdale, GL54 4DN
Tel no: (01451) 860262
www.puesdown.cotswoldinns.com
Modern British

A cleverly rejuvenated Cotswold boozer with a smart, gentrified outlook, the stone-built Puesdown Inn has a liking for local produce and seasonal flavours. Simple pub-style lunches and free-range Sunday roasts give way to more ambitious evening menus featuring a mixed bag of dishes from steamed mussels or duck pancakes (£7.50) to sea bass fillet with crab sauce (£15) or slow-cooked lamb brisket with kidneys, mushrooms, olive mash and rosemary jus. Desserts are workaday offerings such as apple crumble or bread-and-butter pudding. House wine is £13.50. No food Sun D. Accommodation.

Corse Lawn
Corse Lawn House Hotel
Elegance and classic cooking
Corse Lawn, GL19 4LZ
Tel no: (01452) 780771
www.corselawn.com
Anglo-French | £35
Cooking score: 3
£5 OFF 🛏 V

Behind the village green and large ornamental pond lies the elegant Queen Anne house owned since the 1970s by the Hine family. It offers a familiar enough country house package, at the heart of which is a restaurant done in pale peach and blue. The theme is French-influenced classical cooking with some modern touches. A meal opens, perhaps, with an artichoke heart stuffed with mushroom duxelles, served with girolles and hollandaise, or potted crab with mango salsa, then proceeds to char-grilled salmon with crushed peas and chive beurre blanc. More enterprising tastes are served by sautéed calf's brains with caper butter and olive potatoes. Garden fruits such as poached greengages may turn up in season, perhaps with lavender parfait. The Bistro offers simpler dishes. The exhaustive behemoth of a wine list is almost as painstaking outside ancestral France as within. House selections start at £18.50 (£4.90 a glass).
Chef/s: Andrew Poole and Martin Kinahan. **Open:** all week L 12 to 2, D 7 to 9.30. **Closed:** 24 to 26 Dec. **Meals:** alc (main courses £15 to £23). Set L and D £15 (2 courses) to £20. **Service:** not inc. **Details:** 70 seats. 40 seats outside. No music. Wheelchair access. Car parking.

■ Didmarton

ALSO RECOMMENDED
▲ The Kings Arms
The Street, Didmarton, GL9 1DT
Tel no: (01454) 238245
www.kingsarmsdidmarton.co.uk
British

This seventeenth-century coaching inn with its easy-on-the-eye mix of beams and timbers, polished wood tables, oak settles and an open fire is as convivial as country inns should be. The cooking style brings the traditional pub repertoire up to date, with the likes of pigeon with a chorizo and mixed bean casserole (£6.95), rustic fish stew, and minted lamb steak with rosemary and redcurrant sauce (£11.75). House wine is £16. No food Sun D. Accommodation. Reports, please.

■ Ebrington

ALSO RECOMMENDED
▲ The Ebrington Arms
Ebrington, GL55 6NH
Tel no: (01386) 593223
www.theebringtonarms.co.uk
Modern British

A board of home-baked breads sets the tone at this food-loving seventeenth-century inn just a couple of miles from Chipping Campden. Check out the daily specials or settle for something enterprising from the monthly changing menu – perhaps a warm salad of pigeon breast with Puy lentils, parsnip and bread sauce (£6), pan-fried John Dory with crab and chilli risotto (£15) or a char-grilled Longhorn ribeye steak with gratin dauphinois, béarnaise sauce and bourguignon salad, then treacle tart. European wines from £16. Accommodation. Open all week.

■ Eldersfield

The Butchers Arms
Cosy country pub with excellent fish
Lime Street, Eldersfield, GL19 4NX
Tel no: (01452) 840381
www.thebutchersarms.net
Modern British | £42
Cooking score: 4

'We don't mind not having a tablecloth', is how a happy, well-fed fan of the few-frills Butchers Arms at Eldersfield gamely puts it. The absence of crisp linen napery from this cosy country pub is a small price to pay for James Winter's impeccably sourced, assuredly seasonal cooking. Fish dishes 'figure prominently'; day-boat bounty is whizzed up to rural Gloucestershire from Cornwall and Dartmouth. Cornish fish soup of smoked hake, Fowey mussels and scallops is a 'stunning' starter, and, sticking with fish, 'meaty' hake fillets with chorizo and lentils, or turbot on the bone with belly pork and truffle mash demonstrate the chef's success with 'surf and turf' pairings. Desserts are 'equally assured', particularly 'an old favourite' of dark chocolate torte with toffee ice cream. Service is 'first class'. Enjoy traditional ale straight from the cask or wine from a 'short but very well-varied' list (from £19.50).
Chef/s: James Winter. **Open:** Wed to Sun L 12 to 1 (bookings only), Tue to Sat D 7 to 9. **Closed:** Mon, 25 and 26 Dec, 2 weeks Jan, last 2 weeks Aug.
Meals: alc (main courses £20 to £26).
Service: 12.5% for parties over 10. **Details:** 25 seats. Separate bar. No music. No children at D.

Fairford

Simply Allium
Smart but simple cooking
1 London Street, Fairford, GL7 4AH
Tel no: (01285) 712200
www.alliumfood.co.uk
Modern British | £25
Cooking score: 4

Behind the mellow old stone of Simply Allium's frontage is a light, modern dining room with well-spaced tables and simple furnishings. It was previously known as Allium; the change of name reflects James and Erica Graham's change of tack. 'Simply' is the key word now, but that doesn't come at the expense of skilled cooking or first-class produce. A test meal found perfect, fresh-from-the-oven bread, a precise, balanced starter of asparagus and poached egg with simple vinaigrette and a sprinkling of peppery wild garlic flowers, then a main course of roasted suckling pig with pearl barley and artichokes that was a triumph of tender pigginess. For dessert, a crumbly, soft-in-the-middle meringue met its match in tangy passion-fruit cream with a topping of diced pineapple. A short international wine list offers plenty by the glass. Bottles from £14.50.
Chef/s: James Graham. Open: Tue to Sat L 12 to 3, D 6 to 10. Closed: Mon, Sun, 3 weeks Dec to Jan, 1 week Jul. Meals: alc (main courses £10 to £20). Set L £12.50 (2 courses) to £15. Service: not inc. Details: 50 seats. Music.

Symbols

🛏 Accommodation is available

£30 Three courses for less than £30

V Separate vegetarian menu

£5 £5-off voucher scheme

🍷 Notable wine list

Long Ashton

NEW ENTRY
The Bird in Hand
Much improved village pub
17 Weston Road, Long Ashton, BS41 9LA
Tel no: (01275) 395222
www.bird-in-hand.co.uk
British | £25
Cooking score: 2

'We no longer need to get a taxi into Bristol to sample good food' commented one frequent visitor to this much improved village pub, run by the team behind the city's Pump House (see entry). Teal walls covered with pages ripped from Mrs Beeton books and shelves of homemade pickles and chutneys indicate that the kitchen means business, and many of the ingredients are wild or foraged. Seasonal dishes are simple and ingredients-driven: a well-made Old Spot and wood pigeon terrine might be followed by a precisely cooked onglet steak with oxtails, bone marrow and chips. Wines from £15.
Chef/s: Jake Platt. Open: Tue to Sun L 12 to 3, Tue to Sat D 6 to 9. Closed: Mon. Meals: alc (main courses £10 to £16). Service: not inc. Details: 45 seats. 30 seats outside. Music.

Lower Oddington

The Fox Inn
Cotswold inn with commendable food
Lower Oddington, GL56 0UR
Tel no: (01451) 870555
www.foxinn.net
British | £27
Cooking score: 1

Nestling in a genteel Cotswold hamlet, this picture-pretty, ivy-clothed inn comes with a generous slice of hop-garlanded rusticity. The Fox's rambling, stone-floored rooms and alcoves are ideal for holing up with a decent pint and some commendable pub food, and there's a lovely walled garden too. Expect confit duck rillettes with rhubarb compote ahead of char-grilled ribeye steak, risotto nero or roast monkfish with braised fennel and chorizo. For afters, perhaps try honey and pine-nut tart with glazed figs. Well-chosen wines from £15.50.

Chef/s: Phillip Carter. **Open:** all week L 12 to 2 (3 Sun), D 6.30 to 9.30 (10 Fri and Sat, 7 to 9.30 Sun). **Closed:** 25 Dec. **Meals:** alc (main courses £10 to £20). **Service:** not inc. **Details:** 85 seats. 100 seats outside. Separate bar. No music. Car parking.

Northleach

The Wheatsheaf Inn

Captivating Cotswold coaching inn
West End, Northleach, GL54 3EZ
Tel no: (01451) 860244
www.cotswoldswheatsheaf.com
Modern British | £28
Cooking score: 3

Want to find the perfect Cotswold inn? This captivating seventeenth-century coaching inn close to Northleach's pretty market square is a heritage destination beyond compare, offering the comforts and luxury of a small hotel with everything you might expect from a well-to-do country hostelry: bare boards, open fires, real ales. It's fun, wonderfully relaxed and run with positive enthusiasm. The seasonally based cooking delivers the kind of plain-speaking dishes (devilled kidneys on toast, crab risotto with tomato and basil) that respect their ingredients and their natural flavours. Generous, gutsy plates of poached and grilled chicken breast with chorizo, champ potatoes and glazed onions, and beer-battered whiting with frites, crushed peas and a chunky tartare sauce have found favour, as has a hot chocolate mousse with raspberry sorbet. Wines from £16.

Chef/s: Antony Ely. **Open:** all week L 12 to 3 (4 Sat and Sun), D 6 to 10 (9 Sun). **Meals:** alc (main courses £9 to £36). Set L Mon to Fri £12.75 (2 courses) to £15. Sun L £18. **Service:** not inc. **Details:** 60 seats. 60 seats outside. Separate bar. Wheelchair access. Music. Car parking.

Sapperton

The Bell at Sapperton

Perfect country-inn package
Sapperton, GL7 6LE
Tel no: (01285) 760298
www.foodatthebell.co.uk
Modern British | £30
Cooking score: 3

Paul Davidson and Pat Le Jeune have been the driving force behind this amenable country inn since 1999 and they continue to deliver such a convincing package that the place 'is packed with happy, contented customers'. It has 'great character, with welcoming open fires', is run with well-honed professionalism and offers 'fantastic food in a lovely setting'. Visitors have been delighted with the robust flavours, the seasonal game selection and the daily fresh fish. Inspiration comes from near and far: homespun pub diehards ('a rather well-made burger') sit happily beside more up-to-date ideas of warm goats' cheese on toasted brioche with Evesham beetroot chutney, ahead of a perfectly pink breast of local duckling or 'well-cooked sea bass'. Wines from £17.50.

Chef/s: Mike Brindley. **Open:** all week L 12 to 2.15 (2.30 Sun), D 7 to 9.30 (9 Sun). **Closed:** 25 Dec. **Meals:** alc (main courses £12 to £23). Set L and D £12.50 (2 courses) to £15.95. **Service:** not inc. **Details:** 65 seats. 40 seats outside. Wheelchair access. Car parking. Children over 10 yrs only at D.

Stow-on-the-Wold

The Old Butcher's

Straight-talking seasonal flavours
7 Park Street, Stow-on-the-Wold, GL54 1AQ
Tel no: (01451) 831700
www.theoldbutchers.com
Modern British | £31
Cooking score: 3

Peter and Louise Robinson's converted butcher's shop opts for a smart brasserie look that combines creature-comfort niceties and a relaxed atmosphere with swanky furnishings, a cool bar and a bold glass frontage. Straight-talking seasonal flavours come through strongly on the menu, from warm Bath chaps with Scotch quail's egg and salsa verde to grilled loin of roe deer with a little cottage pie. The kitchen also looks across the Channel for plates of endive, pear and Roquefort salad or slow-cooked belly pork with morcilla, chickpeas and chorizo. Desserts bring out tempters such as sherry trifle or pannacotta with blood oranges, although one regular swears by the show-stopping Harry's Bar hot custard pancake. House Duboeuf is £16.50. The Robinsons now run the nearby White Hart too – if you fancy a pie and a pint.

Chef/s: Peter Robinson. **Open:** Tue to Sun L 12 to 2.30, Tue to Sat D 6 to 9.30 (10 Sat). **Closed:** 1 week May, 1 week Oct. **Meals:** alc (main courses £15 to £21). **Service:** not inc. **Details:** 45 seats. 12 seats outside. Wheelchair access. Music.

Tetbury
The Chef's Table
Traditional French deli/bistro
49 Long Street, Tetbury, GL8 8AA
Tel no: (01666) 504466
www.thechefstable.co.uk
French | £34
Cooking score: 4

The Bedfords' multifaceted outfit in a former antiques shop extends over two floors and encompasses a small deli, a fish counter and a modern bistro with bar seating, where you can watch Michael and his team at their labours in the open kitchen. And unabashedly traditional French bistro fare it is, featuring creamy moules marinière, chicken liver parfait with breaded foie gras, and mains such as grilled ribeye and frites with béarnaise. Fish dishes may be less familiar, as when roasted brill turns up with truffled and rosemaried gnocchi and petits pois, while an alternative option might be a porcini risotto with rosemary butter and shaved Parmesan. Finish on a thoroughly indulgent note with a praline soufflé, served with toffee banana and vanilla ice cream. If the carafes of 'French plonk' don't appeal, regular bottles start at £17.25 (£4.20 a glass).

Chef/s: Michael Bedford. **Open:** Tue to Sat L 12 to 2.30, Wed to Sat D 7 to 9.30. **Closed:** Sun, Mon, 25 to 27 Dec, 1 to 3 Jan, bank hols. **Meals:** alc (main courses £17 to £21). **Service:** not inc. **Details:** 54 seats. Music.

Thornbury
Ronnie's of Thornbury
Low-key gem
11 St Mary Street, Thornbury, BS35 2AB
Tel no: (01454) 411137
www.ronnies-restaurant.co.uk
Modern European | £35
Cooking score: 3
£5 OFF

From 'simple lunches to Christmas dinners en masse', Ronnie Faulkner's low-key gem continues to generate salvos of satisfaction from its many contented customers. Originally a school for underprivileged children, this 'quaint but buzzy' place now educates palates rather than minds; it delivers exemplary plates of wild mushroom risotto with Champagne and truffle oil, twice-cooked belly pork, and 'divine' grilled calf's liver with polenta, tomato and salsify chips – not forgetting regularly applauded roast duck breast with rösti, cranberries and spinach. As for dessert, the smart money is on chocolate fondant with cappuccino ice cream – although lemon curd pavlova with orange, mint and poppy-seed gremolata sounds intriguing. Around 20 selections by the glass (from £4.50) top the well-spread wine list, with bottles from £16. Ronnie has also introduced an 'off-licence' range to take home.

Chef/s: Ronnie Faulkner. **Open:** Tue to Sun L 12 to 2.30 (3 Sun), Tue to Sat D 6.30 to 11. **Closed:** Mon, 25 and 26 Dec, 1 and 2 Jan. **Meals:** alc (main courses £16 to £30). Set L £13 (2 courses) to £16. Set D £16 (2 courses) to £19. Sun L £16 (2 courses) to £19. **Service:** 10%. **Details:** 72 seats. Wheelchair access. Music. Car parking.

■ Upper Slaughter
Lords of the Manor
Gorgeous retreat with 'spectacularly good' food
Upper Slaughter, GL54 2JD
Tel no: (01451) 820243
www.lordsofthemanor.com
Modern French | £65
Cooking score: 6
£5 OFF 🍷 🛏

Hollywood location scouts looking for a beautiful English country house hotel for their next *Four Weddings*-esque caper couldn't do much better than the Lords of the Manor. With its golden Cotswold stone and walled gardens, the former rectory is a gorgeous countryside retreat that, thanks to chef Matt Weedon, is also a haven of elegant, subtly progressive cooking. Thick carpets, immaculate tablecloths, plush golden-hued chairs and 'very French and absolutely flawless' service set the scene for a classical experience – though creative use of Cotswolds produce and some powerful flavours result in something more up-to-the-minute. The three-course, fixed-price menu delivers 'spectacularly good' dishes including ravioli of Burford Brown egg yolk, truffled potato, wild mushrooms, artichoke and Parmesan; Longhorn rib with oxtail, chervil roots, snails and salsify, as well as prune and Armagnac soufflé with matching ice cream and Earl Grey mousse. The wine list is so enticing it will have designated drivers cursing. Serious bottles from the big regions – Bordeaux, Burgundy, Piedmont and so on – are counterbalanced by other gems including a 'Sommelier's Value Selection' (a contradiction in terms, you might have thought) from £20, English and French fizz and a superb range of half-bottles.
Chef/s: Matt Weedon. **Open:** all week D 7 to 9.30, Sun L 12 to 2. **Meals:** Set D £65. Tasting menu £90. Sun L £40. **Service:** 10%. **Details:** 52 seats. 28 seats outside. Separate bar. No music. Car parking. No children.

■ Weston Subedge
The Seagrave Arms
A pub success story
Friday Street, Weston Subedge, GL55 6QH
Tel no: (01386) 840192
www.seagravearms.co.uk
Modern British | £26
Cooking score: 3
£5 OFF 🛏 £30

Kevin and Sue Davies have really put this Grade II-listed coaching inn back on the map since taking over and revitalising the place. These days, the Seagrave Arms is a pub success story with 'sympathetically restored' accoutrements, leather armchairs in the bar and a fondness for seasonal Cotswold produce. The kitchen keeps its loyalties close to home, offering locally cured charcuterie with pickles and olives or intense mushroom and rosemary soup, ahead of perfectly timed lamb fillet with crisped-up, creamy sweetbreads, venison bourguignon or juicy Dexter sirloin steak with superb chips (served in a little metal basket). Fish comes up from Cornwall (grilled herrings with white bean stew, for example), while dessert might bring a 'deconstructed' English trifle bavarois or a trip down memory lane for semolina with a dollop of strawberry jam and cookies. House wine is £16.95.
Chef/s: Kevin Harris. **Open:** Tue to Sun L 12 to 2.30, D 6 to 9. **Closed:** Mon. **Meals:** alc (main courses £12 to £19). **Service:** not inc. **Details:** 40 seats. 40 seats outside. Separate bar. No music. Wheelchair access. Car parking.

▮▮● Please send us your feedback
To register your opinion about any restaurant listed in the Guide, or a new restaurant that you wish to bring to our attention, please visit the web address at the bottom of the page. Your feedback informs the content of the book and will be used to compile next year's reviews.

Winchcombe

5 North Street

Pint-sized eatery with stellar food
5 North Street, Winchcombe, GL54 5LH
Tel no: (01242) 604566
www.5northstreetrestaurant.co.uk
Modern European | £45
Cooking score: 6

V

Squeezed into a crooked, half-timbered house on Winchcombe's main drag, 'Gus' and Kate Ashenford's pint-sized eatery continues to thrive as a low-key family affair noted for its comfy, romantic feel, warm heart and 'consistently brilliant' food. It's also a very flexible set-up, with dinner guests offered a choice of three pared-back set menus; mixing and matching is positively encouraged and meals are priced accordingly. After some beautifully crafted mini-loaves and high-end preliminaries, you might be treated to a mousse of line-caught sea bass, crab and grain mustard with a scattering of ginger-infused vegetables, pak choi, lemon oil and sorrel, ahead of an assertive seasonal dish of Dumbleton Estate venison loin with pumpkin purée and caramelised vanilla pear tempered by a lapsang souchong-infused jus. Marcus Ashenford also has a witty, mischievous streak – fashioning a trendy 'breakfast' starter from crispy duck egg, haggis, baked beans, ceps and brown sauce, as well as assembling a 'British dessert' combo of apple crumble, bread-and-butter pudding, rice pud and trifle. Alternatively, finish off with the indulgently exotic thrills of white chocolate, passion-fruit curd, poached mango and Turkish delight with basil and mango sorbet. Service ensures that a happy mood prevails, and the 'nicely varied' wine list covers most bases; prices start at £21. Note that it's essential to book in advance if you fancy lunch.
Chef/s: Marcus Ashenford. **Open:** Wed to Sun L 12.30 to 1.30, Tue to Sat D 7 to 9. **Closed:** Mon, first week Jan, 2 weeks Aug. **Meals:** alc (main courses £20 to £23). Set L £23 (2 courses) to £27. Set D £30 (2 courses) to £49. Sun L £33. Gourmet menu £64 (7 courses). **Service:** not inc. **Details:** 26 seats. Music.

Wesley House

A kitchen in safe hands
High Street, Winchcombe, GL54 5LJ
Tel no: (01242) 602366
www.wesleyhouse.co.uk
Modern European | £25
Cooking score: 3

£5 OFF 🛏 £30

Winchcombe's High Street holds a fabulous collection of ancient buildings, but the half-timbered Wesley House stands out, with its unsymmetrical façade. That it is very old becomes apparent inside, where there are beams, exposed stone and a huge inglenook. It has been run by Matthew Brown as a restaurant-with-rooms for the past 20 years, and though there has been a change of chef since the last edition of the Guide, the kitchen is in safe hands. Reports in the main are positive; a typical, well-praised meal is honey-glazed belly pork with black pudding fritter, apple purée and pear syrup, then caramelised Gressingham duck breast with red cabbage, dauphinois and cherry sauce, and crème brûlée with rhubarb and shortbread. Wines from £16.50.
Chef/s: Cedrik Rullier. **Open:** all week L 12 to 1.45, Mon to Sat D 7 to 9.30. **Closed:** 26 Dec. **Meals:** alc (main courses £12 to £32). Set L £12.95 (2 courses) to £15.95. Set D £19.95 (2 courses) to £25.95. **Service:** not inc. **Details:** 70 seats. Separate bar. Music.

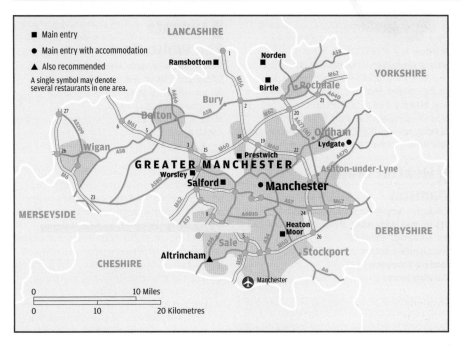

LANCASHIRE

- ■ Main entry
- ● Main entry with accommodation
- ▲ Also recommended

A single symbol may denote several restaurants in one area.

Ramsbottom ■
Norden ■
Birtle
Rochdale
YORKSHIRE

Bury
Bolton
Wigan
Oldham
Lydgate ●
GREATER MANCHESTER
Prestwich
Worsley ■
Salford ■
● Manchester
Ashton-under-Lyne

MERSEYSIDE
Sale
Heaton Moor ■
Stockport
DERBYSHIRE

Altrincham ▲

CHESHIRE

✈ Manchester

0   10 Miles
0   10   20 Kilometres

■ Altrincham

ALSO RECOMMENDED
▲ Dilli

60 Stamford New Road, Altrincham, WA14 1EE
Tel no: (0161) 9297484
www.dilli.co.uk
Indian

Still regarded by many as the best Indian in the South Manchester area, Dilli's kitchen is underpinned by authentic regional dishes from Delhi, Mumbai and Kolkata, and chefs are committed to ancient Ayurvedic principles. There is a lightness of touch with the spicing, whether it's a street food snack of gobi mutter tak-a-tak (cauliflower florets and green peas with cumin, ginger, green chilli and coriander, £8.95) or achari khargosh (rabbit with chillies and spices, £12.95). Wines from £12.95. Open all week.

■ Birtle

The Waggon at Birtle

Hearty Modern British cooking
131 Bury and Rochdale Old Road, Birtle, BL9 6UE
Tel no: (01706) 622955
www.thewaggonatbirtle.co.uk
Modern British | £28
Cooking score: 2

£5 OFF £30

This former pub celebrated its tenth anniversary in 2012 and continues to provide hearty fare to a faithful clientele. On offer is an à la carte and a fixed-price market menu. They take a few twists and turns, with some success, such as duck cassoulet terrine with herb crumb or warm ox tongue with a lemon and caper dressing. Mains might be char-grilled 'melting' salt beef, horseradish mash and parsley, garlic and caper vinaigrette, or tomato and basil risotto cakes with spicy aubergine and onion. Puddings are a little more pedestrian, say ginger sponge and custard. The short wine list offers plenty of interest, starting at £14.50.

Chef/s: David Watson. **Open:** Thur and Fri L 12 to 2, Wed to Sat D 6 to 9.30 (9 Wed and Thur), Sun 12.30 to 7.30. **Closed:** Mon, Tue, 26 to 30 Dec, 23 Jul to 7 Aug. **Meals:** alc (main courses £10 to £23). Set L and D £14.95 (2 courses) to £16.95. Sun L £11.95. **Service:** not inc. **Details:** 50 seats. Separate bar. Wheelchair access. Music. Car parking.

Heaton Moor

Damson

Colourful neighbourhood restaurant
113 Heaton Moor Road, Heaton Moor, SK4 4HY
Tel no: (0161) 4324666
www.damsonrestaurant.co.uk
Modern European | £33
Cooking score: 2

Well-padded and decidedly purple, Damson envelops customers in the experience of a neighbourhood restaurant that would do very well on a bigger stage. British produce is used in modern European dishes; witness salt-and-vinegar cockles added to a Whitby crab and parsley risotto in a house favourite. Standards like sirloin steak with dauphinois potatoes are 'always a winner'. Celebrated local cheesemonger Peter Papprill is in charge of an English and French selection, though inventive desserts including lemon and raspberry posset with lemon meringue pie and marshmallow are also a highlight. Wines are taken seriously without being priced prohibitively; bottles start at £14.95.

Chef/s: Anshul Dhyani. **Open:** Tue to Sat L 12 to 2.30, Mon to Sat D 5.30 to 9.30. Sun 12 to 7.30. **Closed:** 25 and 26 Dec. **Meals:** alc (main courses £15 to £20). Set L and D £14.95 (2 courses) to £17.95. Sun L £14.95. **Service:** 10% for parties of 6 or more. **Details:** 78 seats. 15 seats outside. Separate bar. Music. Children at early D only.

Lydgate

The White Hart

Hilltop inn with some stellar food
51 Stockport Road, Lydgate, OL4 4JJ
Tel no: (01457) 872566
www.thewhitehart.co.uk
Modern British | £32
Cooking score: 4

═ V

Standards remain high at this hilltop inn with brasserie, restaurant and rooms. Head chef Mike Shaw has worked his way back to his nearby Greenfield roots via a recent spell at Gilpin Lodge (see entry). There is some stellar food on the menu. Starters to win praise have been crispy Colchester oysters with olive oil hollandaise and red wine sauce, which offered a 'perfect crispy, salty shell', and morteau sausage on creamy Puy lentils – 'not a great looker, but great taste'. Mains might be local venison, red cabbage, mushrooms and red wine sauce, or pan-fried sea bream with escabèche and tapenade. There are vegetarian dishes, too, perhaps Mediterranean vegetable tart with goats' curd. Desserts are comforters with a twist: cinnamon custard pot with red apple sorbet or silky pannacotta with Agen prunes soaked in Armagnac. A good selection of wines starts at £15.50, with some available by the glass.

Chef/s: Michael Shaw. **Open:** Mon to Sat L 12 to 2.30, D 6 to 9.30. Sun 1 to 8. **Closed:** 26 Dec, 1 Jan. **Meals:** alc (main courses £13 to £26). Set L £13.50 (2 courses) to £16.50. Sun L £19.95. **Service:** not inc. **Details:** 48 seats. 10 seats outside. Separate bar. Wheelchair access. Music. Car parking.

Manchester

Australasia

Cool, big-city pan-Asian
1 The Avenue, Spinningfields, Manchester, M3 3AP
Tel no: (0161) 8310288
www.australasia.uk.com
Pan-Asian | £50
Cooking score: 2

A striking glass pyramid rising from the pavements of the financial quarter leads to a cavernous basement with limewashed brickwork, potted driftwood and tables clustered in open-plan booths. There's a heaving bar, a DJ (not everyone will approve of the decibel level) and an open kitchen producing a medley of pan-Asian cooking where off-piste choices from the Japanese robata grill prove more exciting than sushi. High points have been salt-and-pepper tofu with spiced beetroot, 'subtle' wild mushrooms in delicate tempura with truffle mayonnaise, and mango soufflé and chocolate pavé. Expect a vast wine list presented on iPads, with bottles from £18.
Chef/s: Phil Whitehead. **Open:** Mon to Fri L 12 to 3, D 5.30 to 11. Sat and Sun 12 to 11. **Closed:** 25 and 26 Dec. **Meals:** alc (main courses £14 to £60). **Service:** not inc. **Details:** 150 seats. Separate bar. Wheelchair access. Music. Car parking.

The French at the Midland Hotel

Manchester's grandest dining room
16 Peter Street, Manchester, M60 2DS
Tel no: (0161) 2363333
www.qhotels.co.uk
Anglo-French | £40
Cooking score: 2

£5 OFF 🚅

There's no underestimating the seductive sparkle of Manchester's grandest dining room. Tucked away at the heart of the Midland Hotel, windowless but with so many mirrors and ornate fripperies that diners don't feel the lack of natural light, the French is an 'occasion restaurant' incarnate. Alongside the glamour,

readers like the loaded bread trolley and old-fashioned service, and the food fights off the threat of being lost with 'sharp-intake-of-breath' prices and a Franco-northern slant. To start, there's pork pie with egg and pickle, then Goosnargh duck with foie gras, cherries and chocolate granola. Finish with treacle soufflé and malted milk ice cream. House wine starts at £23.50.
Chef/s: Andrew Matter. **Open:** Tue to Sat D only 7 to 10.30. **Closed:** Sun, Mon, bank hols, 2 weeks Aug. **Meals:** alc (main courses £25 to £33). Set D £29 (2 courses) to £45. **Service:** not inc. **Details:** 40 seats. Separate bar. Wheelchair access. Music.

The Gallery Café

Fresh, simple food and generous cakes
Whitworth Art Gallery, Oxford Road, Manchester, M15 6ER
Tel no: (0161) 2757497
www.themoderncaterer.co.uk
Modern British | £13
Cooking score: 2

£5 OFF £30

As if art wasn't sustenance enough, the Gallery Café feeds the Whitworth's visitors and staff a soul-nourishing diet of fresh, simple food and generous cakes. Though brightened by an open kitchen, art and a shop shelf of gourmet groceries, the café is showing its age, and plans are afoot for a new space. In the meantime, take a seat in the atrium for sweet potato and cumin soup with good bread and butter, bruschetta topped with sweet beetroot and local Blacksticks Blue cheese, or Goosnargh chicken stew with green veg and herbs. Service (order at the counter) is bright and friendly. House wine from £13. Cash only.
Chef/s: Jason Kosh. **Open:** Mon to Sat L only 10 to 3.30 (Sun 12 to 2.30). **Closed:** 23 Dec to 3 Jan. **Meals:** alc (main courses £7 to £9). **Service:** not inc. **Details:** Cash only. 55 seats. 24 seats outside. No music. Wheelchair access. Car parking.

Greens

Well-loved veggie with a thrill-factor
43 Lapwing Lane, West Didsbury, Manchester,
M20 2NT
Tel no: (0161) 4344259
www.greensdidsbury.co.uk
Vegetarian | £22
Cooking score: 2

V

Greens now caters to three times the number of covers it served when it opened in 1990, thanks to successive expansions which show the popularity of Simon Rimmer's inventive vegetarian cookery. In the relaxing wood-toned restaurant, Simon ensures the thrill factor by mixing southern European and south and east Asian traditions with fresh, flavourful vegetables, producing arancini risotto balls with tapenade dip, Indian-spiced chickpea parcel with sweet potato and spinach in tomato and mustard-seed sauce, and red Thai curry with grilled aubergine, pak choi and baby corn. Finish with chocolate and blueberry meringue cheesecake. House Spanish is £13.75 a bottle (£3.95 a glass). **Chef/s:** Simon Rimmer. **Open:** Tue to Sat L 12 to 2 (3 Sat), Mon to Sat D 5.30 to 10.30. Sun 12 to 9.30. **Closed:** 25 and 26 Dec, bank hols. **Meals:** alc (main courses £11 to £13). Set D £17.50. Sun L £17.50. **Service:** not inc. **Details:** 90 seats. 10 seats outside. Music.

The Lime Tree

Long-standing local favourite
8 Lapwing Lane, West Didsbury, Manchester,
M20 2WS
Tel no: (0161) 4451217
www.thelimetreerestaurant.co.uk
Modern British | £30
Cooking score: 3

Consistency is the watchword at this West Didsbury stalwart, which since 1987 has seen trendier venues rise and fall around it. The conservatory is a lovely summer spot in which to try some of the produce raised on the restaurant's Macclesfield Forest smallholding; wood pigeon comes with their own belly pork

and Bury black pudding. Readers appreciate 'great modern classics' like calf's liver with bubble and squeak, while vegetarians will find the lesser-spotted nut roast – here with cashews, chestnuts and mushrooms, baked en croûte – concealed among the rare breeds. Dessert might be warm chocolate torte with pistachio ice cream or straightforward apple crumble with custard. Interesting 'wines of the month' augment a strong list; house bottles start at £13.95. **Chef/s:** Jason Parker. **Open:** Tue to Fri and Sun L 12 to 2.30, all week D 5.30 to 10 (9 Sun). **Closed:** 25 and 26 Dec, 1 Jan. **Meals:** alc (main courses £12 to £21). Set L £10 (2 courses) to £15.50. Set D £13.95 (2 courses) to £15.95. Sun L £19.95. **Service:** 10% for parties of 10 or more. **Details:** 75 seats. 15 seats outside. Music.

Michael Caines at ABode Manchester

Classy city-centre dining
107 Piccadilly, Manchester, M1 2DB
Tel no: (0161) 2477744
www.abodehotels.co.uk
Modern European | £44
Cooking score: 5

Robert Cox now heads the Manchester kitchen and reports suggest that things are moving up a notch with him at the helm. Harmonious flavours abound and can be sampled in a variety of menu combinations. Start with crab ravioli – 'gossamer thin' pasta parcels with a delicately seasoned crab filling with lemongrass and ginger – or a 'fab little dish' of quail with herb purée, potato gnocchi, quail egg and tarragon jus. The list goes on, but does not disappoint: salted hake and crab with lemon purée, chorizo foam and samphire; roasted baby monkfish tail served with Jerusalem artichoke and truffle risotto, roasted chicken wings and chicken jus; ballotine of Goosnargh duck with pain d'épices crumb, black pudding purée, grelot onions and date sauce. Desserts, too, show considerable skill and an eye for detail, witness a signature passion-fruit mousse and creamy rice pudding ice cream, or hot pistachio soufflé. Service is pleasant, knowledgeable and unfussy, and it all takes place in the spacious, atmospheric basement of an old cotton merchant's warehouse. You need to know your stuff with the wine list, but there is plenty of advice on hand; prices from £25.

Chef/s: Robert Cox. **Open:** Mon to Sat L 12 to 2.30, D 6 to 10. **Closed:** Sun. **Meals:** alc (main courses £23 to £27). Set L £14.50. Set D £17.95 (2 courses) to £25. **Service:** 12%. **Details:** 76 seats. Separate bar. Wheelchair access. Music.

NEW ENTRY

The Northern Quarter

Well-established Mancunian brasserie
108 High Street, Manchester, M4 1HQ
Tel no: (01618) 327115
www.tnq.co.uk
Modern European | £29
Cooking score: 2

A buzzing reflection of its vibrant location, The Northern Quarter dispenses easy-to-like European brasserie dishes in a comfortable corner dining room, with a terrace across the street for sunny days. Starters are of the rich variety: try belly pork with fennel and apple or goats' curd with a canary-yellow polenta crust, celeriac rémoulade and crisp, raw stripy beetroot. Mains might be simple plaice with samphire, Morecambe Bay shrimps and lashings of butter, or spring vegetable gnocchi with lemon and basil cream sauce. Dessert (baked cheesecake, sticky toffee) lacks the creative touch. Service can be laggardly, but it's friendly. Wine from £16.

Chef/s: Anthony Fielding. **Open:** all week 12 to 10.30 (7 Sun). **Closed:** 25 and 26 Dec, 1 Jan. **Meals:** alc (main courses £10 to £20). Set L and D £12.95 (2 courses) to £15.95. Sun L and D £14.95 (2 courses) to £18.95. **Service:** 10%. **Details:** 55 seats. 48 seats outside. Wheelchair access. Music.

Second Floor

Fashionable food and rooftop views
Harvey Nichols, 21 New Cathedral Street,
Manchester, M1 1AD
Tel no: (0161) 8288898
www.harveynichols.com
Modern European | £40
Cooking score: 4

Harvey Nichols' Second Floor is very well run, from the popular bar where everybody seems to have a great time, to the more formal restaurant where picture windows capitalise on the rooftop views of Manchester's Wheel, and the black-and-white interior comes with well-spaced, well-dressed tables. Meals comprise a succession of intricate modern European dishes – crab and Morecambe Bay ravioli with celeriac and apple rémoulade and langoustine dressing, for example, or crisp oxtail salad with roast garlic, onion jam and pickled mushroom. Elsewhere, it's accomplished partnerships all the way: rump of lamb with braised shoulder, smoked aubergine purée and a Puy lentil cassoulet, or olive-oil poached cod teamed with saffron broth, mussels, kale and grelot onions. Desserts explore different avenues, from a raspberry and white chocolate soufflé to beetroot parfait with yoghurt mousse, chocolate soil and pickled blackberries. The well-collated wine list features an even-handed selection of countries besides France, from £19.50.

Chef/s: Sam Everett. **Open:** all week L 12 to 3, Tue to Sat D 6 to 9.30. **Closed:** 25 to 27 Dec, Easter Sun. **Meals:** Set L and D £32 (2 courses) to £40. Tasting menu £55. **Service:** 10%. **Details:** 50 seats. Separate bar. Wheelchair access. Music.

ALSO RECOMMENDED
▲ Teacup on Thomas Street
53-55 Thomas Street, Manchester, M4 1NA
Tel no: (0161) 8323233
www.teacupandcakes.com
Modern British

Described by one reporter as 'American downtown café meets English tea room', this buzzy café specialises in tea and cakes but is branching out with 'supper and a cuppa'. Tempting cakes include luxury carrot and 'an amazing Battenburg-style in primary colours'; tea is served with a timer for brewing. Savouries start with breakfast; eggs all ways including Benedict (£7.50), then perhaps a lunchtime 'feather-light haloumi' salad (£8). Supper might be British grub with a twist; homemade fish fingers in Japanese breadcrumbs, say. Wine starts at £17.50. Open all week.

▌Norden
Nutters
Wacky indulgence and serious purpose
Edenfield Road, Norden, OL12 7TT
Tel no: (01706) 650167
www.nuttersrestaurant.co.uk
Modern British | £34
Cooking score: 3

V

'The amazing crispy black pudding won tons and the Goosnargh duck confit with ginger are two of my favourite dishes ever!' confesses a die-hard fan of Andrew Nutter's atmospherically offbeat restaurant. Set in six acres of parkland overlooking Ashworth Moor, the Georgian manor is still a family business, with Andrew's mum and dad playing their part out front and behind the scenes. Wacky indulgence may be part of Nutter's culinary appeal, but there's no arguing with the skill, or the purposeful use of excellent produce – be it crispy lobster fritter with basil emulsion and quinoa salad or a trio of Haresfield lamb with creamy smoked garlic and potato gratin. For afters, don't miss the chocolate délice with peanut brittle shards and honeycomb splinters. Informative service extends to the suitably eclectic wine list; prices from £14.95.
Chef/s: Andrew Nutter. **Open:** Tue to Sun L 12 to 2 (4 Sun), D 6.30 to 9.30 (8 Sun). **Closed:** Mon, 1 or 2 days after Christmas and New Year. **Meals:** alc (main courses £18 to £23). Set L £13.95 (2 courses) to £16.95. Gourmet D £40 (6 courses). Sun L £22.50. **Service:** not inc. **Details:** 146 seats. Separate bar. Wheelchair access. Music. Car parking.

▌Prestwich
Aumbry
Go-to place for classy contemporary dining
2 Church Lane, Prestwich, M25 1AJ
Tel no: (0161) 7985841
www.aumbryrestaurant.co.uk
British | £36
Cooking score: 5

£5 OFF

'My fourth visit to Aumbry and it was as good as ever' enthused one reporter, who liked the fact that the cooking showed 'skill, innovation and no pretension', adding: 'That goes for front-of-house, too'. Mary-Ellen McTague and Laurence Tottingham are now in their third year and have established this intimate, cottage-style dining room as a go-to place for ambitious contemporary dining. The cooking shows real flair and sensitivity when it comes to ingredients and a feel for their impact on the palate. Witness one reporter's account of a rapturous meal that progressed from sautéed snails and wild mushrooms with garlic, parsley and fresh curds rolled in hay ash to a 'delicate but earthy' combination of roast wild turbot, smoked eel pudding ('a little bomb of flavour'), frog's leg and parsley root. Elsewhere, the kitchen proves the point with high quality, locally sourced ingredients in such dishes as Gloucester Old Spot pork served with black peas in vinegar and apple sauce. Desserts such as beetroot and chocolate cake with hazelnut, caraway and bee pollen show classy intent. The wine list travels the world, but for a purpose, offering some unusual choices to complement the food; house selections from £18.

Chef/s: Mary-Ellen McTague and Laurence Tottingham. **Open:** Fri and Sat L 12 to 2.30, Tue to Sat D 6 to 9.30. **Closed:** Sun, Mon, 25 and 26 Dec, first week Jan. **Meals:** Set L £18 (2 courses) to £22. Tasting menus £35, £45 £60. **Service:** not inc. **Details:** 34 seats. Separate bar. Wheelchair access. Music.

▉ Ramsbottom

Hideaway

Good-value Italian gem
16-18 Market Place, Ramsbottom, BLO 9HT
Tel no: (01706) 822005
www.ramsons-restaurant.com
Italian | £24
Cooking score: 1

The setting is a candlelit basement below ramsons (see entry), the menu is set, with prices attuned to a depressed economy. Welcome to Louise Varley's *enoteca con cucina* – earthy Italian food that takes in a shared plate of antipasti, a 'lovely' soup, say spring vegetable with Gorgonzola, rose veal casserole with cheese mash and roasted vegetables, and a cheese plate or pannacotta (or both). Wines from ramsons' magnificent cellar (from £20).

Chef/s: Louise Varley. **Open:** Tue to Sat D 7.30 for 8 (1 sitting). **Closed:** Sun and Mon. **Meals:** Set D £20 to £29 (5 courses). **Service:** not inc. **Details:** 18 seats. Music.

ramsons

Italian fine dining, Piedmont-style
18 Market Place, Ramsbottom, BLO 9HT
Tel no: (01706) 825070
www.ramsons-restaurant.com
Italian | £48
Cooking score: 4

Ramsons has been through many guises over the years, but Chris Johnson's love of all things Italian is what abides. The current incarnation,

with Babak Masoudi heading a new team, now concentrates on the food of the Piedmont region. The kitchen was still finding its feet at a test meal, but the menu demonstrated Johnson's determination to source the best ingredients: witness an antipasto of carpaccio of tuna with Castelfranco leaves dressed with honey and mustard, and Italian staples such as risotto of fava beans with barba di frati (monk's beard) or 'fluffy' gnocchi with leeks and mussels. Follow, perhaps, with silver hake, crushed potato, spinach and parsley sauce. Cheese might be artisan direct from Piedmont or locally sourced British, and tiramisu with espresso granita and Savoy biscuit provides a sweet ending. Chris Johnson's unique front-of-house style is complemented by charming and efficient young staff. The all-Italian wine list reflects a passion for food and wine matching, and for fine quality (and often lesser-known) wines sourced from every region; recommendations are always spot-on. Prices start at £22.50.

Chef/s: Babak Masoudi. **Open:** Wed to Sat L 12 to 2.30 (1 to 3.30 Sun), Tue to Sat D 7 to 9.30. **Closed:** Mon. **Meals:** Set L £26 (2 courses) to £78. Set D £40 to £78. Sat set D £50 (4 courses) to £58. **Service:** not inc. **Details:** 32 seats. Music.

Sanmini's

Terrific Indian with pitch-perfect flavours
7 Carrbank Lodge, Ramsbottom Lane,
Ramsbottom, BLO 9DJ
Tel no: (01706) 821831
www.sanminis.com
Indian | £30
Cooking score: 3

Dr Mini Sankar and her medic husband set up this terrific little restaurant in a handsome stone gatehouse in 2008 and have never looked back. It's a warm, highly personal set-up (don't be surprised if one of the chefs brings out your food) and the cooking is a pitch-perfect distillation of homespun south Indian flavours. The menu may not change much, but it seldom matters when you can feast on zingy cashew and spinach pakoras, pan-fried

mutton varuval or fiery nuggets of marinated 'chicken 65', ahead of ennai kathirikkai (aubergines with roasted lentils and tomatoes) or special minced lamb with potatoes. There's generally an unusual sweet, too – 'I bet the beetroot halva is a killer' exclaimed one fan. House Australian is £13.95. The owners also run Sanmini's Express on Bury Market.
Chef/s: Mr Sundaramoorthy and Mr Sathyanand. **Open:** Sun L 12 to 2.30, Tue to Sun D 6.30 to 9.30 (10.30 Fri to Sun). **Closed:** Mon, 25 and 26 Dec, May bank hols. **Meals:** alc (main courses £9 to £14). Sun L £17.50. **Service:** not inc. **Details:** 40 seats. Separate bar. Wheelchair access. Music.

▌Salford

The Mark Addy

Fashionably old-school vittles
Stanley Street, Salford, M3 5EJ
Tel no: (0161) 8324080
www.markaddy.co.uk
British | £26
Cooking score: 2

'The only place outside of an Oldham chippy that you're going to see rag pudding' enthuses one correspondent of the riverside pub where Robert Owen Brown indulges his taste for the old-fashioned. The surrounds are offally eighties – it lacks sprucing – but the menu is fashionably old-school. Bull's fry with caper butter, wild rabbit and mushroom pie, and baked ham with mead have the air of vittles placed on Mr Bumble's table. To finish, Eccles cake with Lancashire cheese is one of several tributes to St John's Fergus Henderson. It's all nourishing and knowledgeably served. Wine starts at £13.50.
Chef/s: Robert Owen Brown. **Open:** all week L 12 to 3 (5 Sat, 6 Sun), Mon to Sat D 5 to 9 (10 Sat). **Closed:** 25 to 27 Dec. **Meals:** alc (main courses £9 to £17). **Service:** not inc. **Details:** 80 seats. 100 seats outside. Separate bar. Music. Car parking.

▌Worsley

**★ READERS' RESTAURANT OF THE YEAR ★
NORTH WEST**

Grenache

Popular local bistro
15 Bridgewater Road, Walkden, Worsley, M28 3JE
Tel no: (0161) 7998181
www.grenacherestaurant.co.uk
Modern British | £27
Cooking score: 2

'Great to have such a treasure on our doorstep' enthused a regular to Hussein Abbas's small but expansively welcoming restaurant. This year, reporters have applauded the 'ever-changing menu', the 'fantastic scallops, steak and a sharing cheeseboard to die for'. While it may not be daring cooking, dishes are freshly prepared using quality raw materials, from pheasant leg rillettes and seared venison teamed with beetroot, via confit of halibut with lemon broccoli, confit potatoes and red wine jus, to a classic baked egg custard with blackcurrant sauce. The Grenache grape is the star of house recommendations, with bottles from £12.95.
Chef/s: Ken Calder. **Open:** Sun L 1 to 5, Wed to Sat D 5.30 to 9 (9.30 Fri and Sat). **Closed:** Mon, Tue, first 10 days Jan, 1 week Aug. **Meals:** alc (main courses £10 to £23). Set D £14.95 (2 courses) to £17.95. Sun L £10.95 (2 courses) to £14.95. **Service:** not inc. **Details:** 34 seats. Separate bar. Wheelchair access. Music. No children after 7.30pm.

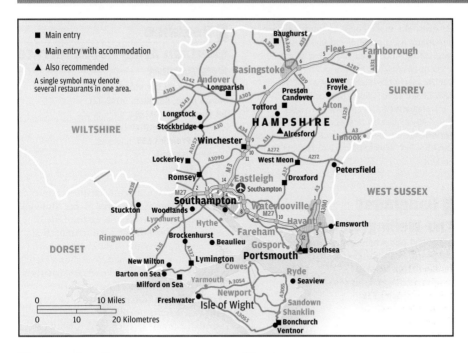

■ Alresford

ALSO RECOMMENDED
▲ Caracoli

15 Broad Street, Alresford, SO24 9AR
Tel no: **(01962) 738730**
www.caracoli.co.uk
Modern British

One of three Caracoli deli/cafés across the
southern counties, this branch serves its
community well. Breakfast provides a daily
wake-up call, brunch delivers lazy treats on
Sunday, and the honest-to-goodness lunch
menu brings some eclectic flavours to the table
– generally a soup (perhaps pumpkin and
roasted garlic), a few salads (anything from
Thai beef to tarragon chicken) and the
occasional hot special. Coffee and cakes also
suit Alresford's shopping crowd. Wines from
£13.50. Other high street outlets in Guildford
and Winchester.

■ Barton on Sea

Pebble Beach

Glorious clifftop eatery with sparkling seafood
Marine Drive, Barton on Sea, BH25 7DZ
Tel no: **(01425) 627777**
www.pebblebeach-uk.com
French | £34
Cooking score: 3

Location is everything at this smart restaurant-
with-rooms, and the ravishing clifftop
location looking out towards the Needles is
hard to beat, especially in fine weather when
visitors pack the terrace. Service is keen as
mustard and in Pierre Chevillard the place has
a talented, conscientious chef. Absolutely
fresh seafood is the main attraction, from
platters of fruits de mer and whole local lobster
thermidor to sea bass papillote, well-timed
lemon sole, and monkfish and squid in a spicy
shellfish sauce. But meat is treated with equal
respect and might include char-grilled veal
cutlet or calf's liver and bacon. Well-made

desserts take in iced banana soufflé dipped in chocolate with caramelised pecan nuts. An interesting, intelligent wine list arranged by style opens at £16.90.

Chef/s: Pierre Chevillard. **Open:** all week L 11 to 2.30 (3 Sat, 12 to 3 Sun), D 6 to 11 (6.30 to 10.30 Sun). **Meals:** alc (main courses £8 to £46). Set L and D £26.50 (2 courses) to £31.50. Sun L £16.95. **Service:** not inc. **Details:** 90 seats. 36 seats outside. Separate bar. Wheelchair access. Music. Car parking.

Baughurst
The Wellington Arms

Delightful pub where everything's done well
Baughurst Road, Baughurst, RG26 5LP
Tel no: (0118) 9820110
www.thewellingtonarms.com
Modern British | £28
Cooking score: 4

£30

'This place is an absolute delight. There may be country pubs that are prettier, but there are not too many places where everything seems to be done so well.' This expresses a feeling shared by many who have eaten at Jason King and Simon Page's country pub-with-rooms over the past eight years. Absolute, untiring devotion, enthusiasm, skill and an innate sense of hospitality – 'very calm and assured, with time for everyone, even with the restaurant being extended into where the outside gents used to be' – make the place memorable. Where possible, ingredients are local (many vegetables are grown on site) and everybody seems to find everything 'delicious'; for example, lobster soup, twice-baked Marksbury Cheddar soufflé, a venison pot pie of 'hearty chunks of meat' where the pastry 'mopped up the juices nicely', and steamed marmalade sponge served with custard made from their own eggs. Wines from £18.

Chef/s: Jason King. **Open:** all week L 12 to 1.30, Mon to Sat D 6.30 to 9 (6 Sat). **Meals:** alc (main courses £11 to £21). Set L £15.75 (2 courses) to £18.75. **Service:** 10%. **Details:** 32 seats. 20 seats outside. Wheelchair access. Music. Car parking.

Beaulieu
Montagu Arms Hotel, Terrace Restaurant

Pulling out all the stops
Palace Lane, Beaulieu, SO42 7ZL
Tel no: (01590) 612324
www.montaguarmshotel.co.uk
Modern French | £55
Cooking score: 6
£5 OFF ▭ V

A brick-built, seventeenth-century country inn not far from the National Motor Museum, the Montagu Arms is in the heart of the New Forest in a splendidly pastoral setting. Its premier dining room is a stately space with oak panelling, gilt-framed mirrors and French windows opening on to the terrace that gives the restaurant its name. Roux graduate Matthew Tomkinson pulls out all the stops with a menu of regionally based food, some of it from the hotel's kitchen garden, with fish from the south coast, and game and pork from the New Forest national park. A six-course *menu surprise* is sorely tempting for anyone not in a hurry, but the carte makes for such good reading that it may well prove hard to resist. Gurnard fillet with crab gratin and pickled samphire offers a taste of the sea to kick things off, while mains give star billing to meats such as Alresford roe deer with a venison croquette, beetroot fondant and parsnip purée, or wild mallard served Wellington-fashion for two, with morteaux, sweet-and-sour cabbage and crab apple jelly. Unusual dessert flavours include quince tart with hazelnut frangipane, or fig and almond Bakewell with fig and vanilla cream. The French-led wine list has plenty under £30; bottles start at £23 (£5.75 a glass).

Chef/s: Matthew Tomkinson. **Open:** Wed to Sun L 12 to 2.30, Tue to Sun D 7 to 9.30. **Closed:** Mon. **Meals:** Set L £19 (2 courses) to £25. Set D £65. Sun L £32.50. Tasting menu £75. **Service:** not inc. **Details:** 50 seats. 25 seats outside. Separate bar. Wheelchair access. Music. Car parking. Children over 8 yrs only.

Brockenhurst

The Pig
Kitchen garden cooking
Beaulieu Road, Brockenhurst, SO42 7QL
Tel no: (01590) 622354
www.thepighotel.co.uk
Modern British | £35
Cooking score: 4

The name might suggest a pub, but nutshell-wise The Pig is a 'budget version of Raymond Blanc's Le Manoir and his kitchen-garden-to-plate philosophy'. Set amid New Forest oaks, the Georgian country house offers a shabby-chic interior and a conservatory restaurant filled with herbs and seedlings, stacked wooden vegetable boxes, flowerpots and climbers. Old tables and chairs, colourful floor tiles and staff in green striped aprons create a laid-back feel – though the place can be high-decibel when busy. James Golding's menu uses produce from the kitchen garden, supplemented by foraged pickings or produce sourced within 25 miles; flexibility comes via small or larger plates. Not surprisingly there are plenty of 'piggy bites' (Saddleback crackling and apple sauce), and slow-roasted belly (with crushed new potatoes, cavolo flowers and apple and mustard sauce). Otherwise expect, say, melt-in-the-mouth roast Hampshire lamb rump with a fine minted broad bean purée and rosemary jus. An inspired wine list opens with house bottles at £16.50.
Chef/s: James Golding. **Open:** all week L 12 to 2.30 (3 Sun), D 7 to 10. **Meals:** alc (main courses £8 to £26). **Service:** 12.5%. **Details:** 65 seats. 30 seats outside. Separate bar. Wheelchair access. Music. Car parking.

Visit us Online
To find out more about
The Good Food Guide, please visit
www.thegoodfoodguide.co.uk

Droxford

The Bakers Arms
Beguiling village pub
High Street, Droxford, SO32 3PA
Tel no: (01489) 877533
www.thebakersarmsdroxford.com
Modern British | £26
Cooking score: 3

Adam and Anna Cordery are splendid custodians of this beguilingly unassuming village inn. Inside, expect a real pub with real ales (from a micro-brewery just one mile away), a cosy vibe, and a short, to-the-point menu that reveals plenty of conscientious sourcing. It's all delivered in an unfussy manner, with good, full flavours coming through in a dish of creamy pheasant and chestnut gratin and a simple main course pork fillet with Puy lentils and kale. Rabbit Wellington with baby carrots, cavolo nero and creamy mustard sauce is worth considering, and desserts are in keeping – especially pear and apple crumble with custard and sticky toffee pudding. House wines are £14.95.
Chef/s: Richard Harrison. **Open:** Tue to Sun L 12 to 2, Tue to Sat D 7 to 9. **Closed:** Mon. **Meals:** alc (main courses £12 to £18). Set L and D £13. Sun L £14.95. **Service:** 10%. **Details:** 40 seats. 20 seats outside. No music. Car parking.

Emsworth

Fat Olives
Homely restaurant with Med-inspired food
30 South Street, Emsworth, PO10 7EH
Tel no: (01243) 377914
www.fatolives.co.uk
Modern British | £35
Cooking score: 3

A former fisherman's cottage by Emsworth quayside is the setting for Lawrence and Julia Murphy's homely but polished set-up. Not surprisingly, local seafood waxes strongly on the seasonal, Med-inspired menu, so look out for dishes such as sea bass with lentils, garlic and Serrano ham or turbot with prawn and caper risotto. Alternatively, keep things fresh with beetroot, orange and Sussex Slipcote cheese salad, move on to a richly flavoured plate of Hyden Farm pork loin with black pudding faggot, quince and trotter sauce, and round off with a dramatic combination of white chocolate pannacotta, poached pear and liquorice sauce. The results are generally pleasing on the palate, although there have been a few issues with seasoning: 'the salt cellar has never been so busy' quipped one reporter. Wines start at £13.95.

Chef/s: Lawrence Murphy. **Open:** Tue to Sat L 12 to 2, D 7 to 9.30. **Closed:** Sun, Mon, 1 week Christmas, 1 week Mar, 2 weeks Jun. **Meals:** alc (main courses £15 to £26). Set L £17.75 (2 courses) to £19.75. **Service:** not inc. **Details:** 25 seats. 10 seats outside. Wheelchair access. Music. Children over 8 yrs only.

36 On The Quay
Destination restaurant-with-rooms
47 South Street, Emsworth, PO10 7EG
Tel no: (01243) 375592
www.36onthequay.co.uk
Modern French | £55
Cooking score: 6

Facing resolutely towards the sparkling serenity of the harbour, amid the squalling of seabirds, in a photogenic Hampshire fishing village, the Farthings' restaurant-with-rooms has been for many years one of the leading lights of the south coast dining scene. It's run with professional attention to detail, and long service has not dulled but rather whetted the edge of Ramon Farthing's culinary ambition. It's modern food, but with the emphasis on old-fangled technique which helps the components of dishes to meld rather than stand combatively off each other. A soft-cooked duck egg appears with Serrano ham on braised Puy lentils, with duck liver torchon and rye bread, for a wholly comforting opener, while the Japanese treatment of scallops (seared or ceviche) sees them partnered with dashi stock soup, shimejis and daikon cress. Mains add more layers still, but always within the bounds of logic, so that

turbot comes on a bed of caponata, with smoked bacon and artichoke mousse and a beignet of orange and basil, or there could be two cuts of lamb – roasted loin and braised brisket – with a caviar of aubergine, tomato and basil and roasted garlic. Finish with a very pretty chocolate cube set about with caramelised banana and mango. The stylistically sorted wine list begins with seasonal house selections from £19.50.

Chef/s: Ramon Farthing. **Open:** Tue to Sat L 12 to 1.45, D 6.30 to 9.30. **Closed:** Sun, Mon, 1 weekend May, 1 week Nov, first 2 weeks Jan. **Meals:** Set L £23.95 (2 courses) to £27.95. Set D £45 (2 courses) to £57. **Service:** not inc. **Details:** 50 seats. Separate bar. No music. Wheelchair access.

Isle of Wight

Appuldurcombe Restaurant
Refined dining and charm aplenty
The Royal Hotel, Belgrave Road, Ventnor, Isle of Wight, PO38 1JJ
Tel no: (01983) 852186
www.royalhoteliow.co.uk
Modern British | £40
Cooking score: 3

The Royal Hotel is one of the island's oldest hotels, and has an appealing way of sticking to established values in everything from service to soft furnishings. The Appuldurcombe is its formal restaurant (the conservatory is reserved for lunch and afternoon tea), and chef Alan Staley is a reassuring presence for its many fans. One of his signatures is a soufflé of the unpasteurised local cheese Gallybagger, a 'miracle of featherweight perfection' according to one smitten reporter. This might be followed by a pork tasting plate, or the lesser-spotted coq au vin, a rare sight on menus these days. Tropical cheesecake with coconut foam or dark chocolate tart with caramel oranges are a bright final note. Reporters praise an experienced, unobtrusive service team. Wine starts from £18.

Chef/s: Alan Staley. **Open:** all week L 12 to 1.45, D 6.45 to 9. **Closed:** 2-3 weeks from 3 Jan. **Meals:** Set L £15 (2 courses) to £19.50. Set D £31 (2 courses) to

£40. Sun L £29. Tasting menu £50. **Service:** not inc.
Details: 100 seats. Separate bar. No music.
Wheelchair access. Car parking. Children over 3 yrs
only at D.

NEW ENTRY
Justin Brown at Farringford
Intelligent cooking at Tennyson's home
Bedbury Lane, Isle of Wight, PO40 9PE
Tel no: (01983) 752700
www.farringford.co.uk
Modern British | £30
Cooking score: 4

£5 OFF 🍽 V

Quotes from Tennyson adorn the walls of this
airy chalet-style restaurant in the grounds of
Farringford, the poet's former home. Now an
upmarket holiday destination with self-
catering accommodation, it aims to please
residents, locals and visiting diners; with that
in mind, young chef Justin Brown has been
installed in the kitchen. The result is a menu
that's broadly classic but rarely predictable.
Take a generous starter of seared king scallops
for example, with golden raisin purée, black
pudding, baby garden herbs and Sauternes
sauce, or a main course of free-range corn-fed
chicken breast with fondant potato, pak choi,
celeriac purée and red wine jus. Flavours are
sometimes too subtle, but when they really
come together – as in a dessert of vanilla
poached pear with pineapple ice cream and
praline crisp – the result is stunning. A wine
list offering plenty of favourites kicks off at
just £14.95.
Chef/s: Justin Brown. **Open:** Tue to Sun L 12 to 2,
Tue to Sat D 6 to 9. **Closed:** Mon, 2 Jan to 2 Feb.
Meals: alc (main courses £17 to £22). Tasting menu
£50. **Service:** not inc. **Details:** 35 seats. 20 seats
outside. Separate bar. Wheelchair access. Music.
Car parking.

The Pond Café
Appealing little village venue
Bonchurch Village Road, Bonchurch, Isle of
Wight, PO38 1RG
Tel no: (01983) 855666
www.robert-thompson.com
Mediterranean | £30
Cooking score: 3

£5 OFF

'The floodlit duck pond opposite is magical,'
comments an observant reader, justifying
Robert Thompson's decision to name this
appealing little village venue after it. Not far
from his nerve-centre at the Hambrough (see
entry), the Café is a more laid-back, everyday
place, with pitch-perfect service and attractive
brasserie food. Serrano ham with pickled
mushrooms or crab and squid linguine are
dazzlingly intense starters. Mains offer royally
treated local ingredients: say cod with leeks in
truffle sauce, or char-grilled leg of island lamb
with roasted beetroot, salsify and lentils. An
intriguing mix of local and Spanish cheeses
allows the chance to taste Isle of Wight Blue
alongside Manchego and Murcía. Plum and
cinnamon tart has proved deservedly popular,
too. A compact wine list offers sound drinking
from £17 (£4 a glass).
Chef/s: Richard Broughton. **Open:** Mon to Thur L 10
to 3, D 6 to 10. Fri to Sun 10 to 10. **Meals:** alc (main
courses £12 to £22). Set L £18. Sun L £18 (2 courses)
to £22. **Service:** not inc. **Details:** 30 seats. 20 seats
outside. Music.

Average Price
The average price listed in main-entry
reviews denotes the price of a three-
course meal, without wine.

Robert Thompson at the Hambrough

Alchemy from an undisputed star
Hambrough Road, Ventnor, Isle of Wight,
PO38 1SQ
Tel no: (01983) 856333
www.robert-thompson.com
Modern French | £60
Cooking score: 7

£5 OFF ⟿ V

A three-storey Victorian villa perched on a clifftop on the sheltered edge of the Isle of Wight, the Hambrough is a masterpiece of modern understatement inside. The high-ceilinged public rooms and the dining room have been left deliberately quite plain, the better to emphasise those bewitching views. Tables are adorned with eye-catching pieces of local glassware, but are principally distinguished by the even more diverting dishes of the island's undisputed culinary star, Robert Thompson. A chorus of acclamation attends the six-course (seven if you take cheese) tasting menus, which marshal signature dishes as well as fresh ideas in a style of memorable contemporary alchemy. The underlying ideas are often perfectly simple, as in an opening salad of Mayan Twilight potato, rainbow chard, artichoke and summer truffle in a hazelnut and crème fraîche dressing. A long-stayer is the majestic terrine comprised of smoked eel, belly pork, foie gras and Granny Smith, garnished with celeriac rémoulade. Fish dishes are defined by strong, assertive flavours, bringing pickled cucumber and white radish, as well as the smoulder of horseradish cream, to mackerel ceviche, but there is still an alertness to the more rounded flavours of meat dishes such as the roasted veal tenderloin that appears with piquillo peppers and white asparagus, as well as a garnish of silky bone marrow, in Madeira and thyme jus. Venison and snails make an interesting partnership, along with roasted chervil roots and field mushroom purée. To finish, there are refined spins on classics such as tarte Tatin and rum baba, as well as Manjari chocolate and

passion-fruit marquise with cocoa nibs and chicory ice cream. Excellent staff pitch the tone just right, and the wine list is a relatively concise but exceptional collection of imaginatively chosen bottles, including a handful of fine Uruguayans (the next big South American thing). Bottles start from £22 (£5 a small glass).
Chef/s: Robert Thompson. **Open:** Tue to Sat L 12 to 1.30, D 7 to 10. **Closed:** Sun, Mon, 2 weeks Nov, 2 weeks Jan, 2 weeks Apr. **Meals:** Set L £32. Set D £60. Tasting menu £70. **Service:** 12.5%. **Details:** 45 seats. Music.

READERS RECOMMEND

Dan's Kitchen
Modern British
Lower Green Road, Isle of Wight, PO33 1TS
Tel no: (01983) 872303
www.danskitcheniow.com
'One of the best meals we have had in terms of the food, atmosphere (relaxed and friendly yet efficient) and very reasonable prices.'

▌Lockerley
The Kings Arms
A cracking village local
Romsey Road, Lockerley, SO51 0JF
Tel no: (01794) 340332
www.kingsarmsatlockerley.co.uk
British | £25
Cooking score: 2

£5 OFF £30

This eighteenth-century pub close to Mottisfont Abbey has had a chequered history, including a period of closure. Reopened in 2010, it's now a bustling village local with a chic new look and an impressive landscaped garden. It not only pulls in drinkers attracted by well-kept real ales, but also diners lured by menus that make the most of local ingredients. A starter of pressed Awbridge pheasant and boiled ham terrine with pear chutney might be followed by caramelised duck breast with braised Puy lentils and Savoy cabbage, then baked chocolate mousse with blackcurrant sorbet. House wines start at £14.95.

Open: all week L 12 to 2 (3 Sat, 4 Sun), Mon to Sat D 7 to 9.30. **Closed:** 25 Dec. **Meals:** alc (main courses £11 to £20) Sun L £21 (2 courses) to £25. **Service:** 12.5% for parties of 10 or more. **Details:** 40 seats. 60 seats outside. Music. Car parking.

▮ Longparish

★ PUB OF THE YEAR ★

NEW ENTRY

The Plough Inn
The perfect village pub
Longparish, SP11 6PB
Tel no: (01264) 720358
www.theploughinn.info
Modern British | £25
Cooking score: 5

'Loved it here', enthused a visitor to this dream setting in a picturesque Test Valley village. The Plough reels in the crowds with its easy-going good looks, highly accomplished food and sunny-natured service. Though dating from 1721, today's inn benefits from a sympathetic makeover that delivers a smart gloss without detracting from the old beams, timbers and fireplaces. With owner and ex-Maze executive chef James Durrant behind the stove, and ex-Maze restaurant manager Janet Cage front-of-house, class is assured. But locals can relax – 'things haven't gone all cheffy'. Instead, the kitchen adopts a simple, accessible approach, using the very best seasonal produce – local and regional wherever possible. An opener of fried duck egg with English asparagus, bacon and burnt butter vinaigrette is typical of the style. Elsewhere, braised shoulder of lamb, with onion pureé, red onions and an accompanying salt-marsh mutton shepherd's pie, delivers more robust, punchy flavours, and there's a 'super' cheese trolley. The blackboard offers a daily special, perhaps local beef fillet (for two), and there are lunchtime sandwiches. The small bar area comes with real ales, and the well-considered wine list features a by-the-glass selection in various measures, or bottles from £12.

Chef/s: James Durrant. **Open:** all week L 12 to 2.30 (4.30 Sun), Mon to Sat D 6 to 9.30. **Meals:** alc (main courses £12 to £21). **Service:** not inc. **Details:** 50 seats. 40 seats outside. Wheelchair access. Music. Car parking.

▮ Longstock

The Peat Spade Inn
Sporty rural retreat
Village Street, Longstock, SO20 6DR
Tel no: (01264) 810612
www.peatspadeinn.co.uk
Modern British | £28
Cooking score: 2

Tricked out in swanky green and brown livery, the Peat Spade promotes itself as a country retreat for sportin' types and anglers (the river Test is nearby). Real ales, pies, ploughman's lunches and bucolic banter set the tone in the bar, but the place also does a decent line in smart regional cooking. Fish is a strong suit (although 'over-cooking' can be a problem), but the kitchen also turns its hand to local pheasant with 'pan-fried' bread sauce or loin of lamb and braised shoulder with Puy lentils, swede and carrot purée. To conclude, expect anything from chocolate and caramel mousse to prune and Armagnac parfait. Wines from £15.

Chef/s: Andy Rolfe. **Open:** all week L 12 to 2.30 (3.30 Sun), D 6.30 to 9.30 (9 Sun). **Closed:** 25 Dec. **Meals:** alc (main courses £10 to £20). Sun L £20 (2 courses) to £25. **Service:** not inc. **Details:** 40 seats. Wheelchair access. Music. Car parking.

⫪ Please send us your feedback

To register your opinion about any restaurant listed in the Guide, or a new restaurant that you wish to bring to our attention, please visit the web address at the bottom of the page. Your feedback informs the content of the book and will be used to compile next year's reviews.

Lower Froyle

The Anchor Inn

Cracking local with well-cooked classics
Lower Froyle, GU34 4NA
Tel no: (01420) 23261
www.anchorinnatlowerfroyle.co.uk
Modern British | £30
Cooking score: 2

The spruced up sixteenth-century Anchor captures the style and atmosphere of an English inn, embracing country pursuits and appealing to the shooting and fishing fraternity. This extends to the resolutely British menu that champions local ingredients and successfully combines traditional and modern ideas. Expect nothing fancy, just satisfying, well-cooked classics: perhaps a starter of ox tongue and salt beef salad, then a good pub staple like steak and ale pie, or halibut with crab risotto and winter greens. With mind-your-head beams, glowing fires, rugs on polished wood floors and candelabras on old dining tables it's still a belter of a local, serving Hampshire-brewed ales. House wine £15.
Chef/s: Kevin Chandler. **Open:** all week L 12 to 2.30 (3 Sat, 4 Sun), D 6.30 to 9.30 (10 Fri and Sat, 7 to 9 Sun). **Closed:** 25 Dec. **Meals:** alc (main courses £12 to £22). **Service:** 10%. **Details:** 100 seats. 60 seats outside. Separate bar. Music. Car parking.

Lymington

Egan's

Enjoyable cooking in an old police station
24 Gosport Street, Lymington, SO41 9BE
Tel no: (01590) 676165
Modern British | £28
Cooking score: 2

Lymington's old police station has been home to John and Debbie Egan's smart but 'unstuffy' restaurant since 1999. The cooking, fittingly, stays on the straight and narrow, featuring tried-and-tested combinations updated just enough. The daily changing menu could kick

off with seared scallops with basil oil, chorizo and fennel purée, ahead of rack and shoulder of lamb with redcurrant and rosemary reduction. An assiette of desserts is the way to go for afters. Service is 'attentive, but not cloyingly so'. Prices are fair – no grumbles about the 'old bill' here – and decent house wine is £17.65.
Chef/s: John Egan. **Open:** Tue to Sat L 12 to 2, D 6.30 to 10. **Closed:** Sun, Mon, 2 weeks from 25 Dec. **Meals:** alc (main courses £15 to £23). Set L £14.95 (2 courses) to £17.95. **Service:** not inc. **Details:** 50 seats. 20 seats outside. Separate bar. No music.

Milford on Sea

The Marine

Stylish Art Deco dining
Hurst Road, Milford on Sea, SO41 0PY
Tel no: (01590) 644369
www.themarinerestaurant.co.uk
Modern British | £27
Cooking score: 2

Rising like a liner from the pebbled seafront at Milford, the Art Deco-styled Marine is a hot ticket, with its clean lines and show-stopping sea views. There's a ground-floor café/bar-cum-bistro and a big rooftop terrace, but for the main action head upstairs to the smart, light-filled restaurant with its leather seating, floor-to-ceiling curving glass wall and terrace. The modern, flavour-driven brasserie approach is seafood-led (Mediterranean fish stew or roasted wild sea bass fillet with champ mash, baby spinach and crayfish bisque), but there are meat offerings – perhaps confit Hampshire belly pork or local lamb hotpot – and a vegetarian menu. Wines from £16.50.
Chef/s: Sam Hughes. **Open:** all week L 12 to 2 (2.30 Sat, 3 Sun), Wed to Sat D 6 to 9.30. **Closed:** first two weeks Jan. **Meals:** alc (main courses £13 to £25). Set L and D £17.50 (2 courses) to £22.50. Sun L £17.50. **Service:** not inc. **Details:** 40 seats. 100 seats outside. Separate bar. Wheelchair access. Music. Car parking.

▌New Milton

NEW ENTRY
Vetiver

Aristocratic retreat with a whole new outlook
Chewton Glen, New Milton, BH25 6QS
Tel no: (01425) 275341
www.vetiverchewtonglen.com
Modern British | £55
Cooking score: 5

£5 OFF 🍴 V

'It's a whole new menu and restaurant at Chewton Glen – absolutely lovely' noted a regular to this aristocratic country retreat complete with sweeping drive, immaculate grounds and a high-end spa. While one reporter thought that the place 'still has that sophisticated air of a playground for the minted fiftysomethings', the elegantly remodelled Vetiver (spread across five rooms) does try hard to offer a more up-to-date country house look, with bold-statement contemporary furnishings. Likewise, the kitchen's modern approach comes underpinned by a classical theme, perhaps roast Devonshire duck breast with chicory tarte Tatin and a blood orange sauce or Dover sole, grilled or meunière. Indeed, fish is a star turn, judging by glowing reports of 'memorable' tempura of monkfish cheeks with a 'creative' Vietnamese salad, or a generous portion of roast halibut with capers, parsley root and preserved Amalfi lemons – 'a great combination'. Praise, too, for Sicilian orange cake with lemon thyme ice cream, and for the 'unobtrusive but highly professional' staff. The wine list runs to 700 bins, with a grand tour of the Old and New worlds. Bottles start at £23, though prices soon escalate.
Chef/s: Andrew Du Bourg. **Open:** all week L 12 to 2.30, D 6 to 10. **Meals:** alc (main courses £20 to £44). Set L £20 (2 courses) to £25. Sun L £35. Tasting menu £79.50 (5 courses). **Service:** not inc. **Details:** 160 seats. 40 seats outside. Separate bar. Wheelchair access. Music. Car parking.

▌Petersfield

NEW ENTRY
Annie Jones

Country town restaurant with unexpected charm
Lavant Street, Petersfield, GU32 3EW
Tel no: (01730) 262728
www.anniejones.co.uk
Modern British | £35
Cooking score: 2

£5 OFF

It's easy to walk past Steven Ranson's unassuming neighbourhood restaurant; it looks much like 'any other country town outfit'. However, the boho-chic of the intimate dining room – done out with red walls, bare floorboards and fashionable high-backed leather chairs alongside cushioned pews – is the charming setting for some modern cooking using top-drawer regional produce. Olives and warm homemade focaccia land as you're seated; openers might include belly pork croquette with wild garlic, cep, celeriac and truffle, and to follow, perhaps butter-poached skate wing with mushrooms and jamón linguine. Wines start at £14.95. Out back, there's a surprise – a large terrace and bar/tapas operation.
Chef/s: Steven Ranson. **Open:** Wed to Sun L 12 to 2, Tue to Sun D 6 to 10. **Closed:** Mon, 25 and 26 Dec. **Meals:** Set L £14.95 (2 courses) to £17.95. Set D £27.50 (2 courses) to £35. Sun L £22.50. **Service:** 12.5%. **Details:** 34 seats. 70 seats outside. Separate bar. Music.

JSW

Less-is-more, fined-tuned artistry
20 Dragon Street, Petersfield, GU31 4JJ
Tel no: (01730) 262030
www.jswrestaurant.com
Modern British | £48
Cooking score: 6

🍴 V

Jake Saul Watkins's charmingly discreet restaurant-with-rooms – though housed in a one-time seventeenth-century coaching inn with a full quota of beams and timbers – is a tour de force of effortless, understated modern design. Jake's equally light, uncluttered modern British cooking matches the surroundings, delivering a classy, less-is-more style – everything on the plate has its place. An opener of scallops teamed with cauliflower cheese and cep pearls showcased this intelligent simplicity perfectly, while another starter of pork cooked two ways (with a black pudding crust and with cumin) displayed the immaculate flavour balance that allows seasonal, top-notch produce (often rooted firmly in the region) to shine. Elsewhere, wild turbot might be teamed with Jersey Royals, asparagus and morels, or slow-cooked lamb may make an appearance with root vegetables and garlic croquettes. Canapés, bread, amuse-bouche and petits fours all deliver the same fine-tuned artistry. The wine cellar is a corker (some 900 bins). Lesser-known labels stand up alongside more starry names; bottles start at an accessible £19, while a splendid choice of half-bottles plus by the glass options don't disappoint either. Out back there is a sheltered alfresco terrace.

Chef/s: Jake Saul Watkins. **Open:** Tue to Sat L 12 to 2, D 7 to 9. **Closed:** Sun, Mon, 2 weeks Jan, 2 weeks Jul/Aug. **Meals:** Set L £17.50 (2 courses) to £22.50. Set D £27.50 (2 courses) to £32.50. Tasting menu £52.50 (5 courses) to £65 (7 courses). **Service:** 10%. **Details:** 50 seats. 28 seats outside. No music. Wheelchair access. Car parking. Children over 8 yrs only at D.

Portsmouth

ALSO RECOMMENDED
▲ Abarbistro
58 White Hart Road, Portsmouth, PO1 2JA
Tel no: (023) 9281 1585
www.abarbistro.co.uk
Modern British

On the cobbled camber of Portsmouth's old docks, this cool eatery has been brightly decked out in New England style. A friendly vibe prevails as the kitchen turns out capable Anglo-European classics ranging from potted salted beef and mackerel escabèche (£5) to

fishcakes with hollandaise, moules marinière and corn-fed chicken breast with wild mushroom risotto (£13). For afters, perhaps try apple and pear crumble. The owners also run Camber Wines from the tasting room and shop upstairs. Mark-ups are very fair, with bottles from £13.50. Open all week.

Preston Candover
Purefoy Arms
Welcoming hostelry with first-class food
Alresford Road, Preston Candover, RG25 2EJ
Tel no: (01256) 389777
www.thepurefoyarms.co.uk
Modern European | £27
Cooking score: 3

 £30

'Really appealing place', noted a reporter of this 'beautiful' restored village hostelry. It's all joyfully warm and welcoming inside, thanks in no small part to chef/patron Andres Alemany. He regularly plunders the Hampshire countryside for first-class seasonal produce ('splendid use of local game', for example), although an assortment of 'properly authentic Spanish tapas' such as chorizo picante, a plate of pata negra ham or Montenebro goats' cheese and truffle honey are part of the broadly European repertoire. Potted shrimps and warm crumpets, Cornish crab gratin, wild venison, and confit duck leg with white beans get votes aplenty. Dessert-wise, churros (Spanish doughnuts) with a rich chocolate sauce go down well. Cheeses are English and French; the wine list offers sound drinking possibilities from Europe with prices from £14.50.

Chef/s: Andres Alemany. **Open:** Tue to Sun L 12 to 3 (4 Sun), Tue to Sat D 6 to 10. **Closed:** Mon, 26 Dec, 1 Jan. **Meals:** alc (main courses £10 to £25). **Service:** not inc. **Details:** 50 seats. 60 seats outside. Music. Car parking. No children after 7pm on Sun.

Romsey
The Three Tuns
Local with updated pub classics
58 Middlebridge Street, Romsey, SO51 8HL
Tel no: (01794) 512639
www.the3tunsromsey.co.uk
Modern British | £25
Cooking score: 2

From the outside the Three Tuns exudes a real sense of tradition. It is still very much a pub, with real ales for those just wanting a drink, plus decent bar snacks, but the dining area moves things up a notch or two with updated pub classics (braised beef, mushroom and horseradish pie, gammon, duck egg and chips) and more ambitious ideas. Expect starters such as salad of Romsey tomatoes with Rosary goats' cheese and Bloody Mary vinaigrette, then hake fillet with potato gnocchi, braised lettuce hearts, peas and baby onions, and lemon shortbread fool for dessert. Wines from £14.50.
Chef/s: Damian Brown and Andrew Freeman. **Open:** all week L 12 to 2.30 (3 Fri, Sat and Sun), D 6 to 9 (9.30 Fri and Sat). **Closed:** 25 Dec. **Meals:** alc (main courses £10 to £19). **Service:** not inc. **Details:** 50 seats. 30 seats outside. Separate bar. Wheelchair access. Music. Car parking.

Southampton
The White Star Tavern
Lively urban bar with all-day food
28 Oxford Street, Southampton, SO14 3DJ
Tel no: (023) 8082 1990
www.whitestartavern.co.uk
Modern British | £25
Cooking score: 1

The White Star was once a hotel for ocean-going passengers; it's now a modern pub-with-rooms. The opened-up space is set around a large bar and blends original features with contemporary design and comforts like chill-out lounges. It has a bustling appeal. All-day brasserie-style menus range from breakfast to small-plate options at lunch (tempura squid with Bloody Mary mayo) and heartier mains like fishcake served with leek purée, spinach, poached egg and hollandaise. A concise global wine list starts at £16.
Chef/s: Stewart Hellsten. **Open:** all week L 12 to 2.20 (3 Fri, 4 Sat and Sun), D 6 to 9.30 (10 Fri and Sat, 9 Sun). **Closed:** 25 to 27 Dec. **Meals:** alc (main courses £11 to £19). Sun L £13. **Service:** not inc. **Details:** 70 seats. 20 seats outside. Wheelchair access. Music.

Southsea
Montparnasse
Smart, inventive and much-loved bistro
103 Palmerston Road, Southsea, PO5 3PS
Tel no: (023) 9281 6754
www.bistromontparnasse.co.uk
Modern European | £38
Cooking score: 4

'A complimentary drink on arrival, delicious amuse-bouches, succulent steaks, unusual little accompaniments, seasonal vegetables, superb local fish' – just some of the things regulars love about this smartly appointed fixture of the Southsea scene. Nikolas Facey's sensibly restrained fixed-price menus show class and invention, moving from scallop velouté with black pudding to fillet steak with Puy lentils and a horseradish and thyme croquette, then on to pomegranate parfait with marshmallow. The kitchen also respects the seasons by offering oxtail and mushroom pudding laced with Guinness gravy or maple-roasted breast of pheasant with caramelised walnuts in winter, and welcoming summer with broad bean, carrot and French bean charlotte or fillet of new season's lamb with herb-crusted shoulder, Anna potatoes and fennel jam. 'It's always just the right amount to savour and enjoy' concluded one devotee. Special occasions and gourmet evenings go down well, helped along by a creditable wine list that offers sound drinking from £18.50.
Chef/s: Nikolas Facey. **Open:** Tue to Sat L 12 to 1.30, D 7 to 9.30. **Closed:** Sun, Mon, 25 and 26 Dec, 1 Jan. **Meals:** Set L and D £32.50 (2 courses) to £37.50. **Service:** not inc. **Details:** 30 seats. Music.

Restaurant 27

High-definition French food to rave about
Burgoyne Road, Southsea, PO5 2JF
Tel no: (023) 9287 6272
www.restaurant27.com
Modern French | £40
Cooking score: 5

In days gone by, 27 was a chapel and, following that, the gymnasium of the local grammar school. Since 2009, it has achieved another kind of apotheosis, having been home to Kevin Bingham's authoritative neighbourhood restaurant, the kind of place that people travel miles for, and write to us copiously about. Bingham's style is all about concentrating the essence of fine ingredients in novel, lightly French-influenced preparations that are described with a minimum of flourish on the tersely written menus. Strange combinations work well, as when delicately melting foie gras is cut with the bright note of passion fruit, and given an extra dimension with chorizo. Another well-worked starter is a chicken and carrot ballottine in crab dressing, with added texture from shallot and chervil granola. Mascarpone may be an odd thing to find in a fish dish, but it lends its gentle richness here to sea bass and langoustine, while the utterly memorable 30-hour pork belly, served perhaps with rhubarb, aubergine and rosemary, is close to becoming one of the south coast's most widely reputed dishes. More rosemary may turn up in the shortbread to accompany a lush, custardy fig trifle, or try poached apple with Gorgonzola ice-cream. A concise, broadly based wine list opens with Languedoc Sauvignon and Merlot at £19.50.
Chef/s: Kevin Bingham. **Open:** Sun L 12 to 2.30, Wed to Sat D 7 to 9.30. **Closed:** Mon, Tue. **Meals:** Set D £40. Sun L £27. **Service:** not inc. **Details:** 34 seats.

▌Stockbridge

The Greyhound Inn

Good looks and foodie aspirations
31 High Street, Stockbridge, SO20 6EY
Tel no: (01264) 810833
www.thegreyhound.info
Modern British | £35
Cooking score: 4

While the name and exterior suggest a traditional hostelry, the Greyhound is in reality a relaxed restaurant-with-rooms. Set on the long main street of England's fly-fishing capital, and with the river Test flowing through the back garden, this former fifteenth-century inn has bucketloads of charm. Beams and timbers, inglenooks and scrubbed-wood tables deliver just the right amount of character, while fashionable leather dining chairs and a lounge kitted out with contemporary sofas tell a different story. The kitchen takes an ambitious modern approach, with a light, clean-cut touch and an eye for presentation, delivering top-drawer braised shin and seared fillet of Hampshire beef teamed with root vegetables, tarragon and oxtail consommé, roasted bone marrow and truffled potato tortellini. Fish has its say too, perhaps featuring seared halibut fillet served alongside salsify, violet artichokes, fennel, and broad bean and tomato salsa. A well-considered global wine list gives France top billing and opens at £15.75.
Chef/s: Alan Haughie. **Open:** all week L 12 to 2 (2.30 Fri to Sun), Mon to Sat D 7 to 9 (9.30 Fri and Sat). **Meals:** alc (main courses £12 to £21). **Service:** not inc. **Details:** 45 seats. 20 seats outside. Separate bar. Car parking.

Stuckton
The Three Lions
Old-fashioned English auberge
Stuckton, SP6 2HF
Tel no: (01425) 652489
www.thethreelionsrestaurant.co.uk
Anglo-French | £40
Cooking score: 5

£5 OFF 🛏 V

Quirky, homely and unashamedly retro, Mike and Jayne Womersley's self-styled 'English auberge' has a special place in the annals of New Forest hospitality – a genial farmhouse in sylvan acres, with fine food, serious wines and a personable frame of mind. Look beyond the unsophisticated, time warp surrounds (garish woodchip walls, Provençal-print curtains, dated pine furniture) and there is much to enjoy here. Mike is unfazed by fashion and does things his own way when it comes to matters gastronomic – from richly nutritious soups (leek, asparagus and chives, say), home-cured gravadlax and homemade vermicelli with ceps, to lime chicken with crispy skin, a dish of Creedy Carver duck with blueberries or a perfectly rendered offal-fest of liver, kidney and faggot with a heap of Puy lentils. Ingredients are superlative and sauces are textbook, although dinky extra helpings of vegetables provide 'more colour than taste or satisfaction'. To finish, the hot chocolate pudding is legendary, but pear and frangipane tart and an up-to-the-minute pairing of seared pineapple with liquorice ice cream have also been deemed 'spectacular'. There are locally brewed Ringwood ales at the refurbished bar, and the auspicious, 150-bin wine list is a model of excellence for serious wine fans and bargain-hunters alike. It features reputable blue-chip growers in abundance, bright young sparks aplenty and a host of prestigious house selections from £14.75 (£3.50 a glass).
Chef/s: Mike Womersley. **Open:** Tue to Sun L 12 to 2, Tue to Sat D 7 to 9. **Closed:** Mon, last 2 weeks Feb.
Meals: alc (main courses £19 to £27). Set L £21.50.

Set D £26.50. **Service:** not inc. **Details:** 60 seats. 10 seats outside. Separate bar. Wheelchair access. Music. Car parking.

Totford
The Woolpack Inn
Stylish pub with alluring food
Totford, SO24 9TJ
Tel no: (0845) 2938066
www.thewoolpackinn.co.uk
Modern British | £25
Cooking score: 2

🛏

Following the departure of Jarina and Brian Ahearn, there has been something of a shake-up at this smart pub-with-rooms. It still has the air of a village local and, with its contemporary look, makes a distinctive yet relaxed hostelry. However, Ryan Stacey has now been promoted to take over the kitchen; his food strikes many alluring British chords, from pub classics of fish and chips and bangers and mash, to carefully worked contemporary ideas such as roasted cauliflower and macaroni cheese with chilli crumb, or sea trout fillet with courgette and carrot linguine, Jersey Royals and watercress pesto. Wines from £16.
Chef/s: Ryan Stacey. **Open:** all week L 12 to 2.30 (3 Sat and Sun), D 6.30 to 9 (5 to 8 Sun). **Meals:** alc (main courses £10 to £12). **Service:** 10%.
Details: 50 seats. 60 seats outside. Music. Car parking.

West Meon
The Thomas Lord
Rustic charm and local fare
High Street, West Meon, GU32 1LN
Tel no: (01730) 829244
www.thethomaslord.co.uk
British | £30
Cooking score: 3

'A real out-and-out pub that does good food – no separate dining room (just a small library room)' enthused one local about this off-the-beaten-track gem. Cricketing memorabilia is a reminder that the hostelry is named after the

founder of Lord's. It's displayed amid a mix of dark beams, scuffed floorboards, scrubbed-wood tables and old chairs, evening candles and winter fires. The unpretentious menu features seasonal ingredients from small-scale producers around Britain (especially Hampshire), with herbs and vegetables from the pub's own potager. These top-notch ingredients star in a starter of potted Hampshire game with redcurrant and rosemary jelly, or an equally big-hearted main of river Test smoked eel and bacon with mash and parsley cream sauce. Local also extends to real ales; wines from £15.75.
Chef/s: Gareth Longhurst. **Open:** Tue to Sun L 12 to 2 (3 Fri and Sat, 4 Sun), Tue to Sat D 7 to 9 (9.30 Fri and Sat). **Closed:** Mon, 25 Dec, 1 Jan. **Meals:** alc (main courses £13 to £21). Set L and D £9.95 (2 courses). **Service:** not inc. **Details:** 70 seats. 40 seats outside. Separate bar. No music. Wheelchair access. Car parking.

Winchester

The Black Rat
Lovely food awaits
88 Chesil Street, Winchester, SO23 0HX
Tel no: (01962) 844465
www.theblackrat.co.uk
Modern British | £40
Cooking score: 5

Don't let the town boozer-like exterior fool you – the interior is a vision of comfortable rural chic, with just a touch of quirkiness. Indeed, the Black Rat is a testament to the single-minded persistence of proprietor David Nicholson and is warmly appreciated by its faithful followers. What awaits, according to one reporter, is 'lovely food'. That report singled out starters of scallops seared in lobster oil and served with cured morcilla, crushed celeriac and lovage velouté, a mirin-glazed smoked mackerel 'matched beautifully' with pork and apple croquettes, and a slow-cooked egg on Périgord truffle with broccoli done three ways – 'all three so enjoyable we wanted to start again'. Main courses capitalise on local (and not so local) supplies, from Balmoral venison Wellington with locally

foraged mushrooms, via lamb neck fillet with seared shoulder, pancetta and potato terrine, spinach and dried onion, to whole roast partridge with morteau sausage, chestnut mushrooms, creamed potatoes, a chicory tarte fine and a sauce of lapsang souchong that 'brought out the delicate flavour of the bird quite amazingly'. Well-constructed desserts draw praise too, including an ingenious blood-orange sorbet with a 'contrasting yet complementary' herb salad. Wines from £21.
Chef/s: Jamie Stapleton-Burns. **Open:** Sat and Sun 12 to 2.15, all week D 7 to 9.30. **Closed:** 23 Dec to 7 Jan, 1 to 21 Apr, first 2 weeks Oct. **Meals:** alc (main courses £17 to £22). Set L £22.95 (2 courses) to £25.95. **Service:** not inc. **Details:** 40 seats. 18 seats outside. Separate bar. Music. Children over 14 yrs only.

The Chesil Rectory
Historical head-turner with modern food
1 Chesil Street, Winchester, SO23 0HU
Tel no: (01962) 851555
www.chesilrectory.co.uk
Modern British | £30
Cooking score: 4

With its centuries-old good looks, the timber-framed Chesil certainly turns heads. The fifteenth-century dwelling was bequeathed to the city by Mary Tudor and it delivers bags of original features across two floors: dark oak beams and timbers, creaking floorboards, ancient doorways and open fireplaces. But that's where ye olde England ends. A thoughtful modern makeover adds style via classily upholstered chairs, buttoned banquettes and vintage chandeliers. Damian Brown's kitchen takes a correspondingly modern approach that's admirably centred around quality regional produce. It delivers punchy flavours in dishes such as roasted rib of Hampshire beef accompanied by cream layered potatoes, spinach and parsley purée and red wine sauce; a lighter touch might be seen in pan-fried organic salmon served alongside potato dumplings, braised lettuce, peas and shallots. Friendly service contributes

to the relaxed vibe, and the wine list has plenty of invigorating drinking. Bottles start at £19.95.
Chef/s: Damian Brown. **Open:** all week L 12 to 2.20 (3 Sat and Sun), D 6 to 9.30 (10 Fri and Sat, 9 Sun). **Closed:** 25 and 26 Dec, bank hols. **Meals:** alc (main courses £13 to £20). Set L and D £15.95 (2 courses) to £19.95. **Service:** not inc. **Details:** 65 seats. Separate bar. Music. Children at L only.

■ Woodlands
Hotel TerraVina
Celebrating the best of food and wine
174 Woodlands Road, Woodlands, SO40 7GL
Tel no: (023) 8029 3784
www.hotelterravina.co.uk
Modern European | £35
Cooking score: 4

🍷 ⊏ V

At ease in its attractive Victorian house on the edge of the New Forest, the Bassets' Californian-style boutique hotel exudes an assured informality and charm. It's an enterprise that enthusiastically celebrates the best in food and wine (Gérard Basset is one of the UK's leading wine experts). On the food front, Neil Cooper opts for distinctly ambitious cooking by bringing on board black olive powder, textures of onion and pear, smoked potato purée and other modish extras. Elsewhere, smoked haddock is given some Asian lustre by being served Thai green curry-style with basil linguine, fennel and brown shrimp butter, while a starter of pigeon is teamed with roasted parsnip purée, kale, red chicory, wild mushrooms, celeriac and dark chocolate. As well as desserts such as lemon sponge roll with passion-fruit gel, there are good regional cheeses. The innovative, gently priced wine list (from £16) is pure delight, arranged by style and plundering the world's vineyards for fascinating flavours.
Chef/s: Neil Cooper. **Open:** all week L 12 to 2, D 7 to 9.45 (9.30 Sun). **Meals:** alc (main courses £20 to £26). Set L £20.50 (2 courses) to £27. Sun L £20.50 (2 courses) to £27. **Service:** not inc. **Details:** 56 seats. 26 seats outside. Separate bar. No music. Wheelchair access. Car parking.

🍴 STREET LIFE

Call it local distinctiveness, call it *terroir*, or simply call it an antidote to supermarket uniformity, but the food at Britain's traditional street markets offers a refreshingly earthy introduction to indigenous produce.

Take the Saturday market at Swaffham in Norfolk, where the fish stalls display Brancaster mussels in winter, marsh samphire in summer, and Cromer crabs whenever the sea's calm enough to land them. Or try Bury market in Greater Manchester, with its bulbous black pudding served hot with mustard and its freshly chopped 'pot herbs' ready for Lancashire hotpots.

There's history aplenty too; many markets date from charters granted over eight centuries ago. Ripon's Thursday market, with its admirable pie-makers and Dales cheeses, is still officially opened by a bell-man at 11am.

Food inextricably linked with an area is proudly exhibited: laverbread in Swansea; pork pies and Stilton in Melton Mowbray. Nothing beats a stroll along the stalls to hone the appetite before lunch.

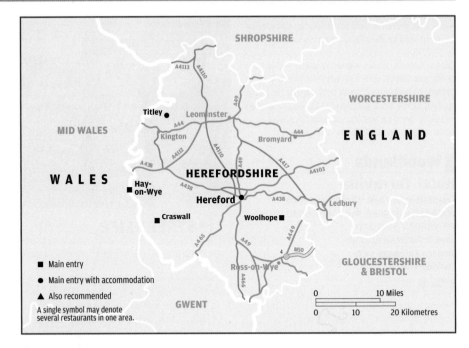

SHROPSHIRE
WORCESTERSHIRE
MID WALES
Titley
Leominster
Kington
A44
Bromyard
ENGLAND
WALES
HEREFORDSHIRE
Hay-on-Wye
Hereford
Ledbury
Craswall
Woolhope
M50
Ross-on-Wye
GLOUCESTERSHIRE & BRISTOL
GWENT

■ Main entry
● Main entry with accommodation
▲ Also recommended
A single symbol may denote several restaurants in one area.

0 ————— 10 Miles
0 —— 10 —— 20 Kilometres

▌Craswall

NEW ENTRY
The Bull's Head
Welcoming inn that's worth seeking out
Craswall, HR2 0PN
Tel no: (01981) 510616
www.bullsheadcraswall.co.uk
Modern British | £28
Cooking score: 2
£5 OFF

It's well worth seeking out this old drovers' inn in the shadows of the Black Mountains just a few miles south-east of Hay. Run by husband and wife team Charles and Kathryn Mackintosh, this simply decorated country pub serves up a short menu of Mediterranean-influenced dishes to appreciative weekenders. Self-taught cook Charles starts with the best-quality ingredients, from Hereford beef to fruity Italian olive oil, and creates rustic favourites such as roasted Piedmont peppers, slow-roast shoulder of lamb or home-cured bresaola. Desserts are a particular highlight, including a clementine cake with candied clementine that could give even a highly trained pâtissier a run for his money. House wine £15.50.
Chef/s: Charles Mackintosh. **Open:** Fri to Sun L 12 to 2, Fri and Sat D 7 to close. **Closed:** Mon to Thur, 3 weeks Jan/Feb. **Meals:** alc (main courses £11 to £23). **Service:** not inc. **Details:** 34 seats. 20 seats outside. No music.

▌Hay-on-Wye

ALSO RECOMMENDED
▲ Richard Booth's Bookshop Café
44 Lion Street, Hay-on-Wye, HR3 5AA
Tel no: (01497) 820322
www.boothbooks.co.uk
Modern British

While away an hour browsing the shelves of Hay's largest bookshop before stopping for lunch in the split-level café. Kick off with a properly spiced Bloody Mary, the perfect accompaniment to a patatas bravas hash with chorizo and bacon. The frequently changing menu features seasonal vegetables in warming soups (£3.75) and vibrant salads, and there's always a fish dish, such as smoked mackerel fishcakes (£6.75) or grilled octopus pepped up with wasabi vinaigrette. Save room for something sweet, perhaps a divine spiced orange brownie, or go savoury with a plate of local cheeses. The town of books has been short on decent eateries, until now, and queues are not unknown. House wine £16.

▌Hereford
Castle House

New twists in a swanky setting
Castle Street, Hereford, HR1 2NW
Tel no: (01432) 356321
www.castlehse.co.uk
Modern British | £32
Cooking score: 3

£5 OFF

Though it sounds like a country estate, Castle House is a Regency town house not far from Hereford's cathedral. The cooking, although based on well-tried combinations, contrives to introduce new twists and original touches, as in scallops teamed with pink peppercorn gnocchi, cauliflower purée and orange sauce, or a chicken breast with vanilla and lime-flavoured sweet potato mash, char-grilled pineapple, sweet-and-sour peppers and pak choi. There are straightforward dishes – reporters have praised a cheese soufflé and 'first-rate meat', perhaps loin and sticky shoulder of lamb with onion purée, fondant potato, spinach and tomato confit. However, there are complaints too, with some dishes' parts not making a ravishingly exciting whole. Service is polite and willing. Wines from £16.50.
Chef/s: Claire Nicholls. Open: all week L 12 to 2 (12.30 Sun), D 6.30 to 9.30 (9 Sun). Meals: alc (main courses £12 to £24). Sun L £27. Tasting menu £50 (7 courses). Service: not inc. Details: 32 seats. 18 seats outside. Separate bar. Wheelchair access. Music. Car parking.

▌Titley
The Stagg Inn

Foodie gem worth travelling to
Titley, HR5 3RL
Tel no: (01544) 230221
www.thestagg.co.uk
Modern British | £33
Cooking score: 5

🛏 V

For the last 15 years, Steve and Nicola Reynolds' pub has been a foodie destination, despite its remote location. It's an unassuming little gem with a homely feel, good-humoured and dedicated to the principles of real food. Steve Reynolds oversees a regularly changing seasonal menu and his cooking gets straight to the point. What he is good at is familiar combinations of quality ingredients, mostly sourced from a network of well-chosen local suppliers and cooked with care. Starters such as a game terrine with horseradish cream and beetroot pickle come with homemade toasted sourdough bread, for example. Main courses are given extra shine by pedigree components, as in a dish of Madgett's Farm duck breast and confit leg served with roast winter vegetables, potato croquette and Robinson's cider. To conclude, there might be a cinnamon rice pudding with mulled wine pear, or chocolate mousse, sorbet and ice cream. This is unaffected cooking where incidentals charm too: good bread, the fantastic regional specimens on the mighty cheese trolley and the care of customers. It's all backed up by local beers, ciders and perrys, and by a quality wine list that offers sound drinking at easy prices (from £14.50).
Chef/s: Steve Reynolds. Open: Tue to Sun L 12 to 2 (2.30 Sun), Tue to Sat D 6.30 to 9 (9.30 Sat). Closed: Mon, 25 to 27 Dec, 2 weeks Jan/Feb, 2 weeks Nov. Meals: alc (main courses £17 to £23). Sun L £19.80. Service: not inc. Details: 70 seats. 20 seats outside. Separate bar. No music. Car parking.

Welwyn

The Wellington

Modern British
1 High Street, Welwyn, AL6 9LZ
Tel no: (01438) 714036
www.wellingtonatwelwyn.co.uk

'A lovely place to go for a meal. It has a relaxed atmosphere and the service is excellent.'

Woolhope

The Butchers Arms

Rustic pub with fresh flavours
Woolhope, HR1 4RF
Tel no: (01432) 860281
www.butchersarmswoolhope.com
Modern European | £23
Cooking score: 4

Stephen Bull's agreeable country boozer plays the part of a busy local, especially when the sun shines and the garden comes into its own, but these days it is better known for its food. When lunch includes 'unusual but very tasty' haggis fritters with beetroot relish and 'a superb meaty game pie with winter vegetable mash', it is clear that cooking is taken seriously. While much is made of local sourcing of ingredients, inspiration for dishes comes from wider-spread European roots, perhaps in the form of boned sardine bruschetta with Sicilian stuffing and olive vinaigrette, or potato gnocchi with tomato sauce, cashew nut and rocket pesto. Elsewhere, 'hearty but precisely cooked' has described roast breast of partridge served with both a winter vegetable and a potato dauphinoise. To finish, there's warm ginger cake and treacle toffee ice cream or a 'quite delicious' almond frangipane and damson sorbet. An interesting wine list starts at £14.
Chef/s: Fran Snell. **Open:** Tue to Sun L 12 to 2, Tue to Sat D 6 to 9. **Closed:** Mon, 25 Dec. **Meals:** alc (main courses £11 to £17). Sun L £18.50 (2 courses) to £24. **Service:** not inc. **Details:** 60 seats. 30 seats outside. Separate bar. Car parking.

GOOD BRITISH PUDS

'What an excellent thing is an English pudding,' wrote a Frenchman in the 17th century. 'They make them 50 several ways'. Indeed we do: be it apple crumble, Sussex pond pudding, junket or Bakewell tart, in recent years traditional British puddings have been making a comeback on menus across the board, from pubs to top-flight restaurants.

St John in Clerkenwell serves apple crumble and custard, or Eccles cakes. **Pollen Street Social** in Mayfair boasts goats' milk rice pudding, and Knightsbridge's **Dinner by Heston Blumenthal** has English desserts spanning four centuries with the likes of taffety tart and lemon suet pudding. You can't eat anywhere in the Lake District without finding sticky toffee pudding on the menu or, as **L'Enclume** call it, 'stiffy tacky pudding', and they've been serving hot marmalade pudding with Drambuie custard at the **Three Chimneys** on Skye ever since they opened in 1984.

These puddings are not just old favourites rediscovered, but honourable traditions refined and reinvented. Forget the stodgy suet roly poly of school dinner memory and think instead of the best of British.

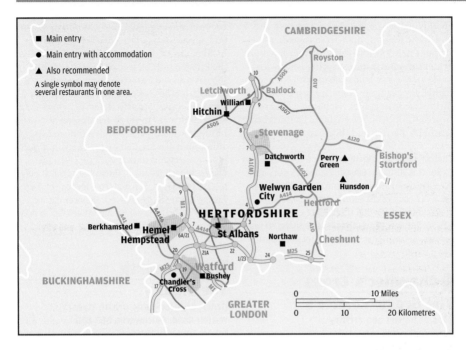

- ■ Main entry
- ● Main entry with accommodation
- ▲ Also recommended

A single symbol may denote
several restaurants in one area.

■ Berkhamsted
The Gatsby
Deco decadence and artful food
Rex Cinema, 97 High Street, Berkhamsted,
HP4 2DG
Tel no: (01442) 870403
www.thegatsby.net
Modern European | £36
Cooking score: 2

Berkhamsted's bright young things mingle
with movie buffs at this upbeat bar/restaurant
within the fabulously restored Rex Cinema –
a wonder of Art Deco flamboyance, complete
with extravagant chandeliers, ornate mirrored
columns and sculpted ceilings. It can get a
touch chaotic when blockbusters are being
screened, and service plays it casual, but the
place holds up well and the kitchen shows its
modern sensibilities with artfully crafted
dishes such as spiced escabèche of mackerel
with pearl barley and coriander or roast duck
breast with sweet pickled beetroot, red onion

tart and orange reduction. To conclude,
Granny Smith tarte fine with Calvados crème
fraîche is a speciality. Wines from £15.95.
Chef/s: Matthew Salt. **Open:** Mon to Sat L 12 to
2.30, D 5.30 to 10.30. Sun 12 to 9.30. **Closed:** 25 and
26 Dec. **Meals:** alc (main courses £16 to £26). Set L
and D £14.95 (2 courses) to £20.90. **Service:** 12.5%.
Details: 106 seats. 56 seats outside. Separate bar.
Music. No children after 6.

■ Bushey
St James
Doing Bushey proud
30 High Street, Bushey, WD23 3HL
Tel no: (020) 8950 2480
www.stjamesrestaurant.co.uk
Modern European | £28
Cooking score: 1

V

'Hallelujahs!' all round for this hard-working
local asset opposite St James' Church, which
has been doing Bushey proud since 1997.
Much is down to gleeful host Alfonso La Cava

and his big personality, but the kitchen also makes the most of super-fresh ingredients – strips of richly sauced calf's liver with red onion compote, rump of spring lamb with sauce vierge or whole sea bass with roasted fennel, for example. There are also some distinctive re-treads of celeb-chef classics (seared scallops on spiced dhal). Desserts bring crumbles, parfaits and cheesecakes. House wine is £15.95.

Chef/s: Matt Cook. **Open:** all week L 12 to 2.30, Mon to Sat D 6.30 to 10. **Closed:** 25 and 26 Dec, bank hols. **Meals:** alc (main courses £17 to £21). Set L £15.95 (2 courses) to £20.95. Set D £17.95 (2 courses) to £22.95. Sun L £20.95 (2 courses) to £25.50. **Service:** 12.5%. **Details:** 100 seats. 20 seats outside. Separate bar. Wheelchair access. Music. Car parking.

▌Chandler's Cross
The Grove, Colette's
Bags of impact and artistry
Chandler's Cross, WD3 4TG
Tel no: (01923) 296015
www.thegrove.co.uk
Modern British | £65
Cooking score: 5
£5 OFF 🛏

Now infamous as a playground for footballers and their wives, the sprawling Grove complex started life as an 'out of town' bolt-hole for the Earls of Clarendon. The old aristocracy wouldn't recognise the place now, especially if they stumbled into Colette's – a bespoke restaurant emblazoned with huge canvases, sculptures and fantastical chandeliers. It may be OTT, but supporters reckon that chef Russell Bateman is at the 'top of his game', delivering highly complex ideas with bags of impact and artistry. He is also fleshing out his network of dedicated suppliers and plundering the Grove's walled garden for seasonal pickings – how about a pretty plate of poached and roasted lobster with heirloom carrots, purple potato, fennel and star anise, or 'eight-spice' squab pigeon with turnip, rocket and honey from the estate? Elsewhere, organic pork gets the jerk treatment with pineapple,

coconut and coriander, and Cumbrian rose veal appears as a tartare with brioche, winter truffles, mustard and quail's egg yolk. Finally, the kitchen puts on its party hat for desserts such as rose and pistachio meringue with rhubarb and rose-scented crème anglaise. The comprehensive wine list deserves a cheer for its commitment to small 'handmade' producers and organic/biodynamic names, although it's bedevilled by premiership prices. House selections start at £27 (£7.50 a glass).

Chef/s: Russell Bateman. **Open:** Tue to Sat D only 6.30 to 10. **Closed:** Sun and Mon. **Meals:** Set D £65. Tasting menu £80 (7 courses). **Service:** not inc. **Details:** 42 seats. Separate bar. Wheelchair access. Music. Car parking. Children over 12 yrs only.

▌Datchworth
The Tilbury
Generous, good-value British classics
Watton Road, Datchworth, SG3 6TB
Tel no: (01438) 815550
www.thetilbury.co.uk
Modern British | £29
Cooking score: 3
£5 OFF   £30 🛐

Regulars are clearly delighted to have Paul Bloxham's village pub close to home. And what's not to like? Real ales on tap mean drinkers are still welcome, and eager diners are drawn by the heavy commitment to local, seasonal produce, generous portions and good pricing. The regularly changing menu is peppered with ideas that attempt to please all palates, a policy that seems to work well. Upbeat British classics could include the likes of whole dressed Dorset crab mayonnaise, a plate of Burnham Green Old Spot pig with sage and onion and cider gravy, or roast rump of Herdwick mutton with braised white onion, spinach and fine capers. Puds are a good call, too – perhaps walnut and treacle tart. The short global wine list opens at £16.95.

Chef/s: Paul Bloxham and Ben Crick. **Open:** all week L 12 to 3 (4 Sun), Mon to Sat D 6 to 11. **Meals:** alc (main courses £11 to £26). Set L and D £13.95 (2 courses) to £17.95. Sun L £17.95. **Service:** not inc. **Details:** 70 seats. 40 seats outside. Separate bar. Wheelchair access. Music. Car parking.

Hemel Hempstead
Restaurant 65
Admirable local eatery with real pride
65 High Street, Old Town, Hemel Hempstead, HP1 3AF
Tel no: (01442) 239010
www.restaurant65.com
Modern British | £27
Cooking score: 2

A godsend on the fringes of Hemel Hempstead's foodie wasteland, Grant and Gina Young's pint-sized restaurant runs along merrily in a converted butcher's shop opposite the Old Town Hall & Arts Centre. The couple take care of just about everything themselves, putting in the hours and delivering capable food with a real sense of pride. Meals may take time, but it's worth the wait – especially when the minuscule kitchen can deliver real value in the shape of roasted beetroot, walnut and goats' cheese tart with beetroot purée, rump of lamb with minted mash or seared sea bream with tapenade, tomato dressing and pumpkin-seed pesto. House wine is £13.95.
Chef/s: Grant Young. **Open:** Tue to Fri and Sun L 12 to 2 (12.30 to 2.30 Sun), Tue to Sat D 7 to 9.30. **Closed:** Mon, first week Jan, second week Jul. **Meals:** Set L £14.95 (2 courses) to £19.95. Set D

£21.95 (2 courses) to £26.95. Sun L £12.95. **Service:** not inc. **Details:** 32 seats. Music. Car parking.

Hitchin
NEW ENTRY
Hermitage Rd
Sparky food and feel-good vibes
20-21 Hermitage Road, Hitchin, SG5 1BT
Tel no: (01462) 433603
www.hermitagerd.co.uk
Modern British | £21
Cooking score: 2

With the White Horse in Brancaster Staithe and the Fox at Willian under their belts (see entries), Cliff Nye and co have transformed Hitchin's legendary Hermitage Ballroom into a feel-good restaurant and all-day bar. The cavernous, high-ceilinged interior with its brick walls and iconic arched window is the setting for sparky brasserie-style food, from deli boards and 'larder' plates (crisp tomato and lemon thyme risotto balls) to grills and seafood – Brancaster bivalves, and seared sea trout with flageolet bean and tomato ragù or grilled hake in a broth with clams, squid and red chard. To finish, try fruit crumble. East Anglian ales, and wines from £16.50.
Chef/s: Kumour Uddin. **Open:** Wed to Sun L 12 to 2.30 (3.30 Sun), D 6.30 to 10 (9 Sun). **Closed:** Mon, Tue. **Meals:** alc (main courses £9 to £21). **Service:** not inc. **Details:** 150 seats. Separate bar. Wheelchair access. Music.

Hogpits Bottom
READERS RECOMMEND
Bricklayers Arms
Modern British
Hogpits Bottom, HP3 0PH
Tel no: (01442) 833322
www.bricklayersarms.com
'The atmosphere was really good, the service excellent and above all the food was outstanding.'

Hunsdon

ALSO RECOMMENDED
▲ Fox & Hounds

2 High Street, Hunsdon, SG12 8NH
Tel no: (01279) 843999
www.foxandhounds-hunsdon.co.uk
Modern European

A summertime terrace and big, child-friendly garden are assets at this terrific, 'happily run' pub/restaurant a few miles from Ware. Eat in the convivial bar or the smart chandeliered dining room from a robust daily menu promising the likes of char-grilled squid with chermoula (£7.95), pappardelle with rich chicken liver ragù or saddle of venison with parsnip purée, red cabbage and wild mushrooms (£19.95). For afters, consider apple tarte fine or homemade ice cream. Well-kept, locally brewed real ales and carefully chosen wines from £15. No food Sun D or Mon.

Northaw

The Sun at Northaw

Terrific inn packed with regional delights
1 Judges Hill, Northaw, EN6 4NL
Tel no: (01707) 655507
www.thesunatnorthaw.co.uk
British | £29
Cooking score: 3

Opened up and remodelled it may be, but there's a friendly, unpretentious charm to this white-painted inn that anchors the village green. Oliver Smith is a fervent supporter of seasonal and regional British ingredients, and most of the kitchen's building blocks come from named suppliers in Hertfordshire and surrounding counties – anything from Mersea Island rock oysters to Suffolk guinea fowl (served with roasted parsnips, bacon and thyme). Salsify fritters with homemade ketchup, smoked cod's roe on toast with watercress and lemon, and mains such as whole roasted lemon sole with sprouting broccoli, fennel and wild chervil help reinforce the comforting, domestic atmosphere. Date pudding with sticky toffee sauce and salted caramel ice cream is as good as it gets. All this, plus good local cheeses, regional ales and handpicked wines (from £17).
Chef/s: Oliver Smith. **Open:** Tue to Sun L 12 to 3 (4 Sun), Tue to Sat D 6 to 10. **Closed:** Mon. **Meals:** alc (main courses £13 to £25). Set L £12.50 (2 courses) to £16.50. Sun L £26.50 (2 courses) to £32.50. **Service:** not inc. **Details:** 80 seats. 60 seats outside. Separate bar. Wheelchair access. Music. Car parking.

Perry Green

ALSO RECOMMENDED
▲ The Hoops Inn

Perry Green, SG10 6EF
Tel no: (01279) 843568
www.hoops-inn.co.uk
British

Dedicated to feeding and watering visitors who descend on the nearby Henry Moore Foundation, this admirable Victorian boozer has a big appetite for honest British grub. Homemade pies are a top call, but the menu also promises seasonal treats including grilled mackerel with heritage beetroot and horseradish (£7.50), 'flavoursome' beef and Adnams ale casserole (£13.95), juicy roe deer burgers, and puds such as rhubarb Bakewell tart. Also look out for chutney contests and other foodie events. Good ales and gluggable wines from £16.95. Closed Mon and Christmas to Easter, though as we went to press the restaurant was considering whether to remain open during this time, so do check their website.

Also Recommended

Also recommended entries are not scored but we think they are worth a visit.

∎ St Albans

Darcy's

A lot to like
2 Hatfield Road, St Albans, AL1 3RP
Tel no: (01727) 730777
www.darcysrestaurant.co.uk
Modern European | £40
Cooking score: 2
£5 OFF

There's a lot to like about Ruth Hurren's restaurant, just off St Albans' main drag. Décor is smart, clean-lined and modern, and the cooking style is all-embracing, a kind of British eclecticism that mixes Pacific rim (fried soft-shell crab and green mango with lime and chilli dressing) with traditional favourites (game terrine with piccalilli). Sea bass, too, makes an impact, served with spiced aubergine and cucumber and mint yoghurt, while a well-reported grilled kangaroo comes teamed with roasted beetroots, Wobbly Bottom goats' cheese and dukkah. For dessert, Oreo cookie bombe has been praised, as has 'charming, friendly and efficient' service. Wines from £15.90.
Chef/s: David Christie. **Open:** all week L 12 to 2.30 (3 Sun), D 6 to 9.30 (9 Sun). **Closed:** 26 Dec, 1 Jan. **Meals:** alc (main courses £12 to £23). Set L and D £12.90 (2 courses) to £15.90. Sun L £16.90 (2 courses) to £19.90. **Service:** 12.5%. **Details:** 93 seats. 20 seats outside. Separate bar. Wheelchair access. Music.

Lussmanns

Smart eatery with something for everyone
Waxhouse Gate, off High Street, St Albans, AL3 4EW
Tel no: (01727) 851941
www.lussmanns.com
Modern European | £25
Cooking score: 1
£5 OFF   £30

An independently owned antidote to bland high street brands, Andrei Lussmann's brasserie continues to please reporters with its relaxed, unfussy dining. 'It's such a refreshing change to encounter excellent customer service' is a typical comment. Provenance and seasonality are at the fore on the approachable menus, which might start with south coast devilled sprats with lemon mayonnaise before moving on to wild rabbit and chestnut mushroom linguine. House wine is £14.95. There is also a branch in Hertford.
Chef/s: Nick McGowan. **Open:** all week 12 to 10 (10.30 Fri and Sat, 9.30 Sun, 9 Mon). **Closed:** 25 and 26 Dec. **Meals:** alc (main courses £10 to £18). Set L and D £10.95 (2 courses) to £13.95. **Service:** not inc. **Details:** 115 seats. 6 seats outside. Wheelchair access. Music.

ALSO RECOMMENDED

▲ The Foragers

The Verulam Arms, 41 Lower Dagnall Street, St Albans, AL3 4QE
Tel no: (01727) 836004
www.the-foragers.com
British £5 OFF

Housed in a backstreet pub, the Foragers is part foodie enterprise, part 'natural roots' community, dedicated to all things wild and edible. Walks, talks and demos are part of the deal, and you can sample the results: expect rough-hewn rusticity in the shape of snails with turnip purée, goosegrass and chickweed (£7.50), venison Wellington with nettle sauce (£16) or salt beef and hogweed crumble, plus wild-flower fritters to finish. Special ales, infused drinks and wines (from £15). No food Mon L and Sun D.

▮▮▯ Please send us your feedback

To register your opinion about any restaurant listed in the Guide, or a new restaurant that you wish to bring to our attention, please visit the web address at the bottom of the page. Your feedback informs the content of the book and will be used to compile next year's reviews.

▌Welwyn Garden City
Auberge du Lac
Flamboyant food in moneyed surroundings
Brocket Hall, Brocket Road, Welwyn Garden City,
AL8 7XG
Tel no: (01707) 368888
www.aubergedulac.co.uk
Modern French | £60
Cooking score: 5

🍽 V

An eighteenth-century country retreat turned gold-standard hospitality venue and golfing complex, Brocket Hall may whiff of corporate money, but it has its human side. In the middle, overlooking a lake, is the Auberge du Lac, a converted hunting lodge that looks like it was built by Hansel and Gretel's rich relations. Phil Thompson's highly worked contemporary food mixes modern French flamboyance with ideas from faraway lands. There is much to applaud, from a standout starter of spiced, Merlot-braised octopus with smoked mussels, chorizo, olives and Mimolette cheese to plaice crusted with pumpkin seeds and garnished with slivers of squid, sprout leaves, butternut squash, salsify and mushrooms. Thompson's convoluted flavours occasionally get confused and sometimes fail to make any impact at all, but the kitchen shows its class more often than not; witness a pitch-perfect plate of venison with chocolate sauce on a bed of spätzle with tiny pear cubes. Home-baked breads shine, the cheeseboard is superb, and desserts have included apple-crumble soufflé with toffee apple parfait and mini-doughnuts. Some have found dinner 'rapaciously priced', but the set lunch (including two glasses of wine) is excellent value. The list of over 400 bins has a French centre and a treasure trove from Austria, Italy, Australia and beyond. Prices from £28.
Chef/s: Phil Thompson. **Open:** Tue to Sat L 12 to 2.30, D 7 to 9.30. **Closed:** Sun, Mon, 27 Dec to 13 Jan. **Meals:** Set L £28.50 (2 courses) to £32.50. Set D £60. Tasting menu £69.50 (6 courses) to £75 (9 courses). **Service:** 10%. **Details:** 60 seats. 30 seats outside. Music. Car parking.

▌Willian
The Fox
Dining-pub gem
Willian, SG6 2AE
Tel no: (01462) 480233
www.foxatwillian.co.uk
Modern British | £28
Cooking score: 2

 £30

The Nye family's mini-empire of dining pubs includes this gem, an eighteenth-century local by the green. There's a contemporary feel to the atrium dining room and the bar, where you can quaff Brancaster Best (brewed by the Nyes in Norfolk; they also own the White Horse in Brancaster Staithe – see entry). Their Norfolk links ensure deliveries of fresh mussels, oysters, crab and fish. These and other top-notch ingredients are cooked simply so flavours shine; witness cod with mussel chowder, or roast venison with confit garlic purée and chocolate jus, plus passion-fruit cheesecake with mango smoothie and lime sorbet. House wine £16.50.
Chef/s: Chris Jones. **Open:** all week L 12 to 2 (3.30 Sun), Mon to Sat D 6.30 to 9.15. **Meals:** alc (main courses £12 to £22). **Service:** 10%. **Details:** 70 seats. 80 seats outside. Separate bar. Wheelchair access. Music. Car parking.

- ■ Main entry
- ● Main entry with accommodation
- ▲ Also recommended

A single symbol may denote several restaurants in one area.

0   10 miles

0   10   20 Kilometres

▮ Alkham

The Marquis at Alkham

Chef with a foodie following
Alkham Valley Road, Alkham, CT15 7DF
Tel no: (01304) 873410
www.themarquisatalkham.co.uk
Modern British | £43
Cooking score: 4

In the four years it has been open, this former roadside pub has established itself as a destination restaurant-with-rooms – a place that's 'simply difficult to fault', according to one reporter. Chef Charlie Lakin certainly has a keen following for his food. What he is good at is sourcing quality ingredients, mostly from a network of well-chosen local suppliers, and cooking them with care. At its best it is cooking that makes a virtue of simplicity. The first course might be ramson (wild garlic) pannacotta with honey-soused vegetables and Berkswell cheese sablé, while main courses could bring neatly judged flavours in a dish of

Godmersham wood pigeon served with black pudding, kohlrabi and rhubarb. Attractive desserts have included lemon parfait with beetroot sorbet and sweet cicely. Minor details, especially bread, are done well and service is 'very polite and professional'. Wines from £17.50.
Chef/s: Charles Lakin. **Open:** Tue to Sun L 12 to 2.30, all week D 6 to 9.30. **Meals:** Set L and D £17.50 (2 courses) to £22.50. Sun L £27.50. **Service:** not inc. **Details:** 74 seats. Separate bar. Wheelchair access. Music. Car parking. Children over 8 yrs only at D.

▯▯ Please send us your feedback

To register your opinion about any restaurant listed in the Guide, or a new restaurant that you wish to bring to our attention, please visit the web address at the bottom of the page. Your feedback informs the content of the book and will be used to compile next year's reviews.

Aylesford

Hengist

Local asset with contemporary food
7-9 High Street, Aylesford, ME20 7AX
Tel no: (01622) 719273
www.hengistrestaurant.co.uk
Modern French | £38
Cooking score: 3

£5
OFF

Aylesford is reputedly the oldest village in England (circa 459AD), although the building that houses Hengist (named after the first king of Kent) dates from the mid-sixteenth century. Age determines the timbers and exposed stone, but it's all overlaid with a cool drop of twenty-first century styling, and the food follows suit with its strong contemporary outlook. French influences are grafted on to spanking fresh ingredients: roast saddle of wild rabbit comes with spiced couscous, marinated carrot and cardamom salad and carrot and orange dressing; daube of beef is teamed with caramelised baby onions and mushroom bourguignon, creamed mousseline potatoes and red wine jus. Reports suggest service is mixed, but this Richard Philips-owned restaurant (see Thackeray's, Tunbridge Wells) remains a good local asset. House wine is £16.95.
Chef/s: Jon Baldock. **Open:** Fri to Sun L 12 to 2.30, Tue to Sat D 6.30 to 10. **Closed:** Mon. **Meals:** alc (main courses £17 to £21). Set L £12.95 (2 courses) to £14.95. Set D £23.50 (2 courses) to £25.50. Sun L £19.95. Tasting menu £48 (7 courses). **Service:** 12.5%. **Details:** 65 seats. 10 seats outside. Separate bar. Wheelchair access. Music. Car parking.

Average Price

The average price listed in main-entry reviews denotes the price of a three-course meal, without wine.

Biddenden

The West House

Innovative cooking in laid-back surrounds
28 High Street, Biddenden, TN27 8AH
Tel no: (01580) 291341
www.thewesthouserestaurant.co.uk
Modern European | £40
Cooking score: 5

There's something very personal about this intimate restaurant housed in a Kentish weaver's cottage, and fans love the warm, laid-back feel of the place – from the glow of the wood-burning stove to the naughtily addictive crackers served between courses. They also appreciate chef-proprietor Graham Garrett's innovative approach and his ability to conjure something quite unexpected from locally sourced ingredients – belly pork coated in miso accompanied by coconut gel, pineapple and salted chilli pork 'scratchings', or 'undulating layers' of warm smoked haddock carpaccio set off by green flashes of pickled rock samphire and pea shoots, for example. Earthy 'concentrated flavours' also shine through in plates of slow-cooked beef cheeks with parsnip purée or roast Huntsham Farm pig with a sausage roll, braised cabbage and verjus caramel. Elsewhere, mackerel kebabs are ingeniously presented with aromatic Middle Eastern accompaniments, while 'rashers' of grilled lamb breast are served 'breakfast-style' with slow-cooked egg, salsa verde and an anchovy fritter. Clearly, Garrett hasn't lost his sense of humour: how about starting with 'Irish coffee' (actually butternut squash soup with Parmesan cream, thyme and cep doughnuts) and rounding off with a deconstructed Crunchie bar or a 'truly remarkable' banana rice pudding soufflé? The French-led wine list has an enterprising showing of 'natural' vintages and a terrific selection by the glass or carafe. Bottles start at £19.
Chef/s: Graham Garrett. **Open:** Tue to Fri and Sun L 12 to 2 (2.30 Sun), Tue to Sat D 7 to 9 (9.30 Fri and Sat). **Closed:** Mon, 24 Dec to 9 Jan, 2 weeks Jul.

Meals: Set L £25. Set D £35 (2 courses) to £40. Tasting menu £50. **Service:** 12.5%. **Details:** 32 seats. Music. Car parking.

ALSO RECOMMENDED
▲ The Three Chimneys
Hareplain Road, Biddenden, TN27 8LW
Tel no: (01580) 291472
www.thethreechimneys.co.uk
Modern British

As country pubs go, the fifteenth-century Three Chimneys has a distinct edge of quaintness, with its timbered façade and extensive gardens. Inside it is full of promise and possibilities, from an ancient bar offering beer tapped from the cask, to the series of atmospheric rooms (culminating in a smart dining room extension) delivering polished pub food – say terrines, Thai-style crab and salmon fishcakes (£8.95) and rack of lamb with its own shepherd's pie (£19.95). Wines from £16. Open all week.

▮ Bodsham
Froggies at the Timber Batts
Country pub, classic French grub
School Lane, Bodsham, TN25 5JQ
Tel no: (01233) 750237
www.thetimberbatts.co.uk
French | £35
Cooking score: 1
£5
OFF

Here's a proper country pub, off a narrow, winding road, full of beams and open fires with fantastic views over the North Downs. It's a surprise, then, to discover a menu that is dyed-in-the-wool Gallic bistro (the chef-proprietor is French). The food is unashamedly traditional; come here for game terrine, rack of lamb, fillet steak with Roquefort sauce, and crème brûlée. Lunch deals expand the core repertoire, there are real ales, and Loire house wines are £18.50. **Chef/s:** Joël Gross and Romuald Laurent. **Open:** Tue to Sun L 12 to 2.30 (12.30 to 3 Sun), Tue to Sat D 7 to 9 (9.30 Fri and Sat). **Closed:** Mon, 25 and 26 Dec,

1 and 2 Jan, bank hols. **Meals:** alc (main courses £15 to £25). Set L £16 (2 courses) to £20. Sun L £20.50 (2 courses) to £25.65. **Service:** not inc. **Details:** 50 seats. 50 seats outside. Separate bar. Music. Car parking.

▮ Broadstairs
NEW ENTRY
Albariño
Finally, a newcomer making waves
29 Albion Street, Broadstairs, CT10 1LX
Tel no: (01843) 600991
www.albarinorestaurant.co.uk
Tapas | £18
Cooking score: 4

£30

Albion Street plays host to a parade of eating places that serve this old-fashioned seaside town, but Alberiño stands out. Not physically, it isn't much of a restaurant – just a small space dominated by a bar and close-packed tables – its credentials lie in bringing serious cooking to a part of Kent that could use more of it. The chef-proprietor is English and his wife French, the food is quintessentially Spanish tapas, from the straightforward (patatas bravas, ham and cheese croquettes, salt cod fritter), to the standout (chickpea and fennel chips, sobrasada sausage with chickpeas and spinach, slow-cooked ox cheek with liquorice). Ingredients are carefully sourced and thoughtfully prepared – fish comes from local day boats, there's local rabbit, lamb, pork belly. And worth a punt, too, are desserts such as olive oil and polenta cake with goats' curd, crystallised orange and walnuts. Service is hard to fault. House wine is £14. **Chef/s:** Steven Dray. **Open:** Mon to Sat L 12 to 3, D 6 to 11. **Closed:** Sun, 25 and 26 Dec, 1 Jan, first 2 weeks Nov. **Meals:** alc (tapas £6 to £8). **Service:** not inc. **Details:** 20 seats. 2 seats outside. Wheelchair access. Music.

▌Canterbury

The Goods Shed
Shedloads of good things
Station Road West, Canterbury, CT2 8AN
Tel no: (01227) 459153
www.thegoodsshed.co.uk
Modern British | £32
Cooking score: 2

The Goods Shed has long been a fierce
champion of local produce, from the stalls of
the six-day-a-week farmers' market to the
dishes in the raised restaurant overlooking this
former railway shed. From the homespun
décor to the seasonal menu, all is as it should
be: sea trout comes with cucumber sauce and
brown shrimps, braised neck of lamb with
white beans and aïoli. The kitchen pleases pud
fans with, say, a textbook dark chocolate
fondant. At lunchtime, look to the market,
too, for stalls selling bespoke sandwiches and
plates of lamb keftes or fish pie. Wines
from £14.50.
Chef/s: Rafael Lopez. **Open:** Tue to Sun L 12 to 2.30
(3 Sat and Sun), Tue to Sat D 6 to 9.30. **Closed:** Mon,
25 to 27 Dec, 1 and 2 Jan. **Meals:** alc (main courses
£12 to £20). **Service:** not inc. **Details:** 75 seats. Car
parking.

Michael Caines at ABode Canterbury
Cooking with considerable panache
High Street, Canterbury, CT1 2RX
Tel no: (01227) 826684
www.michaelcaines.com
Modern European | £45
Cooking score: 5

The renovated former County Hotel on
Canterbury's High Street has become a
modern, stylish hotel, a branch of Andrew
Brownsword's ABode group. A large part of
the ground floor is occupied by a spacious,
contemporary restaurant, which offers well-
spaced crisp-clothed tables and the restrained
cuisine of Michael Caines – interpreted with
vigour and accuracy by long-standing

executive chef Jean-Marc Zanetti. His
cooking displays considerable panache,
focusing largely on fresh regional raw
materials and allying French technique to
modern British sensibility; he teams pan-fried
duck liver with rhubarb and Sauternes jelly,
poached rhubarb and honeycomb, or serves a
main-course aged sirloin steak with truffle
pomme purée, wild mushrooms, shallot
confit and red wine sauce. Elsewhere, silky
crab cannelloni comes with braised fennel,
sauce vierge and shellfish froth, fillet of sea
bass with a Thai purée, stir-fried shiitake
mushrooms, beansprouts and lemongrass
sauce, and a first-class warm banana soufflé is
partnered by a flavour-packed passion-fruit
sorbet. While poor service and
misunderstandings have put some people off,
others contend that it's 'really nice to have a
quality restaurant in the heart of Canterbury'
and praise 'efficient service' and the set meal
deals. The wine list opens at £22.
Chef/s: Jean-Marc Zanetti. **Open:** all week L 12 to
2.30, Mon to Sat D 6 to 10. **Meals:** alc (main courses
£23 to £27). Set L £14.50. Set D £17.95 (2 courses) to
£25. Sun L £14.95. **Service:** 12%. **Details:** 72 seats.
Wheelchair access. Music. Car parking.

▌Cranbrook

Apicius
Big-statement cooking in a tiny space
23 Stone Street, Cranbrook, TN17 3HF
Tel no: (01580) 714666
www.restaurant-apicius.co.uk
Modern European | £40
Cooking score: 6

A converted fifteenth-century weaver's
cottage in one of Kent's most compact market
towns, Apicius is proof positive that small is
not only beautiful, but highly effective too. It's
owned and run by Timothy Johnson and Faith
Hawkins: he cooks, she takes care of front-of-
house. Inside, it's all about unstuffy
informality, with plain walls, some
minimalist furniture and not much else in
between; everything revolves around the food
– and that's exactly how the regulars like it.
Timothy delivers big-statement cooking

defined by bold technique, artistry and gentle innovation, from celeriac and truffle velouté with foie gras tortellini and baby spinach to a frivolous take on banana split with strawberry sauce. Here is a chef who is happy to slow-roast joints of Kentish pork, but also knows how to fashion trendy plates of pan-fried sea bream with radish and carrot 'spaghetti', fennel purée and chorizo. His cep pannacotta with Parmesan crisp, roasted almonds, Jerusalem artichokes and endive salad is a savoury dream ticket for those who want a change from meat or fish, while the sweet brigade go overboard for his white chocolate and lavender cream custard with orange salad, honey ice cream and raspberry coulis. The wine list is a tidy collection of well-chosen bottles, with prices from £18.

Chef/s: Timothy Johnson. **Open:** Wed to Fri and Sun L 12 to 2, Wed to Sat D 7 to 9. **Closed:** Mon, Tue, 2 weeks Jun/Jul, 2 weeks Christmas. **Meals:** Set L £28 (2 courses) to £32. Set D £34 (2 courses) to £40. **Service:** 12.5%. **Details:** 30 seats. No music. Wheelchair access. Children over 8 yrs only.

▌Dargate
The Dove Inn
Cosy pub with top-notch grub
Plum Pudding Lane, Dargate, ME13 9HB
Tel no: (01227) 751360
www.doveatdargate.co.uk
Modern British | £27
Cooking score: 2

This rustic pub is a centre for meeting, eating and drinking, and has an appropriately informal atmosphere; a log fire and worn floorboards create a cosy, lived-in feel. Sit at scrubbed pine tables and order 'top-notch' dishes, many with a Gallic accent: foie gras and chicken liver parfait with toasted hazelnuts and shallot marmalade, for instance, followed by duck breast with braised red cabbage and potato gratin. Dessert lovers will alight on something like triple chocolate brownie with peanut butter and jam ice cream, or cinnamon rice pudding with fig jam to round it all off. Wines start at £14.

Chef/s: Phillip MacGregor. **Open:** Tue to Sun L 12 to 2, Wed to Sat D 7 to 9. **Closed:** Mon, one week Feb. **Meals:** alc (main courses £13 to £19). **Service:** 10%. **Details:** 25 seats. 40 seats outside. Music. Car parking.

▌Dover
The Allotment
Interesting, good-value food
9 High Street, Dover, CT16 1DP
Tel no: (01304) 214467
www.theallotmentdover.com
Modern British | £23
Cooking score: 3

Shored by a good local reputation, the Allotment remains the only option for interesting and good-value food hereabouts. The dining room incorporates an open-to-view kitchen and gives on to a bijou enclosed garden. The relaxed, happy atmosphere is due in part to Dave Flynn's care of customers, but also to the simple cooking of seasonal and local produce. Leek soup followed by a small salad of carrots steeped in orange juice with herbs and home-pickled baby beets, and pot-roasted chicken with vegetables and cider comprised one well-reported meal; garlic and chilli prawns, roast cod, and Moroccan-style lamb have also impressed. A 'superb' almond and raspberry frangipane, apple crumble, and an intense, dark chocolate pot have provided fine notes to end on. Wines from £15.

Chef/s: David Flynn. **Open:** Tue to Sat 8.30am to 11pm. **Closed:** Sun, Mon, 24 Dec to 16 Jan. **Meals:** alc (main courses £8 to £16). **Service:** not inc. **Details:** 26 seats. 24 seats outside. Wheelchair access. Music.

▐❙● Visit us Online
To find out more about *The Good Food Guide*, please visit www.thegoodfoodguide.co.uk

▌Faversham

Read's

Delightful, lovingly polished restaurant-with-rooms
Macknade Manor, Canterbury Road, Faversham, ME13 8XE
Tel no: (01795) 535344
www.reads.com
Modern British | £58
Cooking score: 6

'Excellent service, excellent food, excellent atmosphere' – Rona and David Pitchford's Georgian manor house continues to delight visitors with its disarmingly calm outlook and ever-so-English sense of decorum. It glides along as a lovingly polished restaurant-with-rooms, with much depending on David Pitchford's kitchen and his fruitful connections with the local food network. His cooking is at the gentler end of the modern British spectrum, with combinations that make sense: a hot soufflé of mature Montgomery cheddar, for example, is teamed with smoked haddock glazed in a cream sauce, while twin accompaniments of Cox's apple jelly and pickled vegetables offset a rich potted chicken liver parfait. An occasional foray into Asian ways might bring sea bream on a lightly curried cauliflower couscous with golden sultanas, toasted almonds and onion bhajia, or there could be Kentish lamb – roasted loin and epigrammes (breaded cutlets) of slow-cooked shoulder – served with Jerusalem artichoke purée, fondant potato and rosemary jus. Unwavering consistency and highly skilled executions are also the hallmarks of desserts, say a deep lemon tart with Read's own lemon sorbet and glazed meringue. Lunch is considered 'very good value', the wine list a cracker. France is explored in depth, but imagination is shown elsewhere; and, for those on a budget, there's a digest of 60 'best buys' from £20.
Chef/s: David Pitchford. **Open:** Tue to Sat L 12 to 2, D 7 to 9. **Closed:** Sun, Mon, 25 to 27 Dec, first week Jan, first 2 weeks Sept. **Meals:** Set L £25. Set D £48

(2 courses) to £58. **Service:** not inc. **Details:** 50 seats. 24 seats outside. Separate bar. No music. Wheelchair access. Car parking.

▌Folkestone

ALSO RECOMMENDED
▲ Rocksalt
4-5 Fishmarket Road, Folkestone, CT19 6AA
Tel no: (01303) 884633
www.rocksaltfolkestone.co.uk
Seafood

For the setting, this modern restaurant overlooking Folkestone harbour is hard to beat. However, results from the kitchen have been uneven of late. Successes have included 'tremendous' fish soup (£7.50), Josper-baked mussels, and local mackerel with white beans and herb vinaigrette (£12.50). Salt marsh lamb with rosemary sauce has been both a hit and a miss; vegetable cookery and puddings are not a strong suit. Service is cheerful, but can falter under pressure. Wines from £15.50. Closed Sun D and Mon.

▌Locksbottom

Chapter One
Big-city cooking at local prices
Farnborough Common, Locksbottom, BR6 8NF
Tel no: (01689) 854848
www.chaptersrestaurants.com
Modern European | £36
Cooking score: 5

V

A gastronomic landmark in Kent's commuterland, this handsome mock-Tudor building has accrued a solid reputation since launching in 1996. The attraction is a cocktail of cosmopolitan surroundings and big-city cooking at decidedly local prices. Chef Andrew McLeish knows the ways of the world and invests his dishes with some up-to-the-minute strokes – come here for a cheeky take on kedgeree involving smoked haddock and curry mayonnaise embellished with little rice balls, squid croquettes and red-vein sorrel, or an equally emphatic seasonal pairing of line-caught sea bass with roasted trevise, cauliflower beignets, mushroom purée and a scattering of hazelnuts. As for meat, a thumpingly good Ibérico pork chop served on Savoy cabbage has pleased, although the star turn for one reader was a deeply flavoured plate of jugged South Downs hare with truffle espuma and a little skewer of hare 'satay'. Desserts also maintain the high standard – witness organic lemon tart with passion-fruit mille-feuille and crème fraîche sorbet, or a deconstructed Black Forest gâteau with dark chocolate sorbet. At lunchtime, you can eat even more affordably from a brasserie menu that offers anything from tagliatelle carbonara to Josper-grilled steaks. Serious wines from France and elsewhere are available at very fair mark-ups, with prices starting at £16.50 (£4.75 a glass). **Chef/s:** Andrew McLeish. **Open:** all week L 12 to 2.30 (2.45 Sun), D 6.30 to 11 (9 Sun). **Closed:** first week Jan. **Meals:** alc (main courses £19). Set L £18.95. Sun L £20.95. **Service:** 12.5%. **Details:** 120 seats. 20 seats outside. Separate bar. Wheelchair access. Music. Car parking.

Lower Hardres
The Granville
Pub that consistently delivers
Street End, Lower Hardres, CT4 7AL
Tel no: (01227) 700402
www.thegranvillecanterbury.com
Modern European | £28
Cooking score: 3

This gently upgraded roadside pub, baby sister to the Sportsman in Whitstable (see entry), has few pretensions beyond providing pints of Shepherd Neame ales in the drinkers' bar and impeccably sourced food in the spacious dining room. It consistently delivers on all points. There's no doubt that Jim Shave gets the best from his prime raw materials, with dishes like smoked haddock Welsh rarebit, coq au vin or bream fillet with bouillabaisse sauce and harissa mayonnaise. Roast belly pork with crackling and apple sauce is pretty much a fixture, and commitment to quality sustains

through excellent homemade focaccia to a fulsome dessert menu that has featured cherry Bakewell with Kirsch syrup and sticky toffee pudding with Muscovado ice cream. The keenly priced wine list opens at £15. **Chef/s:** Jim Shave. **Open:** Tue to Sun L 12 to 2, Tue to Sat D 7 to 9. **Closed:** Mon, 26 Dec. **Meals:** alc (main courses £15 to £19). Set weekday L £12.95 (2 courses) to £15.95. **Service:** not inc. **Details:** 55 seats. 30 seats outside. Separate bar. Wheelchair access. Music. Car parking.

Margate
ALSO RECOMMENDED
▲ The Ambrette
44 King Street, Margate, CT9 1QE
Tel no: (01843) 231504
www.theambrette.co.uk
Indian

The building is shabby, the furnishings unassuming, but most reporters rate the modern Indian cooking highly. Sound regional ingredients are used to telling effect. Char-grilled Godmersham pigeon with ginger and aromatic spices (£5.25), brochettes of leg of local lamb, slow-cooked in a Kashmiri-spiced gravy (£14.95) and chocolate samosas have all been hits. Dev Biswal divides his time between here and a second Ambrette in Rye, East Sussex (see entry) with no apparent dip in quality. Wines from £13.95. Closed Mon.

Oare
The Three Mariners
Well beyond the usual pub standard
2 Church Road, Oare, ME13 0QA
Tel no: (01795) 533633
www.thethreemarinersoare.co.uk
Modern British | £25
Cooking score: 3

Still resolutely a pub, complete with drinkers' bar and roaring winter fire, this off-the-beaten-track village inn is also the setting for food that stretches well beyond the usual pub

standard. John O'Riordan's cooking reflects the seasons; his fuss-free approach showcases the very best of local produce. Ideas are straightforward – as in soft herring roes with capers and garlic on toast, or tarte Tatin of shallot with goats' cheese – and much of the food runs along familiar lines, taking in fish soup, local skate wing with brown butter, and gutsy beef two ways (roast fore rib and slow-roast chuck rib). The everyman appeal extends to desserts such as a rich chocolate fondant. Excellent bread has made a positive impression, too. Wines from £13.50.
Chef/s: John O'Riordan. **Open:** all week L 12 to 2.30 (3 Sat, 3.30 Sun), D 6.30 to 9 (9.30 Fri and Sat, 7 to 9 Sun). **Meals:** alc (main courses £10 to £19). Set L £11.50 (Mon to Sat). Set D £16.50 (Mon-Thur). Sun L £16.50. **Service:** not inc. **Details:** 63 seats. 30 seats outside. Separate bar. Music. Car parking.

Ramsgate

Age & Sons
Cut-above café and restaurant
Charlotte Court, Ramsgate, CT11 8HE
Tel no: (01843) 851515
www.ageandsons.co.uk
Modern British | £29
Cooking score: 1

 £30

This Victorian wine warehouse, split into a ground-floor café and formal upstairs restaurant, is a cut above the usual offerings hereabouts. The cooking is fashionably simple and fiercely seasonal, but doesn't hit as many highs as it should – at inspection an otherwise excellent rack of new season's lamb was marred by poor trimming. Typical are local asparagus, ham hock and hollandaise, Aylesbury duck with peas à la française and chicory, and textbook tarte Tatin. Service is charming. Wines from £15.
Chef/s: Toby Leigh. **Open:** Tue to Sun L 12 to 3.30, Tue to Sat D 7 to 9.30. **Closed:** Mon, 25 and 26 Dec, 1 to 11 January. **Meals:** alc (main courses £10 to £22). Set L and Sun L £9.95 (2 courses) to £12.95. Set D £12.95 (2 courses) to £15.95. **Details:** 60 seats. 30 seats outside. Separate bar.

Eddie Gilbert's
A seaside beacon
32 King Street, Ramsgate, CT11 8NT
Tel no: (01843) 852123
www.eddiegilberts.com
Seafood | £30
Cooking score: 1

In a rundown Ramsgate street, Eddie Gilbert's shines. It's known for its fish shop and chippy, and first-floor seafood restaurant. The kitchen cooks competently with good materials, but tries too hard to impress; a superb lobster tart's impact was diminished by melon balls and Parma ham. But there has been good butter-roasted John Dory with scallops, king prawns, crushed potatoes and baby broccoli, as well as rosemary-marinated monkfish with lemon-infused couscous and ratatouille, and fish and seafood fritto misto. Service is pleasant and anxious to please. Wines from £14.
Chef/s: Craig Edgell. **Open:** all week L 12 to 2.30 (3 Sun), Mon to Sat D 5.30 to 9.30. **Closed:** 25 and 26 Dec. **Meals:** alc (main courses £15 to £18). Set L £8.50 (2 courses) to £9.95. Sun L £14.50 (1 course) to £24.50. **Service:** not inc. **Details:** 48 seats.

St Margaret's-at-Cliffe

Wallett's Court
Country house with carefully considered food
Westcliffe, St Margaret's-at-Cliffe, CT15 6EW
Tel no: (01304) 852424
www.wallettscourt.com
Modern British | £40
Cooking score: 2

The Oakley family is rightly proud of the restoration of this ancient manor house and the place is a tribute to serious nurturing. The kitchen doesn't aim for undue sophistication, but it gets the essentials right: prime ingredients range from locally bred pork and Sussex red beef to Kentish cheeses, and ideas are carefully considered. Typical is a starter of courgette, apple and goats' cheese soup with goats' cheese beignet, followed by tender braised shoulder of Romney Marsh lamb with broad beans, pine nuts and mint, and textbook elderflower crème brûlée. Wines are cosmopolitan, well-chosen and reasonably priced (from £18.95).

Chef/s: David Hoseason. **Open:** Sun L 12 to 2.30, all week D 7 to 9. **Meals:** Set D £34.95 (2 courses) to £39.95. Sun L £16.95. **Service:** not inc. **Details:** 60 seats. Separate bar. Music. Car parking.

ALSO RECOMMENDED
▲ The Bay Restaurant
The White Cliffs Hotel, High Street, St Margaret's-at-Cliffe, CT15 6AT
Tel no: (01304) 852229
www.thewhitecliffs.com
Modern British £5 OFF

Standing proud in a village not far from Dover, this weatherboarded inn is a welcoming hostelry with a reputation for reliable food. The bar has a wood-burner and brick walls; the dining room is simple and light. The menu mixes country pub grub such as fish and chips (£9.95) or wild boar bangers, with bistro-style dishes of goats' cheese, Kentish cobnut fritter and baby beet salad (£4.95), alongside Goan fish curry (£15.50). House wine is £12.95. Accommodation. Open all week.

Speldhurst

ALSO RECOMMENDED
▲ George & Dragon
Speldhurst Hill, Speldhurst, TN3 0NN
Tel no: (01892) 863125
www.speldhurst.com
Modern British £5 OFF

Wonky carved beams, flagstones and a massive inglenook fireplace provide the perfect backdrop for sampling local ales and modern pub food at this magnificent thirteenth-century inn, one of the region's oldest hostelries. Daily menus reflect the seasons and showcase local farmers and artisan producers; the choice takes in pub classics like pork sausages, mash and onion gravy (£10.50), steak boards (sirloin with chips and béarnaise,

£21.50) and belly pork with wilted greens and bubble and squeak (£15.50). House wine £14.50.

Stalisfield Green

NEW ENTRY
The Plough
Country pub classics and local ales
Stalisfield Green, ME13 0HY
Tel no: (01795) 890256
www.stalisfieldgreen.co.uk
British | £26
Cooking score: 2
£5 OFF £30

Follow twisting lanes through the Kent countryside to find this centuries-old pub beside an expanse of village green. Beams, standing timbers and locally brewed ales create a suitably rustic mood in the bar, but there's nothing old-fashioned about the food. The kitchen is noted for industrious home production (bread, piccalilli and chutney) and tapping into the local supply network. Seasonal game and fish bolster a menu that might include pork terrine or mussels in Biddenden cider, mains of suet-crusted Romney mutton pie or roasted skate wing with brown butter, and the lightest syrup sponge with oranges. Wines from £15.50.

Chef/s: Alex Windebank. **Open:** Tue to Sun L 12 to 2.30 (4 Sun), Tue to Sat D 6 to 9 (9.30 Sat). **Closed:** Mon, 25 Dec, 2 weeks Aug, bank hols. **Meals:** alc (main courses £11 to £20). **Service:** not inc. **Details:** 55 seats. Separate bar. Music. Car parking.

Tenterden

READERS RECOMMEND
Number 75
Modern British
75 High Street, Tenterden, TN30 6BB
Tel no: (01580) 762075
www.number75.com
'A really lovely dining experience from start to finish... pan-fried scallops with cauliflower purée and chorizo for starter – delicious!'

Tunbridge Wells

Thackeray's

French food with a touch of class
85 London Road, Tunbridge Wells, TN1 1EA
Tel no: (01892) 511921
www.thackerays-restaurant.co.uk
Modern French | £60
Cooking score: 4

 V

Satirical wordsmith William Makepeace
Thackeray wouldn't recognise his old home
these days, but Tunbridge regulars have a soft
spot for its current incarnation. There are
echoes of the past in the dining room's ancient
floorboards and low ceilings, although cool
contemporary design now sets the tone – bag
a table in the Japanese terraced garden if you
fancy eating alfresco. Richard Phillips and his
team apply refined French technique to top-
drawer regional ingredients, and the results
have a touch of class: steamed Dorset crab and
langoustine mousse appears with suitable
companions including braised fennel,
buttered cockles and langoustine beignets,
while Kentish venison might be hot-smoked,
then roasted and served with chestnuts,
ventrèche bacon and beetroot. Also check out
the extravagant assiette of Berkshire pork with
caramelised Roscoff onion, black pudding
tortellini and smoked garlic, and don't miss
the lemon and pineapple Vacherin with
clementine sorbet to finish. Keenly priced set
lunches get the nod, and the stylish global
wine list offers serious drinking from £18.95.
Chef/s: Richard Phillips and Daniel Hatton. **Open:**
Tue to Sun L 12 to 2.30, Tue to Sat D 6.30 to 10.30.
Closed: Mon. **Meals:** alc (main courses £24 to £28).
Set L £16.95 (2 courses) to £18.95. Set D £24.50 (2
courses) to £26.50. Sun L £26.50. Tasting menu £69
(7 courses). **Service:** 12.5%. **Details:** 80 seats. 30
seats outside. Separate bar. Music.

Whitstable

JoJo's

Top-notch tapas by the sea
2 Herne Bay Road, Whitstable, CT5 2LQ
Tel no: (01227) 274591
www.jojosrestaurant.co.uk
Tapas | £25
Cooking score: 4

 £30

'A great combination of fresh, interesting food
made from local produce, friendly, fun
atmosphere and good value'. So writes one
devoted fan, happy to support Nikki
Billington and Paul Watson's casual eatery
overlooking the North Sea. The infectiously
laid-back atmosphere matches the sunny
Mediterranean cooking, while freshness and
timing make the most of excellent ingredients.
Dishes are designed for sharing – favourites
include lamb cannon (seared and thinly sliced
with mint jelly), Nikki's famed beer-battered
calamari, and mutton and feta koftas.
Blackboard specials provide seasonal accents,
say mackerel with horseradish mustard mayo
or red mullet in a rich, rich tomato sauce with
chorizo and thyme. There's often loin of
venison, thinly sliced and seared on the char-
grill, and slow-cooked pig's cheek with 'the
most delicious, meltingly crisp crackling'.
Finish with crème brûlée or a 'fantastic' blood
orange sorbet. Although JoJo's is licensed
(bottles from £14), the popular BYO policy
remains (corkage £2). No credit cards.
Chef/s: Nikki Billington (and team Fran, Jake, Dan,
Nim). **Open:** Wed to Sun L 12.30 to 2.30 (3.30 Sun),
Tue to Sat D 6.30 to 9. **Closed:** Mon. **Meals:** alc
(tapas £4 to £12). **Service:** not inc. **Details:** Cash
only. 60 seats. Wheelchair access. Music.

The Sportsman
Astonishing food in the most congenial pub
Faversham Road, Seasalter, Whitstable, CT5 4BP
Tel no: (01227) 273370
www.thesportsmanseasalter.co.uk
Modern British | £38
Cooking score: 6

Once a rallying point for 'sportsmen' with
their guns and dogs, this weatherbeaten pub
overlooking the blowy salt marshes now
attracts a very different crowd, lured by the
prospect of astonishing food in the most
congenial surroundings you could imagine.
Inside, all is bare boards and wooden tables –
the kind of place where you feel like stretching
your legs, having a natter and supping a pint.
Self-taught chef and heroic artisan Stephen
Harris is doing remarkable things here –
churning his own ambrosial butter, baking
treacle-sweet soda bread and 'sinful' focaccia,
dry-curing hams in his beer cellar, even
producing his own sea salt... in Seasalter. If
you want to know where it all starts, look
outside: lamb is from sheep grazing on the
marshes, seaweed is harvested from the beach
and bivalves are out of the estuary – it's living,
breathing 'terroir' in action. As for ordering,
just head for the daily blackboard menu by the
bar and take your pick: perhaps pickled
herring and cabbage salad followed by slabs of
roast Monkshill Farm lamb or seared skate on
crunchy greens with sweet cockles and
astringent sherry vinegar dressing. It may have
sackfuls of self-sufficient cred, but this is pin-
sharp cooking defined by natural-born
flavours: briny rock oysters with musky-
sweet, hot chorizo; 'unbelievably fresh' miso-
grilled mackerel; crispy duck with smoked
chilli salsa. Alternatively, book ahead in a
group and sample the tasting menu, a multi-
course résumé of Stephen's endeavours,
running from pork scratchings to teasing
desserts such as jasmine tea junket with
rosehip syrup or rhubarb sorbet tingling with
popping candy. Cheery, chatty staff match the
convivial mood, and there are some astute
wines (from £15.95) on the concise list.

Chef/s: Stephen Harris and Dan Flavell. **Open:** Tue
to Sun L 12 to 2 (2.30 Sun), Tue to Sat D 7 to 9.
Closed: Mon, 25 and 26 Dec. **Meals:** alc (main
courses £18 to £23). Tasting menu Tue to Fri £65.
Service: not inc. **Details:** 45 seats. Music. Car
parking.

Wheelers Oyster Bar
Plates of 'immense loveliness'
8 High Street, Whitstable, CT5 1BQ
Tel no: (01227) 273311
Seafood | £38
Cooking score: 4

This striking pink-and-blue painted
restaurant is a Whitstable institution that has
barely changed for 150 years. It encourages
bring-your-own on the wine front (no
corkage) and if you are lucky you might find
one of the four stools at the counter of the tiny
Victorian oyster bar free – only if you book
can you bag a table in the snug back room.
Mark Stubbs deals in modern fish cookery.
His short menus cover a lot of territory and
bristle with bright ideas. As a starter, Rye Bay
scallops with white onion purée, confit rabbit,
chickweed and bacon sauce is an exciting
blend of richness and delicacy, while lemon
sole with purple sprouting broccoli, lobster
and wild garlic dumplings, wilted lettuce,
tartare sauce and lemon oil is 'a plate of
immense loveliness'. Cinnamon pannacotta
with gingerbread ice cream and blood orange
curd is reckoned to be an outstanding dessert.
Unlicensed.
Chef/s: Mark Stubbs. **Open:** Thur to Tue 1 to 7.30 (7
Sun). **Closed:** Wed, 2nd week Jan for 2.5 weeks.
Meals: alc (main courses £19 to £22). **Service:** not
inc. **Details:** Cash only. 16 seats.

RAISE A GLASS TO ENGLAND

Not long ago, English wine was something you might buy a bottle of at a farm-gate in the Home Counties, having raised a dutiful eyebrow at how palatable it tasted.

Fast forward to recent years and you will find that our domestic wine industry is big news. At its forefront are sparkling wines, made across a swathe of the southern UK, from Cornwall to Kent. They are produced by the same methods as Champagne, from the same grape varieties and are grown on similar geological chalk deposits as occur in northern France. Many of these wines are now garlanded with international awards. A number of restaurants are proud to serve these wines, including **Nathan Outlaw at St Enodoc Hotel** at Rock in Cornwall.

Right behind the sparklers is a generation of fragrant and herbaceous white wines. The grape varieties have taken a bit of getting used to (among them Bacchus and Schönburger), but there are increasing plantings of Chardonnay and even Sauvignon Blanc. Reds suitable for the cool climate include Rondo and Regent, and what should in time be some potentially exciting Pinot Noir.

Williams & Brown Tapas
Simple, flavour-packed tapas
48 Harbour Street, Whitstable, CT5 1AQ
Tel no: (01227) 273373
www.thetapas.co.uk
Tapas | £25
Cooking score: 2
£30

Christopher Williams' pint-sized tapas bar is simple and unfussy, with cramped tables and bar stools at counters running the length of the windows. The attraction is exceptional ingredients, many locally sourced, and a kitchen with the self-confidence and skill to prepare them very simply, bringing out their full flavours. Sweet shavings of jamón Serrano, char-grilled mackerel with salsa verde, quail with red onion marmalade, chorizo baked in red wine, patatas bravas – while the core of the menu doesn't change, daily specials keep regulars interested and there's a popular take-away service, too. Spanish house is a reasonable £14.95.
Chef/s: Christopher Williams and Andy Cozens. **Open:** all week L 12 to 2 (2.45 Sat and Sun), D 6 to 9 (9.30 Fri, 9.45 Sat). **Closed:** Sun D, Tue and Wed from Nov to end Mar, 25 and 26 Dec. **Meals:** alc (tapas £4.50 to £17). **Service:** 10%. **Details:** 30 seats. 6 seats outside. Music.

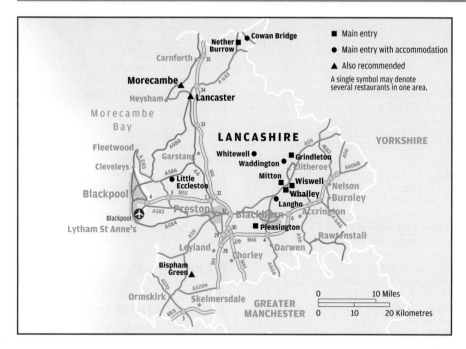

Map legend:
- ■ Main entry
- ● Main entry with accommodation
- ▲ Also recommended

A single symbol may denote several restaurants in one area.

Arkholme

The Redwell Inn
Modern British
Arkholme, LA6 1BQ
Tel no: (015242) 21240
www.redwellinn.net

'A lovely setting with log fires in winter and innovative, genuinely good food using the finest quality ingredients, sourced locally.'

Bispham Green

▲ The Eagle & Child
Malt Kiln Lane, Bispham Green, L40 3SG
Tel no: (01257) 462297
www.eagleandchildbispham.co.uk
Modern British £5 OFF

A bowling green and wildlife area, a thriving farm shop and fine ales from North Country microbreweries are just some reasons to visit this centuries-old country boozer a short drive from the M6. The enterprising food is also a big draw; locally reared steaks line up beside the likes of pigeon breast with black pudding salad (£6.50), roast chicken Rossini (£12) or seared tuna loin with clams and romesco sauce. Good local cheeses, ice creams and homely puds, too. House wine is £14. Open all week.

Cowan Bridge
Hipping Hall
Luxurious ingredients and good ideas
Cowan Bridge, LA6 2JJ
Tel no: (01524) 271187
www.hippinghall.com
Modern British | £50
Cooking score: 4

🛏 V

If a medieval dining room conjures thoughts of uncouth flesh-ripping and rough ale, prepare for something smarter at Hipping Hall. The galleried fifteenth-century dining hall is plain and spare, with wenches replaced by an engaged service team juggling all the little extras required of a small, ambitious Lakes hotel. Chef Brent Hulena frequently brings Cumbrian produce into play alongside luxurious ingredients and good ideas; a first course of ewe's milk custard with truffle and asparagus comes with clever shallot shortbread. There might be some pretty, superfluous folderols, but the cooking is sound; try lamb with kidney, broccoli and pickled red cabbage or red mullet with olive and Parmesan. Wine matches work more often than not, and there's fun to be had in combinations like a passion-fruit and orange dessert with plum-infused saké. There's not a huge amount of wine by the glass, but customers are encouraged to ask about what else is open. Bottles from £21.

Chef/s: Brent Hulena. **Open:** Sat and Sun L 12 to 2, all week D 7 to 9.30. **Meals:** Set L £29.50. Set D £49.50. Tasting menu £65. **Service:** not inc. **Details:** 28 seats. Separate bar. Wheelchair access. Music. Car parking. Children over 12 yrs only.

Grindleton
The Duke of York Inn
Traditional pub with sharp seasonal food
Brow Top, Grindleton, BB7 4QR
Tel no: (01200) 441266
www.dukeofyorkgrindleton.com
Modern British | £30
Cooking score: 3

£5 OFF **V**

As befits its setting deep in the Ribble Valley, this creeper-clad Victorian hostelry makes admirable use of produce from Lancashire's farmers and growers – chef/landlord Michael Heathcote knows the region and a trusted local network keeps him topped up with provisions throughout the year. The result is a sharp seasonal repertoire that wins friends with its restrained creativity and pretty presentation: consider a wintry dish of oxtail soup laced with Black Sheep beer, embellished with crispy kale and horseradish foam, or Goosnargh chicken breast surrounded by black pudding, chicken wing, potato galette

and cauliflower cheese. Fish also gets an airing (cod fillet with artichoke mousse and chanterelles, say), and the North Country cheeseboard is a ripe beauty. 'Outstanding' Sunday roasts, an untarnished pubby atmosphere and cosseting service are plus points, and the well-spread wine list kicks off at £15.25.

Chef/s: Michael Heathcote. **Open:** Tue to Sun L 12 to 2, D 6 to 9 (5 to 7.30 Sun). **Closed:** Mon, 25 Dec. **Meals:** alc (main courses £14 to £27). Set L £12.99 (2 courses) to £14.99. Set D £13.99 (2 courses) to £15.99. Sun L £15.95 (2 courses) to £18.50. Tasting menu £35 (5 courses) to £42.50 (7 courses). **Service:** not inc. **Details:** 70 seats. 20 seats outside. Separate bar. No music. Wheelchair access. Car parking.

Lancaster

ALSO RECOMMENDED
▲ Penny Street Bridge
Penny Street, Lancaster, LA1 1XT
Tel no: (01524) 599900
www.pennystreetbridge.co.uk
Modern British

This spacious bar-cum-brasserie, once a hostelry, sits in the heart of Lancaster, right beside the canal – a pretty spot to meet up for food and drink. The pleasant dining room, with scrubbed tables, offers a menu that ranges from homemade nibbles (pork crackling, perhaps) to more substantial offerings such as local potted shrimps (£6.25), toasted goats' cheese crumpets, or wild boar sausages, mash and crispy onions (£9.75). Service is friendly. A short wine list starts at £13.95. Open all week.

Symbols
🛏 Accommodation is available

£30 Three courses for less than £30

V Separate vegetarian menu

£5 OFF £5-off voucher scheme

🍷 Notable wine list

Langho
Northcote
A smart, timeless retreat
Northcote Road, Langho, BB6 8BE
Tel no: (01254) 240555
www.northcote.com
Modern British | £50
Cooking score: 6
🛏 V

An air of grandeur hangs about Northcote, the small hotel in a nineteenth-century manor house in one of Lancashire's lovelier corners. Last year's refurb brought a crisper look (and a rather large light fitting) to the dining room, but the essential appeal is that of a smart, timeless retreat, where joint proprietor and wine buff Craig Bancroft is likely to be found uncorking something reassuringly celebratory. Co-owner Nigel Haworth's food philosophy – when in Lancashire, eat Lancashire – is very much in evidence, but the head chef is Lisa Allen, and her food, say readers, is 'top-notch'. The relationships forged with local suppliers continue to inform the menu, so a tartare of happy veal is allied with carpaccio of Ascroft's cauliflower, horseradish and cauliflower cream, and marrow bone and caper toast, while a butternut squash risotto billed as 'very runny' fulfils its promise. Main courses such as Bowland venison with faggot, celeriac purée, wild mushrooms and roasted beets have an earthy appeal, and grouse is turned into a Wellington with turnips showcased in a sweet-and-sour purée. Desserts, including melting ginger pudding with iced double cream and caramel custard, hit all the pleasure points. Classy service and a commitment to wine matching complete an experience that reporters unanimously praise as destination stuff; the wine list starts at £23.50 and offers great possibilities.
Chef/s: Lisa Allen. **Open:** all week L 12 to 2, D 7 to 9.30 (6.30 to 10 Sat, 7 to 9 Sun). **Closed:** 25 Dec. **Meals:** alc (main courses £25 to £35). Set L £26. Set D £50 (4 courses) to £58 (5 courses). Sun L £36 (4 courses). Tasting menu £85. **Service:** 10%. **Details:** 60 seats. Separate bar. Wheelchair access. Music. Car parking.

Little Eccleston
The Cartford Inn
Handsome inn serving pub classics
Cartford Lane, Little Eccleston, PR3 0YP
Tel no: (01995) 670166
www.thecartfordinn.co.uk
Modern British | £22
Cooking score: 2
£5 OFF 🛏 £30

'Every detail, from the staff who clearly enjoy their job to the décor and food, makes this establishment well worth a visit' notes one satisfied diner. Patrick and Julie Baume have thrown everything they've got into this handsome pub in a backwater 10 miles from Blackpool. Julie has a 'great, if slightly eccentric, eye' for mixing vintage and contemporary in spaces that include a dining room overlooking the river. The food 'has never failed to impress with its freshness and consistency'. Pub classics abound; belly pork and fish stand out, but watch for unexpected treats, perhaps pigeon breast with rösti potatoes and asparagus. House wine is £14.25.
Chef/s: Ian Manning. **Open:** Tue to Sat L 12 to 2, Mon to Sat D 5.30 to 9 (10 Fri and Sat), Sun all day 12 to 8.30. **Closed:** 25 Dec. **Meals:** alc (main courses £9 to £22). **Service:** not inc. **Details:** 80 seats. 30 seats outside. Separate bar. Music. Car parking.

Mitton
The Three Fishes
Flying the flag for local eating
Mitton Road, Mitton, BB7 9PQ
Tel no: (01254) 826888
www.thethreefishes.com
British | £26
Cooking score: 2
£30

Nigel Haworth's original Ribble Valley Inn flies the flag for good eating hereabouts. There is no fast footwork, just a laudable interpretation of British food – an almost unashamedly nostalgic menu that name-checks local suppliers and kicks off with the likes of Chadwick's Bury black pudding or warm Morecambe Bay shrimps. The theme of posh, patriotic comfort food is reflected in main course haddock and chips ('the best I have eaten'), a signature Lancashire hotpot, and desserts of rice pudding and sticky ginger parkin. Wines from £13.95. Sibling to the Highwayman and the Clog & Billycock (see entries).

Chef/s: Andy McCarthy. **Open:** Mon to Sat L 12 to 2, D 5.30 to 8.30 (9 Fri and Sat). Sun 12 to 8. **Closed:** 25 Dec. **Meals:** alc (main courses £11 to £18). Set L and D Mon to Thur £11.50 (2 courses) to £15. **Service:** not inc. **Details:** 120 seats. 50 seats outside. No music. Wheelchair access. Car parking.

Morecambe

ALSO RECOMMENDED
▲ Sun Terrace Restaurant at The Midland

Marine Road West, Morecambe, LA4 4BU
Tel no: (01524) 424000
www.englishlakes.co.uk
Modern British

A long, glass-fronted restaurant is part of the sympathetic renovation of this Art Deco icon, affording every diner stunning views over Morecambe Bay. Menus boast local delicacies: potted shrimps (£7.25), or perhaps pan-fried mackerel with beetroot salad. Mains stay close to home: lamb rump (£17.50) or a hearty ribeye of beef from the Cumbrian hills that can be spied across the bay. Desserts are familiar, with the likes of sticky toffee pudding. Wines are helpfully grouped into price bands from £16. Open all week.

¡¦ Readers Recommend

A 'readers recommend' review is a genuine quote from a report sent in by one of our readers. We intend to follow up these suggestions throughout the year to come.

Nether Burrow
The Highwayman
A fantastic local asset
Burrow Road, Nether Burrow, LA6 2RJ
Tel no: (01524) 273338
www.highwaymaninn.co.uk
British | £25
Cooking score: 2
£30

Beams, oak floors, blazing fires and locally brewed beer point up the Highwayman's heritage as a country pub, but most people are here to eat, and more regularly 'now that you can book in advance'. It's a fantastic resource for the area, with cooking based on prime seasonal and regional produce. Recent favourites are the local beef burger, cheese and onion pie, fish pie, and bread-and-butter pudding. Asparagus with a poached egg and hollandaise, and a fantastic salad of locally smoked salmon, Morecambe Bay shrimps and seawater prawns are seasonal top shouts. Wines from £15.50. One of Nigel Haworth's Ribble Valley Inns.

Chef/s: Neil Kenny. **Open:** Mon to Sat L 12 to 2, D 5.30 to 8.30 (9 Fri and Sat). Sun 12 to 8. **Closed:** 25 Dec. **Meals:** alc (main courses £10 to £20). **Service:** not inc. **Details:** 110 seats. 60 seats outside. Separate bar. No music. Wheelchair access. Car parking.

Newton-in-Bowland

READERS RECOMMEND
The Parkers Arms
British
Parkers Arms, Newton-in-Bowland, BB7 3DY
Tel no: (01200) 446236
www.parkersarms.co.uk
'The welcome, the open fires, the views and particularly the locally sourced food are well worth travelling any distance for.'

Pleasington
The Clog & Billycock
Welcoming pub that champions local produce
Billinge End Road, Pleasington, BB2 6QB
Tel no: (01254) 201163
www.theclogandbillycock.com
British | £20
Cooking score: 2

Thoroughly rooted in the village of Pleasington, Nigel Haworth's modishly rustic third Ribble Inn (see entries for the Highwayman and the Three Fishes) is so focused on local produce that suppliers' pictures line the walls. It's an upbeat place where a jaunty, smiling welcome greets regulars and visitors, and the atmosphere is 'warm and inviting, whatever season'. Lancashire hotpot remains a firm favourite, but readers have also praised an 'exceptionally well put-together' seafood platter, beef bourguignon on a soft winter mash, and rhubarb jelly and custard. The wine list (from £15) is arranged by style and there are real ales. **Chef/s:** Mark Prescott. **Open:** Mon to Sat L 12 to 2, D 5.30 to 9, Sun 12 to 8. **Closed:** 25 Dec. **Meals:** alc (main courses £9 to £18). Set L and D £11.50 (2 courses) to £15. **Service:** not inc. **Details:** 120 seats. 50 seats outside. Wheelchair access. Car parking.

Waddington
NEW ENTRY
The Waddington Arms
Lovely, welcoming village local
Waddington, BB7 3HP
Tel no: (01200) 423262
www.waddingtonarms.co.uk
Modern British | £21
Cooking score: 1

Waddington is an impossibly pretty village with the welcoming pub at its heart; at a weekday meal everyone was here – locals, be-suited execs and workers in high-vis jackets enjoying a bite before heading home. Oak tables stand on flagstones, fires blaze and a comforting pub-grub menu beckons. Portions are substantial; a starter of mackerel and Lancashire cheese fishcake is a meal in itself, but boeuf bourguignon is hard to resist: deeply rich, with smooth cauliflower mash. Desserts include sticky toffee pudding, if you've room. Wines from £14.25. **Chef/s:** Thomas Steele. **Open:** Mon to Fri L 12 to 2.30, D 6 to 9.30, Sat 12 to 9, Sun 12 to 9.30. **Closed:** 25 Dec. **Meals:** alc (main courses £10 to £15). Sun L £10.95. **Service:** not inc. **Details:** 62 seats. 50 seats outside. No music. Wheelchair access. Car parking.

Whalley
★ BEST CAFÉ ★
Food by Breda Murphy
Café/deli with exciting, fresh cooking
Abbots Court, 41 Station Road, Whalley, BB7 9RH
Tel no: (01254) 823446
www.foodbybredamurphy.com
Modern British | £25
Cooking score: 2

'Never had a bad meal' says one regular of this contemporary café and deli in the pretty hamlet of Whalley. 'Wonderful service' from 'gracious staff' is one plus point, another is the 'innovative, exciting and fresh' cooking. The menu includes favourites such as an 'out of this world' fish pie, and lighter snacks ranging from open sandwiches to salads on toasted soda bread. This is colourful, eclectic cooking, spanning comfort food (beef lasagne) and international flavours, as in pan-fried salmon fillet with curried rice salad. Finish with sticky date parkin with toffee sauce and cream cheese sorbet. A concise international wine list opens at £13.95. **Chef/s:** Gareth Bevan. **Open:** Tue to Sat L 11 to 5.30, occasional evenings 7 to 9. **Closed:** Sun, Mon, 24 Dec to 3 Jan. **Meals:** alc (main courses £11 to £17). Set D £42.50 (5 courses). **Service:** not inc. **Details:** 50 seats. 20 seats outside. Wheelchair access. Music. Car parking.

Whitewell

The Inn at Whitewell

Pleasing inn with bang-up-to-date cooking
Whitewell, BB7 3AT
Tel no: (01200) 448222
www.innatwhitewell.com
British | £30
Cooking score: 3

Charles Bowman imbues this ancient stone inn with warmth, personality, and a pleasing quirkiness. It stands in splendid isolation beside the river Hodder, amid the wild beauty of the Trough of Bowland. Rambling bars and dining rooms have a country-house feel, with heavy beams, antique furnishings and blazing fires, yet the atmosphere is relaxed. Ingredients are local and top-notch, and bang-up-to-date cooking sees both bar meals and carte classics skilfully updated. A starter of scallops with pea purée and watercress dressing could be followed by beef fillet with a cottage pie of braised oxtail and baby onions, celeriac purée and red wine jus. Finish with British and Irish cheeses or a homely pudding. The comprehensive global wine list, strong in France, opens at £14.50.
Chef/s: Jamie Cadman. **Open:** all week L 12 to 2, D 7.30 to 9.30. **Meals:** alc (main courses £15 to £27). **Service:** not inc. **Details:** 150 seats. 30 seats outside. Separate bar. No music. Car parking.

Wiswell

Freemasons Country Inn

Upmarket inn with scores of fans
8 Vicarage Fold, Wiswell, BB7 9DF
Tel no: (01254) 822218
www.freemasonswiswell.co.uk
Modern British | £33
Cooking score: 4

'It's miles from where I live, but I dine there almost every week. All the food is amazing in both flavour and quality, expertly prepared and beautifully presented.' So notes one regular, neatly summing up the reasons to visit this classy country inn-cum-restaurant.

Originally three cottages, one of which was a freemasons' lodge, it is stylishly decorated and exudes warmth and sincerity. Steven Smith does a good line in brasserie dishes and ideas come thick and fast: a starter of tandoori roast scallops with sweet potato, apple and cumin, mains of liver and onions teamed with Savoy cabbage, balsamic and shallot sauce or 'absolutely faultless' butter-poached cod with scampi. It's freewheeling stuff, using a finely honed network of suppliers to provide the best raw materials. Desserts command attention, especially a lovingly prepared rhubarb and custard soufflé. The thoughtful wine list puts France centre stage, but takes pains elsewhere; prices from £14.95.
Chef/s: Steven Smith. **Open:** Tue to Sun L 12 to 2.30, D 5.30 to 9 (6 to 9.30 Fri and Sat). **Closed:** Mon, 1 to 16 Jan. **Meals:** alc (main courses £14 to £29). Set L and D £13.95 (2 courses) to £15.95. Tasting menu £55 (7 courses). **Service:** not inc. **Details:** 70 seats. 16 seats outside. Wheelchair access. Music.

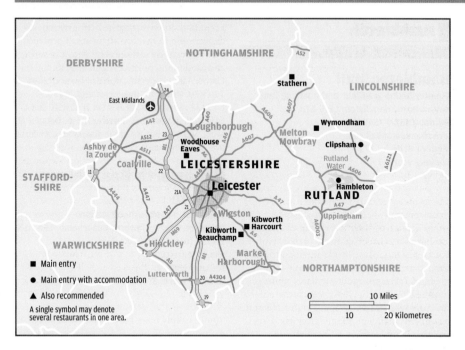

■ Clipsham

The Olive Branch

Perfect country pub with great-value food
Main Street, Clipsham, LE15 7SH
Tel no: (01780) 410355
www.theolivebranchpub.com
British | £31
Cooking score: 3

It seems everyone falls in love with this 'perfect country pub' two miles off the A1 – it's the very image of a lovingly nurtured local hostelry. That said, great-value food is also a big draw. A network of trusted local suppliers provides much of the produce for seasonally inspired menus, and influences come from far and wide: ham hock terrine with piccalilli and crispy bacon sits shoulder-to-shoulder with breast of wood pigeon, date purée, paprika and smoked bacon jus. Mains range from honey-roast belly pork to sea bass with shrimp and mussel tagliatelle, while desserts span everything from treacle tart to vanilla

pannacotta. Drinking extends from a selection of pedigree real ales to a sophisticated wine list that puts the emphasis on affordability; prices start at £16.50.
Chef/s: Sean Hope. **Open:** all week L 12 to 2 (3 Sun), D 7 to 9.30 (9 Sun). **Meals:** alc (main courses £15 to £22). Set L £16.95 (2 courses) to £19.95. Set D £19.50 (2 courses) to £24.50. Sun L £24.50. **Service:** not inc. **Details:** 45 seats. 32 seats outside. Separate bar. Wheelchair access. Music. Car parking.

Please send us your feedback

To register your opinion about any restaurant listed in the Guide, or a new restaurant that you wish to bring to our attention, please visit the web address at the bottom of the page. Your feedback informs the content of the book and will be used to compile next year's reviews.

Hambleton

★ TOP 50 ★

Hambleton Hall
Country house grandeur and amazing food
Ketton Road, Hambleton, LE15 8TH
Tel no: (01572) 756991
www.hambletonhall.com
Modern British | £75
Cooking score: 7

🍽 V

The gardens are only the half of it, a masterpiece of the horticulturist's and landscaper's arts, with something to discover around every corner against a backdrop of Rutland tranquillity. Inside are magnificent rooms, including a lounge in gentle mint green and the appropriately stately dining room, all built in the 1880s for a brewing magnate who liked to ride to hounds. Despite its obvious grandeur, Hambleton has always been run by its owners as a welcoming, unfusty sort of place, which is reflected in the approach of the dining room staff: 'silver service, but with a smile' as one reader neatly puts it. Aaron Patterson has now entered his third decade at the stoves and the place is all the richer for that continuity. The menus don't blind with science; dishes are simply and succinctly described – which is why what appears before you is all the more amazing for the purity, concentration and surprises it contains. An opulent opener might comprise wild mushrooms, Pink Fir Apple potatoes and leeks in a truffled ragoût, or skate in the form of a terrine wrapped in Parma ham, given tang with gherkins and capers. Mains extend the range into the realms of a tronçon of turbot with a multiplicity of onion variations and a fried quail egg, while one regular goes unerringly for anything featuring duck: usually the roast breast and confit leg, perhaps with Japanese artichokes, spiced lentils and pickled mooli. Exciting dessert offerings include pear and blackberry terrine with mini-doughnuts and salted caramel, or the Force 10 intensity of a rich chocolate tart with orange sorbet. The wine list declares: 'We are prejudiced in favour of the little guy', so expect a plethora of excellent small growers, from Burgundy and the Rhône to Carneros and Stellenbosch. Prices open at £20.
Chef/s: Aaron Patterson. **Open:** all week L 12 to 2, D 7 to 9.30. **Meals:** alc (main courses £28 to £39). Set L £22 (2 courses) to £36.50. Set D £38.50. Sun L £45. Tasting menu £67. **Service:** 12.5%. **Details:** 60 seats. Separate bar. No music. Car parking. Children over 7 yrs only at D.

Kibworth Beauchamp

Firenze
Just-right neighbourhood Italian
9 Station Street, Kibworth Beauchamp, LE8 0LN
Tel no: (0116) 2796260
www.firenze.co.uk
Italian | £35
Cooking score: 3

£5 OFF

'Quite simply one of my favourite places to eat' pronounced one reader, and such praise is echoed in many reports for the Polis' small contemporary Italian. People love the way the place strikes just the right note for a neighbourhood restaurant. They applaud pleasant service (led by Sarah) and Lino's seasonal cooking, which takes full advantage of superb seafood. He delivers forthright Florentine flavours – in an open ravioli with red wine-braised oxtail, a 'most amazing' game ragù, squid ink risotto or short rib of beef with cotechino sausage, ox tongue, mustard fruits and green vegetable relish... the hit list goes on. For dessert, consider vanilla and white chocolate spelt pudding. The wine list is an illuminating tour of serious modern Italian drinking. Prices (from £17.50) are wallet-friendly.
Chef/s: Lino Poli. **Open:** Tue to Sat L 12 to 3, D 7 to 11. **Closed:** Sun, Mon, 25 and 26 Dec, 1 Jan, bank hols. **Meals:** alc (main courses £16 to £20). Set L and D £17.50 (2 courses) to £22.50 and £27.50 (4 courses). **Service:** not inc. **Details:** 60 seats. Music.

▌ Kibworth Harcourt

Boboli

All-day Italian bristling with artisan treats
88 Main Street, Kibworth Harcourt, LE8 ONQ
Tel no: (0116) 2793303
www.bobolirestaurant.co.uk
Italian | £25
Cooking score: 1
£5 OFF £30

Like its big brother Firenze in Kibworth
Beauchamp (see entry), Boboli brings some
welcome Italian sunshine to an ancient
English village. The all-day menu bristles
with artisan treats: dip into the list of antipasti
(beef carpaccio with Gorgonzola and
walnuts), order a bowl of beetroot and goats'
cheese risotto or feast on veal milanese with
sauce agrodolce. You can also drop in any time
for some piadini and pasticcini snacks, or
nibble a pizza on the piazza, dreaming of
warmer climes. The zippy little wine list (from
£14.90) is stuffed with Italian regional
goodies from Firenze's outstanding cellar.
Chef/s: Lino Poli and Tom Wilde. **Open:** all week
10am to 9.30pm. **Closed:** 25 and 26 Dec, 1 Jan, bank
hols. **Meals:** alc (main courses £8 to £20). Set L
£13.50 (2 courses) to £18.50. Sun L £14.50 (2
courses) to £22.50 (4 courses). **Service:** not inc.
Details: 90 seats. 28 seats outside. Separate bar.
Music. Car parking.

Symbols

🛏 Accommodation is available

£30 Three courses for less than £30

V Separate vegetarian menu

£5 OFF £5-off voucher scheme

🍾 Notable wine list

▌ Leicester

Entropy

Buzzy all-dayer in an old butcher's
42 Hinckley Road, Leicester, LE3 0RB
Tel no: (0116) 2259650
www.entropylife.com
Modern British | £30
Cooking score: 4
£5 OFF

This nineteenth-century butcher's shop may
occupy a spot in one of Leicester's less
fashionable suburbs, but Tom Cockerill
clearly spotted its potential when he opened
his all-day restaurant and bar in 2000. An
open kitchen and a modern rustic look add to
the unpretentious, relaxed atmosphere, and
the food is just as straightforward and unfussy;
the flexible daily changing menus appeal to
diners who don't want an amuse-bouche
followed by three courses. The cooking is
underpinned by seasonality and careful
sourcing of ingredients, which extends to
lamb and beef from the family farm.
Although one reporter thought the food was a
touch slow emerging from the kitchen, there
were no grumbles over the 'beautifully
cooked' Gloucester Old Spot sausages with
mashed potato and onion gravy. Pineapple
tarte Tatin with lime-chilli caramel and
coconut sorbet is one of the recommended
desserts. House wine is £15.50.
Chef/s: Tom Cockerill. **Open:** Tue to Fri 11.30 to 10,
(10.30am Sat, 10.30 to 5 Sun). **Closed:** 25 and 26
Dec, 1 Jan. **Meals:** alc (main courses £11 to £20).
Service: not inc. **Details:** 36 seats. Separate bar.
Music.

ALSO RECOMMENDED

▲ Maiyango

13-21 St Nicholas Place, Leicester, LE1 4LD
Tel no: (0116) 2518898
www.maiyango.com
Modern European £5 OFF

Exotic coloured lanterns, dark drapes and
luxurious cushions give boutique hotel
restaurant Maiyango a Moroccan air, though

▮▮▮ PAUL LEARY
The Woodhouse

When did you realise you wanted to be a chef?
From the age of 16, when I had a pot washer's job at Hilton Hotels.

Which chefs do you admire, and why?
Nathan Outlaw - he is a very good chef who doesn't brag about it!

What's your earliest food memory?
Eating hot dogs as a 4-year-old.

What food trends are you spotting at the moment?
Everyone is using a water bath, even my mum!

What's your least favourite food?
Anything under seasoned.

Sum up your cooking style in three words
Clean, tasty, perfection (in my eyes!).

What advice would you give a chef starting their career?
Be passionate and dedicated, and be prepared to kiss a few frogs!

What would be your last meal?
A fish-finger sandwich, followed by cherry pie and custard.

the culinary influences are as likely to be Thai or Italian. Expect goats' cheese, tomato and red onion tart in balsamic reduction, trio of tagine-spiced lamb cuts with root vegetable dauphinoise, and dark chocolate fondant with pistachio ice cream and berry compote on the fixed-price dinner menu (£29, or £26.50 for two courses). House Chilean is £17.50. Open Wed–Sat L, all week D.

▮ Stathern
Red Lion Inn
Satisfying, honest grub
2 Red Lion Street, Stathern, LE14 4HS
Tel no: (01949) 860868
www.theredlioninn.co.uk
British | £28
Cooking score: 2

If you are hankering after country pub virtues, this village inn has them in spades: local ales, rustic interiors, wood fires and grub that celebrates local produce – flip over the menu to see it all charted on a map. It's 'very welcoming, comfortable and relaxed'. Satisfaction is guaranteed when it comes to honest dishes such as braised pork fritters with black pudding and apple sauce, toad-in-the-hole or roast breast of chicken with sherry and mushroom sauce. Dessert fans will love coffee pudding with toffee sauce and Amaretto ice cream. Wines from £14.95. Related to the Olive Branch, Clipsham (see entry).
Chef/s: Sean Hope. **Open:** Tue to Sun L 12 to 2 (3 Sun), Tue to Sat D 6.30 to 9.30 (7 to 9.30 Sat). **Closed:** Mon. **Meals:** alc (main courses £11 to £22). Set L £13.50 (2 courses) to £16.50. Set D £15.50 to £19.50. Sun L £19.50. **Service:** not inc. **Details:** 60 seats. 30 seats outside. Separate bar. Music. Car parking.

▌Woodhouse Eaves

Paul Leary at The Woodhouse

Village restaurant with big ideas
43 Maplewell Road, Woodhouse Eaves, LE12 8RG
Tel no: (01509) 890318
www.thewoodhouse.co.uk
Modern British | £38
Cooking score: 3

V

A pretty white cottage with a striking red interior is the setting for Paul Leary's ambitious, sometimes complex, cookery – a far cry from what you might expect in the gentle Leicestershire countryside. Readers report 'smiley' service from a capable young team, and they also love the extra bits that adorn many plates. To start, salmon has a Douglas fir cure and is served with a little crab sandwich and salt-baked beetroot, while offal often partners prime ingredients – as in the Dexter beef plate with ox tongue and an artichoke and truffle purée. Wild greens and other foraged goodies are used with restraint, and dessert sees combinations including hay-infused ice cream with a prune and Armagnac soufflé. Wine, listed by style, is from £18, with plenty under £30.
Chef/s: Paul Leary. **Open:** Tue to Fri and Sun L 12 to 2.30 (4 Sun), Tue to Sat D 6.30 to 10 (7 Sat). **Closed:** Mon, 26 Dec to 2 Jan. **Meals:** Set L £14.95 (2 courses) to £16.50. Set D £16.95 (2 courses) to £21.95. Sun L £24.95. **Service:** not inc. **Details:** 50 seats. Separate bar. Music. Car parking.

▌Wymondham

NEW ENTRY
The Berkeley Arms

Admirable country charmer
59 Main Street, Wymondham, LE14 2AG
Tel no: (01572) 787587
www.theberkeleyarms.co.uk
British | £32
Cooking score: 3

Spruced-up and brimming with country charm, Neil and Louise Hitchen's centuries-old village inn offers a lot more than a 'deep sofa and a pair of well-worn armchairs by the roaring open fire'. The kitchen makes admirable use of local and regional produce, carefully crafting unpretentious dishes with robust Brit overtones. Cream of celery soup with Long Clawson Stilton cheese on toast is one way to start; main dishes run a broad course from 'perfect' fish and chips to 'beautifully cooked' local venison and 'superb' braised shoulder of Launde Farm lamb with ratatouille. Those in the market for top-notch Sunday roast beef and Yorkshire pudding won't go away empty – especially if they conclude with crème brûlée and poached rhubarb. Wines from £15.50.
Chef/s: Neil Hitchen. **Open:** Tue to Sun L 12 to 2 (5 Sun), Mon to Sat D 6 to 9 (9.30 Fri and Sat). **Closed:** first two weeks Jan, 1 week summer. **Meals:** alc (main courses £10 to £21). Set L £14.95 (2 courses) to £17.95. Sun L £17.95. **Service:** not inc. **Details:** 48 seats. Separate bar. No music. Wheelchair access. Car parking.

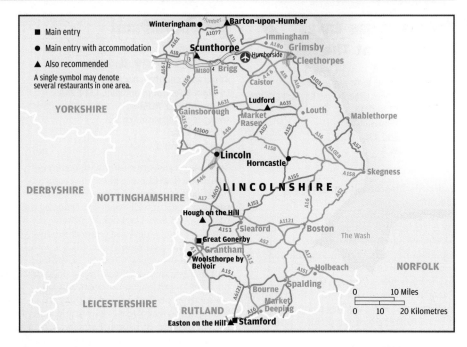

Map legend:
- ■ Main entry
- ● Main entry with accommodation
- ▲ Also recommended

A single symbol may denote several restaurants in one area.

YORKSHIRE

DERBYSHIRE

NOTTINGHAMSHIRE

LEICESTERSHIRE

RUTLAND

Winteringham • ▲ Barton-upon-Humber

Humber

Scunthorpe

Humberside

Immingham
Grimsby
Cleethorpes

Brigg

Caistor

Gainsborough

Ludford

Market Rasen

Louth

Mablethorpe

● Lincoln
Horncastle

Skegness

LINCOLNSHIRE

Hough on the Hill ▲

Sleaford

Boston

The Wash

■ Great Gonerby

● Grantham

Woolsthorpe by Belvoir

Holbeach

NORFOLK

Bourne

Spalding

Market Deeping

Easton on the Hill ▲ ■ Stamford

0   10 Miles

0   10   20 Kilometres

■ Barton-upon-Humber

ALSO RECOMMENDED
▲ Elio's
11 Market Place, Barton-upon-Humber, DN18 5DA
Tel no: (01652) 635147
www.elios-restaurant.co.uk
Italian

Elio Grossi's engaging trattoria-with-rooms has been a fixture of the Humberside scene since 1983, renowned for its congenial family atmosphere, striking alfresco courtyard and fondness for fish. Seafood specials such as salmon en croûte or grilled swordfish are the stars; the menu also trawls its way through the Italian mainstream for mozzarella caprese (£6.55), gnocchi with Gorgonzola, garlicky roast saddle of lamb (£18.95) and calf's liver with polenta. Also note the pizzas and assaggini 'tasters'. Wines from £14.95. Open Mon to Sat D only.

■ Easton on the Hill

ALSO RECOMMENDED
▲ The Exeter Arms
21 Stamford Road, Easton on the Hill, PE9 3NS
Tel no: (01780) 756321
www.theexeterarms.net
Modern British £5 OFF

Something of a dining destination in these parts, the Exeter Arms combines all the best country pub design elements with great alfresco opportunities. Plates of food now take preference over pints of beer, and eager crowds enjoy up-to-the-minute favourites such as oriental fish broth (£6.95) and duck breast with rösti, kale and orange (£16.95). Fish and chips or sausages and mash please pub diehards. Chocolate brownies and banana fritters are typical desserts. House wine is £14.95. Accommodation. No food Sun D.

▋ Great Gonerby

Harry's Place

A rare treasure
17 High Street, Great Gonerby, NG31 8JS
Tel no: (01476) 561780
Modern French | £62
Cooking score: 6

£5
OFF

While others retool, reboot and relaunch, in accordance with this year's concept, Harry and Caroline Hallam remain serenely aloof from it all in their former farmhouse in a village just outside Grantham. They do things pretty much as they have done since 1988. You'd like to look at the website? Don't be silly. There are two possible consequences of sticking rather than twisting in the restaurant world: sinking into a perfunctory rut, or acquiring the burnished patina of long experience. Harry's Place, with its three tables, its warm colours and the positively glowing hospitality of its owners, has matured like old claret, remaining faithful to an essentially French formula that seduces first-timers at once, and ensures the regular return of old friends. The format is a pair of choices at each stage, the descriptions so precise as to amount almost to recipes: fillet of monkfish lightly sautéed and served with beluga lentils, shallots and bacon, with a sauce of red wine, Noilly Prat, a little lemon juice, and basil, thyme and coriander. Seasonal game is often the main-course alternative, perhaps locally shot grey partridge with blueberries and a herb stuffing, in a sauce of white wine, Madeira and Armagnac. Prior to those might have come a gratin of smoked haddock, sweetcorn and chives in a pastry case, or a bowl of truffle-oiled mushroom soup with outstanding homemade bread. Dessert may well be ice cream, made with local damsons, or jelly, a cherry brandy job garnished with peppered yoghurt. That's jelly or ice cream, not an enormous slate of bits and bobs. To those who wish this direct style of readily intelligible cooking had never gone away, the truth is, it didn't quite. The single-page wine list is a brief jumble, opening with white Rioja at £20, and a Douro red at £32.

Chef/s: Harry Hallam. **Open:** Tue to Sat L 12.30 to 2, D 7 to 8.30. **Closed:** Sun, Mon, 1 week from 25 Dec, 1 week Aug, bank hols. **Meals:** alc (main courses £38 to £39). **Service:** not inc. **Details:** 10 seats. No music. Car parking. Children 5 yrs and over only.

▋ Horncastle

Magpies

Brimming with fine things
73 East Street, Horncastle, LN9 6AA
Tel no: (01507) 527004
www.magpiesrestaurant.co.uk
Modern British | £42
Cooking score: 5

🛏 V

Every market town should have one – a family-run restaurant brimming with hospitable cheer, a gentle ambience, assured cooking and fine wines, that is. Magpies is such a place. It is set in a terrace of 200-year-old black-and-cream cottages, and the comfortably furnished, low-ceilinged interior is full of charm. If tables are fairly closely distributed, that only adds to the aura of friendly intimacy. Caroline Gilbert runs the front of house and also whips up the desserts, and Andrew does everything else. Enterprising stuff it is too, drawing inspiration from afar – as in a starter of saddle of rabbit and spiced won ton with Chinese greens and rice-noodle rösti – as well as from the produce close to home. Grimsby crab might turn up dressed in lime mayonnaise with crayfish tortellini and a scallop in lemongrass sauce, while loin of local lamb is teamed with a roast fig and mustard seed tart, roasted cauliflower and walnuts. Puddings take up the rhubarb theme, boozily enough in rhubarb oat crumble with rhubarb and ginger-beer sorbet and rhubarb vodka jelly. A commendable wine list makes concise, sound selections from the principal countries at heart-gladdening prices. House wines start at £17.05.

Chef/s: Andrew Gilbert. **Open:** Wed to Fri and Sun L 12 to 2 (2.30 Sun), Wed to Sun D 7 to 9. **Closed:** Mon, Tue, 26 to 30 Dec. **Meals:** Set L £20 (2 courses) to

£25, Set D £36 (2 courses) to £42. **Service:** not inc. **Details:** 34 seats. 6 seats outside. Wheelchair access. Music. No children at Sat D.

Hough on the Hill

ALSO RECOMMENDED
▲ The Brownlow Arms
Grantham Road, Hough on the Hill, NG32 2AZ
Tel no: (01400) 250234
www.thebrownlowarms.com
British

This well-dressed pub-cum-restaurant-with-rooms makes an exceptional country haven. The kitchen aims for a mix of traditional and modern cooking, so menus run from twice-baked soufflé with crumbled Colston Bassett (£8.95) and fillet steak au poivre (£26.95) to ginger-marinated quail with sweet-and-sour peppers and Puy lentil cassoulet, and turbot with braised fennel, olive oil, orange and aged balsamic dressing (£21.95). Try hot plum tart with Mirabelle plum sorbet for dessert. Wines from £16.50. Open Mon to Sat D and Sun L.

Lincoln

The Old Bakery
Charming restaurant with great ingredients
26-28 Burton Road, Lincoln, LN1 3LB
Tel no: (01522) 576057
www.theold-bakery.co.uk
Modern European | £35
Cooking score: 2
£5 OFF 🍴

'Happy and unpompous' is how one regular described this popular restaurant-with-rooms close to Lincoln Castle. The vibrant cooking draws its inspiration from the Mediterranean, although carefully sourced ingredients come from local, named producers. The 'well-executed' dishes are, according to one, 'not without their sophistication' and a starter of ricotta and spinach fritters with tomato chutney has generated particular praise. A main course grilled fillet of local beef with slow-roasted tomatoes, dried Parma ham, sautéed porcini, mash and beef jus might be

followed by a selection from 20-plus artisan British cheeses. A varied wine list starts at £14.95.
Chef/s: Ivano de Serio. **Open:** Tue to Sun L 12 to 2, Tue to Sat D 7 to 9. **Closed:** Mon, 26 and 27 Dec, 1 Jan. **Meals:** alc (main courses £15 to £25). Set L £12.50 (2 courses) to £16.50. Sun L £17.95 (3 courses). Tasting menu £49. **Service:** not inc. **Details:** 60 seats. Wheelchair access. Music.

ALSO RECOMMENDED
▲ No 14 Bistro
14 Bailgate, Lincoln, LN1 3AE
Tel no: (01522) 576556
www.no14bistro.co.uk
French £5 OFF

'A break from the rigours of shopping' and a favourite with young and old alike, this chirpy, gregarious bistro goes about its business at the heart of old Lincoln. Come here for unreformed bourgeois food along the lines of moules marinière (£5.95), steak tartare, beef bourguignon (£13.95) or confit duck with orange and lentils – not forgetting big helpings of bouillabaisse and cassoulet. Traditional afters include tarte Tatin, crème caramel or spiced pear with madeleines. House wine is £10.95. Open all week.

Ludford

ALSO RECOMMENDED
▲ The Black Horse Inn
Magna Mile, Ludford, LN8 6AJ
Tel no: (01507) 313645
www.blackhorseludford.co.uk
Modern British £5 OFF

The seventeenth-century Black Horse Inn has been smartly refurbished in recent years and continues to undergo improvements. The kitchen looks to local produce for inspiration – as in a starter of white onion soup with Lincolnshire Poacher rarebit (£4.50) or fricassee of Lincolnshire pheasant with apples and prunes in a Skidbrooke cider cream with mashed potatoes (£13.50). For dessert, maybe

Yorkshire rhubarb and ginger crumble (£5.25). A modest selection of international wines starts at £13.20. Open Tue to Sun L.

Scunthorpe

ALSO RECOMMENDED
▲ San Pietro
11 High Street East, Scunthorpe, DN15 6UH
Tel no: (01724) 277774
www.sanpietro.uk.com
Modern European £5 OFF

It's been delighting visitors for 10 years, and the Catalano family's Grade II-listed windmill with courtyard gardens has lost none of its allure. Broadly European cooking delivers the likes of scallops with Jerusalem artichoke (roast and purée) and chorizo (£13.95), stone bass with tiger prawn tempura or game suet pudding with seared foie gras and spiced red cabbage (£23.95), and a hot chocolate pyramid with black cherry compote and mascarpone and Amaretto sorbet. Wines from £16.50. Closed Mon L and Sun.

Stamford

Jim's Yard
Terrific neighbourhood eatery
3 Ironmonger Street, Stamford, PE9 1PL
Tel no: (01780) 756080
www.jimsyard.biz
Modern European | £25
Cooking score: 2

£5 OFF £30

After six years there is a comfortable sense that this charming neighbourhood eatery is here to stay – good news for Stamford. Quality ingredients, like local game, get standard modern treatment: pigeon breast served with confit onion purée and honey-roast chestnuts, or fillet of hare teamed with pearl barley, smoked bacon and root vegetable ragoût. Fish dishes are a sure-fire hit, say sea bream with confit peppers and pepper sauce, while sweet black cherry soufflé with cherry-ripple ice cream is a 'real triumph'. House wine is

£13.50. Sister enterprise the Beehive pub is at 70 Albert Place, Peterborough; tel: (01733) 310600.
Chef/s: James Ramsay. **Open:** Tue to Sat L 12 to 2.30, D 6 to 9.30 (10 Fri and Sat). **Closed:** Sun, Mon, 2 weeks from 25 Dec, last week Jul, first week Aug. **Meals:** alc (main courses £12 to £21). Set L 14.50 (2 courses) to £17.50. Set D £19.50. **Service:** not inc. **Details:** 55 seats. 20 seats outside. Separate bar. Wheelchair access. Music.

Winteringham

Winteringham Fields
A shining star
1 Silver Street, Winteringham, DN15 9ND
Tel no: (01724) 733096
www.winteringhamfields.co.uk
Modern European | £75
Cooking score: 5

£5 OFF 🛏

Colin McGurran writes that he has managed to shrink the food miles for many of the dishes on his menus down to about five. Lots of the materials come from Winteringham's own smallholding, and have been 'grown, reared, picked or produced' by the in-house team, or else foraged from local woods and fields. This converted farmhouse, a stylish restaurant-with-rooms, has long been a shining star amid the North Lincolnshire flatlands. People love the genuine civility and warmth and the clear, expressive cooking, offered as either Menu Surprise or a three-course format in the evenings. One bowled-over reporter opened with a cup of sweetcorn velouté with tarragon foam, passed on to a portion of whitebait from South Ferriby beach, served amid shells, seaweed and pebbles, and then spätzle with a fragrant onion and cardamom purée. So far, so stunning, but then the main course – pork jowl with black pudding cream, caramelised apple and choucroute – raises the game still further. Textural exploration is one of the ways of making food fascinating, seen here again in the crisp-skinned roasted salmon that comes with variations on sweetcorn. It might all close with memorable pineapple and coconut pannacotta with pineapple and basil sorbet.

The extremely professional wine list is an aficionado's delight, in both hemispheres. There are no tasting notes; it's far more useful to talk to the sommelier. Bottles start at £26 (£7.30 a glass).
Chef/s: Colin McGurran. **Open:** Tue to Sat L 12 to 2, D 7 to 9. **Closed:** Sun, Mon, 25 Dec to 10 Jan, 3 weeks Aug. **Meals:** Set L £35 (2 courses) to £39.95. Set D £65 (2 courses) to £75. Tasting menu £79. **Service:** not inc. **Details:** 55 seats. Separate bar. No music. Car parking.

■ Woolsthorpe by Belvoir

Chequers Inn

Honest country pub with no-nonsense victuals
Main Street, Woolsthorpe by Belvoir, NG32 1LU
Tel no: (01476) 870701
www.chequersinn.net
Modern British | £26
Cooking score: 1

Real ales, blazing fires and honest pubby virtues are big selling points at this seventeenth-century village boozer – although the Chequers backs up its offer with Belgian beers, Buck's Fizz and a menu of no-nonsense victuals. The kitchen dishes up plates of beer-battered haddock, salmon fishcakes and homemade pies, but also turns its hand to flashier items such as barbecued quail with sweetcorn purée and pineapple salsa, or crab-crusted salmon with pak choi and ponzu dressing. For afters, try chocolate and chilli crème brûlée. House wine £14.
Chef/s: Mark Nesbit. **Open:** all week L 12 to 2.30 (4 Sun), D 6 to 9.30 (8.30 Sun). **Meals:** alc (main courses £12 to £20). Set L £11.50 (2 courses) to £15. Set D £15 (2 courses) to £17.50. Sun L £13.95. **Service:** not inc. **Details:** 90 seats. 80 seats outside. Music. Car parking.

MICKAEL WEISS
Coq d'Argent

When did you realise you wanted to be a chef?
Really early on, aged five: I was always bothering my mum in the kitchen. I had my first day in a professional kitchen aged 14, then started my apprenticeship the following year.

What's your biggest kitchen bugbear?
Wastage, I simply hate it. I am an ambassador for Action Against Hunger, and I see food as something precious.

What would be your last meal?
Steak & chips with béarnaise sauce, if I can chew it!

Which chefs do you admire, and why?
The Galvin brothers: both are really successful chefs. Their story shows that even as you get older you can start your own business and be very good at it.

What is your 'show-off' dish?
At the moment, due to the season, salt marsh lamb rump with carrot and cumin purée, lavender and London honey yoghurt, pansies and honey cress.

What would you be if you weren't a chef?
An architect or an artist.

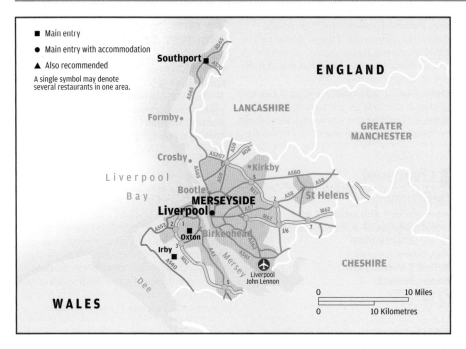

Heswell

Nova
Modern British
68 Pensby Road, Heswell, CH60 7RE
Tel no: (0151) 3429959
www.novarestaurant.co.uk
'Memorable dishes have been ox cheek, oxtail croquette, belly pork, braised shoulder of beef, chunky chips, burnt English cream, panacotta and blood-orange set cream.'

Readers Recommend
A 'readers recommend' review is a genuine quote from a report sent in by one of our readers. We intend to follow up these suggestions throughout the year to come.

Irby
Da Piero
Tasty Italian home cooking
5 Mill Hill Road, Irby, CH61 4UB
Tel no: (0151) 6487373
www.dapiero.co.uk
Italian | £30
Cooking score: 4
£5 OFF **V**

Dawn and Piero Di Bella are creating a loyal following for their 'consistently authentic' Sicilian offerings. In their simple (and now a little more spacious) front room-style restaurant you might try what is fast becoming a signature dish of tuna tartare, or linguine al limone. Mains, too, are faithful to their Sicilian roots, with plenty of seafood: diver-caught scallops with salmoriglio dressing (garlic, lemon and parsley) or a seafood parcel with garlic chilli, for example. Earthier offerings include Sicilian sausages with lentils, or pollo alla Piero – chicken thighs slow-cooked in white wine and cream with Parmesan potatoes. Interesting side dishes include broccoli 'affogati' (drowned) in red wine. As you might expect, gelato (ice cream) features heavily in the desserts. An all-Italian wine list starts at £10.40.

Chef/s: Piero Di Bella. **Open:** Tue to Sat D only 6 to 11. **Closed:** Sun, Mon, 25 and 26 Dec, 1 and 2 Jan. **Meals:** alc (main courses £20 to £42). **Service:** not inc. **Details:** 32 seats. No music.

▌Liverpool

Delifonseca
Wonderful deli with satisfying food
12 Stanley Street, Liverpool, L1 6AF
Tel no: (0151) 2550808
www.delifonseca.co.uk
Modern European | £25
Cooking score: 2

£5 OFF £30

Occupying a mezzanine above a 'wonderful deli', Delifonseca's restaurant is a popular destination for everything from salads, snacks and sandwiches to satisfying blackboard specials. Start with a 'perfectly prepared' ham hock terrine or figs stuffed with Gorgonzola and wrapped in Serrano ham with a watercress and rocket salad. Steamed Scottish venison pudding with wild mushrooms, red cabbage and chunky chips makes a hearty main, while spanakopita with roasted vegetable couscous and leaves is one of many good vegetarian choices. There's a superb range of beers, and wines start at £13.35. If you like this, try Delifonseca Dockside, on Brunswick Quay.

Chef/s: Marc Paley. **Open:** Mon to Fri 8 to 9 (9.30 Fri), 10 to 9.30 Sat, 10 to 5 Sun. **Closed:** 25 Dec to 1 Jan, bank hols. **Meals:** alc (main courses £10 to £15). **Service:** 10%. **Details:** 50 seats. Music.

Average Price
The average price listed in main-entry reviews denotes the price of a three-course meal, without wine.

NEW ENTRY
Hanover Street Social
All-day brasserie with international flavours
Casartelli Building, 16-20 Hanover Street, Liverpool, L1 4AA
Tel no: (01517) 098784
www.hanoverstreetsocial.co.uk
Modern European | £23
Cooking score: 1

£5 OFF £30

Restaurateur Paddy Smith's second venture is opposite his first, Salt House (see entry). The high ceilings, bare bricks and generous space create a relaxed brasserie look, with a semi-open kitchen where chefs 'should mind their language'. An all-day international menu runs from breakfast French toast with blueberries to a salad of radishes, broad beans, feta and herbs, or simple grills and roasts such as roast chicken with tarragon aïoli and fries. A large bar raises noise levels. House wine starts at £13.95.

Chef/s: Simon Wood. **Open:** all week L 12 to 6, D 6 to 10.30. **Closed:** 25 Dec. **Meals:** alc (main courses £7 to £32). Set L £9.95 (2 courses) to £12.95. Sun L £11.95 (2 courses) to £15.50. **Service:** not inc. **Details:** 95 seats. Separate bar. Wheelchair access. Music.

Host
Fast and friendly fusion
31 Hope Street, Liverpool, L1 9HX
Tel no: (0151) 7085831
www.ho-st.co.uk
Pan-Asian | £20
Cooking score: 1

V £30

In a setting of bare refectory tables and brick walls, Host offers pan-Asian fusion served fast and friendly, with plenty of chilli heat, vivid seasonings and Merseyside umami. Crisp-fried squid with chilli mayo or prawn and shiitake tempura with black pepper sauce arrive on small plates; duck red curry with coconut and lychee, or seafood udon noodles in sweet-and-sour sauce on big ones. Finish with cranberry and orange pannacotta and orange sorbet. Veggies are well looked after, there are guest beers, and wines from £14.95. **Chef/s:** Dave Fitzsimmons. **Open:** all week 11am to 11pm. **Closed:** 25 and 26 Dec, 1 Jan. **Meals:** alc (main courses £9 to £12). **Service:** 10%. **Details:** 120 seats. 20 seats outside. Separate bar. Wheelchair access. Music.

The London Carriage Works

Special dinners from treat-filled menus
Hope Street Hotel, 40 Hope Street, Liverpool, L1 9DA
Tel no: (0151) 7052222
www.thelondoncarriageworks.co.uk
Modern European | £35
Cooking score: 3

Still the city centre's no-brainer for dinner with a sense of occasion, the London Carriage Works has a prime corner spot on the loveliest street in town. Chef-patron Paul Askew shops as well as he cooks, filling the menu with local treats and the occasional foreign interloper. Scallops come with braised pork cheek, morcilla, cauliflower purée and a golden raisin dressing; fell-bred beef carpaccio gets a salad of Wirral watercress. There's no trickery here, even with a trio of Herdwick lamb involving confit shoulder, pan-roast loin and liver, Askew's style is essentially simple and likeable. There's an exceptional selection of regional cheeses, but chocolate fondant with salted caramel ice cream is a favourite. Wine is from £16.50; plentiful notes cover wine and beer matches.
Chef/s: Paul Askew. **Open:** all week L 12 to 3, D 5 to 10 (9 Sun). **Meals:** alc (main courses £12 to £29). Set L and D £15 (2 courses) to £20. Sun L £15 (2 courses) to £20. **Service:** not inc. **Details:** 70 seats. Separate bar. Wheelchair access. Music.

PERUVIAN PARTY

Think of South American cuisine and your mind will most likely turn to sizzling slabs of pampas-reared beef or sinfully sticky desserts of dulce de leche. The Noughties saw Argentinian steakhouses, or *parilladas*, springing up across the capital, including Hackney's **Buen Ayre**, where hipsters chow down on prime sirloin and plates of melted provolone cheese.

But now Peruvian food has landed on these shores and it owes as much to the raw fish dishes of Japan as it does to rib-sticking stews and Andean grains. According to Gabriel Gonzalez of Lima London, it's the 2500km of Pacific coastline that led to the creation of Peru's most famous dish, ceviche, slices of raw fish or seafood marinated in citrus juices and chilli.

At **Ceviche** in Soho, they import *aji amarillo*, a special variety of yellow chilli whose sweetness perfectly complements a dish of raw seabass. Beef still features on the menu, but in the form of *anticuchos*, grilled skewers of top rump or tender heart, or appearing in a stir-fry. 'Peruvian cuisine appeals to modern diners because it's simple and fresh,' says Ceviche's owner Martin Morales.

Lunya

Vibrant Spanish eatery and deli
18-20 College Lane, Liverpool One, Liverpool,
L1 3DS
Tel no: (01517) 069770
www.lunya.co.uk
Spanish | £22
Cooking score: 2

Deep in the heart of the Liverpool One
shopping development, Lunya is a vibrantly
busy, warmly run Spanish tapas place and deli
that features some Catalan specialities. Grab a
table upstairs for views of the kitchen action.
Good things at inspection included fine
tomato-smeared bread, brilliant hot-smoked
baby anchovies, plump grilled sardines with
salsa verde, and tender braised ox cheek with
celeriac purée and sticky cinnamon-scented
jus. Cinnamon fans will also love the crema
catalana or there's tarta di Santiago (almond
cake) with vanilla ice cream and raspberry
coulis. Good Spanish wines and sherries
accompany. Prices from £16.95 (£4.75 a
glass).
Chef/s: Dave Upson. **Open:** all week 9 to 9 (10pm
Thur, 11pm Fri and Sat, 10am Sun). **Closed:** 25 Dec.
Meals: alc (tapas £4 to £8). **Service:** not inc.
Details: 150 seats. 30 seats outside. Wheelchair
access. Music. Tapas banquets £15 to £30.

NEW ENTRY

Salt House

One of Liverpool's premier purveyors of tapas
Hanover Street, Liverpool, L1 3DW
Tel no: (0151) 7060092
www.salthousetapas.co.uk
Spanish | £14
Cooking score: 2

Cutlery in paprika tins and sherry behind the
bar are among the few hints that this coolly
pared-back double-height space, complete
with old school chairs and switched-on
service, is one of Liverpool's premier
purveyors of tapas. Attention to detail means
that good bread comes with PX vinegar and

poky olive oil. At lunch, belly pork with
crunchy-chewy ends is served with rhubarb,
and a walnut and apple salad with sea salt
pyramids is generous. Texture reigns in a
bubbly turrón mousse with soft sultanas and
caramel-coated almonds. There are extra
flourishes at dinner, when a cosy buzz
descends. House wine £13.95.
Chef/s: Martin Renshaw. **Open:** all week 12 to 10.30
(11pm Fri and Sat). **Closed:** 25 Dec. **Meals:** alc
(tapas £4 to £7). **Set L** £9.90. **Service:** not inc.
Details: 90 seats. 26 seats outside. Separate bar.
Music.

The Side Door

Welcoming, good-value little bistro
29a Hope Street, Liverpool, L1 9BQ
Tel no: (0151) 7077888
www.thesidedoor.co.uk
Modern European | £27
Cooking score: 2

The 'relaxed, informal atmosphere' of this
characterful bistro is greatly valued by its
regulars. There's comfort in the creaky floors,
reasonable prices and easy welcome, but the
menu doesn't play it particularly safe. To start,
there might be chilli-fried squid with teriyaki
noodles, followed by a mini-frittata of
asparagus, pea and dill, with tender, aïoli-
drizzled patatas bravas. Puddings could be
rhubarb and custard tart or 'pana colada', a
coconut pannacotta with pineapple and rum
sauce. The confidence that comes from
longevity has survived a recent change in
ownership and allows the kitchen to have a
little fun. House wine is £13.95.
Chef/s: Michael Robinson. **Open:** all week L 12 to
2.30 (4 Sun), Mon to Sat D 5.30 to 10. **Closed:** 25 to
28 Dec, 1 and 2 Jan. **Meals:** alc (main courses £12 to
£19). **Set L** £15.95 (2 courses) to £18.95. **Set D** £16.95
(2 courses) to £18.95. **Service:** 10%. **Details:** 52
seats. Music.

60 Hope Street

A go-to address for culture vultures
60 Hope Street, Liverpool, L1 9BZ
Tel no: (0151) 7076060
www.60hopestreet.com
Modern British | £42
Cooking score: 1

A smart cookie on the Liverpool gastro scene for more than 12 years, 60 Hope Street is also a go-to address for the city's culture vultures. Set in a dignified Georgian town house close to the Philharmonic Hall, it offers great lunchtime deals, café/bar options and swanky brasserie dishes in the modern mode: hand-dived scallops are served with smoked potato, red pepper and chorizo; roast rump of lamb is presented with Jerusalem artichokes, anchovy and olive dressing, while desserts play it cheeky with, say, a deep-fried jam sandwich and Carnation Milk ice cream. The appetising, food-friendly wine list is peppered with interesting names and reputable growers from across the planet. House vin de pays is £17.95 (£4.25 a glass).
Chef/s: Damien Flynn. **Open:** Sun to Fri L 12 to 2.30, all week D 5 to 10.30. **Closed:** 26 Dec, 1 Jan. **Meals:** alc (main courses £14 to £30). Set L and D £15 (2 courses) to £20. Sun L £15. **Service:** not inc. **Details:** 180 seats. 20 seats outside. Separate bar. Music.

Spire

Neighbourhood nirvana
1 Church Road, Liverpool, L15 9EA
Tel no: (0151) 7345040
www.spirerestaurant.co.uk
Modern European | £28
Cooking score: 4

Brothers Matt and Adam Locke have achieved neighbourhood nirvana at their bistro close to Penny Lane. Readers report that time spent in the bare-brick dining room, dotted with abstract art, is 'always a joy'. Adam presides over 'attentive' service, while chef Matt's menu (which would benefit from a spell-check)

takes a modern European approach, with texture to the fore. Start with crisp shoulder of salt marsh lamb with shallot purée and wild mushrooms, or a chowder of smoked haddock, scallops and clams, to be followed by a trio of fish (salmon, sea bass and cod) with watercress velouté and a smoked haddock and potato fritter, or Goosnargh chicken with creamed cabbage and mustard and thyme sauce. Puddings including hot chocolate fondant and vanilla cheesecake push pleasure buttons rather than boundaries. House wine is from £13.95, with the majority coming in at under £25.
Chef/s: Matt Locke. **Open:** Tue to Fri L 12 to 2, Mon to Sat D 6 to 9 (9.30 Fri and Sat). **Closed:** Sun, first week Jan. **Meals:** alc (main courses £14 to £20). Set L £10.95 (2 courses) to £13.95. Set D £14.95 (2 courses) to £17.95. **Service:** not inc. **Details:** 68 seats. Music.

Oxton

★ TOP 50 ★

Fraiche

'Who dares wins' extreme cuisine
11 Rose Mount, Oxton, CH43 5SG
Tel no: (0151) 6522914
www.restaurantfraiche.com
Modern French | £48
Cooking score: 7

🍾 V

'A confident, world-class chef... and he's right on our doorstep', yelped one reader from Merseyside who was astonished by Marc Wilkinson's extraordinary one-man show – not least because the whole shebang takes place in pint-sized surroundings close to Birkenhead. Wilkinson is his own man, a notoriously single-minded soul who insists on shaping every detail, from the glass sculptures and suede chairs that grace his intimate dining room to the deliberately abstruse, tersely worded menus that are designed to keep diners guessing. This is highly unorthodox, extreme cuisine – a 'who dares wins' trip inspired by the European avant-garde, driven by hard graft and accommodating the best of regional

British produce. The result is a choice of three pithy menus, moving from 'elements' and 'signature' versions to an open-ended 'bespoke' deal – a surprise package tailored to include some of your favourite things. From the outset you will be shifted out of your comfort zone, as little bowls of 'smoking' olives, slates of unnervingly primeval 'crackling', strange-looking but delectable breads and crazy things on sticks are laid before you. After that, it's wave upon wave of startling innovation and edge-of-your-seat drama – although Wilkinson has dispensed with some of his more outlandish gastronomic trickery of late. Calibrate your taste buds with a morsel of butternut squash, tangerine and yoghurt, or a bowl of deconstructed 'cauliflower cheese' pointed up with mint. Moving on, you may find yourself in slightly more familiar territory as Wilkinson fashions sparsely assembled plates of wild sea bass on puréed aubergine with grains of wild rice, a sprig or two of marsh samphire and a few oyster leaves, or thick slices of pink venison loin with girolles and artichoke 'petals'. Then, as the compass swings towards sweetness, you might be confronted by mouth-tingling 'fizzy grapes', shot glasses of lemongrass pannacotta topped with sour cherry and vanilla or architectural constructions involving chocolate mousse, sea buckthorn sorbet, chocolate 'soil' and shards of sesame biscuit. Matching the culinary extravaganza is a top-class, 300-bin wine list that plunders the world's vineyards and cellars for enlightened and purposeful drinking, as well as celebrating viticulture's new trailblazers – Elena Walch in Alto Adige and Ian Hollick in South Australia, for example. Scores of half-bottles provide an illuminating way in, and there are satisfying house selections from £18.

Chef/s: Marc Wilkinson. **Open:** Fri and Sat L 12 to 1.30, Wed to Sun D 7 to 8.30 (6 to 7.30 Sun). **Closed:** Mon, Tue, 25 Dec, first week Jan, 2 weeks Aug. **Meals:** Set L £20 (2 courses) to £26.50. Set D £48 (3 courses) to £58 (6 courses). Bespoke menu £68. **Service:** not inc. **Details:** 16 seats. 6 seats outside. Separate bar. Wheelchair access. Music. Children over 12 yrs only at D.

▌Southport

Bistrot Vérité

Homely eatery with Gallic classics
7 Liverpool Road, Birkdale, Southport, PR8 4AR
Tel no: (01704) 564199
www.bistrotverite.co.uk
French | £25
Cooking score: 3

The francophiles of Birkdale village head to chef Marc Vérité's 'homely' bistro for a taste of classic French provincial cuisine. You may notice a few English touches on the blackboard – think haddock and chips, or crumble and custard for pudding – but Gallic standards are what it's really all about. Boudin noir with apples and crab thermidor are typically rich starters, perhaps followed by fillet of brill dugléré (in white wine sauce) or the big, bold flavours of ham and morteau sausage, or rabbit leg with Agen prunes. Apple tart makes a fitting finale. Food and service win plaudits; the bustling ambience, however, splits the vote: cramped seating and high noise levels can be a problem. The wine list opens with quaffable French red or white at £16.45.

Chef/s: Marc Vérité. **Open:** Tue to Sat L 12 to 1.30, D 5.30 to 9.30. **Closed:** Sun, Mon, 25 and 26 Dec, 1 Jan, 1 week Feb, 1 week Aug. **Meals:** alc (main courses £12 to £26). **Service:** not inc. **Details:** 45 seats. 14 seats outside. Music.

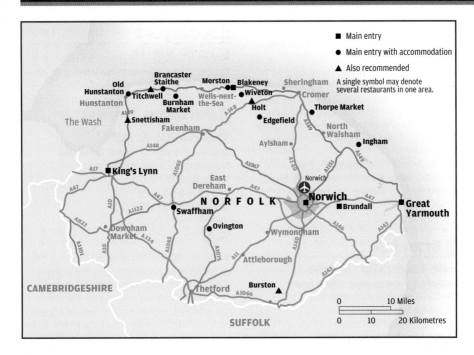

Legend:
- ■ Main entry
- ● Main entry with accommodation
- ▲ Also recommended

A single symbol may denote several restaurants in one area.

■ Blakeney

The Moorings

Lively little café-cum-bistro
High Street, Blakeney, NR25 7NA
Tel no: (01263) 740054
www.blakeney-moorings.co.uk
Modern British | £30
Cooking score: 2

Richard and Angela Long's lively little café-cum-bistro is just a few yards from Blakeney's quay and miles of salt marsh. Expect a laid-back café vibe during the day, when the cheery, sunny-yellow interior draws in coastal path walkers for soups, sandwiches and summer salads. Evening sees more ambition; the big-on-flavour modern British menu brims with seasonal game and locally landed fish and seafood: say, Morston mussel, cockle and shrimp chowder, and cod with chorizo and tomatoes on white bean mash. Leave room for one of Angela's legendary homemade puddings, perhaps rhubarb, honey and saffron tart. House wine £15.

Chef/s: Richard and Angela Long. **Open:** Tue to Sun L 12 to 3, Tue to Sat D 6.30 to 9. **Closed:** Mon to Thur Nov to Mar, 2 weeks Jan. **Meals:** alc (main courses £14 to £21). Sun L £16.95. **Service:** not inc. **Details:** 50 seats. Music.

■ Brancaster Staithe

The White Horse

Simple cooking lets the flavours shine
Brancaster Staithe, PE31 8BY
Tel no: (01485) 210262
www.whitehorsebrancaster.co.uk
Modern British | £30
Cooking score: 3

From the decked terrace and conservatory restaurant there are stunning views across salt marshes to the sea beyond. Unsurprisingly, this popular inn favours fish, much of it landed along the coast, with mussels, oysters and samphire harvested within 150 metres of the inn, and the cooking is simple to allow key flavours to shine through. It's not all fish,

though, and you could start with rabbit and ham hock terrine with Madeira jelly, before going on to wild black bream with saffron, pea and squid risotto and chive beurre blanc, or Holkham venison with wild mushroom suet pudding and juniper jus. To finish, try the hibiscus pannacotta with strawberry salsa. There's a seaside feel to the décor, a cracking bar serving home-brewed ales, and house wine is £16.
Chef/s: Avrum Frankel. **Open:** all week L 12 to 2, D 6.30 to 9. **Meals:** alc (main courses £10 to £21). **Service:** not inc. **Details:** 100 seats. 160 seats outside. Separate bar. Wheelchair access. Music. Car parking.

Brundall
The Lavender House
Delightfully unassuming foodie haven
39 The Street, Brundall, NR13 5AA
Tel no: (01603) 712215
www.thelavenderhouse.co.uk
Modern British | £40
Cooking score: 3

The menu at this delightfully unassuming restaurant on Brundall's quiet main street bursts at the beams with Norfolk's foodie finest. Chef Richard Hughes doesn't have to travel far to fill a shopping bag with gems: a quick sprint to Cromer (warm spiced crab tart with pink grapefruit is a deliciously palate-awakening starter), round the coast to Cley for smoked salmon, before heading inland for Attleborough asparagus. The slow-cooked belly pork, black pudding and pickled pear does require a cross-border trip to Blythburgh, but the flavour-packed tenderness of the meat makes the Suffolk detour admissible. Fragrant local strawberries served with elegant cubes of mint jelly are a refreshing finale to an exquisite meal. A three- or five-glass flight of matched wines is a tempting way of exploring the carefully chosen and well-annotated list, but there is also house wine from £19.95.

Chef/s: Richard Hughes. **Open:** Sun L 12 to 3, Wed to Sat D 6 to 10. **Closed:** Mon, Tue, 26 Dec to 4 Jan. **Meals:** Set D £39.95 (5 courses). **Service:** not inc. **Details:** 50 seats. Separate bar. Wheelchair access. Music. Car parking.

Burnham Market
The Hoste Arms
Gracious inn with brasserie favourites
The Green, Burnham Market, PE31 8HD
Tel no: (01328) 738777
www.hostearms.co.uk
Modern British | £28
Cooking score: 2

When the Whittomes took over this seventeenth-century coaching inn in 1989, they set about fostering a sense of gracious Englishness that has suffused the place ever since. Now Jeanne Whittome has sold up, to Brendan and Bee Hopkins, local residents and long-standing friends. Nothing else has changed. Aaron Smith continues to offer a menu that's a familiar run through the modern brasserie catalogue: Cromer crab with saffron mayonnaise or salmon and prawn fishcakes to start, mains that embrace good steaks, chicken and asparagus pie or lemon sole with samphire and caper butter sauce, and highly rated house ice creams. Wines from £16.60.
Chef/s: Aaron Smith. **Open:** all week L 12 to 2, D 6 to 9. **Meals:** alc (main courses £13 to £22). **Service:** not inc. **Details:** 140 seats. 100 seats outside. Separate bar. Music. Car parking.

Burston
ALSO RECOMMENDED
▲ The Crown
Mill Road, Burston, IP22 5TW
Tel no: (01379) 741257
www.burstoncrown.com
Modern European

A roster of tip-top Norfolk microbrewery ales, regular live gigs and a big blazing inglenook fire add to the fun-loving allure of this amazingly friendly village hostelry. The kitchen also does a good line in food, sending out pub classics alongside more inventive blackboard specials: Greek meze platters (£8.50) start things well, before honey-roast duck with rhubarb and port sauce (£12.50), vodka and soy-cured trout, and puds ranging from chocolate marquise to Pimm's and strawberry jelly. House wine is £15. No food Sun D.

Edgefield

The Pigs

Iffits good local grub you're after...
Norwich Road, Edgefield, NR24 2RL
Tel no: (01263) 587634
www.thepigs.org.uk
British | £25
Cooking score: 1

Well into its third decade, this welcoming seventeenth-century country pub-with-rooms retains a solid commitment to locally sourced produce, with meat from local farms, fish from the North Sea and game from nearby shoots. The real draw here is the 'Iffits' – Norfolk's version of tapas; one reporter heaps particular praise on the 'fantastic' honey, Colman's mustard and marmalade-glazed pork ribs. English rose veal osso buco is one of the more substantial main courses on offer. House wine £15.50.
Chef/s: Tim Abbott. **Open:** Mon to Sat L 12 to 2.30 (3 Sat), D 6 to 9. Sun 12 to 9. **Meals:** alc (main courses £10 to £20). **Service:** not inc. **Details:** 100 seats. 60 seats outside. Separate bar. Wheelchair access. Music. Car parking.

Symbols

⊨ Accommodation is available

£30 Three courses for less than £30

V Separate vegetarian menu

£5 OFF £5-off voucher scheme

🍷 Notable wine list

Great Yarmouth

Seafood Restaurant

Excellent seafood and homemade treats
85 North Quay, Great Yarmouth, NR30 1JF
Tel no: (01493) 856009
www.theseafood.co.uk
Seafood | £35
Cooking score: 2

Christopher and Miriam Kikis have been running their excellent seafood restaurant for more than 30 years and regular customers all seem keen to praise their favourite dishes. These run from curried monkfish, turbot with herb butter, lemon sole with a blue cheese sauce, and Dover sole (possibly served with Dijon mustard and smoked ham) to lobster thermidor, which gets an especially big thumbs-up. 'Everything is homemade, from the bread to the chocolates with the coffee' notes one fan. The restaurant itself is in 'a beautiful old building with lovely high ceilings', where the service is spot-on. Wines start at £14.50.
Chef/s: Christopher Kikis. **Open:** Mon to Fri L 12 to 1.45, Mon to Sat D 6.30 to 10.30. **Closed:** Sun, 24 Dec to 7 Jan, last week May, first week Jun, bank hols. **Meals:** alc (main courses £12 to £33). **Service:** not inc. **Details:** 42 seats. Separate bar. Music. Children over 7 yrs only.

Holt

ALSO RECOMMENDED
▲ Byfords

1 Shirehall Plain, Holt, NR25 6BG
Tel no: (01263) 711400
www.byfords.org.uk
Modern European

Byfords' all-day opening, flexible menus and laid-back atmosphere introduce a lively continental-café style to this pretty Georgian market town. Drop in for breakfast, pick from the user-friendly daytime menu (served 8 to 5.30) or nip in for coffee and cake. Otherwise, explore the versatile carte for shared deli boards (£7.95) or grazing dishes, pizzas topped with, say, chilli chicken and chorizo, or go for Moroccan lamb tagine (£15.95) and East Anglian cheeses. Wines from £14.95. Open all week. Accommodation.

Ingham

The Ingham Swan

A proper hostelry, with modern food
Sea Palling Road, Ingham, NR12 9AB
Tel no: (01692) 581099
www.theinghamswan.co.uk
Modern European | £28
Cooking score: 2

'Lovely location', noted a visitor to this ancient thatched pub in a pretty hamlet. It retains the feel of a proper hostelry – drinkers with their pints of Woodforde's ales, beams, timbers – but Daniel Smith takes a modern view in the kitchen, offering eclectic European combos with a smattering of local produce (local asparagus, Cromer crabs). Lively ideas, colour and flavour distinguish dishes such as seared rare beef fillet with truffle mayonnaise, and whole lemon sole with Brancaster mussel broth, potato purée and spinach. Vanilla pannacotta with blood orange sorbet makes a fine finish. Wines from £19.
Chef/s: Daniel Smith. **Open:** Tue to Sun L 12 to 2 (3 Sun), Tue to Sat D 7 to 9. **Closed:** Mon. **Meals:** alc (main courses £14 to £26). Set L £12.95 (2 courses) to £16.95. Set D £16.95 (2 courses) to £27.50. Sun L £23.50. **Service:** not inc. **Details:** 52 seats. 20 seats outside. Music. Car parking.

King's Lynn

Market Bistro

Enterprising local asset
11 Saturday Market Place, King's Lynn, PE30 5DQ
Tel no: (01553) 771483
www.marketbistro.co.uk
Modern British | £25
Cooking score: 2

Industrious home production is at the heart of this enterprising little bistro on King's Lynn's ancient marketplace. Richard and Lucy

Golding bake bread, cure meats, smoke fish, make pickles and more besides, as well as procuring local seafood and seasonal Norfolk produce for their 'wonderfully tasty' food. The menu moves confidently from braised pork cheeks with pancetta and lentils to slow-cooked lamb shoulder with smoked beets and Chantenay carrots, or pheasant breast and terrine with mushroom pithiviers and kale, and ends with wild-flower honey pannacotta with roasted plum and ginger shortbread. A decked roof terrace adds appeal in summer. Wines from £13.55.
Chef/s: Richard Golding. **Open:** Tue to Sat L 12 to 2, D 6.30 to 9. **Closed:** Sun, Mon, 25 and 26 Dec. **Meals:** alc (main courses £11 to £17). **Service:** not inc. **Details:** 30 seats. 12 seats outside. No music.

Morston

Morston Hall

Accomplished country hotel
The Street, Morston, NR25 7AA
Tel no: (01263) 741041
www.morstonhall.com
Modern British | £62
Cooking score: 5

The ravishing north Norfolk coast has become quite a destination for gastronomes, and Morston Hall is one of the premier stops on the itinerary. The Blackistons acquired the Hall in 1992, and over the years they have honed it into an accomplished country hotel on the human scale (just 13 bedrooms), complete with restful interiors, highly polished service and Galton Blackiston's confident, uncluttered culinary style. The drill is daily changing set dinner menus, plus Sunday lunch, with the option of wine choices to accompany four of the five evening courses. A winter menu opened with a portion of rabbit served with camomile-roasted carrots, and proceeded to cured lobster with chard in leek consommé, and then spiced crown of Gressingham duck with butternut squash and purple sprouting broccoli. A pre-dessert intervenes – perhaps hot chocolate mousse with mango purée – before the only choice of

either a main dessert (maybe rosemary pannacotta with barbecued pear in vanilla sauce) or British cheeses with sultana and walnut bread. The busily informative wine list is well-chosen throughout, and there is enough price relief under £30; it opens with a South African Pinotage (£21) and a Chilean unoaked Chardonnay (£22).
Chef/s: Galton Blackiston and Richard Bainbridge. **Open:** Sun L 12.30 for 1 (1 sitting), all week D 7.30 for 8 (1 sitting). **Closed:** 24 to 26 Dec, Jan. **Meals:** Set D £62. Sun L £35. **Service:** not inc. **Details:** 50 seats. Wheelchair access. Car parking.

▮ Norwich
Roger Hickman's
Clean, clear seasonal flavours
79 Upper St Giles Street, Norwich, NR2 1AB
Tel no: (01603) 633522
www.rogerhickmansrestaurant.com
Modern British | £40
Cooking score: 5
£5 OFF 🍷

The 'first choice' in Norwich by a country mile, Roger Hickman's civilised yet animated gaff is now firmly on the national radar – thanks to its affable demeanour, pleasantly unhurried service and sharply defined seasonal food. Clean, clear flavours are Hickman's culinary trademarks, whether he is fashioning a tiny pot of chicken liver parfait beneath a foamy crown or a broad-shouldered plateful of impressively rich roast duck breast, sweet carrots and a crispy, crunchy egg with a melting yolk ('one of the best things I've eaten all year' exclaimed one reader). He can also conjure up delicacy and spirit-level balance when required, as in an 'incredibly light' combo of crab salad, avocado purée, lemongrass mousse and confit tomatoes, or an earthy warm beef salad with truffled potatoes and pickled mushrooms (a favourite accessory). Desserts show painstaking skill in every department – from the summery freshness of pink-hued poached strawberries etched with golden honeycomb to salted caramel ice cream with caramelised bananas and pecan crumb (a sensation that 'almost

popped in the mouth'). The wine list also comes up trumps, offering an exemplary choice of growers and varietals at eminently fair prices, from a Tokay Pinot Gris to a potent Henschke from Australia's Eden Valley. Fourteen terrific house selections start at £19.
Chef/s: Roger Hickman. **Open:** Tue to Sat L 12 to 2.30, D 7 to 10. **Closed:** Sun, Mon, 1 week Jan, 1 week Aug. **Meals:** Set L £18 (2 courses) to £22. Set D £32 (2 courses) to £40. **Service:** not inc. **Details:** 42 seats. Music.

ALSO RECOMMENDED
▲ The Assembly House
Theatre Street, Norwich, NR2 1RQ
Tel no: (01603) 626402
www.assemblyhousenorwich.co.uk
Modern British

This handsome Georgian building has long been one of Norwich's most prestigious addresses and it is now a multifaceted cultural hot spot. Julia Hetherton's brunch dishes of thick-cut ham and mature Cheddar toasties (£5.95) and black pudding with poached egg and apple salad (£6) make way for lunch options of slow-cooked belly pork, greens and apple sauce (£11.95) or pan-fried lambs' liver, bacon and mash (£9.95). Bookings are essential for the refined afternoon teas. Wines from £15. Open all week.

▲ Shiki
6 Tombland, Norwich, NR3 1HE
Tel no: (01603) 619262
www.shikirestaurant.co.uk
Japanese

Pitched on trendy Tombland opposite the cathedral, this effervescent, young-at-heart Japanese canteen is a hit with students, tourists and foodies. Drop by for dependable sushi, thick-cut sashimi, perfectly timed tempura, wakame salad (£4.90), pork tonkatsu and other carefully made favourites. Lunch also features great-value bento boxes (£10), one-plate meals and street-food staples including nourishing donburi rice bowls; evening brings theatrical teppanyaki menus in addition to the regular offering. Drink green tea, Japanese beer, wine (from £4 a glass) or chuhai (shochu with lemonade). Closed Sun.

▌Old Hunstanton
The Neptune
Expert creations and gorgeous little delicacies
85 Old Hunstanton Road, Old Hunstanton, PE36 6HZ
Tel no: (01485) 532122
www.theneptune.co.uk
Modern British | £50
Cooking score: 5

£5 OFF 🛏

Given the lack of interior design statements and silver service flummery, prices at the Neptune can be eye-opening – but the food has few detractors. Behind its foliage-bedecked exterior, this former village pub, run by chef Kevin Mangeolles and his wife Jacki, is split into a bar for pre-prandial drinks and, up a couple of steps, a little front-room of a dining area decorated in sea-grey hues. Burnham Market second homeowners fill the place at weekends, though weekdays are quieter. It's an intimate setting for Kevin's beautifully presented, expertly balanced creations. Local ingredients figured strongly in an inspection meal, where a 10in strip of guinea fowl terrine provided the base for gorgeous little delicacies: perfectly deep-fried sweetbreads, curled slivers of radish, piquant pickled mushrooms. To follow, baby halibut was as succulent and fresh as a fish can be, ably supported by little crab 'gnocchi' (more like crab cakes), diminutive broad beans and sweet 'cannelloni' of red pepper, filled with seafood rice. Pudding was exemplary: a deconstructed Gariguette strawberry cheesecake on sablé biscuit offset by sharp strawberry sorbet and sweet Campari jelly. Like Jacki Mangeolles's chatty, knowledgeable service, the wine list (from £19.50) is without airs or graces, and gives plenty of choice in the £20-£35 bracket.
Chef/s: Kevin Mangeolles. **Open:** Sun L 12 to 1.30, Tue to Sun D 7 to 9. **Closed:** Mon, 1 week Nov, 26 Dec, 3 weeks Jan. **Meals:** alc (main courses £22 to £29). Sun L £32.50. **Service:** not inc. **Details:** 24 seats. Separate bar. Music. Car parking. Children over 8 yrs only.

▌Ovington
The Café at Brovey Lair
Thrilling gastro-theatre
Carbrooke Road, Ovington, IP25 6SD
Tel no: (01953) 882706
www.broveylair.com
Pan-Asian/Seafood | £53
Cooking score: 6

£5 OFF 🛏 **V**

Years before reality TV cottoned on to the idea of turning your own home into a restaurant, Mike and Tina Pemberton were showing how it should be done. Needless to say, it's a notion that comes with its own quirks and mores – in this case, culinary likes and dislikes are discussed in detail over the telephone and the resulting show is played out as a piece of open gastro-theatre. The thrills, elegance and intimacy of the place invariably impress first-timers, although the spectacle may not always stand up to repeat performances – especially as menus follow a strict format, involving stir-fries, energising salads and teppan grilling, interspersed with 'New Age' soups and desserts that are mostly from the wholefood school (almond-crusted ricotta and mascarpone cheesecake). The world is Tina's larder, so expect daikon, quinoa and miso alongside Norfolk asparagus and samphire, while supplies of seafood go way beyond the North Sea. She conjures up some 'delightfully complex tastes': a Mediterranean beetroot soup with cumin and saba (concentrated grape 'must') that would 'leave borscht lovers open-mouthed with wonderment'; an oft-reported dish of sesame-coated scallops on beanshoot salad, or fillets of Dover sole baked with spicy Thai basil, Kaffir lime and coconut. To get the best from Brovey Lair, stay over; that way you might get to lounge by the swimming pool and enjoy the spoils of the 'deliciously different' Cal-Mex breakfast. Wine from £17.50.

Chef/s: Tina Pemberton. **Open:** all week L by special arrangement, D 7.45 (1 sitting). **Closed:** 25 and 26 Dec. **Meals:** Set L and D £52.50 (4 courses). **Service:** 10%. **Details:** 20 seats. 20 seats outside. No music. Wheelchair access. Car parking. Children over 15 yrs only.

Snettisham

ALSO RECOMMENDED
▲ The Rose & Crown
Old Church Road, Snettisham, PE31 7LX
Tel no: (01485) 541382
www.roseandcrownsnettisham.co.uk
Modern British

All rambling beamed rooms, open fires and low ceilings, this whitewashed fourteenth-century inn is firmly in tune with the times when it comes to food and service. Freshly baked bread sets the tone, and the menu nods to the region with Bingham Blue cheese tartlet (£6.50), bowls of Brancaster mussels or whole plaice with crushed new potatoes and beurre noisette (£12.50). Also expect anything from chicken Caesar burgers to coq au vin or butternut squash risotto. House wine is £14. Accommodation. Open all week.

Swaffham

Strattons
Eco champ with modish menus
4 Ash Close, Swaffham, PE37 7NH
Tel no: (01760) 723845
www.strattonshotel.com
Modern British | £34
Cooking score: 2

Long a champion of prime local ingredients, Strattons continues to win plaudits for its 'extremely high standard of fare'. The Rustic restaurant – in a romantic old hotel just off Swaffham's market place – has dark walls, decorative urns and gilded mirrors. Gilded, too, are the kitchen's modish pastiches of pub food: pâté-like corned beef with runny-yolked Scotch egg; mains of 'divine' cottage pie. Slips aren't unknown, witness an ill-

conceived mackerel 'pasty' stuffed with chorizo-like sausage meat. Nevertheless, creamy blood orange posset and granita with shortbread made some amends. 'Prompt, informative' service and a thoughtful wine list (from £18.50) are further plus points.
Chef/s: Sam Bryant. **Open:** Sun L 12 to 2.30, all week D 6.30 to 9. **Closed:** 1 week Christmas. **Meals:** alc (main courses £14 to £25). Set L £19 (2 courses) to £25. Set D £28.50 (2 courses) to £35. Sun L £25. **Service:** not inc. **Details:** 32 seats. 10 seats outside. Separate bar. Music. Car parking.

Thorpe Market

★ BEST NEW ENTRY ★

NEW ENTRY
The Gunton Arms
Game-changer that fizzes with success
Cromer Road, Thorpe Market, NR11 8TZ
Tel no: (01263) 832010
www.theguntonarms.co.uk
Modern British | £30
Cooking score: 5

A north-east Norfolk game-changer, the Gunton Arms brings modern sensibilities to a classically English setting in the grounds of a country estate. Baronial furnishings in this capacious pub-hotel-restaurant are leavened by witty neon signage and casually dressed (but expertly trained) young staff. Mark Hix protégé Stuart Tattersall runs the kitchen. Local produce – seafood and foraged plants from the coast, venison from the herd that's visible in the distance – in simple but alluring combinations, peppers his menu. Precisely fried duck egg, perfectly counterbalanced by King's Lynn brown shrimps and salty seashore vegetables, might be followed by tender beef flank and ale pie in voluptuous gravy. Roasted meat, cooked over a vast open fire in the Elk Room, is another highlight. Gorgeous, too, are the puds – butterscotch and nut brittle cheesecake is a whisper-light, freshly made masterpiece. Prices are appealingly modest, both for food and the concise but spot-on wine list, which starts at £14. Bar snacks are

on-trend too: pork crackling with apple and gooseberry sauce, for instance, and some of Norfolk's finest real ales are served there. Norfolk's gentry (and others) can't keep away; this place, rightly, fizzes with success.
Chef/s: Stuart Tattersall. **Open:** all week L 12 to 3, D 6 to 10 (9 Sun). **Closed:** 25 Dec. **Meals:** alc (main courses £10 to £45). **Service:** not inc. **Details:** 60 seats. 40 seats outside. Separate bar. Wheelchair access. Music. Car parking.

▌ Titchwell

ALSO RECOMMENDED
▲ Titchwell Manor
Titchwell, PE31 8BB
Tel no: (01485) 210221
www.titchwellmanor.com
Modern European

Transformed by the Snaith family into a chic coastal bolt-hole, the former gentleman's club overlooks wild salt marsh to the sea. Eric Snaith sources top-notch local and seasonal ingredients, and his brasserie-style 'Eating Rooms' menu delivers classics like Dexter beef pie (£10), confit duck (£13) and créme brûlée (£7) alongside fresh fish and seafood. His ambitious seven-course tasting menu (£45), served in the Conservatory Restaurant, pushes boundaries with complex and unusual ingredient combinations. House wine £16.50. Open all week.

▌ Wiveton

Wiveton Bell
Popular pub with well-cooked staples
Blakeney Road, Wiveton, NR25 7TL
Tel no: (01263) 740101
www.wivetonbell.com
Modern British | £28
Cooking score: 1

This is crab country, and you can do worse than visit this pub for a Cromer crab salad and glass of something refreshing on its patio. The menu is too long, and cluttered with pub stables, but at best it provides good local grub

– a hearty Wivvy Bell steak burger with Norfolk Dapple smoked cheese, say, or a starter of asparagus with a beautifully poached egg, 'melt-in-the-mouth' belly pork or a deliciously bitter-sweet coffee pannacotta. House wine £15.95.
Chef/s: Jamie Murch. **Open:** all week L 12 to 2.15 (2.30 Sun), D 6 to 9. **Closed:** 25 Dec. **Meals:** alc (main courses £12 to £21). **Service:** not inc. **Details:** 60 seats. 60 seats outside. No music. Wheelchair access. Car parking.

ALSO RECOMMENDED
▲ Wiveton Farm Café
Wiveton Hall, Wiveton, NR25 7TE
Tel no: (01263) 740515
www.wivetonhall.co.uk/cafe.htm
Modern British

This enterprising, quirky café is set amidst the PYO strawberry and raspberry fields at Wiveton Hall, and it overlooks marshland with views towards the sea. One contented reporter particularly enjoyed the 'relaxed feel and friendly welcome' as much as the generous helpings of 'delicious' Cromer crab salad with new potatoes, and a hazelnut brownie. In fact, the only gripe was the fact the café closes for the winter season. House wine £12.50. Open all week end Mar to end Nov (tapas Fri and Sat D).

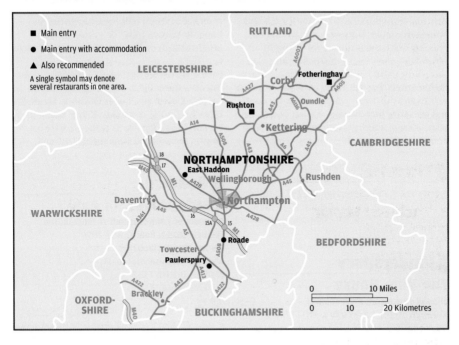

East Haddon

The Red Lion
Reborn country inn
Main Street, East Haddon, NN6 8BU
Tel no: (01604) 770223
www.redlioneasthaddon.co.uk
Modern British | £25
Cooking score: 3

Since its rather grand makeover in 2010, the stone-built Red Lion has reasserted itself as one of Northamptonshire's notable country inns – thanks partly to culinary input from Gary Rhodes' lieutenant Adam Gray (see Rhodes Twenty Four, London). Despite a few unnecessary affectations (pumpkin soup poured over a blue cheese fritter at table, for example), the kitchen generally makes a good fist of mainstream dishes such as a runny free-range pork Scotch egg with caper and parsley mayonnaise, braised ox cheek in red wine with mash, or crispy pollack and chips. Desserts are mostly tweaked-up standards, including

Black Forest cheesecake and banana fool with toffee sauce. Service can veer from 'sharp and urbane' to 'rough and ready' (as befits a born-again hostelry), and the one-page wine list starts at £15.25.
Chef/s: Adam Gray and Anthony Horn. Open: Mon to Sat L 12 to 2.30, D 6 to 10. Sun 12 to 8. Meals: alc (main courses £11 to £18). Service: not inc.
Details: 80 seats. 70 seats outside. Separate bar. Wheelchair access. Music. Car parking.

Fotheringhay

The Falcon Inn
Smart country haven
Fotheringhay, PE8 5HZ
Tel no: (01832) 226254
www.thefalcon-inn.co.uk
Modern European | £37
Cooking score: 2

An exceptional country haven, this stone-built inn stands proud in the shadow of Fotheringhay's great church. It has the air of a smart restaurant, with its elegant garden and classy interior, but a good-value bar menu plus sandwiches reinforce pubby credentials. Otherwise, there's a monthly changing à la carte built securely on fresh materials, perhaps in the form of Portland crab with linguine and a chilli and dill crème fraîche. Clear flavours and attractive presentation are part of the deal, as in a rack of English lamb with dauphinoise potatoes, baby vegetables and red wine jus. Wines start at £13.50.

Chef/s: Danny Marshall. **Open:** all week L 12 to 2.15 (3 Sun), D 6.15 to 9.15 (8.30 Sun). **Meals:** alc (main courses £13 to £19). Set L and D £12.95 (2 courses) to £15.50. **Service:** not inc. **Details:** 70 seats. 80 seats outside. Separate bar. No music. Wheelchair access. Car parking.

Paulerspury
The Vine House
Blissful restaurant-with-rooms
100 High Street, Paulerspury, NN12 7NA
Tel no: (01327) 811267
www.vinehousehotel.com
Modern British | £31
Cooking score: 4

Marcus and Julie Springett's restaurant-with-rooms is the kind of place that wins you over in an instant – especially if the weather's right. It occupies a gorgeous 300-year-old farmhouse, and weaves its magic with a blend of personable courtesy and affection, backed by cooking that knows all about seasonality, balance and flavours that work. Dishes change daily, but local black pudding crops up regularly in different guises – perhaps with shallot cream and mustard pickle purée, or as part of a terrine with a poached egg and homemade ketchup. Lamb from Northamptonshire's rich pastures is also a perennial hit, or perhaps Cornish red mullet accompanied by pea risotto, korma curry emulsion and shellfish oil. To conclude, the kitchen also takes its cue from the calendar – witness a summertime jelly suffused with elderflowers, topped with local honey and finished with lemon syllabub. If you're after

romance as well as culinary contentment, book the garden folly for a dreamy assignation. A drinker-friendly wine list starts at £17.50.

Chef/s: Marcus Springett, Kelly Kerley and Jordan Bateman. **Open:** Tue to Sat L 12 to 1.45, Mon to Sat D 6 to 9. **Closed:** Sun, 1 week Christmas. **Meals:** Set L and D £27.50 (2 courses) to £30.95. **Service:** 12.5%. **Details:** 33 seats. Separate bar. No music. Car parking. Children over 12 yrs only.

Roade
Roade House
An oasis of calmness and respectability
16 High Street, Roade, NN7 2NW
Tel no: (01604) 863372
www.roadehousehotel.co.uk
Modern British | £32
Cooking score: 3

Chris and Sue Kewley's stone-clad 'restaurant and hotel' (in that order) may be within easy reach of Silverstone, but it feels far removed from the fuel-injected, high-octane world of F1. Inside, the Roade House exudes calmness and respectability, with a mood of courteous personal bonhomie matching the innocuous old-style furnishings and fittings. The cooking never offends, and Chris deals professionally with the demands of, say, wild duck breast with confit leg, red cabbage, apple and Calvados, pan-fried sea bass with sweet potatoes, smoked salmon and dill butter sauce, or calf's liver with pancetta, mash and onion confit. Proceedings might open with a bowl of mushroom and Madeira soup, while desserts never stray far from the time-honoured sweetness of lemon tart, rhubarb crumble or chocolate cheesecake. The international wine list (from £16) isn't about to scare the horses either.

Chef/s: Chris Kewley. **Open:** Sun to Fri L 12.30 to 2 (2.30 Sun), Mon to Sat D 7 to 9. **Closed:** 1 week from 26 Dec, bank hols. **Meals:** alc (main courses £15 to £22). Set L £20.50 (2 courses) to £23.50. **Service:** not inc. **Details:** 48 seats. Separate bar. Wheelchair access. Music. Car parking.

Rushton

NEW ENTRY

Rushton Hall, Tresham Restaurant

Satisfying seasonal food in venerable surroundings

Desborough Road, Rushton, NN14 1RR
Tel no: (01536) 713001
www.rushtonhall.com
Modern British | £49
Cooking score: 3

£5
OFF

Built by the landed Tresham family in 1438, Rushton Hall now stands proud as a stately mansion and heritage-strewn leisure retreat. With its carved stonework, tapestries, cloistered hallways and immaculate grass quad, it reminded one visitor of 'a venerable Oxford college' – although things are decidedly dressed-down in the oak-panelled Tresham Restaurant. Polite, personable staff know the ropes and the kitchen delivers satisfying, seasonal dishes with bags of flavour but no shocks to the system. Cumin-crusted scallops are teamed with cauliflower purée and cubes of apple jelly, new season's lamb is accurately poached in a water bath and served alongside a tidy assortment of spring vegetables and wild garlic, while roast day-boat brill might come with squid-ink risotto and lemongrass foam. To finish, a toothsome, technically astute plate of crisp blueberry cannelloni with chocolate sorbet and 'Crunchie bar' honeycomb has lived up to its star billing. Top marks for the breads and ambrosial 'homemade' butter, too. The weighty wine list starts at £18.50.
Chef/s: Adrian Coulthard. **Open:** Sun L 12 to 2, all week D 7 to 9. **Meals:** alc (main courses £20 to £28). Sun L £25. **Service:** not inc. **Details:** 40 seats. 40 seats outside. Separate bar. Wheelchair access. Music. Car parking. Children over 10 yrs only at D.

COOL FOR KIDS

Most temples of gastronomy could do with a lively touch, and restaurants where well-behaved children are welcome have jollity built in. But what do they offer their pint-sized diners? A friendly welcome and good food from their own special menu, in the case of our favourite hot spots for tots.

Le Manoir Aux Quat' Saisons, Great Milton
Children get the royal treatment at Le Manoir, with teddy bears and kitchen tours and a three-course menu (£25) which finishes with Raymond Blanc's favourite childhood desserts. Babies are served organic vegetable purée.

The Bingham, Richmond
While mum and dad are wowed by chef Shay Cooper's intricately presented plates at the riverside hotel, kids are treated to a three-course menu (£20) starring simple fish dishes and rice pudding with a chocolate sauce.

Northcote, Langho
While the children are unable to enjoy Northcote's great cellar, all ages are welcome in the dining room. Mini versions of à la carte main courses are one route, but the kitchen will also knock up something simpler to please the young ones.

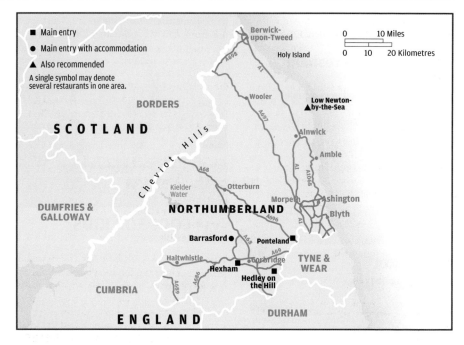

- ■ Main entry
- ● Main entry with accommodation
- ▲ Also recommended

A single symbol may denote several restaurants in one area.

▋Barrasford

The Barrasford Arms

Well-run, no-frills village inn
Barrasford, NE48 4AA
Tel no: (01434) 681237
www.barrasfordarms.co.uk
Modern British | £25
Cooking score: 2

'A no-frills village inn, well-run, with good food to match'. So ran one reporter's summary of this substantial inn with Tyne Valley views. The feeling is relaxed – it's a stone's throw from Hadrian's Wall and there are great facilities for walkers and cyclists. The food is a mix of traditional British with modern European touches, so most people find something they like. Start, perhaps, with crab, chilli and Parmesan tart with garlic and saffron rouille, then veal with braised charlotte potatoes, mushrooms, tarragon and tomato in a white wine sauce; finish with almond and local damson tart. Wines from £13.95.

Chef/s: Tony Binks. **Open:** Tue to Sun L 12 to 2 (3 Sun), Mon to Sat D 6.30 to 9. **Closed:** 25 and 26 Dec, bank hols. **Meals:** alc (main courses £10 to £17). Set L £11.50 (2 courses) to £14.50. Sun L £14 (2 courses) to £16.50. **Service:** not inc. **Details:** 65 seats. Separate bar. Music. Car parking.

▋Hedley on the Hill

The Feathers Inn

Cracking inn that's great value
Hedley on the Hill, NE43 7SW
Tel no: (01661) 843607
www.thefeathers.net
British | £25
Cooking score: 3

'Despite its humble rusticity, this is a tip-top inn in every way, and is run with panache by the owners', enthused one visitor to Rhian and Helen Cradock's cracking 200-year-old drovers' inn. It comes with a full quota of exposed stone walls, beams and simple furnishings, supports local produce in a big

way, and the cooking is accomplished without being pretentious. It is considered 'the best-value food for miles around'. Lunch is simple and straightforward, but there are more complex dishes in the evening. Try John Dory fillet with wild mushrooms and celeriac, and herb velouté to start, follow with roast free-range organic duck with sloe gin, braised white cabbage and rösti potatoes, and finish with burnt Northumbrian cream. Wines on the short blackboard list start at £15.
Chef/s: Rhian Cradock. **Open:** Tue to Sun L 12 to 2 (2.30 Sun), Tue to Sat D 6 to 8.30. **Closed:** Mon, first 2 weeks Jan. **Meals:** alc (main courses £20 to £30). Sun L £17 (2 courses) to £20. **Service:** not inc. **Details:** 45 seats. 15 seats outside. No music. Car parking.

▮ Hexham

Bouchon Bistrot
Proper French cooking at gentle prices
4-6 Gilesgate, Hexham, NE46 3NJ
Tel no: (01434) 609943
www.bouchonbistrot.co.uk
French | £26
Cooking score: 4

Bouchon Bistrot is 'a rare find', serving proper French country cooking at gentle prices. Many of the dishes hail from the Elizabeth David school: think salade landaise with cured magret (duck breast) and gizzards, grilled pork chop with pomme purée and French beans, and mousse au chocolat with sablé Breton (butter biscuit) or 'brilliant' crème brûlée. The few more international touches – perhaps 'subtle, tender' lamb tagine or sea bass tartare – would not raise eyebrows at a similar establishment over the Channel. The brick walls, beamed ceilings and burgundy palette are 'pleasant' and 'restrained', all the better for an evening of convivial, rather than grandstanding, French cuisine. Early-bird and set lunch menus are a steal, and the ever-popular 'steak frites' appears there. Staff are 'friendly without being familiar' and maintain

those standards even on big nights. The wine list (from £13.95), *quelle surprise*, is proudly, but not quite completely, French.
Chef/s: Nicolas Duhil. **Open:** Mon to Sat L 12 to 2, D 6 to 9.30. **Closed:** Sun, 24 to 26 Dec. **Meals:** alc (main courses £12 to £19). Set L £11.95 (2 courses) to £13.95. Set early D £13.95 (2 courses) to £15.50. **Service:** 10% for parties of 6 or more. **Details:** 130 seats. Wheelchair access. Music.

ALSO RECOMMENDED
▲ The Rat Inn
Anick, Hexham, NE46 4LN
Tel no: (01434) 602814
www.theratinn.com
Modern British

This laid-back, ivy-clad inn has a beer garden with views over the Teme Valley, a traditional interior of stone-flagged floors, assorted chairs and open fires – and a knack of attracting the crowds. Blackboard menus in the bar offer simple items such as watermelon and feta salad with pumpkin seeds (£6.50), West Mill Hills lamb chops, roasted carrots and mashed swedes (£14.50), and ginger sponge with stem ginger ice cream (£5.50). Wines from £13.95. No food Sun D and Mon.

▮ Low Newton-by-the-Sea

ALSO RECOMMENDED
▲ The Ship Inn
Newton Square, Low Newton-by-the-Sea, NE66 3EL
Tel no: (01665) 576262
www.shipinnnewton.co.uk
Modern British

This whitewashed pub tucked into a corner of a square yards from the beach ticks all the boxes for friendliness, good beer, comfort, character – and food. Simple, carefully prepared meals are what Christine Forsyth does well: grilled goats' cheese with basil and tomato (£4.50), local sirloin steak with onion marmalade or monkfish with a green pepper and olive tagine (£16.50), and well-made lemon posset or local unpasteurised cheeses. Wines from £14.45. Open all week (check for seasonal variations). Cash only.

∎ Ponteland

Café Lowrey
Setting the bar for neighbourhood eateries
33-35 The Broadway, Darras Hall, Ponteland, NE20 9PW
Tel no: (01661) 820357
www.cafelowrey.co.uk
Modern British | £32
Cooking score: 3

Smart yet relaxed and enduringly popular, Ian Lowery's neighbourhood bistro has settled into a rhythm over the years, delivering 'a wholly satisfying meal in a lovely restaurant', for one visitor. A lot of care and thought have gone into the details and simple classics have a please-all appeal, from cheese and spinach soufflé to lobster bisque, from confit of duck leg with beetroot and lyonnaise potatoes and red wine jus to fishcakes served with buttered spinach and parsley sauce. The food delivers plenty of flavour without pretension, something as simple as 'superb' steak and chips is widely praised, while skilful desserts like chocolate fondant with white chocolate ice cream add a finishing touch. Wines from £15.95.
Chef/s: Ian Lowrey. **Open:** Fri to Sun L 12 to 2.30 (3 Sun), Tue to Sat D 5.30 to 10 (6 Sat). **Closed:** Mon, 25 and 26 Dec, bank hols. **Meals:** alc (main courses £17 to £25). Set L and D £15.95 (2 courses) to £18.95. **Service:** not inc. **Details:** 70 seats. Wheelchair access. Music. Car parking.

⫴● SUPPLY AND DEMAND

Until recently, provenance was a little-known concept in the restaurant world and few UK chefs, let alone diners, gave much thought to the region or producer their ingredients were from. These days, however, suppliers are often listed on a menu, so you can see the precise field where your parsnips were grown, or your pork was reared.

For Kent-born Mark Sergeant, a desire to showcase the fantastic produce of his home county led him to choose local suppliers, many of whom are name-checked on the menu of his **Rocksalt** restaurant in Folkestone. Fish comes from Folkestone Trawlers, yards from his front door, while Monkshill Farm in Faversham supplies much of the meat, and herbs and salads come from the restaurant's own smallholding. When Mark started out in the industry 20 years ago, restaurants would buy from Rungis market outside Paris. Now, they're proud to champion local producers.

Also flying the flag for his region is Sean Hope at the **Olive Branch** in Rutland, who encourages diners to visit suppliers, including the Colston Bassett dairy and Oakham Grainstore Brewery, by following a food trail printed on the back of the menu.

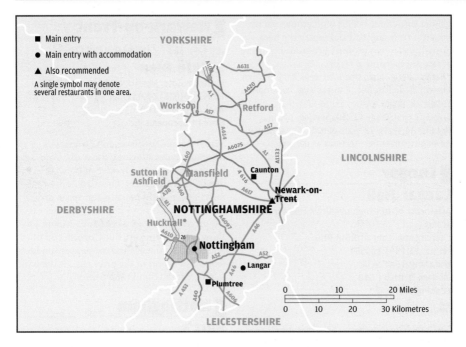

Blyth

READERS RECOMMEND
White Swan at Blyth
British
High Street, Blyth, S81 8EQ
Tel no: (01909) 591222
www.whiteswanblyth.co.uk
'Thoughtfully created food using excellent quality, locally sourced ingredients. A warm welcoming atmosphere with a real roaring fire.'

Readers Recommend
A 'readers recommend' review is a genuine quote from a report sent in by one of our readers. We intend to follow up these suggestions throughout the year to come.

Caunton
Caunton Beck
All-year-round treats aplenty
Main Street, Caunton, NG23 6AB
Tel no: (01636) 636793
www.wigandmitre.com
Modern British | £27
Cooking score: 2

A self-proclaimed 'meeting house, reading room, watering hole and restaurant' noted for its personable all-day hospitality and convivial mood, this sixteenth-century cottage hostelry 'by a beck' offers treats aplenty throughout the week. The kitchen runs 'in perpetual motion', moving from breakfasts of bacon sarnies or poached eggs on toast through to seasonal offerings such as herb-crusted brill with chorizo and 'micro' coriander risotto, or ale-braised beef featherblade with horseradish mash and tarragon jus. Antipasti and ciabattas fill any gaps, while desserts might feature spiced clementine crème brûlée with cinnamon ice cream. 'Freehouse' real ales satisfy the beer crowd, and wines promise generous imbibing at fair prices (from £14.25).

Chef/s: Valerie Hope. **Open:** all week 8am to 10pm. **Closed:** 25 and 26 Dec, 2 weeks Aug, bank hols. **Meals:** alc (main courses £11 to £15). Set L and D £12.95 (2 courses) to £15.50. **Service:** not inc. **Details:** 84 seats. 32 seats outside. Separate bar. No music. Wheelchair access. Car parking.

▌Langar

Langar Hall

Aristocrat of Nottinghamshire's restaurant scene
Church Lane, Langar, NG13 9HG
Tel no: (01949) 860559
www.langarhall.co.uk
Modern British | £40
Cooking score: 4

Set at the end of a shady, lime tree-lined driveway – between a croquet lawn and a country church – Langar Hall has been an aristocrat of the Nottinghamshire restaurant scene for almost three decades. The dining rooms are a study in English country house elegance – Grecian statues watch over white linen tables, while an antique clock quietly tick-tocks on the mantelpiece. The emphasis in the kitchen is on finely tuned British cooking, and accordingly the menu rings like a cadence from *The Lark Ascending* – witness a starter of lamb's tongue with salt-baked celeriac, pears and walnuts. Game from the Vale of Belvoir is a regular fixture; try a hearty main of roast Belvoir partridge, accompanied by bubble and squeak, bread sauce and bacon. Readers continue to praise good-value set lunches, polished service and the owner's wise selections from the extensive wine list, which starts at £20 a bottle.

Chef/s: Gary Booth and Ross Jeffery. **Open:** all week L 12 to 2, D 6 to 10. **Meals:** alc (main courses £13 to £26). Set L £16.50 (2 courses) to £22.50. Set D £20 (2 courses) to £27.50. Sun L £29.50. **Service:** 10%. **Details:** 60 seats. 15 seats outside. Separate bar. Wheelchair access. Music. Car parking.

▌Newark-on-Trent

ALSO RECOMMENDED
▲ Café Bleu

14 Castle Gate, Newark-on-Trent, NG24 1BG
Tel no: (01636) 610141
www.cafebleu.co.uk
Modern European £5 OFF

With baroque fireplaces and canvases of romping nudes adorning the walls, Café Bleu has been a bohemian fixture of Newark's dining scene for years. The menu mixes and matches – mainly modern European dishes, with a few excursions (try a fiery starter of Moroccan spiced split-pea soup). Mains, too, show good intentions, but Cornish cod fillet with curried mussels and red pepper fondue fell slightly short of the price tag. House wine is £14. Closed Sun D and Mon.

▌Nottingham

Hart's

Some very good things to eat indeed
Standard Court, Park Row, Nottingham, NG1 6GN
Tel no: (0115) 9110666
www.hartsnottingham.co.uk
Modern British | £40
Cooking score: 5

Tim Hart's elegant modern restaurant occupies part of the old General Hospital (with rooms in the adjoining hotel). Since opening its doors in 1997, it has established itself as one of the most welcoming and friendly places to eat in Nottingham. Unfussy modern British and French dishes are the kitchen's stock-in-trade, and the menu offers some very good things to eat indeed. Guinea fowl galantine with tea-soaked raisin purée, toasted pistachios and Madeira jus ('just stunning') vies for attention with Tamworth pork belly and black pudding terrine, while main courses offer wild sea bass with mussel and clam velouté, spinach and saffron potatoes alongside Goosnargh duck breast served with a sweet potato gratin, red cabbage and cep purée. The set lunch is excellent value and might offer grilled mackerel with beetroot and tapenade, lamb's shoulder with tomato and white bean cassoulet, and hot chocolate fondant with pistachio ice cream. Service is slick and professional, though for one reader 'a little too quick – perfect for eating alone (which I do a lot) but not for a romantic dinner'. The style-led wine list is a corker – coping with special occasions as well as more humble day-to-day dining at very fair prices (from £20).

Chef/s: Dan Burridge. **Open:** all week L 12 to 1.45, D 7 to 10 (9 Sun). **Closed:** 1 Jan. **Meals:** alc (main courses £16 to £30). Set L £14.95 (2 courses) to £17.95. Set D £26. Sun L £23. **Service:** 12%. **Details:** 80 seats. Separate bar. No music. Wheelchair access. Car parking.

The Larder on Goosegate
Vintage charm and gutsy dishes
1st Floor, 16-22 Goosegate, Hockley, Nottingham, NG1 1FE
Tel no: (0115) 9500111
www.thelarderongoosegate.co.uk
British | £25
Cooking score: 2

Nottingham lad Jesse Boot opened an apothecary's shop in these premises when a certain high-street pharmacy chain was just a twinkle in his eye. Now it's a modern restaurant with a bare-boarded floor and unclothed, well-spaced tables, where the menus specialise in lesser-known meat cuts and unusual ingredients for added personality. Seasonal asparagus comes with a poached duck egg and wild garlic sauce, followed perhaps by dry-rubbed skirt steak with roasted shallots, penny bun mushrooms and chickweed salad, then rhubarb and ginger-beer jelly trifle to finish. A serviceable wine list opens with Côtes de Gascogne at £14.50 (£3.95 a glass). **Chef/s:** Ewan McFarlane. **Open:** Thur to Sat L 12 to 4, Tue to Sat D 6 to 10. **Closed:** Sun, Mon. **Meals:** alc (main courses £13 to £20). Set L and D £13.95 (2 courses) to £15.95. **Service:** not inc. **Details:** 64 seats. Music.

Restaurant 1877
British grub, old and new
128 Derby Road, Canning Circus, Nottingham, NG1 5FB
Tel no: (0115) 9588008
www.restaurant1877.com
British | £20
Cooking score: 2

Restaurant 1877 was a pharmacy in a previous life – these days it prescribes robust British dishes to the denizens of Nottingham. The setting is a grand wedge-shaped building just outside the city centre, where modish interiors feel faintly mismatched with the nineteenth-century architectural plans that hang on the walls. Luckily the menu is built on sturdy foundations – start with salt marsh rabbit and black pudding terrine, before a main of crispy wild sea bass, deftly matched with saffron potatoes and courgette ribbons. Desserts play it straight with the likes of sticky toffee pudding and rhubarb and almond tart. The respectable wine list starts at £16.

Chef/s: Antony Baxter. **Open:** Fri to Sun L 12 to 3, Tue to Sat D 5 to 10.30. **Closed:** Mon, 26 Dec. **Meals:** alc (main courses £11 to £20). Set L and D £9.95. Sun L £6.95. **Service:** 10%. **Details:** 65 seats. Wheelchair access. Music.

★ TOP 50 ★

Restaurant Sat Bains
Razor-sharp imagination combines with peerless technique
Lenton Lane, Nottingham, NG7 2SA
Tel no: (0115) 9866566
www.restaurantsatbains.com
Modern British | £75
Cooking score: 9

Let's get location out of the way first. You or your SatNav will have fun finding the semi-rural, semi-industrial spot on the south-western outskirts of the city where Amanda and Sat Bains run one of the most alluring and impressive restaurants in the UK. It may look and feel like a smart French auberge, yet polished service and awe-inspiring food mean this most ambitious of restaurants delivers serious dining for serious people. Dinner brings a choice of two tasting menus, allowing you to chart paths of seven or ten courses, with succinct, intense add-ons – perhaps an opener of horseradish pannacotta topped by a vivid nettle soup and a crisp croûton, accompanied by an equally memorable mini horseradish ice cream sandwich with the ideal degree of tingle. Sat Bains also knows to pull back and trust in the basic, homespun pleasures of something like freshly baked bread rolls and Lincolnshire Poacher butter. After the overtures, razor-sharp imagination and peerless technique take flight as the kitchen wheels out a procession of dishes of pure brilliance, clarity and cohesion. Scallops, for example, both raw and cooked, come embellished with melon, samphire, caviar and brown butter in a textbook interplay of tart, salty and sweet. Crab mayonnaise takes a predictable partner, avocado, but the base note comes from crunchy shards of peanut brittle, which deftly accentuates the sweetness of the dish. Consider, too, the unconventional construction of duck liver muesli, the richness of the liver cut by the sweetness of dried apricots and cranberries. Or a magnificently tender piece of roe deer served atop venison tartare, all sweetness and softness with earthiness from meaty slices of mushrooms underscored by thyme and chocolate. This is cooking marked by a perfect sense of balance and sheer artistry, which really comes to the fore with desserts. Witness a dainty lollipop of beetroot parfait coated in white chocolate studded with diced, dried raspberry, or a clever chocolate alliance with olive oil, 25-year-old balsamic and an intense coffee-flavoured crisp. But if one dish is going to linger in your thoughts, then an evocative sweet-and-sour assemblage of strawberries, ice cream, meringue, rocket and tarragon imbued with strawberry vinegar could be it. Several reports have praised the seven-course lunch served only at the chef's table (minimum two people), considering it 'a real treat' to watch the kitchen at work and chat with the chefs as they

serve the dishes. Wherever you choose to eat, masterful wine service is on hand to guide you through the impressively arranged list, even if it is just matching a series of glasses. There are no budget options; prices start at £33 for an Italian Valpolicella and £35 for a Chilean Sauvignon Blanc.

Chef/s: Sat Bains. **Open:** Tue to Sat L 12.30 (1 sitting), D 7 to 9. **Closed:** Sun, Mon, 2 weeks winter, 1 week spring, 2 weeks summer. **Meals:** Tasting menu £75 (7 courses) to £89 (10 courses). **Service:** 12.5%. **Details:** 40 seats. Children over 8 yrs only.

World Service

A G8 summit of global flavours
Newdigate House, Castle Gate, Nottingham, NG1 6AF
Tel no: (0115) 8475587
www.worldservicerestaurant.com
Modern British | £35
Cooking score: 3

£5
OFF

Few places embrace eclecticism like World Service – the Nottingham restaurant where a Japanese pebble garden stands alongside a seventeenth-century town house, and where interiors feature sport masks, Buddhas and statues of prancing horses from across the Orient. Accordingly, dishes represent a veritable G8 summit of global flavours, but the kitchen manages to mix and match influences without much getting lost in translation. Start, perhaps, with crispy prawn kataifi with chilli aïoli, then mains conjure up a few unanticipated combinations – lamb rump with sweetbreads and sheep's milk purée, or whole roast plaice with saffron new potatoes, Jerusalem artichokes and hijiki seaweed. Desserts are less exotic (think banana soufflé or rhubarb semifreddo) but the wine list goes in for its fair share of globetrotting; prices from £16.

Chef/s: Jacque Ferreira. **Open:** all week L 12 to 2 (3.30 Sun), Mon to Sat D 7 to 10 (6.30 Mon and Sat). **Closed:** 25 and 26 Dec. **Meals:** alc (main courses £15 to £26). Set L £14.50 (2 courses) to £19.50. Set D

£21.50 (2 courses) to £26.50. Sun L £19.50.
Service: 12%. **Details:** 80 seats. 30 seats outside.
Separate bar. Music. Children over 12 yrs only at D.

ALSO RECOMMENDED
▲ Delilah
15 Middle Pavement, Nottingham, NG1 7DX
Tel no: (0115) 9484461
www.delilahfinefoods.co.uk
Modern European

Delilah is a cheery deli-cum-eatery that
buzzes all day, thanks to its city-centre
location and the fact that it invests in decent
raw materials. There's no shortage of support
for 'great food', so bag one of the nine counter
stools for a breakfast of scrambled eggs, basil
pesto and Alderton marmalade ham on toast
(£6.95), or pop in anytime for a frittata
(£7.50), fried Roquefort sandwich,
charcuterie plate or cheese platter. Wines from
£8.99. Open all week.

▲ Ibérico World Tapas
Shire Hall, High Pavement, Nottingham, NG1 1HN
Tel no: (0115) 9410410
www.ibericotapas.com
Spanish/Tapas

'Really clever and inventive tapas' bring the
crowds to this vaulted basement beneath
Nottingham's old courthouse. Moorish tiles
and ethnic artefacts point up the 'world' of the
name, and the menu follows suit – so expect
spicy miso salmon (£4.95) and truffled onglet
steak with shimeji mushrooms alongside
Spanish charcuterie, triple-cooked patatas
bravas and plates of char-grilled baby chorizo
with smoked aubergine purée or gambas a la
plancha (£7.50). Desserts also mix things up,
from sweet yuzu yoghurt with rhubarb
compote to churros with hot chocolate. Wines
from £15.50. Closed Sun.

▉ Plumtree
Perkins
Good-value family favourite
Station House, Station Road, Plumtree, NG12 5NA
Tel no: (0115) 9373695
www.perkinsrestaurant.co.uk
Modern European | £30
Cooking score: 2

'A lovely experience' is one enthusiastic verdict
on this converted Victorian railway station
where the Perkins family have chalked up 31
years, dishing out hospitality and dependable
brasserie dishes with aplomb. A full menu is
available at both sessions, and the short set
lunch and dinner are particularly good value.
Chicken liver parfait with onion jam is a
typical starter; main courses may range from
an 'absolutely delicious' sea bass fillet with
rosemary fondant potato and shrimp and
caper butter to roast venison haunch with
celeriac gratin and Madeira jus. Desserts may
include well-made bread-and-butter
pudding. House wine is £16.50.
Chef/s: Sarah Newham. **Open:** all week L 12 to 2
(3.30 Sun), Mon to Sat D 6 to 10. **Meals:** alc (main
courses £15 to £23). Set L £14.50 (2 courses) to
£17.95. Set D £16.50 (2 courses) to £18.95. Sun L
£15.50 (2 courses) to £18.95. **Service:** not inc.
Details: 73 seats. 20 seats outside. Separate bar.
Wheelchair access. Music. Car parking.

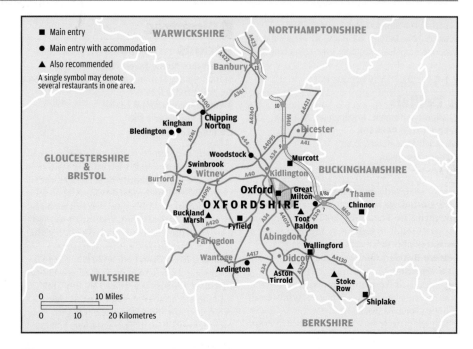

Ardington
The Boar's Head
Assured fish cookery and more besides
Church Street, Ardington, OX12 8QA
Tel no: (01235) 833254
www.boarsheadardington.co.uk
Modern British | £32
Cooking score: 3
£5 OFF

An esteemed timber-framed pub in a
quintessential Oxfordshire village, the Boar's
Head may have boozing in its blood, but food
is what lures the affluent local populace these
days. Since arriving in 2000, chef/proprietor
Bruce Buchan has earned a devoted following
for his assured fish cookery, and readers
continue to cheer precisely timed, full-
flavoured dishes such as spaghetti with crab,
fillet of Newlyn cod with scallop soufflé, and
sea bass with squid tempura, samphire and
pesto dressing. Meat and game are almost as
impressive, whether it's Scotch beef fillet with
seared foie gras and rösti or stuffed saddle of

rabbit with ratatouille. Desserts look to the
seasons for summery strawberry Vacherin
with clotted cream and strawberry sorbet or
comforting date and walnut pudding. The
well-endowed, creditable wine list starts
at £15.
Chef/s: Bruce Buchan. **Open:** all week L 12 to 2
(2.30 Sun), Mon to Sat D 7 to 9.30. **Closed:** 26 Dec, 1
Jan. **Meals:** alc (main courses £16 to £27). Set L
£14.50 (2 courses) to £17.50. Sun L £25. **Service:** not
inc. **Details:** 40 seats. 25 seats outside. Separate
bar. Wheelchair access. Music. Car parking.

Aston Tirrold

ALSO RECOMMENDED
▲ The Sweet Olive
Baker Street, Aston Tirrold, OX11 9DD
Tel no: (01235) 851272
www.sweet-olive.com
Modern British

The Alsatian proprietor at this popular
country pub (serene with its ancient tiled floor
and wood-panelled walls) rustles up well-

wrought versions of Anglo-French classics. The blackboard list – a starter of precisely cooked sweetbreads and wild mushrooms in a creamy mustard sauce (£6.95), for instance – is augmented by plentiful specials, such as delicately cooked panaché of fish (£18.95), or tarte Tatin (£6.50). Alsatian wines star in a list starting at £18.50, or there's real ale in the bar. Closed all day Wed and Sun D.

Bledington
The Kings Head Inn
Textbook village hostelry
The Green, Bledington, OX7 6XQ
Tel no: (01608) 658365
www.thekingsheadinn.net
Modern British | £30
Cooking score: 2

There's much to praise about the Orr-Ewings' lovely old inn, from the village green setting, via the robustly seasonal menus, to the charming service. The cooking more than lives up to expectations in every detail, whether it's flavourful Addlestrop pigeon breast with caramelised red cabbage and redcurrant jus, Cornish crab and chilli linguine, or spiced, braised shoulder of Bledington lamb with home-smoked chump and a salad of warm baby gem, capers, pea and mint. Among straightforward posh comfort desserts, apple charlotte with thyme custard stands out. Wines from £15.50. Related to the Swan Inn, Swinbrook (see entry).
Chef/s: Steven Brookes. **Open:** all week L 12 to 2 (2.30 Sat, 3 Sun), D 6.30 to 9 (9.30 Fri and Sat). **Closed:** 25 and 26 Dec. **Meals:** alc (main courses £11 to £23). Set L and D £15 (2 courses) to £18.50. Sun L £14 to £16. **Service:** not inc. **Details:** 65 seats. 50 seats outside. Separate bar. Wheelchair access. Music. Car parking.

Also Recommended
Also recommended entries are not scored but we think they are worth a visit.

Buckland Marsh
ALSO RECOMMENDED
▲ The Trout at Tadpole Bridge
Tadpole Bridge, Buckland Marsh, SN7 8RF
Tel no: (01367) 870382
www.troutinn.co.uk
British £5 OFF

A dewy-eyed, *Wind in the Willows* setting helps attract visitors to this quaintly named hostelry beside a humpback bridge over the Thames. The kitchen is in tune with the seasons; expect lobster in summer, braised pheasant in winter, pies aplenty and more showy dishes such as Hebridean scallops with celeriac purée and pickled beetroot (£10.50), or slow-cooked rabbit in white wine with confit red cabbage (£13.95). Puds are equally lively offerings, from pistachio pannacotta to black cherry frangipane. House wine is £14.50. Accommodation. Open all week.

Chinnor
The Sir Charles Napier
Freewheeling Falstaffian largesse
Sprigg's Alley, Chinnor, OX39 4BX
Tel no: (01494) 483011
www.sircharlesnapier.co.uk
Modern British | £43
Cooking score: 4

'Ah! The Napier!' swooned one reader after visiting this one-time 'beer house' high up on the blustery expanses overlooking Bledlow Ridge. SCN's pubby days are long gone, but the place is still a rollickingly surreal and instantly seductive prospect – all weird sculptures, pleasure grounds, zany detailing and freewheeling Falstaffian largesse. The kitchen has seasonality in its blood and proves its worth with some stonkingly good game dishes: partridge with choucroute and perry jus; mallard with confit leg and endive tart; loin of venison with beetroot purée. Fish also shows bags of finesse, be it scallops with silky brandade and lentils or outstanding turbot fillet with pumpkin gnocchi, braised celeriac, chanterelles and parsley-root purée. The seasons continue to ring out when it comes to desserts such as pear and lime sponge with bramble compote, while a big tray of ripe cheeses whiffs invitingly. Ever-accommodating Julie Griffiths is the heartbeat of the place, although her well-meaning young charges can let the side down – especially on madcap, sell-out Sundays. Wine is also a passion and the top-drawer list oozes class: note the noble Burgundies, Alsace treasures and pedigree Australians. House selections start at £17.50.

Chef/s: Chris Godfrey. **Open:** Tue to Sun L 12 to 2.30 (3.30 Sun), Tue to Sat D 6.30 to 9.30 (10 Fri and Sat). **Closed:** Mon, 25 to 28 Dec. **Meals:** alc (main courses £20 to £29). Set L and D Tue to Fri £17.50 (2 courses). **Service:** 12.5%. **Details:** 70 seats. 70 seats outside. Separate bar. Music. Car parking. Children over 6 yrs only at D.

▌Chipping Norton

Wild Thyme

Sharply focused seasonal flavours
10 New Street, Chipping Norton, OX7 5LJ
Tel no: (01608) 645060
www.wildthymerestaurant.co.uk
Modern British | £35
Cooking score: 3

This tidy little restaurant-with-rooms is 'a beacon for local food', according to one reader. It is also valued for its unpretentious, warmly welcoming vibes, eclectic interiors and sharply focused seasonal flavours. Venison and partridge from nearby estates could feature in winter, alongside the likes of wild rabbit and mushrooms in puff pastry with Dijon espuma, steamed loin, honey-glazed shoulder and Jerusalem artichoke purée, or a simple dish of Cornish sea bass on brown shrimp risotto with some curly kale. Twice-baked goats' cheese soufflé with roasted beetroot and a dollop of red onion marmalade remains a show-stopping starter. Desserts have ranged from a pitch-perfect chocolate fondant to a fruity

assemblage of banana parfait with caramelised bananas, honey-glazed figs and 'figgy pudding'. Wines start at £14.50.

Chef/s: Nicholas Pullen. **Open:** Tue to Sat L 12 to 2, D 7 to 9. **Closed:** Sun, Mon, first 2 weeks Jan, 1 week May. **Meals:** alc (main courses £13 to £25). Set L £18 (2 courses) to £22.50. Midweek set D £25. **Service:** not inc. **Details:** 35 seats. 10 seats outside. Music.

▌Fyfield

The White Hart

Welcoming, much-loved hostelry
Main Road, Fyfield, OX13 5LW
Tel no: (01865) 390585
www.whitehart-fyfield.com
Modern British | £30
Cooking score: 3

In a village west of Abingdon, Kay and Mark Chandler's fifteenth-century former chantry house is well worth seeking out. Now an upbeat and modishly rustic hostelry with striking original features and a 'superb atmosphere', it's a welcoming place much loved by locals and visitors. Mark's modern menu showcases local (and home-grown) produce and reveals realistic ambition; his clear focus is greatly appreciated. White onion soup with English breakfast garnish, followed by loin of roe deer served with a mini venison cottage pie typifies the predominantly British style, although elsewhere sharing boards of charcuterie or meze have a more Mediterranean feel. There's a good selection of British cheeses if 'scrumptious puddings' such as egg custard and nutmeg tart with poached pineapple don't appeal. Wines from £16.50.

Chef/s: Mark Chandler. **Open:** Tue to Sun L 12 to 2.30 (3.30 Sun), Tue to Sat D 7 to 9.30. **Closed:** Mon (exc bank hols). **Meals:** alc (main courses £14 to £20). Set L £16 (2 courses) to £19. Sun L £21 (2 courses) to £24. **Service:** not inc. **Details:** 65 seats. 50 seats outside. Music. Car parking.

Great Milton

★ TOP 50 ★

Le Manoir aux Quat'Saisons

Unashamed luxury and pure delight
Church Road, Great Milton, OX44 7PD
Tel no: (01844) 278881
www.manoir.com
Modern French | £120
Cooking score: 8

🛏 V

Since launching in 1984, Raymond Blanc's fabulous honey-stone manor house has blossomed into a world-class hospitality package, an exclusive retreat where you can take a trip in a Ferrari or indulge in a little Champagne tasting. But it's also the ultimate dream ticket for those who simply want to taste the good life – if only for a few hours. Despite its French name, there's something very English about the Manoir experience, whether you are playing croquet on the lawn or taking a tour of the ravishing organic gardens. These bounteous acres may be blissful, but their main purpose is to feed the kitchen, which remains the Manoir's workshop and engine room. To appreciate the place at its foodie best, come when the grounds are in full bloom and eat in the tent-like conservatory from a choice of menus that show the breadth of Raymond Blanc's culinary intelligence and creativity. Lightness, balance and intensity are his trademarks, with consummate technique in every department and a talent for exquisite prettiness on the plate. Here is a kitchen that knows how to deliver the ultimate spring vegetable risotto, but can also surprise and delight with more complex creations: a dish of red mullet in bonito and tapioca broth with Asian greens, or an assiette of Pyrenean lamb with quinoa and spring garlic purée, for example. Blanc's respect for the calendar is also writ large in other fastidiously composed plates, from a salad of Cornish crab pointed up with grapefruit and asparagus to Rhug chicken with morels and Jura wine sauce or even a brace of perfectly roasted grouse with classic accoutrements. To conclude, the cheese trolley is a minor miracle of Gallic ripeness (check out the Comté specimens from M. Blanc's native region); otherwise, desserts provide waves of divine patisserie and eye-popping artistry, from La Gariguette ('a theme on the French strawberry') to the exotic thrills of fruit ravioli with Kaffir lime and coconut jus. The hotel staff epitomise courtesy, politeness and polish, although their restaurant counterparts can sometimes seem indifferent, 'remote' and insensitive to customers' demands: one heavily pregnant reader who required specific dietary advice was simply fobbed off with a cursory vegetarian menu. As for the cost of it all, sky-high prices come with the territory and the magisterial wine list is also guaranteed to dent your wallet – although there's a treasure trove to explore if money is no option. Expect French regional diversity, a crusading approach to organic/biodynamic production and some astonishing acquisitions from artisan winemakers across the globe. Bottles start around £40.

Chef/s: Raymond Blanc and Gary Jones. **Open:** all week L 11.45 to 2.15, D 6.45 to 9.30. **Meals:** alc (main courses £48). Set L £75 (5 courses) to £120 (7 courses). Set D £130 (6 courses) to £150 (9 courses). **Service:** not inc. **Details:** 80 seats. Separate bar. No music. Wheelchair access. Car parking.

Kingham

The Kingham Plough

A townie's rural dream
The Green, Kingham, OX7 6YD
Tel no: (01608) 658327
www.thekinghamplough.co.uk
Modern British | £32
Cooking score: 3

 £5 OFF 🛏

Standing proud at the heart of the village, this stone inn feels English to a T. The bar and restaurant make a suitably rustic setting for food that takes account of seasonal supplies and Cotswold produce, and the convivial way the place is run is a great draw. Reporters have been delighted with the honest food ('I ate the best meal I have ever eaten at this pub');

favourites have included spatchcocked quail, pigeon Wellington, and chicken and ham pie. Elsewhere, a crisp Burford Brown egg served with slow-cooked oxtail, chanterelles and tarragon sauce has made an impressive starter, rhubarb and custard trifle with ginger honeycomb a luscious finish. The local cheeseboard is a winner, too. A short European wine list opens at £16.

Chef/s: Emily Watkins and Ben Dulley. **Open:** all week L 12 to 2 (2.30 Sat and Sun), Mon to Sat D 7 to 9 (9.30 Sat, 8 Sun). **Closed:** 25 Dec, last week Jan, 1st week Feb. **Meals:** alc (main courses £12 to £23). **Service:** not inc. **Details:** 74 seats. 25 seats outside. Separate bar. Car parking.

Murcott
The Nut Tree Inn
Picture-perfect, own-producing pub
Main Street, Murcott, OX5 2RE
Tel no: (01865) 331253
www.nuttreeinn.co.uk
Modern British | £38
Cooking score: 5

£5
OFF

A 'picture perfect' thatched pub in Oxfordshire's gentle walking country, the Nut Tree Inn elicits delighted reactions from those prepared to endure the 'pain' of getting there. That's thanks in part to a careful balance of pubby approachability and accurate, grown-up cooking by Mike North and sister Mary. They're living the seasonal sourcer's dream, home-smoking their salmon, raising rare breed pigs for the table, and kneading 'some of the best' bread. You can buy sausages, pies and the like to take home if you just pop in for a pint. But that would be missing a trick. Pan-fried terrine of pig's head with sauerkraut and a fried quail's egg is a staunch favourite with texture fiends, a fillet of Cornish mackerel finds a fresh Med-style accompaniment of tapenade, onion tart and roasted peppers, and others appreciate the charms of a well-balanced and generously proportioned salmon fishcake with creamed spinach and a tomato butter sauce. A 'quite magnificent' sticky toffee pudding with caramelised apple tart boasts

more brilliant texture, and a hot pistachio soufflé with chocolate ice cream also scores well. Service, run by Mike's wife Imogen, is well-judged and wine starts at £16; steer a careful course, as some are 'pricey'.

Chef/s: Michael and Mary North. **Open:** Tue to Sun L 12 to 2.30 (3.30 Sun), Tue to Sat D 7 to 9. **Closed:** Mon. **Meals:** alc (main courses £17 to £27). Set L and D £18 (2 courses). **Service:** not inc. **Details:** 60 seats. 40 seats outside. Separate bar. Music. Car parking.

Oxford
The Anchor
Busy local with polished food
2 Hayfield Road, Oxford, OX2 6TT
Tel no: (01865) 510282
www.theanchoroxford.com
Modern British | £26
Cooking score: 2

£5   £30
OFF

In the leafy reaches of north Oxford, near Port Meadow, the Aristotle Bridge and the Oxford Canal, the Anchor is a busy local pub done in modernised but down-home style, with bare floors and tables. The kitchen supports local suppliers and turns out traditional but polished food. Start with devilled lamb's kidneys and creamed spinach on toast, then mains such as smoked haddock fishcakes and chips with ginger, lime and coriander mayo, or slow-roast belly pork with puréed celeriac, curly kale and root veg; finish with treacle tart and ginger cream. There are bar snacks, dishes for 'little people' and wines from £15.50.

Chef/s: Jamie King. **Open:** all week L 12 to 2.30 (3 Sun), D 6 to 9.30 (6.30 to 8.30 Sun). **Closed:** 25 and 26 Dec. **Meals:** alc (main courses £12 to £17). Sun L £18. **Service:** not inc. **Details:** 70 seats. 50 seats outside. Separate bar. Wheelchair access. Music. Car parking. No children under 12 yrs after 7.30.

Branca

Terrific-value all-day Italian
111 Walton Street, Oxford, OX2 6AJ
Tel no: (01865) 556111
www.branca-restaurants.com
Italian | £23
Cooking score: 1

All-day opening, a buzzy atmosphere and terrific value make this veteran Italian on the fringes of Jericho a sure-fire hit with students, couples and families with kids. Inside, the big open space rings with garrulous *grazies* and the kitchen proves its worth with salads, stone-baked pizzas and a mixed bag of Euro-accented dishes from char-grilled sea bream with saffron mash to macaroni cheese and slow-braised lamb shank. Alternatively, gaze at the stars from the garden terrace (rugs and heaters provided). House wine is £14.95.
Chef/s: E Blandes. **Open:** all week 11am to 11pm. **Closed:** 24 to 26 Dec. **Meals:** alc (main courses £10 to £19). Set L and early D £11.45 (2 courses). Sun L £12.45. **Service:** not inc. **Details:** 100 seats. 70 seats outside. Separate bar. Wheelchair access. Music.

Cherwell Boathouse

Idyllic riverside favourite
50 Bardwell Road, Oxford, OX2 6ST
Tel no: (01865) 552746
www.cherwellboathouse.co.uk
Modern British | £32
Cooking score: 1

As well as being the place for hiring a punt and going for a paddle on the Cherwell, the Verdin family's Victorian boathouse serves Oxford admirably as a contemporary restaurant. The food is upbeat; seasonal menus feature slow-cooked pigeon, chervil root and Madeira jelly; hogget (lamb) spring roll with mint jelly; and beef and winter vegetable casserole with creamed potatoes and horseradish mousse. The lovingly assembled wine list is a joy, with a mouthwatering selection by the glass; bottles from £14.50.

Chef/s: Carson Hill. **Open:** all week L 12 to 2 (2.30 Sat and Sun), D 6 to 9.30. **Closed:** 25 to 30 Dec. **Meals:** alc (main courses £15 to £25). Set midweek L £13.50 (2 courses) to £24.75. Set D £21.25 (2 courses) to £26.75. Sun L £24.75. **Service:** 10% for parties of 6 or more. **Details:** 65 seats. 40 seats outside. Separate bar. Wheelchair access. Car parking.

Gee's

Oxford landmark with easy-going food
61 Banbury Road, Oxford, OX2 6PE
Tel no: (01865) 553540
www.gees-restaurant.co.uk
Modern British | £31
Cooking score: 2

A local landmark for more than two decades, Gee's is the reincarnation of a Victorian florist's emporium – a striking, light-filled conservatory, trendy Gary Hume portraits and a menu of easy-going brasserie food. The kitchen's output can vary from 'utterly memorable' seared scallops with Jerusalem artichokes and salsify to a dish of slow-cooked Rofford beef that reminded one reader of 'over-sauced school food'. However, there are always plenty of takers for its comforting pasta, grills and desserts such as pear tart or chocolate St Emilion. Live jazz suppers also lure Oxford's town and gown. To drink, expect plenty of gluggable wines by the glass or pichet; bottles from £17.50.
Chef/s: Simon Cottrell. **Open:** all week L 12 to 3 (3.30 Sat and Sun), D 5.45 to 11 (11.30 Fri to Sun). **Closed:** 25 and 26 Dec. **Meals:** alc (main courses £16 to £27). Set L £16.95 (2 courses) to £20.95. Sun L £22.95 (2 courses) to £25.95. **Service:** 12.5%. **Details:** 85 seats. 20 seats outside. Separate bar. Music.

Visit us Online
To find out more about *The Good Food Guide*, please visit www.thegoodfoodguide.co.uk

NEW ENTRY
My Sichuan
A no-holds-barred Szechuan adventure
The Old School, Gloucester Green, Oxford,
OX1 2DA
Tel no: (01865) 236899
www.mysichuan.co.uk
Chinese | £20
Cooking score: 3

 £30

Educating Oxford about a cuisine new to the city, My Sichuan inhabits a late-Victorian former school: a capacious three-roomed space incorporating a beautiful stained-glass dome. Chinese students, among others, come to sample the wide repertoire of no-holds-barred Szechuan cookery served by friendly staff. Offal and chillies figure prominently on a menu where many dishes (spicy sea snails, for instance) are fearsomely hot. Nevertheless, there's subtlety too, with little cubes of ham and tiny shrimps enhancing the sweetness of the pea shoots in rich broth, and appealing tanginess in the tender beef in sour sauce – and don't miss anything containing the fragrant, mouth-numbing Szechuan peppercorns. A rare culinary adventure. House wine £13.95. Our questionnaire was not returned, so please check the restaurant's website for details.
Open: all week 9 to 11. **Meals:** alc (main courses £7 to £19)

NEW ENTRY
The Rickety Press
Well-attired pub with fair prices
67 Cranham Street, Oxford, OX2 6DE
Tel no: (01865) 424581
www.thericketypress.com
Modern British | £25
Cooking score: 1

 £30

Snug in the affluent backstreets of Jericho, this well-attired pub reopened in June 2011 and is a hit with chattering thirtysomethings. Even midweek they fill the darkly furnished real ale bar and the contrastingly light conservatory restaurant. Here, a fairly priced monthly menu

of 'sophisticated' modern classics could commence with rather tart beetroot and goats' cheese tart, before luscious ox cheek and tail pie, or sea bass with vanilla butter. Don't miss the salted caramel ice cream. Wine starts at £16.
Chef/s: Andrew Holland. **Open:** all week L 12 to 2.30 (3 Sun), Mon to Sat D 6.30 to 9.30. **Closed:** 25 to 30 Dec. **Meals:** alc (main courses £12 to £19). Sun L £14 to £16. **Service:** not inc. **Details:** 60 seats. 20 seats outside. Separate bar. Wheelchair access. Music. Children allowed under parental supervision.

NEW ENTRY
Turl Street Kitchen
Vibrant charity venue
16-17 Turl Street, Oxford, OX1 3DH
Tel no: (01865) 264171
www.turlstreetkitchen.co.uk
Modern British | £16
Cooking score: 1

 £30

Opened in September 2011, this vibrant bar-café-restaurant raises money for the Oxford Hub, a collection of student-run charities. The bright, split-level venue in a Georgian town house has stripped floorboards and windows looking on to pretty Turl Street. Clued-up staff serve a daily menu of fashionably earthy cooking: brawn with gribiche, or nourishing lentil soup could precede braised wood pigeon or a satisfying beef, tomato and barley pie. House wine by the glass, carafe or bottle (£13.50) encourages the merry hubbub.
Chef/s: Carl Isham. **Open:** all week L 12 to 3, Mon to Sun D 6.30 to 10. **Closed:** 1 week Christmas. **Meals:** alc (main courses £9 to £15). Set D £12.50 (2 courses) to £16. **Service:** not inc. **Details:** 65 seats. Separate bar. Music.

Average Price
The average price listed in main-entry reviews denotes the price of a three-course meal, without wine.

ALSO RECOMMENDED

▲ Ashmolean Dining Room

Beaumont Street, Oxford, OX1 2PH
Tel no: (01865) 553823
www.ashmoleandiningroom.com
Mediterranean

It's a great location in a world-class museum with a spacious, light-filled refectory-style room and a 'perfect' rooftop terrace, but prices are high for a museum café and service 'too studenty' for a serious restaurant. Menus change quarterly and have a strong Mediterranean slant, delivering ripe figs with a plate of Serrano ham (£8) and an enjoyable soft-shell crab with sweet chilli mayonnaise, as well as seafood platters (£17) and braised belly pork with clams. Wines from £15.75. Closed Mon.

▲ Edamamé

15 Holywell Street, Oxford, OX1 3SA
Tel no: (01865) 246916
www.edamame.co.uk
Japanese

See the queue outside tiny premises on Oxford's loveliest street and you've found Edamamé. With no bookings, eccentric opening hours, cramped seating and shared tables, this Japanese café is no place for first dates, but students (including Japanese) love it. Thursday's sushi night brings the freshest raw-fish set meals (£6-£9), with specials like unagi (eel). Otherwise, simple classics – pork curry (£9), chicken yakisoba (£9) – hold sway. Service is congenial, but don't expect to linger. House wine (£12). Open Wed to Sun L, Thur to Sat D.

▲ The Magdalen Arms

243 Iffley Road, Oxford, OX4 1SJ
Tel no: (01865) 243159
www.magdalenarms.com
British

A boon for any neighbourhood, this revitalised hostelry takes a dressed-down, casual approach, with animated local vibes and no standing on ceremony. On the food front,

things kick off simply with a plate of Spanish cured ham and Manchego or deep-fried sprats and tartare sauce (£5), before going on to other modern Brit staples such as roast hake with chorizo potatoes and aïoli, and pot-roast partridge with Savoy cabbage and flageolet beans (£11.80). Wines from £13.80. No food Mon, Tue L.

▲ Sojo

6-9 Hythe Bridge Street, Oxford, OX1 2EW
Tel no: (01865) 202888
www.sojo-oxford.co.uk
Chinese

With its dark good looks and menu of enticing regional Chinese food, Sojo attracts young diners from east and west. A short dim sum list includes a good-value set choice for £10 and is bolstered by congees, rice bowls and soup noodles – say, a large, nourishing bowlful of tender beef flank with udon (£6.50). The full menu features the appealing likes of Shanghai braised sweet soy pork hock. Service is congenial; saké is an alternative to wine (from £15). Open all week.

▮ Shiplake

Orwells

Menus sparkling with culinary fireworks
Shiplake Row, Shiplake, RG9 4DP
Tel no: (01189) 403673
www.orwellsatshiplake.co.uk
Modern British | £34
Cooking score: 5

Ryan Simpson and Liam Trotman's village inn near Henley has been making exciting waves since they took over the lease in 2010. Named after the local-boy author of *Animal Farm*, the place perfectly marries the country pub ethos of exposed walls and low beams with modern tweaks, such as a viewing panel through which you can see the kitchen team at work in their conservatory. We wondered how long the division between the main pub and the Room, the compact fine-dining space, would last, given the popularity of the culinary fireworks that sparkle all over the menus in the latter, and are quite unsurprised to report that the full menu is now available throughout. A spring dinner progressed from a smoothly delicious take on that modern classic, scallops with cauliflower (and peanut) purée, to crab salad with fritter, and then pork-cheek cake with rhubarb and langoustine – 'one of the best dishes I've ever eaten'. Surf-and-turf combinations are a passion, witness the equally stunning roast sea bass with veal sweetbreads, parsnip, spring onion and verjus. By the time a goats' cheesecake arrives under a layer of candyfloss, or a chocolate fondant with Guinness and blackcurrant ice cream and toasted barley, you'll have completed an extraordinary journey. Plenty of affordable wines line up on the thoughtful list, with bottles from £14.95 (£4.50 a glass).

Chef/s: Ryan Simpson and Liam Trotman. **Open:** Tue to Sun L 11.30 to 3 (3.30 Sun), Tue to Sat D 6.30 to 9.30 (10 Sat). **Closed:** Mon, first 2 weeks Jan, 1 week Apr, first 2 weeks Sept. **Meals:** alc (main courses £13 to £24). Set L £10 (2 courses) to £16. Sun L £24.95 (2 courses) to £29.95. Tasting menu £55 (5 courses) to £75. **Service:** not inc. **Details:** 70 seats. 40 seats outside. Separate bar. Wheelchair access. Music. Car parking.

Stoke Row

ALSO RECOMMENDED
▲ The Crooked Billet
Newlands Lane, Stoke Row, RG9 5PU
Tel no: (01491) 681048
www.thecrookedbillet.co.uk
Modern European

Tucked down a winding lane and backed by meadows, this charmingly wonky and timeworn inn was once the hideout of highwayman Dick Turpin. Chef-proprietor Paul Clerehugh cooks up an 'excellent, varied menu' full of local produce. Chilli mussels with green coconut and coriander (£8.30) and sticky glazed slow-roasted honey duck with buttery mash and green beans (£18.90) show the range. Desserts are mostly British classics such as Eton mess or Bakewell tart (£5). Wines start at £20. Open all week.

Swinbrook
The Swan Inn
Idyllic stone pub
Swinbrook, OX18 4DY
Tel no: (01993) 823339
www.theswanswinbrook.co.uk
Modern British | £30
Cooking score: 2

This lovely old inn next to the river Windrush and overlooking a cricket pitch was remodelled some six years ago and now oozes rustic sophistication. While it lives up to its title as an inn, dispensing real ales and pub hospitality, it also puts on a stylish show for customers in search of food. Hits include Dorset crab cannelloni with Parmesan glaze, 'tender and fine-tasting' ribeye steak with Café de Paris butter, 'perfectly cooked' pork chop with flageolet beans and chorizo, and pear and almond tart. Well-priced wines from £15.50. Related to the King's Head Inn, Bledington (see entry).

Chef/s: Richard Burkert. **Open:** all week L 12 to 2 (2.30 Sat, 3 Sun), D 7 to 9 (9.30 Fri and Sat, 8.30 Sun). **Closed:** 25 and 26 Dec. **Meals:** alc (main courses £14 to £21). Set L and D £15 (2 courses) to £18. Sun L £16. **Service:** not inc. **Details:** 60 seats. 60 seats outside. Wheelchair access. Music. Car parking.

Toot Baldon

ALSO RECOMMENDED
▲ The Mole Inn
Toot Baldon, OX44 9NG
Tel no: (01865) 340001
www.themoleinn.com
Modern European

Three centuries of history make this country pub five miles from Oxford a highly attractive prospect. Refurbishment has brought the building up to date, but the interior still has the requisite beams and log fire. Gary Witchalls' cooking is up-to-the-minute, say sautéed lamb's kidneys (£7.95), and grilled haddock with minted curly kale, smoked haddock curry cream and Cheddar mash pie (£16.95) followed by mango and passion-fruit pavlova. There's an atmospheric bar, plus lovely gardens. Wines from £17.50. Open all week.

▌ Wallingford

NEW ENTRY

The Partridge
Refined pub where food's a pleasure
32 St Mary's Street, Wallingford, OX10 0ET
Tel no: (01491) 825005
www.partridge-inn.com
Modern European | £28
Cooking score: 2

Once a town-centre boozer, the Partridge now displays refined plumage. The bar (no real ale) features log fire, pine flooring, beams and opulent wallpaper juxtaposed with brick. To the left, differentiated only by carpeting, is the restaurant. Food is a pleasure, extending from a no-choice two-course lunch – soothing celeriac velouté, perhaps, then pink slices of local steak over lentils – to a menu gourmand. After appetisers, the ambitious carte might continue with duck tortellino topped by duck yolk, surrounded by parsley-root velouté, a main course pollack with beetroot risotto and deep-fried squid, then gooey Nutella soufflé. Wine starts at £18.50.
Chef/s: José Cau. **Open:** Tue to Sun L 12 to 2.30 (3.30 Sun), Tue to Sat D 6 to 9.30. **Closed:** Mon, last 2 weeks Aug. **Meals:** Set L £13.95 (2 courses) to £16.95. Set D £16.95 (2 courses) to £19.95. Sun L £22.95. **Service:** 12.5% for parties of 6 or more. **Details:** 55 seats. 24 seats outside. Music.

▌ Woodstock

The Feathers
Coaching inn with alluring menus
Market Street, Woodstock, OX20 1SX
Tel no: (01993) 812291
www.feathers.co.uk
Modern British | £50
Cooking score: 4

Hushed formality at this traditional coaching inn is leavened by a jazzy carpet lining its venerable wood-panelled, three-roomed dining area. The kitchen, too, is no stick-in-the-mud. Kevin Barrett has created an alluring menu that showcases impeccable ingredients and well-balanced flavours and textures. The set-price meal (there's also a tasting menu) incorporates plenty of extras (amuse-bouche, pre-dessert) and a seasonally adjusted choice of elaborate constructions such as pigeon breasts with beetroot, Stilton and thyme-infused deep-fried oatcake. Mains are equally complex; however an otherwise pitch-perfect seared stone bass with fregola pasta, tomatoes, spinach and butter beans didn't need flavourless puréed potatoes too. Service can be a little green, and the bill rather steep. Nevertheless, chestnut parfait, wittily presented as a mushroom on a meringue 'stalk' surrounded by a forest-floor debris of bitter coffee jelly and pistachios, showed real culinary flair. The 'recommended' wines (from £22) provide a straightforward choice from a complicated list.
Chef/s: Kevin Barrett. **Open:** all week L 12 to 2.30, D 6 to 10. **Meals:** Set L and D £39.95 (2 courses) to £49.95. Sun L £28.50. Tasting menu £65.
Service: 10%. **Details:** 50 seats. 80 seats outside. Separate bar. Wheelchair access. Music.

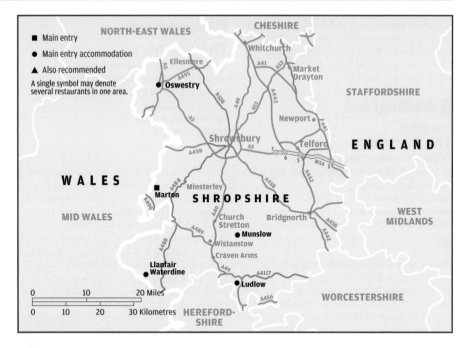

Llanfair Waterdine

The Waterdine

Foodie destination with true Brit flavours
Llanfair Waterdine, LD7 1TU
Tel no: (01547) 528214
www.waterdine.com
Modern British | £33
Cooking score: 4

With its thick stone walls, leaded windows, sturdy wood floors and inglenook, this sixteenth-century thatched long house and drovers' pit-stop on the Anglo-Welsh border may feel like a bucolic watering hole, but these days it does duty as a charmingly rustic restaurant-with-rooms and serious foodie destination (booking essential) known for its love of invigorated British flavours. Dinner is the main event, and the regularly updated menu keeps it tight. Starters of baked black pudding with honey-glazed walnuts and apple or smoked haddock mousse with lemon butter and coriander sauce set the tone, while mains put the emphasis on well-respected native ingredients. Organically reared mountain lamb might be served with boulangère potatoes and creamed leeks; rump of Welsh Black beef is complemented by a mini cottage pie, fine beans and red wine sauce. Fish is often given a flourish (cucumber and wasabi beurre blanc with Cornish brill), and the refreshingly honest, low-key approach also runs through to simple desserts such as orange crème brûlée or lemon syllabub. Around 50 wines from £18.50.

Chef/s: Ken Adams. **Open:** Thur to Sat L (by appointment only), Sun L 12 to 4, Tue to Sat D 7 to 11. **Closed:** Mon, 1 week spring, 1 week autumn. **Meals:** Set L and D £32.50. Sun L £22.50. **Service:** not inc. **Details:** 20 seats. Separate bar. No music. Car parking. Children over 10 yrs only at D.

■ Ludlow

La Bécasse
A commitment to classic modern dishes
17 Corve Street, Ludlow, SY8 1DA
Tel no: (01584) 872325
www.labecasse.co.uk
Modern French | £60
Cooking score: 6

V

This is the most eye-catching of the constituent restaurants in Alan Murcheson's 10 in 8 fine dining collection; the rough stone walls and varnished oak panelling of the original seventeenth-century coaching inn remain intact – as does Will Holland's commitment to classic modern dishes. A summer appetiser of spiced carrots in an intense carrot velouté sprinkled with coriander leaves may leave you never reaching for another supermarket carton again. That meal hadn't quite done with carrots, which also appeared pickled in orange in the opening course, to accompany a fillet of red mullet with battered squid rings and sublime breaded deep-fried brandade. Jellied pig's head ballottine (brawn if you prefer) was a refined version accompanied by chickpea and preserved lemon salsa and and a dab of hummus, while the main course was breast of Welsh lamb with a punchy stuffing of pine nuts, rosemary and capers and a trickle of salsa verde. Dessert might be comprised of a brilliant lemon curd-filled crêpe with strawberry sorbet, black pepper caramel and basil oil. Good Italian and Australasian producers are among the highlights on a basically classical list (from £19) that doesn't offer a great deal of price relief, but is certainly discerning enough.
Chef/s: Will Holland. **Open:** Wed to Sun L 12 to 2, Tue to Sat D 7 to 9 (9.30 Fri and Sat). **Closed:** Mon, 2 weeks Christmas and New Year. **Meals:** Set L £26 (2 courses) to £30. Set D £54 (2 courses) to £60. Gourmand menu £65 (7 courses) to £90 (10 courses). **Service:** 12.5%. **Details:** 35 seats. Separate bar. Music. Car parking.

The Green Café
Lovely cornmill café with tasty lunches
Mill on the Green, Ludlow, SY8 1EG
Tel no: (01584) 879872
www.thegreencafe.co.uk
Modern British | £19
Cooking score: 1

Green by name, green by nature, this cracking café in a converted cornmill beside the river Teme is surrounded by open spaces – complete with clear views of Ludlow Castle and Dinham Bridge. 'So fresh, so tasty' is the verdict on lunches with a spirited seasonal flavour: ox tongue is served with piccalilli, Wyre Forest Pig salami comes with goats' cheeses and medlar paste. Trencherman helpings of confit duck cassoulet and seafood stew satisfy big appetites. To drink, expect local beers and ciders, plus organic wines (from £16.50). Cash or cheques only.
Chef/s: Clive Davis. **Open:** Tue to Sun 10am to 4.30pm. **Closed:** Mon, 24 and 25 Dec, 28 Jan to 14 Feb, bank hols. **Meals:** alc (main courses £7 to £11). **Service:** 10%. **Details:** 30 seats. 25 seats outside. No music. Wheelchair access.

★ TOP 50 ★

Mr Underhill's
Flowing beautifully from start to finish
Dinham Weir, Ludlow, SY8 1EH
Tel no: (01584) 874431
www.mr-underhills.co.uk
Modern European | £63
Cooking score: 6

↹ V

Ludlow old-timer Mr Underhill's is praised year-in year-out for its thoughtful service and personalised bespoke menus by self-taught chef Chris Bradley. The restaurant-with-rooms is dreamily located by the river, and is now set to beat its own high standards after a re-style of the dining room reduced covers to just 24. Open only in the evening, it offers a daily changing 'market menu' of eight courses that 'flows beautifully' from the arrival of, say,

Parmesan and sweet pepper buns right through to petits fours. Signatures such as 'outstanding' duck liver custard appear time and again in new guises (perhaps with sweetcorn cream and lemongrass glaze). Other unusual combinations, such as leek and potato velouté with spiced apple ice cream, 'work perfectly'. Dishes from the proudly sous vide-free menu vary in detail, though the structure changes little. Fish and meat courses such as lemon sole, confit ratte potato and mustard cream, or venison fillet with caper and raisin jus and cauliflower cheese cream give way to a pre-dessert, ahead of a choice of desserts (hot fondant beetroot tart, perhaps) or cheese. Unsnooty service led by Judy Bradley guides guests towards suitable wine pairings, 'modestly marked up' and with plenty by the glass. House wine is £20.

Chef/s: Chris Bradley. **Open:** Wed to Sun D only 7.30 (1 sitting). **Closed:** Mon, Tue, 25, 26 and 31 Dec, 1 Jan, 1 week June, 1 week Oct. **Meals:** Set D £62.50 (8 courses). **Service:** not inc. **Details:** 24 seats. 24 seats outside. No music. Car parking.

Marton

Gartells at the Sun Inn
Pubby hospitality, real ales, honest food
Marton, SY21 8JP
Tel no: (01938) 561211
www.suninn.org.uk
Modern British | £25
Cooking score: 1

The setting is the Shropshire-Powys borders at their prettiest, and the venerable Sun Inn is a sturdy stone hostelry that has not forsaken its pub roots – so expect real ales in the hospitable bar. But the savvy local dining crowd knows it as home to the Gartell family's cordial restaurant, where old favourites include duck breast with clementine and brandy sauce and casserole of venison with port, juniper and thyme. To finish, perhaps chocolate délice. House wine is £13.95.

Chef/s: Peter Gartell. **Open:** Wed to Sun L 12 to 2, Tue to Sat D 7 to 9. **Closed:** Mon. **Meals:** alc (main courses £11 to £16). Sun L £14.95 (2 courses) to £17.95. **Service:** not inc. **Details:** 50 seats. Separate bar. No music. Wheelchair access. Car parking.

Munslow

The Crown Country Inn
Quirky old inn with fresh, simple food
Corvedale Road, Munslow, SY7 9ET
Tel no: (01584) 841205
www.crowncountryinn.co.uk
Modern British | £29
Cooking score: 3

Jane and Richard Arnold's pub-with-rooms is a quirkily traditional, homely place. The former 'hundred house' has its full quota of beams, inglenooks and olde-worlde charm. Richard's food has never fallen victim to fads of fashion either, yet his straightforward approach matches the current vogue for keeping things simple and fresh, with produce almost entirely locally sourced. Kedgeree made with naturally smoked haddock and topped with a poached egg, or faggots with parsnip mash make first-rate lunch dishes in the bar, while dinner in the first-floor dining room could bring a smooth parfait of chicken livers, roast breast and confit leg of Gressingham duck, vegetable selections served on a separate plate, and lemon and mandarin crème brûlée. Wines from £15.75.

Chef/s: Richard Arnold. **Open:** Tue to Sun L 12 to 2, Tue to Sat D 6.45 to 9. **Closed:** Mon, 25 to 27 Dec, 1 to 3 Jan. **Meals:** alc (main courses £15 to £19). Set L and D £19.50. Sun L £20.95. **Service:** not inc. **Details:** 60 seats. 30 seats outside. Separate bar. Music. Car parking.

▌Oswestry

Sebastians

A petit slice of France
45 Willow Street, Oswestry, SY11 1AQ
Tel no: (01691) 655444
www.sebastians-hotel.co.uk
French | £40
Cooking score: 3

Sebastians' crooked beams, wonky floors and wood panelling might suggest a teashop straight out of an Agatha Christie novel, but this chintzy, centuries-old coach house is actually a petit slice of France – with the culinary accents to prove it. Michelle and Mark Sebastian Fisher have carved out their own niche here, matching cordial hospitality with a repertoire of commendable bourgeois food – think affordable haute cuisine dolled up with amuse-bouches and mid-course sorbets. Their monthly menu might turn up anything from loin of lamb accompanied by a mini shepherd's pie, tomato confit and a goats' cheese tarte fine to a take on sole véronique involving cauliflower velouté and pickled grapes. To finish, plump for French cheeses (perversely served with Welsh rarebit) or something sweet – perhaps griottine cherry and almond clafoutis with pistachio ice cream. French regional wines (from £17.95) dominate the well-chosen list.
Chef/s: Richard Jones. **Open:** Tue to Sat D only 6.30 to 9.30. **Closed:** Sun, Mon, 24 to 26 Dec, 1 Jan. **Meals:** Set D £19.95. **Service:** not inc. **Details:** 40 seats. Music. Car parking.

MATT GILLAN
The Pass

When did you realise you wanted to be a chef?
When I was 16, helping out in the kitchen at the Hen & Chicken Inn at Froyle.

Give us a quick culinary tip
Soak pulses in sparkling water overnight. They will cook more evenly.

Which chefs do you admire, and why?
Chefs that have built up their own restaurants to make them successful. It inspires me to keep pushing, so that one day I can do it for myself.

What food trends are you spotting at the moment?
Food has taken a simpler presentation route and restaurants are becoming alot less formal. Foraging is also big at the moment.

Sum up your cooking style in three words
Fun, progressive, British.

What's your 'show-off' dish?
Vanilla pannacotta, popcorn coulis and soy sauce gingerbread.

What's your earliest food memory?
My mum's goat curry.

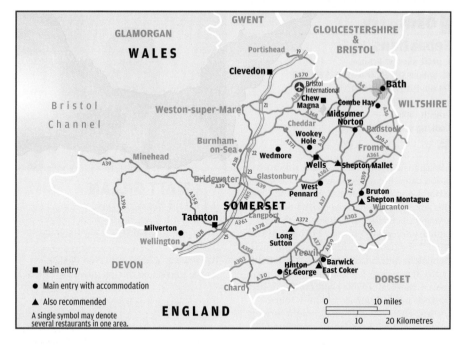

Main entry ■
Main entry with accommodation ●
Also recommended ▲
A single symbol may denote several restaurants in one area.

0   10 miles
0   10   20 Kilometres

▌Barwick

Little Barwick House
An unalloyed rural idyll
Rexes Hollow Lane, Barwick, BA22 9TD
Tel no: (01935) 423902
www.littlebarwickhouse.co.uk
Modern British | £44
Cooking score: 5

Tim and Anna Ford's unalloyed rural idyll sits not far from the Dorset border, set in its own three acres of gardens amid some of the West Country's most seductive landscapes. A soft-toned, elegant dining room is the setting for Tim's classically informed cooking – he did a long stint at Sharrow Bay (see entry, Ullswater) – which draws on local supply lines to great effect. A twice-baked cheese soufflé is lifted out of the airy ordinary by its accompaniment of spiced smoked haddock and mussel ragoût. Main-course flavours are built into streamlined productions; a colour-coordinated dish of pink-cooked roe deer saddle comes with braised red cabbage and beetroot purée, while West Bay sea bass is partnered by roasted fennel and saffron potato in Champagne sauce. Thoroughbred West Country cheeses with raisin bread and quince paste are the alternative to indulgences such as white chocolate and orange mousse with dark chocolate sauce and mandarin sorbet. A wine list brimful of discernment and originality is arranged by style, from 'zesty, crisp and refreshing whites' to 'heavier, full-bodied and rich reds'. Dessert wines and half-bottles in plenty add to the fun. Prices open at £18.95 (£6.50 a glass) for Chile's Ventisquero Merlot Reserva.
Chef/s: Tim Ford. **Open:** Wed to Sun L 12 to 2, Tue to Sat D 7 to 9.30. **Closed:** Mon, 3 weeks from 25 Dec. **Meals:** Set L £23.95 (2 courses) to £27.95. Set D £37.95 (2 courses) to £43.95. Sun L £28.95. **Service:** not inc. **Details:** 40 seats. No music. Car parking. Children over 5 yrs only.

Bath

The Bath Priory
Destination venue with a vivid modern menu
Weston Road, Bath, BA1 2XT
Tel no: (01225) 331922
www.thebathpriory.co.uk
Modern European | £75
Cooking score: 5

 V

Set in pretty gardens a mile from Bath city centre, this handsome hotel is surprisingly relaxed. Despite its luxurious country-house trappings and reputation as one of the region's destination restaurants, staff are cheery and the dining room is more a place of bonhomie than whispering reverence. Michael Caines' protégé Sam Moody has quickly put his stamp on the menu with vivid modern dishes underpinned by sound raw materials. Seafood, delivered daily from Cornwall, is treated innovatively, witness an amuse-bouche of pan-fried scallop with apple and hazelnut salad, confit lemon and veal jus. From a spring lunch menu, a fine starter of caramelised rose veal sweetbreads with mushroom risotto and broad beans was followed by a precisely cooked fillet of Brixham John Dory served with a shellfish bisque and purple sprouting broccoli. Desserts follow the form, a light and airy rhubarb soufflé accompanied by delicate ginger ice cream being one seasonal offering. The exhaustive and intimidating wine list numbers more than 500; France may dominate but there are several top-drawer choices from Australia, California and Italy. Prices start at £28.
Chef/s: Michael Caines and Sam Moody. **Open:** all week L 12.30 to 2.30, D 6.30 to 9.30. **Meals:** Set L £25.50 (2 courses) to £35. Set D £59 (2 courses) to £75. Sun L £42. Tasting menu £90. Signature menu £100. **Service:** not inc. **Details:** 70 seats. 20 seats outside. No music. Wheelchair access. Car parking.

Casanis
Charming bistro with Gallic classics
4 Saville Row, Bath, BA1 2QP
Tel no: (01225) 780055
www.casanis.co.uk
French | £28
Cooking score: 1

£30

'If we lived locally we would enjoy returning to work through the à la carte,' was the verdict from one roving reporter, who thought the set menus at Casanis offered 'excellent value'. Occupying an elegant Georgian building adjacent to Bath's Assembly Rooms, this charming, family-run bistro majors on authentic Gallic classics. A 'properly made' Provençal fish soup could be followed by roasted quail with lentil ragoût, fondant potatoes and rosemary jus, with a well-crafted tarte aux pommes and vanilla ice cream for dessert. House wine from £18.50.
Chef/s: Laurent Couvreur. **Open:** Tue to Sat L 12 to 2, D 6 to 10. **Closed:** Sun, Mon, 25 to 27 Dec, 1 to 14 Jan, 1 week Aug, 3 days Jun. **Meals:** alc (main courses £13 to £25). Set L £14.75 (2 courses) to £18.75. Set D £18.50 (2 courses) to £22.50. **Service:** not inc. **Details:** 54 seats. 16 seats outside. Music.

NEW ENTRY
The Circus Café and Restaurant
Welcoming family-run gem
34 Brock Street, Bath, BA1 2LN
Tel no: (01225) 466020
www.thecircuscafeandrestaurant.co.uk
Modern British | £29
Cooking score: 3

£5
OFF

This family-run restaurant occupies a Georgian building in the street linking The Royal Crescent and The Circus – the perfect location to attract both locals and visitors. 'The welcome is always warm and the service excellent' noted one reader of the compact eatery, which boasts original fireplaces and cornicing. Chef/patron Alison Golden cites

Elizabeth David and Jane Grigson among her influences, and clear, simple flavours certainly shine, witness a comforting starter of Cornish smoked haddock baked with leeks and spinach and topped with Montgomery Cheddar. A main of 'very fresh', accurately timed sea bass fillets with salsa verde and roasted fennel showed respect for the main ingredient, as did a Yorkshire rhubarb fool layered with Amaretto syllabub and ratafia biscuits. The European wine list starts at £14.90.
Chef/s: Alison Golden, Adie Ware and Dicky Simpson. **Open:** Mon to Sat L 12 to 3 (4 Sat), D 5.30 to 10.30. **Closed:** Sun, 24 Dec to 14 Jan. **Meals:** alc (main courses £15 to £20). Set L £15 (2 courses) to £19.70. Set D £24.50 (2 courses) to £29. **Service:** not inc. **Details:** 50 seats. 8 seats outside. Music. Children over 7 yrs only.

The Marlborough Tavern
Stylish, popular food pub
35 Marlborough Buildings, Bath, BA1 2LY
Tel no: (01225) 423731
www.marlborough-tavern.com
British | £28
Cooking score: 3
£5 OFF £30

Just a few paces from Bath's famous Royal Crescent, this once-unloved city centre watering hole has been transformed into a stylish and popular food pub. High ceilings, village hall furniture and plenty of Farrow & Ball paint give it a sophisticated look, although the hand-pulled real ales still attract the drinkers and locals. Richard Knighting's confident cooking makes impressive use of local, seasonal ingredients and the menu name-checks many of the producers. Ingredients are treated with respect and dishes are unfussy, as in a starter of smoked haddock chowder and a main course of beef fillet and braised ox cheek, horseradish and black pudding mash and seasonal greens. For dessert, perhaps spiced Guinness parkin with pear sorbet and salted caramel sauce. House wine £15.90.

Chef/s: Richard Knighting. **Open:** all week L 12.30 to 2.30 (3 Sat, 4 Sun), D 6 to 9.30 (10 Fri and Sat, 9 Sun). **Closed:** 25 Dec. **Meals:** alc (main courses £11 to £22). Set L £12 (2 courses) to £15. **Service:** not inc. **Details:** 76 seats. 90 seats outside. Music. No children after 8.

The Queensberry Hotel, Olive Tree Restaurant
Comfort, quirks and eclectic cooking
4-7 Russel Street, Bath, BA1 2QF
Tel no: (01225) 447928
www.olivetreebath.co.uk
Modern British | £45
Cooking score: 4
£5 OFF

Built in 1771 for the Marquis of Queensberry, this palatial Georgian town house punches well above its weight, and now combines the full-on Bath experience with a heavy dose of boutique pizazz. The hotel's snazzy vibe also permeates down to the Olive Tree – a stylish, white-walled dining room lit by orange lamps. The kitchen applies sharp modern technique to impeccably chosen ingredients – perhaps ravioli of native lobster with ginger and lemongrass velouté or brochette of Creedy Carver duck breast with a spring roll, Alsace cabbage and fondant potato. A fondness for fusion also yields a Thai green curry made with wild rabbit, chermoula-spiced red gurnard with quinoa, and a dish of Cornish sea bass with Bombay potato and tempura skate cheeks. Desserts pick up the eclectic theme for, say, orange and polenta cake with mandarin and pomegranate or passion-fruit bavarois with its own 'curd' and mango sorbet. The invigorating and revelatory wine list puts the fun back into serious imbibing, with colourful notes, easy mark-ups and some mouthwatering categories ('black fruits full of body', anyone?). At the last count, no fewer than 34 top-class house selections were on offer, from £18 (£5 a glass).
Chef/s: Nick Brodie. **Open:** Tue to Sun L 12 to 2 (12.30 to 2 Sun), all week D 7 to 10. **Meals:** alc (main courses £17 to £27). Set L £18.50 (2 courses) to

£22.50. Set D £32.50 (2 courses) to £38.50. Sun L £22.50. **Service:** 10%. **Details:** 60 seats. Separate bar. Music.

The White Hart Inn
Quirky pub with assertive cooking
Widcombe Hill, Widcombe, Bath, BA2 6AA
Tel no: (01225) 338053
www.whitehartbath.co.uk
Modern British | £25
Cooking score: 2

The White Hart's proximity to Bath's railway station makes it a favoured watering hole for locals and visitors. The backpackers' hostel upstairs adds to the quirkiness, but doesn't detract from the assertive cooking of chef Rupert Pitt and his team. Eat in the dining area or the walled garden, and there's lots of choice. Crab and chilli salad with fennel and lemon confit might be followed by roast lamb rump, Mediterranean vegetables and green sauce, and diverting desserts include lemon jelly with lemon posset sorbet. Wines from £15.50.
Chef/s: Rupert Pitt, Jason Horn, Rachel Milsom and Luke Gibson. **Open:** all week L 12 to 2, Mon to Sat D 6 to 10 (9 Mon and Tue). **Closed:** 25 Dec, bank hols. **Meals:** alc (main courses £12 to £18). Set L £12.50. **Service:** not inc. **Details:** 50 seats. 40 seats outside. Wheelchair access. Music.

ALSO RECOMMENDED
▲ The Garrick's Head
7-8 St Johns Place, Bath, BA1 1ET
Tel no: (01225) 318368
www.garricksheadpub.com
British £5 OFF

Pre-show suppers are naturally a top deal at this civilised Georgian hostelry next to the Theatre Royal. Otherwise, eat in the bar or the dining room from a Brit-inspired menu that might promise anything from Cornish crab and apple salad with celeriac rémoulade (£7.95) to spiced orange and bay leaf crème brûlée, via braised Somerset beef shin and horseradish suet pud (£14.95), herb-crusted

sea bream with cauliflower purée or wild mushroom tart with Jerusalem artichoke salad. Wines from £14.50. Open all week.

▲ King William
36 Thomas Street, Bath, BA1 5NN
Tel no: (01225) 428096
www.kingwilliampub.com
British £5 OFF

A short walk from Bath's city centre, this Georgian pub offers no-frills British comfort food in the bar and the more formal dining room. A menu that showcases carefully sourced, seasonal ingredients is illustrated by a starter of home-smoked salmon, beetroot and shallot dressing (£6.75) and a main of confit duck leg, white bean, roast garlic and apple stew with steamed greens (£15.95). Finish with custard tart and poached rhubarb (£5.95). House wine is £14. Closed Mon and Tues L.

▲ Yak Yeti Yak
12 Pierrepont Street, Bath, BA1 1LA
Tel no: (01225) 442299
www.yakyetiyak.co.uk
Nepalese

The basements of three eighteenth-century town houses have been turned into a little piece of Nepal. Whether you opt for conventional chairs and tables or to sit on traditional floor cushions, you will be served authentic Nepalese food. Steamed, spiced pork dumplings with hemp seed chutney (£5.50) open things, then stir-fried lamb with cumin and masala spices (£8.40), or the vegetarian Kathmandu speciality of stir-fried fermented bamboo shoots, new potatoes and black-eyed peas. Wines from £13.20. Open all week.

Menu Gordon Jones

Modern British
2 Wellsway, Bath, BA2 3AQ
Tel no: (01225) 480871
www.menugordonjones.co.uk
'Seven courses and it was sensational!
Definitely worth checking out.'

▌Bruton

At the Chapel

Busy, stylish all-dayer
High Street, Bruton, BA10 0AE
Tel no: (01749) 814070
www.atthechapel.co.uk
Modern British | £24
Cooking score: 2

A restyled coaching inn and chapel makes a
highly singular venue for a bakery, wine shop,
bar and restaurant. The busy day kicks off with
the likes of scrambled eggs and mushrooms on
sourdough toast for breakfast, then motors on
through lunchtime pizzas from the wood-
fired oven, to dinner menus that deal in
modern European thrills aplenty – wood
pigeon with pomegranate, Parma ham and
Parmesan; hake with brown shrimp butter and
sprouting broccoli; baked vanilla cheesecake
with rhubarb. There's a kids' menu, and for
adults some pretty nifty drinking in the shape
of a cocktail list, and wines from £16 (£4 a
glass).
Chef/s: Steven Horrell. Open: all week L 12 to 3, D 6
to 9.30. Meals: alc (main courses £9 to £18).
Service: not inc. Details: 70 seats. 40 seats outside.
Separate bar. No music.

▌Chew Magna

The Pony & Trap

Versatile local food champion
Knowle Hill, Chew Magna, BS40 8TQ
Tel no: (01275) 332627
www.theponyandtrap.co.uk
Modern British | £27
Cooking score: 4

After cooking his way around various Bristol
kitchens, Josh Eggleton took over this country
pub some five years ago. It's a gamble that has
clearly paid off – while it feels very remote, it
is just a 15-minute drive from Bristol and has
become a popular venue for unpretentious but
clever modern cooking. The kitchen responds
to the seasons and sourcing is a strength; much
of the seriously promoted produce is local.
Here you will find pigeon bresaola and char-
grilled pigeon breast with walnuts and carrots
('an innovative dish, both texturally and
flavour-wise'), 'notably fresh' fillet of Cornish
brill with crab and lemon, caper and brown
shrimp butter, and spiced crème brûlée with
apple purée, granola and apple sorbet – 'a
playful, amusing twist on apple crumble'. The
balance between pub and restaurant is spot-
on, too – it's possible to visit for a pint and a
burger or ploughman's. Wines start at £13.50.
Chef/s: Josh Eggleton. Open: Tue to Sun L 12 to 2.30
(3.30 Sun), D 7 to 9.30. Closed: 25 Dec. Meals: alc
(main courses £11 to £20). Service: not inc.
Details: 60 seats. 40 seats outside. Separate bar.
Music. Car parking.

Clevedon

Murrays

All-day Italian café-deli
87-93 Hill Road, Clevedon, BS21 7PN
Tel no: (01275) 341555
www.murraysofclevedon.co.uk
Italian | £25
Cooking score: 3

 £30

Murrays has been delivering Italian flavour to Clevedon for almost three decades. It is now a café-deli with informal service and a flexible menu that runs from breakfast to late afternoon in fashionably unfussy surroundings. There's an awareness of the seasons and a serious commitment to top-drawer produce, and the kitchen's familiar trademark touches continue to delight visitors, from the bread baked each morning to the range of pizzas that are available to take away. It caters for all-comers, with cakes, sandwiches and light lunches of Cornish crab and leek tart with a Parmesan crust, as well as more substantial dishes such as braised ox cheek with a potato, salami and pecorino cake, curly kale and salsa verde. Wines from £12.95.
Chef/s: Reuben Murray. **Open:** Tue to Sat 8.30am to 5pm. **Closed:** Sun, Mon, 25 and 26 Dec. **Meals:** alc (main courses £9 to £23). **Service:** not inc. **Details:** 40 seats. 4 seats outside. Music.

Combe Hay

The Wheatsheaf

Chic inn that oozes rustic sophistication
Combe Hay, BA2 7EG
Tel no: (01225) 833504
www.wheatsheafcombehay.com
Modern British | £32
Cooking score: 4

£5 OFF 🛏

Hidden in a lush and secluded valley, yet just 15 minutes from Bath, this well-groomed sixteenth-century inn oozes rustic sophistication. The chic interior, with its original stone floors, beams and Lloyd Loom chairs, is complemented by a gorgeous three-tiered garden next to an abundant kitchen and the pub's very own chickens and ducks. It all combines to set the stage for what one reader summed up as 'a delicious meal in pleasant surroundings'. Eddy Rains conjures bold, well-defined flavours from top-notch seasonal local produce. Typically, a starter of river Exe mussels in Midford cider could be followed by fillet of Gloucester Old Spot pork, ham hock croquettes, cider vinegar and mustard glaze. Desserts might feature warm treacle tart with white chocolate and crème fraîche sorbet. The 150-strong, European-only wine list offers a well-considered line-up that majors on Bordeaux. House wine starts at £14.95 and there are 14 by the glass.
Chef/s: Eddy Rains. **Open:** Tue to Sun L 12 to 2 (3 Sun), Tue to Sat D 6.30 to 9. **Closed:** Mon, first week Jan. **Meals:** alc (main courses £12 to £22). Sun L £19.50 (two courses) to £24.50. **Service:** 10%. **Details:** 56 seats. 80 seats outside. Music. Car parking.

East Coker

ALSO RECOMMENDED
▲ Helyar Arms

Moor Lane, East Coker, BA22 9JR
Tel no: (01935) 862332
www.helyar-arms.co.uk
British

A well-preserved fifteenth-century hostelry in a handsome Somerset village, the Helyar Arms pleases drinkers and famished punters in equal measure. Plump for 'classic' pub grub such as honey-roast ham and eggs, local sausages with champ, or an aged Somerset ribeye with chunky chips. Alternatively, go posh with confit chicken terrine, quince and baby fig jelly (£6.25) followed by roast Lulworth Estate venison with a mini-cottage pie and celeriac dauphinois (£18.95), plus a helping of trifle or chocolate fondant to finish. Wines from £14.95. Accommodation. Open all week.

Hinton St George

The Lord Poulett Arms

Appealing village pub with seasonal food
High Street, Hinton St George, TA17 8SE
Tel no: (01460) 73149
www.lordpoulettarms.com
Modern British | £26
Cooking score: 2

'Had a lovely evening at this super pub in rural Somerset', noted a visitor to this thatched, hamstone inn, which dates from the seventeenth century. With its roaring log fires, rug-strewn flagstone floors and real ale straight from the barrel, it has all the appeal of a traditional village pub. The menu does feature pub favourites (ham, egg and chips), but there are more contemporary dishes, too, and what's in season is important, so expect the likes of spring pea velouté with crème fraiche and pea bruschetta, and crispy fillet of bream with new potatoes, chorizo and dill and lemon dressed spring vegetables. Wines from £15.
Chef/s: Steven Kiernan. **Open:** all week 12 to 9. **Closed:** 25 and 26 Dec, 1 Jan. **Meals:** alc (main courses £10 to £27). Sun L £19. **Service:** not inc. **Details:** 60 seats. 40 seats outside. Separate bar. No music. Car parking.

Long Sutton

ALSO RECOMMENDED
▲ The Devonshire Arms

Cross Lane, Long Sutton, TA10 9LP
Tel no: (01458) 241271
www.thedevonshirearms.com
British

A greystone country inn-with-rooms overlooking the village green, the Devonshire has a breezily modern feel inside, with a smart restaurant ambience overlaying the pub ethos of bare tables and blackboard menus. Modern British ideas inform the cooking: char-grilled scallops with fennel and bacon velouté (£10.50), beef chuck in port with creamy mash and curly kale (£13.95) and ginger

sticky toffee pudding with lime leaf ice cream and Grand Marnier sauce (£5.95). Wines from £15.95. Accommodation. Open all week.

Midsomer Norton

The Moody Goose at the Old Priory

Serenity and cosmopolitan cooking
Church Square, Midsomer Norton, BA3 2HX
Tel no: (01761) 416784
www.theoldpriory.co.uk
Modern British | £40
Cooking score: 4

There's something tirelessly serene about this ancient stone-built hotel and its beautiful walled garden in the centre of Midsomer Norton. It dates from the twelfth century (reputedly one of the oldest houses in Somerset), and is made up of a warren of tiny rooms with period features including a large inglenook fireplace. On the food front, the main focus is contemporary, cosmopolitan cooking based on a foundation of well-sourced materials. The style is appealing without being flamboyant. Well thought-out combinations range from warm Brixham crab with a tomato and Parmesan tartlet and rocket pesto, via calf's liver and pancetta with roasted shallots and garlic and cream potato, to caramelised plum cream with cinnamon doughnuts. The contemporary list of wines is good value, with prices starting at £19.
Chef/s: Stephen Shore. **Open:** Mon to Sat L 12 to 1.30, D 7 to 9.15 (7.30 Mon). **Closed:** Sun, 1 week Christmas, 1 Jan, bank hols. **Meals:** Set L and D £32.50 (2 courses) to £39.50. **Service:** not inc. **Details:** 30 seats. Wheelchair access. Music. Car parking.

❙❘❙ Also Recommended
Also recommended entries are not scored but we think they are worth a visit.

Milverton
The Globe
Posh comfort food, served generously
Fore Street, Milverton, TA4 1JX
Tel no: (01823) 400534
www.theglobemilverton.co.uk
Modern British | £25
Cooking score: 2

£5 OFF £30

This vigorously refurbished coaching inn nevertheless draws the crowds with a credo of high-quality ingredients cooked simply and served generously. The menu is slightly retro – expect posh comfort food along the lines of wild mushrooms with cream and garlic on toasted brioche or twice-baked Wookey Hole Cheddar soufflé with red onion jam, alongside local ribeye steak with onion rings, peppercorn sauce and chips. Sea bass fillets may be jazzed up with a few exotic flourishes (curried lentils, Thai coconut broth and coriander salad), but it's back to the comfort zone with desserts of apple pie and custard. Wines from £13.50.

Chef/s: Mark Tarry and Kaan Atasoy. **Open:** Tue to Sun L 12 to 2, Mon to Sat D 6.30 to 9. **Meals:** alc (main courses £9 to £19). Sun L £12.95 (2 courses) to £15.95. **Service:** not inc. **Details:** 50 seats. 25 seats outside. Separate bar. Wheelchair access. Music. Car parking.

Shepton Mallet
ALSO RECOMMENDED
▲ Blostin's
29-33 Waterloo Road, Shepton Mallet, BA4 5HH
Tel no: (01749) 343648
www.blostins.co.uk
Modern British £5 OFF

Loyal Shepton Mallet servants for many years, Nick and Lynne Reed aim to please all-comers in their small but perfectly formed restaurant. A short set-price menu (£18/£22) showcases excellent local materials. Praise is heaped on good things such as duck and pork terrine and grilled fillet of hake with wilted spinach and lemon butter sauce. Seasonal specialities could

include Cornish crab tartlets with sauce grelette (£8.25) and pheasant breast in pancetta (£16.95). Wines from £14.75. Open Tue to Sat D only.

Shepton Montague
ALSO RECOMMENDED
▲ The Montague Inn
Shepton Montague, BA9 8JW
Tel no: (01749) 813213
www.themontagueinn.co.uk
Modern European £5 OFF

This laid-back pub in a very rural location is refreshing and likeable – low-key with a robustly seasonal and local attitude to food. The appealing, crowd-pleasing menu keeps things pubby at lunchtime with ploughman's and home-cooked ham, egg and chips (£10.50); dinner could bring confit duck, rack of lamb and blackboard specials, say a tart of feta, beetroot, pea and mint, or wild venison saddle (£18.50). Desserts range from crème brûlée to chocolate brownie. Wines from £14.50. No food Sun D.

Taunton
NEW ENTRY
Augustus Restaurant
Local hero goes solo
3 The Courtyard, St James Street, Taunton, TA1 1JR
Tel no: (01823) 324354
www.augustustaunton.co.uk
Modern British | £25
Cooking score: 5

£5 OFF £30

After more than a decade as head chef at The Castle just around the corner, Richard Guest is now his own man at this intimate, white brick-walled bistro – and such is his local following that tables are hard to secure unless you book. Guest championed great British cooking at The Castle, but takes a simpler French route for this, his first solo venture, although precise technical skills and high-quality seasonal ingredients are still to the fore. A concise menu might offer blackboard specials of duck livers on toast with Calvados cream or Somerset faggots with mash and greens. From the carte, any richness of the precisely cooked smoked eel fishcake with beurre blanc is countered by a delicate garnish of razor-thin slices of radish. A well-judged fillet of exceptionally fresh brill with smoked bacon and impressively light gnocchi is equally accomplished. To conclude, a Yorkshire rhubarb Vacherin achieves the right balance between tart and sweet, the topping of whipped cream being sprinkled with a dusting of crunchy honeycomb. Unobtrusive, knowledgeable staff add to the charm of the place. House wines from £15.

Chef/s: Richard Guest. **Open:** Tue to Sat L 12 to 3, D 6 to 9.30. **Closed:** Mon, Sun, 24 Dec to 3 Jan. **Meals:** alc (main courses £10 to £18). **Service:** not inc. **Details:** 30 seats. 24 seats outside. No music.

The Willow Tree
The best kind of neighbourhood restaurant
3 Tower Lane, Taunton, TA1 4AR
Tel no: (01823) 352835
www.thewillowtreerestaurant.com
Modern British | £34
Cooking score: 5

Tucked down a little alleyway behind the Castle, the Willow Tree is a neighbourhood restaurant of the best ilk, loyally supported by local customers, the kind of place that's full in midweek, no matter what the economic climate. The cottagey feel (low-ceilinged, beamed interiors and log-stuffed fireplace) helps, and so does the supremely professional front-of-house. Darren Sherlock produces simple, direct and classy bistro dishes with a high comfort factor (the Montgomery Cheddar soufflé with walnut and celery cream, and the bread-and-butter pudding at the other end are among the ornaments of modern Taunton). A starter of black bream is accurately timed and comes with finely diced gazpacho vegetables, quivery tomato jelly and wild rocket, while a satisfying main course of roast guinea fowl offers well-seasoned, crisp-skinned meat, with sautéed gnocchi and a

little confit red onion. If you're after something light to finish, slices of peach set in Champagne jelly, alongside a dollop of mascarpone cream, should fit the bill. Wines start at £18.95 (£5.75 a glass).

Chef/s: Darren Sherlock. **Open:** Tue, Wed, Fri and Sat D only 6.30 to 9. **Closed:** Mon, Thur, Sun, 26 to 31 Dec, Jan, Aug. **Meals:** Set D Tue and Wed £27.95, Fri and Sat £29.95. **Service:** 10%. **Details:** 25 seats. 10 seats outside. Separate bar. Music.

Wedmore

NEW ENTRY
The Swan
Simple, satisfying pub food
Cheddar Road, Wedmore, BS28 4EQ
Tel no: (01934) 710337
www.theswanwedmore.com
Modern British | £25
Cooking score: 2

A great-looking pub in a picture-perfect village, The Swan does rustic chic with breezy flair. The obligatory wood-burner, floorboards and quarry tiles are teamed with bare white walls and simple furniture for a subtly modern edge. Service from smart young staff is on-the-money, and the open kitchen keeps pace, turning out simple, stylish food made with excellent ingredients. Crisp smoked pollock croquettes with aïoli are typical finger-licking starters, followed perhaps by Chew Valley steak with a beetroot salad and superb crisp, fluffy chips. A dark chocolate pudding made a memorable dessert. The international wine list opens at £15.35.

Chef/s: Tom Blake. **Open:** all week L 12 to 2.45, Mon to Sat D 6 to 9.45. **Meals:** alc (main courses £11 to £20). **Service:** not inc. **Details:** 120 seats. 64 seats outside. Separate bar. Music. Car parking.

▌Wells

Goodfellows

Astute seafood cookery
5 Sadler Street, Wells, BA5 2RR
Tel no: (01749) 673866
www.goodfellowswells.co.uk
Modern British/Seafood | £39
Cooking score: 5

 £5 OFF

Nestled snugly in the shadow of Wells' mighty cathedral, Goodfellows' two-pronged set-up trades on easy-going flexibility. If you can stand the heat, pitch up on the ground floor with its slate, steel, marble surfaces and open kitchen; otherwise, enjoy the intimacy of the few tables upstairs, crowned with a glass roof. Either way, chef-proprietor Adam Fellows' astute seafood cookery is the main attraction: for the best pickings, trawl the 'market menu', or take the plunge with his six-course tasting extravaganza, which might yield the likes of deep-fried shellfish with croquettes and fennel salad, tuna sashimi with white radish and black sesame, or Brixham crab with sweetcorn purée, chorizo vinaigrette and Parmesan tuile. Good calls from recent meals have included simply cooked Welsh mussels in white wine and a generous, fine-looking dish of sea bream with marinated girolles, broad beans and tomatoes. Pretty presentation is also a feature of regular 'non-fish' dishes such as confit duck with celeriac purée and crispy vine leaves or organic spelt risotto with beetroot and thyme. As for desserts, chocolate, pear and frangipane tart with cinnamon ice cream is a speciality. For something lighter and quicker, check out the Sadler Street Café next door, which deals in cakes, pastries and simpler bistro-style dishes. House wines start at £15.
Chef/s: Adam Fellows. Open: Tue to Sat L 12 to 2, Wed to Sat D 6.30 to 9.30. Closed: Sun, Mon, 25 to 27 Dec, 7 to 20 Jan. Meals: alc (main courses £14 to £24). Set L £20 (2 courses) to £23.50. Set D £39. Tasting menu £58 (6 courses). Service: not inc. Details: 35 seats. Music.

The Old Spot

A supremely accomplished operation
12 Sadler Street, Wells, BA5 2SE
Tel no: (01749) 689099
www.theoldspot.co.uk
Modern British | £28
Cooking score: 4

 £30

The Spot in question overlooks the green of Wells' wonderful cathedral from the back, with a double-fronted Georgian bay window framing the front view. It's a supremely accomplished two-handed operation by wine expert Clare Bates and husband Ian, whose cheffing CV includes stints with Michel Guérard in France and Simon Hopkinson at Bibendum (see entry, London). The name of the game here is precisely defined modern British cooking making optimal use of seasonal flavours. A great chunk of coarse pork terrine with onion confit is a good wintry way to start, following which there may be roast grey mullet with spiced lentils, mussels and coriander, or a regionally unimpeachable dish of pheasant in Somerset cider brandy with bacon and thyme. A fortifying finish sees pear and ginger clafoutis dressed in honey and cream from a local farm. The wine list is a model of clarity and concision, with interesting flavours from all over. Prices start at £16.95.
Chef/s: Ian Bates. Open: Wed to Sun L 12.30 to 2, Tue to Sat D 7.30 to 9. Closed: Mon, 1 week Christmas. Meals: Set L £15.50 (2 courses) to £18.50. Sun L £22.50. Service: not inc. Details: 50 seats. No music.

Symbols

⏺ Accommodation is available

£30 Three courses for less than £30

V Separate vegetarian menu

£5 OFF £5-off voucher scheme

♦ Notable wine list

▌West Pennard

NEW ENTRY

The Apple Tree Inn

Hearty food in a homely roadside inn
West Pennard, BA6 8ND
Tel no: (01749) 890060
www.appletreeglastonbury.co.uk
British | £28
Cooking score: 3

The Apple Tree is a homely roadside pub with
its own bakery and an emphasis on hearty
homemade food. Its interior blends pubby
features (real fires, flagstone floors, brass
ornaments) with arty, homespun touches such
as handmade cushions and collages made from
buttons. Buttery potted pork with cornichons
and wholesome homemade bread is typical of
the simple, comforting style, followed,
perhaps, by tender guinea fowl and wild garlic
Kiev with perfectly cooked spring vegetables
and cider sauce. White chocolate parfait with
macerated strawberries, shortbread and
strawberry and clotted cream ice cream makes
a satisfying dessert. Wines, including lots by
the glass, start at £14.50 a bottle.
Chef/s: Lee Evans. **Open:** Tue to Sun L 12 to 2.30,
Tue to Sat D 6 to 11. **Closed:** 25 Dec, 1 week Jan.
Meals: alc (main courses £10 to £22). Sun L £14.95
(2 courses) to £19.95. **Service:** not inc. **Details:** 40
seats. 40 seats outside. Separate bar. Music. Car
parking.

▌Wookey Hole

The Wookey Hole Inn

Wacky, fun-loving village pub
High Street, Wookey Hole, BA5 1BP
Tel no: (01749) 676677
www.wookeyholeinn.com
Modern British | £30
Cooking score: 1

The good-time vibes and razzmatazz of this
village pub close to the famous caves are
perfectly in tune with the riot of colour,
wacky sculpture garden and promise of love,

peace and great food. The kitchen casts its net
wide, although European flavours feature
strongly. You might kick off with sugar-cured
trout, horseradish pannacotta and pickled
cucumber, before prosciutto-wrapped
chicken with black pudding, parsley mash and
chorizo and butter-bean casserole. Finish with
lemon tart with damson and sloe gin ice
cream. Wines from £14.50.
Chef/s: Adam Kennington. **Open:** all week L 12 to
2.30 (3 Sun), Mon to Sat D 7 to 9.30. **Closed:** 25 and
26 Dec. **Meals:** alc (main courses £12 to £24). Sun L
£16.95 (2 courses) to £19.95. Sun D £13.95 (1 course).
Service: not inc. **Details:** 70 seats. 150 seats
outside. Wheelchair access. Music. Car parking.

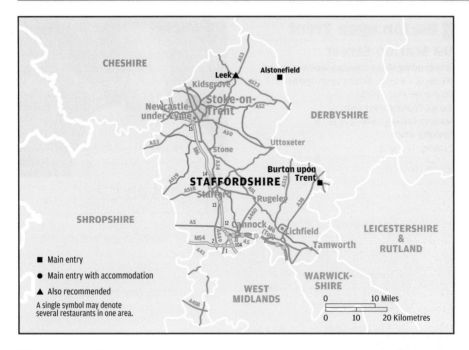

- ■ Main entry
- ● Main entry with accommodation
- ▲ Also recommended

A single symbol may denote
several restaurants in one area.

0   10 Miles

0   10   20 Kilometres

■ Alstonefield

The George
Village local with comfort food
Alstonefield, DE6 2FX
Tel no: (01335) 310205
www.thegeorgeatalstonefield.com
Modern British | £29
Cooking score: 2

£30

It's not just the blazing log fire that ensures a
warm welcome at this unpretentious pub in
the heart of the Peak District. Originally an
eighteenth-century coaching inn, The George
remains the hub of the village, but reporters
are prepared to drive long distances for the
simple and sensibly priced food. A starter of
Scottish scallops wrapped in pancetta with
cauliflower purée has attracted particular
praise, as has steak, Stilton and red wine pie
with buttered greens and gravy. A cherry-
centred dark chocolate fondant served with
honeycomb is one of several desserts not
aimed at calorie-counters. House wine is £14.

Chef/s: Chris Rooney. Open: all week L 12 to 2.30, D
6.30 to 9 (8 Sun). Closed: 25 Dec. Meals: alc (main
courses £11 to £30). Service: not inc. Details: 40
seats. 40 seats outside. Separate bar. Car parking.

■ Bradley

READERS RECOMMEND
The Red Lion
Modern British
Smithy Lane, Bradley, ST18 9DZ
Tel no: (01785) 780297
www.theredlionbradley.co.uk
'Locally sourced meat and vegetables are all
cooked and presented with skill and good
execution.'

**Visit us
Online**
To find out more about
The Good Food Guide, please visit
www.thegoodfoodguide.co.uk

▌Burton upon Trent

99 Station Street

Outstanding value from an old-town asset
99 Station Street, Burton upon Trent, DE14 1BT
Tel no: (01283) 516859
www.99stationstreet.com
Modern British | £30
Cooking score: 1

Top-class service, outstanding value and shrewd sourcing mark out this old-town bistro as a genuine neighbourhood asset. Chef Daniel Pilkington now owns the place and his dedication to the local cause shows in everything from Packington Pork tenderloin on braised leeks with sage and onion purée to 'fantastic' extra-aged rib of Bromley Hurst beef on the bone – although his venison 'mini-burger' with tomato and thyme relish is currently the top shout. Cherry and white chocolate fool hits the sweet spot. House wine is £11.95.
Chef/s: Daniel Pilkington. **Open:** Wed to Sun L 12 to 2, Tue to Sat D 6.30 onwards. **Closed:** Mon, 23 to 28 Dec. **Meals:** alc (main courses £11 to £22). Set L £9.95 (2 courses) to £12.50. Sun L £16.95. **Service:** not inc. **Details:** 44 seats. Separate bar. Wheelchair access. Music.

▌Leek

ALSO RECOMMENDED
▲ Qarma

Cross Mill, Cross Street, Leek, ST13 6BL
Tel no: (01538) 387788
www.the-qarma.com
Indian £5
OFF

Crowds continue to descend on this stylishly revamped textile mill. Much of the large menu is as familiar as chicken tikka or lamb rogan josh; more unusual items include a south Indian-style beetroot and coconut samosa, tuna and crab fishcake (£4.55), coriander fish (£8.45) and the 'chicken served in a fresh pineapple' that has featured in most reports this year. Praise, too, for sizzling brownies, ice cream and chocolate sauce. Wines from £9.95. Open all week, D only.

▌▌● ROSS PIKE
The British Larder

When did you realise you wanted to be a chef?
I was baking cakes for my mum from a very young age and realised it's something I am good at. I went to work at the village pub at the age of 14 washing dishes, and progressed to peeling potatoes and then eventually cooking wonderful food.

Give us a quick culinary tip
Don't buy ready-ground spices, but grind your own from whole spices as and when they are needed. The tastes, aroma and flavour are so different and much better.

What is your earliest food memory?
Enjoying a chip butty with my aunt Vera.

What is your 'show-off' dish?
A tasting of Suffolk pheasant (pheasant Scotch egg, pheasant Kiev and pheasant on horseback).

What would you be if you weren't a chef?
I can't think of any other career I would have rather done, this has always been it for me.

What would be your last meal?
Fish-finger sandwiches with malt vinegar and sea salt.

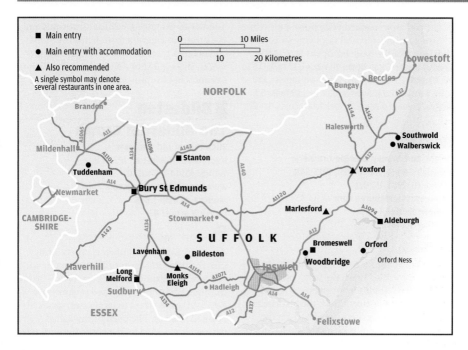

- ■ Main entry
- ● Main entry with accommodation
- ▲ Also recommended

A single symbol may denote several restaurants in one area.

■ Aldeburgh

The Lighthouse

Expect some fine seafood-based cookery
77 High Street, Aldeburgh, IP15 5AU
Tel no: (01728) 453377
www.lighthouserestaurant.co.uk
Modern British | £25
Cooking score: 2

Some Lighthouse customers may be hardy perennials who stop by only when the Festival is in town, but they are nonetheless careful not to miss a booking for 'the best fish and chips I've ever had'. Look for the little white frontage on the High Street, and expect some finely wrought seafood-based cookery – potted shrimp risotto with Parmesan, grilled cod with curried lentils and spinach, sea bass in Thai noodle broth. There are also one or two meat options such as calf's liver and bacon. Sticky treats like boozy banana pancake with toffee crunch ice cream should send you away happy. House French is £15.95.

Chef/s: Guy Welsh and Thierry Aubugeau. **Open:** all week L 12 to 2 (2.30 Sat and Sun), D 6.30 to 10. **Meals:** alc (main courses £11 to £15). **Service:** not inc. **Details:** 90 seats. 16 seats outside. No music. Wheelchair access.

152 Restaurant

Convivial local eatery
152 High Street, Aldeburgh, IP15 5AX
Tel no: (01728) 454594
www.152aldeburgh.com
Modern European | £25
Cooking score: 1

'Very good service – attentive without being fussy', noted one reporter of this rustic, café-style restaurant which is found in an alley between the beach and the High Street. The air of energetic conviviality with which it is run is a great draw, as is cooking that takes in ham hock and confit shallot terrine, grilled local

plaice and slow-cooked belly pork, plus white chocolate truffle tart and raspberry sorbet. A short, workaday wine list opens at £14.95.
Chef/s: Wayne Tong. **Open:** all week L 12 to 3, D 6 to 10. **Closed:** 25 Dec. **Meals:** alc (main courses £10 to £19). Sun L £12.95. **Service:** not inc. **Details:** 53 seats. 20 seats outside. Wheelchair access. Music.

Regatta

Bright and breezy seaside brasserie
171 High Street, Aldeburgh, IP15 5AN
Tel no: (01728) 452011
www.regattaaldeburgh.com
Modern British | £25
Cooking score: 1

The beach is just a stroll away from this bright and breezy seaside brasserie, so it's no surprise that fish from the Aldeburgh boats figures strongly on the menu. Check the blackboard for daily specials, otherwise pick from the likes of grilled sprats with garlic and parsley or roast corn-fed chicken breast on sweet potato purée with a sweetcorn fritter. Items from the smokehouse are always worth ordering. Puds might feature warm almond and marzipan cake with apricot sauce. Wines from £14.50.
Chef/s: Robert Mabey. **Open:** all week L 12 to 2, D 6 to 10. **Closed:** 24 to 26 and 31 Dec, 1 Jan. **Meals:** alc (main courses £11 to £20). **Service:** not inc. **Details:** 95 seats. No music.

ALSO RECOMMENDED

▲ The Aldeburgh Market Café

170-172 High Street, Aldeburgh, IP15 5AQ
Tel no: (01728) 452520
www.thealdeburghmarket.co.uk
Modern British £5 OFF

Owned by Sara Fox of the nearby Lighthouse (see entry), this enterprising set-up comprises a fishmonger's, deli, greengrocer's and livewire daytime café under one roof. The kitchen deals in locally sourced grub with a global slant: order kedgeree with a poached egg (£6.75) for breakfast, fill up on pad thai noodles or fish pie (£9.25) at lunchtime, and get a teatime sugar fix from lemon, almond and polenta cake. Bottled beers, juices and wines (from £13.50). Open all week (till 9pm during school summer hols).

■ Bildeston

The Bildeston Crown

Slick mix of old and new
High Street, Bildeston, IP7 7EB
Tel no: (01449) 740510
www.thebildestoncrown.com
Modern British | £45
Cooking score: 4

A fine example of a timber-framed country inn, the fifteenth-century Bildeston Crown had a sharp makeover some years back – hence the huge paintings, prints and mirrors that now add some pizazz to its ancient, crooked-beamed interior. The pub's bushy-tailed persona is matched by the contemporary fizz of Chris Lee's cooking – a blend of back-to-the-roots familiarity and bouncy modern flavours. Take the 'classic' route with smoked haddock fishcakes, venison ragù or fish pie, otherwise explore the 'select' menu's more complex culinary riffs. Here you might find cumin-roasted scallops with smoked eel and carrot or parsley soup with snails and cured ham, followed by an elaborately worked dish of locally reared Semer lamb with sweetbreads, watercress and turnips, or a pairing of chicken and langoustine with fennel, mushrooms and truffle. To conclude, try chocolate and orange brûlée with Arctic roll and orange sorbet. The substantial, wide-ranging wine list offers plenty of perky drinking at very fair mark-ups. Fifteen house selections start at £17 (£4 a glass).
Chef/s: Chris Lee. **Open:** all week L 12 to 3, D 7 to 10 (9 Sun). **Closed:** 24 to 26 Dec, 1 Jan. **Meals:** alc (main courses £12 to £25). Set L and D £24. Sun L £25. Tasting menu £70 (8 courses). **Service:** not inc. **Details:** 120 seats. 30 seats outside. Separate bar. Wheelchair access. Music. Car parking.

Bromeswell

The British Larder
Seasonal cooking that sings with flavour
Orford Road, Bromeswell, IP12 2PU
Tel no: (01394) 460310
www.britishlardersuffolk.co.uk
British | £30
Cooking score: 3
£5 OFF

One of the many assets of this expertly run pub-cum-restaurant is its roadside location (in an Area of Outstanding Natural Beauty) just two miles from the A12 – if you're travelling, it's well worth the detour. This is a congenial labour of love from Madalene Bonvini-Hamel and Ross Pike, who match bare tables and an unfussy mood with loyalty to local producers, ethically reared meat and sustainable fish. The result is intensely seasonal cooking that sings with flavour, as in a game tasting starter (terrine, venison Scotch egg, pheasant sausage roll, rabbit pasty) or a dessert of forced rhubarb with brown sugar meringue mess. Belly pork with colcannon cake, apple chutney, kale and crackling, an East Anglian cheeseboard, and a modest but snappy wine list (from £16.50) are equally typical.
Chef/s: Ross Pike and Madalene Bonvini-Hamel. **Open:** all week L 12 to 3 (3.30 Sun), Mon-Sat D 6 to 9 (9.30 Fri and Sat), Sun 6-9.30 (May to end Dec). **Closed:** Mon (Jan to first bank hol). **Meals:** alc (main courses £14 to £21). Sun L £22.50 (2 courses) to £27.50. **Service:** not inc. **Details:** 70 seats. 100 seats outside. Separate bar. Wheelchair access. Music. Car parking.

Bury St Edmunds

★ READERS' RESTAURANT OF THE YEAR ★
EAST ENGLAND

Maison Bleue
The freshest fish, worth seeking out
30-31 Churchgate Street, Bury St Edmunds, IP33 1RG
Tel no: (01284) 760623
www.maisonbleue.co.uk
Seafood | £34
Cooking score: 4

Regis Crépy's popular restaurant is well worth seeking out. A fresh, light colour scheme and contemporary artwork create an impression of relaxed chic, matched by attentive service and a menu that specialises in the freshest fish and seafood. Traditional fare, such as fish soup with rouille garlic croûtons and shredded Gruyère, and halibut with cream of mussel and cauliflower and a white wine sauce, is cleverly mixed with some speculative efforts, along the lines of monkfish with shatkora Bangladeshi lemon, coconut and coriander sauce, or yellowfin tuna with spicy tomato concassé and ginger hollandaise. For confirmed meat eaters, there's the option of roasted rack of lamb, or maybe roasted saddle of venison. At other times, enjoy the set lunch ('so good-value it is beyond words'); perhaps 'tasty' mussels with wine, cream and bacon and a 'tender' roast tenderloin and slow-cooked belly pork. Wines from £15.50.
Chef/s: Pascal Canevet. **Open:** Tue to Sat L 12 to 2, D 7 to 9.30. **Closed:** Sun, Mon, 4 weeks Jan, 2 weeks Aug. **Meals:** alc (main courses £16 to £24). Set L £17.50 (2 courses) to £21.95. Set D £31.95. **Service:** not inc. **Details:** 65 seats. Music.

Pea Porridge

Something quite special
28-29 Cannon Street, Bury St Edmunds, IP33 1JR
Tel no: (01284) 700200
www.peaporridge.co.uk
Modern British | £28
Cooking score: 3

'I am addicted' reports one unashamed return visitor to Justin Sharp's former bakery turned simple – but rather special – restaurant. The name comes from the restaurant's location on what was once Pea Porridge Green, and the food is rather more sophisticated than that suggests. Interesting, sometimes folksy, flavours are handled with panache, as in a starter of sautéed snails and bacon with bone marrow, garlic, parsley and capers. There's a wider geographical scope in seared squid with risotto nero and gremolata or a 'very good indeed' fillet of hare with polenta, squash purée, harissa and golden raisins. Dessert might be a clean yoghurt pannacotta with Champagne rhubarb. Wine starts at £14.75 and staff know the keenly priced and idiosyncratically annotated list very well.
Chef/s: Justin Sharp. **Open:** Tue to Sat L 12 to 2, D 6.30 to 9.30 (10 Fri, Sat). **Closed:** Sun, Mon, 2 weeks Christmas, 2 weeks Sept. **Meals:** alc (main courses £13 to £20). Set L and D £11.95 (2 courses) to £15.95. **Service:** 10% for parties over 6. **Details:** 46 seats. 10 seats outside. Music. Children at lunch only.

▌Lavenham
The Great House

Impressive Gallic cooking
Market Place, Lavenham, CO10 9QZ
Tel no: (01787) 247431
www.greathouse.co.uk
Modern French | £40
Cooking score: 4

'Feels like France' noted a visitor to this ever-so-English period house overlooking Lavenham's old market square. The bright and dressed-up pair of dining rooms cleverly dovetail period solidity with up-to-the-moment features, creating a suitably smart backdrop for some very Gallic cooking. After nearly 30 years at the helm, Regis Crépy continues to impress, overseeing food that 'is consistently superb', and directing smartly dressed staff who are 'excellent – very attentive but easy-going'. A typical route in might be fish soup with rouille, garlic croûtons and Gruyère, followed perhaps by roasted French pigeon breasts with red cabbage, glazed apple and red wine and mustard sauce, then passion-fruit and milk chocolate crème brûlée to finish. It's a menu built around established standards, and people return again and again because they know the quality won't waver. The wine list covers the major French regions, with a smattering of international choices; from £18.50.
Chef/s: Regis Crépy. **Open:** Wed to Sun L 12 to 2.30, Tue to Sat D 7 to 9. **Closed:** Mon, Jan, 2 weeks summer. **Meals:** alc (main courses £20 to £24). Set L £17.50 (2 courses) to £21. Set D £31.95. Sun L £31.95. **Service:** not inc. **Details:** 50 seats. Music. Car parking.

▌Long Melford
Scutchers

Quality ingredients and generous portions
Westgate Street, Long Melford, CO10 9DP
Tel no: (01787) 310200
www.scutchers.com
Modern British | £28
Cooking score: 2

The setting is a converted pub in the heart of Long Melford, lovingly nurtured as a country restaurant by Diane and Nick Barrett since 1981. They have restricted the days they open, but it is worth trying to sample Nick's bistro-style cooking. He places much emphasis on quality ingredients and generous portions. Typical choices are scallops on potato purée with crispy bacon and red wine jus, lamb fillet with Toulouse sausage, flageolets and Puy lentils in a thyme gravy, or turbot on a shrimp, leek and lobster chowder. Finish with iced berries with hot white chocolate sauce, say. Wines start at £17.

Chef/s: Nicholas Barrett. **Open:** Fri and Sat L 12 to 2, D 7 to 9.30. **Closed:** Sun to Thur, 24 to 26 Dec, last 2 weeks Aug. **Meals:** alc (main courses £16 to £26). **Service:** not inc. **Details:** 50 seats. 20 seats outside. No music. Wheelchair access. Car parking.

Marlesford

ALSO RECOMMENDED
▲ Farmcafé

Main Road (A12), Marlesford, IP13 0AG
Tel no: (01728) 747717
www.farmcafe.co.uk
Modern British

'Serving local food since 2001', chimes this dedicated refuelling point beside the A12. Breakfast and brunch (from £8.90) are top shouts, while lunchtime brings assorted salads, handmade burgers, tagliatelle carbonara, double-crust pies (free-range chicken and leek or butternut squash and goats' cheese, say) and daily fish specials. Meanwhile, cakes, fruit tarts and summer pudding (£4.90) hit the sweet spot. Drinks range from milkshakes and iced coffees to Suffolk cider and a few wines (from £13.90). Takeaways and a 'foodmarket' too. Open until 3pm all week.

Monks Eleigh

ALSO RECOMMENDED
▲ The Swan Inn

The Street, Monks Eleigh, IP7 7AU
Tel no: (01449) 741391
www.monkseleigh.com
Modern British

The thatched building in the centre of the village is effectively a pub, 'though it doesn't feel like a country pub inside'. But any lack of pubby cosiness is more than made up for by 'exceptionally warm and engaging' service from Carol Ramsbottom. Nigel Ramsbottom's food features carefully sourced ingredients (Cromer crab, Suffolk asparagus,

game) offered on a regularly changing blackboard or set menu (£12.75/£15.75 for two/three courses): say, French onion soup and baked plaice fillets with char-grilled courgettes in Parmesan sauce. Wine from £14. Closed Mon.

Orford
The Trinity, Crown & Castle

Warm vibes and big seasonal flavours
Orford, IP12 2LJ
Tel no: (01394) 450205
www.crownandcastle.co.uk
Modern British | £32
Cooking score: 4

🍴 V

Co-proprietor and hotel guru Ruth Watson has featured in the Guide for 27 years at different establishments, and knows a thing or two about hospitality – no wonder readers are quick to applaud the wonderfully 'relaxed' mood at her gorgeous Suffolk retreat. Seasonal food makes a big impact here, and crab is always a sound bet (perhaps served with leeks and parsley on toast); otherwise look seawards for Orford-landed skate with sautéed grapes and almonds or seared black bream with garlicky saffron mash and gremolata. Meat eaters might veer towards the Middle East for rump of lamb with spiced barberry and pistachio pilaf, while the sweet-toothed brigade should be delighted by poached pear with walnut praline parfait. Despite its name, the Crown & Castle is definitely not a boozer – although you can still roll up for a 'proper pub lunch' of fish soup followed by slow-roast belly pork. Bellinis and elderflower bubbly are zesty alternatives to the well-informed, colourfully annotated wine list, which offers 13 selections by the glass and bottles from £16.95.

Chef/s: Nick Thacker and Ruth Watson. **Open:** all week L 12.15 to 2.15, D 6.30 to 9.15. **Meals:** alc (main courses £15 to £25). **Service:** 10%. **Details:** 50 seats. 40 seats outside. Separate bar. No music. Wheelchair access. Children over 8 yrs only at D.

▌Southwold

The Crown Hotel

Buzzy pub with good food
90 High Street, Southwold, IP18 6DP
Tel no: (01502) 722275
www.adnams.co.uk
Modern British | £30
Cooking score: 2

'There's a buzzy atmosphere whenever you go' is how one reporter summed up the appeal of this long-serving pub-with-rooms. People are drawn by the metropolitan feel of the main bar (no bookings) and the good food. The kitchen buys wisely and notes seasonal shifts. The pig board (braised cheek, black pudding fritter and purée, crispy ears) is a great favourite; you might also see venison terrine, and mains of local pheasant breast with sloe gin jus, or sea bream with mussels, cauliflower risotto and saffron velouté. The stellar Adnams wine list opens with a wide selection by the glass; bottles from £19.95.
Chef/s: Tyler Torrance. **Open:** all week L 12 to 2 (2.30 Sat and Sun), D 7 to 9 (6.30 Sat). **Meals:** alc (main courses £11 to £23). Sun L £19.95. **Service:** not inc. **Details:** 80 seats. 30 seats outside. Separate bar. Wheelchair access. Car parking.

Sutherland House

Oak-beamed heritage and low food miles
56 High Street, Southwold, IP18 6DN
Tel no: (01502) 724544
www.sutherlandhouse.co.uk
Modern British | £30
Cooking score: 2

Bits of this illustrious Southwold landmark date back to 1455, but oak-beamed heritage isn't the only attraction. Food miles mean a lot here, and the menu spells things out in precise detail: locally smoked ham hock terrine with piccalilli clocks up two miles; carpaccio of Red Poll beef comes in at 10 miles, while most veg only travel a few hundred yards. Then there's fish from the local harbour and beyond:

turbot is pan-roasted on the bone with brown shrimp butter; however scallops have a trip from Scotland before appearing with homemade black pudding and teriyaki sauce. Offbeat wines from £17.
Chef/s: Jed Tedjada. **Open:** all week L 12 to 2.30, D 7 to 9. **Closed:** 2 weeks Jan. **Meals:** alc (main courses £12 to £22). Set L £15 (2 courses) to £18. Sun L £18. **Service:** not inc. **Details:** 50 seats. 30 seats outside. Separate bar. Wheelchair access. Music. Car parking.

▌Stanton

The Leaping Hare

Charming vineyard eatery
Wyken Vineyards, Stanton, IP31 2DW
Tel no: (01359) 250287
www.wykenvineyards.co.uk
Modern British | £27
Cooking score: 2

Home-brewed Good Dog Ale and impressive Wyken wines are among the rewards for visitors to Wyken Hall's vineyard café and restaurant. It's housed in an impressively timbered 400-year-old barn, where the bucolic setting charms and the food is just the ticket, with cosmopolitan ideas and plenty of homegrown and local produce. The café deals in salmon fishcakes, gamekeeper's pie and lovely cakes. Lunch and occasional evening options in the restaurant include Ellingham goats' cheese soufflé with red onion sauce, Newmarket lamb rump with gratin and flageolets, and home-reared steaks. Vineyard wines (from £15) head up the short, global wine list.
Chef/s: Jon Ellis. **Open:** all week L 12 to 4, Fri and Sat D 7 to 9.30, café 10 to 6. **Closed:** 25 Dec to 5 Jan. **Meals:** alc (main courses £11 to £22). Set L £16.95 (2 courses) to £18.95. **Service:** not inc. **Details:** 45 seats. 20 seats outside. Separate bar. No music. Wheelchair access. Car parking.

Tuddenham

Tuddenham Mill

Mesmerising skills in a seductive setting
High Street, Tuddenham, IP28 6SQ
Tel no: (01638) 713552
www.tuddenhammill.co.uk
Modern British | £40
Cooking score: 6

It's hard not to be seduced by Tuddenham Mill from the word go. In early summer willows dip into a picture-perfect mill pond, fluffball ducklings ripple the water, and flower-filled meadows stretch into the sunny distance. Add Paul Foster's adventurous cooking and faultless front-of-house team to the mix and you'll want this lunchtime affair to last. Paul's skills at the stove are mesmerising and while the influence of his mentor, Sat Bains, is evident (this is a place of water bath cooking and exact temperatures, startling combinations and deep but clean flavours achieved with few ingredients), Paul's menu embraces rural Suffolk warmly; he noses out the chickweed for a taster menu dish of mackerel 52°C, asparagus and cobnut, or bravely picks sweet-sour sea buckthorn berries to go with burnt meringue and granola. Wild garlic will enliven a tender nugget of West Country lamb, and nettle juice a starter of asparagus, slow-cooked hen's egg and baked oats. Daring touches to main dishes include duck breast and heart 'cooked to perfection' with fennel and quinoa cutting through the meat's richness. A more conventional pudding of bitter chocolate textures, hazelnut, goats' milk and mint is 'sublime'. There's plenty to drink by the glass, competent guidance, and house wine from £22.
Chef/s: Paul Foster. **Open:** all week L 12 to 2.30, D 6.30 to 9.30. **Meals:** alc (main courses £20 to £26). Sun L £25. Tasting menu L £35 and D £65. **Service:** not inc. **Details:** 56 seats. 32 seats outside. Separate bar. Music. Car parking.

Walberswick

The Anchor

Clever, deeply satisfying eco-cooking
Main Street, Walberswick, IP18 6UA
Tel no: (01502) 722112
www.anchoratwalberswick.com
Modern British | £25
Cooking score: 2

Run by a team with honourable green intentions, the eco-friendly Anchor occupies an Arts and Crafts building overlooking Walberswick's dunes and beach huts. Breakfast, daytime tapas and afternoon tea are part of a tourist-friendly offer and Sophie Dorber's clever, rustic cooking is deeply satisfying. She burrows into the world larder, bringing out black pudding ravioli, Peking-style duck leg and plates of roast cod with lentils and chorizo, and revs up beer-battered cod with pease pudding and jalapeño-spiked tartare sauce. Mark Dorber provides imbibing suggestions for each dish: how about a bottle of Goose Island IPA with a bowl of local fish soup, or banana fritters accompanied by a shot of Pedro Ximénez sherry? Adnams wines from £14.50.
Chef/s: Sophie Dorber. **Open:** all week L 12 to 3, D 6 to 9 (10 Fri and Sat). **Closed:** 25 Dec. **Meals:** alc (main courses £14 to £23). **Service:** not inc. **Details:** 100 seats. 150 seats outside. Separate bar. No music. Wheelchair access. Car parking.

Woodbridge

The Crown at Woodbridge

Stylish all-rounder
Thoroughfare, Woodbridge, IP12 1AD
Tel no: (01394) 384242
www.thecrownatwoodbridge.co.uk
Modern European | £26
Cooking score: 3

Happily straddling the roles of pub and town-centre hotel, this modernised seventeenth-century inn is something of an all-rounder. The menu reflects this, ranging from light bites of crab cakes and a whole range of good things on toast, to a magnificent char-grilled veal T-bone. Otherwise, the kitchen's remit spreads over the modern European repertoire, to bring in osso buco of Suffolk Red Poll beef with barley, braised mushrooms, shallots and cavolo nero, and charred marinated squid with pulled pork, peperonata, and harissa potatoes. The look is predictably cool, even if the surroundings are a bit stark – but service is cheerful and keeps up even when the restaurant is 'full and noisy'. The modern wine list (from £16.25) ticks all the boxes for serious intent, quality and value.

Chef/s: Stephen David and Luke Bailey. **Open:** all week L 12 to 2.30, D 6 to 9.30. **Meals:** alc (main courses £13 to £25). Set L and D £18.50 (2 courses) to £23.50. **Service:** not inc. **Details:** 80 seats. 20 seats outside. Separate bar. Wheelchair access. Music. Car parking.

The Riverside
Meals and movies by the river
Quay Street, Woodbridge, IP12 1BH
Tel no: (01394) 382587
www.theriverside.co.uk
Modern British | £25
Cooking score: 1

Special movie deals are the big attraction at this open-plan Woodbridge evergreen by the Deben, and it's also a great alfresco spot. The restaurant runs in tandem with the Riverside theatre/cinema complex and the cooking sits squarely in the modern British camp. Local and seasonal ingredients take to the stage in eclectic dishes such as monkfish, sea bass and red mullet stew with toasted focaccia or spiced rump of Ketley Farm lamb with couscous, harissa and cacik (yoghurt dip). Simple puds and bargain tapas-style lunches too. House wine is £14.

Chef/s: Luke Parsons. **Open:** all week L 12 to 2.15 (12.30 to 2.30 Sun), Mon to Sat D 6 to 9.30 (10 Fri and Sat). **Closed:** 25 and 26 Dec. **Meals:** alc (main courses £9 to £28). Set D with film £30. **Service:** not inc. **Details:** 40 seats. 30 seats outside. Separate bar. Wheelchair access. Music. Car parking.

■ Yoxford

ALSO RECOMMENDED
▲ Main's Restaurant
High Street, Yoxford, IP17 3EU
Tel no: (01728) 668882
www.mainsrestaurant.co.uk
Modern British

Regulars vouch for the 'fantastic' service and 'delicious' food at this well-regarded neighbourhood eatery. Nancy Main's bread has gained such a following that the bakery has been extended so people can enjoy freshly baked goods with coffee on Saturday mornings. Meanwhile, husband Jason's daily menus are built around carefully sourced local produce typified by cauliflower baked custard with Stichelton blue (£6.50) and roast partridge, black pudding, fondant turnip and white wine gravy (£15). Wines from £13.50. Closed Sun and Mon.

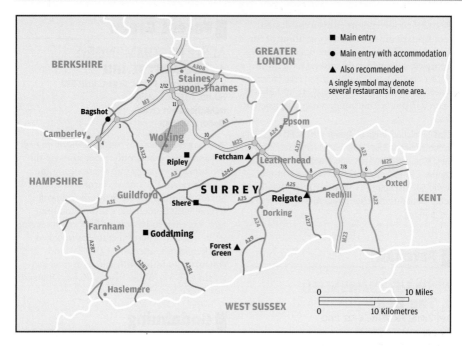

■ Main entry
● Main entry with accommodation
▲ Also recommended

A single symbol may denote
several restaurants in one area.

▮ Bagshot

Michael Wignall, the Latymer at Pennyhill Park Hotel

Carefully crafted food from a culinary star
London Road, Bagshot, GU19 5EU
Tel no: (01276) 471774
www.pennyhillpark.co.uk
Modern European | £60
Cooking score: 7

🛏 V

Pennyhill Park is the very image of soft-focus Home Counties opulence, a creeper-covered house in more than 120 acres of parkland. As a modern destination hotel, not far from Royal Ascot, it comes with exotic spa treatments and a range of mod cons that its Victorian architect could scarcely have imagined. Its principal dining experience is the Latymer restaurant, which is kitted out in gentle green and tawny hues, and incorporates a chef's table area in the kitchen complete with LCD screens of the action. All that announces a culinary presence of some stature and, in Michael Wignall, Pennyhill has just that. Characterising his own food as 'carefully crafted, very technical but not intimidating', Wignall lives up to the rubric by constructing dishes whose prime components are allowed their full integrity, but which are given the kind of intricate framing that encourages them to reveal more about themselves, rather than denaturing them into something else entirely. An opener might see a productive pairing of red mullet and salt cod alongside red endive in bagna cauda with citrus syrup, or a nervelessly complex assemblage of Anjou squab with black pudding and walnut crumble, an open raviolo of confit pigeon leg and kohlrabi and smoked celeriac purée in jasmine-scented jus. At main, Swaledale lamb presents top-drawer roast loin with crisp tongues and shoulder confit amid artichokes and girolles, or there could be seafood in the shape of John Dory, razor clams, palourdes and a poached scallop set alongside texture-varied cauliflower.

Textural counterpoints enliven the desserts too, from praline with a harvest home of oat granola, puffed barley and malt ice cream, to pumpkin cassonade and sponge with burnt butter crumble and lemon thyme ice cream. There are a few wines under £30, and glasses from £7, on the fine but inevitably plutocratic list.

Chef/s: Michael Wignall. **Open:** Wed to Fri L 12.30 to 2, Tue to Sat D 7 to 9.15 (9.30 Fri and Sat). **Closed:** Sun, Mon, first 2 weeks Jan. **Meals:** Set L £26 (2 courses) to £34. Set D £60 (3 courses). Tasting menu £82 (10 courses). **Service:** 12.5%. **Details:** 50 seats. Separate bar. No music. Wheelchair access. Car parking.

Fetcham

ALSO RECOMMENDED
▲ The Bell

Bell Lane, Fetcham, KT22 9ND
Tel no: (01372) 372624
www.bellfetcham.co.uk
British

A new kitchen brigade is starting to up the foodie stakes at this attractive 1930s boozer in the Mole Valley. Bread is baked in-house and well-considered regional sourcing is now high on the agenda – witness Wiltshire wild boar, venison and sloe gin salami with celeriac and pear rémoulade (£5.95), Dingley Dell sausages or slow-braised shoulder of lamb with apricots, wholegrain mustard mash and cavolo nero (£14.95). A smart alfresco terrace, cheery staff, Young's beers and gluggable wines (from £15.90) are further assets. Open all week.

┃┃● Readers Recommend

A 'readers recommend' review is a genuine quote from a report sent in by one of our readers. We intend to follow up these suggestions throughout the year to come.

Forest Green

ALSO RECOMMENDED
▲ The Parrot Inn

Horsham Road, Forest Green, RH5 5RZ
Tel no: (01306) 621339
www.theparrot.co.uk
Modern British

'A very personable inn, with the right mix of old and new' is how one reader sums up this seventeenth-century pub overlooking the village green. The owners farm 500 acres of Surrey, bringing to the menu coarse pork terrine with homemade chutney and toast (£6.25), then rolled loin of lamb with medlar jelly (£15.50). There's fish too, as in baked mackerel with ratatouille (£13.25), and chocolate pudding with salted caramel ice cream (£6.50). Wines from £15.50. Open all week, exc Sun D.

Godalming

La Luna

Well-groomed Italian thoroughbred
10-14 Wharf Street, Godalming, GU7 1NN
Tel no: (01483) 414155
www.lalunarestaurant.co.uk
Italian | £29
Cooking score: 4
£5 OFF £30

Tantalising chickpea panelle, smoked swordfish and other stuzzichini nibbles open the show at Daniele Drago's well-groomed Italian thoroughbred, which has been feeding the inhabitants of Godalming and beyond for more than a decade. Quality means a great deal here, and the kitchen knows how to give British ingredients a bona fide Mediterranean spin: hazelnut-crusted Shackleford pork fillet comes with Sicilian Muscat sauce and barba di frate (wispy green 'monk's beard'), rump of South Downs lamb is paired with Umbrian lentils and a slick of rosemary jus, and baked hake appears in company with soupy clam guazzetto, parsley pesto and sprouting broccoli. Readers have also enthused about sardines stuffed with fennel and sultanas, as well as 'fantastic' vanilla pannacotta with rhubarb sauce – although the chocolate and hazelnut torte with salted caramel truffles and crème brûlée ice cream is also a head-turner. Knowledgeable staff are eager to guide customers through the byways of the stonkingly good Italian regional wine list, which travels from Piedmonte and Veneto to Campania and Calabria in search of fine drinking. A pared-back 'introductory' selection starts at £13.95.

Chef/s: Valentino Gentile. **Open:** Tue to Sat L 12 to 2, D 7 to 10. **Closed:** Sun, Mon, 2 weeks Aug, bank hols. **Meals:** alc (main courses £11 to £20). Set L £11.95 (2 courses) to £14.50. **Service:** not inc. **Details:** 58 seats. Music.

Kingston upon Thames

READERS RECOMMEND
The Canbury Arms
Modern British
49 Canbury Park Road, Kingston upon Thames, KT2 6LQ
Tel no: (020) 8255 9129
www.thecanburyarms.com

'An exquisite broccoli and Stilton soup with homemade bread to die for, followed by steak pudding with mashed potatoes, kale and rib-clinging gravy. For dessert, fig rice-pudding with triangles of brandy snap.'

Reigate

ALSO RECOMMENDED
▲ Tony Tobin @ The Dining Room
59a High Street, Reigate, RH2 9AE
Tel no: (01737) 226650
www.tonytobinrestaurants.co.uk
Modern European

'We could not fault it' was the verdict of one reporter after visiting this bustling first-floor restaurant. Loyal locals still flock here for the relaxed dining room and sharp service. Warm leek and Gruyère tart followed by fillet of lamb with Moroccan spiced aubergines are typical of the à la carte (two courses £31), but

set menus for lunch (two courses £16.95) and weekday dinner (three courses £24.95) are more keenly priced. Wine from £16.95. Closed Sat L and Sun D.

Ripley

★ WINE LIST OF THE YEAR ★

Drake's Restaurant
Picture-perfect modern food
The Clock House, High Street, Ripley, GU23 6AQ
Tel no: (01483) 224777
www.drakesrestaurant.co.uk
Modern British | £60
Cooking score: 6

♦ V

Ever since Steve and Serina Drake turned this clock-fronted Georgian house into a destination restaurant, their ambition has rarely gathered dust. Last year the restaurant was refurbished, a lounge-bar created and they are starting to grow their own herbs and vegetables. In the kitchen, Steve continues to sail confidently through the tricky waters of intricate modern cuisine, fashioning picture-perfect dishes that dovetail artisan British ingredients with contemporary techniques. In a beautiful integration of crisp and soft flavours, red mullet appears strewn with mushroom soil atop a pearl barley pudding flecked with finely chopped truffle with spring onion alongside, and, mindful of the need for some textural contrast, lamb (loin and slow-cooked shoulder) is teamed with courgette, cashew brittle, chicory and pomegranate seeds. Steve also has an inspired way with vegetables (salt-baked kohlrabi, for example, served with poached egg, raw broccoli and sorrel). His creative momentum remains at full throttle for desserts, often focusing on specific ingredients and exploring their textures and contrasts in depth; witness an intricately worked parsnip parfait with blackberry compote, sorrel ice and yoghurt foam. Good-value lunches (including a glass of wine) maintain the tempo, though slow service continues to be a bugbear for some reporters. Not the least glory of the place, however, has always been the fantastic wine list, the work of a true devotee, backed up by sensitively proffered advice. Burgundy leads the way, with rich pickings from the Languedoc, Rhone and Savoie, but also look for idiosyncratic numbers from elsewhere. Prices from £18.

Chef/s: Steve Drake. **Open:** Wed to Sat L 12 to 2, Tue to Sat D 7 to 9.30. **Closed:** Sun, Mon, 25 and 26 Dec, 2 weeks Jan, 2 weeks Aug. **Meals:** Set L £22 (2 courses) to £28. Set D £50 (2 courses) to £60. 'Flavour Journey' menu £60. 'Discovery' menu £80. **Service:** 12.5%. **Details:** 40 seats. Separate bar. Music.

Shere

Kinghams

Relaxed restaurant with creature-comfort niceties
Gomshall Lane, Shere, GU5 9HE
Tel no: (01483) 202168
www.kinghams-restaurant.co.uk
Modern British | £36
Cooking score: 2

Paul Baker's converted cottage has all the creature-comfort niceties of a smart country restaurant, from summer alfresco in a heated gazebo to linen-clad tables and comfortable chairs in the low-beamed rooms within. The mood is relaxed, service on-the-ball and the food strikes a symphony of popular notes: perhaps Cornish crab parcel with red pepper dressing, and a trio of game (venison loin, pigeon breast, braised rabbit filo parcel) with red cabbage and redcurrant sauce. Dessert could be roasted rhubarb and strawberries with crème brûlée. However, readers have flagged up the occasional misfiring dish – more reports please. House wine is £17.50.
Chef/s: Paul Baker. **Open:** Tue to Sun L 12 to 2 (4 Sun), Tue to Sat D 7 to 12. **Closed:** Mon, 25 Dec to 6 Jan. **Meals:** alc (main courses £15 to £21). Set L and D £16.95 (2 courses) to £23.90. Sun L £24. **Service:** not inc. **Details:** 48 seats. 12 seats outside. Music. Car parking.

BREAKFAST OF CHAMPIONS

Since **The Wolseley** in Mayfair opened its doors in 2003, breakfast has become an opportunity for eating out that's every bit as impressive as a lazy lunch or expensive dinner. Why entertain clients over a four-hour boozy lunch when you can clinch that deal over eggs Benedict on your way to work? Hitting the shops or museums? Set yourself up with a full English and you can last right through 'til teatime.

Today, lots of great restaurants serve breakfast, giving diners a chance to sample their cooking for less. At **The Modern Pantry** in Clerkenwell, tuck into the famous sugar-cured prawn omelette at 8am, when you're more likely to wash it down with a green tea than a Grüner Veltliner. The seriously hungry should head to City steakhouse **Hawksmoor Guildhall**, where the sharing breakfast with its piggy treats and unlimited toast will see you through the whole day, if not two. Mix your own Bloody Mary if a strong espresso isn't enough of an eye-opener. For a touch of spice, head to Westminster's the **Cinnamon Club** for uttapam, a South Indian rice pancake enjoyed at breakfast.

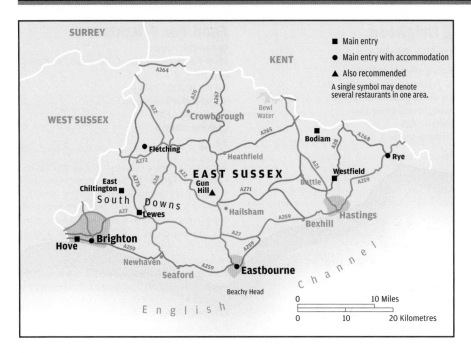

SURREY

KENT

Bewl Water

WEST SUSSEX

Crowborough

Fletching

EAST SUSSEX

East Chiltington

Gun Hill

South Downs

Lewes

Hailsham

Brighton

Hove

Newhaven

Seaford

Beachy Head

Bodiam

Rye

Westfield

Battle

Hastings

Bexhill

Eastbourne

English Channel

A264 A26 A267 A22 A265 A268 A272 A275 A26 A271 A21 A259 A27 A259 A259 A259 A27

■ Main entry
● Main entry with accommodation
▲ Also recommended
A single symbol may denote several restaurants in one area.

0   10 Miles
0   10   20 Kilometres

▌Bodiam

The Curlew

Seriously good stuff
Junction Road, Bodiam, TN32 5UY
Tel no: (01580) 861394
www.thecurlewrestaurant.co.uk
Modern British | £35
Cooking score: 4

V

A country location 'which really takes some effort to find', may not be the first place you'd think of looking for a bullish metropolitan-style restaurant, but Mark and Sara Colley have conjured just such a creation out of an attractive seventeenth-century clapboard coaching inn. Light and air fill the contemporary dining room, while bare wood tables establish the breezy laid-back mood, and the cooking follows through. Neil McCue is a chef who fills his larder with seasonal ingredients and produces inspired combinations, including a modern take on the prawn cocktail (shrimps, langoustine fritter and chilli mayonnaise) and 'chop and chips' (aka Jacob's ladder, dripping potatoes, horseradish and pickled cabbage), both huge hits with readers this year. There's real interest, too, in dishes such as breast of mallard with cranberry, orange, chicory and marmalade potatoes. Clever desserts include a rum-flavoured junket with Eccles cakes. An admirable wine list opens at £17.
Chef/s: Neil McCue. **Open:** Wed to Sun L 12 to 2.30 D 6 to 9.30 (9 Sun). **Closed:** Mon, Tue, two weeks Jan. **Meals:** alc (main courses £12 to £22). Set L £19 (2 courses) to £23. **Service:** not inc. **Details:** 64 seats. 30 seats outside. Music. Car parking.

▌▐ Average Price

The average price listed in main-entry reviews denotes the price of a three-course meal, without wine.

▌Brighton

Chilli Pickle

Buzzy, vibrant Indian
17 Jubilee Street, Brighton, BN1 1GE
Tel no: (01273) 900383
www.thechillipickle.com
Indian | £25
Cooking score: 3
£30

Originally buried in the labyrinth of the Lanes, Brighton's pan-Indian restaurant is now enfolded within the confines of myhotel, but still manages to impersonate the buzz of a Subcontinental city street-market. An array of small nibbles is offered at lunch – vegetable kachoris with tamarind chutney, mutton dumplings with mustard sauce, tandoori chicken drumsticks. In the evenings, dishes grow into vibrant, satisfying main courses like Chennai seafood stew with idiyappam rice noodles and saffron potatoes, or mutton rogan josh with coconut naan, the sauce fragrant with cinnamon, cloves and garam masala. The many vegetarian dishes are equally inspired: try paneer and chickpea kadai in spiced yoghurt gravy with red onion flatbread. Don't miss the homemade ice creams. Cocktails, lassis and beers supplement the wines, which start at £15.50.
Chef/s: Alun Sperring. **Open:** Wed to Mon L 12 to 3, D 6 to 10.30. **Closed:** Tue, 25 and 26 Dec. **Meals:** alc (main courses £9 to £19). Set D £22.25 (2 courses) to £25.50. **Service:** 10% for parties of 8 or more. **Details:** 115 seats. 20 seats outside. Wheelchair access. Music.

Symbols

🛏 Accommodation is available

£30 Three courses for less than £30

V Separate vegetarian menu

£5 OFF £5-off voucher scheme

🍷 Notable wine list

Food For Friends

Urban-chic veggie
17-18 Prince Albert Street, The Lanes, Brighton, BN1 1HF
Tel no: (01273) 202310
www.foodforfriends.com
Vegetarian | £22
Cooking score: 1

V £30

Brighton's veggie veteran hung up its hippie kaftan and binned its sandals some years back, replacing them with a much sharper twenty first-century outfit. Huge glass windows and urban-chic interiors are the setting for a menu that delves into the global melting pot and comes up with Thai sweetcorn fritters, bean mole quesadillas, Moroccan chickpea, aubergine and harissa stew, and salads such as warm haloumi niçoise. Sussex cheeses and desserts in the style of hot gooey chocolate pudding bring it all back home. House wine is £16.95.
Chef/s: Lisa Walker. **Open:** all week 12 to 10 (10.30 Fri and Sat). **Closed:** 25 Dec. **Meals:** alc (main courses £11 to £13). Set L £11.95 (2 courses). Set D £19.95. Sun L £9.95. **Service:** not inc. **Details:** 70 seats. 16 seats outside. Music.

The Ginger Dog

Revamped pub with fashionable local food
12-13 College Place, Brighton, BN2 1HN
Tel no: (01273) 620990
www.gingermanrestaurants.com
Modern British | £25
Cooking score: 3

£5 OFF £30

Ben McKellar has worked wonders with this backstreet Kemptown pub, upgrading and invigorating the place. It is part of his Gingerman group (see entries for Gingerman in Brighton, Ginger Pig in Hove, and Ginger Fox in West Sussex). The starting point is carefully sourced produce for 'good-quality cooking' that fizzes with fashionable flourishes, whether pheasant and roast garlic croquettes with mustard mayonnaise or roast halibut with coconut and cauliflower purée, cauliflower pakora, aubergine pickle, Bombay potatoes and curry sauce. One reporter commended the 'big, flavoursome faggots', others were delighted by the Guinness Welsh rarebit. Sweet things include rhubarb éclair with rhubarb sorbet and Szechuan pepper tuile. Wines from £15.50.

Chef/s: Tom Wright. **Open:** all week L 12 to 2 (3 Sat, 12.30 to 4 Sun), D 6 to 10. **Closed:** 25 Dec. **Meals:** alc (main courses £10 to £19). Set L £12.50 (2 courses). **Service:** not inc. **Details:** 80 seats. Separate bar. Wheelchair access. Music.

Gingerman

Jam-packed foodie hot spot
21a Norfolk Square, Brighton, BN1 2PD
Tel no: (01273) 326688
www.gingermanrestaurants.com
Modern European | £35
Cooking score: 3

Holed up on a side street just off the seafront, Ben McKellar's original restaurant is still a hot ticket with Brighton's foodie throngs. Done out in restrained colours, with high ceilings and cool fittings, it plays to regular full houses who applaud the self-appointed 'Gingerman's' assured take on big-city food. Braised rabbit ravioli, Thai-style mussels and a bourride of South Coast fish add some extra spark to a menu that also offers Sussex beef fillet with an oxtail faggot and cauliflower purée or a fine assembly of roast guinea fowl, Gruyère croquette, crispy Carmarthen ham, spinach purée and Marsala jus. To finish, a 'blissful' dessert of iced caramel parfait with bitter chocolate ganache and coffee tuile almost tempted one reader into some devil-may-care plate licking. The snappy, eclectic wine list opens at £15.50 (£3.90 a glass).

Chef/s: Ben McKellar and Simon Neville-Jones. **Open:** Tue to Sun L 12.30 to 2, D 7 to 10. **Closed:** Mon, 2 weeks Jan. **Meals:** Set L £15 (2 courses) to £18. Set D £30 (2 courses) to £35. Sun L £25. **Service:** not inc. **Details:** 32 seats. Music.

The Restaurant at Drakes

Fine dining at a classy boutique hotel
43-44 Marine Parade, Brighton, BN2 1PE
Tel no: (01273) 696934
www.therestaurantatdrakes.co.uk
Modern British | £40
Cooking score: 6

£5 OFF

A little way to the east of the pierhead, Drakes is a classy boutique hotel that has been the reference for fine dining on the Brighton seafront for a good few years now. It seems a small shame that the restaurant is in the basement, but it's a light-filled room during the day, with a more intimate, low-lit feel in the evenings. Andrew MacKenzie worked for some of the biggest names in London gastronomy (Anton Mosimann, Nico Ladenis) in years gone by, and while there is no 1980s nostalgia about the cooking here, it does nonetheless retain classical technique. Tuna tartare with fleur du sel, dressed in white truffle oil, is a statement starter, or there may be more modish beetroot risotto with goats' cheese, before main courses explore the resonances to be teased from the likes of poulet noir, poached and roasted, served with smoked mash, a braised drumstick and baby leeks and carrots, or turbot fillet accompanied robustly by roast artichoke, crab ravioli and crab cream sauce. Desserts such as chocolate soufflé with pistachio ice cream, or roast peppered pineapple with vanilla, are worth the wait. The wines are classified by style, and open with a page of glass selections from £6.50. Bottles start at £22.

Chef/s: Andrew MacKenzie. **Open:** all week L 12.30 to 2, D 7 to 9.45. **Meals:** Set L £20 (2 courses) to £25. Set D £29.95 (2 courses) to £39.95. Sun L £25. **Service:** 12.5%. **Details:** 38 seats. Separate bar. Music. Car parking.

Sam's of Seven Dials

Buzzy brasserie in an old bank
1 Buckingham Place, Brighton, BN1 3TD
Tel no: (01273) 885555
www.sevendialsrestaurant.co.uk
British | £28
Cooking score: 2

Smack beside Brighton's busy Seven Dials intersection, just a stroll from the railway station, Sam Metcalfe's stylish brasserie occupies a handsome red brick and stone building, formerly Lloyd's bank. The striking interior features big windows, high ceilings, polished floorboards and modern artwork. Expect a lively buzz, a decked terrace and modern brasserie-style dishes on monthly menus and daily chalkboards. Seasonal ingredients are used in, say, squid with risotto nero and paprika roast peppers; gilthead bream with cucumber tagliatelle, chervil velouté and crab beignet; and coconut brioche-and-butter pudding. House wine £15. Sibling Sam's of Brighton is at 1 Paston Place; tel: (01273) 676222.
Chef/s: Sam Metcalfe. **Open:** Mon to Sat L 12 to 3 (4 Sun), D 6 to 10 (10.30 Sat, 9 Sun). **Closed:** 25 and 26 Dec. **Meals:** alc (main courses £12 to £19). Set L and early D £12 (2 courses) to £14. **Service:** 12.5%. **Details:** 60 seats. 40 seats outside. Separate bar. Wheelchair access. Music.

Terre à Terre

Funky vegetarian maverick
71 East Street, Brighton, BN1 1HQ
Tel no: (01273) 729051
www.terreaterre.co.uk
Vegetarian | £30
Cooking score: 3
V

Terre à Terre's funky, maverick pose and left-field boho vibe are pure Brighton – so it's no surprise that it has bedded in comfortably since launching itself on the local scene back in 1993. This colourful veggie still plunders the world larder for inspiration and has never lost its oddball sense of humour – 'rösti revisited'

or 'nosey parkin', anyone? Other 'outstandingly creative' goodies from the gloriously jumbled melting pot might range from smoked sun-dried tomatoes with walnut and parsley tarator to tandoori haloumi with chilli pineapple and coriander salad – not forgetting 'frangipane sizzle dates' with mint-tea granita and pomegranate gazpacho. Extras such as the 'amazing' deep-fried olives, salted caramel truffles and wacky cocktails are regularly cheered, and the organically minded drinks list also embraces trendy world beers, nectars and wines (from £17.50).
Chef/s: Dino Pavledis. **Open:** all week 12 to 10.30 (11 Sat, 10 Sun). **Closed:** Mon (Oct to Apr), 25 and 26 Dec. **Meals:** alc (main courses £14 to £16). Set D £30. **Service:** not inc. **Details:** 100 seats. 15 seats outside. Wheelchair access. Music.

East Chiltington
The Jolly Sportsman

Cheery hostelry that fits the bill
Chapel Lane, East Chiltington, BN7 3BA
Tel no: (01273) 890400
www.thejollysportsman.com
Modern British | £29
Cooking score: 2

Bruce Wass's 'lovely, attractively done-up pub' is a cheery, modern-day country hostelry that has won plenty of followers for the sensible, regularly changing menu underpinned by a classical theme. It fits the bill perfectly. Local produce from well-chosen suppliers is used to good effect; one winter visitor enjoyed boudin blanc with Madeira and wild mushroom sauce, and seared calf's liver with a beef-cheek faggot, horseradish mash and Savoy cabbage. At other meals there have been crab cakes with chilli jam and pickled ginger; seasonal game; brill fillet with smoked celeriac purée and braised salsify, and chocolate sea-salt tart. Wines from £16.50.
Chef/s: Anthony Masters and Bruce Wass. **Open:** all week L 12.15 to 2.30 (3 Sat, 3.30 Sun), Mon to Sat D 6.30 to 9.30 (10 Fri and Sat). **Closed:** 25 Dec. **Meals:** alc (main courses £12 to £20). Set L £13.50 (2 courses) to £16.75. Set D £19.50. Sun L £19.50.

Service: not inc. **Details:** 100 seats. 40 seats outside. Separate bar. No music. Wheelchair access. Car parking.

Eastbourne
The Grand Hotel, Mirabelle
Gloriously traditional seafront hotel
King Edward's Parade, Eastbourne, BN21 4EQ
Tel no: (01323) 412345
www.grandeastbourne.com
Modern European | £45
Cooking score: 5

One of the last truly grand seafront hotels left in England, the Eastbourne Grand stares impassively over the Channel, a tiered wedding-cake of an edifice, within the confines of which little orchestras play the tunes of yesteryear, and the mood of gay abandon is fixed at somewhere around the time of the end of postwar rationing. It's glorious, and all the more so for having a fine dining restaurant, the Mirabelle, that has more assiduously moved with the gastronomic times. Gerald Röser has clocked up a decade here now, and continues to impress with menus that dexterously balance traditional technique with a modern approach to flavours and seasonings. A soufflé of pike with a portion of buttered lobster and sea urchin sauce is virtually Gavroche-like in its unabashed classicism, and may be followed by roast loin of Sussex Marsh lamb with minted pea purée and truffled dauphinois. But then you might come across duck magret in tamarind and five-spice sauce with baby pak choi, lotus root and a kind of orientally seasoned risotto. Desserts aim to swathe you in richness, à la Madagascar chocolate fondant with pain d'épices and honey ice cream. A top-drawer wine list does France exhaustively and expensively, but has good value in the southern hemisphere. Prices open at £24.50.
Chef/s: Gerald Röser. **Open:** Tue to Sat L 12.30 to 2, D 7 to 10. **Closed:** Sun, Mon, first 2 weeks Jan.
Meals: Set L £20 (2 courses) to £24.50. Set D £40.

Tasting menu £58.50. **Service:** not inc. **Details:** 50 seats. Separate bar. Wheelchair access. Car parking. Children 12 and over only.

Fletching
The Griffin Inn
Recipe for a quality day out
Fletching, TN22 3SS
Tel no: (01825) 722890
www.thegriffininn.co.uk
Modern British | £30
Cooking score: 3

Little changes at this ancient country pub: winter visitors are always welcomed by crackling log fires, in summer the view over the Ouse Valley from the splendid tiered garden never fails to delight. Bang-up-to-date cooking pulls in the crowds, too; the kitchen draws on excellent seasonal produce for dishes such as braised oxtail with piquillo peppers and saffron risotto, and venison loin with Jerusalem artichokes, beetroot, cavolo nero and shallot purée. Reporters have praised carpaccio of beef with red onion jam and rocket, and 'a good paella with fish fillets, mussels, clams, prawns and chorizo'. Elsewhere, Rye Bay fish and chips (from the bar menu) shows respect for pub tradition. The strong wine list hits the spot – short on pretention, long on quality and reasonably priced (from £14.90).
Chef/s: Matthew Sandells. **Open:** all week L 12 to 2.30 (3 Sat and Sun), Mon to Sat D 7 to 9.30.
Closed: 25 Dec. **Meals:** alc (main courses £12 to £25). Set L £13.50 (2 courses) to £18.50. Sun L £25 (2 courses) to £30. **Service:** 10%. **Details:** 65 seats. 30 seats outside. Separate bar. No music. Wheelchair access. Car parking.

Gun Hill

ALSO RECOMMENDED
▲ The Gun

Gun Hill, TN21 0JU
Tel no: (01825) 872361
www.thegunhouse.co.uk
Modern British £5 OFF

Way out in the sticks, just off the Wealden Way, this seriously expanded sixteenth-century watering hole now attracts a foodie crowd with its generous modern pub cooking. Top ingredients feature strongly, from Old Spot pork pie with scratchings or potted Dorset crab (£6.95) to stuffed spring rabbit with wild mushrooms (£13.50) or a trio of Sussex salt marsh lamb. Duck egg custard tart with poached rhubarb is a winning dessert. Terrific home-baked bread, real ales and gluggable wines (from £16.95). Open all week.

Hove

The Foragers

Agreeable local with good, tasty flavours
3 Stirling Place, Hove, BN3 3YU
Tel no: (01273) 733134
www.theforagerspub.co.uk
Modern British | £23
Cooking score: 2

£30

This agreeable backstreet local has an infectiously laid-back atmosphere. It's all very casual, an easy mix of mismatched tables and a partial view of the chefs at work from the front bar. The menu is short and to the point; for instance, a simple dish of home-cured gravadlax with dill, horseradish and fresh bread. Good, tasty flavours come through in main courses of braised squid and chorizo stew with garlic bruschetta, or braised venison haunch with red cabbage, celeriac and truffled potato purée, and sloe berry jus. For dessert, lemon meringue pie with foraged blackberry ice cream is a winner. Wines from £13.95.

Chef/s: Josh Kitson. **Open:** all week L 12 to 3 (4 Sat and Sun), Mon to Sat D 6 to 10. **Meals:** alc (main courses £9 to £15). Set L and D £12 (2 courses). **Service:** not inc. **Details:** 90 seats. 90 seats outside. Separate bar. Music.

The Ginger Pig

All-rounder with some terrific dishes
3 Hove Street, Hove, BN3 2TR
Tel no: (01273) 736123
www.gingermanrestaurants.com
Modern British | £30
Cooking score: 4

Occupying the shell of a defunct hotel just off Hove seafront, this was 'Gingerman' Ben McKellar's first foray into the world of foodie pubs. These days, the Pig is a 'top-class' all-rounder, delivering exactly what is required when it comes to relaxed vibes, good drinking and big-hearted food. A strong local supply network is at the heart of things, and the kitchen makes the most of the exceptional bounty for some terrific dishes. Crispy pig's head is a favourite opener, with mustard, turnips and apple, or you might fancy a fusion plate of tuna tartare with watermelon, wasabi, coriander and spiced cereal. After that, big seasonal flavours prevail, from oxtail and kidney suet pie to roast haunch of venison with pressed shoulder, prune purée and creamed Brussels tops. To finish, try the mischievous popcorn pannacotta with a peanut butter bar and chocolate sorbet. Service is really friendly, and the global wine list provides admirable drinking at fair prices (from £15.50).

Chef/s: Marek Mislan and Ben McKellar. **Open:** all week L 12 to 2 (3 Fri and Sat, 12.30 to 4 Sun), D 6.30 to 10. **Closed:** 25 Dec. **Meals:** alc (main courses £11 to £19). Set L and D £12.50 (2 courses). **Service:** not inc. **Details:** 70 seats. 40 seats outside. Separate bar. Wheelchair access. Music.

Graze Restaurant

Well-sourced tasting menus
42 Western Road, Hove, BN3 1JD
Tel no: (01273) 823707
www.graze-restaurant.co.uk
Modern British | £32
Cooking score: 3

V

This opulent, though petite, Regency-style dining room in well-heeled Hove is lavish with burgundy velvet and gilt mirrors. It styles itself as a tasting-menu restaurant, though softens this approach by offering standard à la carte and set menus for keener budgets. Head chef Will Stanyer sends out impeccable produce: refined carpaccio of tuna, squid ink jelly and grapefruit caviar, or charred mackerel, horseradish pannacotta, hazelnuts and beetroot sorbet – a regular feature on the seven-course tasting menu – rounded off with palate-cleansing chilled strawberry soup. Accomplished Sunday roasts and elegant plates are testimony to Stanyer's extensive training in French technique. However, while Graze remains a restaurant for Hove to be proud of, flavours, service and the décor could do with sharpening up. Wines from £18.
Chef/s: Will Stanyer. **Open:** all week L 12 to 2 (12.30 to 3 Sun), D 6.30 to 9 (9.30 Fri and Sat, 8.30 Sun). **Closed:** 1 to 4 Jan. **Meals:** Set L £16 (2 courses) to £20. Set D £26 (2 courses) to £32. Sun L £15. Tasting menu £45 (7 courses). **Service:** 12%. **Details:** 50 seats. 4 seats outside. Music.

The Hove Kitchen

A buzzing hub for Hove
102-105 Western Road, Hove, BN3 1FA
Tel no: (01273) 725495
www.thehovekitchen.com
Modern European | £25
Cooking score: 2

Breakfast and brunch kick off the day's proceedings at this energetic addition to the Hove scene, and HK's alfresco tables are much in demand when the sun's out. Inside, there's also a buzz as the kitchen knocks up an array of exact, vigorous dishes with a strong Mediterranean slant. Veggie tapas plates, Sardinian prosciutto or local pheasant breast with confit leg, cavolo nero, chestnuts and quince steal the limelight from cheeseburgers, char-grilled pork fillet or roast pollack with mash, parsley and capers. Desserts also mix things up, so take your pick from treacle tart or pannacotta with caramelised clementines and grappa. Wines from £13.50.
Chef/s: Steve Beadle. **Open:** all week L 12 to 3 (4 Sat, 5 Sun), Tue to Sat D 5.30 to 10. **Closed:** 25 and 26 Dec. **Meals:** alc (main courses £11 to £19). Set L and early D £10 (2 courses). **Service:** not inc. **Details:** 85 seats. 40 seats outside. Separate bar. No music. Wheelchair access.

■ Lewes

The Kings Head

Foodie pub for our times
9 Southover High Street, Lewes, BN7 1HS
Tel no: (01273) 474628
Modern British | £22
Cooking score: 2

Pitched close to Southover Priory and Anne of Cleves House, with views of Lewes Castle from the garden, this Victorian boozer has been dusted down and reconfigured as a proper foodie pub for our times. The kitchen mixes home-grown and European flavours for a raft of thoroughly modern dishes with an upbeat accent – think smoked eel with crispy bacon, Jerusalem artichoke and fennel or slow-braised rabbit in cider with new season's leeks and truffle mash. For afters, steamed apple pudding with caramelised pears and ice cream is one for the Brits. House wine is £14.35. Related to the Foragers in Hove (see entry).
Chef/s: Jon Aldridge. **Open:** all week L 12 to 3 (4 Sun), Tue to Sat D 6 to 10. **Meals:** alc (main courses £10 to £20). Set L and D £12 (2 courses). Bar menu available. **Service:** 10%. **Details:** 80 seats. 75 seats outside. Separate bar. Wheelchair access. Music.

Rye

NEW ENTRY

The Ambrette at Rye
Cracking Indian in a fine old house
White Vine House, 24 High Street, Rye, TN31 7JF
Tel no: (01797) 222043
www.theambrette.co.uk
Indian | £25
Cooking score: 1
£5 OFF V £30

This new venture from the Ambrette in Margate, Kent (see entry), is off to a cracking start. Expect the same menu but grander surrounds; the panelled rooms of venerable White Vine House make a fitting setting for Dev Biswal's modern Indian food. Ramsgate crab meat stir-fried with mustard oil, cinnamon and cardamom, and spiced loin of Kentish pork with an aromatic Goan sauce of malt vinegar and garlic wine use regional produce impressively. Spicing is spot-on, prices remarkably fair. Wines from £14.95.
Chef/s: Dev Biswal. **Open:** Tue to Sun L 11.30 to 3.30, D 6 to 9.30. **Closed:** Mon, 25 and 26 Dec. **Meals:** alc (main courses £9 to £16). Set L £14.95 (2 courses) to £19.95. Tasting menu £40 (6 courses). **Service:** not inc. **Details:** Wheelchair access. Music.

The George Grill
Bolt-hole with quality crowd-pleasers
The George Inn, 98 High Street, Rye, TN31 7JT
Tel no: (01797) 222114
www.thegeorgeinrye.com
Modern European | £25
Cooking score: 2

Lovingly restored, with a smart contemporary feel, this sixteenth-century coaching inn has become a favoured Sussex coast bolt-hole for the down-from-London crowd. Like the locals, they love the George Tap, the classic pub at its heart, and the restyled, informal Grill Restaurant, which really hits the mark with its menu of quality local ingredients cooked simply and well in the charcoal oven. Crowd-pleasers combine classics (club sandwich and

chips) with Angus steaks, Rye Bay fish and seafood (perhaps lobster with chilli, garlic and parsley), and Romney Marsh lamb rump served with smoked aubergine purée and braised leeks. House wine £19.50.
Chef/s: Gabriel Ilinca. **Open:** all week 12 to 10. **Meals:** alc (main courses £8 to £19). Set L £12.95 (2 courses) to £15.95. **Service:** 7.5%. **Details:** 80 seats. 20 seats outside. Separate bar. Music.

Landgate Bistro
Landmark bistro that champions local food
5-6 Landgate, Rye, TN31 7LH
Tel no: (01797) 222829
www.landgatebistro.co.uk
Modern British | £27
Cooking score: 3
V £30

A faithful contributor to Rye's culinary reputation for many a year, this landmark neighbourhood bistro stands proud by one of the town's ancient gateways. Current chef/proprietor Martin Peacock is something of a hero when it comes to supporting local food, and he makes fine use of the region's ample harvest: potted Camber rabbit is served with homemade piccalilli, and rump of Romney Marsh lamb might be given an aromatic Moroccan lift with baba ganoush, harissa and couscous. 'Wonderfully tender' Winchelsea pork also puts in an occasional appearance, while desserts could feature iced nut parfait with Amaretto ice cream and Frangelico liqueur jellies. Front-of-house has been deemed 'outstanding' in every department. Real ales from Harveys and Shepherd Neame are on tap, and the modest wine list offers sound drinking from £14.60.
Chef/s: Martin Peacock. **Open:** Sat and Sun L 12 to 2.15, Wed to Sat D 7 to 9 (6.30 to 9.15 Sat). Sun D 7 to 9 (bank hols only). **Closed:** Mon, Tue, 24 to 26 and 31 Dec, 1 Jan, 1 week Jun, bank hols. **Meals:** alc (main courses £13 to £19). Set L £13.50 (2 courses) to £16.50. Set D (Wed and Thur only) £16.80 (2 courses) to £19.80. **Service:** not inc. **Details:** 32 seats. Separate bar. Music.

Webbe's at the Fish Café

Easy-going eatery with good local produce
17 Tower Street, Rye, TN31 7AT
Tel no: (01797) 222226
www.webbesrestaurants.co.uk
Seafood | £25
Cooking score: 2

£5 OFF £30

The style here is simple: an unusual Edwardian four-storey building housing a fairly minimalist ground-floor café with its open-plan kitchen. As the name implies, fish is a strong (though not exclusive) suit. It is not the most ambitious cooking around, but the food is prepared using good local produce. Start with Rye Bay scallops with cauliflower purée and curry and lime oil, before grilled plaice fillets with cider sauce, smoked bacon and pan-fried potatoes, or slow-cooked ox-cheek in claret and thyme. Desserts range from raspberry crème brûlée with Drambuie ice cream to pear and blackcurrant crumble. House wine is £15.95.
Chef/s: Matthew Drinkwater. **Open:** all week L 12 to 2.30, D 6 to 9.30. **Closed:** 24 to 26 Dec, 2 Jan for two weeks. **Meals:** alc (main courses £10 to £19). **Service:** not inc. **Details:** 54 seats. No children after 7.

■ Westfield

The Wild Mushroom

Civilised country restaurant
Woodgate House, Westfield Lane, Westfield, TN35 4SB
Tel no: (01424) 751137
www.webbesrestaurants.co.uk
Modern British | £28
Cooking score: 2

£5 OFF £30

Paul Webbe's rural Sussex outpost is a red-brick late Victorian farmhouse on the edge of Westfield, seven miles from his Fish Café in Rye (see entry). Canapés are served with drinks in the conservatory bar or the garden. At linen-clothed tables in the civilised dining room, locals enjoy well-presented dishes

prepared from quality seasonal ingredients by a competent kitchen team. Typical offerings are homemade breads and a starter of crab, broad bean and wild mushroom risotto with shellfish sauce, then belly pork with Rye Bay scallops and celeriac and Bramley purée, and chocolate fondant with pistachio ice cream. House wine is £16.95.
Chef/s: Chris Weddle. **Open:** Wed to Sun L 12 to 2.30, Wed to Sat D 7 to 9.30. **Closed:** Mon, Tue, 25 and 26 Dec, first 2 weeks Jan, bank hols. **Meals:** alc (main courses £13 to £20). Set L £16.95 (2 courses) to £19.95. Sun L £23. Tasting menu £34. **Service:** not inc. **Details:** 40 seats. Separate bar. Wheelchair access. Music. Car parking.

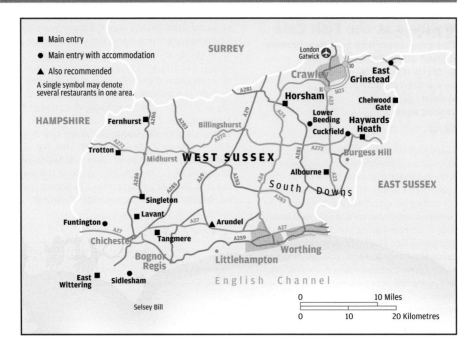

Albourne

The Ginger Fox

The complete package
Muddleswood Road, Albourne, BN6 9EA
Tel no: (01273) 857888
www.gingermanrestaurants.com
Modern British | £25
Cooking score: 4

 £30

The West Sussex branch of Ben McKellar's growing empire (see Gingerman, Ginger Dog and Ginger Pig in Brighton) is a handsome, thatched South Downs pub offering the complete package when it comes to rural conviviality. Whether you are relaxing in a colourful armchair by the open fire or taking advantage of the pleasant garden, it all sets the scene for straightforward seasonal cooking. The kitchen plunders the Sussex larder for tip-top local ingredients, which may appear in the form of pan-fried Rye Bay scallops with cauliflower purée and cauliflower pakoras, or braised rabbit with potato and aged pecorino gnocchi and chorizo. Follow with pan-fried salmon fillet, glazed salsify, salmon roe and tarragon velouté or a more traditional braised venison suet pastry pie with honey-roasted parsnips, horseradish mash and red wine gravy. Steamed marmalade pudding with whisky custard is a good way to conclude. House wine starts at £15.50.

Chef/s: James Dearden. **Open:** all week L 12 to 2 (3 Sat, 4 Sun), D 6 to 10 (6.30 to 10 Sat, 6 to 9 Sun). **Closed:** 25 Dec. **Meals:** alc (main courses £12 to £19). Set L £12.50 (2 courses). **Service:** 12.5% for parties of 6 or more. **Details:** 55 seats. 80 seats outside. Separate bar. Wheelchair access. Music. Car parking.

Visit us Online

To find out more about
The Good Food Guide, please visit
www.thegoodfoodguide.co.uk

Arundel

ALSO RECOMMENDED
▲ The Town House
65 High Street, Arundel, BN18 9AJ
Tel no: (01903) 883847
www.thetownhouse.co.uk
Modern British

'Good value, beautifully presented food and excellent service' noted one reporter of this restaurant-with-rooms run by chef/proprietor Lee Williams. Located opposite Arundel Castle, the handsome Georgian townhouse boasts a sixteenth-century ceiling imported from Italy, which adds to the charm of the comfortable dining room. The set-price menu (lunch £19.50, dinner £29 for three courses) might offer seared foie gras with grape chutney and roasted chateaubriand before chocolate fondant and honeycomb ice cream. House wine is £15.50. Closed Sun and Mon.

Chelwood Gate
Red Lion
Inviting pub with fine food
Lewes Road, Chelwood Gate, RH17 7DE
Tel no: (01825) 740265
www.raffansredlion.co.uk
Modern British | £28
Cooking score: 4

£30

Mark Raffan made his name amid the stately Elizabethan grandeur of Gravetye Manor (see entry), but gave it all up to take charge of this inviting country pub a few miles down the road. Humble cuts may have replaced haute cuisine, but there's no shortage of determination, style or classy technique in the kitchen – whether Raffan is fashioning a terrine of rabbit, confit pork and foie gras or knocking up a terrific rump-steak burger with smoked Goodwood cheese. His warm crab tart with white crab salad and mango salsa is regularly mentioned in despatches; other top-end dishes include crisp duck confit with a cassolette of chickpeas and chorizo. To finish,

try the autumnal delights of cinnamon-scented pannacotta with mulled pears. Food aside, the Red Lion is still a proper Sussex hostelry, with a crackling fire in winter, jazz and barbecues in the summer garden, and a battalion of Shepherd Neame ales to sup. There are two dozen wines; prices start at £16 (£4 a glass).
Chef/s: Mark Raffan. Open: Tue to Sun L 12 to 2.30 (3 Sun), Tue to Sat D 6.30 to 9.30. Closed: Mon. Meals: alc (main courses £12 to £23). Service: not inc. Details: 80 seats. 50 seats outside. Separate bar. Wheelchair access. Music. Car parking.

Cuckfield
Ockenden Manor Hotel & Spa
High-impact cooking in a lovely setting
Ockenden Lane, Cuckfield, RH17 5LD
Tel no: (01444) 416111
www.hshotels.co.uk
Modern French | £55
Cooking score: 5

The setting – an extended seventeenth-century manor house – is lovely, with its attractive gardens, neat lawns and splendid views. In fine weather a pre-dinner drink alfresco is a must. In the kitchen Stephen Crane likes to keep things simple, using pinpoint accuracy of timing, careful balance and pretty much faultless composition to make an impact. Expect a bedrock of modern Anglo-French ideas with additions from Italy in starters such as braised hare with a tangle of fresh pasta, glazed root vegetables and horseradish. For main course, saddle of venison might arrive with its own pasty, while a fine piece of sea bass might be voguishly accompanied by smoked bacon, potato gnocchi, purple sprouting broccoli and grain mustard sauce. Desserts bring on vibrant assemblies; a technically perfect caramelised lemon tart with an intense blackcurrant sorbet is once again a highlight in reports this year. Immense effort and care have gone into the wine list, which picks first names from France and beyond. It can contribute energetically to

the cost of it all, but there's relief in a line-up of house selections at £23, plus a batch of decent bottles at the lower end of the scale.
Chef/s: Stephen Crane. **Open:** all week L 12 to 2, D 6.30 to 9. **Meals:** Set L £16.50 (2 courses) to £23. Set D £55. Sun L £34.50. **Service:** not inc. **Details:** 70 seats. Separate bar. No music. Wheelchair access. Car parking.

East Grinstead
Gravetye Manor
Enchanting Elizabethan charmer
Vowels Lane, East Grinstead, RH19 4LJ
Tel no: (01342) 810567
www.gravetyemanor.co.uk
Modern British | £55
Cooking score: 4

V

Gravetye Manor appeals on many fronts, from the beautiful gardens and elegant Elizabethan architecture to Rupert Gleadow's forward-thinking but generally restrained cooking, which works well within the soft-centred country house environment. A Gallic pairing of ballottine of foie gras with pickled girolles turns up among starters with salted grapes, hazelnuts and celeriac, or there may be a skilfully straightforward dish of scallops teamed with black pudding, rumbledethumps (potato, cabbage and onion) and sage butter. Mains show a fondness for intense flavours in well-balanced combinations, say spiced fillet of pork served with an apple and sage sausage, rösti potato, kale and white port sauce. Intricately wrought desserts could include a hot beetroot soufflé with sage ice cream and cocoa jelly. The top-drawer wine list has France in the ascendancy on its global tour. Expect a broad sweep of grape varieties and good by-the-glass and half-bottle choices; prices from £26.
Chef/s: Rupert Gleadow. **Open:** all week L 12 to 2, D 6.30 to 9.30. **Meals:** Set L £22.50 (2 courses) to £27.50. Set D £33 (2 courses) to £40. Sun L £35. **Service:** 12.5%. **Details:** 40 seats. 15 seats outside. Separate bar. No music. Car parking. Children over 7 yrs only.

East Wittering
Samphire
A super little find
57 Shore Road, East Wittering, PO20 8DY
Tel no: (01243) 672754
www.samphireeastwittering.co.uk
Modern British | £23
Cooking score: 2

Just fifty metres from Wittering beach, Samphire is 'a super little find' and fits its village setting perfectly. From the mini-terrace with driftwood-style tables to the small dining room sporting scrubbed tables and cushioned benches, it's rustic through and through. Chef-proprietor David Skinner makes everything from bread to ice cream in his tiny, open-to-view kitchen, and conjures cracking dishes from local, seasonal and sustainable produce. Typical are: Almodington asparagus with Scotch pheasant egg and balsamic and rocket salad, then wild sea bass with garlic purée, crushed Jersey Royals and tomato, fennel and bacon butter, and rhubarb, apple and berry crumble. House wine £14.
Chef/s: David Skinner. **Open:** Mon to Sat L 12 to 2, D 6 to 9 (9.30 Fri and Sat). **Closed:** Sun, 25 and 26 Dec, 2 weeks Jan. **Meals:** alc (main courses £12 to £20). Set L £13 (2 courses) to £16. **Details:** 30 seats. 12 seats outside. Music.

Fernhurst
The Duke of Cumberland Arms
The perfect country pub
Henley, Fernhurst, GU27 3HQ
Tel no: (01428) 652280
www.dukeofcumberland.com
Modern British | £32
Cooking score: 4

'What a country pub should be' states a visitor to this sympathetically extended sixteenth-century hostelry. Our reporter was pleased to find the Duke adheres firmly to the old-fashioned values of inn-keeping, offering

warmth, comfort, real ales and good food. Choose between the ancient bar (for many readers 'the best place') or the more contemporary restaurant (with a terrace taking in stunning views). While ales tapped from the cask suggest an olde-worlde outlook, the cooking takes a modern approach, with a nod to the Mediterranean and a reliance on first-rate produce. Scallops with chorizo, garlic, pomme purée and truffle oil, and confit belly pork with apple and Calvados glaze are 'particularly good'; smoked haddock with cabbage, lardons and cream sauce has also been praised. Mount Gay Rum pineapple, coconut ice cream, chilli and peanut praline is quite a finale. Sunday lunch 'is a must', service 'excellent', and in fine weather the terraced garden with streams and pools comes into its own. House wine is £14.50.
Chef/s: Simon Goodman. **Open:** all week L 12 to 2, Tue to Sat D 7 to 9. **Meals:** alc (main courses £16 to £30). **Service:** not inc. **Details:** 54 seats. 117 seats outside. Music. Car parking.

▌Funtington
Hallidays
Village restaurant with good-value food
Watery Lane, Funtington, PO18 9LF
Tel no: (01243) 575331
www.hallidays.info
Modern British | £35
Cooking score: 2

£5
OFF

The ancient thatched cottage (which was once three) is a quietly confident, personally run restaurant set in a prosperous rural village not far from Chichester. It's an affectionately nurtured set-up, with low-beamed ceilings lending an intimate, homely feel. Andrew Stephenson has been at the stove for some 16 years, and people return enthusiastically for his good-value, seasonally inspired menus. Start with scallops with purple sprouting broccoli and Seville oranges, motor on to baked local gurnard with mussels, prawns and vermouth, or honey-roast duck breast with

lentils, herbs and sherry vinegar, then finish with vanilla crème brûlée and blood-orange sorbet. Wines from £17.50.
Chef/s: Andrew Stephenson. **Open:** Wed to Fri and Sun L 12 to 2. Wed to Sat D 7 to 9.30. **Closed:** Mon, Tue, 1 week Mar, 2 weeks Aug. **Meals:** alc (main courses £17 to £20). Set L £15 (2 courses) to £20. Set D £21 (2 courses) to £26. Sun L £23. **Service:** not inc. **Details:** 28 seats. Separate bar. No music. Wheelchair access.

▌Haywards Heath

★ READERS' RESTAURANT OF THE YEAR ★
SOUTH EAST

Jeremy's Restaurant
Special occasion dining at everyday prices
Borde Hill Garden, Balcombe Road, Haywards Heath, RH16 1XP
Tel no: (01444) 441102
www.jeremysrestaurant.co.uk
Modern European | £36
Cooking score: 4

£5
OFF

'Every town could do with a restaurant of this standard' coos a reader – not that Jeremy's, with its captivating setting within historic Borde Hill Garden, could ever be replicated. It's quite the 'special occasion' restaurant, boasting a smart but relaxed dining room and even lovelier alfresco tables, though one needn't save it for best, given that the three-course menu du jour is just £18. Owner Jeremy Ashpool, now joined in the kitchen by chef Jimmy Grey, 'innovates continuously'; he offers globe and Jerusalem artichoke salad with smoked salsify and cep oil, say, or sea bass with polenta cake, smoked tomatoes and balsamic jelly. Or there might be something more classic, such as home-cured mackerel, beetroot and horseradish or Balcombe Estate partridge with pearl barley and smoked bacon. As for desserts, sticky toffee pudding 'is always a winner'. The reasonably priced global wine list, from £17, is commendably food-friendly.
Chef/s: Jeremy Ashpool and Jimmy Grey. **Open:** Tue to Sun L 12.30 to 2.30, Tue to Sat D 7 to 9.30. **Closed:** Mon, first 2 weeks Jan. **Meals:** alc (main

courses £15 to £26). Set L and D £15 (2 courses) to £18. Sun L £29.50. **Service:** 10%. **Details:** 60 seats. 40 seats outside. Separate bar. Wheelchair access. Music. Car parking.

Horsham

Restaurant Tristan

Outstanding cooking at modest prices
3 Stans Way, Horsham, RH12 1HU
Tel no: (01403) 255688
www.restauranttristan.co.uk
Modern European | £40
Cooking score: 5

Despite its reputation as one of Sussex's culinary highlights, Restaurant Tristan refuses to rest on its laurels, and a new ground-floor bar and café has given it added presence in Horsham's old town. Upstairs in the oak-beamed dining room, chef-patron Tristan Mason continues to turn out 'outstanding and consistent' modern cooking that makes good use of luxury ingredients despite modest prices. The menu may read simply – a dessert titled 'milk chocolate' gives little away, for example – but the kitchen's obvious talent and a willingness to play around with flavour combinations help exceed expectations. A good-value lunch kicked off with gazpacho accompanied by gently spiced crab, tomato consommé, a skinned heritage tomato and micro basil leaves, followed by a hearty summer main that showed real finesse: chicken with Jerusalem artichokes, wild mushrooms, delicate lobster velouté dressing and some sprightly shiso leaves. To finish, the mysterious 'milk chocolate' was revealed to be an excellent, dense ball of chocolate mousse, milk ice cream and vanilla mousse. Service is 'attentive and friendly'. An expertly annotated wine list starts at £19 and offers a superb range around the £20-£30 mark.
Chef/s: Tristan Mason. **Open:** Tue to Sat L 12 to 2.30, D 6.30 to 9.30. **Closed:** Sun, Mon, first week Jan, 2 weeks Aug. **Meals:** Set L £16 (2 courses) to £20. Set D £32 (2 courses) to £40. **Service:** 12.5%. **Details:** 38 seats. Separate bar. Music.

Lavant

The Earl of March

Historic inn with forthright seasonal food
Lavant Road, Lavant, PO18 0BQ
Tel no: (01243) 533993
www.theearlofmarch.com
Modern British | £30
Cooking score: 4

£5
OFF

William Blake coined the phrase 'England's green and pleasant land' while marvelling at the undulating prospect of the South Downs from this very spot back in 1803. The vistas that inspired *Jerusalem* haven't changed a great deal since then, but the breathtaking views now play second fiddle to Giles Thompson's highly assured, twenty-first century food. Knowledgeably sourced regional produce is the jumping-off point for forthright seasonal dishes such as steamed mussels with Sussex cider and parsley cream, grilled Rother Valley steaks, loin of venison with celeriac dauphinois and sweet beetroot ripple or pan-seared halibut with chive mash and wilted spinach, sauced with crayfish and watercress. Slates of charcuterie or goats' cheese and walnut crostini start things off well, while top desserts have included autumn fruit crumble and a cleverly crafted white chocolate and orange 'brioche-and-butter' pudding with white chocolate ice cream. Upbeat pub lunches and Sussex real ales are served in the bar, while the wine list offers good pickings from £16 (£3.90 a glass).
Chef/s: Giles Thompson and Luke Gale. **Open:** all week L 12 to 2.30 (3 Sun), D 5.30 to 9.30 (6 to 9 Sun). **Meals:** alc (main courses £14 to £23). Set L and D £18.50 (2 courses) to £21.50. **Service:** not inc. **Details:** 70 seats. 60 seats outside. Separate bar. Wheelchair access. Music. Car parking.

Lower Beeding

★ TOP 50 ★

The Pass

Fireworks and fun in the kitchen
South Lodge Hotel, Brighton Road, Lower
Beeding, RH13 6PS
Tel no: (01403) 891711
www.southlodgehotel.co.uk
Modern British | £60
Cooking score: 7

 V

It may sound like a gimmicky novelty – an
entire restaurant housed within the confines of
a kitchen, complete with CCTV monitors for
those sitting with their backs to the action –
but the Pass is a serious gastronomic
contender. In case you were wondering, the
name is chef-speak for that hallowed ground
between the stove and the table, where
finished dishes are inspected (or binned) by
the head chef before making their way to the
customer. It's normally a hot-tempered,
tyrannical place – although things have been
calmed down for Joe Public here, and
expletives are strictly deleted. The designers
have gone for a garish, chilly look, with fierce
lighting, sparkly surfaces, sickly green seating,
green glasses and banquettes in a row. The
kitchen sets out its stall with three kinds of
salt, tremendous home-baked breads and a
series of tasting menus promising anything
from mushrooms with chocolate oil and
walnut jelly or confit trout with celery sorbet
to yoghurt parfait with cherry compote,
yoghurt meringue and pink peppercorns.
Flavours could easily run riot here, but chef
Matt Gillan and his brigade manage to roll out
a procession of acutely calibrated, harmonious
dishes full of ingenious contrasts and textures
– a 'brilliantly presented' display of culinary
fireworks, but without the scary bangs or
damp squibs. Consider a plate of crab
mayonnaise with char-grilled pineapple,
burnt coconut and green tea, or oat-crusted
halibut with chervil root purée, roasted
chervil root and chicken skin. Moving on,
goats' cheese gets cheeky with pickled apple
and celery popcorn, and you might find
pumpkin pannacotta among the risqué
desserts. Despite the anti-comfort ambience,
eating here is 'great fun' and service is good-
humoured – 'even when a fire alarm caused us
all to decamp to the lawn for 15 minutes and a
brief burst of hyperactivity ensued'. Wine
prices reflect the fact that the Pass is part of a
five-star country house hotel; bottles start
at £24.50.
Chef/s: Matt Gillan. **Open:** Wed to Sun L 12 to 2, D 7
to 9. **Closed:** Mon, Tue, first 2 weeks Jan. **Meals:** Set
L £25. Set D £60 (6 courses). Sun L £35 (5 courses)
to £55 (7 courses). **Service:** 10%. **Details:** 22 seats.
Separate bar. No music. Car parking.

Sidlesham

The Crab & Lobster

Contemporary seafood by a nature reserve
Mill Lane, Sidlesham, PO20 7NB
Tel no: (01243) 641233
www.crab-lobster.co.uk
Modern European | £35
Cooking score: 3

There are two experiences to be had at this
revived 350-year old inn. Outdoor seating
overlooks the marshes and flats of Pagham
Harbour nature reserve, while under the low
beams in the dining room there's a smarter, less
rustic feel. Not surprisingly, shellfish is given a
thorough outing on a contemporary, but not
overcomplicated, menu. Selsey crab and
crayfish is bundled into a parcel of smoked
salmon, and later a saffron seafood risotto
comes with scallops and a crab mascarpone,
while Brixham brill has a thoroughly modern
garnish of seaweed beignets. One visitor
found that battered cod cheeks suffered
slightly on the way to the table, but a dessert of
deep-fried coconut ice cream could never be
kept waiting. House wine is £15.85 from a
two-tier list with a heftier 'special selection'
area.
Chef/s: Malcolm Goble. **Open:** Mon to Fri L 12 to
2.30, D 6 to 9.30 (10 Fri), Sat and Sun 12 to 10 (9
Sun). **Meals:** alc (main courses £16 to £29). Set L

£19.50 (2 courses) to £23. **Service:** 10% for parties of 7 or more. **Details:** 58 seats. 40 seats outside. Wheelchair access. Music. Car parking.

Singleton
The Partridge Inn
A satisfying foodie package
Grove Road, Singleton, PO18 0EY
Tel no: (01243) 811251
www.thepartridgeinn.co.uk
British | £25
Cooking score: 1

Owned by Giles and Ruth Thompson from the auspicious Earl of March in nearby Lavant (see entry), this friendly South Downs boozer also aims to please – although its intentions are much more pubby. The kitchen takes an open-minded approach to things, offering deep-fried whitebait, O'Hagan's sausages and 'sizzling steaks' alongside tomato and herb bruschetta, macaroni cheese and pan-fried sea bream with wilted spinach and creamed leeks. Lunchtime sarnies, Sunday roasts and blackboard specials complete a satisfying foodie package, while drinkers can sup Sussex real ales or workmanlike wines (from £15.50). **Chef/s:** Achim Klein. **Open:** all week L 12 to 2 (3 Sat and Sun), D 6 to 9 (9.30 Sat). **Meals:** alc (main courses £13 to £20). **Service:** not inc. **Details:** 65 seats. 90 seats outside. Separate bar. Wheelchair access. Music. Car parking.

Tangmere
Cassons
A love of all things French
Arundel Road, Tangmere, PO18 0DU
Tel no: (01243) 773294
www.cassonsrestaurant.co.uk
Anglo-French | £39
Cooking score: 2

Vivian and 'Cass' Casson will soon be gearing up to celebrate their first decade at this country restaurant not far from Goodwood and Chichester. A love of all things French

underpins their 'excellent-value' menus, although they also pay their respects to indigenous British ingredients: witness a warm mackerel and Bayonne ham 'sandwich' with lemon gel, or venison fillet with cauliflower and Parmesan purée, black pudding, wild mushrooms, Parmentier potatoes and truffle jus. Some reports suggest that the kitchen over-eggs its dishes and falls down on the details, but desserts always finish strongly – perhaps peanut butter mousse with caramelised bananas, banana sherbet and caramel sauce. Well-chosen wines from £20. **Chef/s:** Vivian Casson. **Open:** Wed to Sun L 12 to 2, Tue to Sat D 7 to 10. **Closed:** Mon, 26 to 30 Dec. **Meals:** Set L £15 (2 courses) to £20. Set D weekdays £24 (2 courses) to £31. Set D weekends £31 (2 courses) to £39. Sun L £22.50 (2 courses) to £28. **Service:** not inc. **Details:** 36 seats. 16 seats outside. Separate bar. Wheelchair access. Music. Car parking.

Trotton
The Keepers Arms
Appealing ancient hostelry
Terwick Lane, Trotton, GU31 5ER
Tel no: (01730) 813724
www.keepersarms.co.uk
Modern British | £25
Cooking score: 1

A cottage façade and backdrop of stunning countryside add to this ancient hostelry's appeal. Although still a pub (especially when the sun shines and the garden comes into its own), this is also a forward-looking restaurant with a liking for seasonal produce. Look for ham hock rillettes with a burnt chilli and courgette salad, and roasted belly and braised shoulder of pork with celeriac dauphinois, then local ice creams or salted peanut parfait with caramelised bananas. Wines from £17. **Chef/s:** Sharon McGrath. **Open:** all week L 12 to 2.30 (11 to 4 Sun), Mon to Sat D 6 to 10. **Meals:** alc (main courses £9 to £24). Sun L £13.50. **Service:** not inc. **Details:** 50 seats. 40 seats outside. Separate bar. Wheelchair access. Music. Car parking.

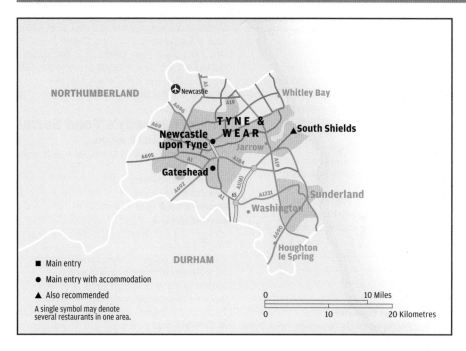

- ■ Main entry
- ● Main entry with accommodation
- ▲ Also recommended

A single symbol may denote
several restaurants in one area.

■ Gateshead
Eslington Villa
Dependable cooking and a caring heart
8 Station Road, Low Fell, Gateshead, NE9 6DR
Tel no: (0191) 4876017
www.eslingtonvilla.co.uk
Modern British | £25
Cooking score: 2

'We stayed here for two nights, and found the hotel very personal and friendly', noted visitors to Nick and Melanie Tulip's Victorian villa. Part of the attraction is that you can eat in the dining room or in the conservatory overlooking the gardens; chef Jamie Walsh's cooking is also solidly dependable. Lunch and early-bird menus offer crowd-pleasers such as spiced chicken, fennel and watercress salad, moules marinière with skinny chips and sticky toffee pudding with toffee sauce. Dinner sees more ambitious dishes, say pork tenderloin with haggis, potato cake and leeks with red wine jus. Wines from £17.50.

Chef/s: Jamie Walsh. **Open:** all week L 12 to 3 (4 Sun), D 5.30 to 10 (6.30 to 10 Sat, 9 Sun). **Closed:** 25 and 26 Dec. **Meals:** Set L £13.95 (2 courses) to £16.95. Set D £20.95 (2 courses) to £24.95. Sun L £19.75. **Service:** not inc. **Details:** 85 seats. 20 seats outside. Separate bar. Wheelchair access. Music. Car parking.

■ Newcastle upon Tyne
Blackfriars Restaurant
Modern food where medieval monks dined
Friars Street, Newcastle upon Tyne, NE1 4XN
Tel no: (0191) 2615945
www.blackfriarsrestaurant.co.uk
British | £30
Cooking score: 3

£5
OFF

A reliable fixture on the Newcastle dining scene, this relaxed, bistro-style restaurant scores with its easy-going attitude, good food and 'the best historical city-centre location' – in the former refectory of a Dominican priory dating from 1239. The cooking takes its cue

from Britain's regional larder. Ingredients are given forthright modern treatments, say steamed mussels and clams with dry vermouth, garlic and tarragon, or wild mushroom pancake with Mordon blue cheese and walnut dressing. The signature fishcakes and duck egg with black pudding and homemade brown sauce feature in starter or main course sizes. Braised beef shin with glazed carrots, red cabbage and horseradish mash makes a gutsy main course. For pudding you might consider lemon and vanilla tart. Wines start at £16.50.
Chef/s: Troy Terrington. **Open:** all week L 12 to 3 (4 Sun), Mon to Sat D 5.30 to 10. **Closed:** 25 and 26 Dec, bank hols. **Meals:** alc (main courses £9 to £21). Set L, D and Sun L £12 (2 courses) to £15. **Service:** 10%. **Details:** 72 seats. 24 seats outside. Music.

Café 21
Stylish quayside favourite
Trinity Gardens, Quayside, Newcastle upon Tyne, NE1 2HH
Tel no: (0191) 2220755
www.cafetwentyone.co.uk
Modern British | £38
Cooking score: 3

V

Local food-hero Terence Laybourne's stylish quayside brasserie remains a favourite with the city's foodie crowd. They love the dynamism of the place, the sharp service, the easy-going, metropolitan approach and the kitchen's impressively stamped culinary passport. Its fancy-free, border-hopping sorties might yield various French 'café salads', Asian spiced belly pork with pak choi and fragrant rice, fresh crab lasagne or braised monkfish with pipérade and chorizo, as well as plates of Lindisfarne oysters, Northumbrian pheasant terrine and fishcakes with parsley cream and chips. After that, knickerbocker glory or hot lemon curd soufflé might hit the spot for a fun-loving finale. The carefully assembled wine list offers an admirable selection by the glass or carafe; bottle prices start at £16.95.

Chef/s: Chris Dobson. **Open:** all week L 12 to 2.30 (3 Sun), D 5.30 to 10.30 (9.30 Sun). **Closed:** 25 and 26 Dec, 1 Jan, Easter Mon. **Meals:** alc (main courses £16 to £30). Set L and D £16.50 (2 courses) to £20. Sun L £22. **Service:** 10%. **Details:** 128 seats. Separate bar. Wheelchair access. Music.

David Kennedy's Food Social
Prime food to suit all pockets
Biscuit Factory, Stoddart Street, Newcastle upon Tyne, NE2 1AN
Tel no: (0191) 2605411
www.foodsocial.co.uk
Modern British | £25
Cooking score: 4

As the name suggests, there is something very sociable about eating here. The spacious dining room with its bare brick walls and wooden floor blends well with the Biscuit Factory (the largest commercial art emporium in the UK). Service is brisk and friendly, and there is a menu to suit all pockets: 'social nibbles' (a take on Spanish tapas), early evening set menu and a fuller à la carte (also reasonably priced). Andrew Wilkinson cooks in a straightforward manner, but there is more to his technique than meets the eye. At a test meal, tempura of king prawns with chilli jam and coriander was a good curtain-raiser. This was followed by rump of lamb, crushed heritage potatoes, foraged greens and thyme, and the meal finished with a properly wobbly vanilla pannacotta with rhubarb and sablé biscuit. There are no unnecessary flourishes here. Wines from £13.95. David Kennedy has also opened River Café, 51 Bell Street, Fish Quay, North Shields; tel: (0191) 2966168.
Chef/s: David Kennedy and Andrew Wilkinson. **Open:** all week L 12 to 2 (3 Sat and Sun), Mon to Sat D 6 to 9 (10 Sat). **Closed:** 25 and 26 Dec, 1 and 2 Jan. **Meals:** alc (main courses £12 to £15). Set L £10 (2 courses) to £12.95. Set D £12.95 (2 courses) to £15. Sun L £9.95. **Service:** 10%. **Details:** 80 seats. 25 seats outside. Separate bar. Wheelchair access. Music. Car parking.

Jesmond Dene House
Refined twirls and no-holds-barred flavours
Jesmond Dene Road, Newcastle upon Tyne,
NE2 2EY
Tel no: (0191) 2123000
www.jesmonddenehouse.co.uk
Modern European | £51
Cooking score: 5

As close to a self-appointed 'country house in
the city' as you could imagine, Jesmond Dene
is a grandiose Arts and Crafts mansion
overlooking the sylvan expanses of the
landscaped park after which it is named.
Newcastle's beating heart is within easy reach
– although it might seem a world away.
Following a lavish conversion, contemporary
fabrics and design flourishes now sit cheek-by-
jowl with stolid stonework and heavy
panelling, while the sedate dining room opens
into a pretty conservatory overlooking the
gardens. North Country ingredients are given
a refined twirl in the kitchen, and many dishes
come prettily embroidered with tiny flowers
and herbs (check out grower Ken Holland's
organic vegetable salad pointed up with sorrel
emulsion). Elsewhere, there is a fondness for
no-holds-barred flavours (Northumbrian
corned beef hash with homemade ketchup and
truffled egg) as well as precise modern
detailing (a loin of veal with parsley root,
grapes, walnuts and watercress, for example).
Named fishermen also get in on the act –
Robert Latimer's wild turbot might be served
with Périgord truffle, Swiss chard and local
chanterelles – while desserts venture into the
tricksy world of iced lemon and honey parfait
with honeycomb, lemon sponge and parsnip
ice cream. A commendable selection of wines
by the glass or carafe head up the
knowledgeably chosen, quality-driven wine
list. Bottles start at £18.
Chef/s: Michael Penaluna. **Open:** all week L 12 to 2
(12.30 to 2 Sat, 12.30 to 3.15 Sun), D 7 to 9.30 (6.30
to 10 Fri and Sat). **Meals:** alc (main courses £16 to
£35). Set L £16.95 (2 courses) to £22.95. Set D and
Sun L £25 (2 courses) to £28. Tasting menu £55. Bar
menu available. **Service:** 10%. **Details:** 70 seats. 28
seats outside. Separate bar. Wheelchair access.
Music. Car parking.

Pan Haggerty
Suave city eatery with ambitious food
21 Queen Street, Newcastle upon Tyne, NE1 3UG
Tel no: (0191) 2210904
www.panhaggerty.com
Modern British | £35
Cooking score: 2
£5 OFF

The high-ceilinged dining room is awash
with natural light and accented with deep red
walls, exposed brickwork and wood, and
there is a casual neighbourhood vibe. It's a
British bistro of sorts, a speciality is pan
haggerty (a Northumberland dish of potatoes,
onions and cheese), but on the whole the
cooking fuses some very English ingredients
with Italian and French culinary traditions.
The result is very effective: Alnwick pigeon
breast Kiev with confit leg and white onion
purée to start, then fillet of sea trout with
pumpkin and Parmesan gnocchi and salsa
verde, while sweet things could include white
chocolate and cherry fondant. Wines
from £16.50.
Chef/s: Kelvin Linstead. **Open:** all week L 12 to 2.30
(2 Sat, 3.30 Sun), Mon to Sat D 5.30 to 9.30 (5 Sat).
Closed: 25 and 26 Dec, bank hols. **Meals:** alc (main
courses £14 to £21). Set L and D £14.95 (2 courses)
to £17.95. **Service:** 10%. **Details:** 65 seats. Music.

ALSO RECOMMENDED
▲ Caffè Vivo
29 Broad Chare, Newcastle upon Tyne, NE1 3DQ
Tel no: (0191) 2321331
www.caffevivo.co.uk
Italian

Terence Laybourne's all-day eatery stands next
to Newcastle's Live Theatre and is a boon for
cast and audience alike. It's a smart-casual kind
of place with a light, stylish look and a menu
dedicated to straightforward Italian cooking.
Alongside standard fare of seafood fritto misto
(£7.50) and rigatoni with Italian sausage

(£12.50), there are more interesting options: spaghetti with 'prawn meatballs' and shellfish sauce, say, and venison with Parmesan-mascarpone polenta and wild mushrooms. Wines from £15.95. Closed Sun and Mon.

▲ Sky Apple Café
182 Heaton Road, Heaton, Newcastle upon Tyne, NE6 5HP
Tel no: (0191) 2092571
www.skyapple.co.uk
Vegetarian

Totally unpretentious surroundings and good vegetarian food at reasonable prices guarantee regular full houses at this Heaton favourite. It's a bubbly, elbow-to-elbow place, family-friendly and serving everything from cups of coffee to huge vegetarian breakfasts (£5.60) and lunches of salads, sandwiches and curries. Evening menus follow the seasons, with crowd-pleasers running from artichoke and onion tart (£5.50) via steamed leek and goats' cheese pudding (£8.80) to lemon meringue pie. House wine is £10. Closed D Sun and Mon.

∎ North Shields

READERS RECOMMEND
Irvins Brasserie
Modern British
Union Road, The Fish Quay, North Shields, NE30 1HJ
Tel no: (0191) 2963238
www.irvinsbrasserie.co.uk
'I like the relaxed atmosphere, the space, the fact that you can have most dishes as a starter or a main course...but mostly...I like the food'

▮▮ Readers Recommend
A 'readers recommend' review is a genuine quote from a report sent in by one of our readers. We intend to follow up these suggestions throughout the year to come.

∎ South Shields

ALSO RECOMMENDED
▲ Colmans
182-186 Ocean Road, South Shields, NE33 2JQ
Tel no: (0191) 4561202
www.colmansfishandchips.com
Seafood £5 OFF

Expect a 'friendly, smiling welcome' at this smart fish and chip restaurant, plus details of when and where your fish was caught. For all its simple modern styling, Colmans is a venerable institution, having passed through five generations of the same family. 'Highest quality' fish and chips remain the mainstay – pollack and chips (£7.95) is a typical offering, but there are also specials such as scampi (£9.95), calamari (£12.95) or Dover sole. International wines start at £12.95. Open all week.

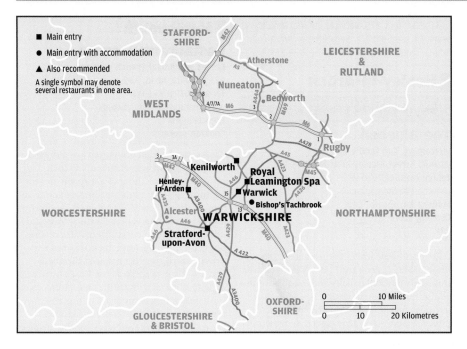

■ Bishop's Tachbrook

Mallory Court, Main Dining Room

Pedigree package for country house fans
Harbury Lane, Bishop's Tachbrook, CV33 9QB
Tel no: (01926) 330214
www.mallory.co.uk
Modern British | £60
Cooking score: 5

£5 OFF ☐ V

A pedigree package for fans of the full-dress country manor experience, Mallory Court remains an independent house of distinction – just look at the alluring terraces, trademark topiary and immaculately landscaped gardens surrounding this Lutyens-style mansion. Inside, aristocratic elegance reigns supreme – especially in the swish panelled dining room, with its mullioned windows, drapes and tapestry carpets. Long-serving chef Simon Haigh matches the august backdrop with cooking that rejects luxurious overkill in favour of seasonality and sharp contemporary ideas – perhaps a ballottine of rabbit with carrots, brown beech and violet mustard ice cream, or gurnard fillet with chorizo, squid and soy-tinged poultry jus. Readers have also relished humbler, more robust dishes, from chicken, leek and prune terrine with a vibrant salad of pickled vegetables to a punchy plate of pigeon breast, served pink with 'fall-apart' ox cheek, red cabbage and tiny mushrooms, or a duo of pork with parsnip purée, apples and sage-scented jus. When it comes to dessert, the kitchen lets rip, serving rhubarb and yoghurt cannelloni with pistachio crumble and advocaat ice cream, or reinventing lemon meringue pie with a dressing of pine-nut butter. Guests also appreciate the finer points, from aperitifs and canapés in the library to coffee with a multitude of petits fours. Wines from nearby Welcombe Hills Vineyard open the wide-ranging list; prices from £21.
Chef/s: Simon Haigh and Andrew Scott. **Open:** Sun to Fri L 12 to 1.30, all week D 6.30 to 9. **Meals:** Set L £27.50 (2 courses) to £32.50. Set D £45 (2 courses)

to £59.50. Sun L £35. **Service:** not inc. **Details:** 60 seats. 24 seats outside. Separate bar. Wheelchair access. Music. Car parking.

Henley-in-Arden

★ READERS' RESTAURANT OF THE YEAR ★
MIDLANDS

The Bluebell
Welcoming, fun foodie inn
93 High Street, Henley-in-Arden, B95 5AT
Tel no: (01564) 793049
www.bluebellhenley.co.uk
Modern European | £28
Cooking score: 3

'Warm and welcoming atmosphere . . . service impeccable . . . great fun'. That is the feel that this richly decorated, half-timbered Tudor inn engineers without appearing to try. Reporters have also been quick to sing the praises of Simon Malin – Guide readers may remember him from his time at Malbec in Stratford-on-Avon. He has taken charge of the kitchen and his cooking suits the mood: simple, familiar and as ambitious as it needs to be, whether coarse country pâté with Cumberland sauce, a 'delicious and very generous' tian of Cornish crab, with avocado and red pepper coulis or a 'full of flavour' Warwickshire lamb and pearl barley pie ('with a scrumptious suet crust'). For dessert, homemade ice creams (especially an 'unusual' nutmeg) and crème brûlée are particular delights. Wines from £15.50.
Chef/s: Simon Malin. **Open:** Tue to Sun L 12 to 2.30 (3.30 Sun), Tue to Sat D 6 to 9.30. **Closed:** Mon. **Meals:** alc (main courses £13 to £19). Set L and D £15 (2 courses) to £18. Sun L £13.75. **Service:** not inc. **Details:** 50 seats. 50 seats outside. Separate bar. Wheelchair access. Music. Car parking.

Kenilworth

Restaurant Bosquet
Earthy provincial French cuisine
97a Warwick Road, Kenilworth, CV8 1HP
Tel no: (01926) 852463
www.restaurantbosquet.co.uk
French | £40
Cooking score: 3

The warm-hearted domesticity of Bernard and Jane Lignier's determinedly French restaurant is something of a surprise on a busy Leamington thoroughfare, but step inside and you are immediately in a cosseted, comforting world of silk drapes, pretty prints, treasured knick-knacks and curios. Bernard's cooking respects ingredients and the kind of earthy provincial cuisine that inspired Elizabeth David – be it sweetbreads and pig's trotter on asparagus purée with truffle sauce, loin of veal with wild mushrooms or a traditionally glazed tarte au citron. Occasionally the kitchen breaks free from the old ways, as in a pairing of belly pork and lobster on celeriac and horseradish purée with a sauce of sweet wine and grapefruit, but it's not about to ruffle any feathers. The modest wine list also keeps its feet firmly on French soil, with prices from £18.50.
Chef/s: Bernard Lignier. **Open:** Tue to Fri L 12 to 1.15 (bookings only), Tue to Sat D 7 to 9.30. **Closed:** Sun, Mon, 1 week Christmas, 2 weeks Jul/Aug. **Meals:** alc (main courses £21 to £23). Set L and D Tue to Fri £32.50. **Service:** not inc. **Details:** 26 seats. No music.

Leamington Spa

Restaurant 23

Cooking that fizzes with bright ideas
34 Hamilton Terrace, Leamington Spa, CV32 4LY
Tel no: (01926) 422422
www.restaurant23.co.uk
Modern European | £39
Cooking score: 4

£5
OFF

This new incarnation of Restaurant 23 –
following the unabated success of the original
in Dormer Place – is a 'stunning' affair. The
open kitchen that put Peter Knibb centre stage
has been lost, but the ambitious new setting
speaks volumes for his intentions. Overblown
light fixtures and centrepiece wine displays
blend surprisingly well with the towering
pillars and ornate architraves of the listed
Victorian building. But there's substance as
well as style, thanks to contemporary cooking
that fizzes and pops with bright ideas. Set
menus are startlingly good value: crisp parcels
of rabbit confit perched on white beans and
chorizo, or salmon ravioli napped with bisque
and onion jam are both intricate enough to
belie such kind pricing. Ingredients, too, are
out of the top drawer – navarin of Lighthorne
lamb and turnips, for example, or Blythburgh
pork loin with sage gnocchi both showcase
British meat. However, over-smoked apple
purée or unpeeled carrots reflect a brigade in
transition. Service perched precisely between
friendly and formal. The French-led wine list
starts at £19.90.
Chef/s: Peter Knibb. **Open:** all week L 12 to 2 (3
Sun), Mon to Sat D 6.15 to 9.30. **Closed:** 25 and 26
Dec, 1 Jan. **Meals:** alc (main courses £17 to £26). Set
L £14.50 (2 courses) to £16.95. Set D £25. Sun L £25.
Service: 12.5%. **Details:** 64 seats. 30 seats outside.
Separate bar. Music. No children after 7.

LET THEM EAT STEAK

Whilst it's no surprise that the recession has
heralded a trend for thrift and the arrival of
discount dining cards, the rising popularity
of steak houses would have been much
harder to predict. According to Richard
Turner, executive chef at **Hawksmoor** in
London, 'during a recession, diners want
to eat something familiar, something
they remember from childhood.' Turner
should know - Hawksmoor has opened
three sites in five years, serving 35-day
aged prime cuts at around £30 a pop to
an appreciative audience. 'People may be
spending £50 or £60 a head,' he says, 'but
they come away feeling full and happy.'

In the Midlands, Andreas Antona, chef-
patron of **Simpson's**, has tapped in
to the nostalgia for a good steak in
simple surroundings by opening Beef in
Kenilworth. Here you'll find cuts from
British rump to South American Wagyu
sirloin, all served with double-cooked beef
dripping chips. French chain Le Relais de
Venise has opened a fourth UK branch in
Manchester. The no-choice menu, which
includes a green salad and steak frites for
£21, keeps prices low and demand high,
while the no-bookings policy often sees
diners queuing out the door.

Stratford-upon-Avon

No 9 Church St

Skilful cooking at very fair prices
9 Church Street, Stratford-upon-Avon, CV37 6HB
Tel no: (01789) 415522
www.no9churchst.com
Modern British | £30
Cooking score: 1
£5 OFF

A quaint listed building in Stratford's old town, this local favourite is a regular hit with tourists, shoppers and Bard worshippers looking for skilful cooking at very fair prices. Recent successes from the lively evening menu have included char-grilled squid with sea vegetables on bulgur wheat salad, wholesome braised pig's cheeks with grilled black pudding and apples, and a cute pairing of îles flottantes with Pimm's and strawberry jelly. Set lunches and pre-theatre suppers are a snip, and the concise wine list promises decent drinking from £14.50.
Chef/s: Wayne Thomson. **Open:** all week L 12 to 2 (3.30 Sun), Mon to Sat D 5 to 9.30. **Closed:** 25 to 28 Dec, bank hols. **Meals:** alc (main courses £12 to £21). Set L and pre-theatre D £12.50 (2 courses) to £16.50. Sun L £18.95. **Service:** not inc. **Details:** 40 seats. Separate bar. Music.

ALSO RECOMMENDED

▲ The Rooftop Restaurant

The Royal Shakespeare Theatre, Waterside,
Stratford-upon-Avon, CV37 6BE
Tel no: (01789) 403449
www.rsc.org.uk
British

A year after opening, the dramatic wraparound eatery/bar above the Royal Shakespeare Theatre has attracted a few 'slings and arrows'. The operation is geared for the theatre crowd; at other times diners report 'zilch atmosphere' and 'poor service'. At its best, dishes such as scallop and confit duck with lentils (£7.95) and a classic sole véronique (£17.50) are 'still good' and the set lunch and early-bird dinner (4.30–6.15) are good value at £15.50 for 2 courses and £18.50 for 3. Closed Sun D.

Warwick

Tailors

Dynamic duo's ritzy, glory-stealing food
22 Market Place, Warwick, CV34 4SL
Tel no: (01926) 410590
www.tailorsrestaurant.co.uk
Modern British | £35
Cooking score: 3
£5 OFF **V**

Culinary sidekicks Dan Cavell and Mark Fry are making quite an impact at this converted tailor's shop shoehorned into Warwick's market square. 'Entertaining' service plays its part, but their ritzy, highly embellished food steals most of the glory – think confit rabbit and butternut squash cannelloni with date purée, onion foam and garlic crisps. They also indulge in some playful trickery, adding pineapple foam and liquorice to their take on smoked salmon and scrambled eggs, matching 'Cheddar cheese spaghetti' with fig and almond bolognese, and reinventing sole véronique with a little help from salted grapes and grape jelly; also check out their marrowfat pea 'custard'. On safer ground, rump steak with chunky chips is regularly applauded, likewise Parma ham with marinated beetroot and creamed goats' cheese. Desserts dip into the past for 'Black Forest' or 'Jammie Dodger'. House wines start at £16.50.
Chef/s: Dan Cavell and Mark Fry. **Open:** Tue to Sat L 12 to 2, D 6.30 to 9.30. **Closed:** Sun, Mon, 25 to 31 Dec. **Meals:** Set L £12.95 (2 courses) to £16.90. Set D £29.50 (2 courses) to £34.50. **Service:** not inc. **Details:** 28 seats. Music.

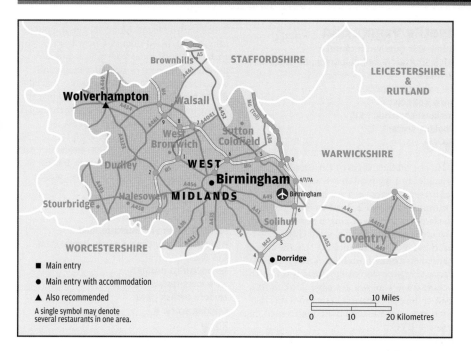

STAFFORDSHIRE

Brownhills

LEICESTERSHIRE
&
RUTLAND

Wolverhampton

Walsall

West
Bromwich

Sutton
Coldfield

WARWICKSHIRE

Dudley

WEST

Birmingham

MIDLANDS

Birmingham

Halesowen

Stourbridge

Solihull

Coventry

WORCESTERSHIRE

Dorridge

■ Main entry

● Main entry with accommodation

▲ Also recommended

A single symbol may denote
several restaurants in one area.

| 0 | | 10 Miles |
| 0 | 10 | 20 Kilometres |

Birmingham

NEW ENTRY

The Asquith and Ginger's Bar

Accomplished, affordable cooking with sizzle
11 Newhall Street, Birmingham, B3 3NY
Tel no: (0121) 2001588
www.theasquith.com
Modern French | £30
Cooking score: 4

Just round the corner from his flagship
Purnell's (see entry) in Birmingham's financial
district, Glynn Purnell's second restaurant is a
vibrant mix of slick, spacious cocktail bar and
more understated restaurant tucked behind.
Although the dining room is 'nothing to get
excited about', it's the accomplished,
affordable cooking that grabs the attention.
There's 'a real sense of sizzle' to the cooking,
and while dishes such as a crispy egg bathed in
gooey cheese on toast foam may hint at
trademark Purnell humour, the kitchen's real
strength lies in making familiar dishes special

while keeping the final bill in check. Witness
the delicate quail and sweetcorn ballottine
made lively by chorizo nuggets and crunchy
hazelnuts, or braised lamb shoulder and pink
slices of rump, carrot dauphinoise and little
spikes of coriander shoots, then caramelised
banana and chocolate mousse with banana
sorbet. Engaging staff match the informal
premises, as do affordable wines (from
£15.95).
Chef/s: Jason Eaves. **Open:** Tue to Sat L 12 to 1.45, D
6.30 to 9. **Closed:** Sun, Mon, Christmas to early Jan
(excl 31 Dec), 1 week Aug. **Meals:** alc (main course
£13 to £20). Set L £14.99 (2 courses) to £19.99.
Tasting menu £42.95 (5 courses). **Service:** 12.5%.
Details: 40 seats. Separate bar. Wheelchair access.
Music.

Visit us
Online

To find out more about
The Good Food Guide, please visit
www.thegoodfoodguide.co.uk

Jyoti's Vegetarian

Admirable family-run canteen
1045 Stratford Road, Hall Green, Birmingham,
B28 8AS
Tel no: (0121) 7785501
www.jyotis.co.uk
Indian/Vegetarian | £15
Cooking score: 1

V

It may be on the fringes of Birmingham's 'balti triangle', but the food in this admirable family-run canteen is a world away from Brummie clichés. The kitchen is overseen by the ladies of the house, and the menu promises a selection of potently flavoured Gujarati street snacks at rock-bottom prices – try the crisp pani puri, steamed patra leaves, deep-fried cassava chips or aloo tikki. Dosas and assorted veggie curries are also available: look for the best-selling potato version served with crisp fried breads and mango pulp. Unlicensed, but you can BYO wine.
Chef/s: Harsha and Bhavna Joshi. **Open:** all week 12.30 to 9 (7 Sun). **Closed:** 25 and 26 Dec, 1 to 4 Jan. **Meals:** alc (main courses £6 to £13). Set L and D £13. **Service:** not inc. **Details:** 40 seats. Wheelchair access. Music.

Lasan

Stylish Indian eatery
3-4 Dakota Buildings, James Street, St Paul's Square, Birmingham, B3 1SD
Tel no: (0121) 2123664
www.lasan.co.uk
Indian | £47
Cooking score: 3

 V

The menu in this stylish Indian restaurant sensibly straddles familiar favourites such as onion bhajia or chicken jalfrezi and lesser-known dishes, ranging from nali nihari (a traditional Awadhi-style dish of slow-cooked lamb shank in smooth onion and bone-marrow gravy flavoured with curd, mace and elephant cardamom) to modern creations such as 'delicious, flavourful' konkan kekada (soft shell crab dipped in crispy ajwain and chilli

batter with a Devonshire crab, pea and potato cake) or pan-fried fillet of Cornish sea bass on garlic-scented tender leaf spinach and new potatoes simmered in Bengali tomato and coriander-scented broth. Appealing vegetable dishes include sweet potato kofta and baigan ka bartha (north Indian smoked aubergine). A snappy wine list kicks off at £16.50.
Chef/s: Aktar Islam. **Open:** Sun to Fri L 12 to 2.30, all week D 6 to 11. **Closed:** 25 Dec. **Meals:** alc (main courses £13 to £26). **Service:** not inc. **Details:** 64 seats. Separate bar. Wheelchair access. Music.

Loves

Intimate vibes and intricate food
Browning Street, Canal Square, Birmingham, B16 8FL
Tel no: (0121) 4545151
www.loves-restaurant.co.uk
Modern British | £42
Cooking score: 4

 V

With its unassuming frontage, smoked glass and chocolate-toned wallpaper, Steve and Claire Love's restaurant keeps a low profile, but there's no denying its personable vibe or seriously accomplished cooking. A regularly endorsed starter of yellowfin tuna with feta and beetroot in various forms rightly deserves its 'signature' status, but Steve's kitchen has also produced a host of intricate, thoughtful dishes with lots of 'feel-good touches': braised pig's head with crispy pig's ear, pickled mussels, apple and black pudding crumb; a sharing dish of Herefordshire 'centre ribeye' with pickled carrots, Paris mushrooms and béarnaise sauce, and some brilliant veggie offerings. Elsewhere, banana and lime sorbet with pork scratchings should raise a smile, while desserts have included a 'fabulous' medley of chocolate and superbly crafted white rum cake with coconut, lime curd and palm-sugar ice cream. 'Utterly charming' Claire Love is the brains and passion behind the thrilling, hand-picked wine list – a compendium of innovative and revelatory stuff from some of the planet's most forward-looking producers. House recommendations start at £20 (£5 a glass).

The only downside appears to be a rather tricky, hard-to-find location, five minutes' walk from trendy Brindleyplace.
Chef/s: Steve Love. **Open:** Fri and Sat L 12 to 2, Tue to Sat D 7 to 9.30 (6.30 Fri and Sat). **Closed:** Sun, Mon, 2 weeks Jan, 2 weeks Aug/Sept. **Meals:** Set L and midweek D £20 (2 courses) to £25. Set D £38 (2 courses) to £42. Tasting menu £68 (8 courses). **Service:** 10%. **Details:** 44 seats. 16 seats outside. Separate bar. Wheelchair access. Music. Children over 8 yrs only at D.

Opus

Welcoming city brasserie
54 Cornwall Street, Birmingham, B3 2DE
Tel no: (0121) 2002323
www.opusrestaurant.co.uk
Modern British | £37
Cooking score: 2

Butch and brash it may be, but Opus' sprawling, red-walled interior also feels comfortable, with a warm buzz that never tips into boisterousness. Readers report being 'made to feel very welcome' by engaging service, and heap praise on a bargain three-course market menu (wine and coffee included), which might yield chicken liver parfait with crab apple jelly, braised pork collar with carrot purée, mash and cider cream sauce, then rhubarb pannacotta. The à la carte pricing can seem steep, with few mains below £20, but the quality of Fingask Farm beef fillet, Balmoral venison or Cornish monkfish represents good value, and wines starting at £16.50 soften the blow.
Chef/s: David Colcombe. **Open:** Mon to Fri L 12 to 2, Mon to Sat D 6 to 9.30. **Closed:** Sun, 24 Dec to 8 Jan, bank hols. **Meals:** alc (main courses £16 to £38). Set L and D £24.50. **Service:** 12.5%. **Details:** 80 seats. Separate bar. Wheelchair access.

★ TOP 50 ★

Purnell's

Intricate cooking with a sense of humour
55 Cornwall Street, Birmingham, B3 2DH
Tel no: (0121) 2129799
www.purnellsrestaurant.com
Modern British | £50
Cooking score: 6

Birmingham's premier restaurant this may be, but what really puts Purnell's on the culinary map is the way Glynn Purnell weaves his huge personality and unique sense of fun into his intricate, modern cooking. Humour is a constant, with goats' cheese bavarois and pineapple jelly on cocktail sticks as pure 1970s nostalgia, or smoked haddock foam and a single egg yolk sprinkled with curry oil and cornflakes in witty homage to the British breakfast. Japery aside, this is serious, complex cooking that rarely fails to delight — it may be amusing to coat a nugget of salt beef in Oxo granules and serve alongside slithers of raw fillet, charred tentacles of octopus and onion chutney, but it's also delicious. Elsewhere Birmingham's Indian heritage is referenced with poached monkfish and pickled carrots made punchy by lentils intense with lime, chilli and coriander, or a butternut squash soup re-energised through ginger, sesame and cubes of pickled feta. Come dessert and burnt English custard surprise is not only a lusciously smooth crème brûlée but, served in a plinth-mounted egg shell, visually arresting, too. The dining room is, in contrast, sombre and uncharacteristically restrained, and service hops from confused to compelling — for one reporter 'too starchy', another 'the antithesis of stuffy'. Wines from £22.95 balance French big-hitters against value-rich picks from around the world.
Chef/s: Glynn Purnell. **Open:** Tue to Fri L 12 to 1.30, Tue to Sat D 7 to 9. **Closed:** Sun, Mon, 24 Dec to first week Jan, 1 week Easter, first 2 weeks Aug. **Meals:** Set L £22 (2 courses) to £27. Set D £40 (2 courses) to £50. Tasting menu £80 (8 courses). **Service:** 12.5%. **Details:** 45 seats. Separate bar. Wheelchair access. Music. Children over 7 yrs only.

Saffron

Glitzy, creative Indian
909 Wolverhampton Road, Oldbury, Birmingham,
B69 4RR
Tel no: (0121) 5521752
www.saffron-online.co.uk
Indian | £20
Cooking score: 2

£5 OFF **V** £30

'Quality from the moment you walk through the door'enthuses one of Saffron's many fans. This glitzy, clean-cut Indian certainly knows how to impress with its bold, clubby interiors, 'starlit' ceiling and creative, 'beautifully seasoned' food. A signature starter of sea bass marinated in the golden spice shows the kitchen's intentions, likewise succulent rabbit varuval, kadhai lamb hyderabadi and a cheffy assemblage of spiced red mullet with chickpea and spinach gâteau, cumin and coriander-scented beurre blanc. Masala dosas and biryanis strike a more familiar note. Don't miss the poached pears with kheer (rice pudding) to finish. Attentive staff are up to the task, and there's a choice of great-value wines from £10.50.
Chef/s: Sudha Shankar Saha and Avijit Mondal.
Open: all week L 12 to 2.30, D 5.30 to 11. **Meals:** alc (main courses £8 to £20). **Service:** not inc.
Details: 92 seats. Wheelchair access. Music. Car parking.

Simpsons

Formidably accomplished suburban restaurant
20 Highfield Road, Edgbaston, Birmingham,
B15 3DU
Tel no: (0121) 4543434
www.simpsonsrestaurant.co.uk
Modern French | £49
Cooking score: 6

The refreshing setting in the suburb of Edgbaston is just one of the draws of Andreas Antona's formidably accomplished restaurant. Tables outside, surrounded by Greek landscaped gardens and waterfall art may not quite be what you're expecting amid the hustle

CASUAL DINING, INDIAN STYLE

As cash-strapped diners continue to embrace the trend for casual dining, the nation's Indian restaurants have been swift to respond. All-day menus, small plates, street food and cocktails are on offer at this new breed of eatery, without a tablecloth or plush banquette in sight.

London's **Dishoom** models itself on the Persian cafés popular in 1960s Bombay, where diners meet in its funky brasserie-style surroundings over Anglo-Indian breakfasts, salads, snacks and grills. At **Roti Chai** in London's West End, the ground-floor 'street kitchen' serves up samosas and buns from an open hatch in a room modelled on an Indian railway station. Brighton's **Chilli Pickle** offers a menu of thalis, street food and roti rolls in a setting that owes more to a hip urban canteen than a traditional curry house, while at **Guchhi** in Leith, sharing is encouraged with a lunchtime selection of seafood tapas and platters, Indian style.

According to Vivek Singh, the chef behind **Cinnamon Club**, 'there is so much more appreciation and awareness of Brand India that it was only a matter of time before it would translate into the casual dining sector.'

and bustle of Birmingham. This is a relaxing, expansive venue, though, stylishly designed with lots of natural light and a smart monochrome look in the dining room. The cooking, under executive chef Luke Tipping and his head chef Adam Bennett, delivers plenty of substantial flavour, often in delicately conceived packages. The overall impact of a three-course meal (there are seven-course tasting menus, too) was resoundingly positive. A pair who think nothing of the hour-and-a-quarter drive here began lunch with 'superbly moist and tender' venison carpaccio with salt-baked celeriac and mustard, before proceeding to equally impressive cod on yellow lentil dhal with cauliflower, coconut and coriander. Dinner menus might bring on halibut in seaweed butter with burnt cabbage heart and avruga caviar, followed perhaps by squab pigeon on toasted cracked wheat with roasted carrots and date and lemon purée. Stimulating flavour combinations distinguish desserts such as lemon tartlets served with cashews, honey mousse, mango sorbet and basil. A very old-school wine list features lots of serious French gear at three and four figures, and the base price for the rest is high; glasses start at £8, bottles north of £30. Beef Restaurant (it's business is steak) is a new opening from Simpson's owner Andreas Antona: 11 Warwick Road, Kenilworth, Warwickshire CV8 1HD; tel: (01926) 863311.

Chef/s: Luke Tipping. **Open:** all week L 12 to 2 (2.30 Sun), Mon to Sat D 7 to 9.30. **Closed:** 25 and 26 Dec, 1 Jan. **Meals:** alc (main courses £23 to £25). Set L £38. Tasting menu £85 (8 courses). **Service:** 12.5%. **Details:** 70 seats. 20 seats outside. No music. Wheelchair access. Car parking.

Turners

A truly joyous surprise
69 High Street, Harborne, Birmingham, B17 9NS
Tel no: (0121) 4264440
www.turnersrestaurantbirmingham.co.uk
Modern European | £60
Cooking score: 5

Its unpromising location in a suburban concrete shopping parade makes Turners, with its creative contemporary cooking, a truly joyous surprise. The mirrored room, all pressed cloths, high-backed velvet seating and plush pile, strikes a serious note, echoed by 'extremely formal' service ('almost standoffish'), but this culinary outpost can dazzle. An amuse-bouche of well-made Jerusalem artichoke velouté beneath hazelnut foam gives way to a treatment of rabbit and langoustine, which sees silky confit supporting bacon-wrapped loin and plump shellfish, their sweetness picked up by vanilla jelly and celeriac purée and tartly emphasised by slivers of pickled onion. Elsewhere, seasonality was deployed too early in a mid-March meal that saw peas, broad beans and morels make a bland addition to a dish of creamy sweetbreads and pink veal fillet. However, a generous pre-dessert of pannacotta, passion-fruit jelly and orange granita, and a faultless dessert of intense chocolate délice with caramel pannacotta and peanut ice cream more than made up for any inconsistencies. The eclectic wine list is sorted by varietal, with prices from £25.

Chef/s: Richard Turner. **Open:** Tue to Sat L 12 to 2, D 7 to 9.30. **Closed:** Sun, Mon. **Meals:** Set L £29.95 (2 courses) to £34.95. Set D £47.50 (2 courses) to £60. 'Taste of Turners' menu (Tue only) £30 (5 courses). Du Jour menu (Wed and Thur) £37.95 (5 courses). Tasting £75 (8 courses). **Service:** 12.5%. **Details:** 26 seats. Wheelchair access. Music. Car parking.

ALSO RECOMMENDED
▲ Bank

4 Brindleyplace, Birmingham, B1 2JB
Tel no: (0121) 6334466
www.bankrestaurants.com
Modern British £5 OFF

This very modern British brasserie is to be found in the stylish Brindleyplace complex, and it makes a good fist of being all things to all-comers through its revolving doors – whether it be chic cocktailers, plate-sharers, brunch trysters, or kids hanging out for pasta and toffee pudding. The principal menu serves up chilli squid on Thai noodles (£7.95), beef bourguignon (£17.95) and lemon crème brûlée with ginger shortbread (£6.50). Wines from £16.25 (£4.75 a glass). Open all week.

READERS RECOMMEND
Carters of Moseley

Modern British
2c Wake Green Road, Moseley, Birmingham, B13 9EZ
Tel no: (0121) 4498885
www.cartersofmoseley.co.uk
'The food was tremendous, the flavours and presentation wonderful, the atmosphere relaxed and unpretentious.'

▌Dorridge
The Forest

A beacon of hospitality
25 Station Approach, Dorridge, B93 8JA
Tel no: (01564) 772120
www.forest-hotel.com
Modern European | £28
Cooking score: 3

 £30

Once Dorridge's railway hotel, the Forest has maintained its role as beacon of hospitality into the twenty-first century in the capable hands of Gary and Tracy Perkins. An informal dining room with foliage-patterned décor and bare tables is the setting for some modern brasserie food; a goats' cheese soufflé with beetroot and walnuts might be followed by sea bass with a scallop, crisp oysters, fennel and cauliflower. Meat mains aim directly for the comfort zone with duck breast, chestnuts and truffled mash, or hare Wellington. Scotch rump steak comes with béarnaise and chips done in beef dripping. Pub-style classics and a kids' menu leave no bases uncovered, and neither does the dessert repertoire – try plum tarte Tatin with cinnamon ice cream. Wines open at £13.95.
Chef/s: Dean Grubb. Open: all week L 12 to 2.30 (3 Sun), Mon to Sat D 6.30 to 10. Closed: 25 Dec. Meals: alc (main courses £12 to £18). Set L and D £13.45 (2 courses) to £15.90. Sun L £14.95 (2 courses) to £17.95. Service: 10%. Details: 65 seats. 30 seats outside. Separate bar. Wheelchair access. Music. Car parking.

▌Wolverhampton
ALSO RECOMMENDED
▲ Bilash

2 Cheapside, Wolverhampton, WV1 1TU
Tel no: (01902) 427762
www.thebilash.co.uk
Indian

Diners are 'absolutely delighted' with Bilash's 'stunningly creative food' which looks to Indian home cooking for inspiration. It offers up classics like chicken biryani alongside the chef's inventions such as the Bilash super (a spin on chicken tikka masala). Start with maacher shami kebab (minced fish with herbs and spices, served with tamarind sauce, £6.50) followed by spicy lamb tikka hasina (£14.50) or – from an excellent selection of vegetarian mains – paneer chilli masala (£10.50). Wines start at £18. Closed Sun.

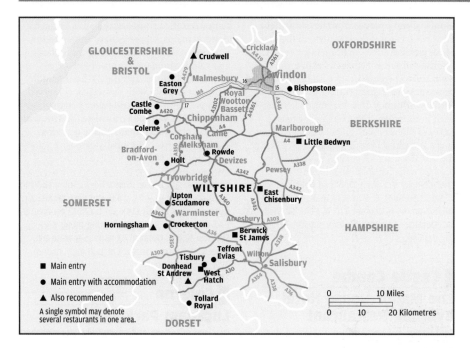

Main entry

● **Main entry with accommodation**

▲ **Also recommended**

A single symbol may denote several restaurants in one area.

▌Berwick St James
The Boot Inn
Appealing pub with home cooking
High Street, Berwick St James, SP3 4TN
Tel no: (01722) 790243
www.bootatberwick.co.uk
British | £24
Cooking score: 1

 £5 OFF £30

Tenacious travellers stopping off on their way to and from the West Country continue to sing the praises of Giles and Cathy Dickinson's appealing rural pub, with its bare tables and chalkboard menus offering unfussy home cooking. A reporter eating in winter was delighted by celeriac and wild mushroom soup, and steak with Gentleman's Relish. Others have enjoyed baked cod with brown shrimp butter and parsley mash, and marmalade bread-and-butter pudding with orange custard. Wines from £14.35.

Chef/s: Giles Dickinson. **Open:** Tue to Sun L 12 to 2.15 (2.30 Sun), Tue to Sat D 6.30 to 9.15 (9.30 Sat). **Closed:** Mon, 1 to 10 Feb. **Meals:** alc (main courses £10 to £16). Sun L 12.50 (2 courses) to £16.50. **Service:** not inc. **Details:** 35 seats. 25 seats outside. Wheelchair access. Music. Car parking.

▌Bishopstone
Helen Browning at the Royal Oak
Cheery organic pub-cum-B&B
Cues Lane, Bishopstone, SN6 8PP
Tel no: (01793) 790481
www.royaloakbishopstone.co.uk
British | £27
Cooking score: 3

£5 OFF 🛏 £30

A free Land Rover taxi service, live blues gigs, Arkell's ales and bartering deals on fruit and veg... just some of the prime assets at this cheerily revitalised pub-cum-B&B. Helen Browning is one of England's organic pioneers, and produce from her showpiece Eastbrook Farm is the star turn on the menu. Steak pies and cracking burgers get top marks, but the daily menu covers a lot of ground: from seared pigeon breast with home-pickled beetroot salad to roast squash and chickpea fritters with spicy dips, via soused herrings with horseradish crème fraîche, or roast gurnard fillets on saffron potatoes with fennel, curry and mussel broth. For afters, try one of the buffalo-milk ice creams. A zesty little organic wine list starts at £19.50.

Chef/s: Ricky McCowen. **Open:** all week L 12 to 2.30 (3 Sat, 3.30 Sun), D 6 to 9.30 (6.30 to 8 Sun). **Meals:** alc (main courses £10 to £24). **Service:** not inc. **Details:** 50 seats. 25 seats outside. No music. Car parking.

Castle Combe
The Manor House Hotel, Bybrook Restaurant
Real verve and versatility
Castle Combe, SN14 7HR
Tel no: (01249) 782206
www.manorhouse.co.uk
Modern British | £60
Cooking score: 5

Set amid the Cotswolds at their most smoothly contoured, the Manor House is the centrepiece of an unspoiled medieval village that looks, as Steven Spielberg commented when filming *War Horse* here, 'like Hollywood built it'. Dating back to the fourteenth century, the Manor is a handsome building that pushes all the right buttons inside, from wood panelling to mullioned windows and rapturous views over the gardens from the Bybrook dining room. Richard Davies has brought a real sense of verve to the menus here, drawing richly on local produce and happily rolling up his sleeves to help tend the hotel's own vegetable patches. His culinary style is versatile, bringing a touch of Mediterranean sun to starters such as Salcombe Bay crab tian with guacamole in gazpacho, and achieving resonant depth in the

famous truffled risotto with oyster beignet. Among mains, reporters have eulogised the roast sea bass that comes with spiced aubergine and celeriac fondant in a jus of sun-dried tomato and lemon, and the 24-hour Middle White pork belly with braised cheek, served with pak choi, lentils and sweet potato purée. To conclude, Valrhona chocolate fondant with salted caramel and crème fraîche ice cream slips down a treat. A globally extensive wine list starts at £24.50 for Sicilian white or Portuguese red.

Chef/s: Richard Davies. **Open:** Tue to Sun L 12.30 to 2, all week D 7 to 9 (9.30 Fri and Sat). **Meals:** alc (main courses £10 to £14). Set L £25 (2 courses) to £30. Set D £60. Sun L £35. Tasting menu £72. **Service:** 12.5%. **Details:** 70 seats. Separate bar. Wheelchair access. Music. Car parking. Children over 11 yrs at D only.

Colerne
Lucknam Park
Discreet grandeur and supremely accomplished food
Colerne, SN14 8AZ
Tel no: (01225) 742777
www.lucknampark.co.uk
Modern British | £70
Cooking score: 6

Cloth merchants, clothiers, coffee planters, Victorian philanthropists: the story of Lucknam's ownership down the centuries has been a colourful one. It has been a country hotel only since the 1980s, and is one of the less ostentatious of English Palladian mansions, although it lacks nothing in discreet grandeur. What is now the Park restaurant was once the ballroom, its fine views over the grounds framed by elaborately swagged drapes, but the ambience on a candlelit evening can be surprisingly intimate. Staff ensure everything runs seamlessly, as well they might, for Hywel Jones's supremely accomplished, innovative cooking brooks no distractions. There is a wealth of choice on the main carte, which might open with port-marinated duck liver with pickled cherries and hazelnut praline.

Main courses are constructed of elements that work together harmoniously and interestingly, but without the need to throw in unexpected ingredients: Cornish brill comes with smoked sausage, girolles and Puy lentils in red wine sauce; the Brecon venison from over the border arrives honour-guarded with butternut squash and chestnut cannelloni in a sloe gin sauce. Finish in classical style with raspberry feuillantine and vanilla cream. A wine list of transcendent opulence also has fair choice between £25 and £30.

Chef/s: Hywel Jones. **Open:** Sun L 12 to 2, Mon to Sat D 6 to 10. **Meals:** Set D £70 to £90. Sun L £39. **Service:** not inc. **Details:** 60 seats. No music. Wheelchair access. Car parking.

Crockerton

The Bath Arms
Popular pit-stop
Clay Street, Crockerton, BA12 8AJ
Tel no: (01985) 212262
www.batharmscrockerton.co.uk
Modern British | £25
Cooking score: 2
£5 OFF 🛏 £30

The crew behind this coaching inn certainly know what's required when it comes to feeding and watering Crockerton's locals and the droves of sightseeing families who descend on neighbouring Longleat. There's usually a welcoming fire, fine local ales including Crockerton Classic and 'buckets of chips' to go with everything from breaded plaice to grilled sirloin steak or even chicken nuggets. But it's not all run-of-the-mill pub grub: if you fancy testing the kitchen's mettle, order fillet of hake with crushed peas and pecorino or the best-selling 'sticky beef' with braised red cabbage. Puds are out of the chocolate brownie/apple crumble mould. Wines start at £15.95.
Chef/s: Dean Carr. **Open:** all week L 12 to 2, D 6.30 to 9. **Meals:** alc (main courses £12 to £16). **Service:** not inc. **Details:** 100 seats. 40 seats outside. Separate bar. Music. Car parking.

Crudwell

ALSO RECOMMENDED
▲ The Potting Shed
The Street, Crudwell, SN16 9EW
Tel no: (01666) 577833
www.thepottingshedpub.com
British

Formed from roadside cottages, this ancient pub has been tweaked for the twenty-first century and is a highly attractive prospect. The interior still has a sense of deep-rooted antiquity, but the cooking is thoroughly up-to-the-minute. Menus have a seasonal ring; a meal in February produced hand-picked crab and pomegranate rillettes with avocado mousse (£6.50), game sausages with colcannon and onion gravy (£13.95), jugged hare, and a trio of rhubarb with cinnamon biscuit for dessert. Wines from £15.50. Open all week.

Donhead St Andrew

ALSO RECOMMENDED
▲ The Forester
Lower Street, Donhead St Andrew, SP7 9EE
Tel no: (01747) 828038
www.theforesterdonheadstandrew.co.uk
Modern European

Chris and Lizzie Matthews' thatched, stone-built village pub does the local community proud. Menus deliver plenty of choice; crowd-pleasing dishes are backed up by good flavours from well-sourced ingredients. Crab soup with rouille and croûtons (£6) has been praised, followed perhaps by duck leg with mash, Savoy cabbage, wild mushrooms and mixed roast beetroots (£13), then lavender pannacotta with honeycomb, or artisan cheeses. Weekday lunch and dinner deals are a snip (from £15.50). Wines from £14.95. No food Sun D.

East Chisenbury

The Red Lion

Much more than your average freehouse
East Chisenbury, SN9 6AQ
Tel no: (01980) 671124
www.redlionfreehouse.com
Modern British | £32
Cooking score: 5

£5 OFF

Picture the scene: a wickedly pretty, immaculately thatched pub in a remote village on the fringes of Salisbury Plain's military wasteland. Pies and pints, you might think, but the Red Lion is much more than your average beer-fuelled freehouse. Yes, it has its quota of beams, open fires, local ales, lunchtime sarnies and even a pet dog called Stowford, but 'consistently extraordinary' cooking is what inspires crowds to programme their SatNavs. Guy and Brittany Manning came here with gold-plated CVs and have worked hard ever since: they bake breads, cure charcuterie, make condiments and even grow some stuff in their greenhouse. The result is a rolling repertoire of big, bold food with uncluttered flavours and emphatic cosmopolitan oomph. Consider their sought-after seasonal tasting menus: spring might herald lamb served two ways with confit cherry tomatoes, Jersey Royals and asparagus; summer could promise wild salmon (cooked rare) with bean cassoulet and nasturtium leaves, while the darker months invite plates of roast venison adorned with Jerusalem artichokes, pickled rhubarb and Roscoff onion. To finish, Brittany's training as a pastry chef under superstar Thomas Keller shows in, say, a voluptuous Valrhona chocolate crémeux with cocoa crumbs and crunchy fleur de sel. The 40-bin wine list (from £15) packs oodles of artisan class on to two sides of A4. And with luxury bedrooms now in place, you don't have to rush home.
Chef/s: Guy Manning. **Open:** all week L 12 to 2 (3 Sun), D 6 to 9 (8.30 Sun). **Meals:** alc (main courses £13 to £20). Sun L £18 (2 courses). **Service:** 12.5%. **Details:** 50 seats. 20 seats outside. Separate bar. Music. Car parking.

Easton Grey

★ TOP 50 ★

Whatley Manor, The Dining Room

Some truly astounding food
Easton Grey, SN16 0RB
Tel no: (01666) 822888
www.whatleymanor.com
Modern French | £76
Cooking score: 8

£5 OFF 🍴

A Cotswold manor house built in the eighteenth century as part of a farming estate, this was originally called Twatley Manor. Whatley's better. In the 1920s it was acquired by a Canadian owner who was a keen huntsman, and he added the hunting lodge that now houses the dining room. It has been a hotel only since the 1980s. The entire place exudes upmarket class, from the immaculately manicured lawns to the spa facilities, the oak-panelled public rooms to the restaurant where, against a backdrop of cream walls and striped seating, some truly astounding food is served. Martin Burge is one of the handful of first-division country-house practitioners. Where other such venues encourage a homogeny of style, with creamy richness and undemanding textures to the fore, his is absolutely cutting-edge, the sort of laser-like precision and skill you expect to find in the big cities. Dishes are composed in accordance with the mixture of classical technique and modern technology now familiar at this level, but they look as near-perfect as food produced to order is capable of getting, and are full of complex, dynamic taste sensations. A portion of pig cheek is braised in Thai spices and served with caramelised langoustine tails and a resonant shellfish purée. Loin of local hare appears as a starter too, roasted and dressed in smoked shallot purée with confit red cabbage and poached raisins. Main courses are full of depth-charge flavours, as when 100 per cent cocoa bitter chocolate is grated on to roast venison with its own sausage in reduced Shiraz, or a cannelloni of oysters and lime

appears alongside a construction of compressed cucumber for sea bass in Champagne caviar sauce. Discoveries continue into the innovative desserts, such as the celebrated cheese plate that combines creamed Roquefort and deep-fried goats' cheese with black truffle ice cream and candied walnuts, or there might be lemon ravioli with clementine sorbet and olive oil ice cream under a foaming layer of pine nuts. The wines are not bargain-bins, but the mark-ups are not as painful as you might fear in the context. Selections zip briskly across the planet (not forgetting the owners' native Switzerland) pulling in plenty of pedigree growers in the process. Glasses start at £5, bottles at £21.50, and there's an extensive range of half-bottles.
Chef/s: Martin Burge. **Open:** Wed to Sun D only 7 to 10. **Closed:** Mon, Tue. **Meals:** Set D £76. Tasting menu £96 (7 courses). **Service:** 10%. **Details:** 40 seats. Separate bar. Wheelchair access. Music. Car parking. Children 12 yrs and over only.

▌Foxham

READERS RECOMMEND
The Foxham Inn
Modern British
Foxham, SN15 4NQ
Tel no: (01249) 740665
www.thefoxhaminn.co.uk
'Excellent food: lobster, mango and avocado salad; mackerel with aubergine purée and tomato salsa; salt cod croquettes with aioli; apple tart with passion fruit and clotted cream – all delicious. Excellent service.'

¶¶ Readers
¶¶ Recommend
A 'readers recommend' review is a genuine quote from a report sent in by one of our readers. We intend to follow up these suggestions throughout the year to come.

▌Holt
The Tollgate Inn
A bonanza of locally sourced produce
Ham Green, Holt, BA14 6PX
Tel no: (01225) 782326
www.tollgateholt.co.uk
Modern British | £27
Cooking score: 2

£5 OFF ⊨ £30

In its time, this sturdy stone building has done duty as a school, Baptist reading room and weaving shed (the upstairs restaurant occupies the workers' old chapel). These days, however, chef Alexander Venables treats visitors to a bonanza of locally sourced produce ranging from Limpley Stoke lamb to hand-reared beef from the lush pastures of Broughton Gifford. Game terrine with homemade chutney or bresaola with truffle dressing could lead on to a char-grilled steak, chicken breast stuffed with olives and goats' cheese on tomato ragoût, or even a hotpot of Cornish fish. Refreshment comes from the region's microbreweries and a thoughtfully assembled wine list (from £14.50). A trip to the pub's own food shop is also recommended.
Chef/s: Alexander Venables. **Open:** Tue to Sun L 12 to 2 (2.30 Sun), Tue to Sat D 7 to 9 (9.30 Fri and Sat). **Closed:** Mon, 25 Dec, 1 Jan. **Meals:** alc (main courses £13 to £20). Set L £15.50 (2 courses) to £17.95. Set D £19.95 (2 courses) £22.95. **Service:** not inc. **Details:** 60 seats. 60 seats outside. Separate bar. Wheelchair access. Music. Car parking.

▌Horningsham

ALSO RECOMMENDED
▲ The Bath Arms
Longleat Estate, Horningsham, BA12 7LY
Tel no: (01985) 844308
www.batharms.co.uk
Modern British

Standing proud by the gates to Longleat House, this creeper-clad eighteenth-century inn is a rambling hostelry with a reputation for reliable food and classy drinking opportunities. Menus are priced at one, two or three courses (£16.50/£24.40/£29.50) and output from the cosmopolitan kitchen ranges from crab bisque or Creedy Carver duck pudding with pickled cherries and walnuts to sea bass with white bean cassoulet and brown shrimps, and rhubarb and coconut crumble with coconut ice cream. Wines from £17. Open all week.

Little Bedwyn
The Harrow at Little Bedwyn
Stunning food and quality quaffing
Little Bedwyn, SN8 3JP
Tel no: (01672) 870871
www.theharrowatlittlebedwyn.co.uk
Modern British | £55
Cooking score: 6

♦ V

It's important to note that the Harrow is not, as it once was, the Harrow Inn, for all that its two-toned brick and stone façade may lead you to expect a village hostelry. In fact, the place illuminates Little Bedwyn – and much of Wiltshire – with Roger and Sue Jones' concerted commitment to small producers, wild foraging and the noble art of food and wine matching, the last celebrated all through John Brown's menus, with their alliances of sharply delineated modern British dishes and quality quaffing. The vogue for Indian seasonings is acknowledged in a starter of Pembrokeshire lobster with tarka dhal and coriander chutney in carrot jus, while a contemporary classic matching of foie gras, black pudding and a scallop in a 1927 PX caramel dressing is the last word in opulence. Mains feature some of the best real meats to be found anywhere. The new season's Welsh mountain lamb comes as rack, fillet and faggot with mushy peas, or there may be Northumberland roe deer with chestnuts and ceps. Desserts might return to the Indian axis for poached pear with Asian rice pudding and cardamom ice cream. The wines, served in Riedel glassware, could hardly wish for more enthusiastic exponents than here. A particular love for great Australian growers is evident, as is the cream of the German regions and aged

Spanish Reservas. Prices are by no means hellish, given the fabulous credentials of so many of the producers, with bottles from £19 (£6 a small glass).
Chef/s: Roger Jones and John Brown. **Open:** Wed to Sat L 12 to 3, D 7 to 9. **Closed:** Sun to Tue, 25 Dec to 6 Jan. **Meals:** alc (main courses £30). Set L £35. Tasting menu £50 (4 courses) to £75. **Service:** not inc. **Details:** 34 seats. 24 seats outside. Music.

Rowde
The George & Dragon
Proper period local with star seafood
High Street, Rowde, SN10 2PN
Tel no: (01380) 723053
www.thegeorgeanddragonrowde.co.uk
Modern British | £25
Cooking score: 4

A sixteenth-century coaching inn complete with carved Tudor rose, original beams and open fireplaces, the George & Dragon is a proper period local. The dining experience is a cut above, with rugs on the floors, crisp table linen, and fish and seafood delivered daily from St Mawes in Cornwall. Specials of the day appear on the blackboards, and there are fixed-price menus too. The food is a mix of traditional and modern, so choices range from spicy fishcakes with hollandaise, char-grilled scallops and black pudding brochette, and beer-battered whiting with tartare sauce and chunky chips, to salmon teriyaki with soy and ginger. If you're not a fishie, try roast chicken breast with black pudding and potato cake in red wine jus. Good pubby sweets include lemon posset, and a version of bread-and-butter pudding fabulised up with chocolate and orange. Wines start at £13, with glasses from £3.90 (standard) or £4.90 (large).
Chef/s: Christopher Day. **Open:** all week L 12 to 3 (4 Sat and Sun), Mon to Sat D 6.30 to 10. **Meals:** alc (main courses £14 to £30). Set L and D £16.50 (2 courses) to £19.50. Sun L £19.50. **Service:** 10%. **Details:** 35 seats. 50 seats outside. Separate bar. Music. Car parking.

◼ Teffont Evias

Howard's House Hotel
Country comforts and quietly confident food
Teffont Evias, SP3 5RJ
Tel no: (01722) 716392
www.howardshousehotel.co.uk
Modern European | £45
Cooking score: 3

Built in 1623, this gently extended dower house is a charmer, guaranteed to elicit 'oohs' from first-timers and regulars alike – a pastoral idyll pointed up with tiny streams, gorgeous gardens and undulating topiary. The whole place glides along unhindered, and nothing disturbs its pastel-hued vision of genteel country comforts allied to quietly confident cooking. Chef Nick Wentworth keeps one eye on the calendar and the other on his home patch, serving up, say, free-range chicken and Sauternes consommé with wild mushroom tortellini, ahead of mallard breast and confit leg enriched with red cabbage and spiced orange jus. His refreshingly concise menu also finds room for fish (wild sea bass with mussel and saffron stew), while Agen prune and Armagnac soufflé with pistachio ice cream is a winning dessert. Wines from all quarters start at £16.75.
Chef/s: Nick Wentworth. **Open:** all week L 12.30 to 2, D 7 to 9. **Closed:** 1 week Christmas. **Meals:** Set L £24 (2 courses) to £28.50. Set D £36 (2 courses) to £45. Sun L £28.50. **Service:** not inc. **Details:** 40 seats. 24 seats outside. Music. Car parking.

Symbols
🛏 Accommodation is available
£30 Three courses for less than £30
V Separate vegetarian menu
£5 OFF £5-off voucher scheme
🍷 Notable wine list

◼ Tisbury

NEW ENTRY
Beckford Arms
Upmarket rural inn
Fonthill Gifford, Tisbury, SP3 6PX
Tel no: (01747) 870385
www.beckfordarms.com
British | £25
Cooking score: 3

With its log fires and cosy country luxe décor, Charlie Luxton's eighteenth-century hostelry offers the comforts and luxury of a small and very relaxing hotel, the 'perfect pub' after a walk through the surrounding Fonthill Estate. The kitchen showcases some of our best native ingredients – Exmoor venison terrine and Laverstoke Farm mozzarella, for example. The clear British tone of the seasonal menus is tempered by a 'hint of Scandinavian simplicity' from Swedish chef Pravin Nayar; witness dishes such as seared Cornish mackerel with pickled cucumber, dill mayonnaise and shallots, the balance of the smoky, rich fish with the piquant, crunchy vegetables wonderfully executed. The well-priced wine list (from £15.50) includes a Seyval Blanc from nearby Fonthill Gifford.
Chef/s: Pravin Nayar. **Open:** all week L 12 to 2.30 (3 Sat and Sun), D 6 to 9.30 (9 Sun). **Closed:** 25 Dec. **Meals:** alc (main courses £10 to £22). **Service:** 10%. **Details:** 65 seats. 25 seats outside. Separate bar. Music. Car parking.

◼ Tollard Royal
The King John Inn
Popular village inn with unusual flair
Tollard Royal, SP5 5PS
Tel no: (01725) 516207
www.kingjohninn.co.uk
Modern British | £35
Cooking score: 3
🛏

You can see why this place is popular. A village inn with unusual flair, it can be thought of as a gentrified pub in two parts: one where drinkers are welcome, and an informal dining room delivering a menu of contemporary brasserie-style dishes. Basic materials are well-sourced and well-handled. The unpretentious approach is matched by some appealing, soothing food along the lines of moules marinière and pig's head hash with fried egg and parsley sauce, ahead of whole Poole Bay Dover sole with Pink Fir Apple potatoes, sprouting broccoli and hollandaise, or venison haunch with beetroot pearl barley and greens. Desserts are uncomplicated offerings such as rum baba with vanilla ice cream or sticky toffee pudding with butterscotch sauce. House wines are £16.95.

Chef/s: Simon Trepess. **Open:** all week L 12 to 2.30 (3 Sat and Sun), D 7 to 9.30 (9 Sun). **Closed:** 25 and 31 Dec. **Meals:** alc (main courses £13 to £29). **Service:** not inc. **Details:** 70 seats. 40 seats outside. No music. Wheelchair access. Car parking. Children at L only.

Upton Scudamore

The Angel Inn
Homely and professional village hostelry
Upton Scudamore, BA12 OAG
Tel no: (01985) 213225
www.theangelinn.co.uk
Modern British | £25
Cooking score: 2

This 'homely and professional' sixteenth-century coaching inn has a walled garden and a sheltered terrace where you can dine on balmy summer days. After complimentary homemade breads, expect inventive food like flaked ham hock with minted pea pannacotta, brown Melba toast and egg yolk jam, followed by venison loin on sweet-and-sour red cabbage with celeriac gratin and cranberry jus. Fish is a strong suit – perhaps sea trout fillet with fennel, citrus fruit and ginger concasse, sesame seed broad beans and oyster sauce noodles. Desserts include cappuccino crème brûlée with lemon and cinnamon shortbread. International wines start at £14.

Chef/s: Peter Laurenson. **Open:** all week L 12 to 3, D 6 to 11. **Closed:** 26 Dec, 1 Jan. **Meals:** alc (main courses £15 to £24). Set L £10 (2 courses) to £15. Set D £25. Sun L £12. **Service:** not inc. **Details:** 60 seats. 40 seats outside. Separate bar. Music. Car parking.

West Hatch

NEW ENTRY
Pythouse Kitchen Garden Shop and Café
Quaint kitchen garden eatery
West Hatch, SP3 6PA
Tel no: (01747) 870444
www.pythouse-farm.co.uk
British | £20
Cooking score: 2

This charming foodie gem, in the ex-potting shed of the picturesque Victorian Pythouse kitchen garden, is by no means your average garden centre café. There are flagstone floors, exposed bricks and beams and a dresser laden with homemade cakes, plus a shop displaying pickles, preserves, veg and other goodies. The daily changing menu uses garden produce and local supplies in dishes like a smoked salmon salad of home-grown leaves dressed with apple, ginger and poppy seed and pink grapefruit, or artichoke, pepper and roasted red onion tart; broccoli and Cheddar soup has a rich base and full, savoury flavour. Well-selected wines from £4.50 a glass.

Chef/s: Matthew Trendall. **Open:** Wed to Mon L 12 to 2.30, D (Thur only) 7 to 8.30. **Closed:** Tue, 25 and 26 Dec, 1 Jan. **Meals:** alc (main courses £6 to £10). Set D £20. **Service:** not inc. **Details:** 40 seats. 30 seats outside. Wheelchair access. Music. Car parking.

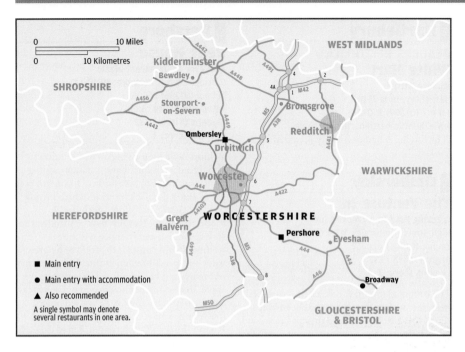

▌Broadway

Russell's

Inviting boutique brasserie
20 High Street, Broadway, WR12 7DT
Tel no: (01386) 853555
www.russellsofbroadway.co.uk
Modern British | £35
Cooking score: 4

As a boutique-style brasserie-with-rooms, Russell's has always been seen as a refreshingly modern contrast to its olde-worlde Cotswold village setting. The former headquarters of renowned furniture designer Gordon Russell is now an appealing, beautifully renovated Cotswold-stone building that mixes beams and exposed stone with polished wood floors and bare tables. The look is 'inviting more than showy' and complements Damian Clisby's accessible, bistro-orientated cooking perfectly. While essentially simple, there's razor-sharp technique behind dishes like stuffed rabbit saddle with confit shoulder,

rosemary gnocchi and spring vegetables, 'delicate' butterflied sardines grilled on tomato-braised fennel, or silky chocolate délice with griottine cherries. Prices, which seem reasonable, may dip further for lunch and early evening set menus, from which asparagus and potato minestrone, roasted pollack and mussels in tomato broth, then a classic Bakewell tart might prove particularly good value. Service can range from 'well-meaning' to stretched at busier times. House wines are £15.95.

Chef/s: Damian Clisby. **Open:** all week L 12 to 2.30, Mon to Sat D 6 to 9.30. **Meals:** alc (main courses £14 to £23). Set L and D £14.95 (2 courses) to £17.95 (Mon to Thur). Set D £21.95 (Fri and Sat). Sun L £23.95. **Service:** not inc. **Details:** 60 seats. 30 seats outside. Separate bar. Wheelchair access. Music. Car parking.

Hartlebury

READERS RECOMMEND
White Hart
Modern British
Hartlebury, DY11 7TD
Tel no: (01299) 250286
www.thewhitehartinhartlebury.co.uk
'The food is delicious, freshly prepared and cooked.'

Ombersley
The Venture In
Cracking food in a crooked inn
High Street, Ombersley, WR9 0EW
Tel no: (01905) 620552
Anglo-French | £37
Cooking score: 3

The timbered inn may look a little crumpled from the outside, but then it has been here since 1430. Inside, there are ancient beams and uneven floors, a log fire burns when needed to bestow cheer, and Toby Fletcher is on hand to provide some gently modernised British cooking that also draws on French influences. A pre-Christmas pair enjoyed generous duck confit, followed by hake with Puy lentils in mushroom sauce, or there might be seared scallops with pea and ham fricassee in parsley emulsion, then pan-roasted pheasant with a mini-game pie and wilted Savoy cabbage. Round things off richly with prune and Armagnac tart and a good dollop of clotted cream. An enterprising, nicely balanced wine list opens at £16 (£4.50 a glass).
Chef/s: Toby Fletcher. **Open:** Tue to Sun L 12 to 2, Tue to Sat D 7 to 9. **Closed:** Mon, 25 Dec to 2 Jan, 1 week Feb, 1 week June, 2 weeks Aug, Tue after bank hols. **Meals:** Set L £24 (2 courses) to £28. Set D £38. **Service:** not inc. **Details:** 28 seats. Children over 10 yrs only.

Pershore
Belle House
Purveyor of upmarket meals
5 Bridge Street, Pershore, WR10 1AJ
Tel no: (01386) 555055
www.belle-house.co.uk
Modern British | £32
Cooking score: 3

Behind Belle House's big arched windows you'll find a restaurant and a traiteur selling upmarket meals to take home. Dining in, you get to enjoy the sleek interior, which blends original Georgian features with simple modern touches. Readers have applauded the service ('warm and friendly without stuffiness') and consider the food to be 'great value' – especially at lunchtime. Expect plenty of French and Italian influences: porcetta with apple, shallot and potato crisps, say, then breast and leg of guinea fowl with braised pulses, roasted vegetables and creamed potatoes. Round things off with peanut, salted caramel and chocolate tart. Wines are drawn from small, quality-conscious producers worldwide, and include an impressive selection by the glass. Bottles start at £18.50.
Chef/s: Steve Waites. **Open:** Tue to Sat L 12 to 2, D 7 to 9.30. **Closed:** Sun, Mon, first 2 weeks Jan. **Meals:** Set L £16 (2 courses) to £24. Set D £25 (2 courses) to £32. Tasting menu £45. **Service:** not inc. **Details:** 80 seats. Separate bar. Wheelchair access. Music.

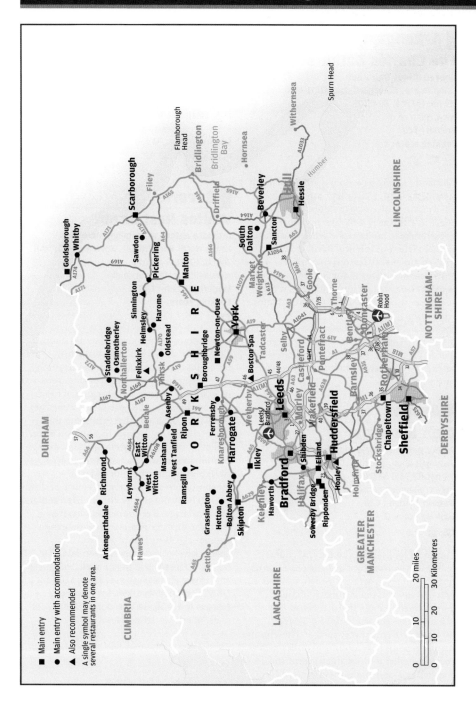

Arkengarthdale
The Charles Bathurst Inn
Unpretentious Dales pub
Langthwaite, Arkengarthdale, DL11 6EN
Tel no: (01748) 884567
www.cbinn.co.uk
British | £25
Cooking score: 1

The Cody family have done a remarkable job, creating a warm, welcoming inn in such a lonely spot. With wooden floors, beams and open fires, this may look like any other rural Yorkshire pub, but the food sets it apart. The kitchen sends out robustly flavoured dishes that rely on quality seasonal ingredients – a hearty curried parsnip soup, say, followed by pheasant (breast and ragù) with red cabbage and mash, then sticky toffee pudding. House wine from £15.95.
Chef/s: Gareth Bottomley. **Open:** all week L 12 to 2, D 6.30 to 9. **Closed:** 25 Dec. **Meals:** alc (main courses £12 to £20). Sun L £13.50 (2 courses). **Service:** not inc. **Details:** 100 seats. Music. Car parking.

Asenby
Crab & Lobster
Quirky pub with some pleasing fish
Dishforth Road, Asenby, YO7 3QL
Tel no: (01845) 577286
www.crabandlobster.co.uk
Modern British | £28
Cooking score: 2

Outside it looks like an archetypal country pub, with thatched roof and creeper-covered walls, set in seven acres of garden. Inside is a different story, as one reporter's 'unique, quirky surroundings' translates as an extraordinary clutter, with bric-à-brac seemingly covering every surface. The lengthy repertoire leans heavily on fish; dishes such as crispy fishcakes with creamed greens and a poached egg, and tandoori-marinated monkfish with a tomato, onion and coriander

salad, spiced wedges and mint and cucumber yoghurt have pleased visitors. Otherwise, you might find twice-baked Yorkshire Cheddar soufflé or game pie, and sticky date and toffee pudding. Wines from £24.
Chef/s: Steve Dean. **Open:** all week L 12 to 2.30, D 7 to 9. **Meals:** alc (main courses £18 to £30). Set L £15.95 (2 courses) to £18.95. Sun L £15.50 (1 course). **Service:** not inc. **Details:** 120 seats. 60 seats outside. Separate bar. Wheelchair access. Music. Car parking.

Beverley
Whites Restaurant
Intimate eatery with imaginative food
12-12a North Bar Without, Beverley, HU17 7AB
Tel no: (01482) 866121
www.whitesrestaurant.co.uk
Modern British | £30
Cooking score: 2

John Robinson's intimate 28-seat restaurant close to Beverley's old town walls is refreshingly lacking in pomp and ceremony, which is probably why one reporter so enjoyed its 'good atmosphere and exceptional food'. There may not be the posh table settings or frippery of other establishments, but this owner/chef is not lacking in ambition when it comes to imaginative, well-considered combinations such as a starter of lamb's sweetbreads with chestnut and wild mushroom cream, and a main course of slow-cooked belly pork, pork cheeks, hazelnuts and Savoy cabbage. Recommended desserts include rosewater pannacotta with orange sesame cake. Wines from £16.95.
Chef/s: John Robinson. **Open:** Tue to Sat L 12 to 2, D 6.30 to 9. **Closed:** Sun, Mon, 1 week Dec, 1 week Aug. **Meals:** alc (main courses £18 to £20). Set L £15.50 (2 courses) to £17.95. Set D £18.50 (2 courses) to £22.50. **Service:** not inc. **Details:** 28 seats. Wheelchair access. Music.

▌Bolton Abbey

The Burlington at the Devonshire Arms

A premier Yorkshire destination
Bolton Abbey, BD23 6AJ
Tel no: (01756) 710441
www.burlingtonrestaurant.co.uk
Modern French | £65
Cooking score: 6

The Duke of Devonshire's flagship hotel has a degree of timeless authority that puts it in the premier league of Yorkshire destinations. At its heart is the Burlington restaurant – an elegant room of soft lights, pale aubergine walls hung with historic architectural drawings, and designer silverware. By contrast, Steve Smith's menus immediately catapult guests into the modish world of textures, foams and arty dabs, with a full battery of amuse-bouches, smoke-filled cloches and shots to ram home the message. A 'pig's head' starter comprises a highly complex, intricately worked plate of slow-cooked, pressed *tête* with langoustine, carrot, horseradish and Joselito ham. Other specialities are also flagged with their cherry-picked primary protein – Hebridean lamb, Cumbrian venison, Brixham red mullet, and so on. Some idea of Smith's broad palette can be gauged from smoked Angus beef sirloin and braised cheek with parsley risotto, snails and red wine, or a dish of roast Limousin veal with sweetbreads, pumpkin and lemon, shin cannelloni, trompette mushrooms and tonka bean froth. As for desserts, how about 'chocolate mayhem' with peanut, caramel and lime? The recently introduced 'pescetarian' tasting menu is also proving popular with fish-loving visitors who appreciate Smith's meticulous attention to detail. And then there's the Burlington's 2,000-bin wine list – a veritable *Encyclopaedia Britannica* encompassing the great, the good and the exceedingly rare from all corners of the wine-making planet. No fewer than 82 house selections in three price bands (from £18) offer a snapshot of glorious things to come – although it isn't all dusty, four-figure vintages.
Chef/s: Steve Smith. **Open:** Sun L 12 to 2.30, Tue to Sun D 7 to 9.30. **Closed:** Mon, 7 to 15 Jan. **Meals:** Set D £65. Sun L £35. Tasting menu £72 (9 courses). Prestige menu £80 (12 courses). **Service:** 12.5%. **Details:** 60 seats. Separate bar. No music. Car parking. No children under 7 yrs after 7.

The Devonshire Brasserie

Ducal eatery with a metropolitan edge
Bolton Abbey, BD23 6AJ
Tel no: (01756) 710710
www.devonshirebrasserie.co.uk
Modern British | £30
Cooking score: 2

If the Devonshire Arms evokes antiques, wellies and Barbours, its brasserie may surprise. Here is a bold, colourful modern restaurant with a metropolitan edge and a modern brasserie menu; potted duck confit with pickled vegetables and chicken liver parfait with red onion marmalade are regularly endorsed starters. Main courses embrace good steaks, braised lamb shank hotpot or oxtail stew with sage dumplings. To finish, the house cheesecake is highly rated, or try cherry clafoutis with almond ice cream. The Brasserie really scores with its astutely chosen wine list, which offers an enticing global range and ungreedy mark-ups (bottles from £16.95).
Chef/s: Daniel Field. **Open:** all week L 12 to 2.30 (4 Sun), D 6 to 9 (6.30 to 10 Fri and Sat, 6.30 to 9 Sun). **Meals:** alc (main courses £13 to £24). **Service:** 12.5%. **Details:** 70 seats. 40 seats outside. Wheelchair access. Music. Car parking.

Visit us Online
To find out more about
The Good Food Guide, please visit
www.thegoodfoodguide.co.uk

▌Boroughbridge

The Dining Room
Welcoming family-run restaurant
20 St James Square, Boroughbridge, YO51 9AR
Tel no: (01423) 326426
www.thediningroomonline.co.uk
Modern British | £30
Cooking score: 4

£5
OFF

This comfortable and welcoming Queen Anne house overlooking Boroughbridge's market square has no pretension or grandeur, since it is a well-run family enterprise. Meals might begin with a drink on the terrace (weather permitting) or in front of the fire in the lounge, while in the kitchen Chris Astley's fixed-price menus deal in tried-and-trusted preparations, underpinned by the wholesome feeling of good ingredients. Evening choices have included cream of white onion soup with crumbled Stilton croûtons or chicken liver parfait. Main courses take in the likes of lemon sole fillets with Morecambe Bay shrimps and herb butter, or confit of duck with black pudding, cider sauce and Bramley apple. Awaiting you at meal's end will be something like homemade meringues with vanilla cream, bitter chocolate and cherries in Kirsch. A decent selection of wines opens at £17.50.
Chef/s: Chris Astley. **Open:** Wed to Fri L 12 to 2, Sun L 12 to 2, Tue to Sat D 7 to 9.15. **Closed:** Mon, 26 Dec, 1 Jan, bank hols. **Meals:** alc (main courses £15 to £19). Set L £20 (2 courses) to £26.50. Set D £26 (2 courses) to £29.95. Sun L £27. **Service:** not inc. **Details:** 34 seats. 22 seats outside. Separate bar. Music. Children over 3 yrs only at D.

||| Also
||| Recommended
Also recommended entries are not scored but we think they are worth a visit.

▌Boston Spa

ALSO RECOMMENDED
▲ The Fish House
174 High Street, Boston Spa, LS23 6BW
Tel no: (01937) 845625
www.fishhouseboston.com
Seafood £5
OFF

The Fish House overlooks the high street of this pretty Yorkshire village and comprises three beamed rooms decorated with an airy blue-and-white seaside theme. Although one reporter felt the service was a touch inattentive, there have been no complaints about the quality of the seafood, which might include a starter of crispy breaded monkfish scampi (£7.50) followed by fillet of sea bass, crab and chive risotto and lobster bisque (£16.50). Wines start at £12.95. Closed Sun D and Mon.

▌Bradford

Prashad
Cut-above veggie Indian
86 Horton Grange Road, Bradford, BD7 2DW
Tel no: (01274) 575893
www.prashad.co.uk
Indian Vegetarian | £18
Cooking score: 3

£5 **V** £30
OFF

By the time you read this, it is possible that Prashad will have moved from its current unprepossessing site to larger, licensed premises, doubling the seating capacity – good news for those who have had to endure the 'holding pen across the road'. As we went to press Prashad told us it was about to sign, but was unable to divulge the new address. Do phone ahead to check. For many, Kaushy Patel and her daughter-in-law Minal's distinctive Gujarati vegetarian food 'really is a cut above most Indian restaurants'. Expect a fascinating mix of samosas, pakoras and puris, plus exquisite masala dosas (crisp rice pancake filled with potato and onion curry and served

with a spicy lentil soup and coconut and yoghurt chutney). Finish with kulfi or shrikand. Unlicensed.
Chef/s: Minal Patel. **Open:** Tue to Sun L 11 to 3 (4 Sat and Sun), D 6 to 10.30. **Closed:** Mon, 25 Dec, 1 Jan. **Meals:** alc (main courses £8 to £14). **Service:** not inc. **Details:** 40 seats. Music.

Chapeltown
Greenhead House
Cottagey favourite with alluring menus
84 Burncross Road, Chapeltown, S35 1SF
Tel no: (0114) 2469004
www.greenheadhouse.com
Modern European | £40
Cooking score: 2

Occupying a cottagey seventeenth-century dwelling in a leafy Sheffield suburb, Neil and Anne Allen's long-serving restaurant is still befriended by the food-loving local populace. It may have limited opening times and an out-of-the-way location, but there's no lack of enthusiasm or flair in the kitchen. Neil is forever ringing the changes on his monthly menus. Meals run to four courses; starters of pappardelle with hare ragù or pheasant and pistachio ballottine give way to a soup or sorbet; then expect anything from game pie to paupiettes of lemon sole with lobster sauce and lobster risotto. For afters, poached pear with zabaglione mousse might hit the spot. House wine is £20.50.
Chef/s: Neil Allen. **Open:** Fri L 12 to 1, Wed to Sat D 7 to 8.30. **Closed:** Sun to Tue, 1 week Christmas and New Year, 2 weeks Jun, 2 weeks Aug. **Meals:** Set D £46.95 to £47.95 (4 courses). **Service:** not inc. **Details:** 32 seats. No music. Wheelchair access. Car parking. Children over 5 yrs only.

❚❙❘ Average Price
The average price listed in main-entry reviews denotes the price of a three-course meal, without wine.

East Witton
The Blue Lion
Dales inn with hearty pub food
East Witton, DL8 4SN
Tel no: (01969) 624273
www.thebluelion.co.uk
Modern British | £33
Cooking score: 3
🛏 V

The hefty blackboard menus in this long-loved Dales inn range wider than ever under chef Michael McBride. Langoustine with saffron aïoli, and slow-braised pig's cheek with five-spice jus are among the starters; mains of belly pork with sage and apple sauce, wild rabbit, venison, halibut and steak continue the hearty take on pub food. Desserts include the likes of warm banana cake, banana mousse and rum and raisin syrup, or rhubarb crumble and custard. It's all served in the wonderfully atmospheric bar, a classic of stone-flagged floors, mighty fireplace and country furniture, or in the relaxed dining room. House wines start at £17.65, but with Theakston and Black Sheep breweries down the road in Masham, you may prefer to sup the local brews.
Chef/s: Michael McBride. **Open:** all week L 12 to 2, D 6 to 9. **Closed:** 25 Dec. **Meals:** alc (main courses £13 to £27). **Service:** not inc. **Details:** 70 seats. 20 seats outside. Separate bar. No music. Wheelchair access. Car parking.

Elland
La Cachette
Happy-go-lucky hideaway
31 Huddersfield Road, Elland, HX5 9AW
Tel no: (01422) 378833
www.lacachette-elland.com
Modern European | £25
Cooking score: 2
£5 OFF £30

Take some pubby accoutrements (a stag's head and a large bar), add bistro blackboards, cosy candlelit booths and a French name (it means 'hiding place'), and leaven the mix with assorted Anglo-European flavours. The result is La Cachette – a happy-go-lucky venue with local cred and a wide-ranging menu that yo-yos from meaty pigeon and pheasant faggots on mushy peas, fishcakes with tartare sauce, and calf's liver with splendid dripping chips to moules marinière, butternut squash risotto and a 'great-looking' dish of pan-fried halibut atop a mix of artichokes, chorizo and peas. For afters, try a slice of rich fruitcake with a slab of Wensleydale cheese. Carefully chosen wines (from £12.95) also get the nod.

Chef/s: Jonathan Nichols. **Open:** Mon to Sat L 12 to 2.30, D 6 to 9 (10 Fri and Sat). **Closed:** Sun, 2 weeks Aug, 1 week Jan, bank hols (exc 25 and 26 Dec). **Meals:** alc (main courses £11 to £25). Set L and D £12.95 (2 courses) to £21.95. **Service:** not inc. **Details:** 85 seats. Separate bar. Wheelchair access. Music.

▌Felixkirk

ALSO RECOMMENDED
▲ The Carpenters Arms
Felixkirk, YO7 2DP
Tel no: (01845) 537369
www.thecarpentersarmsfelixkirk.com
Modern British

The bar at this well-heeled country pub dispenses real ales, and drinkers are made very welcome – but value-for-money cooking is the thing, and people come from miles around to eat here. Plenty of local connections show up in the likes of game terrine (£5.95) or a rack of spicy, sticky pork ribs served with homemade spicy beans, fries and coleslaw (£13.95). There are Yorkshire cheeses or pear and blackberry Bakewell tart with custard to finish. Wines from £13.95. Open all week.

▌Ferrensby
The General Tarleton
High-profile foodie beacon
Boroughbridge Road, Ferrensby, HG5 0PZ
Tel no: (01423) 340284
www.generaltarleton.co.uk
Modern British | £28
Cooking score: 4

Since launching in 2003, the General Tarleton has served as a beacon out on the country roads off the A1, evolving along similar lines to its high-profile cousin the Angel at Hetton (see entry). It's quite a leap from North Country drinking den to prestigious bar/brasserie, but long-standing chef/proprietor John Topham has preserved the hospitable, egalitarian tone of the place despite high culinary ambitions. Menus touting 'food with Yorkshire roots', 'pub classics' and 'family suppers' show that GT's heart and soul are in the right place, and the kitchen aims to please. Those after fish and chips, burgers and char-grilled steaks receive their full dues, while sophisticates can consider the finer points of seared scallops with slow-braised belly pork and butternut squash purée, or fillet of Dales beef with foie gras tortellini and veal consommé. After that, look to lemon tart or a tasting of Yorkshire rhubarb for sweet satisfaction. The wine list oozes cosmopolitan quality, with house recommendations from £18.

Chef/s: John Topham. **Open:** all week L 12 to 2, D 5.30 to 9.15 (8.30 Sun). **Meals:** alc (main courses £13 to £28). Set L and D £15 (2 courses) to £18.50. Sun L £22.50. **Service:** not inc. **Details:** 120 seats. 60 seats outside. Separate bar. Music. Car parking.

▌Goldsborough

The Fox & Hounds

No fuss, just high-quality food
Goldsborough, YO21 3RX
Tel no: (01947) 893372
www.foxandhoundsgoldsborough.co.uk
Modern European | £32
Cooking score: 5

This former country pub – 'in a rural and breathtaking setting' – has been converted to create several small dining rooms. While the setting is decidedly country-restaurant, the food is unmistakably modern, with no unnecessary fuss or trimmings, just high-quality ingredients lightly and confidently handled by Jason Davies. The place is small enough to allow Jason to do almost all the work in the kitchen himself, and his brief, to-the-point menus move along gently, changing with the seasons. In winter, you could expect bruschetta with burrata cheese, purple sprouting broccoli and prosciutto, and an impressive dry-aged fillet steak with chips, grilled radicchio and horseradish cream. Contrasts are handled well: king scallops come with borlotti beans, wild rocket and red chilli; turbot with porcini potatoes, Swiss chard and lemon oil; while calf's liver is served alongside Puy lentils, curly kale, sage, lemon and capers. Desserts shine too, in the form of almost teasingly straightforward lemon tart with crème fraîche or blood-orange sorbet. Equally impressive are good bread and amiable service from Sue Davies. For a small restaurant, the wine list features some well thought-out bottles and fair value. Prices start at £16.
Chef/s: Jason Davies. **Open:** Wed to Sat D only 6.30 to 8. **Closed:** Sun to Tue, 24 to 28 Dec, 2 weeks Jan. **Meals:** alc (main courses £16 to £26). **Service:** not inc. **Details:** 22 seats. Music. Car parking.

▌Grassington

Grassington House Hotel

Impressive field-to-fork food
5 The Square, Grassington, BD23 5AQ
Tel no: (01756) 752406
www.grassingtonhousehotel.co.uk
Modern British | £27
Cooking score: 3

£5 OFF 🛏 £30

Chef/proprietor John Rudden's home-reared, rare breed pork is one of the star attractions at this confidently run Georgian town house in a delightful Dales village. Inside, the old conservatory can be a tad 'draughty', but comfort appears in the shape of perky 'taster slates' and impressively crafted dishes that are true to the spirit of the Yorkshire larder: consider Yellison's goats' cheese délice with pickled vegetables, ahead of pan-roasted Thirsk lamb loin and slow-cooked shoulder with artichoke purée and a potato crisp, or grilled fillet of cod with seared queenie scallops and citrus-braised fennel. Otherwise, order a locally reared, 28-day aged steak with Wensleydale cheese dauphinois, before rounding off with artisan regional cheeses or apple and apricot strudel with eggnog and gingerbread ice cream. Wines start at £15.25 (£4.15 a glass).
Chef/s: John Rudden. **Open:** Mon to Sat L 12 to 2.30 (4 Sat), D 6 to 9.30, Sun 12 to 8. **Meals:** alc (main courses £12 to £24). Set L and D £14.50 (2 courses) to £16.50. Sun L £14.50. Bar menu also available. **Service:** not inc. **Details:** 58 seats. 24 seats outside. Separate bar. Wheelchair access. Music. Car parking.

Harome
The Pheasant Hotel
A tempting package all round
Mill Street, Harome, YO62 5JG
Tel no: (01439) 771241
www.thepheasanthotel.com
Modern British | £36
Cooking score: 5

🛏 V

Sharing ownership with the nearby Star Inn (see entry below), the Pheasant ensures that lucky Haromians are permanently spoiled for choice. Amalgamated into a country inn from what were once a blacksmith's, village shop and barns, it's a tempting package all round, with a coffee-coloured, low-ceilinged dining room, conservatory extension and a terrace overlooking the village duck pond. Peter Neville's impeccably modern menu approach, which incorporates wild foraged materials from woodland and shore, follows the ingredient-listing template, so that you might start with smoked cod mousse, piccalilli, oat crumble, pistachio, and follow on with Saddleback pork belly, Granny Smith apple, artichoke purée, shrimp, scratchings, and be sure that each dish is an enlightening exploration of the taste potentials of its various components. A floral tendency brings begonia and a courgette-flower fritter on to a main course of John Dory with Alsace bacon and carrot, but there is a soundness to the conception of these dishes that is powerfully convincing. Good farmhouse cheeses trundle by on their trolley, and desserts avoid the temptation to relapse into the obvious, so that egg custard tart is garnished with blueberry and juniper sorbet and wood sorrel. Wines are an international miscellany in ascending price order, beginning with South African Chenin and Chilean Cabernet at £19.

Chef/s: Peter Neville. **Open:** all week L 12 to 2, D 6.30 to 9. **Meals:** alc (main courses £18 to £24). Set L £23.50 (2 courses) to £28.50. Set D £36. Sun L £34. Tasting menu £65. **Service:** not inc. **Details:** 40 seats. 20 seats outside. Separate bar. Wheelchair access. Music. Car parking.

The Star Inn
Proper English pub with serious food
High Street, Harome, YO62 5JE
Tel no: (01439) 770397
www.thestaratharome.co.uk
Modern British | £40
Cooking score: 5

🛏

Last year's Guide highlighted serious inconsistencies in the Perns' thatched inn on the edge of the North York Moors. This year, we are happy to report greater steadiness in the kitchen. Indeed, on a bitter mid-winter lunchtime, it's hard to match the no-booking, atmospheric bar with a fire in the grate and just enough beam and brass to remind you you're in a proper English pub. Of course, when you are offered partridge with truffle risotto you know this isn't any old pub, and that is the contradiction. Is it a 'vastly overpriced' pub, as one reader suggests, or a serious restaurant? A bar and two dining rooms, all with the same menu, confirm the latter. A chef's table raises expectations even higher. Wherever you eat, there is no arguing with Andrew Pern's commitment to showcasing local produce and his astute matching of ingredients. His black pudding, foie gras and apple is deservedly legendary. Local suckling pig with roast apples and smoked pork Scotch egg is satisfying; baked ginger parkin with rhubarb ripple ice cream and hot spiced syrup work in perfect harmony. There are two dozen wines by the glass and a noteworthy list starting at £18.95.

Chef/s: Andrew Pern. **Open:** Tue to Sun L 12 to 2 (12 to 6 Sun), Mon to Sat D 6.30 to 9.30. **Closed:** 1 Jan. **Meals:** alc (main courses £17 to £26). Set L and D £20 (2 courses) to £25. **Service:** not inc. **Details:** 100 seats. 30 seats outside. Separate bar. Music. Car parking.

Harrogate

Orchid Restaurant
Well-crafted oriental cooking
Studley Hotel, 28 Swan Road, Harrogate, HG1 2SE
Tel no: (01423) 560425
www.orchidrestaurant.co.uk
Pan-Asian | £30
Cooking score: 2

Over the years Kenneth Poon and his team
have turned this contemporary restaurant in
the basement of the Studley Hotel into a
bastion of reliable oriental cooking – offering
a well-crafted menu that reaches out to China,
Malaysia, Thailand, Singapore, Hong Kong,
Korea, even Japan. Starters are given up-to-
the-minute presentation. King scallops
steamed with garlic, spring onions, coriander
and glass noodles; and roasted, sliced belly
pork with crispy crackling and yellow bean
and honey dip have been particularly
impressive. More substantial dishes include a
rich massaman lamb curry, crispy tamarind sea
bass, and kung po chicken. Spice-friendly
wines open at £17.60.
Chef/s: Kenneth Poon. **Open:** Mon to Fri and Sun L
12 to 2, all week D 6 to 10. **Closed:** 25 and 26 Dec.
Meals: alc (main courses £8 to £20). Set L £9.95 (2
courses) to £12.95. Set D £21.95. Sun L £16.70.
Service: 10%. **Details:** 76 seats. 24 seats outside.
Separate bar. Music. Car parking.

Sasso
Sound regional Italian cooking
8-10 Princes Square, Harrogate, HG1 1LX
Tel no: (01423) 508838
www.sassorestaurant.co.uk
Italian | £25
Cooking score: 3

Secreted in an uncluttered basement on one of
Harrogate's Georgian terraces, Sasso plies its
trade in a low-key setting of polished tables
and contemporary artwork. Chef Stefano
Lancellotti proves his worth with some
trademark pasta dishes (perhaps lobster ravioli

with courgettes and shallots), but it's also
worth considering the sweet Gorgonzola and
mascarpone terrine served as a starter, and
'secondi' such as rabbit leg stuffed with Italian
sausage on a cinnamon-spiked sauce. Specials
ranging from Venetian-style grilled sardines
with sweet-and-sour vegetables to sea bass
fillet wrapped in Tuscan lardo di colonnata
point up the kitchen's regional appetite.
Desserts keep it classic with sound renditions
of tiramisu, pannacotta and semifreddo with
toffee and Amaretto sauce. The international
wine list also has a strong regional Italian slant,
with prices from £13.95 (£3.75 a glass).
Chef/s: Stefano Lancellotti. **Open:** Mon to Sat L 12
to 2 (2.30 Sat), D 6 to 10 (5.45 to 10.30 Fri and Sat).
Closed: Sun, 25 and 26 Dec, 1 Jan. **Meals:** alc (main
courses £10 to £22). Set L and early D £8.95 (2
courses). **Service:** not inc. **Details:** 80 seats. 16
seats outside. Music.

**★ READERS' RESTAURANT OF THE YEAR ★
NATIONAL WINNER**

Van Zeller
A chef firing on all cylinders
8 Montpellier Street, Harrogate, HG1 2TQ
Tel no: (01423) 508762
www.vanzellerrestaurants.co.uk
Modern British | £40
Cooking score: 4

£5 OFF **V**

Harrogate deserves a high-quality restaurant
and Van Zeller is just that. Found in the
historic centre of town, it's an intimate,
narrow dining room on two levels (bag a table
by the window for a street view), with a sleek
vibe. Judging by reader reports this year, Tom
Van Zeller is firing on all cylinders, delivering
smart, contemporary dishes full of vibrancy,
bold strokes and ambition – even at a humble
Sunday lunch there were 'impressive canapés
and a pre-dessert'. Startling combinations
include nori-cured whiting with pickled
mooli and cucumber, miso, borage, mirin and
sesame dressing and wasabi ice cream, and a
'decidedly brill' main course of brill from
Brixham market, which came with pea purée,
broccoli, lollo bionda, tahini yoghurt, dukkah

and pomegranate. Prodigious technical skill is a given, and desserts are bang on target, with passion-fruit cannelloni more complex than the name suggests. Service is 'attentive, friendly', pricing 'didn't seem excessively expensive', and the wine list opens at £21.
Chef/s: Tom Van Zeller. **Open:** Tue to Sun L 12 to 2 (2.30 Sun), Tue to Sat D 6 to 10. **Closed:** Mon, first week Jan, first week Aug. **Meals:** Set L £25. Set D £39.50. Tasting menu £55. **Service:** 10%. **Details:** 36 seats. Music. Children allowed 'subject to availability'.

▎Haworth

Weavers

Amiable Brontë stop-off
15 West Lane, Haworth, BD22 8DU
Tel no: (01535) 643822
www.weaverssmallhotel.co.uk
Modern British | £30
Cooking score: 3

After 34 years at their restaurant-with-rooms, Jane and Colin Rushworth can consider themselves old hands at the catering game. But despite their longevity (and the formidable tourist footfall drawn by the nearby Brontë Parsonage Museum), they remain as enthusiastic as ever. The restaurant – three knocked-together weavers' cottages – is cosy with a jumble of furniture and warm lighting. The mood is easy and the cooking takes full account of the region's good things, from allotment vegetables, via Nidderdale trout, Yorkshire-cure collar bacon and Goosnargh duck, to Sandham's Lancashire cheese. Slow-cooked shank of lamb served with hotpot potato makes a notable main course, while forced rhubarb and custard meringue with a crumble dust is simply sublime. House wine is £14.95.
Chef/s: Colin Rushworth and Ross Swinson. **Open:** Tue to Fri L 11.30 to 2, Tue to Sat D 6.30 to 8.30. **Closed:** Sun, Mon, 2 weeks Christmas. **Meals:** alc (main courses £13 to £20). Set L and D £15 (2 courses) to £17.50. **Service:** not inc. **Details:** 60 seats. Separate bar. Music.

TOM VAN ZELLER
Van Zeller

When did you realise you wanted to be a chef?
Long after I had started my apprenticeship! I picked up a copy of *White Heat* and suddenly found some direction.

Which chefs do you admire, and why?
My own team! They are talented, creative, hard working and above all great team players. I am very proud of them.

What food trends are you spotting at the moment?
Clever understatement.

What's your biggest extravagance in the kitchen?
Time off.

What advice would you give a chef starting their career?
Keep your head down. Accept everything that comes your way and form your own opinions later.

What is your 'show-off' dish?
Turbot. Very expensive but very worth it!

What would be your last meal?
The food would be insignificant compared to the company.

■ Helmsley
Feversham Arms Hotel
Personable ex-coaching inn
High Street, Helmsley, YO62 5AG
Tel no: (01439) 770766
www.fevershamarmshotel.com
Modern European | £45
Cooking score: 4

Grown-up chic is what you get the moment you walk through the doors of the Feversham Arms Hotel. The former coaching inn offers just the sort of hospitality and facilities that travellers appreciate. Nothing is too posh or too grand, indeed the scale is personable, from the beautifully designed garden to the pub-like bar and elegant conservatory dining room that looks out over the swimming pool and courtyard. Simon Kelly continues to haul in the best seasonal produce and by a mixing and melding of culinary styles produces first courses such as tandoori salmon with crème fraîche and samphire, and mains of Yorkshire lamb loin with cashew nut, broccoli and potato dauphinois. Reporters have been equally content with a grazing plate of smoked salmon, Serrano ham, lime-cured sea bass and bresaola, served with fresh bread and olive oil from the very good-value lounge lunch menu. Wines from £28.50.
Chef/s: Simon Kelly. **Open:** all week L 12 to 2 (12.30 to 2.30 Sun), D 6.45 to 9.30. **Meals:** alc (main courses £18 to £24). Set L £27.50 (2 courses) to £32.50. Set D £45 (3 courses). Sun L £19.50 (2 courses) to £25. Tasting menu £32.50. **Service:** not inc. **Details:** 80 seats. 40 seats outside. Wheelchair access. Car parking. No children after 8.

■ Hessle
Artisan
Impressive performance from a solo chef
22 The Weir, Hessle, HU13 0RU
Tel no: (01482) 644906
www.artisanrestaurant.com
Modern European | £50
Cooking score: 5

Richard and Lindsey Johns' restaurant lies by the side of the weir in a peaceful East Riding suburb, in an elegantly decorated Georgian town house that also happens to be their home. With understated décor, well-upholstered seating and smartly dressed tables, it's a suitably chic setting for Richard's carefully constructed modern dinner menus (plus Sunday lunch once a month). Following an appetiser and homemade bread, a four-course format might offer smoked haddock and saffron risotto topped with a poached egg and caviar, slow-roast ballottine of chicken in butternut squash velouté, dressed in orange oil, and then roast rump and best end of Nidderdale lamb served with gnocchi, creamed cabbage, mushrooms and bacon in a truffled red wine sauce. Excellent artisan (what else?) cheeses with tomato chutney are the savoury alternative to a plate of assorted mini-desserts that might include Belgian white chocolate and raspberry pot and orange-curd yoghurt ice cream. The whole performance is all the more impressive when you consider that Richard Johns works alone in the kitchen. A well-chosen, compact wine list opens with a pair of southern French specialities, a Picpoul de Pinet at £22 and a red Côtes Catalanes blend at £22.50.
Chef/s: Richard Johns. **Open:** last Sun of every month L 1 to 2, Wed to Sat D from 7. **Closed:** Mon, Tue. **Meals:** Sun L £25. Tasting menu £50 (4 courses). **Service:** not inc. **Details:** 16 seats. Wheelchair access. Music. Car parking.

Hetton
The Angel Inn
Honest-to-goodness country pub for foodies
Hetton, BD23 6LT
Tel no: (01756) 730263
www.angelhetton.co.uk
Modern British | £28
Cooking score: 3

🛋 V £30

It's a tribute to the Watkins family's dedication that they have preserved the Angel as an honest-to-goodness country pub while maintaining its reputation as a dining destination. A fixture in the Guide for more than a quarter of a century, its enduring appeal shows no sign of diminishing. It's a 'happy, buzzing place', with blazing winter fires and dishes like little money-bags of seafood with lobster sauce that have been a feature since the beginning. Seasonal menus burst with sharply executed ideas – excellent fish specials as well as rare breed suckling pig with Bramley apple potato, swede and pepper purée, Yorkshire kale, black pudding and cider sauce. There are home-baked rolls, local cheeses and a quality wine list, without eye-watering mark-ups. Prices from £15.75.
Chef/s: Mark Taft and Bruce Elsworth. **Open:** Mon to Sat L 12 to 2, D 6 to 9.30, Sun 12 to 8. **Closed:** 25 Dec, 3 days Jan. **Meals:** alc (main courses £13 to £27). Set L and D £12.95 (2 courses) to £15.95. Sun L £27.50. **Service:** not inc. **Details:** 65 seats. 20 seats outside. Separate bar. No music. Wheelchair access. Car parking.

Honley
ALSO RECOMMENDED
▲ Mustard and Punch
6 Westgate, Honley, HD9 6AA
Tel no: (01484) 662066
www.mustardandpunch.co.uk
British

Locals know how lucky they are to find Mustard and Punch on their doorstep, and they praise the relaxed atmosphere. Owners and chefs Richard Dunn and Wayne Roddis

have their eye on food trends and food traditions; the menu might feature haslet with sippets of bread (£6) lamb rump with kidney pudding (£14.50) and Yorkshire parkin with rhubarb and ginger sorbet. It's all priced to encourage return custom; the 'exceedingly good-value', three-course set dinner menu (£20) includes wine. House wine is £14.50. Closed Sun.

Huddersfield
Bradley's
Boisterous basement brasserie
84 Fitzwilliam Street, Huddersfield, HD1 5BB
Tel no: (01484) 516773
www.bradleysrestaurant.co.uk
Modern European | £25
Cooking score: 2

£5 OFF £30

Gastronomic themed nights, quizzes, terrific early-bird menus and 'prime time' deals (with wine included) are just some of the reasons why Huddersfield's bargain-hunting foodies continue to pack Andrew Bradley's boisterous brasserie. Set in the basement of a converted mill and spread over three levels, it promises good-time vibes, great value and a menu of lively, eclectic food ranging from chicken satay or devilled whitebait with curry mayonnaise to braised lamb shank, haunch of venison with wild mushrooms and whisky sauce or king prawn, pancetta and chorizo tagliatelle. For afters, take a punt on stem ginger fool or cherry and almond Bakewell tart. House wine is £15.45. There's a branch at 46-50 Highgate, Heaton, Bradford; tel (01274) 499890.
Chef/s: Jamie Rylance. **Open:** Tue to Fri L 12 to 2, Tue to Sat D 6 to 10 (5.30 Fri and Sat). **Closed:** Sun, Mon, bank hols. **Meals:** alc (main courses £10 to £21). Set L £7.50 (2 courses) to £9.50. Set D £14.95 (2 courses) to £18.95. **Service:** not inc. **Details:** 120 seats. Separate bar. Wheelchair access. Music.

NEW ENTRY
Eric's

Quality built into every element
75 Lidget Street, Huddersfield, HD3 3JP
Tel no: (01484) 646416
www.ericsrestaurant.co.uk
Modern British | £28
Cooking score: 2

The location is very handy for the M62 (junctions 23/24), but Eric Paxman's restaurant has charms besides convenience. There is quality built into every element, from the light dining rooms to the excellent produce on the seasonal menus. These menus may not startle you with originality, but they do deliver consistently good food. Duck liver parfait or curried parsnip soup, say, may be followed by roast fillet of hake with Lyonnaise potatoes, buttered greens and avocado mayonnaise, or slow-braised pork shank with dauphinois. Desserts include sticky toffee and date pudding with butterscotch sauce and crème chantilly. House wine is £14.95.
Chef/s: Eric Paxman. **Open:** Tue to Fri L 12 to 2, Tue to Sat D 6 to 10 (5.30 Fri and Sat), Sun 12 to 6. **Closed:** Mon, 1 to 10 Jan. **Meals:** alc (main courses £13 to £25). Set L £12.95 (2 courses) to £24.95. Set early D £17.95 (2 courses) to £21.95. Sun L £17.95 (2 courses) to £21.95. **Service:** not inc. **Details:** 80 seats. Separate bar. Music. No children at Fri and Sat D.

ALSO RECOMMENDED
▲ T&Cake

91a Northgate, Almondbury, Huddersfield, HD5 8RX
Tel no: (01484) 430005
www.t-and-cake.co.uk
British

Stephen and Tracy Jackson last appeared in the Guide in 2010 at the Weavers Shed in Golcar. They have downsized to this daytime café, but local and home-grown ingredients still drive the simple menu of soup, sandwiches, things on toast like devilled lamb's kidneys (£7), superb savoury tarts and quiches, and classics

like eggs Benedict or roast chicken Caesar salad (£8). Chocolate torte (£2.50) is one of many luscious homemade cakes. You'll also find speciality teas, and wines from £16. Closed Sun.

■ Ilkley

★ TOP 50 ★

The Box Tree

One of Yorkshire's very finest destinations
35-37 Church Street, Ilkley, LS29 9DR
Tel no: (01943) 608484
www.theboxtree.co.uk
Anglo-French | £55
Cooking score: 6

It's 50 years since Malcolm Reid and Colin Long turned a cute roadside tea room into one of Britain's legendary restaurants. After their retirement in 1986 the Box Tree slipped into a decline and near bankruptcy until 2004, when Simon and Rena Gueller put it firmly back on the culinary map. With new head chef Dan Birk alongside, and the Guellers' own drive and talent married to attention to detail and classical skills, the Box Tree is once again a thoroughbred destination, one of Yorkshire's very finest. A spring lunch was characterised by fresh, clean, clear flavours: a ballotine of salmon wrapped in herbs is a Box Tree classic, and deservedly so. The just-cooked salmon with a crème fraîche accompaniment was superb. Similarly a pea velouté was bursting with fresh pea flavour, nicely finished with pea shoots and heady shavings of truffle. Mains follow the same pattern: rounded dishes that deploy knowing skill and a light touch. So red mullet 'à la niçoise' comes with finely chopped olives, peppers, aubergine, garlic, soft-boiled quails' eggs, shaved courgettes, turned potatoes and basil with a sauce vierge. There's a lot going on, yet with no confusion of flavours; it's all beautifully composed and expertly delivered. Décor apart (some of it is beginning to look dated), readers have been overwhelmingly positive: 'exemplary service, perfect food'. The distinctive wine list is knowledgeably managed by sommelier Didier de Costa; it starts at £19 for a Pinot Grigio and has plenty of interest by the glass. **Chef/s:** Simon Gueller and Dan Birk. **Open:** Fri to Sun L 12 to 2, Tue to Sat D 7 to 9.30 (6.30 Sat). **Closed:** Mon, 26 to 30 Dec, 1 to 6 Jan. **Meals:** Set L £25. Set D £35. Sun L £32.50. Gourmand menu £65. **Service:** not inc. **Details:** 60 seats. Separate bar. Music. No children at D.

Farsyde

Long-running favourite with value specials
1-3 New Brook Street, Ilkley, LS29 8DQ
Tel no: (01943) 602030
www.thefarsyde.co.uk
Modern British | £25
Cooking score: 3

Cherished for its personal charm and welcoming atmosphere, this long-running Ilkley restaurant is a favourite destination. On the food front, Gavin Beedham's cooking has lots of bright, contemporary accents, though there is always enough familiarity to keep the old guard satisfied. To begin, tortellini of pheasant and squash with walnut and Taleggio salad might appear alongside deep-fried calamari with chilli jam and a roast pepper, mango and Brie salad. Mains could embrace everything from rump of lamb with pearl barley and bacon stew to sea bass wrapped in basil pesto and Parma ham. Sweet-toothed offerings include Belgium waffles served with caramelised bananas in toffee sauce with liquorice ice cream. Good-value set lunches and early-bird dinners are popular, and the fairly priced wine list offers bottles from £14.90.
Chef/s: Gavin Beedham. **Open:** Tue to Sat L 9.30 to 2, D 6 to 10. **Closed:** Sun, Mon, 25 and 26 Dec, 1 and 2 Jan. **Meals:** alc (main courses £10 to £22). Set L £15.85. Early-evening set D £16.95 (2 courses). **Service:** not inc. **Details:** 80 seats. Separate bar. Wheelchair access. Music.

Ilkley Moor Vaults

Pub with plenty to please
Stockeld Road, Ilkley, LS29 9HD
Tel no: (01943) 607012
www.ilkleymoorvaults.co.uk
Modern British | £22
Cooking score: 2

The Vaults was originally the billiard room of a Victorian spa hotel that burned down in the 1960s. It is divided between a proper bar and a wood-floored, spacious and pleasantly informal dining room. The star starter is a homemade charcuterie board laden with sausage, salami, pâté, terrine and pickles, or you might begin traditionally, with Yorkshire pudding and gravy. Mains offer plenty to please, from poached salmon and salsa verde to beef and ale pie with mash. Sticky toffee pudding and ice cream is a good way to round it all off, or perhaps Yorkshire cheeses. House French is £13.90.
Chef/s: Sabi Janak. **Open:** Tue to Sat L 12 to 2.30 (3 Sat), Tue to Sat D 6 to 9, Sun 12 to 7. **Closed:** Mon. **Meals:** alc (main courses £10 to £19). **Service:** not inc. **Details:** 60 seats. 40 seats outside. Separate bar. No music. Wheelchair access. Car parking.

Leeds

Anthony's

Complex, fiercely contemporary cooking
19 Boar Lane, Leeds, LS1 6EA
Tel no: (0113) 2455922
www.anthonysrestaurant.co.uk
Modern European | £45
Cooking score: 6

When local boy and El Bulli apprentice Anthony Flinn set up shop in nightclub premises once owned by hard man Vinnie Jones, it raised more than a few eyebrows; eight years on, the venue still suffers because of its insalubrious location near Leeds railway station: 'a high-end restaurant on a low-end street', observed one who knows. That said, Anthony's basement dining room exudes a calm, urbane vibe, allowing the kitchen full rein to express itself with waves of complex, fiercely contemporary dishes. Some ideas continue to triumph – notably the white onion risotto with foamy Parmesan air and espresso topped with coffee beans; a dish of duck five ways (breast, tongue, liver, leg and web); and a plate of pork that gets its smoky fragrance from a coating of Earl Grey tea. There are also cheers for Flinn's take on surf and turf: a short rib of beef (complete with a garnish of charred bone) on a bed of shredded crustacea with langoustine bisque. This is cooking as alchemy, although not everything gels – witness a failed marriage of 'beautiful' smoked goose with cockles, coconut mousse and lychee jelly. Meals come with audacious distractions, and desserts pile on the zany thrills – note the chocolate chiboust with cherry sorbet, chicory foam and liquorice, or the 'lemon textures' offset by honey parfait and black olive. Staff seem to have sharpened up their act, and drinkers can look forward to some fascinating beer flights and a slate of creditable wines; prices from £16 (£4.40 a glass).

Chef/s: Anthony Flinn. **Open:** Tue to Sat L 12 to 2, D 7 to 9 (10 Fri and Sat). **Closed:** Sun, Mon, 25 Dec. **Meals:** Set L £21 (2 courses) to £24. Set D £36 (2 courses) to £45. Tasting menu £65 (7 courses). **Service:** not inc. **Details:** 40 seats. Separate bar. Wheelchair access. Music.

Brasserie Forty 4

A nice place to be
44 The Calls, Leeds, LS2 7EW
Tel no: (0113) 2343232
www.brasserie44.com
Modern European | £28
Cooking score: 2

Once at the forefront of the city-centre regeneration and with an inventive menu to match, Brasserie 44 has settled into a more sedate, middle-aged rhythm. Its charms remain: riverside location, rough grain mill aesthetic and decent value, but there are fewer surprises and variable delivery. One reporter found a duck starter and sea bass main 'excellent'. Another declared poached squid in

a herb dressing spot-on, but mushroom risotto too stodgy. Lamb rump with pearl barley was first-rate; however 'we were not the only table to return untouched a dish of unadorned boiled veg'. A broad wine list starts at £16.50.

Chef/s: David Robson. **Open:** Mon to Sat L 12 to 2 (1 to 3 Sat), D 6 to 10 (5 Sat). **Closed:** Sun, 25 and 26 Dec, bank hols (exc Good Friday). **Meals:** alc (main courses £12 to £22). Set L £12.50 (2 courses) to £18.10. Set D £23.95. **Service:** 10%. **Details:** 120 seats. 18 seats outside. Separate bar. Wheelchair access. Children over 2 yrs only.

NEW ENTRY
City Café at Double Tree by Hilton

Stylish eatery with unique taste sensations
Granary Wharf, 2 Wharf Approach, Leeds, LS1 4BR
Tel no: (0113) 2411000
Modern British | £25
Cooking score: 2

Chef Leah Jensen's mentors include Richard Corrigan and Gary Rhodes, and influences from both can be detected in her modern menu at this stylish hotel restaurant. Local meat and game are showcased; quail tart, pheasant terrine and trio of venison feature on a short menu that also includes interesting vegetarian choices – smoked potato gnocchi with butternut squash dressed with Puy lentil vinaigrette is a winner. Pontefract liquorice rice pudding with candied clementine delivers a unique taste sensation and, together with tiny peppermint macaroons full of eye-popping space dust, provides a fitting finale to 'a dinner you won't forget in a hurry'. House wine is £17.75.

Chef/s: Leah Jenson. **Open:** all week L 12 to 2.30 (1 to 3 Sat and Sun), D 5.30 to 10. **Meals:** alc (main courses £11 to £19). Set L £15.50. Set D £19.50. **Service:** 10%. **Details:** 150 seats. 50 seats outside. Separate bar. Wheelchair access. Music. Car parking.

NEW ENTRY

Create

31 Kings Street, Leeds, LS1 2HL
Tel no: (0113) 2420628
www.foodbycreate.co.uk
Modern British | £23
Cooking score: 2

'From the moment we entered Create, the welcoming staff provided excellent service,' said one impressed diner. Located in the stately old Bank of Ireland building, Create aims to help people back into work. It was opened by a social-enterprise outside catering company; the surprise signing was Richard Walton-Allen, former executive chef at Harvey Nichols, Leeds. He has shaped a colourful contemporary restaurant and a strong, seasonally changing menu. Starters such as potted duck and pickled plums, spelt risotto, and mackerel with Yorkshire rhubarb are sharply priced. And among mains including salt beef with braised celeriac or fish pie with Wensleydale mash, only skirt steak tops £12. Wines start at £14.
Chef/s: Edward Lee. **Open:** Mon to Sat L 12 to 2.30, Tue to Sat D 5 to 10. **Closed:** Sun, bank hols. **Meals:** alc (main courses £11 to £13). Set L £10.95 (2 courses) to £13.95. Set D £13.95 (2 courses) to £16.95. **Service:** not inc. **Details:** 130 seats. Separate bar. Wheelchair access. Music.

Fourth Floor

Cityscape views and new menus
Harvey Nichols, 107-111 Briggate, Leeds, LS1 6AZ
Tel no: (0113) 2048000
www.harveynichols.com
Modern European | £30
Cooking score: 2

Harvey Nichols' in-house restaurant has always worn the prestige of its location lightly, with cityscape views and the open kitchen contributing to its enduring appeal. There have been changes; new chef Paul Cunliffe has remodelled the menu with added flourishes, though the hit rate remains less consistent than some readers would like. Successful flavour combinations appeared in a starter of pigeon with Puy lentils and an old-school main course of chicken thighs stuffed with Boursin. Pastry skills need work, though an anise biscuit barrel containing hazelnut foam worked wonders for an overset caramel mousse. Wine is from £17, with heftier possibilities up to £195.
Chef/s: Paul Cunliffe. **Open:** all week L 12 to 3 (4 Sun), Tue to Sat D 5.30 to 10. **Closed:** 25 Dec, 1 Jan, Easter Sun. **Meals:** alc (main courses £13 to £23). Set L and D £20 (2 courses) to £25. **Service:** 10%. **Details:** 90 seats. 20 seats outside. Separate bar. Wheelchair access. Music.

Salvo's

Fantastic pizzas and budget prices
115 Otley Road, Headingley, Leeds, LS6 3PX
Tel no: (0113) 2755017
www.salvos.co.uk
Italian | £28
Cooking score: 2

With a new extension and the introduction of a booking policy for part of the restaurant (Salvo's wouldn't be Salvo's without a queue), this perfectly charming Italian continues to attract everyone from large families to cosy dates. The draw? The Dammone family's fantastic pizzas, although the budget prices of the broad-appeal menu also help. Very good mainstream dishes are based on quality ingredients and range from whole grilled sardines via ziti al'forno to roast belly pork in a sweet-and-sour red pepper and caper confit. Well-priced wines open at £16.75. Sibling Salvo's Salumeria at 107 Otley Road delights with its homely cooking.
Chef/s: Gip Dammone and Giuseppe Schirripa. **Open:** Mon to Sat L 12 to 2, D 6 to 10.30 (5.30 to 11 Fri and Sat). Sun 12 to 9. **Closed:** 25 and 26 Dec, 1 Jan. **Meals:** alc (main courses £9 to £19). Set L £10.50 (2 courses). Set D £14.50 (2 courses) to £17.50. **Service:** not inc. **Details:** 88 seats. Separate bar. Wheelchair access. Music.

ALSO RECOMMENDED

▲ Hansa's

72-74 North Street, Leeds, LS2 7PN
Tel no: (0113) 2444408
www.hansasrestaurant.com
Indian vegetarian £5 OFF

Hansa's has been a Leeds favourite since 1986, and the excellent Gujarati cooking goes from strength to strength. The vegetarian menu is overseen by Mrs Hansa Dabhi and service is from an all-female team. Curries, say chickpea koftas with potatoes (£7.25), are characterised by clear spicing and complemented by bhatura bread and plain and pilau rice. Start with samosa chaat or chilli paneer (£4.25) and finish with the wonderful curd cheese-based shrikand. Organic wines from £13.95. Open Sun L and Mon to Sat D.

▲ Kendells Bistro

St Peters Square, Leeds, LS9 8AH
Tel no: (0113) 2436553
www.kendellsbistro.co.uk
French

'Real food cooked with great skill and love' trumpets a fan of this honest-to-goodness French bistro. The menu is written on a blackboard each day (use the binoculars provided, if necessary) and there's always plenty to enjoy – from rich, velvety soupe de poissons (£8.50) or goats' cheese tart with roast beetroot, to confit duck with Cassis (£14.90), côte de boeuf and belly pork boulangère. Portions are generous, prices are very fair and warm-hearted cordiality prevails. French regional wines from £17.95. Open Tue to Sat D only.

▲ Sukhothai

8 Regent Street, Chapel Allerton, Leeds, LS7 4PE
Tel no: (0113) 2370141
www.sukhothai.co.uk
Thai

This impeccably turned out Thai favourite is a boon for Chapel Allerton. The broad menu offers plenty of choice for vegetarians, and jogs around the mainstays of the cuisine, stopping off for well-reported classic hot-and-sour salads like som tum (£6.95) and appetisers including duck spring rolls and soups, then the usual red and green coconut milk-based curries, stir-fries and grills (whole sea bass in banana leaves £14.95). Wine from £13.95. Closed Mon to Wed L. Branches in Headingley and Harrogate.

■ Leyburn

The Sandpiper Inn

Highly polished Dales inn
Market Place, Leyburn, DL8 5AT
Tel no: (01969) 622206
www.sandpiperinn.co.uk
Modern British | £29
Cooking score: 3

Jonathan and Janine Harrison run a highly polished operation at the Sandpiper, a seventeenth-century inn set in the heart of a Dales market town. Menus are built on expert local sourcing, and Jonathan keeps things simple – the impact comes from big, punchy flavours. He serves a warm salad of poached egg, black pudding, smoked bacon and sauté potatoes, dishes up grilled ribeye steak with traditional garnish, and isn't afraid to offer fish and chips on the lunchtime menu. Elsewhere, his cheffing background shows in pressed Dales lamb served with celeriac purée, carrots and potato gnocchi in a smoked garlic jus, and a dessert of fruit salad with bitter lemon sorbet and caramelised meringue. Thirty or so affordable wines start at £14.50.
Chef/s: Jonathan Harrison. **Open:** Tue to Sun L 12 to 2.30 (2 Sun), D 6.30 to 9 (9.30 Fri and Sat). **Closed:** Mon. **Meals:** alc (main courses £12 to £20). **Service:** not inc. **Details:** 40 seats. 20 seats outside. Separate bar. Music.

¶│● Also Recommended

Also recommended entries are not scored but we think they are worth a visit.

▌Malton

NEW ENTRY

Talbot Hotel

Revamped hotel with flair and care
Yorkersgate, Malton, YO17 7AJ
Tel no: (01653) 639096
www.talbotmalton.com
Modern British | £29
Cooking score: 3

This was a seriously faded hotel until the
Fitzwilliam Estate resumed control 18 months
ago and restored it to the tune of £4 million.
Much of that went on hiring TV chef James
Martin as executive chef, and the menu he's
created is a good fit with the new Talbot:
conservative with a safe modern edge. Salmon
comes with curried mussels and samphire;
beef with spelt risotto; lamb is roasted in
lavender and hay. Head chef Craig Atchinson
(formerly of Swinton Park, see entry) is
comfortably on top of Martin's creations,
serving an agreeable Whitby kipper cake in
cream and butter sauce, then cod and brown
shrimps with crushed Jersey Royals. Local
produce dominates – as does Malton's horsey
tradition on the walls. Wine from £16 typifies
square value.
Chef/s: Craig Atchinson. **Open:** Sun L 12 to 2.30, all
week D 6.30 to 9.30. **Meals:** Set D £24 (2 courses)
to £29. Sun L £20 (2 courses) to £25. **Service:** not
inc. **Details:** 46 seats. Separate bar. No music.
Wheelchair access. Car parking.

▌Masham

Samuel's at Swinton Park

Exhilarating cooking and Gothic grandeur
Swinton Park, Masham, HG4 4JH
Tel no: (01765) 680900
www.swintonpark.com
Modern British | £52
Cooking score: 5

A grandiose, castellated leviathan surrounded
by a 20,000-acre estate complete with a deer
park, an ornamental lake and a four-acre

walled garden, the Cunliffe-Listers' sprawling
Gothic pile does country-house splendour
with gold-leaf knobs on. Brace yourself for a
weighty procession of family portraits and
treasured antiques, plus enormous windows
and ornate ceilings in the palatial dining room
(built by the owner's great-great-great
grandfather). Amid this vision of unbridled
aristocracy, chef Simon Crannage conjures up
serious food with modern inflections, from
beetroot-cured salmon with cucumber sorbet,
beetroot jelly and oyster vinaigrette to cherry
soup accompanied by an almond and pistachio
parfait and dark chocolate crémeux.
Complexity is a given, but there is also room
for rich seasonal pickings from the
surrounding countryside and the estate itself –
perhaps confit belly and cheek of Wateredge
Farm pork with garden celeriac purée, sage
buckwheat and compressed apple, or an earthy
dish of partridge with glazed turnips, Savoy
cabbage and game chips. Fish also receives
high-end treatment: witness line-caught sea
bass with artichoke purée, charred leeks,
wilted kale and Pink Fir Apple potatoes,
moistened with a luxurious reduction of
roasted chicken and truffles. The Castle menu
offers simpler, brasserie-style food, and the
wine list is a suitably auspicious tome
peppered with interesting names; prices
from £19.
Chef/s: Simon Crannage. **Open:** Tue to Sun L 12.30
to 2, all week D 7.30 to 9.30 (10 Fri and Sat).
Meals: alc brasserie menu (£11 to £16). Set L £22 (2
courses) to £25.95. Set D £52. Sun L £28. Tasting
menu £60 (7 courses) to £70 (10 courses).
Service: not inc. **Details:** 60 seats. Separate bar.
Wheelchair access. Music. Car parking. Children
over 8 yrs only at D.

Symbols

⮌ Accommodation is available

£30 Three courses for less than £30

V Separate vegetarian menu

£5 OFF £5-off voucher scheme

🍾 Notable wine list

Vennell's

Metropolitan makeover for a Dales favourite
7 Silver Street, Masham, HG4 4DX
Tel no: (01765) 689000
www.vennellsrestaurant.co.uk
Modern British | £28
Cooking score: 5

 £30

The big news is that Jon and Laura Vennell have given their formerly chintzy, but highly personal, restaurant a full-dress makeover. In place of the rather uncomfortable layout, the spanking new interior is spread over two levels, with sociable drinks now served in the upstairs bar. The whole place breathes sleek metropolitan chic, with deep aubergine walls, grey paintwork, oversized lampshades, sparkling gold mirrors and fig-motif wallpaper – although Jon has resisted the temptation to needlessly reinvent his menus. On offer is a tight repertoire of meticulously crafted, classy dishes that never play to the gallery; the much-loved beef Wellington and trencherman oxtail and mushroom suet pudding still flex their muscles, although the kitchen can also apply a lighter touch when needed – especially when it comes to fish. Olive oil-poached salmon appears with salmon tartare, beetroot wafers and lemon dressing, while seared sea bass might be served with crushed potato, tomato concassé, crab tortellini and basil oil. After that, there is always a plate of fine Yorkshire cheeses to assuage savoury palates, while sweet-toothed diners might look to warm chocolate fondant with passion-fruit sorbet or a trio of iced desserts for sugary satisfaction. The wine list has also been retuned, with more emphasis on appropriate food-friendly tipples; 11 house selections start at £17.75.
Chef/s: Jon Vennell. **Open:** Sun L 12.30 to 4, Wed to Sat D 7.15 to 11.30. **Closed:** Mon, Tue, 26 to 29 Dec, 1 to 14 Jan, 1 week Jun. **Meals:** Set D £24.50 (2 courses) to £28. Sun L £18.50 (2 courses) to £21.50. **Service:** not inc. **Details:** 30 seats. Separate bar. Music.

▮ Newton-on-Ouse

The Dawnay Arms

Brit cooking with verve and gusto
Newton-on-Ouse, YO30 2BR
Tel no: (01347) 848345
www.thedawnayatnewton.co.uk
British | £25
Cooking score: 4

 £30

The bright lights of Leeds must seem a long way away as city chef-turned-country innkeeper Martel Smith enters his fifth year at this eighteenth-century boozer with gardens running down to the river Ouse. Inside, beams, flagstone floors and shades of grey set the tone for his skilful cooking, which deploys regional ingredients with verve and gusto. Black pudding is made on the premises and served with braised belly pork and apple, ballottine of ham hock is perked up with pineapple pickle and a Scotch quail's egg, and plates of beef bourguignon are accompanied by parsnip mash. On the fish front, chunks of crab-crusted Whitby cod enriched with fresh tagliatelle, spinach and shellfish cream show Smith's high-end background, while battered haddock with chunky chips and mushy peas is pure pub grub. To conclude, it's unfussy satisfaction all the way, from caramelised apple tart with honeycomb ice cream to ginger crème brûlée accompanied by a helping of Yorkshire rhubarb. Ten house wines start at £14.95.
Chef/s: Martel Smith. **Open:** Tue to Sun L 12 to 2.30 (6 Sun), Tue to Sat D 6 to 9.30. **Closed:** Mon. **Meals:** alc (main courses £12 to £21). Sun L £14.95 (2 courses) to £17.95. **Service:** not inc. **Details:** 60 seats. 40 seats outside. Separate bar. Wheelchair access. Music. Car parking.

Oldstead
The Black Swan
From family inn to garlanded restaurant
Oldstead, YO61 4BL
Tel no: (01347) 868387
www.blackswanoldstead.co.uk
Modern British | £45
Cooking score: 4

 V

The Black Swan has enjoyed a startling trajectory from simple family-run inn to garlanded restaurant in just five years. The elegant, understated style – big oak tables, sturdy chairs, sporting prints and Turkish rugs – extends to the food, which one reader describes as 'not overly inventive, but done very well indeed.' Ham hock terrine has its profile raised with a smooth pease pudding and sharp piccalilli. Equally uplifting is homemade black pudding with Jerusalem artichoke purée and chestnuts, plates of roast beef, pig's cheek, and halibut are accompanied by good English vegetables – celeriac, parsnips, sprouts – while Parmesan gnocchi is given extra oomph by a shot of wild garlic and shaved black truffle. As a finale, crisp filo sandwiching a lemon and honey parfait with a dusting of honeycomb and pine nuts 'sealed a classy meal throughout'. A thorough wine list includes interesting choices by the glass. House wine starts at £19.
Chef/s: Adam Jackson. **Open:** Thur to Sun L 12 to 2 (3 Sun), all week D 6 to 9. **Closed:** 1 week Jan.
Meals: alc (main courses £19 to £26). Set L £20 (2 courses) to £25. Sun L £28. **Service:** not inc.
Details: 50 seats. 24 seats outside. Separate bar. Music. Car parking.

Average Price
The average price listed in main-entry reviews denotes the price of a three-course meal, without wine.

Osmotherley
Golden Lion
Warmhearted Yorkshire watering hole
6 West End, Osmotherley, DL6 3AA
Tel no: (01609) 883526
www.goldenlionosmotherley.co.uk
Anglo-French | £26
Cooking score: 3

Still a proper Yorkshire watering hole complete with real ales and blazing fires, this eighteenth-century village pub manages to pack 'em in with its easy-going approach and all-round food. Eager crowds get full satisfaction from goats' cheese, chorizo and red pepper salad with harissa dressing or salmon fishcake with chive beurre blanc, but the kitchen also assuages pub diehards with steak and kidney with a suet crust, fried fillets of plaice and chips, and sirloin steak with pepper sauce, all served with warm-hearted Yorkshire generosity. Leave room for one of the hearty desserts – they don't stray much further than bread-and-butter pudding with lashings of cream. Prices are reasonable, and that also goes for the short wine list, which opens at £15.95.
Chef/s: Chris and Judith Wright. **Open:** Wed to Sun L 12 to 2.30, all week D 6 to 9. **Closed:** 25 Dec.
Meals: alc (main courses £10 to £21). **Service:** not inc. **Details:** 68 seats. 16 seats outside. Wheelchair access. Music.

Pickering
The White Swan Inn
Oozing big-hearted Yorkshire hospitality
Market Place, Pickering, YO18 7AA
Tel no: (01751) 472288
www.white-swan.co.uk
Modern British | £35
Cooking score: 3

It's been going a long time – the Buchanan family has been cosseting visitors for nigh on 30 years. They place comfort at the heart of their sixteenth-century inn-with-rooms, which is a delight to behold, cleverly reworked without losing any of its period charm. Food is a key part of the operation. The cooking is underpinned by well-sourced ingredients and a sound knowledge of the classics: Whitby fishcakes with herbed shrimp salad and tartare sauce to start, a trio of game (venison haunch, teal and widgeon) with game chips, redcurrant jelly and bread sauce, or braised lamb shoulder shepherd's pie with a Fountains Gold cheese glaze and clapshot for mains, then perhaps chocolate cake and boozy cherries to finish. House wine is £15.95. **Chef/s:** Darren Clemmit. **Open:** all week L 12 to 2, D 6.45 to 9. **Meals:** alc (main courses £13 to £22). **Service:** not inc. **Details:** 55 seats. 20 seats outside. Separate bar. No music. Wheelchair access. Car parking.

▌Ramsgill

★ TOP 50 ★

The Yorke Arms

A chef with stellar talents
Ramsgill, HG3 5RL
Tel no: (01423) 755243
www.yorke-arms.co.uk
Modern British | £65
Cooking score: 6

£5 OFF 🛏

From a classical base, Frances Atkins has crafted a refined contemporary restaurant in this ivy-covered former hunting lodge in the tranquil Nidderdale valley. It is all managed with great warmth and dedication and there are gastronomic pleasures in abundance for those making the trip. The regularly changing menu, inspired by top-class seasonal ingredients (the inn has its own productive kitchen garden) and a meticulous attention to detail, place Frances at the top of her game. The menu comprises tried and trusted 'Yorke Arms Classics' like a potage of shellfish with Whitby crab and salt cod, Wensleydale soufflé with scallops, and slow-cooked lamb shoulder and loin with sweetbread. These are supplemented with 'Dishes of the Day', which might be slow-cooked hare, wild sea bass with langoustine or, memorably, boned and truffle-

stuffed quail with honey, walnuts, celery and apple. Basil and lemon tart matched with sharp blackcurrants and a dash of liquorice is among a carte of artfully composed desserts. The wine list is pure delight for aficionados, with top-flight French names and a contingent of serious, wallet friendly goodies from further south. Bottles start at a manageable £19.50, with 20 by the glass. **Chef/s:** Frances Atkins. **Open:** all week L 12 to 1.30, Mon to Sat D 7 to 8.30 (Sun reservations only). **Meals:** alc (main courses £24 to £43). Set L £35. Sun L £40. Tasting menu £85. **Service:** not inc. **Details:** 40 seats. 20 seats outside. Separate bar. Music. Car parking.

▌Richmond

The Punch Bowl Inn

Popular Dales refuelling point
Low Row, Richmond, DL11 6PF
Tel no: (01748) 886233
www.pbinn.co.uk
Modern British | £24
Cooking score: 1

£5 OFF 🛏 £30

A striking location in the Swaledale valley makes the Codys' seventeenth-century pub-with-rooms a popular refuelling point for outdoor types touring the Dales. At its best it mixes straightforward country-pub cooking with heart-warming generosity, and seems to please on both fronts. A bowl of cauliflower and Cheddar soup might open proceedings, followed by braised beef and vegetable casserole or belly pork with spiced red cabbage, then Yorkshire parkin with apple compote and custard to finish. Wines from £15.95. **Chef/s:** Andrew Short. **Open:** all week L 12 to 2 (2.30 Sun), D 6 to 9. **Closed:** 25 Dec. **Meals:** alc (main courses £12 to £20). Sun L £10.45 (1 course). **Service:** not inc. **Details:** 60 seats. Music. Car parking.

Ripon

Lockwoods

All-dayer that aims to please
83 North Street, Ripon, HG4 1DP
Tel no: (01765) 607555
www.lockwoodsrestaurant.co.uk
Modern British | £27
Cooking score: 1

This smart all-purpose eatery close to the city centre gets a lot of footfall; shoppers and tourists drop in for coffee, cakes, sandwiches or meals. The kitchen mixes regional produce with ideas from further afield in lively style: lamb rump and crispy breast with white bean stew and salsa verde, say, or the roast loin of venison that gave a French visitor a 'home from home experience'. Desserts jump from homely (treacle tart) to exotic (spiced roast pineapple). The global wine list starts at £14.95.
Chef/s: Ronayut Grimshaw. **Open:** Tue to Sat L 12 to 2.30, D 6 to 9.30 (10 Fri and Sat). **Closed:** Sun, Mon, 25 and 26 Dec, 1 Jan. **Meals:** alc (main courses £9.50 to £22). Set D £17.50 (2 courses) to £19.95. **Service:** not inc. **Details:** 60 seats. Wheelchair access. Music.

Ripponden

El Gato Negro

No clichés, just sharp, honest tapas
1 Oldham Road, Ripponden, HX6 4DN
Tel no: (01422) 823070
www.elgatonegrotapas.com
Spanish | £25
Cooking score: 5

It may not inhabit the moody backstreets of Barcelona, but Simon Shaw has injected some Iberian vim and vigour into this defunct boozer since decamping to Ripponden in 2005. His lucky 'black cat' (el gato negro) is a down-home kind of place, with rustic good looks, an easy-going vibe and jaunty paper menus doubling as place mats (simply tick the boxes, and scribble any requests on the 'chest'

of the cartoon feline). There are no castanet clichés here, just sharp, honest tapas based on impeccably sourced ingredients – from the finest acorn-fed jamón Ibérico, Catalan bread and regional cheeses to North Country meats and seafood. Signature daily specials add a few challenges, otherwise there is little to frighten the shire horses. Croquetas, patatas bravas, tortillas and roast baby chicken with paprika and romesco sauce join forces with 12-hour belly, cheek and morcilla, rabo de toro (oxtail) with horseradish mash or pinto beans with parsley root purée. As for fish, expect anything from char-grilled gambas (large prawns) with chorizo and chilli butter to baby monkfish tails with shellfish paella. The revamped wine list straddles Spain and the 'Spanish New World', with intelligent pickings and fair prices from £14.95 (£3.75 a glass).
Chef/s: Simon Shaw. **Open:** Sat L 12 to 2, Tue to Sat D 6 to 11. **Closed:** Sun, Mon, 25 Dec to 6 Jan, 2 weeks summer, 2 weeks winter, bank hols. **Meals:** alc (tapas £5 to £16). Set D £35 for 2 (inc wine). **Service:** not inc. **Details:** 52 seats. Wheelchair access. Music.

Sancton

NEW ENTRY

The Star @ Sancton

Appealingly local menus and sound cooking
King Street, Sancton, YO43 4QP
Tel no: (01430) 827269
www.thestaratsancton.co.uk
Modern British | £30
Cooking score: 3

Ever more people are finding their way to the Yorkshire Wolds in the wake of the David Hockney exhibition – and they should also find their way to Ben and Lindsey Cox's smartly upholstered roadside pub/restaurant. An appealingly local menu offers wild rabbit three ways or Yorkshire pudding and oxtail confit, and rose veal calf's liver with bubble and squeak. Cooking is sound, but there's a fondness for crisp coatings, as in crab fishcake, rabbit rissole and cod cheek fritter. Ben's food

works best when at its simplest, as in the sea bream with sautéed new potatoes and wild garlic butter tried at a test meal. Desserts are bountiful, as in Yorkshire parkin ice cream with chocolate honeycomb. House wine starts at £14.95 and prices rise alongside interest and quality.
Chef/s: Ben Cox. **Open:** Tue to Sun L 12 to 2 (3 Sun), D 6 to 9.30 (8 Sun). **Closed:** Mon. **Meals:** alc (main courses £10 to £25). Set L £15 (2 courses) to £18. **Service:** not inc. **Details:** 80 seats. 36 seats outside. Separate bar. Wheelchair access. Music. Car parking.

Sawdon
The Anvil Inn
Former forge with up-to-the-minute food
Main Street, Sawdon, YO13 9DY
Tel no: (01723) 859896
www.theanvilinnsawdon.co.uk
Modern European | £28
Cooking score: 2

A village forge in the eighteenth century, this comfortably renovated pub on the edge of Dalby Forest still sports the original furnace and blacksmith's tools. But that's where the nostalgia ends, for the kitchen is thoroughly up to date when it comes to cooking. Chef/proprietor Mark Wilson makes a good fist of things; he's especially adept at handling local game, say terrine of confit hare with wood pigeon breast, roast beetroot with red wine, grape and juniper chutney. Otherwise loin of Whitby cod with Parmesan crust, fricassee of leek, peas and dry-smoked bacon has gone down well. For afters, perhaps try bitter chocolate marquise. Wines start at £14.95.
Chef/s: Mark Wilson. **Open:** Wed to Sun L 12 to 2 (2.30 Sun), D 6.30 to 9 (8 Sun). **Closed:** Mon, Tue, 25 and 26 Dec, 1 Jan. **Meals:** alc (main courses £12 to £20). **Service:** not inc. **Details:** 36 seats. Separate bar. Music. Car parking.

Scarborough
Lanterna
A proper Piedmontese ristorante
33 Queen Street, Scarborough, YO11 1HQ
Tel no: (01723) 363616
www.lanterna-ristorante.co.uk
Italian | £40
Cooking score: 3

Giorgio and Rachel Alessio run the illustrious Lanterna as a full-on, dyed-in-the-wool 'ristorante', rejecting pizzeria clichés in favour of Piedmontese truffles and spanking fresh seafood from the Scarborough boats. Seasonal feasts are staged in honour of the princely subterranean fungus, while the sea yields ozone-fresh plates of langoustine, sea bass, turbot, lobster — or whatever the nets and pots can provide. Handmade pasta is also a reliable call if your fancy turns to spaghetti with locally gathered winkles or ravioli stuffed with venison, eggs and spinach. Those in the mood for meat might consider chicken breast with Gorgonzola and Parma ham or medallions of fillet steak, cooked rare with butter and garlic in true Piedmontese style. After that, genuine zabaglione and wobbly pannacotta await. The wine list is a treasure trove of directly imported bottles from the Italian regions, with prices from £14.95.
Chef/s: Giorgio Alessio. **Open:** Mon to Sat D only 7 to 9.30. **Closed:** Sun, 25 and 26 Dec, 1 Jan, last 2 weeks Oct. **Meals:** alc (main courses £8 to £45). **Service:** not inc. **Details:** 35 seats. Music.

Sheffield
Artisan
Sharp neighbourhood eatery
34 Sandygate Road, Crosspool, Sheffield, S10 5RY
Tel no: (0114) 2666096
www.artisansheffield.co.uk
Modern British | £28
Cooking score: 3

Standing proud in Sheffield's oldest 'village', Artisan proves its worth as a sharp neighbourhood eatery with an eye for native

produce. Local boy and owner Richard Smith has honed his supply network since pitching camp here in 1995 and his menus add some timely tweaks to seasonal produce. Black pudding tarte Tatin with sautéed calf's liver, apples and a boozy, sticky reduction; roast lamb rump with a miniature Lancashire hotpot and crushed cauliflower; and warm chocolate tart with peanut ice cream are typical of the kitchen's honest, big-flavoured output. Artisan also has its own steak menu (the house chateaubriand has been enthusiastically received), and there are plans to develop the cheese trolley. Richard is also keen on beer and has introduced some intriguing food-matching ideas – although the cosmopolitan wine list (from £14) offers satisfaction too.
Chef/s: Ian Robley. **Open:** all week L 12 to 3, D 5 to 10 (9 Sun). **Meals:** alc (main courses £16 to £24). Set L £12 (2 courses) to £15. Set D £15 (2 courses) to £20. Sun L £23. **Service:** not inc. **Details:** 80 seats. 6 seats outside. Separate bar. Wheelchair access. Music.

Kitchen

Big-on-flavour bistro food
762 Ecclesall Road, Sheffield, S11 8TB
Tel no: (0114) 2671351
www.sheffieldkitchen.com
Modern European | £20
Cooking score: 3

'Farm to table' food isn't quite the tall order it might be in many another English city; Sheffield has always had its green side. John Parsons is an assiduous sourcer and hands-on kitchen presence, overseeing in-house butchery, bread baking and much more. It all gets turned into refined bistro cookery that's big on strong, true flavour. A platter of smoked and cured fish with beetroot and cream cheese is a generous opener, then pork three ways (belly, fillet and cheek), mixed grilled fish (sea bass, salmon, cod and prawns), or beef fillet in blue cheese with smoked ham, asparagus and celeriac. One satisfied customer concluded with 'hearty and exceptional sticky

toffee pudding with lashings of caramel sauce', and couldn't have been happier. A tiny wine list starts at £14.
Chef/s: John Parsons. **Open:** Wed to Sat L 12 to 3, D 6.30 to 9.30. **Closed:** Sun to Tue, 25 and 26 Dec, 1 Jan, Easter. **Meals:** alc (main courses £8 to £18). Set D £12 (2 courses) to £15. **Service:** not inc. **Details:** 40 seats. Wheelchair access. Music.

The Milestone

Buzzy pub with kaleidoscope cooking
84 Green Lane, Sheffield, S3 8SE
Tel no: (0114) 2728327
www.the-milestone.co.uk
British | £25
Cooking score: 2

'Amazing dining experience, worth a massive detour, putting Sheffield on the map' sums up the unwavering local support given to Matt Bigland and Marc Sheldon's laid-back pub. The kitchen adds to the buzz, pumping out a kaleidoscope of ingredients and flavours: carrot and coriander soup that 'never tasted so good'; some 'beautiful beef served with a kidney shepherd's pie'; pot-roast chicken with bacon, fried potatoes, spinach and onion purée; an 'amazing' hot pear crumble served with a 'vibrant green' apple sorbet. In general prices are modest, but lunch and early-bird menus are a steal. Wines from £14.50. Related to the Wig and Pen by The Milestone (see entry).
Chef/s: Matt Hodkin. **Open:** Mon to Fri L 12 to 4, Sat and Sun 11 to 4, all week D 5 to 10 (9 Sun). **Closed:** 25 and 26 Dec, 1 Jan. **Meals:** alc (main courses £13 to £17). Set L and early D £16 (2 courses) to £18. Sun L £14 (2 courses) to £16.50. **Service:** not inc. **Details:** 120 seats. Separate bar. Wheelchair access. Music.

Visit us Online

To find out more about
The Good Food Guide, please visit
www.thegoodfoodguide.co.uk

Moran's Restaurant

Characterful and rewarding local restaurant
289b Abbeydale Road South, Dore, Sheffield,
S17 3LB
Tel no: (0114) 2350101
www.moranssheffield.co.uk
Modern European | £30
Cooking score: 4

£5 OFF

Tucked away in Sheffield's wooded Dore district, Moran's is a characterful neighbourhood restaurant, all dark wood and low lighting, with jazz dinners on certain dates. Its informality extends to a cheery ambience of everybody mucking in (you may have to ask your neighbours to move if you want to nip to the loo), but the food rewards those who enter into the spirit. It can be as simple as the asparagus and poached egg, calf's liver with mustard mash, and strawberry cheesecake that placated one pair who had waited a while for a table to free up. When the kitchen takes wing in full British mode, expect king prawn tempura with crab cakes; chilli jam and lime mayo; roast local venison with braised red cabbage and parsnip purée in port and redcurrant; and warm carrot cake with carrot and orange jelly and milk ice cream. A well-written, fairly priced wine list opens at £12.95.
Chef/s: Bryan Moran. **Open:** Sat and Sun L 12 to 2.30 (3 Sun), Tue to Sat D 6 to 9 (7 to 9.30 Fri and Sat). **Closed:** Mon, first 2 weeks Jan. **Meals:** alc (main courses £15 to £26). Sun L £23.95. **Service:** not inc. **Details:** 60 seats. Separate bar. Wheelchair access. Music. Car parking.

Symbols

🛏 Accommodation is available

£30 Three courses for less than £30

V Separate vegetarian menu

£5 OFF £5-off voucher scheme

🍾 Notable wine list

Wig & Pen by The Milestone

Good eating and good value
44 Campo Lane, Sheffield, S1 2EG
Tel no: (0114) 2722150
www.the-wigandpen.co.uk
British | £28
Cooking score: 2

£5 OFF   £30

There's good eating to be had at this venerable city pub, a sibling of the Milestone (see entry). Overlooking Paradise Square, it's a welcoming place complete with attentive service, sound cooking and good value. Part of the appeal is the set-price two-course menu and the excellent comfort food on the carte. Modern brasserie cooking deploys quality materials in dishes like a starter of ham hock ballottine with green apple and black pudding crumb, main of pork loin and confit belly with crispy squid and root vegetable stew, and dessert of rhubarb frangipane and cardamom ice cream. House wine is £14.50.
Chef/s: Matt Hodkin. **Open:** all week L 12 to 4, Mon to Sat D 5 to 10. **Closed:** 25 and 26 Dec, 1 Jan. **Meals:** alc (main courses £11 to £17). Set L and D £20 (2 courses, plus half-bottle wine) to £24. Sun L £14.95 (2 courses) to £18.95. **Details:** 120 seats. 20 seats outside. Separate bar. Wheelchair access. Music.

ALSO RECOMMENDED

▲ Lokanta
478-480 Glossop Road, Sheffield, S10 2QA
Tel no: (0114) 2666444
www.lokanta.co.uk
Turkish £5 OFF

'A well-balanced menu, good wine list, warm family atmosphere, excellent service and good value for money': Lokanta clearly ticks all the boxes for readers. It's a welcoming Turkish eatery majoring in satisfying meze – aubergine and pepper in garlic yoghurt (£5.50), lamb köfte in onion and sumac (£5.60) – as well as full dishes like grilled whole sea bass with potato salad (£14.50).

Finish classically with nutty, honey-drenched baklava (£5.50). Turkish wines from £14. Open Tue-Sun D and Sun L.

▲ Rafters

220 Oakbrook Road, Nether Green, Sheffield, S11 7ED
Tel no: (0114) 2304819
www.raftersrestaurant.co.uk
Modern British

'An exceptional and thoroughly enjoyable experience' exclaimed one visitor to this neighbourhood favourite in the leafy suburb of Nether Green. One reader praised chef/proprietor Marcus Lane's assured cooking as 'beautifully presented', another noted the 'friendly, efficient and respectful' service. From the fixed-price dinner menu (£36.95), the pan-fried fillet of Angus beef with oxtail, thyme-roasted sweet potato and Shiraz jus has attracted plaudits, as have desserts such as Black Forest terrine. House wine is £15.50. Open Mon and Wed to Sat D only.

▲ Silversmiths Restaurant & Bar

111 Arundel Street, Sheffield, S1 2NT
Tel no: (01142) 706160
www.silversmiths-restaurant.com
Modern British £5 OFF

Justin Rowntree's vibrant restaurant is a delight, from the way it 'utilises available space without creating a cramped feel' to the 'fantastic dining experience' that puts provenance at the heart of the menu. Wild mushroom soup, and pulled pork with black pudding bonbon, sausage patty, crackling and homemade piccalilli (£5.95), have been particularly enjoyed, ditto 'awesome' braised pheasant, slow-braised beef short rib and ox cheek cottage pie (£13.50), plus great cocktails; try the rhubarb Martini. Wines from £15.95. Closed Sun and Mon.

The Street Food Chef
98 Pinstone Street, Sheffield, S8 7UE
www.streetfoodchef.co.uk
'Takeaway breakfast or lunch – burrito, taco, quesadilla or empanadas – are fresh and tasty and cooked in front of you. Pork shoulder comes from Moss Valley farm 3 miles away; all the other meats from within a 30 mile radius.'

▌ Shibden
Shibden Mill Inn
Captivating inn with solid cooking
Shibden Fold, Shibden, HX3 7UL
Tel no: (01422) 365840
www.shibdenmillinn.com
Modern British | £23
Cooking score: 3
🛏 V £30

Set deep in a lush green valley, with an old mill stream bubbling away contentedly, this captivating seventeenth-century inn is a delight to behold. Naturally it's a heritage destination par excellence – all beams, open fires and tiny rooms – but the food lives in the present. Chef Darren Parkinson delivers 'good solid cooking' pointed up with plenty of elaborate detailing. A 'belting braise' of beef short ribs (aka Jacob's ladder) comes with kale, two kinds of beetroot, a punchy horseradish risotto and a tangy local cheese fritter. North Country ingredients also take centre stage in, say, an assiette of Yorkshire game accompanied by Brussels sprout coleslaw or grilled Peterhead mackerel with scallop and coriander ravioli, rémoulade and caper velouté. Artisan cheeses are true to the region, while the wine list casts its net across the globe (prices from £15.65).
Chef/s: Darren Parkinson. **Open:** Mon to Sat L 12 to 2 (2.30 Fri and Sat), D 6 to 9.30. Sun 12 to 7.30. **Closed:** 24 to 26 Dec, 1 Jan. **Meals:** alc (main courses £16 to £20). Set L £12 (2 courses) to £15. **Service:** not inc. **Details:** 90 seats. 80 seats outside. Separate bar. No music. Car parking.

■ Sinnington

ALSO RECOMMENDED
▲ Fox & Hounds

Main Street, Sinnington, YO62 6SQ
Tel no: (01751) 431577
www.thefoxandhoundsinn.co.uk
Modern British £5 OFF

Tucked away in a peaceful little village, this
solid stone inn has warmth and charm to
spare. The menu celebrates trustworthy
sourcing, relishable cooking and strong
flavours, perhaps twice-baked Lincolnshire
Poacher Cheddar soufflé (£6.25), lamb hotpot
with red cabbage or prime ribeye steak with
all the trimmings (£18.95). Desserts stay
dependably in the comfort zone of lemon
meringue tart, apple and plum crumble and
bread-and-butter pudding. Wines from
£15.95. Open all week. Accommodation.

■ Skipton

Le Caveau

Gutsy bistro cooking in a secret cellar
86 High Street, Skipton, BD23 1JJ
Tel no: (01756) 794274
www.lecaveau.co.uk
Anglo-French | £32
Cooking score: 2
£5 OFF

Hidden down a stone stairway beneath the
High Street, this vaulted sixteenth-century
cellar makes an appealing, other-worldly
venue. Once used to lock up sheep-rustlers, it
is now the place for gutsy, French-accented
bistro cooking, ably rendered by Richard
Barker. Typical dishes are a starter of pigeon
breast with caramelised onions and black
pudding in red wine jus, then halibut fillet on
shrimp and tarragon risotto with crab butter
sauce. Round things off with winter berry
mascarpone cheesecake in berry coulis. An
informal jumble of international drinking
opens at £15.50 (£4.10 a glass) for Duboeuf
and Concha y Toro house wines.

Chef/s: Richard Barker. Open: Tue to Fri L 12 to 2,
Tue to Sat D 7 to 9.30 (5 to 9.45 Sat). Closed: Sun,
Mon, 25 and 26 Dec, first week Jan, first week Jun,
first 2 weeks Sept. Meals: alc (main courses £13 to
£23). Set L £9.95 (2 courses) to £13.95. Set D £15.95
(2 courses) to £20. Service: not inc. Details: 24
seats. Separate bar. Music.

■ South Dalton

The Pipe & Glass Inn

Appealing tavern with memorable cooking
West End, South Dalton, HU17 7PN
Tel no: (01430) 810246
www.pipeandglass.co.uk
Modern British | £30
Cooking score: 5

🛏 V

The Pipe and Glass stands in attendance at the
gateway to Lord Hotham's estate, on the site of
the original gatehouse. An appealing
whitewashed country tavern, it has been
smartly modernised inside, with burnished
wood surfaces and buttoned leather sofas. It
hasn't stopped being a local hostelry – witness
the regional guest ales and daily specials
board, featuring the likes of scallops baked in
the shell with creamed leeks and smoked
bacon. Is that a proper prawn cocktail being
carried to the next table? It is. It's in the
understated elegant dining room, with its
framed pictures and hanging copper utensils,
that James Mackenzie really spreads his wings
to produce memorable, creative dishes that
capitalise on superb local supplies. Seasonal
asparagus comes with a crispy duck egg,
Yorkshire chorizo and lovage for one spring
starter, or there may be salt beef rissole with
piccalilli and ale jelly. Mains maintain the pace
with grilled Barnsley lamb chop and devilled
kidney in mint and nettle sauce, with pickled
red cabbage and Jersey Royals. A roll-call of
comfort-zone afters includes sticky toffee
pudding with stout ice cream and walnut
brittle. Wines from a useful list start at £14.95
(£4.10 a glass).

Chef/s: James Mackenzie. Open: Tue to Sun L 12 to
2 (4 Sun), Tue to Sat D 6.30 to 9.30. Closed: Mon
(exc bank hols), first 2 weeks Jan. Meals: alc (main

courses £10 to £26). **Service:** not inc. **Details:** 100 seats. 50 seats outside. Separate bar. Wheelchair access. Music. Car parking.

Sowerby Bridge

Gimbals

Upbeat neighbourhood bistro
76 Wharf Street, Sowerby Bridge, HX6 2AF
Tel no: (01422) 839329
www.gimbals.co.uk
Modern European | £33
Cooking score: 3

'The complete package', according to one local admirer, Simon and Janet Baker's upbeat neighbourhood bistro scores heavily with its cordial atmosphere and fabulous interiors (think metallic sculptures, mosaics, a mirrored staircase and 'snowflake' displays courtesy of Blackpool illuminations). It can also deliver reliably good food in the shape of, say, grilled scallops with coriander and Gruyère gratin, venison fillet on bubble and squeak with Madeira syrup and parsnip crisps, or turbot with smoked potato purée, samphire and Morecambe Bay shrimps. Steaks and lamb kleftiko are also praised by reporters. Desserts generally involve neat riffs on fruit and chocolate (try one of the 'petite' assiettes). House wine is £14.90.
Chef/s: Mark Ferrier. **Open:** Mon to Sat D only 6.30 to 9 (9.30 Fri and Sat). **Closed:** Sun, 24 to 26 Dec. **Meals:** alc (main courses £13 to £22). Set D £16.90 (2 courses) to £19.90. **Service:** not inc. **Details:** 50 seats. Separate bar. Wheelchair access. Music.

Staddlebridge

McCoys at the Tontine

A delightfully eccentric destination
Staddlebridge, DL6 3JB
Tel no: (01609) 882671
www.theclevelandtontine.co.uk
Modern British | £40
Cooking score: 3

A gold-plated Yorkshire eccentric of the best sort, this quirkily reconfigured Victorian coaching inn just off the A19 has been the McCoy brothers' pride and joy for more than 35 years – and it just keeps rolling along. There are plenty of oddball spaces for private bashes, but the bistro-style restaurant also puts on a wacky show with its vintage lamps, huge mirrors and antique sideboards. The kitchen whisks punters down memory lane for seafood pancakes, braised beef with suet dumplings and jam roly-poly, but also doffs its cap to the British renaissance by offering scallops with crispy pork and pumpkin risotto, slow-cooked cod with braised endive and razor clams or citrus terrine with sparkling rosé and clementine sherbet. The wine list is a typically offbeat trek through the winemaking world, with prices from £19.95.
Chef/s: James Cooper. **Open:** all week L 12 to 2 (2.30 Sun), D 6.30 to 9 (9.45 Fri and Sat, 8.30 Sun). **Closed:** 25 and 26 Dec, 1 and 2 Jan. **Meals:** alc (main courses £20 to £33). Set L £17.95 (2 courses) to £19.95. Sun L £22.50. **Service:** not inc. **Details:** 60 seats. Music. Car parking.

West Tanfield
The Bruce Arms
Striking pub with splendidly rustic food
Main Street, West Tanfield, HG4 5JJ
Tel no: (01677) 470325
www.thebrucearms.com
Modern British | £29
Cooking score: 3

This attractive eighteenth-century village pub-with-rooms manages a successful mix of old and new. Log fires burn, beams are exposed, tables are polished and paintings are contemporary – the whole effect is quite striking. Chef Hugh Carruthers used to work with Frances Atkins (see Yorke Arms, Ramsgill) and his menus contain much to catch the eye. Fresh flavours and seasonality are driving forces, and the cooking has a splendidly rustic edge, from the excellent homemade brawn with pickles and toast to orange pannacotta with poached plums. In between, fillet of silver mullet is served appealingly with asparagus, peas, clams, jamón Ibérico, butter beans, olive oil and parsley, while grilled rump of beef is perked up with mustard hollandaise. House wine is £15.50.
Chef/s: Hugh Carruthers. **Open:** Tue to Sun L 12 to 2.30 (3.30 Sun), Tue to Sat D 6 to 10. **Closed:** Mon, 2 weeks March. **Meals:** alc (main courses £13 to £33). Set L £12.95 (2 courses) to £15.95. Sun L £16.95. **Service:** not inc. **Details:** 45 seats. 20 seats outside. Wheelchair access. Music. Car parking.

West Witton
The Wensleydale Heifer
Seafood and chic vibes in the country
Main Street, West Witton, DL8 4LS
Tel no: (01969) 622322
www.wensleydaleheifer.co.uk
Seafood | £35
Cooking score: 3

A Wensleydale landmark since the 1600s, the once-bucolic Heifer is now a country-chic boutique hotel with foodie aspirations. Despite the bovine name, seafood is the kitchen's main business and visitors can choose to eat informally in the bare-tabled 'fish bar' or splash out amid the 'contemporary decadence' of the main restaurant. Chocolate leather chairs, linen cloths and vibrant artwork set the scene for a raft of classic and modern ideas ranging from gravlax, retro prawn cocktail and fish pie to chilli salt squid with marinated fennel salad, pesto-crusted cod with saffron mash or maple-roasted Whitby lobster salad with scallops and crispy belly pork. Steaks and slow-roast lamb shoulder with Jerusalem artichoke cassoulet please the carnivores. Those wanting a sweet hit could opt for banana sticky toffee pudding or the renowned 'Snickerbocker glory'. House wine is £20.50.
Chef/s: David Moss. **Open:** all week L 12 to 2, D 6 to 9.30. **Meals:** alc (main courses £17 to £43). Set L and D £19.75 (2 courses) to £21.75. **Service:** 10%. **Details:** 62 seats. 30 seats outside. Separate bar. Wheelchair access. Music. Car parking.

Whitby

Green's
When the boat comes in...
13 Bridge Street, Whitby, YO22 4BG
Tel no: (01947) 600284
www.greensofwhitby.com
Seafood | £30
Cooking score: 2

 V

Although this seafood restaurant goes out of
its way to advertise Wednesday as 'grill night',
there are plenty of meat dishes on the daily
menu anyway. Feedback has been mixed this
year, with some finding it 'expensive' and a
'disappointing experience', while others
judging it 'excellent'. There is much to tempt
on the menu: oysters aplenty, served with
various sauces, grilled queen scallops in their
shell with Parmesan, pesto and cured ham,
moules marinière, bouillabaisse, Thai-style
seafood broth, or Green's fish pie. Surf and turf
is popular here. Service is smiling, but not
always knowledgeable. House wine is £15.75.
Chef/s: Rob Green and Ryan Osbourne. **Open:** Mon
to Fri L 12 to 2, D 6.30 to 9.30. Sat and Sun 12 to
9.30. **Closed:** 25 and 26 Dec, 1 Jan. **Meals:** alc (main
courses £12 to £23). Sun L £11.95. **Service:** not inc.
Details: 50 seats. Separate bar. Music.

Magpie Café
Fish-and-chip champ
14 Pier Road, Whitby, YO21 3PU
Tel no: (01947) 602058
www.magpiecafe.co.uk
Seafood | £25
Cooking score: 2

Fish and chips rule in this distinctive black-
and-white building overlooking Whitby
harbour – and the owners have acquired a
fishmonger's, along with an experienced
buyer, thus ensuring a ready supply of top-
notch ingredients. After starters such as
fishcakes or sautéed squid, the 'whale-sized'
haddock and chips comes highly
recommended, as does the 'Magpie Trio' of sea

bass, salmon and scallops, which arrives with
chips, potatoes or a 'wonderful' mixed salad.
Non-fishy options might include coq au vin
or creamy mushroom gnocchi with a garlic
baguette. The international wine list offers
plenty by the glass, with bottles starting
at £13.95.
Chef/s: Ian Robson and Paul Gildroy. **Open:** all week
11.30 to 9. **Closed:** 25 Dec, 7 to 31 Jan. **Meals:** alc
(main courses £7 to £23). **Service:** not inc.
Details: 120 seats. Wheelchair access. Music.

NEW ENTRY
The Woodlands Cafébar
Charming eatery by the sea
East Row, Sandsend, Whitby, YO21 3SU
Tel no: (01947) 893438
thewoodlands-sandsend.com
Modern British | £25
Cooking score: 1

Tartan walls, Verner Panton chairs and stags'
antlers set the tone for this chic sandstone
cottage by the sea. Potted shrimps on toast
followed by Barnsley chop, boulangère
potatoes and devilled kidneys top the evening
menu. Wrap up with lemon posset or
elderflower rice pudding. By day it's
sandwiches, Welsh rarebit, scones and cakes
and perhaps a special of seafish stew or pigeon
breast. Eat in or out in the delightful gravel
garden with deckchairs, parasols, drifts of
lavender and a glimpse of the sea. Wine starts
at £14.50.
Chef/s: Alexander Perkins. **Open:** Tue to Sun L 12 to
3, Wed to Sun D 6 to 9. **Closed:** Mon (exc bank hols),
25 Dec. **Meals:** alc (main courses £8 to £18).
Service: not inc. **Details:** 40 seats. 34 seats
outside. Music. Car parking.

> ### Average Price
> The average price listed in main-entry
> reviews denotes the price of a three-
> course meal, without wine.

York

de'Clare Café

Flexible café with its heart in Spain
1 Peter Lane, York, YO1 8SW
Tel no: (01904) 652920
www.declaredeli.co.uk
Spanish | £18
Cooking score: 2

 £30

What is on offer at this modern café set in a quiet lane ('one of the oldest "snickleways" in York') is very much in tune with the current times: simple, affordable, flexible. The Spanish-inspired cooking is clean and vibrant, from revuelta chorizo, potato and smashed eggs for breakfast, through to lunches (and weekend dinners) of plancha-grilled sea bass fillet with chickpea, coriander and spring onion salad. Share platters of Spanish hams and cheeses or tuck into an open sandwich of escalivada aubergine and red pepper stew with hot goats' cheese; finish with chocolate and orange cake. Spanish wines from £14.
Chef/s: Mark Anthony Lees. **Open:** all week 9 to 5 (10.30pm Fri and Sat, 9.30 to 5 Sun). **Closed:** 25 and 26 Dec, Easter Sun. **Meals:** alc (main courses £8 to £10). **Service:** not inc. **Details:** 36 seats. Wheelchair access. Music.

J. Baker's Bistro Moderne

Serious big-city food... and fun
7 Fossgate, York, YO1 9TA
Tel no: (01904) 622688
www.jbakers.co.uk
Modern British | £33
Cooking score: 5

 £5 OFF

The J is for Jeff, whose moderne outfit occupies what was once a hardware store in York centre, a hop from the shopping on Parliament Street. Bare tables and humorous prints set a pleasingly light-hearted tone, and the food has a big-city feel to it; the simply written menus belie a serious approach to quality materials. Whitby crab with curried granola and textures of apple is the kind of starter that stimulates both taste-buds and imagination (though one reporter thought it was perhaps served a mite too cold). Mains might offer venison chop in 99 per cent chocolate with chopped mushrooms and an exotic vegetable bouquet of black carrots and green cauliflower. A fish option might be sea bass on Indian-spiced mussel stew. For vegetarians, a 'mock risotto' made with spiced beetroot and red wine is given richness with Butler's Blacksticks Blue. Grazing menus will suit the snackers. The chocolate menu allows you to fix your percentages (can you handle the 72 per cent Kayambe Noir sorbet?), or else go with spotted dick in bay-leaf custard, doused in Pedro Ximénez syrup. A well-chosen international wine list tries to keep prices on a leash; bottles start at £15.50 (£4.50 a small glass).
Chef/s: Jeff Baker. **Open:** Tue to Sat L 12 to 2, D 6 to 9.30. **Closed:** Sun, Mon, first week Jan. **Meals:** alc (main courses £10). Set L £12 (3 small plates) to £20 (5 small plates). Set D £25 (2 courses) to £45.00 (8 small plates). **Service:** not inc. **Details:** 52 seats. Separate bar. Music.

Le Langhe

Artisan foodie enterprise
The Old Coach House, Peasholme Green, York, YO1 7PW
Tel no: (01904) 622584
www.lelanghe.co.uk
Italian | £35
Cooking score: 4

 £5 OFF

Given that it takes its name from Piedmont's Langhe Hills (home of the Slow Food movement), it's no surprise that the spirit of *cucina rustica* is alive and well at Ottavio Bocca's remarkable foodie enterprise. The place has blossomed since bedding in at Peasholme Green, and a new wine bar is the latest addition to its all-purpose deli/eatery. Lunch in the airy mezzanine or alfresco courtyard is the main event, with bespoke menus created from top-drawer artisan ingredients. How about this for a 'wholly satisfying' repast: smoked duck and warm duck confit with

lamb's lettuce followed by silky handmade pasta with monkfish and a dish of pheasant with mash and foie gras velouté. Two evenings a week, the kitchen raises its game for grander, osteria-style dinners in the affable upstairs dining room. Here you might find line-caught sea bass with warm lentil salad and hazelnut tapenade, slow-cooked hare with polenta, and desserts such as yoghurt pannacotta. The food is matched by a stellar list of directly imported wines from small-scale vineyards across Italy, with bottles from £15 and loads of fabulous stuff by the glass.
Chef/s: Ottavio Bocca. **Open:** Mon to Sat L 12 to 3, Fri and Sat D 7 to 10. **Closed:** Sun, 25 to 28 Dec, 1 to 20 Jan, bank hols. **Meals:** alc (main courses £20 to £38). Set L £22.50 (4 courses). Set D £35 (6 courses). **Service:** not inc. **Details:** 60 seats. 25 seats outside. Wheelchair access. Music.

Melton's
Dressed-up British flavours
7 Scarcroft Road, York, YO23 1ND
Tel no: (01904) 634341
www.meltonsrestaurant.co.uk
Modern British | £32
Cooking score: 5

One of York's big players, Michael and Lucy Hjort's unassuming restaurant in a Victorian terrace continues to feed the crowds with impressively good food. 'Excellent regional provenance' is a hallmark of the kitchen's dexterous endeavours. Dressed-up British flavours dominate the menu, from a trio of parsnips that adds 'new dimensions to an unloved root' to a fabulous dish of rose veal with parsley mash and girolles. Also check out blockbusters such as the 'whole hog' – trotter, belly and hock with bigos (pork and cabbage stew) and Madeira jus – or the 'truly divine' fish medley with mussels, cauliflower mousse, fennel and new potatoes. Occasionally the kitchen gets itchy feet, heading east for the likes of crisp Lebanese pastries with blood-orange granita, or partridge breast with Moroccan salad and harissa dressing. As for dessert, puffed-up, boozy seasonal soufflés are

worth the wait (the prune and brandy number is 'exceptional'). Otherwise, it's back to the North Country with a vengeance for the slate of artisan cheeses. Lunch and early evening deals are 'amazing value'; the same can be said for Lucy Hjort's cannily assembled global wine list. Food-matching suggestions earn bonus points and sub-£20 bottles get a good airing – although big spenders will also find plenty to savour. House recommendations are £16 (£3.80 a glass).
Chef/s: Michael Hjort. **Open:** Tue to Sat L 12 to 2, D 5.30 to 9.30. **Closed:** Sun, Mon, 2 weeks Dec. **Meals:** alc (main courses £15 to £20). Set L and early D £21 (2 courses) to £25. Tasting menu £35 (5 courses). **Service:** not inc. **Details:** 42 seats. Music.

Melton's Too
Flexible drop-in/bistro with freewheeling food
25 Walmgate, York, YO1 9TX
Tel no: (01904) 629222
www.meltonstoo.co.uk
Modern European | £23
Cooking score: 2

Housed in an atmospheric seventeenth-century building that was once a saddler's and agricultural emporium, this boisterous, bare-boarded sibling of Melton's (see entry) plies its trade as a flexible drop-in/bistro that's equally handy for coffee with the papers or something more filling. The menu spells out the provenance of each dish (chicken thighs from Loose Birds of Harome, say) and it's a freewheeling affair: expect tapas sharing plates, Russian koulibiac (salmon pie), slow-roast rare breed pork with mulled pears, and homespun puds. Brunch, all-day lunches and teatime snacks are part of the offer, and it's worth looking out for regular foodie events. Drinks run from real ales and world beers to good-value wines from £14.50.
Chef/s: Michael Hjort. **Open:** all week 10.30am to 10.30pm (9.30pm Sun). **Closed:** 25 and 26 Dec, 1 Jan. **Meals:** alc (main courses £10 to £17). Set L and early D £10.90 (2 courses) to £12. **Service:** 10%. **Details:** 120 seats. Separate bar. Wheelchair access. Music.

SCOTLAND

Borders, Dumfries & Galloway,
Lothians (inc. Edinburgh),
Strathclyde (inc. Glasgow), Central, Fife,
Tayside, Grampian, Highlands & Islands

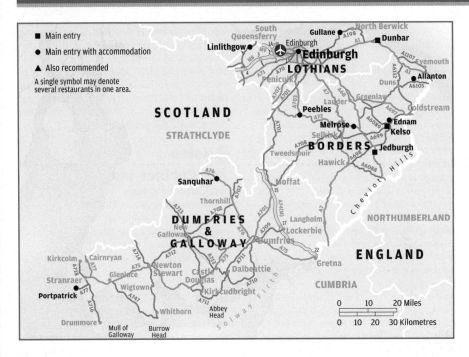

▌Allanton

The Allanton Inn
Hearty food and an eye for detail
Allanton, TD11 3JZ
Tel no: (01890) 818260
www.allantoninn.co.uk
Modern British | £28
Cooking score: 3

A dark stone Borders inn on the outside, this village eatery has a surprisingly bright and modern interior, overseen by warmly welcoming staff. Big flavours and big portions are the order of the day; a basket of springy home-baked bread got things off to a good start, and a dish of tender, steamed Shetland mussels with white wine, garlic and herbs delivered on that promise. Also satisfying was a main of pesto-coated free-range chicken breast on a warm salad of green beans, cherry tomatoes and croûtons, with sautéed baby potatoes; gnocchi with wild mushrooms,

pecorino cream sauce and truffle oil was intense and rounded. Desserts such as baked lemon and lime cheesecake with ginger syrup and berries are unmissable. International wines start at just £13.95.
Chef/s: Katrina Reynolds. **Open:** all week L 12 to 2, D 6 to 9. **Closed:** 25 and 26 Dec. **Meals:** alc (main courses £10 to £24). **Service:** not inc. **Details:** 55 seats. 56 seats outside. Music.

▌Ednam

Edenwater House
Personally run borderland retreat
Ednam, TD5 7QL
Tel no: (01573) 224070
www.edenwaterhouse.co.uk
Modern British | £40
Cooking score: 4

Squirrelled away in the borderlands of the Upper Tweed valley, this four-square converted manse is house and home to Jeff and Jacquie Kelly; he plays host, while she takes care of business in the kitchen. Although it's primarily geared to residents, dinner in the couple's Lilliputian four-table restaurant is well worth seeking out. Seasonal ingredients are used with skill and imagination, from roast monkfish with crispy pancetta on braised leeks and olives with aïoli to loin of roe deer accompanied by a spinach and cauliflower galette, stuffed Savoy cabbage, roasted beetroot and port jus. Flavours from the world larder also add some zing to proceedings – witness tartare of tuna with coconut and wasabi sorbet and pickled radish. Meanwhile, dessert could be as reassuring as apple and custard tartlets or as lively as lychee, lime and ginger parfait with a pavé of rich chocolate brownie. Regular 'wine shed' tastings and themed weekends show the couple's interest in all things vinous; their well-structured list starts at £19.50.

Chef/s: Jacquie Kelly. **Open:** all week D only 7, 1 sitting (non-residents Wed, Fri and Sat only). **Closed:** 16 Dec to 31 Jan. **Meals:** Set D £40. **Service:** not inc. **Details:** 16 seats. No music. Car parking. Children over 12 yrs at D only.

▌Jedburgh
The Caddy Mann
Quaint and much-loved local restaurant
Mounthooly, Jedburgh, TD8 6TJ
Tel no: (01835) 850787
www.caddymann.com
Modern British | £22
Cooking score: 2

Reporters exude nothing but good will towards Ross Horrocks' quaintly old-fashioned Jedburgh restaurant. They love the 'warm, comfortable, informal' setting and friendly service, but it's the food that 'never fails to impress'. The emphasis is, as one would wish, on seasonal Borders produce. A duo of the local lamb with mashed tatties and shallot confit is a firm favourite. Starters of spelt risotto with chorizo, squash and crispy pig's trotters or haggis spring roll with neeps 'n' tatties croquette clearly demonstrate Ross's

'imaginative' streak, though fish and chips and Sunday's rib of beef remain staunchly traditional. House wine is £12.95.

Chef/s: Ross Horrocks. **Open:** all week L 12 to 2, Fri and Sat D 7 to 10. **Closed:** 25 and 26 Dec, 1 to 3 Jan. **Meals:** alc (main courses £10 to £19). **Service:** not inc. **Details:** 50 seats. 12 seats outside. Wheelchair access. Music. Car parking.

▌Kelso
The Cobbles Inn
Local beer and victuals
7 Bowmont Street, Kelso, TD5 7JH
Tel no: (01573) 223548
www.thecobblesinn.co.uk
Modern European | £20
Cooking score: 1

Drinkers and diners generate a buzz at this vibrant Victorian coaching inn, drawn by the full range of Tempest ales from chef-proprietor Gavin Meiklejohn's microbrewery and by pub and brasserie classics jazzed up with voguish flourishes. Local game terrine, deep-fried squid with black pepper and lime mayonnaise, steaks with peppercorn sauce, and roast saddle of roe deer with a mini-Wellington, beetroot cornichons, port jus and dauphinoise potatoes show the range. House wine is £13.95.

Chef/s: Gavin Meiklejohn and Karol Giachera. **Open:** Tue to Sun L 12 to 2 (2.30 Sat), D 6 to 9 (9.30 Fri and Sat, 8 Sun). **Closed:** Mon, 25 and 26 Dec. **Meals:** alc (main courses £8 to £22). Set D £20.95 (2 courses) to £24.95. Sun L £15.95 (2 courses) to £19.95. **Service:** not inc. **Details:** 65 seats. 20 seats outside. Separate bar. Wheelchair access. Music. Car parking.

Average Price
The average price listed in main-entry reviews denotes the price of a three-course meal, without wine.

Melrose

Burt's Hotel

Grand old inn with excellent ingredients
Market Square, Melrose, TD6 9PL
Tel no: (01896) 822285
www.burtshotel.co.uk
Modern British | £36
Cooking score: 2

A grand old inn in the centre of Melrose, Burt's offers bar food in its comfortably traditional front rooms. There's a more ambitious restaurant menu in the large, country house-style dining room. Expect classically-based dishes made with excellent fresh ingredients: a starter of wild mushroom and truffle velouté, full-flavoured and generous, a main course of grilled halibut with shallot purée, spinach, saffron potatoes and a chive butter sauce, and desserts such as passion-fruit mousse with caramelised pineapple and tangy sea buckthorn sorbet. A substantial wine list kicks off at £16.25.
Chef/s: Trevor Williams. **Open:** all week L 12 to 2, D 7 to 9. **Closed:** 26 Dec, 3 to 9 Jan. **Meals:** alc (main courses £11 to £22). Set L £23.50 (2 courses) to £27.75. Set D £29.50 (2 courses) to £36. **Service:** not inc. **Details:** 60 seats. 24 seats outside. Music. Car parking. Children over 8 yrs only in restaurant.

Peebles

Cringletie House

Sumptuous country house hotel
Edinburgh Road, Peebles, EH45 8PL
Tel no: (01721) 725750
www.cringletie.com
Modern British | £45
Cooking score: 2

Cringletie began life as a Victorian architect's idea of a castle; now it's a sumptuous hotel, whose dining room comes complete with ceiling fresco, log fire in winter and rug-covered oak floor. Patrick Bardoulet arrived in 2011, and began settling into the modern Scottish style the place is famed for: a wild garlic velouté may open proceedings, before delicate, complex lobster consommé with carrot and courgette under puff pastry, then, perhaps, ballottine of guinea fowl with asparagus and baby onions in liquorice and coffee sauce. Desserts include reimagined Black Forest gâteau with cherry confit and vanilla cream. House wines from £18.50.
Chef/s: Patrick Bardoulet. **Open:** all week L 12.30 to 2.30, D 6.30 to 9. **Closed:** 3 weeks Jan. **Meals:** alc (main courses £21 to £25). Set L £17.50 (2 courses) to £22.50. Set D £27.50 (2 courses) to £33. **Service:** 10%. **Details:** 34 seats. Separate bar. Wheelchair access. Music. Car parking.

Osso

Impeccably modern café and restaurant
Innerleithen Road, Peebles, EH45 8AB
Tel no: (01721) 724477
www.ossorestaurant.com
Modern British | £28
Cooking score: 3

A bold blue-and-white frontage catches the eye at this impeccably modern venue in the Borders. Osso metamorphoses from daytime caff ('Where better to enjoy a delicious homemade scone and pot of tea after an eight-mile walk along the Tweed?', or tapas and meze, for that matter) into an accomplished contemporary restaurant in the evenings. Inventive modern brasserie dishes include a starter of smoked eel with ham croquette, cauliflower and mustard, and mains like hake with kale, leeks and lobster macaroni, or sirloin steak with duck-fat chips, onion rings and béarnaise. Fixed-price menus offer particularly good value. Finish with chocolate mousse, griottine cherries and pistachios, or poached rhubarb seasoned with vanilla and ginger. The short wine list offers thrifty drinking from £13.50 (£3.60 a glass).
Chef/s: Ally McGrath. **Open:** all week L 11 to 4.30, Tue to Sat D 6 to 9. **Closed:** 25 Dec, 1 Jan. **Meals:** alc (main courses £14 to £22). Set D £19.50 (2 courses) to £25. **Service:** not inc. **Details:** 37 seats. 4 seats outside. Wheelchair access. Music.

▌Portpatrick

Knockinaam Lodge

Thrilling, windswept views and refined food

Portpatrick, DG9 9AD

Tel no: (01776) 810471

www.knockinaamlodge.com

Modern British | £58

Cooking score: 5

£5 OFF ⇌ V

Built as a hunting lodge in 1869, Knockinaam Lodge comes with lavish gardens, its own private beach and thrilling, windswept views over the Irish Sea – although the 20-seater dining room promises intimate calm rather than cloche-lifting ostentation. Long-serving chef Tony Pierce knows the game and feeds his guests from a refined repertoire of quietly assured cooking; Scotland provides much of the produce and France chips in with fastidious culinary technique. Arrive in August and you might progress from a delicate chicken and basil sausage with grilled black pudding and wild mushroom reduction to a bowl of Knockinaam leek, pea and truffle soup. After that, roast fillet of Luce Bay turbot with a potato crust, cauliflower purée and broad beans could give way to something sweet (perhaps a three-toned chocolate terrine with a tuile basket of raspberry sorbet) or some Anglo-French cheeses. Dinner always closes with coffee and petits fours in the comfy lounge. Owner David Ibbotson is a serious wine enthusiast and his authoritative list spans the globe, cherry-picking everything from rare French vintages to exciting Antipodean discoveries. Half-bottles abound, and house recommendations start at £23.

Chef/s: Tony Pierce. **Open:** all week L 12 to 1.30, D 7 to 9. **Meals:** Set L £40 (4 courses). Set D £58 (5 courses). Sun L £30 (4 courses). **Service:** not inc. **Details:** 20 seats. Separate bar. Music. Car parking. No children at D.

▌Sanquhar

Blackaddie House Hotel

Going from strength to strength

Blackaddie Road, Sanquhar, DG4 6JJ

Tel no: (01659) 50270

www.blackaddiehotel.co.uk

Modern British | £48

Cooking score: 4

⇌

'Blackaddie is the one for me!' exclaimed a returning Caledonian native of this revitalised sixteenth-century manse on the banks of the Nith. Since staking his claim here, doughty chef/proprietor Ian McAndrew has worked wonders, making the most of the region's abundant seasonal larder. 'We loved his commitment to supporting the local economy' commented one visitor, who also appreciated the 'immense care and attention to detail' evident in highly worked specialities such as seared scallops with cauliflower in four different forms, a blast of fennel foam and shards of pancetta. Elsewhere, expect satisfaction from a complex plate of lamb (cannon, tongue and a warm terrine with broccoli purée) or an equally involved trio of dry-aged Scotch beef comprising fillet, slow-braised and deep-fried shin, and a Moroccan-style salad. Desserts also ramp up the thrills – witness a walnut tart with roasted pear and parsnip cappuccino. Service is unfailingly courteous, and the food is matched by a strong, food-friendly wine list with house recommendations from £19.95 (£5.25 a glass).

Chef/s: Ian McAndrew. **Open:** all week L 12.30 to 2 (3 Sun), D 6.30 to 9. **Meals:** alc (main courses £16 to £29). Set L £20.50 (2 courses) to £26.50. Set D £48. Sun L £26.50. **Service:** not inc. **Details:** 20 seats. Separate bar. Music. Car parking.

▌Dunbar

The Creel

Spanking-fresh food and keen prices
25 Lamer Street, Dunbar, EH42 1HJ
Tel no: (01368) 863279
www.creelrestaurant.co.uk
Modern British | £25
Cooking score: 4

The Creel is just a few yards from Dunbar's pretty little harbour and you might even feel you are moored there, so ship-like is the entirely wooden interior. Logan Thorburn's keenly priced menu is perfectly pitched, offering a fail-safe repertoire of spanking fresh fish and meat. 'Simple but fresh' starters of roasted local crab claws with a lemon and dill dressing, hot shell-on prawns with homemade mayonnaise, or cappuccino of local fish soup, 'in which the balance of tomato, paprika and sesame oil enriched the broth' are typical choices. Mains might combine Belhaven beer-battered Eyemouth haddock for a fine fish and chip lunch, or a seared gigot of Borders lamb with a blue cheese sauce, while grilled sea bass on a bed of rice is elevated by smoked pimento, sherry vinegar and 'the all-essential dab of sour cream'. A 'perfectly judged' vanilla pannacotta is a superb finale. Wines from £16.95.
Chef/s: Logan Thorburn. **Open:** Wed to Sun L 12 to 2.30, D 6.30 to 9. **Closed:** Mon, Tue. **Meals:** Set L £14.50 (2 courses) to £18.50. Set D £21.50 (2 courses) to £25.50. **Service:** not inc. **Details:** 36 seats. Wheelchair access. Music. No children under 14 yrs after 7.30.

Symbols

🛏 Accommodation is available

£30 Three courses for less than £30

V Separate vegetarian menu

£5 £5-off voucher scheme

🍷 Notable wine list

▌Edinburgh

Angels with Bagpipes

Old Town meets the 21st century
343 High Street, Royal Mile, Edinburgh, EH1 1PW
Tel no: (0131) 2201111
www.angelswithbagpipes.co.uk
Modern European | £31
Cooking score: 3

Readers continue to enjoy the contrast between this atmospheric, classy proposition from Marina Crolla (of the famous deli dynasty) and the rest of the Royal Mile. The angels of the name come from a carving spotted by Marina in St Giles' Cathedral across the way. Chef Paul Whitecross's menu is proudly Scottish and contemporary in approach, and might feature Mull scallops with a pig's head terrine, black pudding and parsnip, while wild goodies like sea lettuce add extra interest to simple sea bass with a stuffed razor clam. Desserts balance nostalgia with on-trend details, as in Arctic roll with fennel pollen ice cream. 'Excellent' service and a piece of tablet with coffee leave readers in a sweet – perhaps angelic – mood. House wine is £18.
Chef/s: Paul Whitecross. **Open:** all week 12 to 10. **Closed:** 24 to 26 Dec. **Meals:** alc (main courses £13 to £21). Set L £11.95 (2 courses) to £15.95. **Service:** not inc. **Details:** 70 seats. 24 seats outside. Wheelchair access. Music.

Café St Honoré

A little bit of Paris
34 North West Thistle Street Lane, Edinburgh, EH2 1EA
Tel no: (0131) 2262211
www.cafesthonore.com
French | £34
Cooking score: 3
£5 OFF

Not far from Princes Street, the Café maintains the distinctive air of Parisian times gone by, with its rickety chairs, black-and-white tiles and many mirrors. All it lacks is the fog of Gauloises (or maybe not). Amid such thoroughgoing Francophilia, Neil Forbes maintains a neat balance between classic French brasserie fare and more home-grown ideas. A starter terrine is composed of smoked salmon, anchovy butter and capers, and served with pickled cucumber and beetroot, before duck breast with Stornoway black pudding rösti and wild greens ups the ante. Scotch beef-shin stew with buttery mash is a signature dish to save for a rainy day. The balancing act concludes with a choice between textbook crème brûlée or custard tart with sloe-berry clotted cream. The French-led wines start at £17.90.

Chef/s: Neil Forbes. **Open:** all week L 12 to 2, D 5.15 to 10 (6 Sat and Sun). **Closed:** 24 to 26 Dec, 1 to 2 Jan. **Meals:** alc (main courses £14 to £23). Set L £15.50 (2 courses) to £19.50. Set D £18 (2 courses) to £22.50. **Service:** 10%. **Details:** 48 seats. Music.

★ TOP 50 ★

Castle Terrace
Superlative cooking, sensational food
33-35 Castle Terrace, Edinburgh, EH1 2EL
Tel no: (0131) 2291222
www.castleterracerestaurant.com
Modern British | £52
Cooking score: 6

The range of outstanding cookery that's going on in Edinburgh makes outsiders envy the city's residents; there is far too much for mere weekenders to fit in. This inviting venue, a Georgian townhouse beneath the Castle Mound, has been subtly decorated in modern style. Dominic Jack, once a rising star of the Parisian firmament, is now firmly established as a supernova in his own right, with a style of brightly imaginative and flawlessly executed modern Scottish food. A couple who took the tasting menu were regaled with seven courses of excellence, among them a ceviche of North Sea halibut presented à la sushi, with wasabi ice cream, stunning Crowdie cheese and herb ravioli in tomato sauce ('we know we're in the presence of greatness when something as simple as that is as astonishing as it was'), crispy ox tongue and veal heart confit in spelt

risotto, and roast grouse with sautéed girolles, watercress and bread sauce. The exalted level is maintained with desserts such as pear poached in hibiscus, served with nougatine, pear sorbet and coriander syrup. A serious wine list climbs through the classics, but has a fair few under £30. Fine house varietals from Maurel Vedeau in the Languedoc are £20.

Chef/s: Dominic Jack. **Open:** Tue to Sat L 12 to 2, D 6.30 to 10. **Closed:** Sun, Mon, Christmas and New Year. **Meals:** alc (main courses £24 to £34). Set L £24. Tasting menu £70 (6 courses). **Service:** 10% for parties of 8 or more. **Details:** 60 seats. Separate bar. Wheelchair access. Music. Children over 5 yrs only.

Centotre
Lively all-day Italian eatery
103 George Street, Edinburgh, EH2 3ES
Tel no: (0131) 2251550
www.centotre.com
Italian | £30
Cooking score: 1

This lively all-day city-centre eatery is run by Victor and Carina Contini (whose family established Valvona & Crolla – see entry). Following this tradition, they source fine Scottish and Italian produce and offer a menu mainly of pizza and pasta. More evolved dishes, such as slow-roasted rabbit with olives and lemon, are done well; desserts like crema cotta and tiramisu are 'creamy and delicious'. At busy times, service can be affected as the friendly, informative staff come under pressure. Wines from £14.95.

Chef/s: Carina Contini. **Open:** all week 12 to 11 (Thur to Sat midnight, Sun 9pm). **Closed:** 25 and 26 Dec. **Meals:** alc (main courses £9 to £23). **Service:** not inc. **Details:** 100 seats. 36 seats outside. Wheelchair access. Music.

Visit us Online
To find out more about
The Good Food Guide, please visit
www.thegoodfoodguide.co.uk

David Bann

Awesome contemporary veggie
56-58 St Mary's Street, Edinburgh, EH1 1SX
Tel no: (0131) 5565888
www.davidbann.co.uk
Vegetarian | £22
Cooking score: 2

This modern, minimalist vegetarian restaurant on the edge of the Old Town oozes friendly charm. There's a happy buzz about the place – David Bann could turn the head of the staunchest meat eater as he brings vegetarian cooking to life with an 'awesome' soufflé of apple, beetroot and Dunsyre Blue cheese, and a chilli filo tart with smoked sweet potato and courgettes drizzled with a spiced chocolate sauce. Desserts include rhubarb sponge cake with vanilla cream and, like everything else on the menu, are labelled if they are vegan. The wine list is a decent selection and opens at £13.95.
Chef/s: David Bann. **Open:** all week 12 to 10 (10.30 Fri, 11 to 10.30 Sat, 11 to 10 Sun). **Closed:** 25 and 26 Dec, 1 Jan. **Meals:** alc (main courses £10 to £13). Set L and D £16.50 (2 courses) to £21.50. **Service:** not inc. **Details:** 80 seats. No music.

The Dogs

Hearty casual dining
110 Hanover Street, Edinburgh, EH2 1DR
Tel no: (0131) 2201208
www.thedogsonline.co.uk
Modern British | £22
Cooking score: 2

Now established as one of the leaders of Edinburgh's casual dining pack, The Dogs continues to produce hearty, flavoursome food. The quirky Victorian décor of the high-ceilinged dining room is matched by an eclectic menu, ranging from devilled liver to stargazy pie, from pan-fried salmon to succulent ribeye steak (both 'precisely timed'). Elsewhere, belly pork cooked in cola and fried lamb breast with butternut squash and rosemary are interesting and successful

combinations. Desserts such as lemon posset and banoffi pie are more conventional. Grooming is required – some dishes are distinctly shaggy around the edges – but service is friendly. Wines start at £14.95.
Chef/s: Aitor Rodrigo. **Open:** all week L 12 to 4, D 5 to 10. **Closed:** 25 Dec, 1 Jan. **Meals:** alc (main courses £7 to £18). **Service:** not inc. **Details:** 60 seats. Separate bar.

Fishers Bistro

Quirky nautical bistro with quality seafood
1 The Shore, Leith, Edinburgh, EH6 6QW
Tel no: (0131) 5545666
www.fishersrestaurantgroup.co.uk
Seafood | £27
Cooking score: 1

Although one of a trio, this quirky little venue on Leith Shore has a character all its own. There's a multi-level arrangement of bar, bistro and box-sized open kitchen, all pleasantly ramshackle and thrown together. You'll also find nautical art and a menu dictated by quality seafood. Set lunches – smoked haddock kedgeree, mussels in wine and cream, or plaice goujons on sugar-snap and sesame salad, then rice pudding with plums, say – seem more appropriate in this simple setting than £36 lobster-frites luxury. Wines start at £14.95.
Chef/s: Andrew Bird. **Open:** all week 12 to 10.30 (12.30 Sun). **Closed:** 25 and 26 Dec, 1 Jan. **Meals:** alc (main courses £10 to £40). Set L £12.95 (2 courses) to £15.95. **Service:** not inc. **Details:** 40 seats. 20 seats outside. Separate bar. Music.

> ### Please send us your feedback
> To register your opinion about any restaurant listed in the Guide, or a new restaurant that you wish to bring to our attention, please visit the web address at the bottom of the page. Your feedback informs the content of the book and will be used to compile next year's reviews.

Forth Floor

Ambitious cooking, glorious views and shopping
Harvey Nichols, 30-34 St Andrew Square, Edinburgh, EH2 2AD
Tel no: (0131) 5248350
www.harveynichols.co.uk
Modern European | £42
Cooking score: 3

A subtle refurbishment of Forth Floor's glass-fronted dining room should prove just chic enough for Harvey Nics shoppers, although it can't compete with the spectacular views of the Firth of Forth and Edinburgh Castle. However, Stuart Muir's ambitious cooking *is* captivating enough to distract. At inspection, pressed chicken dotted with syrupy prunes, wrapped in leeks and stabbed with a crisp shard of skin, was served with a good date chutney and crunchy caramelised pecans; pigeon came sous vide in Shiraz and aniseed with beetroot and pear. Simpler efforts, such as hake on a fricassee of broccoli, broad beans and asparagus and served with a poached egg, let quality Scottish produce shine. The modern approach occasionally backfires; an overworked carrot cake draped in anonymous orange foam failed to impress. Wines start at £16.50.
Chef/s: Stuart Muir. Open: all week L 12 to 3 (3.30 Sat and Sun), Tue to Sat D 6 to 10. Closed: 25 Dec, 1 Jan. Meals: alc (main courses £18 to £24). Set L £24 (3 courses). Set D £40 (2 courses) to £45.
Service: 10%. Details: 47 seats. 10 seats outside. Separate bar. Wheelchair access. Music. Car parking. Children over 12 yrs only.

La Garrigue

Authentic French food with real aplomb
31 Jeffrey Street, Edinburgh, EH1 1DH
Tel no: (0131) 5573032
www.lagarrigue.co.uk
French | £30
Cooking score: 3

£5 OFF

Not far from Waverley station and the Royal Mile is this tub-thumpingly patriotic French bistro. Jean-Michel Gauffre does the ancestral things with real aplomb, offering casseroled snails and gésiers (gizzards) in spicy tomato sauce to start, followed, perhaps, by garlicky bourride with white fish, mussels and spring vegetables. Reporters have enjoyed the honest simplicity of baked goats' cheese coated in almonds and accompanied by puréed beetroot, and the melt-in-the-mouth joue de boeuf (beef cheeks) in tomatoes, olives and red wine with gratinated macaroni. Just to show off, the chocolate fondant oozes both dark and white filling, and comes with sharon-fruit and orange coulis. Otherwise, finish with cheeses and chestnut bread. Wines celebrate the pick of the Midi appellations: Corbières, Minervois, Faugères, St-Chinian, Costières de Nîmes, Fitou. Prices open at £15.50. A second branch is at 88 Commercial Street, Leith; tel: (0131) 553 5933.
Chef/s: Jean-Michel Gauffre. Open: all week L 12 to 2.30, D 6 to 9.30. Closed: 26 Dec to 1 Jan. Meals: Set L £12.50 (2 courses) to £15.50. Set D £24.50 (2 courses) to £30. Sun L £12.50.
Service: 10%. Details: 45 seats. No music. Wheelchair access. Car parking.

Guchhi Indian Seafood & Bar

Clubby vibes and trendy Indian food
9-10 Commercial Street, Leith, Edinburgh,
EH6 6JA
Tel no: (0131) 5555604
www.guchhi.com
Indian/Seafood | £21
Cooking score: 2

This trendy Indian hybrid is lighting up the re-energised Leith scene with its combination of clubby vibes, tapas-style bites and bright, bouncy seafood cookery. Small plates are the thing – clams in coconut and green masala, gravlax with curried cauliflower and horseradish, for example – but you can also feast on big helpings of baked scallops with 'Bombay duck' sauce or fiery lobster iguru. Away from the sea, the kitchen knocks out trademark biryanis and other curry house staples, plus novelties such as artichoke pakoras or '1947 bannu kebabs' (egg-and-breadcrumbed chicken 'nuggets'). Sip groovy cocktails at the bar or dip into the fish-friendly wine list (from £14.25).

Chef/s: Sachin Dhanola. **Open:** all week 12 to 11. **Meals:** alc (main courses £10 to £36). Set L and D £8.95 (2 courses) to £10.95. Set D £15.95. **Service:** not inc. **Details:** 72 seats. 16 seats outside. Separate bar. Music.

★ TOP 50 ★

The Kitchin

Star player on the waterfront
78 Commercial Quay, Leith, Edinburgh, EH6 6LX
Tel no: (0131) 5551755
www.thekitchin.com
Modern European | £60
Cooking score: 7

V

A star player on Leith's scrubbed-up waterfront, Tom Kitchin's punningly named restaurant occupies an old whisky warehouse that has been gentrified for Edinburgh foodies and others wanting to glimpse a celeb chef on his home turf. Inside, the dining room maintains that 'special occasion' feel with plush velveteen chairs, polished mahogany tables and snazzy wooden wine displays – although the lack of natural light isn't to everyone's taste. 'From nature to plate' is the mantra, and Kitchin is at pains to pinpoint every piece of fish, slab of meat and wild picking on his seasonal menus and 'surprise' tasting packages. Here you will find seafood from the Orkneys, Scrabster and Eyemouth, game from the Borders, lamb from the Highlands (cooked in local hay), sea buckthorn from East Neuk and more besides. The result is a highly personal style defined by textbook technique, finesse and a visually stunning approach to presentation: consider a signature dish of fat Arisaig razor clams ('spoots'), sliced to order and warmed in a stock-based sauce with chorizo, confit lemon and chives; or seared hand-dived scallop with a ragoût of sea kale; or even a precise, disarmingly simple dish of roast hake with braised carrots, turnips, peas and fennel. This is Scottish seafood cookery at its most convincing and sensitive, but Kitchin is equally smart when it comes to composing blockbusters from fastidiously sourced meat and game. Mallard en croûte, crispy veal sweetbreads with salsify, and beef pot-au-feu show his orthodox side, although he pulls a few tricks out of the hat when it comes to handling rabbit: a plate of poached and roasted saddle and kidney alongside crisped-up confit legs, endive, broad beans and wilted wild garlic hit the spot for one reader. Finally, desserts bring mouthfuls of happiness in the shape of lemon tart with a 'crisp-gooey' lemon macaroon, rhubarb crumble soufflé or a swollen prune steeped in syrupy tea with Armagnac ice cream. Service is engaging, friendly and clued-up – in fact the only downsides appear to be a lack of home-baked bread and an occasional heavy hand with the salt cellar. Elite French producers steal most of the glory on the auspicious wine list, although there is gold-standard ballast from elsewhere. Bottles start at £27, but don't miss the seasonal by-the-glass selections (from £9.50).

Chef/s: Tom Kitchin. **Open:** Tue to Sat L 12 to 2.15, D 6.30 to 10. **Closed:** Sun, Mon. **Meals:** alc (main courses £31 to £36). Set L £26.50. Tasting menu £70

(6 courses). **Service:** not inc. **Details:** 55 seats. 32 seats outside. Separate bar. Wheelchair access. Music. Children over 5 yrs only.

Restaurant Mark Greenaway

A classy joint
12 Picardy Place, Edinburgh, EH1 3JT
Tel no: (0131) 5570952
www.no12picardyplace.com
Modern British | £39
Cooking score: 3

Mark Greenaway's restaurant is on the ground floor of a boutique hotel opposite the Omni Complex, in what was the Hawke and Hunter restaurant. It's a 'classy joint'. Stone, leather and brass create a sleek look, and the cooking is British eclectic. Contrasting flavours are juggled in dishes such as braised pork cheek pavé with hot apple jelly, sea buckthorn and wild herbs, and mains of honey-roasted Gressingham duck breast with a sausage roll, tarragon croquette, watermelon, celeriac purée, roasted salsify and tarragon jus. That same complexity is maintained in desserts such as a jam jar filled with rice pudding, rhubarb jelly and compote, with a ripple ice cream served in the upturned lid. The set lunch has been well reported. Wines start at £18.
Chef/s: Mark Greenaway. **Open:** Tue to Sat L 12 to 2.30, D 5.30 to 9.45. **Closed:** Sun, Mon. **Meals:** alc (main courses £18 to £28). Set L and D £16.50 (2 courses) to £20. Set D £35. **Service:** 10%. **Details:** 60 seats. Separate bar. Music. No children in the bar.

¶¶| **Visit us**
||| **Online**
To find out more about
The Good Food Guide, please visit
www.thegoodfoodguide.co.uk

number one

Subtly inventive cooking that really surprises
The Balmoral, 1 Princes Street, Edinburgh,
EH2 2EQ
Tel no: (0131) 5576727
www.restaurantnumberone.com
Modern European | £64
Cooking score: 6

On entry, descend a velveteen-carpeted staircase into an encased glass box of a bar, then through into the hushed, cocoon-like dining room where tables are metres apart, walls mirrored, double tablecloths pleated and carpets deadening. It all feels conventionally grand and there is an army of very agreeable and friendly staff hanging on your every move. So far so fine dining, but Billy Boyter's subtly inventive cooking really surprises. Foie gras set as silk on a strip of blood-orange gel may read as conventional luxe, but candied kumquats, crisp oxtail sandwich and shavings of cobnut nullify any sense of the predictable. Where familiar ideas are employed – goats' cheese alongside ubiquitous beetroot – they're charged up, the cheese set as a wobbly pannacotta getting a shot of bitterness from baby turnips, sweetness from carrots, and lively zing from redcurrant syrup. Sea trout cooked in lemon verbena oil becomes almost gel-like alongside poached oysters and celeriac, and rib and braise of beef with veal sweetbreads on luscious pearl barley risotto are a true showcase for Scottish ingredients. Desserts can pale by comparison, with multifarious combinations of rhubarb and crème fraîche appearing somewhat overworked. Wines start at £26 but choice is regrettably slim below £40.
Chef/s: Billy Boyter and Jeff Bland. **Open:** all week D only 6.30 to 10 (6 Sat). **Closed:** first 2 weeks Jan. **Meals:** Set D £64. Tasting menu £70. **Service:** not inc. **Details:** 55 seats. Separate bar. Wheelchair access. Music.

Ondine

Sustainable seafood favourite
2 George IV Bridge, Edinburgh, EH1 1AD
Tel no: (0131) 2261888
www.ondinerestaurant.co.uk
Seafood | £45
Cooking score: 4

'Special but not stuffy' and 'relaxing', note visitors to one of Edinburgh's best-loved restaurants, which specialises in seafood, sustainability and making customers feel 'well looked after'. The first-floor position and full-height windows ensure elegant city views, and such is Ondine's reputation that the atmosphere suffers not a jot from its being tucked away upstairs. Reporters reserve particular praise for the salt-and-pepper squid tempura with Vietnamese sauce and a main course of fish curry with raita and basmati. Simple grilled dishes also demonstrate the kitchen's skill. At the crustacean bar, staff prepare oysters to be served raw or cooked, and spectacular fruits de mer, all eaten with a clean conscience due to Ondine's careful sourcing policy. To finish, treacle tart is a hit, while the coconut pannacotta with mango salsa is declared a 'dessert made in heaven'. White wines dominate a list that starts at £16.50.
Chef/s: Roy Brett. **Open:** all week L 12 to 3, D 5.30 to 10. **Closed:** 24 to 27 Dec, 2 to 4 Jan. **Meals:** alc (main courses £15 to £42). Set L and D £16.95 (2 courses) to £19.95. **Service:** not inc. **Details:** 74 seats. Wheelchair access. Music.

Plumed Horse

Aiming way above mere satisfaction
50-54 Henderson Street, Edinburgh, EH6 6DE
Tel no: (0131) 5545556
www.plumedhorse.co.uk
Modern European | £55
Cooking score: 5

Housed in a red sandstone building on the approach to the Leith Shore, Tony Borthwick's modern European restaurant is an elegant and relaxing place to eat. Tables are reasonably well-spaced in the irregularly shaped

interlinked rooms, which are done in gentle shades of green, with contemporary artwork. The cooking continues to aim way above mere satisfaction, with surprises and delights along the way. The late-summer tasting menu was 'one of the meals of my life' for one reporter: the three ways with foie gras (cromesqui, ice cream and with Armagnac-soaked dates) 'each a masterpiece, cumulatively staggering'. Confidence with seafood produces a tian of white crabmeat, offset with high tang in the shapes of pickled cucumber and a mango and pineapple salsa. Veal is accorded its full nobility: the Wellington treatment for the fillet, together with a crépinette of truffled shin, accompanied by spinach and wild leeks. Dornoch lamb is also a thing of two halves – roast loin and braised flank – served with red pepper custard and couscous. The tang tendency continues into desserts such as cherry soufflé with chocolate vinegar sorbet, or you could opt for the silkier route with clementine mousse and candied almonds. Service flows 'seamlessly, smoothly and elegantly', and there are some great wines, from £20.
Chef/s: Tony Borthwick. **Open:** Tue to Sat L 12.30 to 1.30, D 7 to 9. **Closed:** Sun, Mon, Christmas, 2 weeks summer. **Meals:** Set L £26. Set D £55. **Service:** not inc. **Details:** 40 seats. Wheelchair access. Music.

★ TOP 50 ★

Restaurant Martin Wishart

Complex food from an inspirational chef
54 The Shore, Leith, Edinburgh, EH6 6RA
Tel no: (0131) 5533557
www.martin-wishart.co.uk
Modern French | £65
Cooking score: 7
V

Martin Wishart opened here in 1999, setting what was then the shiny new redevelopment of the Leith port area of the Scottish capital on a course for the stars. The ripples that have flowed out from this suave, understated dining room (refurbished in 2012 in a brighter, less formal livery with stripped pine boards on the walls, but still hinting at grandeur with its deep-pile carpet and double-clothed tables) helped inspire a whole new generation of Edinburgh chefs in and near this fashionable quarter. Wishart's menus deal in complex treatments of highly refined ingredients in a rarefied style that balances ingenious presentation and intricate flavour construction. North Berwick lobster appears as a starter with smoked haddock gratin and creamed parsley, spiked with grain mustard and Espelette pepper, to be followed, perhaps, by blade and braised crispy short rib of Wagyu beef, alongside pumpkin, salsify and truffled potato confit. There's a bravura and confidence about the best dishes, seen to best effect in the full elaboration of the tasting menus. However, it is sometimes felt, particularly in the case of the less highly worked dishes, that the production can drop weirdly below what is expected. An experience with the cheaper lunch menu wasn't happy. A more or less disastrous opening effort of smoked haddock, leeks and poached egg in mustard cream with a dribble of syrupy fish stock contained a fair few bones and a badly undercooked egg. Dessert, however, restored our faith in the form of superb praline parfait with bitter chocolate sorbet. Service is deeply congenial, keeping things relaxed and fluid while maintaining the sense of a special occasion, and wines are very fine. The opening glass selection is full of character and purpose, from Bründlmayer's Grüner Veltliner (at £7.50) to Vergelegen Merlot, and the main list teems with modern thinking – interesting growers are the key, not just vintage runs of famous classed growths. Bottles start at £27.

Chef/s: Martin Wishart. **Open:** Tue to Sat L 12 to 1.30, D 7 to 9 (6.30 to 9.30 Fri and Sat). **Closed:** Sun, Mon, 25 and 26 and 31 Dec, 2 to 3 weeks Jan. **Meals:** Set L £28.50. Set D £65. Sun L £60. Tasting menu £70 (6 courses). **Service:** not inc. **Details:** 45 seats. Wheelchair access. Music.

Rhubarb at Prestonfield

Magnificent interiors and head-turning cooking
Prestonfield House, Priestfield Road, Edinburgh, EH16 5UT
Tel no: (0131) 2251333
www.prestonfield.com
Modern British | £50
Cooking score: 4

It's not exactly a castle, but the splendour certainly falls on this extravagantly modernised baroque pile, judging by reports of Prestonfield's magnificently fashioned interiors and legions of smart staff in kilts. Occupying two oval-shaped Regency rooms, the Rhubarb restaurant makes its own design statement with exotic colour schemes and dusky fabrics, but it's the cooking that really turns heads. Here is a kitchen that knows how to transform native produce and foraged pickings into plates of fancy contemporary food: hand-dived scallops come with cauliflower purée, alexanders, chorizo and confit lemon; roast Arctic char might crop up with two kinds of asparagus, pea purée, wild garlic and laver, and St Bride's free-range chicken is arrayed with Puy lentils, hazelnut paste and kohlrabi. Rhubarb was famously cultivated at Prestonfield during the eighteenth century, and it regularly stars in desserts – perhaps with a yoghurt pannacotta and sablé 'sandwich' and a ball of lime and beetroot sorbet. A mighty international wine list opens with house recommendations from £23.

Chef/s: John McMahon. **Open:** all week L 12 to 2 (3 Sat and Sun), D 6 to 10 (11 Fri and Sat). **Meals:** alc (main courses £14 to £35). Set L £16.95 (2 courses) to £30. Set D £30. **Service:** not inc. **Details:** 90 seats. 20 seats outside. Separate bar. Wheelchair access. Music. Car parking. No children after 7.30.

NEW ENTRY

Tanjore

Authentic Tamil cooking at bargain prices
6-8 Clerk Street, Edinburgh, EH8 9HX
Tel no: (0131) 4786518
www.tanjore.co.uk
Indian | £15
Cooking score: 2

Tanjore's unassuming cafeteria interior and the longish waits for food are no problem for fans of the authentic Tamil cooking to be found here. Owner Boon Ganeshram is happy to advise on specialities that make Tanjore such a haven for veggies and vegans, including idli (steamed rice and lentil cakes) and vadai (crunchy lentil doughnuts). Outstanding are the dosas, which are large, thin and delicately crisp and served with sambar and subtle mint, tomato and coconut chutneys, all based on roasted lentils. Spicing, as in fish or crab curry, is subtle and breads are delightfully soft and fluffy. BYO or drink refreshing mango lassi.
Chef/s: Boon Ganeshram. **Open:** all week L 12 to 2.30 (3.30 Sat and Sun), D 5 to 10. **Meals:** alc (main courses £6 to £10). **Service:** not inc. **Details:** 40 seats. 10 seats outside. No music.

21212

Kooky contemporary cuisine
3 Royal Terrace, Edinburgh, EH7 5AB
Tel no: (0131) 5231030
www.21212restaurant.co.uk
Modern French | £68
Cooking score: 5

'Possibly the most beautifully quirky dining room in the UK' purred one reader after visiting this shrine to kooky contemporary cuisine in a high-ceilinged Georgian town house. Renegade chef Paul Kitching has been ruffling feathers for years, and 21212 finds him still playing tricks and applying his own culinary logic to a truckload of ingredients. The restaurant's regimented name isn't a musical countdown in reverse, but a reference to the menu choices: two starters, one soup,

two mains, one cheese, two desserts. Kitching has toned down his zany dish names, but there's no let-up when it comes to the shopping-list descriptions: look at 'smoked saffron baked haddock, spicy scallop ratatouille', a riotous assembly involving aubergines, apricots, sticky onion rice, red pepper fondant, yeast cream and more besides. Depending on the season, you might also find sea bass 'blanc' (an exploration of all things white, from beansprouts to bread sauce) or a 'meat feast' of corn-fed chicken, barley pudding, haggis, mustard and other trencherman staples. Risky stuff indeed, but that's how Kitching works; at best, the whole shebang gels into a sublime gustatory helter-skelter; at worst, it can seem like an overblown jumble of ill-suited flavours. To finish, readers have been underwhelmed by the 'post-exams glazed custard and wintry trifle'. Staff get top marks for their enthusiasm and helpful attitude, but coffee 'in plastic cups' has raised a few eyebrows. Daily selections by the glass offer the best value on the grown-up wine list; bottles from £20.50.
Chef/s: Paul Kitching. **Open:** Tue to Sat L 12 to 1.45, D 6.45 to 9.30. **Closed:** Sun and Mon, 10 days Jan, 10 days summer. **Meals:** Set L £28 to £52 (5 courses). Set D £68 (5 courses). **Service:** not inc. **Details:** 38 seats. Separate bar. No music. Children over 5 yrs only.

Valvona & Crolla Caffè Bar

Showcasing fine ingredients
19 Elm Row, Edinburgh, EH7 4AA
Tel no: (0131) 5566066
www.valvonacrolla.co.uk
Italian | £27
Cooking score: 3

An Edinburgh institution, Valvona & Crolla Caffè Bar is tucked away at the back of a deli where the range of Italian meats, cheeses, wine, fresh fruit and vegetables is 'staggering'. The caffè is understated (small pine tables, slim green wood chairs, wood-effect lino, local art on the walls) with a casual honesty that fits the simple Italian food and range of cakes. Toasted sourdough with San Marzano tomatoes, capers, anchovies, basil and olive oil showcases fine ingredients, while orecchiette pasta in tomato and pork sugo (sauce) combines freshness with intense flavour. The wine selection is compact – understandable for a café – but V&C manages to pack a lot into the 10 or so all-Italian bottles (from £13.95) and every main course has a suggested wine match. **Chef/s:** Mary Contini. **Open:** Mon to Thur 8.30 to 5.30, Fri and Sat 8 to 6pm, Sun 10.30 to 3.30. **Closed:** 25 and 26 Dec, 1 and 2 Jan. **Meals:** alc (main courses £10 to £15). **Service:** 10%. **Details:** 60 seats. Music.

The Witchery by the Castle
Some fancy trickery with Scottish produce
Castlehill, Royal Mile, Edinburgh, EH1 2NF
Tel no: (0131) 2255613
www.thewitchery.com
Modern British | £50
Cooking score: 2

The name of this dramatically atmospheric rendezvous by the gates of Edinburgh Castle immediately summons up hubble-bubble images of Gothic theatricality, and the Witchery doesn't disappoint. Sculptural excesses, tapestries, acres of buttoned leather and even the odd bagpipe-playing cherub greet visitors to the oak-panelled dining room – or you can enjoy the enchantingly romantic Secret Garden. Either way, expect a riot of Scottish produce and some fancy trickery: haggis blended with chicken mousse; Tweeddale pigeon breast with a salad of pickled girolles; hot-smoked Loch Duart salmon served with sweet potatoes. The wine list is a baronial grandee that majors on fine Champagnes, illustrious Burgundies and Bordeaux, but also gives full weight to Spain, Italy and the New World. Prices start at £23. **Chef/s:** Douglas Roberts. **Open:** all week L 12 to 4, D 5.30 to 11.30. **Closed:** 25 Dec. **Meals:** alc (main courses £16 to £39). Set L and pre-theatre D £15.95 (2 courses) to £33. Set D £33. Sun L £33. **Service:** not inc. **Details:** 110 seats. 20 seats outside. Music. Children over 12 yrs only after 7.30.

ALSO RECOMMENDED

▲ John Hope Gateway Restaurant
Royal Botanic Garden, Arboretum Place, Edinburgh, EH3 5LR
Tel no: (0131) 5522674
www.gatewayrestaurant.net
Modern European £5 OFF

This relaxed restaurant is set within the Royal Botanic Gardens, and many of the fruit and vegetables it uses are grown there. Such seasonality is reflected in the regularly changing menu; sandwiches and sharing platters sit alongside main courses such as braised ox cheek in red wine with horseradish and wilted spinach (£10.50). Finish with cardamom rice pudding with pear, blueberry and apple jam and whisky cream (£4.95). House wine is £15.95. Open all week for L.

▲ Kalpna
2-3 St Patrick Square, Edinburgh, EH8 9EZ
Tel no: (0131) 6679890
www.kalpnarestaurant.com
Indian vegetarian

Now entering its fourth decade, Kalpna was the first restaurant to promote Indian vegetarian food in Edinburgh. It draws on Punjabi, Gujarati and south Indian cooking; highlights are 'Kalpna favourites' (from £7.95) like Mughal kofta (cheese, onion, nut and potato fritters in a spicy sauce) or saam savera (spinach leaves wrapped around homemade paneer, saffron, ginger and vegetables). Lunch is a buffet, the dosas (from £8.95) are good, and there's lassi, beer or house wine (£13.95). Closed Sun.

READERS RECOMMEND

The Mulroy
Modern British
11a-13a William Street, Edinburgh, EH3 7NG
Tel no: (0131) 2256061
www.themulroy.co.uk
'One of the best dining spots in Edinburgh – in my humble opinion.'

▌Gullane

NEW ENTRY

Chez Roux

Graceful villa with Albert Roux menus
Greywalls Hotel, Muirfield, Gullane, EH31 2EG
Tel no: (01620) 842144
www.greywalls.co.uk
French | £39
Cooking score: 4

£5 OFF ☰ V

Now that Albert Roux has his fingerprints all over the menu, this graceful Edwardian villa is enjoying a new lease of life. Service is *comme il faut* and the dining room, with views across Muirfield golf course and the Firth of Forth, is relaxed yet suitably formal for this genteel enclave. Derek Johnstone interprets the Roux style perfectly. Soufflés abound, mousseline of lobster and 'salade de crabe' are both popular, but there are some sharp contemporary ideas too, say Saddleback pig's head with cured ox tongue in a beetroot glaze. Elsewhere, shellfish and fish stew in cider sauce has been 'sweet and rich, yet far from cloying, thanks to delicately balanced herbs and a well-judged measure of aniseed'. Other hits include roast saddle of rabbit with kidneys and carrot mousse, and the signature Rothschild omelette: peaches steeped in peach liqueur and sautéed in Champagne, topped with a saucer-sized soufflé. The impressive wine list starts at £22.
Chef/s: Derek Johnstone. **Open:** all week L 12 to 2.30, D 6.30 to 10. **Meals:** alc (main courses £16 to £24). Set L £21 (2 courses) to £25. Set D £24 (2 courses) to £28. Sun L £25. **Service:** 10%.
Details: 60 seats. 25 seats outside. Separate bar. No music. Car parking.

▮▮ Readers
▮▮ Recommend

A 'readers recommend' review is a genuine quote from a report sent in by one of our readers. We intend to follow up these suggestions throughout the year to come.

La Potinière

A cavalcade of immensely pleasurable food
34 Main Street, Gullane, EH31 2AA
Tel no: (01620) 843214
www.la-potiniere.co.uk
Modern British | £43
Cooking score: 6

A singular-looking, bow-fronted building with bedding plants out front, La Potinière nonetheless maintains a low profile in pretty little Gullane. 'Quiet and gentle' sums up the mood in the restrained dining room, with its cream and pink colour schemes, impeccably laid tables and extremely cordial atmosphere. No one is about to rush or get too excited here – although the cooking is immensely pleasurable from start to finish. A list of local suppliers sits quite naturally on the menu, and the Mary Runciman/Keith Marley double act is capable of transforming top-class raw materials into an easy-paced cavalcade of highly polished, beautifully turned-out dishes. Choice is limited, but the lunch menu elicits glowing tributes for its exceptional value and sheer satisfaction – just consider a 'properly flavoured' pea mousse alongside some poached peas, spiky leaves and minted crème fraîche, or an equally summery dish of crisp-skinned, coral-pink sea trout with crushed dill potatoes, steamed asparagus, green beans and a perfectly rendered, creamy shellfish reduction. Dinner sees a fleshed-out repertoire involving the likes of Gorgonzola, chestnut and honey tart, Thai coconut soup with poached scallops, and desserts such as cherry and Kirsch crème brûlée with warm cherry compote. Details such as 'outstandingly good' breads, unsalted butter, fine cheeses and coffee with traditional tablet are just so, and the thoughtful wine list is helpfully divided into different price brackets. Half-bottles abound and house recommendations start at £16.75.
Chef/s: Mary Runciman and Keith Marley. **Open:** Wed to Sun L 12 to 1.30, D 7 to 8.30. **Closed:** Mon, Tue, Jan. **Meals:** Set L £19.50 (2 courses) to £25. Set D £43 (5 courses). **Service:** not inc. **Details:** 24 seats. No music. Wheelchair access. Car parking.

Linlithgow

Champany Inn

Pioneering steakhouse
Champany Corner, Linlithgow, EH49 7LU
Tel no: (01506) 834532
www.champany.com
Scottish | £73
Cooking score: 3

Long before the current fashion for steakhouses, Anne and Clive Davidson were showing how it should be done. Over the years the couple have fostered a polished, old-fashioned Scottish air in their sympathetically run, professional restaurant, housed in a group of sixteenth-century farm buildings. They have built their reputation on Scottish-reared beef, aged for three weeks in an ionised chill room and cooked on specially designed stoves. However, if you are not in the mood for a porterhouse, prime rib or entrecôte, there's always butter-poached lobster, grilled salmon or organic cod and chips. The execution impresses mightily, and that goes for desserts such as rhubarb cannelloni with rhubarb and ginger sorbet. An epic wine list opens at £20.50. For something more affordable, try the adjoining Chop and Ale House.
Chef/s: Clive Davidson and David Gibson. **Open:** Mon to Fri L 12.30 to 2, Mon to Sat D 7 to 10 (6.30 Sat). **Closed:** Sun, 25 and 26 Dec, 1 and 2 Jan. **Meals:** alc (main courses £29 to £49). Set L £22.50 (2 courses) to £30.50. Set D £42.50. **Service:** 10%. **Details:** 54 seats. 12 seats outside. Separate bar. No music. Wheelchair access. Car parking. Children over 8 yrs only.

MARTIN WISHART
Restaurant Martin Wishart

Give us a quick culinary tip
Always use the freshest ingredients and be patient - don't rush the cooking process.

What's your biggest kitchen bugbear?
Untidiness in the kitchen; you cannot cook or think properly if your kitchen is not organised.

What food trends are you spotting at the moment?
There is a big trend for foraging for wild plants at the moment. As with any trend, I think it should not be over-used.

Sum up your cooking style in three words
Seasonality, freshness and flavour-intensity.

What's your biggest extravagance in the kitchen?
My love of truffles; every time the season comes along I must buy some.

What would you be if you weren't a chef?
I would have loved to be involved in sailing, perhaps as a professional skipper.

What would your last meal be?
Reestit mutton and tattie soup from Shetland. Every mouthful brings a good memory of my deepest roots.

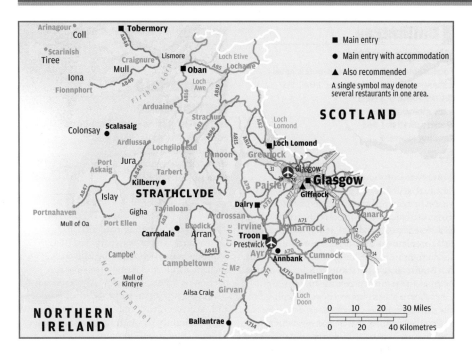

▮ **Annbank**

Enterkine House

Splendour, charm and fine-tuned cooking
Enterkine Estate, Annbank, KA6 5AL
Tel no: (01292) 520580
www.enterkine.com
Modern European | £30
Cooking score: 4

£5 OFF 🛏

'What a lovely setting for a restaurant' exclaimed a visitor who managed to bag a window table at this immaculate 1930s residence with views over the river Ayr. Squirrelled away in a 310-acre estate, Enterkine has splendour and personal charms in abundance, bolstered by food of a high order. Chef Paul Moffat is cementing his reputation here with some fine-tuned contemporary dishes involving broad culinary brush strokes. His savoury soufflés are a dream (try the goats' cheese version enlivened with red pepper and Meaux mustard), or you could begin in luxurious style with cured foie gras, morel relish and Sauternes jelly. To follow, moist local sea trout might be served with purple potatoes, while a dish of lamb and sweetbreads receives a heady Middle Eastern lift from quinoa, squash and ras-el-hanout. Cutely embellished macaroons are something of a speciality to finish, otherwise delve into the slate of Scottish cheeses. House wines start at £21.95.
Chef/s: Paul Moffat. **Open:** all week L 12 to 2, D 7 to 9. **Meals:** Set L £16.50 (2 courses) to £18.50. Set D £30 (2 courses) to £40. Sun L £18.50. **Service:** not inc. **Details:** 40 seats. 20 seats outside. Music. Car parking.

Average Price

The average price listed in main-entry reviews denotes the price of a three-course meal, without wine.

Ballantrae

Glenapp Castle

Formidable cooking at a top-notch hotel
Ballantrae, KA26 0NZ
Tel no: (01465) 831212
www.glenappcastle.com
Modern British | £65
Cooking score: 6

£5 OFF 🛏

This grandiose Victorian Gothic castle is baronial exuberance personified – a mighty vision in stone, all turrets, castellated walls and high battlements looking out towards the Irish Sea. As a top-notch hotel, it also parades the full complement of antiques, portraits and lavish trappings – although the food served in its two extravagantly furnished dining rooms belongs firmly in the twenty-first century. Chef Adam Stokes knows how to deploy the latest techniques and gizmos, especially in his six-course evening extravaganzas, which are strewn with 'formidable', startlingly presented contemporary dishes. Consider a playful, multicoloured assemblage of pigeon with spring onion 'milk', black pudding, carrot sorbet and pistachio, or fillet of John Dory with saffron-infused buckwheat, anchovy beignet and cauliflower. Or take things up another notch with a serving of milk-fed pork thoughtfully partnered by trotter cromesquis, grelot onions, Parma ham and a herb crumb. Dinner climaxes with a choice of two desserts: perhaps a 'breathtaking' soufflé or a milk chocolate and Grand Marnier mousse with cinnamon ice cream and burnt orange syrup (a triumph of the chocolatier's craft, according to one recipient). Refined details add a special frisson to the gastronomic trip, from the tiny, outrageously addictive beetroot meringues filled with cream cheese and served as canapés, to the Scottish cheeses with white truffle honey and the Sumatran coffee accompanied by ever-so-dainty petits fours. Burgundy and Bordeaux claim pole position on the international wine list; prices open at £27.
Chef/s: Adam Stokes. **Open:** all week L 12.30 to 2, D 7 to 10. **Closed:** Christmas week, 3 Jan to mid Mar. **Meals:** Set L £39.50. Set D £65 (6 courses).

Service: not inc. **Details:** 34 seats. No music. Wheelchair access. Car parking. Children over 5 yrs only at D.

Carradale

Dunvalanree

Enchanting clifftop home-from-home
Port Righ, Carradale, PA28 6SE
Tel no: (01583) 431226
www.dunvalanree.com
Modern British | £28
Cooking score: 2

£5 OFF 🛏 V

The 'long and winding road' that leads to Dunvalanree's door is actually the B842/879, which eventually reaches the Milsteads' enchanting clifftop home-from-home overlooking Port Righ Bay. Alyson M has always been keen on native Scottish produce, and she takes care of the culinary details while tripping lightly through an easy-to-manage seasonal repertoire – serving confit of Carradale salmon with dill vinaigrette and chilli jam, matching honey-roast duckling with blueberries poached in bramble wine, and enriching rack of Saddell lamb with a garlicky Marsala gravy. Expect old-fashioned desserts such as bananas in rum and maple syrup, or the deceptively named Dunvalanree cream ('essentially chocolate and alcohol', according to the menu). Wines from £14.75.
Chef/s: Alyson Milstead. **Open:** all week D only 7 to 9. **Closed:** 24 to 29 Dec. **Meals:** Set D £23.50 (2 courses) to £28. **Service:** not inc. **Details:** 20 seats. Wheelchair access. Music. Car parking.

Symbols

🛏 Accommodation is available

£30 Three courses for less than £30

V Separate vegetarian menu

£5 OFF £5-off voucher scheme

🍾 Notable wine list

Dalry
Braidwoods

Precision-tuned cooking and incisive flavours
Drumastle Mill Cottage, Dalry, KA24 4LN
Tel no: (01294) 833544
www.braidwoods.co.uk
Modern British | £43
Cooking score: 6

A pair of 200-year-old whitewashed millers' cottages set in Ayrshire farmland have been home to Keith and Nicola Braidwood's polished operation for nigh on 20 years. Both are Master Chefs and they show no sign of flagging, despite all the hard work and dedication that running a relatively remote place brings. Local produce is the kitchen's mainstay, but there is nothing rustic about its preparation. Classical skills underpin the production, from the painstaking clarification of stocks to the making of breads and pasta, and the canny use of unusual herbs and seasonings gives the cooking distinction. One windblown pair were glad of a starter of fortifying butternut squash soup with ginger, 'just the correct balance of flavour and spice on a very wild day'; or there could be a fishcake of lightly smoked salmon with poached quail egg on pea purée. An intermediate course crops up at dinner, before something like mushroom-stuffed roast loin of rabbit wrapped in Parma ham, with spinach and a thyme jus. Favoured finales might include bread-and-butter pudding with caramel sauce. A discriminating wine list has been written with passion and care, and contains plenty of good-value bottles. House selections are from £23.95 (£5.95 a glass).
Chef/s: Keith and Nicola Braidwood. **Open:** Wed to Sun L 12 to 1.30, Tue to Sat D 7 to 9. **Closed:** Mon, 25 Dec to 22 Jan, first 2 weeks Sept. **Meals:** Set L £23 (2 courses) to £26. Set D £43. Sun L £30.
Service: not inc. **Details:** 24 seats. No music. Car parking. Children over 5 yrs only at L, over 12 yrs only at D.

⫷ GIN O'CLOCK

Recent years have seen a distilling revival and Great Britain is leading the charge with 'boutique' gin brands like Sipsmith, Sacred and Six O'Clock gaining popularity and awards.

For Dominic Jacobs at the **Harvey Nichols Fifth Floor Bar**, the emergence of new British spirits like Williams Gin from Herefordshire's Chase distillery taps into our love of hand crafted, home-grown products. The base spirit is made from organic cider apples, so Jacobs serves it in a Hereford Martini with apple juice from the Chase estate and a splash of Chase rhubarb liqueur for a truly British cocktail.

For the largest gin collection around, head to the **Feathers Hotel** in Woodstock, where a record-breaking 162 varieties await you. A special seven-course tasting menu sees dishes like a ceviche of yellow-fin tuna, scallop and lime jelly paired with Tanqueray's lime-infused Rangpur gin. The hotel's ultimate G&T combines Blackwoods 2007 from the Shetlands with Brooklyn-born Q tonic and ice made from Blenheim Palace water.

Giffnock

ALSO RECOMMENDED
▲ The Giffnock Ivy

219 Fenwick Road, Giffnock, G46 6JD
Tel no: (0141) 6201003
www.giffnockivy.co.uk
Modern European

This simple, stylish, suburban restaurant is a reliable Glasgow crowd-pleaser offering dishes that are gently familiar. Chicken liver parfait and red onion marmalade (£5.95), mussels in white wine, garlic and parsley, and chicken suprême with chorizo, chickpea and potato stew (£13.95) may seem predictable, but they are well made and there is no arguing with the sheer value for money. For pud, try the vanilla crème brûlée. Wines from £13.95. Closed Mon.

Glasgow

Brian Maule at Chardon d'Or

French food that is very pleasing indeed
176 West Regent Street, Glasgow, G2 4RL
Tel no: (0141) 2483801
www.brianmaule.com
French | £40
Cooking score: 4

V

'Brilliant service, food is consistently excellent' is the heartfelt declaration of one reader, summing up the fondness with which regulars view Brian Maule's elegant town house restaurant. His cooking is measured but effective, a series of well-judged dishes whose cumulative effect is very pleasing indeed. Pickled cucumber and basil dressing are counterpoints to baked smoked haddock, and a dish of scallops with spätzle, chorizo and beetroot essence plays with earthy notes. To follow, roast lamb fillet is given Mediterranean tones with aubergine caviar, garlic purée and courgette beignet; braised beef cheek with a red wine sauce and winter vegetables has a British feel. To conclude, there might be a tarte Tatin with vanilla ice cream and butterscotch sauce. The wine list does the job at prices that rarely get silly (from £19). Consideration is given to organic and biodynamic producers as well as pedigree growers and top vintages.
Chef/s: Brian Maule. Open: Mon to Sat L 12 to 3 (5 Sat), D 5 to 10. Closed: Sun, 25 and 26 Dec, 1 and 2 Jan, bank hols. Meals: alc (main courses £22 to £27). Set L and D £17.50 (2 courses) to £20.50. Tasting menu £58 (6 courses). Service: not inc. Details: 150 seats. Separate bar. Music. No children after 8.

Gamba

Smart restaurant with 'lip-smacking' seafood
225a West George Street, Glasgow, G2 2ND
Tel no: (0141) 5720899
www.gamba.co.uk
Seafood | £38
Cooking score: 3

£5
OFF

It's not Spanish, but it is seafood: this smart, softly lit basement restaurant is guided by Derek Marshall's chefly appetite for fish, and in particular his penchant for teaming it with Asian flavours. A 'superb' fish soup features crab, ginger and coriander and a buoyant cargo of prawn dumplings, and there's a 'lip-smacking' cocktail of crayfish, prawn and crab with chilli and lime. Whole fish might be steamed en papillote with scallops, ginger and spring onions. There are earthier options – duck roast with apple and pancetta, or a mushroom risotto – but why miss out? Pudding could be a warm cherry Bakewell or chocolate tart with Nutella crème fraîche. 'Sharp' pricing makes the market and lunch menus a particularly good idea. Wine is from £19.
Chef/s: Derek Marshall. Open: Mon to Sat L 12 to 2.15, all week D 5 to 10 (9 Sun). Closed: 25 and 26 Dec, 1 to 9 Jan. Meals: alc (main courses £17 to £25). Set L and D £16.95 (2 courses) to £19.95. Service: not inc. Details: 65 seats. Separate bar. Music.

Stravaigin

Global food from good Scottish ingredients
28 Gibson Street, Glasgow, G12 8NX
Tel no: (0141) 3342665
www.stravaigin.com
Modern European | £25
Cooking score: 2

'We love this place for a lazy Sunday brunch with the newspapers' writes a reporter of this buzzy, extravagantly friendly venue, which serves global dishes made with good Scottish ingredients. Think coconut and curry leaf pancakes with dhal, pepper salsa and raita, then red pepper-crusted hake with chorizo, purple potato and broad beans in garlic and almond sauce, or nasi goreng made with Carluke bacon, king prawns and a poached egg. Pudding could be lemongrass polenta with ginger sabayon, caramelised tamarind and pineapple. Wines from £15.95 a bottle (£3.95 a glass). Sibling Stravaigin 2 is at 8 Ruthven Lane, Glasgow; tel: (0141) 3347165. Its speciality is Rijsttafel nights, a sort of Indonesian thali, served on the second Tuesday of the month.

Chef/s: Douglas Lindsay. Open: Sat and Sun L 12 to 5, all week D 5 to 11. Closed: 25 Dec, 1 Jan. Meals: alc (main courses £9 to £23). Set L £11.95 (2 courses) to £14.95. Set pre-theatre D £13.95 (2 courses) to £15.95. Service: not inc. Details: 46 seats. Separate bar. Music. No children after 10pm.

★ READERS' RESTAURANT OF THE YEAR ★
SCOTLAND

Ubiquitous Chip

Glasgow icon
12 Ashton Lane, Glasgow, G12 8SJ
Tel no: (0141) 3345007
www.ubiquitouschip.co.uk
Modern British | £40
Cooking score: 4

'This is why I love dining in Glasgow' confessed one reader after a visit to the city's most redoubtable gastronomic veteran. Of course, the Chip has always been in it for the long haul, expanding its horizons without ever seeming mawkishly trendy. The sprawling, labyrinthine interior comprises four different zones for eating and drinking (plus a sought-after roof terrace), while the kitchen mixes past and present with real gusto. Scottish provenance remains the mantra, although you'll now find pistachio-dusted Islay scallops with pickled apple purée and crisp belly pork, or a tian of smoked beetroot and Morangie Brie with cannellini beans and dill gremolata alongside old-timers such as the legendary venison haggis (circa 1971) and a kilt-swirling Caledonian take on surf and turf. Fans also appreciate the kitchen's 'little intricacies', from the espresso cups of Cullen skink to the ever-present oatmeal ice cream. The Chip's monumental wine list is a national treasure in its own right – a veritable encyclopaedia of mature clarets and Burgundies matched by gold-standard offerings from boutique wineries across the globe. Restaurant prices start at £18.85, although there are bargains aplenty in the bar/brasserie.

Chef/s: Andrew Mitchell. Open: Restaurant: all week L 12 to 2.30 (12.30 to 3 Sun), D 5 to 11. Brasserie: all week 11 to 11. Closed: 25 Dec, 1 Jan. Meals: Set L £15.95 (2 courses) to £19.95. Set D £34.95 (2 courses) to £39.95. Sun L £19.95. Service: not inc. Details: 170 seats. 49 seats outside. Separate bar. Wheelchair access. Music. No children after 10.

La Vallée Blanche

Neighbourhood French bistro
360 Byres Road, Glasgow, G12 8AY
Tel no: (0141) 3343333
www.lavalleeblanche.com
French | £28
Cooking score: 3

Although French bistro cooking is the style at this first-floor, Swiss chalet of a restaurant off the busy Byres Road, the kitchen takes a fairly broad-brush approach. Starters range from a straightforward shellfish bisque to a hare, rabbit and foie gras terrine teamed with sauce gribiche and port jelly; mains take in roast ribeye of rose veal (with pomme purée, wild mushrooms, spinach and Arran mustard sherry cream), and halibut (with onion soubise, braised chicken wings, leeks and salsa verde). Desserts have included blood-orange posset, and hot apple soufflé with salted caramel ice cream. House wine is £17.95. **Chef/s:** David Maxwell. **Open:** Tue to Sun L 12 to 2.15 (3.15 Sat and Sun), D 5.30 to 9.30 (8.45 Sun). **Closed:** Mon, 25 Dec, 1 Jan. **Meals:** alc (main courses £11 to £25). Set L £14.95 (2 courses) to £17.95. **Service:** not inc. **Details:** 78 seats. Music. No children after 9.

ALSO RECOMMENDED
▲ Number 16
16 Byres Road, Glasgow, G11 5JY
Tel no: (0141) 3392544
www.number16.co.uk
Modern British £5 OFF

'Small restaurant with very pleasant staff' noted one reporter; 'highly, highly recommended' exclaimed another. This intimate, two-tiered bistro continues to please, offering surroundings that are clean-cut, modern and well dressed. Sound cooking, based on prime ingredients, spans everything from thyme gnocchi with blue cheese, walnuts and red wine reduction (£6.95) to slow-cooked belly pork, and Vietnamese fish broth with ginger and mustard vegetables (£17.50). Set lunch and pre-theatre deals have been praised. House wines are £14.95. Open all week.

▲ Red Onion
257 West Campbell Street, Glasgow, G2 4TT
Tel no: (0141) 2216000
www.red-onion.co.uk
Global £5 OFF

'Friendly staff, great décor, good range on menu for all tastes' just about sums up John Quigley's flexible all-day eatery. His unfussy cooking displays a real fusion of flavours in an aromatic chicken salad with crispy noodles,

mandarins and spicy peanut dressing (£6) or a mixed grill of harissa loin of lamb, merguez sausages, smoked aubergine, tzatziki and couscous (£17.50), but he can also deliver a textbook French onion soup or wild mushroom risotto with spinach and Parmesan. Wines from £15.95. Open all week.

READERS RECOMMEND
City Merchant
Seafood
97-99 Candleriggs, Glasgow, G1 1NP
Tel no: (0141) 5531577
www.citymerchant.co.uk
'The grilled seafood platter was excellent, the freshest fish I have had in many years.'

Isle of Colonsay
The Colonsay
Good stuff at an island getaway
Scalasaig, Isle of Colonsay, PA61 7YP
Tel no: (01951) 200316
www.colonsayestate.co.uk
Modern British | £25
Cooking score: 2

'Produced a delicious meal for a very modest price' noted one intrepid reporter of this eighteenth-century inn on the remote Isle of Colonsay. It's hard not to like this far-flung outpost, run with pioneering zeal for the best things this piece of God's acreage can offer – local fish and shellfish, home-grown salad leaves and vegetables. Simple, attractive bar lunches (soups, sandwiches, terrines and casseroles) make way for two or three-course dinners. It's good stuff: Colonsay oysters, mussels, langoustine, even fish and chips and steaks, with Colonsay wild-flower honey and vanilla ice cream to finish. Wines from £11.50. **Chef/s:** Robert Smyth. **Open:** all week L 12 to 3, D 5.30 to 9.30. **Closed:** Nov to Feb. **Meals:** alc (main courses £9 to £20). Set D £12.95 (2 courses) to £15.95. **Service:** not inc. **Details:** 40 seats. 20 seats outside. Separate bar. Wheelchair access. Car parking.

Isle of Mull
Café Fish
Fantastic no-frills seafood
The Pier, Main Street, Tobermory, Isle of Mull,
PA75 6NU
Tel no: (01688) 301253
www.thecafefish.com
Seafood | £27
Cooking score: 3

 £30

'Fantastic seafood, cooked simply and effectively. Very limited space, so can feel crowded, but this all adds to the feeling of relief that you managed to get a table – book early'. So ran a confirmation of the quality of this small, no-frills restaurant housed in former ferry offices overlooking Tobermory Harbour. The catch of the day is always worth going for, and oysters and crab are particularly good – especially crab cakes with 'no skimping on the crab'. Otherwise, there's 'hearty and bursting with flavour' fish stew or a 'magic' fish pie, creel-caught squat lobster and langoustine, queen scallops sautéed with bacon, and homely sticky ginger pudding for afters. The wine list opens at £14.90, or there's locally brewed beer – 'a pleasant surprise'.
Chef/s: Liz McGougan. **Open:** all week L 12 to 3, D 5.30 to 10. **Closed:** Jan and Feb. **Meals:** alc (main courses £6 to £28). **Service:** not inc. **Details:** 36 seats. 30 seats outside. Music.

Kilberry
The Kilberry Inn
Dream destination with divine seafood
Kilberry Road, Kilberry, PA29 6YD
Tel no: (01880) 770223
www.kilberryinn.com
Modern British | £35
Cooking score: 3

A 'holiday highlight' for one couple, the rose-clad Kilberry Inn is strung out on a single-track road between Tarbert and Lochgilphead. It's a trek, but those who make it can look forward to dream hospitality, Hebridean

views and some fine, eclectic cooking inspired by Scottish produce. 'Divine' seafood always shows up well, from surf clams cooked with manzanilla and chorizo to Gigha halibut with fennel confit, lemon and black olives. The owners even have their own smokehouse for locally landed mackerel and suchlike. Meat eaters have been well pleased with flavoursome plates of Sika deer, ribeye with Café de Paris butter, and marinated rack of Edinvale lamb with herb-tinged couscous salad, while luscious homemade ice creams, gooey treacle tart and 'floating' meringues provide an irresistible sugar rush. Wines are categorised by style ('green and tangy'), with prices from £17.
Chef/s: Clare Johnson and Hugh McShannon. **Open:** Tue to Sun L 12 to 2, D 6.30 onwards. **Closed:** Mon, Jan to mid Mar. **Meals:** alc (main courses £14 to 22). **Service:** not inc. **Details:** 32 seats. 8 seats outside. Wheelchair access. Music. Car parking.

Loch Lomond
NEW ENTRY
Martin Wishart at Loch Lomond
Wishart's stylish lochside venture
Loch Lomond, G83 8QZ
Tel no: (01389) 722504
www.martinwishartlochlomond.co.uk
Modern French | £65
Cooking score: 6

V

This lochside outpost of Martin Wishart's acclaimed Edinburgh restaurant has much in common with its big brother, which has contributed staff, the design team and, of course, Wishart's watchful guidance to the mix. The décor has gravitas – napkins and napery, chocolate wood floors and panelling, high-backed chairs and sparkling glassware – but the scene-stealer is the view of Loch Lomond. Those familiar with Wishart's style will see it mirrored here in Graham Cheevers' endlessly diverting cooking. Nothing feels laboured, no combination strained, yet there are surprises and revelations – as in an astonishingly light amuse-bouche of beetroot macaroons with a horseradish filling. Other openers (a crisply coated salsify stick with curried mayonnaise dip; cauliflower cream topped with golden raisins) matched crunchy with tender and savoury with sweet, with breezy flair. A starter of perfectly timed winter truffle risotto topped with a caramelised scallop took savoury to new, musky depths, while a galette of braised oxtail 'Auvergnate' with sweetbreads roasted in buckwheat, glazed chestnuts, baby onions and ham ran the full gamut of flavours, from the intensely salty ham to the caramel sweetness of the chestnuts. In between came the meaty intensity of oxtail and plump sweetbreads of almost buttery richness. Valrhona chocolate mousse with Sacher sponge and orange ice cream balanced sweet, bitter and tangy with sure-footed ease. Service is leisurely and unobtrusive and there's an expert sommelier on hand to give recommendations from a list that is full of interesting finds, including biodynamic options and plenty from France. Bottles start at £27.

Chef/s: Graham Cheevers. **Open:** Sat and Sun L 12 to 2 (2.30 Sun), Wed to Sun D 6.30 to 9.30 (7 to 9.30 Sun). **Closed:** Mon, Tue, 25 and 26 Dec, 1 Jan. **Meals:** Set L £25. Set D £50 (2 courses) to £65. Sun L £25. Tasting menu £70. **Service:** 10%. **Details:** 40 seats. Separate bar. Wheelchair access. Music. Car parking. No children at D.

Oban

Waterfront Fishouse Restaurant

Minimal-frills, super-fresh seafood
1 Railway Pier, Oban, PA34 4LW
Tel no: (01631) 563110
www.waterfrontoban.co.uk
Seafood | £24
Cooking score: 1

The former Waterfront, a versatile first-floor seafooder near the ferry terminal, has a proud new owner in the shape of long-standing manager Alex Needham (who has wisely

CHOCOLATE REVOLUTION

William Curley, award-winning British pâtissier chocolatier, has brought the joys of fine chocolate to the masses. Here, he reveals his favourite chocolate flavour combinations: 'Chocolate is fantastic to work with as it is so versatile and blends well with a broad variety of ingredients. My wife, Suzue, is Japanese and has introduced me to many exciting flavours such as Yuzu, Wasabi, Kinako and Matcha. You may wonder how such strong, independent flavours will work with chocolate, but we use a subtle infusion which complements the chocolate to bring out the flavours. Mustard and tarragon combine well with chocolate; the aniseed notes from the tarragon and the heat from the mustard create a unique and delicious experience on the palate. Another interesting combination is soy and tomato; the saltiness from the soy and the sweet acidity of the tomato blend beautifully.

There is a chocolate revolution taking place, with chocolate being regarded as a more sophisticated treat than your average sugary bar. We are now realising the potential of fine chocolate, through including it in savoury dishes or experimenting with unusual flavour combinations.'

retained the head chef of three years' standing). The kitchen is well-practised at serving minimal-frills, daisy-fresh fish and seafood, from fish and chips to whole local langoustine, from local mussels to halibut fillet in lemon and tarragon cream sauce. There's also good homemade bread, sticky toffee pudding and fish-friendly wines from £14.99.

Chef/s: Roy Stalker. **Open:** all week L 12 to 2.15, D 5.30 to 9.30. **Closed:** 25 Dec. **Meals:** alc (main courses £9 to £20). Set L and D £9.95 (2 courses). **Details:** 80 seats. 16 seats outside. Music.

ALSO RECOMMENDED

▲ Ee-Usk

North Pier, Oban, PA34 5QD
Tel no: (01631) 565666
www.eeusk.com
Seafood

Great views of the Argyll coast are a big selling point at this popular eatery by Oban harbour, and the place also scores with its flappingly fresh local seafood. The kitchen deals in fish cookery of the old school; think scallops Mornay (£8.95), mussels with chips, battered haddock, and sea bass with creamed leeks and savoury mash (£17.95). Huge seafood platters go down well and staff are charming, although high prices and uneven cooking have disappointed some readers. House wine £14.95. Open all week.

▮ Troon

MacCallums Oyster Bar

No fancy posturing, just prime seafood
The Harbour, Troon, KA10 6DH
Tel no: (01292) 319339
Seafood | £27
Cooking score: 2

 £30

Plot a course for Troon harbour to find this converted hydraulic pump house stuffed with America's Cup sailing memorabilia. Owners John and James MacCallum are fish merchants by trade, so there are no prizes for guessing that prime maritime pickings are the mainstay

of the menu. The kitchen rejects fancy posturing in favour of direct, upfront flavours – perhaps grilled langoustine with garlic butter ahead of Parmesan-crusted roast pollack or whole sea bream with herb oil and lemon dressing. At lunchtime, you can also drop in for an open sandwich of pan-fried mackerel with beetroot coleslaw, and perhaps a pud of crème brûlée. House wine is £15.95 (£4.55 a glass).

Chef/s: Phillip Burgess. **Open:** Tue to Sun L 12 to 2.30 (3 Sun), Tue to Sat D 6.30 to 9.30. **Closed:** Mon, 3 weeks from 25 Dec. **Meals:** alc (main courses £10 to £28). **Service:** not inc. **Details:** 43 seats. Music. Car parking.

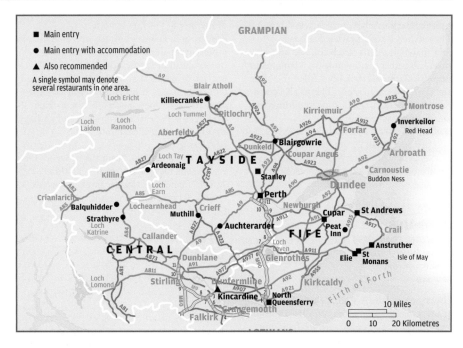

▮ Ardeonaig

NEW ENTRY
Ardeonaig Hotel
Deft loch-side cooking
South Loch Tay Side, Ardeonaig, FK21 8SU
Tel no: (01567) 820400
www.ardeonaighotel.co.uk
Modern British | £45
Cooking score: 4

🛏 V

A pre-dinner drink in the cottagey front rooms of this smart but homely hotel does nothing to prepare you for the colonial grandeur of the dining room, with its tall windows, terracotta floors and picture-perfect loch views. With new owners and a new chef, early reports have been ecstatic: 'probably the finest food we have ever eaten on our frequent trips to Scotland' is typical. One reporter's lunch came up trumps: Ibérico ham with langoustine, baby artichokes and red wine sauce was an intelligent combination of top-notch ingredients; a beautifully fresh piece of Gigha halibut with chive beurre blanc, crushed potatoes and broccoli made a precise and comforting main course, while a deeply savoury wild mushroom and truffle risotto was perfectly seasoned and timed. Homemade sorbets impressed at dessert, as did truffly Amedei chocolate slices. Service is 'excellent – very polished'. A substantial wine list, divided by type, starts at £15.
Chef/s: David Maskell. **Open:** Thur to Sun L 12 to 3 (2 Thur), Wed to Sun D 6.30 to 9.30. **Closed:** Mon, Tue, 3 Jan to 3 Feb. **Meals:** Set L £22.50. Set D £45. Tasting menu £60. **Service:** not inc. **Details:** 35 seats. 20 seats outside. Separate bar. Wheelchair access. Music. Car parking.

Average Price
The average price listed in main-entry reviews denotes the price of a three-course meal, without wine.

█ Balquhidder
Monachyle Mhor
Family enterprise with a foodie heart
Balquhidder, FK19 8PQ
Tel no: (01877) 384622
www.mhor.net
Modern British | £47
Cooking score: 5

Pink-washed Monachyle Mhor is the foodie heart of a family enterprise that now incorporates a fishmonger's/chippie, bakery and tea room dotted around the Trossachs National Park. It stands invitingly at the end of a winding six-mile track by the shores of Loch Voil. This is Rob Roy country, although in recent years chef Tom Lewis and his unofficial clan have made it their very own. 'Few venues can rate higher on provenance' observed one visitor, and Tom certainly knows his own backyard. Meat from its livestock pastures, plus seasonal game and foraged pickings provide the backbone for five-course dinners full of invention, artistry and 'light modern touches'. Flavours always ring true, whether it's a dish of home-reared Tamworth pork with salsify and cassoulet beans or saddle of mountain hare allied to Puy lentils, steamed greens, coriander and ginger. Fish is also a star turn, judging by glowing reports of mackerel with fennel, capers and sorrel or halibut with tarragon-flecked pasta. To finish, try something humble such as apple pie with oatmeal crumble and raisin purée. Tom Lewis is a generous host 'who always seems to be laughing', and the whole place is imbued with a spirit of genial bonhomie. 'Brilliant' dessert wines are just one feature of a fascinating, highly personal list that gives prominence to unusual varietals and self-styled 'oddballs' alongside gold-star vintages. Prices start at £22 (£5.50 a glass).
Chef/s: Tom Lewis. **Open:** all week L 12 to 2, D 7 to 9. **Closed:** 7 to 31 Jan. **Meals:** alc (main courses £16 to £27). Set D £47 (5 courses). Sun L £32. **Service:** not inc. **Details:** 40 seats. Separate bar. Music. Car parking.

█ Strathyre
Creagan House
Delightful farmhouse with standout food
Strathyre, FK18 8ND
Tel no: (01877) 384638
www.creaganhouse.co.uk
French | £32
Cooking score: 4

Surrounded by Highland scenery, this baronial-style restaurant-with-rooms is 'an absolute delight', thanks to the 'care and attention' and 'total dedication' of owners Gordon and Cherry Gunn. You'll find Cherry front-of-house, overseeing a dining room with polished wood floors, a grand fireplace and a magnificent vaulted ceiling. Gordon has been chef here for more than 23 years and 'continues to excel' in the role, turning out modern European dishes brimming with local ingredients – breast of grouse with boudin of grouse leg, compote of grouse liver and apple and smoked bacon for instance, or cutlets of local lamb, leg patty with mint and ginger, and redcurrant lamb gravy. Bittersweet chocolate cake with Baileys ice cream and chocolate sauce is a typical dessert. Cherry oversees the 'very fairly priced' wine list, which is weighted towards France and includes a good selection by the glass and 500ml carafe. Bottles start at £18.40.
Chef/s: Gordon Gunn. **Open:** Fri to Tue D only 7.15 for 8 (1 sitting). **Closed:** Wed, Thur, 24 to 26 Dec, 18 Jan to 7 Mar, 6 to 21 Nov. **Meals:** Set D £32.50. **Service:** not inc. **Details:** 14 seats. Separate bar. No music. Wheelchair access. Car parking. Children over 10 yrs only.

Visit us Online
To find out more about
The Good Food Guide, please visit
www.thegoodfoodguide.co.uk

Anstruther

The Cellar

Sparkling-fresh seafood favourite
24 East Green, Anstruther, KY10 3AA
Tel no: (01333) 310378
www.cellaranstruther.co.uk
Seafood | £40
Cooking score: 6

Peter and Susan Jukes's evergreen seafood restaurant is a local institution; the thoroughly welcoming atmosphere, the interior of beams, polished tables, open fires and gentle lighting all testify to years of hands-on dedication. The kitchen continues to keep customers satisfied with the straightforward cooking of sparklingly fresh fish. Simplicity is evident, whether dressed local crab, fish soup or lobster and smoked salmon tart, but this indicates that attention is focused where it should be – raw materials are of the very highest quality, and technique is sound. The short menu brims with local flavours and acute seasonal detailing, be it a never-off-the-menu smoked haddock omelette or a half-lobster and diver-caught scallops with herb and garlic butter, Jersey Royals and tossed leaves. Visitors have also raved about Scottish asparagus risotto served with a poached egg, the 'herring and gravadlax which set the tone for the wonderful meal which followed', and the signature grilled halibut (on this occasion served on a bed of cabbage, bacon, pine nuts, and basil mash). Gressingham duck and fillet of beef are alternatives for those who must. Rhubarb pavlova with lemon curd ice cream is a brilliant conceit if you fancy finishing on a sweet note. Excellent house wines start at £18.50.
Chef/s: Peter Jukes. **Open:** Fri and Sat L from 12.30, Tue to Sat D 6.30 to 9. **Closed:** Sun, Mon, 24 to 26 Dec. **Meals:** Set L £19.95 (2 courses) to £24.95. Set D £34.95 (2 courses) to £39.95. **Service:** not inc. **Details:** 40 seats.

Cupar

Ostlers Close

Characterful cooking from a local hero
25 Bonnygate, Cupar, KY15 4BU
Tel no: (01334) 655574
www.ostlersclose.co.uk
Modern British | £42
Cooking score: 5

The Close is a snug little alleyway off Cupar's main street, and it's where Jimmy and Amanda Graham's intimate, smartly appointed restaurant – now in its fourth decade and still bounding youthfully along – is to be found. The russet décor and crisp table linen speak of old-school elegance, and there's an atmosphere of cultivated civility. Jimmy is a dedicated supporter of local suppliers, more so than many who make the claim. He draws on seafood from East Neuk, meats from Fife farms, fruit and veg from his own plots, and wild mushrooms that he gathers himself. It's this commitment that lends such character to the cooking, which has the air of a chef who's confident enough to try new things as well as revisiting successful ideas. Monkfish fillets on Spanish-style open pastry, accompanied by stir-fried sultanas, pine nuts and Serrano ham, are a favourite; they could be followed by pot-roast breasts of wood-pigeon with black pudding mash and red cabbage in a game stock reduction. Game is a strong point in the season, best taken as a 'Gamekeeper's Bag' selection of roast items in a juniper-scented sauce. Lemon coconut tart with pineapple and coconut ice cream and Earl Grey syrup is a fine finish, or Scottish cheeses with mirabelle plum paste. House Chilean is £18 (£4.50 a glass).
Chef/s: Jimmy Graham. **Open:** Sat L 12 to 1.30, Tue to Sat D 7 to 9.30. **Closed:** Sun, Mon, 25 and 26 Dec, 1 and 2 Jan, 2 weeks Apr, 2 weeks Oct. **Meals:** alc (main courses £19 to £24). **Service:** not inc. **Details:** 28 seats. No music.

Elie
Sangster's
Appealing Fife fixture
51 High Street, Elie, KY9 1BZ
Tel no: (01333) 331001
www.sangsters.co.uk
Modern British | £40
Cooking score: 5

'Small, intimate and on form' was one visitor's verdict on this appealing fixture of the Fife restaurant scene. Inside, Bruce and Jacqueline Sangster's personable and homely town house has been treated to a gentle dose of cosmopolitan chic – a feature that also applies to the food. Seared hand-dived scallops ('of the highest standard') continue to hit the mark – often invigorated with chilli, galangal and coriander – and Bruce's twice-baked Tobermory cheese soufflé is never off the menu. The kitchen's devotion to Scottish produce also shows in heartily endorsed, robust dishes of slow-cooked pork cheek with roast black pudding and an apricot-stuffed chunk of fillet, or roast monkfish with braised fennel and langoustine sauce. Low-key craftsmanship is the hallmark of desserts such as vanilla pannacotta with rhubarb compote, or a 'trough' of raspberry crème brûlée accompanied by raspberries in crème anglaise. Dinner comes with most of the bells and whistles you might expect at this level (amuse-bouches, pre-desserts, assorted bread rolls), although the cooking is unlikely to set the pulse racing – 'pitch-perfect, but uninspiring' commented one reader. Knowledgeably selected wines from Europe share the bill with equally inviting choices from the New World, and the choice of growers is exemplary across the board. House recommendations start at £19.50 (£6.50 a glass).
Chef/s: Bruce Sangster. **Open:** Sun L 12.30 to 1.30, Tue to Sat D 7 to 8.30. **Closed:** Mon, 25 and 26 Dec, Jan, first 2 weeks Nov. **Meals:** Set D £32.50 (2 courses) to £39.50. Sun L £27.50. **Service:** not inc. **Details:** 28 seats. No music. Children over 12 yrs only.

Kincardine
ALSO RECOMMENDED
▲ The Unicorn Inn
15 Excise Street, Kincardine, FK10 4LN
Tel no: (01259) 739129
www.theunicorn.co.uk
Modern British £5 OFF

'A gem in our community', say regulars who support this revamped seventeenth-century hostelry at the heart of historic Kincardine. It may be an ancient inn, but the adjoining brasserie cuts a contemporary dash: expect clean-lined interiors, tapas sharing plates (£8.50), char-grilled Aberdeen Angus steaks and dishes such as rack of Borders lamb with truffled potatoes, wilted greens and lavender-scented jus (£17.50). Lemon curd cheesecake with gingerbread ice cream is a typical dessert. House wine is £13.95. Brasserie closed Sun D and Mon.

North Queensferry
The Wee Restaurant
A diamond under the Forth Bridge
17 Main Street, North Queensferry, KY11 1JG
Tel no: (01383) 616263
www.theweerestaurant.co.uk
Modern European | £32
Cooking score: 3

With a capacity of just 26 covers, this aptly named neighbourhood restaurant beneath the Forth Bridge has been well supported since it opened in 2006. In a former life, the 100-year-old building was a jail and ironmonger's, but now it is one of Fife's culinary gems. 'A warm welcome and cosy atmosphere' was the lasting impression for one satisfied reporter, who also commented on the 'exceptionally reasonable' prices of Craig Wood's set-price menus. The modern Scottish food looks to France and Italy for inspiration, and flavours are well-defined. A starter of rabbit boudin might be served with black pudding and celeriac rémoulade, whilst pan-fried brill arrives with

linguine, wilted greens and lobster bisque. Finish with hot chocolate fondant and Grand Marnier ice cream. House wine is £16.75.
Chef/s: Craig Wood. **Open:** all week L 12 to 2, D 6 to 9. **Closed:** 25 and 26 Dec, 1 and 2 Jan. **Meals:** Set L £16.75 (2 courses) to £20. Set D £26 (2 courses) to £32. **Service:** not inc. **Details:** 36 seats. Music.

Peat Inn

★ TOP 50 ★

The Peat Inn

Oozing comfort and class
Peat Inn, KY15 5LH
Tel no: (01334) 840206
www.thepeatinn.co.uk
Modern European | £55
Cooking score: 7

From the well-drilled front-of-house team and a kitchen that can send out an immaculate six-course tasting menu, calmly adapting three of the courses for a guest with a shellfish allergy, to the young waitress who 'talked us effortlessly through 25 prime Scottish cheeses', the Peat Inn oozes comfort and class. It's six years since Geoffrey and Katherine Smeddle took over this much-loved restaurant-with-rooms in east Fife and they are operating at the top of their game. The smart three-winged dining room pays more than lip service to seasonality, with a spring menu that on inspection offered beetroot cured salmon with langoustine and horseradish, and lemon sole with lobster, fennel confit and young leeks. A plate of pork managed to pack in cheek, fillet, trotter and belly, was tender enough to eat with a spoon, and still found space for crackling and wild garlic sauce. The cheese trolley covered the breadth of the country, from neighbouring Anstruther's unpasteurised Anster cheese to creamy Hebridean Blue, while a plate of desserts delivered pistachio cream, blood orange sorbet, coffee mousse and a show-stopping salted Amadei chocolate pavé. A well-constructed list of classic wines with a bias

towards France starts at £29 with a Domaine de Ricaud Entre-Deux-Mers and a broad choice of half-bottles.
Chef/s: Geoffrey Smeddle. **Open:** Tue to Sat L 12.30 to 1.30, D 7 to 9. **Closed:** Sun, Mon, Christmas, 2 weeks Jan, 1 week Nov. **Meals:** alc (main courses £23 to £26). Set L £19. Set D £40. **Service:** not inc. **Details:** 40 seats. Separate bar. No music. Wheelchair access. Car parking.

St Andrews

The Seafood Restaurant

Sustainable seafood in a spectacular setting
The Scores, Bruce Embankment, St Andrews, KY16 9AB
Tel no: (01334) 479475
www.theseafoodrestaurant.com
Seafood | £45
Cooking score: 3

In a cube-like glass box right on the shoreline, The Seafood Restaurant serves sustainable fish with a formal flourish. High-backed chairs, clothed tables and proudly announced amuse-bouches set a special-occasion tone that's softened by the activity in a completely open kitchen. Plump west coast oysters and a vast seafood platter aside, cooking takes a complex, creative tack. Scallops are paired with five-spiced belly pork, sour carrot purée and pickled fennel, a fat tranche of halibut is served alongside celeriac dauphinoise, meaty oyster mushrooms and artichoke purée, and from St Andrews Bay lobsters to Pittenweem crab, quality is consistently high. To finish, rich chocolate délice might be balanced by marinated cherries and honeycomb. Wines start at £22.
Chef/s: Colin Fleming. **Open:** all week L 12 to 2.30 (12.30 to 3 Sun), D 6 to 10. **Closed:** 25 and 26 Dec, 1 Jan. **Meals:** Set L £22 (2 courses) to £26. Set D £38 (2 courses) to £45. Sun L £12.95. **Service:** not inc. **Details:** 60 seats. 24 seats outside. No music. Wheelchair access. Car parking.

ALSO RECOMMENDED

▲ The Doll's House

3 Church Square, St Andrews, KY16 9NN
Tel no: (01334) 477422
www.dollshouse-restaurant.co.uk
Modern European

A family-friendly attitude is one of the virtues of this cheerful, casual Old Town eatery. It's a popular place, there's lots of animated chatter and tables are constantly in demand – not surprising when the kitchen delivers such value for money (note the two-course set lunch for £6.95). Elsewhere, there's warm salad of smoked brisket with butter beans and pancetta (£6.25) and Carnoustie pork fillet with braised prunes and brandy sauce (£14.95). Wines from £14.95. Open all week.

▲ The Vine Leaf

131 South Street, St Andrews, KY16 9UN
Tel no: (01334) 477497
www.vineleafstandrews.co.uk
Modern British

The Hamiltons opened their restaurant in the centre of St Andrews in 1986 and their fixed-price, dinner-only format (£26.50/£29.95 for two/three courses) has worked as smoothly as a well-oiled machine ever since. The menu is as arresting as the colourful 'artsy' décor with generous dishes such as crab baked in the shell with mustard and Cheddar, crispy pollack in pakora batter with pineapple pickle and cucumber salad, and pecan and maple tart. Wines from £16.75. Open Tue to Sat D only.

Symbols

🛏 Accommodation is available

🍷 Three courses for less than £30

V Separate vegetarian menu

£5off £5-off voucher scheme

🍾 Notable wine list

▌St Monans

Craig Millar @ 16 West End

Special seafood and spectacular harbour views
16 West End, St Monans, KY10 2BX
Tel no: (01333) 730327
www.16westend.com
Seafood | £40
Cooking score: 5
£5off

Fill your lungs on the windswept Fife coast before seeking refuge in the modernised fisherman's cottage that is Craig Millar's gorgeously sited restaurant. Seafood is the principal suit, though not to the exclusion of all else, and the friendly but efficient approach complements those spectacular harbour views to a T. A reporter awards her 'all-time favourite starter ever' citation to Millar's Thai mussel broth with its warming palette of coconut, spring onion and chilli – and the main-course halibut, presented 'simply but exquisitely', wasn't far behind. More involved presentations might see stone bass partnered with chorizo, shiitakes and stewed borlottis, while the often overlooked coley appears with Puy lentils and cauliflower purée in a curry dressing. Meat lovers should enjoy roast pork loin, traditionally attended by buttered cabbage, creamed potato, spiced apple purée and sage jus. Desserts bring on some contemporary classics in the way of chocolate ganache with salted caramel ice cream, or lemon polenta cake with lemon curd and Earl Grey sorbet. A commendably imaginative wine list majors on whites, finding some variation beyond the usual Chardonnay-Sauvignon axis, and is particularly good in the southern hemisphere. House selections from £20 (£5 a glass).
Chef/s: Craig Millar. **Open:** Wed to Sun L 12.30 to 2, D 6.30 to 9. **Closed:** Mon, Tue, 25 and 26 Dec, 1 Jan, 2 weeks Jan. **Meals:** Set L £22 (2 courses) to £26. Set D £35 (2 courses) to £40. Sun L £26. **Service:** not inc. **Details:** 35 seats. 20 seats outside. Separate bar. No music. Wheelchair access. Car parking. Children over 12 yrs only at D.

Auchterarder

Andrew Fairlie at Gleneagles

Awe-inspiring, luxurious French cuisine
Auchterarder, PH3 1NF
Tel no: (01764) 694267
www.andrewfairlie.co.uk
Modern French | £85
Cooking score: 7

Everyone has heard of Gleneagles – Scotland's most famous tourist icon, a French-style château resplendent in 850 acres of landscaped grounds, including a world-class golf resort. Deep in the corporate heart of this gilt-edged pageant is Andrew Fairlie's restaurant – a slightly unnerving, windowless room hidden behind swathes of ecru curtain, with pitch-black walls, dim lights and a portrait of the man himself in his whites. It's a subdued sanctum, dedicated to wealthy indulgence and the serious business of proper 'fine dining' – so brace yourself for some truly frightening prices. In return, you will be treated to the finest ingredients that Scotland and Rungis Market in Paris can muster, as Fairlie contrives a procession of refined contemporary dishes with awe-inspiring attention to detail in every department. A resounding French accent is applied to everything from the signature home-smoked lobster (cured over old whisky barrels and dressed with warm lime and herb butter) to masterful desserts such as hot almond praline 'coulant' with black-treacle ice cream or pear and almond tart with poached pear and quince sorbet. In between, luxuries are strewn liberally over the plate as themes are deconstructed, reinvented and turned on their head: ballotine of duck foie gras nestling beside apple and buckthorn purée and mulled apple; roast fillet of sea bass with smoked eel, parsley quinoa and red wine jus, or poached and roast quail with artichoke and foie gras velouté, for example. But there's also unabashed wholesomeness in the form of an assiette of Gascony pork moistened with jus rôti, slow-cooked beef cheeks with creamed parsnip, or loin of Highland roe deer in familiar company with dauphinois potatoes and confit pear – not forgetting the prospect of wallowing in the ripe pleasures of some glorious artisan cheeses. The international wine list takes no prisoners, and you'll need more than pocket money to appreciate its range; a couple of sub-£30 bottles are barely visible as prices zoom skywards.
Chef/s: Andrew Fairlie. Open: Mon to Sat D only 6.30 to 10. Closed: Sun, 25 and 26 Dec, 3 weeks Jan. Meals: Set D £85 (3 courses) to £125 (6 courses). Service: not inc. Details: 50 seats. Wheelchair access. Music. Car parking. Children over 12 yrs only.

Blairgowrie

Kinloch House Hotel

Prime ingredients treated with care and flair
Dunkeld Road, Blairgowrie, PH10 6SG
Tel no: (01250) 884237
www.kinlochhouse.com
Modern British | £53
Cooking score: 5

A stuffed bear greets visitors to this dignified Victorian mansion, and the 'hunting lodge' theme continues with a full quota of stags' heads and trophies in the hotel's panelled rooms. Kinloch also flaunts its baronial pedigree with a portrait gallery, stunning antique furniture, glittering crystal chandeliers and panoramic views of the Perthshire hills. In the kitchen, chef Steve MacCallum 'knows exactly what he wants to achieve', according to a reader who rates the restaurant as 'one of the top places on Tayside'. There's nothing revolutionary about the food, but native ingredients are treated with respect, great assurance and more than a modicum of flair – especially when it comes to seasonal game: sweet roe deer has been 'beautifully cooked', while breast of mallard might appear in a wintry collation with wild mushrooms, chestnuts, creamed pearl barley, prune and apple sauce. Fish also receives appropriate treatment, from Arbroath lobster with roast fennel, chicory and citrus dressing to fillet of

Loch Duart salmon with a fishcake, sea spinach, asparagus and buttery lemon sauce. To finish, readers have applauded hot chocolate fondant with milk ice cream, but you might also fancy iced mango parfait with a lime muffin and honeycomb. The serious Francophile wine list includes bottles from Sir David Murray's estates, a big Burgundian contingent and also some intriguing stuff from top Chilean producer Viña Ventisquero. Prices start at £26.50 (£6.50 a glass).
Chef/s: Steve MacCallum. **Open:** all week L 12.30 to 1.45, D 7 to 8.30. **Closed:** 13 to 29 Dec. **Meals:** Set L £19.50 (2 courses) to £25.50. Set D £53. Sun L £30. **Service:** not inc. **Details:** 34 seats. Separate bar. No music. Wheelchair access. Car parking. Children over 7 yrs only at D.

▌Inverkeilor

Gordon's
Cooking with vitality and dazzle
Main Street, Inverkeilor, DD11 5RN
Tel no: (01241) 830364
www.gordonsrestaurant.co.uk
Modern British | £48
Cooking score: 5

🍴

'A class act at a fair price' just about sums up the appeal of this family-run restaurant-with-rooms in a sympathetically restored Victorian residence near Lunan Bay. This is a close-knit enterprise that sings of tidy, personable hospitality, although some readers reckon the rather 'mausoleum-like' interior could do with freshening up. Maria Watson is a warm, cheery and welcoming presence out front, while Gordon and his son Garry hold sway in the kitchen. Their menus may be short, but there is plenty of vitality and dazzle about the cooking, from the regularly applauded twice-baked Tobermory Cheddar soufflé to Drambuie-laced hot chocolate pudding with honeycomb ice cream and a cherry and basil compote. Recent meals have delivered some highly impressive dishes with pitch-perfect flavours and bags of confidence: quail with black pudding and lentils; 24-hour, slow-cooked featherblade of Forfar beef with seared

fillet, vanilla, parsnip and red onion confit; meltingly tender Perthshire roe deer with ox cheek and butternut squash; and a plate of pan-fried hake with langoustine cannelloni, carrot tagliatelle and sauce vierge. Top desserts have included chocolate pudding, and a delectable iced orange parfait with orange syrup and Amaretto dust. The wine list is well chosen and informative, with prices from £17.50.
Chef/s: Gordon and Garry Watson. **Open:** Wed to Fri and Sun L 12.30 to 1.45, Tue to Sun D 7 to 9. **Closed:** Mon, Jan. **Meals:** Set L £28. Set D £48 (4 courses). **Service:** not inc. **Details:** 24 seats. No music. Wheelchair access. Car parking. Children over 9 yrs only at D.

▌Killiecrankie

Killiecrankie House
Personally run Victorian retreat
Killiecrankie, PH16 5LG
Tel no: (01796) 473220
www.killiecrankiehotel.co.uk
Modern British | £42
Cooking score: 3

🍴 **V**

'Proof that country house cooking is alive and well' concluded one happy visitor after dining at this personally run Victorian retreat in sylvan grounds overlooking the Pass of Killiecrankie. Chef Mark Easton has been manning the stoves since 1996 and has built up strong Scottish supply lines over the years. The results speak for themselves – from seared king scallops with chorizo risotto or Highland venison fillet with turnip fondant, red cabbage and sloe gin jus, to a 'thoroughly enjoyable' 80s throwback in the shape of chicken breast stuffed with a lemon and thyme mousse. Desserts such as richly sweet honey and walnut tart are followed by help-yourself British cheeses arrayed on the sideboard. Service is tickety-boo, although the waiters 'must despair at their joke tartan trousers'. House wine is £18.50.

Chef/s: Mark Easton. **Open:** all week D only 6.30 to 8.30. **Closed:** 3 Jan to mid Mar. **Meals:** Set D £42 (4 courses). Bar menu also available. **Service:** not inc. **Details:** 34 seats. Separate bar. No music. Wheelchair access. Car parking.

Muthill
Barley Bree
Congenial venue with French connections
6 Willoughby Street, Muthill, PH5 2AB
Tel no: (01764) 681451
www.barleybree.com
Anglo-French | £32
Cooking score: 3

Take one seventeenth-century coaching inn with an emphatically Scottish name, add an enthusiastic French couple with bags of personality and you have Barley Bree – a congenial restaurant-with-rooms in a Tayside conservation village. The cooking reflects Fabrice Bouteloup's roots, although he leavens his dishes with some Caledonian flavours and seasonal ingredients. Seared red mullet with gremolata and beetroot fondant lines up alongside wild garlic and pea soup, while Aberdeen Angus ribeye comes to the table with lyonnaise potatoes, wild mushroom fricassee and black peppercorn sauce. Elsewhere, wild sea bass fillet is paired with Vitelotte potato and aubergine caviar, and slow-cooked belly pork gets an exotic makeover with sweet potato, pak choi and soy dressing. To finish, perhaps consider pot au chocolat coulant (chocolate fondant) with lychees and kiwi sorbet. Wines start at £15.95.
Chef/s: Fabrice Bouteloup. **Open:** Wed to Sat L 12 to 2, D 6.45 to 9. Sun 12 to 7.30. **Closed:** Mon, Tue, 25 to 27 Dec, 1 week Feb, 2 weeks Oct. **Meals:** alc (main courses £17 to £21). **Service:** not inc. **Details:** 35 seats. No music. Car parking.

Perth
Deans @ Let's Eat
Smart restaurant with eclectic flavours
77-79 Kinnoull Street, Perth, PH1 5EZ
Tel no: (01738) 643377
www.letseatperth.co.uk
Modern British | £29
Cooking score: 3

Willie and Margo Deans are firm favourites with Perth's smart set, and they continue to play to full houses. Their restaurant may be classically attired in thoroughly traditional garb, but Margo's accommodating presence out front helps to dispel any feelings of stuffy sobriety. Meanwhile, Willie cooks with flair and confidence, piling on the eclectic flavours but keeping a sure hand on things – witness a main course of John Dory fillets on couscous with lemon thyme, corn kernels, samphire and wild mushrooms. To start, the orient beckons with a salad of slow-cooked, hoisin-glazed belly pork, pak choi, chilli and miso dressing, while dessert might promise a comforting 'jam jar' of vanilla and star anise rice pudding with prunes and chocolate ice. The wine list opens with a clutch of recommendations from £16 (£4 a glass).
Chef/s: Willie Deans. **Open:** Tue to Sat L 12 to 2.15, D 6 to 9.15. **Closed:** Sun, Mon, first 2 weeks Jan. **Meals:** alc (main courses £14 to £21). Set L £12.50 (2 courses) to £16.95. Set D £15.50 (2 courses) to £20.50. **Service:** not inc. **Details:** 70 seats. Wheelchair access. Music.

The North Port
Confident performer in an arty location
8 North Port, Perth, PH1 5LU
Tel no: (01738) 580867
www.thenorthport.co.uk
Modern British | £25
Cooking score: 2

Pitched close to Perth's Concert Hall and the nearby Museum & Art Gallery, this confident culinary performer occupies rather cramped, wood-panelled quarters in an eighteenth-century town house. Despite the historical surrounds, the kitchen works to a modern remit, serving steamed mussels in a Thai curry broth and matching Cajun-spiced sea bream fillets with a green bean, tomato and olive salad. Away from the sea, expect anything from veggie haggis with neeps 'n' tatties to a trio of game birds, or braised pork cheeks with black pudding and caramelised apples. Chocolate and orange pot or big wedges of strawberry cheesecake bring up the rear. Wines from £14.95.

Chef/s: Kevin Joubert. **Open:** Fri and Sat L 12 to 2.30, Tue to Sat D 6 to 9.30. **Closed:** Sun, Mon, 25 and 26 Dec, first 2 weeks Jan, second week Jul. **Meals:** alc (main courses £10 to £18). Set L £9.95 (2 courses). Pre-theatre D £13.95. **Service:** not inc. **Details:** 55 seats. Music.

63 Tay Street
Local food that's big on flavour
63 Tay Street, Perth, PH2 8NN
Tel no: (01738) 441451
www.63taystreet.com
Modern British | £37
Cooking score: 3

Positioned between the Queens Bridge and the rail bridge on the west shore of the Tay, Graeme Pallister's city restaurant is a light-filled place done in neutral hues. 'Local, honest, simple' are the watchwords printed at the top of the various menus; they denote a style of modern Scottish cooking that's big on flavour and doesn't look too far afield to source most of its materials. Marinated Scotch beef tartare with celeriac rémoulade and pickled beetroot could be the opener for mains that see plaice fillets parsley-crumbed and partnered with a brandade fritter, or roast quail given a texturally satisfying counterpoint of crisp polenta, with bass notes of black pudding and confit garlic. Sticky toffee pudding comes with ice cream and butterscotch sauce. A thoroughly conscientious effort has been made with wines, introducing some pedigree

Spanish, Italian and even German bottles alongside the French classics, and with lots of half-bottles, too. Prices open at £19.

Chef/s: Graeme Pallister. **Open:** Tue to Sat L 12 to 2, D 6.30 to 9. **Closed:** Sun, Mon, 26 to 29 Dec, 1 to 8 Jan, 3 to 7 July. **Meals:** alc (main courses £19 to £20). Set L £19.50 (2 courses) to £25. Set D £29 (2 courses) to £37. **Service:** not inc. **Details:** 32 seats. Music.

▮ Stanley
The Apron Stage
Small is beautiful
5 King Street, Stanley, PH1 4ND
Tel no: (01738) 828888
www.apronstagerestaurant.co.uk
Modern British | £28
Cooking score: 3

'This tiny restaurant has never failed to delight us', enthused one regular. 'It's a favourite for special occasions', added another, impressed by affable service and consistent output from the kitchen. The weekly changing menu, while short on choice (one meat and one fish at main course), is always 'highly imaginative and creative', and there's no stinting on generosity. Starters of potted duck with spiced peas and toasted brioche or smoked trout and avocado soup set the tone, before bourride of halibut, monkfish, king scallop and mussels, or roast rack of lamb teamed with twice-cooked shoulder. Desserts are palate-pleasing standards like chocolate fondant with coffee bean sauce and the short, easy-going wine list is fairly priced, with bottles starting at £15.

Chef/s: Shona Drysdale and Tony Heath. **Open:** Fri L 12 to 2, Wed to Sat D 6.30 to 9.30. **Closed:** Mon, Tue, 1 week May, 1 week Sept. **Meals:** alc (main courses £14 to £19). Set L £13.75 (2 courses) to £16.75. **Service:** not inc. **Details:** 18 seats. Wheelchair access. Music. No children.

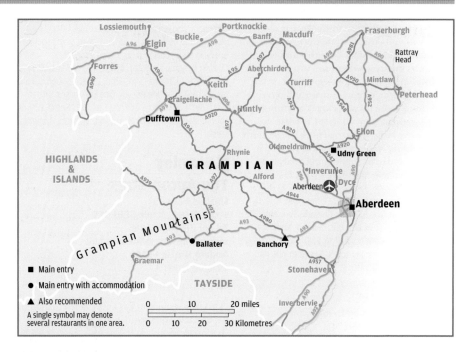

Aberdeen

Silver Darling

Fish-loving harbourside evergreen
Pocra Quay, North Pier, Aberdeen, AB11 5DQ
Tel no: (01224) 576229
www.thesilverdarling.co.uk
Seafood | £44
Cooking score: 4

Deep in the docks and with excellent harbour views, this first-floor restaurant has been pulling in punters for 26 years. It's moved with the times, though, and feels crisply modern inside, with pale wood floors, linen-clad tables and lots of glass to make the most of those watery views. The theme is fish and seafood, although appetisers of gazpacho, confit duck and ceviche showed confidence across the board. However, a starter of lightly pickled mackerel with crunchy diced vegetables and horseradish cream, although generous, proved surprisingly subtle for one reporter. Ditto a shyly flavoured main of steamed rock turbot with cockles, seafood risotto and grilled

spring onions. This is food for delicate palates – although a dessert of summer berry crumble with yoghurt and honey sorbet ('a perfect balance of sweet and tart') simply sang with flavour. The short wine list is mostly French and starts at £19.50.
Chef/s: Didier Dejean. **Open:** Sun to Fri L 12 to 1.45 (2.30 Sun), Mon to Sat D 6.30 to 9.30. **Closed:** 2 weeks Christmas and New Year. **Meals:** alc (main courses £17 to £29). Set L £19.50 (2 courses) to £23.50. **Service:** 10%. **Details:** 50 seats. Music. No children after 8.

Please send us your feedback

To register your opinion about any restaurant listed in the Guide, or a new restaurant that you wish to bring to our attention, please visit the web address at the bottom of the page. Your feedback informs the content of the book and will be used to compile next year's reviews.

▌Ballater

Darroch Learg

Bastion of Scottish hospitality
56 Braemar Road, Ballater, AB35 5UX
Tel no: (013397) 55443
www.darrochlearg.co.uk
Modern British | £45
Cooking score: 5

The Gaelic name translates as 'the oak wood on a sunny hillside' – a romantic prospect that has served the Franks family well over the last 50 years or so. Since becoming custodians of Darroch Learg in 1961, they have turned this Victorian residence into a bastion of personal hospitality on fashionable Deeside. Long-serving sous-chef John Jeremiah has been promoted to main man in the kitchen, but the food is largely unchanged – a pedigree country house repertoire founded on carefully sourced ingredients from the region's farms and waters. Following a little 'taster', dinner might open with a wholesome north-east fishcake alongside crushed peas and a buttery caper and shallot sauce, or slow-cooked belly pork with confit garlic and a carrot and coriander purée. After that, Deeside venison could put in an appearance with goats' cheese gnocchi, or you might prefer a slab of prime Scotch beef fillet embellished with wild mushroom tortellini, a blob of beetroot and horseradish relish and a deep, boozy oxtail sauce. Proceedings draw to a close with desserts from the classic school of patisserie – think lemon tart or apple and cinnamon pithiviers with crème anglaise. The wine list is also steeped in the old ways, parading fine vintage Burgundies, Bordeaux and Rhônes as well as flirting with the New World. Prices start at £23 (£7 a glass).
Chef/s: John Jeremiah. **Open:** Sun L 12 to 2, all week D 7 to 9. **Closed:** 1 week Christmas, last 3 weeks Jan. **Meals:** Set D £45. Sun L £24. **Service:** not inc. **Details:** 48 seats. No music. Wheelchair access. Car parking.

The Green Inn

Warmly welcoming restaurant-with-rooms
9 Victoria Road, Ballater, AB35 5QQ
Tel no: (013397) 55701
www.green-inn.com
Modern European | £43
Cooking score: 4

When a meal kicks off with a 'cappuccino' of garden peas that tastes like the very essence of pea, with a tender sliver of melt-in-the-mouth quail filling the role usually played by bacon (imagine a posh take on pea and ham soup), you know you're in for a treat. In truth, by the time you've made it to the appetiser you've already got a fair idea that chef Chris O'Halloran and family mean business. The Green Inn is a warmly welcoming, homely restaurant-with-rooms with just a handful of tables in the comfortable conservatory dining room. Seasonal produce is close to the kitchen's heart; diners are wowed by everything from red mullet with broad beans, spring onion and radish salad, soy and orange sauce, to fall-apart tender, slow-braised Aberdeen Angus beef with spinach, smoked potato purée, baby onions, wild mushrooms, foie gras and red wine jus. Wines from a balanced international list open at £19.95.
Chef/s: Chris O'Halloran. **Open:** Wed to Sat D only 7 to 9. **Closed:** Sun, Mon, Tue, Nov, Dec. **Meals:** Set D £42.50. **Service:** not inc. **Details:** 20 seats. Separate bar. Music.

▌Banchory

ALSO RECOMMENDED
▲ Cow Shed Restaurant

Raemoir Road, Banchory, AB31 5QB
Tel no: (01330) 820813
www.cowshedrestaurant.co.uk
Modern British

'What a find this is', enthuse visitors to this slick, bright and unfussy country restaurant with views over the Hill of Fayre. Graham Buchan has stamped his mark on the place, drawing praise for his 'superb' bread, a cheese pudding with apple and thyme (£7.50), and belly pork with vegetable fricassee, broccoli purée and prune tapenade (£18.50). A dessert of rhubarb, pineapple, coconut ice cream and crumble has found particular favour. Wines from £18. Closed Sun to Tue. More reports, please.

Dufftown
La Faisanderie
Confident French cooking
2 Balvenie Street, Dufftown, AB55 4AD
Tel no: (01340) 821273
www.lafaisanderie.co.uk
French | £34
Cooking score: 2

Untouched by chain stores, Dufftown can feel like you've stepped back a decade or two. La Faisanderie fits in nicely, having the confidence of a place that's been filling bellies for years. Its menu is reminiscent of rural France, as is the look of the place; assorted antiques add character to an otherwise simple interior. The food is equally straightforward: confit duck leg with a rocket and orange salad to start, followed perhaps by venison in a rich red wine sauce with spätzle noodles. The freshly baked tarte Tatin with crisp, light pastry, is excellent. The French wine list starts at £14.80.
Chef/s: Eric Obry. Open: all week L 12 to 2, D 5.30 to 8.30 (8 Wed). Closed: 16 Dec to 12 Feb. Meals: alc (main courses £19 to £23). Set L £14.20 (2 courses) to £18.50. Set D £34. Service: not inc. Details: 28 seats. Wheelchair access. Music.

Udny Green
Eat on the Green
Likeable village restaurant with sound cooking
Udny Green, AB41 7RS
Tel no: (01651) 842337
www.eatonthegreen.co.uk
Modern European | £38
Cooking score: 2
V

Sound cooking and unhurried vibes are the trump cards at Craig Wilson's likeable village restaurant, housed in Udny Green's old post office. There are some fancy ideas on the menu – from a tian of crab with potato pancakes, avocado and ginger pannacotta to baked sea bass with mussel and chickpea curry – although no-nonsense plates of char-grilled Aberdeen Angus sirloin with chunky chips and béarnaise also get an emphatic thumbs-up. Desserts play it straight, with the likes of crème brûlée or rhubarb crumble and ice cream. A new 'tasting room' is the setting for multi-course extravaganzas served in cocooned, chandelier-lit surroundings. The global wine list offers decent drinking from £17.95.
Chef/s: Craig Wilson. Open: Wed to Fri and Sun L 12 to 2, Wed to Sun D 6.30 to 8.30 (6 to 9 Fri and Sat). Closed: Mon and Tue. Meals: alc (main courses £23 to £26). Set L £21.95 (2 courses) to £24.95. Sat D £52 (4 courses). Sun L £24.95 (2 courses) to £29.95. Tasting menu £95 (10 courses). Service: not inc. Details: 65 seats. Music. Car parking. No children after 10pm.

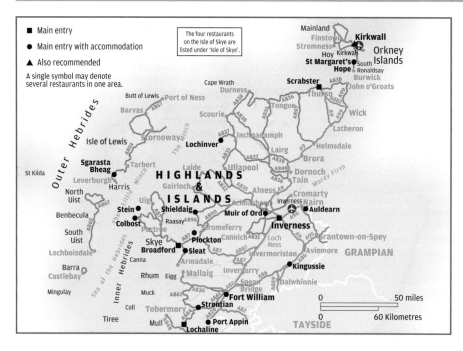

Map legend:
- ■ Main entry
- ● Main entry with accommodation
- ▲ Also recommended

A single symbol may denote several restaurants in one area.

The four restaurants on the Isle of Skye are listed under 'Isle of Skye'.

▌Applecross

READERS RECOMMEND

Applecross Inn
Modern British
Applecross, IV54 8LR
Tel no: (01520) 744262
www.applecross.uk.com
'Of particular delight was the fresh caught haddock and chips, the local shellfish and the amazing steaks.'

❘❘❘ Please send us your feedback

To register your opinion about any restaurant listed in the Guide, or a new restaurant that you wish to bring to our attention, please visit the web address at the bottom of the page. Your feedback informs the content of the book and will be used to compile next year's reviews.

▌Auldearn

Boath House

Country house with own-grown produce
Auldearn, IV12 5TE
Tel no: (01667) 454896
www.boath-house.com
Modern European | £70
Cooking score: 5

A fine porticoed Regency manor set amid manicured grounds in the north east of Scotland, Boath House offers the full country-house deal, including a refreshing dining room done in summery hues of rose and lilac, overlooking the gardens. Charlie Lockley's kitchen is run as a tight ship; much of the produce comes from the hotel's own vegetable plots and orchards, supplemented by a nearby organic dairy farm and superb Highland seafood. A shopping-list approach to the six-course dinner menu descriptions tells you what you'll get, but not how, so that pheasant, apple, sorrel turns out to be a coarse-textured terrine with puréed apple, sorrel leaves and a savoury biscuit. Turbot, lentils, pork belly, fennel offers gently cooked fish with an unadvertised and slightly jarring addition of chorizo, and brittle texture from fennel crisps. Duck, carrot, Savoy, rosemary features breast meat coated in five-spice and poached, alongside potato and carrot purée, crisp-cooked cabbage and rosemary foam, while dessert brings on sublime chocolate fondant with salted caramel ice cream and cocoa nibs. Before dessert, a serving of one of the new generation of Scottish cheeses – Corra Linn, Arran Mist, Bonnet – comes with oatmeal biscuits or crispbreads. The resourceful wine list contains some real gems; glasses from £7.50, bottles from £21.

Chef/s: Charlie Lockley. **Open:** all week L 12.30 to 1.15, D 7 (1 sitting). **Meals:** Set L £24 (2 courses) to £30. Set D £70 (6 courses). **Service:** not inc. **Details:** 26 seats. Separate bar. Wheelchair access. Car parking.

Aviemore

READERS RECOMMEND
Mountain Café
Eclectic
111 Grampian Road, Aviemore, PH22 1RH
Tel no: (01479) 812473
www.mountaincafe-aviemore.co.uk
'The coffee is outstanding, food delicious and good value. The service is great, atmosphere lovely.'

Delny

READERS RECOMMEND
Birch Tree
Modern British
Delny Riding Centre, Delny, IV18 ONP
Tel no: (01349) 853549
www.the-birchtree.com
'A hidden gem! Cannot fault anything with this restaurant. Friendly welcome, lovely décor and good menu with a good choice.'

Fort William

Crannog
Fun fish restaurant on the pier
Town Pier, Fort William, PH33 6DB
Tel no: (01397) 705589
www.crannog.net
Seafood | £31
Cooking score: 1

£5 OFF

Crannog has 'a dream location' right on the shore. It's a fun red-and-white wooden building that doubles as a fish restaurant and a pier; the owner's boat runs cruises round the loch. The set lunch has produced mussels with wine and cream followed by grilled salmon. Recommended, too, is Cullen skink, skate wing with capers and an orange and fennel side salad, and a dessert of rich strawberry and vanilla custard tart with 'excellent thin, crisp pastry'. Wines from £16.20.
Chef/s: Stewart MacLachlan. **Open:** all week L 12 to 2.30, D 6 to 9.30. **Closed:** 25 and 26 Dec, 1 Jan. **Meals:** alc (main courses £15 to £20). Set L £11.95 (2 courses). **Service:** not inc. **Details:** 55 seats. Separate bar. Wheelchair access. Music. No children after 8pm.

Inverlochy Castle
Baronial pile with high-end contemporary food
Torlundy, Fort William, PH33 6SN
Tel no: (01397) 702177
www.inverlochycastlehotel.co.uk
Modern British | £67
Cooking score: 6

🛏 V

The remnants of Inverlochy's medieval castle pale into insignificance beside the high-Victorian opulence and castellated battlements of its namesake hotel, tucked into the foothills of Ben Nevis. Dolled up to the nines in baronial garb, its portrait-lined rooms resonate with echoes of the past: Queen Victoria recorded that it was one of the loveliest, most romantic places imaginable. It takes the notion of the upper-crust country house party to new levels of pampering –

especially in the full-dress restaurant (jacket and tie please, gentlemen). However, crystal chandeliers and priceless antiques probably won't prepare you for Philip Carnegie's elaborately worked contemporary food – seared skate with speck-wrapped fennel and chorizo foam, anyone? Despite the occasional hiccup (gritty sorbets, 'poorly balanced' petits fours), he is capable of great things – witness an outstanding dish of crispy Gressingham duck breast with spiced lentils and foie gras ('the best food of my trip'). Scottish ingredients are given a bold spin – Loch Linnhe prawns with smoked eel tortellini, beetroot carpaccio and horseradish foam, perhaps, or slow-cooked beef shoulder with a Parmesan crust, wild mushrooms and quail's egg. Extravagant desserts include sweet potato cake with candied walnuts and rosemary sorbet. The wine list is a country house heavyweight, dripping with pedigree vintages; prices from £28.

Chef/s: Philip Carnegie. **Open:** all week L 12 to 1.45, D 6 to 10. **Meals:** Set L £28 (2 courses) to £38. Set D £67 (4 courses). **Service:** not inc. **Details:** 45 seats. Wheelchair access. Music. Car parking. Children over 8 yrs only.

The Lime Tree
'Wonderful from start to finish'
The Old Manse, Achintore Road, Fort William, PH33 6RQ
Tel no: (01397) 701806
www.limetreefortwilliam.co.uk
Modern British | £30
Cooking score: 4

'We have never had a bad experience in all of the 20 times we've visited' reports one fan of this smart but informal restaurant at the foot of Ben Nevis. The Lime Tree is a handsome former manse with an interior that is all soft lighting and bare wood furniture, and it delivers a 'wonderful experience from start to finish', with 'memorable' and 'inspiring' food. Some dishes reference Scottish traditions – as in a starter of haggis, neeps and tatties or a dessert of rhubarb and ginger cranachan.

Others take a broader view (sweet potato, cumin and coconut soup, for instance), but the emphasis is on modern British ideas – maybe slow-roasted belly pork with Stornoway black pudding, braised red cabbage and apple and cider jus, or pan-fried fillet of sea bass with butternut squash, braised fennel and rocket pesto. A substantial wine list, divided by style, favours Europe. Bottles start at £20.

Chef/s: John Wilson. **Open:** all week D only 6 to 9. **Closed:** 24 to 26 Dec. **Meals:** Set D £27.95 (2 courses) to £29.95. **Service:** not inc. **Details:** 32 seats. Wheelchair access. Music. Car parking.

Inverness
Rocpool
Eye-catching riverside restaurant
1 Ness Walk, Inverness, IV3 5NE
Tel no: (01463) 717274
www.rocpoolrestaurant.com
Modern European | £31
Cooking score: 2

An eye-catching contemporary venue by the river, Rocpool's glass frontage lets the light pour in during the day, and then provides dramatic views of the Ness and the illuminated castle after sunset. It's a thoroughly modern setting for thoroughly modern brasserie food, with combinations such as king scallops and chorizo with spring onion crème fraîche, Indian-influenced chicken with cauliflower fritters, spinach and lentil dhal and raita, or halibut with Arbroath smokie risotto, spinach and a poached egg. Finish with passion-fruit pavlova or affogato. Thirteen choices by the glass from £4.95 head up a well-constructed wine list, with bottles from £16.50.

Chef/s: George Fleet. **Open:** Mon to Sat L 12 to 2.30, D 5.45 to 10. **Closed:** Sun, 25 and 26 Dec, 1 to 3 Jan. **Meals:** alc (main courses £12 to £23). Set L £13.95 (2 courses). Set D £15.95 (2 courses). **Service:** not inc. **Details:** 55 seats. Wheelchair access. Music.

Isle of Harris

Scarista House

Gorgeous getaway showcasing island bounty
Scarista, Isle of Harris, HS3 3HX
Tel no: (01859) 550238
www.scaristahouse.com
Modern British | £43
Cooking score: 2

☐ V

A miraculously remote getaway with glorious
sunsets, sandy beaches and views of the rolling
Atlantic, this converted Georgian manse is a
haven for all things local, organic and home-
grown. Long-serving custodians Tim and
Patricia Martin make telling use of the island's
bounty for all-inclusive dinner menus with
strong connections to the land and sea. When
the boat comes in they respond by offering
John Dory with saffron risotto, lovage-
crusted cod with rosemary potatoes or scallops
with sauce vierge and artichoke purée, but you
can also expect plates of Argyll smoked ham
with quail's egg, Aberdeen Angus beef fillet
and desserts such as marmalade tart with plum
compote. House wine is £17.
Chef/s: Tim and Patricia Martin. **Open:** all week D
only 8 (1 sitting). **Meals:** Set D £43 to £49.50 (4
courses). **Service:** not inc. **Details:** 25 seats. No
music. Car parking.

Isle of Skye

Creelers of Skye

Delightful French-style seafood
Broadford, Isle of Skye, IV49 9AQ
Tel no: (01471) 822281
www.skye-seafood-restaurant.co.uk
French | £28
Cooking score: 2

£5 OFF £30

A foursome reeling through a deluge on Skye
found themselves U-turning outside Creelers,
in desperate search of a bowl of soup. They
looked at the menu and, some time after,
emerged full of three courses of delight. David
and Ann Wilson's Broadford Bay kitchen does
rustical French things to local seafood, to

striking effect. Expect big bowls of mussels
landaise with aïoli, salmon poached in
Chardonnay with watercress and tarragon
crème fraîche sauce, whole pan-roasted sea
bass, and a cornucopia of a bouillabaisse for
two, redolent with saffron. There are meats
and pasta dishes too, and clootie dumpling
with cranachan. House Muscadet is £14.50.
Chef/s: David Wilson. **Open:** Mon to Sat L 12 to 5, D
5 to 9.30. **Closed:** Sun, 1 Nov to 1 Mar. **Meals:** alc
(main courses £12 to £18). Set L £14 (2 courses) to
£18. Set D £20 (2 courses) to £28. **Service:** not inc.
Details: 28 seats. Wheelchair access. Music. Car
parking. No children after 7.

Kinloch Lodge

Remote retreat with finely crafted food
Sleat, Isle of Skye, IV43 8QY
Tel no: (01471) 833214
www.kinloch-lodge.co.uk
Modern British | £60
Cooking score: 5

☐ V

The seat of the Macdonald clan for
generations, this enviably remote,
seventeenth-century hunting lodge combines
elemental Highland vistas with ancestry,
portraits and blazing fires. Kinloch is still a
family affair – albeit one with a lordly
pedigree – and Claire Macdonald's culinary
nous is apparent behind the scenes: from the
'amazing' flavoured butters and little 'soupçon'
to start, through to the finely crafted petits
fours. Recent high points have included a
faultless pairing of sea bream and monkfish
wrapped in Parma ham with a 'phenomenal'
lime and coconut sauce, and a dish of Skye
lamb fillet accompanied by caramelised apples
and pears, shallots and perfect dauphinois
potato. Chef Marcello Tully also deals in
Mallaig skate wings with slow-roast Moray
belly pork, pea and an oriental sauce, or fillet
of hake with Drumfearn mussels, carrot rösti
and caper pesto. Dessert might be an orange
crème with warm chocolate sauce and apricot
fudge, although the wicked caipirinha sorbet
planted beside a vanilla crème fraîche
pannacotta took one recipient straight back to

a holiday in Rio. Service is polished and unobtrusive from start to finish, and the owners' magisterial wine list brings together the great and the good from gold-standard producers across the planet. Mark-ups are very accommodating (even at the top end), with house selections starting at £24. Also check out the bespoke beer and whisky flights.
Chef/s: Marcello Tully. **Open:** all week L 12 to 2, D 6 to 9. **Meals:** Set L £29.99 (2 courses) to £34.99. Set D £55 (2 courses) to £65. Sun L £29.99. **Service:** not inc. **Details:** 38 seats. Separate bar. Wheelchair access. Music. Car parking.

Loch Bay

No flimflam, just spanking fresh fish
1-2 Macleod Terrace, Stein, Isle of Skye, IV55 8GA
Tel no: (01470) 592235
www.lochbay-seafood-restaurant.co.uk
Seafood | £30
Cooking score: 2

£5 OFF

Loch Bay bills its seafood as 'simply sublime'. A reporter declares it 'uncompromised', meaning: spanking fresh fish cooked without flimflam. The exclusively fishy menu delivers superb Skye shellfish such as Loch Bay langoustine and hand-dived scallops, alongside catch-of-the-day specials from the blackboard, perhaps whole young turbot or pan-fried hake. Most mains come ultra-simply dressed, brushed with little more than olive oil and lemon. 'A touch plain' sometimes, but the raw materials and the setting – 'remote and gorgeous' – dazzle regardless. For a patriotically inclined pudding, go for clootie dumpling, steamed for three hours, with cream. Wine from £17.25.
Chef/s: David Wilkinson. **Open:** Tue to Sat L 12 to 2, D 6.15 to 9. **Closed:** Mon, Sun, Nov to week before Easter. **Meals:** alc (main courses £12 to £23). **Service:** not inc. **Details:** 23 seats. 8 seats outside. No music. Car parking. Only children over 8 at dinner

The Three Chimneys

Seductively isolated hotel
Colbost, Isle of Skye, IV55 8ZT
Tel no: (01470) 511258
www.threechimneys.co.uk
Modern British | £60
Cooking score: 6

We reckon it takes about 90 minutes to drive from the Skye Bridge, via lonely roads sparsely speckled with crofters' cottages, against a mountainous backdrop, to the shore of Loch Dunvegan where the Spears' hotel stands in seductive isolation. Uneven door frames and low ceilings, exposed brick and seagrass flooring await within, the loch view peeping through little windows in the dining room. Highland produce pours forth from Michael Smith's menus, which also employ some nods to Scottish tradition in light, modernised guises. A seafood platter for one is hard to resist: seared scallops, dressed mussels, prawns, oysters, potted crab, fish salad and a shot-glass of Skye winkles. Otherwise, seafood might form the centrepiece of a starter such as grilled sea trout with mussel and fennel risotto, garnished with apple sorrel and spiced oil. Big-hearted main courses showcase island Blackface lamb (loin, rib and pressed shoulder) with miniature neeps, haggis and tattie scones, while Lochalsh beef comes with pearl barley in vegetable broth for a winter warmer. The signature finale is a riotously rich marmalade pudding with Drambuie custard, or there may be a witty take on hot toddy, an iced version singing with honey and whisky, with pink grapefruit and aniseed brittle. The wine list features a gin section, which includes some of Scotland's finest; the wines themselves are teeming with interest, from Japanese Koshu to fine Australasians, an Oregon Gewürztraminer and one of the vanishingly rare white wines of Irouléguy in the French Basque country. Bottles start at £22 (£5.50 a glass).
Chef/s: Michael Smith. **Open:** Mon to Sat L 12.15 to 1.45, all week D 6.15 to 9.45. **Closed:** 1 to 24 Jan. **Meals:** Set L £28.50 (2 courses) to £37. Set D £60.

Tasting menu £90. **Service:** not inc. **Details:** 44 seats. No music. Wheelchair access. Car parking. Children over 5 yrs only at L, over 8 yrs only at D.

Lochaline

NEW ENTRY
The Whitehouse Restaurant
Local fare with harbour views
Lochaline, PA80 5XT
Tel no: (01967) 421777
www.thewhitehouserestaurant.co.uk
Seafood | £30
Cooking score: 3

£5
OFF

Not far from the ferry at Lochaline, The Whitehouse makes the most of coastal ingredients but stops short of being a seafood restaurant, preferring to focus on the full gamut of ingredients available locally. A cosy, rustic-chic space with sturdy pine furniture, lavender-painted walls, an abundance of fresh flowers and lots of evening candlelight, it feels like a home-from-home, but offers cooking with a sense of occasion. The wide open kitchen allows some tables a view of the action; here scallops are roasted and served in a velvety cauliflower velouté; just-caught plaice is teamed with surf clams, butter, tender asparagus, leeks and puréed potato; and luxuriantly creamy rice pudding is coupled with tart, fall-apart rhubarb. An international selection of wines kicks off at £15.95.
Chef/s: Mike Burgoyne. **Open:** Tue to Sat L 11.30 to 2.30, D 6 to 10. **Closed:** Sun, Mon, Nov to Easter. **Meals:** Set L and D £25.99 (2 courses) to £29.99. **Service:** not inc. **Details:** 24 seats. 10 seats outside. No music. Wheelchair access.

Also Recommended
Also recommended entries are not scored but we think they are worth a visit.

Lochinver
Albannach
Solace, sustenance and fine hospitality
Baddidarroch, Lochinver, IV27 4LP
Tel no: (01571) 844407
www.thealbannach.co.uk
Modern British | £61
Cooking score: 6

Remoteness is a virtue at Albannach – a tall white house standing proud among the wild and bracing moors above Lochinver harbour. Since 1990, this windswept retreat has been home to Colin Craig and Lesley Crosfield – dedicated providers of solace, sustenance and fine hospitality to hardy outdoor types and those who simply want to indulge in some serene R&R. The couple's dedication to local sourcing and home-production is admirable, and they now close on Mondays so that they can attend to their poly-tunnel and other foodie matters. They also make a formidable double act in the kitchen, delivering a procession of skilfully crafted dishes bursting with limpid natural flavours. On a September evening, dinner might begin with a plate of pan-fried duck breast with confit leg, some fresh chard from a local croft, orange and Madeira sauce, before a wee beetroot soufflé. After that, proceedings move at a leisurely pace towards a centrepiece of, say, seared hand-dived scallops and monkfish with braised fennel, leeks, sorrel and beurre blanc; then it's on to cheeses (organic Dunlop and Gorgonzola, perhaps), before sweetness arrives in the shape of caramelised apple tart with apple crisp and an apple and Calvados 'gelato'. Finally, things wind down with coffee and petits fours as guests drift from the cocooned dining room. Colin Craig's highly personal, cleverly chosen wine list avoids florid notes and simply lets the bottles do the talking. France is the main focus, but there are also pages of glorious stuff from elsewhere. Prices start at £17, and you can also drink seriously by the glass.

Chef/s: Colin Craig and Lesley Crosfield. Open: Tue to Sun D only 8 (1 sitting). Closed: Mon to Wed in Nov and Dec, Jan to mid Mar. Meals: Set D £61 (6 courses). Service: not inc. Details: 20 seats. No music. Car parking. Children over 12 yrs only.

Muir of Ord
The Dower House
Inviting Highland hideaway
Highfield, Muir of Ord, IV6 7XN
Tel no: (01463) 870090
www.thedowerhouse.co.uk
Modern British | £42
Cooking score: 2

More of a cottage orné than a hotel, this early-Victorian dower house is still a picture of pampered domesticity and politesse, thanks to dedicated custodians Robyn and Mena Aitchison. Eating at their homely hideaway is akin to a sedate country house dinner party – a touch of full-dress formality here, some unbuttoned bonhomie there. The evening's no-choice menu might run from a salad of scallops and black pudding to coffee with homemade tablet. In between, guests can expect anything from local beef fillet with port and anchovy sauce to grilled 'mint-studded' sea bass with lemon potatoes, plus puds such as chilled baked peaches with Amaretto. House wine is £19.
Chef/s: Robyn Aitchison. Open: all week D only 7.30 (1 sitting). Closed: 25 Dec, 2 weeks Nov. Meals: Set D £38. Service: not inc. Details: 16 seats. 4 seats outside. No music. Wheelchair access. Car parking. Children over 4 yrs only at D.

Symbols
🛏 Accommodation is available
£30 Three courses for less than £30
V Separate vegetarian menu
£5 OFF £5-off voucher scheme
🍷 Notable wine list

Oban
Seafood Temple
Seafood
Dungallan Park, Gallanach Road, Oban, PA34 4LS
Tel no: (01631) 566000
www.obanseafood.com
'A small restaurant with sea views. The lobster is very good, and friendly and attentive staff made for a very agreeable experience.'

Orkney Islands
★ TOP 50 ★
The Creel
Orcadian oasis dedicated to island produce
Front Road, St Margaret's Hope, Orkney Islands, KW17 2SL
Tel no: (01856) 831311
www.thecreel.co.uk
Modern British | £39
Cooking score: 6

There's something irresistibly appealing about Alan and Joyce Craigie's far-flung Orcadian oasis: perhaps it's the magical sunsets and views over the bay; perhaps it's the quirky dining room festooned with artworks and tapestries; perhaps it's simply the mood of congenial hospitality that suffuses every corner of this tribute to tranquillity. Since setting up shop here in 1985, the couple have also established the Creel as a provider of exquisitely fresh island produce and fish from the Orkney boats: hand-dived scallops paired with lemon sole and spiced cauliflower; a chunk of roasted hake with squid and lentil casserole; diver-caught scallops and langoustine sharpened up with rocket and pine-nut pesto – even megrim, torsk and wolf-fish get an outing (the latter presented with spinach and roasted courgettes). Alan Craigie's way with seafood may be effortlessly harmonious, but he is equally adept at extracting maximum value and flavour from locally reared meat – especially seaweed-fed Ronaldsay mutton, which might appear in a salad with ham 'hough' terrine and plum chutney or as a burnished pithiviers ringed by parsnip purée and barley gravy. Cheeses are some of Scotland's finest, while those with a sweet tooth regularly get excited about the pitch-perfect glazed lemon tart with homemade marmalade ice cream. Other details also suggest serious dedication to the cause – home-baked bannocks and soda bread, real ales from Orkney's own brewery, island malts and a carefully constructed wine list with sound drinking from £15.

Chef/s: Alan Craigie. **Open:** Wed to Sun D only 7 to 8. **Closed:** Mon, Tue, mid-Oct to Easter. **Meals:** Set D £32 (2 courses) to £39. **Service:** not inc. **Details:** 24 seats. No music. Wheelchair access. Car parking.

ALSO RECOMMENDED

▲ Dil Se

7 Bridge Street, Kirkwall, Orkney Islands, KW15 1HR
Tel no: (01856) 875242
www.dilserestaurant.co.uk
Indian

Tucked away behind Kirkwall harbour, this glass-fronted restaurant is the most northerly outpost of Indian/Bangladeshi cooking in the UK. Locally reared meats are put to good use in a menu that runs from 'old flames' such as rogan josh and prawn dhansak (£9.95) to tandooris, tikkas (from £11.95) and signature dishes including chicken chilli balti or creamy Kashmiri chasni with bananas and a touch of red wine. To finish, keep it local with an Orkney ice cream. House wine is £11.95. Open all week from 4pm.

¶¶ Please send us your feedback

To register your opinion about any restaurant listed in the Guide, or a new restaurant that you wish to bring to our attention, please visit the web address at the bottom of the page. Your feedback informs the content of the book and will be used to compile next year's reviews.

▌Plockton
Plockton Inn
Proving that simple can be best
Innes Street, Plockton, IV52 8TW
Tel no: (01599) 544222
www.plocktoninn.co.uk
Seafood | £21
Cooking score: 2
£5 OFF 🍴 £30

In a village setting, just 100 metres from the harbour, this long-standing family-run inn has a homely atmosphere. Fresh raw ingredients – there are venison medallions, lamb shank and homemade burgers if you are in the mood for meat – are treated simply. Wonderfully fresh Plockton prawns with hot garlic butter, or a platter of seafood from the inn's own smokery, followed by skate wing with black butter, has proved that simple can be best. There are no-frills salads and basic desserts such as sticky toffee pudding or lemon and ginger crunch pie, and a short, affordable wine list with prices from £14.50.

Chef/s: Mary Gollan. **Open:** all week L 12 to 2.15, D 6 to 9.30. **Closed:** 25 and 26 Dec. **Meals:** alc (main courses £16 to £34). **Service:** not inc. **Details:** 60 seats. 16 seats outside. Separate bar. Wheelchair access. Music. Car parking.

▌Port Appin
Airds Hotel
Former ferry inn full of delights
Port Appin, PA38 4DF
Tel no: (01631) 730236
www.airds-hotel.com
Modern British | £53
Cooking score: 5
🍴 V

This former ferry inn has a great position – by the shore of Loch Linnhe – but the unpretentious exterior scarcely hints at the delights within. The decoration, personal attention and overall comfort, even luxury, come as a surprise to first-time visitors. Everyone praises the view and the fact that the place is 'delightfully, efficiently' run. Much depends on the output of Robert MacPherson's kitchen and his fruitful connections with local and regional producers. Game always gets a good outing in season, perhaps pheasant, truffle and oyster mushroom pithiviers with roasted shallots and chestnut velouté, or roast saddle of Kingairloch roe deer (with braised red cabbage, quince curd, fondant potatoes and juniper jus). For those who fancy fish, Isle of Luing scallops come teamed with a parsley, Parmesan and lemon risotto, or Mallaig cod with a risotto of oyster mushroom and parsley and Loch Morar broth. Highly skilled execution is also the hallmark of desserts such as vanilla bavarois with poached rhubarb and Champagne jelly. Light meals and sandwiches are served at lunchtime. France and other major producing countries share out the spoils on the varietally arranged wine list, which is notable for its helpful notes, ungreedy prices and knowledgeable selections; prices start at £20.

Chef/s: Robert MacPherson. **Open:** all week L 12 to 1.45, D 7.30 to 9.30. **Closed:** 2 days each week Nov to Jan. **Meals:** alc L (main courses £7 to £23). Set D £53 (5 courses). Sun L £21.95. Tasting menu £70 (7 courses). **Service:** not inc. **Details:** 32 seats. No music. Car parking. Children over 8 yrs only at D.

∎ Scrabster
The Captain's Galley
Terrific harbourside eatery with sustainable seafood
The Harbour, Scrabster, KW14 7UJ
Tel no: (01847) 894999
www.captainsgalley.co.uk
Seafood | £47
Cooking score: 3

'It's not a meal – it's a whole evening out', exclaims an ardent fan of Jim and Mary Cowie's terrific neighbourhood eatery in Scrabster's old salmon 'bothy' and icehouse. People come here for sustainable seafood cooked with minimum intervention but bags of culinary acumen – from Orkney razor clams ('spoots'), ling and langoustine to baked loin of hake with borlotti bean and mussel

broth, or smoked pollack (cured overnight) served on leek mash with a poached egg and grain-mustard sauce. Meat and game also get the vote (the venison is 'out of this world') and you can hit the sweet button with 'an appreciation of raspberries' or the Galley's 'infamous' chocolate fondant. Fish-friendly wines start at £15.55. There are plans to create an informal patio/seafood bar outside the kitchen.

Chef/s: Jim Cowie. **Open:** all week L 12 to 2, Tue to Sat D 6.30 to 9. **Closed:** 25, 26 and 31 Dec, 1 Jan. **Meals:** Set D £35 (4 courses) to £47 (5 courses). Tasting menu £57 (7 courses). **Service:** not inc. **Details:** 25 seats. 25 seats outside. Wheelchair access. Music. Car parking.

∎ Shieldaig
Tigh an Eilean Hotel
Enchanting refuge in a fishing village
Shieldaig, IV54 8XN
Tel no: (01520) 755251
www.tighaneilean.co.uk
Modern British | £43
Cooking score: 3

An enchanting refuge in a thriving fishing village by the shores of Loch Torridon, Tigh an Eilean is house and home to Chris and Cathryn Field, who have imbued the place with a spirit of cordial, domestic hospitality. She meets and greets, while he does good things with locally sourced produce in the kitchen. Seafood from the jetty and beyond might appear on the evening menu (grilled West Coast halibut with spaghetti nero, brown shrimps and asparagus velouté, for example), while meat eaters might be treated to tenderloin of outdoor-reared pork on juniper-braised Savoy cabbage with Dijon mustard sauce. To finish, try a galette of traditional raspberry cranachan. House wine is £16.50. For lunch and more casual meals (Torridon langoustine 'scampi' and chips, say), head to the adjoining Shieldaig Bar & Coastal Kitchen.

Chef/s: Christopher Field. **Open:** all week L 12 to 3 (bar only), D 6 to 9 (12 to 9 in high season). **Closed:** 25 Dec. **Meals:** Bar: alc (main courses from £6 to £17). Restaurant: set D £45 (4 courses). **Service:** not inc. **Details:** 54 seats. 50 seats outside. Separate bar. No music. Car parking.

▌Strontian

Kilcamb Lodge

Welcoming retreat of the best Highland kind
Strontian, PH36 4HY
Tel no: (01967) 402257
www.kilcamblodge.co.uk
Modern European | £50
Cooking score: 4

£5 OFF 🛏 V

This stately eighteenth-century lodge by the shores of Loch Sunart is claimed to be one of the oldest stone houses in Scotland. It has been home to all manner of high-ranking and high-minded people, including the naturalist/philosopher Sir Fraser Darling – whose books can still be seen in Kilcamb's library. It's a graciously welcoming retreat of the best Highland kind, and the kitchen applies some cheffy flourishes to its larder of Scottish ingredients: Orkney crab and Inverawe smoked salmon come together in a salad; loin of lamb is offset by apricot mousse, goats' cheese mash, caper and mint butter; twice-cooked Duroc pork is partnered by spinach, celeriac and wild mushrooms. Four-course dinners always open with a little amuse-bouche (perhaps hot-smoked trout with dips), while dessert might bring something homely such as pear and quince crumble with home-churned vanilla ice cream or white chocolate, banana and peanut bread-and-butter pudding. Salads, burgers and pasta dominate the all-purpose lunch menu. A clutch of house wines starts at £22.50 (£5.70 a glass).
Chef/s: Gary Phillips. **Open:** all week L 12 to 2 (3 Sun), D 7 to 8.30. **Closed:** Jan, Mon and Tue in Feb, Nov and Dec. **Meals:** Set L £18.50. Set D £49.50 (4 courses). Sun L £15.50. **Service:** not inc. **Details:** 26 seats. 8 seats outside. Separate bar. Music. Car parking. Children over 10 yrs only at D.

⑪ LIZ McGOUGAN
Café Fish

When did you realise you wanted to become a chef?
I took a part-time job in a kitchen when I was 14 and have been hooked ever since.

What food trends are you spotting at the moment?
People want to know the provenance of their food and are very aware of sustainable fishing methods in particular.

What advice would you give a chef starting their career?
Start off as a kitchen porter in a good kitchen, work hard and be persistent, so when a commis vacancy comes up you're better placed to apply for it.

What is your 'show-off' dish?
Our roast shellfish platter is very visually arresting and always catches the customer's eye.

What's your earliest food memory?
My dad was a fisherman and when we were growing up he'd always bring home fresh scallops, queenies, herring and prawns.

What's your least favourite food?
Anything processed.

WALES

Glamorgan, Gwent, Mid-Wales, North-East Wales, North-West Wales, West Wales

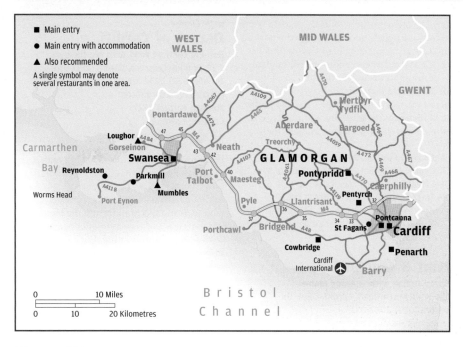

- ■ Main entry
- ● Main entry with accommodation
- ▲ Also recommended

A single symbol may denote
several restaurants in one area.

▌Cardiff

NEW ENTRY

Bully's

Long-running family-owned gem
5 Romilly Crescent, Cardiff, CF11 9NP
Tel no: (029) 2022 1905
www.bullysrestaurant.co.uk
Modern British | £30
Cooking score: 2

A gem of a family-run restaurant in suburban
Cardiff, Bully's has been going strong for over
15 years. Its homespun interior is crammed
with everything from gilt-framed mirrors to
receipts and menus gathered on the owners'
own gastronomic travels, and the repertoire,
while broadly French, does pack in a few
international flavours. A generous portion of
pan-fried spiced foie gras may come with
forced rhubarb compote and Japanese saké
dressing, for example, or seared loin of
yellowfin tuna with braised fennel, confit
potatoes and Madagascan green peppercorn

sauce. For dessert, look out for the pear tarte
Tatin with peardrop ice cream. Wines kick off
at £17.
Chef/s: Gareth Farr. **Open:** Wed to Sun L 12 to 2
(3.30 Sun), Wed to Sat D 7 to 9 (10 Fri and Sat).
Closed: Mon, Tue, 1 week Jan, 1 week Jun, 1 week
Sept. **Meals:** alc (main courses £14 to £25). Set L
£14 (2 courses) to £17.50. Sun L £16 (2 courses) to
£19.50. **Service:** 10%. **Details:** 40 seats. Music.

ffresh

Flag-waving minimalist eatery
The Wales Millennium Centre, Bute Place, Cardiff,
CF10 5AL
Tel no: (029) 2063 6465
www.ffresh.org.uk
Modern British | £27
Cooking score: 1

There's a strong sense of national identity
about this cool, minimalist eatery within the
Wales Millennium Centre. Floor-to-ceiling
windows provide enviable views of Cardiff

Bay, the menu proudly touts its wares in Welsh as well as English, and native ingredients show up strongly across the board – from Perl Lâs cheese and elderberry mousse with candied walnuts to bread-and-butter pud laced with Brecon gin marmalade. In between, Wales meets the world in the shape of venison with shallot and thyme purée or confit belly pork paired with chilli and garlic squid. Wines from £14.95.

Chef/s: Kurt Fleming. **Open:** Tue to Sun L 12 to 2.30 (3.30 Sun), Tue to Sat D 5 to 9.30. **Closed:** Mon, 25 Dec. **Meals:** alc (main courses £12 to £19). Set L £15.50 (2 courses) to £18.50. Set D £18.50 (2 courses) to £22.50. **Service:** not inc. **Details:** 130 seats. 50 seats outside. Separate bar. Wheelchair access. Music.

Mint & Mustard

Buzzy Indian with winning menus
134 Whitchurch Road, Cardiff, CF14 3LZ
Tel no: (029) 2062 0333
www.mintandmustard.com
Indian | £22
Cooking score: 2

A relaxed and buzzy Indian restaurant in suburban Cardiff, Mint and Mustard offers a winning mix of familiar favourites, traditional Keralan dishes and modern inventions. Starters range from nandu (crispy soft-shell crab) to chicken tikka, and the signature main of tiffin sea bass (pan-seared on curry leaf-infused mash in a raw mango, ginger and coconut sauce) is a must – that is, if you can tear yourself away from the likes of chicken tikka masala and Syrian beef curry. Also unmissable are the chocolate samosas with caramelised banana and pistachio ice cream. A simple selection of international wines starts at £15.

Chef/s: Pramod Nair. **Open:** all week 2 to 11. **Closed:** 25 and 26 Dec, 1 Jan. **Meals:** alc (main courses £8 to £17). Tasting menu £39.95. **Service:** 10% for parties of 10 or more. **Details:** 58 seats. Separate bar. Music.

Oscars of Cardiff

Homely comfort food with big flavours
6-10 Romilly Crescent, Cardiff, CF11 9NR
Tel no: (029) 2034 1264
www.oscarsofcardiff.com
Modern British | £27
Cooking score: 2

Formerly Le Gallois, this smart but laid-back suburban restaurant has slipped comfortably into its new role as a purveyor of simple food with big flavours. Inside it's grey walls, bare table tops and lots of light, and the menu trawls trends and classics to offer hearty dishes with a high comfort rating. Juicy fried buttermilk chicken, for instance, was teamed with sweet chilli and smoked garlic to make a generous starter, while hearty roast belly pork came with good salty crackling, homely bubble and squeak, and sensibly sour apple and cherry relish. Apple frangipane tart with custard rounded things off. International wines open at £14.95.

Chef/s: John Cook. **Open:** Tue to Sun L 12 to 6 (5 Sun), Tue to Sat D 6 to 9.30 (10 Sat). **Closed:** Mon, 25 and 26 Dec. **Meals:** alc (main courses £9 to £24). Set L £13 (2 courses) to £17. **Service:** not inc. **Details:** 60 seats. 20 seats outside. Separate bar. Music. Car parking.

The Potted Pig

Snappy cooking and divine desserts
27 High Street, Cardiff, CF10 1PU
Tel no: (029) 2022 4817
www.thepottedpig.com
Modern British | £25
Cooking score: 2

A darkly atmospheric former bank vault has been stripped back to its bare walls to create this trendily utilitarian restaurant. Snappy modern cooking delivers the likes of char-grilled squid, perfectly seasoned and 'full of flavour', teamed with a pleasantly punchy aïoli, a 'beautifully balanced' main course of 'very fresh' crisp-skinned hake with bacon, peas, Little Gem and potato, and 'show-stopping desserts' such as a dense, intensely chocolatey mousse with a layer of salted caramel underneath and brandy cream on top – 'divine'. Service is slick and an international wine list opens at £15.

Chef/s: Gwyn Myring and Tom Furlong. **Open:** Tue to Sun L 12 to 2.30, D 7 to 9 (6.30 to 9.30 Fri and Sat). **Closed:** Mon. **Meals:** alc (main courses £8 to £25). Set L £10. Sun L £15. **Details:** 60 seats. Wheelchair access. Music.

Woods Brasserie

British classics, taken seriously
The Pilotage Building, Stuart Street, Cardiff, CF10 5BW
Tel no: (029) 2049 2400
www.knifeandforkfood.co.uk
Modern British | £25
Cooking score: 3

Affable service and consistent output from the kitchen is what Woods is all about. Revamped in the best possible taste, this one-time pilotage building by Cardiff Bay offers light, space and plenty of outdoor seating. The atmosphere might be relaxed, but food is taken seriously. The menu is focused on British classics; this may translate (sometimes a little loosely) as anything from fish and chips with hand-cut chips, sausages with potato purée, Savoy cabbage and red wine jus, and good steaks, to roasted cured salmon fillet with panzanella salad, squid ink and olive oil emulsion. Start with a soft Scotch egg teamed with smoked bacon pannacotta and finish with lemon, pistachio and poppy seed cake with tarragon mascarpone. Wines from £17.

Chef/s: Steve Raisis. **Open:** all week L 12 to 2 (2.30 Sat, 3 Sun), Mon to Sat D 5.30 to 10. **Closed:** 25 and 26 Dec. **Meals:** alc (main courses £9 to £24). Set L and D £20. Sun L £16.95. **Service:** not inc. **Details:** 90 seats. 40 seats outside. Separate bar. Wheelchair access. Music.

▌Cowbridge

NEW ENTRY
Oscars of Cowbridge

Bright, breezy and imaginative cooking
65 High Street, Cowbridge, CF71 7AF
Tel no: (01446) 771984
www.oscarsofcowbridge.com
Modern British | £22
Cooking score: 1

A bright, cheery restaurant with lime-green walls covered in modern artwork, Oscars has a breezy menu full of salads, international dishes and favourites such as steak or burger and chips. A sprightly purple potato and green bean salad with egg and roasted garlic mayonnaise is one of many good meat-free options. For a bit of spice, try chicken kofta with bulgur wheat and salad. Desserts range from homemade cakes to strawberry mess. International wines open at £14.95. Closed Sun.

Chef/s: John Cook. **Open:** Mon to Sat 10am to 11pm. **Closed:** Sun, 25 and 26 Dec. **Meals:** alc (main courses £9 to £24). **Service:** 12.5%. **Details:** 60 seats. 12 seats outside. Wheelchair access. Music. Car parking.

ALSO RECOMMENDED

▲ Bar 44

44c High Street, Cowbridge, CF71 7AG
Tel no: (01446) 776488
www.bar44.co.uk
Tapas £5 OFF

Described as a 'modern bar and restaurant with a tapas-style menu' by one visitor (who reckoned two to three dishes per head made up a very adequate meal), Bar 44 offers some surprises. As well as familiar dishes like a plate of jamón Ibérico, cider-poached chorizo (£4.25) or tortilla, there are really eye-catching items like oxtail-stuffed piquillo peppers, or baked Cañarejal cheese with rosemary, country bread and olive jam (£4.95) and a dessert of sangria granita. Wines from £13.50. Closed Mon D.

Loughor

ALSO RECOMMENDED
▲ Hurrens Inn on the Estuary

13 Station Road, Loughor, SA4 6TR
Tel no: (01792) 899092
www.hurrens.co.uk
Modern European

Tucked up a steep, winding lane near Loughor Castle, Hurrens is a great spot on sunny days, when you can settle outdoors and enjoy estuary views. The interior is smart and homely, and the menu references pub food, say maple-glazed bacon steak with mango salsa, tempura pineapple and chips (£8.50), pan-fried sea bass with prawn and crab risotto (£16.50), and an excellent apple and berry crumble. A short international wine list opens at £15.95. Closed Sun D and Mon.

Mumbles

ALSO RECOMMENDED
▲ Out of the Blue

698 Mumbles Road, Mumbles, SA3 4EH
Tel no: (01792) 361616
www.outofthebluerestaurant.co.uk
Seafood £5 OFF

The seafront setting with calming views across Swansea Bay is spot-on for a lively fish restaurant. Inside, the exposed stone walls, tiled floor and sea-blue colour scheme are the backdrop for generous, tomatoey bouillabaisse (£6.95), seared king scallops with smoked salmon mash and lemon vinaigrette (£21.95), or the odd meat dish such as slow-roast belly pork in honey jus (£15.95). Afters could be a pear poached in mulled wine with mascarpone (£4.95). House Chilean is £13.95. Open Tue-Sat.

Parkmill
Maes-Yr-Haf

Boutique interiors and big-city food
Parkmill, SA3 2EH
Tel no: (01792) 371000
www.maes-yr-haf.com
Modern European | £30
Cooking score: 3

Don't be fooled by its bucolic 'heritage' surroundings, this boutique restaurant-with-rooms lives in the cool, contemporary comfort zone. Since arriving in 2010, owner Patty Ford and chef Ben Griffiths have 'turned the place around', according to correspondents with their eye on the local scene. The kitchen is prepared to take chances and invest seasonal Welsh ingredients with some creative, big-city oomph – witness exceptional duck liver arancini, a dish of monkfish and glazed sweetbreads with artichoke purée and chicken jus, or an anatomical bonanza of local pork 'head to toe'. But it also knows how to comfort traditional tastes, serving up the likes of dry-aged Welsh ribeye with oxtail pudding, or bara brith apple and pear charlotte with hot toddy ice cream. Sunday roasts receive glowing reviews too. Service is spot-on, and there's plenty of good drinking from £14.95.
Chef/s: Ben Griffiths. **Open:** Tue to Sun L 12 to 2, Tue to Sat D 7 to 9 (6.30 Fri and Sat). **Closed:** Mon, 1 week Jan. **Meals:** alc (main courses £15 to £23). Set L £16.95 (2 courses) to £20.95. **Service:** not inc. **Details:** 44 seats. Separate bar. Wheelchair access. Music. Car parking.

▌Penarth

The Fig Tree

Panoramic seaside views and sheer value
The Esplanade, Penarth, CF64 3AU
Tel no: (029) 2070 2512
www.thefigtreepenarth.co.uk
Modern British | £28
Cooking score: 2

'Has the best location of any I've seen in or around Cardiff', reported a visitor to this converted Victorian beach shelter with views of Penarth Pier and out across the Bristol Channel. What impresses, too, is Mike Caplan-Hill's no-nonsense cooking, his eye for seasonal ingredients and the sheer value. Reports have praised a host of things, from 'possibly the best scallops I've ever had' (with sweet potato purée and chorizo crisps), and spring rolls with dipping sauce and wilted spinach salad, to 'spot-on' Welsh Black sirloin steak with chips. For afters, treat yourself to rhubarb and ginger bread-and-butter pudding with rhubarb compote. Wines from £13.50.

Chef/s: Mike Caplan-Hill. **Open:** Tue to Sun L 12 to 3 (4 Sun), Tue to Sat D 6.30 to 9.30. **Closed:** Mon, 25 and 26 Dec, 1 Jan. **Meals:** alc (main courses £11 to £19). Set L £11 (2 courses) to £13.50. Sun L £17.95. **Service:** not inc. **Details:** 54 seats. 28 seats outside. Wheelchair access. Music.

ALSO RECOMMENDED

▲ Pier 64

Penarth Marina, Penarth, CF64 1TT
Tel no: (029) 2000 0064
www.pier64.co.uk
Modern British

A stylish waterside eatery with plenty of alfresco seating, Pier 64 has slotted seamlessly into Penarth's slick marina development. Run by the team behind the late, great Cardiff restaurant Le Gallois, it represents a decisive change of tack, with a focus on down-to-earth cooking. The menu features classics like chicken liver and foie gras parfait (£6.95),

favourites including grilled steaks (from £16.95) and fish and chips (£14.95), then maybe pistachio crème brûlée (£5.95). A French-weighted wine list opens at £14.95.

▌Pentyrch

Kings Arms

Worth a special journey
Church Road, Pentyrch, CF15 9QF
Tel no: (029) 2089 0202
www.kingsarmspentyrch.co.uk
Modern British | £25
Cooking score: 2

This charming village inn does a steady trade as a local, but its restaurant is worth a special journey. A whitewashed, slate-floored garden room with reclaimed furniture, it maintains the pub's attractive rustic look yet has a sense of occasion. The menu follows suit, offering hearty food with one nod to tradition and another to classic French techniques: pheasant and pork rillettes with tangy, thick-cut onion chutney; a tender chicken breast stuffed with asparagus and served with pommes pailles (skinny fries) and an Otley ale, shallot and mustard jus. Rhubarb and sherry trifle closes things nostalgically. The short international wine list starts at £14.95.

Chef/s: Ken Bell. **Open:** all week L 12 to 2.30 (3 Sat, 3.30 Sun), Mon to Sat D 6.30 to 9 (9.30 Sat). **Meals:** alc (main courses £11 to £15). Sun L £12.50 (2 courses) to £15.50. **Service:** not inc. **Details:** 40 seats. 20 seats outside. Separate bar. Music. Car parking.

🍴 Please send us your feedback

To register your opinion about any restaurant listed in the Guide, or a new restaurant that you wish to bring to our attention, please visit the web address at the bottom of the page. Your feedback informs the content of the book and will be used to compile next year's reviews.

Pontcanna

NEW ENTRY
The Conway
Imaginative pub food
58 Conway Road, Pontcanna, CF11 9NW
Tel no: (029) 2022 4373
www.knifeandforkfood.co.uk/conway
Modern European | £27
Cooking score: 2

Still a real pub despite its airy good looks, the Conway has a convivial front bar and spacious dining area with white walls, bookshelves, a real fire and an artfully mismatched collection of modern and reclaimed furniture. Choices from the blackboard menu range from modern pub dishes (such as an excellent Scotch egg, crisp on the outside and runny in the middle) to Eurozone-inspired options such as succulent chicken breast with chorizo, black pudding and chickpea ragù. A dessert of Nutella bread-and-butter pudding is a 'decadent take on Nutella sandwiches'. There are excellent real ales, and an international wine list starting at £14.95.
Chef/s: Stefan Nilsson. **Open:** Mon to Sat 12 to 9.30 (10pm Fri and Sat), Sun L 12 to 4, D 5 to 9. **Meals:** alc (main courses £10 to £17). **Service:** not inc. **Details:** 66 seats. 40 seats outside. Separate bar. Wheelchair access. Music.

Pontypridd
Bunch of Grapes
Hostelry that does the neighbourhood proud
Ynysangharad Road, Pontypridd, CF37 4DA
Tel no: (01443) 402934
www.bunchofgrapes.org.uk
Modern British | £25
Cooking score: 1

Down by the old canal, the 'Bunch' is a local hostelry that does its neighbourhood proud. You won't see many navvies or narrowboat workers these days, but the place still knows how to nourish its customers with generous platefuls of devilled lamb's kidneys on focaccia, poached fillet of sea trout in farmhouse cider or braised lamb shank with celeriac mash. Alternatively, sit in the cosy revamped bar and order a pint of Otley's ale to go with your ploughman's. House wine is £14.80.
Chef/s: Sebastien Vanoni. **Open:** all week L 12 to 2.30 (3.30 Sun), Mon to Sat D 6.30 to 9.30. **Meals:** alc (main courses £10 to £25). **Service:** not inc. **Details:** 80 seats. 30 seats outside. Separate bar. Wheelchair access. Music. Car parking.

Reynoldston
Fairyhill
Smart hotel with an excellent chef
Reynoldston, SA3 1BS
Tel no: (01792) 390139
www.fairyhill.net
Modern British | £45
Cooking score: 4

A reporter notes that in the past Fairyhill's prices 'have raised eyebrows', then adds 'but now that it offers some of the most intelligent, satisfying food in the area, people will no doubt reach for their wallets more willingly'. It seems the kitchen at this smart country house hotel is excelling in the hands of chef Neil Hollis. Begin in the bar or lounge, and enjoy canapés such as laverbread quiche, cured salmon with crème fraîche and rare beef with horseradish. Then, in the classically elegant dining room, superb home-baked breads are followed by deceptively simple dishes made with top-notch ingredients: soused mackerel with pickled cucumber, radish and crispy shallots; crisp-skinned sea bass fillets with green beans, crushed new potatoes and sauce vierge that 'simply bursts with lemony flavour'; then tangy apple and tarragon tart with thick clotted cream ice cream. The impressive wine list covers the major French regions in detail before striking out. Bottles from £19.50.
Chef/s: Neil Hollis. **Open:** all week L 12 to 2, D 7 to 9. **Closed:** 26 Dec, first 3 weeks Jan. **Meals:** Set L £20 (2 courses) to £25. Set D £35 (2 courses) to £45.

Sun L £27.50. **Service:** not inc. **Details:** 60 seats. 30 seats outside. Separate bar. Music. Car parking. Children over 8 yrs only at D.

▌St Fagans
The White House
A fusion of old and new
Greenwood Lane, St Fagans, CF5 6EL
Tel no: (029) 2056 5400
www.white-house-restaurant.co.uk
Modern European | £30
Cooking score: 3

Having run the Old Post Office as a hospitable restaurant-with-rooms since 2006, Simon Kealy decided it was time for a new name. Apart from that, little else has changed: the interior is all chic, contemporary minimalism, and culinary matters still focus on the cool conservatory dining room. Like the building itself, Kealy's food is a fusion of old and new, and he brings a sure culinary intelligence to the table. A starter of warm pig's head salad might appear alongside a plate of 'dad's' pickled beetroot with anchovies and tenderstem broccoli, pork comes from the grounds of the nearby Natural History Museum (try the slow-roast belly with mustard mash), and there are fishy outings for, say, roast hake with brown shrimp dressing. To finish, have fun stuffing jam and chocolate into the DIY doughnuts. House wine is £17.95.
Chef/s: Simon Kealy. **Open:** Thur to Sun L 12 to 2 (3 Sun), Tue to Sat D 7 to 9.30. **Closed:** Mon, 31 Dec to 15 Jan. **Meals:** alc (main courses £11 to £25). Set L £12.95 (2 courses) to £15.95. Sun L £14.95 (2 courses) to £17.95. **Service:** not inc. **Details:** 36 seats. 20 seats outside. Separate bar. Wheelchair access. Music. Car parking.

▌Swansea
Didier & Stephanie
Tasteful French cuisine
56 St Helen's Road, Swansea, SA1 4BE
Tel no: (01792) 655603
French | £30
Cooking score: 4

Swansea's workaday St Helen's Road is an unlikely spot for fine French dining, but Didier and Stephanie's restaurant has been going strong here for over a decade. Buttery yellow walls and acres of stripped wood make it a tranquil, timeless setting, and smart, attentive staff (headed by Stephanie) get things off to a splendid start. In the kitchen Didier delivers, turning out intelligent, contemporary French food that tastes as good as it looks. Dense, crusty oven-fresh bread delighted at inspection, as did a smartly judged prawn risotto, and a croustillante of black pudding (a favourite with regulars). An excellent piece of beef fillet (served with smooth, creamy mash and green peppercorn sauce) was punchily flavoured and accurately cooked, while a waffle with thick chestnut cream brought things to a devilishly good close. The wine list covers all the major French regions before striking out for the New World. Bottles start at £14.90.
Chef/s: Didier Suvé. **Open:** Tue to Sat L 12 to 2, D from 7 onwards. **Closed:** Sun, Mon, Christmas to New Year, 2 weeks summer. **Meals:** alc (main courses £16 to £19). Set L £14.50 (2 courses) to £17.50. **Service:** not inc. **Details:** 25 seats. Music. Car parking.

Hanson at the Chelsea

Convivial haven with moreish food
17 St Mary Street, Swansea, SA1 3LH
Tel no: (01792) 464068
www.hansonatthechelsea.co.uk
Modern European | £35
Cooking score: 3

£5 OFF

This thriving little restaurant occupies an unlikely spot on a lane just off Swansea's Wind Street, the city's main bar and nightclub district. Once inside you could be miles from the hustle and bustle; the restaurant exists in its own bubble of convivial chatter. The simple, cheery décor includes a large chalkboard listing the day's specials (there's always a good fresh fish option). A creamy take on moules marinière made a satisfying starter, with its moreishly moppable liquor. Also enjoyable was a main course of fresh hake with beautifully fresh asparagus and a good hollandaise. Desserts are a highlight – if you can't choose, opt for the trio of mini versions: crème brûlée, apple crumble and a chocolate orange pot. A simple international wine list starts at £13.95.
Chef/s: Andrew Hanson. **Open:** Mon to Sat L 12 to 2, D 6.30 to 9.30. **Closed:** Sun, bank hols. **Meals:** alc (main courses £12 to £25). Set L £12.95 (2 courses) to £16.95. Set D £19.95. **Service:** not inc. **Details:** 40 seats. Music.

Pant-y-Gwydr Restaurant

French cooking that hits the spot
Oxford Street, Swansea, SA1 3JG
Tel no: (01792) 455498
www.pantygwydr.co.uk
French | £30
Cooking score: 3

This charmer of a restaurant in the heart of Swansea has been drawing appreciative crowds since it opened in 2010. Reporters approve of the resolutely French approach to things, in what was once a public house (now boldly renovated to achieve a stylish blend of old and new). Jacques Abdou's 'deliciously presented fresh food' draws on local supplies as well as those from further afield and his classic ideas sure hit the spot. These might come in the form of fish soup or frogs' legs, boned and cooked in a marinière sauce, and mains of coq au vin or medallions of veal served with cocotte potatoes, chestnuts, mushrooms and glazed button onions. It's no surprise to find the short wine list is all-French; prices from £13.95.
Chef/s: Jacques Abdou. **Open:** Tue to Sat L 12 to 2.15, D 6 to 10. **Closed:** Sun, Mon, 2 weeks from 4 Sept. **Meals:** alc (main courses £7 to £27). **Service:** not inc. **Details:** 48 seats. Wheelchair access. Music.

Slice

Personal service and menus that work
73-75 Eversley Road, Swansea, SA2 9DE
Tel no: (01792) 290929
www.sliceswansea.co.uk
Modern British | £34
Cooking score: 3

Restaurants come in all shapes and sizes, but there can't be many quite like Slice – a wedge-shaped building with Philip the chef in the 'shop window' and partner Helen running the minuscule restaurant on the first floor. They've made a virtue of the unusual set-up, offering service with a personal touch and carefully composed menus that, quite simply, 'work'. The cooking is 'fresh, vibrant and seasonal'. The three-course menu (£34) might see trout raviolo with leek ragoût and lemon oil ('a masterclass in simplicity') followed by duck breast with sweet potato cake and Seville orange sauce, then comforting bara brith pudding with vanilla ice cream. Cellar space is minimal, so the wine list has to be short and versatile (from £14).
Chef/s: Philip Leach. **Open:** Thur to Sun D only 6.30 to 9. **Closed:** Mon to Wed, 4 weeks Dec to Jan. **Meals:** Set D £34. **Service:** not inc. **Details:** 16 seats. Music.

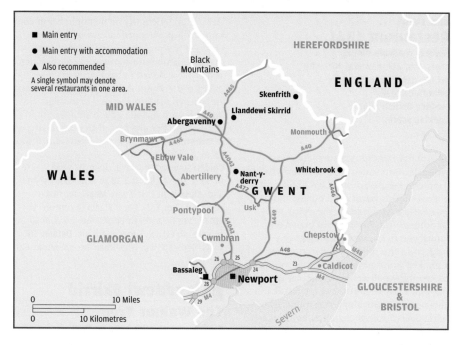

- ■ Main entry
- ● Main entry with accommodation
- ▲ Also recommended

A single symbol may denote several restaurants in one area.

HEREFORDSHIRE

Black Mountains

ENGLAND

Skenfrith ●

MID WALES

Llanddewi Skirrid ●

Abergavenny ●

Monmouth

Brynmawr

WALES

Ebbw Vale

Abertillery

● Nant-y-derry

Whitebrook ●

GWENT

Pontypool

Usk

GLAMORGAN

Cwmbran

Chepstow

0   10 Miles

0   10 Kilometres

Bassaleg

26   25

Newport

24

23

Caldicot

GLOUCESTERSHIRE & BRISTOL

28

29

Severn

▋Abergavenny

The Hardwick

A winner all round
Old Raglan Road, Abergavenny, NP7 9AA
Tel no: (01873) 854220
www.thehardwick.co.uk
Modern British | £35
Cooking score: 5

This amiable, rustic-hued venue still knows how to extol pubby generosity – even if the place now blends low beams and red-tiled floors with varnished wood and leathery affluence. Main man Stephen Terry thinks big when it comes to local sourcing, flavours and choice – around a dozen starters head a line-up that appeals to diehards craving pressed ham hock with Welsh rarebit or chicken and leek pie, while satisfying bucolically minded foodies with ravioli of roast Middle White pork and fennel with creamed endive, or pan-fried Gower sea bass with chorizo, saffron potatoes and new season's broad beans. This

may be Wales, but Mediterranean riffs play out everywhere – from a panzanella salad 'of utmost seasonality and freshness' involving three varieties of heritage tomatoes, to a 'butch' dish of linguine with crab, courgettes, anchovy and chilli. Presentation comes with lots of effort but a merciful lack of pomposity – witness a tripartite dish of rabbit on a wooden board, with sautéed potatoes in their own 'fiercely hot pan' and another vessel for the sauce. To finish, readers adore the tip-top Welsh cheeses and the prospect of dunking wickedly indulgent churros (Spanish doughnuts) into hot chocolate sauce with some sweetly tart marmalade ice cream on the side. A raft of admirable wines (from £18.50) also makes the Hardwick 'a winner all round'.
Chef/s: Stephen Terry. **Open:** all week L 12 to 3, D 6.30 to 10 (6 to 9 Sun). **Closed:** 25 Dec, second week Jan. **Meals:** alc (main courses £16 to £29). Set L £16.50 (2 courses) to £21. Sun L £23 (2 courses) to £28. **Service:** not inc. **Details:** 100 seats. 40 seats outside. Separate bar. Wheelchair access. Music. Car parking. No children under 8 yrs after 8 in restaurant.

NEW ENTRY
Restaurant 1861
Homely roadside dining
Cross Ash, Abergavenny, NP7 8PB
Tel no: (0845) 3881861
www.18-61.co.uk
Modern British | £37
Cooking score: 3

£5 OFF **V**

This pretty roadside restaurant has black-and-white décor to match the beams that crisscross its internal walls. Softened by candlelight, the overall effect is warm and homely, and co-owner Kate King adds to the charm with smooth service. An amuse of brawn with a punchy grain mustard dressing got an inspection visit off to a good start, followed by a smoked venison consommé that conjured forests and wood smoke with every spoonful. Flavours here are sometimes too subtle ('this chef needs to learn about seasoning!'), but ingredients are deftly handled, as in a main course of perfectly cooked hake with scallop ravioli. The real show-stoppers, however, are desserts such as a perfectly risen passion-fruit soufflé with passion-fruit syrup and white chocolate ice cream. A worldwide wine list kicks off at £17. **Chef/s:** Simon King. **Open:** Tue to Sun L 12 to 2, Tue to Sat D 7 to 9. **Closed:** Mon, first 2 weeks Jan. **Meals:** alc (main courses £18 to £23). Set L £19 (2 courses) to £24.50. Set D £36. Sun L £25. Tasting menu £49.50 (7 courses). **Service:** not inc. **Details:** 35 seats. Music. Car parking.

Bassaleg
Junction 28
A lot to choo-choose from
Station Approach, Bassaleg, NP10 8LD
Tel no: (01633) 891891
www.junction28.com
Modern European | £30
Cooking score: 2

Just outside Newport, overlooking the river Ebbw, Junction 28 is a converted railway station, its lower section dressed up to look like an old-fashioned carriage from the great days of rail. A lengthy menu might begin with king scallops wrapped in Parma ham on creamed Savoy cabbage, and go on to cannon of Welsh lamb with cumin-roasted shoulder and provençale veg in basil-scented jus, or baked cod with smoked salmon in lemongrass and chervil velouté. Desserts to indulge yourself with include a chocoholic's baked Alaska with brandy-flamed crème anglaise, or a citrus trio of tart, posset and ice cream. Wines from £15.95. **Chef/s:** Simona Bordeianu. **Open:** all week L 12 to 2 (4 Sun), Mon to Sat D 5.30 to 9.30 (9.45 Fri and Sat). **Closed:** 26 Dec, 1 Jan. **Meals:** alc (main courses £12 to £22). Set L £12.95 (2 courses) to £14.95. Set D £16.95 to £19.95. Sun L £13.95 (2 courses) to £15.95. **Service:** not inc. **Details:** 160 seats. Separate bar. Wheelchair access. Music. Car parking.

Llanddewi Skirrid
The Walnut Tree
Famous eatery with bang-on food
Llanddewi Skirrid, NP7 8AW
Tel no: (01873) 852797
www.thewalnuttreeinn.com
Modern British | £45
Cooking score: 6

For years the Walnut Tree has had pilgrimage status, and with cottage accommodation now available, 'get a room' takes on a whole new urgency when thinking about this low-ceilinged, farmhouse-chic eatery deep in the Monmouthshire foothills. On the food front, Shaun Hill is a master of plain-speaking dishes, the kind of stuff that respects ingredients and their natural flavours: 'bang-on' red mullet invigorated with tomato, chilli and ginger; woodpigeon with a boudin of sweetbreads; a plate of skirt steak, cooked rare with ceps, Parmentier potatoes and a punchy, anchovy-toned salsa verde. When it comes to desserts, the artless touch shines through yet again – readers have cheered his miraculous mirabelle fool ('plums and cream, nothing more needed'), and a dramatic monochrome assemblage of nectarines and whimberries

with a glossy, almost black sauce. The kitchen never soft-pedals, even when it comes to amazing-value set lunches, judging by glowing tales of skate with shrimps and dill, rabbit liver parfait with damson chutney, and pollack accompanied by a serving of petits pois in a cast-iron pot. Everything is handled with 'efficiency and cheer', from the moreish bread (walnut, of course) right down to the unmissable petits fours. The wine list is a 100-bin beauty offering everything from pitch-perfect 'classic' varietals and a host of shining stars to top-end vintages without top-end price tags. Bottles start at £18.
Chef/s: Shaun Hill and Roger Brook. **Open:** Tue to Sat L 12 to 2.30, D 6.30 to 9.30. **Closed:** Sun, Mon, 1 week Christmas. **Meals:** alc (main courses £15 to £25). Set L £20 (2 courses) to £26. **Service:** not inc. **Details:** 50 seats. 15 seats outside. Separate bar. No music. Wheelchair access. Car parking.

▌Nant-y-derry
The Foxhunter
Sheer indulgence and thoughtful food
Nant-y-derry, NP7 9DN
Tel no: (01873) 881101
www.thefoxhunter.com
Modern British | £30
Cooking score: 4

🍴 V

A reader who endured five hours on public transport to reach this one-time station-master's house in the tiny village of Nant-y-Derry was bowled over by the owners' kindness, sincerity and genuine desire to please: 'I was looking for sheer indulgence and laughter... and that's exactly what I had'. Much depends on Matt Tebbutt's generous, easy-going and thoughtful food: ham hock with 'mustard fruits' and fresh herb sauce; cep soup garnished with walnuts; lamb steak with anchovy and rosemary butter, and a gutsy dish of pork loin with Toulouse sausage have all gone down a storm. The kitchen treats carefully sourced produce with confidence and respect, whether it's local woodcock with celeriac purée, choucroute and bacon or John Dory with salt cod brandade, purple

sprouting broccoli and black olive dressing. After that, desserts such as poached pear with crumbly blue cheese and honeycomb, orange and cardamom posset or grilled panettone with new season's rhubarb and crème fraîche promise a perky, satisfying finale. The wide-ranging, knowledgeably chosen wine list balances quality and value, with some tremendous stuff from rock-solid producers. Prices start at £16.95 (£4.65 a glass).
Chef/s: Matt Tebbutt. **Open:** Tue to Sun L 12 to 2, Tue to Sat D 7 to 9. **Closed:** Mon, 25 and 26 Dec, bank hols. **Meals:** alc (main courses £17 to £22). Set L £20.95 (2 courses) to £25.95. Sun L £22.95 (2 courses) to £27.95. **Service:** not inc. **Details:** 50 seats. 12 seats outside. Separate bar. Wheelchair access. Music. Car parking.

▌Skenfrith
The Bell at Skenfrith
Riverbank inn with a kitchen garden
Skenfrith, NP7 8UH
Tel no: (01600) 750235
www.skenfrith.co.uk
Modern British | £35
Cooking score: 4

£5 🍴
OFF

Lush green hills surround the tiny village of Skenfrith and this fertile land provides much of what's on the menu at The Bell, including game shot by owner William Hutchings. The pub has an organic kitchen garden, and raises its own pigs; these appeared at a test meal as slow-braised cheek of Saddleback pork with black pudding ravioli, crackling, parsnip 'cake' and apple sauce. The meat was tender and flavourful, the ravioli rich and perfectly executed. Also impressive was a starter of beef carpaccio with sweet, spicy pickled mushrooms and horseradish cream. Try to leave room for dessert (difficult if you've overindulged on hot, crusty bread rolls) because this a highlight, perhaps perfect bittersweet chocolate 'soup' with cinnamon doughnuts and creamy peanut parfait. Also unmissable is the phenomenal wine list, a weighty international tome that includes everything from keenly priced house wines to luxurious Bollinger and Taittinger. Prices start at £15.

Chef/s: Kristian Greenwell. **Open:** all week L 12 to 2.30, D 7 to 9.30. **Closed:** Tue (Nov to Mar), last week Jan, first week Feb. **Meals:** alc (main courses £15 to £20). **Service:** not inc. **Details:** 60 seats. 30 seats outside. Separate bar. No music. Wheelchair access. Car parking. Children over 8 yrs only at D.

Whitebrook

★ TOP 50 ★

The Crown at Whitebrook

Premier-league cooking and superlative wines
Whitebrook, NP25 4TX
Tel no: (01600) 860254
www.crownatwhitebrook.co.uk
Modern British | £55
Cooking score: 7

🛏 V

'Magical' is a word that crops up frequently when readers are describing the remarkable Crown at Whitebrook. Set on a steep, heavily wooded hillside close to the river Wye, this converted seventeenth-century inn feels more like an amorous French auberge, full of romantic promise and courteous gestures – although everyone is here to sample James Sommerin's premier-league cooking. The best approach is to plunge straight into the extravagant nine-course tasting menu – an endlessly fascinating lucky dip that throws up a sackful of surprises every night. One couple who indulged themselves on two consecutive evenings picked out their highlights from Sommerin's gastronomic mystery tour: a perfectly balanced starter of fresh, flavourful grey mullet with a 'cannelloni' of smoked eel, shiso and avocado; a clever dish of poached and roasted sea bass with langoustine, artichoke and butternut squash; a 'fine pot-pourri of Welsh lamb' comprising loin and chop served with spiced tomato, potatoes and red wine jus, and more besides. Others have found pleasures aplenty in clear-flavoured, seasonal plates of heritage tomatoes, goats' cheese, cucumber and tarragon, hay-baked

venison with celeriac, and true-Brit combos of pan-fried turbot, crab, asparagus and samphire. 'James delivers every time' concluded yet another satisfied customer – although some of the most fulsome praise is reserved for beautifully crafted, sweet delectations such as Agen prune and vanilla flan with nutmeg ice cream and tangerine or a duo of pannacotta cream with bread and banana soufflé ('a magnificent example of top-notch cooking'). Meals are interspersed with all manner of fashionable extras, from exquisite canapés, amuse-bouches and between-course sorbets to delightful petits fours (presented with post-prandial coffee in the lounge). Everyone agrees that service is 'exceptional', and well-informed staff also know their way around the superlative 300-bin wine list – a 'fabulous combination of soil, climate and savoir faire' dispensed in the finest Riedel glassware. 'Terroir' is now the watchword, and the choice runs from forward-looking artisan names to gilt-edged obscurities from across the globe; sommelier's selections start at £19.

Chef/s: James Sommerin. **Open:** all week L 12 to 2, D 7 to 9.30. **Closed:** 2 weeks Christmas. **Meals:** Set L Mon to Thur £24.50 (2 courses) to £34.50. Set D £55. Tasting menu £62.50 (6 courses), £75 (9 courses). **Service:** not inc. **Details:** 30 seats. Music. Car parking. Children over 12 yrs only at D.

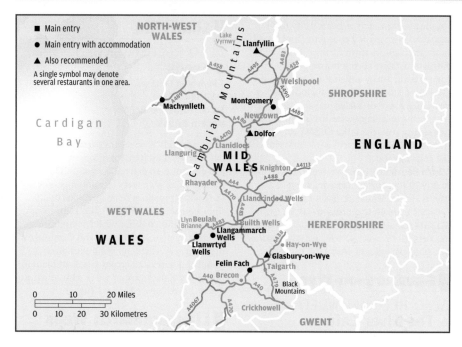

■ Main entry
● Main entry with accommodation
▲ Also recommended

A single symbol may denote
several restaurants in one area.

Dolfor

ALSO RECOMMENDED
▲ The Old Vicarage Dolfor
Dolfor, SY16 4BN
Tel no: (01686) 629051
www.theoldvicaragedolfor.co.uk
Modern British £5 OFF

Built as a vicarage in 1880, Tim and Helen
Withers' Welsh hideaway is now making quite
an impact as a 'country guest house' with a
penchant for smart provincial cooking.
Seasonal, organic and local ingredients are the
building blocks for fixed-price dinner menus
(from £30) that might yield Llyn plaice and
prawn terrine, followed by braised Bryn
Derw duck with ginger, lemongrass, noodles
and butternut squash, plus farmhouse cheeses
and bread-and-butter pudding. Organic
wines (from £15) dominate the savvy little
drinks list. All week D only.

Felin Fach

The Felin Fach Griffin
A beacon of Brecon hospitality
Felin Fach, LD3 0UB
Tel no: (01874) 620111
www.felinfachgriffin.co.uk
Modern British | £32
Cooking score: 4

£5 OFF

This heart-warming country inn extols the
virtues of eating, drinking and sleeping – and
it is 'everything you imagine a good pub to be',
according to a reader who drove down from
Edinburgh for the privilege of staying here.
The place itself has done duty as a dance hall
and farm building, and it's still closely
connected to the Brecon countryside –
especially on the food front. Recent hits have
included baked goats' cheese with roasted
beetroot, tomato and fried bread, ham hock
terrine with gooseberry chutney, and a
thumpingly good plateful of slow-roast belly
pork with garlicky pomme purée, girolles and

thyme jus. Fish such as 'beautifully fresh' mackerel with grilled courgettes and broad bean pesto comes from further afield, while 'bargain' desserts keep it homespun (marmalade bread-and-butter pudding with cinnamon custard). Drinks include an ever-changing roster of Welsh real ales and cider. The well-considered wine list is dominated by interesting stuff from the Old World. Bottles start at £16.50, and there's a splendid choice by the glass or carafe.

Chef/s: Ross Bruce. **Open:** all week L 12 to 2.30, D 6 to 9 (9.30 Fri and Sat). **Closed:** 24 and 25 Dec, 4 days early Jan. **Meals:** alc (main courses £15 to £20). Set L £16.50 (2 courses) to £19.50. Set D £21.95 (2 courses) to £27. Sun L £23.50. **Service:** not inc. **Details:** 45 seats. 30 seats outside. Separate bar. Wheelchair access. Music. Car parking.

Glasbury-on-Wye

ALSO RECOMMENDED
▲ The River Café

Glasbury-on-Wye, HR3 5NP
Tel no: (01497) 847007
www.therivercafeglasbury.co.uk
Italian

There's a jovial buzz to this quirky restaurant where staff gamely wheel a vast blackboard menu from table to table. The location is delightful: the river Wye flows outside and alfresco seating looks over the water. Inside it's bright, with wooden furniture and artwork. There's an Italian flavour to dishes such as pappardelle with crab sauce (£11.50); a starter of goats' cheese, beetroot and salad (£6.50) and lemon tart also hit the spot. Wines from £14.50. Open Wed to Sun.

Also Recommended

Also recommended entries are not scored but we think they are worth a visit.

Llanfyllin

ALSO RECOMMENDED
▲ Seeds

5 Penybryn Cottages, High Street, Llanfyllin, SY22 5AP
Tel no: (01691) 648604
Modern British £5 OFF

Mark and Felicity Seager's cottage restaurant has been feeding locals and tourists since 1991, and continues to deliver the goods. The simple dining room is a cheery bastion of good value; the evening menu is fixed-price for two or three courses (£23.50/£27.50). Expect unpretentious cooking with Mediterranean accents: oven-baked tomato and Gorgonzola in puff pastry, chicken breast with black pudding, sherry and cream sauce, and lemon posset with blackcurrant sauce. House wine is £12. Closed Sun, Mon and Tue.

Llangammarch Wells

Lake Country House

The perfect place for a celebration
Llangammarch Wells, LD4 4BS
Tel no: (01591) 620202
www.lakecountryhouse.co.uk
Modern British | £39
Cooking score: 2

This nineteenth-century former hunting lodge standing in 50 acres of parkland is the perfect place for a celebration; polished wood, antiques and spacious rooms create a real sense of occasion. In the dining room, the repertoire may hold few surprises but it certainly doesn't lack interest. A spring menu might bring pigeon breast with pea risotto and pea shoots, then rump of Welsh lamb, roast belly pork or supreme of salmon with cockles, broad beans, fennel and herb broth. Wines from £21.50. More reports, please.

Chef/s: Russell Stach. **Open:** all week L 12 to 2, D 7 to 9. **Meals:** Set L £17.50 (2 courses) to £22.50. Set D £38.50. **Service:** not inc. **Details:** 80 seats. Separate bar. No music. Wheelchair access. Car parking. No children under 8 yrs.

Llanwrtyd Wells
Carlton Riverside
Smart yet homely riverside retreat
Irfon Crescent, Llanwrtyd Wells, LD5 4ST
Tel no: (01591) 610248
www.carltonriverside.com
Modern European | £44
Cooking score: 5

Alan and Mary Ann Gilchrist have
transformed this centuries-old building by
the banks of the Irfon into a smartly attired but
homely restaurant-with-rooms. There's a
bustling bar/bistro down in the cellar, but the
serious culinary action takes place in the
deeply relaxing surrounds of the refined
dining room overlooking the river. Dinner
brings a choice of two fixed-price menus that
tap into the pan-European mainstream for
twice-baked goats' cheese and apple soufflé,
Dover sole with salmon mousse, spinach and
chive beurre blanc or plates of seared beef fillet
perked up with oxtail bonbons and a dinky
cottage pie. The kitchen has also delivered an
'explosion of tongue-tickling enticement' in
the form of tiger prawns with fish sausage and
pea risotto, as well as a clever lamb dish
involving roast loin, slow-cooked breast and
devilled kidneys with red wine jus. Mary Ann
is a talented, perceptive chef with a devoted
following, but her cooking can sometimes
lack that extra 'panache' – desserts such as
sticky toffee pudding and lemon meringue
have struck some readers as rather mundane,
and there have been question marks about
freshness in the fish department. Service is
always friendly and accommodating,
although staff occasionally reveal a lack of
experience. House wine is £16.50.
Chef/s: Mary Ann Gilchrist. Open: Mon to Sat D only
7 to 8.30. Closed: Sun, 23 to 30 Dec. Meals: Full
menu £37.50 (2 courses) to £43.50. Set D £21.50 (2
courses) to £27.50. Service: not inc. Details: 20
seats. Separate bar. Music. Children over 8 yrs only.

Lasswade Country House
Hugely appealing country house
Station Road, Llanwrtyd Wells, LD5 4RW
Tel no: (01591) 610515
www.lasswadehotel.co.uk
Modern British | £36
Cooking score: 2

Not far from Builth Wells and the Royal
Welsh Showground, the Stevens' hugely
appealing Edwardian country house looks out
over ravishing views of the Cambrians. In the
high-toned dining room, with its burnished
mahogany, Roger's menus deal in refined
country house style. Expect home-smoked
trout with potato and radish salad in lemon
thyme oil to start, and then rabbit loin
wrapped in Parma ham with a faggot of rabbit,
Savoy cabbage and a port reduction, closing
majestically with bara brith bread-and-butter
pudding. Good homemade breads add class.
Wines start at £12.50 for South African
Chenin, or £14.25 for Chilean Merlot.
Chef/s: Roger Stevens. Open: all week D only 7.30
to 9.30. Closed: 25 and 26 Dec, bank hols.
Meals: Set D £36. Service: not inc. Details: 20
seats. No music. Car parking.

Machynlleth
The Wynnstay Hotel
Eminently affable Welsh champion
Maengwyn Street, Machynlleth, SY20 8AE
Tel no: (01654) 702941
www.wynnstay-hotel.com
Modern British | £28
Cooking score: 1

Whether you opt for the scrubbed pine tables
by the inglenook fire, or the back room with
its egg-yolk walls and parquet floors, the
friendly staff at this relaxed hotel will make
you feel at home. Local ingredients are name-
checked on a seasonal menu that might feature
Tywyn lobster or Clywedog trout.
Presentation can be overly simple, and more
attention should be paid to the vegetable

accompaniments, but the base ingredients are sound and well cooked. Save room for ambitious desserts of, say, rich chocolate truffle terrine with cumin caramel. Wines from £13.95.

Chef/s: Gareth Johns. **Open:** all week L 12 to 2, D 6.30 to 9. **Closed:** 1 week around New Year. **Meals:** alc (main courses £11 to £17). Set L £10 (2 courses) to £12.50 (market day only). Set D £27.50. Sun L £15.95. **Service:** not inc. **Details:** 80 seats. 40 seats outside. Separate bar. No music. Wheelchair access. Car parking.

Montgomery

NEW ENTRY
The Checkers
Faultless French food
Broad Street, Montgomery, SY15 6PN
Tel no: (01686) 669822
www.thecheckersmontgomery.co.uk
French | £40
Cooking score: 5

The first sign that the Checkers is rather more than a local hostelry is the discreet sign above the door: 'The Frenchman and the farmer's daughters'. This whitewashed former boozer in the pretty town of Montgomery was taken over by Stéphane Borie and partner Sarah (one of the farmer's daughters) in 2010. Today, a cosy front bar complete with wood-burning stove gives way to two dining areas, tastefully decorated with antique French chairs and eau de nil panelling. The other farmer's daughter, Kathryn, ably runs front-of-house. From amuse-bouches to petits fours, the Checkers delivers faultless dishes: mussel and saffron soup boasts a light, frothy texture combined with real depth of flavour, enhanced by fine julienne of chorizo and carrot; a perfectly risen smoked cheese soufflé arrives with a smoked cheese cream to pour into the fluffy centre; roasted loin of lamb is actually three dishes in one – crispy-skinned cutlet; roasted tomato stuffed with aubergine, goats' cheese and confit lamb; pink slices of loin. The menu descriptions only hint at the skill and

complexity of the finished dishes, so prepare to be very pleasantly surprised. Wines from £14.

Chef/s: Stéphane Borie. **Open:** Wed to Sat L 12 to 2, Tue to Sat D 6 to 10. **Closed:** Sun, Mon, 3 weeks Dec, 1 week Aug. **Meals:** alc (main courses £15 to £27). **Service:** not inc. **Details:** 40 seats. 15 seats outside. Separate bar. Children over 8 yrs only at D.

Pennal

READERS RECOMMEND
Glan Yr Afon
Modern British
Pennal, SY20 9DW
Tel no: (01654) 791285
riversidehotel-pennal.co.uk
'The traditional pub atmosphere is quite simply brilliant, a must for anyone passing through or near the Pennal area...or even make a trip especially; it's worth it.'

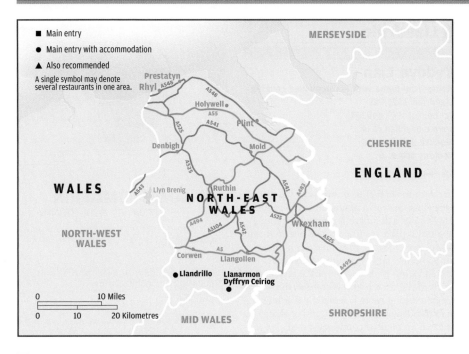

- ■ Main entry
- ● Main entry with accommodation
- ▲ Also recommended

A single symbol may denote several restaurants in one area.

Llanarmon Dyffryn Ceiriog

The West Arms Hotel

Characterful inn with fine local food
Llanarmon Dyffryn Ceiriog, LL20 7LD
Tel no: (01691) 600665
www.thewestarms.co.uk
Modern British | £23
Cooking score: 3

The West Arms is a drovers' inn near Wrexham, built in 1570. Today, it's all sparkling white on the outside (the better to stand out against the Berwyn Mountains backdrop) but full of bygone character within. Slate-flagged floors, low beams and inglenook fireplaces make for the proper country-inn setting, but the dark-walled dining room, with its crisply dressed tables, is full of sophisticated elegance. Grant Williams cooks a modern Welsh menu using lots of fine local produce. Start, say, with home-smoked trout tartare with prawn and cucumber salsa and lemongrass vinaigrette, then move on to thoroughbred Welsh black beef wrapped in Carmarthenshire ham with wild mushroom confit in a thyme-scented burgundy sauce. Finish with plum and pear crumble and vanilla ice cream. House Chilean is £15.95.
Chef/s: Grant Williams. **Open:** all week L 12 to 2.30, D 6 to 9. **Meals:** alc (main courses £10 to £19). Set D £27.95 (2 courses) to £32.95. Sun L £22.85.
Service: not inc. **Details:** 68 seats. 40 seats outside. Separate bar. Wheelchair access. Music. Car parking.

Symbols

🛏 Accommodation is available

£30 Three courses for less than £30

V Separate vegetarian menu

£5 OFF £5-off voucher scheme

🍷 Notable wine list

Llandrillo

★ TOP 50 ★

Tyddyn Llan

Home-from-home with accomplished cooking
Llandrillo, LL21 0ST
Tel no: (01490) 440264
www.tyddynllan.co.uk
Modern British | £55
Cooking score: 6

£5 OFF

Set deep in the Welsh countryside, the Webbs' appealing Georgian restaurant-with-rooms has become a destination venue. Everything about this place is authentic and heartfelt, and it is many loyal followers' idea of a home-from-home – always assuming you have Bryan Webb's highly accomplished cooking skills to call on at home. A comfortable, elegant dining room is served by confident staff (headed by Susan Webb) and cooking that is based on familiar combinations of impeccably sourced ingredients (mostly from a network of well-chosen local suppliers). The food makes a virtue of simplicity and economy and seems to please the great majority on both fronts. A first course might be something as simple as dressed crab with fennel and pea shoot salad, while generous mains shine, thanks to pedigree ingredients; witness a dish of local organic pork comprising a roast fillet, belly with black pudding, braised cheek and breaded trotter, or a simple but stunning sea bass with laverbread buerre blanc. Desserts promise pinpoint flavours – as in rhubarb and blood orange Champagne trifle – and there are always good cheeses from Neal's Yard Dairy. The wine list is an all-round cracker, with well-chosen bottles starting at £21 and decent choice under £30.
Chef/s: Bryan Webb. **Open:** Fri to Sun L 12.30 to 2, all week D 7 to 9 (9.30 Fri and Sat). **Closed:** weekdays 2 Jan to 10 Feb. **Meals:** alc (main courses £20 to £28). Set L £19.50 (2 courses) to £25.50. Set D £45 (2 courses) to £55. Sun L £38. **Service:** not inc. **Details:** 40 seats. 12 seats outside. Separate bar. Wheelchair access. Car parking.

JAMES SOMMERIN
The Crown at Whitebrook

When did you realise you wanted to be a chef?
When I was about 12, after discovering a passion for cooking from my grandmother.

What's your biggest kitchen bugbear?
Mess and working untidily.

Which chefs do you admire, and why?
The Roux Brothers, for their classic perfection, and René Redzepi for his take on national excellence and his witty cooking.

Sum up your cooking style in three words
Fresh, bold and fun.

What's your biggest extravagance in the kitchen?
Liquid nitrogen.

What is your 'show-off' dish?
Lemon and raspberry cheesecake with scented smoke. It's a really fun dish.

What would be your last meal?
My grandmother's chicken and asparagus bake and my wife, Louise's, sherry trifle.

What would you be if you weren't a chef?
A policeman.

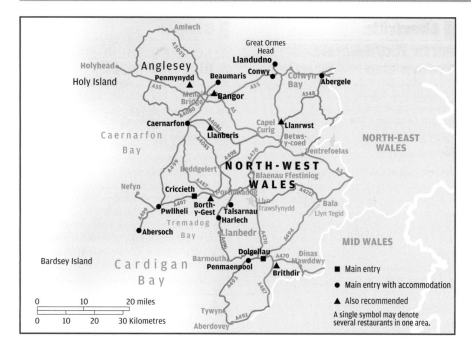

Abergele

The Kinmel Arms

Revitalised inn with fulfilling Welsh food
St George, Abergele, LL22 9BP
Tel no: (01745) 832207
www.thekinmelarms.co.uk
Modern British | £30
Cooking score: 4

A highly personal labour of love, this cleverly revitalised sandstone inn now plays out as a contemporary restaurant-with-rooms offering ebullient hospitality and food with deeply fulfilling Welsh roots. Given the location – within ozone-sniffing distance of Colwyn Bay – it's no surprise that the Kinmel gets top marks for seafood. King scallops with red chard, beetroot coulis, chervil and orange foam, battered cod fillet, and an elegant combo of wild sea bass with ginger-spiced squid and a saffron, chorizo and butter bean dressing show a sure, sympathetic touch. Gwyn Roberts is 'incredibly knowledgeable'

when it comes to local game, and makes admirable use of Welsh meats, too; try the rack of spring lamb with cabbage, bacon, smoked parsnip purée and a minted lamb pasty. To finish, opt for Welsh cheeses or some patriotic sweetness in the shape of roast pear with bara brith ice cream. Lighter, brasserie-style dishes take precedence at lunchtime. The thoughtful wine list opens with house recommendations from £16.95.

Chef/s: Gwyn Roberts. **Open:** Tue to Sat L 12 to 2, D 6 to 9.30. **Closed:** Sun, Mon, 25 Dec, 1 Jan, bank hols. **Meals:** alc (main courses £15 to £23). **Service:** not inc. **Details:** 88 seats. 24 seats outside. Separate bar. No music. Wheelchair access. Car parking. No children after 9.

Visit us Online

To find out more about
The Good Food Guide, please visit
www.thegoodfoodguide.co.uk

▌Abersoch

Porth Tocyn Hotel

Relaxing, welcoming hotel with bay views
Bwlch Tocyn, Abersoch, LL53 7BU
Tel no: (01758) 713303
www.porthtocynhotel.co.uk
Modern European | £44
Cooking score: 3

In the hands of the Fletcher-Brewer family
since 1948, Porth Tocyn is Abersoch's long-
standing 'smart' option, but remains relaxing
and notably child-friendly. In prime position
above Cardigan Bay, the hotel's dining room
hosts a much-loved Sunday lunch buffet, but
individual dishes might be confit belly pork
with vanilla and apple purée, faggot and
redcurrant syrup, or smoked salmon with
pickled cucumber, followed, perhaps, by veal
loin with veal and onion pie, dauphinois
potatoes and mustard cream sauce. Desserts
include strawberry parfait with raspberry
sorbet, and savouries, such as devils on
horseback, are a rare treat. Some dishes, like
some of the décor, would benefit from polish
in places, but the welcome is genuine and
reflected in the care lavished on details such as
good homemade bread. Wine is from £16.95.
Chef/s: Louise Fletcher-Brewer and Charlie Wild.
Open: all week L 12.15 to 2.30, D 7.15 to 9 (9.30 in
high season). **Closed:** Nov to week before Easter.
Meals: Set D £36 (2 courses) to £43.25. Sun L £25.
Service: not inc. **Details:** 50 seats. 30 seats outside.
Car parking. Children over 6 yrs only at D. (Please
check by telephone when booking.)

▐▌● Please send us your feedback

To register your opinion about any
restaurant listed in the Guide, or a new
restaurant that you wish to bring to our
attention, please visit the web address at
the bottom of the page. Your feedback
informs the content of the book and will
be used to compile next year's reviews.

▌Bangor

ALSO RECOMMENDED
▲ Blue Sky Café

Ambassador Hall, 236 High Street, Bangor,
LL57 1PA
Tel no: (01248) 355444
www.blueskybangor.co.uk
International £5 OFF

'There's just something about Blue Sky' says
one reporter. 'Whenever I go, I feel like I'm
eating something truly unique to the café.'
Personal touches abound, in everything from
homemade falafel with pitta bread, organic
yoghurt and mint dip (£4.45) to a shortbread
heart with your coffee. In between might
come char-grilled haloumi with quinoa,
roasted vegetables and chilli sauce (£7.15) or
burgers made from Welsh beef. Finish with
pistachio meringue, whipped cream and fresh
fruit salad (£4.45). Wines start at £11.25.
Open Mon to Sat 9.30 to 5.30.

▌Beaumaris

NEW ENTRY
Cennin

Mecca for local meat
31 Castle Street, Beaumaris, LL58 8AP
Tel no: (01248) 811230
www.restaurantcennin.com
Modern British | £35
Cooking score: 4
£5 OFF **V**

Modestly housed in an old building opposite
Ye Olde Bull's Head (see entry), Cennin
(meaning leek) is a small, beamed dining
room with cattle-themed artwork, above a
butcher's shop and deli. Shop and restaurant
belong to Brian and Ffiona Thomas, who have
won many accolades for their Beef Direct
farm business; Aled Williams is head chef and
manager of the restaurant. Tip-top local
ingredients are the cornerstone of the menu
and the unfussy seasonal style has impressed
reporters. You might start with lemon-grilled
sardine fillets teamed with local feta cheese
salsa, slow-roasted cherry tomatoes, radish,

sourdough wafer and micro cress. Roast loin of Carwyn's lamb with shoulder meat and kidney suet pudding, confit artichokes, broccoli purée and minted jus is a typical main course, which might be followed by buttermilk pannacotta with fennel pollen, served in a jar alongside raspberry sorbet and jelly. Wines from £14.95. Café MooBaaOinc downstairs serves L Tue to Sun.

Chef/s: Aled Williams. **Open:** Tue to Sun D only 6 to 9. **Closed:** Mon. **Meals:** alc (main courses £18 to £27). Set D £29.95. **Service:** not inc. **Details:** 50 seats. Separate bar. Music.

Ye Olde Bull's Head Inn, Loft Restaurant

Bull with pull
Castle Street, Beaumaris, LL58 8AP
Tel no: (01248) 810329
www.bullsheadinn.co.uk
Modern British | £43
Cooking score: 5

An aristocratic beast, this Olde Bull was born in 1472 and 'improved' in 1617. Over the centuries it has played host to literati, politicians and a parade of famous faces, and it still knows how to pull the crowds. Much attention now centres on the aptly named Loft Restaurant – a dramatic, eyrie-like space squeezed into the eaves, with circular mirrors, arty partitions and a raftered ceiling. Chef Hefin Roberts impresses visitors with his respect for ingredients, pin-sharp technique and eye for detail. He intersperses dinner with fashionable extras but keeps his feet firmly on Welsh soil when it comes to sourcing. A signature starter is seared Anglesey scallops with curried mussels, a crisp crab fritter, langoustines and lemon hollandaise; wild duck breast might appear in company with wild garlic, cumin-spiked carrots and sprout tops glazed with foie gras butter. Welsh beef receives suitably bullish treatment, while fish is often given a freewheeling, eclectic spin – witness steamed black bream with crisp lemon polenta, feta ravioli, fennel and pak choi. Desserts also pull off some clever ploys,

matching roast peanut cake with lemon pannacotta, burnt orange and cardamom meringue, for example. Shrewdly chosen wines from big-hitting French regions lead the impressive list, although those wanting to veer off-piste will also find ample rewards. Classy house selections start at £19.50 (£4.90 a glass). For more casual dining, try the slate-floored brasserie at the back of the hotel.

Chef/s: Hefin Roberts. **Open:** Tue to Sat D only 7 to 9.30 (6.30 Fri and Sat). **Closed:** Sun, Mon, 25 and 26 Dec, 1 Jan. **Meals:** Set D £42 (3 courses). **Service:** not inc. **Details:** 45 seats. Separate bar. No music. Car parking. Children over 10 yrs only.

Borth-y-Gest

ALSO RECOMMENDED
▲ Moorings Bistro
4 Ivy Terrace, Borth-y-Gest, LL49 9TS
Tel no: (01766) 513500
www.mooringsbistroborthygest.com
Modern British

This former shipbuilder's house overlooks Borth-y-Gest harbour and makes a super little eatery. Steve Williams' straightforward cooking makes the most of local produce, including fish. Start, perhaps, with well-reported braised chicken livers in a Marsala sauce, served on black pudding (£5.50), then sea bass with creamed leeks and chives (£14.95); finish with lemon and lime tart with a salted caramel wafer and berry sorbet. Wines from £14.95. Open Wed to Sat D, also L on Sun and bank hols.

Brithdir

ALSO RECOMMENDED
▲ Cross Foxes
Brithdir, LL40 2SG
Tel no: (01341) 421001
www.crossfoxes.co.uk
British £5 OFF

Rescued from dereliction and spruced up in style, this listed pub-with-rooms stands within striking distance of the Cader Idris mountain range. It puts on a classy show, with slate floors and granite walls, and operates as a lively all-rounder, opening for breakfast and providing brasserie-style food all day. Lunch or dinner may offer light bites (toasted Welsh rarebit £4.95), classics (Welsh Black beef, mushroom and ale pie £12.95), and well-hung steaks. Finish with dark chocolate torte. Wines from £12.95. Open all week.

▌Caernarfon

Rhiwafallen

Homely hospitality and glorious sea views
Llandwrog, Caernarfon, LL54 5SW
Tel no: (01286) 830172
www.rhiwafallen.co.uk
Modern British | £35
Cooking score: 2

The immaculate interior of Kate and Rob John's Welsh farmhouse tells its own story about their dedication to the principles of good, homely hospitality – although there is much to be said for the glorious sea views and Rob's sharply tuned cooking. Dinner is the main event in this amicable restaurant-with-rooms, and the kitchen takes care with the details: a starter called 'orchard floor' comprises wild mushrooms, goats' cheese croustade, candied walnuts and quince, while dessert might bring cinnamon-spiked apple crumble with scorched vanilla cream and bramble sorbet. In between, expect anything from butter-roast Welsh beef fillet to sea bass with braised cannellini beans and chorizo. House wine is £15.95.
Chef/s: Robert John. **Open:** Sun L 12 to 3, Tue to Sat D 7 to 11. **Closed:** Mon, 25 and 26 Dec. **Meals:** Set D £35. Sun L £19.50. **Service:** not inc. **Details:** 30 seats. Music. Car parking.

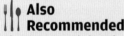

¶¶● Also Recommended
Also recommended entries are not scored but we think they are worth a visit.

ALSO RECOMMENDED

▲ Castell
33 Y Maes, Caernarfon, LL55 2NN
Tel no: (01286) 677970
www.castellcaernarfon.co.uk
Modern British £5 OFF

Reporters have commented that management has been rather uncertain at this Georgian hotel recently – the promised rooms have not come on-stream. Yet Daniel ap Geraint still produces noteworthy food, and it can still be thought of as 'a gem' with reasonably priced, flexible menus. Try, perhaps, salmon three ways – fishcake, fennel-cured, pâté (£6.50), rack and shoulder of lamb, fondant potato, spring greens, Madeira and mint (£16.50) then bara brith butter pudding with Penderyn whisky ice cream (£5.75). Wines from £13.95. Open all week.

▲ Oren
26 Hole in the Wall Street, Caernarfon, LL55 1RF
Tel no: (01286) 674343
Modern European £5 OFF

Tucked down an alleyway facing the medieval town wall, this quirky little bistro run by Dutchman Gert Vos punches above its weight when it comes to culinary ambition. Although one reporter thought the service 'painfully slow', dishes like mackerel with rhubarb and horseradish, Moorish pork chops with sherry and raisins, and lemon almond cake more than made up for it, especially considering the price tag of £15 for three courses. Wines from £12.50. Open Thur to Sat L and D.

READERS RECOMMEND

Stones Bistro
Modern British
4 Hole in the Wall Street, Caernarfon, LL55 1RF
Tel no: (01286) 676097
www.stonesbistro.co.uk
'Nice atmosphere, lovely chicken liver pâté, perfectly cooked sea bass, nice chocolate and almond tart, all at a very good price.'

Conwy

Dawson's at the Castle Hotel

Rejuvenated dining room with local produce
High Street, Conwy, LL32 8DB
Tel no: (01492) 582800
www.castlewales.co.uk
Modern British | £28
Cooking score: 2

A timely formula of all-day opening, flexible menus and relaxed ambience has gone a long way to making this rejuvenated dining room in the Castle Hotel 'seem more inviting' – although regulars are still wincing at the busy wallpaper, which they feel does a disservice to the Shakespearean paintings by Victorian illustrator John Dawson-Watson. Fresh ingredients lay a secure foundation for the food, with plenty of local produce – from a starter of Conwy mussels to a main of Welsh lamb rump with a mint and parsley crust or a leek and Llanrwst Cheddar cheese tart. The same food is served in the popular bar. Wines from £15.90.
Chef/s: Andrew Nelson. **Open:** all week 12 to 9.30 (10 Sat, 9 Sun). **Meals:** alc (main courses £16 to £23). Sun L £16.95 (2 courses) to £19.95. **Service:** 10%. **Details:** 73 seats. 30 seats outside. Separate bar. Music. Car parking.

Criccieth

Tir a Môr

Corner bistro with comforting local food
1-3 Mona Terrace, Criccieth, LL52 0HG
Tel no: (01766) 523084
www.tiramor-criccieth.co.uk
European | £26
Cooking score: 2

The name translates as 'land and sea' – an epithet that sums up Tir a Môr's location and the scope of its menu. This family-run bistro is pitched on a street corner not far from Tremadog Bay, and the local catch is put to good use in dishes such as grilled plaice with lemon and caper butter or seared fillets of sea bass with sweet pepper essence and pistou. As for the 'land', Welsh beef makes a big impression (perhaps served with rosemary and red wine sauce). Desserts take a broad-minded spin through pear financier, lemon posset and banana sticky toffee pudding. House wine is £16.50.
Chef/s: Laurent Hebert. **Open:** Tue to Sat D only 6 to 9. **Closed:** Sun, Mon, 25 Dec to Feb. **Meals:** alc (main courses £14 to £23). Set D £19.50 (2 courses) to £21.50. **Service:** not inc. **Details:** 40 seats. No music. Wheelchair access.

Dolgellau

Bwyty Mawddach

A great find, with excellent ingredients
Llanelltyd, Dolgellau, LL40 2TA
Tel no: (01341) 424020
www.mawddach.com
Modern British | £28
Cooking score: 2

A 'great find' housed in a 'beautiful farm barn conversion' overlooking the river Mawddach, this family venture relies on excellent local ingredients to fuel a menu of modern classics such as chicken liver pâté with Bramley apple fruit cheese and toasted sourdough, or slow-cooked local Welsh Black beef and red wine with herb dumplings. Expect occasional Mediterranean influences in the form of risottos or pressed and grilled breast of local lamb with soft polenta and rosemary and anchovy sauce. Orange and almond cake is a typical dessert. The international wine list opens at £14.75 and offers plenty for under £25.
Chef/s: Ifan Dunn. **Open:** Wed to Sun L 12 to 2.30 (3.30 Sun), Wed to Sat D 6 to 9.30. **Closed:** Mon, Tue, 26 Dec, first week Jan, 1 week Apr, 2 weeks Nov. **Meals:** alc (main courses £11 to £18). Sun L £14 (2 courses) to £18. **Service:** not inc. **Details:** 75 seats. 25 seats outside. Separate bar. Wheelchair access. Music. Car parking.

Dylanwad Da

Busy all-day asset
2 Ffôs-y-Felin, Dolgellau, LL40 1BS
Tel no: (01341) 422870
www.dylanwad.co.uk
Modern British | £28
Cooking score: 1

Dylan Rowlands' relaxed all-day café-bar-bistro has been Dolgellau's focal point for 25 years. It's a busy place, serving everything from daytime soups and tapas to three-course meals. Well-wrought cooking keeps things within sensible bounds. Good local ingredients are used in tried-and-trusted combinations, say salmon fishcake with tartare sauce or pheasant breast wrapped in Serrano ham with orange-scented gravy, and there's always a couple of steaks. Dylan is an independent wine merchant, too, and there are lots of interesting tipples to sample on a list that includes cherry-picked beauties imported directly from European growers. Prices from £15.
Chef/s: Dylan Rowlands. **Open:** Tue to Sat L 10 to 3 (Tue and Wed high season only), D 7 to 9. **Closed:** Sun, Mon, Feb. **Meals:** alc (main courses £14 to £20). Set L and D £20 (2 courses) to £25. **Service:** not inc. **Details:** 28 seats. Separate bar. Music.

▌Harlech

Castle Cottage

Accomplished restaurant-with-rooms
Y Llech, Harlech, LL46 2YL
Tel no: (01766) 780479
www.castlecottageharlech.co.uk
Modern British | £40
Cooking score: 2

Down a narrow lane just a stone's throw from the thirteenth-century castle (a World Heritage Site), this tiny, granite former coaching inn (now a restaurant-with-rooms) looks cottagey from the outside, but has been totally modernised within, taking in a small bar and L-shaped dining room. Jacqueline Roberts runs front-of-house with brisk efficiency, husband Glyn heads the kitchen. From the canapés in the bar, through the chef's appetiser (maybe seafood bisque), to almond and raspberry tart, dinner is an accomplished affair. Dishes are multifaceted: 'carefully assembled' scallops with belly pork and black pudding, say, followed by generously portioned Gressingham duck (roasted breast, confit leg, mushroom lasagne). Wines from £16.
Chef/s: Glyn Roberts. **Open:** all week D only 7 to 9. **Closed:** 3 weeks Nov, 3 days Christmas. **Meals:** Set D £39.50 (3 courses). **Service:** not inc. **Details:** 35 seats. Separate bar. Music. Car parking.

▌Llanberis

ALSO RECOMMENDED
▲ The Peak

86 High Street, Llanberis, LL55 4SU
Tel no: (01286) 872777
www.peakrestaurant.co.uk
Modern British £5 OFF

Excellent local produce is at the heart of this unpretentious modern village restaurant in Snowdonia. From the open kitchen, chef/proprietor Angela Dwyer sends out dishes with a global influence – typical choices are Welsh lamb koftas with roasted cherry tomatoes, cucumber, red onion and mint Greek yoghurt (£5.95), then maybe locally smoked haddock chowder with saffron and crispy pancetta (£14.95). To finish, try apple crumble tartlet and cream. Wines from £12.95. Closed Mon, Tue, Sat L and Sun L.

Symbols

🛏 Accommodation is available

💲30 Three courses for less than £30

V Separate vegetarian menu

£5 OFF £5-off voucher scheme

🍾 Notable wine list

▌Llandudno

Bodysgallen Hall, The Dining Room

A glorious garden and complex dinners
Llandudno, LL30 1RS
Tel no: (01492) 584466
www.bodysgallen.com
Modern British | £41
Cooking score: 4

🛏 V

The core of this country house hotel dates from the thirteenth century, but the most glorious feature is the garden, with its long terrace and far distant views of Conwy Castle and Snowdonia. Michael Cheetham now heads the kitchen, having worked with his two predecessors for many years. Lunch is simple, dinner is more complex; things might start with seared hand-dived scallops, Oakwood Park belly pork, golden raisins and caramelised cauliflower, then a palate-cleansing sorbet before a main of, say, poached fillet of Llanfair Hall Farm beef, paired with compressed ox cheeks and served with stewed celeriac and a marrow bone fritter. Finish, perhaps, with confit banana, cinder toffee espuma and bitter chocolate mousse. The impressive wine list features a sound base of classical French wines, complemented by bottles from around the globe; house selection starts at £20. Note: lighter, cheaper meals are served at the 1620 Bistro in the converted coach house.
Chef/s: Michael Cheetham. Open: Tue to Sun L 12.30 to 1.45, Tue to Sat D 7 to 9. Closed: Mon. Meals: Set L £19.50 (2 courses) to £22.50. Set D £41. Sun L £27. Service: not inc. Details: 50 seats. Separate bar. No music. Wheelchair access. Car parking. Children over 6 yrs only.

🍴 Average Price

The average price listed in main-entry reviews denotes the price of a three-course meal, without wine.

St Tudno Hotel, Terrace Restaurant

Traditional hotel with well-judged dishes
Promenade, Llandudno, LL30 2LP
Tel no: (01492) 874411
www.st-tudno.co.uk
Modern British | £35
Cooking score: 2

£5 OFF 🛏

The St Tudno is an old school hotel (it's been around for four decades) and the Terrace Restaurant is enlivened by colourful murals of Lake Como, well-dressed tables and flowers. Andy Foster is well established in the kitchen, and continues to pursue a mature modern British style which still finds an appreciative local audience. Expect well-judged dishes such as Anglesey scallops with slow-cooked belly pork, apples and crackling, and pot-roast guinea fowl breast with shallots, bacon, mushrooms, Parisienne potatoes and Burgundy jus. Finish with honey mousse wrapped in brandy-snap, pears and ice cream. The well-researched wine list starts at £16.50.
Chef/s: Andrew Foster. Open: all week L 12 to 2 (1.45 Sun), D 6.30 to 9.30 (9 Sun). Meals: alc (main courses £17 to £25). Set L and early set D £16.95 (2 courses) to £20. Sun L £18.95. Service: not inc. Details: 65 seats. 18 seats outside. Separate bar. Music. Car parking. Children over 5 yrs only. Families can have full dinner in coffee lounge area.

▌Llanrwst

ALSO RECOMMENDED
▲ Y Tanerdy

Willow Street, Llanrwst, LL26 0ES
Tel no: (01492) 641655
www.ytanerdy.net
Modern British £5 OFF

Gerwyn Williams is a local lad who worked at Odette's in London before opening this informal first-floor restaurant overlooking the river Conwy. Start with seared scallops with chickpea purée, fennel salad, chorizo and picked leaves (£6.75) before loin of local lamb and lamb faggot, with pea purée, in a light broth, plus fondant potato and lamb jus (£17.95). Finish with coconut pannacotta with pineapple. The short wine list starts at £13.95. Open Thur to Sat D, also Sun L, light meals served during the day Wed to Sat.

▌Penmaenpool
Penmaenuchaf Hall
Oak-panelled opulence and modern menus
Penmaenpool, LL40 1YB
Tel no: (01341) 422129
www.penhall.co.uk
Modern British | £43
Cooking score: 2

Sheltering in the foothills of Cader Idris, Penmaenuchaf Hall is a Victorian house of oak-panelled opulence, impeccably renovated to be both full of character and extremely stylish. The kitchen produces a well-wrought version of modern British cooking. Parmesan and asparagus tart with hollandaise sauce is a typically plain-speaking starter or you might prefer belly pork with steamed broccoli, chilli and lime caramel syrup. To follow, local cod is teamed with ratatouille vegetables and a spicy tomato sauce, while desserts can be as simple as apple and pear clafoutis with cinnamon ice cream. An exemplary wine list uncoils generously over the globe, taking in regional Italian specialities and mouthwatering names from the USA and Australia as well as plenty of classic claret; prices from £19.95.
Chef/s: Justin Pilkington. **Open:** all week L 12 to 2, D 7 to 9.30 (9 Sun). **Meals:** alc (main courses £25 to £28). Set L £16.50 (2 courses) to £18.50. Set D £42.50. Sun L £18.75. **Service:** not inc. **Details:** 32 seats. 16 seats outside. Separate bar. Wheelchair access. Music. Car parking. Children over 6 yrs only.

⫴ Visit us Online
To find out more about
The Good Food Guide, please visit
www.thegoodfoodguide.co.uk

▌Penmynydd
ALSO RECOMMENDED
▲ Neuadd Lwyd Country House
Penmynydd, LL61 5BX
Tel no: (01248) 715005
www.neuaddlwyd.co.uk
Modern British

Beautiful views of Snowdonia from the dining room delight guests at this handsome country rectory turned restaurant-with-rooms on Anglesey. Chef Susannah Woods champions Anglesey produce and has a deft touch with it. The no-choice, four-course daily menu (£42) is attractively presented and might include summer herb risotto with feta and courgette, sea bass with new potatoes and broad beans, then chocolate mousse with Chantilly cream, followed by good Welsh farmhouse cheeses. Wines from £14.95. Open Thur to Sat D only.

▌Pwllheli
Plas Bodegroes
Landmark hotel with impressive food
Nefyn Road, Pwllheli, LL53 5TH
Tel no: (01758) 612363
www.bodegroes.co.uk
Modern British | £45
Cooking score: 5

Famed for its location on the Llyn Peninsula, this wonderfully secluded Georgian manor house has become a landmark hotel in the dutiful hands of Chris and Gunna Chown, who are now into their third decade as custodians. Avenues of beech trees, flower-strewn woodland paths and an amazing art collection may distract the eye, but the main focus is on the food. Chris was serving salmon sashimi with beetroot pickle back in 1986, but since then his cooking has become more conventional as he applies impeccable technique and years of experience to thoughtfully sourced produce: a routine teaming of seared scallops and cauliflower purée with crispy Carmarthen ham say, or a well-reported starter of crispy belly pork with a black pudding Scotch egg and Puy lentil dressing. Char-grilled Welsh Black beef and roast loin of mountain lamb have also elicited rave reviews (the latter served with devilled kidney, confit rib and mint jus), while fish fans with a taste for the old ways might be drawn to grilled fillet of turbot with smoked haddock mash and parsley sauce. Desserts generally feature a seasonal fruit tart with a matching 'ripple' ice cream (the damson version has been endorsed), and it's worth concluding with a savoury flourish in the shape of Welsh rarebit on walnut toast. Treasures from French regional vineyards loom large on the authoritative wine list, although New World contenders also have their say. Prices start at £18, and there's a brilliant collection of around 100 half-bottles, plus 20 selections by the glass.

Chef/s: Chris Chown. **Open:** Sun L 12 to 2, Tue to Sat D 7 to 9. **Closed:** Mon, 30 Nov to 1 Mar. **Meals:** Set D £45. Sun L £22.50. **Service:** not inc. **Details:** 40 seats. Separate bar. No music. Wheelchair access. Car parking.

▌Talsarnau

Maes-y-Neuadd
Medieval manor with own-grown produce
Talsarnau, LL47 6YA
Tel no: (01766) 780200
www.neuadd.com
Modern European | £35
Cooking score: 3

£5 OFF 🍴

This impressive mansion in a wild location looms into view after driving up a narrow winding lane. Dating from the fourteenth century, it has been added to over the centuries. Vegetables, fruits and herbs come from the walled garden. The five-course dinner includes amuse-bouche, a starter such as salmon tartare with citrus yoghurt and garden greens, followed by a fish course (perhaps fishcake with sautéed leek and lobster cream). The main course might be loin of

venison with root vegetables, braised shallots, lentil casserole and chocolate jus, and the 'Grand Finale' brings a Welsh cheeseboard and three different desserts. The winelist now includes German vintages, and bottles chosen by the proprietors from New Zealand vineyards, plus new dessert wines. Prices from £16.95.

Chef/s: John Owen Jones. **Open:** all week L 12 to 1.30, D 7 to 8.45. **Meals:** alc L (main courses £10 to £15). Set D £30 (2 courses) to £35. Sun L £17.95. **Service:** not inc. **Details:** 65 seats. 20 seats outside. Separate bar. Wheelchair access. Car parking. Separate family dining room.

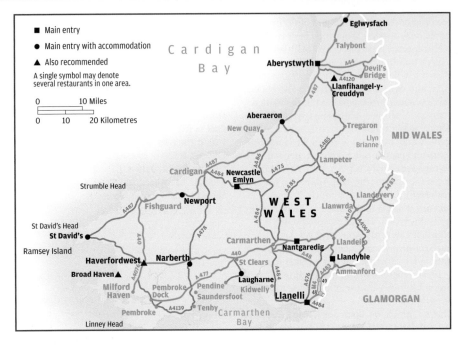

Aberaeron

Harbourmaster

Sleek harbourside hotel
Pen Cei, Aberaeron, SA46 OBT
Tel no: (01545) 570755
www.harbour-master.com
Modern British | £30
Cooking score: 2

It's more than a decade since Glyn and Menna Heulyn bravely took on this early nineteenth-century harbourmaster's residence. Set in a cracking position on the water's edge, the hotel offers décor that is elegant but not stiff and a crowd-pleasing repertoire of dishes. In the bar expect a mix of pizzas and upmarket pub grub (haddock and chips, steaks, chicken Caesar salad), while dinner in the restaurant has a more modern edge, say Cardigan Bay crab cake with tamarind ketchup, mint and coriander salad, and Welsh venison loin with roasted celeriac, apple and Madeira purée, toasted walnuts and port jus. House wine is £14.50.

Chef/s: Kelly Thomas. **Open:** all week L 12 to 2.30, D 6.30 to 9. **Closed:** 25 Dec. **Meals:** alc (main courses £11 to £25). Set D £25 (2 courses) to £30. Sun L £16 (2 courses) to £21. **Service:** not inc. **Details:** 95 seats. 15 seats outside. Separate bar. No music. Wheelchair access. Car parking.

ALSO RECOMMENDED

▲ Ty Mawr Mansion

Cilcennin, Aberaeron, SA48 8DB
Tel no: (01570) 470033
www.tymawrmansion.co.uk
Modern British £5 OFF

'Great location . . . little hidden gem' is how one traveller summed up the special appeal of the McAlpines' Georgian mansion deep in the Aeron Valley. He also praised the 'great service and food'. Dinner is the main event; the kitchen turns its hand to Cardigan Bay scallops with cauliflower risotto, chorizo and tempura caperberries (£9.95) and Welsh Black beef sirloin with dauphinois potatoes, smoked hickory onion purée, red wine jelly and horseradish jus (£24.95). Wines from £16.95. Mon to Sat D only. Accommodation.

Aberystwyth
Ultracomida
Delicious deli dining
31 Pier Street, Aberystwyth, SY23 2LN
Tel no: (01970) 630686
www.ultracomida.co.uk
Spanish | £20
Cooking score: 2

V

Ogling the stock at Ultracomida is as much a joy as sampling the array of tapas on offer at the cramped, bare tables. The well-endowed deli, based around produce from Spain, France and Wales, drives the kitchen, so expect to find plates of acorn-fed jamón Ibérico, French saucisson and Glamorgan sausages (made with Welsh farmhouse cheeses) served alongside albondigas (Spanish meatballs in a rich tomato sauce), paella, and Ceredigion Bay dressed crab with salad and aïoli. A scoop of Welsh ice cream with Pedro Ximénez sherry sums it all up deliciously. Wines from £11.75. Ultracomida has a branch in Narberth (see entry).
Chef/s: Aled Jones. **Open:** all week L 10 to 4.30 (3.30 Sun), Mon to Sat D 5 to 9. **Closed:** Dec 25. **Meals:** alc (tapas from £5 to £10). Set L £11 (2 courses) to £13. Tapas menu £19.50 (6 courses). **Service:** not inc. **Details:** 32 seats. Wheelchair access. Music. Car parking.

ALSO RECOMMENDED
▲ Treehouse
14 Baker Street, Aberystwyth, SY23 2BJ
Tel no: (01970) 615791
www.treehousewales.co.uk
Global £5

The menu at this former pub lets quality organic ingredients and largely vegetarian or vegan dishes speak for themselves. The

upstairs dining room (the ground floor is a well-stocked organic food shop) opens from breakfast to afternoon tea. Lunch delivers 'honest and genuine' dishes, say carrot, beetroot and red lentil soup (£3.75), Angus beef and kalamata olive koftas or Jerusalem artichoke dauphinois with a creamy Perl Las cheese sauce (£7.10) and apple and raspberry crumble. Wines from £9.95. Open all day Mon to Sat.

Broad Haven
ALSO RECOMMENDED
▲ The Druidstone
Broad Haven, SA62 3NE
Tel no: (01437) 781221
www.druidstone.co.uk
Global

A veteran of Pembrokeshire's holiday scene for four decades, the Bell family's quirky boho hotel is renowned for its idyllic views over St Brides Bay, its cottage accommodation, drama workshops, kids' junketings, art exhibitions and cheeky global food. On offer might be spiced baked pineapple (£6.50), pinto bean and vegetable lasagne, Medieval baked chicken (£10.50), Iranian spinach and potato tortillas, cottage pie, slow-roast leg of Welsh lamb and desserts from banoffi pie to sticky toffee pudding. House wine £11.80. Open all week.

Eglwysfach
Ynyshir Hall
Cooking with real potential
Eglwysfach, SY20 8TA
Tel no: (01654) 781209
www.ynyshirhall.co.uk
Modern European | £73
Cooking score: 4

£5 OFF

This lovely old house sits in sweeping grounds on the edge of an RSPB reserve. Joan and Rob Reen established the hotel's reputation before selling to the von Essen group. Joan remained in charge, and bought the hotel back on von

Essen's demise. The look is much as before, apart from some fresh colour schemes, but there's been a change of chef. Paul Croasdale shows real potential, creating menus that are full of interest and invention. An amuse of potted Morecambe Bay shrimps with lobster mousse impressed at inspection, as did a starter of hay-smoked asparagus with a crispy egg, wild duck ham and morels. Balanced flavours and interesting textures were repeated in a main course of thyme roasted fillet of line-caught Borth bass with spring-vegetable minestrone and lobster. A take on Eton mess (raspberry marshmallows, caramel coated raspberries, dabs of lemon curd) made a successful dessert. The thorough and interesting wine list opens at £23.
Chef/s: Paul Croasdale. **Open:** all week L 12.30 to 2, D 7 to 9. **Meals:** alc (main courses £13 to £19). Set L £25 (2 courses) to £29.50. Set D £72.50 (5 courses). Tasting menu £90 (8 courses). **Service:** not inc. **Details:** 28 seats. 12 seats outside. Separate bar. Wheelchair access. Music. Car parking. Children under 9 yrs allowed at D by arrangement.

Haverfordwest

ALSO RECOMMENDED
▲ Black Sheep
Shire Hall, High Street, Haverfordwest, SA61 2BN
Tel no: (01437) 767017
www.blacksheeprestaurant.co.uk
Modern British £5 OFF

Originally two separate restaurants with the same owners, the Black Sheep recently absorbed the neighbouring Mambo Italiano to offer a menu that combines the Black Sheep's hearty traditional cooking with pizza and pasta dishes. Italian-style fishcakes (£6) has a foot in both camps, while chicken stuffed with leek and bacon with a layered potato cake and thyme butter (£13.50) is typical of the Black Sheep's homely fare. Finish with cherry and white chocolate cheesecake (£5). Wines from £14. Closed Sun. As we went to press a possible change of location was in the offing.

Johnston

READERS RECOMMEND
Silverdale Inn & Lodge
Modern European
Johnston, SA62 3NZ
Tel no: (01437) 890943
www.silverdaleinn.co.uk
'Overall a great find. Well-cooked locally sourced food, friendly staff in a nice setting, and good value for money.'

Laugharne
The Cors
Romantic restaurant-with-rooms
Newbridge Road, Laugharne, SA33 4SH
Tel no: (01994) 427219
www.thecors.co.uk
Modern British | £36
Cooking score: 3
£5 OFF

Idiosyncratic and highly romantic, Nick Priestland's restaurant-with-rooms occupies a rambling Victorian villa surrounded by a luxuriant fairy glade of a garden. The house is full of boho arty flourishes and curios, with a grotto-like dining room at the centre of things. Nick divides his time between the garden and the kitchen, and feeds his guests well from a menu of indulgent, skilfully crafted dishes based on top-notch ingredients. Smoked haddock crème brûlée is a slightly surprising starter, but it's back to more familiar patriotic themes for rosemary and garlic-crusted rack of lamb (from Barhedyn Farm, Aberhosan), locally reared Welsh Black beef (courtesy of Mr James of Penrhyncoch) or char-grilled smoked salmon with Puy lentils, roasted cherry tomatoes and salsa verde. To finish, keep it simple with lemon tart. Twenty wines start at £14.95.
Chef/s: Nick Priestland. **Open:** Thur to Sat D only 7 (1 sitting). **Closed:** Sun to Wed, 25 Dec, first 2 weeks Nov. **Meals:** alc (main courses £15 to £26). Set D £30 (2 courses) to £36. **Service:** not inc. **Details:** 28

seats. 12 seats outside. Separate bar. Wheelchair access. Music. Car parking. Children over 12 yrs only.

Llandybie

Valans

Good-looking neighbourhood eatery
29 High Street, Llandybie, SA18 3HX
Tel no: (01269) 851288
www.valans.co.uk
Modern European | £31
Cooking score: 2

As much a feature of local life as the nearby village church, Dave and Remy Vale's neighbourhood restaurant cuts quite a dash, with its striking red and black chairs, crisp napery and smart interiors. The kitchen flaunts its specialist suppliers, offering line-caught sea bass landed by the boat *Popso* and salt marsh lamb from Weobley Castle Farm, as well as dishes such as medallions of pork in a sauce of honey and Welsh cider with caramelised apples and white pudding. Easy-going, bistro-style lunches also hit the spot, judging by reports of spiced chicken meatballs, fishcakes and gooey, oozing hot chocolate pudding. House wine is £13.85.
Chef/s: Dave Vale. **Open:** Tue to Sat L 12 to 3, D 7 to 11. **Closed:** Sun, Mon. **Meals:** alc (main courses £13 to £23). Set L and D £10.95 (2 courses) to £15.50. Set D (Sat only) £18.50 (2 courses) to £21.95. **Service:** not inc. **Details:** 35 seats. Wheelchair access. Music.

Llanelli

NEW ENTRY

Sosban

Slick new dockside contender
North Dock, Llanelli, SA15 2LF
Tel no: (01554) 270020
www.sosbanrestaurant.com
Modern British | £35
Cooking score: 3

A space so vast could feel sterile, but the converted pumphouse glitters warmly, its high ceiling adorned with lights that resemble falling autumn leaves. The lounge bar is all slate floors and chesterfields, while the cathedral-like dining area has well-spaced tables, exposed stone walls and a happy buzz from the diners. Hunks of homemade focaccia set the scene for an uncluttered, European style of cooking. A starter of crab lasagne oozed buttery warmth, while a main course of Towy sewin (sea trout) came very lightly cooked on a nicely executed pea risotto, with a crunchy sprinkling of pea shoot salad. Desserts are a strength here – look out for the tarte Tatin with vanilla ice cream. An international wine list kicks off at £15.
Chef/s: Sian Rees. **Open:** all week L 12 to 2.45, Mon to Sat D 6 to 9.45. **Meals:** alc (main courses £12 to £21). Set L and D £15 (2 courses) to £18. Sun L £23.50. **Service:** not inc. **Details:** 90 seats. 90 seats outside. Wheelchair access. Music. Car parking.

Llanfihangel-y-Creuddyn

ALSO RECOMMENDED
▲ Y Ffarmers

Llanfihangel-y-Creuddyn, SY23 4LA
Tel no: (01974) 261275
www.yffarmers.co.uk
Modern British £5 OFF

A thoroughly updated village pub, Y Ffarmers is as much a drop-in drinking establishment as a destination local restaurant. Expect a regularly changing, market-led menu majoring in Welsh produce, and surprisingly good cooking, from smoked mackerel and horseradish fishcake with beetroot salsa (£5) to chicken breast and Penlan treacle bacon in red wine (£13.50). There are Welsh cheeses or the likes of hot chocolate fondant with vanilla ice cream to finish. Wines from £13.50. No food Sun D, Mon, and Tue L.

¡¡• Also Recommended
Also recommended entries are not scored but we think they are worth a visit.

▮▮● VEG OUT

Forget the homogeneous sludge that once passed for the dreaded vegetarian option, today's chefs are working harder than ever to create meat-free dishes that will delight even the most committed carnivore.

Andrew Dargue at vegetarian restaurant **Vanilla Black**, based in Farringdon, believes around 50 per cent of his customers are meat eaters. He mimics the structure of meat or fish dishes by creating definition on the plate so, for example, seared seaweed and pickled potatoes are offset by soda bread sauce and wilted turnip tops.

At Yotam Ottolenghi's Soho restaurant **Nopi**, the humble carrot is elevated to star status: four heritage varieties are marinated in orange vinaigrette and served with chicory and black olive powder. For Simon Rogan at **L'Enclume** in Cartmel, the real skill lies in presenting dishes in such a way that the customer doesn't realise they comprise only vegetables. Landmark Brighton restaurant **Food for Friends** prides itself on its sophisticated veggie fare which fuses Middle Eastern, North African and Mediterranean influences.

▮ Nantgaredig

★ READERS' RESTAURANT OF THE YEAR ★
WALES

Y Polyn

Superb local food with flair
Capel Dewi, Nantgaredig, SA32 7LH
Tel no: (01267) 290000
www.ypolynrestaurant.co.uk
Modern British | £30
Cooking score: 3

Gutsy, down-to-earth dining would be reason enough to visit Y Polyn, but it succeeds in all areas, from the warm, relaxed welcome to the rustic, slightly arty interior and, of course, the kitchen, which serves up superb local ingredients with minimal fuss and a flair for flavour. Take a starter of Carmarthen ham with coarse and creamy celeriac rémoulade for example, or a sprightly salad of shaved raw asparagus with rocket, Parmesan and shallot vinaigrette. A generous piece of Towy sewin (sea trout), pan-fried and served with a perfect beurre blanc made a satisfying main course, and accompanying vegetables (ratatouille, cauliflower gratin, creamy mash) were nostalgic and comforting. A gargantuan rhubarb and ginger crumble knickerbocker glory made a shamelessly indulgent dessert. The international wine list opens at £14.
Chef/s: Susan Manson and Alix Alliston. **Open:** Tue to Sun L 12 to 2 (2.30 Sat and Sun), Tue to Sat D 7 to 9 (6.30 to 9.30 Fri and Sat). **Closed:** Mon. **Meals:** alc (main courses £11 to £17). Set L £12 (2 courses) to £14.50. Set D £24 (2 courses) to £30. Sun L £18.50 (2 courses) to £23.50. **Service:** not inc. **Details:** 60 seats. 12 seats outside. Separate bar. Wheelchair access. Music. Car parking.

Narberth

The Grove

Assured cooking in an idyllic setting
Molleston, Narberth, SA67 8BX
Tel no: (01834) 860915
www.thegrove-narberth.co.uk
Modern European | £45
Cooking score: 5

Coddled in a Pembrokeshire valley, with views of the Preseli mountains beyond, this boutique hotel occupies a highly desirable, white-painted residence flanked by trim lawns, flower borders and meadows. Warm intimacy prevails in the traditional dining room, where guests can savour Duncan Barham's assured and highly complex take on contemporary cuisine – an approach that depends on top-drawer local produce, foraged snippets and seasonal pickings from the Grove's bountiful kitchen garden. Arrive in autumn and you might be treated to 'mellow fruitfulness' in the shape of hazelnut-crusted loin of Brecon venison with braised shin dumpling, celeriac, pear and a slug of Brecon gin jus, or butter-roasted skate with honey and clove-spiked pig's cheek, swede fondant and sprouting broccoli. Readers have also been blown away by superb poached Caldey Island lobster, impeccably cooked Preseli Bluestone lamb and plates of elaborately embellished, 'bone-in' Welsh beef. Subtle, highly worked artistry is also the hallmark of cute, boozy desserts such as William pear steeped in homemade sloe gin, accompanied by pain perdu and set ginger cream. Service is intelligent and helpful – particularly when it comes to the mightily impressive, 200-bin wine list. Bottles from Wales, eastern Europe and the Middle East now compete with high-fliers from France and elsewhere, and prices (from £18) are extremely competitive.
Chef/s: Duncan Barham. **Open:** all week L 12 to 2.30, D 6 to 9.30. **Meals:** Set L £15 (2 courses) to £19. Set D £35 (2 courses) to £45. Sun L £25. **Service:** not inc. **Details:** 70 seats. 30 seats outside. Separate bar. Music. Car parking.

Ultracomida

Unpretentious tapas and great charcuterie
7 High Street, Narberth, SA67 7AR
Tel no: (01834) 861491
www.ultracomida.co.uk
Spanish | £20
Cooking score: 2

£30

A sister to Aberystwyth's Ultracomida (see entry), this deli-cum-tapas bar sits in the middle of Narberth's High Street, opposite the Queen's Hall. First-timers may discover that half the fun of visiting lies in working their way through the deli's feast of sights and smells to reach the unpretentious tapas bar with its communal seating. Indeed, Ultracomida's well-endowed larder drives the kitchen, supplying all manner of charcuterie (Serrano ham, chorizo, French saucisson) and a changing cheeseboard selection, as well as straightforward tapas like patatas bravas and albondigas (meatballs). 'Splendid' set lunches, weekend evening deals and daily breakfasts (not Sun) complete the package. Spanish wines from £11.75.
Chef/s: Padraig Nallen. **Open:** Mon to Sat 10 to 4.30, Fri and Sat D 7 to 9. **Closed:** Sun, Dec 25. **Meals:** alc (main courses £7 to £10). Set L £11 (2 courses) to £13. Tapas menu £19.50 (6 courses). **Service:** not inc. **Details:** 34 seats. Wheelchair access. Music.

Newcastle Emlyn

Ludo's at The Coopers

Seasonal Welsh food with a French spin
Station Road, Newcastle Emlyn, SA38 9BX
Tel no: (01239) 710588
Modern French | £25
Cooking score: 3

£30

A converted pub on the outskirts of a bustling market town, the Coopers Arms is home to Ludovic Dieumegard and Lowri Jones's stripped-down restaurant operation. The bare floors and stone walls reflect the straightforward intention – to offer seasonal modern Welsh food, drawing a little on Ludo's Breton background. Salmon cheesecake with pickled beetroot and Melba toast gets things started, or there may be fried gnocchi with black pudding, cockles and spring onion. Mains might see sea bream turn up with chorizo and spinach linguine and herb vinaigrette, while a spin on duck à l'orange finds new soulmates for the old-timer in the shapes of carrot and cardamom purée and pilau rice. Bara brith tart with vanilla ice cream is a signature finisher. The little wine list starts at £13.95.

Chef/s: Ludovic Dieumegard. **Open:** Wed to Sun L 12 to 2, D 6 to 9. **Closed:** Mon, Tue, first 2 weeks Jan. **Meals:** alc (main courses £6 to £21). Set L £11.50 (2 courses) to £12.50. **Service:** 10% for parties of 7 or more. **Details:** 42 seats. Separate bar. Wheelchair access. Music. Car parking. No children at D.

▌Newport

Cnapan

Home-from-home with excellent ingredients
East Street, Newport, SA42 0SY
Tel no: (01239) 820575
www.cnapan.co.uk
Modern British | £32
Cooking score: 2
£5 OFF 🍽 V

Occupying a Grade II-listed Georgian house in the centre of Newport, Cnapan is a long-running restaurant-with-rooms, noted for its relaxed, home-from-home atmosphere. Dinner starts with drinks in the bar before moving through to the dining room. The cooking makes use of excellent local ingredients and pulls together a variety of influences, from Mediterranean (as in a starter of vegetable tapas) to classic – maybe honeyed duck confit with bitter orange sauce and red onion marmalade. Finish with creamy vanilla pod rice pudding with cinnamon spiced pear. The international wine list opens at £14.50.

Chef/s: Judith Cooper. **Open:** Wed to Mon D only 6.30 to 9.30. **Closed:** Tue, mid Dec to mid Mar. **Meals:** Set D £26 (2 courses) to £32. **Service:** not inc. **Details:** 35 seats. Separate bar. Music. Car parking.

▌St David's

Cwtch

Hearty, wholesome local food
22 High Street, St David's, SA62 6SD
Tel no: (01437) 720491
www.cwtchrestaurant.co.uk
Modern British | £29
Cooking score: 3
£5 OFF 🍽 £30

An uncluttered, rough-hewn interior (wood floors, heavy beams, whitewashed stone walls) sets the scene here for a hearty and deceptively simple style of cooking, with local ingredients very much to the fore. At lunch expect the likes of wholesome cream of chestnut mushroom soup with big chunks of granary bread and Parmesan croûtons, followed by rustic ham hock and pistachio terrine with piccalilli and salad. The same dish might double as an evening starter, ahead of fillet of sea bass with Penclawdd laverbread and salsa verde. For dessert, look out for the silky crème brûlée with melt-in-the-mouth shortbread, or maybe lemon posset with blood orange sorbet and flapjack. A simple international wine list kicks off at £17; alternatives include Pimm's and cocktails.

Chef/s: Andy Holcroft. **Open:** all week L 12 to 2.30, D 6 to 9.30. **Closed:** Sun and Mon (1 Nov to 31 Mar). **Meals:** alc (main courses £14 to £20). **Service:** not inc. **Details:** 50 seats. Wheelchair access. Music.

CHANNEL ISLANDS

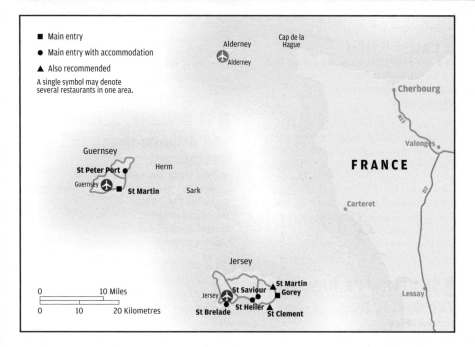

▌ Gorey, Jersey

Sumas

The best of land and sea
Gorey Hill, St Martin, Gorey, Jersey, JE3 6ET
Tel no: (01534) 853291
www.sumasrestaurant.com
Modern European | £34
Cooking score: 5

£5
OFF

Sumas is genteel yet informal, laid-back yet on-the-ball, a place where old ladies rub shoulders with suits. A small terrace gives on to the palm-fronded harbour, with its bobbing boats; above looms the imposing form of Mount Orgueil Castle. This stark contrast of land and sea is admirably reflected in Daniel Ward's menu, where loin of venison and various cuts of Aberdeen Angus appear alongside Jersey's rich marine harvest, perhaps line-caught brill with scallops, or sea bass with crab croquettes and Savoy cabbage. The cooking is measured and doesn't puff itself up, but dishes are never ordinary or ill-conceived

– witness beef salad, the meat sweet and succulent, offset by perfect locally grown cherry tomatoes and deep-fried beetroot and parsnip, or textbook ginger-braised belly pork and fondant potato. The mini-pudding plate (including fig pie, perfectly judged lemon tart with raspberry crisps, and an apple sorbet that 'summoned the very essence of the fruit') hit just the right notes. The wine list, though global, is biased towards France, with house selections from £16.
Chef/s: Daniel Ward. **Open:** all week L 12 to 2.30 (4.30 Sun), Mon to Sat D 6 to 9.30. **Closed:** 21 Dec to mid Jan. **Meals:** alc (main courses £15 to £25). Set L and D £17.50 (2 courses) to £20. Sun L £18.50 (2 courses) to £22.50. **Service:** not inc. **Details:** 40 seats. 16 seats outside. Music.

 Visit us Online
To find out more about *The Good Food Guide*, please visit www.thegoodfoodguide.co.uk

ALSO RECOMMENDED

▲ Castle Green

La Route de la Côte, Gorey, Jersey, JE3 6DR
Tel no: (01534) 840218
www.castlegreenjersey.co.uk
Modern British

You can enjoy the fabulous views at this modern pub secure in the knowledge that what you order from the blackboard will be worthwhile. Local oysters are a given (you can see the beds in the bay); there's also a generous tapas-style platter ('a meal in itself') for £12.50 that includes a fine ham hock terrine with piccalilli, Ibérco ham with rocket, and a lustrous crab hummus. Elsewhere, scallop and crab risotto in a shellfish bisque (£14.95) scores. Wines from £14. Open all week.

▌St Brelade's Bay, Jersey

The Oyster Box

Seafood haven
St Brelade's Bay, Jersey, JE3 8EF
Tel no: (01534) 743311
www.oysterbox.co.uk
Seafood | £40
Cooking score: 3

An enviable beachside location and breezy good looks are not the only charms of The Oyster Box. The majority of the fish and seafood that dominates the menu is very local, and handled with care to produce likeable modern European dishes. To start, try sautéed scallops with smoked pancetta or confit of duck with ballottine of foie gras and beetroot mayo. Follow either with one of the chunkier mains (fish and chips, steak and chips) or a perfectly executed shellfish risotto with lobster bisque, squid and firm Dover sole. Dessert might be a dark chocolate, prune and Armagnac feuilletine tart or, if the holiday spirit needs further evocation, piña colada parfait with lime marshmallow and banana and passion-fruit sorbet. House wine is from £15.

Chef/s: Patrick Tweedie. **Open:** Tue to Sun L 12 to 2.30 (3 Sun), all week D 6 to 9 (9.30 Fri and Sat). **Closed:** 25 and 26 Dec. **Meals:** alc (main courses £10 to £42). **Service:** not inc. **Details:** 120 seats. 80 seats outside. Separate bar. Wheelchair access. Music.

▌St Brelade, Jersey

The Atlantic Hotel, Ocean Restaurant

Holiday views and serious food
Le Mont de la Pulente, St Brelade, Jersey, JE3 8HE
Tel no: (01534) 744101
www.theatlantichotel.com
Modern British | £65
Cooking score: 4

🍴 V

Outside there's a holiday landscape of palm trees and blue water, but there are no lighthearted frolics in the kitchen at the Atlantic Hotel. Mark Jordan is serious about the food served in the Ocean Restaurant's white-shuttered dining room, and so are the front-of-house staff. There's a legion of them, attentive and pinafored, proffering, perhaps, an amuse-bouche of intensely rooty celeriac velouté. To start, try a perfectly al dente risotto of Jersey crab, delicately spiced with curry oil in a shellfish reduction. Other dishes on a wide-ranging menu might include thyme-roasted sea bass with wild mushroom jus, or Jersey beef done three ways. To finish, there's a 'superlative' crème brûlée offset by the tangy cut of a raspberry sorbet. The wine list, with a strong bias towards France, is thicker than the Jersey phone book. House wines start at £25, and there are 19 served by the glass.

Chef/s: Mark Jordan. **Open:** all week L 12.30 to 2.30, D 6.30 to 10. **Closed:** 2 Jan to 3 Feb. **Meals:** Set L £20 (2 courses) to £25. Table d'hôte £55. Set D £65. Sun L £30. Tasting menu £75. **Service:** not inc. **Details:** 60 seats. Separate bar. Music. Car parking.

ALSO RECOMMENDED
▲ Wayside Café
Le Mont Sohier, St Brelade, Jersey, JE3 8EA
Tel no: (01534) 743915
Global

With a large alfresco dining area overlooking St Brelade's vast expanse of sand, the refurbished Wayside seems to be pulling in the beach crowd in ever-larger numbers. The menu takes a something-for-everyone approach; yummy-looking home-baked cakes and pastries are perfect with morning coffee, then lunch brings fragrant Thai and seafood soups (£5.95) and a busy blackboard whose frequent changes wait for time nor tide. Try, say, scallops on Spanish-style risotto with garlic butter and rocket (£14.50). House wine from £11.95. Closed Mon L and Wed D.

▮ St Clement, Jersey
ALSO RECOMMENDED
▲ Green Island Restaurant
Green Island, St Clement, Jersey, JE2 6LS
Tel no: (01534) 857787
www.greenisland.je
Seafood

Slap-bang at the end of the slipway above Green Island's sandy bay, you'll find this stylish dining room – though the temptation is to eat al fresco whatever the weather. The theme is Mediterranean and 'there's clearly a lot of passion at work'. Expect Greek vine leaves stuffed with lamb kofta, tzatziki and hummus (£9.50), followed, perhaps, by a tarragon-crusted rack of lamb, plus shank, with boulangère potatoes, roasted salsify and red wine and shallot purée (£26.95). House wines £16.25. Closed Sun and Mon.

▮ St Helier, Jersey
★ TOP 50 ★
Bohemia
Innovation and great flavour
The Club Hotel & Spa, Green Street, St Helier, Jersey, JE2 4UH
Tel no: (01534) 880588
www.bohemiajersey.com
Modern European | £55
Cooking score: 6
🛏 V

An 'exciting whiff of originality' pervades Shaun Rankin's confident spa hotel restaurant, where a teak-and-leather dining room feels surprisingly unstuffy, and a plethora of menus allows room for financial manoeuvre. A dish eliciting regular praise (and demonstrating the kitchen's comfort with a variety of styles) is roast curry-salted Jersey scallops with coconut dhal, onion bhajia, coriander and apple salad, while innovation comes knocking courtesy of Anjou pigeon breast with Roquefort creamed rice, Roquefort beignet and pressed pear, with a rich jus spiked with star anise. An original take on surf and turf comes in the form of slow-cooked, perfectly caramelised ox cheek, with cod as a beignet, popcorn and purée. Dessert might be the celebrated house treacle tart or a prune and Armagnac pannacotta coupled with chocolate tart. Shaun Rankin's long service – he's been here nine years – is an advantage, though readers report momentary lapses in focus over the past year. Staff are solicitous without being overbearing, and wine service is a highlight. There's plenty by the glass and some great matches from a precise list. House wine starts at £18.
Chef/s: Shaun Rankin. **Open:** all week L 12 to 2.30, D 6.30 to 10. **Closed:** 25 to 31 Dec. **Meals:** alc (main courses £30 to £34). Set L £22.50 (2 courses) to £27.50. Set D £46 (2 courses) to £55. Sun L £35. **Service:** 10%. **Details:** 60 seats. Separate bar. Wheelchair access. Music. Car parking.

NEW ENTRY

Tassili

Headline restaurant at a luxury spa hotel
Grand Jersey, 9 Esplanade, St Helier, Jersey,
JE2 3QA
Tel no: (01534) 722301
www.grandjersey.com
Modern British | £49
Cooking score: 4

🛏 V

Overlooking St Aubin's Bay, just a short
sashay from the beach, is a modest exterior
concealing a *grand luxe* spa hotel with all the
amenities, including a headline restaurant in
the shape of Tassili. A light, faintly
anonymous room with pale peach napery
provides a neutral backdrop for Richard
Allen's pyrotechnically inventive cooking.
Marinated foie gras and smoked duck with 100
per cent-cocoa bitter chocolate, peanut butter,
pain d'épices and Pedro Ximénez vinegar jelly
is a bravura opener, as is the partnering of
confit pork belly and langoustine in shellfish
cappuccino, with purées of chorizo and squash
and a smattering of popcorn ('a much better
idea than it sounds'). Mains might offer
bracingly fresh turbot alongside spider crab in
mayonnaise, sauced with saffron-scented crab
essence. Desserts sustain the heroic
complexity, with the likes of excellent
pistachio and olive oil cake, served with an
orange macaroon and chocolate sorbet. A
commendable wine list features plenty of
quality producers (Luquet's Pouilly-Fuissé,
Chignard's Fleurie, Lageder, Ata Rangi,
Catena) as well as lots of choice below £30;
bottles open at £20.
Chef/s: Richard Allen. **Open:** Thur and Fri L 12 to 2,
Tue to Sat D 7 to 10. **Closed:** Mon, Sun, 25 Dec, first
2 weeks Jan. **Meals:** Set L £18.95. Set D £49. Tasting
menu £67 (5 courses) to £89. V tasting menu £57.
Service: not inc. **Details:** 24 seats. Separate bar.
Wheelchair access. Music. Car parking.

ALSO RECOMMENDED

▲ The Green Olive

1 Anley Street, St Helier, Jersey, JE2 3QE
Tel no: (01534) 728198
www.greenoliverestaurant.co.uk
Mediterranean £5 OFF

'Great food, great service, great ambience' just
about sums up Paul and Anna Le Brocq's
charming restaurant. Bread is straight from
the oven, while the menu deals in triple dips of
guacamole, tapenade and chickpea or scallops
with sweetcorn purée, apricot salsa and a hint
of pancetta (£8.95). Mains include gilthead
bream with flageolet, a zingy pesto and
cauliflower purée (£16.95) and there's lemon
posset, strawberry salsa and mint sorbet
(£5.95) for dessert. Wines from £16.95.
Closed Sat L, Sun and Mon.

▌St Martin, Guernsey

The Auberge

Clifftop dining with dramatic views
Jerbourg Road, St Martin, Guernsey, GY4 6BH
Tel no: (01481) 238485
www.theauberge.gg
Modern British | £30
Cooking score: 4

Perched in its eyrie on a Guernsey clifftop, the
Auberge has commanding views of the
neighbouring Channel Islands, as well as St
Peter Port below. On a summer evening, the
terrace and garden make one of the most
dramatic settings on the island, and the menu
of traditional and modern British dishes does
the rest. A serving of beef carpaccio is
sprinkled with chilli flakes, sea salt and ginger
as well as lemon and shallot vinaigrette, while
a suitably sea-themed main course might be
scallops and king prawns in garlic butter with
spring onion mash, smoked bacon and pesto.
Finish with pear poached in Champagne and
vanilla, served with thick local cream, or a
selection of local, French and Irish cheeses.
Wines start at £18 (£6.25 a glass).

Chef/s: Daniel Green. **Open:** all week L 12 to 2, Mon to Sat D 6.30 to 10. **Closed:** 23 Dec to 1 Feb. **Meals:** alc (main courses £13 to £30). Set L £14.95. Set D £18.95. Sun L £24.95. **Service:** not inc. **Details:** 70 seats. 25 seats outside. Separate bar. Wheelchair access. Music. Car parking.

St Martin, Jersey

ALSO RECOMMENDED
▲ Feast
Gorey Pier, St Martin, Jersey, JE3 6EW
Tel no: (01534) 611118
www.feast.je
Modern European

Stashed at the foot of the Mont Orgueil Castle on the edge of Gorey harbour, Feast offers a curiously rustic atmosphere, friendly staff and a hearty, no-nonsense approach. Starters include scallops with chorizo and red pepper hollandaise (£9), 'sensational' sticky pork ribs, and 'totally moreish' squid. Among mains, Argentine sirloin with garlic and parsley chimichurri sauce (£17.50) has been described as 'stunning, cooked to absolute perfection'. Wines from £14.50. Closed Mon.

St Peter Port, Guernsey

La Frégate
Stunning seascapes and complex cooking
Beauregard Lane, Les Cotils, St Peter Port, Guernsey, GY1 1UT
Tel no: (01481) 724624
www.lafregatehotel.com
Modern British | £37
Cooking score: 4

High above the narrow streets of St Peter Port – but easily accessed via its private gardens – this elegantly extended eighteenth-century manor house makes the most of its harbour views and fascinating glimpses of ancient Castle Cornet. Inside, the dining room's arched windows, fashionable floral arrangements and abstract artwork chime well with Neil Maginnis's highly detailed cooking. Local seafood and meat appear in equal measure, from lobster velouté (enriched with Guernsey cream, of course), lightly curried scallops with cauliflower purée or sea bass with Thai-spiced crabmeat, soy dressing and coriander butter to pistachio-crusted lamb fillet served with tomato and chickpea cassoulet, or saddle of venison accompanied by a horseradish rösti, parsnip purée and beetroot jus. Steak tartare and crêpes suzette are prepared at the table with much theatrical brio; otherwise finish with the signature coconut mousse – a complex composition involving a dark chocolate shell, banana and passion-fruit sorbet and a warm chocolate brownie. Wines from France dominate the unchallenging list, with prices from £18.
Chef/s: Neil Maginnis. **Open:** all week L 12 to 2, D 7 to 10. **Meals:** alc (main courses £16 to £25). Set L £23.50. Set D £33.50. Sun L £22.50. **Service:** not inc. **Details:** 70 seats. 25 seats outside. Separate bar. No music. Car parking.

ALSO RECOMMENDED
▲ Da Nello
46 Lower Pollet, St Peter Port, Guernsey, GY1 1WF
Tel no: (01481) 721552
www.danello.gg
Italian £5 OFF

'Hugely popular' and always on the money, Da Nello has been doing Guernsey proud for more than three decades – no wonder readers adore its warm feel, professional outlook, attention to detail and canny use of island produce (especially seafood). Linguine nero with scallops and vermouth (£11.95), and a dish of sea bass with mussels, tomatoes and white wine have been abundantly endorsed, while meat eaters look to the char-grill – perhaps rack of lamb or paillard of veal (£14.95). House wines from £15.95. Open all week.

Also Recommended
Also recommended entries are not scored but we think they are worth a visit.

St Peter, Jersey

Mark Jordan at the Beach
Modern British
La Plage, La Route de la Haule, St Peter, Jersey, JE3 7YD
Tel no: (01534) 780180
www.markjordanatthebeach.com
'Just what we were looking for: classic food, beautifully cooked.'

St Saviour, Jersey
Longueville Manor
A special place
St Saviour, Jersey, JE2 7WF
Tel no: (01534) 725501
www.longuevillemanor.com
Modern British | £58
Cooking score: 4

There is no doubt that this small, ancient manor, with its manicured lawns and cultivated woodlands, is a special place. A phalanx of discreet, well-groomed staff lurks in the nooks and crannies, surveying the scene from the poolside terrace to the cocktail bar. This solicitousness wafts its way through the airy, informal Garden Room to the darkly panelled sepulchral calm of the venerable dining room. Here the inspiration of chef Andrew Baird, who has long championed local and home-grown produce, is realised with brisk efficiency. Perhaps a bonbon of chancre crab, pine nuts, coriander and guacamole might combine with an assiette of local pork; or a duo of poached lobster with cream caviar and a main course of sea bass and grilled squid. A humble coq au vin proved a let-down for one reporter, but was compensated for by a dark chocolate praline parfait and a splendid cheeseboard. Wines, from a colossal list, start at £25.

Chef/s: Andrew Baird. **Open:** all week L 12 to 2, D 7 to 10. **Meals:** Set L £22.50 (2 courses) to £27.50. Set D £50 (2 courses) to £57.50. Sun L £35. Tasting menu £75. **Service:** not inc. **Details:** 90 seats. 35 seats outside. Separate bar. Music. Car parking.

Sark

Maison Pommier
French
Rue du Fort, Sark, GY10 1SF
Tel no: (01481) 832643
www.maisonpommier.com
'Superb French chef uses local ingredients so fresh that in the morning they were still growing or swimming.'

NORTHERN
IRELAND

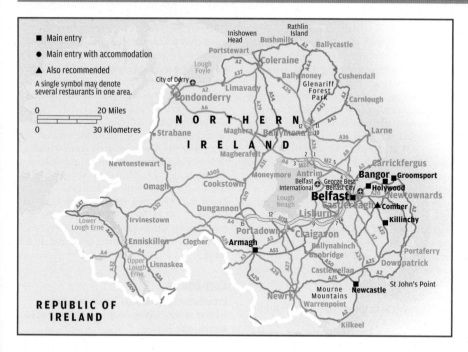

Legend:
- ■ Main entry
- ● Main entry with accommodation
- ▲ Also recommended

A single symbol may denote several restaurants in one area.

0 — 20 Miles
0 — 30 Kilometres

▌Armagh, Co Armagh

NEW ENTRY
Uluru Bistro
An Aussie-in-Armagh experience
16 Market Street, Armagh, Co Armagh, BT61 7BX
Tel no: (028) 3751 8051
www.ulurubistro.com
Australian | £28
Cooking score: 2

V

This casual Australian-owned bistro has built up a loyal following in Armagh city since it opened in 2005. The kitchen makes good use of a mix of local ingredients alongside a few exotic imports to deliver an Antipodean-in-Armagh experience. Local seafood is the star in dishes such as 'fisherman's basket' of beer-battered cod, scampi, prawns, and mini-fishcakes served with a lemon caper mayo. Elsewhere, a trademark main of kangaroo is a seared ribbon-cut served with a red wine sauce and kumera (sweet potato) chips. House wine is £13.50.

Chef/s: Dean Coppard. **Open:** Tue to Sat L 12 to 3, Tue to Sun D 5 to 8.30 (9.30 Fri and Sat). **Closed:** Mon, 25 and 26 Dec. **Meals:** alc (main courses £13 to £22). Early D £16.50 (2 courses). **Service:** not inc. **Details:** 34 seats. Separate bar. Wheelchair access. Music.

▌Bangor, Co Down

NEW ENTRY
The Boat House
Dutch harbourside gem
1a Seacliff Road, Bangor, Co Down, BT20 5HA
Tel no: (028) 9146 9253
www.theboathouseni.co.uk
Modern British | £38
Cooking score: 6

Housed in the Victorian harbourmaster's office overlooking Bangor Marina's boatyard, the Boat House is run by a pair of Dutch brothers; the ambitious cooking is overseen by Joery Castel and younger brother Jasper heads up the front-of-house. The boxy stone building's interior has been given a modern makeover

that, like Dr Who's Tardis, makes it feel roomier inside than seems possible. You climb the stone stairs to the entrance and, once inside, descend to the dining room, which, despite offering no clear view of the water, still charms. Menus take a sophisticated approach to Ulster ingredients, with seafood from the local loughs (Belfast and Strangford) and the Atlantic to the fore. The à la carte and tasting menus – an accompanying wine flight is available with the latter – are priced for special occasions. However, the set menu, available at lunch and dinner, offers a more affordable way in on a regular basis. Typically elaborate dishes such as pan-fried Carlingford Lough sea trout with hollandaise, potato pancakes, Italian summer truffle, braised courgette, pine nuts and golden raisin with North Sea brown shrimp are far too good to be left to the have-yachts. The thoughtful wine list starts at £16.50 a bottle (£4.50 a glass).
Chef/s: Joery Castel. **Open:** Wed to Sat L 12.30 to 2.30, D 5.30 to 9.30, Sun 1 to 8. **Closed:** Mon, Tue. **Meals:** alc (main courses £19 to £22). Set L £17.50 (2 courses) to £21.50. Set D £21 (2 courses) to £25. Tasting menu £55. **Service:** not inc. **Details:** 36 seats. 8 seats outside. Separate bar. Music. Car parking.

▌Belfast, Co Antrim

NEW ENTRY
The Bar & Grill at James Street South
Simple menu based around a Josper grill
21 James Street South, Belfast, Co Antrim, BT2 7GA
Tel no: (028) 9560 0700
www.belfastbargrill.co.uk
Modern British | £25
Cooking score: 3

£30

Opened in late 2011 as a casual counterpoint to Niall McKenna's James Street South (see entry), the Bar & Grill is sited in the previously derelict (a spell as an illegal nightclub notwithstanding) other half of the Victorian linen mill that the former has occupied since

2003. Upstairs there's a spanking new all-mod-cons private dining room and cookery school. Downstairs, in a stripped-back dining room that combines exposed brickwork with cool Irish Sea-blue wood-panelling and leather banquettes, the menu is built around the Josper grill. There's comfort and nostalgia in simply presented dishes such as crab on toast, macaroni cheese and knickerbocker glory. But the steaks, expertly cooked with a choice of eight different house-made sauces, are the main event. The smart, sharp wine list starts at £15 for a bottle (£4 a glass).
Chef/s: Carl Johannsen. **Open:** all week 12 to 9.30. **Closed:** 25 and 26 Dec, 1 Jan, 12 July. **Meals:** alc (main courses £10 to £22). **Service:** not inc. **Details:** 60 seats. Separate bar. Wheelchair access. Music.

Cayenne
Established globetrotter raises its game
7 Ascot House, Shaftesbury Square, Belfast, Co Antrim, BT2 7DB
Tel no: (028) 9033 1532
www.cayenne-restaurant.co.uk
Global | £30
Cooking score: 4
V

It could be argued that the downsizing of chef Paul Rankin's once extensive Belfast empire to just this restaurant, while unfortunate for him, is a selfish gain for Belfast diners, as he's now forced to focus his undeniable talents here. There are those who would say that the cooking at Cayenne is again reaching the heights that it did when it opened with a splash in 1999 on what had been the site of Rankin's original award-winning restaurant, Roscoff. The globetrotting menu makes use of prime local produce – particularly seafood – while veering from France (braised chicken leg stuffed with foie gras) via the Mediterranean (seafood linguini with chilli gremolata and white wine cream) to Asia (miso-glazed salmon with pickled ginger and radish salad, and sticky sesame rice balls). The set lunch and

early evening menus offer good value, while the house wine comes in at a reasonable £16 a bottle.
Chef/s: Paul Rankin, Paul Waterworth and Dave O'Callaghan. **Open:** Thur to Sun L 12 to 2.30 (8 Sun), Wed to Sat D 5 to 11. **Closed:** Mon, Tue, 25 and 26 Dec, 1 Jan, Easter Mon and Tue, 12 and 13 Jul. **Meals:** alc (main courses £12 to £22). Set L £13.95 (2 courses) to £16.95. Set D £16.95 (2 courses) to £23.95. **Service:** 10%. **Details:** 120 seats. Separate bar. Wheelchair access. Music.

Deanes

Versatile upscale brasserie
36-40 Howard Street, Belfast, Co Antrim, BT1 6PF
Tel no: (028) 9033 1134
www.michaeldeane.co.uk
Modern European | £44
Cooking score: 5

Chef-restaurateur Michael Deane currently has six very different outlets across Belfast – seven if you count The Circle at Deanes, the upstairs dining room here at his Howard Street headquarters, which has a separate menu from Deanes, the upscale brasserie downstairs. The latter remains his flagship. The smart modern dining room succeeds in being as many things as possible to as many people as possible, by offering a series of different menus at different price points to suit most budgets. The prix-fixe menu is a bargain for those who can't stretch to the à la carte or the five- or eight-course 'Titanic tasting menu'. The cooking is accomplished across the board, pays attention to the seasons and makes good use of Ulster's rich larder. A trademark starter might combine Strangford Lough scallops with chorizo, celeriac purée and smoked paprika; a main course could see smoked belly pork appear in company with poached lobster and a rich shellfish bisque. Desserts are particularly strong, as is the cheese plate selection. Service is polished, informed and friendly. The extensive wine list trawls the globe and does both Old and New Worlds justice, with entry-level bottles priced at £19.50; there's also a satisfying number by the glass.

Chef/s: Simon Toye. **Open:** Mon to Sat L 12 to 3, D 5.30 to 10. **Closed:** Sun, 25 to 26 Dec, 1 Jan, Easter Mon, 12 Jul. **Meals:** alc (main courses £11 to £25). Set L and early D £14.95 (2 courses) to £19.95. Tasting menu £65 (7 courses). **Service:** 10%. **Details:** 80 seats. Wheelchair access. Music.

NEW ENTRY
Il Pirata

Clever, casual Italian
279-281 Upper Newtownards Road, Ballyhackamore, Belfast, Co Antrim, BT4 3JF
Italian | £20
Cooking score: 3
£30

Occupying what was previously a KFC branch, Il Pirata is an indication of where this part of East Belfast seems to be going. It's a modish, casual Italian, of the sort familiar to London (the owners are most probably admirers of Polpo, see entry), and the menu's a fashionable mixture of small plates and larger dishes for sharing. There's no pizza, as nearby Little Wing (see entry) has that covered; instead the white-tiled interior's wooden tables are given over to the serving of sliders, fried fish, bruschettas, salads, pasta dishes and polenta chips. Add to that service from an enthusiastic young team, reasonably priced Italian wines (bottles begin at £15; carafes, £10; glasses, £3.75), and a drinks list that includes well-made cocktails, the restaurant's own beer and local cider. Walk-in only; no reservations.
Chef/s: Jonny Davidson. **Open:** all week 12 to 10 (11 Fri and Sat). **Closed:** 25 Dec. **Meals:** alc (main courses £8 to £12). **Service:** not inc. **Details:** 75 seats. Wheelchair access. Music. Car parking.

Average Price
The average price listed in main-entry reviews denotes the price of a three-course meal, without wine.

James Street South
Serious cooking at accessible prices
21 James Street South, Belfast, Co Antrim,
BT2 7GA
Tel no: (028) 9043 4310
www.jamesstreetsouth.co.uk
Modern European | £35
Cooking score: 6

A decade after it opened on a then-scruffy
city-centre backstreet, Niall McKenna's James
Street South has established itself as arguably
Belfast's most serious restaurant. Housed in
one half of an old linen mill – the other half is
McKenna's recently opened and more casual
Bar & Grill (see entry) – the impressive
contemporary dining room, with its
whitewashed walls hung with colourful
modern art, would not look out of place in any
major city. So, too, the cooking – assured
French technique applied to the best produce
that Northern Ireland has to offer. Prices have
been adjusted since Belfast's bubble burst in
the downturn and the set lunch and pre-
theatre menu options make it a lot more
accessible. The à la carte and wine list have also
come down in price. Typical dishes of finely
finessed local ingredients, combined with the
occasional imported touch, include Lough
Neagh smoked eel with Bayonne ham and
rosemary custard; Mourne lamb loin with
confit rib, radishes and butternut squash; and
treacle tart with Earl Grey ice cream to finish.
Wine starts at £16.50 a bottle.
Chef/s: Niall McKenna. **Open:** Mon to Sat L 12 to
2.45, D 5.45 to 10.45. **Closed:** Sun, 25 and 26 Dec, 1
Jan, 12 to 15 Jul. **Meals:** alc (main courses £14.50 to
£22). Set L £14.95 (2 courses) to £16.95. Pre-theatre
D £16.95 (2 courses) to £18.95. Tasting menu £55.
Service: not inc. **Details:** 60 seats. Separate bar.
Wheelchair access. Music.

Also Recommended
Also recommended entries are not scored
but we think they are worth a visit.

Molly's Yard
Unpretentious bijou bistro
1 College Green Mews, Botanic Avenue, Belfast, Co
Antrim, BT7 1LW
Tel no: (028) 9032 2600
www.mollysyard.co.uk
Modern Irish | £29
Cooking score: 3

Tucked away in a converted Victorian stable in
a courtyard off Botanic Avenue, the bijou
Molly's Yard borrows the title of a Thomas
Hardy novel for its tagline, the hard-to-
argue-with 'far from the madding crowd'. It's
owned by pioneering Irish microbrewery
Hilden, which also has the Tap Room on the
Lisburn site where it makes its beer – which,
naturally enough, is found behind Molly's bar.
Non-beer drinkers can take comfort in the
compact wine list, where bottles start at £15.
The unpretentious bistro menu (the only
choice at lunch) sits alongside a marginally
more elaborate dinner menu. Typically
satisfying dishes include hot smoked salmon
on chive fadge (potato cake); Fermanagh
chicken stuffed with pork and leek; and Irish
whiskey and tiramisu sundae.
Chef/s: Ciarán Steele. **Open:** Mon to Sat 12 to 9
(9.30 Fri and Sat). **Closed:** Sun, 25 and 26 Dec, 1
Jan, 12 Jul. **Meals:** alc (main courses £9 to £20).
Service: 10%. **Details:** 45 seats. 20 seats outside.
Wheelchair access. Music.

★ READERS' RESTAURANT OF THE YEAR ★
NORTHERN IRELAND

Mourne Seafood Bar
Local seafood hero
34-36 Bank Street, Belfast, Co Antrim, BT1 1HL
Tel no: (028) 9024 8544
www.mourneseafood.com
Seafood | £25
Cooking score: 3

Fresh local seafood at affordable prices is the
Mourne's mission statement, and in delivering
that it succeeds with gusto. The original

branch lies on the picturesque County Down coast at Dundrum, but this Belfast sibling has been the flagship since opening in 2006. In 2011 the owners added a more casual no-reservations oyster bar with a separate entrance, and a cooking school upstairs from the main restaurant. The short menu of what they call 'Mourne Classics' – various treatments of local oysters, crab claws with chilli butter, and mighty portions of beer-battered fish and chips – is backed up by a lengthy roll call of daily specials. The wine list, which starts at £15, is similarly supplemented by a series of even more affordable special-offer bottles.

Chef/s: Andy Rea. **Open:** all week L 12 to 5 (4 Fri and Sat, 1 to 6 Sun), Tue to Sat D 5 to 9.30 (10.30 Fri and Sat). **Closed:** 24 to 26 Dec, 1 Jan, 17 Mar, 12 Jul. **Meals:** alc (main courses £9 to £19). **Service:** not inc. **Details:** 74 seats. Separate bar. Music. No children after 9.

NEW ENTRY
The Potted Hen
Pick of Cathedral Quarter's new arrivals
Edward Street, Belfast, Co Antrim, BT1 2LR
Tel no: (028) 9023 4554
www.thepottedhen.co.uk
Modern British | £25
Cooking score: 3

 £30

The pick of the new restaurants in what's now known as the Cathedral Quarter, the Potted Hen is a handsomely appointed modern bistro. With its high ceiling, slate floor and iron beams, it's a good-looking, casual dining room that doesn't take itself too seriously. It's a sibling to Oregano, which lies in the Antrim countryside north of Belfast, and the menu ploughs similar territory. There's good technique from the kitchen in a rich chicken liver parfait served with a fantastic piece of freshly baked brioche. An Indian-tinged special of roast monkfish with a korma sauce, bhajia and crispy crab claws is perfectly executed, likewise a refreshing pink grapefruit posset. The wine list starts at £16.95 a bottle (£4.50 a glass).

Chef/s: Marty Murphy. **Open:** Mon to Sat L 12 to 2.45, D 5 to 9.30 (10 Fri and Sat), Sun 12 to 9. **Closed:** 24 to 27 Dec, 1 and 2 Jan, 11 to 13 Jul. **Meals:** alc (main courses £11 to £19). Early D £15.95 (2 courses) to £17.95. Sun £18.95 (2 courses) to £21.95. **Service:** not inc. **Details:** 75 seats. 40 seats outside. Wheelchair access. Music.

ALSO RECOMMENDED
▲ The Ginger Bistro
7-8 Hope Street, Belfast, Co Antrim, BT12 5EE
Tel no: (028) 9024 4421
www.gingerbistro.com
Modern European

Opened back in 2004, this lovable, keenly priced bistro has a big heart and a nice line in good-value modern European cooking. Starters of smoked mackerel pâté and toast, and warm chorizo salad with pesto, baby potatoes, mozzarella and roast peppers both come in at £6. Main courses of roast Saddleback pork loin with Parmesan risotto (£9) and crispy-skinned sea bass on a creamy celeriac and crayfish casserole (£10) show that the kitchen has imagination. Wines from £15.

▲ Nick's Warehouse
35 Hill Street, Belfast, Co Antrim, BT1 2LB
Tel no: (028) 9043 9690
www.nickswarehouse.co.uk
Modern European

Back in 1989, long before the rundown cobbled streets behind St Anne's had been rebranded as the Cathedral Quarter and post-ceasefire pounds were poured into the area, chef Nick Price opened in a red-brick warehouse, built in 1832 as a bonded storage for Bushmills. He wasn't mad, as some said at the time, but a pioneer and a prophet. The compact menu does modern European with the odd touch of Asian. The wine list, with lots of selections by the glass from £4.25, has bottles starting at £16.45. Closed Sun and Mon.

Little Wing
Italian
201 Upper Newtownards Road, Ballyhackamore,
Belfast, Co Antrim, BT4 3JD
Tel no: (028) 9065 1555
www.littlewingpizzeria.com
'Proper wood-fired pizzas, friendly service,
cool atmosphere and good tunes.'

▌Comber, Co Down
ALSO RECOMMENDED
▲ The Old Schoolhouse Inn
100 Ballydrain Road, Comber, Co Down, BT23 6EA
Tel no: (028) 9754 1182
www.theoldschoolhouseinn.com
Modern British £5 OFF

The Old Schoolhouse opened more than 30
years ago in Castle Espie near Strangford
Lough. The recent return of the owners' son,
rising young chef Will Brown (who worked
in London at The Square, Maze and The
Glasshouse) as chef-proprietor, marks a clear
rise in ambition. Barring Sunday lunch, it's a
dinner-only destination; an eight-course
tasting menu at £55 (£80 with the matching
wine flight) runs alongside the à la carte.
Wines start at £13.95 a bottle. Closed Mon
and Tue.

▌Groomsport, Co Down
NEW ENTRY
Strudel Bistro
Sharp seaside café-cum-bistro
39 Main Street, Groomsport, Co Down, BT19 6JR
Tel no: (028) 9145 6758
www.strudelbistro.com
Modern European | £25
Cooking score: 3
V

The husband and wife team behind this
attractive café-cum-bistro in Groomsport
previously ran the likeable, pocket-sized Café
Strudel in Bangor. Chef-owner Fritz Machala
was born in Vienna before his family moved to

Northern Ireland, where he met his wife
Sharon. Open throughout the week for
breakfast, lunches, tea and cakes (apple strudel
being a speciality), Machala also does dinner
on Friday and Saturday evenings, when he
serves a more ambitious à la carte and offers
five- or seven-course tasting menus. The
kitchen makes use of local seafood (the crab is
landed in Groomsport) and Germanic touches
appear in dishes such as pork with sauerkraut,
rösti, carrots and thyme velouté. BYO, £2
corkage, free if you buy from the
neighbouring off-licence.
Chef/s: Fritz Machala. **Open:** Tue to Sun L 12 to 3
(10am Sun), Fri and Sat D 6.30 to 9. **Closed:** Mon, 3
days Christmas, 12 and 13 Jul, bank hols. **Meals:** Set
D £21.50 (2 courses) to £24.95. Tasting menu £34.95
(5 courses) to £39.95. **Service:** not inc. **Details:** 46
seats. 8 seats outside. Wheelchair access. Music.

▌Holywood, Co Down
The Bay Tree
Quirky quality café
118 High Street, Holywood, Co Down, BT18 9HW
Tel no: (028) 9042 1419
www.baytreeholywood.co.uk
Irish | £25
Cooking score: 2

The unpretentious Bay Tree packs the punters
into its basically decorated dining room –
terracotta tiles on the floor, whitewashed walls
– for breakfast, lunch and the occasional
dinner. The day is best started with its
celebrated cinnamon scones or its take on the
Ulster Fry. Lunch offers a simple menu built
around soups, salads and filled baked potatoes.
It's only on Friday evenings, when it opens for
dinner, that the kitchen's ambition stretches
beyond that of a café, with hearty staples such
as roast chicken, rack of lamb and salmon,
usually sitting alongside a couple of clever,
Mediterranean-inspired vegetarian dishes.
Wines from £13.50.

Chef/s: Sue Farmer. **Open:** Mon to Fri B from 8 (Sat 9, Sun 10), all week L 12 to 3.45, Fri only D 5.30 to 9.30. **Closed:** 25 and 26 Dec, 12 and 13 Jul. **Meals:** alc (main courses £10 to £16). **Service:** not inc. **Details:** 60 seats. Music. Car parking.

▌Killinchy, Co Down

NEW ENTRY
Balloo House
Classy old coaching inn
1 Comber Road, Killinchy, Co Down, BT23 6PA
Tel no: (028) 9754 1210
www.ballooinns.com
Irish | £22
Cooking score: 3

This County Down coaching inn, not far from Strangford Lough, dates back to the late 1600s. Danny Millar, who also oversees the menu at the well-regarded Parson's Nose in Hillsborough, has run the kitchen since 2006. The ground floor houses what's still a lively bar, and what staff call their 'bistro', and some might describe as a pub. Upstairs lies the more grown-up, dinner-only dining room, which has a separate, more ambitious menu. But the craic is invariably down below, where, particularly with a roaring fire in winter, the welcome is warm. Well-executed, heartily proportioned dishes include smoked haddock, bacon and scallion chowder (perfect with the Guinness wheaten bread); Lissara Farm duck breast, fried duck egg and duck-fat chips; and sticky toffee pudding with Bushmills butterscotch sauce. The wine list starts at £14.95.
Chef/s: Danny Millar. **Open:** all week 12 to 9 (9.30 Fri and Sat). **Closed:** 25 Dec. **Meals:** alc (main courses £6 to £19). Set L £8.95 (1 course) to £16.95. **Service:** not inc. **Details:** 70 seats. Separate bar. Wheelchair access. Music. Car parking.

▌Newcastle, Co Down

NEW ENTRY
Vanilla
Local classics meet exotic fare
67 Main Street, Newcastle, Co Down, BT33 0AE
Tel no: (028) 4372 2268
www.vanillarestaurant.co.uk
Global | £26
Cooking score: 3

In the seaside resort of Newcastle, 'where the Mountains of Mourne sweep down to the sea', as the ol' Percy French song goes, local chef Darren Ireland opened this pleasing bistro in the autumn of 2009. The menu mixes local favourites – smoked bacon chop, fish and chips, seafood pie – with the more exotic and well-travelled. There's a love of Spain evident in a perfectly executed main of Ibérico Secreto black pig, the succulent shoulder-cut served pink. Elsewhere the kitchen touches on various parts of Asia with a Thai-tinged roast monkfish and salt-and-pepper squid in a light batter laced with curry powder. The lunch and early-bird menus offer exceptional value, while the compact wine list opens at £14.50 a bottle (£4.50 a glass).
Chef/s: Darren Ireland. **Open:** all week L 12 to 3.30, D 5 to 9.30 (6 Fri and Sat, 9 Sun). **Closed:** 25 to 27 Dec, 1 Jan. **Meals:** alc (main courses £14 to £19). Early D £14.95 (2 courses) to £18.95. **Service:** not inc. **Details:** 40 seats. 2 seats outside. Wheelchair access. Music.

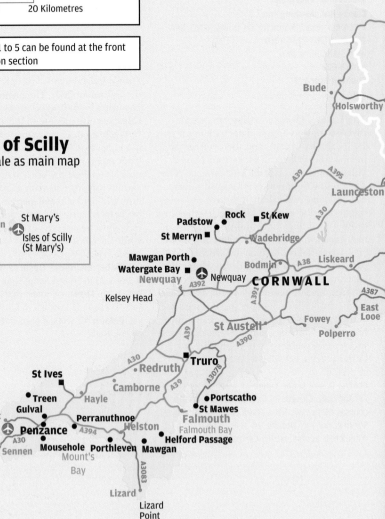

MAP 6

- ■ Main entry
- ● Main entry with accommodation
- ▲ Also recommended

A single symbol may denote
several restaurants in one area.

0   10 Miles
0   10   20 Kilometres

Note: Maps 1 to 5 can be found at the front
of the London section

Isles of Scilly
Same scale as main map

Hugh Town St Mary's
Isles of Scilly
(St Mary's)

Lundy

Bude
Holsworthy

A39   A395

A39   A30

Launceston

Padstow   Rock   ■ St Kew
St Merryn ■   Wadebridge

Mawgan Porth ●
Watergate Bay ■   Bodmin ●   A38 Liskeard
Newquay   A392 Newquay   CORNWALL
Kelsey Head   A387

East
St Austell   Fowey   Looe
A391   A390   Polperro

A30   Redruth   ■ Truro
St Ives ■   A3078
Camborne   A39
Treen   Hayle
Gulval   Portscatho ●
St Just   Perranuthnoe   ● St Mawes
Land's End   Penzance   A394 Helston Falmouth
                              Falmouth Bay
Land's End   A30   Helford Passage ●
         Sennen Mousehole Porthleven Mawgan
                 Mount's
                  Bay
                          A3083
         Lizard ●
              Lizard
              Point

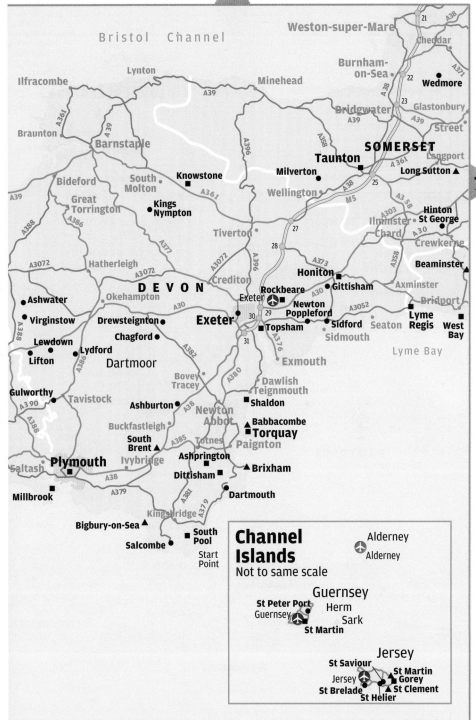

Bristol Channel

Weston-super-Mare

21

Cheddar

A38

A371

Lynton

Ilfracombe

Minehead

Burnham-on-Sea

22

Wedmore

23

A39

Bridgwater

Glastonbury

Braunton

Barnstaple

A361

A39

A39

South Molton

Knowstone

Milverton

SOMERSET

Taunton

A361

Long Sutton

A58

Langport

Street

25

Bideford

Great Torrington

Kings Nympton

A361

Wellington

M5

A303

Ilminster

Chard

A30

Hinton St George

Crewkerne

A39

A386

A388

Tiverton

27

A358

Beaminster

Hatherleigh

A3072

A3072

Crediton

28

A373

Honiton

Gittisham

Axminster

Bridport

A3072

DEVON

Okehampton

Rockbeare

Newton Poppleford

A3052

Lyme Regis

West Bay

Ashwater

Virginstow

Drewsteignton

A30

Exeter

30

29

Topsham

Sidford

Seaton

Exeter

Chagford

31

A376

Sidmouth

Lyme Bay

Lewdown

Lifton

Lydford

A386

Dartmoor

A382

Exmouth

Gulworthy

A390

Tavistock

Bovey Tracey

A380

Dawlish
Teignmouth

Shaldon

Plymouth

Saltash

Ashburton

A38

Newton Abbot

Babbacombe

Torquay

Buckfastleigh

South Brent

A385

Totnes

Paignton

Millbrook

A38

A379

Ivybridge

Ashprington

Dittisham

Brixham

A381

Dartmouth

Kingsbridge

A379

Bigbury-on-Sea

South Pool

Salcombe

Start Point

Channel Islands

Not to same scale

Alderney

Alderney

Guernsey

St Peter Port

Guernsey

Herm

Sark

St Martin

Jersey

St Saviour

Jersey

St Martin

Gorey

St Brelade

St Clement

St Helier

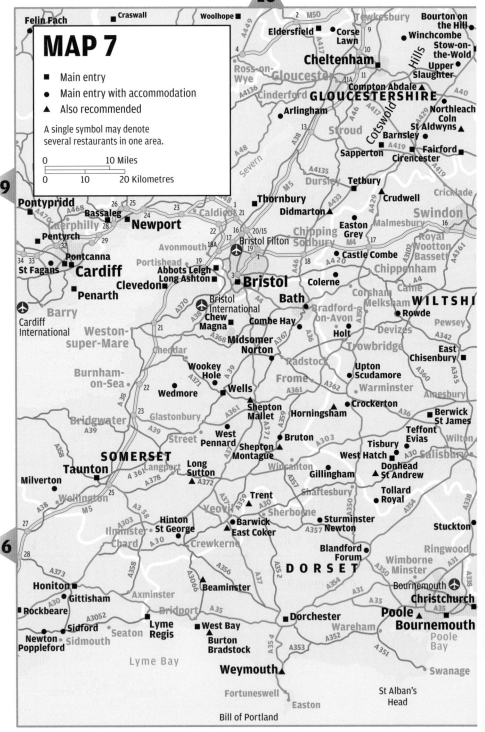

10

MAP 7

■ Main entry

● Main entry with accommodation

▲ Also recommended

A single symbol may denote
several restaurants in one area.

0   10 Miles
0   10   20 Kilometres

9

6

Felin Fach   Craswall   Woolhope   Eldersfield   Corse Lawn   Bourton on the Hill   Winchcombe   Stow-on-the-Wold   Upper Slaughter

M50   Tewkesbury

Cheltenham

Ross-on-Wye   Gloucester   Compton Abdale   GLOUCESTERSHIRE   Northleach   Coln   St Aldwyns

Cinderford   Arlingham   Stroud   Barnsley   Cirencester   Fairford

Severn   Dursley   Tetbury   Crudwell   Cricklade

Sapperton

Thornbury   Didmarton   Easton Grey   Malmesbury   Swindon

Caldicot   Chipping Sodbury   Royal Wootton Bassett

Pontypridd   Bassaleg   Newport   Avonmouth   Bristol Filton   Castle Combe   Chippenham

Caerphilly   Pentyrch   Portishead   Abbots Leigh   Long Ashton   Bristol   Colerne   Corsham   Calne   WILTSHIRE

Pontcanna   St Fagans   Cardiff   Clevedon   Penarth   Bath   Bradford-on-Avon   Melksham   Rowde

Barry   Cardiff International   Weston-super-Mare   Cheddar   Bristol International   Chew Magna   Combe Hay   Holt   Devizes   Pewsey

Burnham-on-Sea   Midsomer Norton   Radstock   Trowbridge   East Chisenbury

Wookey Hole   Frome   Upton Scudamore   Warminster   Amesbury

Wedmore   Wells   Shepton Mallet   Horningsham   Crockerton   Berwick St James

Bridgwater   Glastonbury   Street   West Pennard   Bruton   Teffont Evias   Tisbury   Wilton

SOMERSET   Shepton Montague   Wincanton   West Hatch   Donhead St Andrew   Salisbury

Taunton   Long Sutton   Trent   Gillingham   Tollard Royal

Milverton   Wellington   Yeovil   Sherborne   Shaftesbury   Stuckton

Ilminster   Chard   Hinton St George   Barwick   East Coker   Sturminster Newton   Ringwood

Crewkerne   Blandford Forum   Wimborne Minster   Bournemouth

Honiton   Gittisham   Axminster   Beaminster   DORSET   Christchurch

Rockbeare   Sidford   Seaton   Lyme Regis   West Bay   Burton Bradstock   Dorchester   Poole   Bournemouth

Newton Poppleford   Sidmouth   Lyme Bay   Wareham   Poole Bay

Weymouth   Swanage

Fortuneswell   Easton   St Alban's Head

Bill of Portland

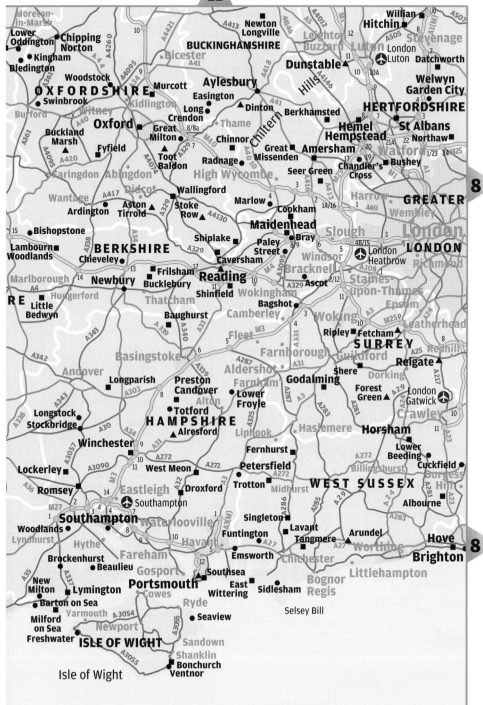

8

8

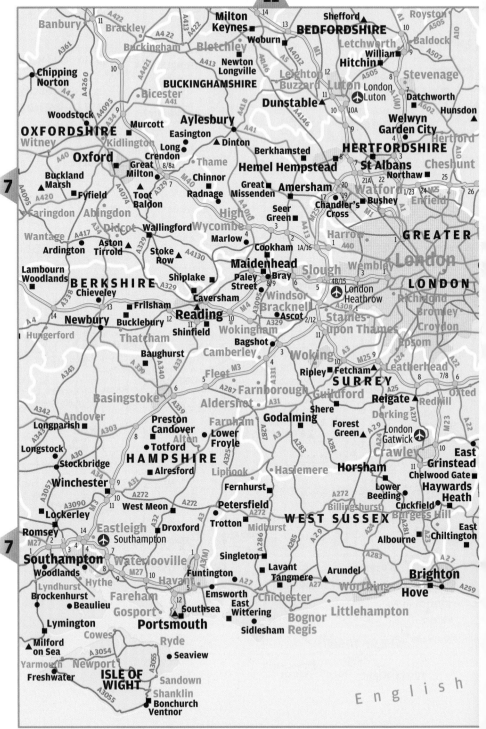

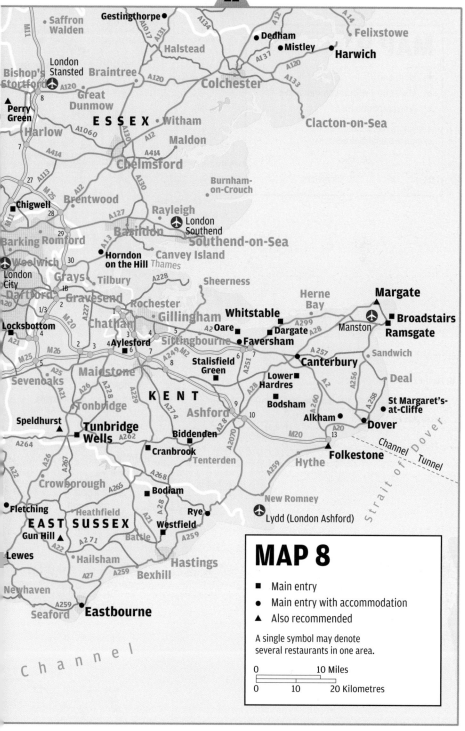

MAP 8

■ Main entry

● Main entry with accommodation

▲ Also recommended

A single symbol may denote
several restaurants in one area.

0   10 Miles

0   10   20 Kilometres

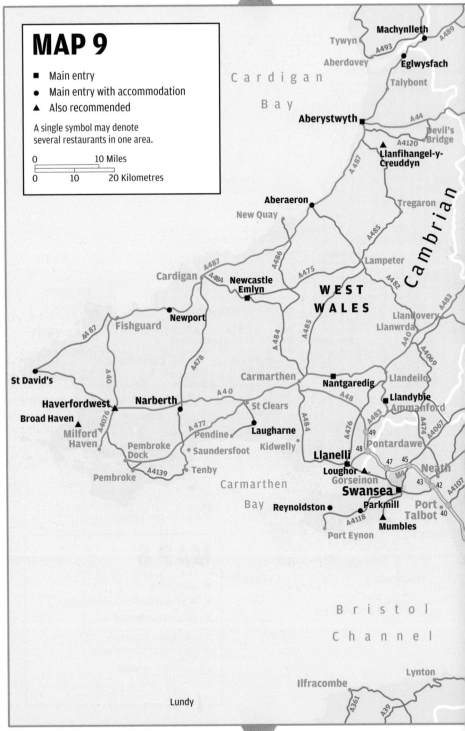

MAP 9

- ■ Main entry
- ● Main entry with accommodation
- ▲ Also recommended

A single symbol may denote
several restaurants in one area.

```
0               10 Miles
0        10       20 Kilometres
```

Machynlleth
Tywyn   A493   A489
Aberdovey   Eglwysfach
Cardigan   Talybont
Bay
        Aberystwyth ■   A44
                    A4120 Devil's
                    ▲   Bridge
                  Llanfihangel-y-
                  Creuddyn
        Aberaeron ●
New Quay
                  Tregaron
                  A485
                          Cambrian
                  Lampeter
Cardigan A487 A486 A475
        A484 Newcastle A482
              Emlyn ■   WEST
                        WALES   A483
Fishguard Newport ●   Llandovery
A4 87   Llanwrda   A40
                    A484 A485   A4069
St David's ●   Carmarthen Nantgaredig ■ Llandeilo
Haverfordwest ▲ Narberth A40   Llandybie ■
Broad Haven ▲   St Clears   Ammanford
Milford   A4076 A477 Pendine Laugharne ● 49 Pontardawe A474 A4067
Haven   Pembroke Saundersfoot Kidwelly 48   47 45
         A4139 Dock Tenby   Llanelli ■   M4 43 42 Neath
Pembroke   Loughor ▲   A4107
                  Carmarthen   Gorseinon   40
                  Bay Reynoldston ● Swansea ■ Port
                          Parkmill ▲ Talbot
                  A4118   Mumbles
                  Port Eynon

B r i s t o l
C h a n n e l

                          Lynton
        Ilfracombe   A361 A39
Lundy
```
```

Mountains

Montgomery
Marton
Minsterley
SHROPSHIRE
Wolverhampton
A488
A490
A458
A41
A442
A489
Newtown
Church Stretton
Bridgnorth
A489
A458
Dudley
Halesowen
Dolfor
Munslow
Wistanstow
Stourbridge
Craven Arms
A442
A491
Llanidloes
Llanfair Waterdine
A449
Kidderminster
Bewdley
A448
4
Llangurig
A4117
Ludlow
Stourport-on-Severn
A443
Bromsgrove
4A
1
MID WALES
A4113
A456
A488
Knighton
A4110
Droitwich
5
Rhayader
A44
Ombersley
WORCESTER-SHIRE
A422
Llandrindod Wells
A483
Titley
Leominster
A44
Kington
A4112
Bromyard
A44
A417
Worcester
6
7
Beulah
Builth Wells
HEREFORDSHIRE
A4110
A49
Great Malvern
A4103
A438
Pershore
8
Llangammarch Wells
A438
Hay-on-Wye
Hereford
Ledbury
A438
M50
1
M5
Llanwrtyd Wells
Glasbury-on-Wye
Craswall
Woolhope
Eldersfield
Tewkesbury
2
Corse Lawn
9
A40
Felin Fach
Talgarth
A465
A449
Ross-on-Wye
Gloucestershire
Cheltenham
10
Brecon
A479
A40
Skenfrith
A466
4
A417
Gloucester
11A
11
Crickhowell
Abergavenny
Llanddewi Skirrid
A4136
GLOUCESTERSHIRE
A46
Brynmawr
Monmouth
A40
Cinderford
Arlingham
13
Sapperton
A470
Ebbw Vale
Nant-y-derry
GWENT
A466
Stroud
Merthyr Tydfil
Aberthaw
A472
Whitebrook
A48
Dursley
Aberdare
Bargoed
A469
Pontypool
Usk
A449
Severn
A4135
Tetbury
Crudwell
Treorchy
A4059
Cwmbran
Chepstow
M48
M5
Didmarton
Malmesbury
A433
GLAMORGAN
A472
A468
26 25
A48
2
Thornbury
Easton Grey
A435
Pontypridd
Caerphilly
Bassaleg
28
24
23
Caldicot
21
Chipping Sodbury
Castle Combe
M4
17
Llantrisant
Pentyrch
29
22
16
20/15
Castle Combe
A420
Chippenham
B6
35
32
18A
Bristol Filton
19
18
Colerne
Bridgend
34 33
Pontcanna
19
1
A46
Corsham
northcawl
A48
St Fagans
Abbots Leigh
3
Bristol
Melksham
Cowbridge
Penarth
Clevedon
Long Ashton
Bath
Bradford-on-Avon
A350
Cardiff
Barry
Bristol International
Chew Magna
A4
Combe Hay
A36
Holt
Cardiff International
Weston-super-Mare
21
A368
A367
Trowbridge
Upton Scudamore
Cheddar
Midsomer Norton
Radstock
Burnham-on-Sea
22
A371
Wookey Hole
A39
Frome
Warminster
A362
Minehead
Wells
A361
Horningsham
Crockerton
A39
23
Glastonbury
Shepton Mallet
A361
A359
Bridgwater

10
8

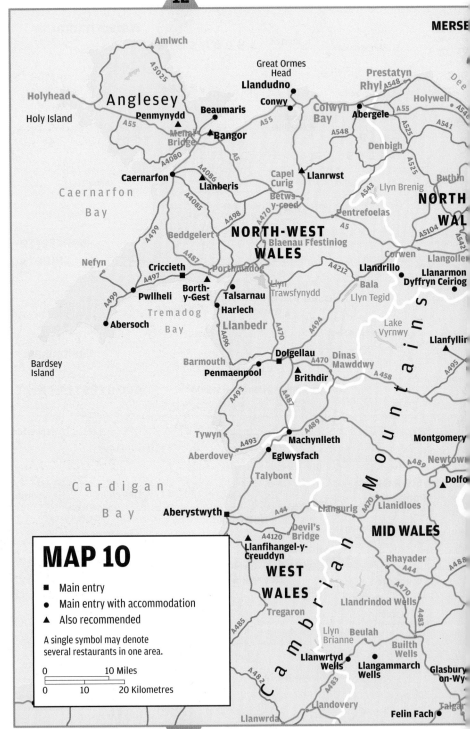

MERSE

Dee

Amlwch

A5025

Anglesey

Holyhead
Holy Island
Penmynydd
A55

Beaumaris

Great Ormes
Head
Llandudno
Conwy
**Colwyn
Bay**
Abergele

Prestatyn
Rhyl A548
Holywell
A55
A548
A541
A548

A55

Menai
Bridge
Bangor
A5

Denbigh

A525

C a e r n a r f o n
Caernarfon
A4080

A4086
Llanberis

Capel
Curig
Betws-
y-coed
Llanrwst

Llyn Brenig
A543
Ruthin

NORTH

B a y
A499
A4085
A4098
A470
A5
Pentrefoelas
A5104
A542
WAL

Beddgelert
**NORTH-WEST
WALES**

Blaenau Ffestiniog
Corwen
Llangollen

Nefyn
A487
A4212
Llandrillo
**Llanarmon
Dyffryn Ceiriog**

Criccieth
A497
Porthmadog
Llyn
Trawsfynydd
Bala

Pwllheli
**Borth-
y-Gest**
Talsarnau
Llyn Tegid
Lake
Vyrnwy
Llanfyllin

A499
Abersoch
T r e m a d o g
Harlech
Llanbedr
A496
A470
A494
A458
A495

Bardsey
Island
B a y
Barmouth
Penmaenpool
Dolgellau
A470
Dinas
Mawddwy

Brithdir
A493
A487

M
o
u
n
t
a
i
n
s

Tywyn
A493
A489
Machynlleth
Montgomery
Newtow

Aberdovey
Eglwysfach
A489
Dolfo

Talybont

C a r d i g a n
B a y
Aberystwyth
A44
Llangurig
A470
Llanidloes

MID WALES

Devil's
Bridge
A4120
**Llanfihangel-y-
Creuddyn**

Rhayader
A44
A488

C
a
m
b
r
i
a
n

**WEST
WALES**
Llandrindod Wells
A470
A483

Tregaron
A485
Llyn
Brianne
Beulah
Builth
Wells

**Llanwrtyd
Wells**
**Llangammarch
Wells**
A483
**Glasbury
on-Wy**

A482
Llandovery
Felin Fach
Talgar

Llanwrda

MAP 10

- ■ Main entry
- ● Main entry with accommodation
- ▲ Also recommended

A single symbol may denote
several restaurants in one area.

0   10 Miles

0   10   20 Kilometres

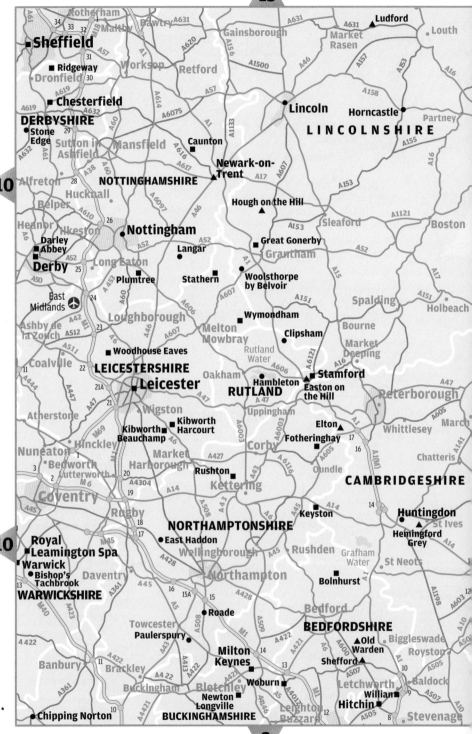

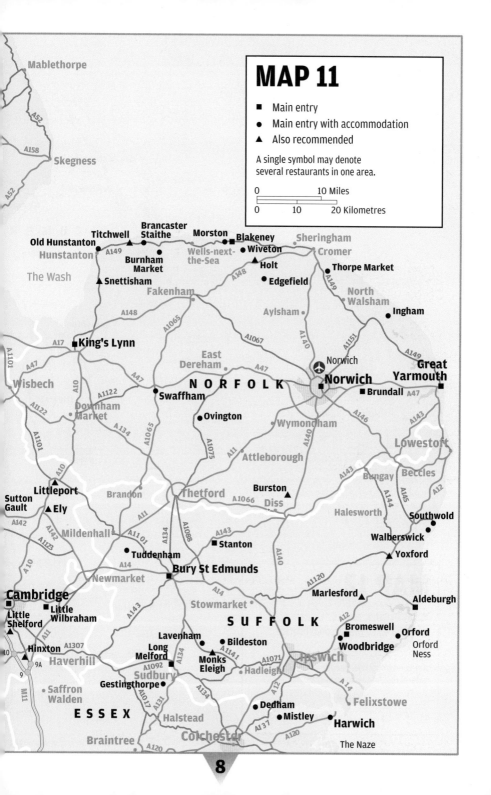

MAP 11

- ■ Main entry
- ● Main entry with accommodation
- ▲ Also recommended

A single symbol may denote
several restaurants in one area.

0	10 Miles	
0	10	20 Kilometres

Mablethorpe

A52

A158

Skegness

A52

Old Hunstanton
Hunstanton
The Wash

Titchwell
A149

Brancaster
Staithe
Burnham
Market

Morston
Blakeney
Wells-next-
the-Sea

Wiveton
Holt
Edgefield

Sheringham
Cromer

Thorpe Market

Snettisham
Fakenham
A148

North
Walsham

Ingham

A1065

A148

King's Lynn
A17

A1101

A47

East
Dereham

A1067

A140

A1151

A149

Norwich

Great
Yarmouth

Wisbech

A10

A1122

N O R F O L K
Swaffham

A47

Norwich

Brundall
A47

A11122

A1101

Downham
Market

A134

A1065

Ovington

Wymondham

A146

A143

Lowestoft

A11

A1075

Attleborough

A140

A143

Beccles

A10

Littleport

Brandon

Thetford

Burston

Bungay

A144

A145

A12

Sutton
Gault

A42

Ely

A11

A1101

A134

A11

A1066

Diss

Halesworth

Southwold

A1123

Mildenhall

A1088

A143

Stanton

A140

Walberswick

Yoxford

A10

Tuddenham
A14

Newmarket

Bury St Edmunds

A1120

Marlesford

Aldeburgh

Cambridge
Little
Shelford
Little
Wilbraham

A143

Stowmarket

S U F F O L K

A12

Bromeswell
Woodbridge

Orford

Orford
Ness

Hinxton
A1307

Haverhill

Lavenham
Long
Melford

Bildeston

A1141

Monks
Eleigh

A1071

Hadleigh

Ipswich

M11

9A

9

Saffron
Walden

A1092

Gestingthorpe

Sudbury

A1017

A131

A134

A14

Felixstowe

E S S E X

Halstead

Dedham

Mistley

Harwich

Braintree
A120

Colchester

A137

A120

The Naze

8

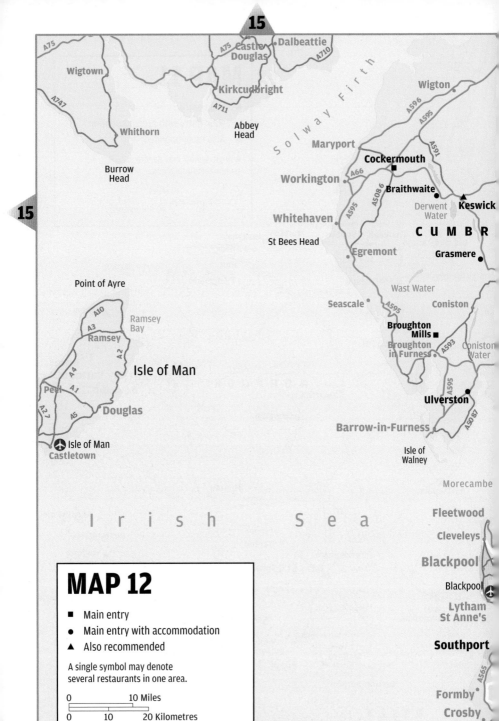

Bishop Auckland
Redcar
Aycliffe
Stockton-on-Tees
Middlesbrough
Romaldkirk
59
A688
Guisborough
Goldsborough
Barnard Castle
Summerhouse
58
A67
A66
Darlington
A171
A174
Winston
57
Hutton Magna
A66
56
Hurworth-on-Tees
Durham Tees Valley
A172
Brough
Kirkby Stephen
A167
Arkengarthdale
Richmond
Staddlebridge
A684
Osmotherley
A169
Hawes
A684
Leyburn
A684
Bedale
A168
Northallerton
Sinnington
12
West Witton
East Witton
A6108
Felixkirk
Helmsley
Pickering
A170
A170
Masham
West Tanfield
Asenby
Thirsk
Harome
Oldstead
A168
Malton
Ramsgill
Ripon
49
A61
A19
A64
Y O R K S H I R E
Boroughbridge
A166
Settle
A65
Grassington
Ferrensby
Knaresborough
47
A59
Newton-on-Ouse
A166
Hetton
Bolton Abbey
Harrogate
A59
A658
A661
46
Boston Spa
York
A1079
Skipton
Wetherby
A1(M)
Grindleton
A59
A682
Ilkley
A65
A658
Tadcaster
A19
Keighley
A6068
Leeds/Bradford
A64
45
Clitheroe
Haworth
A629
A658
44/48
Selby
Wiswell
Nelson
Bradford
Leeds
A63
M62
Burnley
A6033
3
46
37
Accrington
A646
Halifax
Shibden
26
27
1
Morley
A1041
Goole
A6
Rawtenstall
Sowerby Bridge
Batley
29
Castleford
36
A65
Elland
Wakefield
33/41
Pontefract
A63
7/35
Ramsbottom
Ripponden
23
Dewsbury
A638
34
A161
Norden
24
Huddersfield
39
A628
A1
6
Thorne
A18
Bury
Birtle
Honley
38
A629
5
1
A58
M66
2
Rochdale
Holmfirth
37
Barnsley
A635
Bentley
4
A614
2
A161
3
15
M60
18
19
20
Oldham
37
Doncaster
Worsley
Prestwich
Ashton-under-Lyne
A628
36
2/35
A1(M)
Salford
Lydgate
Stocksbridge
35
Rotherham
3
Robin Hood
A631
Gainsborough
Manchester
Glossop
Chapeltown
A61
Bawtry
A159
8
Sale
A57
34
33
Maltby
A620
A156
Heaton Moor
Stockport
A625
32
A57
A1
Altrincham
A6
Bradwell
Sheffield
31
Worksop
Retford
A57
7
M56
Manchester
A624
Ridgeway
30
NOTTINGHAMSHIRE
Wilmslow
Knutsford
Alderley Edge
Chapel-en-le-Frith
A623
Dronfield
A619
A614
Macclesfield
Buxton
Baslow
Chesterfield
A632
A6075
A1133
A34
A537
A6
Bakewell
A619
A60
18
A54
Beeley
Stone Edge
29
Mansfield
A616
Congleton
DERBYSHIRE
M1
A61
Caunton
17
A53
Matlock
A632
A515

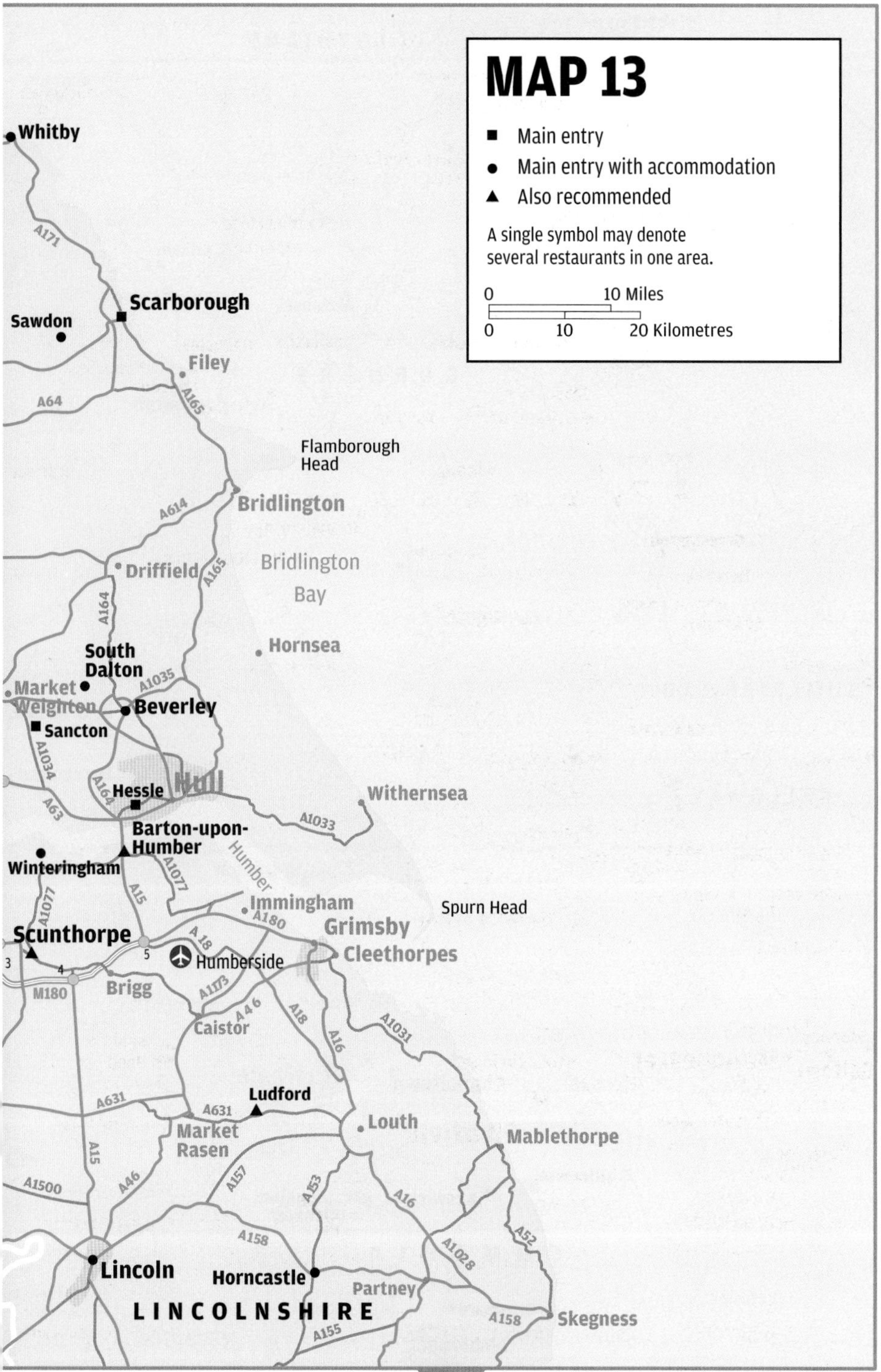

MAP 13

- ■ Main entry
- ● Main entry with accommodation
- ▲ Also recommended

A single symbol may denote
several restaurants in one area.

```
0                    10 Miles
0        10          20 Kilometres
```

Whitby

A171

Scarborough

Sawdon

Filey

A64

A165

Flamborough
Head

A614

Bridlington

Driffield

A165

Bridlington
Bay

A164

South
Dalton

A1035

Hornsea

Market
Weighton

Beverley

A1034

Sancton

A164

Hessle

Hull

Withernsea

A63

A1033

Barton-upon-
Humber

Winteringham

Humber

A1077

A15

Immingham

A1077

A180

Spurn Head

Scunthorpe

A18

Grimsby

3   4   5

Humberside

Cleethorpes

M180

Brigg

A1173

Caistor

A46

A18

A16

A1031

A631

Ludford

A631

Louth

Mablethorpe

Market
Rasen

A15

A46

A157

A153

A16

A52

A1500

A158

A1028

Lincoln

Horncastle

Partney

LINCOLNSHIRE

A158

Skegness

A155

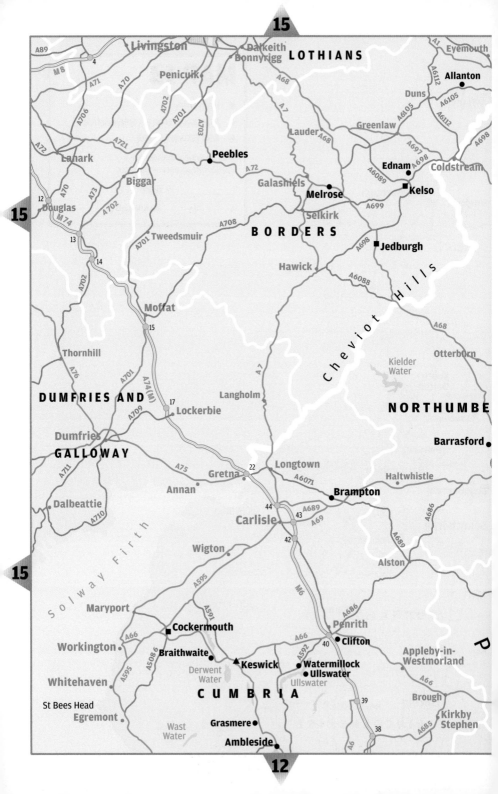

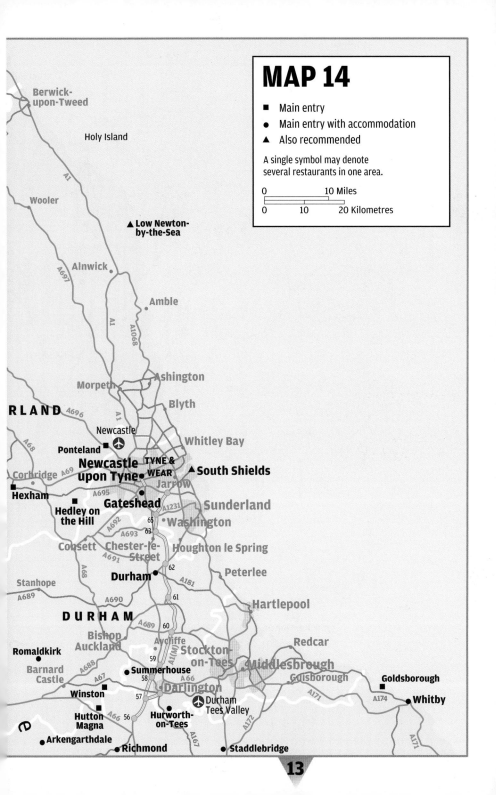

MAP 14

- ■ Main entry
- ● Main entry with accommodation
- ▲ Also recommended

A single symbol may denote
several restaurants in one area.

```
0                10 Miles
0        10        20 Kilometres
```

Berwick-
upon-Tweed

Holy Island

Wooler

▲ Low Newton-
by-the-Sea

Alnwick

Amble

Morpeth

Ashington

RLAND A696

Blyth

Newcastle

Ponteland ■

Whitley Bay

Newcastle
upon Tyne

TYNE &
WEAR

▲ South Shields

Corbridge A69

Jarrow

Hexham ■

A695

Gateshead

Sunderland

Hedley on
the Hill

65

Washington

63

Consett Chester-le-
Street

Houghton le Spring

A691

62

Stanhope

Durham ●

Peterlee

A689

A690

61

Hartlepool

DURHAM

A689

60

Bishop
Auckland

Aycliffe

Redcar

Romaldkirk ●

59

Stockton-
on-Tees

Middlesbrough

Barnard
Castle

A688

Summerhouse

A66

Guisborough

Goldsborough

Winston ●

58

Darlington

A171

A174

Whitby ●

57

Durham
Tees Valley

Hutton
Magna

A66

56

Hurworth-
on-Tees

A172

Arkengarthdale ●

Richmond

Staddlebridge ●

A167

A171

13

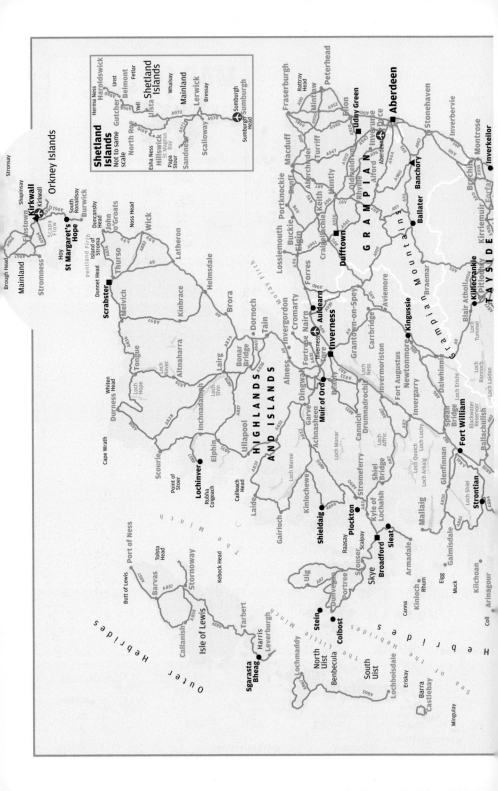

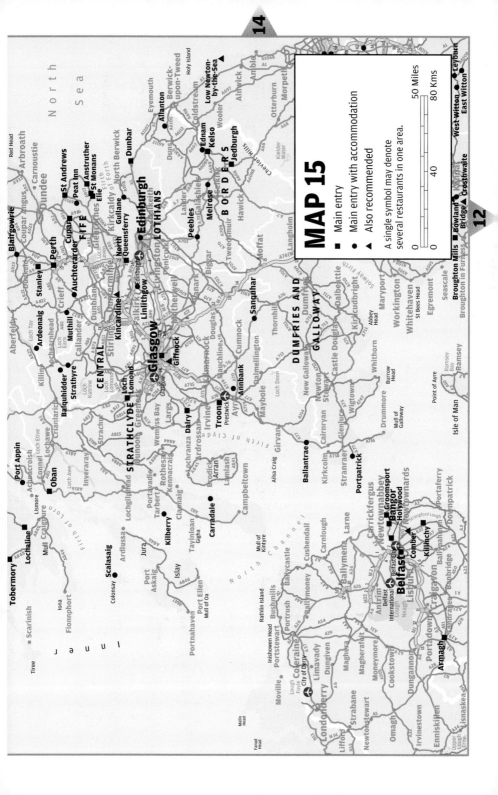

Note: The INDEX BY TOWN does not include London entries.

Abbots Leigh	265	Barton-upon-Humber	336	Broad Haven	557
Aberaeron	556	Barwick	380	Broadstairs	315
Aberdeen	514	Baslow	232	Broadway	443
Abergavenny	537	Bassaleg	538	Brockenhurst	291
Abergele	547	Bath	381	Bromeswell	395
Abersoch	548	Baughurst	290	Broughton Mills	222
Aberystwyth	557	Beaminster	252	Brundall	348
Albourne	414	Beaulieu	290	Bruton	384
Aldeburgh	393	Beaumaris	548	Buckland Marsh	367
Alderley Edge	201	Beeley	233	Bucklebury	183
Alkham	313	Belfast, Co Antrim	574	Bunbury	202
Allanton	479	Berkhamsted	307	Burnham Market	348
Alresford	289	Berwick St James	435	Burston	348
Alstonefield	391	Beverley	446	Burton Bradstock	254
Altrincham	281	Biddenden	314	Burton upon Trent	392
Ambleside	220	Bigbury-on-Sea	238	Bury St Edmunds	395
Amersham	188	Bildeston	394	Bushey	307
Annbank	495	Birmingham	429	Caernarfon	550
Anstruther	506	Birtle	281	Cambridge	195
Applecross	517	Bishopstone	435	Canterbury	316
Ardeonaig	504	Bishop's Tachbrook	425	Cardiff	529
Ardington	366	Bispham Green	325	Carradale	496
Arkengarthdale	446	Blairgowrie	510	Cartmel	222
Arkholme	325	Blakeney	347	Castle Combe	436
Arlingham	265	Blandford Forum	252	Caunton	361
Armagh, Co Armagh	573	Bledington	367	Caversham	183
Arundel	415	Blyth	361	Chagford	239
Ascot	180	Bodiam	405	Chandler's Cross	308
Asenby	446	Bodsham	315	Chapeltown	449
Ashbourne	231	Bollington	202	Cheltenham	271
Ashburton	237	Bolnhurst	177	Chelwood Gate	415
Ashprington	238	Bolton Abbey	447	Chester	202
Ashwater	238	Boroughbridge	448	Chesterfield	234
Aston Tirrold	366	Borth-y-Gest	549	Chew Magna	384
Auchterarder	510	Boston Spa	448	Chieveley	183
Auldearn	517	Bournemouth	253	Chigwell	262
Aviemore	518	Bourton on the Hill	266	Chinnor	367
Aylesbury	189	Bowland Bridge	221	Chipping Campden	273
Aylesford	314	Bowness-on-Windermere	221	Chipping Norton	368
Babbacombe	238	Boylestone	233	Christchurch	254
Bagshot	401	Bradford	448	Cirencester	273
Ballantrae	496	Bradley	391	Clevedon	385
Ballater	515	Bradwell	233	Clifton	224
Balquhidder	505	Braithwaite	221	Clipsham	331
Banchory	515	Brampton	222	Cockermouth	224
Bangor	548	Brancaster Staithe	347	Colerne	436
Bangor, Co Down	573	Bray	181	Coln St Aldwyns	274
Barnsley	266	Brighton	406	Combe Hay	385
Barrasford	358	Bristol	267	Comber, Co Down	578
Barton	201	Brithdir	549	Compton Abdale	274
Barton on Sea	289	Brixham	239	Congleton	204

Conwy	551	Eglwysfach	557	Harrogate	453
Cookham	184	Eldersfield	275	Hartlebury	444
Corse Lawn	274	Elie	507	Harwich	263
Cotebrook	204	Elland	449	Haverfordwest	558
Cowan Bridge	325	Elton	197	Haworth	454
Cowbridge	531	Ely	197	Hay-on-Wye	304
Cranborne	254	Emsworth	291	Haywards Heath	417
Cranbrook	316	Epping	263	Heatley	205
Craswall	304	Exeter	242	Heaton Moor	282
Criccieth	551	Fairford	276	Hedley on the Hill	358
Crockerton	437	Faversham	318	Helford Passage	206
Crosthwaite	225	Felin Fach	541	Helmsley	455
Crudwell	437	Felixkirk	450	Hemel Hempstead	309
Cuckfield	415	Fernhurst	416	Hemingford Grey	198
Cupar	506	Ferrensby	450	Henley-in-Arden	426
Dalry	497	Fetcham	402	Hereford	305
Dargate	317	Fletching	409	Hessle	455
Darley Abbey	234	Flitton	178	Heswell	341
Dartmouth	240	Folkestone	318	Hetton	456
Datchworth	308	Forest Green	402	Hexham	359
Dedham	262	Fort William	518	Hinton St George	386
Delny	518	Fotheringhay	355	Hinxton	198
Derby	235	Foxham	439	Hitchin	309
Didmarton	275	Frilsham	184	Hogpits Bottom	309
Dinton	189	Funtington	417	Holt	349
Dittisham	241	Fyfield	368	Holywood, Co Down	578
Dolfor	541	Gateshead	421	Honiton	244
Dolgellau	551	Gestingthorpe	263	Honley	456
Donhead St Andrew	437	Giffnock	498	Horncastle	337
Dorchester	254	Gillingham	255	Horndon on the Hill	264
Dorridge	434	Gittisham	243	Horningsham	439
Dover	317	Glasbury-on-Wye	542	Horsham	418
Drewsteignton	242	Glasgow	498	Hough on the Hill	338
Droxford	291	Godalming	402	Hove	410
Dufftown	516	Goldsborough	451	Huddersfield	456
Dunbar	483	Gorey, Jersey	565	Hunsdon	310
Dunstable	178	Grasmere	225	Huntingdon	199
Durham	258	Grassington	451	Hurworth-on-Tees	259
Easington	190	Great Gonerby	337	Hutton Magna	260
East Chiltington	408	Great Milton	369	Ilkley	457
East Chisenbury	438	Great Missenden	190	Ingham	350
East Coker	385	Great Shefford	185	Inverkeilor	511
East Grinstead	416	Great Wilbraham	197	Inverness	519
East Haddon	355	Great Yarmouth	349	Irby	341
East Wittering	416	Grindleton	326	Isle of Colonsay	500
East Witton	449	Groomsport, Co Down	578	Isle of Harris	520
Eastbourne	409	Gullane	493	Isle of Mull	501
Easton Grey	438	Gulval	206	Isle of Skye	520
Easton on the Hill	336	Gulworthy	243	Isle of Wight	292
Ebrington	275	Gun Hill	410	Jedburgh	480
Edgefield	349	Hambleton	332	Johnston	558
Edinburgh	483	Harlech	552	Kelso	480
Ednam	479	Harome	452	Kenilworth	426

Keswick	225	Lochinver	522	Narberth	561
Keyston	199	Lockerley	294	Near Sawrey	226
Kibworth Beauchamp	332	Locksbottom	318	Nether Burrow	328
Kibworth Harcourt	333	Long Ashton	276	New Milton	297
Kilberry	501	Long Crendon	190	Newark-on-Trent	362
Killiecrankie	511	Long Melford	396	Newbury	185
Killinchy, Co Down	579	Long Sutton	386	Newcastle, Co Down	579
Kincardine	507	Longparish	295	Newcastle Emlyn	561
Kingham	369	Longstock	295	Newcastle upon Tyne	421
King's Lynn	350	Loughor	532	Newport	562
Kings Nympton	244	Low Newton-by-the-Sea	359	Newton-in-Bowland	328
Kingston upon Thames	403	Lower Beeding	419	Newton Longville	193
Kirkby Lonsdale	226	Lower Froyle	296	Newton-on-Ouse	463
Knowstone	244	Lower Hardres	319	Newton Poppleford	246
Lambourn Woodlands	185	Lower Oddington	276	Norden	286
Lancaster	326	Ludford	338	North Queensferry	507
Langar	362	Ludlow	377	North Shields	424
Langho	327	Lydford	246	Northaw	310
Laugharne	558	Lydgate	282	Northleach	277
Lavant	418	Lyme Regis	255	Norwich	351
Lavenham	396	Lymington	296	Nottingham	362
Leamington Spa	427	Lymm	205	Oare	319
Leeds	458	Machynlleth	543	Oban	502
Leek	392	Maidenhead	185	Old Hunstanton	352
Leicester	333	Malton	462	Old Warden	178
Lewdown	245	Manchester	283	Oldstead	464
Lewes	411	Margate	319	Ombersley	444
Leyburn	461	Marlesford	397	Orford	397
Lifton	245	Marlow	191	Orkney Islands	523
Lincoln	338	Marton	378	Osmotherley	464
Linlithgow	494	Masham	462	Oswestry	379
Little Bedwyn	440	Mawgan	207	Ovington	352
Little Eccleston	327	Mawgan Porth	207	Oxford	370
Little Shelford	199	Melrose	481	Oxton	345
Little Wilbraham	200	Midsomer Norton	386	Padstow	209
Littleport	200	Milford on Sea	296	Paley Street	186
Liverpool	342	Millbrook	208	Parkmill	532
Llanarmon Dyffryn		Milton Keynes	193	Paulerspury	356
Ceiriog	545	Milverton	387	Peat Inn	508
Llanberis	552	Mistley	264	Peebles	481
Llanddewi Skirrid	538	Mitton	327	Penarth	533
Llandrillo	546	Monks Eleigh	397	Penmaenpool	554
Llandudno	553	Montgomery	544	Penmynydd	554
Llandybie	559	Morecambe	328	Pennal	544
Llanelli	559	Morston	350	Pentyrch	533
Llanfair Waterdine	376	Mousehole	208	Penzance	211
Llanfihangel-y-Creuddyn	559	Muir of Ord	523	Perranuthnoe	212
Llanfyllin	542	Mumbles	532	Perry Green	310
Llangammarch Wells	542	Munslow	378	Pershore	444
Llanrwst	553	Murcott	370	Perth	512
Llanwrtyd Wells	543	Muthill	512	Petersfield	297
Loch Lomond	501	Nant-y-derry	539	Pickering	464
Lochaline	522	Nantgaredig	560	Pleasington	329

The Good Food Guide 2013

Plockton	524	Salcombe	248	Sturminster Newton	256
Plumtree	365	Salford	288	Summerhouse	261
Plymouth	247	Sancton	466	Sutton Gault	200
Pontcanna	534	Sanquhar	482	Swaffham	353
Ponteland	360	Sapperton	277	Swansea	535
Pontypridd	534	Sark	570	Swinbrook	374
Poole	256	Sawdon	467	Talsarnau	555
Port Appin	524	Scarborough	467	Tangmere	420
Porthleven	212	Scholes	178	Taunton	387
Portpatrick	482	Scrabster	525	Teffont Evias	441
Portscatho	213	Scunthorpe	339	Tenterden	321
Portsmouth	298	Seer Green	194	Tetbury	278
Preston Candover	298	Shaldon	249	Thornbury	278
Prestwich	286	Sheffield	467	Thorpe Market	353
Pwllheli	554	Shefford	178	Tisbury	441
Radnage	194	Shepton Mallet	387	Titchwell	354
Ramsbottom	287	Shepton Montague	387	Titley	305
Ramsgate	320	Shere	404	Tollard Royal	441
Ramsgill	465	Shibden	470	Toot Baldon	374
Reading	187	Shieldaig	525	Topsham	250
Reigate	403	Shinfield	187	Torquay	251
Reynoldston	534	Shiplake	373	Totford	301
Richmond	465	Sidford	249	Treen	218
Ridgeway	235	Sidlesham	419	Trent	256
Ripley	403	Singleton	420	Troon	503
Ripon	466	Sinnington	471	Trotton	420
Ripponden	466	Skenfrith	539	Truro	218
Roade	356	Skipton	471	Tuddenham	399
Rock	213	Snettisham	353	Tunbridge Wells	322
Rockbeare	248	South Brent	250	Udny Green	516
Romaldkirk	260	South Dalton	471	Ullswater	226
Romsey	299	South Pool	250	Ulverston	227
Rowde	440	South Shields	424	Upper Slaughter	279
Rushton	357	Southampton	299	Upton Scudamore	442
Rye	412	Southport	346	Virginstow	251
St Albans	311	Southsea	299	Waddington	329
St Andrews	508	Southwold	398	Walberswick	399
St Brelade, Jersey	566	Sowerby Bridge	472	Wallingford	375
St Brelade's Bay, Jersey	566	Speldhurst	321	Warwick	428
St Clement, Jersey	567	Staddlebridge	472	Watergate Bay	219
St David's	562	Stalisfield Green	321	Watermillock	228
St Fagans	535	Stamford	339	Wedmore	388
St Helier, Jersey	567	Stanley	513	Wells	389
St Ives	215	Stanton	398	Welwyn	306
St Kew	217	Stathern	334	Welwyn Garden City	312
St Margaret's-at-Cliffe	320	Stockbridge	300	West Bay	256
St Martin, Guernsey	568	Stoke Row	374	West Hatch	442
St Martin, Jersey	569	Stone Edge	236	West Meon	301
St Mawes	217	Stow-on-the-Wold	277	West Pennard	390
St Monans	509	Stratford-upon-Avon	428	West Tanfield	473
St Peter, Jersey	570	Strathyre	505	West Witton	473
St Peter Port, Guernsey	569	Strontian	526	Westfield	413
St Saviour, Jersey	570	Stuckton	301	Weston Subedge	279

Weymouth 257
Whalley 329
Whitby 474
Whitebrook 540
Whitewell 330
Whitstable 322
Willian 312
Winchcombe 280
Winchester 302
Windermere 228
Winster 230
Winston 261
Winteringham 339
Wiswell 330
Wiveton 354
Woburn 179
Wolverhampton 434
Woodbridge 399
Woodhouse Eaves 335
Woodlands 303
Woodstock 375
Wookey Hole 390
Woolhope 306
Woolsthorpe by Belvoir 340
Worsley 288
Wymondham 335
York 475
Yoxford 400

Features

The American Dream 174
Breakfast of Champions 404
Casual Dining, Indian Style 432
The Chocolate Revolution 502
Cool for Kids 357
Gin o'Clock 497
Good British Puds 306
Let them Eat Steak 427
A Match Made in Heaven 205
Peruvian Party 343
Raise a Glass to England 324
Street Life 303
Supply and Demand 360
Veg Out 560

Chef Interviews

Andy Appleton, Fifteen, Cornwall 219
Hélène Darroze, The Connaught 161
Craig Dunn, Michael Caines at ABode Exeter 247
Matt Gillan, The Pass 379
Mark Jordan, Ocean Restaurant 257
Paul Leary, The Woodhouse 334
Bruno Loubet, Bistrot Bruno Loubet 93
Liz McGougan, Café Fish 526
Ross Pike, The British Larder 392
Simon Rogan, L'Enclume 227
Hans Schweitzer, Cotto 198
James Sommerin, The Crown at Whitebrook 546
Tom Van Zeller, Van Zeller 454
Mickael Weiss, Coq d'Argent 340
Alyn Williams, Alyn Williams at the Westbury 179
Martin Wishart, Restaurant Martin Wishart 494

A

Abarbistro, Portsmouth 298
L'Absinthe, Primrose Hill 83
Abu Zaad, Shepherd's Bush 133
Adam Simmonds at
    Danesfield House,
    Marlow 191
The Admiral Codrington,
    Chelsea 133
Agaric, Ashburton 237
Age & Sons, Ramsgate 320
Airds Hotel, Port Appin 524
Alain Ducasse at the
    Dorchester, Hyde Park 28
Alba, St Ives 215
Albannach, Lochinver 522
Albariño, Broadstairs 315
Albert's Table, Croydon 165
The Albion, Islington 83
Albion, Shoreditch 94
The Aldeburgh Market
    Café, Aldeburgh 394
Alderley Edge Hotel,
    Alderley Edge 201
Alfresco, St Ives 215
The Allanton Inn, Allanton 479
The Allotment, Dover 317
Almeida, Islington 83
Alyn Williams at the
    Westbury, Mayfair 28
Amaranto, Mayfair 29
Amaya, Knightsbridge 133
The Ambrette, Margate 319
The Ambrette at Rye, Rye 412
Amico Bio, Barbican 94
The Anchor, Oxford 370
The Anchor, Walberswick 399
The Anchor & Hope, South
    Bank 116
The Anchor Inn, Lower
    Froyle 296
The Anchor Inn, Sutton
    Gault 200
Anchorstone Café,
    Dittisham 241
Andrew Edmunds, Soho 29
Andrew Fairlie at
    Gleneagles, Auchterarder 510
The Angel, Dartmouth 240
The Angel Inn, Hetton 456
The Angel Inn, Upton
    Scudamore 442
Angel Restaurant, Long
    Crendon 190
Angels with Bagpipes,
    Edinburgh 483
Angels and Gypsies,
    Camberwell 116

Angelus, Lancaster Gate 30
Anglesea Arms, Shepherd's
    Bush 133
L'Anima, City 94
Annie Jones, Petersfield 297
Anthony's, Leeds 458
The Anvil Inn, Sawdon 467
Apicius, Cranbrook 316
The Apple Tree Inn, West
    Pennard 390
Applecross Inn, Applecross 517
Appuldurcombe
    Restaurant, Isle of Wight 292
The Apron Stage, Stanley 513
Apsleys, Hyde Park 30
Arbutus, Soho 31
Ardeonaig Hotel,
    Ardeonaig 504
The Ark, Notting Hill 134
The Artichoke, Amersham 188
Artisan, Hessle 455
Artisan, Sheffield 467
The Arundell Arms, Lifton 245
Ashmolean Dining Room,
    Oxford 373
The Asquith and Ginger's
    Bar, Birmingham 429
Assaggi, Notting Hill 134
The Assembly House,
    Norwich 351
At the Chapel, Bruton 384
L'Atelier de Joël Robuchon,
    Covent Garden 31
The Atlantic Hotel, Ocean
    Restaurant, St Brelade,
    Jersey 566
L'Auberge, Putney 116
The Auberge, St Martin,
    Guernsey 568
Auberge du Lac, Welwyn
    Garden City 312
Augustus Restaurant,
    Taunton 387
Aumbry, Prestwich 286
Aurelia, Mayfair 32
Australasia, Manchester 283
L'Autre Pied, Marylebone 32
Axis at One Aldwych,
    Covent Garden 33

B

Babur, Forest Hill 116
The Bakehouse, Penzance 211
The Bakers Arms,
    Droxford 291
The Balcon, St James's 33
Balloo House, Killinchy,
    Co Down 579

Baltic, Southwark 117
Bank, Birmingham 434
Bar Battu, City 95
Bar Boulud, Knightsbridge 134
The Bar & Grill at James
    Street South, Belfast, Co
    Antrim 574
Bar Shu, Soho 33
Bar Trattoria Semplice,
    Mayfair 34
Bar 44, Cowbridge 531
Barley Bree, Muthill 512
Barrafina, Soho 34
The Barrasford Arms,
    Barrasford 358
Barrica, Fitzrovia 34
The Bath Arms,
    Crockerton 437
The Bath Arms,
    Horningsham 439
The Bath Priory, Bath 381
The Bay, Penzance 211
The Bay Horse, Hurworth-
    on-Tees 259
The Bay Horse, Ulverston 227
The Bay Restaurant, St
    Margaret's-at-Cliffe 321
The Bay Tree, Holywood,
    Co Down 578
La Bécasse, Ludlow 377
Beckford Arms, Tisbury 441
The Bell, Fetcham 402
The Bell Inn, Horndon on
    the Hill 264
The Bell at Sapperton,
    Sapperton 277
The Bell at Skenfrith,
    Skenfrith 539
Bell's Diner, Bristol 267
Belle House, Pershore 444
Benares, Mayfair 35
Bentley's Oyster Bar &
    Grill, Piccadilly 35
The Berkeley Arms,
    Wymondham 335
Bibendum, South
    Kensington 135
Bilash, Wolverhampton 434
The Bildeston Crown,
    Bildeston 394
The Bingham, Richmond 165
Birch Tree, Delny 518
The Bird in Hand, Long
    Ashton 276
Bistro 21, Durham 258
Bistro Union, Clapham 117
Bistrot Bruno Loubet,
    Clerkenwell 95

Bistrot Vérité, Southport 346
The Black Horse, Shefford 178
The Black Horse Inn,
  Ludford 338
The Black Rat, Winchester 302
The Black Rock, St Ives 215
Black Sheep,
  Haverfordwest 558
The Black Swan, Oldstead 464
Blackaddie House Hotel,
  Sanquhar 482
Blackfriars Restaurant,
  Newcastle upon Tyne 421
Blacksmiths Arms,
  Broughton Mills 222
The Bladebone Inn,
  Bucklebury 183
Blagdon Manor, Ashwater 238
Blas Burgerworks, St Ives 216
Blostin's, Shepton Mallet 387
The Blue Lion, East Witton 449
Blue Sky Café, Bangor 548
The Bluebell, Chigwell 262
The Bluebell, Henley-in-
  Arden 426
The Boar's Head,
  Ardington 366
The Boat House, Bangor,
  Co Down 573
Boath House, Auldearn 517
The Boathouse, Ely 197
Boboli, Kibworth
  Harcourt 333
Bocca di Lupo, Piccadilly 36
Bodysgallen Hall, The
  Dining Room,
  Llandudno 553
La Boheme, Heatley 205
Bohemia, St Helier, Jersey 567
Bombay Brasserie, South
  Kensington 135
Bonds, City 96
The Boot Inn, Berwick St
  James 435
Boqueria Tapas, Brixton 118
Bordeaux Quay, Bristol 267
Bouchon Bistrot, Hexham 359
Boulters Riverside
  Brasserie, Maidenhead 185
The Box Tree, Ilkley 457
Bradley's, Huddersfield 456
Bradleys, Swiss Cottage 84
Braidwoods, Dalry 497
Branca, Oxford 371
Brasserie Forty 4, Leeds 459
Brasserie Vacherin, Sutton 166
Brawn, Shoreditch 96

Bread Street Kitchen, St
  Paul's 97
Brian Maule at Chardon
  d'Or, Glasgow 498
Bricklayers Arms, Hogpits
  Bottom 309
The Bridgewater Arms,
  Winston 261
Brilliant, Southall 166
Brinkley's Kitchen,
  Wandsworth 118
The British Larder,
  Bromeswell 395
The Brixham Deli,
  Brixham 239
Brompton Bar & Grill,
  South Kensington 136
The Brown Dog, Barnes 166
The Brown Horse Inn,
  Winster 230
The Brownlow Arms,
  Hough on the Hill 338
The Bruce Arms, West
  Tanfield 473
Brula, Twickenham 167
Brunswick House Café,
  Vauxhall 118
The Bull & Last,
  Hampstead 84
The Bull's Head, Craswall 304
Bully's, Cardiff 529
Bumbles, Belgravia 36
Bunch of Grapes,
  Pontypridd 534
Burger & Lobster, Mayfair 36
The Burlington at the
  Devonshire Arms,
  Bolton Abbey 447
Burt's Hotel, Melrose 481
The Butchers Arms,
  Eldersfield 275
The Butchers Arms,
  Woolhope 306
La Buvette, Richmond 167
Bwyty Mawddach,
  Dolgellau 551
Byfords, Holt 349

C
La Cachette, Elland 449
The Caddy Mann,
  Jedburgh 480
Le Café Anglais, Notting
  Hill 136
Café Bleu, Newark-on-
  Trent 362
The Café at Brovey Lair,
  Ovington 352

Café Fish, Isle of Mull 501
Café Japan, Golders Green 84
Café Lowrey, Ponteland 360
Café St Honoré, Edinburgh 483
The Café at Sotheby's,
  Mayfair 36
Café Spice Namasté, Tower
  Hill 97
Café 21, Newcastle upon
  Tyne 422
Caffè Vivo, Newcastle upon
  Tyne 423
Cambio de Tercio, Earl's
  Court 136
The Canbury Arms,
  Kingston upon Thames 403
Cantinetta, Putney 119
Canton Arms, Stockwell 119
Capote y Toros, South
  Kensington 137
Le Caprice, Mayfair 37
The Captain's Galley,
  Scrabster 525
Caracoli, Alresford 289
Carlton Riverside,
  Llanwrtyd Wells 543
Carnevale, Barbican 97
The Carpenters Arms,
  Felixkirk 450
The Carpenters Arms,
  Great Wilbraham 197
The Carpenter's Arms,
  Hammersmith 137
Carters of Moseley,
  Birmingham 434
The Cartford Inn, Little
  Eccleston 327
The Cary Arms,
  Babbacombe 238
Casa Brindisa, South
  Kensington 138
Casanis, Bath 381
Cassis, South Kensington 138
Cassons, Tangmere 420
Castell, Caernarfon 550
Castle Cottage, Harlech 552
Castle Green, Gorey, Jersey 566
Castle House, Hereford 305
Castle Terrace, Edinburgh 484
Castleman Hotel,
  Blandford Forum 252
Caunton Beck, Caunton 361
Le Caveau, Skipton 471
Cây Tre Soho, Soho 37
Cayenne, Belfast, Co
  Antrim 574
The Cellar, Anstruther 506
A Cena, Twickenham 165

Cennin, Beaumaris 548
Centotre, Edinburgh 484
Le Cercle, Belgravia 138
Ceviche, Soho 38
Chabrot Bistrot d'Amis,
  Knightsbridge 139
Chakra, Notting Hill 139
Champany Inn, Linlithgow 494
Le Champignon Sauvage,
  Cheltenham 271
The Chancery, Holborn 38
Chapter One, Locksbottom 318
Chapters All Day Dining,
  Blackheath 119
Le Chardon, East Dulwich 120
The Charles Bathurst Inn,
  Arkengarthdale 446
The Charles Lamb Pub and
  Kitchen, Islington 85
Charlotte's Bistro,
  Chiswick 140
Charlotte's Place, Ealing 140
The Checkers,
  Montgomery 544
The Chef's Table, Tetbury 278
Chequers Inn, Woolsthorpe
  by Belvoir 340
Cherwell Boathouse,
  Oxford 371
The Chesil Rectory,
  Winchester 302
Chez Bruce, Wandsworth 120
Chez Jerome, Dunstable 178
Chez Roux, Gullane 493
Chilli Cool, King's Cross 85
Chilli Pickle, Brighton 406
China Tang at the
  Dorchester, Hyde Park 38
Chinese Cricket Club,
  Blackfriars 97
Chisou, Mayfair 39
Chiswell Street Dining
  Rooms, City 98
La Chouette, Dinton 189
The Church Green, Lymm 205
Chutney Mary, Fulham 140
Cigala, Bloomsbury 39
Cigalon, Holborn 39
Cinnamon Club,
  Westminster 40
Cinnamon Kitchen, City 98
Cinnamon Soho, Soho 40
The Circus Café and
  Restaurant, Bath 381
City Café at Double Tree by
  Hilton, Leeds 459
City Merchant, Glasgow 500
Clarke's, Notting Hill 141

The Clog & Billycock,
  Pleasington 329
Clos Maggiore, Covent
  Garden 41
Club Gascon, City 98
Cnapan, Newport 562
The Coach & Horses,
  Clerkenwell 99
The Cobbles Inn, Kelso 480
The Cock, Hemingford
  Grey 198
The Cock O' Barton,
  Barton 201
Colchis Bar and
  Restaurant, Notting Hill 141
The Coldstreamer Inn,
  Gulval 206
Colmans, South Shields 424
Le Colombier, Chelsea 141
The Colonsay, Isle of
  Colonsay 500
Combe House, Gittisham 243
Comptoir Gascon,
  Clerkenwell 99
The Conway, Pontcanna 534
Copita, Soho 41
Coq d'Argent, City 100
Corner Room, Bethnal
  Green 100
Corrigan's Mayfair,
  Mayfair 41
The Cors, Laugharne 558
Corse Lawn House Hotel,
  Corse Lawn 274
Cotswold House, Chipping
  Campden 273
The Cottage in the Wood,
  Braithwaite 221
Cotto, Cambridge 195
Cow Shed Restaurant,
  Banchory 515
The Crab at Chieveley,
  Chieveley 183
Crab House Café,
  Weymouth 257
Crab & Lobster, Asenby 446
The Crab & Lobster,
  Sidlesham 419
Craig Millar @ 16 West
  End, St Monans 509
Crannog, Fort William 518
Creagan House, Strathyre 505
Create, Leeds 460
The Creel, Dunbar 483
The Creel, Orkney Islands 523
Creelers of Skye, Isle of
  Skye 520
Cringletie House, Peebles 481

The Crooked Billet,
  Newton Longville 193
The Crooked Billet, Stoke
  Row 374
The Crooked Well,
  Camberwell 120
Cross Foxes, Brithdir 549
The Crown, Burston 348
The Crown Country Inn,
  Munslow 378
The Crown Hotel,
  Southwold 398
The Crown Inn, Elton 197
The Crown at Whitebrook,
  Whitebrook 540
The Crown at Woodbridge,
  Woodbridge 399
The Curlew, Bodiam 405
CUT at 45 Park Lane,
  Mayfair 42
Cwtch, St David's 562

D
Dabbous, Fitzrovia 42
The Daffodil, Cheltenham 272
Damson, Heaton Moor 282
Dan's Kitchen, Isle of
  Wight 294
Darcy's, St Albans 311
Darleys, Darley Abbey 234
Darroch Learg, Ballater 515
The Dartmoor Inn,
  Lydford 246
David Bann, Edinburgh 485
David Kennedy's Food
  Social, Newcastle upon
  Tyne 422
The Dawnay Arms,
  Newton-on-Ouse 463
Dawson's at the Castle
  Hotel, Conwy 551
de'Clare Café, York 475
Dean Street Townhouse,
  Soho 43
Deanes, Belfast, Co Antrim 575
Deans @ Let's Eat, Perth 512
Dehesa, Oxford Circus 43
The Delaunay, Covent
  Garden 44
Delifonseca, Liverpool 342
Delilah, Nottingham 365
The Depot, Barnes 167
Les Deux Salons, Covent
  Garden 44
The Devonshire Arms,
  Beeley 233
The Devonshire Arms,
  Long Sutton 386

The Devonshire Brasserie, Bolton Abbey 447
Didier & Stephanie, Swansea 535
Dil Se, Orkney Islands 524
Dilli, Altrincham 281
The Dining Room, Ashbourne 231
The Dining Room, Boroughbridge 448
Dinings, Marylebone 45
Dinner by Heston Blumenthal, Knightsbridge 142
Dishoom, Covent Garden 45
The Dogs, Edinburgh 485
The Doll's House, St Andrews 509
The Don, City 101
Dosa World, Bournemouth 253
The Dove Inn, Dargate 317
The Dower House, Muir of Ord 523
Drake's Restaurant, Ripley 403
Driftwood, Portscatho 213
The Druidstone, Broad Haven 557
The Drunken Duck Inn, Ambleside 220
Ducksoup, Soho 45
The Duke of Cumberland Arms, Fernhurst 416
The Duke of York Inn, Grindleton 326
Dunvalanree, Carradale 496
Dylanwad Da, Dolgellau 552

E
e&o, Notting Hill 143
The Eagle & Child, Bispham Green 325
The Earl of March, Lavant 418
Eat on the Green, Udny Green 516
Eat17, Walthamstow 168
The Ebrington Arms, Ebrington 275
Ebury Restaurant & Wine Bar, Belgravia 143
Edamamé, Oxford 373
Eddie Gilbert's, Ramsgate 320
Edenwater House, Ednam 479
Ee-Usk, Oban 503
Ees Wyke, Near Sawrey 226
Egan's, Lymington 296
The Elephant, Torquay 251
Elio's, Barton-upon-Humber 336

Elliot's Café, Borough 121
Emile's, Putney 121
L'Enclume, Cartmel 222
L'Endroit, Congleton 204
Enoteca Turi, Putney 121
Enterkine House, Annbank 495
Entrée, Battersea 122
Entropy, Leicester 333
Eric's, Huddersfield 457
Eslington Villa, Gateshead 421
L'Etranger, South Kensington 143
The Exeter Arms, Easton on the Hill 336
The Exhibition Rooms, Crystal Palace 168
Eyre Brothers, Shoreditch 101

F
Fairyhill, Reynoldston 534
La Faisanderie, Dufftown 516
The Falcon Inn, Fotheringhay 355
Farlam Hall, Brampton 222
Farmcafé, Marlesford 397
Farsyde, Ilkley 458
The Fat Duck, Bray 181
Fat Olives, Emsworth 291
Feast, St Martin, Jersey 569
The Feathers, Woodstock 375
The Feathers Inn, Hedley on the Hill 358
The Felin Fach Griffin, Felin Fach 541
The Fen House, Littleport 200
Fernandez & Wells, Covent Garden 46
Ferryboat Inn, Helford Passage 206
Feversham Arms Hotel, Helmsley 455
Y Ffarmers, Llanfihangel-y-Creuddyn 559
ffresh, Cardiff 529
Fifteen Cornwall, Watergate Bay 219
Fifteen London, Shoreditch 101
1539 Restaurant & Bar, Chester 202
Fifth Floor, Knightsbridge 144
The Fig Tree, Penarth 533
Fino, Fitzrovia 46
Firenze, Kibworth Beauchamp 332
Fischer's Baslow Hall, Baslow 232
Fish & Grill, Croydon 168

The Fish House, Boston Spa 448
Fishers Bistro, Edinburgh 485
Fitzbillies, Cambridge 195
5 North Street, Winchcombe 280
500 Restaurant, Archway 85
Flinty Red, Bristol 267
Food by Breda Murphy, Whalley 329
Food For Friends, Brighton 406
The Foragers, Hove 410
The Foragers, St Albans 311
The Forest, Dorridge 434
The Forester, Donhead St Andrew 437
Forth Floor, Edinburgh 486
La Fosse at Cranborne, Cranborne 254
four o nine, Clapham 122
Fourth Floor, Leeds 460
The Fox, Willian 312
Fox & Barrel, Cotebrook 204
The Fox & Grapes, Wimbledon 122
The Fox & Hounds, Goldsborough 451
Fox & Hounds, Hunsdon 310
Fox & Hounds, Sinnington 471
The Fox Inn, Lower Oddington 276
The Foxham Inn, Foxham 439
The Foxhunter, Nant-y-derry 539
Fraiche, Oxton 345
Franco Manca, Brixton 123
Franklins, East Dulwich 123
Freemasons Country Inn, Wiswell 330
La Frégate, St Peter Port, Guernsey 569
The French at the Midland Hotel, Manchester 283
The French Table, Surbiton 168
Froggies at the Timber Batts, Bodsham 315
La Fromagerie, Marylebone 46

G
The Gallery Café, Manchester 283
Galvin Bistrot de Luxe, Marylebone 47
Galvin La Chapelle, Spitalfields 102
Galvin at Windows, Mayfair 46

Galvin's Café à Vin, Spitalfields 102
Gamba, Glasgow 498
The Garrick's Head, Bath 383
La Garrigue, Edinburgh 486
Gartells at the Sun Inn, Marton 378
Gastronomica, Pimlico 144
The Gate, Islington 86
El Gato Negro, Ripponden 466
The Gatsby, Berkhamsted 307
Gauthier Soho, Soho 47
Le Gavroche, Mayfair 48
Gee's, Oxford 371
The General Burgoyne, Ulverston 228
The General Tarleton, Ferrensby 450
The George, Alstonefield 391
George & Dragon, Clifton 224
The George & Dragon, Rowde 440
George & Dragon, Speldhurst 321
The George Grill, Rye 412
The George Inn, Abbots Leigh 265
The Giaconda Dining Room, Soho 49
Gidleigh Park, Chagford 239
The Giffnock Ivy, Giffnock 498
The Gilbert Scott, Euston 86
Gilbey's, Amersham 189
Gilpin Hotel & Lake House, Windermere 228
Gimbals, Sowerby Bridge 472
The Ginger Bistro, Belfast, Co Antrim 577
The Ginger Dog, Brighton 406
The Ginger Fox, Albourne 414
The Ginger Pig, Hove 410
Gingerman, Brighton 407
Glan Yr Afon, Pennal 544
The Glasshouse, Kew 169
Glenapp Castle, Ballantrae 496
The Globe, Milverton 387
Golden Lion, Osmotherley 464
Goodfellows, Wells 389
The Goods Shed, Canterbury 316
Gordon's, Inverkeilor 511
Gourmet Spot, Durham 259
The Grand Hotel, Mirabelle, Eastbourne 409
The Granville, Lower Hardres 319
Grassington House Hotel, Grassington 451

Gravetye Manor, East Grinstead 416
Graze Restaurant, Hove 411
Great Eastern Dining Room, Shoreditch 103
The Great House, Lavenham 396
Great Queen Street, Covent Garden 49
The Green Café, Ludlow 377
The Green Inn, Ballater 515
Green Island Restaurant, St Clement, Jersey 567
The Green Olive, St Helier, Jersey 568
Green's, Whitby 474
Greenhead House, Chapeltown 449
The Greenhouse, Green Park 49
Greens, Manchester 284
Greens' Dining Room, Bristol 268
Grenache, Worsley 288
The Greyhound Inn, Stockbridge 300
The Griffin Inn, Fletching 409
The Grove, Narberth 561
The Grove, Colette's, Chandler's Cross 308
The Grove Inn, Kings Nympton 244
Guchhi Indian Seafood & Bar, Edinburgh 487
Guildhall Tavern, Poole 256
The Guinea Grill, Mayfair 50
The Gun, Canary Wharf 103
The Gun, Gun Hill 410
Gung-Ho, West Hampstead 86
The Gunton Arms, Thorpe Market 353
The Gurnard's Head, Treen 218

H

Haandi, Knightsbridge 144
The Hackney Pearl, Hackney Wick 103
Hakkasan, Fitzrovia 50
Hakkasan Mayfair, Mayfair 50
Hallidays, Funtington 417
Halsetown Inn, St Ives 217
Hambleton Hall, Hambleton 332
The Hand & Flowers, Marlow 192
Hanover Street Social, Liverpool 342
Hansa's, Leeds 461

Hanson at the Chelsea, Swansea 536
Haozhan, Soho 51
Harbourmaster, Aberaeron 556
The Hardwick, Abergavenny 537
The Hare, Lambourn Woodlands 185
Hare & Hounds, Bowland Bridge 221
Hare & Hounds, Old Warden 178
The Harris Arms, Lewdown 245
Harris's, Penzance 211
Harrison's, Balham 123
The Harrow at Little Bedwyn, Little Bedwyn 440
Harry's Place, Great Gonerby 337
Hart's, Nottingham 362
Hartwell House, Aylesbury 189
The Harwood Arms, Fulham 145
The Havelock Tavern, Shepherd's Bush 145
Hawksmoor, City 104
Hawksmoor Guildhall, City 103
Hawksmoor Seven Dials, Covent Garden 51
Hedone, Chiswick 145
Helen Browning at the Royal Oak, Bishopstone 435
Hélène Darroze at the Connaught, Mayfair 52
Helyar Arms, East Coker 385
Hengist, Aylesford 314
Hereford Road, Notting Hill 146
Hermitage Rd, Hitchin 309
The Herring, Mawgan Porth 207
Hibiscus, Mayfair 52
Hideaway, Ramsbottom 287
The Highwayman, Nether Burrow 328
The Hinds Head, Bray 182
Hipping Hall, Cowan Bridge 325
Hive Beach Café, Burton Bradstock 254
Hix, Soho 53
Hix at the Albemarle, Mayfair 53
Hix Oyster & Chop House, Clerkenwell 104

Hix Oyster & Fish House, Lyme Regis 255
Holbeck Ghyll, Windermere 229
The Hole in the Wall, Little Wilbraham 200
The Holt, Honiton 244
Homa, Stoke Newington 86
The Hoops Inn, Perry Green 310
The Horn of Plenty, Gulworthy 243
Horse & Groom, Bourton on the Hill 266
Host, Liverpool 342
The Hoste Arms, Burnham Market 348
Hotel TerraVina, Woodlands 303
Hotel Tresanton, St Mawes 217
The House, Scholes 178
The Hove Kitchen, Hove 411
Howard's House Hotel, Teffont Evias 441
Hunan, Chelsea 146
Hurrens Inn on the Estuary, Loughor 532

I

Ibérica, Canary Wharf 105
Ibérica, Fitzrovia 54
Ibérico World Tapas, Nottingham 365
Ilkley Moor Vaults, Ilkley 458
Incanto, Harrow-on-the-Hill 169
Indian Zilla, Barnes 170
Indian Zing, Hammersmith 147
The Ingham Swan, Ingham 350
The Inn at Whitewell, Whitewell 330
Inside, Greenwich 123
Inverlochy Castle, Fort William 518
Irvins Brasserie, North Shields 424
The Ivy, Covent Garden 54

J

J. Baker's Bistro Moderne, York 475
J. Sheekey, Covent Garden 54
J. Sheekey Oyster Bar, Covent Garden 55
The Jack in the Green, Rockbeare 248

James Street South, Belfast, Co Antrim 576
Jeremy's Restaurant, Haywards Heath 417
Jerichos at the Waverley, Windermere 229
Jesmond Dene House, Newcastle upon Tyne 423
Jesse's Bistro, Cirencester 274
The Jetty, Christchurch 254
Jim's Yard, Stamford 339
Jin Kichi, Hampstead 87
John Hope Gateway Restaurant, Edinburgh 492
JoJo's, Whitstable 322
The Jolly Cricketers, Seer Green 194
The Jolly Sportsman, East Chiltington 408
José, Bermondsey 124
Joseph Benjamin, Chester 202
JSW, Petersfield 297
The Jumble Room, Grasmere 225
Junction 28, Bassaleg 538
Justin Brown at Farringford, Isle of Wight 293
Jyoti's Vegetarian, Birmingham 430

K

Kalpna, Edinburgh 492
Karpo, King's Cross 87
Kasturi, Whitechapel 105
The Keepers Arms, Trotton 420
Kendells Bistro, Leeds 461
Kenny Atkinson at The Orangery, Hurworth-on-Tees 259
Kensington Place, Notting Hill 147
Kentish Canteen, Kentish Town 88
Kerbisher & Malt, Hammersmith 147
Kêu!, Shoreditch 105
Kiku, Mayfair 55
The Kilberry Inn, Kilberry 501
Kilcamb Lodge, Strontian 526
Killiecrankie House, Killiecrankie 511
The King John Inn, Tollard Royal 441
King William, Bath 383
The Kingham Plough, Kingham 369
Kinghams, Shere 404

The Kings Arms, Didmarton 275
The Kings Arms, Lockerley 294
Kings Arms, Pentyrch 533
The Kings Head, Lewes 411
The Kings Head Inn, Bledington 367
Kinloch House Hotel, Blairgowrie 510
Kinloch Lodge, Isle of Skye 520
The Kinmel Arms, Abergele 547
Kiraku, Ealing 148
Kitchen, Sheffield 468
Kitchen W8, Kensington 148
The Kitchin, Edinburgh 487
Knockinaam Lodge, Portpatrick 482
Koffmann's, Belgravia 148
Koh Thai Tapas, Bournemouth 253
Kota, Porthleven 212
Koya, Soho 55

L

Lake Country House, Llangammarch Wells 542
Lamberts, Balham 124
Landgate Bistro, Rye 412
Langar Hall, Langar 362
Le Langhe, York 475
Lantana Café, Fitzrovia 56
Lanterna, Scarborough 467
The Larder on Goosegate, Nottingham 363
Lasan, Birmingham 430
Lasswade Country House, Llanwrtyd Wells 543
Latium, Fitzrovia 56
Launceston Place, South Kensington 149
The Lavender House, Brundall 348
The Lawn Bistro, Wimbledon 124
The Leaping Hare, Stanton 398
The Ledbury, Notting Hill 149
Lemon Tree Café & Bistro, Plymouth 248
Lewtrenchard Manor, Lewdown 245
Lido, Bristol 268
Light House, Wimbledon 125
The Lighthouse, Aldeburgh 393
The Lighthouse Restaurant, Boylestone 233

The Lime Tree, Fort William 519
The Lime Tree, Manchester 284
Linthwaite House, Bowness-on-Windermere 221
Little Barwick House, Barwick 380
Little Wing, Belfast, Co Antrim 578
Lobster Pot, Elephant and Castle 125
Locanda Locatelli, Marble Arch 57
Loch Bay, Isle of Skye 521
Lockwoods, Ripon 466
Lokanta, Sheffield 469
Lola Rojo, Battersea 125
Lola & Simon, Hammersmith 150
The London Carriage Works, Liverpool 343
London Street Brasserie, Reading 187
Longueville Manor, St Saviour, Jersey 570
The Lord Clyde, Bollington 202
The Lord Poulett Arms, Hinton St George 386
Lords of the Manor, Upper Slaughter 279
Loves, Birmingham 430
Lucknam Park, Colerne 436
Ludo's at The Coopers, Newcastle Emlyn 561
Lumière, Cheltenham 272
La Luna, Godalming 402
Lunya, Liverpool 344
Lussmanns, St Albans 311
Lutyens, City 105

M
Ma Cuisine, Kew 170
MacCallums Oyster Bar, Troon 503
Made by Bob, Cirencester 273
Made in Camden, Camden 88
Madhu's, Southall 170
Madsen, South Kensington 150
Maes-y-Neuadd, Talsarnau 555
Maes-Yr-Haf, Parkmill 532
Magdalen, Southwark 126
The Magdalen Arms, Oxford 373
Magpie Café, Whitby 474
Magpies, Horncastle 337
Main's Restaurant, Yoxford 400

Maison Bleue, Bury St Edmunds 395
Maison Pommier, Sark 570
Maiyango, Leicester 333
Maliks, Cookham 184
Malina, Hammersmith 150
The Mall Tavern, Notting Hill 150
Mallory Court, Main Dining Room, Bishop's Tachbrook 425
Mandarin Palace, Gants Hill 171
Mangal 1 Ocakbasi, Stoke Newington 88
Mango Tree, Belgravia 57
Le Manoir aux Quat'Saisons, Great Milton 369
The Manor House Hotel, Bybrook Restaurant, Castle Combe 436
Marcus Wareing at the Berkeley, Belgravia 151
Mari Vanna, Knightsbridge 152
The Marine, Milford on Sea 296
The Mark Addy, Salford 288
Mark Jordan at the Beach, St Peter, Jersey 570
Market, Camden 89
Market Bistro, King's Lynn 350
The Marlborough Tavern, Bath 382
The Marquis at Alkham, Alkham 313
Martin Wishart at Loch Lomond, Loch Lomond 501
Masa, Derby 235
The Masons Arms, Knowstone 244
Mazi, Notting Hill 152
McCoys at the Tontine, Staddlebridge 472
Meatballs, Clerkenwell 106
Mehek, Moorgate 106
Mele e Pere, Soho 57
Melton's, York 476
Melton's Too, York 476
Mennula, Fitzrovia 57
Menu Gordon Jones, Bath 384
Meza, Tooting 126
Michael Caines at ABode Canterbury, Canterbury 316
Michael Caines at ABode Chester, Chester 203
Michael Caines at ABode Exeter, Exeter 242

Michael Caines at ABode Manchester, Manchester 284
Michael Wignall, the Latymer at Pennyhill Park Hotel, Bagshot 401
Midsummer House, Cambridge 196
The Milestone, Sheffield 468
The Millbrook Inn, South Pool 250
Mint & Mustard, Cardiff 530
Mishkin's, Covent Garden 58
The Mistley Thorn, Mistley 264
The Modern Pantry, Clerkenwell 106
The Mole & Chicken, Easington 190
The Mole Inn, Toot Baldon 374
Molly's Yard, Belfast, Co Antrim 576
Mon Plaisir, Covent Garden 58
Monachyle Mhor, Balquhidder 505
Montagu Arms Hotel, Terrace Restaurant, Beaulieu 290
The Montague Inn, Shepton Montague 387
Montparnasse, Southsea 299
The Moody Goose at the Old Priory, Midsomer Norton 386
Moores', Newton Poppleford 246
The Moorings, Blakeney 347
Moorings Bistro, Borth-y-Gest 549
Moran's Restaurant, Sheffield 469
Morgan M, Barbican 107
Morito, Clerkenwell 107
Moro, Clerkenwell 108
Morston Hall, Morston 350
Mosaica @ the Factory, Wood Green 171
Moti Mahal, Covent Garden 58
Mountain Café, Aviemore 518
Mourne Seafood Bar, Belfast, Co Antrim 576
Mr Kong, Soho 59
Mr Underhill's, Ludlow 377
The Mulroy, Edinburgh 492
Mumbai Chilli, Derby 235
Murano, Mayfair 59
Murrays, Clevedon 385

The Muset by Ronnie,
Bristol 269
Mustard and Punch,
Honley 456
My Sichuan, Oxford 372
Mya Lacarte, Caversham 183

N
Nathan Outlaw Seafood &
Grill, Rock 213
National Portrait Gallery,
Portrait Restaurant,
Trafalgar Square 60
Da Nello, St Peter Port,
Guernsey 569
The Neptune, Old
Hunstanton 352
Neuadd Lwyd Country
House, Penmynydd 554
The New Inn, Coln St
Aldwyns 274
New Yard Restaurant,
Mawgan 207
Nick's Warehouse, Belfast,
Co Antrim 577
99 Station Street, Burton
upon Trent 392
No 14 Bistro, Lincoln 338
No 9 Church St, Stratford-
upon-Avon 428
Nobu Berkeley St, Mayfair 60
Nobu London, Mayfair 60
Non Solo Vino,
Chesterfield 234
Nopi, Soho 61
The North Port, Perth 512
North Road, Clerkenwell 108
Northcote, Langho 327
The Northern Quarter,
Manchester 285
Notting Hill Brasserie,
Notting Hill 152
Noura Brasserie, Belgravia 61
Nova, Heswell 341
number one, Edinburgh 488
Number 16, Glasgow 500
Number 75, Tenterden 321
The Nut Tree Inn, Murcott 370
Nutters, Norden 286

O
The Oak Tree Inn, Hutton
Magna 260
Ockenden Manor Hotel &
Spa, Cuckfield 415
Ode, Shaldon 249
Odette's, Primrose Hill 89
The Old Bakery, Lincoln 338

The Old Bridge Hotel,
Huntingdon 199
The Old Butcher's, Stow-
on-the-Wold 277
The Old Coastguard,
Mousehole 208
The Old Inn,
Drewsteignton 242
The Old Passage,
Arlingham 265
The Old Schoolhouse Inn,
Comber, Co Down 578
The Old Spot, Wells 389
The Old Vicarage,
Ridgeway 235
The Old Vicarage Dolfor,
Dolfor 541
The Olive Branch,
Clipsham 331
Ondine, Edinburgh 489
152 Restaurant, Aldeburgh 393
One-O-One,
Knightsbridge 153
Opera Tavern, Covent
Garden 62
Opus, Birmingham 431
Orchid Restaurant,
Harrogate 453
Oren, Caernarfon 550
L'ortolan, Shinfield 187
Orwells, Shiplake 373
Oscars of Cardiff, Cardiff 530
Oscars of Cowbridge,
Cowbridge 531
Osso, Peebles 481
Ostlers Close, Cupar 506
Ottolenghi, Islington 90
Out of the Blue, Mumbles 532
The Oyster Box, St
Brelade's Bay, Jersey 566
The Oyster Shack,
Bigbury-on-Sea 238

P
Pan Haggerty, Newcastle
upon Tyne 423
Pant-y-Gwydr Restaurant,
Swansea 536
El Parador, Camden 90
Paris House, Woburn 179
The Parkers Arms,
Newton-in-Bowland 328
The Parrot Inn, Forest
Green 402
The Partridge, Wallingford 375
The Partridge Inn,
Singleton 420
The Pass, Lower Beeding 419

Paul Ainsworth at No. 6,
Padstow 209
Paul Leary at The
Woodhouse, Woodhouse
Eaves 335
Pea Porridge, Bury St
Edmunds 396
The Peak, Llanberis 552
Pearl, Holborn 62
The Peat Inn, Peat Inn 508
The Peat Spade Inn,
Longstock 295
Pebble Beach, Barton on
Sea 289
Penmaenuchaf Hall,
Penmaenpool 554
Penny Street Bridge,
Lancaster 326
Percy's, Virginstow 251
Perkins, Plumtree 365
Petersham Nurseries Café,
Richmond 171
La Petite Auberge, Great
Missenden 190
La Petite Maison, Topsham 250
Pétrus, Knightsbridge 153
The Pheasant,
Gestingthorpe 263
The Pheasant, Keyston 199
The Pheasant Hotel,
Harome 452
Phoenix Palace,
Marylebone 63
Pied-à-Terre, Fitzrovia 63
The Pier at Harwich,
Harbourside Restaurant,
Harwich 263
Da Piero, Irby 341
Pier 64, Penarth 533
The Pig, Brockenhurst 291
The Pigs, Edgefield 349
The Pipe & Glass Inn,
South Dalton 471
Il Pirata, Belfast, Co
Antrim 575
El Pirata Detapas, Notting
Hill 154
Pizarro, Southwark 126
Pizza East, Shoreditch 109
Pizza East Portobello,
Ladbroke Grove 154
Plas Bodegroes, Pwllheli 554
Platform, Southwark 127
Plockton Inn, Plockton 524
The Plough, Bolnhurst 177
The Plough, Stalisfield
Green 321

The Plough Inn, Longparish 295
Plumber Manor, Sturminster Newton 256
Plumed Horse, Edinburgh 489
Pollen Street Social, Mayfair 64
Da Polpo, Covent Garden 42
Polpo, Soho 64
Y Polyn, Nantgaredig 560
The Pond Café, Isle of Wight 293
Le Pont de la Tour, Bermondsey 127
The Pony & Trap, Chew Magna 384
Popeseye, Olympia 154
La Porte des Indes, Marble Arch 65
Porth Tocyn Hotel, Abersoch 548
Porthmeor Beach Café, St Ives 217
Porthminster Beach Café, St Ives 216
Portobello Ristorante Pizzeria, Notting Hill 155
The Pot Kiln, Frilsham 184
The Potager Restaurant, Barnsley 266
La Potinière, Gullane 493
Potli, Hammersmith 155
The Potted Hen, Belfast, Co Antrim 577
The Potted Pig, Cardiff 530
The Potting Shed, Crudwell 437
Prashad, Bradford 448
Prego, Bristol 269
The Princess Victoria, Shepherd's Bush 155
Princi, Soho 65
The Print Room, Bournemouth 253
The Providores, Marylebone 65
The Puesdown Inn, Compton Abdale 274
The Pump House, Bristol 269
The Punch Bowl, Crosthwaite 225
The Punch Bowl Inn, Richmond 465
Purefoy Arms, Preston Candover 298
Purnell's, Birmingham 431

Pythouse Kitchen Garden Shop and Café, West Hatch 442

Q

Qarma, Leek 392
The Queensberry Hotel, Olive Tree Restaurant, Bath 382
Quilon, Westminster 65
Quince & Medlar, Cockermouth 224
Quirinale, Westminster 66
Quo Vadis, Soho 66

R

The Raby Hunt, Summerhouse 261
Racine, Knightsbridge 156
Rafters, Sheffield 470
Railroad, Hackney 109
The Raj, Epping 263
Rampsbeck Country House Hotel, Watermillock 228
ramsons, Ramsbottom 287
Ransome's Dock, Battersea 127
Rasoi, Chelsea 156
The Rat Inn, Hexham 359
Read's, Faversham 318
The Red Fort, Soho 67
The Red Lion, Bradley 391
Red Lion, Chelwood Gate 415
The Red Lion, East Chisenbury 438
The Red Lion, East Haddon 355
Red Lion Bar & Bistro, Stone Edge 236
The Red Lion Inn, Hinxton 198
Red Lion Inn, Stathern 334
Red Onion, Glasgow 500
The Redwell Inn, Arkholme 325
Refettorio, City 109
Regatta, Aldeburgh 394
Restaurant Alimentum, Cambridge 196
Restaurant Bosquet, Kenilworth 426
Restaurant Coworth Park, Ascot 180
The Restaurant at Drakes, Brighton 407
Restaurant Gordon Ramsay, Chelsea 157

Restaurant Mark Greenaway, Edinburgh 488
Restaurant Martin Wishart, Edinburgh 489
Restaurant Michael Nadra, Chiswick 157
Restaurant Nathan Outlaw, Rock 214
The Restaurant at the Petersham, Richmond 172
Restaurant Sat Bains, Nottingham 363
Restaurant Stock Hill, Gillingham 255
Restaurant Tristan, Horsham 418
Restaurant 1877, Nottingham 363
Restaurant 1861, Abergavenny 538
Restaurant 65, Hemel Hempstead 309
Restaurant 27, Southsea 300
Restaurant 23, Leamington Spa 427
Retro Bistrot, Teddington 172
Rhiwafallen, Caernarfon 550
Rhodes Twenty Four, City 110
Rhodes W1 Restaurant, Marble Arch 67
Rhubarb at Prestonfield, Edinburgh 490
Richard Booth's Bookshop Café, Hay-on-Wye 304
Rick Stein's Café, Padstow 209
The Rickety Press, Oxford 372
Rick's Restaurant, Tooting 128
The Riding House Café, Fitzrovia 68
Ristorante Semplice, Mayfair 68
The River Café, Glasbury-on-Wye 542
The River Café, Hammersmith 158
The Riverside, Woodbridge 400
Riverside Restaurant, West Bay 256
riverstation, Bristol 270
Rivington Grill, Shoreditch 110
Roade House, Roade 356
Roast, Southwark 128
Robert Thompson at the Hambrough, Isle of Wight 294
Rochelle Canteen, London 110

Rockfish Grill, Bristol 270
Rockfish Seafood and
  Chips, Dartmouth 241
Rocsalt, Folkestone 318
Rocpool, Inverness 519
Rogan & Company,
  Cartmel 223
Roganic, Marylebone 68
Roger Hickman's,
  Norwich 351
Rojano's in the Square,
  Padstow 210
Roka, Fitzrovia 69
Ronnie's of Thornbury,
  Thornbury 278
The Rooftop Restaurant,
  Stratford-upon-Avon 428
The Rose & Crown,
  Romaldkirk 260
The Rose & Crown,
  Snettisham 353
The Rose & Crown, Trent 256
Rosevine, Portscatho 213
Roti Chai Street Kitchen,
  Marylebone 69
Roux at the Landau,
  Oxford Circus 70
Roux at Parliament Square,
  Westminster 69
Rowley's, Baslow 232
The Royal Oak, Paley
  Street 186
RSJ, Southwark 128
Rules, Covent Garden 71
Rushton Hall, Tresham
  Restaurant, Rushton 357
Russell's, Broadway 443

S
Saffron, Birmingham 432
St Andrew's Street Bistro,
  St Ives 216
St James, Bushey 307
St John, Clerkenwell 111
St John Bread & Wine,
  Spitalfields 111
St John Hotel, Leicester
  Square 74
St Kew Inn, St Kew 217
St Petroc's Bistro, Padstow 210
St Tudno Hotel, Terrace
  Restaurant, Llandudno 553
Salloos, Knightsbridge 158
Salt House, Liverpool 344
Salt Yard, Fitzrovia 71
The Salty Monk, Sidford 249
Salvo's, Leeds 460

Sam's Brasserie & Bar,
  Chiswick 159
The Samling, Windermere 230
Samphire, East Wittering 416
Sam's of Seven Dials,
  Brighton 408
The Samuel Fox Inn,
  Bradwell 233
Samuel's at Swinton Park,
  Masham 462
San Pietro, Scunthorpe 339
The Sandpiper Inn,
  Leyburn 461
The Sands End, Fulham 159
Sangster's, Elie 507
Sanmini's, Ramsbottom 287
Sasso, Harrogate 453
Savoy Grill, Covent
  Garden 71
Scarista House, Isle of
  Harris 520
Scott's, Mayfair 72
Scutchers, Long Melford 396
Seafood Restaurant, Great
  Yarmouth 349
The Seafood Restaurant,
  Padstow 210
The Seafood Restaurant, St
  Andrews 508
Seafood Temple, Oban 523
Seagrass Restaurant, St Ives 217
The Seagrave Arms, Weston
  Subedge 279
The Seahorse, Dartmouth 241
Searcy's, Barbican 111
Seasons.Casamia, Bristol 271
Sebastians, Oswestry 379
Second Floor, Manchester 285
Seeds, Llanfyllin 542
Serpentine Bar & Kitchen,
  Hyde Park 72
Seven Park Place, Mayfair 72
Sharrow Bay, Ullswater 226
Shayona Restaurant,
  Neasden 90
Shibden Mill Inn, Shibden 470
Shiki, Norwich 351
The Ship Inn, Low
  Newton-by-the-Sea 359
Shrimpy's, King's Cross 90
Siam Café, Soho 73
The Side Door, Liverpool 344
Sienna, Dorchester 254
Silver Darling, Aberdeen 514
Silverdale Inn & Lodge,
  Johnston 558
Silversmiths Restaurant &
  Bar, Sheffield 470

Simon Radley at the
  Chester Grosvenor,
  Chester 203
Simply Allium, Fairford 276
Simply Thai, Teddington 173
Simpsons, Birmingham 432
Singapore Garden, Swiss
  Cottage 91
The Sir Charles Napier,
  Chinnor 367
60 Hope Street, Liverpool 345
63 Tay Street, Perth 513
Sketch, Lecture Room &
  Library, Mayfair 73
Sky Apple Café, Newcastle
  upon Tyne 424
Skylon, South Bank 129
Slice, Swansea 536
Soif, Battersea 129
Sojo, Oxford 373
Sonny's Kitchen, Barnes 173
Sosban, Llanelli 559
South Sands Beachside
  Restaurant, Salcombe 248
Spire, Liverpool 345
The Sportsman, Whitstable 323
Spuntino, Soho 73
The Square, Mayfair 73
The Stagg Inn, Titley 305
The Star @ Sancton,
  Sancton 466
The Star Inn, Harome 452
Stones Bistro, Caernarfon 550
Strattons, Swaffham 353
Stravaigin, Glasgow 499
The Street Food Chef,
  Sheffield 470
Strudel Bistro,
  Groomsport, Co Down 578
Sukhothai, Leeds 461
Sumas, Gorey, Jersey 565
Sumosan, Mayfair 75
The Sun Inn, Dedham 262
The Sun Inn, Kirkby
  Lonsdale 226
The Sun at Northaw,
  Northaw 310
Sun Terrace Restaurant at
  The Midland,
  Morecambe 328
Sushi-Say, Willesden 91
Sushi of Shiori, Euston 92
Sutherland House,
  Southwold 398
The Swan, Wedmore 388
The Swan Inn, Great
  Shefford 185

The Swan Inn, Monks Eleigh 397
The Swan Inn, Swinbrook 374
The Sweet Olive, Aston Tirrold 366
Swinside Lodge, Keswick 225
Sycamore House, Little Shelford 199

T
T&Cake, Huddersfield 457
Tabb's, Truro 218
Tailors, Warwick 428
Taipan, Milton Keynes 193
Talbot Hotel, Malton 462
Tamarind, Mayfair 75
Y Tanerdy, Llanrwst 553
Tangawizi, Richmond 173
Tanjore, Edinburgh 491
Tanners, Plymouth 247
Tapas Brindisa, Southwark 130
Tapas Brindisa Soho, Soho 76
Tassili, St Helier, Jersey 568
The Tavern, Cheltenham 272
Tayyabs, Whitechapel 112
Teacup on Thomas Street, Manchester 286
10 Greek Street, Soho 76
Tentazioni, Bermondsey 130
Terre à Terre, Brighton 408
Terroirs, Covent Garden 76
Texture, Marble Arch 77
Thackeray's, Tunbridge Wells 322
Theo Randall at the InterContinental, Mayfair 77
34, Mayfair 78
36 On The Quay, Emsworth 292
The Thomas Cubitt, Belgravia 159
The Thomas Lord, West Meon 301
The Three Chimneys, Biddenden 315
The Three Chimneys, Isle of Skye 521
The Three Fishes, Mitton 327
The Three Horseshoes, Radnage 194
The Three Lions, Stuckton 301
The Three Mariners, Oare 319
The Three Tuns, Romsey 299
Tigh an Eilean Hotel, Shieldaig 525
The Tilbury, Datchworth 308
Timo, Kensington 160

Tinello, Pimlico 160
Tir a Môr, Criccieth 551
Titchwell Manor, Titchwell 354
The Tollgate Inn, Holt 439
Tom Aikens, Chelsea 160
Tom Ilic, Battersea 130
Tom's Kitchen, Chelsea 162
Tony Tobin @ The Dining Room, Reigate 403
Tosa, Hammersmith 162
The Town House, Arundel 415
Towpath Café, Dalston 112
Treehouse, Aberystwyth 557
Trinity, Clapham 131
The Trinity, Crown & Castle, Orford 397
Trishna, Marylebone 78
Les Trois Garçons, Shoreditch 112
La Trompette, Chiswick 162
The Trout at Tadpole Bridge, Buckland Marsh 367
Trullo, Islington 92
Tsunami, Clapham 131
Tuddenham Mill, Tuddenham 399
Turl Street Kitchen, Oxford 372
Turners, Birmingham 433
The Turtley Corn Mill, South Brent 250
28°-50°, City 113
22 Mill Street, Chagford 240
2 Fore Street, Mousehole 209
21212, Edinburgh 491
Ty Mawr Mansion, Aberaeron 556
Tyddyn Llan, Llandrillo 546

U
Ubiquitous Chip, Glasgow 499
Ultracomida, Aberystwyth 557
Ultracomida, Narberth 561
Uluru Bistro, Armagh, Co Armagh 573
Umu, Mayfair 78
The Unicorn Inn, Kincardine 507
Untitled by Robert Wright, Penzance 212

V
Le Vacherin, Chiswick 163
Valans, Llandybie 559
La Vallée Blanche, Glasgow 499
Valvona & Crolla Caffè Bar, Edinburgh 491
Van Zeller, Harrogate 453

Vanilla, Newcastle, Co Down 579
Vanilla Black, Farringdon 113
The Vanilla Pod, Marlow 192
Vasco & Piero's Pavilion, Soho 79
Veeraswamy, Piccadilly 79
Vennell's, Masham 463
The Venture In, Ombersley 444
Vetiver, New Milton 297
Viajante, Bethnal Green 113
The Victoria, East Sheen 174
Victoria Inn, Perranuthnoe 212
Viet Grill, Shoreditch 114
The View, Millbrook 208
Village East, Southwark 131
The Village Pub, Barnsley 266
The Vine House, Paulerspury 356
The Vine Leaf, St Andrews 509
The Vineyard Café, Ashprington 238
The Vineyard at Stockcross, Newbury 185
Vinoteca, Farringdon 114
Vinoteca, Marylebone 79

W
The Waddington Arms, Waddington 329
The Waggon at Birtle, Birtle 281
Wallett's Court, St Margaret's-at-Cliffe 320
The Walnut Tree, Llanddewi Skirrid 538
Wapping Food, Wapping 115
The Waterdine, Llanfair Waterdine 376
Waterfront Fishouse Restaurant, Oban 502
The Waterside Inn, Bray 182
Wayside Café, St Brelade, Jersey 567
Weavers, Haworth 454
Webbe's at the Fish Café, Rye 413
The Wee Restaurant, North Queensferry 507
The Wellington, Welwyn 306
The Wellington Arms, Baughurst 290
The Wensleydale Heifer, West Witton 473
Wesley House, Winchcombe 280

The West Arms Hotel,
 Llanarmon Dyffryn
 Ceiriog 545
The West House,
 Biddenden 314
WestBeach, Bournemouth 253
Whatley Manor, The
 Dining Room, Easton
 Grey 438
The Wheatsheaf, Combe
 Hay 385
The Wheatsheaf Inn,
 Northleach 277
Wheelers Oyster Bar,
 Whitstable 323
The White Hart, Flitton 178
The White Hart, Fyfield 368
White Hart, Hartlebury 444
The White Hart, Lydgate 282
The White Hart Inn, Bath 383
The White Horse,
 Brancaster Staithe 347
The White House, St
 Fagans 535
The White Oak, Cookham 184
The White Star Tavern,
 Southampton 299
The White Swan, Holborn 79
White Swan at Blyth, Blyth 361
The White Swan Inn,
 Pickering 464
Whitechapel Gallery
 Dining Room,
 Whitechapel 115
The Whitehouse
 Restaurant, Lochaline 522
Whites Restaurant,
 Beverley 446
Wig & Pen by The
 Milestone, Sheffield 469
The Wild Garlic,
 Beaminster 252
Wild Honey, Mayfair 80
The Wild Mushroom,
 Westfield 413
Wild Thyme, Chipping
 Norton 368
Williams & Brown Tapas,
 Whitstable 324
The Willow Tree, Taunton 388
Wiltons, Mayfair 80
Winteringham Fields,
 Winteringham 339
The Witchery by the Castle,
 Edinburgh 492
Wiveton Bell, Wiveton 354
Wiveton Farm Café,
 Wiveton 354

The Wolseley, Mayfair 81
The Woodlands Cafébar,
 Whitby 474
Woods Brasserie, Cardiff 531
The Wookey Hole Inn,
 Wookey Hole 390
The Woolpack Inn, Totford 301
World Service,
 Nottingham 364
Wright Brothers, Soho 81
Wright Brothers Oyster &
 Porter House, Southwark 132
The Wynnstay Hotel,
 Machynlleth 543

X

XO, Belsize Park 92

Y

Yak Yeti Yak, Bath 383
Yalla Yalla, Piccadilly 81
Yashin Sushi, Kensington 163
Yauatcha, Soho 81
Ye Olde Bull's Head Inn,
 Loft Restaurant,
 Beaumaris 549
The Yew Tree Inn, Bunbury 202
Ynyshir Hall, Eglwysfach 557
The York & Albany,
 Camden 92
The Yorke Arms, Ramsgill 465

Z

Zafferano, Belgravia 82
Zaika, Kensington 163
Zest, Derby 235
The Zetter Townhouse,
 Clerkenwell 115
Zucca, Bermondsey 132
Zuma, Knightsbridge 164

The Good Food Guide 2013

THANK YOUS

This book couldn't happen without a cast of thousands. Our thanks are due to the following contributors. A full list can be found at www.thegoodfoodguide.co.uk

Mr Raficq Abdulla
Mr David Abell
Mr Eric Abell
Mr Demi Abiola
Mr Anthony Abrahams
Mr Garth Abram
Mr James Ackrill
Miss Michelle Acton
Mr Alasdair Adam
Mr David Adam
Mr Frank Adams
Mr Scott Adams
Mrs Kay Adam-Smith
Mr Michael Adamson
Mr Ralph Adedeji
Miss Cherene Aggarwal
Mr John Aird
Mr John R Aird
Mr Johnny Aisher
Mr Peter Aitken
Mrs Andrea Alcock
Mrs Patricia Alderman
Ms Melanie Alderson
Mr Michael Alebon
Dr Ilene Alexander
Ms Liza Alexandra
Mr Asim Ali
Dr Ali A Alibhai
Mrs Anna Allen
Mr Edward Allen
Mr Henry Allen
Mr Ian Allen
Mrs Janice Allen
Mr Mark Allen
Mrs Melanie Allen
Mrs Rachel Allen
Mr Bob Allenby
Mrs Jeanne Allerston
Dr Hilary Allison
Mr Nicola Alvin-Smith
Mr Oliver Amann
Mr Tim Ambrose
Mr Steve Ambrose-Jones
Mr Mourad Amellal
Mrs Avril Anderson
Mr Jason Anderson
Mr Mark Anderson
Ms Marnie Anderson
Ms Oana Andrei
Mrs Alyson Andrew
Miss Elizabeth Andrewartha
Mrs Lorna Andrews
Mr Claudia Angelilli
Mr Sebastian Anstey
Mr Shem ap Geraint
Mrs Elizabeth Archer
Mrs Karen Archer
Mr Mark Archer
Mrs Jessica Armfelt
Mr Barrie Armstrong
Ms Sally Arnison
Mr Rainer Arnold
Mr Roshan Arya
Mrs Linda Ash
Mr Barry James Ashcroft
Mr Gareth Ashington
Ms Pauline Ashley
Miss Lisa Ashurst
Mr Paul Ashurst
Mr Chris Ashworth
Mrs Hazel Askey
Mrs Tracy Atchison
Mr Henry Atherton
Ms Margaret Atherton
Ms Kate Atkins
Mr Paul Atkins
Mr J Atkinson
Mr Frank Attwood
Miss Charlotte Austin
Mrs Leigh Austin
Mrs Denise Avent
Mrs Christina Avis
Mr Charles Ayovi
Mr George Ayres
Miss Neelam Azim
Dr Fiona Bach
Mrs Andrena Backhouse
Miss Kristyna Baczynska
Mr Bradley Baddams
Mr Marco Baggioli

Mrs Catherine Baigent
Mr Christopher Baigent
Mrs Ali Bailey
Mr C Bailey
Miss Clare Bailey
Mr Kimball Bailey
Mr Mark Bailey
Mrs Rita Bailey
Mr James Baird
Ms Catherine Baker
Mrs Lesley Baker
Mrs Mandy Baker
Mrs Niki Baker
Miss Sharron Baker
Mrs Paola Baldovin
Mrs Jessica Balfour
Mr Andrew Ball
Mr Duncan Ball
Mrs Heather Bamford
Mrs Rose Marie Bancroft
Mrs Sonia Banks
Mrs Margaret Banksma
Mr Donald Baptie
Mr Chris Baranov
Mrs Kathryn Barber
Mr Rick Barber
Mr Sarah Barber
Mrs Diana Barclay
Mr James Barclay
Miss Rachael Barham
Mr Greg Barker
Ms Anne Barlow
Mr Christopher Barlow
Mrs Genevieve Barnard
Mr David Barnes
Mrs Jan Barnes
Miss Rebecca Barnes
Mr Richard Barnes
Mrs Louise Barnett
Mr Stephen Barnett
Miss Jane Barnett-Roberts
Mrs P Baron
Dr Ross Barrand
Miss Keely Barrett
Mrs Liz Barrett
Mr Olly Barrett
Ms Andrea Barron
Mrs Liz Barron
Mrs Jane Barry
Mrs Cherry Bartles-Smith
Ms Hilary Bartlett
Miss E Barton
Mr Martin Bashall
Mrs Geraldine Batchelor
Mrs Layla Batchelor
Mr Nigel Batchelor
Mr David Bate
Mr Anthony Bates
Mrs Jane Bates
Mr Keith Bates
Mr Ryan Bates
Ms Lyn Bates
Mrs Marta Bau
Mr Benjamin Baumguertel
Miss Amanda Baxter
Mrs Liane Baxter
Mrs Kristin Bayes
Mr Jim Beach
Ms Lesley Beach
Mr Owen Beacock
Mrs Jacqueline Beagle
Miss Hannah Beal
Mr Duncan Beales
Mrs Sarah Beall
Miss Natalie Beard
Mr James Beardon
Miss Claire Beatty
Mrs Irene Becker
Mr Chris Beckham
Miss Alison Beckwith
Mr Robert Bedford
Mrs Tracey Beesley
Dr Simon Begnor
Mr David Bell
Mrs Gemma Bell
Mrs Liz Bell
Mrs Maria Bell
Mrs Nicola Bell
Miss Stephanie Bell
Mr Trevor Bell

Mrs Hannah Bellefontaine
Miss Catherine Belsten
Mr Jean-Luc Benazet
Mrs Karen Bennett
Ms Kathy Bennett
Miss Alexandra Benson
Mr Paul Bentall
Ms Abby Bentham
Miss Victoria Bentley
Mrs Rachel Benton
Mr Chris Berry
Mr Martin Berry
Mr Alan Bertram
Miss Alexandra Bertram
Mrs Elizabeth Bertram
Mr Renaud Besnard
Mrs Helen Bessemer-Clark
Miss Chloe Best
Mr Charles Betts
Mr Liam Betts
Mr Richard Beverley
Mr Mattia Bianchi
Mr Anthony Bickers
Mrs Susan Bickle
Ms Irena Biedka
Mr Steven Biggs
Miss Laura Bignell
Mr John Billett
Miss Nikki Billington
Mr Ryan Birch
Mr Craig Birchall
Mr Jeff Bird
Ms Lucy Bird
Ms Rosie Birkett
Mr Matt Birtwistle
Miss Lauren Bishop
Mr Alistair Black
Miss Natasha Black
Mr Stuart Black
Mr Arthur Blackburn
Miss Leila Blackburn
Ms Caroline Blackburn-Huijgen
Mrs Susan Blacker
Mr Patrick Blake
Mrs Sheila Blake
Mr Tony Blakeson
Mr Kevin Blakey
Mrs Susan Blakey
Mr Paul Blanc
Ms Wendy Blann
Mrs Sophie Blatchford
Mrs Jane Blewitt
Miss Naomi Bloomer
Mrs Bonita Bloor
Mr Jamie Bluck
Mrs Kerry Blunt
Miss Joanna Blythe
Mr Andy Boase
Mrs Barbara Boden
Ms Anastasia Bogacheva
Ms Anouke Bokkerink
Mr Jon Bolter
Mrs Rozalina Boneva
Mr Steven Bonfield
Mr Matthew Bonnaud
Mr Neil Bonsall
Mrs Susan Bonsor
Mr John Boon
Mrs Angela Booth
Mr Ben Booth
Mr Pippa Booth
Mr Hylton Boothroyd
Miss Anjuli Borgonha
Mr Emile Borgonha
Mr Brian Borjesson
Mrs Lucy Bostock
Mr J Roderick Boswell
Miss Samara Bott
Mr Simon Bottomley
Mrs Vanessa Boukharouba
Mr Darren Boulding
Mr Adrian Boulton
Mr Kate Boutinot
Mrs Suzanne Bowden
Mr Travis Bowland
Mrs Tatty Bowman
Mr K Bowra
Mrs Laura Boyce
Mr Nick Boyd

Mr Grant Boyd-Hall
Ms Gill Bracey
Dr Valerie Bradburn
Mr Matt Bradbury
Mrs Lynne Bradey
Mr Andrew Bradley
Ms Jean Bradley
Mrs Nancy Bradley
Mrs Beverley Bradshaw
Mr Guy Brady
Mrs R Brady
Dr Karen Braithwaite
Mr Alastair Bramley
Mrs Victoria Bramwell
Miss Jennifer Brannan
Mr Harry Bratley
Miss Sarah-Jayne Bray
Mr Michael Braziel
Mr Ken Brazier
Miss Xanthe Breen
Mrs Joan Brennan
Mrs Sarah Brennan
Miss Anne Brewer
Mrs M Elizabeth Brewington
Mr Geoffrey Bridge
Mr Alec Briggs
Mr David Briggs
Mr Simon Bristow
Ms Zoe Britton
Dr Jane Broadbent
Ms Adelina Broadbridge
Mr Simon Broady
Mr Paul Brodie
Mrs Polly Brookes
Mr Nigel Brooke-Smith
Mrs Amanda Brooking
Mr Simon Brookland-Beck
Mrs Ellenor Brooks
Ms Mary Brooks
Mr Paul Brooks
Ms Theresa Brosnan
Mrs Helen Brough
Dr Ellie Broughton
Miss Amanda Brown
Mr Chris Brown
Mr Colin Brown
Mr Dennis Brown
Miss Emma Brown
Mrs Gillian Brown
Mrs Joan Brown
Ms Kate Brown
Miss Laura Brown
Mrs Leanne Brown
Miss Lisa Brown
Mrs Marian Brown
Mr Peter W Brown
Mr Roger Brown
Mrs Tina Brown
Mr Peter Brownjohn
Mr Mike Brownlow
Mr Peter Brunnen
Ms Nicola Brunning
Mr Michael Brunt
Mrs Caroline Bryan
Mr John Bryant
Mr Philip Bryant
Mrs Sally Bryce
Mrs Gillian Buchan
Mr Ian Buchan
Mrs Jennifer Buck
Ms Caroline Bull
Mr Ian Bull
Mrs Jennie Bullen
Mr Walter Bullen
Mrs Carole Bullock
Mr Mike Bunce
Mr James Bunn
Mr Stephen Burcham
Ms Michelle Burden
Mr Peter Burfoot
Mr Andrew Burge
Mr Richard Burger
Mrs Daphne Burgess
Mrs Fran Burgess
Mr Paul Burke
Miss Kate Burne
Mrs Clare Burnell
Mrs Donna Burnett
Mr Mark Burnett
Mr Tom Burnham

Mrs Jenny Burnley
Mrs Kirsten Burns
Miss Megan Burns
Mr Ian Burrell
Mrs Jill Burrington
Mr Geoffrey Burt
Mrs Susan Burton
Mr Zak Burton
Mrs Cara Buswell
Miss Felicity Butcher
Dr Isabella Butcher
Mr Peter Butler
Mr Toby Butler
Mrs Zara Butler
Mr Ahmad Butt
Mrs Ruth Buttery
Mrs Ann Buxton
Mr Chris Byrne
Mrs Judith Byrne
Miss Sharon Byrne
Mrs Janet Caborn
Mrs Janice Cade
Miss Kay Cadman
Mr Nicholas Caiger
Miss Nichola Cain
Mrs Caroline Caird
Mr Gilles Caisey
Mrs Brenda Calder
Mr Colin Calder
Ms Emma Callery
Ms Romina Calvet
Mrs Keely Cambell
Mr George Cameron
Mr Giancarlo Camilleri
Dr Tiziana Camilleri
Mrs Lucy Campbell
Mr Paul Campy
Mrs Carole Candish
Ms Jane Canessa
Mrs Hiroko Canning
Miss Carly Capper
Mr James Cardwell
Mrs Charlotte Carew Pole
Mrs Sarah Carlon
Mr Dean Carney
Mr Michael Carney
Miss Rachel Carney
Miss Amy Carr
Mr David Carr
Mrs Jane Carr
Mr Jerry Carr-Brion
Mr Mark Carroll
Mrs Rebecca Carroll
Mr Alastair Carson
Mr Graham Carson
Miss Catherine Carswell
Mr Eddie Carswell
Miss Amy Carter
Mr David Carter
Miss Laura Carter
Miss Lucy-Jane Carter
Mrs Abigail Cartledge
Mr Paul Caruana
Mr Dennis Carvell
Mrs Lynne Carville
Mr Mike Carwithen
Mr Colin Case
Miss Rebecca Casey
Mrs Wendy Cash
Mr David Cassidy
Mrs Rebecca Castle
Mr Chris Catelani
Mr Neil Cater
Dr Susannah Cater
Mrs Jane Caunce
Mr Philip Caveney
Mr Mark Cawood
Ms Diane Cesar
Miss Lizie Cha
Mrs Sylvia Chadwick
Mrs Janet Chainey
Mr Fred Chamberlain
Mr Alan Champion
Mr Bee J Chandaria
Mrs Janet Chandler
Mr Jamie Chapman
Miss Jo Chapman
Dr Keith Chapman
Mrs Maureen Chapman
Mr Robin Chapman

THANK YOUS

Ms Sharon Charteress
Miss Louise Chatfield
Mr Shahzad Chaudhry
Mrs Michelle Cheeseman
Miss Angela Cheetham
Mr Stefano Chessa
Miss Leonie Chettle
Mrs Tess Chidgey
Mr Richard Chinnock
Miss Alexandra Chisholm
Mr Shahad Choudhury
Mrs Anne Chowne
Mrs Carol Christie
Mr Othon Christodolou
Mr Luke Churchill
Mr Michael Cinnamond
Mrs Margaret Clancy
Mrs Joan Clapham
Mrs Aileen Clark
Ms Alison Clark
Mr Andrew Clark
Mr Dan Clark
Mrs Kathryn Clark
Mr Anthony Clarke
Miss Helen Clarke
Mr J Clarke
Miss Katie Clarke
Mr Nigel Clarke
Mr Richard Clarke
Mr Robert Clarke
Mrs Sarah Clarke
Mrs Susan Clarke
Mr Donald Clayton
Mr Steve Clayton
Mrs Suzanne Clayton
Miss Victoria Clayton
Mrs Hilary Claytonsmith
Ms Jane Cleary
Mrs Gillian Cleeve
Mr Mark Clemence
Ms Anne Clements
Mr Paul Clery
Mr Ivor Cleves
Mrs June Clewley
Miss Lisa Clewley
Mr Colin Clowes
Mrs Fiona Coad
Mrs Wilma Cochrane
Mrs Julie Cockell
Miss Gillian Codd
Ms Emma Cogan
Mrs Claire Coghlin
Mrs Wendy Coke
Mrs Susan Colebrook
Mr Adam Coleman
Mr David Coleman
Mr John Coleman
Mr Michael Colley
Mrs Naomi Colley
Mrs Helen Colling
Mr Duncan Collins
Miss Rebecca Collins
Mrs Angela Collum
Mr Kevin Connell
Mrs Susan Connington
Mr Alex Connolly
Mr Ronald Graham
    Connolly
Mrs Emma Connor
Mr Steve Connor
Miss Catherine Conroy
Mrs Dawn Convery
Mr Glenn Cook
Mr Martin Cooke
Mr Adrian Cooling
Ms Nicky Cooney
Dr Adam Cooper
Miss Anna Cooper
Mrs Chrissa Cooper
Mrs Lisa Cooper
Mr Michael Cooper
Mr Philip Cooper
Dr Rob Cooper
Mr William Cooper
Mrs Caroline
    Cooper-Charles
Miss Federica Corbetta
Miss Christine Corbiere
Mr Dan Corcoran
Mr Peter Corey
Mr Andrew Cornick
Miss Alison Cornock
Mrs Sarah Cost
Dr Christopher Costello
Mrs Pamela Cottam
Miss Sophie Cottam

Mr Gary Cotterill
Mrs Christine Couchman
Mrs Sally Counsell
Mrs Karen Courtney
Mr Hugh Cousins
Dr Graeme Cowan
Miss Nicola Cowburn
Mr Paul Cowell
Mrs Penny Cowing
Mr Elliot Cox
Mr Jon Cox
Mrs Karen Cox
Mr Mark Cox
Mr Matthew Cox
Mrs Theresa Cox
Miss Michelle Coxall
Mr Nigel Coxhead
Mr Jason Cozens
Mr Anthony Crabtree
Mr John Crabtree
Mrs Marion Cracknell
Mrs Suzanne Crafer
Mr David Craig
Mrs Diane Craig
Miss Hannah Craig
Mr Robert Craig
Miss Stacey Craigie
Miss Hannah Craker
Mrs Ann Crane
Mrs Clio Crane
Mrs Jane Craven
Mrs Michaela Craven-Smith
Mr Andy Crawford
Mr Gary Crawford
Miss Hannah Crawley
Mr Evan Crichton
Mr James Crichton
Mrs Helen Crichton Jenner
Mr Stephen Crick
Mr John Crider
Mr David Crimble
Miss Lyndsey Crook
Mr Alasdair Crooks
Mr Paul Cross
Mrs Ruth Cross
Mr Jack Crossley
Mr Jonathan Crowther
Mr Sebastian Crowther
Mrs Jane Crudace
Mr Michael Crulley
Mr Richard Crulley
Mr Robert Cuin
Mrs Marion Cullen
Mr Richard Cullen
Mrs Clare Culliney
Mrs Sarah Cunliffe
Miss Francesca Curland
Ms Jan Curle
Mr Ian Curtis
Mrs Margaret Curtis
Mr Nick Curtis
Mr Michael Cuschieri
Mr Nicholas Cushion
Mrs Corrie Cuthbertson
Mr Mariusz Czapla
Mr Gary Da Costa
Mrs Alyson d'Adamo
Mr Will Dale
Miss Dianne Daley
Dr Matteo Dalla Valle
Mrs C Dallimore
Ms Amber Dalton
Mr Ewan Daniel
Mr Phil Daniels
Mr Cory Danks
Mr Christian Dannemann
Ms Susan d'Arcy
Mr Paul Darken
Mr Daniel Darwood
Mr Nikhil Das
Mrs Loraine Davenport
Mrs Alison Davey
Mr Christopher Davey
Ms Heidi Davey
Mrs Margaret Davey
Dr Peter Davey
Mr Craig Davidson
Mrs Debra Davies
Mrs Jill Davies
Mr John Davies
Ms Judith Davies
Mr Keith Davies
Ms Linda Davies
Mr Michael Davies
Mr Mike Davies
Mr Paul Davies

Mrs Pauline Davies
Mr Peter Davies
Mr Richard Davies
Miss Sam Davies
Ms Ann Davis
Mrs Clare Davis
Dr Julian Davis
Mrs Keren Davis
Mr Broch Davison
Miss Coralie Davison
Mrs Kate Davison
Mrs Michelle Davy
Mr Nick Dawe
Mrs Michelle Dawson
Mr Neil Dawson
Mr Chris Day
Mr Joff Day
Mr Jon Day
Mr Pod Day
Mr Ranulph Day
Mrs Suzanne Day
Mrs Norma de Bidaph
Mrs Anne de Salis
Mrs Annette Deakin
Mr Carl Dean
Mrs Heather Deans
Mr Subhankar Debnath
Mr Jacob Dee
Mr Nicholas Dee
Mr Chris Deller
Miss Imelda Dempsey
Mr Geoffrey Dence
Mr S Denham
Mrs Sarah Dent
Mrs Alex Dentith
Mr Roy Denton
Mr Nilesh Desai
Mrs Anne Devlin
Mrs Angela Dewey
Mr Stephen Dewhirst
Mrs Pamela Dewhurst
Mr Jasneet Dhingra
Mrs Jeanie Dick
Mrs Monique Dick
Dr Steve Dickinson
Mr Richard Dilks
Mrs Rhiannon Dillon
Mr Robert Dillon
Mr Matthew Dix
Mrs Jan Dixcey
Mrs Julien Dixon
Mrs Suzanne Dixon
Ms Julie Dobson
Mrs Maggie Dobson
Miss Rachael Dobson
Mr Martin Dodd
Ms Orla Doherty
Mr Clifford Dolley
Mr Andrew Donaldson
Mrs Liz Donnelly
Mrs Susy Donoghue
Mr Jane Donovan
Mr Kevin Donovan
Mr William Donovan
Ms Patricia
    Dopping-Hepenstal
Mr Frank Doran
Mr James Doran
Mr Struan Douglas
Dr Rhid Dowdle
Miss Wendy Downie
Miss Kathryn Doyle
Dr Lisa Doyle
Mrs Sheila Doyle
Miss Florence Drake
Mrs Lesley Draper
Mr Dudley Drayson
Mrs Angie Drew
Mr Brian Drury
Ms Sharron D'Souza
Mr John Ducker
Mrs Nicola Duckett
Mr Colum Duffy
Mr Kevin Duggan
Mrs Sue Dulley
Mr Andrew Duncan
Miss Jade Duncan
Miss Regan Duncan
Mrs Louise Dunkley
Mr Graeme Dunn
Mrs Anne Dunne
Miss Anouska Dunne
Mr Guy Dunphy
Mrs Cathy Durham
Mrs Joanna Durham
Mrs Pamela Dutson

Mr Geoffrey Dutton
Mrs Cecilia Dyckhoff
Dr Roy Dyckhoff
Mrs Barbara Dye
Miss Kimberley Dye
Mrs Rosie Dymond
Miss Elizabeth Eagles
Dr Jeremy Eakin
Dr Lindsay Easton
Mrs Jane Ebberson
Mr John Ebo
Mrs Kathleen Eccles
Mrs Amanda Eccleston
Mrs Susan Edgar
Mr A Edwards
Mrs Janice Edwards
Mr Julie Edwards
Mrs Sandra Edwards
Mr Simon Edwards
Mr Kevin Egan
Mr Francisco Egana
Mr Gary Elffett
Miss Faith Elkan
Ms Therese Ellard
Mrs Marie Ellenthorpe
Mr Michael Ellery
Mr Phillip Elliot
Mrs Jo Elliott
Mr Mike Elliott
Mrs Frances Ellis
Miss Josephine Ellis
Mr Lyn Ellis
Ms Sheila Ellis
Mrs Tessa Ellis
Mr Tim Ellis
Mrs Emma Ellison
Ms Margaret Else
Mr Daniel Eltringham
Mr Jonathon Elwood
Mrs Jenny Emberey
Mr Gavin Emmett
Ms Vicky Endersen
Mr Sally Engelbert
Ms Jane England
Dr John England
Mr Richard England
Mr Graham English
Mr Craig Ennis
Mr Timothy Eppel
Miss Isabelle Epps
Mrs Joyce Epps
Mr Bertrand Escoffier
Mr Christopher Escott
Mr Adrian Esland
Miss Safah Essa
Mrs Cheryl Essam
Mr Lewis Esson
Mr Louise Esterson
Ms Carolina Etty
Ms Alex Evans
Ms Amanda Evans
Mrs Angela Evans
Mrs Cath Evans
Mr Dafydd Evans
Mrs Iona Evans
Miss Megan Evans
Mrs Sandra Evans
Mr Wayne Evans
Mr Jon Everall
Mr and Mrs J Ewan
Mr Keith Exford
Mr Matt Fagan-Curry
Mr Tom Fahey
Mr Mike Fairclough
Mr John Fairley
Mr Rambaut Fairley
Mr M F Fakhru
Mr Matthew Fallen
Mrs Jacqueline Faller
Mr D Falzani
Mrs Jane Fardon
Miss Nicola Farge-Bennett
Mr Clive Farmer
Mrs Michelle Farmer
Mr Chris Farmery
Mr John Farndell
Mrs Pauline Farnsworth
Mr George Farquharson
Mr Peter Farrell
Mr T Fathers
Ms Emma Faulkner
Mrs Angela Fawcett
Miss Fiona Feeney
Mr Mary Fei
Ms Penny Feltham
Mrs Lisa Fenner

Mr Steve Fenwick
Mrs Iffat Ferdinand
Miss Sarah Ferguson
Mrs Sarah Ferguson
Mrs Stevie Ferguson
Mr Gavin Fernandes
Dr Ranil Fernando
Mrs Anna Ferrara-Oldfield
Mrs Emma Ferres
Mrs Elizabeth Ferrigno
Mrs Lisa Ferrol
Mrs Sarah Fiedosiuk
Mr Anthony Field
Mr Neville Filar
Mr David Finch
Mr Graham Findlay
Mr Cliff Finn
Mrs Janet Firth
Mr Ben Fisher
Mr Brian Fisher
Mrs Katherine Fisher
Miss Marion Fisher
Mr Andy Fitchet
Mr Shane Fitzpatrick
Mr Kierann Flatt
Mrs Gillian Flegg
Mr Jordan Fleming
Mr Andrew Fletcher
Miss Chloe Fletcher
Mr Edward Fletcher
Mrs Maria Flewitt
Mrs Joanne Flieming Kirwan
Mr Adam Flint
Mrs Carol Flockhart
Mr James Flockhart
Mr David Flynn
Mr Kevin Flynn
Ms Anna Foalks
Mrs Gillian Forbes
Mr Stephen Forbes
Miss Alison Ford
Miss Elle Ford
Miss Emma Ford
Mrs Susan Ford
Mrs Claudine Foskett
Mrs Nicola Foster
Dr Paul Foster
Dr Kate Fothringham
Mr Richard Foulkes
Miss Sue Foulston
Mr Mike Fountain
Mr David Fowler
Mr John Fowler
Mrs Debbie Fox
Miss Rachel Fox
Mr Sebastian Fox
Mrs Tessa Fox
Miss Lottie-Daisy Francis
Ms Tazina Frank
Mrs Di Franklin
Mr John Fraser
Miss Catharine Frediani
Mr Paul Fredrick
Mr Jennifer Freeman
Mrs Karen Freeman
Mrs Isobel French
Mr Chris Frost
Mr Harriet Frost
Mrs Lorraine Frost
Mr Roger Frost
Mr Jason Fudge
Mr Edward Fulcher
Mrs Teresa Fullalove
Mr Alastair Fuller
Mr Keir Fuller
Mrs Kate Fulwell
Mr Gareth Furse
Mr Ian Fyfe
Miss Loulou G Smith
Mr Philip Gadsby
Mr Mark Gainford
Ms Denise Gale
Mrs Karenna Galer
Mr Rod Galilee
Mr Mick Gallagher
Miss Ruth Gallagher
Mrs Sharon Gallagher
Mrs Caron Galloway
Mrs Mary Galt
Mrs Debbie Gamble
Dr Vijeya Ganesan
Miss Olivia Gannon
Mr Richard Gapper
Mr Carla Gardiner
Mrs Rebecca Gardiner
Mrs Amanda Gardner

Mrs Carole Gardner
Mrs Kathryn Gardner
Mrs Emma Gargett
Mr David Garner
Miss Sue Garton
Mr Joshua Gartside
Mrs Charlotte Gather
Mr Tim Gay
Miss Elizabeth Gayther
Mr Geoff Geary
Mr Alan Gent
Mr Tony Gentil
Mr Tony Georgakis
Miss Alicia George
Mr Simon George
Mr Stephen Gerrard
Mr Gianpaolo Giancovich
Miss Samantha Gibbons
Mr Gordon Gibbs
Miss Dianne Gibson
Dr Hervey Gibson
Miss Jo Gibson
Miss Lisa Gibson
Mr Neil John Gibson
Mrs Melanie Gifford
Mr Chas Gilbert
Mr John Gilder
Miss Lindsay Giles
Dr Sukhdev Gill
Mr Murdo Gillanders
Mr Matt Giordano-Bibby
Mr Duncan Girling
Mrs Lois Gishen
Mr Robert Glasier
Mrs Moira Glass
Mr Peter Glazer
Mr Keith Gleadall
Ms Adrianna Glover
Mr Roger Glover
Mr Christopher Glynn
Mr R S Goddard
Mr Dave Godfrey
Mrs Lucy Gofton
Mr David Gold
Miss Cara Golden
Mr Richard Golding
Mr Richard Golland
Miss Sally Gomersall
Mrs Carole Gomez
Ms Sandrine Gonnet
Mr Keith Good
Mr Michael Goodacre
Mr Richard Goodall
Mr George Goodey
Miss Frances Goodfellow
Miss Liza Goodier
Mr Grant Goodlad
Mr David Goodship
Mr Matthew Goodwill
Mr Michael Gordge
Miss Christine Gordon
Mrs Abbe Gordziejko
Dr James Gore
Mrs Anne Gornall
Mr William Gornall-King
Mr Angus Gosman
Mr Richard Goss
Mr Kieron Goulden
Mr Robert Goundry
Ms Gillian Gove
Mr Chris Gower
Mrs Julie Gowland
Mrs Karen Grace
Mr Fraser Graham
Mrs Wendy Graham
Mr David Grant
Miss Louise Grant
Mrs Nicola Grant
Mr Richard Grant
Mrs Christine Granville-Edge
Miss Catherine Gray
Mr James Gray
Mrs Karen Gray
Mr Philip Gray
Ms Stephanie Gray
Mrs Sylvia Gray
Mrs Lavinia Greacen
Mrs Fiona Green
Mr Michael Green
Mr Nick Green
Mr Nigel Green
Mr Tony Green
Mr Nick Greenan
Mr Peter Greene
Mrs Alla Greenfield
Mrs Janet Greenhill

Mr Alan Greening
Mr James Greenlees
Miss L Greenwell
Mrs Camilla Greenwood
Miss Miriam Greenwood
Miss Rhian Greenwood
Mrs Roslin Greenwood
Ms Ebonee Gregory
Mr John Gregory
Mrs Susan Greig
Dr David Grey
Mrs Louisa Grey
Mr Antony Griew
Mr James Griffin
Mr Mark Griffin
Mr Nikki Griffith
Mrs Gillian Griffiths
Miss Jessica Griffiths
Mr Michael Griffiths
Mr Richard Griffiths
Mr Barry Griggs
Mr Steve Grimble
Mrs Janie Grimes
Mr Aidan Grimshaw
Mr Mark Grimshaw
Ms Nicola Grimshaw
Mr Brian Grimward
Mrs Kate Grogan
Mr William Grove
Miss Katherine Groves
Mr Vic Groves
Mrs Lorena Guedes
Miss Danielle
 Guildford-Sharp
Mr Iain Gunn
Mr Jon Gunn
Mr Tony Guntrip
Mr Alan Gurnett
Mr Meirion Guyon
Mr Elliott Hackney
Mr Richard Haes
Mrs Elizabeth Hagerty
Miss Rumana Haider
Mr Alan Haimes
Mr Christopher Haine
Mr Greg Hainess
Mr Chris Hall
Mr Daniel Hall
Mr James Hall
Mrs Lynn Hall
Mr Sam Hall
Miss Simona Hall
Mrs Linda Halliday
Miss Katherine Halls
Ms Lynne Hallums
Ms Nana Ham
Mrs Sara Hamer
Mr Ella Hamilton
Mrs Sue Hamilton
Mrs Valerie Hamilton
Mrs Amanda Hammond
Mr James Hammond
Miss Kate Hammond
Mr Phil Hampson
Mr David Hancock
Miss Riena-Jade Hancox
Mrs Deborah Handley
Mrs Sheelagh Handy
Ms Siobhan Hanley
Miss Sarah Hannell
Ms B Hansen
Mr S Hansford
Mr John Hanson
Mrs Margaret Hanson
Mr David Harber
Mrs Deborah Harding
Mrs Diane Harding
Mr John Harding
Dr K Harding
Mrs Liz Harding
Miss Lucy Hardman
Miss Faye Hardwick
Mrs Sarah Hargreaves
Miss Ellie Hargreaves
Mr Tom Hargreaves
Mr Harold Harland
Dr Linda Harland
Mr Sean Harley
Mr Anthony Harling
Mr David Harman
Miss Annabel Harmer
Miss Joan Harper
Ms Kathryn Harper
Mr Harry Harrington
Mr Alan Harris

Mrs D Harris
Mr Giles Harris
Mrs Natalie Harris
Mr Simon Harris
Mr Steve Harris
Miss Heather Harrison
Mr James Harrison
Ms Jessica Harrison
Mrs Samantha Harrison
Mr Stuart Harrison
Ms Yvonne Harrop
Ms Elizabeth Hart
Dr Stephanie Hart
Mrs Helen Hartley
Mr John Hartley
Mr Ben Harvey
Mr Julian Harvey
Ms Kathleen Harvey
Mr John Harwood
Dr Barbara Haskew
Ms Jasmine Hatami
Mr Phil Hatton
Mr Charles Hawes
Miss Amie Hawker
Ms Glyn Hawker
Mrs Verity Hawkes
Mrs Emma Hawkins
Miss Rebecca Haworth
Mrs Joanne Haydon
Mr Alan Hayes
Mrs Nicola Hayes
Miss Teresa Hayes
Mr Andy Hayler
Miss Helen Hayward
Ms Monica Hayward
Miss Louise Hazard
Mrs Joanne Hazel
Miss Rebekah Heald
Miss Gillian Healey
Ms Bairbre Healy
Mrs Gillie Healy
Mr James Heaney
Mr David Heath
Mr John Heath
Mr Terence Heath
Mr Robert Heed
Mrs Christina Helps
Miss Laura Helsby
Mr Dale Hemming-Tayler
Mr David Henderson
Dr Robert Henderson
Mr Ross Henderson
Mr Stuart Henderson
Ms Helga Henry
Mr David Hensley
Dr Davina Hensman
Mrs Donna Hepworth
Mr Jeremy Herbert
Ms Jo Jo Hernandez
Dr Michael Hession
Mrs Beverly Hetherington
Mr Gad Heuman
Mr Anthony Hewett
Mr James Hewines
Mrs Yvonne Hewins
Mrs Angela Hewitt
Ms Nicki Hewitt
Mr Terry Hewitt
Mr Gary Hibbard
Mr Ray Hickling
Mr John Hicks
Mrs Catherine Higgins
Mr Chris Highton
Dr Peter Higson
Mrs A Hill
Mr Bernard Hill
Mr Bob Hill
Mr John Hill
Mrs Sarah Hill
Mr Simon Hill
Mrs Wendy Hill
Mrs Sally Hilton
Miss Katie Himsworth
Mrs Janet Hinchliffe
Mr Susan Hind
Mr Darren Hine
Mr John Hippisley
Mr Jonathan Hird
Mr Roger Hird
Mr Peter Hirschmann
Mr Morton Hirst
Mrs Lucie Hoar
Mrs Linda Hobbis
Mr Martin Hobbs
Mr Robert Hobbs
Mrs Sarah Hobbs

Mr Clive Hodgetts
Mr Ben Hodgkinson
Mr Nick Hodgsom
Mr David Hodgson
Mr Philip Hodgson
Mr Matt Hodkin
Mrs Elaine Hoffman
Ms Helen Hogh
Miss Lucy Holburn
Mr James Holden
Mr Trevor Holden
Mr Graeme Holdsworth
Mr Ian Holland
Mr Nevander Holland
Mr Al Holliman
Mr Francis Holly
Mrs Belinda Hollyer
Miss Angela Holmes
Mr Brian Holmes
Mrs Fiona Holmes
Mrs Joy Holmes
Mrs Liz Holmes
Mr Simon Homes
Mr Colin Honey
Miss Katie Honeyborne
Miss Barbara Hood
Mr George Hooper
Mr Graham Hooper
Mrs Keri Hopkins
Dr Paul Hopkins
Miss Zoe Hopkins
Mr Andy Hopkinson
Miss Polly Horn
Mr Andrew Hornby
Ms Zoe Horwich
Mrs J Hosegood
Mr Graham Hoskins
Ms Diana Houghton
Mrs Kim Houghton
Mr Peter Houghton
Mr Rebekkah Houghton
Miss Zara Houghton
Mr Robin Houldsworth
Mr Malcolm Houston
Mr Dean Howard
Mr Ken Howard
Mrs Sheila Howarth
Mrs Elizabeth Howe
Mr Nicholas Howe
Mr Christopher
 Howes-Burrows
Ms Caroline Howlett
Mrs Carol Hubbard
Miss Lisa Hubber
Dr Annie Hughes
Mr Charles Hughes
Miss Emma Hughes
Mrs Joanne Hughes
Miss Sian Hughes
Mrs Susan Hughes
Mrs Alwena Hughes Moakes
Mr Royden Hukin
Miss Rebecca Hull
Mrs Enid Hume
Mrs Ann Humphrey
Mr Joe Humphries
Mr Mark Hunsley
Dr Amelia Hunt
Mr Brian Hunt
Mr Jason Hunt
Mrs Sonia Hunt
Mr Suzanne Hunt
Mr Chris Hunter
Mr Craig Hunter
Mr Mark Hunter
Mrs Melissa Hunter
Mrs Myra Hunter
Mr Neil Hunter
Mr Oliver Hunter
Mrs Claire Hurst
Mr Tom Hurst
Mr Anamul Hussain
Mr Paul Hussein
Mrs Jayne Hustwick
Mrs Katherine Hutchins
Mr Gordon Hutchison
Mrs Louise Hynard
Mr Paul Ibbetson
Mr Adam Ibrahim
Miss Joana Idoate
Mr Philip Igoe
Mr Mark Illman
Mr Andrew Imm
Mr Alexander Ingram
Mr Steven Isaacs
Mr David Jackson

Mr Dominic Jackson
Mrs Elizabeth Jackson
Miss Lyndsey Jackson
Mr Paul Jackson
Mr Kenneth Jacobs
Mrs Kate Jacobson
Dr Douglas Jaenicke
Mr Paul Jakubovic
Miss Fiona Jalil
Mrs Claire James
Miss Emma James
Ms Julie James
Mrs Leigh James
Miss Robyn Jankel
Mr Ajit Jansari
Mr R Janzen
Mr Adrian Jaques
Mr Stephen Jardine
Mrs Claire Jarmain
Miss Sarah Jarman
Mr Simon Jarrold
Ms Fiona Jarvis
Mrs Samantha Jarvis
Mr Bharat Jashanmal
Mr Frank Jeffries
Mrs Jeanette Jemson
Mr Chris Jenkins
Ms Jenni Jenkins
Mr Steve Jenkins
Mr J Peter Jenkinson
Mr David Jervis
Mr Paul Jervis
Mr Oliver Jessel
Mrs Laura Jessop
Mrs Julie Jewers
Mr Clive John
Mr Edward John
Miss Emma Johnson
Miss Julie Johnson
Mr Leo Johnson
Mr Robert Johnson
Mr Simon Johnson
Mrs Teresa Johnson
Mr Andrew Johnston
Mrs Anne Johnston
Mrs Anneme Johnston
Miss Clare Johnston
Mrs Clare Johnston
Mrs Natasha Johnston
Mrs Jane Johnstone
Mr Peter Jolly
Miss Amy Jones
Mrs Avril Jones
Miss Bethan Jones
Miss Catherine Jones
Mrs Christine Jones
Mr David Jones
Mrs Elizabeth Jones
Mr Gordon Jones
Ms Heather Jones
Mr Hugh Jones
Mr James Jones
Mr John Jones
Mrs Judith Jones
Miss Kate Jones
Miss Kay Jones
Miss Maud Jones
Miss Meg Jones
Mrs Patricia Jones
Mr Paul Jones
Mr Peter Jones
Mr Simeon Jones
Mrs Stephanie Jones
Mr Steve Jones
Miss Lucie Jordan
Miss Rickie Josen
Mrs Melanie Josling
Mr Jonathan Jowitt
Miss Erika Juan
Mrs Samantha Judge
Mr Simon Jukes
Mrs Julie Julian
Miss Aleksandra Jurczak
Mr Mohiuddin Kakiwala
Ms Christine Kaltoft
Mr John Kandel
Mr Roland Kandiah
Ms Julia Kanger
Mrs Deborah Karavias
Mr Richard Katz
Dr Leon Kaufman
Mr Bill Kawai-Calderhead
Mr Andrew Kay
Miss April Keech
Mr Eric Keeler
Mrs Bronwen Keeling

THANK YOUS

Mr Peter Keenan
Mrs Alison Keith
Mr Paul Keith
Dr Bernard Kelly
Mr Bernard Kelly
Mr David Edward Kelly
Mr Julian Kelly
Miss Hilary Kelly
Mrs Lyndsey Kelly-Aberle
Mr Gail Kelsing
Miss Ceildh Kemp
Mr Jon Kempner
Mr Cavan Kendall
Mrs H Kendall-Elcock
Mr Tom Kendle
Mrs Nicola Kenn
Mr Adam Kennard
Mrs Joanne Kennedy
Mr John Kennedy
Mrs Hilary Kennedy
Ms Katisha Kenyon
Mr Lawrence Kershen
Mr Mohammad Khan
Mr Gary Kidd
Ms Christine Kieran
Mr John Kilby
Mr Servet Kilic
Miss Susan Killeen
Mr Charles King
Mr David King
Mr Gerard King
Miss Julie King
Mrs Julie King
Mr Steve King
Mr Stuart King
Mr Timothy King
Mrs Nadine Kingsley
Mr David Kirby
Mr Chris Kirk
Mrs Jean Kirk
Mr Stuart Kirk
Mrs Natalie Kirsch
Miss Minka Kishneva
Miss Martina Klimentova
Mrs Heather Knapton
Mr Elliott Knight
Miss Michelle Knight
Dr Simon Knight
Mr Steve Knight
Mr Alan Knighting
Mr John Knowles
Miss Clare Knowles-Brown
Mrs Rachel Knox
Mr Theo Kortland
Mrs Marysia
  Korzeniowska-Olmi
Mr Stefan Kosciuszko
Mrs Patricia Koza
Mr Piers Krause
Miss Melissa Kroc
Miss Leena Kuusniemi
Ms Lai Kwan
Mrs Donna Kynaston
Mr Darren Ladbury
Miss Jag Lagah
Mr Ian Laidlaw-Dickson
Mr Jonathan Lake
Mrs M Lakhani
Mr Mohan Lal
Mr Indy Lally
Mr Benoit Lamaudiere
Mr Andrew Lamb
Mr Christopher Lamb
Mr Stephen Lamb
Ms Linda Lambert
Mrs Rachel Lampen
Mrs Jean Lancaster
Mr F Javier Lancina
Miss Louise Land
Mrs Marjorie Lane
Miss Rebecca Lane
Mrs Gemma Langley
Miss Katharine Larkin
Miss Kate Larner
Ms Joanne Latta
Ms Fay Lau
Mr Tim Lau
Mrs Judith Lavender
Miss Mary Lavin
Mr John Law
Miss Carole Lawford
Mrs Caroline Law-Irish
Mrs Anne Lawley
Miss Denise Lawrence
Mrs Julie Lawrence
Dr Thomas Lawrence

Mr Kim Lawson
Mr Anthony Lawton
Dr Richard Layfield
Mrs Hazel Lazenby
Mr Alan Le Cornu
Mr Doug Lea
Mrs Linda Lea
Ms Aida Leal
Ms Brianne Leary
Mr Justin Leclair
Mrs Kerryanne Ledwidge
Mrs Gloria Lee
Miss Sue Lee
Mr Peter Leek
Mrs Diane Leeson
Mr Timothy Leeson
Mr John Legg
Dr Didier Leibovici
Mrs Paula Leigh
Mr Peter Leigh-Quine
Mrs Ann Leitch
Mrs Joanna Leitch
Miss Ewa Lelontko
Mr Janet Lennon
Mr Nosh Lentin
Mrs Rachel Leon-Wardrop
Miss Jill Leopold
Mr Rex Lerego
Mrs Harrie Lerman
Mr Holger Levey
Mr Anthony Lewis
Mr Chris Lewis
Mr David Lewis
Mr Hugh Lewis
Ms J Lewis
Ms Jill Lewis
Ms Jo Lewis
Mrs Nia Lewis
Mrs Paula Lewis
Mr Philip Lewis Williams
Mrs Donna Lightbody
Mr Stafford Lightman
Mr Renars Likansis
Ms Rowann Limond
Mrs Carole Lindey
Mr George Lindfield
Mrs Katherine Lindop
Mr Roy Lindop
Mrs Teresa Linford
Mrs Ruth Lingwood
Mrs Lisa Linton
Mrs Gail Lithgow
Mrs Kirsty Littlewood
Mr Matt Littlewood
Mr David Llewellyn
Mr Simon Llewellyn
Ms Carrie Lloyd
Mr David Lloyd
Mrs Dereda Lloyd
Mr Gareth Lloyd
Mrs Helen Lloyd
Mr John Lloyd
Miss Joanna Lloyd-Jones
Mrs Amy Lobley
Mr Roz Lobo
Mrs Liz Lock
Mrs Doreen Lockett
Mr Paul Lockett
Mr Clive Lockyer
Mr Adrian Lodge
Mrs Charlotte Lodge
Mrs Norma Lodge
Mr Mark Loftus
Mrs Evelyne Loible
Miss Claire Longfield
Mrs Maria Fe Lopez
Mr Dave Lord
Mr Geoffrey Lord
Mrs Cecilia Lowe
Mrs Diane Lowe
Mr Norman Lowe
Miss P M Lowe
Miss Rachel Lowe
Mr Richard Lowy
Mr Gary Lucas
Mrs Sylvia Lucas
Mrs June Lucock
Miss Sarah Lumb
Mr A Lunan
Mr Mark Lunn
Mrs Chloe Luxton
Mr Frank Luxton
Mrs Valerie Luxton
Mrs Karen Lynch
Dr Natalie Lynch
Miss Sarah Lynsdale

Mr John Lyon
Ms Ali Lyons
Mrs Hilary Lyons
Mrs Sammy Maccallum
Mr David Macdonald
Mr Iain Macdonald
Mrs Jane Macdonald
Mr Stewart Macdougall
Mrs Leah Macgilp
Mrs Samantha MacGowan
Miss Paula Machado
Mr Steve Machin
Mr Ian Maciver
Miss Clare Mackay
Mrs Elizabeth MacKenzie
Mr Richard Mackey
Mr Bruce MacKinnon
Ms Alex Maclavertuy
Mr John Macleod
Mr Ross Macleod
Mrs Kate Macpherson
Mr Iain MacRae
Mr Ruairidh MacRae
Mrs Nicola Madan
  Schiannini
Dr George Madden
Mrs Vivienne Madden
Mrs Joanne Madeira
Mr Robert Madeira
Mr Sam Madison
Miss Madelaine Maguire
Mr Fazal Mahboob
Mr Syed Mahmud
Mr Stephen Makin
Ms Susanna Malkakorpi
Miss Laura Malster
Mr Simon Malton
Mrs Heather Manceau
Mrs Margaret Manchester
Mr Edward Manders
Mr James Manger
Mrs Sarah Mann
Mr Tom Mann
Mrs Susan Mannion
Mr Glenn Mansfield
Mr Steve Manson
Mr Christophe Mansour
Miss Alexandra Manton
Mr Arthur Manuel
Mr Stuart Manuel
Mrs S Marchal
Ms Jane Mardon
Mr Adrian Markley
Mr Lewis Marks
Dr Charles Markus
Mrs Louise Markus
Mrs J M W Marley
Miss Vanessa Marriott
Miss Niki Marsden
Miss Victoria Marsden
Miss Andrea Marshall
Mrs Glynis Marshall
Mr St John Marston
Mr Craig Martin
Mr Graham Martin
Mr Jason Martin
Mr John Martin
Mr Phil Martin
Mrs Sandra Martin
Mrs Anne Martin-Coyle
Mr B R Martinez
Miss Sara Martinez
Mr John Martyn
Mr Andrew Masacz
Mr Richard Mash
Mr Adrienne Mason
Mrs Anne Mason
Mr Clive Mason
Mr Denis Mason
Mr Kevin Mason
Mr Roy Mason
Mr Christopher Mason-Watts
Mrs Abbi Massey
Mr Trevor Massey
Mrs Helen Masters
Mr Paul Masters
Mr Craig Mather
Mr Brian Mathers
Mr James Matheson
Mr Murdo Mathewson
Ms Sue Matthew
Mr Leigh Matthews
Dr R Bob Matthews
Mr John Maudsley
Mrs Ruth Mauritzen
Mr David May

Mr Michael May
Mr Matthew Maynard
Mr Alex Mazaraki
Miss Rupa Mazumder
Mr Matty McArdle
Mrs Elaine McArthur
Mr Fiona McBain
Miss Mags McBride
Miss Laura McCallion
Mr Scott McCallum
Mrs Kate MccGwire
Mr Gary McClarnan
Mrs Ashley McClements
Miss Louise McCloskey
Mr K McCormick
Mr Mark McCourt
Mrs Margaret McCoy
Mrs Allison
  McDonald-Brandes
Dr Barry McDonnell
Mrs Claire McDonnell
Miss Lynne McDougall
Mr Michael McDowell
Mrs Wendy McDowell
Mr Tony McEvoy
Mr Dugald McGarry
Mr Duncan McGill
Mr Daniel McGinty
Miss Joanne McGrath
Mr Andrew McGuinness
Ms Rebecca McGuinness
Ms Jan McIntosh
Mr Stuart McIntosh
Mrs Susan McIntyre
Ms Jen McKevitt
Miss Rachel McKillop
Mrs Jane McLaughlin
Mrs Sophie McLoughlin
Mrs Martine McMaster
Mrs Kay McMenamin
Mr Richard McMenemy
Mr Keith McMonies
Miss Lindsay McNaughton
Mr John McNerney
Mr Gordon McPhie
Mr Malcolm McSwan
Mrs Jane Meadows
Mr James Meager
Mr Tanya Mealey
Mrs Joanne Mears
Mrs Cheryl Meek
Mr Alan Meekings
Mrs Gina Megeary
Mrs Lynda Meikle
Mr Mike Meineck
Mrs N Mellins-Cohen
Mrs Amanda Mellor
Miss Sarah Melville
Mrs Romy Melville-Evans
Mrs Danielle Menage
Mr Robin Menzies
Mrs Deborah Mercandelli
Mr Beverley Merry
Mr Rumel Miah
Mr Coll Michaels
Mr Jay Michaels
Mr Donald Michie
Mrs Dee Midgley
Mr Antoni Mikulski
Mr Jon Miles
Mrs Jane Milford
Miss Sarah Milford
Mr Debbie Millard
Mr Barbara Miller
Mrs Claire Miller
Miss Sarah Miller
Mrs Yvonne Miller
Mr Mary Millichip
Miss Lindsey Millington
Miss Tima Millington
Miss Cathy Millis
Mr Chris Mills
Mrs Michelle Mills
Mrs Beth Milner
Mr Stefan Mineur
Mrs Lauren Misiukanis
Mrs Annie Mitchell
Mrs Lilian Mitchell
Miss Olivia Mitchell
Mrs Valerie Mitchell
Ms Bonnie Mockett
Ms Joanna Moffatt
Mr Marc Moffatt
Mrs Louise Anne
  Mohammed
Mr Marsh Mokhtari

Miss Frances Molloy
Mrs Joy Moloney
Mrs Joanne Molyneux
Miss Kate Monaghan
Mr Peter Monks
Mr Richard Monnington
Mr Drew Montague
Dr Alan Montgomery
Ms Andrea Montgomery
Mrs Hazel Moody
Mr Lou Mooney
Mr Terence Mooney
Mr Peter Moore
Mrs Rachael Moore
Mr Simon Moore
Mr Simon Moorhead
Mrs Lynne Moralee
Mrs Bev Morgan
Mr Carl Morgan
Mrs Shirley Morgan
Mrs Stephy Morgan
Miss Ellena Moriarty
Mr Colin Morison
Mr Dennis Morley
Mrs Emma Morris
Mr Ian Morris
Mr Leuan Morris
Ms Tanya Morris-Davis
Ms Esther Morrison
Mr Ian Morrison
Mr David Morton
Mr Graham Morton
Mrs Dee Moss
Mrs Diane Moss
Mrs Katy Moss
Miss Stephanie Moss
Mr Trevor Moss
Mr Chris Mounsor
Ms Jean Mountford
Mr Luccas Moura
Mrs Susan Moyler
Mr Martin and Anne Muers
Mr Peter Mullen
Ms Michelle Muller
Ms Areej Muneeb
Mrs Alicia Munson
Mr Izidor Muraben
Mr Steven Murgatroyd
Mrs Belinda Murphy
Mr Craig Murphy
Mr Jon Murphy
Mr Michael Murphy
Mrs Sylvia Murphy
Mrs Valerie Murphy
Mrs Helen Murray
Mr Ian Murray
Mr James Murray
Miss Jane Murray
Ms Katrina Murray
Mr Simon Murray
Mrs Tracey Murray
Mrs Sue Murray-Johnson
Miss Francesca
  Murray-Smith
Mr Rick Murrier
Mrs Carla Musgrove
Mr Rich Musgrove
Miss Kathryn Mutch
Ms Ella Myles
Mr Richard Nagy
Mr Tony Nakhimoff
Mr Richard Napier
Mrs Anna Nash
Mrs Maria Nawaz
Dr Andrew Naylor
Mrs Gemma Neal
Mr David Neale
Miss Stacey Nelligan
Mrs Christine Nelson
Mr Colin Nelson
Ms Sally Neocosmos
Mr Marian Nerpas
Mr Iain Nesbitt
Mr Stephen Netherwood
Mrs Ann Neville
Miss Philippa Neville
Mr Paul New
Mr Alex Newby
Dr Tabetha Newman
Mr Richard Newton
Mrs Amanda Nichol
Mr Robert Nicholds
Mr Chris Nichols
Ms Laura Nickoll
Mrs Karen Ninnis
Dr Paul Nischal

Mrs Marina Niven
Mr Rolf Noble
Mrs Jane Noddings
Mr Adrian Nolan
Mr Asad Noorani
Mr Leslie Norman
Mr Reg Norman
Mr J G Norris
Mrs Deborah Norton
Mr Steve Norton
Miss Louise Norval
Mr David Nossiter
Mr Marc Notenbomer
Mr Roger Nowell
Miss Rosie Noyce
Mr F Nuha
Mrs Jacquie Nuttall
Ms Lyn Oates
Miss Nicola O'Brien
Miss Olivia O'Brien
Mrs Tosin O'Callaghan
Mr Ray O'Connell
Miss Carly O'Connor
Mrs Janet O'Connor
Mrs Kirsty O'Connor
Mrs Liz O'Daly
Mr Graham Oddey
Miss Helen O'Donnell
Mr Nigel O'Donoghue
Mrs Lizzie O'Donohoe
Mr Glenn Ogden
Mr Peter O'Grady
Mr Jun Ogura
Mrs Annette O'Hara
Mrs Stephanie O'Hara
Miss Rachael O'Kane
Mr Andy Oldham
Mr Daniel O'Leary
Miss Bryony Oliver
Mrs Sandra Oliver
Mr Jonathan Olney
Dr James Olsen
Miss Marian O'Neill
Miss Matilda O'Neill
Mr William O'Neill
Mr Steve Ongeri
Mr Ken Onion
Mrs Heather Ootam
Ms Esther Oppenheim
Ms Donna Orchard
Mr Andrew Ormerod
Mrs Audrey Ormes
Mr Roderic Osbaldeston
Mr Zeke Osho
Ms Renata Ostrowska
Dr Kirstine Oswald
Miss Jess Oundjian
Mr Michael Ousby
Miss Sophie Outhwaite
Mrs Anna Overton
Miss Amanda Owen
Mrs Charlotte Owens
Mrs Judy Owens
Mr Graham Oxlade
Mrs Alex Packman
Mr Chris Packman
Mr Martin Padilla
Mr John Page
Dr Louise Page
Miss Nicola Palethorpe
Mr Richard Paley
Mr Desmond Palmer
Mrs Maureen Palmer
Mr Graham Pape
Mr Daniel Pardoe
Mrs Liz Pardon
Miss Claire Parker
Mrs Adele Parkes
Mr Julian Parkin
Miss Liz Parkin
Mr Paul Parkinson
Mr Tom Parkinson
Mrs Barbara Parry
Mr Rob Parry
Mr Christopher Parsons
Dr Quentin Parsons
Mrs Rosemarie Partlett
Mr Jeff Parton
Miss Laura Partrudge
Mrs Carolyn Pascall
Dr Jennifer Pascoe
Mr Lorraine Pauley
Mrs Carol Paxton De Acosta
Mrs Laura Payne
Mr Nick Payne

Mrs Lorraine Payton
Mrs Karen Peach
Mr Roger Peach
Mr Gary Pearson
Mrs Joanne Pearson
Mr John Pearson
Mr Michael Pearson
Miss Nicola Pearson
Mrs Shamsi Pearson
Mrs Tracey Pearson
Mrs Sarah Peck
Mrs Pamela Peek
Mrs Natalie Pemberton
Miss Emma Elizabeth Penney
Ms Anne Pennington
Mr Alan Penny
Mr Simon Penrhyn
Mr Peter Perchard
Miss Rosa Perez
Mrs Deborah Perfect
Mrs Natalie Perillo
Mrs Susan Perkes
Mr Nicholas Perkin
Ms Jane Perkins
Mr T R Perry
Mrs Rosemary Persi
Mr Stephen Perugi
Mrs Heather Peters
Mr Mark Peters
Mr Martyn Peters
Mr Nick Peters
Mrs Susan Peters
Mr John Peterson
Miss Frances Petipher
Mr William Petrie
Mr David Phillips
Mr Kane Phillips
Ms Liz Phillips
Miss Natasha Phillips
Mr Robert Phillips
Mr Thomas Phillips
Mrs Zoe Phillips
Mrs Sue Philp
Mr Simon Philpot
Mr David Pickup
Dr Lloyd Pietersen
Ms Tanya Piggins
Mr Alastair Pike
Mrs Fran Pike
Miss Ophelie Pimaud
Mr Anthony Pine
Miss Eroney Pinnock
Mr Stefan Piotrowski
Mrs Abigail Pitcher
Mr Martin Pitcher
Mr Harry Pitt
Mrs Sara Pizzey
Mr Terry Pleace
Miss Sarah Plumley
Mr David Pocock
Mr Chris Poles
Mr Tony Pooke
Mr Mark Porter
Mr Alan Portwood
Mr Alan Potter
Mr David Potter
Mrs Jody Potter
Mr Marc Poulaud
Mr Martin Pounce
Mrs Chantal Powell
Mr Chris Powell
Mrs Emma Powell
Mrs Heather Powell
Mr Michael Powell
Mr David Pratt
Mr Ian Pratt
Miss Tina Pratt
Mr John Precious
Ms Jane Preston
Mr Nick Preston
Mr Chris Price
Mr Michael Price
Mr Mark Prince
Dr Julian Procter
Mr Paul Proctor
Mr Darren Prosser
Mrs Tracey Prosser
Mr Matthew Prouten
Ms Deborah Prynne
Mr Alon Prytherch
Dr John Prytherch
Mrs Beverley Pugh
Mr Matthew Pullara
Mr Gareth Purnell
Mr Steve Putman

Mr Douglas Pye
Ms Claire Pyke
Miss Jessica Pyne
Mr Moin Qazi
Mr Michael Quaife
Mr Julian Quantrill
Mr Peter Quantrill
Miss Suzanne Quarmby
Mr Pedro Quartin Graca
Mr Keith Quinn
Mrs Margaret Quinn
Miss Deena Quinnell
Dr Gillian Raab
Ms Yvonne Rabek
Ms Lesley Rackley
Mr Charley Radcliffe
Mrs Helen Rae
Dr Tom Rafferty
Mr Limon Rahman
Miss Nadia Rahman
Mr Nadia Rahman
Mr Lyle Rainey
Mr Giri Rajaratnam
Miss Kimberlea Ralph
Mr Rajinder Ram
Mr Sally Randall
Mrs Tracey Randall
Mrs Joanne Randell
Mrs Gayle Randle
Mrs Jane Ranzetta
Mr Alexander Rast
Mr Dean Ratcliffe
Mrs Carol Rawlings
Mrs Susan Rawson
Mrs Fiona Raymond
Mr Mike Rea
Mr Peter Read
Mrs Sue Read
Ms Suzanne Reade
Mr Harry Readman
Mr Paul Reaney
Mrs Delphine Rech
Mr Kumar Reddy
Mr Jason Redgers
Mrs Jennifer Redman
Mr John Reed
Mr Thomas Reed
Mr David Rees
Mrs Val Rees
Mr Sam Rees-Adams
Miss Amanda Claire Reeve
Mrs Penny Reeves
Mr Alan Reid
Mrs Jane Reid
Mr Mike Reid
Mr Raymond Reid
Miss Susan Reid
Mr Andrew Rendall
Mrs Nicola Renshaw
Mrs June Retter
Mrs Olivia Retter
Mr Anthony Revington
Mr Alan Reynolds
Mrs Georgina Reynolds
Mr James Reynolds
Mrs Julia Reynolds
Miss Stephanie Rhodes
Mr Tony Rhodes
Mr Peter Ribbins
Mrs Laurie Rice-Coxall
Mrs Elizabeth Richards
Mrs Jeanette Richards
Miss Rebecca Richards
Mrs Andrea Richardson
Mrs Barbara Richardson
Mr C John Richardson
Mrs Camilla Richardson
Mrs Johanna Riches
Mr Tim Richman Gadoffre
Miss Maria Rico
Mrs Carol Riddick
Mrs Pam Ridgway
Mr Angelo Rigali
Mr Adam Rigby
Mrs Heather Rigby
Mr Juli Riley
Mr Robert Riley
Mrs Anne Rimer
Mr Oliver Rimmell
Mr Keith Rimmer
Mr B J Ripley
Mr Mike Rippon
Mrs Ruth Roadnight
Mr Liam Roarty
Ms Cecily Roberts
Mr Charles Roberts

Mr Geoffrey Roberts
Ms Jenny Roberts
Miss Judith Roberts
Mr Kenneth Roberts
Mrs Meg Roberts
Miss Anna Robertson
Mrs Debbie Robertson
Mr Gary Robertson
Mrs Jane Robertson
Mrs Julie Robertson
Mr Kerr Robertson
Mr David Robinson
Mr James Robinson
Mr Jonathan Robinson
Dr Peter Robinson
Mr Stuart Robinson
Ms Susan Robinson
Mr Nicolas Robin
Mrs Angela Robson
Miss Dale Anne Robson
Mrs Jacqueline Robson
Mrs Lorraine Robson
Miss Louise Rockerfeller
Mrs Leanne Rockingham
Miss Hayley Roddwell
Ms Samantha Rodgers
Mr Bruce Roe
Miss Emma Rogers
Mr Geoffrey Rogers
Mr Peter Rogers
Mr Stephen Rogers
Mr Tom Rogers
Mr Trevor Rogers
Mr Phillip Roles
Mr Paul Rollings
Mr Carlos Roobrouck
Mrs Alison Rooker
Mrs Tracey Rose
Mr Alan Rosher
Mr Antonio Rosignoli
Mrs Jackie Ross
Dr James Ross
Mr John Ross
Mr Paul Ross
Miss Sidney Celia Ross
Mr Thomas Ross
Dr Janice Rossen
Dr Colin Roth
Mr Mark Rothwell
Mrs Nicola Round
Mr David Rouson
Mrs Valerie Rousseau
Mrs Janice Rowe
Mrs Angie Rowland
Mr Malcolm Rowlands
Mr Richard Rowlands
Mr Simon Rubin
Mr David Ruddock
Mr John Rudkin
Mr Michael Rugman
Mr Ben Russell
Mrs Bev Russell
Mrs Kate Russell
Mr Robert Russell
Mr Adrian Ruthen
Mr Chris Ryan
Mr Gerald Ryan
Mr Henry Rymill
Mr Nigel Sadler
Miss Emily Sage
Mr Mark Salter
Mrs Nicki Salter
Ms Bernice Saltzer
Mr Keith Salway
Mrs Lesley Samms
Mr Irene Sampson
Ms Lisa Samuelson
Mrs Catherine Sander
Miss Kimberley Sander
Mrs Carol Sanders
Dr Catherine Sanders
Mrs David Sanders
Mr Matthew Sanders
Dr Ian Sanderson
Mr Nishul Saperia
Mr James Saul
Mrs Susan Saul
Mrs Angela Saunders
Mrs Rebecca Saunders
Miss Lucy Savage
Ms Selaine Saxby
Miss Sian Saxton
Mr Iain Sayer
Mrs Janet Sayers
Miss Lizzie Scanlan
Mr Rory Scarfe

Mr Peter Scherschel
Ms Teresa Schrezenmaier
Mrs Cornelia Scott
Mr Karl Scott
Dr Nicola Scott
Mr Sam Scott
Mr Peter Scott-Edeson
Mrs Nicola Scrivener
Miss Victoria Scrope
Ms Helen Seale
Mrs Sara Searle
Mr Steven Searle
Mrs Jane Seddon
Miss Joanne Seddon
Mr Jonathan Paul Seedall
Mrs Dee Selby
Miss Ellie Selby
Mr Jack Selby
Mrs Jennie Selman
Mrs Kelly Service
Ms Jackie Severn
Mr Richard Severn
Miss Gillian Seville
Mr Nicholas Shanahan
Mr Clive Share
Mr Anil Sharma
Mr Geoffrey Sharp
Mr William Sharp
Mr Alec Sharpe
Mrs Alyson Sharpe
Dr Heather Sharrock
Mr Bertram Shaw
Ms Liz Shaw
Mr Robert Shaw
Miss V Shaw
Mrs Norma Sheard
Mrs Fiona Sheehy
Mrs Mandy Shenton
Mrs Jo Shepherd
Mr Nic Sheppard
Mr Paul Sherburn
Mr Bernard Sheridan
Mr C Sheridan
Mrs Pauline Sheridan
Mr Alan Sherlock
Dr Alan Sherratt
Mr Warren Sherratt
Mrs Danielle Sherson
Ms Jill Sherwin
Miss Siobhan Sherwin
Mrs Amanda Sherwood
Mr Adam Shilling
Mr Neil Shilling
Ms Akiko Shimamura
Ms Sue Shone
Mr Gilbert Short
Miss Karen Shorter
Mr Mark Shorting
Mrs Karen Shufflebotham
Mr Andrew Shuttleworth
Mr Joe Shyne
Miss Saima Sid
Mrs Sultana Siddiki
Mr Mam Sidke
Mr Stewart Sim
Miss Kylie Simmonds
Mr Mervyn Simmonds
Mr Peter Simmonds
Mr Paul Simmons
Mrs Naomi Simons
Mr Scott Simons
Miss Astrid Simonsen
Ms Anna Simpson
Ms Julia Simpson
Mr Roger Simpson
Miss J Simpson
Mr Andrew Sinclair
Mr Andy Sinclair
Miss Emily Sinclair
Mr Keith Sinclair
Mr Roy Sinclair
Mr Greg Sinfield
Mr Stuart Singer
Mr Jasbinder Singh
Mr S Singh
Ms Tracey Sisley
Mr Michael Skeemer
Mr Alexander Skinner
Mr Ivan Skinner
Mrs Poppy Skinner
Mrs Sian Skinner
Mr Stephen Skinner
Miss Kerrie Skipsey
Mr Bryan Skull
Mrs Sally Slade
Mrs Christine Slater

Mrs Ella Slater
Miss Hannah Slater
Ms L Slater
Mrs Helen Slinger
Miss Amanda Slorach
Mr Anthony Small
Mr Brian Small
Mr David Small
Mrs Pamela Small
Mr Chay Smalls
Miss Caroline Smart
Mrs Pamela Smart
Mr Phillip Smart
Mr Rodney Smelt
Dr John Roderic Smethurst
Ms Josee Smets
Mr Aidan Smith
Mr Andrew Smith
Miss Carol Smith
Mr Clive Smith
Mrs Frances Smith
Mr Greg Smith
Mrs Hilary Smith
Dr Hillas Smith
Mr I Smith
Mr Jason Smith
Mrs Jayne Smith
Ms Jayne Smith
Miss Jillian Smith
Mrs Judith Smith
Mrs Lesley Smith
Miss Lindsay Smith
Mr Martin Smith
Mr Richard Smith
Mrs Sandra Smith
Miss Sarah Smith
Mrs Sarah Smith
Mr Steven Smith
Mr Stuart Smith
Mr Chris Smithson-Connelly
Mr Frank Smits
Mrs Senga Smykala
Mrs Sandra Snelling
Mrs Diane Snelson
Miss Vanessa Snook
Mr Paul Somerville
Ms Katherine Sorrell
Mrs Joanne Southall
Mrs Patricia Southern
Mr Anton Sowden
Miss Yolande Sowerby
Mrs Pauline Sowry
Mr Ian Sparks
Mr Graham Spaull
Mrs Emma Spencer
Mrs Janet Spencer
Dr Mark Spencer
Mrs Kate Spicer
Mrs Judith Spiers
Miss Anna Splain
Mr Jeremy Spring
Mr Ian Springall
Mrs Sarah Sprong
Mr Rory Squires
Mr Stephen Squires
Mr Stuart Squires
Mrs Mandi St Clair Down
Mr Simon Stagnell
Mr Edward Staines
Mr Andrew Stalker
Miss Jessica Standen
Ms Cressida Stanley-Williams
Mrs Beryl Stanniland
Mr Andy Statham
Mr Richard Staton
Mr Glen Staunton
Mr Martin Steadman
Mr Drew Steanson
Mr Andrew Stedman-Keeble
Mrs J Steele
Mr Paul Steele
Mrs Ellen Stephens
Mrs Margaret Stephens
Ms Andrea Stephenson
Dr Andrew Stevenson
Miss Rosemary Stevenson
Mrs Georgina Stewart
Mrs Jacky Stewart
Mrs Janet Stewart
Miss Jo Stewart
Mrs Josephine Stibbards
Mr Allen Stidwill
Mr James Stillwell
Mr Simon Stillwell

Ms Caroline Stirling
Mr David Stirling
Mrs Chris Stockbridge
Mr Freddie Stockdale
Mr Roy Stockwell
Mr Richard Stok
Mr Adrian J R Stokes
Miss Laura Stolper
Mr David Stone
Mrs Sonia Stone
Mrs Sue Stone
Mr Terence Stone
Mr Peter Storey
Mr Paul Stower
Mrs Sheila Stowers
Ms Laura Stratford
Ms Ro Strawson
Mr Craig Street
Mrs Judith Stringer
Mr Matthew Strong
Mrs Karen Stubbings
Miss Kate Sturley
Miss Bonnie Styles
Miss Katie Sullivan
Mr Terence Sullivan
Mrs Sofia Sultana
Ms Judy Summers
Mrs Nicky Summers
Mrs Patricia Sunley
Mrs Bridgette Sunman
Mr Duncan Sutcliffe
Mr John Sutcliffe
Miss Katie Sutcliffe
Mr Michael Sutcliffe
Mr Andrew Swan
Ms Margaret Sweet
Mr Martin Sykes
Mrs Sabrina Sykes
Mrs Vivien Symons
Mr Aumar Taib
Mrs Emma Tait
Mr Douglas Talintyre
Miss Naomi Tamplin
Mr John Tanburn
Mrs Sian Taplin
Mr David Tapper
Miss Lauren Tasker
Mr Rodney Tatman
Mrs Judy Tayler-Smith
Mr Alan Taylor
Miss Amy Taylor
Ms Bo Taylor
Mrs Carol Taylor
Mrs Caroline Taylor
Mrs Caz Taylor
Mr Darren Taylor
Miss Georgina Taylor
Mr Harvey Taylor
Ms Helen Taylor
Mr Ian Taylor
Mr J Taylor
Mrs Karen Taylor
Mr Kevan Taylor
Mrs Kim Taylor
Ms Lee Taylor
Miss Lyndsay Taylor
Mr Mark Taylor
Mr Mike Taylor
Mrs Morwen Taylor
Miss Rachel Taylor
Mr Robert Taylor
Ms Sally Taylor
Mr Sandy Taylor
Mrs Sara Taylor
Mrs Sheila Taylor
Mr Tim Taylor
Mr Livio Te
Miss Gemma Teal
Mr Christopher Teatum
Mr Geoff Tedstone
Mr William Tempest
Mr William Templeton
Dr Robin Tems
Mr Christopher Terry
Ms Patricia Terry
Mr Michael Theobald
Mrs Eileen Thistlethwaite
Mr Russell Thom
Mrs A C Thomas
Mr Ian Thomas
Mr Mark Thomas
Mrs Melinda Thomas
Mr Paul Thomas
Mr Simon Thomas
Dr Walter Thomas
Mr Gary Thomassen

Mr Jane Thompson
Miss Lisa Thompson
Mr Matt Thompson
Mr Paul Thompson
Miss Rhianna Thompson
Mrs Rocio Thompson
Mr Roger Thompson
Mr Thomas Thompson
Mrs Tina Thompson
Mrs Val Thompson
Mrs Angela Thomson
Mr Michael Thomson
Mrs Tracey Thomson
Mr Christopher Thornes
Mrs Janette Thornton
Mrs Jill Thornton
Mr Robert Thurlow
Mr Frederick Tickell
Mr John Tickle
Mr Nick Tiley
Mr Adrian Tindall
Mr Barry Tipple
Mrs Jan Todd
Ms Ilina Todorovska
Mrs Cyrena Tomlin
Mr Michael Tomlinson
Mr J P Toole
Mr Scott Torrance
Ms Rosemary Towler
Mr Ian Townsend
Mr Peter Townsend
Mrs Marion Tracey
Mrs Geraldine Trafford
Mrs Sara Trentini
Mr Ian Trinder
Mr Uttam Tripathy
Mr Leslie Tritton
Mr Richard Troman
Mr Liam Trotman
Mr Paul Trott
Mr David Tryon
Mr David Tuck
Mr Chris Tucker
Mrs Helen Tucker
Miss Vikki Tucker
Mr Brian Turner
Mr Darren Turner
Mr David Turner
Mr John Turner
Mrs Jill Turton
Mrs Pauline Twigg
Mr Andrew Tye
Mr Mark Tyrrell
Mr James Underwood
Mr Dixon Upcott
Mrs Janice Urquhart
Mrs Anne Ursell
Ms Susan Usher
Mrs Christine Vallely
Mr Pim van Baarsen
Mr Martin van der Stijl
Mrs Katrina van Pelt
Mrs Lynn-mari van Wyk
Mrs Victoria van Wyk
Mr Dick Vardy
Mr Jonathan Varey
Miss Jill Vasey
Mr John Vaughan
Mr Robin Vaughan
Mr Tom Vaughan
Mr Ben Vaux
Dr David Vaux
Mrs Suzanne Vinall
Miss Angela Vinci
Mrs Anita Vine
Miss Sarah Vine
Mrs Gill Vlasto
Ms Louise Voss
Mrs Maureen Wagstaff
Mr Lee Waites
Mr Charles Wake
Mrs Fiona Wales
Mr Ian Walker
Ms Lucy Walker
Ms Lyn Walker
Mr Pat Walker
Mr Steve Walker
Mr Tom Walker
Ms Wendy Walker
Mr Richard Wall
Mr Brian Wallace
Mrs Catherine Waller
Mr Ian Waller
Dr Graham Wallis
Mr Christopher Walls
Mr Peter Wallum

Mrs Ulrike Walther
Mr Robert Walton
Mr Stuart Warburton-Smith
Mrs Hannah Ward
Mrs Jill Ward
Mr John Ward
Mr Malcolm Ward
Mrs Liz Warden
Mrs Alena Wardle
Mr Rodney Wardle
Mrs Josie Wareing
Mr Steve Warner
Mrs Dragica Warren
Miss Lottie Warren
Mr Joe Warwick
Mr William Wass
Mr Phillip Waters
Mr James Watkins
Mr Joseph Watkinson
Mrs Bridget Watson
Mr David Watson
Mrs Dawn Watson
Miss Melissa Watson
Mr Nigel Watson
Mr Brian Watt
Mr James Watt
Mr John Watt
Mr David Watters
Mrs Alice Watts
Mr Chris Waugh
Mrs Jill Waugh
Mrs Elizabeth Way-Rider
Mr Mark Weatherill
Mr Nicholas Weaver
Mr Paul Weaver
Dr Gillian Webb
Mr Graham Webb
Mr Peter Webb
Mr Alistair Webster
Mr James Webster
Mrs Karis Webster
Mrs Jane Weightman
Mr Neil Weightman
Mr Helen Weir
Mr Derek Weldon
Miss Patricia Welford
Dr Alastair Wells
Miss Gemma Wells
Mrs Alison Welsford
Mr Tomasz Wencel
Miss Jayne Wenlock
Mrs J W West
Mr Jake West
Mr M West
Mrs Christine Westerland
Mrs Karen West-Jubb
Mr Kevin Westland
Miss Rosie Weston
Miss Susan Weston
Ms Jenni Wetters
Mrs Penny Whale
Mr Steven Whalley
Mrs Sandra Wharton
Mrs Kathryn Whawell
Mrs Catherine Wheatley
Miss Jeanette Wheeler
Mrs Kay Whelpdale
Mrs Susan Whiston
Mr Colin White
Mrs Dawn White
Miss Estela White
Miss Jackie White
Mr John White
Miss Julie White
Miss Laura White
Mr Mark White
Mr Paul White
Mr Richard White
Mrs Ruth White
Mrs Sara White
Mr Tony Whitehouse
Mr Paul Whitfield
Mr James Whittaker
Mr Michael Whittall
Mr Ian Whittingham
Mr Robert Whittingham
Miss Paula Whittle
Miss Claire Whomes
Mrs Taoa Widdall
Mr Chris Wigg
Mrs Lucy Wiggins
Mrs Clare Wight
Mr Ian Wilcox
Mr Andrew Wilde

Mrs Elaine Wild-Jones
Mr Brian Wiles
Mr Jim Wilkie
Mr John Wilkinson
Mrs Julia Wilkinson
Mr Richard Wilkinson
Mr Sam Willacy
Mr Alan Williams
Dr Anthony Williams
Mr Arnold Williams
Ms Barbara Williams
Mrs Christina Williams
Mrs Drena Williams
Mr Edwyn Williams
Mrs Emma Williams
Ms Jackie Williams
Mrs Jenny Williams
Mr Jon Williams
Mrs June Williams
Mrs Kath Williams
Miss Lesley-Anne Williams
Mr Mark Williams
Mrs Niki Williams
Ms Sharon Williams
Mr Stephen Williams
Miss Claire Williamson
Mr Harris Williamson
Mrs Carol Wilson
Mr James Wilson
Miss Meg Wilson
Miss Sophie Wilson
Mrs Stella Wilson
Mrs Susan Wilson
Mr Trevor Wilson
Mrs Polly Winder
Mrs Bev Wingate
Mrs Karen Winslade
Mrs Chris Winter
Mr John Winter
Mr George Wirgman
Mr Mike Wise
Mr Andrew Wiseman
Ms Fiona Wiseman
Dr Paul Withers
Miss Emma Witort
Miss Jemma Witting
Mr Paul Witrey
Mr Nicky Wolfe
Mrs Sue Womack
Mrs Sophie Wonghen
Mr Chris Wood
Mr Claire Wood
Mr Graeme Wood
Mrs Janet Wood
Miss Kirsty Wood
Mr Martin Wood
Mr Simon Wood
Mrs Jenny Woodbridge
Ms Mary Woodburn
Mr Harry Woodmass
Miss Steph Woodley
Mr Mark Woodward
Mr Mike Woollam
Ms Linda Woolston
Mr Michael Worley
Mrs Trudi Worner
Mrs Margaret Worsley
Mrs Sue Worthington
Miss Jo Woulfe
Mr Peter Wozencroft
Ms Amanda Wragg
Ms Berni Wright
Ms Catherine Wright
Mr Chris Wright
Mrs Denise Wright
Mr Derek Wright
Mrs Deborah Wrightson
Mrs Helen Wrightson
Mr James Wrigley
Mr Will Wyatt
Mr Ian Wyles
Dr David Wyllie
Miss Cat Yaffe
Mrs Hilary Yarnall
Mr Steve Yates
Mrs Jana Yell
Mr Tristan Yelland
Miss L Yevtushenko
Mr Alex Young
Mrs Deirdre Young
Mrs Jodene Young
Dr Simon Young
Mrs Uruj Zahid
Miss Lucia Zelieskova
Miss Amna Zulfiqar

Special Thanks

We would like to extend special thanks to the following people: Kirstie Addis, Hilary Armstrong, Iain Barker, Lily Bowden, Emily Brunwin, Ruth Coombs, Mark Griffiths, Alan Grimwade, Ros Mari Grindheim, Phil Harriss, Ben Kay, Muireann Kirby, Janice Leech, Angela Newton, Jeffrey Ng, John Rowlands, Neil Simpson, Emma Sturgess, Kerenza Swift, Mark Taylor, Stuart Walton, Jenny White, Gemma Wilkinson, Blanche Williams, Jane Wilson and Zeren Wilson.

Picture credits
Illustrations for features courtesy of Shutterstock
Andy Appleton courtesy of David Griffen
Tom Van Zeller courtesy of Javan Liam
Restaurant of the Year winners courtesy of Duncan Soar

Map credits
Maps designed and produced by Cosmographics Ltd, www.cosmographics.co.uk
UK digital database © Cosmographics Ltd, 2012
Greater London Map © Cosmographics Ltd, 2012
North and South London maps © Collins Bartholomew, 2012
West, Central and East London maps © BTA (trading as VisitBritain), 2012, produced by Cosmographics Ltd and used with the kind permission of VisitBritain.

Please send updates, queries, menus and wine lists to:
editors@thegoodfoodguide.co.uk or write to:
The Good Food Guide, 2 Marylebone Road, London, NW1 4DF

Please leave restaurant feedback at: www.thegoodfoodguide.co.uk/feedback

Online: www.thegoodfoodguide.co.uk
Twitter: @GoodFoodGuideUK

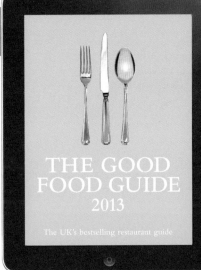